State and Local Gover
in a Federal Syste

State and Local Government in a Federal System

NINTH EDITION

Daniel R. Mandelker
Howard A. Stamper Professor of Law
Washington University in St. Louis School of Law

Judith Welch Wegner
Burton Craige Professor of Law Emerita
University of North Carolina School of Law

Janice C. Griffith
Professor of Law
Suffolk University Law School

Evan C. Zoldan
Professor of Law
University of Toledo College of Law

Cynthia Baker
Clinical Professor of Law
Director, Program on Law and State Government
Indiana University Robert H. McKinney School of Law

Carolina Academic Press
Durham, North Carolina

ISBN 978-1-5310-1487-2
eISBN 978-1-5310-1488-9
LCCN 2020939747

Carolina Academic Press
700 Kent Street
Durham, North Carolina 27701
Telephone (919) 489-7486
Fax (919) 493-5668
E-mail: cap@cap-press.com
www.cap-press.com

Printed in the United States of America

To my children, John, Amy, and Daniel
-D.R.M.-

To Daniel Mandelker, mentor extraordinaire
and
To Frayda Bluestein & Robert Hagemann, exceptional students, colleagues and friends
-J.W.W.-

To Weston Jr., Mary Robin, Frank, and Heidi
-J.C.G.-

To Ariel and Charlie
-E.C.Z.-

To Tim and our children, the loves of my life, and in memory of my father, Ernest F. Oppliger
-C.A.B.-

Contents

Table of Cases

Preface

Viewpoints, Objectives, and Emphasis

The Preface to the first edition of this casebook by its two original co-authors stated our purpose in ways that continue to ring true:

> It is reasonable to assume that every casebook has a point of view; it is an equally safe assumption that no casebook could satisfy the point of view, needs, or objectives of every teacher of state and local government law. Within these boundary conditions we have constructed a casebook which has a modest and frequently unobtrusive point of view and which at the same time attempts to provide materials adequate to satisfy the needs and objectives of other teachers.
>
> This point of view is relatively simple and essentially structural. The study of state and local government for law students should be built on a framework of the tri-partite distribution of powers, both vertically and horizontally: the federal-state-local levels of government and their interrelationship, the legislative-executive-judicial branches of government and their interaction.
>
> The book has two principal objectives. First, it focuses on government powers: where they come from, how they operate, and how disputes about such powers are resolved. Second, it addresses the participants in the governance process: who they are, and how they play their roles as entities and individuals. Inevitably, reflection on the governance process results in reflection on the political process, and the interaction of legislators, judges, and members of the executive branch (mayors, governors, and administrative officers). Attention to this intra-governmental distribution of powers stems, of course, from American separation of powers.
>
> Students will also find a good deal more state government law and somewhat less municipal law than is traditional in courses in this area. That also reflects our structural preoccupation. Now, perhaps more than in the latter half of the twentieth century, states occupy a pivotal role in our multi-level structural system. The rhetorical depiction of states as "laboratories" of democracy has never rung more true.
>
> The book is designed for the generalist in state and local government law rather than for the municipal law practitioner. The reasons are twofold.

> First, and we concede that this is a complaint heard from every law teacher, the time allotted is inadequate: rarely more than three hours, sometimes only two hours. The pressure has been somewhat relieved by the practice in some law schools in recent years of creating a separate course for land use issues and sometimes also for state and local taxation. On the other hand, while some of the content may have moved on to other offerings, new problems have more than replaced them—metropolitan government, reapportionment, school finance, etc. Even by our standard of selectivity, there are more materials than a three-hour course will comfortably contain—which allows room for free choice. We feared that if we expanded coverage the doctrines would pass by so fast that what remained for the student would be a blur.
>
> In addition, more than is true for most public law courses, the students who elect state and local government law often do not intend to practice in this area, or to confront state or local government problems other than those that arise in the context of land disputes. Teachers of state and local government courses are nevertheless accustomed to hearing from former students that there was more "practical use" for clients from the course than they would have guessed. A substantial number are also likely to find that their extracurricular professional activities—as school board members, combatants in a neighborhood zoning or highway or environmental dispute—require a legal understanding of local, state, and federal governments. It is important for the course to meet their needs also. Many students enter law school hoping to contribute to the good of their communities and the cause of justice, and such students may be particularly drawn to take state and local government law or other similar courses.
>
> The decision to write for the generalist meant that we do not purport to include all of the subjects and issues which might be covered, or to cover the topics which we have included exhaustively (with perhaps a few exceptions). We have omitted such areas as the duties and rights of office holders, government contract powers, and state legislative reapportionment. Nonetheless, we believe that our materials offer an opportunity to explore a variety of engaging questions in areas of emerging importance.

Despite the burgeoning law in this field, we have endeavored to maintain concise coverage and to continue the book's long-standing commitment to "teachability." To that end, we continue to employ framing problems at the outset and at some other strategic points in the chapters. In addition, the notes following principal cases are formatted to allow both teachers and students to grasp the application of related questions to timely situations that should spark engaged classroom discussion. We have also continued to shift certain coverage to expanded Notes that instructors may elect to assign for more in-depth consideration of particular topics, while making it easy for others to pick and choose areas they wish to cut in the interests of time. We hope that this approach will allow instructors to engage students more actively, particularly since the state and local government course is an elective taken in the second or third year of school, when a fresh pedagogical approach is likely to be more interesting to all concerned. To that end, we have endeavored to identify opportunities to introduce discussions and instruction relating to various kinds of professional skills and insights (such as professional responsibility and drafting) in various contexts as discussed in the teachers' manual.

Ninth Edition

The Ninth Edition of this book reflects a number of important changes. We continue to miss two of our senior authors. Professor Dawn Netsch retired from Northwestern School of Law and subsequently died before work on the Eighth Edition began. Professor Peter Salsich also retired and took emeritus status at Saint Louis University School of Law before the Eighth Edition commenced. We miss both of these significant contributors and friends very much. We appreciate that Professor Daniel Mandelker continued to serve as a sounding board and reviewer of the Ninth Edition, even though he passed on writing obligations to others and the role of senior editor to Judith Wegner.

The Ninth Edition has added two new authors, University of Toledo's Professor Evan Zoldan (who covered federalism, special legislation and delegation) and Indiana-Indianapolis Professor Cynthia Baker (who covered government powers). Janice Griffith continued to handle the chapter on alternate forms of government. Judith Wegner took on additional responsibilities for chapters (including public finance and government liability) covered by two departing authors who had played a role in the Eighth Edition.

You will notice a number of substantive changes and shifts in emphasis in this Edition. All parts of the book have been thoroughly updated. Chapter 2 has been updated to reflect new thinking from the National League of Cities (and associated scholars) on best practices in crafting home rule authority for local governments, and significant and worrisome trends involving state preemption of local government decision-making. Especially substantial changes have been made in Chapter 4, relating to public finance, to update and streamline coverage. Policy developments in this area have been significant, as sources of and strategies for government funding have shifted, tax laws have changed, and financial practices once embraced as "accepted wisdom" have been found in some cases to be less than transparent or have benefited the private sector more than taxpayers. Other important updates address evolving patterns regarding types of local governments, and trends in alternate and regional forms of government. The update also addresses evolving issues affecting public employees, government liability, licensure, voting, and education. It likewise updates coverage on such issues as gubernatorial vetoes, forms of action in suits against local governments, initiatives and referenda.

Coverage Choices and Continuing Themes

More than ever, the range of fascinating issues potentially encompassed by the course in state and local government provides faculty and students with hard choices about balancing breadth and depth of inquiry. We believe the first two chapters provide necessary and essential background no matter what the length of the course. Reasonable decisions can then be made whether to emphasize the material in Part I, which deals primarily with governmental structure, powers and intergovernmental problems, or Part II, which deals primarily with internal governmental functions, judicial review issues and access to the courts.

Those who have previously taught the course in state and local government undoubtedly emphasize selected themes as a unifying force. We offer several possibilities for consideration, based on our own ongoing work in the field and with this book.

An initial important theme is the way in which discrete pockets of doctrine seem inevitably to come together in operation, since most problems facing state and local governments raise a multitude of issues at once. For example, questions of municipal liability are likely to require an appreciation for the scope of authority under which an employee functioned, the range of discretion involved, the place of the employee in the organizational structure, the relation of the diverse branches of government, and the interplay of state tort law and federal and state constitutions.

Another unifying pattern is the simplicity and one might say the crudeness of doctrine in this field. State and local government legal issues often are solved through the application of "tired" two-way classifications that are conclusory and do not really explain results. The time-worn governmental-proprietary distinction is an example. One of the more vibrant trends in state and local government law is the rejection of these ancient classifications and the substitution of new doctrine. The question is whether some of this new doctrine, such as the "balancing test" now applied to a variety of issues, is really an improvement. The same point applies to the ministerial-discretionary distinction often used in local government tort law.

It is also possible to trace the tension between responsiveness on the part of local government and parochialism. There is a constant search for boundaries that delineate community identity. The geographic scope of municipalities must be defined at the time of incorporation and may be expanded through annexation. Broader community links are increasingly forged through intergovernmental cooperation designed to address shared possibilities or concerns. On the other hand, certain populations may be "fenced out" even as others are brought in. Government authority may be used to favor some (be they particular homeowners, businesses, older or younger individuals) at the expense of others (who may carry a differential tax load).

In addition, of course, there is the perennial question of the role of the courts in the state and local government system, and the extent to which they should review state and local government actions. Here, there is a notable contrast between the judicial reserve characteristic of cases raising substantive issues with the more active judicial role in issues, like voting rights, where the structure of the governmental system and the fairness of the governmental process are at issue. These patterns reflect something more subtle than constitutional concern for separation of powers, since there are substantive patterns at work. In addition, one must wonder about the ways in which the closeness of state court judges to local and state-wide politics informs their judgment in ways that may float to the surface now and again.

Then, too, there are the interesting questions of how theory informs practice and how practice informs theory. This theme is increasingly evident in the aftermath of the "devolution" frenzy evident in congressional and presidential policy-making over the last two decades and the resulting growth of discrete state-based and localized solutions to major social problems, crafted more often in the legislatures than in the courts. The range of empirical studies on such topics as welfare and educational reform and the growing sophistication of academic theory on local governments more generally create a beneficial counterpoint.

Emerging Issues

Each time we update this book, we endeavor to think ahead about where the future will likely lead. Here is some food for thought as the Ninth Edition goes to press.

- *COVID-19 pandemic implications.* This edition was written and submitted in large part prior to the emergence of the COVID-19 pandemic in early 2020. The experience of the pandemic has had profound effects on many aspects of civic life in the United States and beyond. Education has changed, and law schools have embraced new forms of instruction. The public has been challenged to rethink the social compact in significant ways as citizens have been called to comply with "stay at home" orders so as to protect not only their own health and well-being but the health and well-being of others. Federalism has been cast in a different light as state and local governments have found the federal response wanting in terms of providing emergency assistance and guidance in trying times. New strategies have been developed on the fly to address massive unemployment, health needs, and business downturns. The relationships between Wall Street and Main Street, and between urban and rural interests have frayed more significantly. So, too, understandings about the responsibilities of state governors, local officials, and state legislatures on matters such as constraints on church gatherings or definitions of essential businesses have become increasingly fraught, casting in sharp relief the nation's political divisions. So too, have divisions between state branches of government and the federal courts, as demonstrated in decisions regarding how elections can and should be held in a time of pandemic. Although it will take some years to sort out the implications of the fallout from these events, it is likely that the United States, government practices, and public assumptions about the role of diverse governments (local, state, and federal) will never be the same. While it is impossible to predict all the consequences of the COVID-19 pandemic, where possible, the authors have added relevant questions and examples in strategic points throughout this edition of the casebook.

- *Local government powers and state preemption.* As discussed in Chapter 2, perhaps the most significant development in recent years has been the growing tendency of state legislatures to preempt local government powers. This development may well reflect political gerrymandering practices, in which state legislatures dominated by rural interests have sought to bring urban and suburban governments with differing policy views to heel. It remains to be seen whether the 2020 Census and 2020 election will affect the balance of power in state houses and attention to urban views and concerns. The recent National League of Cities report on reformulating home rule authority may play an important role in coming years.
- *Financial deficits.* As discussed in Chapter 4, the overpowering federal deficit that resulted from recent federal tax cuts and federal spending practices may have a significant "ripple down" effect that results in the federal government's limiting funding to states and localities, or taking over traditional sources of state and local revenue. Much has been written about the squeeze placed on state and local governments as a result of state taxation and expenditure limits. Localities have increasingly tried to avoid such limits by turning to special districts with Balkanized responsibilities and limited transparency and accountability. It remains to be seen how these significant cross-currents can be resolved.
- *Structural deficiencies and infrastructure needs.* There is significant evidence that state and local governments lack funds needed to address deteriorating public infrastructure, even as greater stress is placed on that infrastructure as a result of climate change. It is unclear whether and how resources can be mustered to address such crucial problems. New approaches will surely be needed, but it may be difficult for localities to find solutions without state enabling authority and federal reform (including reform of the federal flood insurance policy).
- *Deadlocked government.* The Eighth Edition highlighted concerns about deadlocked government, but related issues have grown even more significant in ensuing years. At this juncture, it appears that at least some government officials are no longer committed to telling the truth about facts affecting their constituents, or allowing those with expertise to share their knowledge in

times of public emergency. While the U.S. Congress seems most afflicted by such problems, there is clear evidence that state legislatures are adopting the congressional playbook by, for example, forbidding legislation that engages with issues of climate change and by limiting the extent to which facts and expertise (rather than opinion) can be brought to bear on public policy deliberations. With a new census on our doorstep, and incumbent protection a guiding force during redistricting, it is unclear whether there's "some way out of here" as Bob Dylan sang years ago.

- *Economic and racial disparities.* As noted in the Preface to the Eighth Edition, the last few years have witnessed growing division between the "1%" and everyone else. As the nation has experienced a growing concentration in wealth, the plight of those with limited means has increased. All levels of government will be called upon to maintain a "safety net" for those who lack the financial wherewithal to weather storms, or deal with basic necessities such as food and shelter. How such dilemmas are handled will determine what sort of nation the United States will be. Economic disparities have other implications and causes. In the spring of 2020 the nation exploded with protests about racial injustices evident in practices of some police departments, as well as in housing, schooling, and employment opportunities. Related issues are addressed throughout the book in coverage relating to state constitutions, municipal underbounding, government liability, voting rights and school finance.
- *Technology and community.* This issue was also noted in the Preface to the Eighth Edition. All levels of government have increasingly embraced advanced technology as a means of communicating with citizens and gathering their points of view. As technology advances, virtual communities may take the place of traditional meetings and face-to-face interaction. The courts have begun to grapple with such questions as how freedom of information laws should be interpreted, and how search and seizure requirements should be implemented. These new pressures may ultimately result in rebalancing of authority and financial frameworks at federal, state and local government levels.

Conventions and Thanks

Only selected footnotes from the cases and other reprinted materials are reproduced. These footnotes retain their original numbering. Ellipses are used within cases to indicate omitted textual material only and are not used to indicate deleted case citations. Internal citations to Supreme Court cases in reproduced decisions are cited only to the official reporter where available. Statutes cited and quoted in the text were current as of the date of publication, so dates are not given.

The authors wish to thank the following individuals:

- Diane D'Angelo, Legal Reference Librarian, Moakley Law Library, Suffolk University Law School for Professor Griffith.
- Susan deMaine, Associate Director and Lecturer in Law, Ruth Lilly Law Library, Indiana University Robert H. McKinney School of Law for Professor Baker.

We also wish to thank our colleagues who teach in this area across the country and our students who each year engage with us in addressing challenging legal and policy questions in hopes of building a better world.

DANIEL R. MANDELKER
JUDITH WELCH WEGNER
JANICE C. GRIFFITH
EVAN C. ZOLDAN
CYNTHIA A. BAKER

Part One

The Governmental System

Chapter 1

An Overview of State and Local Government in a Federal System

Introduction

State and Local Government Responses to the Mortgage Meltdown

A number of factors fueled the international economic crisis that began in 2008 and continues in significant respects today. The United States experienced a significant housing "bubble," as prices rose rapidly and as housing became viewed as a safe form of investment (rather than simply a place to live). Unsophisticated first-time homebuyers were lured to participate through aggressive lender practices (such as marketing of risky "subprime" loans with low down payments, high rates, hidden fees, and adjustable features). More experienced homebuyers were encouraged to establish and draw down "home equity loans" in order to purchase vacation homes or pay for other substantial expenses such as college tuition. Sophisticated investors were encouraged by investment banks and other financial advisers (who received substantial bonuses) to purchase shares in trusts holding pooled mortgage assets of varying quality, while ratings agencies closed their eyes to possible financial troubles ahead.

As mortgage interest rates rose (particularly when adjustable rates reset), mortgage defaults and foreclosures began to rise. Major investment institutions such as Lehman Brothers faltered when they could not sustain their financial positions in light of substantial holdings of subprime bonds. The economy softened further. Businesses began to shed jobs, unemployment rose, and credit became hard to get. The mortgage meltdown accelerated as many homeowners lost jobs or faced higher mortgage rates when adjustable mortgages reset. Even those who were better positioned found themselves "underwater" (that is, the cost of repaying their mortgages exceeded the market values of the homes they had purchased). They faced the quandary of trying to sell their homes in a declining market, covering unpaid principal out of pocket, or simply walking away in hopes lenders would not seek a personal recovery. Often, homeowners in distress fell into even more difficulties, as lenders refused to reduce principal due or agree to mortgage modifications. Property owners with mortgages held by investment trusts also found it impossible to locate or engage with the numerous parties with shares in related debt (who asserted they were entitled to full repayment of even risky loans and resisted bargaining for possible "workout" solutions).

Against this complex background, consider some of the questions posed by this Chapter and the course in state and local government as a whole:

Problem 1-1

Middletown is a middle-sized city, in the State of West Utopia that has seen a large number of mortgage defaults. Local property tax revenues have fallen substantially as homeowners have abandoned property and moved away, while lenders have delayed foreclosures in hopes that property values will gradually rise again and allow them to recoup more on their investments. Members of the city council are considering the following options:

> Requiring property owners and financial institutions with interests in real property to provide the town with contact information, carry insurance on the property, maintain the property in good condition, and keep all taxes and assessments current.
>
> Establishing a "land bank" that would employ the power of eminent domain to condemn selected abandoned residential properties for their current market value (which is less than remaining loan value), thereby clearing the property of mortgage debt. It would then resell the property at a lower current market rate (and repay the amount realized to the lender) in order to stabilize neighborhoods at risk of becoming derelict.
>
> Placing a "moratorium" on new "annexations" (expansion of municipal boundaries to encompass nearby land currently in county jurisdiction) and extension of public water and sewer services, because of declines in tax revenue and an unwillingness to absorb adjacent poor and minority areas given the fiscal problems currently facing the existing population.
>
> Suing major financial institutions in the state under a public nuisance theory because those institutions contributed to the dereliction of local property and loss of property tax and register of deeds revenues due to alleged deliberate action or gross negligence in targeting subprime loans to unsophisticated minority purchasers. They also failed to use due care in securing accurate ratings of mortgage securities in the city's public employee pension investment fund.

West Utopia's General Assembly has also been concerned about the mortgage meltdown and its legislators have a mix of views. Bills have been proposed that would:

> Require operating subsidiaries of all banks that do business in the state (including subsidiaries of nationally chartered banks) to register in the state and operate under state requirements.
>
> Prohibit high-interest loans by federally chartered banks, their subsidiaries, state chartered banks, credit unions, and all other lenders

(including payday lenders and lenders who specialize in automobile loans), even though such loans are not prohibited under federal law.

Prohibit the state's governor from applying for or accepting funds available from the federal government for economic development, until the governor approved legislation creating a consumer protection agency that would be responsible for establishing a mortgage refinance mediation program and would assist federal agencies in documenting instances of consumer abuse relating to home loans.

Consider which, if any, of these possible initiatives can be pursued consistent with the law and what questions you might ask to reach related conclusions. If Middletown were not a "home rule" city, could it take the proposed actions if state statutes authorized it to act on behalf of the "general welfare," to engage in "urban redevelopment," abate "public nuisances," or "maintain a secure pension fund"? Would it matter whether Middletown is a "home rule" city? Can Middletown decline to annex and bring public water and sewer to poor areas in light of its current plight? Would a claim of public nuisance be strengthened or weakened by concerns for minority purchasers or the pension fund?

Would the actions proposed by Middletown or West Utopia run risks of violating provisions of the state or federal constitutions? When is concurrent regulation by state and federal authorities appropriate? Would it matter if there were federal legislation authorizing certain activities by federally chartered banks (the National Bank Act authorizes federally chartered banks to engage in "real estate lending," and gives them "incidental powers" to carry on the business of banking, including conducting activities through operating subsidiaries)? What if federal regulations set specific standards for federally chartered banks and limited the power of states to regulate, but not regulate or constrain state action as to credit unions or other lenders?

What issues does the proposed legislation raise that would tie federal funds to creating a state agency with particular responsibilities and bar a state's Governor from accepting federal funds?

A. The Federal Government

The federal role. Students with previous courses in constitutional law are used to believing the federal government is the critical government in our federal system. That may be true to the extent the federal government is the central government in our governmental system, but it is not the central source of authority for state and local government. The federal government is a government of limited power as defined by the Constitution. It has no express constitutional authority to intervene or participate in state or local government matters, so any authority Congress can exercise over state or local matters comes either from the spending power, Art. I, § 8, cl. 1, or the power to regulate interstate commerce, Art. I, § 8, cl. 3. Congress also has the power to adopt laws to implement the Fourteenth Amendment. For discussion of congressional authority under the Commerce Clause, see *United States v. Lopez*, 514 U.S. 549 (1995).

The politics of federal intervention. The political landscape has changed. At one time, a Democratic-controlled Congress linked to counterpart city political machines set the national agenda for intervention in state and local affairs. Political rhetoric concentrated on inequality, such as the unequal distribution of fiscal resources in metropolitan areas among local governments. The great reform movements of the last century, such as school finance reform, arose out of this rhetoric.

Changing demographics and politics have changed the rhetoric and balance of political power. The largest group of Americans now lives in the suburbs and exurban areas, many of the large inner cities continue to decline, and population has shifted dramatically to the south and west. With the decline in national political strength of the larger cities, congressional attention to city problems has also declined. Bipartisan agreement has reduced federal financial aid to state and local governments, and has restructured that aid to deliver it with reduced federal influence. Some of the largest federal payments now take the form of payments to individuals, such as Social Security and Medicare.

Federal financial assistance affects state and local governments in a number of ways. At the state level, the common federal statutory requirement that states designate a single state agency to administer federal assistance shapes the organization of state governments. Similar responses occur at the local level, where special local government units form to provide the necessary statutory authority and fiscal powers to administer federally aided programs. Federal assistance also affects state and local budgeting and spending priorities. Conditions attached to federal assistance mandate federal requirements ranging from civil rights and equal opportunity responsibilities to minimum wage and maximum hour requirements. New state legislation and local ordinances are needed to provide the enabling authority to meet these conditions.

B. State Government

Structure and function. State government is essentially a mirror image of the federal government. There is a similar tripartite division of authority among legislative, administrative and judicial branches, and the separation of powers doctrine applies. There are differences, however. One is that state governments are governments of plenary, not limited, authority. They possess the full residual authority of governmental power, which they delegated up to the federal government in the federal Constitution, and which they can delegate down to local governments through the state constitution and state statutes. The role of the state in shaping local government is explained in a report by the former Advisory Commission on Intergovernmental Relations (ACIR):

> As decisionmakers for local governments, states determine—either through the state constitution, or by statute or charter—what local governments there will be; the proper allocation of powers to and among them; their functional assignments; their internal structure, organizations, and procedures for local operations; their fiscal options in regard to revenue, expenditures, and debt; the extent of the interlocal cooperation; how their boundaries can be expanded or contracted; and to some degree their land-use patterns. When one government exercises this kind of influence over others, its decisions affect those subordinate governments critically. [STATE AND LOCAL ROLES IN THE FEDERAL SYSTEM 151 (1982).]

State governments are also major service providers, and provide a majority of governmental expenditures in most states for highways, welfare, hospitals, health, natural resources, and corrections. Local governments may provide matching funds for some of these services, but the state share usually dominates.

State governments are much less centralized than the federal government. State governors are usually weaker than the President. In many states, there are elected boards or commissions that administer important government programs, such as the highway and transportation program. These boards and commissions create a multi-headed state executive, and are outside political control because they are not appointed by the governor. Major state officials, such as the auditor and attorney general, may also be separately elected and may not be of the same political party as the governor. Texas has 27 elected state officials, for example. Unlike the President, however, most governors can exercise a line item veto of budget items passed by the legislature.

Trends in state government. Major trends in state government include the modernization of many state constitutions and changes that have strengthened state governors. For a general survey, see Morehouse & Jewell, *States as Laboratories: A Reprise*, ANN. REV. POL. SCI. 7 (2004): 177–203, at 184–90. Governors in all but a few states now serve four-year terms. Almost all governors control the budget process and nearly all appoint their cabinet. A majority of the states have also carried out substantial administrative reorganizations. Gubernatorial authority has increased but has leveled off in recent years. See Beyle, *Being Governor, in* THE STATE OF THE STATES 53 (Van Horn, ed. 2006). This trend has become even more pronounced in an era in which the federal government has become notably dysfunctional. See Seifter, *Gubernatorial Administration*, 131 HARV. L. REV. 483 (2017). Professor Seifter argues that governors have increasingly acted to address pressing issues such as clean energy, voting rights, disaster relief and discrimination; and to mobilize state governments to support or redress federal actions in areas such as climate change. At the same time, Professor Seifter emphasizes that state agencies may require more oversight than has usually accorded them because of their relative lack of transparency, and the limited oversight available from local press and advocacy groups at the state level. See Seifter, *Further from the People? The Puzzle of State Administration*, 93 N.Y.U. L. Rev. 107 (2018).

State legislatures have also grown in strength. In most states they are no longer a "sometime government," meeting only a few weeks every other year, poorly paid, poorly staffed, and badly apportioned. Court decisions have required apportionment, and all states now have legislative reference libraries, legislative drafting services, and fiscal policy and review analysis. Legislative leadership is critical; most state legislative leaders have more power than their congressional counterparts and committee chairs have considerable control. Term limits, first introduced in the 1990s, may affect leadership roles. For a study finding that legislators believe there is a proper balance of power between legislators and the governor, see Bernick & Bernick, *Executive-Legislative Relations: Where You Sit Really Does Matter*, 89 Soc. Sci. Qtly. No. 4 (2008): 969–86. One of the most notable changes in the last decade has been the growing polarization within state legislatures. See Jordan & Bowling, *Introduction: The State of Polarization in the States*, 48 State & Local Gov't Rev. No. 4 (2016) 220–26 (summarizing symposium papers). The authors identify a growing pattern of single-party control (both houses of state legislatures and governors in individual jurisdictions), and the ascendency of Republican control, particularly following the 2010 Census. Polarization also leads to delays in budget decision-making. Individuals do not seem to disapprove of legislatures that are highly polarized if they share the views of those in control. A growing trend among state legislatures to preempt more progressive local ordinances both fosters and results from this polarization. See Phillips, *Impeding Innovation: State Preemption of Progressive Local Regulations*, 117 Colum. L. Rev. 2225 (2017).

State finance. The "Great Recession" that began in 2008 had a significant impact on state finances. A sharp decrease in tax revenues left many states with million- or billion-dollar budget deficits in 2009. The Center on Budget and Policy Priorities (CBPP) found that budget gaps resulted principally from weak tax collections, while health and education expenses continued to grow. See Oliff *et al.*, *States Continue to Feel Recession's Impact* (June 27, 2012), available at http://www.cbpp.org/cms/index.cfm?fa=view&id=711. There have been a number of post-mortems on the implications of the Great Recession and developments in its aftermath. See, e.g., Williamson, *Emerging from the Great Recession: The View from Local Government*, 46 State & Local Gov't Rev. No. 4 (2014) 232–35 (considering such options as "contracting out" of services, implications for property tax revenues, and spending choices); Alm & Sjoquist, *State Government Revenue Recovery from the Great Recession*, 46 State & Local Gov't Rev. No. 3 (2014) 164–72 (finding that some states have recovered revenue lost during the Great Recession, but that the pattern of recovery is mixed, with no clear explanation applicable to all states apart from general economic growth). The Pew Charitable Trusts concluded that states continue to live with the legacy of the "lost decade" between 2008 and 2018. https://www.pewtrusts.org/en/research-and-analysis/data-visualizations/2014/fiscal-50#ind0 (finding that state revenues are up, but personal income varies by locale, debt and unfunded pension costs loom, 10 states lacked sufficient revenue to cover costs, Medicaid costs raise flags in some places, 9 states lost population in 2018, and reliance on federal revenue sharing varies significantly as does tax volatility).

State constitutions. State constitutions differ significantly from the federal Constitution. State constitutions are generally longer than the federal Constitution, and some are much longer. They are more specific, and there may be many detailed provisions that even go into policy details usually handled by the legislature. For example, the Maryland Constitution addresses off-street parking. This specific listing of requirements and delegated authority affects the authority of state legislatures to enact laws. Like the federal constitution, the state constitutions also prescribe the basic governmental structure for the state, delegate authority to the state legislature and provide for the organization of local governments. The Virginia Constitution is an example:

> The General Assembly shall provide by general law for the organization, government, powers, change of boundaries, consolidation, and dissolution of counties, cities, towns, and regional governments. The General Assembly may also provide by general law optional plans of government for counties, cities, or towns to be effective if approved by a majority vote of the qualified voters voting on any such plan in any such county, city, or town. [VA. CONST. Art. VII, § 2.]

Because state legislatures have plenary power, they do not need to draw authority from the state constitution, but state constitutions can specify how delegated authority should be exercised. The Virginia Constitution, like many others, provides the following rule for the assessment of property for property taxes: "All assessments of real estate and tangible personal property shall be at their fair market value, to be ascertained as prescribed by law." VA. CONST. Art. X, § 2. The Virginia legislature and its local governments are restricted by this constitutional provision and may not adopt another measure of property tax assessment.

Notes and Questions

1. *Who does what?* An important threshold question is to decide how we should distribute authority among different government levels. One traditional basis for distributing governmental authority is to assign functions to governmental units that can capture the benefits of a governmental activity while at the same time accepting its costs. A local government would not be expected to accept the cost of raising an army, for example, because its benefits are more than local. The cost-benefit internalization criterion suggests that one way to allocate governmental responsibilities is to consider what economists call spillover effects. Providing local roads comes close to an activity whose costs and benefits are both recognized locally.

2. *The Winter Commission report and government reform.* An important report by the Winter Commission in 1993, the National Commission on the State and Local Public Service, HARD TRUTHS/TOUGH CHOICES: AN AGENDA FOR STATE AND LOCAL REFORM, recommended several reforms in state and local government. The following article summarizes the report's recommendations, and discusses whether they have been followed:

> The commission's recommendations targeted (1) the political context of state and local governance, with a particular focus on executive leadership, campaign finance reform, and citizen engagement; (2) the specifics of public administration, with primary emphasis on empowering managers through internal deregulation and bolstering human resource capacity; and (3) the nature of the relationship between the national government and the states in a key policy arena. Significant changes in the fabric of state and local governance have occurred in each of these three areas over the last 15 years. Many of these modifications are consonant with the thrust of the Winter Commission report, but [they are limited]. Further reform initiatives should be built on systematic efforts to advance knowledge concerning the origins, nature, and outcomes of the array of institutions and processes present at the state and local levels. [Thompson, *State and Local Governance Fifteen Years Later: Enduring and New Challenges*, 68 PUB. ADMIN. REV. (Nov. 2008): S8 (Abstract).]

3. *Centrist vs. dispersed authority.* State government is decentralized. Most commentators find fault with dispersed authority in state governments and argue that centralized structures, with more power in the governor, are preferable. Robinson, *The Role of the Independent Political Executive in State Governance: Stability in the Face of Change*, 58 PUB. ADMIN. REV. NO. 2 (1998): 119–28, takes a different view. Professor Robinson argues that the dispersal of authority to independent executives provides stability in state government, improves responsiveness, and guarantees diversity in opinion. By contrast, a centrist system in which a governor would have full appointment power would politicize the system because state executives would then mirror the political values of the chief executive. Can you think of any other advantages and disadvantages of a centrist governmental system?

The political issues arising out of the dispersal of power in state government arise at several places in this book, as in Chapter 5, which considers patronage discharges, and Chapter 10, which considers the role of the chief executive. Ask yourself, as you study these materials, whether greater centralization of power at the state level would change the way these outcomes are handled.

4. *The Advisory Commission on Intergovernmental Relations.* The Advisory Commission on Intergovernmental Relations (ACIR) was a congressionally created, federally funded agency that conducted important research on issues affecting state and local government. Its termination by Congress several years ago was unfortunate, and we cite studies done by the ACIR throughout this book.

C. Constitutional Limitations on State and Local Legislation

[1] Equal Protection and Substantive Due Process

Constitutional limitations must now be considered, because state and local legislation is subject to attack under federal and state constitutions when it applies to private entities and individuals. The constitutional limitations that most often apply in these cases are the Equal Protection and Due Process Clauses. Equal protection requires equal treatment and prohibits unreasonable classifications. The substantive element of due process requires legislation to advance a legitimate governmental interest. Due process issues can arise when courts consider whether a program of public spending serves a public purpose and whether a statute licensing trades and professions is constitutional. Equal protection issues arise throughout this casebook, especially in taxation and voting rights cases, and in state school finance programs. There are other examples. Consider the following:

- A state licensing statute provides that dental hygienists cannot do dental fillings.
- A local ordinance provides a lower pay scale for female nurses in city hospitals than it does for male nurses.
- A state statute restricts the vote in municipal bond elections to property owners.

These regulations may not be treated the same under the federal and state constitutions. A prohibition against special legislation included in most state constitutions is also an equal protection equivalent.

1. *The Federal Constitution: Equal Protection.* The Supreme Court has adopted a three-tiered set of judicial review standards it applies under the Equal Protection Clause. The standards a court applies will often determine the outcome in a case. One court has nicely summarized these standards:

> Equal protection claims under the Fourteenth Amendment to the United States Constitution are analyzed under a three tier approach. "A statute that regulates a 'fundamental right' or a 'suspect class' is subject to 'strict scrutiny.'" A statute regulating a "semi-suspect" class or substantially but indirectly affecting a fundamental right will be subject to "intermediate scrutiny." All other statutes are subject to rational basis scrutiny, meaning it must be "rationally related to the achievement of a legitimate state interest." [Citation omitted.] [*Brown v. State*, 811 A.2d 501, 505, 506 (N.J. L. Div. 2002).]

Rational basis. The rational basis standard applies to social and economic legislation, such as the licensing statute in the examples above. The *Brown* decision provided this explanation of rational basis judicial review:

> Statutes carry a strong presumption in favor of constitutionality, and the proponent of invalidity bears the heavy burden of overcoming that presumption. The Legislature has wide discretion in determining the perimeters of a classification. "In considering the constitutionality of legislation, courts do not weigh its efficacy or wisdom." "The problems of government are practical ones and may justify, if they do not require, rough accommodations—illogical, it may be, and unscientific." A court will not second guess the Legislature's policy decisions regarding the "intractable economic, social and philosophical problems presented by employee pension programs."
>
> Nor will "a classification . . . be set aside if any state of facts reasonably may be conceived to justify it." An adequate factual basis for the legislative judgment is presumed to exist. "A statute satisfies the rational basis test even if the classification it makes is imperfect." [Citations omitted.] [*Id.* at 506.]

This standard provides substantial judicial deference to legislative decisions. The court upheld an amendment to a pension system for firefighters and police officers that allowed only retirees to calculate their pension later if this would lead to an increase in the pension amount. The court accepted the legislative justification for the amendment, which was to preserve the fiscal integrity of the system by limiting the number of employees who could claim increased benefits.

Although the most lenient rational relationship standard of judicial review is highly deferential to government regulation, the Supreme Court has occasionally invalidated state and local legislation under this standard in what has been called equal protection review "with a bite." See *City of Cleburne v. Cleburne Living Center*, 473 U.S. 432 (1985) (invalidating denial of special use permit for group home for mentally retarded). However, the Court held in *Board of Trustees v. Garrett*, 531 U.S. 356 (2001), that *Cleburne* did not alter the traditional rational-basis review standard. See also Saphire, *Equal Protection, Rational Basis Review, and the Impact of Cleburne Living Center, Inc.*, 88 Ky. L.J. 591 (1999–2000). The *Cleburne* decision has a good discussion of the varying standards of judicial review.

> *Intermediate scrutiny.* The Supreme Court applies an intermediate "means-focused" equal protection review standard that lies between strict scrutiny and rational relationship review only to classifications based on gender, alienage, and illegitimacy. The second example given above is in this category. State courts seldom apply it. Gunther, *In Search of Evolving Doctrine on the Changing Court: A Model for a Newer Equal Protection*, 86 Harv. L. Rev. 1 (1972), is the best explanation of this intermediate standard. The New Mexico court has described the level of judicial review required by the intermediate scrutiny standard:

Intermediate scrutiny is the next level of equal protection analysis after rational basis scrutiny. The analysis is more probing and requires higher evidentiary burdens than rational basis scrutiny. For a statute to pass constitutional muster under intermediate scrutiny, the government must demonstrate that the classification is substantially related to an important government interest. The intermediate scrutiny standard is used to assess legislative classifications "infringing important but not fundamental rights, and involving sensitive but not suspect classes." [Citations omitted.] [*Trujillo v. City of Albuquerque*, 965 P.2d 305, 310 (N.M. 1998).]

The court, reversing an earlier case, upheld legislation placing a cap on damages awards, and held the intermediate scrutiny standard applied in an earlier case to invalidate such legislation was incorrect. The court held that the constitution's guarantee of access to the courts did not create a right to unlimited government tort liability that triggered intermediate scrutiny review. Rational basis review applied.

Strict scrutiny. Under strict scrutiny, a court will strike down legislation unless government can show it is precisely tailored to serve a compelling governmental interest. This rule means that there is a presumption against the legislation that is overcome only by a compelling interest to support it as well as by the closest possible fit between governmental means and purposes. Strict scrutiny applies when a classification is based on a suspect class or when it impairs the exercise of a fundamental constitutional right. The third example given above is in this category because the right to vote, which is a fundamental right, is improperly restricted to property ownership. Race is an example of a suspect class. A classification based on race is subject to strict scrutiny.

Catch-22. Though intended only to establish standards of judicial review, the multi-tiered federal structure has been a rigid Catch-22. Strict scrutiny is strict in theory but usually fatal in fact. Governments can rarely come up with a governmental interest that is so compelling that it can justify legislation subject to the strict scrutiny test. Rational basis review is theoretically minimal but in practice is deceptive. Legislation is rarely held unconstitutional under this review standard. Intermediate scrutiny was supposed to provide more flexibility in review standards, but the Court has not extended it beyond limited narrow categories.

2. *The Federal Constitution: Substantive Due Process.* The Fourteenth Amendment provides that no person shall be denied the due process of law. Due process has a procedural and substantive dimension. The substantive dimension means that legislation must serve a legitimate governmental purpose, but the Court has also applied a lenient standard to these claims. It has long retreated from its earlier aggressiveness in the *Lochner* era, see *Lochner v. State of New York*, 198 U.S. 45 (1905), where the Court struck down a law limiting hours of work. The following quotation sums up the Court's contemporary views on the application of substantive due process to legislative regulation:

> This Court beginning at least as early as 1934, . . . has steadily rejected the due process philosophy enunciated in [*Lochner* and similar cases]. In doing so it has consciously returned closer and closer to the earlier constitutional principle that states have power to legislate against what are found to be injurious practices in their internal commercial and business affairs,

> so long as their laws do not run afoul of some specific federal constitutional prohibition, or of some valid federal law. Under this constitutional doctrine the Due Process Clause is no longer to be so broadly construed that the Congress and state legislatures are put in a strait jacket when they attempt to suppress business and industrial conditions which they regard as offensive to the public welfare. [*Lincoln Federal Labor Union v. Northwestern Iron & Metal Co.*, 335 U.S. 525, 536–537 (1949) (upholding Right-to-Work law).]

In cases involving executive, rather than legislative, action the Court has adopted an equally deferential "shocks the conscience" test. *City of Cuyahoga Falls v. Buckeye Community Hope Foundation*, 538 U.S. 188 (2003) (rejecting challenge against referendum on affordable housing project). Many state courts follow the Supreme Court's lead and take a similarly deferential view when legislation is challenged as a violation of substantive due process. See *Board of County Comm'rs v. Crow*, 65 P.3d 720, 727–28 (Wyo. 2003) (upholding ordinance limiting size of dwellings). For discussion of recent trends, see Hacker, *The Return to Lochnerism? The Revival of Economic Liberties from David to Goliath*, 52 DePaul L. Rev. 675, 686 (2002). It is important to remember that socially beneficial legislation is sometimes attacked as unconstitutional, and that deferential review protects its constitutionality. See *Kaveny v. Town of Cumberland Zoning Bd. of Review*, 875 A.2d 1 (R.I. 2005) (upholding low- and moderate-income housing act).

For an argument that the modern interpretation of rational basis review fails adequately to describe relevant history and application of related doctrine, see Eyer, *The Canon of Rational Basis Review*, 93 Notre Dame L. Rev. 1317 (2018). Professor Eyer argues that modern review of rational basis review has lost the doctrine's nuanced history, and that history includes a range of more meaningful forms of review. In her view, contemporary portrayals fail to adequately describe how social movements achieve meaningful review under equal protection principles, misdescribe cases involving successful rational basis review by portraying them as only "purporting" to apply such review, ignore the range of lower, state court, and legislative decisions, and oversimplify related review.

3. *State Constitutions.* A substantial number of state courts have not adopted the deferential view the Supreme Court takes to economic legislation. This has occurred in substantive due process and equal protection cases. The following excerpt from a Pennsylvania decision indicates why some state courts have rejected the Court's views on substantive due process. The Pennsylvania court held unconstitutional a state law prohibiting drug price advertising. What criteria did the court use to hold these statutes unconstitutional?

> While . . . in the federal courts the "due process barrier to substantive legislation as to economic matters has been in effect removed," the same cannot be said with respect to state courts and state constitutional law. This difference between federal and state constitutional law represents a sound development, one which takes into account the fact that "state courts

may be in a better position to review local economic legislation than the Supreme Court. State courts, since their precedents are not of national authority, may better adapt their decisions to local economic conditions and needs. . . . And where an industry is of basic importance to the economy of a state or territory, extraordinary regulations may be necessary and proper." Hetherington, *State Economic Regulation and Substantive Due Process of Law*, 53 Nw. U. L. Rev. 226, 250 (1958) (footnote omitted).

Thus Pennsylvania, like other state "economic laboratories," see *New State Ice Co. v. Liebmann*, 285 U.S. 262, 280–311 (1932) (Brandeis, J., dissenting), has scrutinized regulatory legislation perhaps more closely than would the Supreme Court of the United States. We have held unconstitutional, for example, an act regulating car rental agencies as a public utility, see *Hertz Drivurself Stations, Inc. v. Siggins*, 58 A.2d 464 (Pa. 1948), an act forbidding gasoline stations from displaying price signs in excess of a certain prescribed size, see *Gambone v. Commonwealth*, 101 A.2d 634 (Pa. 1954), an act forbidding the sale of carbonated beverages made with sucaryl, see *Cott Beverage Corp. v. Horst*, 110 A.2d 405 (Pa. 1955), an act forbidding the sale of ice-milk shakes, see *Commonwealth ex rel. Woodside v. Sun Ray Drug Co.*, 116 A.2d 833 (Pa. 1955), and an act forbidding nonsigners from selling fair traded items below the price specified in price maintenance contracts, see *Olin Mathieson Chemical Corp. v. White Cross Stores, Inc.*, 199 A.2d 266 (Pa. 1964).

Through all these cases we have been guided by the proposition that "a law which purports to be an exercise of the police power must not be unreasonable, unduly oppressive or patently beyond the necessities of the case, and the means which it employs must have a real and substantial relation to the objects sought to be attained." *Gambone v. Commonwealth*, 101 A.2d at 637. It is with this test, and the above principles, in mind that we now move to consider the constitutionality of the instant statute. [*Pennsylvania State Bd. of Pharmacy v. Pastor*, 272 A.2d 487, 490–91 (Pa. 1971).]

More rigorous application of state constitutional guarantees was advocated by Supreme Court Justice William Brennan in an influential article. Brennan, *State Constitutions and the Protection of Individual Rights*, 90 Harv. L. Rev. 489 (1977). The Supreme Court cited Brennan in a case that recognized this state court option:

As a number of recent state court decisions demonstrate, a state court is entirely free to read its own constitution more broadly than this Court reads the federal Constitution, or to reject the mode of analysis used by this Court in favor of a different analysis of its corresponding constitutional guarantee. [*City of Mesquite v. Aladdin's Castle, Inc.*, 455 U.S. 283, 293 (1982).]

State courts have also been uncomfortable with the Supreme Court's three-tiered system of equal protection review and its refusal to extend strict scrutiny review to legislation affecting other classes that might be suspect. The following case is an example:

Baker v. State

744 A.2d 864 (Vt. 1999)

AMESTOY, C.J.

May the State of Vermont exclude same-sex couples from the benefits and protections that its laws provide to opposite-sex married couples? That is the fundamental question we address in this appeal, a question that the Court well knows arouses deeply-felt religious, moral, and political beliefs. Our constitutional responsibility to consider the legal merits of issues properly before us provides no exception for the controversial case. The issue before the Court, moreover, does not turn on the religious or moral debate over intimate same-sex relationships, but rather on the statutory and constitutional basis for the exclusion of same-sex couples from the secular benefits and protections offered married couples.

We conclude that under the Common Benefits Clause of the Vermont Constitution, which, in pertinent part, reads,

> That government is, or ought to be, instituted for the common benefit, protection, and security of the people, nation, or community, and not for the particular emolument or advantage of any single person, family, or set of persons, who are a part only of that community....

Vt. Const., ch. I, art. 7, plaintiffs may not be deprived of the statutory benefits and protections afforded persons of the opposite sex who choose to marry. [The trial court held the state's marriage statutes could not be construed to permit the issuance of a marriage license to same-sex couples and, as so read, were constitutional. The supreme court reversed.] We hold that the State is constitutionally required to extend to same-sex couples the common benefits and protections that flow from marriage under Vermont law....

II. The Constitutional Claim

Assuming that the marriage statutes preclude their eligibility for a marriage license, plaintiffs contend that the exclusion violates their right to the common benefit and protection of the law guaranteed by Chapter I, Article 7 of the Vermont Constitution....

In considering this issue, it is important to emphasize at the outset that it is the Common Benefits Clause of the Vermont Constitution we are construing, rather than its counterpart, the Equal Protection Clause of the Fourteenth Amendment to the United States Constitution. It is altogether fitting and proper that we do so. Vermont's constitutional commitment to equal rights was the product of the successful effort to create an independent republic and a fundamental charter of government, the Constitution of 1777, both of which preceded the adoption of the Fourteenth Amendment by nearly a century. As we explained in *State v. Badger*, 450 A.2d 336,

347 (Vt. 1982), "our constitution is not a mere reflection of the federal charter. Historically and textually, it differs from the United States Constitution. It predates the federal counterpart, as it extends back to Vermont's days as an independent republic. It is an independent authority, and Vermont's fundamental law."

As we explain in the discussion that follows, the Common Benefits Clause of the Vermont Constitution differs markedly from the federal Equal Protection Clause in its language, historical origins, purpose, and development. While the federal amendment may thus supplement the protections afforded by the Common Benefits Clause, it does not supplant it as the first and primary safeguard of the rights and liberties of all Vermonters. . . .

A. Historical Development

In understanding the import of the Common Benefits Clause, this Court has often referred to principles developed by the federal courts in applying the Equal Protection Clause. At the same time, however, we have recognized that "although the provisions have some similarity of purpose, they are not identical." *Benning v. State*, 641 A.2d 757, 764 n.7 (Vt. 1994). Indeed, recent Vermont decisions reflect a very different approach from current federal jurisprudence. That approach may be described as broadly deferential to the legislative prerogative to define and advance governmental ends, while vigorously ensuring that the means chosen bear a just and reasonable relation to the governmental objective.

Although our decisions over the last few decades have routinely invoked the rhetoric of suspect class favored by the federal courts, there are notable exceptions. The principal decision in this regard is the landmark case of *State v. Ludlow Supermarkets, Inc.*, 448 A.2d 791 (Vt. 1982). There, Chief Justice Albert Barney, writing for the Court, invalidated a Sunday closing law that discriminated among classes of commercial establishments on the basis of their size. After noting that this Court, unlike its federal counterpart, was not constrained by considerations of federalism and the impact of its decision on fifty varying jurisdictions, the Court declared that Article 7 "only allows the statutory classifications . . . if a case of necessity can be established overriding the prohibition of Article 7 by reference to the "'common benefit, protection, and security of the people.'" *Id.* at 795. Applying this test, the Court concluded that the State's justifications for the disparate treatment of large and small businesses failed to withstand constitutional scrutiny. *Id.*

Ludlow, as we later explained, did not alter the traditional requirement under Article 7 that legislative classifications must "reasonably relate to a legitimate public purpose." *Choquette* [*v. Perrault*, 569 A.2d 455, 459 (Vt. 1989)]. Nor did it overturn the principle that the justifications demanded of the State may depend upon the nature and importance of the benefits and protections affected by the legislation; indeed, this is implicit in the weighing process. It did establish that Article 7 would require a "more stringent" reasonableness inquiry than was generally associated with rational basis review under the federal constitution. *Ludlow* did not override the traditional deference accorded legislation having any reasonable relation to a legitimate public purpose. It simply signaled that Vermont courts—having "access to specific legislative history and all other proper resources" to evaluate the object and effect of state laws—would engage in a meaningful, case-specific analysis to ensure that any exclusion from the general benefit and protection of the law would bear a just and reasonable relation to the legislative goals.

Although it is accurate to point out that since *Ludlow* our decisions have consistently recited the federal rational-basis/strict-scrutiny tests, it is equally fair to observe that we have been less than consistent in their application. Just as commentators have noted the United States Supreme Court's obvious yet unstated deviations from the rational-basis standard, so have this Court's holdings often departed from the federal test....

Thus, "labels aside," Vermont case law has consistently demanded in practice that statutory exclusions from publicly-conferred benefits and protections must be "premised on an appropriate and overriding public interest." *Ludlow*, 448 A.2d at 795. The rigid categories utilized by the federal courts under the Fourteenth Amendment find no support in our early case law and, while routinely cited, are often effectively ignored in our more recent decisions.... The balancing approach utilized in *Ludlow* and implicit in our recent decisions reflects the language, history, and values at the core of the Common Benefits Clause. We turn, accordingly, to a brief examination of constitutional language and history.

B. Text

...

The words of the Common Benefits Clause are revealing. While they do not, to be sure, set forth a fully-formed standard of analysis for determining the constitutionality of a given statute, they do express broad principles which usefully inform that analysis. Chief among these is the principle of inclusion.... The affirmative right to the "common benefits and protections" of government and the corollary proscription of favoritism in the distribution of public "emoluments and advantages" reflect the framers' overarching objective "not only that everyone enjoy equality before the law or have an equal voice in government but also that everyone have *an equal share in the fruits of the common enterprise.*" W. Adams, The First American Constitutions 188 (1980) (emphasis added).... Thus, at its core the Common Benefits Clause expressed a vision of government that afforded every Vermonter its benefit and protection and provided no Vermonter particular advantage.

C. Historical Context

Although historical research yields little direct evidence of the framers' intentions, an examination of the ideological origins of the Common Benefits Clause casts a useful light upon the inclusionary principle at its textual core. Like other provisions of the Vermont Constitution of 1777, the Common Benefits Clause was borrowed verbatim from the Pennsylvania Constitution of 1776, which was based, in turn, upon a similar provision in the Virginia Declaration of Rights of 1776. . . .

Although aimed at Great Britain, the American Revolution—as numerous historians have noted—also tapped deep-seated domestic antagonisms. The planter elite in Virginia, the proprietors of Eastern Pennsylvania, and New Yorkers claiming Vermont lands were each the object of long-standing grievances. . . . While not opposed to the concept of a social elite, the framers of the first state constitutions believed that it should consist of a "natural aristocracy" of talent, rather than an entrenched clique favored by birth or social connections. As the preeminent historian of the ideological origins of the Revolution explained, "while 'equality before the law' was a commonplace of the time, 'equality without respect to the dignity of the persons concerned' was not; [the Revolution's] emphasis on social equivalence was significant." B. Bailyn, The Ideological Origins of the American Revolution 307 (1967). . . .

Vermont was not immune to the disruptive forces unleashed by the Revolution. . . . [T]he Pennsylvania Constitution's egalitarianism was arguably eclipsed the following year by the Vermont Constitution of 1777. In addition to the commitment to government for the "common benefit, protection, and security," it contained novel provisions abolishing slavery, eliminating property qualifications for voting, and calling for the governor, lieutenant governor, and twelve councilors to be elected by the people rather than appointed by the legislature. These and other provisions have led one historian to observe that Vermont's first charter was the "most democratic constitution produced by any of the American states." R. Shalhope, Bennington and the Green Mountain Boys: The Emergence of Liberal Democracy in Vermont 1760–1850 172 (1996). . . .

The concept of equality at the core of the Common Benefits Clause was not the eradication of racial or class distinctions, but rather the elimination of artificial governmental preferments and advantages. The Vermont Constitution would ensure that the law uniformly afforded every Vermonter its benefit, protection, and security so that social and political preeminence would reflect differences of capacity, disposition, and virtue, rather than governmental favor and privilege. . . .

D. Analysis Under Article 7

. . . .

We must ultimately ascertain whether the omission of a part of the community from the benefit, protection and security of the challenged law bears a reasonable and just relation to the governmental purpose. Consistent with the core presumption of inclusion, factors to be considered in this determination may include: (1) the significance of the benefits and protections of the challenged law; (2) whether the omission of members of the community from the benefits and protections of the challenged law promotes the government's stated goals; and (3) whether the classification is significantly underinclusive or overinclusive. . . .

[The court next quoted from a Supreme Court opinion by Justice Souter, where he stated that the adjudication of constitutional claims calls for the assessment of the weights and dignities of competing interests as informed by history and tradition. Ultimately, what is required is an exercise of "reasoned judgment."] The balance between individual liberty and organized society which courts are continually called upon to weigh does not lend itself to the precision of a scale. It is, indeed, a recognition of the imprecision of "reasoned judgment" that compels both judicial restraint and respect for tradition in constitutional interpretation.

E. The Standard Applied

With these general precepts in mind, we turn to the question of whether the exclusion of same-sex couples from the benefits and protections incident to marriage under Vermont law contravenes Article 7. The first step in our analysis is to identify the nature of the statutory classification. As noted, the marriage statutes apply expressly to opposite-sex couples. Thus, the statutes exclude anyone who wishes to marry someone of the same sex.

Next, we must identify the governmental purpose or purposes to be served by the statutory classification. The principal purpose the State advances in support of the excluding same-sex couples from the legal benefits of marriage is the government's interest in "furthering the link between procreation and child rearing." The State has a strong interest, it argues, in promoting a permanent commitment between couples who have children to ensure that their offspring are considered legitimate and receive ongoing parental support. The State contends, further, that the Legislature could reasonably believe that sanctioning same-sex unions "would diminish society's perception of the link between procreation and child rearing . . . [and] advance the notion that fathers or mothers . . . are mere surplusage to the functions of procreation and child rearing." The State argues that since same-sex couples cannot conceive a child on their own, state-sanctioned same-sex unions "could be seen by the Legislature to separate further the connection between procreation and parental responsibilities for raising children." Hence, the Legislature is justified, the State concludes, "in using the marriage statutes to send a public message that procreation and child rearing are intertwined."

Do these concerns represent valid public interests that are reasonably furthered by the exclusion of same-sex couples from the benefits and protections that flow from the marital relation? It is beyond dispute that the State has a legitimate and long-standing interest in promoting a permanent commitment between couples for the security of their children. It is equally undeniable that the State's interest has been advanced by extending formal public sanction and protection to the union, or marriage, of those couples considered capable of having children, i.e., men and women. And there is no doubt that the overwhelming majority of births today continue to result from natural conception between one man and one woman.

It is equally undisputed that many opposite-sex couples marry for reasons unrelated to procreation, that some of these couples never intend to have children, and that others are incapable of having children. Therefore, if the purpose of the statutory exclusion of same-sex couples is to "further[] the link between procreation and child rearing," it is significantly under-inclusive. The law extends the benefits and protections of marriage to many persons with no logical connection to the stated governmental goal.

Furthermore, while accurate statistics are difficult to obtain, there is no dispute that a significant number of children today are actually being raised by same-sex parents, and that increasing numbers of children are being conceived by such parents through a variety of assisted-reproductive techniques. Thus, with or without the marriage sanction, the reality today is that increasing numbers of same-sex couples are employing increasingly efficient assisted-reproductive techniques to conceive and raise children. The Vermont Legislature has not only recognized this reality, but has acted affirmatively to remove legal barriers so that same-sex couples may legally adopt and rear the children conceived through such efforts . . . [and] has also acted to expand the domestic relations laws to safeguard the interests of same-sex parents and their children when such couples terminate their domestic relationship.

Therefore, to the extent that the state's purpose in licensing civil marriage was, and is, to legitimize children and provide for their security, the statutes plainly exclude many same-sex couples who are no different from opposite-sex couples with respect to these objectives. If anything, the exclusion of same-sex couples from the legal protections incident to marriage exposes their children to the precise risks that the State argues the marriage laws are designed to secure against. In short, the marital exclusion treats persons who are similarly situated for purposes of the law, differently. . . . [The court then held the state had offered no "persuasive reasoning" for a claim "that because same-sex couples cannot conceive a child on their own, their exclusion promotes a 'perception of the link between procreation and child rearing,' and that to discard it would 'advance the notion that mothers and fathers . . . are mere surplusage to the functions of procreation and child rearing.'" The court then discussed a number of statutes that give protection to marriage and continued:]

While other statutes could be added to this list, the point is clear. The legal benefits and protections flowing from a marriage license are of such significance that any statutory exclusion must necessarily be grounded on public concerns of sufficient weight, cogency, and authority that the justice of the deprivation cannot seriously be questioned. Considered in light of the extreme logical disjunction between the classification and the stated purposes of the law—protecting children and "furthering the link between procreation and child rearing"—the exclusion falls substantially short of this standard. The laudable governmental goal of promoting a commitment between married couples to promote the security of their children and the community as a whole provides no reasonable basis for denying the legal benefits and protections of marriage to same-sex couples, who are no differently situated with respect to this goal than their opposite-sex counterparts. Promoting a link between procreation and childrearing similarly fails to support the exclusion. We turn, accordingly, to the remaining interests identified by the State in support of the statutory exclusion. . . .

The most substantive of the State's remaining claims relates to the issue of childrearing. It is conceivable that the Legislature could conclude that opposite-sex partners offer advantages in this area, although we note that child-development experts disagree and the answer is decidedly uncertain. The argument, however, contains a more fundamental flaw, and that is the Legislature's endorsement of a policy diametrically at odds with the State's claim. In 1996, the Vermont General Assembly enacted, and the Governor signed, a law removing all prior legal barriers to the adoption of children by same-sex couples. At the same time, the Legislature provided additional legal protections in the form of court-ordered child support and parent-child contact in the event that same-sex parents dissolved their "domestic relationship." In light of these express policy choices, the State's arguments that Vermont public policy favors opposite-sex over same-sex parents or disfavors the use of artificial reproductive technologies are patently without substance.

Similarly, the State's argument that Vermont's marriage laws serve a substantial governmental interest in maintaining uniformity with other jurisdictions cannot be reconciled with Vermont's recognition of unions, such as first-cousin marriages, not uniformly sanctioned in other states. . . .

The State's remaining claims (*e.g.*, recognition of same-sex unions might foster marriages of convenience or otherwise affect the institution in "unpredictable" ways) may be plausible forecasts as to what the future may hold, but cannot reasonably be construed to provide a reasonable and just basis for the statutory exclusion. The State's conjectures are not, in any event, susceptible to empirical proof before they occur. [The court then rejected a claim by the state "that the long history of official intolerance of intimate same-sex relationships cannot be reconciled with an interpretation of Article 7 that would give state-sanctioned benefits and protection to individuals of the same sex who commit to a permanent domestic relationship."]

F. Remedy

. . . .

[In discussing an appropriate remedy the court held that]

While the State's prediction of "destabilization" cannot be a ground for denying relief, it is not altogether irrelevant. A sudden change in the marriage laws or the statutory benefits traditionally incidental to marriage may have disruptive and unforeseen consequences. Absent legislative guidelines defining the status and rights same-sex couples, consistent with constitutional requirements, uncertainty and confusion could result. Therefore, we hold that the current statutory scheme shall remain in effect for a reasonable period of time to enable the Legislature to consider and enact implementing legislation in an orderly and expeditious fashion....

JUSTICE DOOLEY concurring in part and dissenting in part

[Justices Dooley and Johnson each wrote extensive separate opinions in which they concurred in part and dissented in part. Justice Dooley noted the court had rejected the federal three-tier standard for equal protection review and commented:]

It is ironic that in a civil rights case we overrule our precedent requiring the State to meet a higher burden in civil rights cases, but still conclude, under the lower standard, that the State has not met its burden....

The effect of the majority decision is that the State now bears no higher burden to justify discrimination against African-Americans or women than it does to justify discrimination against large retail stores as in *Ludlow*. I doubt that the framers of our Constitution, concerned with preventing the equivalent of British royalty, would believe that the inevitable line-drawing that must occur in economic regulation should be equated with the denial of civil and human rights. I do not believe that the new standard is required by, or even consistent with, the history on which the majority bases it.

Notes and Questions

1. *State court views on an independent state constitutional jurisprudence.* The Vermont court later qualified *Baker*, holding that the plaintiffs had put too much emphasis on the word "necessary" in that decision. "Indeed, an inquiry into necessity would contravene the deference which must control our inquiry and place us in the position of reviewing the wisdom of legislative choices." *Badgley v. Walton*, 10 A.3d 469, 478 (Vt. 2010) (upholding exception to Fair Employment Practices Act for law enforcement officers that required them to retire at age 55, notwithstanding claim that such requirements violated the "common benefit clause" central to *Baker*).

Other state courts declined to follow federal doctrine on equal protection. The Alaska court, in a case invalidating personnel regulations that gave an absolute hiring preference to persons who had resided in the state for at least one year, specifically adopted a more stringent rational basis test.

> Under the rational basis test, in order for a classification to survive judicial scrutiny, the classification 'must be reasonable, not arbitrary, and must rest upon some ground of difference having a fair and substantial relation to the object of the legislation, so that all persons similarly circumstanced shall be treated alike.' [Citing cases.] [*State v. Wylie*, 516 P.2d 142, 145 (Alaska 1973).]

The court retained the strict scrutiny test as developed by the U.S. Supreme Court. Yet, in later cases, the Alaska court has treated the state constitution as providing more extensive protection than the federal constitution. See, e.g., *Brewer v. State*, 341 P.3d 1107 (Alaska 2014) (interpreting state takings clause to provide greater protection to property owners than the federal Takings Clause). Are there particular reasons that state courts might interpret state constitutional provisions unrelated to equal protection more stringently?

Some courts that rejected the federal multi-tiered approach have adopted a flexible balancing test:

> The crucial issue under New Jersey case law is "'whether there is an appropriate governmental interest suitably furthered by the differential treatment'" involved. Three factors considered under this balancing test are 'the nature of the affected right, the extent to which the governmental restriction intrudes upon it, and the public need for the restriction.' Our equal protection analysis requires "'a real and substantial relationship between the classification and the governmental purpose which it purportedly serves.'" [Citing cases.] [*Rutgers Council of AAUP Chapters v. Rutgers*, 689 A.2d 828, 832–33 (N.J. 1997).]

The Louisiana Supreme Court rejected the U.S. Supreme Court's multi-tiered approach for equal protection cases and adopted its own categories in which courts should strike down statutes because of classifications adopted by statute. For example, "[w]hen the statute classifies persons on the basis of birth, age, sex, culture, physical condition, or political ideas or affiliations, its enforcement shall be refused unless the state or other advocate of the classification shows that the classification has a reasonable basis." *State v. Expunged Record 249,044*, 881 So. 2d 104, 110 (La. 2004).

These tests elevate judicial scrutiny when legislation is challenged as unconstitutional. Review the three examples given at the beginning of this section and decide how they would be decided under each of these formulations. Many state courts do not agree with this approach. For a case reviewing the history of state judicial activism and refusing to apply a state substantive due process clause to invalidate economic legislation, see *Alabama Power Co. v. Citizens of Alabama*, 740 So. 2d 371, 381 (Ala. 1999): "The lessons of our federal counterpart's activist substantive-due-process experiment are clear. The Constitution of Alabama of 1901 does not vest the Judiciary with the essentially legislative power to reevaluate the broad policy considerations inherent in crafting economic policy."

2. *Approaches to applying state constitutions.* Three approaches to interpreting state constitutional law have been identified—lockstep, primacy and interstitial. The lockstep approach does not give state constitutions an independent interpretation. Under the primacy approach, a court does not examine the federal Constitution if the right is protected under the state constitution, and applies the federal Constitution if the right is not protected under state law. Here is a statement from the New Hampshire Supreme Court on how this approach is applied:

> Since *State v. Ball*, 471 A.2d 347 (N.H. 1983), we have consistently followed the "primacy" approach to adjudication of constitutional issues. This means that when a defendant specifically invokes the State Constitution, we will consider those constitutional claims before addressing federal claims. Nonetheless, decisions from the United States Supreme Court are important in our State constitutional analysis. We scrutinize these decisions and, if they are logically persuasive and well reasoned, paying due regard to precedent and policies underlying specific constitutional guarantees, such decisions may properly claim persuasive weight as guideposts when interpreting State constitutional guarantees. As our former colleague, Justice Souter, observed, "If we place too much reliance on federal precedent we will render the State rules a mere row of shadows; if we place too little, we will render State practice incoherent." *State v. Bradberry*, 522 A.2d 1380 (N.H. 1986) (Souter, J., concurring). [*State v. Beauchesne*, 868 A.2d 972, 975–976 (N.H. 2005).]

Accord, *American Legion Post No. 149 v. Department of Health*, 192 P.3d 306, 324 (Wash. 2008).

Under the interstitial approach

> [A] party must fairly invoke a ruling that our constitution provides greater protection than its federal counterpart. If the relevant state constitutional provision has previously been interpreted to provide greater rights, the litigant need only: "(1) assert[] the constitutional principle that provides the protection sought under the New Mexico Constitution, and (2) show[] the factual basis needed for the trial court to rule on the issue." Where, however, there is no established precedent for interpreting the relevant state constitutional provision differently from its federal counterpart, "a party also must assert in the trial court that the state constitutional provision at issue should be interpreted more expansively than the federal counterpart and provide reasons for interpreting the state provision differently from the federal provision." [Citations omitted.] [*Maso v. State Taxation & Revenue Dep't*, 96 P.3d 286, 288 (N.M. 2004).]

How does the interstitial approach differ from the judicial review tests adopted in *Baker* and the cases discussed in Note 1? How would it be applied to the examples given at the beginning of this section? For an extensive discussion by the Wyoming Supreme Court applying interstitial reasoning, see *In re Neely v. Wyoming Comm'n on Judicial Conduct and Ethics*, 390 P.3d 728, (Wyo. 2017) (examining Wyoming Constitution's freedom of religion provisions and contrasting them with those in the federal Constitution, but declining to find state constitution controlling in case involving magistrate judge who declined to marry same-sex couples based on her religious beliefs). For a scholarly justification of active interpretation of state constitutions rather than lockstep deference, see Boldt & Friedman, *Constitutional*

Incorporation: A Consideration of the Judicial Function in State and Federal Constitutional Interpretation, 76 Md. L. Rev. 309 (2017).

3. *Court decisions and statutes on same-sex marriage after Baker.* It may seem that same-sex marriages were destined to be recognized and that *Baker* simply acknowledged the now-prevailing view. But *Baker*, with its reliance on the state constitution, was a harbinger that led to actions by other state courts in relying on their own constitutions to reach similar results, well before the United States Supreme Court reached a similar conclusion. See, e.g., *Goodridge v. Dep't of Pub. Health*, 798 N.E.2d 941 (Mass. 2003); *Kerrigan v. Comm'r of Pub. Health*, 957 A.2d 407 (Conn. 2008); *Varnum v. Brien*, 763 N.W.2d 862 (Iowa 2009). Vermont became the first state to recognize same-sex marriages by statute. Vt. Stat. Ann. tit. 15, § 8. Other states followed, including New Hampshire, New York, and Rhode Island, while yet others took opposing views.

In June 2015, a divided United States Supreme Court reached a result similar to that in *Baker* under the federal Constitution. *Obergefell v. Hodges*, 135 S. Ct. 2584 (2015). Justice Kennedy's controlling opinion rested on both due process and equal protection grounds. In his due process analysis, Justice Kennedy concluded that marriage is a fundamental right for four major reasons. In his view, the right to personal choice regarding marriage is inherent in the concept of individual autonomy. In addition, the right to marry is fundamental because it supports a two-person union unlike any other in its importance to the committed individuals. The right to marry is also protected as a means of safeguarding children and families, and draws meaning from related rights of childbearing, procreation, and education. It is also important in protecting children from the stigma of being raised in a "lesser" family whose adults are not allowed to marry. Justice Kennedy also explained that since marriage is a keystone to the country's social order, and states have treated it as a central principle, same-sex couples cannot be locked out of this central institution. Turning to equal protection analysis, he explained that same-sex couples wishing to marry may not be prohibited from enjoying the benefits and rights associated with marriage. The Court ultimately held that states must allow same-sex couples to marry and recognize marriages of same-sex couples that had previously been recognized in other states. Notably, *Obergefell* build upon the earlier decision in *United States v. Windsor*, 133 S. Ct. 2675 (2013), which had struck down the federal Defense of Marriage Act in part on federalism grounds. *Windsor* had concluded that the DOMA legislation reflected deliberate action by Congress to intervene in a punitive way to deny states' longstanding role in defining marriage and addressing family issues (by allowing other states to deny marriages sanctioned by fellow states) and to purposely and irrationally disadvantage same-sex married couples authorized to marry under state law.

A Note on Whether an Independent State Constitutional Law Is Justified or Necessary

Though some state courts have been willing to provide an independent interpretation of state constitutions, a respectable number have not, and so an important question is whether a state constitutional law is justified. This issue raises important questions of federalism and the role of states and the federal government in our federal system that is the focus of this book. Gardner, *The Failed Discourse of State Constitutionalism*, 90 Mich. L. Rev. 761 (1992), is a well-known broadside attack arguing that state constitutional law is unprincipled and that a separate state constitutional law is not justified by the distinctiveness of state constitutions. He claimed that principles of federalism and congruity in the interpretation of constitutional limitations argued against differences in state constitutional law, and that the inclusion of statutory detail in state constitutions and the frequency with which they are amended argued against a separate state constitutional law. He also contended, "the communities in theory defined by state constitutions simply do not exist, and debating the meaning of a state constitution does not involve defining an identity that any group would recognize as its own."

State constitutionalism and the Gardner article have spawned a vast literature, and the justifications for an independent state constitutional law in rebuttal to the Gardner thesis vary considerably. One commentator has stated the most common justification for the "judicial federalism" that underlies an independent state constitutional law:

> Most arguments in favor of judicial federalism arise from a strong belief in the basic principle of constitutional federalism: The idea that state courts are legitimately the final arbiters of the meaning of their own constitutions and need not defer to federal decisions when interpreting them. Advocates of judicial federalism argue that too much deference to the Supreme Court reflects an insufficient appreciation of state sovereignty. State courts must, they claim, interpret their state constitutions independently rather than taking a 'relational' approach centering on Supreme Court jurisprudence. [Note, *Neither Icarus Nor Ostrich: State Constitutions as an Independent Source of Individual Rights*, 79 N.Y.U. L. Rev. 1833, 1841 (2004).]

Rodriquez, *State Constitutional Theory and Its Prospects*, 28 N. Mex. L. Rev. 271 (1998), provides another perspective. The author noted that one important difference between the federal and state constitutions is that the state constitutions are constitutions of limitation, not grant. This issue is explored elsewhere in this Chapter. Rodriguez concluded this difference means "public policymaking in state government is, on the whole, a much richer, expansive pro-active enterprise than the national government." *Id.* at 293. He added:

> Given the absence of the principle of limited government in the state constitutional system, the responsibility falls even more squarely than at the

> federal level on judges to evaluate the scope of individual rights and to enforce their protection against state and local encroachment. [*Id.* at 299.]

Subsequently, a growing number of judges have weighed in on related issues. See, e.g., Liu, *State Constitutions and the Protection of Individual Rights: A Reappraisal*, 92 N.Y.U. L. Rev. 1307 (2017) (contending that the legitimacy of state constitutional law does not depend primarily upon the development of a distinctive, state-centered jurisprudence, or issues of interpretive methodology, but instead upon an understanding of the structure of the federal system of government); J. Sutton, Imperfect Solutions: States and the Making of American Constitutional Law 51 (2018) (contending that state constitutions should not be interpreted in lockstep, giving examples in a range of areas including school finance, free speech, and search and seizure, and suggesting that state law claims should be given priority). For additional scholarly views, see Calabresi, Lindgren, Begley, Dore & Agudo, *Individual Rights Under State Constitutions in 2018: What Rights are Deeply Rooted in a Modern-Day Consensus of the States?* 94 Notre Dame L. Rev. 49 (2018) (comparing individual rights that exist in state constitutions in 2018 and those that existed in state constitutions in 1868 when the Fourteenth Amendment was adopted, and arguing that originalist and "living constitution" theorists should recognize that there is much in common between these eras); Calabresi, Agudo & Dore, *The U.S. and the State Constitutions: An Unnoticed Dialogue*, 9 N.Y.U. J. L. & Liberty 685 (2015) (discussing how state and federal constitutional law interpretations have borrowed from each other).

[2] State Legislative Power: Grant Versus Limitation

Problem 1-2

The Constitution of the State of Metro provides as follows:

> The legislature is authorized to create a Department of Finance to administer the financial affairs of the state.

The legislature created a Department of Finance some time ago pursuant to this constitutional provision. A new governor decided that problems of municipal finance in the state required attention from a specialized department. Some municipalities were experiencing financial problems, and other municipalities were interested in new borrowing and financing strategies. At his request, the legislature created a Department of Municipal Finance and assigned to that department all matters of municipal finance that previously were the responsibility of the Department of Finance.

You are the city attorney for Metro City, one of the cities covered by this law. You have learned the Department is considering adoption of a regulation that would prohibit your city from investing municipal funds in certain types of securities. What are the possibilities for a suit against the Department in state or federal court challenging the statute? If either court took your case, would you prevail?

As noted in the text above, one of the functions of a state constitution is to delegate power to the state legislature. The state constitution operates differently than the federal constitution. Congress can only exercise powers granted by the federal constitution. State legislatures have plenary power, except as limited by the state constitution. The case that follows considers the role of state constitutions as a limit on the state legislature:

Utah School Boards Association v. Utah State Board of Education

17 P.3d 1125 (Utah 2001)

RUSSON, ASSOCIATE CHIEF JUSTICE:

The Utah School Boards Association ("Boards Association") appeals the third district court's summary judgment decision in favor of the Utah State Board of Education ("State Board") declaring the Utah Charter Schools Act constitutional. We affirm.

Background

In 1998, the Utah Legislature passed the Utah Charter Schools Act (the "Act") as part of the Schools for the 21st Century initiative to better address the individual needs of Utah students. *See* Utah Code Ann. § 53A-1a-502(1). The Act authorized the creation of "up to eight charter schools [in Utah] for a three-year pilot program." *Id.* The charter schools are part of the state's public education system, *see id.* § 53A-1a-502(2), and are meant to contribute to the improvement and customization of public education programs, *see id.* § 53A-1a-401(1).

Under the Act, the legislature authorized the State Board to act in a supervisory role. The State Board was given the authority to review charter school applications and either approve or deny each one. *See id.* § 53A-1a-505(2)(b). Approved applicants were to work with the State Board in formulating a school's charter that, when signed, served as a contractual agreement. *See id.* § 53A-1a-505(3). The charter may be modified only upon the mutual agreement of the school's governing body and the State Board. *See id.* § 53A-1a-508(4). However, the legislature enumerated in the Act a number of reasons for which the State Board could terminate or refuse to renew a charter. *See id.* § 53A-1a-510. During the term of a charter, a charter school was given certain reporting requirements. These reports were to be sent to the State Board, local school boards, and the legislature. *See id.* §§ 53A-1a-507(4), -509. The State Board also was given the responsibility of developing rules to provide for specific aspects of charter school funding distribution. *See id.* § 53A-1a-513.

In August 1998, the Boards Association filed a complaint for declaratory relief against the State Board, challenging the Act's constitutionality. The Boards Association alleged in its complaint that the Utah Constitution limits the authority the legislature may grant to the State Board. The Boards Association asserted that because the state constitution vested the State Board with the "general control and supervision of the public education system," Utah Const. art. X, § 3, the legislature could authorize the State Board to act only for the whole system. Accordingly, the Boards Association claimed that the legislature violated the constitution by passing the Act, which granted local and specific controls to the State Board.

The State Board denied the Boards Association's allegations and requested that the Act be declared constitutional. The State Board then moved for summary judgment, arguing that the Boards Association had not met its burden of proof in challenging the constitutionality of the Act. The State Board asserted that the Utah Constitution did not preclude it from exercising direct control over specific schools or programs if authorized by the legislature because the greater power expressed by "general control" includes the lesser power of specific control.

The Boards Association made a cross-motion for summary judgment, arguing that general control and supervision meant universal or central control as opposed to particularized or local control; it meant control and supervision directed only to the whole of the public education system. In March 1999, the third district court granted summary judgment in favor of the State Board, holding that the Act did not violate the state constitution. The Boards Association appealed to this court.

On appeal, the Boards Association argues that article X, section 3 of the Utah Constitution limits the authority the legislature may grant to the State Board, and that with the Act, the legislature overreached this authority. Specifically, the Boards Association claims that because the state constitution vested the State Board with only general control and supervision over the public education system, the legislature can authorize the State Board to act only in ways that affect the entire system. The Boards Association argues that this restriction prohibits the legislature from authorizing the State Board to act with specific or local supervision and control. The Boards Association avers that the Act unlawfully authorized the State Board to (1) approve or deny charter applications, (2) work with applicants in setting terms and conditions for operation of specific charter schools, (3) terminate a school's charter, and (4) redirect local school district revenues—all controls specific and local in nature.

The State Board counters that the state constitution's grant of general control and supervision cannot reasonably be interpreted as a limitation on legislative power. Instead, the State Board argues that the legislature has plenary powers and that when read in conjunction with the other relevant constitutional provisions the only reasonable inference of the disputed language is that the legislature is restricted from assigning general supervision and control for the public education system to any other agency or official.

Scope of Review

The power and duty of ascertaining the meaning of a constitutional provision resides exclusively with the judiciary. The issue of whether a statute is constitutional is a question of law that we review for correctness, "affording no particular deference to the trial court's ruling." *Bd. of Comm'rs v. Petersen*, 937 P.2d 1263, 1266 (Utah 1997). Furthermore, "[a] statute is presumed constitutional, and 'we resolve any reasonable doubts in favor of constitutionality.'" *Id.* at 1267.

Analysis

The Act clearly grants the State Board specific and local controls. *See* Utah Code Ann. §§ 53A-1a-504, -505, -508 to -510, -513 (Supp. 2000). Therefore, the essential question before us is whether the legislature had authority to pass the Act giving the State Board the designated supervisory powers.

The Utah Constitution is not one of grant, but one of limitation. "'The state having thus committed its whole lawmaking power to the legislature, excepting such as is expressly or impliedly withheld by the state or federal constitution, it has plenary power for all purposes of civil government.'" *Univ. of Utah v. Bd. of Examiners*, 295 P.2d 348, 361 (Utah 1956) (citing cases); *see also* 16 C.J.S. Constitutional Law § 58, at 150 (1984) ("As a general rule, the legislature possesses and may exercise all legislative power, or power to enact statutes, of the state or people of the state, subject only to the limitations or prohibitions imposed by the state constitution."). Therefore, if the legislature is to be "restricted in educational as well as all other matters, it is imperative that the Legislature be restricted expressly or by necessary implication by the Constitution itself." (citing cases). As a result, the Act at issue must be deemed constitutional unless an examination of the Utah Constitution reveals limitations upon the legislature with respect thereto.

The Utah Constitution provides in relevant part:

> The Legislature shall make laws for the establishment and maintenance of a system of public schools, which shall be open to all the children of the State and be free from sectarian control.

Utah Const. art. III, ord. 4. Accordingly, article X, which provides for Utah's system of education, states:

> The Legislature shall provide for the establishment and maintenance of the state's education systems including: (a) a public education system, which shall be open to all children of the state; and (b) a higher education system. Both systems shall be free from sectarian control.

Id. art. X, § 1. In addition,

> The public education system shall include all public elementary and secondary schools *and such other schools and programs as the Legislature may designate.* The higher education system shall include all public universities and colleges and such other institutions and programs as the Legislature may designate. Public elementary and secondary schools shall be free, except the Legislature may authorize the imposition of fees in the secondary schools.

Id. § 2 (emphasis added).

In considering the meaning of a constitutional provision, the analysis begins with the plain language of the provision. We need not look beyond the plain language unless we find some ambiguity in it. *See id.*

The legislature has plenary authority to create laws that provide for the establishment and maintenance of the Utah public education system. This includes any other schools and programs the legislature may designate to be included in the system. However, its authority is not unlimited. The legislature, for instance, cannot establish schools and programs that are not open to all the children of Utah or free from sectarian control, and it cannot establish public elementary and secondary schools that are not free of charge, for such would be a violation of articles III and X of the Utah Constitution.

However, the Boards Association argues that it is another provision of the constitution that serves as a restriction on the powers of the legislature as applied to this case. That provision states:

> The *general control and supervision* of the public education system shall be vested in the State Board of Education. The membership of the board shall be established and elected as provided by statute. The State Board of Education shall appoint a State Superintendent of Public Instruction who shall be the executive officer of the board.

Utah Const. art. X, § 3 (emphasis added). The Boards Association contends that the phrase "general control and supervision" restricts the legislature by limiting the authority the legislature may grant to the State Board.

In analyzing the plain meaning of a constitutional provision, the words used must be given their ordinary and "'commonly understood meaning.'" (citing cases). Therefore, we must look at the ordinary and commonly understood meaning of the words "general control and supervision" to determine the intent of the provision.

As the following evidence provides, the term is understood to mean the direction and management of *all* aspects of an operation or business. Shortly after adoption of the Utah Constitution, the legislature understood general control and supervision to mean management of *all* aspects of the public education system when it required the State Board superintendent to advise with county superintendents and local school boards "upon *all* matters involving the welfare of the schools." Free School System Act, ch. XIX, ch. 2, § 4, 1897 Utah Laws 107, 112 (emphasis added). In fact, it is with this understanding that the legislature has also passed the following legislation that grants the State Board specific and local authority (1) to approve or deny applications from individual school districts for school nursing services incentive program monies; (2) to select particular schools to participate in extended school year programs; (3) to control and manage applied technology centers; (4) to select particular schools that qualify for additional resources as highly impacted schools; (5) to select a group of rural schools to participate in a modified school week pilot program; (6) to select an urban school district, specific individual urban schools, and specific individual rural schools to participate in the arts in elementary schools pilot program; (7) to approve or deny applications from individual school districts for the classification of particular schools as necessarily existent small schools; and (8) to approve or deny applications from individual school districts for alternative language services funding. (citing statutes).

In addition, this court clearly understood general control and supervision to apply to all aspects of an operation when it held the term "is plenary." *In re Woodward*, 384 P.2d 110, 112 (Utah 1963) (finding statute unconstitutional that gave general control and supervision over juvenile courts to probate commission).

Analogously, because general control applies to all aspects of an operation or a business, a manager or supervisor exercising general control assumes liability for the actions of an employee. (citing cases).

The Boards Association argues that the term "general control and supervision" means that the State Board may be granted authority only to manage the public education system uniformly and universally as a whole. This is unreasonable. It is beyond question that the State Board has always been able to manage separate types of schools and programs differently. For example, the accreditation rules propagated by the State Board for elementary schools are different from those for junior high and middle schools, and the accreditation rules propagated for junior high and middle schools are different from those for secondary schools and special schools. *See* Utah Admin. Code R277-411 to -413. In addition, it is beyond doubt that the State Board can manage vocational programs differently from athletic programs differently from educational programs. *See, e.g., id.* R277-502, -517, -518.

Using the Boards Association's logic, the State Board would have to control and supervise all schools and programs, whether they be elementary or secondary, scholastic or vocational, identically across all classes or types. This would be not only unreasonable but ineffectual. Each class of school and each type of program has specific needs and must be managed to those needs.

From the common and ordinary understanding of the plain language of the Utah Constitution, it is clear that the State Board has been vested with the authority to direct and manage all aspects of the public education system in accordance with the laws made by the legislature. This must include not only the laws regarding the public elementary and secondary schools, but also the laws regarding any other schools and programs that the legislature designates as part of the public education system.

Accordingly, the legislature has used its plenary authority to establish charter schools as a means of pursuing the goal of continually improving and customizing public educational programs. The charter school program is part of the public education system, and the State Board has been given authority to supervise the charter school program in accordance with the Act. Article X, section 3 of the Utah Constitution does not prohibit the legislature from authorizing the State Board to exercise the control and supervision provided in the Act. We affirm the district court's decision that the Act is constitutional.

Justice Durham, Justice Durrant, and Justice Wilkins concur in Associate Chief Justice Russon's opinion.

Chief Justice Howe concurs in the result.

Notes and Questions

1. *The power of plenary legislative power.* The doctrines discussed in the case—that state legislatures have plenary power, that a grant of power from the state constitution is not necessary, and that the state constitution is only a limit on legislative power—are powerful ones. This quotation from an early Michigan case makes the point by contrasting the role of the federal and state constitutions:

> A different rule of construction applies to the Constitution of the United States than to the Constitution of a State. The Federal government is one of delegated powers, and all powers not delegated are reserved to the States or to the people. When the validity of an act of congress is challenged as unconstitutional, it is necessary to determine whether the power to enact it has been expressly or impliedly delegated to congress. The legislative power, under the Constitution of the State, is as broad, comprehensive, absolute and unlimited as that of the parliament of England, subject only to the Constitution of the United States and the restraints and limitations imposed by the people upon such power by the Constitution of the State itself. [*Young v. City of Ann Arbor*, 255 N.W. 579, 581 (Mich. 1934).]

The principle of plenary state legislative power is so basic that the litany of which it is a part is recited in countless decisions. *E.g.*, *Iberville Parish School Board v. Louisiana State Board of Elementary and Secondary Education*, 248 So. 3d 299 (La. 2018) (citing principle in explaining state legislature could allocate funds to "type 2" charter schools); *Cooper v. Berger*, 822 S.E.2d 286 (N.C. 2018) (citing principle in concluding that state legislature could authorize itself to approve members of Governor's cabinet who were statutory rather than constitutional officers); *Oswald v. Hamer*, 115 N.E.3d 181 (Ill. 2018) (citing principle in upholding statute governing property tax exemptions relating to access to hospital and health care services against facial constitutional challenge). Much of the time, the recitation appears to be primarily background and orientation that does not directly affect the outcome of the case. As in the principal case, however, the constitution's failure to describe the full extent of the legislature's power is critical to the result. But see *Cave Creek Unified Sch. Dist. v. Ducey*, 308 P.3d 1152 (Ariz. 2013), holding that nothing in the constitution prohibited a voter-adopted requirement directing the legislature to annually increase base level education funding.

It is important to distinguish two types of constitutional provisions when considering limitations in a state constitution on state legislative power. One type of provision, like that in the principal case, is an explicit delegation of legislative authority. The other type of provision is a limitation on how legislative authority can be exercised. Examples are an equal protection clause and a due process clause, which most state constitutions have. Equal protection and due process are discussed earlier in this Chapter. See also *Fransen v. City of New Orleans*, 988 So. 2d 225 (La. 2008) (constitution authorizes only tax sales as remedy to collect delinquent property taxes).

2. *Expressio unius.* Constitutional provisions often are ambiguous and incomplete. A familiar rule of statutory construction, *expressio unius est exclusio alterius*, holds that a delegation of authority must be found within the statute: the mention of one thing implies the exclusion of another. If this strict rule of construction were applied to state constitutions, the absence of a delegation of authority would mean the legislature does not have this authority, and since state constitutions are often spare, the result would be that legislative power would be severely limited. The principal case makes the point, however, that the *expressio* rule is not applied to state constitutions. Moreover, though the state constitution may limit the legislature's authority, a court will not find limitations lightly:

> [A]ll intendments favor the exercise of the Legislature's plenary authority: 'If there is any doubt as to the Legislature's power to act in any given case, the doubt should be resolved in favor of the Legislature's action. *Such restrictions and limitations* [*imposed by the Constitution*] *are to be construed strictly, and are not to be extended to include matters not covered by the language used.*' [Citations, emphasis in original.] [*Pacific Legal Foundation v. Brown*, 624 P.2d 1215, 1221 (Cal. 1981) (italics added).]

3. *Qualifications for office.* Most courts hold the legislature may not add to qualifications for office. See *Gerberding v. Munro*, 949 P.2d 1366 (Wash. 1998), holding unconstitutional a statute adopted by initiative that put term limits on officeholders, and collecting and discussing the cases. The court reviewed the history of constitutional provisions establishing qualifications for office, and held the clear intent was to allow the legislature to add to constitutional qualifications only when the constitution conferred that authority. Can you see a reason why qualifications for office should be treated differently from other constitutional provisions? *Contra Bysiewicz v. Dinardo*, 6 A.3d 726 (Conn. 2010) (office of attorney general).

4. *Debt and tax limitations.* Constitutional debt limitations for both state and local governments are frequently written in the language of negative command, *e.g.*, "no debt shall be issued except. . . ." The exceptions are usually referendum approval or a requirement that the debt not exceed a stated percentage of local assessed valuation for property taxation. When debt limitations prove unduly burdensome, as they frequently do, state legislatures have sometimes sought ways to avoid them. The principle that state legislative power is plenary except for specific constitutional prohibitions has often served to support the validity of financing methods that do not precisely fit the constitutional mold. In *State Bond Comm'n v. All Taxpayers, Property Owners & Citizens of La.*, 510 So. 2d 662 (La. 1987), for example, the court upheld a statute that authorized the State Bond Commission to issue revenue anticipation notes. It held the constitutional provision prohibiting

the state from issuing debt except by a law adopted by two-thirds of the legislature did not apply. The notes were not debt because they were issued in anticipation of revenues and that "the word [debt] is . . . to be interpreted according to its received meaning." Debt and tax limitation questions are covered in greater detail in Chapter 4.

5. *Campus carry.* A growing number of state legislatures have directed that college campuses must allow those on their premises to carry firearms. See http://www.ncsl.org/research/education/guns-on-campus-overview.aspx. Students and faculty have expressed strong views about the risks associated with such practices, particularly in light of the growing number of shootings on campuses. Another important Utah case addressed these issues. See *University of Utah v. Shurtleff,* 144 P.3d 1109 (Utah 2006). *Shurtleff* involved a claim by University officials that the University was an autonomous constitutional entity that could enforce a policy prohibiting students, faculty, and staff from carrying guns, notwithstanding the fact that state legislation prohibited any restriction on carrying guns on public or private property. The court concluded that under the state constitution, the legislature could not limit the right to bear arms, and that only the legislature could define the lawful use of arms.

A Note on Delegation of Power and Special Legislation

This Note briefly introduces two other constitutional limitations on state legislation as it affects state and local governments. These issues are given more detailed attention later in this casebook in Chapter 8, but they require comment now because they affect legal questions that are discussed earlier.

Delegation of power. State legislatures and local legislative bodies are the sources of legislative power. Though there is no explicit provision in state constitutions that contains this limitation, an important implicit constitutional limitation prohibits the delegation of legislative power to non-legislative agencies. At the state level, a delegation of legislative power can occur when the legislature authorizes a state administrative agency to carry out a program authorized by a statute. An example is the law authorizing the Department of Municipal Finance to adopt regulations that "will secure the financial integrity of cities with a population in excess of 1,000,000" described in Problem 1-2 earlier in this Chapter. The usual rule is that the legislature has unconstitutionally delegated legislative power to the Department unless the statute contains adequate standards that can guide the Department's exercise of this authority.

State legislation may also confer authority on local governments. For example, a state statute can authorize local governments to borrow money or to regulate by ordinance, such as an ordinance prohibiting smoking in restaurants. Though there is no clear reason for it, most courts treat this kind of delegation as an exception to the doctrine that state legislatures may not delegate legislative authority without adequate standards.

A delegation of legislative authority can occur in local governments. State statutes provide the necessary authority for local agencies, but local governing bodies can delegate authority to them. A common example is the delegation of authority in a housing code to require the maintenance and rehabilitation of housing. This type of delegation also requires the enactment of adequate standards.

Special legislation. Return again to Problem 1-2 and the question whether the legislation can delegate authority to remedy fiscal problems but only in municipalities with populations of over 1,000,000. A typical state constitutional provision provides that "No special law shall be passed when a general law can be made applicable." The purpose of this provision is to prohibit special legislation limited to one or only a few local governments which is considered an unacceptable form of favoritism. Courts uphold special legislation only if there is a reasonable basis for classifying the favored class of local governments differently from others. They review the classification of local governments under a special legislation clause similarly to the way they review legislative classifications under an equal protection clause. Equal protection is discussed earlier in this Chapter.

Legislation that applies only to one or a few municipalities is common because legislators from elsewhere in the state may be willing to support it only if it is limited to the affected municipalities. This is especially true when the statute covers large urban areas, and legislators from other parts of the state do not want it to cover their communities. In other instances, a special law may be required for a local government because it has a localized problem that only needs attention there.

D. Local Government

[1] Local Government Types and Organization

> A basic fact about local governments in the United States is their great diversity with respect to such matters as legal nature, size, area, functions, and organizations, both within and among states. . . . [Local governments] may be divided between municipal corporations and quasi-municipal corporations. Or, on the basis of the number of functions, a differentiation may be made between general-purpose governments, such as municipalities and counties, providing a range of services and special-purpose governments, such as school districts, limited to one or a few services. [ACIR, STATE AND LOCAL ROLES IN THE FEDERAL SYSTEM 227 (1982).]

The "quasi-municipal" versus "municipal" distinction made in the ACIR report is widely used but does not always have legal significance. Cities and other incorporated local governments are called "municipal" corporations because they exercise local functions. Counties and townships are called "quasi-municipal" because they carry out state functions at the local level as well as exercising local government powers. An example is county administration of a state welfare assistance program. For a discussion of quasi-municipal corporations, see 1 McQuillin Mun. Corp. § 2:17 (3d ed. 2019) (explaining that quasi-municipal corporations resemble municipal corporations in some respects, but are merely public agencies with the attributes of a municipality that are necessary to meet limited objectives, that is, public agencies "created or authorized by the legislature to aid the state in, or to take charge of, some public or state work, other than community government, for the general welfare").

Local governments, their design, characteristics, and powers, have increasingly drawn scholarly attention. For important insights, see, e.g., Davidson, *Localist Administrative Law*, 126 Yale L.J. 564 (2017) (offering a descriptive account of local administration and related structures and operation, identifying salient factors that should inform judicial review, and exploring the intersection of local government law and administrative law); Saiger, *Local Government as a Choice of Agency Form*, 77 Ohio St. L.J. 423 (2016) (exploring choices in allocation of local government functions and related rationales); Kazis, *American Unicameralism: The Structure of Local Legislatures*, 69 Hastings L.J. 1147 (2018) (exploring why local governments do not employ bicameral legislature structures and related consequences).

[a] Municipalities

"A municipality is defined . . . as a political subdivision within which a municipal corporation has been established to provide general local government for a specific population concentration in a defined area." ACIR, *supra*, at 240. The incorporated status of municipalities distinguishes them from counties. Most municipalities are called cities, but they may also be legally designated as villages, towns (except in New England), or boroughs (except in Alaska).

Municipalities are the dominant form of local government below the county level. They have legislative powers and are authorized to provide the most comprehensive set of governmental services. They dominate local government expenditure on highways, police and fire protection, parking, libraries, housing and urban redevelopment, and sewerage and sanitation. In practice, however, many municipalities are quite small and may provide a limited number of services. Counties may provide more extensive services than many suburban municipalities in some metropolitan areas, and municipalities may contract with county government to provide many municipal services in these areas.

There are two standard organizational forms for municipalities. According to a 2018 survey of municipal forms of government, by the International City/County Management Association, the mayor-council form is common and used by about 38% of all cities. https://icma.org/blog-posts/municipal-form-government-numbers. There is an elected legislative body, often called the city council, and an elected mayor, though the mayor can also be appointed from the council. A strong mayor is the local equivalent of a governor and is typical in the northeast and Midwest. Mayors often are weak executives, however, and weaker than governors. In weak mayor systems, the mayor's role is primarily ceremonial rather than policymaking. Mayors may only be authorized to preside over council meetings and may or may not have veto powers. The council-manager form retains the mayor and council but confers administrative responsibilities on a city manager. This form is used in about 40% of all cities. *Id.* The remaining municipalities use commission, town meeting, or representative town meeting forms of government. *Id.* Careful analysis has shown that cities with the council-manager form of government have a 57% lesser likelihood of corruption convictions than those with the mayor-council form of government. See Nelson & Afonso, *Ethics by Design: The Impact of Form of Government on Municipal Corruption*, 79 Pub. Admin. Rev. No. 4 (2019): 591–600.

The city manager is a professionally-trained employee often appointed by the council who is responsible for the administration of the municipality. About half of all mayor-council cities that do not have managers have an appointed chief administrative officer (CAO) whose duties are similar to those of a manager. In this system, the mayor has executive authority over city departments and has a great deal of power to enforce policy decisions, but the CAO has most of the responsibilities of managing the city on a day-to-day basis. See Frederickson, Logan & Wood, *Municipal Reform in Mayor-Council Cities: A Well-Kept Secret*, 34 State & Local Gov't Rev. No. 2 (2002): 95–104; Moulder, *Municipal Form of Government: Trends in Structure, Responsibility, and Composition, in* ICMA, Municipal Yearbook, at 28 (2008); DeSantis & Renner, *City Government Structures: An Attempt at Clarification*, 34 State & Local Gov't Rev. No. 2 (2002): 95–104.

[b] Counties

The county was well established in seventeenth century England and was brought to the United States as a government type by the colonists. As the ACIR points out, counties are "first of all local units for state purposes." ACIR, *supra*, at 236. Counties provide a number of state-related services at the local level. They include property tax assessment and collection, deed recording, law enforcement, jails, courts, highways, public works, welfare and social services, health care and Medicaid, and agricultural and economic development. Urban counties may provide a large number of additional services in addition to the traditional state services, such as mass transit, parks and recreation, airports, planning, zoning and regional governance. Many states authorize home rule for counties, though only about 10% of the counties that can adopt home rule have done so. *See* J. Benton, Counties as Service Delivery Agents (2002) (discussing changes in county services).

With a couple of exceptions, counties cover the entire area of a state. This means that unincorporated areas as well as incorporated municipalities are within county limits (Virginia is an exception). Counties differ considerably in size, form, and function. Counties in lightly-populated territory in rural areas usually provide only state-related functions, do not have legislative powers, and may have a simplified organization. In the mid-South, for example, county judges may also be the administrative body for the county and may not have legislative powers. Counties are vestigial units of government in the New England and Middle Atlantic states, where incorporated governments and townships are the major local governments. Counties are a dominant form of local government in the south, southwest, and west, and (with exceptions in Texas and some southern states) are substantial in size. They are also important units of government in the mountain states and the Midwest.

Counties can levy taxes within incorporated areas, but cannot legislate within incorporated areas, which may take up much of their area. Counties traditionally provided services only in their unincorporated areas, though this pattern is changing. Especially in metropolitan areas, they may provide services throughout their area, including incorporated municipalities, which may contract for county services instead of providing their own. Counties may be a preferred service provider because they enjoy economies of scale, and have a more extensive and varied tax base. Yet they face increasing financial pressures because they are responsible for the fastest-growing and most costly government programs, such as welfare.

County forms of government vary. See International City/County Managers Association, *County Form of Government 2014 Survey Results*, https://icma.org/documents/form-government-statistics-counties-2014. As of 2014, ICMA reported that of 3031 total counties, 1724 (more than half) used a "commission" form of government in which each commissioner is the administrative head of one or more departments. 819 used a commission-administrator or commission-manager, and 488 used a council-elected-executive form. While a majority of counties with populations of less than 50,000 tended to employ the "commission" form, in those with populations of 50,000 or more, commission-administrator/manager and council-elected executive predominated.

For discussion of county government, see de la Cruz, *County Form of Government: Trends in Structure and Composition, in* ICMA, MUNICIPAL YEARBOOK, at 21 (2009); COUNTY GOVERNMENTS IN AN ERA OF CHANGE (D. Berman ed. 1993); Cigler, *County Government in the 1990s*, 27 STATE & LOCAL GOV'T REV. No. 1 (1995): 55–70. For discussion of the roles of the county executive and legislative body, see *Prunetti v. Mercer County Bd. of Chosen Freeholders*, 794 A.2d 278 (N.J. L. Div. 2001).

[c] Townships

Twenty states in the New England, Central Atlantic and Northwest Territory states have about 16,500 local governments organized as townships. The Northwest Territory states include Ohio, Michigan, Indiana, Illinois, Wisconsin, and Minnesota. Townships are not incorporated. They usually cover all of the county area outside the incorporated municipalities where they exist, and include rural areas as well as unincorporated settlements. Townships are known as "towns" in New York and the New England states. Their origins are colonial:

> As colonial America grew and developed, two major local government models developed, one in the more densely settled areas of the northern colonies (the New England model), and another one in the less densely settled plantation areas of the southern colonies (the Virginia model).

> The New England model called for strong local government autonomy and small area government units, while the Virginia model consisted of extensive government authority residing in larger geographical units. In New England, townships and municipalities were the basic functioning units of general-purpose government. The southern colonies, following the Virginia model, did not establish townships, and counties were given considerable local government authority. [Hamilton, *Township Government: A Tale of One State*, 97 NAT'L CIVIC REV. No. 3 (2008): 37–49].

The northeastern and some north central states are "strong township" states where townships have powers and functions not unlike those possessed by municipalities. The other north central states are "rural township" states in which townships have limited powers to tax and limited service functions. Roads are traditionally their major responsibility. Rural townships have been declining in importance. For a discussion of townships, see Stephens, *The Least Glorious, Most Local, Most Trivial, Homely, Provincial, and Most Ignored Form of Local Government*, 24 URB. AFF. Q. No. 4 (1989): 501–12; Manners, *The Township, the Hope of Democracy? History as Moral Act*, 70 VAND. L. REV. EN BANC 69 (2017) (discussing related historical developments in North Carolina and New England).

[d] Special Districts

Special districts are organized to perform one or at most a few public functions, and are usually established with the approval of local voters under state enabling legislation. Most special districts are single-function districts. Fire protection, water supply, soil conservation, housing and urban renewal, and drainage are the services most usually provided.

Two thirds of all special districts are in rural areas. They are popular because they provide an alternative to municipal incorporation, can provide services where they are needed, and have independent fiscal powers. Multipurpose special districts in metropolitan areas can also provide a more acceptable alternative to metropolitan government, and many serve an entire metropolitan area. Special districts usually raise revenue through user fees for services they provide or special assessments. They do not usually have the power to tax or legislative powers.

Special districts are either independent or dependent. Independent districts are governed by appointed or elected boards and usually can be organized only in unincorporated areas. Dependent special districts are organized by a parent municipality, which also appoints its board. A municipal public housing authority is an example. The special district is the most rapidly expanding local government unit. For a study exploring whether the increase in special districts reflects efforts by general purpose governments to avoid constraints on their fiscal autonomy, see Goodman & Leland, *Do Cities and Counties Attempt to Circumvent Changes in Their Autonomy by Creating Special Districts?* 49 AM. REV. PUB. ADMIN. No. 2 (2019): 203–17 (concluding that restrictions on the fiscal autonomy of cities are linked to creation of new special districts where functional autonomy also exists, but finding no such correlation among counties).

[e] School Districts

School districts are a form of special district, but are universal; every part of a state is organized into school districts. Education is a major local government function, as education accounts on average for over one third of all governmental expenditures at the local level. Older inner cities may spend twice as much on education as their suburbs, however.

Like other special districts, school districts are either independent or dependent. The vast majority of school districts are independently organized and may serve and overlap more than one municipality. Dependent school districts are agencies of other local governments, such as counties or municipalities, and serve only their local government jurisdiction. In metropolitan areas, the inner city is usually served by a single dependent school district, while several independent school districts may cover the suburbs and unincorporated county areas. This geographical separation reinforces fiscal and social disparities in metropolitan areas. Unlike other special districts, school districts have declined rapidly in recent years, almost entirely because of school district consolidation in rural areas. For a discussion of the history of the school district, see Shoked, *An American Oddity: The Law, History, and Toll of the School District*, 111 Nw. U. L. Rev. 945 (2017).

[f] Local Government Trends

The table that follows indicates trends in local government numbers in recent years. The significant trend is the stability in numbers of most local government units. The exception is the continuing and rapid growth in special districts.

Local Government Units: 1972 to 2017

	1972	1982	1992	2012	2017
Local Governments	79,269	81,831	85,006	89,004	90,075
Counties	3,044	3,041	3,043	3,031	3,031
Municipal governments	18,517	19,076	19,279	19,522	19,495
Town or townships	16,991	16,734	16,656	16,364	16,253
School districts	15,781	14,851	14,422	12,884	12,754
Special districts	23,885	28,078	31,555	37,203	38,542

Source: U.S. Census Bureau, https://www.census.gov/data/tables/2017/econ/gus/2017-governments.html.

Notes and Questions

1. *Trends in local government patterns.* This country entered the twentieth century with a simple nineteenth century government model. Counties were the basic building block and provided essential but minimal governmental services throughout the state. Municipalities organized to provide a more complete range of urban services as rural areas urbanized and expanded through annexation as their fringe areas urbanized.

This simple pattern changed with extensive suburbanization at the close of the twentieth century. Inner cities in metropolitan areas could not annex quickly enough to keep up with urbanization at their edges, and in some states, annexation statutes created legal barriers to annexation. Permissive incorporation laws led to the extensive incorporation of new municipalities in suburban areas. The inner city became surrounded by a checkerboard of suburban municipalities that limited growth through annexation. Annexation became possible only by suburban municipalities on the urban edge. In many metropolitan areas, the county organized as an urban government to provide urban services in outlying unincorporated areas.

A new trend that became evident in the 1990s was the growth of population beyond established metropolitan areas. In Missouri, for example, "[f]ully 60 percent of the state's growth in the 1990s took place *outside* the St. Louis and Kansas City metro areas. The result: Forty-five percent of Missouri's population now lives outside the major metropolises compared with 41 percent in 1970." Center for Metropolitan Policy, Brookings Institution, *Growth in the Heartland: Challenges and Opportunities for Missouri* 17 (2002). This decentralization placed substantial population in areas where county government may be minimal and where there are few organized municipalities. More recent analysis by William H. Frey, of the Brookings Institution, offers a number of important observations. By the mid 2010s, big cities (those over 500,000 in population) had a rate of growth that exceeded that of the period 2000–2010, with sunbelt and west coast cities having the greatest growth rates. Between 2011 and 2016, suburban growth trailed that in primary cities. See Frey, *Mid-decade big-city growth continues*, www.brookings.edu/blogs/the-avenue/posts/2016/05/23-mid-decade-big-city-growth-frey. By 2019, the picture was quite different. Major cities with more than 250,000 population saw a significant decline in rate of population growth, and in some cases (Chicago, New York, and San Jose), experienced net losses in population. Suburbs in the Sunbelt and Rustbelt rebounded with increased growth rates. See also Frey, *Big City Growth Stalls Further as the Suburbs Make a Comeback*, https://www.brookings.edu/blog/the-avenue/2019/05/24/big-city-growth-stalls-further-as-the-suburbs-make-a-comeback/; Frey, *U.S. Population Disperses to Suburbs, Exurbs, Rural Areas and Middle of the Country Metros*, https://www.brookings.edu/blog/the-avenue/2018/03/26/us-population-disperses-to-suburbs-exurbs-rural-areas-and-middle-of-the-country-metros/.

The governmental balkanization pattern typical of most metropolitan areas is illustrated in schematic form in the following diagram. Though the diagram is over-simplified, it illustrates the distribution of local government entities which is typical in metropolitan areas around the country. The critical point made by the diagram is the absence of horizontal linkages among governmental units at the local level.

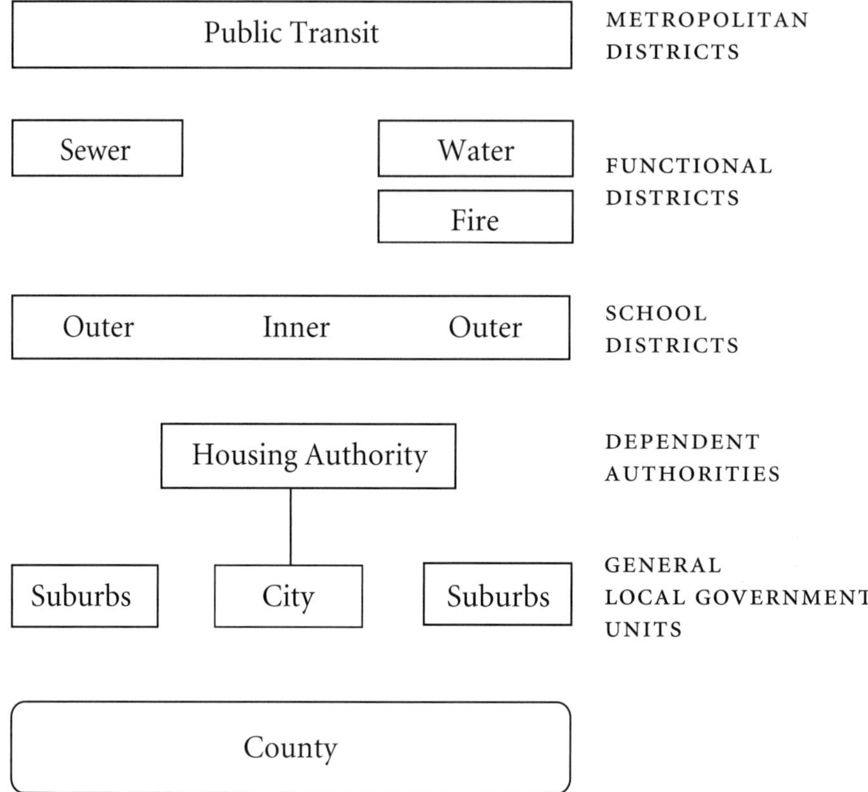

This fragmented local government structure is reinforced by strong vertical links between local governments and the federal and state agencies that provide assistance for local programs. Each state and federal assistance program is functionally specialized. Assistance is provided by a functional agency at the federal or state level to a comparable functional agency at the state or local level, such as a state highway agency. Problems in intergovernmental coordination at the local level prompted a governmental reform movement that calls for the integration and consolidation of local government in metropolitan areas, which has lagged in recent years. It is discussed in Chapter 3. For an important study of local government fragmentation, see Goodman, *Local Government Fragmentation: What Do We Know?* 51 State & Local Gov't Rev. No. 2 (2019): 134–44 (finding that growing fragmentation in local government is associated with growth in special districts, and exploring the implications of fragmentation with an eye to public expenditures and revenues, public employment, and economic growth).

2. *Regional variations.* As this discussion has indicated, local government patterns vary in different parts of the country. The local government pattern is least complex in the south and southwest, and in the southern middle Atlantic region beginning with Maryland. County governments are strong, and townships do not exist. Metropolitan areas also are less balkanized in some parts of the south and southwest. The Midwest has comparatively strong county government, but an intermediate township layer exists in some states. Counties are not as well organized in the border area from Kentucky to Arkansas. Local government patterns are more complicated in the northeast and upper middle Atlantic region. Counties are vestigial units of local government in these areas. Metropolitan areas are often highly balkanized. Towns and townships have a wide range of government functions. They are often quite small and create a complex checker-board pattern in some states and many metropolitan areas. For a review of local government forms, see FORMS OF LOCAL GOVERNMENT: A HANDBOOK ON CITY, COUNTY AND REGIONAL OPTIONS (R. L. Kemp, ed. 2007). For more specific information about particular state variations in local governance, see U.S. Census Bureau, 2017 Census of Governments, Individual State Descriptions 2017, available at https://www.census.gov/library/publications/2019/econ/2017isd.html.

3. *Trends in local governance.* Klase, *New Perspectives on Municipal Government Structure, Performance Management, and Change*, 38 STATE & LOCAL GOV'T REV. No. 2 (2006): 120–25, found that the "differences between traditional structural forms of cities [mayor-council and council-manager] have diminished over time and . . . they have come to resemble each other." Mayor-council cities have adopted administrative characteristics of council-manager cities to enhance efficiency, and council-manager cities have adopted political characteristics to increase representation and responsiveness. Svara, *Strengthening Local Government Leadership: Reexamining and Updating the Winter Commission Goals*, PUB. ADMIN. REV. 68, No. S1 (2008): S27–S49, notes that mayors have expanded the institutional powers of their office in a number of cities and have broadened the scope of governmental authority. He also finds that council performance is enhanced under both forms of government if mayors show leadership. For case studies of conflict and controversy in Los Angeles, New York City, and Washington, D.C., see F. Siegel, THE FUTURE ONCE HAPPENED HERE (1997).

A Note on Reforming Local Government

The administrative city-manager form of government reflects the Progressive concept of government reform that dominated the early twentieth century. That reform movement saw corruption and political control as major evils that required correction in local government. Its response was to remove government from politics. Cities would be run by a citizen legislative body, the office of mayor would be weakened and downgraded, and day-to-day administration would be carried out by city managers who were expected to provide government services in an efficient manner.

Some cities have moved away from the administrative model to adopt a form of government that resembles the political model in which the mayor has greater executive authority. The evolution of governmental structure in Los Angeles illustrates how models of city governance have changed. The city originally adopted a charter in 1925 based on the Progressive model but modified it substantially in 1999, as the following account explains:

> The 1925 charter was heavily influenced by the ideas of the Progressives, reformers who had dominated much of state and local politics in California for the previous two decades. The Progressives wanted to eliminate the mayor's position altogether, and govern the city through what amounted to, in essence, a board of citizen directors....
>
> [T]here was a compromise: retain a weak mayor, create a City Council of 15 members elected by district, and hand off operational control of city departments to citizen "boards of commissioners" and professional "general managers." Under the 1925 charter, commissions have been appointed by the mayor, but most budget and policy decisions have been made by the council. The general managers—that is, the city department heads—have had civil-service status.... [A]ll local elections were nonpartisan.
>
> This diffuse and complicated political structure has always left much of the city wondering exactly where political power lay. The thrust was that it lay everywhere—and nowhere. With no fear of getting fired by politicians, the department heads quietly ruled via bureaucratic control. With no strong executive power to answer to—and representing districts of about 200,000 people each—members of the City Council gradually emerged as little mayors, exerting control over even the smallest details if they chose.
>
> Because there was no clear division between the executive and legislative branches, department heads reported to both the mayor and the council—meaning council members issued orders on administrative matters especially in their districts. [Fulton & Shigley, *Putting Los Angeles Together*, GOVERNING, June 2000, at 21, 22].

In this kind of fragmented governmental structure it is difficult to know what municipal policy is, and who makes it. This governmental chaos led to the creation of two charter revision commissions in the late 1990s, one elected by the voters at the urging of the mayor, and one appointed by the council. Remarkably, they came up with a new charter that the voters approved:

> [T]he charter takes influence away from the council and drives it both upward and downward at the same time. In both cases, the council is the likely loser.... [D]epartment heads will now report to the mayor only.... [T]his change gives the mayor true authority over executive branch departments for the first time....

> At the same time, garden-variety land use decisions . . . will be transferred to seven newly formed "area" planning commissions representing different parts of the city. Members of these commissions will be appointed by the mayor, although with council confirmation. [*Id.* at 24.]

On the possibilities for reform, see Saltzstein *et al.*, who find that urban government reform is hampered by the American local government structure in *Visions of Urban Reform: Comparing English and U.S. Strategies for Improving City Government*, Urb. Aff. Rev. 44, No. 2 (2008): 155–81, at 175–77. They state that "[r]epublican values of individual citizenship in a federal system present an impediment to realizing the four visions" of urban reform: efficient public interest management, improved representation, local political leadership, and metropolitan-wide governance. The authors conclude that the American system, although "built for enhanced representation through its small-area focus[,] has difficulty . . . dealing with issues to do with distributional questions and metropolitan-wide externalities."

Shragger, *Can Strong Mayors Empower Weak Cities? On the Power of Local Executives in a Federal System*, 115 Yale L.J. 2542 (2006), discusses the origins of weak mayor systems and the ability of reform measures to change them. He notes:

> The weakness of the mayoralty illustrates a number of features of American political organization: the elite skepticism of democracy, a belief in technocracy as a solution to political failures, an emphasis on legal decentralization over political decentralization, and a federal system that fractures local power. More so than the presidency or the governorship, the mayoralty was shaped by an abiding ambivalence about the exercise of political power. Municipal policymakers came to believe that the professionalization of city management would do more to promote city efficiency than its politicization. [*Id.* at 2576.]

For a retrospective on earlier efforts at municipal government reform, including the model city charter, the council-manager plan, city management professionalism, and bureaucratic service delivery, see Wheeland, Palus & Wood, *A Century of Municipal Reform in the United States: A Legacy of Success, Adaptation, and the Impulse to Improve,* Am. Rev. Pub. Admin. 44, No. 4S (2014): 11S–28S (observing that the reform impulse continues to operate and noting that there are now both a la carte and a prix fixe approaches to government structure, city managers now must address both good government and governance, and that local governments will need to use fresh approaches to facilitate multi-organizational approaches to problem solving).

Another area of significant reform involves neighborhood governance, a matter discussed in Chapter 3.

[2] Sources of Local Government Authority

The legal status of local governments. Local governments have an entirely different legal status than state governments, which have plenary power that the state constitution can only limit. Local governments do not have plenary power. Any powers that local governments possess must be delegated by the state, either by state statute or by a constitutional home rule provision. Chapter 2 discusses these methods of delegating power, but a discussion of how the legal status of local governments came to be is presented here.

Counties and townships are not incorporated entities, but the key to the legal status of cities lies in their status as organized municipal corporations. Professor Gerald Frug, in his City Making 39–42 (1999), shows how courts developed their legal status in the early nineteenth century. He points out that legal doctrine at that time "divided the corporation into two different entities, one assimilated to the role of an individual in society and the other assimilated to the role of the state. . . . The very purpose of the distinction was to ensure that some corporations, called 'private,' would be protected against domination by the state, and that others, called 'public,' would be subject to such domination." *Id.* at 39. He also noted "[t]he scope of property rights divided private from public corporations, private corporations being those founded by individual contributions of property, and public corporations being those founded by the government without such individual contributions." *Id.* at 41. Yet Frug quotes a passage from Chancellor Kent's Commentaries on American Law 275 (3d ed. 1836), which noted that public corporations also have a public and a private aspect: "They may also be empowered to take or hold private property for municipal uses, and such property is invested with the security of other private rights." These ambiguities led him to conclude that courts at this time had great difficulty making the distinction between public and private corporations.

This history makes the important point that municipal corporations, unlike private corporations, were subject to state control and domination. It also suggests that municipal corporations have a dual status that distinguishes between their public and proprietary dimension, a distinction that occurs repeatedly throughout this book and that affects the outcome of legal disputes. It occurs for the first time in the famed *Hunter* decision, which is reproduced *infra*.

Statutes and charters. State control over municipal corporations is exercised through statutes and charters, and all municipal power must find its source in either type of delegation. Local governments are governments of grant, not limitation. State legislatures often granted charters to municipalities in the colonial period and may still incorporate municipalities in some states, but today the incorporation of municipalities is governed by statutory procedures and criteria. Statutes also delegate authority to local governments, such as the authority to regulate and the authority to borrow and tax.

A number of states now have home rule provisions in their state constitutions. They are called "home rule" because they delegate authority directly to local governments, and statutory intervention is not necessary if the authority is included within the constitutional home rule grant. Constitutions can grant home rule to both cities and counties. Under most home rule provisions, the local government must adopt a home rule charter to make home rule apply. The charter determines what home rule authority the local government can exercise. The validity of a local ordinance then depends on whether the authority to enact it is included in the charter, and whether the charter provides for an authority included within the constitutional home rule grant. Statutes are still important, and a statute may also grant authority to a home rule municipality.

E. Constitutional Limitations on the Authority of States Over Local Governments

Local governments must get their legal authority from the state legislature, and the next question is whether there are any constitutional limits on that authority. The next case, which is the leading case on this problem, answers that question.

Hunter v. City of Pittsburgh

207 U.S. 161 (1907)

Mr. Justice Moody ... delivered the opinion of the court.

The plaintiffs in error seek a reversal of the judgment of the Supreme Court of Pennsylvania, which affirmed a decree of a lower court, directing the consolidation of the cities of Pittsburgh and Allegheny. This decree was entered by authority of an act of the General Assembly of that State, after proceedings taken in conformity with its requirements. The act authorized the consolidation of two cities, situated with reference to each other as Pittsburgh and Allegheny are, if upon an election the majority of the votes cast in the territory comprised within the limits of both cities favor the consolidation, even though, as happened in this instance, a majority of the votes cast in one of the cities oppose it. The procedure prescribed by the act is that after a petition filed by one of the cities in the Court of Quarter Sessions, and a hearing upon that petition, that court, if the petition and proceedings are found to be regular and in conformity with the act, shall order an election. If the election shows a majority of the votes cast to be in favor of the consolidation, the court "shall enter a decree annexing and consolidating the lesser city ... with the greater city." The act provides, in considerable detail, for the effect of the consolidation upon the debts, obligations, claims and property of the constituent cities; grants rights of citizenship to the citizens of those cities in the consolidated city; enacts that "except as herein otherwise provided, all the property ... and rights and privileges ... vested in or belonging to either of said cities ... prior to or at the time of the annexation, shall be vested in and owned by the consolidated or united city," and establishes the form of government of the new city. This procedure was followed by the filing of a petition by the City of Pittsburgh; by an election in which the majority of all the votes cast were in the affirmative, although the majority of all the votes cast by the voters of Allegheny were in the negative, and by a decree of the court uniting the two cities.

Prior to the hearing upon the petition the plaintiffs in error, who were citizens, voters, owners of property and taxpayers in Allegheny, filed twenty-two exceptions to the petition. These exceptions were disposed of adversely to the exceptants by the Court of Quarter Sessions, and the action of that court was successively affirmed by the Superior and Supreme courts of the State. The case is here upon writ of error, and the assignment of errors alleges that eight errors were committed by the Supreme Court of the State. This assignment of errors is founded upon the dispositions by the state courts of the questions duly raised by the filing of the exceptions under the provisions of the Act of the Assembly....

After thus eliminating all questions with which we have no lawful concern, there remain two questions which are within our jurisdiction. There were two claims of rights under the Constitution of the United States which were clearly made in the court below and as clearly denied. They appear in the second and fourth assignments of error. Briefly stated, the assertion in the second assignment of error is that the Act of Assembly impairs the obligation of a contract existing between the City of Allegheny and the plaintiffs in error, that the latter are to be taxed only for the governmental purposes of that city, and that the legislative attempt to subject them to the taxes of the enlarged city violates Article I, section 9, paragraph 10, of the Constitution of the United States. This assignment does not rest upon the theory that the charter of the city is a contract with the State, a proposition frequently denied by this and other courts. It rests upon the novel proposition that there is a contract between the citizens and taxpayers of a municipal corporation and the corporation itself, that the citizens and taxpayers shall be taxed only for the uses of that corporation, and shall not be taxed for the uses of any like corporation with which it may be consolidated. It is not said that the City of Allegheny expressly made any such extraordinary contract, but only that the contract arises out of the relation of the parties to each other. It is difficult to deal with a proposition of this kind except by saying that it is not true. No authority or reason in support of it has been offered to us, and it is utterly inconsistent with the nature of municipal corporations, the purposes for which they are created, and the relation they bear to those who dwell and own property within their limits. This assignment of error is overruled.

Briefly stated, the assertion in the fourth assignment of error is that the Act of Assembly deprives the plaintiffs in error of their property without due process of law, by subjecting it to the burden of the additional taxation which would result from the consolidation. The manner in which the right of due process of law has been violated, as set forth in the first assignment of error and insisted upon in argument, is that the method of voting on the consolidation prescribed in the act has permitted the voters of the larger city to overpower the voters of the smaller city, and compel the union without their consent and against their protest. The precise question thus presented has not been determined by this court. It is important, and, as we have said, not so devoid of merit as to be denied consideration, although its solution by principles long settled and constantly acted upon is not difficult. This court has many times had occasion to consider and decide the nature of municipal corporations, their rights and duties, and the rights of their citizens and creditors. It would be unnecessary and unprofitable to analyze these decisions or quote from the opinions rendered. We think the following principles have been established by them and have become settled doctrines of this court, to be acted upon wherever they are applicable. Municipal corporations are political subdivisions of the State, created as convenient agencies for exercising such of the governmental powers of the State as may be entrusted to them. For the purpose of executing these powers properly and efficiently they usually are given the power to acquire, hold, and manage personal and real property. The number, nature and duration of the powers conferred upon these corporations and the territory over which they shall be exercised rests in the absolute discretion of the State. Neither their charters, nor any law conferring governmental powers, or vesting in them property to be used for governmental purposes, or authorizing them to hold or manage such property, or exempting them from taxation upon it, constitutes a contract with the State within the meaning of the Federal Constitution. The State, therefore, at its pleasure may modify or withdraw all such powers, may take without compensation such property, hold it itself, or vest it in other agencies, expand or contract the territorial area, unite the whole or a part of it with another municipality, repeal the charter and destroy the corporation. All this may be done, conditionally or unconditionally, with or without the consent of the citizens, or even against their protest. In all these respects the State is supreme, and its legislative body, conforming its action to the state constitution, may do as it will, unrestrained by any provision of the Constitution of the United States. Although the inhabitants and property owners may by such changes suffer inconvenience, and their property may be lessened in value by the burden of increased taxation, or for any other reason, they have no right by contract or otherwise in the unaltered or continued existence of the corporation or its powers, and there is nothing in the Federal Constitution which protects them from these injurious consequences. The power is in the State and those who legislate for the State are alone responsible for any unjust or oppressive exercise of it.

Applying these principles to the case at bar, it follows irresistibly that this assignment of error, so far as it relates to the citizens who are plaintiffs in error, must be overruled.

It will be observed that in describing the absolute power of the State over the property of municipal corporations we have not extended it beyond the property held and used for governmental purposes. Such corporations are sometimes authorized to hold and do hold property for the same purposes that property is held by private corporations or individuals. The distinction between property owned by municipal corporations in their public and governmental capacity and that owned by them in their private capacity, though difficult to define, has been approved by many of the state courts (1 Dillon, Municipal Corporations, 4th ed., sections 66 to 66a, inclusive, and cases cited in note to *State ex rel. Buckley v. Williams*, 48 L.R.A. 465), and it has been held that as to the latter class of property the legislature is not omnipotent. If the distinction is recognized it suggests the question whether property of a municipal corporation owned in its private and proprietary capacity may be taken from it against its will and without compensation. Mr. Dillon says truly that the question has never arisen directly for adjudication in this court. But it and the distinction upon which it is based has several times been noticed. Counsel for plaintiffs in error assert that the City of Allegheny was the owner of property held in its private and proprietary capacity, and insist that the effect of the proceedings under this act was to take its property without compensation and vest it in another corporation, and that thereby the city was deprived of its property without due process of law in violation of the Fourteenth Amendment. But no such question is presented by the record, and there is but a vague suggestion of facts upon which it might have been founded. In the sixth exception there is a recital of facts with a purpose of showing how the taxes of the citizens of Allegheny would be increased by annexation to Pittsburgh. In that connection it is alleged that while Pittsburgh intends to spend large sums of money in the purchase of the water plant of a private company and for the construction of an electric light plant, Allegheny "has improved its streets, established its own system of electric lighting, and established a satisfactory water supply." This is the only reference in the record to the property rights of Allegheny, and it falls far short of a statement that city holds any property in its private and proprietary capacity. Nor was there any allegation that Allegheny had been deprived of its property without due process of law. The only allegation of this kind is that the taxpayers, plaintiffs in error, were deprived of their property without due process of law because of the increased taxation which would result from the annexation—an entirely different proposition. Nor is the situation varied by the fact that, in the Superior Court, Allegheny was "permitted to intervene and become one of the appellants." The city made no new allegations and raised no new questions, but was content to rest upon the record as it was made up. Moreover, no question of the effect of the act upon private property rights of the City of Allegheny was considered in the opinions in the state courts or suggested by assignment of errors in this court. The question is entirely outside of the record and has no connection with any question which is raised in the record. For these reasons we are without jurisdiction to consider it, and neither express nor intimate any opinion upon it.

The judgment is

Affirmed.

Notes and Questions

1. *The iron grip of Hunter.* The *Hunter* decision, if absolutely followed, blocks litigation by local governments that challenges state legislation under the federal Constitution. Today there are federalism issues that did not exist when the Court decided *Hunter.* The Court can invalidate federal legislation that interferes with the reserved power of the states under the Tenth Amendment. See Chapter 7.

There is also ambiguity about the constitutional basis for *Hunter.* Is it lack of standing, justiciability and separation of powers, a decision on substantive law, or a decision that local governments cannot invoke the Fourteenth Amendment against states because they are state "creatures"? The New York Court of Appeals considered this problem in a suit that claimed the state's school finance system was unconstitutional:

> The lack of capacity of municipalities to sue the State is a necessary outgrowth of separation of powers doctrine: it expresses the extreme reluctance of courts to intrude in the political relationships between the Legislature, the State and its governmental subdivisions. [*City of New York v. State of New York*, 655 N.E.2d 649, 654 (N.Y. 1995).]

In other words, is there no constitutional restraint on how states organize their local government system? Is this wholly not justiciable?

Some state courts continue to cite *Hunter* as a boilerplate basis for denying federal constitutional relief in equal protection and due process cases. See, e.g, *Pritchett. v. City of Hot Springs*, 514 S.W.3d 447, 449 (Ark. 2017) (denying property owner's assertion that annexation was unconstitutional under the Equal Protection Clause on grounds that *Hunter* signifies that "a state may enlarge a municipality 'with or without the consent of its citizens.'"). Others have concluded that *Hunter* has fallen into disuse. See *Board of Water Works Trustees of the City of Des Moines v. Sac County Board of Supervisors*, 890 N.W.2d 50, 99–101 (Iowa 2017). The *Board of Water Works* cased involved suit by a water utility against upstream drainage districts, seeking damages for costs associated with removing nitrates from drinking water. The court concluded that broad immunity of drainage districts did not violate equal protection and did not create an unconstitutional taking of the water utility board's property. The court cited *Gomillion*, discussed below, as limiting *Hunter.* It also stressed that *Hunter* involved a restriction on the ability of a local government subdivision to sue in federal court to protect its asserted rights under constitutional provisions guaranteeing individual rights, not a suit in state court to vindicate state rights under state law.

For an interesting critique of *Hunter* that at the same time seeks to illuminate its core purpose, see Bendor, *Municipal Constitutional Rights: A New Approach*, 31 Yale L. & Pol'y Rev. 389 (2013) (criticizing *Hunter* for "purposelessness, inconsistency, and overbreath," while also finding that the decision seeks to maintain "state flexibility over powers and contours of its municipalities," and suggesting that it be limited accordingly).

2. *A different view of the Constitution.* The *Hunter* case set off a debate in the federal courts over the role of the federal Constitution in state and local government structure. Most federal courts view *Hunter* as an absolute bar to litigation over federal constitutional issues. See *State of Virginia v. Reinhard*, 568 F.3d 110 (4th Cir. 2009) ("the Supreme Court has held repeatedly that political subdivisions of states could not obtain relief under federal law against the application of state statutes...."), *rev'd & remanded on other grounds*, 563 U.S. 247 (2011); *Henley v. City of Johnson City*, 2012 WL 3027948 (E.D. Tenn. July 24, 2012) (rejecting due process challenge to annexation statute).

Some federal courts refuse to apply *Hunter* when a local government sues to claim a state statute violates the Supremacy Clause of the federal Constitution. *Branson School District RE-82 v. Romer*, 161 F.3d 619 (10th Cir. 1998), held that the *Hunter* line of cases

> stand only for the limited proposition that a municipality may not bring a constitutional challenge against its creating state when the constitutional provision that supplies the basis for the complaint was written to protect individual rights, as opposed to collective or structural rights. Neither the ... [*Hunter*] line of cases nor any other subsequent Supreme Court case has held that a political subdivision is barred from asserting the structural protections of the Supremacy Clause of Article VI in a suit against its creating state. [*Id.* at 628.]

The Fifth Circuit reached the same conclusion but for a different reason, holding that "the Constitution does not interfere with the internal political organization of states." *Rogers v. Brockette*, 588 F.2d 1057, 1069 (5th Cir. 1979). A student note claims it is "antithetical to the supremacy of federal law" to forbid a court from deciding such cases if a party meets standing requirements. Keenan, *Subdivisions, Standing and the Supremacy Clause: Can a Political Subdivision Sue Its Parent State Under Federal Law?*, 103 MICH. L. REV. 1899, 1927 (2005). Could a local government challenge the action of its parent state under provisions of the federal Constitution other than those that typically protect individual rights? See *Kerr v. Polis*, 930F.3d 1190 (10th Cir. 2019). In *Kerr*, Colorado political subdivisions, elected officials, educators and citizens challenged the constitutionality of the Taxpayer's Bill of Rights (TABOR), which limited the power of state and local governments to impose any new tax unless previously approved by voters. The plaintiffs claimed that TABOR denied them a republican form of government as guaranteed by Congress in the Colorado Enabling Act, in violation of the Guarantee Clause. The court concluded that dismissal for lack of subject matter jurisdiction was improper, concluding that political subdivisions had Article III standing and that consideration of the meaning and purpose of the phrase "republican government" was required before consideration of a motion to dismiss. The dissent contended that it was instead well-settled that a political subdivision may not sue its parent state on the basis of certain constitutional provisions.

For an interesting article advocating the overruling of *Hunter* on *Erie* grounds, see Morris, *The Case for Local Constitutional Enforcement*, 47 HARV. C.R.-C.L. L. REV. 1 (2012). The author argues that *Hunter* was poorly reasoned from the start, and that its assumptions fail. See also Reynolds, A *Role for Local Government Law in Federal-State-Local Disputes*, 43 URB. LAW. 977 (2011). Professor Reynolds argues the *Hunter* rule should no longer be followed:

> Although the Supreme Court currently stresses the importance of state sovereignty and . . . states' plenary control over their political subdivisions, its narrow reliance on *Hunter's* broad "creature of the state" language ignores the important fact that state-local relations no longer reflect that one-sided power structure. Rather, in numerous situations and in all states, the state has transferred local independence and initiative to many of its political subdivisions. Once accomplished, that transfer means that the local government is no longer subject to the state's unlimited *Hunter* discretion, at least so long as those enabling laws are in force. Relying on *Hunter*'s emphasis on broad state discretion and flexibility as the sole indicator of the state's sovereignty interest when a state seeks to prohibit local action in spite of a countervailing federal intent to empower the local government, then, ignores the readily available state law evidence that delineates the terms of the intrastate governmental relationship and in many cases confers substantial local freedom from state control. [Thus], the Court improperly assumes the applicability of a principle that in many cases would not be the basis of a state court's own analysis of a purely intrastate dispute pitting local government against its state creator. [*Id.* at 992.]

For an argument that cities should be able to challenge statutes as unconstitutional, see Barron, *Why (and When) Cities Have a Stake in Enforcing the Constitution*, 115 YALE L.J. 2218 (2006). See also Bendor, *supra* (arguing that the *Hunter* rule is still useful as giving states flexibility in state policymaking).

For a holding that the independent nature of a special district exempts it from the *Hunter* rule, see *Housing Auth. v. Fetzik*, 289 A.2d 658 (R.I. 1972). Contra *Spence v. Boston Edison Co.*, 459 N.E.2d 80 (Mass. 1983). The home rule status of a municipality did not make a difference in *Village of Arlington Heights v. Regional Transp. Auth.*, 653 F.2d 1149 (7th Cir. 1981). Compare *City of Chicago v. Lindley*, 66 F.3d 819 (7th Cir. 1995) (contra, where a city sued in its capacity as area agency for the aging, not as a municipal entity). If this is a federal constitutional issue, why should the legal status of a municipality make a difference? See § 1983 of the Federal Civil Rights Act, which authorizes suits against "persons." Is a local government suable as a "person" under this act? See Chapter 6.

3. *Hunter ignored or qualified?* The Court ignored *Hunter* in *Washington v. Seattle Sch. Dist. No. 1*, 458 U.S. 457 (1982), which invalidated under the Equal Protection Clause a state referendum that put school integration programs at a disadvantage by allowing students to attend neighborhood schools. See also *Board of Education*

v. Allen, 392 U.S. 236 (1968) (*Hunter* not discussed, and accepting case challenging under First Amendment a state statute requiring free textbooks for children in public and private schools, but holding statute constitutional). Today the facts of the *Hunter* case could raise equal protection problems under the Supreme Court's voting rights cases. See Chapter 9.

Some state courts recognize exceptions when a fundamental right is involved. *City of Seattle v. State*, 694 P.2d 641 (Wash. 1985) (city had interest in fairness and constitutionality of annexation process, which implicated the right to vote). But see *Wilkerson v. City of Coralville*, 478 F.2d 709 (8th Cir. 1973) (refusal to annex because of poverty did not raise fundamental right). A statute may also confer standing to sue to challenge the constitutionality of a statute. *City of Cave Springs v. City of Rogers*, 37 S.W.3d 607 (Ark. 2001) (statute authorized "any person" to bring a declaratory judgment action).

4. *Extending Hunter.* Later Supreme Court cases extended *Hunter* to other constitutional claims. In *City of Newark v. State of New Jersey*, 262 U.S. 192 (1923), the Court rejected a Contract Clause claim against a New Jersey statute that imposed a charge on the diversion of water from streams in excess of the amount diverted by these cities on a named day. One city argued it had a prior grant from the state to take free and without limitation all the water it required. In *Williams v. Mayor & City Council of Baltimore*, 289 U.S. 36 (1933), the City of Baltimore challenged a state law under the Equal Protection Clause that exempted a railroad from general property taxation by the city. Writing for the Court, Justice Cardozo stated clearly that a municipal corporation may assert no privileges or immunities against the state as its creator. For a review of the *Hunter* doctrine, see *Town of Charlestown v. United States*, 696 F. Supp. 800 (D.R.I. 1988). How do these cases affect your interpretation of *Hunter*?

5. *The proprietary exception?* The *Hunter* opinion suggested in dictum that municipalities might be able to invoke constitutional protections when property held by them in their proprietary as distinguished from their governmental capacity was taken from them by the state without compensation. This kind of property transfer can occur in governmental reorganization when one governmental unit is merged with another. State legislation may provide that property owned by one of the governmental units is transferred to the consolidated unit without compensation. That government unit may object that an unconstitutional taking of property held in a proprietary capacity has occurred.

The proprietary property argument was raised in *Trenton v. New Jersey*, 262 U.S. 182 (1923), but rejected. Noting the *Hunter* dictum that proprietary property is protected, the Court nevertheless said, with reference to the cases relied upon by *Hunter* to support its dictum, that "[i]n none of these cases was any power, right or property of a city or other political subdivision held to be protected by the Contract Clause or the Fourteenth Amendment. This Court has never held that these subdivisions may invoke such restraints upon the power of the State." 262 U.S. at 188.

The Supreme Court has not reconsidered this question. But see *Kerr v. Polis, supra* (focusing in part on the proprietary-governmental distinction but ultimately finding no taking of water utility board's property).

Most state courts follow the Supreme Court's lead on the compensation issue, even when property is held in a proprietary capacity. *Moses Lake School Dist. No. 161 v. Big Bend Community College*, 503 P.2d 86 (Wash. 1972) (statutory transfer of school district property to community college district without compensation upheld). See also *City of Cambridge v. Commissioner of Pub. Welfare*, 257 N.E.2d 782 (Mass. 1970) (city liens subject to legislative control, including right to abolish them without compensation to the municipalities if done for accomplishment of a public purpose). Compare *Texas Antiquities Comm. v. Dallas County Community College Dist.*, 554 S.W.2d 924 (Tex. 1977), where the court held an order by the committee prohibiting the district from demolishing buildings owned by it was an unconstitutional diversion of school property to noneducational purposes. The court refused to apply *Hunter*, holding that "[o]ne agency of the state does not possess powers to divest vested property and contract rights of another state agency 'unrestrained by the particular prohibitions of the constitution.'" Notice how this case reflects the dual nature of local governments noted by Professor Frug. The governmental vs. proprietary distinction, as will be seen in these pages, is an important principle in state and local government law.

6. *State constitutions.* Most state courts apply the *Hunter* rule to claims based on a state constitution. See *Kenai Peninsula Borough v. State Dep't of Community & Reg'l Affairs*, 751 P.2d 14 (Alaska 1988). The court pointed out that "the purpose of the Alaska due process and equal protection clauses is to protect people from abuses of government, not to protect political subdivisions of the state from the actions of other units of state government." Some state courts will hear a claim based on a state constitutional provision without considering the *Hunter* rule, if the local government meets the requirements for standing to sue. See *Kennecott Corp. v. Salt Lake County*, 702 P.2d 451 (Utah 1985). New York allows municipalities to sue the state when there is express authority to do so, where state legislation affects a municipal proprietary interest, where a statute affects municipal home rule powers, or where compliance with a state statute would be unconstitutional. See *City of New York v. State of New York*, 655 N.E.2d 649 (N.Y. 1995). Accord, *Town of Andover v. State*, 742 A.2d 756 (Vt. 1999). A state may allow a municipality to challenge a state statute if it believes that otherwise the merits of a public policy controversy would not be considered at all. See *City of Jersey City v. Farmer*, 746 A.2d 1018 (N.J. L. Div. 2000).

A Note on *Gomillion v. Lightfoot*

In 1960, a case came to the Supreme Court that qualified the absolute nature of the *Hunter* rule. In *Gomillion v. Lightfoot*, 364 U.S. 339 (1960), the state of Alabama had passed a statute that deannexed territory from the City of Tuskegee. The deannexation was structured in such a way that only areas with African-American voters were removed, which altered the shape of the city from a square "to an uncouth twenty-eight-sided figure." The Court, in an opinion by Justice Frankfurter, held the Fifteenth Amendment was violated. Referring to the allegations in the complaint, he stated:

> These allegations, if proven, would abundantly establish that [the deannexation] Act 140 was not an ordinary geographic redistricting measure even within familiar abuses of gerrymandering. If these allegations upon a trial remained uncontradicted or unqualified, the conclusion would be irresistible, tantamount for all practical purposes to a mathematical demonstration, that the legislation is solely concerned with segregating white and colored voters by fencing Negro citizens out of town so as to deprive them of their pre-existing municipal vote. [*Id.* at 341.]

Justice Frankfurter added that the city had never suggested "any countervailing municipal function which Act 140 is designed to serve." He pointed out that cases involving legislation by states concerning their political subdivisions had raised either Contract Clause questions, or cases "in which it is claimed that the State has no power to change the identity of a municipality whereby citizens of a pre-existing municipality suffer serious economic disadvantage." He concluded:

> [A] correct reading of the seemingly unconfined dicta of *Hunter* and kindred cases is not that the State has plenary power to manipulate in every conceivable way, for every conceivable purpose, the affairs of its municipal corporations, but rather that the State's authority is unrestrained by the particular prohibitions of the Constitution considered in those cases. [*Id.* at 344.]

Notes and Questions

1. *What does the case mean? Gomillion* is a transitional case in equal protection and Fifteenth Amendment law, but is important to local government law because it limits the *Hunter* rule in racial discrimination cases. Justice Frankfurter avoided Fourteenth Amendment problems by placing the decision on the Fifteenth Amendment, but subsequent decisions have treated *Gomillion* as a Fourteenth Amendment case. See *Shaw v. Reno*, 509 U.S. 630 (1993). The Supreme Court now requires proof of discriminatory intent in Fifteenth Amendment cases, *Wright v. Rockefeller*, 376 U.S. 52 (1964), and in Fourteenth Amendment cases, *Washington v. Davis*, 426 U.S. 229 (1976). In *Village of Arlington Heights v. Metropolitan Hous. Dev. Corp.*, 429 U.S. 252 (1977), the Court cited *Gomillion* for the following proposition: "Sometimes a clear pattern, unexplainable on grounds other than race, emerges from the effect of state action even when the governing legislation appears neutral on its face."

Lower courts have treated *Gomillion* as a decision vindicating individual equal protection rights, rather than as one that accorded cities a right to assert First Amendment rights on behalf of themselves as entities. See, e.g., *State v. Birmingham*, ___So. 3d___ , 2019 WL 6337424 [at 7–8] (Ala. Nov. 27, 2019) (discussing *Gomillion* and *Hunter*, and rejecting city's assertion that it could contest state statute mandating maintenance of confederate statute because state was forcing it to engage in speech with which it disagreed). See also *Honors Academy, Inc. v. Texas Education Agency*, 555 S.W.3d 54, 65–67 (Tex. 2018) (in case involving discontinuation of charter school contract, discussing *Hunter* and *Gomillion,* and characterizing *Hunter* as disallowing suits by government subdivisions based on individual contract and due process rights, while *Gomillion* involved rights asserted by individuals where important federal interests in nondiscrimination were also at stake).

2. *Gomillion restricted.* The courts have not extended *Gomillion* to uphold claims made against annexations and incorporations. *Enlargement of the Boundaries of Yazoo City v. City of Yazoo City*, 452 So. 2d 837 (Miss. 1984), dismissed without discussing *Gomillion* a Fifteenth Amendment challenge to a municipal annexation that did not change the racial makeup of the population. The court held that "[w]e know of no case which holds that a municipality has a constitutional obligation to maximize the voting strength of a particular racial or ethnic minority." *Id.* at 843. See also *LeBlanc-Sternberg v. Vertullo*, 922 F. Supp. 959 (N.D.N.Y. 1996), which held there was no constitutional obligation to redistrict a religious minority back into a municipality.

The court refused to apply *Gomillion* in a case where plaintiffs claimed a refusal to annex a black area was racially discriminatory because the shape of the municipality was bizarre, and had been created in part by an earlier refusal to annex black areas. *Burton v. City of Belle Glade*, 178 F.3d 1175 (11th Cir. 1999). The court noted there was an affirmative legal duty to redistrict based on population changes.

> In sharp contrast, however, is a city's right to determine if and when it will expand its municipal boundaries. Although the City of Belle Glade may well be bizarrely shaped, its contours were created over an extended time period as hundreds of individual parcels were brought into its ambit incrementally; it was not created by a single scheme designed to exclude property on the basis of race. [*Id.* at 1191.]

Similarly, a court upheld an incorporation against claims that the village boundaries were "consciously drawn . . . to impermissibly exclude . . . Black, Mexican-American and poor citizens who have historically been deemed an integral part of the 'natural community of Dickinson.'" *Caserta v. Village of Dickinson*, 491 F. Supp. 500 (S.D. Tex. 1980), *aff'd*, 672 F.2d 431 (5th Cir. 1982). The court noted in part that the size and population of the village were limited by statute, that the incorporators wanted to include the heart of "old downtown Dickinson," that the village area was based on natural and topographic boundaries, and that the facts were a "far hue and cry" from the *Gomillion* gerrymander. For another incorporation case in which a *Gomillion* violation was not found, see *Taylor v. Township of Dearborn*, 120 N.W.2d 737 (Mich. 1963), *noted*, 48 MINN. L. REV. 604 (1964). See also *Friends of Lake View Sch. Dist. Incorporation No. 25 v. Beebe*, 578 F.3d 753 (8th Cir. 2009) (dismissing a claim that a facially neutral school consolidation discriminated against African-American school districts).

3. *Hunter overruled?* In a case in which the court invalidated a gerrymander that excluded voters who were expected to vote against an annexation, the court made this comment on the *Hunter* rule:

> That was the law when eight of the present members of this Court were law students. But it is not now the law and has not been since 1960, when the U.S. Supreme Court modified its stance in *Gomillion.* [*City of Birmingham v. Community Fire Dist.*, 336 So. 2d 502, 507 (Ala. 1976).]

F. Local Government Incorporation and Annexation

Where incorporation and annexation occur and why. Municipal corporations are created by incorporation, and they grow through annexation. Despite some notable suburban incorporations in recent years, incorporation declined sharply after a major incorporation boom in the 1950s. Annexation is active, as the U.S. Census reported more than 93,000 annexations between 2000 and 2010 that added over eight million acres to existing municipalities. Because most of the largest cities in the country are surrounded by incorporated suburban communities, incorporations and annexations usually occur on the suburban fringe in metropolitan areas, although a number of smaller freestanding cities still have room to annex. For a historical review of incorporation and annexation, see Briffault, *Our Localism: Part II—Localism and Legal Theory*, 90 Colum. L. Rev. 346 (1990).

The interests at stake. Understanding the legal issues in incorporation and annexation requires an understanding of the interests at stake. They usually include the following:

(1) The primary parties are those who initiate an incorporation or annexation. In an incorporation, this is a group of property owners in the area to be incorporated. In an annexation, this is the municipality or an adjacent landowner.

(2) Landowners and residents may oppose an incorporation or annexation. They may live within or adjacent to the area to be incorporated or annexed, and may be concerned that incorporation or annexation will adversely affect their land.

(3) Other governments in the area may oppose an incorporation or annexation because they will lose tax base, zoning, and other regulatory controls over the area. The objecting county or town may also believe it can better provide services and regulatory controls to the area than another municipality or a new specially formed municipality or special district.

Incorporation and annexation procedures. The entity that has an interest in the incorporation or annexation, such as a group of incorporators or an adjacent landowner petitioning for annexation, usually initiates these procedures. The initiating entity defines the incorporation or annexation, which then may go to a county legislative board if it is an incorporation, or to a court if it is an annexation. Neither may modify the proposal. It must be accepted or rejected.

Incorporation and annexation standards and judicial review. These may be minimal, such as a minimum population requirement for incorporations, or a contiguity requirement for annexations. Judicial review is then limited and cannot consider the substantive and policy issues raised by the proposal. P. Steinbauer, et al., An Assessment of Municipal Annexation in Georgia and the United States 17–18 (2002), states that 70% of the states provide for some level of judicial involvement in the annexation process, ranging from appellate review to exercising actual decision-making authority. In most instances, the court's role is to review and determine whether there has been procedural and substantive compliance with statutory requirements. Some courts apply a "rule of reason" to decide on the acceptability of an incorporation or annexation, which is similar to the rule of some courts that they may decide whether a proposal is "reasonable" or "arbitrary and capricious." However, the usual rule of procedure that gives preference to the petition filed first limits any attempt by a court to arbitrate between competing incorporation petitions, or between competing incorporation and annexation petitions.

Policy analysis regarding municipal annexation and incorporation. A growing body of scholarship has explored the implications of municipal and incorporation policy with an eye to exclusion of minority populations and disadvantaged areas. See, e.g., Durst, *Race and Municipal Annexation After the Voting Rights Act,* J. Amer. Plan. Assn. 85, No. 1 (2019): 49–59; Purifoy, *North Carolina [Un]incorporated: Place, Race, and Local Environmental Inequity,* Amer. Behav. Sci. (2019): 1-32.

Areas in decline. A complete picture of local government can no longer focus only on establishment of municipalities and their expanding borders. Some cities (particularly in the snow belt) and local governments (particularly in rural areas) have faced significant decline in population and resulting imperatives to cut costs and restructure. Related issues are discussed in Chapter 4, relating to public finance. For scholarly exploration of associated topics, see, e.g., Anderson, *Dissolving Cities,* 121 Yale L.J. 1364 (2012); Ostrow, *Emerging Counties? Prospects for Regional Governance in the Wake of Municipal Dissolution,* 122 Yale L.J. Online 187 (2013).

[1] Incorporation

Problem 1-3

A foreign manufacturer of automobiles has acquired 200 acres of land on which it proposes to build an assembly plant. The plot is about one-half mile from a small unincorporated settlement of 500. The settlement consists of a main street with a few stores, surrounded by residential dwellings. About one-quarter mile outside of the settlement, a developer has built a large subdivision of 200 single-family homes. All of the surrounding area is agricultural, but some of the agricultural land near the settlement is held by developers who plan to build residential subdivisions.

Residents of the settlement propose to incorporate and to include the settlement, the automobile assembly plant land, the nearby subdivision, and agricultural land extending about one-half mile out from the perimeter of the settlement. Should the area be incorporated?

Statutory and judicial requirements for incorporation. As noted earlier, statutory requirements for incorporation in most states are minimal, and may only require a minimum population and compliance with statutory procedures. Some may also require a minimum population density. Other incorporation statutes go beyond minimal requirements and impose substantive requirements for incorporation. For example, they may require that an incorporation must be "right and proper" or "reasonable," or that a proposed municipality must be a "community." Some states authorize the incorporation of "villages," or "towns," and courts have interpreted these statutes to mean that the area seeking incorporation must be a town or village in the ordinary sense of the term. See Mandelker, *Standards for Municipal Incorporation on the Urban Fringe*, 36 Tex. L. Rev. 271 (1958). Here are some of the requirements that courts and statutes impose on incorporations:

a. *Urban territory.* The courts regularly put a limit on the amount of non-urban or "agricultural" land that may be included in a new municipality. Usually the new municipality attempts to include undeveloped rural land along with the developed portions of the territory that are to be included in the new incorporation. Judicial reluctance to allow too much undeveloped land in a new incorporation may indicate judicial sensitivity to the taxes and benefits issue, because the new municipality may not be able to provide services to the undeveloped areas even though they are fully taxed at the municipal tax rate. Is the area proposed for incorporation in the Problem "urban in character"?

b. *Provision of services.* Many statutes require a showing of how a newly-incorporated municipality will provide and pay for services. See, e.g., La. Rev. Stat. § 33:1(A)(4). Some require a showing that incorporation is a reasonable way of providing services and that there is no other reasonable alternative. See, e.g., Ky. Rev. Stat. § 81.060(1)(b). Statutes like this prevent the incorporation of municipalities that provide no benefits in return for taxation. What should the incorporators in the Problem do to make these showings?

c. *Comprehensive statutory controls on incorporation.* A growing number of states have statutes that contain comprehensive controls on incorporation. The Indiana statute for the incorporation of towns requires a showing that the town is compact and contiguous; that it will be developed for urban uses; that at least six major services will be provided at a reasonable tax rate; and that incorporation is in the "best interests" of the territory. This last specification requires consideration of the expected growth and governmental needs of the surrounding area, and the extent to which another governmental unit "can more adequately and economically provide essential services and functions." IND. CODE ANN. § 36-5-1-8. Would the incorporation proposed in Problem 1-3 be allowed under this statute? What additional information do you need to answer this question? See also the Wisconsin statute for the incorporation of villages, quoted and applied in *Walag v. Wisconsin Dep't of Admin.*, 634 N.W.2d 906 (Wis. App. 2001) (lack of homogeneity, compactness and a reasonably developed community center, and proposed village's roadways do not readily connect the commercial center to residential developments).

Notes and Questions

1. *Why municipalities incorporate.* Reasons why municipalities incorporate change over time. Extensive incorporation in the 1950s, for example, may have been a response to rapid population change in suburban areas. Rice, Waldner & Smith, *Why New Cities Form: An Examination into Municipal Incorporation in the United States 1950–2010*, J. PLAN. LIT. 29, No. 2 (2014): 140–154, reviewed the literature and media articles discussing individual incorporations. They found, as might be expected, that spatial reasons such as growth control, and political reasons, such as defensive incorporations to prevent annexation, were important. Incorporations may also be economically driven, as by an interest in lowering taxes; may be motivated by an interest in better services or by racial exclusion; or may simply be a response to the creation of other new municipalities in the area. There is no single explanation. How should statutes respond to these motivations?

For an important study of factors influencing municipal incorporations, see Leon-Moret, *Municipal Incorporation: Socioeconomic and Policy Factors of Influence*, STATE & LOC. GOV'T REV. 47, No. 4 (2015): 255–70. This study reviewed data from the 2000 and 2010 census and found that the there has been an overall decline in incorporations with the largest numbers occurring in the west and south. Factors predicting incorporation included income heterogeneity, higher per capita revenue, relatively low levels of growth regulation, and growth in county areas. See also Leon-Moret, *Municipal Incorporation in the United States*, URBAN STUDIES 52, No. 16 (2015): 3160-180 (finding that income heterogeneity raises the probability of municipal incorporation and state restrictions on local government autonomy lower that probability); Leon-Moret, *Municipal Incorporation: Socioeconomic and Policy Factors of Influence*, STATE & LOC. GOV'T REV. 47, No. 4 (2015): 255–70 (demonstrating that income heterogeneity raised the probability of incorporation, particularly where municipal per capita revenue is greater, land-use regulation is nonrestrictive, and population growth is rising).

2. *Growth zones.* Several states have adopted statutes that establish "growth zones" around existing cities in order to provide an area for their expansion and to prevent fringe incorporations. These statutes usually prevent the incorporation of a new municipality within a specified distance of the protected city, unless that city consents to the incorporation. *E.g.*, ARIZ. REV. STAT. ANN. § 9-101.01 (generally three to

six miles). Some of these statutes also prohibit annexations within the growth zone. The policy behind these statutes is to prevent incorporation so that protected cites may annex additional land as an alternative.

Does preventing incorporation raise constitutional problems? *Kaltsas v. City of North Chicago*, 513 N.E.2d 438, 442 (Ill. App. 1987), relied on *Hunter v. City of Pittsburgh* to hold the Illinois growth zone statute did not violate equal protection, because it did not involve "the gerrymandering of political districts so as to discriminate against a certain class of voters . . . but rather the location of a new municipality, the control of which is firmly within the hands of the legislature." Accord, *City of Tucson v. Pima County*, 19 P.3d 650 (Ariz. App. 2001) (right to vote not violated).

[2] Annexation by Municipalities

Annexation is a frequently-used strategy for municipal expansion, but its use and the structure of annexation statutes vary widely. All of New England, New Jersey, New York, and Pennsylvania are divided among municipalities, for example, and there is no unincorporated land. Annexation methods can be divided into five categories: popular determination, municipal action by ordinance or resolution, legislative determination, determination by regional or statewide boundary review commissions, and judicial determination. Tyson, *Annexation and the Mid-Size Metropolis: New Insights in the Age of Mobile Capital*, 73 U. Pitt. L. Rev. 505 (2012). Professor Tyson adds:

> Thirty-four states allow the annexation process to be initiated by a petition of property owners in the areas to be annexed. In nine of these states, annexation can be initiated only by property owner petition. . . . Fourteen states require the approval of the affected voters. Eleven states require that the affected county government must approve any municipal annexation. Twenty-nine states provide for an election in the area to be annexed at some point in the annexation process. [*Id.* at 514.]

Annexation is clearly limited when an election or county approval is required.

Basic statutory requirements for annexation vary, but all states have a contiguity requirement, and many states require the annexing city to provide municipal services to the annexed area and may require the development of a plan for such services. Some statutes have urbanization criteria, such as a minimum density, urban zoning, or subdivision of a majority of the land.

Historically, the principal motive for annexation has been to offset the fiscal impact of middle- and upper-income people fleeing cities by recapturing tax base, though some critics have challenged improving fiscal advantage as a proper motive. Annexation is also used to assure orderly growth, to prevent government fragmentation in metropolitan areas, and as a defensive strategy against incorporation.

Annexation may also have racial motivations, as the annexation of white areas may dilute the minority vote in the annexing city. Residents outside a city may seek annexation to get city services or more favorable zoning. Edwards, *Understanding the Complexities of Annexation*, J. PLAN. LIT. 23, No. 2 (2008): 119–35. See also Reynolds, *Rethinking Municipal Annexation Powers*, 24 URB. LAW. 247 (1992) (identifying interests local government has in annexing adjacent areas). The statutes are not generally responsive to motivation issues, though racial discrimination is actionable, and some states have boundary commissions, discussed *infra*, that can provide more comprehensive reviews.

For additional discussion, see Tyson, *Localism and Involuntary Annexation: Reconsidering Approaches to New Regionalism*, 87 TUL. L. REV. 297 (2012) (discussing broad trends); Wegner, *North Carolina's Annexation Wars: Whys, Wherefores, and What Next*, 91 N.C. L. REV. 165 (2012) (discussing North Carolina developments); Bell, *Municipal Annexation Reform in Texas: How a Victory for Property Rights Jeopardizes the State's Financial Health*, 50 ST. MARY'S L.J. 711 (2019) (discussing Texas developments).

Judicial Review Under the Rule of Reason. Some courts review annexations under a "rule of reason." This is a judicially implied standard that allows courts to determine whether the power delegated to the local government to annex has been abused. The annexation typically must meet three requirements: (1) exclusions and irregularities in boundary lines must not be the result of arbitrariness; (2) some reasonable present or demonstrable future need for the annexed property must be shown; and (3) no other factors must exist which would constitute an abuse of discretion on the part of the municipality. As noted by the court in *Town of Baraboo v. W. Baraboo*, 699 N.W.2d 610 (Wis. 2005), however, the rule does not authorize a court to question the wisdom of an annexation. This issue is inherently legislative. See *City of Birmingham v. Mead Corp.*, 372 So. 2d 825 (Ala. 1979) (annexation legislative; if reasonableness of proposed annexation fairly debatable, court must defer to judgment of local legislative body).

Problem 1-4

Reconsider the automobile plant incorporation Problem 1-3 at the beginning of the section on incorporation. Now assume the developed part of the small settlement is incorporated. It plans to extend its boundaries to include all of the land proposed in that Problem for incorporation. What issues would have to be considered under the annexation statutes discussed above? Under the rule of reason?

Annexation petitions by adjacent property owners who want to receive city services or who need a rezoning are common. The question then is whether this private motive invalidates the annexation. The following case, in a state that has the rule of reason, considers this and other questions arising out of an annexation in response to a private petition.

Town of Pleasant Prairie v. City of Kenosha

75 Wis. 2d 322, 249 N.W.2d 581 (1977)

Abrahamson, Justice.

This is an appeal in a declaratory judgment action brought by the Town of Pleasant Prairie. The issue presented is whether annexation by the City of Kenosha of certain land in the Town of Pleasant Prairie violated the rule of reason established in decisions of this court to test the validity of municipal annexations. We conclude that the annexation is valid.

I

On September 4, 1973, Robert E. and Doris P. Gangler filed with the Kenosha city clerk a petition seeking direct annexation by the City of a 28 acre parcel of land, roughly rectangular in shape, then located in the Town of Pleasant Prairie. On the following day the Ganglers petitioned the City to rezone most of the proposed annexation for industrial use.

Along its northern boundary the parcel described in the annexation petition was contiguous to existing city limits, which in this region coincided with the northern boundary of a railroad right-of-way owned by the Chicago & Northwestern Railroad. The proposed annexed territory included 2.9 acres of right-of-way owned by the railroad, 2.6 acres owned by Mr. William Kaphengst, 7.7 acres owned by Mr. Timothy Lawler, and 14.8 acres owned by the Ganglers. No electors lived within this territory. Only the Ganglers, who owned more than half of the land in area, signed the annexation petition.

An ordinance annexing the territory was approved by the Common Council of the City of Kenosha on October 1, 1973. At the same meeting, the Council referred the zoning petition to the City Plan Commission for reconsideration. Three days later the Town of Pleasant Prairie filed the complaint by which the action now before the court was commenced. The action proceeded to trial in the circuit court in November of 1974, and the Town has taken this appeal from a judgment upholding the validity of the annexation....

The claims made are (1) that in several ways matters respecting industrial zoning for the annexed land so infected the annexation as to render it arbitrary, capricious and an abuse of discretion; (2) that the City had no reasonable need for the territory annexed; and (3) that the boundaries of the territory were arbitrarily and capriciously fixed.

II

In ch. 66, Stats., the legislature has conferred upon cities and villages broad powers to annex unincorporated territory. This court has often stated that in determining the validity of annexations it is committed to the doctrine which has come to be known as the "rule of reason." We have stated the rule of reason, which has as its essential purpose the ascertainment whether the power delegated to the cities and villages has been abused in a given case, in the following terms:

> Under this rule, (1) exclusions and irregularities in boundary lines must not be the result of arbitrariness, (2) some reasonable present or demonstrable future need for the annexed property must be shown, and (3) no other factors must exist which would constitute an abuse of discretion. [Citing *Town of Lafayette v. City of Chippewa Falls*, 235 N.W.2d 435 (Wis. 1975) in footnote].

When attacked under the rule of reason, annexation ordinances, like legislative enactments in general, enjoy a presumption of validity, and the burden of overcoming this presumption with proof that the ordinance is invalid rests on the party so claiming. The rule of reason does not authorize a court to inquire into the wisdom of the annexation before it or to determine whether the annexation is in the best interest of the parties to the proceeding or of the public. These matters are inherently legislative and not judicial in character. . . .

III

The Town advances several arguments related to zoning which it claims show the annexation herein to be invalid. It is first claimed that annexation was improperly used for the sole purpose of effecting rezoning of the land involved.

The evidence showed that the Ganglers' chief motive for seeking annexation was to enable industrial development of their property, which was zoned for agricultural use while located in the Town under zoning ordinances of Kenosha county. The Ganglers had approached John Maurer, Town Chairman of Pleasant Prairie, concerning the possibility of industrial development of their land. At the trial Robert Gangler testified that Maurer had told him that he considered the Gangler land to be good industrial property, but that the Town could not then provide it with sewer and water services. Maurer himself testified in substance that he had simply told Gangler that the land was not and would not be zoned for industrial development. In any event, the record shows that the Ganglers desired industrial development for their land before annexation to the City was sought and that neither the zoning nor the municipal services that would be necessary to such development were then available in the Town.

When it appeared that their plans for development could not be realized in the Town, the Ganglers initiated contact with Robert F. Kolstad, City Planner for the City of Kenosha, regarding the possibility of annexing their land to the City. Several meetings were had at which Kolstad explained statutory annexation procedures and advised and assisted the Ganglers in preparing the necessary documents and maps. As stated above, on September 4, 1973, the Ganglers' annexation petition was filed and by letter dated September 5, 1973, Mr. Gangler petitioned the Kenosha Common Council to have most of the annexation rezoned for heavy industrial use. Gangler's letter stated that "the purpose of annexation and rezoning is to permit the development of this property for industrial purposes," and for this reason he requested that the annexation and zoning petitions be considered together. Such joint consideration was in fact undertaken. At its October 1, 1973, meeting the Kenosha Common Council adopted the annexation ordinance and voted to refer the matter of zoning for the annexed area "back to City Plan Commission for reconsideration—to eliminate all heavy industrial zoning and to provide for a proper buffer zone between the industrial and residential areas."

We find nothing in this state of affairs which would justify invalidating the annexation now before the court. The Town's assertion that the sole purpose behind the annexation was to obtain a change in zoning is misleading. The Ganglers' purpose was to develop their land, preferably for industrial use, which required zoning and municipal services not available in the Town. It cannot be doubted that a purpose to develop one's land is legitimate, and this court has stated that property owners may seek annexation in pursuit of their own perceived best interests. *Cf. Town of Madison v. City of Madison*, 106 N.W.2d 264 (Wis. 1960), in which the court recognized that removal of the burden of town zoning ordinances on property in the town owned by the City of Madison was a legitimate goal of the annexation proceeding. We hold that a direct annexation not otherwise in conflict with the rule of reason is not invalidated because the petitioners are motivated by a desire to obtain a change in the zoning of their land.

Nor is this annexation condemned by the existence of a desire or intent to rezone the property on the part of the City of Kenosha. The City sought to justify this annexation by showing that it had a need for land with potential for industrial development. As discussed later, we conclude that a reasonable need for such land was shown to exist. It would be manifestly unreasonable then to say that the annexation is invalidated because of an intent to rezone the land so as to allow it to serve the very need the annexation was designed to fulfill.

The Town next claims that the ordinance is invalid because the City used the economic benefits of rezoning to induce the Ganglers to petition for annexation and because the City in effect delegated its zoning power to the Ganglers. Running through both of these arguments is the Town's assertion that use of the annexed territory for industrial development represents poor urban planning....

The record in this case shows without contradiction that the Ganglers desired annexation by reason of their own self-interest, and that the Ganglers, not the City, initiated the annexation process and made the decision to seek rezoning. Kolstad testified that simultaneous petitioning for annexation and rezoning is a common practice. There is no suggestion in this record that any coercion was practiced upon the Ganglers by the City or that any special economic considerations of the type involved in [an earlier] case were given or promised to the Ganglers.

We decline the Town's suggestion that we infer from the facts that some kind of promise of industrial zoning was made by the City, that industrial zoning was used as a "bribe" to induce the Ganglers to petition for annexation, or that the City somehow "delegated" its zoning powers to the Ganglers.

It may be that the City Planner informed the Ganglers that he personally felt industrial zoning would be appropriate for the annexed area or that he thought the Common Council would probably approve such zoning. However, there is no evidence to show that anyone acting on behalf of the City promised any type of rezoning or otherwise purported to commit the City in this regard. Moreover, as we have noted, the Common Council has already partially refused Mr. Gangler's rezoning petition, which requested that the property be rezoned for heavy industrial use. Speculative characterizations such as the Town has advanced cannot serve to overcome the presumed validity of the annexation ordinance here. The expert testimony and documentary evidence adduced with respect to the alleged impropriety, from the standpoint of sound land use, management and urban planning, of developing the annexed territory for industrial use do not, as the Town contends, establish the Town's assertions of arbitrary economic inducement and invalid delegation of zoning power. The area immediately to the north of the annexation is already industrial, while a residential subdivision is located southeast of the annexation, and nearby lands in other directions are for the most part undeveloped. Without describing the evidence in detail, which would serve no useful purpose, it suffices to say that the conflict between the parties came down to this: The Town took the position that industrial activity should be confined to the area north of the Chicago & Northwestern Railroad tracks—i.e., to the area which is already industrial—with the area south of the tracks, including the annexation here, to be used ultimately for residential development. The railroad tracks would provide a buffer zone between the industrial and residential areas. The City asserted that the railroad was not a good buffer and that light industrial activity should extend south of the railroad tracks with the needed buffer to be provided by a wide boulevard coupled with setback requirements. Both parties produced expert testimony and studies to support their positions.

Under the circumstances we believe the trial court was correct in declining to involve itself in weighing the relative merits of the parties' positions respecting industrial development of the annexed territory. In essence this phase of the trial was an attempt to litigate in court the question of what zoning was best for the territory affected. . . . In *In re City of Beloit*, 155 N.W.2d 633 (Wis. 1968), we held unconstitutional an attempt by the legislature to delegate to the courts determination of whether an annexation was "in the public interest."

It is for the Common Council of the City of Kenosha to weigh competing data and theories bearing on what zoning is best for the area in which this annexation is located. It cannot be said that industrial development of the annexation here would be arbitrary, capricious or an abuse of discretion, and this being so, judicial inquiry on this issue is at an end. . . .

[The court then held the city had demonstrated a need for the annexation and that the boundaries were not arbitrary.]

Notes and Questions

1. *Annexing to develop.* For a similar case upholding an annexation to escape restrictive zoning, see *In re Annexation of Territory in Olmstead Township to City of Olmstead Falls,* 470 N.E.2d 912 (Ohio App. 1984). The court applied the Ohio rule, that personal benefit to the owner of annexed land is sufficient, though not necessarily enough, as proof that the annexation served the "general good of the territory," as required by the annexation statute. Compare *Village of Skaneateles v. Town of Skaneateles,* 456 N.Y.S.2d 185 (App. Div. 1985). The court held the annexation would not be in the "overall public interest" as required by the New York statute because its sole reason was to avoid the restrictive effect of the town zoning ordinance. "We have found no precedent approving the use of annexation as a device by which the owner of land in one municipality may escape the effect of that municipality's local legislation by having the land transferred to an adjoining municipality." *Id.* at 186. For an argument that private interests are an important factor motivating boundary changes, see Fleischmann, *The Goals and Strategies of Local Boundary Changes: Government Organization or Private Gain?* 8 J. URB. AFF., No. 4 (1986): 63–76.

2. *Reviewing annexations.* Courts in some states review the merits of an annexation. Whether there is a need for an annexation, as in the principal case, can be an important critical factor. See *Town of Sugar Creek v. City of Elkhorn,* 605 N.W.2d 274 (Wis. App. 1999) (need for parcel to maintain economic and social well-being); *City of St. Peters v. Ronald A. Winterhoff Living Trust,* 117 S.W.3d 698 (Mo. App. 2003) (need for property zoned industrial along a highway, applying factors to consider in need determination). New York courts applying the public interest test will approve an annexation when they find a positive benefit. *City of Fulton v. Town of Granby,* 984 N.Y.S.2d 778 (App. Div. 2014) (city better to provide services; annexation of treatment plant would stabilize rates and encourage development; city and annexed area were a community).

The Mississippi court adopted 12 factors to determine the reasonableness of an annexation. They include whether there is a need to expand, whether the area is in the city's path of growth, whether there is a need for services, and the impact of the annexation on the voting strength of protected minority groups. *City of Saltillo v. City of Tupelo (In re of the extension of the boundaries of the City of Tupelo),* 94 So. 3d 256 (Miss. 2012) (approving annexation). Compare *City Horn Lake v. Town of Walls (In re Enlarging, Extending & Defining the Corporate Limits & Boundaries of the Horn Lake),* 57 So. 3d 1253 (Miss. 2011) (nine of 12 factors not met, city was experiencing economic problems and did not have a need to expand).

3. *The contiguity problem.* A municipality may want to annex noncontiguous land, such as valuable industrial or commercial property, but avoid annexing contiguous intervening land, either to avoid providing services or to exclude opposition from the annexation election. Noncontiguous annexations may be accomplished by a "strip" annexation in which the noncontiguous land is connected by a strip, such

as a highway. Is this type of annexation bad? Statutes often require annexed areas to be contiguous to a municipality, presumably to provide a community of interest and ensure the provision of services. Quite often the term "contiguity" is not defined, and courts must interpret this ambiguous word.

The contiguity requirement is more difficult to interpret than it appears because only that land adjacent or near to the annexing municipality can be "contiguous," and the question becomes how "contiguous" the annexation must be. The majority view is that annexed land must touch at every point or at least share a substantial common boundary. *Carolina Power & Light Co. v. City of Asheville*, 597 S.E.2d 717 (N.C. 2004) (land must be contiguous to city's boundary, or contiguous to area developed for urban purposes, on at least 60% of external boundary). The minority view is that the annexed land need only touch at some point, no matter how small or narrow. *Glick v. Town of Gilbert*, 599 P.2d 848 (Ariz. 1979); *Town of Campbell v. City of La Crosse*, 634 N.W.2d 840 (Wis. App. 2001). Both rules apply a geographic homogeneity test that does not consider the reasonableness of the annexation. Other courts adopt a more flexible "reasonableness" test, as in *Mutz v. Municipal Boundary Comm'n*, 688 P.2d 12 (N.M. 1984). The court noted it had invalidated annexations for lack of contiguity when the municipality was interested only in annexing the noncontiguous land, and the "strip" was added only for this reason. Which view is correct, and how would you codify the view you prefer to make the contiguity requirement clearer?

4. *Considering the impact of proposed annexations on other governments.* Should and can courts consider the effect of an annexation on other local governments? In *West Mead Township v. City of Meadville*, 294 A.2d 600 (Pa. Commw. 1972), the court rejected a township claim that an annexation raised a threat of "piecemeal annexation township suicide." Although large blocs of township acreage and tax revenue had been taken from the township in recent years, neither township debt nor tax rate had increased. In the *City of Fulton* case, *supra*, the court did not find the impact on the town substantial enough to require invalidation of the annexation.

The priority in time rule can figure here. In *In re Enlargement and Extension of Mun. Boundaries of City of D'Iberville*, 867 So. 2d 241 (Miss. 2004), the Mississippi Supreme Court acknowledged the existence of the rule (that prior in time is prior in jurisdiction), but held it was outdated and overruled it for annexation litigation. The court said the ultimate determination must be whether the annexation is reasonable under the totality of the circumstances. But see *Town of Campbell v. City of La Crosse*, 667 N.W.2d 356 (Wis. Ct. App. 2003) (an annexation proceeding that commences prior to an incorporation proceeding takes precedence).

A Note on Annexation Agreements

Many annexations occur through annexation agreements between landowners and municipalities. They often are used when a developer wishes to develop land that requires city services or, as in the *Pleasant Prairie* case, when the landowner needs a rezoning from the annexing municipality. Agreements are popular with developers because they eliminate the concern that the necessary zoning will not be forthcoming after annexation because neighbors may protest, or the city may have a change of heart. The agreement usually provides that the developer will not protest annexation in return for the municipality's promise to provide necessary services and, if necessary, to rezone the developer's land. It may also provide for fees and site improvements to be provided by the developer. A Maryland statute restricts the zoning classification into which a municipality may place newly annexed property for a period of five years following annexation, unless permission is first obtained from the pre-annexation county. MD. ANN. CODE art. 23A, § 9.

Some states authorize annexation agreements. E.g., 65 ILL. COMP. STAT. 5/11-15.1-1, -2 (agreement may cover zoning of land). See MacNeill & Nissenbaum, *Annexation Agreements*, 15 MGT. INFO. SERV. REP. No. 3 (ICMA, 1986) (includes six successful case studies). State law provisions are important, since they may or may not cover disputes between different cities that seek to annex a particular area. See, e.g., *In re Annexation of Certain Real Property to the City of Proctor from Midway Township*, 925 N.W.2d 216 (Minn. 2019) (Minnesota's "orderly annexation" provisions for annexation agreements does not preclude otherwise lawful annexations by ordinance by other non-party jurisdictions).

Annexation agreements can raise objections that a municipality has bargained away its police power if it agrees to a rezoning in the annexation agreement. *City of Louisville v. Fiscal Court*, 623 S.W.2d 219 (Ky. 1981), invalidated an annexation agreement in which it promised to "assist and cooperate fully" with the property owners in securing any necessary zoning changes, set tax rates and provide for de-annexation at the option of the property owner:

> [T]he city is required to cooperate . . . in matters which fall within the duty and responsibility of the city. . . . It is very conceivable (and even likely) that the obligations of the City under the agreement would create a conflict between the constitutional and statutory duties of the City and its contractual obligations.
>
> . . . [T]he contract . . . also creates an obligation to legislate in the future. . . . A contract which binds a legislative body, present or future, to a course of legislative action is void against public policy. [*Id.* at 225.]

The court did not apply the *Louisville* case where city officials negotiated an agreement with a developer but the agreement was not approved by the local legislative body until after this body had approved the annexation, that there was no improper bargaining away of local power. City officials were not authorized to bind the city contractually and the agreement was not binding until approved by the common council. See *Town of Brockway v. City of Black River Falls*, 702 N.W.2d 418 (Wis. 2005). Other courts have upheld annexation agreements when the municipality did not promise to rezone. *City of Springfield ex rel. Burton v. City of Springfield*, 2000 WL 799727 (Ohio App. 2000). This rule is consistent with cases upholding agreements to rezone when there is no explicit promise to rezone by the municipality.

D. Mandelker, Land Use Law §§6.60–6.61 (2019). Note the uncertainty, however, when there is no explicit rezoning promise in an annexation agreement. Would you advise a client to agree to an annexation without such a promise? A court will enforce an annexation agreement when there has been performance on both sides, *Morrison Homes Corp. v. City of Pleasanton*, 130 Cal. Rptr. 196 (Cal. App. 1976), but if the municipality does not make a definite promise, then what?

What if a city pressured a developer to sign an annexation agreement as a condition to the city's approving the rezoning? *Hoepker v. City of Madison Plan Comm'n*, 563 N.W.2d 145 (Wis. 1997), invalidated an annexation agreement signed under these circumstances because it was held to be the result of direct economic pressure. But see *Yakima County (West Valley) Fire Protection Dist. No. 12 v. City of Yakima*, 858 P.2d 245 (Wash. 1993), where the court approved an agreement by the city to provide sewer services in return for an agreement not to oppose annexation where there was no duty to provide the service. The provision of services was a benefit to the landowners. A request to promote annexation violated First Amendment rights. Are the cases distinguishable?

What happens when developments facilitated by annexation agreements turn sour because a major real estate development fails? See *In re the Banning Lewis Ranch Co. v. City of Colorado Springs, Co.*, 532 B.R. 335 (Bankr. D. Colo. 2015) (debtors who purchased substantial acreage and entered into annexation agreement calling for payment of proportionate share of infrastructure costs could not avoid related obligations in bankruptcy action where annexation agreement was not executory contract; debtor's property could not be sold free and clear of annexation agreement under changed circumstances doctrine).

A Note on Racial Discrimination in Annexations

Annexation can raise a racial discrimination problem if a city with a minority population dilutes the minority vote by annexing an area with a white population. *Holt v. City of Richmond*, 459 F.2d 1093 (4th Cir. 1972), upheld under the Fifteenth Amendment an annexation by Richmond, Virginia that reduced a marginal black majority to a minority. *Gomillion* was distinguished as a case whose "sole or clearly dominant purpose was both obvious and constitutionally impermissible." *Id.* at 1097. For a study of related issues, see Durst, *Race and Municipal Annexation After the Voting Rights Act*, 85 J. Amer. Plan. Ass'n, No. 1 (2019): 49–59 (discussing issues of municipal underbounding).

Racial dilution through annexation questions also arose under §5 and §2 of the federal Voting Rights Act. Section 5, 42 U.S.C. §1973c, required that "covered" jurisdictions obtain a declaratory judgment from the federal District Court for the District of Columbia, or a preclearance from the Attorney General, that any change in "voting qualification, prerequisite, standard, practice, or procedure [with respect to voting] does not have the purpose and will not have the effect of denying or abridging the right to vote on account of race or color." A "covered" jurisdiction was one where there had been a history of discrimination. In *Shelby County v. Holder*, 570 U.S. 529 (2013), the Court invalidated § 4 of the act, under which coverage determinations were made, making § 5 inoperable. Section 2 of the act, 42 U.S.C. § 1973(a), which authorizes litigation to similarly invalidate a "standard, practice, or procedure," was not affected. In *Perkins v. Matthews*, 400 U.S. 379 (1971), the Supreme Court held that annexations fell under § 5 because they had a "sufficient potential" for denying or abridging the right to vote because of race or color. They would also fall under § 2. However, the standards for vote dilution are not the same under § 2 as they are under § 5. *Holder v. Hall*, 512 U.S. 874 (1994).

The Court applied a "fairly reflect" standard in § 5 annexation cases. In *City of Richmond v. United States*, 422 U.S. 358 (1975), the annexation reduced the minority population from 56 to 47 percent. The Court noted the annexation would impair the ability of blacks to elect candidates, but upheld the annexation if the city would adopt a voting system that "fairly reflects" the strength of the black community after the annexation. *Compare City of Rome v. United States*, 446 U.S. 156 (1980), where only 20.6 percent of the pre-annexation population was black, and the annexation resulted in only a 1% drop in the number of blacks in the total population. However, the Court applied *Richmond*, and invalidated the annexation because voting in the city was racially polarized, and because the annexation substantially enlarged the number of white voters without increasing the number of black voters.

Can the Voting Rights Act be used to mandate an annexation when there is racial discrimination? *City of Pleasant Grove v. United States*, 479 U.S. 462 (1987), suggested minority communities may have a right under § 5 to be annexed under the Voting Rights Act, but the cases have not gone this far. The Court there felt the record showed the refusal to annex was racially motivated, and that the city did not show the annexation did not have a purpose of abridging or denying the right to vote on account of race. It affirmed a judgment denying preclearance to the city. *Burton v. City of Belle Glade*, 178 F.3d 1175 (11th Cir. 1999), rejected a § 2 Voting Rights Act challenge to a refusal to annex a black public housing project, though objectors argued a discriminatory intent was supported circumstantially by de jure segregation in the city's housing projects and the city's bizarre shape. In dictum, the Supreme Court in *Holder, supra*, said

> we think it quite improbable to suggest that a § 2 dilution challenge could be brought to a town's existing political boundaries [in an attempt to force it to annex surrounding land] by arguing that the current boundaries dilute a racial group's voting strength in comparison to the proposed new boundaries." [*Id.* at 884.]

A Note on Boundary Review Commissions

Several states have created boundary review commissions to manage formation and annexations by local governments. The boundary review commissions usually have a broad jurisdiction over all local government organization and boundary problems. Special districts may be included along with municipalities. Approval of a commission's decision in an election may be required. Courts have rejected constitutional objections to the commissions. See *Mid-County Future Alternatives Comm. v. City of Portland*, 795 P.2d 541 (Or. 1990) (rejecting home rule and equal protection objections).

Boundary review commission legislation substitutes an agency with expertise and continuing jurisdiction over local government incorporations for bodies like a county board, which considers incorporation petitions infrequently and has no expertise on incorporation problems. For annexations, the commission is a substitute for an annexation process which would otherwise be initiated by a municipality or adjacent property owners for reasons that may be self-serving. Because the commission is an administrative agency with original jurisdiction, it can take an assertive policymaking role that is forbidden to most courts because of limitations on judicial powers. For example, a commission can be given the power to modify proposals submitted to it and to resolve conflicts over territory between competing jurisdictions. Courts cannot exercise these powers. See *Fallbrook Sanitary Dist. v. San Diego Local Agency Formation Comm'n*, 256 Cal. Rptr. 590 (Cal. App. 1989) (commission can modify proposal for special district reorganization); *Village of Farmington v. Minnesota Municipal Comm'n*, 170 N.W.2d 197 (Minn. 1969) (commission not bound by priority in time rule).

Rationale. A study by the Advisory Commission on Intergovernmental Relations could not determine whether boundary review commissions are effective, but offered these comments on their performance:

> The fact that most BRC [boundary review commission] work involves annexation, combined with the fact that many local jurisdictions in metropolitan areas share boundaries with other incorporated governments, like a jigsaw puzzle, keeps most BRC activity incremental. In general, BRCs respond to individual proposals for boundary changes rather than initiating studies of broader strategies for governmental boundary reform. This situation is simultaneously a disappointment to those who hope for a "rationalization" of local government patterns and a comfort to those who believe that an electoral-legal marketplace of boundary decisions is preferable to a centrally planned pattern. [ACIR, LOCAL BOUNDARY COMMISSIONS: STATUS AND ROLES IN FORMING, ADJUSTING AND DISSOLVING LOCAL GOVERNMENT BOUNDARIES 24 (1992).]

California legislation authorizing county boundary review commissions, known as Local Agency Formation Commissions (LAFCOs), resolves competition by municipalities for territory by requiring the adoption by the commissions of "spheres of influence" for local governments within the county. CAL. GOV'T CODE § 56425. For criticism, see Reynolds, *Rethinking Annexation Powers*, 24 URB. LAW. 247, 264–65 (1992).

Statutory review criteria. Because boundary review commissions are viewed as a method of providing an orderly and comprehensive boundary change review process, statutes commonly provide an expansive list of review criteria that require consideration of the merits of a proposal, and a comparative review of which local government in the area is best suited to provide public services and protect public welfare. These statutes may list factors or objectives the commission is to consider but do not "dictate particular decisions," as the court pointed out in *Multnomah Cty. Rural Fire Protection Dist. No. 10 v. Portland Metropolitan Area Local Gov't Boundary Comm'n*, 868 P.2d 783 (Or. 1994). The Washington statute is typical:

> The decisions of the boundary review board shall attempt to achieve the following objectives:
>
> (1) Preservation of natural neighborhoods and communities;
>
> (2) Use of physical boundaries, including but not limited to bodies of water, highways, and land contours;
>
> (3) Creation and preservation of logical service areas;
>
> (4) Prevention of abnormally irregular boundaries;
>
> (5) Discouragement of multiple incorporations of small cities and encouragement of incorporation of cities in excess of ten thousand population in heavily populated urban areas;
>
> (6) Dissolution of inactive special purpose districts;
>
> (7) Adjustment of impractical boundaries;
>
> (8) Incorporation as cities or towns or annexation to cities or towns of unincorporated areas that are urban in character; and
>
> (9) Protection of agricultural and rural lands which are designated for long term productive agricultural and resource use by a comprehensive plan adopted by the county legislative authority. [Wash. Rev. Code § 36.93.180.]

The courts will uphold board decisions if they balance the statutory factors properly. See *Stewart v. Washington State Boundary Review Bd.*, 996 P.2d 1087 (Wash. App. 2000).

G. Special Districts

[1] Nature and Function of Special Districts

A special district or authority is a government corporation, usually created to provide a single function or service. Unlike a general purpose government (a county, town, village or city) which uses its delegated authority to protect the health and welfare of its residents, these government corporations have features of both private and public sectors. They operate similarly to a private corporation because they are often free of many of the restrictions placed on public corporations, yet they are at least indirectly accountable to the public. There is tremendous diversity in purpose, size, and powers of special districts and authorities, as reflected in the legislation under which they are created. Although there is wide variety in the degree of dependence or independence in their governing authority and ability to tax or assess fees to support their activities, most have substantial administrative and fiscal independence, whether created to serve a state or local purpose. Because of this, they are generally touted as being free of politics.

Government corporations are thus owned by the government, yet governed and managed in the manner of a private corporation; they are designed to separate politics from administration, yet in a way that keeps them indirectly accountable to the public; and they are expected to be entrepreneurial, yet with a sense of fiscal responsibility. J. Mitchell, The American Experiment with Government Corporations 11 (1999). Another way of viewing the distinctions between general purpose local governments and special districts is expressed by Professor Christopher Goodman in his study of local government fragmentation. See Goodman, *Local Government Fragmentation: What Do We Know*? State & Loc. Gov't Rev. 51, No. 2 (2019) 134–44. Goodman observes:

> An area is considered "fragmented" if it has a large number of local government units, measured in absolute or per capita terms. The opposite of fragmentation is consolidation and is typified by a small number of units (and in the extreme one unit) of local government. Fragmentation is but one attribute of local government structure. Potentially just as important is the distribution of service delivery and/or revenue generation responsibilities. [Scholars] refer[] to this as concentration.
>
> Those who follow public choice theory suggest the proliferation of vertical tiers of local government allow for the separation of the production of local public services from the provision of such services. The institutional reformers see the proliferation of vertically stacked local governments as a source of inefficiency due to duplication of services and a lack of administrative efficiencies. [citations omitted].
>
> While many overlapping special districts may not be the most efficient system, there is some evidence that local governments use such arrangements to circumvent state-level restrictions on their actions. If this evidence is correct, it would suggest the proliferation of overlapping governments is a means for local governments to continue to provide public services demanded by its citizens, albeit more inefficiently than if those services were produced in house. Coupled with the less than stellar transparency records of many special districts it is difficult to endorse the proliferation of special districts as a means to deal with restrictions on general-purpose governments. [citations omitted]

Types of districts and authorities. The label given a particular government corporation is confusing, whether it be "special district" or "authority." Often both are categorized as "special districts." Generally, however, there are two basic differences. Special districts most often have elected governing boards and are financed through special tax assessments. As noted by Professor K. Foster in THE POLITICAL ECONOMY OF SPECIAL-PURPOSE GOVERNMENT 7–14 (1997):

> The first type of [special district] ... comprises local government entities with the power to tax and levy special assessments. For many taxing districts, user charges may and often do supplement other revenues. Nearly all taxing districts have elected governing boards....

Authorities usually have appointed boards, no taxing authority and are most often supported by user fees, grants, and tax-exempt revenue bonds. Authorities are used at both the state and local level to address large- and small-scale needs. As explained by Foster, *id.*:

> The second type of special-purpose government, known as *public authorities*, comprises government corporations without property-taxing powers. Public authorities raise most revenues through user fees, grants, and private revenue bonds. Authorities tend to provide services that are divisible and chargeable ..., that is, those for which the benefits of a service can be attributed to specific individuals (for example, tolls for road users).... [They] are also common providers of large-scale, typically costly capital projects that might go wanting under a pay-as-you-go system....

Why created? There are numerous reasons for the creation of a special district. A municipality may create a special district because it is limited in its own authority to tax or incur debt necessary to finance a particular service that is needed, but it can create a special district capable of accomplishing the task. In addition, some local governments want to impose the cost of a particular service on an area of their jurisdiction that will benefit from the service, particularly if other areas of the community will not benefit. Drawing the boundaries of the special district to include just those needing it accomplishes this purpose. The size and location of the geographic region within a special district is directly related to the purpose for which it has been created. The district may be located in an unincorporated area (to provide a needed service that is not provided by a municipality); it may encompass part of or all of a local government; or it may include multiple local government boundaries. There is also a growing popularity of large master-planned special district communities in some areas of the country. The number of special districts continues to grow significantly, and as of 2017, stood at 38,542 according to data from the Census of Governments. Numerous states have more than 1000 special districts.

Upsides and downsides. As discussed below, special districts are often used to foster economic development. When municipalities face financial distress, they may instead be used as a means of preserving important services that are at risk. For a useful perspective about the role of special districts in this "downside" context, see Sawyer, *Special Assessment Districts: Neighborhood-Driven Improvements in Distressed Cities*, 63 WAYNE L. REV. 705 (2018) (discussing use of special districts in Detroit for mosquito abatement, snow removal, and private security services).

Notes and Questions

1. *The role of special districts.* Studies of special districts suggest they are more likely to form when states limit local fiscal powers and municipal opportunities to annex land, when there is a need to meet demands for services, and when entrepreneurs see a need to form special districts to provide services for new developments. McCabe, *Special-District Formation Among the States*, 32 State & Loc. Gov't Rev., No. 2 (2000): 121–31. There are many examples of developers seeking the creation of special districts, particularly to gain the ability to have the special district issue revenue bonds to build needed infrastructure. As noted by Professor Burns, in The Formation of American Local Governments (1994), the Reedy Creek Improvement District in Orlando, Florida, was created for Walt Disney World. For scholarly discussions of the recent evolution of special districts, see Shoked, *Quasi-Cities*, 93 B.U. L. Rev. 1971 (2013) (discussing special districts, their history, and their role as an alternative to city formation); Shoked, *The New Local*, 100 Va. L. Rev. 1323 (2014) (discussing special district issues with an eye to school districts and historic districts). Should certain functions not be provided through special district structures? See Kazis, *Special Districts, Sovereignty, and the Structure of Local Police Services*, 48 Urb. Law. 417 (2016) (discussing provision of police services). Should certain types of districts operate with special restrictions? See Bumgardner & Hemyari, *Dodging Mud Slingers: An Analysis and Defense of Texas Municipal Utility Districts*, 21 Tex. Rev. L. & Pol. 377 (2017) (considering the special characteristics of utility districts).

2. *Accountability.* Special districts clearly have an effect on government spending priorities and spending, but they present an accountability problem because they

> have an advantage in that they enable functions to be distanced from the political arena and performed in a manner that meets technical requirements. However, democracy is weakened and accountability is reduced. This may not be a problem for services such as sewerage and water supply where technical requirements usually have priority, but it can easily be a problem for services such as police protection and libraries; and certainly it is a problem if a significant proportion of local government functions are performed by such authorities. [I.M. Barlow, Metropolitan Government 7 (1991).]

[2] Organization of Special Districts

Legislation authorizing special districts usually allows their formation by referendum or by resolution of a municipal governing body, and does not usually contain standards governing the formation of districts that allow for the exercise of discretion. As a result, there is little or no discretionary control over the formation of special districts if a referendum is favorable or if a municipal legislative body decides to create one. This decentralization of authority to form special districts is another reason why they can proliferate without control in metropolitan areas. Like many municipal incorporation statutes, laws providing for the formation of special districts may make the establishment of a district mandatory if it is approved in a referendum, and the statute may include only minimal requirements, such as a minimum number of petitioners to call an election.

Judicial review will be available if the statute authorizing the creation of a district has substantive standards. In *Reilly Tar & Chemical Corp. v. City of St. Louis Park*, 121 N.W.2d 393 (Minn. 1963), for example, a statute authorized a city to organize a housing and redevelopment authority if it found "blighted" areas within a city. The court held that organization of a district would be in "excess" of the city's powers if blighting conditions did not exist. A court may imply a "reasonableness" standard if a statute does not have standards that govern district formation. See *State Farm Mut. Auto. Ins. Co. v. City of Lakewood*, 788 P.2d 808, 816 (Colo. 1990) (holding decision to form district was quasi-legislative, and that a "narrow review of quasi-legislative action is available in a declaratory judgment action").

Judicial review of the formation of a special district may be more assertive if a court believes the special district does not comply with the law, as the next case illustrates.

City of Scottsdale v. McDowell Mountain Irrigation & Drainage District

107 Ariz. 117, 483 P.2d 532 (1971)

WILLIBY E. CASE, JR., JUDGE OF THE COURT OF APPEALS.

This is an appeal from an order granting appellees' motion for summary judgment in an action wherein appellants sought to test the validity of the organization of the McDowell Mountain Irrigation and Drainage District (hereinafter referred to as the District).

Two issues are presented on appeal. First, do any or all of the appellants have standing to test the validity of the District's organization? Second, did the jurisdictional prerequisites exist for the Board to authorize the organization of the District?

The facts necessary for a determination of these issues are as follows.

In the summer of 1968, a petition was filed with the Maricopa County Board of Supervisors, (hereinafter referred to as the Board), pursuant to Title 45, Chapter 6, A.R.S., seeking the organization of certain described land into the McDowell Mountain Irrigation and Drainage District. The land consisting of 11,420 acres was located within Maricopa County and part thereof was situated within six miles of the Scottsdale city limits. . . .

[The city appeared in opposition to the formation of the district, but the board granted the petition for organization. The city appealed, the board moved to dismiss, and the trial court granted the motion. The city then appealed to the supreme court. It held that the city had standing to appeal. The state had a growth zone statute which prohibited the formation of new cities and towns within five miles of cities over 5,000, such as Scottsdale. This statute indicated a legislative intent to allow cities of this size to expand without conflicts from newly created municipalities.]

2. *Did the Jurisdictional Prerequisites Exist for the Board to Authorize the Formation of the District?*

The Court's role in the creation of cities, towns or irrigation districts is limited to determining whether the jurisdictional facts necessary for the Board to act existed.

The statutes defining the jurisdictional prerequisites pertinent herein are as follows:

> § 45-1503. Organization of district
>
> > A. When a majority of the holders of title or evidence of title, including receipts or other evidence of the rights of entrymen on lands under any law of the United States or of this state, to lands in a designated area desire to provide for the irrigation of lands in the area, they may propose the organization of an irrigation district under the provisions of this chapter. When organized the district shall have all powers conferred by law upon irrigation districts.'
>
> § 45-1505. Petition for organization; inclusion of power of drainage
>
> > A. For the purpose of organizing an irrigation district as provided by this chapter, a petition signed by a majority of the resident owners of real property to which they hold title or evidence of title in the proposed district shall be filed with the board of supervisors of the county in which the greater portion of the proposed district is located. Each signer of the petition shall describe the lands to which he holds title or evidence of title in the proposed district.'

The final issue to be decided is whether an irrigation district can be formed wherein the primary intent is not to irrigate arid lands but to develop a planned urbanized community.

In *Post v. Wright*, 289 P. 979 (Ariz. 1930), this Court stated:

> ... Petitioners for the organization of districts must always indicate the purpose of the organizers to be to provide water for the irrigation of their lands....

The Court further declared:

> It goes without saying that an irrigation district may not enter into business of laying out and promoting town sites. Such business is foreign to any of the purposes for which it is organized ...

Appellees indicate that *Post* would control had it not been abrogated by a statutory amendment to what is presently Section 45-1578 A.R.S. Appellees cite the 1931 Amendment to Section 3341, Rev. Code 1928, which added to the District's delineated powers the power "to engage in any and all activities, enterprises and occupations within the powers and privileges of municipalities generally." This language, adopted after *Post*, persists today. Appellees' reliance on the above amendment is misplaced as they fail to appreciate the significance of the language which prefaces the above delegation of power and all other powers of the District. The preface recites: "In order to accomplish the purposes of the district the board may:" (then follows the individual powers). Obviously, the power to engage in activities of municipalities generally is proper only when acting pursuant to the purpose of irrigating arid lands.

Appellees further urge that irrigation be interpreted so as to encompass providing water for city needs such as watering lawns. The cases cited by appellees for this proposition do not deal with irrigation districts and accordingly are inapplicable. In *Post* this Court quoted at length from the California case of *In re Central Irrigation District*, 49 P. 354 (Cal. 1897), which discussed the Wright Act. That case indicated that a drugstore owner, a blacksmith or a town resident could not "desire" to irrigate their lands in the sense the word was used in the Wright Act. That Court further noted that the purpose of the Irrigation District Act was to improve agricultural and farming lands by conveying an adequate supply of water to the soil....

Accordingly, we reverse and remand for proceedings not inconsistent with this opinion.

Notes and Questions

1. *What the case means.* What is the basis for the court's decision? If a local government acts "in excess of its powers," is it necessary to determine whether the local action was "legislative" or "quasi-judicial"? How could the state statute be amended to address the problem raised in the case?

2. *Organizing to exclude.* The question of what powers may be exercised by a special district is closely linked to the question of whether a district may be organized at all. See *Wilson v. Hidden Valley Mun. Water Dist.*, 63 Cal. Rptr. 889 (Cal. App. 1967). This district was formed to prevent the introduction of water and thus the urbanization of the valley. Certain landowners sought to be excluded from the district, but the board of directors denied their petition without reasons. The court upheld the board as a quasi-legislative decision. Whether the petition should be granted raised "political" questions, and was part of an ongoing struggle between an overwhelming majority and a very small minority over the district's basic policies. A later decision explained this case as involving "fundamentally political questions" exercised through quasi-legislative powers. *Anaheim Redevelopment Agency v. Dusek*, 239 Cal. Rptr. 319 (Cal. App. 1987). Compare *Petition of Lower Valley Water & Sanitation Dist.*, 632 P.2d 1170 (N.M. 1981), in which landowners argued that they had no need for sewer improvements to be provided by a proposed sewer and sanitation district. The court upheld a lower court decision excluding their land for sewer but retaining it for water improvement purposes.

3. *Need and comparative advantage.* As some states have done with their annexation laws, Colorado requires consideration of the need and comparative advantage

of a proposed special district. Petitioners for any proposed special district must file a service plan with the board of county commissioners:

> The board of county commissioners shall disapprove the service plan unless evidence satisfactory to the board of each of the following is presented:
>
> (a) There is sufficient existing and projected need for organized service in the area to be serviced by the proposed special district;
>
> (b) The existing service in the area to be served by the proposed special district is inadequate for present and projected needs;
>
> (c) The proposed special district is capable of providing economical and sufficient service to the area within its proposed boundaries.
>
> (d) The area to be included in the proposed district has, or will have, the financial ability to discharge the proposed indebtedness on a reasonable basis. [Colo. Rev. Stat. § 32-1-203(2).]

The law also authorizes a board to disapprove a service plan in its discretion if, *inter alia*, other local governments can provide adequate service or if the service to be provided by the proposed district is not compatible with service provided by other local governments. *Id.* § 32-1-203(2.5). The law is an attempt to provide criteria that will prevent the formation of unnecessary and poorly financed special districts. See *Millis v. Board of County Comm'rs*, 626 P.2d 652 (Colo. 1981) (upholding finding that proposed water district's service plan was adequate).

4. *Annexation*. Special districts may also annex land. Legislatures which create districts by special act may expand them in the same manner. Legislation authorizing annexation through local initiative follows the municipal annexation pattern. Few or no standards are provided, judicial review is minimal, and voter consent usually is necessary. Municipalities may annex land within special districts. This type of annexation creates unique problems. Annexation may not leave the district as a viable unit, or the municipality may annex the capital facilities of the district but leave service lines within the remaining district boundaries. For a discussion of judicial and statutory solutions to this problem, see Note, *Problems Created by Municipal Annexation of Special District Territory*, 1967 Wash. U. L. Q. 560.

A Note on the Use of Special Districts for Economic Development

Local industrial development authorities (IDAs). These vary from state to state but generally they are established by or according to state legislation with a purpose to promote, encourage, and develop various types of industrial, manufacturing, warehousing, commercial, recreation, research, civic, and pollution control facilities. The IDA customarily issues tax-exempt or taxable bonds, real estate tax abatement, and tax exemptions (sales, mortgage recording taxes, etc.). The proceeds from IDA-issued bonds may be loaned to private or not-for-profit developers to be used to finance costs of eligible projects. Even if the bonds are not exempt from federal taxation, and therefore a higher rate of interest is charged, they may be exempt from state taxation and sales taxes on materials used to build the project and other costs such as mortgage recording taxes. A loss of income to a local government from the abatement of real property taxes on IDA projects may be offset by a Payment-in-Lieu-of-Tax agreement (PILOT), requiring the developer to pay a stated amount to the municipality. These entities have become increasingly popular and are felt necessary by many communities in order to compete effectively with other local governments which have them and are engaged in offering their benefits to private developers. Chapter 4 contains information on local bond financing.

Business improvement districts (BIDs). These have been created in many cities, primarily to foster an improved commercial atmosphere in a specific area. As noted by Professor Briffault:

> A BID is a territorial subdivision of a city in which property owners or businesses are subject to additional taxes. The revenues generated by these district-specific taxes are reserved to fund services and improvements within the district and to pay for the administrative costs of BID operations. BIDs' services are provided in addition to those offered by city governments. Most BIDs focus on services, infrastructure and events, such as garbage collection, street maintenance, and security patrols. A few provide assistance to the homeless. Some engage in street repairs, undertake landscaping, provide street furniture, maintain parks, and create public amenities. Many sponsor street fairs and special events, produce promotional brochures, and engage in other direct efforts to draw shoppers, tourists, and businesses into their districts. [Briffault, *A Government for Our Time? Business Improvement Districts and Urban Governance*, 99 COLUM. L. REV. 365, 368–69 (1999).]

Some BIDs have progressed beyond their initial focus to work collaboratively with preservation advocates on preservation and design issues involving historic buildings and streetscapes. See Maley et al., *Safe and Clean*, URBAN LAND, Feb. 2002, at 71–76. BIDs have been criticized. Professor Briffault notes the problems they create and argues for greater public accountability, but believes that their public benefits outweigh their disadvantages and that BIDs are "net contributors to urban life." *Id.* at 477. For additional discussion, see Batchis, *Business Improvement Districts and the Constitution: The Troubling Necessity of Privatized Government for Urban Revitalization*, 38 HASTINGS CONST. L.Q. 91 (2010); Davies, *Business Improvement Districts*, 52 WASH. U. J. URB. & CONTEMP. L. 187 (1997).

How the book is organized. Part I deals with the governmental system. This Chapter reviewed some of the basic constitutional principles that determine the legal status of state and local government, as well as incorporation and annexation by local governments. The rest of Part I considers the structure and powers of local government, including taxing and spending powers, and then looks at internal governmental management, governmental liability, and federalism issues. Part II shifts focus to look at the legislative, judicial, and executive branches of government and the authority they can assume. We use the judicial chapter in Part II to raise major policy questions concerning the distribution of school finance and the guarantee of voting rights in a democratic system.

Chapter 2

Local Government Powers and State Preemption

A. The Distribution of Power Problem

> The subject of state and local government is less about substantive legal doctrine than about institutional design. Decisions that affect localities can be made at a variety of levels—federal, state, or local—and by any of a variety of institutions—administrative, legislative, or judicial—within each level. State and local government law involves the location of decision-making authority within this matrix. [Gillette, *Expropriation and Institutional Design in State and Local Government*, 80 Va. L. Rev. 625, 625 (1994).]

This Chapter considers issues that arise from the distribution of power between state and local governments. While many citizens (and law students) have some understanding about the balance of power between the federal government and the states, there is typically a much less well-developed understanding about the balance of state and local powers and constraints. During the COVID-19 pandemic, related issues have increasingly come to the fore. When can local governments declare states of emergency, and with what associated constraints? How dependent are their actions on actions at the state level by governors and state legislatures? When and to what extent can states or local governments mandate associated actions or limitations on action in the face of a significant public health threat? How do the powers of municipalities and counties bear on decisions such as these?

In framing the core questions addressed in this Chapter, consider the following issues. (1) What authority do local governments of various sorts possess and where does that authority come from? (2) How should grants of authority to local governments be interpreted in situations where there is ambiguity (and what counts as ambiguity)? (3) When can states limit the authority that local governments might otherwise possess and under what circumstances? Note, from this formulation, that at core, three crucial policy issues need to be addressed: when can local governments take the "initiative" (or initiate desired actions), when are they "immune" from state interference including efforts to preempt their powers to initiate governmental actions, and how should ambiguous questions or authority or preemption be resolved?

This Chapter offers insights on each of these questions, insofar as it considers statutory and home rule authority, questions of interpretation raised by frameworks such as "Dillon's Rule" dating from the 19th century, and recent actions by state legislatures, controlled in many cases since the 2010 Census by rural Republican interests that have sought to constrain urban Democratic initiatives. Putting aside partisan viewpoints, it is critically important to understand these core principles, powers, and constraints in order to help future government clients comply with legal requirements.

[1] Introduction to Local Government Powers and State Constraints

[a] Basic Concepts

As discussed in Chapter 1, state legislatures have plenary power over local governments, except as qualified by exceptions to the *Hunter* doctrine or by limitations in state constitutions. This means that local governments, in some way, must receive all the powers they exercise from the state. State legislatures have historically conferred powers on local governments through "enabling" legislation (legislative enactments that authorize specific local action) and through local government charters. During the late 19th and then the 20th century, more and more states adopted local "home rule" constitutional provisions or statutes, conferring more comprehensive powers on at least some local governments (which may be defined by specific characteristics or tied to local actions such as referenda through which voters in the jurisdiction opt to request their local government to exercise broader powers). The term "home rule" implies a broad delegation of general authority for the local government to exercise a degree of control over its form of government and local affairs, and at the same time, may provide limited protection to the local government from state legislative interference.

Many states authorize municipal home rule, with a smaller number authorizing county home rule. For a study summarizing developing patterns regarding home rule, see Svara, *Strengthening Local Government Leadership and Performance: Reexamining and Updating the Winter Commission Goals*, 68 PUB. ADMIN. REV. No. S1 (2008): S37–S49. Even in some of the so-called "non-home rule" states, some level of home rule is abided at one or another level of local government. See Diller, *The City and the Private Right of Action*, 64 STAN. L. REV. 1109, 1129 (2012) (citing D. Krane et al., HOME RULE IN AMERICA: A FIFTY STATE HANDBOOK 24–25, 50, 270, 278, 419, 433, 446, 468 (2001)). A grant of home rule may expand powers given to local governments by specific statutes, but these powers are not unlimited; rather, they are defined by the grant of authority and the interpretation of that grant by the state's courts.

Whether a local government exercises power through a statutory or a state constitutional grant of home rule, a state legislature may preempt the exercise of local power by adopting legislation covering an area of concern also covered by a local ordinance. That is, legislative preemption may occur even though a local government enjoys constitutional home rule. One exception is that a legislature may not preempt powers which are deemed "exclusively" local under a constitutional home rule clause. However, the home rule powers which are exclusively local are limited in scope. For a critique of the implications of the "outmoded conception of home rule," one that preserves the boundaries of the state, the market, and the family, see Stahl, *Local Home Rule in the Time of Globalization*, 2016 B.Y.U. L. Rev. 177, 185 (2016).

The choice of criteria to make distribution of power decisions is the critical issue that constitution-drafters, legislatures, and courts must face. As you study these materials, ask what criteria are being used to make these decisions, and whether you favor categorical fixed rules or more flexible open-ended standards as the basis for decision-making. It is first necessary to look at historic attempts to establish local autonomy before moving on to the modern law of local government powers.

For a thoughtful re-evaluation of local government powers, structure, state constitutions, and the historical trajectories of economic growth, see Schragger, *Decentralization and Development*, 96 Va. L. Rev. 1837 (2010) (reviewing historical trends in relationship between states and local governments and related patterns of economic growth). An empirical study sought to determine whether the balance of state and local power had shifted since the turn of the 21st century, drawing on surveys of state legislators, municipal leagues, city managers, and county association officials. See Bowman & Kearney, *Are U.S. Cities Losing Power and Authority? Perceptions of Local Government Actors*, 48 Urb. Aff. Rev., No. 4 (2012) 528–46 (concluding, in the view of city managers, that cities in the past decade experienced an erosion of authority and increased obligations to manage pursuant to state mandates, while state representatives were much less likely to perceive such trends).

For an interesting statistical analysis of state courts' responses to local government decisions that are at odds with state positions, see Swanson & Barrilleaux, *State Government Preemption of Local Government Decisions Through the State Courts*, 56 Urb. Aff. Rev. 56, No. 2 (2020) 671-697 (reviewing data from 404 state court challenges to local government action and finding less likelihood of preemption when there is greater autonomy accorded to local governments, for example, through some forms of home rule). It is likely that in the wake of the 2020 Coronavirus pandemic, understandings about the role of local, state, and federal governments will evolve and change significantly in coming years. See also Davidson, *The Dilemma of Localism in an Era of Polarization,* 128 Yale L.J. 954 (2019) (arguing that the normative dimensions of localism must be engaged more seriously; state constitutional provisions relating to individual rights must be considered as well as attention given to the broader general welfare of the state in order to avoid dangers of parochialism; outlining different concepts of localism; endeavoring to draw lines between defensible and indefensible localism).

As you begin consideration of the ways that governmental powers can and should be allocated between competing levels of governments, what normative considerations seem especially important? How can normative considerations be clearly framed and embodied in legal principles?

[b] Historical Context

Philosophers, politicians, historians and academics have often extolled the benefits and purpose of local self-government. *Hunter* firmly delivers the law that there is no federal right to local self-government, but the states have sovereign authority to deem otherwise. Through the years, the philosophical question at the state level has been, "Is a sphere of autonomy at the level of local government an inherent right or one that must be delivered through the respective state constitution and its interpretation by the courts?" A brief legal history of the evolution of answers to this question follows.

The "Inherent Right" to Local Self-Government

At one time, local governments were thought to have an "inherent right" to self-government that provided autonomy from state interference and presumably gave them inherent governmental powers as well. The inherent right doctrine arose in the nineteenth century when state legislatures frequently attempted to intervene in local government affairs. For example, state legislatures would create state-appointed commissions with authority to govern in areas of local concern. These interventions did not always amount to state interference. In some cities, states intervened at the request of local politicians to control emerging political groups who threatened existing political power.

Two of the most notable incidents occurred in Michigan. Both incidences resulted in common law, provided by the Michigan Supreme Court, that recognized the critical role of local autonomy and, in fact, the inherent right to local self-governance. In one case, the state legislature created a commission to control a Detroit public park and at the same time appointed the commissioners who were to exercise this function. The Michigan Supreme Court invalidated this legislation in an opinion that recognized an inherent right of local government to be free of state intervention in the control of municipal facilities. *People ex rel. Board of Park Comm'rs v. Common Council*, 28 Mich. 228 (1873). In an earlier decision, the Michigan Supreme Court invalidated a state law that also replaced locally selected officials with state appointees (this time, for a local water district). In so doing, the court stated,

> But when we . . . ask ourselves the question, whether [the framers and the adopters of the Michigan Constitution intended to] vest in the legislature the appointment of all local officers . . . and even in defiance of the wishes [of the local officers]—thus depriving the people of such localities of the most essential benefits of self-government enjoyed by other political subdivisions of the state— . . . the conclusion becomes very strong that nothing of this kind could have been intended. . . . We cannot, therefore, suppose it [the state legislation replacing locally selected public officials with state appointed officials] was intended to deprive cities and villages of the like

> benefit of the principle of local self-government enjoyed by other political subdivisions of the state. [*People ex rel. Le Roy v. Hurlburt*, 24 Mich. 44, 65–66 (1871)].

The concurring of opinion of Justice Thomas Cooley crystallized the idea that locally based independence and self-control demands judicial obligation to read such rights into the law. Justice Cooley wrote, "local government is a matter of absolute right, and the state cannot take it away." *Id.* at 96, 107–08.

Subsequent decades have not been kind to the inherent right doctrine. Repudiation of the doctrine in almost every jurisdiction in which it was accepted is now practically complete. For example, the Kentucky Court of Appeals refused to strike down an act establishing a new retirement and pension system for police and fire departments and stated: "We have concluded that the time has come for this Court to reject, positively and unequivocally, the theory that a right of local self-government inheres in Kentucky municipalities." *Board of Trustees v. City of Paducah*, 333 S.W.2d 515, 518 (Ky. App. 1960). Even in Michigan, where the inherent right doctrine originated, it has lost its vitality. In *City of Highland Park v. Fair Employment Practices Comm'n*, 111 N.W.2d 797, 798 (Mich. 1961), the city claimed that applying a fair employment law to it would invade "the rights of self-government granted municipalities under the provisions of the Constitution." The court found no such provisions, assumed that the reference was to the constitutional home rule clause, but noted that under that provision, Michigan municipalities were subject to the "general laws" of the state. See also *Sussex Woodlands, Inc. v. Mayor & Council*, 263 A.2d 502 (N.J. L. Div. 1970). The rejection of the inherent right doctrine is the basis for the well-accepted rule that local governments enjoy only those powers expressly or impliedly granted, either by statute or by a constitutional home rule provision.

However, the persistence of the importance of, if not an inherent right to, self-government permeates state and local governments' expressions of democracy through state statutes, local ordinances, and the balance of state and local powers. For example, local citizens on both ends of the political spectrum continue to galvanize to make their respective cities sanctuary cities, to create local autonomy, or even a feeling of local autonomy, at the local government level; on the left, these cities want to provide sanctuaries from local government collaboration with aggressive immigration enforcement; on the right, from stricter gun laws and abortion clinics. Searcy, *'Sanctuary Cities' for Unborn Reflect a Nation's Rising Walls.*, N.Y. Times, Mar. 4, 2020 at A1, available at https://www.nytimes.com/2020/03/03/us/politics/texas-abortion-sanctuary-cities.html. In contrast, some suggest that "there is no substantial link" between local autonomy realized and the substantive laws addressing local autonomy in that particular jurisdiction. See Russell & Bostrom, *Federalism, Dillon Rule, and Home Rule, white paper published by the American City County Exchange 4* (2016), available at https://www.alec.org/app/uploads/2016/01/2016-ACCE-White-Paper-Dillon-House-Rule-Final.pdf (expressing views of a conservative lobbying organization that has had a growing influence in urging adoption of legislation limiting local government authority).

The "Special Commission" Problem

Arising out of and closely linked to the inherent right doctrine was the adoption by several states, mostly in the west (California, Colorado, Montana, New Jersey, Pennsylvania, South Dakota, Utah, and Wyoming), of a constitutional provision providing something similar: "[t]he Legislature shall not delegate to any special commission, private corporation or association, any power to make, supervise or interfere with any municipal improvement, money, property or effects . . . to levy taxes . . . or to perform any municipal functions." UTAH CONST. art. VI, § 28. Thus, even without a common law recognition of an inherent right to local government, judiciaries in states with a prohibition on special commissions to interfere with municipal governance or functions have a tool to analyze state legislative efforts requiring local governments to submit to state policy.

This constitutional limitation provides less protection for local governments from state interference than might be imagined. In *City of West Jordan v. Utah State Retirement Bd.*, 767 P.2d 530 (Utah 1988), for example, the city challenged a state statute that required municipalities to participate in the state retirement system if they wanted to provide retirement benefits, arguing that the state agency regulating local retirement systems was performing a municipal function. In rejecting this argument, the court decided not to adopt "hard and fast" categories to decide this question, and instead adopted a balancing test that specified a number of factors that determine when functions should be considered as municipal:

> These include, but are not limited to, the relative abilities of the state and municipal governments to perform the function, the degree to which the performance of the function affects the interests of those beyond the boundaries of the municipality, and the extent to which the legislation under attack will intrude upon the ability of the people within the municipality to control through their elected officials the substantive policies that affect them uniquely. [*Id.* at 534.]

The court then held that retirement systems are not a municipal function, because the state has a legitimate interest in the minimum level of retirement benefits and the financial health of local retirement systems. See also *Winslow Constr. Co. v. City & County of Denver*, 960 P.2d 685 (Colo. 1998) (appellate procedure for local sales and use tax is state function); *Specht v. City of Sioux Falls*, 526 N.W.2d 727 (S.D. 1995) (emergency medical service is local function and cannot be given to regional authority); *Utah Associated Mun. Power Sys. v. Public Serv. Comm'n*, 789 P.2d 298 (Utah 1990) (building of transmission line by agency representing more than 20 local governments not municipal function because of effect of line on state power supply).

Do these cases suggest a general rule for making this distinction? Similar problems of distinguishing between state and local affairs arise under constitutional home rule clauses, where they also serve to determine areas of municipal autonomy.

[c] The Role of the Police Power

Because understandings of the police power are so fundamental to understandings of government powers, it is helpful to keep in mind historical and evolving notions of that power insofar as it affects the distribution of power between state and local governments. See Ohm, *Some Modern Day Musings on the Police Power*, 47 URB. LAW. 625 (2015). See also Miller, *Community Rights and the Municipal Police Power*, 55 SANTA CLARA L. REV. 675 (2015) (providing an historical overview of evolving understandings of local police power and considering issues posed by recent efforts in some local jurisdictions to articulate "community rights" such as a "right to pure water").

Dean Daniel Rodriguez has also weighed in with a modern-day reconception of the police power, but in his case, the focus is on the role of the police power as to the states. See Rodriguez, *The Inscrutable (Yet Irrepressible) State Police Power*, 9 N.Y.U. J. L. & LIBERTY 662 (2015). Dean Rodriguez argues that scholarly literature on state police power has "withered away" and needs to be re-engaged by a consideration of both internal (structural limits and specific provisions regarding rights and liberties), and external limits (federalism) on state authority. In addition, attention needs to be paid, in his view, to states' regulatory objectives (perhaps distinguishing safety, health, and welfare), and techniques (perhaps distinguishing between different approaches to regulation and delegation of authority).

Based on these considerations, Dean Rodriguez urges that more attention be paid to the implications of differences between federal and state constitutions (the federal Constitution involves a grant of power, while states enjoy inherent powers subject only to limitation under state constitutions). He also argues for greater attention to the linkage between how positive rights are defined and fostered, and the extent of the police power as a source of power to achieve such ends. He suggests that more attention needs to be paid to the relationship between economic liberties and the extent of the police power. Dean Rodriguez further contends that consideration should be given to regulatory tactics and institutional choices made by the states, particularly in light of the more elaborate and nuanced details embodied in state constitutions. Ultimately, in his view, the most significant safeguards bearing on state police power are those provided by structural provisions of state constitutions as interpreted by the courts.

[d] Fresh Thinking

A landmark study by the National League of Cities has documented significant aspects of the historical factors leading to the establishment of home rule conventions in the United States, as well as framing forward-looking principles about how policies underlying home rule practices should inform the future of local governments in the 21st century. See NATIONAL LEAGUE OF CITIES, PRINCIPLES OF HOME RULE FOR THE 21ST CENTURY (February 2020), available at https://www.nlc.org/sites/default/files/2020-02/Home%20Rule%20Principles%20ReportWEB-2.pdf (hereinafter referred to as "NLC Home Rule 2020"). The NLC report was developed by a team of distinguished scholars (including Nestor Davidson, Richard Briffault, Paul Diller, Sarah Fox, Laurie Reynolds, Erin Adele Scharff, Richard Schragger, and Rick Su). At the time of the report (before the full implications of the COVID-19 pandemic were considered), major urban areas in the United States were playing an outsized role in the global and state economies. *Id.* at 13–14. Urban areas were also particularly diverse and potentially more responsive to local concerns. *Id.* at 15–16. This study provides an extensive and important update on the National League of City's recommendations regarding home rule authority and preemption, as is discussed in more detail below. For additional insights on changing views about home rule, see Su, *Have Cities Abandoned Home Rule?* 44 Fordham Urb. L.J. 181 (2017) (discussing history and potential for home rule).

Problem 2-1

The state recently passed a comprehensive statute addressing short-term rental use by its citizens, including the permitted length of time a city resident may rent their home to a non-permanent resident and what fees a city may impose on its residents who regularly list their homes on such platforms. The statute authorizes cities to impose short-term rental platform regulations more restrictive than those imposed under the state statute. No other state statute authorizes cities to regulate short-term rental platform use.

In an attempt to deter outside investors from only buying city property for purposes of listing it on short-term rental platforms such as Airbnb and VRBO, the City of Spring Valley adopted an ordinance that prohibits its residents from renting out their home residences to non-permanent visitors for periods less than 30 days. The General City Law, which applies to Spring Valley, authorizes cities to "adopt regulations in order to promote and encourage local investment in the community."

There are two constitutional home rule clauses in the state constitution. The Class A home rule clause authorizes cities adopting charters to "enact regulations concerning their municipal affairs." The Class B home rule clause authorizes cities to "exercise any power not denied by state law." Class B home rule cities need not adopt charters.

Is the short-term rental prohibition authorized if Spring Valley is not a home rule city? Is the short-term rental platform prohibition authorized if Spring Valley is a Class A home rule city? Assume the charter authorizes the city to "adopt regulations in order to promote and encourage local investment in the community." Is the short-term rental platform prohibition authorized if Spring Valley is a Class B home rule city? Does the short-term rental platform law preempt the Spring Valley prohibition on short-term rental platforms? How would you draft a statute specifically authorizing the municipality to adopt this ordinance? Would you recommend such a statute if the city is a home rule city?

B. Local Government Powers and Dillon's Rule

As just discussed, local governments derive their authority to engage in municipal and regulatory activities from the states in which they are located. Historically, such authority was accorded localities based on general statutes and local charters, but was subsequently enhanced by provisions extending home rule authority and protections beginning in the late 19th century. Local government lawyers accordingly typically need to inquire initially about whether the governments they represent can assert authority to act based on general statutes, constitutional or statutory home rule provisions, or local charters.

An additional dimension of such legal analysis should be borne in mind, however. State courts have developed special rules to guide their interpretation of possible sources of authority available to local governments. Rather than adopting a presumption that local governments should be accorded authority to act in cases of uncertainty, state courts over many decades have frequently applied a strict construction rule, known as "Dillon's Rule," when asked to decide whether the local government had the authority to pass the local ordinance in question. It is worth considering the basis for Dillon's Rule and its continuing relevance. Dillon's Rule appeared in the following form in the first published text on local government law, which was authored by Judge Dillon of the Iowa Supreme Court:

Dillon, Municipal Corporations
(1st ed. 1872)

> Sec. 55. It is a general and undisputed proposition of law that a municipal corporation possesses, and can exercise, the following powers, and no others: First, those granted in *express words;* second, those *necessarily or fairly implied in,* or *incident* to, the powers expressly granted; third, those essential to the declared objects and purposes of the corporation—not simply convenient, but indispensable. Any fair, reasonable doubt concerning the existence of power is resolved by the courts against the corporation, and the power is denied.... These general principles of law are indisputably settled, but difficulty is often experienced in their application.

The meaning of Dillon's Rule must be understood against the pattern of statutory enabling authority for local government which was common in Dillon's day. State legislatures typically enacted a list of local government powers which were quite specific. A licensing enabling law, for example, might have authorized municipalities to license peddlers, candle-makers, and a number of other occupations. Dillon apparently concluded from this typical enumeration of powers that any powers not clearly conferred by the legislation were not granted.

Modern enabling legislation for local governments often takes a different form. The legislature may enact a broad and comprehensive enabling act authorizing the exercise of local powers in an area of regulatory concern. A number of examples come to mind, including enabling legislation for zoning, special assessments for public facilities, and housing and community development programs. Although comprehensive enabling legislation also specifies the powers to be exercised by municipalities, it avoids the specific listing of enumerated powers which may have prompted Dillon's Rule. For a discussion of the role of Dillon's Rule in the ostensibly home rule state of Washington, see Spitzer, *"Home Rule" vs. "Dillon's Rule" for Washington Cities*, 38 Seattle U. L. Rev. 809 (2015). Professor Spitzer's article suggests that the "zombie-like" reappearance of Dillon's Rule through common law is a function of 1) the vitality and usefulness of the rule with regard to special districts, 2) appellate judges choosing to apply the rule to support particular cases' outcomes, and 3) a combination of doctrinal forgetfulness and carelessness. Reviewing eighteen cases decided by the supreme and appellate courts in Washington in the last five decades, Spitzer found that "court opinions have moved back and forth between reciting home rule doctrines and repeating Dillon's Rule, depending on which approach best assisted the opinion's drafter in developing an effective rationale for the desired outcome." Spitzer, *supra,* at 843.

A renowned article by Professor Gerald Frug, *The City as a Legal Concept*, 93 Harv. L. Rev. 1057 (1980), provides additional insight on the problem of municipal autonomy and Dillon's Rule. Professor Frug argues that municipalities originally had full legal autonomy, and that the concept of subordination to the state developed only in the 19th century. He traces the origins of Dillon's Rule to Dillon's concept of local government. Dillon believed that cities were not managed by those "best fitted" by intelligence, experience, capacity and moral character. Municipal management often was unwise and extravagant. A major change in city government was needed to achieve local governments dedicated to the public good. *Id.* at 1111.

Frug asserts that Dillon believed that these goals could be achieved through state control of cities, a restriction of cities to "public" functions and a strict judicial construction of municipal powers. *Id.* at 1112. Frug adds that "[i]t is hard for us to comprehend fully Dillon's confidence in *noblesse oblige* and in the expectation that state and judicial control would help ensure the attainment by cities of an unselfish public good." *Id.* Frug also notes that "Dillon's vision of society may be gone forever." *Id.* Supporting Professor Frug's idea are data that demonstrate US citizens' trust in their respective local governments remains high. See Perlman, *The Illusion of Local Control: The Paradox of Local Government Home Rule*, 48 State & Loc. Gov't Rev., No. 3 (2016): 189–93. Perlman notes that this level of confidence in local governments has remained fairly level over the last 40 years and has increased somewhat both historically and recently. *Id.*

However, others contend that the Dillon's Rule's ability to impose consistent uniformity is a "prerequisite for statewide stability and prosperity," and suggest that Dillon's vision of society is, in fact, alive and well, long, long after it was articulated by the judge. See Russell & Bostrom, *Federalism, Dillon Rule, and Home Rule, supra*. Indeed, efforts by state legislatures to impose harsh fiscal penalties on local governments that pass laws subject to preemption (e.g., local firearm regulations or declarations of sanctuary city status) effectively return states that have accorded some measure of local autonomy to their local governments to the Dillon's Rule philosophy of limited local delegation dating from the 19th century. See *infra*, Section D.

Notes and Questions

1. *Dillon's Rule applied.* Dillon's Rule is still applied full-blown by some courts. In *Board of Supvrs. v. Horne*, 215 S.E.2d 453 (Va. 1975), *reaffirmed in Board of Supvrs. v. Countryside Investment Co.*, 522 S.E.2d 610 (Va. 1999), the court applied the rule to hold that an Interim Development Order (IDO) adopted by Fairfax County, substantially freezing all development permission pending a comprehensive revision of the zoning ordinance, was unauthorized by its enabling legislation. It noted:

> In Virginia the powers of boards of supervisors are fixed by statute and are limited to those conferred expressly or by necessary implication. This rule is a corollary to Dillon's Rule that municipal corporations have only those powers expressly granted, those necessarily or fairly implied therefrom, and those that are essential and indispensable. . . .
>
> The Commission on Constitutional Revision recommended inclusion of a provision to reverse Dillon's Rule as to cities and certain counties in order to relax the constraints on local government. Report of the Commission on Constitutional Revision at 228–231 (1969). This recommendation, however, was rejected by the General Assembly, and was not incorporated in the revised Constitution which became effective July 1, 1971. We must conclude, therefore, that, regardless of its fate in other jurisdictions, Dillon's Rule remains in effect in this state. Accordingly, the Board could not enact the IDO under its general police power. [*Id.* at 455–56.]

In a subsequent case, the Virginia Supreme Court rejected efforts by the City of Hampton to establish resource protection areas in harmony with state legislation to protect the Chesapeake Bay and the federal Coastal Barrier Resources Act. See *Marble Technologies, Inc. v. City of Hampton*, 690 S.E.2d 84 (Va. 2010). The Court, citing Dillon's Rule, held that the City lacked express or implied power to consider the federal legislation when making decisions pursuant to the state Chesapeake Bay Protection Act. *Amin v. County of Henrico*, 755 S.E.2d 482 (Va. App. 2014), affirmed the continuing applicability of Dillon's Rule. See also Lineberry, *Payne v. City of Charlottesville and the Dillon's Rule Rationale for Removal*, 104 Va. L. Rev. Online 45 (2018) (arguing that Charlottesville, Virginia's Lee Monument is not authorized under state law as interpreted through the lens of Dillon's Rule).

2. *Inconsistent interpretation.* The application of Dillon's Rule often is inconsistent, when similar issues are faced in different states, or even within the same state. Compare the following cases which consider the question of statutory authority for local ordinances, in two different states, both of which recognize Dillon's Rule, requiring a cash deposit on soft drink containers. In *Bowie Inn, Inc. v. City of Bowie*,

335 A.2d 679 (Md. 1975), the court held that the ordinance was authorized. The court quoted Dillon's Rule, and noted that it had "repeatedly" been applied by the court. It then held that the ordinance was "expressly" authorized by a state statute enabling municipalities "[t]o regulate or prevent the throwing or depositing of any dirt, garbage, trash, or liquids in any public place and to provide for the proper disposal of such material." In *Tabler v. Bd. of Supvrs.*, 269 S.E.2d 358 (Va. 1980), the court held that a similar local ordinance was not authorized by similar enabling legislation, noting that "Virginia follows the Dillon Rule." See Note 1, *supra*. Citing legislative history, the court held that the legislature did not intend to confer this power (to require a cash deposit on soft drink containers) upon local governing bodies. See also *Davis v. City of Blytheville*, 478 S.W.3d 2014 (Ark. 2015) (citing Dillon's Rule but holding that city had implied authority to impose late fee for water services provided).

3. *Criticisms of the rule.* The ambiguities inherent in Dillon's Rule give considerable freedom to the courts:

> If the Court wants to restrict municipal power, adherence to the express language of the statute is a convenient means of doing so. [If] the Court wants to find an implicit grant of municipal power behind the statutory language, it must assume a quasi-legislative stance, because there will be little to guide its search. This purely result-oriented jurisprudence, however, defies principled reconciliation with Dillon's Rule of strict construction. [A.E.S., *Dillon's Rule: The Case for Reform*, 68 Va. L. Rev. 693, 703, 704 (1982).]

Professor Gillette has noted that the consequence of this type of unprincipled interpretation "is subordination of local decision-making to other institutions and a correlative decline in municipal autonomy, political participation, and self-determination by residents. . . . [Courts can] require localities to seek specific enabling acts from the state. A rule that limits local initiative, therefore, implies that local constituents cannot be trusted to sort out those policies that are and are not detrimental to the locality. . . ." Gillette, *In Partial Praise of Dillon's Rule, or, Can Public Choice Theory Justify Local Government Law?*, 67 Chi-Kent L. Rev. 959, 966 (1991). Gillette, however, defends Dillon's Rule as "a judicial check on local tendencies to cater to special interests." Why is this so? If the effect of Dillon's Rule is to reinforce the supremacy of the legislature in municipal affairs, is this desirable?

Depending on one's political and philosophical viewpoint, Dillon's Rule may not be all bad. See, e.g., Taylor, *Dillon's Rule: A Check on Sheriffs' Authority to Enter 287(G) Agreements*, 68 Am. U. L. Rev. 1053 (2019) (arguing that sheriffs' authority to enter into agreements with federal authorities to engage in immigration enforcement should be interpreted and limited through the lens of Dillon's Rule).

4. *Repealing Dillon's Rule.* Some state constitutional grants of home rule authority have been held to be a repeal of Dillon's Rule. For example, Alaska Const., art. X, § 1, provides that "[t]he purpose of this article is to provide for maximum local

self-government. . . . A liberal construction shall be given to the powers of local government." The court read this section as a repeal of Dillon's Rule in *Liberati v. Bristol Bay Borough*, 584 P.2d 1115 (Alaska 1978). The court quoted a statement made at the constitutional convention that the purpose of the article was "to provide the maximum powers to the legislature and to the local government." See *City of New Orleans v. Bd. of Comm'rs*, 640 So. 2d 237 (La. 1994) ("the text of the constitutional provisions and their drafting history clearly indicate that the drafters and ratifiers intended to emancipate home rule governments as fully as possible, not to return them to subjugation under the Dillon rule.").

Other states have repealed Dillon's Rule by statutory grants of home rule. In *Tippecanoe County v. Ind. Manufacturer's Ass'n*, 784 N.E.2d 463 (Ind. 2003), the Indiana court held that the legislature "[i]n 1980, . . . put a stake through the heart of the Dillon Rule by adopting the Home Rule Act," reaffirmed in *City of North Vernon v. Jennings Northwest Regional Utilities*, 829 N.E.2d 1 (Ind. 2005). *General Bldg. Contractors v. Bd. of Shawnee County Comm'rs*, 66 P.3d 873 (Kan. 2003), held that the granting of legislative home rule powers to counties repealed Dillon's Rule. *See also City of Clinton v. Sheridan*, 530 N.W.2d 690 (Iowa 1995) (discussing legislation repealing Dillon's Rule).

Some states have adopted constitutional or legislative provisions requiring a liberal interpretation of local government powers, and courts have held that this is a repeal of Dillon's Rule. See *Hospitality Ass'n v. County of Charleston*, 464 S.E.2d 113 (S.C. 1995). For articles indicating that a repeal of Dillon's Rule does not solve all of the problems of statutory authority, see Lorensen, *Rethinking the West Virginia Municipal Code of 1969*, 97 W. Va. L. Rev. 653 (1995); Owens, *Local Government Authority to Implement Smart Growth Programs: Dillon's Rule, Legislative Reform, and the Current State of Affairs in North Carolina*, 35 Wake Forest L. Rev. 671 (2000).

Under some enabling legislation it is clear the legislature has granted a power to local governments. The question is the extent of the power granted, and the authority of the local government to elaborate on the statutory grant. The following case illustrates this problem:

Early Estates, Inc. v. Housing Board of Review

93 R.I. 227, 174 A.2d 117 (1961)

Paolino, Justice

This is a petition for certiorari to review the decision of the housing board of review of the city of Providence denying the petitioner's appeal from a compliance order of the director of the division of minimum housing standards pursuant to the provisions of chapter 1040 of the ordinances of said city, entitled the Minimum-Standards Housing Ordinance. Pursuant to the writ the board has certified the pertinent records to this court.

The petitioner owns a three-tenement house. Public Laws 1956, chap. 3715, is the enabling act which authorizes the city of Providence to enact a minimum standards housing ordinance. The question presented by this petition is whether the act as written vests the city with power to enact an ordinance requiring petitioner to provide a rear hallway light in its premises and to install hot water facilities in the third-floor tenement, and, if so, whether such requirements are valid.

Sections 7 and 8 of article 4 of the act delegate to the city council power to enact minimum housing standards. Section 7 provides that: "The city council of the city of Providence is authorized to pass, ordain, establish and amend ordinances, rules and regulations for the establishment and enforcement of minimum standards for dwellings." In defining this general grant of power the legislature provided as follows in sec. 8:

> Without limiting the generality of the foregoing, such ordinances, rules and regulations may include:
>
> (a) Minimum standards governing the conditions, maintenance, use and occupancy of dwellings and dwelling premises deemed necessary to make said dwellings and dwelling premises safe, sanitary and fit for human habitation.

Pursuant to the provisions of the enabling act the city council enacted chapter 1040, the Minimum-Standards Housing Ordinance. The provisions involved in the instant proceeding are subsecs. 8.8, entitled "Lighting of Public Spaces," and 6.4, entitled "Hot Water." Subsection 8.8 provides that:

> Every public hall and common stairway used primarily for egress or ingress in connection with two or more dwelling units shall be supplied with a proper amount of natural or electric light at all times; provided that such public halls and common stairways in structures containing not more than three dwelling units shall be deemed to have fulfilled such requirement if they are properly supplied with conveniently located switches, controlling an adequate electric lighting system which may be turned on when needed; and provided that all common stairways not used primarily for egress or ingress in all dwellings shall be properly supplied with such switches.

Subsection 6.4 provides that:

> Within three (3) years following the effective date of this Ordinance every kitchen sink, lavatory basin, and bathtub or shower bath required under the provisions of Subsections 6.1, 6.2 and 6.3 of this section shall be properly connected to hot as well as cold water lines.

The petitioner concedes that subsecs. 8.8 and 6.4, if valid, apply to its premises. However, with respect to the requirements of 8.8, it contends that under the common law of this state as declared in *Capen v. Hall*, 43 A. 847 (R.I. [1899]), and followed by other later cases, there is no duty on a property owner to provide artificial light or switches in common hallways and stairways. The petitioner also contends that the council, absent legislative authority, is without power to change the common law relating to hallway lights; that the act as written contains no language vesting the council with such power; and that consequently subsec. 8.8 is invalid and the director's compliance order requiring such hallway light is null and void.

After careful consideration it is our opinion that the enabling act clearly vests the council with power to legislate on the subject of lighting for common hallways and stairways. The legislature therein declared in art. 2, sec. 2, that "the establishment of minimum standards for dwellings is essential to the protection of the public health, safety, morals and general welfare." Such language clearly indicates a legislative intent to vest in the council power to require minimum standards dealing with factors relating to safety.

Again, in carrying out such intent, the legislature provided in art. 4, sec. 8, that the ordinances which the council was empowered to enact might include, without limiting the generality of the language in sec. 7, minimum standards governing the conditions, maintenance, use and occupancy of dwellings and dwelling premises deemed necessary to make said dwellings and dwelling premises safe, sanitary and fit for human habitation. The use of such language makes it abundantly clear that the legislature clearly intended to vest the council with power to require hallway lights as a safety measure. We are satisfied that the council had legislative authority to enact subsec. 8.8 and that the requirements therein are reasonable and therefore are a proper exercise of the police power. The cases cited by petitioner are not in point and require no discussion.

We come now to a consideration of the provisions of subsec. 6.4 requiring the installation of hot water facilities in the third-floor tenement of petitioner's property. Its principal contentions with respect thereto are that the act is silent on the subject of hot water; that there is no language therein vesting the council with power to legislate on the subject; and that therefore the council acted in excess of its jurisdiction.

At this point we are not concerned with the wisdom or desirability of the requirements in question. It may very well be that hot water facilities in a dwelling are convenient and desirable, but the only question before us is whether the act as written vests the council with power to require the installation of such facilities. The act contains no express grant of such power.

In art. 2 the legislature declares that it has found that there exist in the city of Providence numerous dwellings which are substandard due to "uncleanliness" and lack of adequate "sanitary facilities," and that the establishment of minimum standards for dwellings is essential to the protection of the public health, safety, morals and general welfare. Under sec. 8 the council is vested with power to enact minimum standards governing the conditions, maintenance, use and occupancy of dwellings deemed necessary to make said dwellings safe, sanitary and fit for human habitation.

In the absence of an express grant of legislative authority, the determination of the issue raised by petitioner's instant contentions depends wholly upon the question whether the statutory language discussed in the preceding paragraph indicates a clear legislative intent to delegate the power in question. In other words, is the use of such language equitable to a grant of power to the council empowering it to require the installation of hot water facilities? Is the requirement of hot water facilities related to the "uncleanliness" of dwellings and dwelling premises? Is such requirement related to sanitation or public health and welfare? Keeping in mind that chap. 3715 involves a delegation of power relating to *minimum* housing standards, can it reasonably be said that by empowering the council to enact minimum standards necessary to make dwellings and dwelling premises "fit for human habitation," the legislature meant that the installation of hot water facilities is necessary to achieve the desired purpose? Can it be said that dwellings and dwelling premises lacking such facilities are unfit for human habitation?

Prior to the enactment of chap. 3715, in the absence of contractual obligations to the contrary there was no duty on a property owner to provide hot water facilities under the law of this state. After careful consideration it is our opinion that the act contains no language indicating a legislative intent to create such a duty or to vest the council with power to enact an ordinance requiring the installation of hot water facilities. The requirement of those facilities is not necessarily related to sanitation or public health and welfare, nor is such requirement reasonably necessary to make dwellings and dwelling premises fit for human habitation. We cannot read into the act that which is not there.

From what we have stated, it is clear that in enacting subsec. 6.4 the council exceeded its jurisdiction. That portion of the ordinance is therefore invalid and the decision of the board based thereon is in error. In view of this result it becomes unnecessary to discuss or consider the petitioner's other contentions. . . .

Roberts, Justice (dissenting). . . .

The enabling act confers upon the city council authority to establish by ordinance minimum standards for dwellings. In art. 4, sec. 8 thereof, after expressly stating it to be the legislative policy that the generality of the grant of such authority is not limited thereby, the legislature provided that such an ordinance could set out certain specific provisions, among which were included "Minimum standards governing the conditions, maintenance, use and occupancy of dwellings and dwelling premises deemed necessary to make said dwellings and dwelling premises safe, sanitary and fit for human habitation."

Clearly, it was the intention of the legislature to confer upon the city council comprehensive authority to provide minimum standards for dwelling premises. The subsequent enumeration of norms to be observed by the city council in its exercise of the police power thus delegated to it was not intended to diminish the scope of that authority. Because the legislature intended to bestow upon the city council such a broad power to provide for minimum dwelling standards, I am persuaded that the legislature also intended to leave to the discretion and judgment of the local legislature the nature of the precise minimum standards to be established. If the specific requirements thus prescribed as minimum standards by the city council bear a reasonable relationship to the public health, morals, and welfare, the enactment thereof constituted a valid exercise of the police power delegated to it.

I am unable to perceive that the action of the city council requiring the connecting of kitchen sinks, lavatory basins, and bathing facilities to hot water lines was violative of the norms set out in art. 4, sec. 8(a), of the enabling act. Nor do I think it reasonable to conclude that the providing of lines which would serve to give the occupant of the dwelling access to an appliance that would, if utilized, make available to him a supply of hot water may not be deemed necessary to promote sanitation in dwelling premises or to render such premises fit for human habitation.

That a definite relationship exists between the maintenance of an adequate condition of sanitation in a community and the availability of access to a supply of hot water in the dwelling units in that community has been given judicial recognition in *City of Newark v. Charles Realty Co.*, 74 A.2d 630 (N.J. L. Div. 1950). In that case, on the basis of the evidence adduced, the court found that where a supply of hot water is not readily available in dwellings by reasons of a failure to have access to facilities for supplying such hot water, the danger of production and spread of disease in the community tends to increase. Without intending to unduly extend this dissenting opinion, I quote in part from that case at page 635 of 74 A.2d: "For instance, as to gastro-intestinal diseases, there have been 'outbreaks of that disease because hot water was not available for that purpose,' the testimony instancing as typical, the spread of such disease throughout the city from a restaurant, an employee of which fails to properly wash his hands due to the lack of hot water at home, and thus spreads this diarrheal disease." While it may be possible to maintain adequate sanitation in a community where there is a lack of readily available supplies of hot water for use in personal hygiene by the residents thereof, it is manifestly clear that a high degree of sanitation would be promoted and more effectively maintained when access to adequate supplies of hot water is provided for in the dwellings in that community.

Neither do I believe that the requirement of subsec. 6.4 for the connecting of hot water lines to kitchen sinks, lavatory basins, and bathing facilities may not reasonably be deemed necessary to render a dwelling fit for human habitation. To attribute to the legislature an intention to use the phrase "fit for human habitation" as meaning any structure that suffices to give one shelter from the elements so as to survive the vicissitudes and hardships of life in a climate such as ours is to attribute to the legislature an intent to have its enactment result in an absurdity. It is my belief that a dwelling fit for human habitation within the contemplation of the legislature was a dwelling so built and equipped as to afford the occupants thereof access to those conveniences and amenities that, in this day of social enlightenment, are considered as the responsibility of the property owner to the welfare of the community. When the city council included within the ordinance provisions requiring the connecting of kitchen sinks, lavatory basins and bathing facilities with hot water lines, it was acting well within the norm inherent in the legislative phrase "fit for human habitation."

Notes and Questions

1. *Applying Dillon. Early Estates* illustrates the problems that arise when a state statute covering a complex problem is incomplete. Municipal housing codes apply to existing housing, and are viewed as an essential strategy in housing conservation efforts. They generally require the maintenance of buildings, specify minimum facilities (such as hot water), and impose minimum occupancy space requirements. They came into vogue in the late 1960s under prompting from a requirement then contained in the federal urban renewal legislation that required the adoption of local housing codes as a condition to the receipt of federal urban renewal assistance. Perhaps for this reason, most states did not have enabling legislation for local housing codes and most did not provide the necessary statutory authority.

Early Estates poses an important dilemma. A court may interpret a broadly stated grant of authority to exclude necessary powers of implementation. The alternative is detailed specification in the statute, which the legislature may not wish to undertake, although the Rhode Island legislature subsequently adopted legislation overruling *Early Estates.*

A more detailed delegation of authority may be enough to overcome the limits imposed by Dillon's Rule. For example, in *Berberian v. Hous. Auth.*, 315 A.2d 747 (R.I. 1974), the same court held that a state statute authorizing "minimum standards . . . containing provisions" to keep a dwelling "watertight" and "airtight," along with other detailed maintenance provisions, authorized, even under Dillon's Rule, a local ordinance requiring the painting of "all exposed surfaces which have been adversely affected by exposure or other causes." However, *Amin v. County of Henrico*, 63 Va. App. 203 (2014), held that when a county in a Dillon's Rule state incorporated a state statute into a county ordinance, the county acted beyond its authorized local government powers. In *Amin*, a criminal defendant was charged and convicted of carrying a concealed weapon without a permit in violation of "Henrico County Ordinance 22-2 incorporating Virginia Code Section 18.2-308." Applying Dillon's Rule, the Court of Appeals held that the county did not have the authority to incorporate a state criminal law into a local ordinance, and therefore, the local ordinance upon which Amin was convicted was a legally insufficient basis for a criminal conviction. As a result, Amin's conviction was void *ab initio* (it was without effect from the moment it came into existence).

2. *Selecting the correct power: "general welfare" provisions and more.* An important statutory authority problem arises when a municipality attempts to avoid limitations imposed under one statutory power by relying on another. Most states have adopted legislation authorizing municipalities to adopt ordinances necessary to serve the "general welfare." Can local governments rely upon their "general welfare"

powers or other sources of authority to augment more specific powers or to avoid constraints incorporated into other more specific statutory authorizations? Consider the following scenarios:

(a) *Campaign disclosures and financial contributions.* See *State v. Hutchinson*, 624 P.2d 1116 (Utah 1980). In *Hutchinson*, a candidate for office challenged an ordinance adopted by the Salt Lake County Commissioners that required candidates to file statements regarding campaign contributions, asserting that the County lacked authority to impose such requirements. The County relied upon powers to pass ordinances "necessary and proper to provide for the safety, and preserve the health, promote the prosperity, improve the morals, peace and good order, comfort and convenience of the county and the inhabitants thereof" as a basis for the ordinance. The Utah court treated the statutory "general welfare" provision both as a means for implementing specific grants of authority and as "an independent source of power to act for the general welfare of . . . citizens." In the court's view, "the Dillon Rule of strict construction is not to be used to restrict the power of a county under a grant by the Legislature of general welfare power or prevent counties from using reasonable means to implement specific grants of authority." Is this assessment justified?

(b) *Rent control.* Other courts have also taken an expansive view of the authority granted by a general welfare clause. In *Inganamort v. Borough of Fort Lee*, 303 A.2d 298 (N.J. 1973), the court held that a local rent control ordinance was authorized by a general welfare clause. The statute authorized municipalities to adopt ordinances as they "may deem necessary and proper for the good government, order and protection of persons and property, and for the preservation of the public health, safety and welfare of the municipality and its inhabitants." The court in *Inganamort* did, however, suggest some limitations on the exercise of delegated municipal authority, noting that the state could not leave to localities judgments regarding what constitutes robbery or whether it should be punished, since such matters do not vary locally in their nature or intensity. Municipal action would not be useful, and indeed diverse local decisions could be mischievous or even intolerable. *Id.* at 302. New Jersey also has a constitutional provision requiring that laws "concerning" municipal corporations should be "liberally construed in their favor," a repeal of Dillon's Rule. What explains this result?

(c) *Fair housing ordinances.* Some states follow the familiar *ejusdem generis* rule of statutory construction. This rule states that the grant of specific powers excludes any powers not specifically granted. These states hold that a "general welfare" grant of power cannot add to specific enabling grants of power appearing elsewhere in the statutes. See *City of Stuttgart v. Strait*, 205 S.W.2d 35 (Ark. 1947) (no power to establish setback lines); *KN Energy, Inc. v. City of Casper*, 755 P.2d 207 (Wyo. 1988) (utility licensing). In *Anderson v. City of Olivette*, 518 S.W.2d 34 (Mo. 1975), the city relied on a general welfare delegation authorizing it to enact ordinances for the "good government" of the city to pass a municipal fair housing ordinance applicable to real estate brokers and aimed at preventing discrimination in the sale or rental of housing. The court found that the ordinance was not authorized by this statute.

It noted that cities of this class had been authorized to license and regulate certain businesses, but real estate brokers were not among the businesses that the city was authorized to regulate. For other classes of cities, the power to regulate real estate brokers was expressly granted. It then noted this legislative classification of powers and held the specific grant to the City of Olivette, which did not include the power to regulate, "may not be expanded to authority to license and regulate by reference to the general police power statutes." *Id.* at 39. The court also referred to the strict construction rule that applies to municipal powers, which Missouri still recognizes. How would the New Jersey courts react to this ordinance? If the regulation of blockbusting is a "local" matter, what about a fair housing ordinance?

(d) *City/County funding disputes.* In *Coffee County Bd. of Education v. City of Tulahoma*, 574 S.W.3d 832 (Tenn. 2019), the Tennessee Supreme Court concluded that the city was not required to share proceeds from "liquor by the drink" taxes with the county. Should special rules of thumb or interperative standards apply to disputes between different levels of local governments?

3. *Statutory home rule.* The delegation of legislative power under a general welfare grant is very similar to the delegation of power that occurs under either a constitutional or statutory home rule clause. For example, an Oregon statute provides: "Except as limited by express provision or necessary implication of general law, a city may take all action necessary or convenient for the government of its local affairs." Or. Rev. Stat. § 221.410(1). This grant of statutory home rule is similar to a general welfare provision, but the intent is to delegate a broad sweep of powers subject only to legislative preemption. In *Davidson Baking Co. v. Jenkins*, 337 P.2d 352 (Or. 1959), the court relied on this provision to uphold a local ordinance licensing bakeries and bakery distributors. Would such a provision change your analysis of the scenarios summarized above?

4. *Constitutional questions.* These questions often lurk behind statutory power problems. Some courts, for example, have struck down housing code provisions requiring hot water facilities as an unconstitutional taking of property. They hold these facilities are a matter of convenience, not necessity. See *City of St. Louis v. Brune*, 515 S.W.2d 471 (Mo. 1974); *Gates Co. v. Hous. Appeals Bd.*, 225 N.E.2d 222 (Ohio 1967). A local government's use of its statutory eminent domain authority to take unblighted private property for the purpose of economic development, even though not all the property will be opened to public use, has been sustained as constitutional by the United States Supreme Court. *Kelo v. City of New London*, 545 U.S. 469 (2005) (citing an earlier holding that "[I]t is within the power of the legislature to decide that a community should be beautiful as well as healthy, spacious as well as clean, well-balanced as well as carefully patrolled."). The court's decision in *Early Estates* avoided the constitutional problem. This judicial response is typical, as courts will not decide constitutional questions unless they are necessary to a resolution of the litigation.

See also *Itzen & Robertson v. Bd. of Health*, 215 A.2d 60 (N.J. L. Div. 1965), *subsequent proceeding*, 222 A.2d 769 (N.J. L. Div. 1966). The court held unauthorized an ordinance requiring septic tank installers to post a one-year maintenance bond. The court noted that the installer might be liable on the bond for acts of homeowners or third parties over which she had no control. What constitutional problem does this contingency raise? Is the "reasonable relationship" standard adopted in the *Early Estates* dissent a camouflage for substantive due process review?

C. Constitutional Home Rule

Students of local government need to appreciate the fluidity of critical issues regarding local government authority (autonomy and risk of state preemption) in the present moment. The National League of Cities, a nonpartisan advocacy organization that represents over 19,000 member cities, villages, and towns, has historically had a powerful influence on development of state constitutional home rule provisions. Two major variations on National League of Cities models have been widely adopted: the "*imperio*" model and the "legislative model," as discussed in more detail below. In February 2020, the National League of Cities proposed a new model, based on scholarly analysis of developments regarding local government powers and the growing tendency for states to adopt strong preemption provisions limiting the authority of cities to address issues of particular concern to those in urban or suburban areas in ways with which more rural and conservative interests might disagree. This section initially considers the history of home rule, before exploring in depth both *imperio* (defied) home rule and legislative home rule provisions. After laying the foundation of past efforts to provide local governments with autonomy to address local concerns and to protect against state intervention, it concludes by discussing the way forward as mapped in the new 2020 National League of Cities home rule model.

[1] Home Rule: History and Forms

Why constitutional home rule? The constitutional home rule movement arose in the late nineteenth century as an attempt to overcome the limitations inherent in statutory grants of power, and to provide local governments autonomy in local affairs. In order to curtail judicial decisions that had placed limitations on local autonomy, home rule advocates sought to place home rule authority in the state constitution. Home rule, as noted earlier, is one way of repealing Dillon's Rule. Home rule advocates sought "good government" reforms. They wanted to change the balance of state-local authority in order to halt the proliferation of special state legislation sought by special interest groups that had created higher levels of local taxing and spending. Barron, *Reclaiming Home Rule*, 116 HARV. L. REV. 2255 (2003). Missouri adopted the first municipal home rule provision in 1875 (applicable only to the City of St. Louis). Most states now authorize home rule for some, if not all, of their local governments. In some states, however, the constitutional home rule clause only authorizes the legislature to adopt legislation conferring local home rule powers. For a discussion comparing Dillon's Rule and home rule, and discussing their respective implications for local government autonomy, see Richardson, Jr., *Dillon's Rule Is from Mars, Home Rule Is from Venus: Local Government Autonomy and the Rules of Statutory Construction*, 41 PUBLIUS, No. 4 (2011): 662–685. As of 2020, only nine states lack constitutional home rule provisions: Alabama, Delaware, Indiana, Kentucky, Mississippi, Nevada, North Carolina, Vermont, and Virginia (NLC HOME RULE 2020, *supra*, at 12).

Types of home rule. Constitutional home rule clauses have historically taken two forms. The original form, dubbed "*imperium in imperio*"—a "state within a state"—grants a defined scope of power to local governments. This form of home rule usually grants local governments powers over "municipal" affairs, or over their "property, affairs and government." In this Chapter, it is referred to as "defined (or *imperio*)" home rule. Despite the original expectation, courts have come to play an important role under this form of home rule, since it leaves to the courts the question of determining what is included within the granted scope of local power. Uncertainties prevail because the scope of home rule power requires judicial interpretation.

A more recent form of constitutional home rule, proposed by the late Dean Jefferson Fordham, was given the title of "legislative" home rule. Under this form of home rule, the constitution grants local governments all powers the legislature is capable of delegating, but the legislature is authorized to withdraw or limit home rule powers by statute. National municipal organizations fostered this proposal, and several states have since added it to their state constitutions. In this Chapter, it is referred to as "total unless limited" home rule. Proponents of this "total unless limited" delegation of home rule argued for its adoption because they believed courts had limited the "defined" (or *imperio*) home rule; however, a careful review of this problem concluded courts had not been as restrictive as some believed. Sandalow, *The Limits of Municipal Power Under Home Rule: A Role for the Courts*, 48 MINN. L. REV. 643 (1964). Judicial interpretation is still important under "total unless limited" home rule because courts must decide whether state legislation has limited the exercise of home rule powers. But it is important to recognize that there are significant nuances from state to state, even within the broad categories or "defined" ("*imperio*") and "total unless limited" constitutional frameworks. See NLC HOME RULE 2020, *supra*, at 12 (observing that "constant contestation over the purposes of home rule and the nature of the local role has generated targeted state interventions alternating between particular grants of, and limitations on, local authority. These legal structures have been designed not to vindicate some general theory of the allocation of power between states and local governments, but generally to advance specific policy or governance goals" and citing Barron, *Reclaiming Home Rule*, 116 HARV. L. REV. 2255, 2296–2321 (2003)).

As noted above, the vast majority of states have constitutional home rule provisions (states are roughly evenly divided with slightly more states having provisions employing the "defined"/"*imperio*" home rule model and slightly fewer having legislative home rule). See Baker & Rodriguez, *Constitutional Home Rule and Judicial Scrutiny*, 86 Denv. L. Rev. 1337, 1338–39 (2009). Home rule powers are not exercised vigorously in every state, however. That is, within home rule states, only a limited number of local governments may actually be exercising home rule powers. While a substantial number of the nation's larger cities have home rule charters, many cities and counties with such power have declined to embrace them in their charters.

Delegating power and protecting local autonomy. The important point to note is that home rule, whether by the state constitution or local charter, both *delegates* power to local governments and *protects* local governments from being preempted by the state in the exercise of delegated power. In "defined" (or *imperio*) home rule states, the extent of the delegation and the degree of protection depends on the language of the constitutional home rule grant. The constitutional home rule clause often states that the exercise of local home rule is subject to "general" laws adopted by the state legislature, and courts imply this limitation even if it is not included. This exception allows state legislatures to preempt home rule municipalities through "general" legislation unless the home rule power is exclusively of local concern, in which case preemption may not be possible. See N.Y. Const, Art. IX, § 3.(d)(1) (a general law is one which in terms and in effect applies alike to all of a particular type of local government). In "total unless limited" (or legislative) home rule states, the delegation of power is complete, but the legislature retains full plenary power to prohibit its use in any area it deems appropriate.

Delegation of power and state preemption problems are combined in practically all of the home rule cases. The state legislature has usually enacted a statute covering a problem on which the home rule municipality has also legislated under its constitutional home rule powers. The court may concentrate on the state preemption problem and not consider the delegation of power problem directly. Even when the legislature has not acted, the court may confuse the two sides of home rule.

Equal protection due to source and scope of powers granted. Is there a constitutional problem if home rule local governments are granted powers not conferred on statutory local governments? The court thought not in *Save Palisade FruitLands v. Todd*, 279 F.3d 1204 (10th Cir. 2002). All counties in Colorado are initially created as statutory counties which may become home rule counties, thus increasing the scope of their power of initiative. "Save Palisade FruitLands," a group that wanted to place a measure on a statutory county's ballot, was refused and argued that statutory counties have been denied the equal protection of the laws. The court held that the classification of counties need only bear a rational relation to some legitimate end to satisfy the Equal Protection Clause and that the legitimate end here is that, in Colorado, home rule counties have a broader range of powers than statutory counties. Indeed, another federal court has held that there is no constitutional problem if a state grants no initiative and referendum powers to the citizens of local government. *City of Greensboro v. Guilford County Bd. of Elections*, 248 F. Supp. 3d 692 (M.D. N.C. 2017).

For discussion of home rule generally, see NLC Home Rule 2020, *supra*, at 9–17 (discussing history and imperatives for home rule reform); G. Frug & D. Barron, City Bound: How States Stifle Urban Innovation 60–74 (2008) (discussing home rule in several major cities); *Symposium: Home Rule*, 86 Denv. U.L. Rev. 1239 *et seq.* (2009).

[2] Defined (or *Imperio*) Home Rule Powers

The critical home rule issue in the "defined" (or *imperio*) states is the scope of the delegated local home rule power. The representative state constitutional home rule provisions that follow indicate typical "defined" home rule language, and the tendency of these constitutional provisions to delegate home rule power in areas of "local" concern. Courts usually impose this "areas of local concern" limitation even where the constitution does not expressly provide it.

Most of the home rule constitutional provisions reproduced below are self-executing, which means that they do not require state legislative action prior to their use by the local government. However, the Connecticut provision is non-self-executing. Do you see the difference? Consider the following provisions:

New York Constitution, Art. 9, § 2:

(c) In addition to powers granted in the statute of local governments or any other law, (i) every local government shall have the power to adopt and amend local laws not inconsistent with the provisions of this constitution or any general law relating to its property, affairs or government and, (ii) every local government shall have power to adopt and amend local laws not inconsistent with the provisions of this constitution or any general law relating to the following subjects, whether or not they relate to the property, affairs or government of such local government, except to the extent that the legislature shall restrict the adoption of such a local law relating to other than the property, affairs or government of such local government. . . .

Connecticut Constitution, Art. X, § 1:

The General Assembly shall by general law delegate such legislative authority as from time to time it deems appropriate to towns, cities and boroughs relative to the powers, organization, and form of government of such political subdivisions. The general assembly shall from time to time by general law determine the maximum terms of office of the various town, city and borough elective offices.

Ohio Constitution, Art. XVIII:

Sec. 3. Municipalities shall have authority to exercise all powers of local self-government and to adopt and enforce within their limits such local police, sanitary and other similar regulations, as are not in conflict with general laws.

Sec. 7. Any municipality may frame and adopt or amend a charter for its government and may, subject to the provisions of section 3 of this article, exercise thereunder all powers of local self-government.

Washington Constitution, Art. XI, § 11:

Any county, city, town or township may make and enforce within its limits all such local police, sanitary and other regulations as are not in conflict with general laws.

California Constitution, Art. XI:

Sec. 5. (a) It shall be competent in any city charter to provide that the city governed thereunder may make and enforce all ordinances and regulations in respect to municipal affairs, subject only to restrictions and limitations provided in their several charters and in respect to other matters they shall be subject to general laws. City charters adopted pursuant to this Constitution shall supersede any existing charter, and with respect to municipal affairs shall supersede all laws inconsistent therewith.

(b) It shall be competent in all city charters to provide, in addition to those provisions allowable by this Constitution, and by the laws of the State for: (1) the constitution, regulation, and government of the city police force (2) subgovernment in all or part of a city (3) conduct of city elections and (4) plenary authority is hereby granted, subject only to the restrictions of this article, to provide therein or by amendment thereto, the manner in which, the method by which, the times at which, and the terms for which the several municipal officers and employees whose compensation is paid by the city shall be elected or appointed, and for their removal, and for their compensation, and for the number of deputies, clerks and other employees that each shall have, and for the compensation, method of appointment, qualifications, tenure of office and removal of such deputies, clerks and other employees.

Sec. 7. A county or city may make and enforce within its limits all local, police, sanitary, and other ordinances and regulations not in conflict with general laws.

Note

The delegation of home rule power over "local" affairs, and the implicit limitation of that power over "state" affairs not delegated, creates a three-part taxonomy of local home rule powers:

(a) Some powers are exclusively of state concern. Home rule municipalities may not act.

(b) Some powers are shared between the states and local governments. Home rule municipalities may act, but they may also be preempted by the state. Most home rule powers fall in this category.

(c) Some powers are exclusively of local concern. Home rule municipalities may act, and may not be preempted by the state. The cases and comments that follow illustrate these three home rule power categories. The home rule authority problem arises when the state prohibits what a municipality attempts to do. Consider that issue in reading the following materials.

Another set of issues relates to the judicial role in making decisions about the distribution of governmental power. As framed in an important article by Professors Lynn Baker and Daniel Rodriguez,

> [W]e believe that courts are undertaking and accomplishing three objectives when they resolve constitutional home rule controversies: first, they are dividing the total sum of governmental power between two levels of government and thereby assigning functions (and, indeed, responsibilities) to these separate governments. Second, in defining and delimiting the categories of local and statewide affairs, the courts are making analytical judgments about which institutions are, and traditionally have been, best suited to perform certain tasks and functions. And, lastly, the courts are unavoidably making substantive regulatory choices. Whether or not intentionally, judges are choosing one regulatory result over another by the act of assigning the regulatory prerogative to one level of government, or governmental institution, rather than another. [Baker & Rodriguez, *Constitutional Home Rule and Judicial Scrutiny*, *supra* at 1344–45].

Consider the distribution of powers issues as well as the role of the judiciary in deciding the boundaries of distribution as you read the next case.

City and County of Denver v. State

788 P.2d 764 (Colo. 1990)

En Banc.

Justice Mullarkey delivered the Opinion of the Court.

This is an appeal from a summary judgment and permanent injunction issued in the Denver District Court finding unconstitutional section 8-2-120, 3B C.R.S. (1989 Supp.), which forbids municipalities, with few exceptions, from adopting residency requirements for municipal employees. The court permanently enjoined the state from enforcing section 8-2-120 against the appellees, the City and County of Denver and the City of Durango, finding that it violated Article XX, Section 6(a) of the Colorado Constitution by improperly interfering with the power of home rule municipalities to determine conditions of employment for their employees. We affirm.

I.

On September 12, 1978, Denver voters approved an initiative amending the City Charter to require that all employees hired after July 1, 1979 become residents of the City and County of Denver as a condition of continued employment with the city. . . . Effective January 1, 1980, the City Council of the City of Durango enacted Rule 4.1 of its personnel rules which requires residency in certain instances as a condition of continued employment.

Since being adopted, the residency requirements have been enforced by both Denver and Durango. On April 11, 1988, Governor Roy Romer signed House Bill 1152, codified at section 8-2-120, 3B C.R.S. (1989 Supp.), which purports to preempt residency rules such as those of Denver, Durango and other cities and local governments in Colorado. . . . [Denver and Durango filed suit, trial court granted a preliminary and then a permanent injunction, and the state took a direct appeal.]

II

Once again this court is required to delineate the limits of the power of a home rule municipality to adopt charter provisions and ordinances which are in conflict with state statutes. We often have stated the principles under which we resolve conflicts between provisions of state statutes and home rule charters or ordinances. A brief review is proper here. Article XX, Section 6, of the state constitution, adopted by the voters in 1912, granted "home rule" to municipalities opting to operate under its provisions and thereby altered the basic relationship of such municipalities to the state.[5] It abrogated "Dillon's Rule" . . . .

The effect of the amendment was to grant to home rule municipalities "*every power* theretofore possessed by the legislature to authorize municipalities to function in local and municipal affairs." *Four-County Metro. Capital Improvement Dist. v. Board of County Comm'rs*, 369 P.2d 67, 72 (Colo. 1962) (emphasis in original). Although the legislature continues to exercise supreme authority over matters of statewide concern, a home rule city is not inferior to the General Assembly with respect to local and municipal matters. In determining the respective authority of the state legislature and home rule municipalities, we have recognized three broad categories of regulatory matters: (1) matters of local concern; (2) matters of statewide concern; and (3) matters of mixed state and local concern.

---

5. Colorado Constitution, Article XX, Section 6 states in relevant part:

Home rule for cities and towns. The people of each city or town of this state, having a population of two thousand inhabitants . . . are hereby vested with, and they shall always have, power to make, amend, add to or replace the charter of said city or town, which shall be its organic law and extend to all its local and municipal matters.

Such charter and the ordinances made pursuant thereto in such matters shall supersede within the territorial limits and other jurisdiction of said city or town any law of the state in conflict therewith. [omission by court.]

. . . [After the secretary of state approves a charter, the] city or town, and the citizens thereof, shall have the powers set out in sections 1, 4 and 5 of this article, and all other powers necessary, requisite or proper for the government and administration of its local and municipal matters, including power to legislate upon, provide, regulate, conduct and control:

a. The creation and terms of municipal officers, agencies and employments; the definition, regulation and alteration of the powers, duties, qualifications and terms or tenure of all municipal officers, agents and employees; . . . .

In matters of local concern, both home rule cities and the state may legislate. However, when a home rule ordinance or charter provision and a state statute conflict with respect to a local matter, the home rule provision supersedes the conflicting state provision. In matters of statewide concern, the General Assembly may adopt legislation and home rule municipalities are without power to act unless authorized by the constitution or by state statute. Finally, we have held that in matters of mixed local and state concern, a charter or ordinance provision of a home rule municipality may coexist with a state statute as long as there is no conflict, but in the event of conflict the state statute supersedes the conflicting provision of the charter or ordinance.

Although we have found it useful to employ the "local," "mixed," and "statewide" categories in resolving conflicts between local and state legislation, these legal categories should not be mistaken for mutually exclusive or factually perfect descriptions of the relevant interests of the state and local governments. Those affairs which are municipal, mixed or of statewide concern often imperceptibly merge. To state that a matter is of local concern is to draw a legal conclusion based on all the facts and circumstances presented by a case. In fact, there may exist a relatively minor state interest in the matter at issue but we characterize the matter as local to express our conclusion that, in the context of our constitutional scheme, the local regulation must prevail. Thus, even though the state may be able to suggest a plausible interest in regulating a matter to the exclusion of a home rule municipality, such an interest may be insufficient to characterize the matter as being even of "mixed" state and local concern.

We have not developed a particular test which could resolve in every case the issue of whether a particular matter is "local," "state," or "mixed." Instead, we have made these determinations on an ad hoc basis, taking into consideration the facts of each case. We have considered the relative interests of the state and the home rule municipality in regulating the matter at issue in a particular case. [The court cited cases comparing state and local interests in water projects, control of outdoor advertising, the construction of viaducts and the safety of railroad crossings.]

Although other asserted state interests may be relevant, in determining whether the state interest is sufficient to justify preemption of inconsistent home rule provisions, there are several general factors which are useful to consider. These include the need for statewide uniformity of regulation [citing cases holding that uniform regulation of highway advertising signs by the state is necessary to preclude a potential loss of federal revenue, that state residents have an expectation of uniformity in local criminal laws], and the impact of the municipal regulation on persons living outside the municipal limits [citing a case holding that Denver's decision to construct a viaduct had an important impact on people residing beyond municipal limits, and a law review article stating that "'statewide concern' means those things which are of significant interest to people living outside the home rule municipality."]

Also relevant to this determination are historical considerations, i.e., whether a particular matter is one traditionally governed by state or by local government; 1 C. Antieau, Municipal Corporation Law § 3.40, at 3–115 (1989) (hereinafter Antieau). Further, "where not only uniformity is necessary, but cooperation among governmental units, as well, and where action of state and county officials within the limits of the city is imperative to effectuate adequate protection outside the city, the matter will in all likelihood be considered a state concern." Antieau, § 3.40 at pp. 3–119 to 3–120. Finally, we have considered relevant the fact that the Colorado Constitution specifically commits a particular matter to state or local regulation. [Citing a case considering a constitutional grant to Denver of the right to determine the duties of its officers, on the question of whether Denver or the state controlled the right of Denver sheriff deputies to exercise police power.]

We now apply these principles to the present case to determine whether the issue of the residency of municipal employees is of state, local, or of mixed state and local concern.[6]

1. Uniformity

The state has not asserted any particular state interest in uniformity of regulation with respect to residency requirements for municipal employees, nor do we perceive one. The Denver residency rule has been in existence since 1979. The fact that other municipalities may have declined to adopt such a requirement presents no special difficulties. In this regard we agree with the decision of the Oregon Supreme Court upholding a municipal residency requirement in *State ex rel. Heinig v. City of Milwaukee*, 373 P.2d 680, 684 (Or. 1962):

> In the appropriate case the need for uniformity in the operation of the law may be a sufficient basis for legislative preemption. But uniformity in itself is no virtue, and a municipality is entitled to shape its local law as it sees fit if there is no discernible pervading state interest involved.

There are many differences in the terms and conditions of employment among Colorado's municipalities, yet such inconsistencies alone do not require that we find municipal residency requirements to be of state concern.

2. Extraterritorial Impact

The state argues that the home rule residency requirements have an adverse economic impact beyond the borders of the particular municipalities. The state claims, for example, that by requiring its employees to live in Denver, the city makes it more

---

6. The state also notes that we have given great weight to legislative declarations that a particular matter is of statewide concern. Here the legislature declared in section 8-2-120 that "the right of the individual to work in and or for any local government is a matter of statewide concern. . . ." While the statutory declaration is relevant, it is not binding. If the constitutional provisions establishing the right of home rule municipalities to legislate as to their local affairs are to have any meaning, we must look beyond the mere declaration of a state interest and determine whether in fact the interest is present.

difficult for the surrounding communities to compete for property tax and sales tax revenues, arguing that "for every economic gain caused by a person moving into Denver there is a corresponding loss of revenue in the municipality from which the person moved." . . .

[The court was not convinced that the residency requirement caused Denver employees to live inside, rather than outside, the city, and concluded:] With respect to potential sales tax revenues, there is no evidence as to what extent Denver employees residing within the city limits of Denver spend dollars solely at commercial establishments in Denver rather than in the surrounding communities. Further, even if the state's assertions respecting the desired residency and the consumer spending of Denver employees were true, the state has not shown that such an impact is significant. To the contrary, Denver for its part presented evidence, which was not challenged by the state, that Denver employees comprise merely one-seventh of one percent of the total workforce in the state. In light of this fact, we conclude that the economic impact of the Denver residency requirement on the remainder of the state is de minimis. We also find unconvincing the state's condemnation of "interjurisdictional competition for tax money." Municipalities compete in numerous ways for tax dollars. For example, they may offer tax preferences to encourage industries to relocate to the municipalities. In a more general sense the development of recreational, educational, and cultural facilities also serves to attract businesses and residents. Thus, we are unpersuaded that the impact of the residency requirement on other communities is so significant as to make the residency of a home rule municipality's employees a matter of state concern.

3. Other State Interests

The state, citing *Shapiro v. Thompson*, 394 U.S. 618 (1969), argues that it has an interest in allowing every citizen the right to reside at the place of his or her choosing. While disclaiming any intent to challenge the constitutionality of the municipal residency requirements, the state argues that because courts have recognized a right to reside where one wishes and because municipal residency requirements "burden" that right, the General Assembly may act to protect such right by forbidding municipal residency requirements. . . . [The court noted, however, that the Supreme Court had held residency requirements constitutional, and that the Colorado court of appeals had held the Denver requirement constitutional. Chapter 5 discusses the constitutionality of residency requirements.]

. . . [W]e [also] note that the Colorado Constitution itself recognizes the value of residency provisions, requiring residence as a condition of employment in the state government. Colo. Const., Art. XII, § 13(6). Thus, to the extent that the state denies the legitimacy of the appellees' proferred policy reasons in support of their residency requirements, the state's position is inconsistent with the very policy advanced by our constitution.

4. Local Interests

In contrast to the asserted state interests in forbidding municipal residency rules, the asserted local interests here are substantial. We first note that Article XX, Section 6(a) by its terms grants to home rule cities the power to legislate upon, provide, regulate, conduct and control

> the creation and terms of municipal officers, agencies and employments; the definition, regulation and alteration of the powers, duties, qualifications and terms or tenure of all municipal officers, agents and employees....

Thus, the cities' claim that the residency of municipal employees is a matter appropriate for local regulation finds direct textual support in Section 6(a). Further, our cases have supported a broad interpretation of this provision.

On the other hand, the authority granted to home rule municipalities in Section 6(a) is not unlimited. For example, the cities do not dispute the applicability of laws which implement the state's general public policy regarding such matters as workers' compensation or employment discrimination even though such laws may interfere with a municipality's right to determine the "terms or tenure" of municipal employment. This result follows because, with respect to aspects of municipal employment which are of statewide concern, state statutes may supersede inconsistent municipal provisions.

Although we agree with the state that the enumeration in Section 6 of matters subject to regulation by home rule municipalities is not dispositive, we also agree with the cities that it is significant. If the state is unable to demonstrate a sufficiently weighty state interest in superseding local regulation of such areas, then pursuant to the command of Section 6, statutes in conflict with such local ordinances or charter provisions are superseded.

In addition to the textual support found in Section 6, Denver offered other reasons supporting local control of city employee residency. Denver Mayor Federico Peña testified before the district court and explained the policy reasons behind Denver's residency requirement. First, according to the Mayor, the residency requirement was intended to increase the investment of city tax dollars in the community under the assumption that Denver workers living in Denver are more likely to pay taxes in Denver. For example, as property owners, they will pay Denver property taxes and as consumers they will pay the sales tax. Second, Pena testified that requiring employees to live within the city limits would make them more readily available in the event of a civic emergency. Third, requiring city residency for workers will make them more attentive, compassionate and diligent in their work.[11]

---

11. Other reasons which have been advanced for municipal residency requirements include promotion of ethnic balance in the community, reduction of high unemployment rates among inner city minority groups, and reduction in absenteeism and tardiness among municipal personnel. *Ector v. City of Torrance*, 514 P.2d 433 (Cal. 1973). In *Ector*, the California Supreme Court held that municipal home rule provisions governing residency superseded a conflicting state statute. As

We find all these reasons to be valid. Although the ready availability of employees for an emergency may be most applicable to a relatively small number of employees, such as fire fighters and police officers, the other legitimate reasons offered by the city apply equally to all city employees. Particularly, we are impressed with Denver's argument that requiring municipal employees to reside within the city limits will instill a sense of pride in their work by guaranteeing that the employees have a stake in the common enterprise of municipal government and thereby may make them more attentive, compassionate and diligent in the way that they provide municipal services to Denver residents. . . .

[The court distinguished several of its earlier cases, including the following case:]

In *Huff v. Mayor of Colorado Springs*, 512 P.2d 632 (Colo. 1973), we held that the matter of fire fighters' pensions is one of statewide interest and concern. In *Huff*, we noted that fire fighting was a hazardous employment which required a great deal of physical strength, intelligence and skill. In order to attract the caliber of individuals necessary, municipalities must offer a competitive pension plan. Thus, we held that although the city had an interest in fire fighters' pensions, the state statute governing such pensions superseded municipal home rule provisions because the matter was of statewide concern. The establishment of a uniform fireman's pension plan statewide was "in the exercise of the police powers of this state for the purpose of protecting the health, peace, safety and general welfare of the people of this state." *City of Colorado Springs v. State*, 626 P.2d 1122, 1129 (Colo. 1980) [citing legislative declaration]. The state in this case cannot point to any similar state purpose in enacting section 8-2-120 . . . .[12]

Notes and Questions

1. *What is local?* The decision on what is a "local" matter subject to exclusive local control is an important one because generally only "local" powers are exempt from state statutory limitations or prohibitions. Do the tests approved by the Colorado court adopt the criterion (discussed in Chapter 1) that a function should be assigned to the level of government that can internalize both its costs and its benefits? The court clearly indicates it wishes to retain flexibility in drawing the line between state and local affairs rather than creating airtight categories, which makes the scope of local home rule more uncertain. Is uncertainty desirable in making these decisions? Most constitutions do not contain provisions delegating specific powers, like the

---

with our constitution, the California Constitution specifically granted home rule cities the power to prescribe in their charters the qualifications of their employees. *But see Uniformed Firefighters Assoc. v. City of New York*, 405 N.E.2d 679 (N.Y. 1980) (court finds municipal home rule residency requirements superseded by inconsistent state statute).

12. Thus we reject the argument of the intervenors the Denver Police Protective Association and the Colorado Professional Fire Fighters that even if the municipal residency requirements are valid as to other employees they must be struck down as to police officers and fire fighters because police and fire protection are matters of state interest. We have never held that every aspect of police and fire protection is of state concern. *See Huff*. . . .

provision in the Colorado constitution delegating authority over municipal employees. To what extent did that provision control the outcome in the case?

In *City of New York*, cited in the *Denver* case, the court, in a brief *per curiam* opinion, said that "while the structure and control of the municipal service departments in issue here may be considered of local concern within the meaning of municipal home rule, the residence of their members, unrelated to job performance or departmental organization, is a matter of State-wide concern not subject to municipal home rule. The city offers nothing to show the insubstantiality of the State's interest in affording residential mobility to members of the civil service." *Id.* at 680.

The Colorado court held that an ordinance that prohibited unrelated, registered sex offenders from living together in a single family residence implicated a matter of state concern in *City of Northglenn v. Ibarra*, 62 P.3d 151 (Colo. 2003). The court reaffirmed the principles it had adopted in *City of Denver*, and noted the "totality of circumstances" rule. Considering the totality of the circumstances by looking at certain factors, the court held this was a matter of statewide concern in that there is a need for statewide uniformity, the ordinance has an extraterritorial impact or ripple effect that impacts state residents outside the municipality, the subject matter is one traditionally governed by state government, and the Colorado Constitution does not specifically provide that the city may regulate the number of registered child sex offenders living in foster care homes. Why is living together in a residence a matter of state concern while a requirement about where people can live is not?

2. *Shared concerns.* Most matters on which home rule governments may wish to legislate are matters of shared state and local concern. As the principal case indicated, home rule governments can legislate on these matters but the state legislature can also preempt. Therefore courts often must first determine which level of government may act if a matter is arguably one of both local and state concern. If it is found to be both, they then address the preemption question

As the principal case establishes, Colorado allows home-rule regulations to coexist with state regulations so long as there is no conflict. If there is a conflict, the state statute supersedes the conflicting local regulation to the extent of the conflict. In *Webb v. City of Black Hawk*, 295 P.3d 480 (Colo. 2013), the Colorado Supreme Court held, in light of the state's long-standing recognition of bicycling as a protected mode of transportation, that a city's bicycle prohibition ordinance failed the conflict test. The ordinance prohibited bicycling without providing a suitable alternate route where the state statute authorized such a prohibition only when an alternate route was established. The court found that the city did not have the authority, in a matter of mixed state and local concern, to negate a specific provision that the general assembly enacted in the interest of statewide uniformity.

A national or state interest in a problem does not prevent it from being a matter of local concern. Billboards are an example, as pointed out in *Scadron v. City of Des*

Plaines, 606 N.E.2d 1154 (Ill. 1992). There, the court held a local billboard ordinance was not preempted by state law.

In *California Fed. Savings & Loan Ass'n v. City of Los Angeles*, 812 P.2d 916 (Cal. 1991), the California court held a local tax on financial corporations was of statewide concern because of its "accumulated impact intrastate," and provided the following analysis of the statewide-local affairs problem:

> The phrase "statewide concern" is thus nothing more than a conceptual formula employed in aid of the judicial mediation of jurisdictional disputes between charter cities and the Legislature, one that facially discloses a focus on extra-municipal concerns as the starting point for analysis. By requiring, as a condition of state legislative supremacy, a dimension demonstrably transcending identifiable municipal interests, the phrase resists the invasion of areas which are of intramural concern only, preserving core values of charter city government. [*Id.* at 925.]

The court added it would not "compartmentalize" these decisions by declaring particular areas not of local concern, and stated its decisions would be based on "historical circumstances" and would affect only the immediate case. Legislative supersession must be based on "sensible, pragmatic considerations."

Later, in *Johnson v. Bradley*, 841 P.2d 990 (Cal. 1992), the court added that if a state statute qualifies as a matter of state concern, the court must determine whether it is "reasonably related" to a determination of that concern, and whether it is "narrowly tailored" to limit "incursion into legitimate municipal interests." The court concluded that local funding of campaigns is a matter of statewide concern but the state statute was not reasonably related to the statewide concern of enhancing the integrity of the electoral process. The local charter amendment was enforceable. How do you suppose the California court would have decided the *Denver* case? For a case distinguishing *Johnson* and applying a state "meet and confer" statute to a city, see *Int'l Assn. of Firefighters Local Union 230 v. City of San Jose*, 125 Cal. Rptr. 3d 832 (Cal. App. 2011).

In the case that is foundational to New York home rule, Judge Benjamin Cardozo recognized the difficulty in categorizing government action into local or state concerns. He established the test that is used in New York, and often viewed as limiting protection for local governments from state interference. In his concurring opinion in *Adler v. Deegan*, 167 N.E. 705 (N.Y. 1929), he wrote:

> There are some affairs intimately connected with the exercise by the city of its corporate functions, which are city affairs only.... There are other affairs exclusively those of the State.... A zone, however, exists where State and city concerns overlap and intermingle. The Constitution and the statute will not be read as enjoining an impossible dichotomy.... How great must be the infusion of local interest before fetters are imposed? There is

> concession even by the plaintiff that if the subject be 'predominantly' of State concern, the Legislature may act according to the usual forms. But predominance is not the test. The test is rather this, that if the subject be in a substantial degree a matter of State concern, the Legislature may act, though intermingled with it are concerns of the locality.

3. *State legislative action by general law.* Some home rule states expressly permit state legislative action in areas of local concern, provided the legislative action is by general law, meaning it applies to all local governments of the same type. For example, Article 13, section 4 of the Rhode Island Constitution provides:

> The general assembly shall have the power to act in relation to the property, affairs and government of any city or town by general laws which shall apply alike to all cities and towns, but which shall not affect the form of government of any city or town. . . .

The Rhode Island court in *Moreau v. Flanders*, 15 A.3d 565 (R.I. 2011), held that a statute authorizing the appointment of a receiver for a city facing insolvency did not violate home rule. The statute permitting the appointment of the receiver applied to all cities and towns and did not affect the municipality's form of government.

4. *Local elections and qualifications for office.* Whether these issues are a matter of a local concern depends on how the court views the problem. *In re Advisory Opinion to the House of Representatives*, 628 A.2d 537 (R.I. 1993), held a state reapportionment statute for a local government which would have resulted in the removal of current office holders from the school committee, the water board, the budget board would violate home rule. In *State ex rel. Haynes v. Bonem*, 845 P.2d 150 (N.M. 1992), a city changed the number of councilmen to improve minority voting rights in response to a federal court decree. The court held this was "precisely" the sort of matter intended to be a local concern.

5. *Implementing home rule by statute.* Some state constitutions, like the Connecticut constitution reproduced *supra*, include a constitutional home rule provision authorizing the legislature to implement home rule through legislation. South Carolina is another example. How this type of non-self-executing provision works is explained in *Hospitality Ass'n v. County of Charleston*, 464 S.E.2d 113 (S.C. 1995). The county and some cities adopted various fees, including a fee imposed on rental accommodations for transients. The constitution authorizes the legislature to provide for "[t]he structure and organization, powers, duties, functions, and responsibilities of the municipalities . . . by general law." S.C. Const. Art. VIII, § 9. The constitution also abolishes Dillon's Rule by providing that "[t]he provisions of [the] Constitution and all laws concerning local government shall be liberally construed in their favor" and that any powers granted local government by the constitution and laws "shall include those fairly implied and not prohibited by [the] Constitution." *Id.* § 17. These and related provisions are the constitutional home rule authority.

The legislature implemented this authority by adopting statutes granting powers to local governments such as the following: "All counties of the State . . . have authority to enact regulations, resolutions, and ordinances . . . respecting any subject as appears to them necessary and proper for the . . . security, general welfare, and convenience of counties or for preserving health, peace, . . . order, and good government in them." S.C. Code Ann. § 4-9-25. The court held this section authorized the ordinance imposing the fees. Note how the constitutional and statutory provisions aggregate a number of reforms intended to repeal Dillon's Rule and enlarge the scope of local government powers. How do they compare with "defined" (or *imperio*) home rule provisions authorizing home rule governments to specify their powers in their charters? With a general welfare clause that does not have constitutional support?

6. *State-based nuances.* There are a number of helpful studies of home rule in different states. See, e.g., Mahoney, *Home Rule in Ohio: General Laws, Conflicts, and the Failure of the Courts to Protect the Ohio Constitution*, 67 Clev. St. L. Rev. 117 (2019) (considering home rule in Ohio); Cardozo & Klinger, *Home Rule in New York: The Need for a Change*, 38 Pace L. Rev. 90 (2017) (considering home rule in New York).

Home rule power questions may also turn on the scope of authority contained in a local charter, as affected by the court's view of the local home rule power. The following case considers these problems:

City of Miami Beach v. Fleetwood Hotel, Inc.

261 So. 2d 801 (Fla. 1972)

Roberts, Chief Justice

We here review by direct appeal a decision of the Circuit Court, Dade County, holding unconstitutional an Ordinance of the City of Miami Beach purporting to regulate rents. In rendering his opinion and making his decision the trial judge construed a controlling provision of the Constitution, namely, Section 2, Article VIII, Constitution of Florida. F.S.A. Ordinance No. 1791, entitled "Housing and Rent Control Regulations," provides for regulation of rents in all housing with four or more rental units except for hospitals, nursing homes, retirement homes, asylums or public institutions, college or school dormitories or any charitable or educational or non-profit institutions, hotels, motels, public housing, condominiums and cooperative apartments, and any housing accommodations completed after December 1, 1969.

The City Council enacted the Ordinance in October, 1969 after making a determination that an inflationary spiral and a housing shortage existed in the City which required the control and regulation of rents. The City contends that it acted with the intent and purpose of protecting its residents from exorbitant rents.

Several lessors, who were directly affected, filed a complaint seeking declaratory judgment and injunctive relief and attacking the validity on constitutional grounds. After considering motions for summary judgment filed by both parties, the Circuit

Court, Dade County, declared the Ordinance invalid, holding, inter alia that the Ordinance was an unlawful delegation of legislative authority by the City Council and construed Section 2, Article VIII, *supra*. This appeal followed and we affirm. . . .

The legal issues involved in this case are as follows:

> (1) Whether or not the City of Miami Beach has the power to enact this rent control ordinance? . . .

The first issue must be answered in the negative. The City of Miami Beach does not have the power to enact the ordinance in question. This Court recognizes that the language in the Florida Constitution which governs the powers exercisable by municipalities has been changed by Article VIII, Section 2(b), 1968 Florida Constitution.

Article VIII, Section 8 of the Constitution of 1885 reads,

> The Legislature shall have power to establish, and to abolish, municipalities to provide for their government, to prescribe their jurisdiction and powers, and to alter or amend the same at any time. . . .

Section 2, Article VIII of our new 1968 Constitution provides,

> (a) Establishment. Municipalities may be established or abolished and their charters amended pursuant to general or special law. . . .
>
> (b) Powers. Municipalities shall have governmental, corporate and proprietary powers to enable them to conduct *municipal* government, perform *municipal* functions and render *municipal* services, and may exercise any power for *municipal* purposes except as otherwise provided by law. (Emphasis supplied.)

Although this new provision does change the old rule of the 1885 Constitution respecting delegated powers of municipalities, it still limits municipal powers to the performance of *municipal* functions.

That the paramount law of a municipality is its charter (just as the State Constitution is the charter of the State of Florida) and gives the municipality all the powers it possesses, unless other statutes are applicable thereto, has not been altered or changed. The powers of a municipality are to be interpreted and construed in reference to the purposes of the municipality and if reasonable doubt should arise as to whether the municipality possesses a specific power, such doubt will be resolved against the City. "Municipal corporations are established for purposes of local government, and, in the absence of specific delegation of power, cannot engage in any undertakings not directed immediately to the accomplishment of those purposes." *Hoskins v. City of Orlando, Florida*, 51 F.2d 901 (5th Cir. 1931). The aforestated holding of the United States Fifth Circuit Court is entirely consistent with the 1968 change in our Constitution.

The Charter of the City of Miami Beach does not authorize the City of Miami Beach the power to enact a rent control ordinance. Section 6 of the Code contains no mention of such a power. The only possible source of such a power is Section 6(x) which permits the City "to adopt all ordinances or do all things deemed necessary or expedient for promoting or maintaining the general welfare, comfort, education, morals, peace, health and convenience of said city, or its inhabitants and to exercise all of the powers and privileges conferred upon cities or towns by the General Law of Florida when not inconsistent herewith."

The weight of authority is that without specific authorization from the state, the cities cannot enact a rent control ordinance either incident to its specific municipal powers or under its General Welfare provisions. [Citing cases, including *Wagner v. Mayor and Municipal Council of City of Newark*, 132 A.2d 794 (N.J. 1957).]

Local governments have not been given omnipotence by home rule provisions or by Article VIII, Section 2 of the 1968 Florida Constitution. "Matters that because of their nature are inherently reserved for the State alone and among which have been the master and servant and landlord and tenant relationships, matters of descent, the administration of estates . . . and many other matters of general and statewide significance, are not proper subjects for local treatment. . . ." *Wagner v. Mayor and Municipal Council of City of Newark, supra* at 800. Mr. Justice Cardozo, in *Adler v. Deegan*, 167 N.E. 705, 713 (N.Y. 1929) made the following statement which is in support of the above-stated proposition,

> There are other affairs exclusively those of the state. . . . None of these things can be said to touch the affairs that a city is organized to regulate, whether we have reference to history or to tradition or to the existing forms of charters.

Furthermore, since the inception of federal controls after the beginning of World War II, legislative history and the development of case law shows a recognition that rent control was not a matter within the realm of municipal power without express authority from the state and the existence of an emergency—as hereinafter discussed. *Wagner v. Newark, supra.* The Supreme Court of Errors of Connecticut has held that a city charter conferring police power in general terms did not empower the city to adopt a rent control ordinance. *Old Colony Gardens, Inc., et al. v. City of Stamford*, 156 A.2d 515 (Conn. 1959).

The State of Florida through legislative action has enacted statutory provisions to regulate the landlord-tenant relationship. Chapter 83, Fla. Stat. Ann. Absent a legislative enactment authorizing the exercise of such a power by a municipality, a municipality has no power to enact a rent control ordinance.

[The court then reaffirmed the rule, that rent control ordinances must be founded on emergency conditions, and refused to find an emergency condition in this case.]

Notes and Questions

1. *Understanding and applying Fleetwood.*

(a) *Regulating rentals.* Is the Florida court simply holding that the Miami Beach charter does not confer the authority to enact the rent control ordinance, or is it holding that the charter could not even be amended to confer this power? Is its holding that a "legislative enactment" is needed to confer the power on Miami Beach to regulate rents, by implication, a holding that the power to regulate rents is not included in the home rule grant? Or is the reference to the state landlord and tenant law by implication a holding that the power to regulate rents has been preempted by that statute? See *Fisher v. City of Berkeley*, 693 P.2d 261 (Cal. 1984) (rent control law is not preempted by state law), *aff'd on other grounds*, 475 U.S. 260 (1986).

See also *Rental Housing Assn. of Northern Alameda County v. City of Oakland*, 90 Cal. Rptr. 3d 181 (Cal. App. 2009). In this latter case, the court upheld nearly all aspects of the city's "good cause for eviction" ordinance adopted in order to curb evictions spurred by landlords' decisions to engage in "move in" evictions (often motivated by desire to raise rents for subsequent tenants). The ordinance required landlords to have good faith and proper motives for eviction, created a presumption of violation if landlord moved in but failed to occupy for at least 36 months, placed the burden of proof on the landlord, provided tenant with opportunity to cure offending conduct before eviction, and provided for damage awards. The court concluded that the 36 month occupancy requirement was preempted insofar as it shifted the burden of proof, but concluded that the ordinance provisions were otherwise not preempted under the state fair housing and unlawful detainer statutes. Compare *Larson v. City & County of San Francisco*, 123 Cal. Rptr. 3d 40 (Cal. App. 2011) (provisions allowing rent control board to grant rent reductions for quantifiable losses were not facially invalid, but provisions relating to reductions for nonquantifiable losses were invalid under judicial powers clause; city lacked authority to require attorney's fees to be awarded to prevailing tenants in unlawful detainer actions).

(b) *Authority of cities to conduct immigration inquiries and to use local resources and personnel to participate in certain immigration enforcement activities. City of Huntington Beach v. Becerra*, 257 Cal. Rptr. 3d 458 (Cal. Ct. App. 2020), *review filed* (February 19, 2020), concerned efforts by the state to enforce provisions of the California Values Act (CVA), restricting the ability of local enforcement agencies to conduct immigration inquiries or use local resources and personnel to participate in certain immigration enforcement activities. The City claimed that the CVA unconstitutionally impinged on its home rule authority to "create, regulate, and govern" its own police force and to allow the police force to cooperate with the federal Immigration and Customs Enforcement agency (ICE). The court applied a four-part analytical framework to determine whether the state statute unconstitutionally infringed on the home rule authority of the city, concluding that the inclusion of the regulation of the city police force within the category of "municipal affairs" in the state constitution did not preclude such matters from being viewed as matters of statewide concern. Based on the legislative history of the CVA and expert evidence introduced at trial, the court of appeals noted that (1) "when immigrants hear about the CVA, they have [a] deeper belief that . . . California's laws can protect the confidentiality of witnesses to crimes, even if they are undocumented" and (2) "[w]hen undocumented immigrants hear about the CVA, they are more likely to engage in a broad range of public institutions. . . ." *Id.* at 485. In effect, the court concluded that there is a statewide concern in *limiting* local police involvement with federal immigration enforcement to serve the legitimate effect of *enhancing* public safety and the CVA was, therefore, constitutional. "The need for immigrants to report crimes, work with law enforcement, and serve as witnesses, is therefore a statewide, and not purely local, concern." *Id.* at 487. The court of appeals ultimately concluded that the state statute did not unconstitutionally infringe the City's home rule authority, and thus did not need to reach the question of preemption.

(c) *Domestic partner benefits.* Local governments' interests in legislating the area of domestic affairs (i.e., a city providing benefits to same-sex partners in a state that may not recognize same-sex marriages) has changed since *Obergefell v. Hodges*, 135 S. Ct. 2584 (2015), ruled that the fundamental right to marry is guaranteed to same-sex couples. However, looking to pre-*Obergefell* cases sheds light on how the courts are, intentionally or not, making substantive choices by holding that one level of government, versus the other, has the authority to regulate an activity.

For example, *Lowe v. Broward County*, 766 So. 2d 1199 (Fla. App. 2000), distinguished *Fleetwood.* The court upheld the county's domestic partnership ordinance, finding that it did not legislate in the area of domestic affairs inherently reserved to the state. In the court's view, the ordinance did not elevate non-traditional personal relationships to a status equal to that of marital relationships created by statute. The major effect of the ordinance was to extend benefits and privileges to a domestic partner or to a dependent of a domestic partner on the same basis as the dependent of any other employee. A county employee could also use all forms of leave provided by the county, such as sick leave, annual leave, family illness leave and bereavement leave to care for his or her domestic partner or the dependent of the domestic partner.

Devlin v. City of Philadelphia, 862 A.2d 1234 (Pa. 2004), held that the city had home rule authority to designate and give benefits to same-sex "life partners" which was not deemed to be the functional equivalent of "marriage" but merely supplements the categories as another unmarried status. However, the city could not prohibit discrimination which would reach beyond its border, nor could it exempt life partners from real estate transfer tax in violation of the Uniformity Clause. See also *Heinsma v. City of Vancouver*, 29 P.3d 709 (Wash. 2001) (city's extension of benefits to domestic partners was sustained).

(d) *Employee protections.* Efforts by local governments to protect employees have included action to require employers within their jurisdictions to provide paid sick leave. For a discussion of related issues, see *Metropolitan Milwaukee Ass'n of Commerce, Inc. v. City of Milwaukee*, 798 N.W.2d 287 (Wis. App. 2011) (rejecting various challenges including constitutional and preemption challenges, to requirement that, pursuant to local initiative, employers provide sick leave to employees); Watson, *Defending Paid Sick Leave in New York City*, 19 J.L. & Pol'y 973 (2011) (discussing provisions in Milwaukee, New York City, Washington, D.C., and San Francisco; focusing in particular on New York City home rule authority; and concluding that state and federal law does not preempt municipal discretion to adopt such ordinances). For a further discussion of preemption of state and local legislation relating to labor and employment, see Sachs, *Despite Preemption: Making Labor Law in Cities and States*, 124 Harv. L. Rev. 1153 (2011) (considering in particular state and local discretion in the face of federal law). In addition, some jurisdictions have endeavored to protect employees' jobs by providing a grace period after a business is acquired by another entity. See *California Grocers Ass'n v. City of Los Angeles*, 254 P.3d 1019 (Cal. 2011) (finding no preemption under state or federal law and no equal protection violation).

2. *Exclusively for the state: additional examples.* Deciding what is inherently a matter for the state is contentious in a number of other areas.

(a) *Judicial remedies.* The judicial system is a matter of statewide concern and home rule governments may not create rights of appeal to state courts or confer jurisdiction on local courts. There are still complications in drawing lines, however. Compare *Molitor v. City of Cedar Rapids*, 360 N.W.2d 568 (Iowa 1985) (municipal power over local affairs does not include authority to provide in an ordinance that appeals may be taken to a state court); with *Lee v. Sauvage*, 689 P.2d 404 (Wash. App. 1984) (ordinance regulating eviction from houseboats does not interfere with jurisdiction of state courts).

(b) *Judicial remedies and civil rights.* Local government attempts to combat discrimination have also raised issues concerning the boundary of "private law" (therefore out of bounds for local government regulation) and "public law of local concern" (therefore within the realm of local government regulation). In *Sims v. Besaw's Cafe*, 997 P.2d 201 (Or. App. 2000), the court upheld a local ordinance that created a cause of action for discrimination based on sexual orientation. The court held the ordinance did not confer jurisdiction on state courts but simply provided that people harmed by violations of it "shall have a cause of action in any court of competent jurisdiction." The court concluded that the state court had been given its own power to adjudicate civil, or private-law, disputes without regard to the source of the law. In the absence of a provision authorizing a suit for enforcement, what could someone claiming discrimination do to enforce the ordinance in court?

Compare *McCrory Corp. v. Fowler*, 570 A.2d 834 (Md. 1990), involving an ordinance creating a private judicial cause of action against employment discrimination.

The court said that it was a statewide problem traditionally viewed as within the sole province of the General Assembly and the ordinance is not an appropriate "local law" under the constitutional home rule clause. In response to the case, the state legislature enacted a statute delegating authority to the county to provide that "a person who is subjected to an act of discrimination prohibited by the county code may bring and maintain a civil action against the person who committed the alleged discriminatory act for damages, injunctive relief, or other civil relief." The statute and the county ordinance were later upheld in *Edwards Sys. Tech. v. Corbin*, 841 A.2d 845 (Md. 2004). The court said that the county always had authority to prohibit discrimination but the constitutional problem identified in *McCrory* was that it had created a new cause of action in the courts, which was a matter for the state legislature. That defect had now been remedied by statute. *Washington Suburban Sanitary Comm'n v. Phillips*, 994 A.2d 411 (Md. 2010).

(c) *Licensing.* What about licensing powers? *Nugent v. City of East Providence*, 238 A.2d 758 (R.I. 1968), held a constitutional home rule provision delegating authority over "property, affairs and government" did not authorize a local ordinance licensing cable TV systems. The constitutional provision did not delegate powers "reserved to the general assembly," and the court held that the power to license businesses was a reserved power. It did indicate that the licensing power could be delegated to municipalities by statute. Contra, *Capitol Cable, Inc. v. City of Topeka*, 495 P.2d 885 (Kan. 1972). The Supreme Court in *Nixon v. Mo. Mun. League*, 541 U.S. 125 (2004), held that states are not preempted under the Federal Telecommunications Act from prohibiting their local governments from entering into the telecommunications field as service providers, even though the federal law states that no state or local statute or regulation may prohibit "any entity" from providing telecommunications service. A state may also attach conditions to licenses. See *Amico's Inc. v. Mattos*, 789 A.2d 899 (R.I. 2002) (no-smoking ban). Strong pressure from the tobacco industry and restaurant associations may block such legislation. Berman, *State-Local Relations: Partnerships, Conflict, and Autonomy, in* The Municipal Year Book 43–61 (2005).

(d) *Living wage.* Minimum or "living" wage ordinances also raise questions about local authority. Compare *New Orleans Campaign for a Living Wage v. City of New Orleans*, 825 So.2d 1098 (La. 2002) (holding that statute prohibiting local governments from establishing a minimum wage which a private employer would be required to pay employees is a legitimate exercise of the state's police power and local enactment (imposing a living wage of $1.00 above the federal minimum wage) is unconstitutional; however, an amendment to the home rule charter establishing a minimum wage for individuals employed by the city sustained), with *RUI One Corp. v. City of Berkeley*, 371 F.3d 1137 (9th Cir. 2004) (upholding authority of local government to adopt living-wage ordinance applicable to certain parts of the city). Is this a matter of state concern? Should local governments be permitted to impose higher requirements than state minimum wage restrictions or is this a conflict with state law? See Dalmat, *Bringing Economic Justice Closer to Home: The Legal Viability of Local Minimum Wage Laws Under Home Rule*, 39 Colum. J.L. & Soc. Probs.

93 (2005); Burchill, *Madison's Minimum-Wage Ordinance, Section 104.001, and the Future of Home Rule in Wisconsin*, 2007 Wis. L. Rev. 151 (discussion of minimum-wage ordinance, state's response, and Wisconsin's experience with home rule).

3. *Powers of taxation.* The power to tax is closely guarded. Courts may not be willing to recognize a power to tax along with a home rule power, and the constitutional home rule grant may limit it. If a grant of authority is necessary, an explicit authority to tax must be in the charter. But see *Union Transportes v. City of Nogales*, 985 P.2d 1025 (Ariz. 1999) (charter expressly granted authority to tax, and noting earlier case holding general welfare clause in charter did not authorize tax), *Jachimek v. State of Arizona*, 74 P.3d 944 (Ariz. App. 2003) (city's pawnbroker transaction fee is not an unconstitutional tax). Compare *Dooley v. City of Detroit*, 121 N.W.2d 724 (Mich. 1963) (local income tax authorized under home rule statute that authorized "excise taxes"); with *Carter Carburetor Corp. v. City of St. Louis*, 203 S.W.2d 438 (Mo. 1947) (no authority to levy income tax in charter). Problems may also arise because the constitution may prohibit local governments from levying certain types of taxes, while permitting others.

Some constitutional home rule provisions resolve power to tax problems explicitly. For example, the Illinois home rule provision expressly includes the power to tax and incur debt but only grants the power to license for revenue and impose income, earnings or occupation taxes as the General Assembly may provide by law. Ill. Const. art. VII, §§6(a), 6(e). However, the Illinois courts have had difficulty distinguishing between taxes that are authorized and taxes that are prohibited. For example in *Meites v. City of Chicago*, 540 N.E.2d 973 (Ill. App. 1989), the court held the city's transaction tax on online database searches on the Mead Data Central Lexis-Nexis computerized legal library system was not a service tax because "Mead does not perform a service by providing its subscribers with databases which the subscriber may use to do legal research."

Kan. Const. art. 12, §5(b) authorizes home rule cities to levy "taxes, excises, fees, charges and other exactions except when ... limited or prohibited by enactment of the legislature applicable uniformly to all cities of the same class." *Callaway v. City of Overland Park*, 508 P.2d 902 (Kan. 1973), held this provision authorized the levy of a business occupation tax. What explains the different result? How would you handle the power to tax problem in a home rule constitutional provision?

For an analysis of the extent to which home rule jurisdictions are limited by various provisions and interpretations in their taxing and borrowing capacity, see Gillette, *Fiscal Home Rule*, 86 Denv. U.L. Rev (2009) (arguing that constraints on revenue-raising by home rule municipalities are "oxymoronic" since without freedom to generate revenues, home rule cities are unable to exercise the freedom of action contemplated by their status). See also Sciarfe, *Powerful Cities? Limits on Municipal Taxing Authority and What to Do about Them*, 91 N.Y.U. L. Rev. 292 (2016) (arguing that state law should grant municipal governments "presumptive taxing authority" that parallels municipal regulatory authority and that should be similarly subject to state preemption law).

A Note on the Comparative Autonomy of Local Governments in Home Rule States and Non-Home Rule States

Do home rule municipalities in home rule states have more autonomy in self-government than in states where all local powers are conferred by specific enabling legislation? Consider the following additional cases relating to civil rights.

Home Rule Jurisdictions

Marshall v. Kansas City, 355 S.W.2d 877 (Mo. 1962). The court relied on a number of provisions in a home rule charter authorizing the regulation of business for the public welfare to uphold a public accommodation ordinance. It held the ordinance did not improperly regulate private relationships.

Holiday Universal Club v. Montgomery County, 508 A.2d 991 (Md. App. 1986). The court held that a charter home rule county has the authority to adopt an ordinance prohibiting discrimination in public accommodations. The constitution granted charter home rule counties the power to adopt ordinances for the good government and welfare of the county. The court relied on an earlier Maryland case, which held "that since the State's police power to enact legislation for the public good allows for passage of legislation to prohibit discrimination in public accommodations and housing, and that since the express powers granted Montgomery County include a co-extensive police power, the County can also enact such a provision." *Id.* at 994. Accord, *City of Atlanta v. McKinney*, 454 S.E.2d 517 (Ga. 1995) (antidiscrimination ordinance).

Midwest Employers Council, Inc. v. City of Omaha, 131 N.W.2d 609 (Neb. 1964). The court held a home rule charter did not authorize a fair employment practices ordinance. It noted that Nebraska followed the rule that a charter was a grant of power, applied the strict construction rule it applied to statutory grants of power, and found no express or fairly implied authority for the ordinance. The court added that civil rights and fair employment were matters of statewide concern.

Statutory Powers

On the question of statutory authority to adopt civil rights ordinances, see *Anderson v. City of Olivette*, 518 S.W.2d 34 (Mo. 1975). There, the city relied on a general welfare provision, authorizing it to enact ordinances for the "good government" of the city, to pass a municipal fair housing ordinance applicable to real estate brokers and aimed at preventing discrimination in the sale or rental of housing. The court found that the ordinance was not authorized by the "good government" statute. It noted that cities of this class had been authorized to license and regulate certain businesses, but real estate brokers were not among the businesses that the city was authorized to regulate. For other classes of cities, the power to regulate real estate brokers was expressly granted. It then noted this legislative classification of powers and held the specific grant to Olivette, which did not include the power to regulate, "may not be expanded to authority to license and regulate by reference to the general police power statutes." *Id.* at 39. See also Note, *Local Government Anti-Discrimination Laws: Do They Make a Difference?*, 31 U. Mich. L. Rev. 777 (1998) (reviewing difficulties in enforcing local ordinances prohibiting discrimination in employment, and arguing that federal government is better suited to address this problem); Wood, *The Propriety of Local Government Protections of Gays and Lesbians from Discriminatory Employment Practices*, 52 Emory L. J. 515, 548 (2003) ("The validity of local ordinances enacted to counter . . . discrimination . . . is a direct function of both the degree of power entrusted to local governments, and the extent to which legislative limitation and judicial strict constructionism exert limits on that power.").

The Choice between Statutory and Home Rule Powers

A home rule municipality does not always gain more power by acting under its home rule rather than its statutory authority. Berman notes that local officials may wonder whether home rule governments actually have greater authority than those without it. Berman, *State-Local Relations: Partnerships, Conflict, and Autonomy, in* The Municipal Year Book 47 (2005). Zoning is an example. All states have comprehensive enabling legislation authorizing the adoption of zoning ordinances, but a municipality may wish to adopt a zoning requirement that is not authorized by the enabling act. If zoning is a local rather than a state matter, a home rule municipality may clearly adopt a zoning requirement that is not authorized by the zoning enabling act. *Ayres v. City Council*, 207 P.2d 1 (Cal. 1949) (ordinance requiring street dedications); *Moore v. City of Boulder*, 484 P.2d 134 (Colo. App. 1971) (ordinance authorizing low-cost housing).

How can a home rule municipality decide whether to use its home rule or statutory powers? Some states have provided by statute for an election to use home rule powers. See Wis. Stat. § 61.0101(4), applied in *Gloudeman v. City of St. Francis*, 422 N.W.2d 864 (Wis. App. 1988). See also *Nelson v. City of Seattle*, 395 P.2d 82 (Wash. 1964), holding that reliance on the zoning enabling act was optional with the home rule city, which had taken "no action" to use the powers conferred by the statute. Sometimes, even if a home rule city has a number of statutory options on which to base its action, constitutional limitations and statutory interpretation intervene.

How would you now answer the question raised by this Note? Do home rule municipalities necessarily have more autonomy in self-government than municipalities in states where all local powers are conferred by enabling legislation? Berman expresses the view that local authority varies by region (New England has stronger local self-government than Southern states), type of local government (counties have less than municipalities), and function (all have more discretion in structure and functions than they have in raising funds and spending). Berman, *supra*. See also Bluestein, *Do North Carolina Local Governments Need Home Rule?* 84 N.C. L. Rev. 1983 (2006) (discussing North Carolina's experience as a non-home rule state where a legislative directive for broad construction has replaced Dillon's Rule).

[3] Total Unless Limited (or Legislative) Home Rule

A more comprehensive form of home rule, "total unless limited" (or legislative) home rule, grants all powers to home rule governments the state legislature would be capable of granting, subject to statutory limitations. The following excerpts illustrate the "total unless limited" model as previously adopted by the two national municipal organizations, and in Illinois, South Dakota, and Pennsylvania.

National Municipal League (National Civic League) Alternative Model

Sec. 8.02. *Powers of Counties and Cities.* A county or city may exercise any legislative power or perform any function which is not denied to it by its charter, is not denied to counties or cities generally, or to counties or cities of its class, and is within such limitations as the legislature may establish by general law. This grant of home rule powers shall not include the power to enact private or civil law governing civil relationships except as incident to an exercise of an independent county or city power, nor shall it include power to define and provide for the punishment of a felony.

South Dakota Constitution, Art. IX, § 2

A chartered governmental unit may exercise any legislative power or perform any function not denied by its charter, the Constitution or the general laws of the state. The charter may provide for any form of executive, legislative and administrative structure . . . provided that the legislative body so established be chosen by popular election and that the administrative proceedings be subject to judicial review.

Powers and functions of home rule units shall be construed liberally.

Pennsylvania Constitution, Art. 9, § 2

Municipalities shall have the right and power to frame and adopt home rule charters. . . . A municipality which has a home rule charter may exercise any power or perform any function not denied by this Constitution, by its home rule charter or by the General Assembly at any time.

Notes and Questions

1. *What was intended?* The "total unless limited" (or legislative) home rule model was intended to avoid or at least dilute the judicial role in interpreting the "defined" (or *imperio*) home rule provisions by eliminating the option to invoke the state-local distinction used to define home rule powers. As noted by the Alaska Supreme Court, "It was hoped that the constitutional delegation . . . would lead the courts of this jurisdiction to take a new and independent approach when conflicts inevitably arose between the municipalities and the state." *Native Village of Eklutna v. Alaska R.R. Corp.*, 87 P.3d 41 (Alaska 2004). It requires a denial of home rule power by the legislature or the home rule charter, a reversal of the presumption usually applied under the "defined" (or *imperio*) model. The "defined powers" home rule

provisions interpreted as limitations, not grants, of authority could have been given this interpretation, but the drafters of the "total unless limited" (or legislative) model apparently believed that the courts had not adopted this view.

Even the "total unless limited" (or legislative) model does not fully delegate all powers to home rule municipalities. If a home rule unit under this model were to attempt to legislate on divorce, for example, the courts probably would not allow it, even in the absence of a clause denying local authority to act in civil relationships matters. The courts must also determine what is denied by state law. They may rely on the state-local distinction in making this decision, although they should be less restrictive than courts in "defined" (or *imperio*) states if they respect the intent of the "total unless limited" (or legislative) home rule model.

2. *Does state versus local survive under "total unless limited" (or legislative) home rule?* The answer to that question would seem obvious. See *Jefferson v. State*, 527 P.2d 37 (Alaska 1974), where the court interpreted a legislative home rule provision to hold that "[t]he test we derive from Alaska's constitutional provisions is one of prohibition, rather than traditional tests such as statewide versus local concern." *Id.* at 43. *Ortiz v. Commonwealth*, 681 A.2d 152 (Pa. 1998), held a state statute could preempt a local ordinance regulating firearms both because the state had expressly prohibited local regulation and since this subject was a matter of state concern. New Mexico applies the state versus local distinction under its "total unless limited" (legislative) home rule clause to determine whether a law is "general." See *Cottrell v. Santillanes*, 901 P.2d 785 (N.M. App. 1995) (constitutional clause on qualification for office is general law prohibiting municipal charter from limiting terms of councilmen). Old ideas die slowly.

3. *Hybrids.* The Illinois home rule provision exemplifies a combination of a constitutional recognition of home rule and the "total unless limited" (or legislative) approach. Remember, "total unless limited" home rule recognizes the state legislature's nearly plenary power to act in areas of local concern if it so chooses.

Illinois Constitution, Art. VII, § 6(a)

> [A] home rule unit may exercise any power and perform any function pertaining to its government and affairs including, but not limited to, the power to regulate for the protection of the public health, safety, morals and welfare; to license; to tax; and to incur debt.

Can you see why? Its drafters offered the following explanation of their intent:

> [The home rule clause] is designed to be the broadest possible description of the powers that the receiving units of local government may exercise. It is clear, however, that the powers of home-rule units relate to their own problems, not to those of the state or the nation. Their powers should not extend to such matters as divorce, real property law, trusts, contracts, etc. which are generally recognized as falling within the competence of state rather than local authorities. Thus the proposed grant of powers to local

> governments extends only to matters "pertaining to their government and affairs." [Record of Proceedings, Sixth Illinois Constitutional Convention 1621 (1972).]

How does this provision handle the division of authority between state and local affairs? The Illinois Supreme Court has applied the traditional state versus local distinction to municipal home rule powers. See *Kalodimos v. Village of Morton Grove*, 470 N.E.2d 266 (Ill. 1984) (handgun control a matter of local concern). A few other states have hybrid provisions that include the "total unless limited" (or legislative) model's broad grant of authority but also make vague grants of specific powers. *E.g.*, HAWAI'I. CONST. art. VIII, § 2 ("executive, legislative and administrative structure and organization shall be superior to statutory provisions"); LA.CONST. art. VI, § 6 ("legislature shall enact no law [that affects] the structure and organization or . . . distribution . . . [of] powers").

4. *Statutory implementation.* Some states modified the "total unless limited" (or legislative) home rule model to convert it into a home rule provision which is non-self-executing, thus requiring a legislative grant of authority, which some states have done with "specifically defined" (or *imperio*) home rule. For example, the North Dakota home rule provision states that the legislature "may authorize [home rule governments] to exercise all or a portion of any power or function which the legislative assembly has power to devolve." In *Litten v. City of Fargo*, 294 N.W.2d 628 (N.D. 1980), the court noted that the "constitutional provision in itself does not grant any powers to home rule cities. Whatever powers home rule cities may have are based upon statutory provisions."

The following case illustrates the interplay between the plenary grant of authority and the statutory authority to limit home rule powers in states which have adopted the "total unless limited" (or legislative) home rule model as proposed by its drafters:

Cape Motor Lodge, Inc. v. City of Cape Girardeau

706 S.W.2d 208 (Mo. 1986)

HIGGINS, CHIEF JUSTICE.

The City of Cape Girardeau appeals summary judgment for Cape Motor Lodge, et al., declaring that the City lacked authority to construct and operate a multi-use center jointly with the Board of Regents of Southeast Missouri State University [SEMO]. . . . The judgment is reversed and remanded.

The City of Cape Girardeau is a constitutional charter city. Mo. Const. art. VI, § 19. In 1982, an advisory committee composed of City officials, SEMO officials and members of the City's business community proposed that SEMO and the City jointly finance, construct and operate a $12.9 million Multi-Use Center, the City to finance $5 million of the cost with general obligation bonds and SEMO to finance the remaining $7.9 million of the cost with state appropriations. On April 5, 1983, the people of the city approved the proposition by a vote of 72.8% to 27.2%.

On September 21, 1983, the City Council enacted ordinance 101 which levied a license tax on hotels and motels in an amount equal to 3% of gross receipts derived from sleeping accommodations and on restaurants in an amount equal to 1% of gross receipts derived from food sales, the revenues to be used to retire the bonds and promote conventions, tourism and economic development. The people of the City approved the tax by a vote of 61.4% to 38.6%.

The City and SEMO then drafted the Multi-Use Center Agreement. The agreement provided: SEMO and the City will jointly design, construct, furnish and equip the Multi-Use Center with 5/13 of the costs to be borne by the City and 8/13 by SEMO; upon the recommendation of a citizens' advisory committee, the Multi-Use Center will be located on SEMO campus and SEMO will hold title to the property and own the building; the Multi-Use Center will be available for a variety of SEMO and community uses, supervised by a six-member Board of Managers, three to be appointed by the City and three by SEMO; and SEMO will be responsible for the costs of operating and maintaining and building. SEMO approved and authorized execution of the Multi-Use Center Agreement; the City Council did the same by enacting ordinance 174. On October 31, 1984, the agreement was executed and the City enacted ordinance 190 authorizing issuance of its general obligation bonds in the amount of $5 million.

On December 26, 1984, respondents, a group of local hotel, motel and restaurant owners and operators, sought declaratory judgment and injunction alleging: the City has no authority to enter into the agreement and therefore the agreement and ordinance 174 authorizing the agreement, are invalid.... The trial court enjoined the City from implementing the agreement and the ordinances.

The City contends that this Court should be guided by Missouri's constitutional home rule provision set forth in Mo. Const. art. VI, § 19(a), and that execution of the Multi-Use Center Agreement between the city and SEMO and ordinance 174 were proper exercises of the City's powers derived from the home rule provision. Section 19(a) of article VI of the constitution provides:

Power of charter cities, how limited.

> Any city which adopts or has adopted a charter for its own government, shall have all powers which the general assembly of the state of Missouri has authority to confer upon any city, provided such powers are consistent with the constitution of this state and are not limited or denied either by the charter so adopted or by statute. Such a city shall, in addition to its home rule powers, have all powers conferred by law.

Section 19(a) grants to a constitutional charter city all the power which the legislature could grant.

Prior to the adoption of section 19(a) in 1972, this Court felt compelled to find some grant of authority in the constitution, statutes or the charter. Under section 19(a), in the absence of an express delegation by the people of a home rule municipality in their charter, the municipality possesses all powers which are not limited or denied by the constitution, by statute, or by the charter itself. Recognizing the City's power is derived from section 19(a), the question becomes: Are the agreement and ordinance 174 "consistent with the constitution of this state and . . . not limited or denied either by the charter so adopted or by statute."? Mo. Const. art. V, § 19(a). See *Frech v. City of Columbia*, 693 S.W.2d 813 (Mo. 1985). Respondents argue that the City is without authority to enter into the Multi-Use Center Agreement with SEMO by the terms of Mo. Const. article VI, section 16, and section 70.220, R.S. Mo. 1978. Section 16 of article VI of the constitution provides:

> *Cooperation by local governments with other governmental units.* Any municipality or political subdivision of this state may contract and cooperate with other municipalities or political subdivisions thereof, or with other states or their municipalities or political subdivision[s], or with the United States, for the planning, development, construction, acquisition or operation of any public improvement or facility, or for a common service, in the manner provided by law."

The enabling statute, section 70.220, R.S. Mo. 1978, provides:

> *Political subdivisions may cooperate with each other, with other states, the United States or private persons.*—Any municipality or political subdivision of this state, as herein defined, may contract and cooperate with any other municipality or political subdivision, . . . for the planning, development, construction, acquisition or operation of any public improvement or facility, or for a common service; provided, that the subject and purposes of any such contract or cooperative action made and entered into by such municipality or political subdivision shall be within the scope of the powers of such municipality or political subdivision.

Respondents argue that the City did not have the power to enter into the Multi-Use Center Agreement because SEMO is neither a "municipality or political subdivision" under the constitution and section 70.220, nor a "duly authorized agency of this state" under section 70.220. Respondents assert that section 16 of article VI and section 70.220 delineate with particularity the entities which may enter into cooperative agreements with a municipality; and that section 70.220 and section 16 of article VI do not provide for cooperative agreements with state colleges. Therefore, respondents contend that the City has exercised a power limited by statute and the constitution—thereby directly violating Mo. Const. art. VI, § 19(a).

This analysis was rejected in *Frech.* The City of Columbia had enacted an ordinance which authorized the municipal judge to issue search warrants for administrative searches conducted in connection with the City's licensing procedure of apartment houses and rooming houses. Plaintiffs contended that because the subject matter of the ordinance was not included in chapter 542, R.S. Mo. 1978, which governs the procedure applicable to the issuance of search warrants in criminal proceedings, the City had therefore exercised a power limited by statute; further, plaintiffs contended that the ordinance was inconsistent with this Court's constitutional authority to promulgate rules of practice and procedure for Missouri courts. This Court determined that chapter 542 neither expressly nor implicitly prohibits what the ordinance permits and that the ordinance neither impinges upon nor conflicts with this Court's constitutional authority to promulgate rules of practice and procedure for municipal courts. Accordingly, the ordinance was held not to violate article VI, section 19(a).

Under section 19(a), the emphasis no longer is whether a home rule city has the authority to exercise the power involved; the emphasis is whether the exercise of that power conflicts with the Missouri Constitution, state statutes or the charter itself. Conflicts between local enactments and state law provisions are matters of statutory construction. Once a determination of conflict between a constitutional or statutory provision and a charter or ordinance provision is made, the state law provision controls.

The test for determining if a conflict exists is whether the ordinance "permits what the statute prohibits" or "prohibits what the statute permits." [Citing Missouri cases.] Article VI, section 16, and section 70.220 each provide "[a]ny municipality . . . may contract and cooperate with . . . ;" ordinance 174 provides "[t]he City Manager on behalf of the City of Cape Girardeau, Missouri, is authorized to enter into an Agreement with Southeast Missouri State University. . . ." None of these provisions is written in the form of a prohibition or limitation; each of these is written as an affirmative grant of permission. Ordinance 174 does not expressly prohibit what the state law provisions permit; nor do article VI, section 16, and section 70.220 expressly prohibit what the ordinance permits. The language of these provisions is not expressly inconsistent, nor in irreconcilable conflict.

Statutory cities, acting without a constitutional home rule charter, cannot act without specific grants of power; section 70.220 is such a grant of power. In commenting on whether statutes that grant powers to municipalities are to be construed under article VI, section 19(a), to limit power to the particular way provided in the statute, the drafters of the amendment expressed:

> Since constitutional charter cities would no longer need statutory authorization to exercise a wide range of powers, such cities could elect to establish their own procedures and limitation unless the statute in question was so comprehensive and detailed as to indicate a clear intent that it should operate as both authorization and limitation. [Missouri Local Government at the Crossroads: Report of the Governor's Advisory Council on Local Government Law, p. 5 (1968).]

In carrying out the intent behind section 19(a), caution should be exercised in finding that a power granted to non-home rule cities places an implied limitation on the powers derived from section 19(a), unless such an intent is clear from the constitution or statute itself.

Section 70.220 and section 16 of article VI do not "operate as both authorization and limitation." These provisions contain no indication that the express enumerations of the entities named are to be considered as the exclusion of others not named. Section 70.220 contains no expressions that the legislature intended to preempt the area by limiting cooperative agreements to only those entities named in the statute. If this had been legislative intent it could have so stated. Comment, *State-Local Conflicts Under the New Missouri Home Rule Amendment*, 37 Mo. L. Rev. 677 (1972). Ordinance 174 proposes a cooperative agreement which was determined to be the most practical and economic method for this particular municipality. The legislature could not have intended for municipalities to be precluded from financing and constructing this public multi-purpose center in the most practical and economic fashion. In keeping with the spirit and letter of section 19(a), this Court has studied section 70.220 and article VI, section 16, and is unable to find any provision or language which is susceptible to the restrictive meaning respondents would read into the statute.

Article VI, section 16, and section 70.220 are relevant to a home rule city only to the extent that a local enactment cannot prohibit a municipality from entering into cooperative arrangements otherwise permitted by these state law provisions. This Court holds therefore that ordinance 174 does not violate Mo. Const. art. VI, § 19(a), because the state law provisions and the charter itself neither expressly nor implicitly prohibit the City from entering into the Multi-Use Center Agreement with SEMO.

Section 19(a) provides that home rule cities "shall have all powers which the general assembly of the state of Missouri has authority to confer upon any city. . . ." Mo. Const. art. VI, § 19(a). This grant of power will not be undermined by a determination that the general assembly could not grant a city the power to contract with a state college for the purpose of jointly constructing a multi-purpose building for their mutual benefit. . . . This Court finds no constitutional provisions prohibiting the general assembly from authorizing cooperative agreements between the City and SEMO. By enacting section 70.220, the legislature has stated its intent to enable municipalities to effect economic development and facilitate the performance of their related functions. Ordinance 174 is not inconsistent with this purpose and authorization by the legislature, and the ordinance does not "clearly and undoubtedly contravene some constitutional provisions." . . .

The judgment is reversed and the cause is remanded for further proceedings not inconsistent with this opinion.

All concur.

Notes and Questions

1. *Do statutes count?* What principle does the *Cape Girardeau* case adopt for determining when statutes place limitations on the home rule power? Does the court hold that silence is not denial under this type of home rule? That a "denial" is harder to

prove than "preemption" when there is no constitutional home rule? How does this analysis compare with the analysis we would expect from a court in a "defined" (or *imperio*) home rule state? Note that the court appears to reject the *exclusio* rule in its interpretation of the interlocal cooperation statute. Compare the application of the "limit-not-grant" rule to state constitutions in Chapter 1. Is the holding that the municipality may not prohibit what the interlocal cooperation statute permits an inversion of the intent behind the "total unless limited" (or legislative) home-rule provision? Is a failure to authorize a local ordinance a denial? See *Neuner v. City of St. Louis*, 536 S.W.3d 750 (Mo. Ct. App. 2017) (holding no, and upholding the city's ordinance adopting a payroll tax).

The same court reached a different conclusion in *City of Springfield v. Brechbuhler*, 895 S.W.2d 583 (Mo. 1995), where the city sought to condemn land outside the county in which it was located for natural gas easements that would connect to a publicly operated power facility. The court found a state statute to be "both authorizing and limiting" in its grant of condemnation authority to a home rule city. It said that, unlike the statutory provisions construed in *Cape Girardeau* which contained a list of several types of unrelated entities with which cities may contract, the condemnation statute in this case contains a single, conditional basis for the authorization as opposed to an open-ended list. This difference, combined with its recognition that the power of condemnation is to be strictly construed, led to its conclusion. In *City of Kansas City v. Carlson*, 292 S.W.3d 368 (Mo. App. 2009), the court held upheld the city's prohibition on smoking in bars and billiard halls, even though state law expressly exempted such facilities from no-smoking requirements, stating that home rule ordinances should be upheld unless expressly inconsistent or in irreconcilable conflict with general law.

How can these decisions be reconciled? Does the court's application of the permit-prohibit rule require a precise and explicit prohibition of municipal power? Note the suggestion that a "comprehensive and detailed" statute would be prohibitive. How could the interlocal cooperation statute be amended to meet this test? For more on interlocal cooperation, see Chapter 3.

Some cases recognize an implied statutory denial. Illinois requires an explicit denial, *City of Chicago v. Roman*, 705 N.E.2d 81 (Ill. 1998), as do some state statutes, *e.g.*, Fla. Stat. Ann. § 166.021(1).

2. *Does the "total unless limited" (or legislative) model always create more local autonomy?* With the *Cape Girardeau* case compare *State ex inf. Hanna v. City of St. Charles*, 676 S.W.2d 508 (Mo. 1984). A home rule charter city proposed amendments to its charter annexing two areas to the city. In an annexation election a majority of the voters in the city voted for the annexations, but a majority of the voters in the annexed area voted against the annexations. A state statute required a majority vote in both areas. Prior to Missouri's adoption of a "total unless limited" (legislative) home rule constitutional provision, the court had held that annexations

carried out by an amendment to a home rule charter were not subject to statutory requirements.

The court overruled these decisions. It held that under the "total unless limited" (or legislative) home rule constitutional provision a home rule city did not have to adopt a charter amendment to carry out an annexation because the home rule provision directly granted the power to annex. Because the home rule provision prohibited a city from exercising a home rule power in a manner inconsistent with state law, the St. Charles annexation was subject to the statutory voting requirements. Are the cases distinguishable? Is local autonomy under legislative home rule more or less expansive than in *imperio* states?

3. *Interpreting the "total unless limited" (or legislative) home rule model.* The cases that follow illustrate the variety of approaches courts take when they consider the exercise of home rule powers under this model:

Schwanda v. Bonney, 418 A.2d 163 (Me. 1980). The Maine statutory home rule provision, based on the "total unless limited" (or legislative) home rule model, authorizes a denial of home rule power "either expressly or by clear implication." A statute authorized municipalities to grant a concealed weapons license to persons of good moral character. A city ordinance added requirements that the weapon must be required for personal safety and protection or employment. The court held that the ordinance was prohibited by "clear implication" by the state statute, which was intended to "control all aspects of the licensing of the carrying of concealed weapons to the exclusion of additional local regulations." *Id.* at 166.

City of Boca Raton v. State, 595 So. 2d 25 (Fla. 1992). The constitution grants municipalities "governmental, corporate and proprietary powers," and also provides they "may exercise any power for municipal purposes except as otherwise provided by law." Fla. Const. art. VIII, § 2(b). The court held the city could levy a special assessment under its home rule powers, and did not have to comply with the requirements for special assessments contained in the statute. Although a statute authorized special assessments, it did not limit the home rule power because the statutory method was only one way to carry out this function. See also *City of Ocala v. Nye*, 608 So. 2d 15 (Fla. 1992), holding a home rule city could condemn an entire tract of land to avoid paying business damages on the remainder. The court held the city has the same power the state has to save money in road acquisition costs. But see contra *West Villages Imp. Dist. v. N. Port Rd. & Drainage Dist.*, 36 So. 3d 837 (Fla. App. 2010), *approved sub nom., North Port Rd. & Drainage Dist. v. W. Villages Improvement Dist.*, 82 So. 3d 69 (Fla. 2012) (statute required to impose assessment on public property).

In *Beard v. Town of Salisbury*, 392 N.E.2d 832 (Mass. 1979), the town adopted an ordinance prohibiting the removal of any sand, loam or gravel from the town. The court held that the ordinance regulated "intermunicipal" traffic and concluded that "[a]lthough the Home Rule Amendment confers broad powers on municipal governments, . . . it does not appear to be so expansive as to permit local ordinances . . .

that, as here, regulate areas outside a municipality's geographical limits." The court also noted that the power to regulate traffic was vested in the legislature, and that "it is inconsistent with the present statutory scheme for a town to assume this power on its own."

Compare these cases with the cases on statutory preemption in the next section.

4. *Taxation.* The drafters of the "total unless limited" (or legislative) home rule model intended it to cover financial affairs. Courts have taken this position in states where there is no constitutional or legislative denial of the taxing power, and hold the power to tax is conferred. *City of Anchorage v. Baker*, 376 P.2d 482, 483 n.7 (Alaska 1962). Some "total unless limited" (or legislative) home rule states, however, limit the power to tax by constitutional provision or legislation. MASS. CONST. Art. II, §7 (no power to levy or assess taxes); MONT. CODE ANN., §7-1-112(1) ("unless ... specifically delegated by law," there is no "power to authorize a tax on income or the sale of goods or services"). Municipalities in these "total unless limited" (or legislative) home rule states may have more restricted taxing powers than municipalities in "specifically defined" (or *imperio*) home rule states and may have to obtain legislative authority to tax. See *Montana Innkeepers Ass'n v. City of Billings*, 671 P.2d 21 (Mont. 1983) (city's hotel and motel tax held a prohibited sales tax); *Montana-Dakota Utilities Co. v. City of Billings*, 80 P.3d 1247 (Mont. 2003) (holding that gross-revenue fee for use by utility of right of way was an impermissible tax on goods or services).

5. *Civil relationships—causes of action in torts, contracts, etc.* The National Municipal League model prohibits the enactment of "private or civil law governing civil relationships except as an incident to an exercise of an independent municipal power." Some state constitutions adopting this model, including, e.g., New Mexico and Massachusetts, incorporate this provision, which codifies the idea that home rule governments may not adopt laws regulating civil affairs. This language still lacks direction regarding a clear demarcation between actionable torts and contracts recognized by state law and those which are incident to an exercise of existing municipal power. In deciding these matters, the judiciary has restricted municipal home rule powers in unexpected ways.

The Massachusetts court held this provision prohibited the adoption of a rent control ordinance. *Marshal House, Inc. v. Rent Review & Grievance Bd.*, 260 N.E.2d 200 (Mass. 1970). The court, after noting that the civil relationships clause was vague, rejected an argument the local ordinance was a "public law" governing economic relationships as a substitute for temporarily distorted market forces. Neither was rent control an incident of some other public power. See also *CHR General, Inc. v. City of Newton*, 439 N.E.2d 788 (Mass. 1982) (invalidating ordinance regulating condominium conversions). Compare *City of Atlanta v. McKinney*, 454 S.E.2d 517 (Ga. 1995) (civil relationships clause prohibits local ordinances regulating family relationships), with *City of Atlanta v. Morgan*, 492 S.E.2d 193 (Ga. 1997) (upholding revised Atlanta ordinance enacted pursuant of state statute authorizing local governments to provide insurance to employees and "dependents," without defining "dependents").

After *Fleetwood*, reproduced *supra*, Florida enacted a statutory home rule provision patterned after the National Municipal League's "total unless limited" (or legislative) model. The statute authorizes municipalities to "exercise any power for municipal purposes, except when expressly prohibited by law." In *City of Miami Beach v. Forte Towers, Inc.*, 305 So. 2d 764 (Fla. 1974), the court held the statute authorized a local rent control ordinance, and noted that bringing the ordinance under the "municipal purposes" clause presented no "judicial problem." Local rent control is now prohibited by statute in Florida. For an in-depth review of the "private" or "civil relationships" provisions in home rule jurisdictions, see Diller, *The City and the Private Right of Action*, 64 Stan. L. Rev. 1109 (2012) (arguing that such provisions unduly limit local policy experiments).

6. *Licensing power.* On a certified question from a U.S. District Court to the Arkansas Supreme Court, the court addressed whether a local moratorium on the issuance of building permits was within the power of the City of Elkins. *First State Bank v. City of Elkins*, 546 S.W.3d 477 (Ark. 2018). The city was concerned about the condition of the development's detention ponds owned by an entity not a party to the lawsuit. The owner of adjacent property, which took possession after a default on financing by the initial developer, refused to address the failing retention ponds. The city then issued a moratorium on building. The court held that by conferring power to issue or refuse to issue building permits and to regulate the building of houses to cities of the first class, the legislature denies such power to cities of the second class, like the City of Elkins. The court further held that the "general powers" of home rule provided no such authority.

A New Model: National League of Cities Home Rule 2020

As explained above, in February 2020 the National League of Cities issued an important new proposal for reformulating home rule authority, which more clearly integrated consideration of local government authority and autonomy with issues of state preemption. The new proposal has not yet been adopted but provides a template for possible future amendments to state constitutions and for ongoing consideration of the balance of power between states and local governments.

A Model Constitutional Home Rule Article[1]

Section A. Home Rule and Local Self-Government

1. The state shall provide for the establishment of general-purpose home rule local governments that provide the people with local self-government under the terms of this Article.

Section B. Local Authority

1. Quoted with permission of the National League of Cities and authors.

1. A home rule government may exercise any power within its territorial limits not prohibited by this constitution or by a state law that complies with Section C of this Article. This grant of authority to home rule governments includes the authority both to raise and to spend funds, as well as to determine the provision of public goods and services. . . .

3. Interpretation of Local Authority
   a. The rule of law that any doubt as to the existence of a power of a home rule government shall be resolved against its existence is abrogated, to the extent that any such rule was ever recognized in this jurisdiction.
   b. Any doubt as to the existence of a power of a home rule government shall be resolved in favor of its existence. This rule applies even when a statute granting the power in question has been repealed.

Section C. The Presumption Against Preemption

1. The state shall not be held to have denied a home rule government any power or function unless it does so expressly.
2. The state may expressly deny a home rule government a power or function encompassed by Section B of this Article only if necessary to serve a substantial state interest, only if narrowly tailored to that interest, and only by general law pursuant to Section C. 3 of this Article.
3. To constitute a general law, a statute must
   a. be part of a statewide and comprehensive legislative enactment;
   b. apply to all parts of the state alike and operate uniformly throughout the state;
   c. set forth police, sanitary, or similar regulations, rather than purport only to grant or limit legislative power of a home rule government to set forth police, sanitary, or similar regulations; and
   d. prescribe a rule of conduct upon citizens generally.
4. A home rule government may exercise and perform concurrently with the state any governmental, corporate, or proprietary power or function to the extent that the Legislature has not preempted local law pursuant to the preceding paragraphs. In exercising concurrent authority, a home rule government may not set standards and requirements that are lower or less stringent than those imposed by state law, but may set standards and requirements that are higher or more stringent than those imposed by state law, unless a state law provides otherwise.

Section D. Local Democratic Self-Government

1. The lawmaking body of every home rule government shall be locally elected.
2. A home rule government shall have the power to determine the structure and organization of its government, including providing for local offices and

determining the powers, duties, manner of selection, and terms of office of its officers; the power to determine the terms and conditions of its employees; and the proprietary power. . . .

Notes and Questions

1. *Similarities and differences generally.* Review the new National League of Cities model constitutional provisions, concentrating for now on parts A, B, and D (we will return to preemption later). In what ways does the new model differ from earlier models?

2. *Local authority.* Focus in particular on part B relating to local authority.

(a) *Local and statewide powers.* The drafters' comments indicate that they intended to do away with distinctions between "local" and "statewide" powers. NLC Home Rule 2020, *supra*, at 40. Why would they want to abolish this distinction? How does their draft address this problem?

(b) *Types of powers.* Is the proposal limited to protecting local "police powers" or does it go further? See *id.* at 40–41.

(c) *Private law exception.* How does the new proposal address the "private law exception" considered above? See *id.* at 41.

(d) *Fiscal authority.* How does the new proposal address local governments' capacity to raise and spend funds? See *id.* at 42–45.

(e) *Enforcement authority.* How does the proposal address the means by which local governments can enforce ordinances (for example by making certain matters misdemeanors or requiring payment of fines)? See *id.* at 46–48.

(f) *Dillon's Rule.* How does the new proposal address Dillon's Rule? See *id.* at 51–52.

3. *Local self-government.* Why did the drafters include Part D relating to local governments, elections, and structure? See id. at 53–60 (citing examples of state interference with local government structures and elections, as well as punitive state preemption measures that effectively denied local voter control over municipal regulatory functions and proprietary activities).

Problem 2-2

You are the attorney for your state's League of Municipalities. Your state does not have constitutional home rule, and the League has asked you to draft a home rule provision for inclusion in the state constitution, based on current best practices. A number of recent events have prompted interest in constitutional home rule. One is the adoption of statutes in the latest legislative session that prohibit municipalities from legislating on a number of matters, including rent control and accessory dwelling units (ADUs). Another is a campaign by environmental rights groups to get municipalities to adopt ordinances prohibiting plastic bags, plastic straws, and polystyrene. Advocates for workers in a number of localities are pushing for towns to impose requirements on local contractors to pay higher minimum wages. In the face of protests about #blacklivesmatter, several jurisdictions wish to assure they have authority to reorganize their police forces significantly, create citizen review boards, and remove Confederate monuments. What constitutional language would you recommend? What are the advantages and disadvantages to your client if your proposed language were to be adopted into your state's constitution?

D. Statutory Preemption and Conflict

Fix This Now

> We are at a critical moment in Indiana's history. And much is at stake. Our image. Our reputation as a state that embraces people of diverse backgrounds and makes them feel welcome. And our efforts over many years to retool our economy, to attract talented workers and thriving businesses, and to improve the quality of life for millions of Hoosiers. All of this is at risk because of a new law, the Religious Freedom Restoration Act, that no matter its original intent has done enormous harm to our state and potentially our economic future. The consequences will only get worse if our state leaders delay in fixing the deep mess created.[2]

The law at issue in the above example, Indiana's Religious Freedom Restoration Act (RFRA), preempted local governments from enforcing local ordinances to protect members of the LGBTQ+ community. As the statute's title suggests, its intent was to protect religious freedoms of private shopholders and business owners. However, looked at from a different perspective, Indiana's RFRA allowed discrimination, on religious grounds, against the LGBTQ+ community. Regardless of its intent or effect, the act "caused an immediate economic backlash, losing or putting at risk $250 million dollars of the state's economy. At the time of the initial RFRA passage, twelve cities in Indiana already had LGBTQ protection ordinances." Boswell, *How State Legislative Preemption in Indiana Bars Local Governments from Building a Positive Economic Future*, 51 IND. L. REV. 471, 487 (2018).

In 2016, North Carolina passed House Bill 2, the Public Facilities and Privacy Act (otherwise known as the "bathroom bill"). This bill essentially required citizens to use the public restroom that corresponded to with their "biological" gender as listed on their birth certificate, "thus barring transgender [people] from using the bathroom consistent with their gender identities." Boswell, at 487–88, citing Epps, *North Carolina's Bathroom Bill Is a Constitutional Monstrosity*, https://www.theatlantic.

---

2. Editorial on the front page of the Indianapolis Star opposing Indiana legislature's Religious Freedom Restoration Act, seen by many to facilitate private discrimination against gay, lesbian, bisexual and transsexual individuals, and urging then-governor Mike Pence to intervene (March 5, 2015), available at https://www.indystar.com/story/opinion/2015/03/30/editorial-gov-pence-fix-religious-freedom-law-now/70698802/.

com/politics/archive/2016/05/hb2-is-a-constitutional-monstrosity/482106/. The Atlantic (May 10, 2016). Like Indiana's RFRA, North Carolina's bathroom bill preempted existing local ordinances protecting the LGBTQ+ community (the City of Charlotte, for example, was in the process of passing such an ordinance), but also barred any community from enacting new ones. The North Carolina legislation resulted in the potential loss of billions of dollars to the state economy due to corporate cancellations of expansions and events, which spurred the North Carolina state legislature to repeal the bill. Ultimately, a federal judge in North Carolina approved a settlement that prohibited the state from banning transgender people from using bathrooms in state buildings that match their gender identity.

Both of these examples demonstrate how issues of local control and state preemption storm, sometimes in unexpected ways, to the forefront of state politics, national news, and divisive cultural debates. Indeed, a new term has emerged to describe the growing pattern of intervention by states in areas that might previously have been regarded as local. See Scharff, *Hyper Preemption: A Reordering of the State-Local Relationship*? 106 Geo. L.J. 1469, 1470 (2018) (using the term "hyper preemption" to refer to efforts that not only curtail specific local policies but "chill local policymaking" by "punish[ing] local governments or their public officials for taking policy positions and deny[ing] access to the typical legal processes for determining the legality of local ordinances").

For other important scholarly analysis of mandatory state preemption of local government actions, see Briffault, *The Challenge of the New Preemption*, 70 Stan. L. Rev. 1995, 1999–2002, 2022–25 (2018) (providing examples of preemption relating to firearms, labor issues, public health initiatives, control of plastic bags, and management of Confederate monuments; punitive actions against local governments involving financial burdens and "nuclear" preemption that bans local action in broad categories; observing that to comport with home rule requirements courts should strike down punitive preemption, prohibit nuclear preemption, limit occasions in which states can prohibit any local regulation without imposing alternative regulatory regimes, and require that preemptive state action be narrowly tailored to state substantive concerns); Schragger, *The Attack on American Cities*, 96 Tex. L. Rev. 1163 (2018) (highlighting the significant implications arising from the divide between urban areas as drivers of state economies and non-urban areas; arguing that American federalism is anti-urbanist by nature; highlighting implications of gerrymandering and malapportionment; contending that home rule limits local autonomy rather than advancing it; and explaining other anti-urbanism dynamics); Diller, *The Political Process of Preemption*, 54 U. Rich. L. Rev. 343 (2020) (considering the interplay between *Hunter v. City of Pittsburgh*, 207 U.S. 161 (1907) (discussed in Chapter 1), and *Reynolds v. Sims*, 377 U.S. 533 (1964) (establishing one-person-one-vote requirements and discussed in Chapter 9); arguing that not all preemption is the same and that tailored solutions to associated issues such as gerrymandering are needed). A few states (Alabama, Delaware, Indiana, Kentucky, Mississippi, Nevada, North Carolina, Vermont, and Virginia) have no constitutional home rule provision, which leaves the respective local governments' authority completely in the state legislatures' hands.

Enabling legislation is rarely complete, and municipalities often adopt regulations and requirements that supplement state statutes. Until recently, it was seldom that state legislation would clearly indicate an intent to preempt existing local ordinances. Even addressing classic preemption and conflict issues arising from statutory grants of home rule power and subsequently passed local ordinances (challenged as preempted), these provisions require judicial interpretation and, as a California case notes, there are two possible conceptual issues with classic preemption:

> Conceptually, however, an explicit contradiction between an ordinance and a state statute can take either of two forms. One is where the language of the ordinance directly contradicts the operative language of the statute, *e.g.*, by penalizing conduct which the state law expressly authorizes, or by purporting to permit conduct which the statute forbids. The other form occurs when the regulatory language of the ordinance does not contradict any specific portion of the statutory regulation, but the passage of the ordinance itself contradicts the Legislature's intent, expressly stated in the statute, that no local government shall regulate conduct within that same "field" or subject matter. [*Bravo Vending v. City of Rancho Mirage*, 20 Cal. Rptr. 2d 164 (Cal. App. 1993).]

The next two cases illustrate each alternative:

Miller v. Fabius Township Board

366 Mich. 250, 114 N.W.2d 205 (1962)

Kavanagh, Justice.

Plaintiff filed a bill of complaint in chancery in the circuit court for the county of St. Joseph naming the Fabius township board as defendant under the Michigan declaratory judgment statute, Comp. Laws 1948, § 691.501 et seq. He sought a decree finding the following ordinance adopted by defendant board to be void and unconstitutional:

> Effective August 25, 1959, powerboat racing and water skiing shall be prohibited on Pleasant Lake in Fabius township, St. Joseph county, Michigan each day after the hour of 4:00 p.m. until the following day at 10:00 a.m. Any person who violates, disobeys or refuses to comply with or who resists the enforcement of the provisions of this ordinance shall upon conviction, be fined not less than $25 nor more than $100 for such offense, or imprisonment in the county jail until such fine and costs shall be paid and such imprisonment shall be paid for a period not to exceed 30 days.

Defendant board appeared and filed an answer to the bill of complaint alleging that the ordinance in question was valid and praying for dismissal of the bill of complaint.

Plaintiff claims he is one of a number of people who own land or cottages on the shores of Pleasant Lake and who enjoy the sport of water skiing during the summer months.

Plaintiff alleges that he, like many other summer lake vacationers, due to employment, is unable to arrive at his property on Pleasant Lake until after 5:00 p.m. He desires to take advantage of the recreational facilities of Pleasant Lake and participate in the sport of water skiing during the daylight hours, which last until approximately 9:00 p.m.

Plaintiff claims he is deprived of water skiing by reason of the ordinance adopted by the local township board.

In 1959 the Michigan legislature enacted Act 55, P.A. 1959, amending Act 246, P.A. 1945, the title of which reads as follows:

> An act to authorize the township boards of certain townships to adopt ordinances and regulations to secure the public peace, health, safety, welfare and convenience; to provide for the establishment of a township police department; to provide for policing of townships by the county sheriff; to provide penalties; and to repeal all acts and parts of acts in conflict therewith.

Section 1 of the act, as amended, reads in pertinent part as follows:

> The township board of any township may, at any regular or special meeting by a majority of the members elect of such township board, adopt ordinances regulating health and safety of persons and property therein. . . .

The case came on for hearing in the circuit court for St. Joseph county. After proofs and briefs, the trial court in his opinion found the ordinance constitutional and valid and entered an order dismissing the bill of complaint.

Plaintiff appeals claiming the ordinance is void because the statutes—Act 215, P.A. 1931 and Act 310, P.A. 1957—have preempted the field of regulating motorboating and water skiing on Michigan's inland lakes.

Plaintiff alleges the ordinance is void because it prohibits that which the state statutes permit and exceeds the powers granted townships by Act 246, P.A. 1945, as amended. Plaintiff also claims the ordinance is void because it treats motorboating and water skiing as a local regulatory problem when, in fact, such activities are not local but are state-wide in scope and require uniform state-wide regulation.

Plaintiff argues that in 1931 the legislature undertook regulation of motorboating and water skiing activities on inland lakes when it enacted section 1 of Act 215, P.A. 1931. The act required motorboats and other watercraft to be equipped with mufflers and other devices to deaden the sound. It also purported to regulate the speed and use of motorboats on inland lakes.

Plaintiff further alleges that 26 years later a second statute—Act 310, P.A. 1957—was enacted by the legislature which recognized the need for more comprehensive regulation of boating and water activities on our inland lakes. This statute made certain changes in the regulation of motorboating and provided limitations on water skiing activities.

Section 3 of the 1957 act relates to persons operating watercraft under the influence of intoxicating liquor or narcotic drugs. Section 4 of the act relates to the speed of watercraft. Section 5 of the act as amended by Act 208, P.A. 1958, for the first time took recognition of the problem of water skiing and other water surface sports, and provides as follows:

> Any person who operates any watercraft, or who navigates, steers or controls himself while being towed on water skis, water sleds, surfboards or similar contrivances, upon any of the waterways of this state carelessly and heedlessly in disregard of the rights or safety of others, or without due caution and circumspection and at a speed or in a manner so as to endanger or be likely to endanger any person or property, shall be guilty of reckless operation of a watercraft and upon conviction shall be punished as provided in section 16 of this act.

Section 8 of the act specifically relates to restrictions on the periods when water skiing is prohibited and reads as follows:

> No operator of any watercraft shall have in tow or shall otherwise be assisting in the propulsion of a person on water skis, water sled, surfboard, or other similar contrivance during the period 1 hour after sunset to 1 hour prior to sunrise. Any person permitting himself to be towed on water skis, water sleds, surfboards or similar contrivances in violation of any of the provisions of this act shall be guilty of a misdemeanor.

It is contended the 1957 act was to cover on a state-wide basis the entire field of prohibitory regulation of motorboating and water skiing on our inland lakes.

The trial court rejected plaintiff's claim in this regard. On appeal we are asked to determine whether the ordinance conflicts with the state statutes.

Concerning this problem, 37 Am. Jur., Municipal Corporations, § 165, p. 790, states the following:

> It has been held that in determining whether the provisions of a municipal ordinance conflict with a statute covering the same subject, the test is whether the ordinance prohibits an act which the statute permits, or permits an act which the statute prohibits. . . .
>
> The mere fact that the state, in the exercise of the police power, has made certain regulations does not prohibit a municipality from exacting additional requirements. So long as there is no conflict between the two, and the requirements of the municipal bylaw are not in themselves pernicious, as being unreasonable or discriminatory, both will stand. The fact that an

> ordinance enlarges upon the provisions of a statute by requiring more than the statute requires creates no conflict therewith, unless the statute limits the requirements for all cases to its own prescription. Thus, where both an ordinance and a statute are prohibitory and the only difference between them is that the ordinance goes further in its prohibition, but not counter to the prohibition under the statute, and the municipality does not attempt to authorize by the ordinance what the legislature has forbidden or forbid what the legislature has *expressly* licensed, authorized, or required, there is nothing contradictory between the provisions of the statute and the ordinance because of which they cannot coexist and be effective. Unless legislative provisions are contradictory in the sense that they cannot coexist, they are not deemed inconsistent because of mere lack of uniformity in detail. (Emphasis supplied.)

This court has followed the above rule holding portions of a field not covered by state law are open to local regulation. See *City of Howell v. Kaal*, 67 N.W.2d 704 [(Mich. 1954)]; *People v. McGraw*, 150 N.W. 836 [(Mich. 1915)].

The rule has long been recognized that municipalities are not divested of all control even where the legislature has enacted laws.

This court said in *People v. McGraw, supra*:

> ... the municipality retains *reasonable control* of its highways, which is such control as cannot be said to be unreasonable and inconsistent with regulations which have been established, or may be established, by the state itself with reference thereto. This construction allows a municipality to recognize local and peculiar conditions, and to pass ordinances, regulating traffic on its streets, which do not contravene the state laws. The congested condition of traffic on many of the streets of the city of Detroit is a matter of common knowledge, and these conditions make it absolutely necessary, for the protection of pedestrians and the drivers of vehicles, to enact rules and regulations peculiarly adapted to the conditions there found, and to enact ordinances to diminish the danger. ...

The question we have to determine, then, is whether the state has so preempted the field that it would be unconstitutional for the township to attempt to regulate water skiing by ordinance.

The legislation relied upon by plaintiff merely relates to various phases of the operation of watercraft, including its speed and use upon inland lakes. Section 8 of the 1957 statute only prohibits water skiing during the period one (1) hour after sunset to one (1) hour before sunrise. It, therefore, certainly cannot be said that the legislature intended to preempt the entire field or activity of water skiing. If the legislature so intended, it could have expressly stated preemptive control. It logically follows, then, that the portions of the township ordinance which endeavor to regulate water skiing, if not in conflict with the state law, are valid so far as the preemption doctrine is concerned.

It is obvious the ordinance was enacted to prevent the many dangers and alleviate the congested local conditions that existed on Pleasant Lake.

In *City of Howell v. Kaal, supra* this court held that an ordinance may not invade a field completely occupied by statute but may enter an area not preempted by the state act, and further held that what the state law expressly permits an ordinance may not prohibit.

Since the cited statutes do not expressly control the period of regulation covered by the ordinance, it must be concluded there is no conflict. The ordinance speaks only where the statutes are silent. . . .

The remaining question deals with the subject of whether the ordinance can be sustained on the reasoning it deals with a local regulatory problem which the township has the authority to regulate under the 1959 amendatory act relating to "health and safety of persons and property" if the activity is in fact not local but state-wide. Plaintiff cites several cases in other states which seem to indicate support of his position. However, the cited cases do not deal with acts similar to the ones we are here asked to construe.

While the general problem with reference to water skiing and motorboating and the use of our inland lakes by different classes of sportsmen are state-wide problems, there are peculiar circumstances that are local in character—such as the number of boat users on the lake; the amount of fishing on the lake; the congestion and conflict between fishermen and water skiers; the location of the lake to densely populated areas—which the 1959 amendment authorizes townships to deal with under the "health and safety of persons and property" clause.

A comparison might be made between traffic ordinances of a city and the state traffic statutes. Densely populated cities with large numbers of automobiles require more local regulation, even to a greater reduction in speed, than do rural communities. The state prescribes by its statutes the general provisions with respect to problems, and this court has upheld the right of municipalities to further regulate as long as there is no conflict between the state statute and the municipal ordinance. We believe this rule of law equally applicable to the regulation of boating and water skiing on inland lakes.

The trial court reached a correct conclusion in finding the ordinance was valid as having a reasonable relation to the health and safety of persons and property of the area involved.

Under the facts in this particular case, we do not find the ordinance unconstitutional or invalid for the reasons claimed by plaintiff.

The decree of the lower court is affirmed. A public question being involved, no costs are allowed.

Dethmers, Carr, Kelly, Black and Adams, JJ., concurred with Kavanagh, J.

Souris, Justice (for reversal). I read the township ordinance to prohibit from 4:00 p.m. until one hour before sunset and from one hour after sunrise to 10:00 a.m. that which the state statute *permits* to be done during a period which includes those hours. The ordinance conflicts with the statute and, therefore, necessarily is invalid. . . .

I would reverse, but would not award costs.

Smith, J., concurred with Souris, J.

Notes and Questions

1. *Permit/prohibit.* Why do the state statute and the township ordinance overlap? Is it possible to argue that the state statute permitted what the ordinance prohibited because it implicitly authorized water skiing outside the hours the statute prohibited? Why do you suppose the township enacted the ordinance? Does it matter that the Fabius Township Board is on the Indiana-Michigan border or that South Bend, Indiana, is the closest large city and is an hour and 20 minute drive away?

The Michigan Supreme Court has stated that "examination of relevant Michigan cases indicates that where the nature of the regulated subject matter calls for regulation adapted to local conditions, and the local regulation does not interfere with the state regulatory scheme, supplementary local regulation has generally been upheld," citing several cases, including *Fabius. People v. Llewellyn*, 257 N.W.2d 902 (Mich. 1977). Does this statement explain the *Fabius* holding? How does the analysis in *Fabius* compare with the treatment of the permit versus prohibit problem in the *Cape Girardeau* case, *supra*? See also *DJL Restaurant Corp. v. City of New York*, 749 N.E.2d 186 (N.Y. 2001) (local zoning resolution aimed at alleviating effects of all adult establishments not preempted by state's Alcoholic Beverage Control law; state statutes having a tangential effect do not necessarily preempt local enactments).

In *Michigan Restaurant Ass'n v. City of Marquette*, 626 N.W.2d 418 (Mich. App. 2001), the court held an ordinance prohibiting smoking in restaurants was preempted by a state statute requiring a specified number of seats for smokers in restaurants. The court discussed *Fabius*, held that smoking was a statewide rather than a local concern, and concluded the ordinance did more than "merely extend" the state statute, as was done in *Fabius*. It created a general ban on smoking rather than, for example, reducing the number of smoking seats.

Compare *McNeil v. Charlevoix County*, 741 N.W.2d 27 (Mich. App. 2007). In *McNeil*, a multi-county health department issued regulations, approved by the related counties, prohibiting smoking in "public places" and protecting employees who asserted the right to a smoke-free environment. Business owners and citizens claimed that the regulations were preempted by statutory provisions that allowed owners and operators of public places the discretion to choose whether to maintain a smoking section (with physical barriers) or go smoke-free. The court concluded that the local regulations did not conflict directly with the legislation because the statute expressly offered an option for smoking except in public places where "smoking is prohibited by law" (as was the case under the local regulations). The court also found that the state statute did not "occupy the field," since there was no indication of an express intent to preempt local regulation, no indication of an intent to preempt by implication in the statute's legislative history, the state scheme was not so pervasive as to suggest an intent to preempt, and there was no evidence of a need for state-wide uniformity. The court distinguished the statement in the *Michigan Restaurant Ass'n* case that "[s]moking is a statewide issue that is not local in character" as "mere dictum." The court concluded its preemption analysis by stating that "we agree with the majority in *Marquette* that smoking is inherently an issue of statewide concern that does not necessarily call for regulation adapted to local conditions [but that] ... there is nothing in the legislative declaration accompanying the enactment of the [state statute] to indicate legislative concern for statewide, uniform regulation of that subject matter." *Id.* at 37.

Legislation authorizing state or local regulation of recreational activities on local waters is common. Legislation enacted in Michigan subsequent to *Fabius* authorizes the state natural resources department to regulate activities on the "waters of this state," which may include a prohibition on water skiing. The statute also provides that "[t]he department shall prescribe special local regulations in such a manner as to make the regulations uniform with other special local regulations established on other waters of this state insofar as is reasonably possible." MICH. COMP. LAWS ANN. § 324.80108. How else would you resolve this state-local conflict?

2. *More examples.* When a state statute prohibits some but not all types of conduct without indicating whether the legislative prescription is complete, the inference to be drawn from the legislative failure to specify its intent is not clear. Consider the following cases, and ask whether they are consistent with *Fabius*, and whether there are any principles they provide for deciding preemption cases of this type:

(a) *Deterring trafficking in stolen goods.* Can a city deter trafficking in stolen goods by requiring secondhand merchants to submit electronic reports of transactions involving secondhand goods to the chief of police and to pay $2 per transaction, when the state statute regarding secondhand merchants allows either paper or electronic submission, requires reports less frequently and does not impose fees? See *USA Cash #1, Inc. v. City of Saginaw*, 776 N.W.2d 346 (Mich. App. 2009) (holding that there was no preemption since the ordinance imposed more specific requirements, did not conflict with state statute, and charge constituted a user fee rather than an illegal tax). Can a city, concerned with sale of stolen copper, prohibit metal recyclers from paying cash in connection with any purchase of used copper and direct that merchants hold checks for purchase of copper for 24 hours (where the state statute did not regulate purchases below $100 and did not address question of holding checks)? See *Alabama Recycling Assn., Inc. v. City of Montgomery*,

24 So. 3d 1085 (Ala. 2009) (holding that local ordinance did not conflict with state statute since it did not prohibit anything the statute expressly permitted or permit anything expressly prohibited).

(b) *Fireworks.* Can a chartered county require sellers of fireworks to secure insurance policies (in the amount of $1 million) as a condition of selling fireworks and retaining business permits? See *Phantom of Brevard, Inc. v. Brevard County*, 3 So. 3d 309 (Fla. 2008) (upholding requirement, after determining that state statute regulating sale of fireworks included statement that it should be applied uniformly and did not include an insurance requirement, but concluding that local ordinance did not directly conflict with state statute). What if a state statute regulates fireworks but says nothing about sales from temporary structures? A local ordinance requires sales in temporary structures. The court did not find preemption in *Z & Z Fireworks v. City of Roseville*, No. 333642, 2017 WL 2302587 (Mich. App. May 25, 2017).

(c) *Obesity and soft drinks.* Some cities, such as New York, San Francisco, and Baltimore have tried to intervene by regulating portions of soft drinks made available to their citizens or by requiring disclosures on advertisements for sugar-sweetened beverages (SSBs) on certain advertisements or in businesses that sell SSBs. See *New York Statewide Coalition of Hispanic Chambers of Commerce v. New York City Dept. of Health and Mental Hygiene*, 970 N.Y.S.2d 200 (N.Y. App. Div. 2013) (holding that New York City board of health exceeded its delegated authority as an administrative agency in promulgating soft drink portion cap). Can the states preempt local government regulations of soft drink portions? See Steel, *Obesity Regulation Under Home Rule: An Argument that Regulation by Local Governments Is Superior to Administrative Agencies*, 37 CARDOZO L. REV. 1127 (2016) (considering New York City's portion cap on soft drinks and suggesting alternative strategies for local governments to act under home rule); Sivin, *Striking the Soda Ban: The Judicial Paralysis on the Department of Health*, 28 J.L. & HEALTH 247 (2015) (arguing that the New York court erred in its interpretation of delegation doctrine).

(d) *Fracking.* Fracking (fracturing of subsurface minerals layers by hydraulic means to release oil and gas) has become an important arena in which state and local government authority has been contested. Local governments have been concerned by the impacts of fracking on local water quality, while states have sought to foster uniform approaches to "fracking" in order to foster economic development. See, e.g., *City of Longmont v. Colorado Oil & Gas Ass'n*, 369 P.3d 573 (Col. 2016) (striking down home rule city's incorporation of a ban on hydraulic fracking into its charter, on grounds that fracking concerned matters of both state and local concern and was preempted because in operation it conflicted with state's oil and gas conservation statute and regulations; rejecting claim that preemption must be shown "beyond a reasonable doubt"); *City of Fort Collins v. Colorado Oil & Gas Ass'n*, 369 P.3d 586 (Col. 2016) (finding that five-year moratorium on fracking established through a citizen initiative involved matter of mixed state and local concern, was not impliedly preempted by state law, but operationally conflicted with state law and was accordingly invalid).

As discussed in the *Longmont* case, Colorado's constitutional home rule provision states

> The people of each city or town of this state . . . are hereby vested with, and they shall always have, power to make, amend, add to or replace the charter of said city or town, which shall be its organic law and extend to all its local and municipal matters.
>
> Such charter and the ordinances made pursuant thereto in such matters shall supersede within the territorial limits and other jurisdiction of said city or town any law of the state in conflict therewith.
>
> [Colo. Const. art. XX, § 6.]

Would the results of a preemption challenge differ in states that rely on statutory powers, differently framed imperio home rule, legislative home rule, or the new NLC model? Might other state law or constitutional provisions have a bearing? See Fox, *Home Rule in an Era of Local Environmental Innovation*,44 Ecology L.Q. 575 (2017) (arguing that state constitutional provisions protecting natural resources and public trust doctrine should be considered in analyzing local authority); *Robinson Township v. Commonwealth*, 83 A.3d 901 (Pa. 2013) (finding that state provisions purporting to preempt local actions to plan for environmental concerns relating to fracking and to require that fracking be allowed in all zoning districts were inconsistent with state constitution's environmental rights amendment); D. Mandelker & M. Wolf, 1 Land Use Law § 4.32 (6th ed. 2019).

3. *Preemption, state and local concerns.* The issue of whether the regulation of water skiing is a state or local concern was a factor in the court's decision on preemption and the scope of local powers in the *Fabius* case. Other courts are more willing to find preemption when they hold a matter is one of state concern. See *Lilly v. City of Minneapolis*, 527 N.W.2d 107 (Minn. App. 1995), holding that a court must narrowly construe home rule powers when a matter is of state concern and an ordinance conferring health benefits on same-sex partners was preempted. Deciding whether a matter is of state or local concern arguably is implicit in any decision considering a preemption question, and the California Supreme Court has made this inquiry explicit. An ordinance is preempted when:

> (1) the subject matter has been so fully and completely covered by general law as to clearly indicate that it has become exclusively a matter of state concern; (2) the subject matter has been partially covered by general law couched in such terms as to indicate clearly that a paramount state concern will not tolerate further or additional local action; or (3) the subject matter has been partially covered by general law, and the subject is of such a nature that the adverse effect of a local ordinance on the transient citizens of the

state outweighs the possible benefit to the municipality. [*In re Hubbard*, 396 P.2d 809, 815 (Cal. 1964).]

This approach to the preemption problem seems influenced by the rule that home rule municipalities in the "defined" (or *imperio*) states have only powers over local affairs. It should not apply in the "total unless limited" (or legislative) home rule states. Can you see why? Note, however, that the municipality in *Fabius* was legislating under a "general welfare" clause.

4. *Express v. implied.* The assumption in most of the cases is that preemption may be implied. Recall that home rule grants almost always allow implied preemption. Then what is the meaning of the statement in *Fabius* that the legislature could have "expressly stated preemptive control" if it had so intended? Is this a holding that preemption must be express? Would you favor this view? A few cases take this position. See *Cincinnati Bell Tel. Co. v. City of Cincinnati*, 693 N.E.2d 212 (Ohio 1998) (holding under state constitutional home rule clause that legislative preemption of municipal powers to tax must be express).

What if taxation is not involved? Can a home rule city enact regulations limiting campaign contributions to candidates for municipal office, where the state legislature had enacted modest limitations on the manner in which interested parties could contribute to campaigns for state or local office but had not imposed limitations on amounts of contributions? See *Nutter v. Dougherty*, 938 A.2d 401 (Pa. 2007) (finding no conflict with state constitution provisions requiring uniformity in laws regulating the "holding of elections," and rejecting arguments that state elections code occupied the field since state elections code did not address the amount of contributions but did regulate other aspects of elections with specificity, where ambiguity should be resolved in favor of authority of Philadelphia as home rule city).

5. *Preemption in the time of pandemic: the role of executive orders.* The 2020 COVID-19 pandemic has stressed state and local government relations in numerous ways. Consider, for example, the Mississippi Governor's Executive Orders prohibiting local governments from interfering with his mandate that a wide array of businesses should remain open, notwithstanding local governments' concerns that allowing such operations would spread the virus and lead to more deaths. See Mississippi Executive Order 1463 (Supplement), available at https://www.sos.ms.gov/content/executiveorders/ExecutiveOrders/SupplementEO1463.pdf (last accessed June 25, 2020). In your view, are judgments regarding the definition and continued operation of "essential businesses" during the pandemic a state-wide issue or a local issue? Should it matter that many states give exceptionally expansive powers to local public health authorities to address associated public health emergencies?

6. *Preemption: good or bad?* As discussed at the outset of this section, and as the cases cited illustrate, local governments often chafe at preemption by the state. What is your judgment about the policy considerations that drive such assessments

of preemption? Under what circumstances is preemption by the state justified? Under what circumstances is it most problematic?

Other policy advocates would argue that state preemption is necessary in some cases, especially when local governments adopt exclusionary zoning ordinances, refuse to prohibit discrimination, or allow environmentally harmful development. Indeed, state preemption and regulation of land use and environmental problems has been a major and much-applauded trend, in recent years. The following case reviews and distinguishes preemption and conflict issues in the context of environmental regulation:

Board of Supervisors of Crooks Township v. ValAdCo

504 N.W.2d 267 (Minn. App. 1993) (review denied)

Holtan, Judge

A township appeals from summary judgment prohibiting enforcement of its ordinance regulating pollution from animal feedlots. We affirm the district court's decision that the ordinance is preempted by and in conflict with Minn. Stat. § 116.07, subd. 7 (1992).

Facts

ValAdCo, a cooperative of thirty-eight farm families, sought state and county approval to build two hog confinement facilities on land zoned for agricultural uses in Crooks Township. The Renville County Board of Commissioners approved permits for both sites.

The Minnesota Pollution Control Agency (MPCA) prepared and distributed an Environmental Assessment Worksheet. During the public comment period, the MPCA received correspondence from local residents and state agencies.

The MPCA responded to concerns expressed about ground water availability and contamination, and odors. The MPCA concluded that the ValAdCo project as modified during the review process did not have the potential for significant environmental effects and did not require an Environmental Impact Statement. The MPCA issued the feedlot permits and the Department of Natural Resources issued a water appropriation permit.

After application but prior to approval and issuance of the county and MPCA permits, Crooks Township enacted Ordinance No. 1991-1. The ordinance requires anyone desiring to operate an animal feedlot or livestock sewage lagoon to obtain a permit from the township. ValAdCo never applied for a township permit.

After ValAdCo obtained the county and MPCA permits and began construction, Crooks Township sought declaratory and injunctive relief to prohibit construction of the hog confinement facilities. The district court denied injunctive relief and granted summary judgment for ValAdCo, finding the ordinance invalid because it was preempted by and in conflict with Minn. Stat. § 116.07, subd. 7. Crooks Township appeals.

Issue

Is the Crooks Township ordinance preempted by or in conflict with Minn. Stat. § 116.07, subd. 7 (1992)?

Analysis

The Minnesota Supreme Court has defined preemption as the "occupying the field" concept. *Mangold Midwest Co. v. Village of Richfield*, 143 N.W.2d 813, 819 (Minn. 1966). A state law may fully occupy a particular field of legislation so that there is no room for local regulation. *Id.* If a local ordinance attempts to impose additional regulation in that field it is void, even if it does not duplicate or directly conflict with any express provision of the state law. *Id.*

Four questions are relevant to determining whether there is preemption:

(1) What is the subject matter being regulated?

(2) Has the subject matter been so fully covered by state law as to have become solely a matter of state concern?

(3) Has the legislature in partially regulating the subject matter indicated that it is a matter solely of state concern?

(4) Is the subject matter itself of such a nature that local regulation would have unreasonably adverse effects upon the general population?

Id. at 358, 143 N.W.2d at 820.

The subject matter of the ordinance is the control of pollution from manure produced in animal feedlots. That is the very subject regulated under state law by Minn. R. 7020.0100-.1900 (1991) promulgated to comply with state pollution control policies expressed in Minn. Stat. Chapters 115 and 116. We are convinced that the nature of this subject matter as well as the comprehensive statutory scheme demonstrates the legislature's intent to preempt local enactments on this subject.

Pollution by its very nature is difficult to confine to particular geographical areas. For that reason the state has set up a statutory structure for issuing animal feedlot permits that provides for local input but retains ultimate control in the state. This promotes uniform interpretation and application of state rules and allows the state to take into account the environmental and economic welfare of the state as a whole.

The breadth of the statutory scheme is demonstrated by the thorough review undertaken by the MPCA. The MPCA permit application required ValAdCo to provide information on the number and type of animals to be confined; the location of the feedlot; soil and hydrogeological conditions; a map or aerial photograph of all wells, buildings, lakes and watercourses within 1,000 feet of the proposed feedlot; a manure management plan, including handling and application techniques, acreage available for manure application, and plans for any manure storage structure;

and any additional site-specific or project-specific information requested by the MPCA. Minn. R. 7020.0500, subpt. 2 (1991). [This is a reference to the regulations that implement the statute. There are also references to these regulations later in the case.—Eds.]

Next the MPCA completed an Environmental Assessment Worksheet (EAW) and solicited public comment pursuant to Minn. R. 4410.1000-.1700 (1991). [This is required by the state law requiring environmental impact assessment.—Eds.] The MPCA received letters from 37 local residents, the Department of Natural Resources (DNR), the Minnesota Historical Society, and the Minnesota Department of Health concerning odors and ground water availability and contamination. The MPCA specifically responded to the comments and addressed the concerns in its findings and conclusions.

After pumping tests were conducted, the DNR concluded that ValAdCo's project would not jeopardize ground water supplies. The MPCA approved ValAdCo's manure management plan, which included provisions for waste and soil testing, a 100-foot setback between any residence and landspreading operation, sewage lagoon linings that meet MPCA guidelines, and MPCA-recommended setbacks from residences and surface waters when applying wastes.

The MPCA also approved ValAdCo's proposed measures to minimize odor problems. The agency noted that landspreading of animal wastes is very common in the area around the ValAdCo sites and that the odors from its project should not be any worse than those from existing operations.

The MPCA issued the permits based on information specific to the ValAdCo project as well as its experience in monitoring similar facilities in the state. It stated:

> The nature of the project has been fully examined and all significant environmental effects have been identified and evaluated. The potential environmental effects have also been evaluated in previous environmental review of similar projects, and have been found to be subject to effective regulatory controls.

The MPCA also noted that the ValAdCo operation would be subject to continued monitoring by state agencies.

In the midst of the MPCA review process, Crooks Township enacted its own ordinance with different pollution control requirements for animal feedlots. The ordinance requires anyone who wants to maintain a feedlot or livestock sewage lagoon to obtain a township permit in addition to the county and state permits. Facilities already in existence on the date of enactment are exempt from its provisions. The ordinance contains guidelines for waste application rates and establishes setback distances for sewage lagoons. It also requires anyone constructing a sewage lagoon to file a surety bond or cash with the township board of supervisors. The parties stipulated that the bond required of ValAdCo would total $1,350,000 for the two sites. Any violation of the ordinance is a misdemeanor, and each day any violation continues constitutes a separate offense.

The ordinance's bond requirement presents an issue somewhat different from the setback requirements. In contrast to the MPCA's thorough evaluation of the sewage lagoon and manure application issues, there is no indication that the MPCA considered requiring a bond or making other arrangements to cover costs of cleaning up any spills or of closing the facilities if ValAdCo turns out to be financially irresponsible. A bond is not, strictly speaking, a measure to control pollution from animal feedlots. Rather, it is a way to hold owners financially responsible, in advance, for pollution that may occur in the future.

Nonetheless, we view the absence of a bond requirement in the statutory scheme for issuing animal feedlot permits as an indication of the legislature's judgment that the MPCA application review process provides adequate protection to the public and the environment. The statutory provisions reflect the balance struck by the legislature between the need to control pollution from manure, and the desire to foster a healthy agricultural economy. See Minn. R. 7020.0100 ("An adequate supply of healthy livestock, poultry, and other animals is essential to the well-being of Minnesota citizens and the nation.... [A] joint county-state program is desirable because it will insure local involvement, minimal disruption to agricultural operations and protect the environment from further degradation.").

We are not persuaded by Crooks Township's argument that its ordinance must be upheld because it regulates the health and safety of the people and environment of the township. The township cites Minn. Stat. § 365.10, subd. 17 (1992) as authority for its ordinance. That statute allows town voters to grant the town board the authority to provide for specific activities within certain categories, such as the protection of public and private property, the promotion of health, safety, order, and convenience, and the general welfare. *Id.*, subd. 17(d), (f), (g).

The fact that health and safety concerns provided the motivation for enacting the ordinance does not make the ordinance valid. Although municipalities have the power to regulate in the interest of public health, safety, and welfare, a township cannot invoke "police power" to accomplish what is otherwise preempted by state statute.

If every township were allowed to set its own pollution control conditions, the result could be a patchwork of different rules. Compliance with varying local rules would be burdensome and would have a detrimental effect on the efficient operation of the state's agricultural industry.

We also reject the township's argument that state pollution control laws themselves specifically authorize the type of ordinance enacted here. The township points to language in Minn. R. 7020.0100 that "in repealing the old rules controlling pollution from animal feedlots . . . , the agency will look to local units of government to provide adequate land use planning for residential and agricultural areas. It has been the agency's experience that residential and agricultural uses of land are often incompatible and that the best forum for resolving the conflicting use of land is at the local level. However, in promulgating these rules the agency does not seek to abdicate its mandate. . . ."

Contrary to the township's position, this language focuses only on the local government's designation of land as residential or agricultural. It says that local government is the best forum for resolving conflicts over the best type of use for land. It does not express the intention that, once land has been properly zoned for agricultural use, local government may impose specific requirements on the construction and operation of animal feedlots.

Furthermore, Minn. R. 7020.0100 specifically discusses a cooperative program between the MPCA and counties. It refers to "local" input in the context of county actions. The rule notes that "a joint county-state program is desirable because it will insure local involvement." The counties' role in processing animal feedlot applications is set forth in detail in Minn. Stat. § 116.07, subd. 7 and Minn. R. 7020.1500-.1900 (1991). In all cases the MPCA retains ultimate reviewing authority over county decisions. . . .

Finally, we find the ordinance not only preempted by state law but also in conflict with it. The Minnesota Supreme Court distinguishes the preemption doctrine of "occupying the field" from the doctrine of "conflict," under which a local ordinance is invalid only if the express and implied terms of the ordinance and the state statute are irreconcilable. 143 N.W.2d at 816, 819.

The ordinance conflicts with state law because its setback requirements would prohibit construction of the ValAdCo facilities, which the MPCA and county have already approved. The ordinance's fixed setback requirements run contrary to the MPCA's focus on site- and project-specific determinations of what are appropriate pollution control measures. The ordinance is not merely complementary to and in furtherance of state regulations. ValAdCo could be in compliance with MPCA requirements yet be prosecuted under the local ordinance.

We recognize that local communities have important concerns about pollution and the extent to which they can impose their own regulations. The legislature could help eliminate uncertainty and forestall litigation by explicitly stating when particular legislation preempts local regulations. [The court noted a statute that expressly preempts local ordinances]. The fact that the legislature explicitly preempts local enactments in one statute but not in another can raise doubts about whether preemption is intended in the latter case. Nonetheless, we are persuaded here that the nature of the matter regulated, together with the comprehensive statutory scheme, evidence the legislature's intent to preempt local regulation of pollution from animal feedlots. . . .

Notes and Questions

1. *Regulation of environmental facilities.* The state statute in *ValAdCo* neither authorized nor prohibited local regulation. Isn't this like the problem raised by the motorboating and waterskiing ordinance in *Fabius*? Does the court adequately explain why it believed the legislature struck the right "balance"? Accord *Adams v. State Livestock Facilities Siting Review Bd.*, 820 N.W.2d 404 (Wis. 2012).

Courts are divided on whether state laws licensing environmental facilities preempt local ordinances, and the court's view of legislative purpose is often a deciding factor. For example, in *IT Corp. v. Solano County Bd. of Supervisors*, 820 P.2d 1023 (Cal. 1991), the court held the state hazardous waste disposal law did not preempt county efforts to enforce a requirement prohibiting the disposal of wastes within setback "buffer" zones long established by county land use permits. The court decided the state statute was only a "minimum standards" program, and implied "no general purpose to strip local entities" of their land use regulation powers. Why didn't *ValAdCo* adopt the same view? Accord *Sandlands C&D, LLC v. County of Horry*, 716 S.E.2d 280 (S.C. 2011). For discussion of preemption under state environmental regulation, see D. Mandelker & M. Wolf, Land Use Law §§4.28, 4.32 (6th ed. 2019).

For other examples of cases relating to preemption of environmental requirements, compare *Syngenta Seeds, Inc. v. County of Kauai*, 842 F.3d 669 (9th Cir. 2016) (in challenge by companies that supplied seeds for genetically engineered plants, concluding that state scheme regulating use of pesticides preempted county ordinance restricting application of restricted use pesticides by commercial agricultural entities), with *Montgomery County, Md. v Complete Lawn Care, Inc.*, 207 A.3d 695 (Md. App. 2019) (finding no preemption of county ordinance restricting use of pesticides for cosmetic purposes, particularly when pesticide interests had unsuccessfully lobbied to include local preemption provision in state legislation).

2. *Other licensing programs.* The extent to which a state license can preempt local regulation arises in other programs. For example, courts usually hold that state public utility regulation preempts local ordinances requiring the under-grounding of utility lines, for reasons one court explained:

> Were each municipality through which a power line has to pass free to impose its own ideas of how the current should be transmitted through it, nothing but chaos would result, and neither the utility nor the state agency vested with control could be assured of ability to fulfill its obligations of furnishing safe, adequate and proper service to the public in all areas. [*In re Public Service Electric & Gas Co.*, 173 A.2d 233, 239 (N.J. 1961).]

Accord *Howard County v. Potomac Electric Power Co.*, 573 A.2d 821 (Md. 1990). See also *Detroit Edison Co. v. Township of Richmond*, 388 N.W.2d 296 (Mich. App. 1986) (township may not regulate safety aspects of transmission lines). On zoning, see *Citizens Utils. Co., Kauai Elec. Div. v. County of Kauai*, 814 P.2d 398 (Hawai'i 1991) (county may not regulate height of utility poles); Mass. Gen. Laws ch. 40A, §3 (authorizes state utility agency to preempt zoning, as explained in *Planning Bd. of Braintree v. Dep't of Public Utilities*, 647 N.E.2d 1186 (Mass. 1995)). Can you think of any reasons for allowing local governments to regulate overhead transmission lines?

State licensing of occupations and professions is less comprehensive than utility regulation because it is usually limited to certification, maintenance of standards, and protection of the profession or occupation from competition. See Chapter 9.

Courts are often willing to allow local ordinances containing health regulations that supplement the state law. See *State v. Westrum*, 380 N.W.2d 187 (Minn. App. 1986) (food vendors at fairs); *Department of Licenses & Inspections v. Weber*, 147 A.2d 326 (Pa. 1959) (beauty parlors). A court will preempt a local ordinance that adopts a conflicting basis for licensing or prohibits what the state license permits. See *Blanton v. Amelia County*, 540 S.E.2d 869 (Va. 2001) (preempting ordinance that prohibited application of bio-solids authorized by state). From these cases and the principal case can you develop some idea of what kinds of licensing programs will preempt local regulation?

3. *Traffic control.* When a state statute prohibits some but not all types of conduct without indicating whether the legislative prescription is complete, the inference to be drawn from the legislative failure to specify its intent is not clear. Consider the following cases, and ask whether they are consistent with *Fabius*, and whether they offer helpful principles for deciding preemption cases of this type.

Sometimes local governments attempt to use additional technologies or impose additional fees as further deterrents to driving practices already prohibited as a matter of state law. Compare *Mendenhall v. City of Akron*, 881 N.E.2d 255 (Ohio 2008) (holding that a local home rule government could adopt a camera system for identifying and fining speeders in school zones, where system of civil fines supplemented state law), and *City of Davenport v. Seymour*, 755 N.W. 2d 533 (Iowa 2008) (upholding city's use of red light cameras in face of preemption challenge), with *State v. Kuhlman*, 729 N.W.2d 577 (Minn. 2007) (city ordinances involving use of photo-enforcement of traffic control signals held to conflict with and thus be tacitly preempted by state traffic regulations). See also *Sauby v. City of Fargo*, 747 N.W.2d 65 (N.D. 2008) (holding that the local government could not impose higher fees than provided for violations of the state statute mandating drivers to control their vehicles).

Could a local government adopt its own ordinance prohibiting "driving while dialing or texting" after a series of significant injuries? Would it matter if it were a college town known for its somewhat distracted younger drivers, and applied such requirements only to drivers under 25? Would it matter if the state legislature had recently adopted legislation prohibiting texting while driving but not driving while talking on a cell phone? *See* Noder, *Talking and Texting While Driving: A Look at Regulating Cell Phone Use Behind the Wheel?* 44 VAL. U. L. REV. 237, 257–262 (2009) (summarizing state and local initiatives, and related preemption issues).

4. *When is a law "comprehensive"?* Whether a state statute enacts a comprehensive code preempting local regulation is always a matter of statutory interpretation that produces conflicting results:

Pesticide Pub. Policy Found. v. Village of Wauconda, 510 N.E.2d 858 (Ill. 1987). A local ordinance regulating the use of pesticides was held preempted by the state pesticide statute, which the court characterized as a "broad and detailed scheme designed to regulate the field of pesticide use in all respects." *Id.* at 862. "Diverse pesticide regulations by numerous local governments in Illinois would entirely frustrate the potential for uniformity between Illinois and other States or the Federal government." *Id.* at 863. Accord, *Town of Wendell v. Attorney General*, 476 N.E.2d 585 (Mass. 1985).

Arthur Whitcomb, Inc. v. Town of Carroll, 686 A.2d 743 (N.H. 1996). A local zoning ordinance regulating excavation was held preempted by a state statute that required a permit for excavation after an extensive application. The statute also contained detailed operational and reclamation standards. Such "exhaustive treatment" of the field indicated an intent to preempt. The court noted the statute was passed to decrease the cost of construction materials and the cost of roads and other governmental infrastructure by curtailing simultaneous state and local regulation.

Hertz Corp. v. City of New York, 607 N.E.2d 784 (N.Y. 1992). The court held a city ordinance prohibiting rate discrimination against residents of the city by rental car companies was not preempted by a state law regulating these companies. The court reached this conclusion even though the state statute prohibited other kinds of discriminatory practices, such as discrimination based on age and race, and fuel and airport surcharges. The statutory scheme was not so "broad in scope or so detailed" that it precluded all local regulation.

5. *Statutory purpose.* As the cases indicate, statutory purpose can be an important factor in deciding preemption cases. A court may not find preemption if the statute and a local ordinance serve different purposes:

(a) *Zoning and off-road vehicles. Town of Lyndeborough v. Boisvert Properties*, 846 A.2d 1187 (N.H. 2004). The New Hampshire Supreme Court found no preemption of a local zoning requirement of site plan review before owners of property could open their land to off-highway recreational vehicles, even though they had already listed their land as an open trail with the state Department of Resources and Economic Development, pursuant to state law. See also *Thayer v. Town of Tilton*, 861 A.2d 800 (N.H. 2004) (town ordinance regulating use of sludge not preempted by federal or state law).

(b) *Nudity and beaches. Eckl v. Davis*, 124 Cal. Rptr. 685 (Cal. App. 1975). A local ordinance prohibiting nudity on public beaches was held not preempted by a state statute covering the same subject matter which had been limited to sexually-motivated nudity. The purpose of the ordinance was "to insure the peaceful and undistracted enjoyment of the parks and public beaches of the city."

(c) *Protecting animals and regulating veterinarians.* Can a city prohibit the practice of nontherapeutic declawing of animals within its jurisdiction, where state statute prohibited cities from "prohibit[ing] a person authorized . . . to engage in a particular business, from engaging in that business . . . or profession or any portion thereof," and where state veterinary licensure statute and regulations did not prohibit declawing? See *California Veterinary Medical Ass'n v. City of West Hollywood*, 61 Cal. Rptr. 3d 318 (Cal. App. 2007) (finding no express preemption, and no implied preemption by virtue of licensure of veterinarians where focus of ordinance was on preventing animal cruelty). Can a city adopt an "ethical and humane animal regulations and treatment" (HEART) ordinance, that stated a premise that citizens "should treat animals as more than just lifeless, inanimate chattel property," required owners of companion animals to obtain permits, and limited the number of intact (unneutered) companion animals to four, where state livestock act stated that animals were "chattels" and state veterinary act did not impose such requirements? See *RIO Grande Kennel Club v. City of Albuquerque*, 190 P.3d 1131 (N.M. App. 2008) (in suit by dog owners, veterinarians, and kennel owners, finding no state or federal preemption on the record, but noting that additional factual development was required before reaching takings and other constitutional questions).

(d) *Food sovereignty.* To allay harms to public health and the environment by industrial agricultural practices and the American centralized food system culture, some local governments have passed ordinances to improve local residents' ability to produce and consume locally grown food. Whether such "cottage food laws," laws that allow open air slaughter and processing of poultry or laws that allow production and sale of raw milk, are about democratic self-determination or the desire to avoid food safety regulation fuels the tension between states and their local governments. Countering the trend of state government preemption of local government regulations, the state of Maine, in 2011, passed a resolution recognizing the food sovereignty of its local governments and provided that the state would "oppose any federal statute, law or regulation that attempts to threaten our basic human right to save seed and grow, process, consume and exchange food and farm products within the state of Maine." H.R.J. Res. 1176, 125th Leg., 1st Reg. Sess.

Local ordinances and at least one litigated case followed. See *State v. Brown*, 95 A.3d 82 (Me. 2014) (in suit by state against milk producer who sold "raw milk" and failed to comply with state labeling and licensing requirements, holding that state law "occupied the field" notwithstanding home rule authority of municipality that authorized direct sale for home consumption). Despite traditional notions of federal preemption (under voluminous federal laws to protect the nation's food supply and public health), in 2017 the Maine legislature took another step and adopted "An Act to Recognize Local Control Regarding Food Systems," which acknowledged municipalities' interest in food sovereignty ordinances and that the state would recognize these local laws. For an excellent article on this topic, see Schindler, *Food Federalism: States, Local Governments, and the Fight of Food Sovereignty*, 79 Ohio State L.J. 761 (2018).

6. *Uniformity.* The need for statewide uniformity is often an important factor in preemption cases. Some statutes contain a clear indication that statewide uniformity is an important purpose in the adoption of the state law. The Uniform Motor Vehicle Code adopted by many states is an example. It states that its provisions are uniform throughout the state and that a municipality may not adopt an ordinance that is inconsistent with it or with regulations adopted under it. For a case relying on this statutory purpose to hold a local ordinance modifying the statutory definition

of drunk driving preempted, see *Simpson v. Municipality of Anchorage*, 635 P.2d 1197 (Alaska 1981). See also *Klingbeil Management Group Co. v. Vito*, 357 S.E.2d 200 (Va. 1987), where the court held an ordinance requiring a dead bolt on apartment doors was preempted by a state law with similar requirement because state law was intended as uniform landlord-tenant act. The state law contained a provision stating it was intended to "establish a uniform body of law relating to landlord and tenant relations throughout the Commonwealth."

7. *State preemption legislation.* State legislation can go further and define when preemption occurs. For example, Mont. Code Ann. § 7-3-708(1) provides that home rule "charter provisions may not conflict with . . . statutory limitations on the powers of self-government units." Section 7-1-114(1)(f) is one of these limitations, and provides that self-government powers are subject to any law requiring a "local government to carry out any function or provide any service." *Billings Firefighters Local 521 v. City of Billings*, 973 P.2d 222 (Mont. 1999), applied this provision to hold the city had to follow mandatory suspension procedures contained in a state statute that required a hearing before the city council. Would this statute have made a difference in any of the cases discussed in these Notes?

Other states have similar legislation. Indiana requires an express delegation by prohibiting "[t]he power to regulate conduct that is regulated by a state agency, except as expressly granted by statute." Ind. Code Ann. § 36-1-3-8(a)(7). Statutes can also specify whether local regulation is allowed. *Rabon v. City of Seattle*, 957 P.2d 621 (Wash. 1998) (statute expressly provided that local governments had sole jurisdiction over dangerous dogs).

8. *Mandates vs. preemption.* Some state statutes raise preemption problems by regulating private activities also regulated by local governments, while some impose obligations on municipalities, such as hearing requirements for employee disciplinary proceedings. This second type of statute is sometimes called a state mandate. The municipal interest in seeking exemption from a state mandate is obviously quite different from the municipal interest in regulating conduct also regulated at the state level. Do you see any indication in the cases that the courts recognize this difference? State (as well as federal) mandates are controversial because they can impose costs on municipalities without their consent.

States may also direct local governments to regulate private activities. Environmental land use legislation is one example. Several states, for example, have legislation for wetlands, floodplains and shoreland management that requires local governments to adopt land use regulations for these areas that comply with state statutory standards. State coastal programs, usually adopted to satisfy the requirements of a federal law, are another example. State coastal legislation may contain policies that are binding on local land use regulation in coastal areas. *Gherini v. California Coastal Comm'n*, 251 Cal. Rptr. 426 (Cal. App. 1988), upheld a state coastal commission disapproval of a local coastal plan required by the California law and indicates the extent of state review under the state coastal act. For discussion of these programs, see L. Malone, Environmental Regulation of Land Use (2014).

See Comment, *Federal and State Preemption of Environmental Law: A Critical Analysis*, 24 Harv. Envtl. L. Rev. 237 (2000) (author notes that preemption issues should be decided by considering role differentiation, the need for uniformity and the need for efficiency).

9. *Predatory lending.* Local governments in areas hard hit by predatory lending have at times attempted to add protections for local citizens that go beyond the requirements imposed by state and federal law. For recent discussions of predatory lending, foreclosure problems, and related issues, see Walsh, *The Finger in the Dike: State and Local Laws Combat the Foreclosure Tide*, 44 Suffolk L.Rev. 139 (2011) (discussing the foreclosure crisis of recent years, considering state and federal constitutional provisions that affect the prerogatives of state and local governments in dealing with related issues, and concluding that the states have not yet approached the limits of their powers to deal with related problems); Fennell & Roin, *Controlling Residential Stakes*, 77 U. Chi. L. Rev. 143 (2010) (proposing creation of housing equity markets for local residents, with the help of local governments, in local and nearby jurisdictions); Altier, *Municipal Predatory Lending Regulation in Ohio: The Disproportionate Impact of Preemption on Ohio's Cities*, 59 Clev. St. L. Rev. 125 (2011) (discussing Ohio predatory lending legislation and its implications). The introductory problem to Chapter 1 explores these issues.

10. *Preemption of local criminal offenses.* Local governments have used their delegated authority to protect the health and welfare of citizens by adopting ordinances prohibiting harmful conduct and prescribing sanctions. Of course these local efforts must meet the constitutional standards imposed on all legislative enactments and not suffer from such common deficiencies as overbreadth or vagueness. See *City of Chicago v. Morales*, 527 U.S. 41 (1999) (a Chicago ordinance was held to have violated the Due Process Clause of the Fourteenth Amendment and was unconstitutionally vague because there was no adequate notice of the proscribed conduct that prohibited "criminal street gang members" from loitering in public and it did not establish minimal guidelines for law enforcement). Courts often view local criminal provisions as merely expanding upon state statutes. See *Gibson v. City of Alexander*, 779 So. 2d 1153 (Ala. 2000) (local ordinance prohibiting state licensed establishment from permitting the consumption of alcohol between 12:00 midnight and 7 a.m. and imposing a fine for a violation merely enlarges upon and is not inconsistent with state law); *State v. S.L.S.*, 777 So. 2d 318 (Ala. Crim. App. 2000) (city ordinance providing that giving a "false name or address" to a law enforcement officer is a misdemeanor is not inconsistent with but merely expands upon state law).

Problems arise, however, when local ordinances ease problems of proof and conviction by modifying the elements of a crime defined by a state statute. Upholding the local ordinance would then "work a substantive change in the criminal law and in the powers of law enforcement agencies." Blease, *Civil Liberties and the California Law of Preemption*, 17 Hastings L.J. 517, 563 (1966). See also *State of New Jersey v.*

Paserchia, 813 A.2d 556 (N.J. App. Div. 2003) (finding preemption when ordinance deals with same criminal conduct in a different manner).

Constitutional issues underlie the criminal prohibition problem. Dealing with obscenity provides a good example. See, e.g., *People v. Llewellyn*, 257 N.W.2d 902 (Mich. 1977) (holding state obscenity statute preempted municipality from providing its own definition of obscenity).

What is the assumption underlying a holding that the state legislature is better able to resolve delicate constitutional issues in the definition of a crime? How would you handle this problem? See also *Michigan Gun Owners, Inc. v. Ann Arbor Public Schools,* 918 N.W.2d 756 (Mich. 2018) (finding that school districts were not prohibited by "field preemption" from regulating firearms, since they were not included in precise list of governmental entities prohibited from engaging in such activity).

As a related matter, questions of double jeopardy may arise. See *Waller v. Florida*, 397 U.S. 387 (1970) (defendant who stripped canvas mural from city hall convicted under local ordinance prohibiting destruction of city property; state supreme court concluded that federal Double Jeopardy Clause prohibited successive prosecutions for the same conduct; but on remand the court concluded that municipal offenses were not assumed to be included under state crime). Subsequently the state constitution was amended, superseding the case. Compare *Gamble v. United States*, 139 S. Ct. 1960 (2019) (holding double jeopardy does not prevent prosecutions by dual sovereigns, in this case, the state of Alabama and the U.S.).

Some local governments have banned marijuana use in response to state efforts to decriminalize such use. Others have decriminalized marijuana use despite the fact that such use is a crime under state and federal criminal law. Such local government efforts have been ameliorated or stanched entirely by both targeted and blanket preemption. See Rohrer, *Governor Rick Scott Signs Medical Marijuana Bill into Law,* ORLANDO SENTINEL (June 23, 2017), at B3 (state law preempted county governments from enacting local marijuana regulations). Under these circumstances, what are the legal arguments or strategies to allow such local ordinances? See *Kirby v. County of Fresno*, 195 Cal. Rptr. 3d 815 (Cal. App. 2015) (upholding county ordinance treating medical marijuana storage or cultivation as public nuisance against claim that state law preempted county regulation). See also Chumbler, *Land Use regulation of Marijuana Cultivation: What Authority is Left to Local Government*, 49 URB. LAW. 505 (2017) (discussing practices by states in allowing or preempting local government regulation relating to marijuana growth and sales).

A Note on New National League of Cities Home Rule 2020 Preemption Provisions

The National League of Cities Home Rule 2020 proposal quoted above addresses issues of preemption head-on and comprehensively. See *supra*. Consider the implications of its various provisions by addressing the following questions.

1. *Requiring express preemption.* Why should state legislation be required to address preemption of local action explicitly?

2. *Additional requirements relating to express preemption.* The 2020 proposal would only allow denial of a power or function to a home rule government "if necessary to serve a substantial state interest, only if narrowly tailored to that interest, and only by general law." What is the rationale for such requirements? Are they justified?

3. *General law requirement.* Under the 2020 proposal, a "general law" would involve a statute that is "part of a statewide and comprehensive legislative enacement," "apply to all parts of the state alike and operate uniformly," "set forth police, sanitary, or similar regulations, rather than purport only to grant or limit legislative power of a home rule government to set forth police, sanitary, or similar regulations"; and "prescribe a rule of conduct upon citizens generally." What is the basis for such requirements? Are they justified?

4. *Concurrent authority.* The 2020 model also provides that a home rule government "may exercise and perform concurrently with the state any governmental, corporate, or proprietary power or function to the extent that the Legislature has not preempted local law pursuant to the preceding paragraphs." It further specifies that "in exercising concurrent authority, a home rule government may not set standards and requirements that are lower or less stringent than those imposed by state law, but may set standards and requirements that are higher or more stringent than those imposed by state law, unless a state law provides otherwise." What is the basis for such requirements? Are they justified?

Problem 2-3

You have been asked by a state senator to draft legislation that would contain a comprehensive test for the preemption of local ordinances in your state. Some of the municipalities are home rule municipalities and some are not. Your state is a legislative home rule state.

What issues would you take into account in drafting the statute? Should it apply to local criminal offenses? Should it exclude statutes that enact comprehensive state programs, such as licensing programs? Would it be better to draft a statute indicating when municipalities can legislate rather than when they are preempted? Would your proposed statute be different if you were in a state with *imperio* home rule? In a state that has no constitutional home rule?

How does the preemptive test you have drafted compare to Dillon's Rule?

Would your proposed statute be strengthened if it imposed civil fines on local governments for harms resulting from preempted local laws? What if it allowed a civil cause of action against local government leaders or the unit of local government who acted to pass laws in defiance of the preemption test? What if it prohibited the local government and its elected officials from using public funds to defend the local ordinance from litigation seeking to strike it down as violative of your preemption statute?

Finally, how might you take into account the fact that demographers recognize the metropolitan share of state economic activity far outpaces the nonurban contribution in the majority of states? Note that, before the COVID-19 pandemic, it was projected that by 2050, 90% of the U.S. population would live in cities. Should demographics and economic contribution of local governments influence legal and policy decisions about any legislative preemption test?

Chapter 3

Alternate Models for Local Government

A. Introduction

The clear lines of authority flowing from states to cities and counties suggested by the home rule (cities) and administrative agency (counties) models of local government belie the realities of twenty-first century America. Familiar patterns of urban out-migration in the decades following World War II have resulted in metropolitan areas with staggering numbers of separate governmental units and great disparities in quality of public services. This chapter studies alternate models of governance to handle problems that cannot be solved within the boundaries of general-purpose local governments. Because no local government covers an entire metropolitan area in the United States, a number of different regional governance structures and cooperative arrangements have been created to address issues requiring regional solutions.

A few parts of the United States have been structured to provide governance over a larger metropolitan, regional area. These structures include

(1) one-or two-tier metropolitan governments;

(2) city-county consolidations; and

(3) multi-purpose regional districts.

Other alternate bodies created to perform a regional function consist of:

(1) single-purpose metropolitan authorities and districts (reviewed in Chapter 2);

(2) metropolitan planning organizations, known as MPOs; and

(3) other regional councils and councils of government.

In the absence of an available body to perform a function that needs to transcend local political boundaries, governmental bodies may seek non-structural integration measures that are less complete. They include interlocal agreements for the provision of governmental services, service compacts, public-private nonprofit partnerships, and privatization. K. Foster, Regionalism on Purpose 7 (2001) (outlining the above structural and non-structural classifications).

As you read the materials in this chapter, evaluate whether these tools are well adapted to solving metropolitan-wide problems. What tools work the best for one or several of the problems metropolitan areas face today? Can these tools overcome the metropolitan political fragmentation next described?

[1] Political Fragmentation, the Decline of Central Cities, Continuing Suburban Growth and Sprawl

Metropolitan areas in the United States coexist with the numerous local governments and municipalities comprising them. In the absence of a single governmental body with jurisdiction over the area as a whole, considerable political fragmentation occurs as each municipality exercises governmental authority over only a fraction of the urban area. I. Barlow, METROPOLITAN GOVERNMENT 18–19 (1991). In addition to this territorial fragmentation, functional division also occurs when the performance of a specific governmental function crosses local boundary lines in order to be undertaken on a regional basis. Numerous special-purpose authorities have been created such as transit authorities, water and sewer commissions, and planning agencies, to operate on a regional basis in different parts of a metropolitan area. *Id.* Generally they focus on the delivery of a singular service without necessarily coordinating their activities with other authorities or municipalities. In sum, most metropolitan areas contain both territorial and functional fragmentation. *Id.*

In 1950, most urban dwellers lived in central cities. D. Rusk, CITIES WITHOUT SUBURBS 5 (1993). By 1990, however, more than 60% of those residing in metropolitan areas lived in suburbs in which the majority of jobs were also located. *Id.* As metropolitan regions have expanded over larger territorial areas in response to demographic, economic, political, social, and technological changes since World War II, the number of central city residents has declined. From 2010 to 2014, city growth increased more rapidly than suburban growth, but with an improving economy, that trend was reversed in 2015. Frey, *City Growth Dips Below Suburban Growth, Census* (Brookings Institution, 2017). We have become a country of suburban communities that has led to greater local governmental fragmentation.

Suburbanization changed the landscape of many areas undergoing development. Sprawl became a dominant pattern. Described as development that spreads out geographically in an unplanned and uncoordinated way, sprawl results in low density, scattered development lacking a functional mix of uses. A. Nelson & J. Duncan, GROWTH MANAGEMENT PRINCIPLES AND PRACTICES 1 (1995). Low-density sprawl is viewed as unsustainable development because it (1) necessitates costly infrastructure expenditures to provide services over a larger geographical area; (2) depends upon a car-dominated transportation system that degrades air quality and increases fossil fuel consumption; (3) prematurely consumes greenfields, which otherwise could be kept as open space for wildlife habitat, recreational use, and watershed preservation; and (4) adversely affects the environment by increasing carbon dioxide emissions, energy production, and natural resources depletion.

In response to this geographical spreading out beyond any proportion to population growth, the number of municipal governments and special authorities increased. Pursuant to the public choice doctrine championed by Charles Tiebout in his seminal work, *A Pure Theory of Local Expenditures*, 64 J. Pol. Econ., No. 5 (1956): 416–424, this movement to the suburbs provided an opportunity for multiple jurisdictions to tailor varied services to suit a range of preferences. Suburban development led to incorporation by smaller communities who desired to set their own fiscal, economic, and social priorities. Cashin, *Localism, Self-Interest, and the Tyranny of the Favored Quarter: Addressing the Barriers to New Regionalism*, 88 Geo L. J. 1985, 1991–93 (2000).

Migrants to the suburbs in the post-World War II era tended to be more affluent than the citizenry left behind in the inner cities, many of whom were poor and members of minority groups. Suburbanization thus led to economic and racial segregation in the central cities, which faced rising social costs and a declining tax base. Cashin, *supra*, at 1995. Local land use control contributed to this segregation by race and class. Because local governments traditionally have been empowered to control land uses within their jurisdictions, they have the ability, in the absence of other legal restraints, to establish exclusionary zoning practices that result in racial exclusion and decrease the supply of affordable housing units. *Id.* at 1992–95. [The author argues that state laws encouraging municipal incorporation, delegating land use regulatory power to local governments, and relying on local property taxes for public services (Ch. 4) fostered a "systematic practice of exclusion."—Eds.] Anti-development sentiments have risen in urban areas as well. The movement of wealthier households back to cities has created pressure for the imposition of more stringent zoning, parking, historic preservation, and environmental regulations. See Been, *Environmental Distinguished Lecture: City NIMBYS*, 33 J. Land Use & Envtl. L. 217, 222–23 (2018).

In addition to systematic practices of exclusion, one researcher has demonstrated that political boundaries facilitate a recruitment and selection process that also contributes to economic and racial stratification. G. Weiher, The Fractured Metropolis (1991). In short, political boundaries, by providing crucial, geographically identifiable information, make it easier for people to make locational decisions based on factors of race and income. And the recent empirical literature on locational choice suggests that race, as opposed to the mix of services and taxes a jurisdiction offers, is the strongest of the factors that influence locational decisions.

Even prior to the pandemic, two significant economic downturns in the first decade of the twenty-first century resulted in increased poverty in both large cities and suburbs, but between 2000 and 2015, the growth of suburban poverty in the United States outpaced that of large cities, rural areas, and small metro areas, growing by 57% during this period. Kneebone, *The Changing Geography of US Poverty* (Brookings Institution, 2017). Suburbs accounted for 48% of the country's increase in the poor population during this time period. *Id.* This growth in suburban poverty resulted in the suburbs becoming home to more poor residents than cities. *Id.* Metro areas with higher levels of employment decentralization tended to show a greater suburbanization of poverty. *Id.*

[2] Localism Versus Regionalism

In response to the above urban conditions, disparate groups have come together to revitalize interest in regional concerns and to present solutions for new forms of governance over sprawling suburbs and the central city. Sometimes called the "New Regionalists," they urge new regional approaches to stimulate economic growth, protect the environment, and address economic and racial inequities produced by the concentration of minority and impoverished people in the central cities. Advocates for the new regionalism include leaders of regional business civic organizations who point out that the metropolitan region, rather than the central city, has become the primary economic unit in the global and digital economy. The economy operates on a regional basis because its larger scale provides greater networking opportunities for a specialized workforce in proximity to each other. P. Calthorpe & W. Fulton, The Regional City 17–19 (2001). Business leaders also argue that an unnecessary duplication of facilities and effort results in economic inefficiency when scale of size economies in public service cannot be realized. I. Barlow, *supra*, at 19.

Another regional advocacy group believes that quality of life and environmental issues should be addressed on a regional basis. The last decade has brought renewed attention to the dangers of global warming and the need to reduce the world's carbon footprint. The link between urban sprawl and increased carbon dioxide emissions is clear. See Boudreaux, *The Impact XAT: A New Approach to Charging for Growth*, 43 U. Mem. L. Rev. 35, 79 (2012). Sprawl has its roots in the use of the automobile that enables disperse developments. Municipalities often give little consideration to the impact of their land use practices upon regional welfare and may even zone undesirable uses near their borders so as to directly affect adjacent localities. Further, zoning at the local level has proved ineffective in addressing problems caused by sprawl. *Id.* The inability of localities to protect the environment leads to a more urgent plea for the creation of alternative regional structures empowered to enforce state and regional land use goals that take into consideration the metropolitan-wide welfare.

A third regional advocacy group argues that resources must be shared on a metropolitan basis to address inner-city poverty problems and to help finance the crumbling infrastructure found in central cities. This group believes that each locality must provide its fair share of fiscal resources needed on a regional basis to achieve fiscal equity. See M. Pastor Jr. et al., This Could Be the Start of Something Big: How Social Movements for Regional Equity Are Reshaping Metropolitan America (2009), describing social movements for regional equity and the implementation of community-based regionalism. In summary, economic growth, the environment, and concerns for equity have all shaped the new regionalism.

Advocates for localism argue that a regional government is too large in scale to promote democracy and to give people the variety of choices they seek in public services. One advocacy group argues that localism results in the efficient allocation of public services, the so-called "public choice" approach urged by Charles Tiebout. A separate doctrinal camp defends limited-size governments as essential to increasing the ability of the citizenry to participate in public decision making, which results in greater self-determination and community building around shared concerns and values. G. Frug, City Making: Building Communities without Building Walls 20–21 (1999).

The financial crisis beginning in 2008 has spurred renewed interest in igniting economic growth and finding innovative solutions to large-scale problems on a regional basis. The nation's top 100 metropolitan areas, in which two thirds of the nation's population resides, generate 75% of its gross domestic product. B. Katz & J. Bradley, The Metropolitan Revolution 1 (2013). Given this reality, federal and state leaders must now address how these areas can be better supported and leveraged to fulfill their role as engines for economic development, innovation, the exportation of goods, and sustainability. *Id.* at 191. Twenty-first century problems, such as climate change, water scarcity, new sources of energy, effective transportation systems, and food production most likely will be solved at the metropolitan level with its networked economy and concentration of expertise. *Id.* at 38–40.

States have responded to concerns for economic growth and environmental protection. They are now implementing programs calling for planning, economic development, and water resource management on a regional basis. Georgia, for example, has created 12 regional commissions to help develop and coordinate comprehensive planning relative to economic development, information technology, land use, the environment, transportation, and historic preservation. The commissions have a territorial reach of from 10 and 18 counties. Ga. Code Ann. § 50-8-4 (2013). Georgia has also divided the state into 11 regions for water resource planning and management.

The long-standing debate between localists and regionalists will undoubtedly continue. The vision of the New Regionalists, including their focus on revitalizing the central city, remains to be fulfilled. Federal and state incentive programs and regulations, however, will continue to spur stronger regional developments. The earlier focus on governmental consolidation and regional governance has now shifted to an interest in regional-scale policy and problem solving. Foster & Barnes, *Reframing Regional Governance for Research and Practice*, 48 Urb. Aff. Rev. 272, 272 (2012). Regionalism now embraces more than structure or governance—it is viewed as the collaboration that takes place among multiple private, non-profit, and public actors to solve regional-scale problems. See id. at 273. See generally A. Nelson & R. Lang, Megapolitan America (2011) and B. Katz & J. Bradley, *supra*.

The forces of localism nonetheless remain much stronger than regionalism. Why should this be true? Do the legal doctrines examined in earlier chapters provide a secure footing for localism? For a discussion of how fragmented units of local governments are rooted in state law, see Reynolds, *Intergovernmental Cooperation, Metropolitan Equity, and the New Regionalism*, 78 Wash. L. Rev. 93, 97 (2003). For an analysis of a new trend to localize local government further below the municipal level through the empowerment of sub-areas or neighborhoods, see Shoked, *The New Local*, 100 Va. L. Rev. 1323 (2014). What legal obstacles face the regionalists, who endorse varying degrees of curtailment of local autonomy in favor of region-wide regulatory, fiscal, or general governmental mechanisms? See Reynolds, *supra*, at 98. Although suburban-urban mistrust is pervasive, can city-suburban coalition building succeed in advancing metropolitan agendas at state capitols? See Weir, Wolman, & Swanstrom, *The Calculus of Coalitions: Cities, Suburbs, and the Metropolitan Agenda*, 40 Urb. Aff. Rev. 730 (2005).

Structurally integrated government is another way to address political fragmentation. This Chapter begins by examining several alternate forms of regional governance to traditional local government approaches discussed earlier: (a) metropolitan governance, (b) regional multi-purpose districts, (c) regional single-purpose districts, and (d) councils of government and metropolitan planning organizations (MPOs). Discussion of alternative governmental forms is followed by an examination of how local governments have institutionalized neighborhood level governance to achieve greater citizen participation. The Chapter then examines non-structural cooperative mechanisms to achieve greater efficiency in the delivery of services and to solve problems that span local government boundary lines. These include service contracts, joint service contracts, contracts for the transfer of functions, the creation of new governmental agencies pursuant to an intergovernmental contract, and privatization of services such as education, law enforcement, public safety and public utilities. The Chapter also examines how the judiciary, in the absence of cooperative local action, resolves typical conflicts among local government agencies over land use and development policies.

Expanding the size of a local government can decrease local government fragmentation. Annexation is one way to increase local government size. Consolidation to effectuate governance over a larger portion of a metropolitan area has been achieved in a few areas, primarily in the South and Midwest, but the consolidation movement has not caught on nationally. The successful vote on November 7, 2000, to merge Louisville and Jefferson County, Kentucky, effective January 1, 2003, has sparked renewed interest. Multi-purpose districts, exemplified by Portland, Oregon's Metro and the Minneapolis-St. Paul Metropolitan Council would seem to offer more realistic models for greater regional control over functions having a region-wide impact, but their use has not spread either. Formation of a regional identity is essential to the development of regionalism. For a review of governmental reform efforts concluding that regional government structures will not be supported unless people are persuaded that they share common interests and concerns with people in other parts of the region, see Briffault, *Localism and Regionalism*, 48 Buff. L. Rev. 1 (2001).

For some additional literature on regionalism and the "New Regionalists," see Angarola, *Ohio's Home-Rule Amendment: Why Ohio's General Assembly Creating*

Regional Governments Would Combat the Regional Race to the Bottom Under Current Home-Rule Principles, 63 Clev. St. L. Rev. 865 (2015) (urging authorization for the creation of Ohio regional governments to ensure greater inter-local coordination and to make metropolitan areas more globally competitive); Aoki, *All the King's Horses and All the King's Men: Hurdles to Putting the Fragmented Metropolis Back Together Again? Statewide Land Use Planning, Portland Metro and Oregon's Measure 37*, 21 J.L. & Pol. 397 (2005) (discussing interlocal competition and the tension between localism and regionalism); Crowder, *(Sub)Urban Proverty and Regional Interest Convergence,* 98 Marq. L. Rev. 763 (2014) (presenting regional interest convergence as a framework to address regional inequities); Frisken & Norris, *Regionalism Reconsidered*, 23 J. Urb. Aff., No. 5 (2001): 467–479 (comparing new and old regionalists); Gottlieb, *Regional Land Use Planning: A Collaborative Solution for the Conservation of Natural Resources,* 29 J. Envtl. L. & Litig. 35 (2014) (arguing in favor of controlling land uses by a regional land use agency, but urging a collaborative method of decision making among all stakeholders, including local governments); Griffith, *Regional Governance Reconsidered*, 21 J.L. & Pol. 505, 514–40 (2005) (discussing future regionalism growth, barriers that impede regional governance, and existing regional structures); Pearson, *Metropolitan Regions as Governance Systems: Metropolitan Governance: A Framework for Capacity Assessment*, Deutsche Gesellschaft fur Internationale Zusammenarbeit (2016); Reynolds, *Local Governments and Regional Governance*, 39 Urb. Law. 483, 501–21 (2007) (evaluating regional governance).

Problem 3-1

Metro City, a 200-year-old municipality that has been a manufacturing and transportation center for most of its life, fell on hard times during the latter part of the twentieth century and into the present century. Its population dropped from near 900,000 in 1950 to under 400,000 in 2020. It is landlocked in the center of a metropolitan area that has grown from a population of slightly over 1,000,000 in 1950 to more than 2,500,000 in 2020. The six counties surrounding Metro City have over 100 incorporated municipalities, 50 school districts and a corresponding number of special districts providing public services such as fire protection, library resources, neighborhood development, sewage disposal and water supply.

Over the years, as a result of several migrations (rural to urban, city to suburb, rust belt to sunbelt and new waves of immigration) as well as extraordinary changes in macro and micro economics, Metro City found itself housing a disproportionate share of the region's poor of all races in structures that are disproportionately old and deteriorating. An increasingly sharp "location" mismatch developed between the need for public services (schools, health care, housing, public transportation, etc.) in Metro City and the resources to provide these services through local tax revenues.

Since 2010, however, some professionals, young families, and empty nesters have decided to either stay in Metro City or move back to it. As a result, some of the housing stock close to Metro City's downtown area has improved and new housing construction is taking place in an area near the waterfront that contains vacant parcels of land. This new construction meets Metro City's new standards for green building and energy efficiency. Jobs created by the "new economy" of information management and services, which in the past migrated to Metro's outer suburbs, are now being created in Metro City, which is promoting itself as an "Innovation City" following its receipt of such a classification by a national organization.

The older cities immediately surrounding Metro City (the "inner ring suburbs") are now experiencing similar problems of increased demand for public services and shrinking tax bases that have plagued Metro City. Some of Metro City's less advantaged citizens have moved to these suburbs because the demand for housing in Metro City has driven up the costs of living there. Many of the single family homes in these inner ring suburbs are too small to meet the current demand for larger living quarters and open style floor plans. At the same time, however, wealthy communities on the outer fringes of the metropolitan area continue to form and grow. They possess land not yet developed.

The constitution of the State of Metro authorizes cities and counties in metropolitan areas to consolidate territories and governments, to adjust relationships between cities and counties, to establish metropolitan districts for functional administration of common services, and to adopt "any other plan for partial or complete" metropolitan government. As city attorney, you have been asked by the newly elected mayor to make recommendations concerning new approaches for responding to metropolitan problems in the 21st century. What do you recommend? [Suggested by M. Orfield, METROPOLITICS (1997), and D. Rusk, BALTIMORE UNBOUND (1996).]

B. Metropolitan Governance

[1] Consolidation and Federation

Major forces of decentralization, including the globalization of the economy, the rise of e-commerce, and the continued exodus of jobs, homes and families to the far reaches of suburbia, have triggered renewed calls for local government reform. Somewhat paradoxically, these forces of decentralization have restored the concept of local government centralization to the national agenda. Voter approval of the merger of the city of Louisville and Jackson County, Kentucky in November 2000 (effective January 1, 2003) coupled with creation of the Georgia Regional Transportation Authority ("GRTA," pronounced "Gret-a") in 1999 demonstrate two approaches to local government centralization: consolidation of general purpose governments and creation of public agencies with power to act throughout a region. The "New Regionalism" reform movement discussed at the Introduction to this chapter focuses on the need for new forms of regional governance to make the metropolitan economy competitive, to improve the quality of life through environmental controls and incentives, and to allocate resources for central city revitalization. Many of the "New Regionalists" advocate cooperative regional arrangements although cooperation alone is not sufficient to achieve regional governance. Norris, *Prospects for Regional Governance Under the New Regionalism: Economic Imperatives Versus Political Impediments*, 23 J. URB. AFF., No. 5 (2001): 557, 559–60. Following a review of the history of "metropolitan regionalism," this section will consider the consolidation and federation movement. It will be followed by sections on multi-purpose and single-purpose regional agencies as instruments of regional governance.

Evolution of Metropolitan Regionalism

The Industrial Revolution in the latter half of the nineteenth century resulted in rapid population growth in cities across the United States as workers migrated to urban areas for employment generated by industrial growth. These laborers, as well as newly arrived immigrants, frequently experienced overcrowded, unhealthy, and unsafe working and living conditions. City crime, congestion, and corruption stood in stark contrast to the earlier agrarian way of life. Metropolitan regionalism first arose to address urban problems. Mitchell-Weaver, Miller & Deal, *Multilevel Governance and Metropolitan Regionalism in the USA*, 37 URB. STUDIES No. 4/5 (2000): 851–876, at 852.

Various reform movements speeded the evolution of metropolitan planning in the United States. Housing reform was the first effort. *Id.* at 852–53. The Cities Beautiful Movement, which occurred in the 1890s and early years of the twentieth century, focused on the beautification of cities. This movement ushered in park and boulevard planning as distinct components of metropolitan planning. *Id.* at 853. The tradition of metropolitan park building began with Frederick Law Olmsted's design for Central Park in New York City and was further promoted by the Chicago World's Fair in 1893, the purpose of which was to show that cities in the United States could aspire to be as beautiful as their European counterparts. *Id.* Government reform became the fourth and last theme of metropolitan planning with twin goals: professionalization of local government and the territorial expansion of cities to reflect the reality of metropolitan growth. *Id.*

Metropolitan regionalism's twentieth century history did not waiver from the conviction that the fragmentation of urban areas into numerous subdivisions causes a host of serious problems, including racial, income, and resource imbalance in the metropolis; lack of housing affordability and homelessness; lack of rational land use planning; and environmental degradation. *Id.* at 854–55. Suburban autonomy, however, resisted calls for greater resource sharing throughout the metropolis or for regional land use controls to prevent sprawl. The landscape became increasingly decentralized with the creation of edge cities, which have become centers of employment and function as market places to service suburban living. J. Garreau, EDGE CITY: LIFE ON THE NEW FRONTIER 4 (1991). Suburbanization has now moved from the older inner suburbs to greenfield developments in exurbia beyond the suburban fringe.

Despite further metropolitan area fragmentation and suburbanization, support for metropolitan planning continued in the twentieth century. The federal government played a key role in encouraging more planning on a regional basis through tailored incentives. Under the Housing Act of 1954, the federal government made monies available under its "701" program for planning. The Federal-Aid Highway Act of 1962 required a comprehensive planning process as a prerequisite to the receipt of federal funds for interstate highway development in metropolitan areas. The creation of regional councils was spurred by federal housing legislation in 1965 that made these entities eligible to receive federal funds. Federal funding for multi-county economic development districts and federal authorization for the creation of multi-state river basin commissions also spurred the creation of different forms of regional planning agencies among the states. Regional agencies gained further status upon the promulgation by the U.S. Office of Management and Budget of Circular A-9, which mandated the review by a state, regional, or metropolitan clearinghouse of all applications for federal monies. See American Planning Association, Regional Planning, *The Origins of Regional Planning Agencies*, available at [https://perma.cc/8QZX-CKQZ].

The election of President Ronald Regan began a retreat in the 1980s from intergovernmental approaches to local problems. His Executive Order 12372 ended the required A-95 review, but most states designed their own review process to coordinate federal grant funding as authorized by this executive order. The regional focus of federal transportation funding also continued to encourage more metropolitan-wide planning. Today, the federal government encourages and highlights measures to support coordination on a regional basis within states. The Department of Housing and Urban Development on its web site, for example, provides numerous examples of regional planning efforts for the solution of problems crossing local boundary lines. See U.S. DEPARTMENT OF HOUSING AND URBAN DEVELOPMENT, *Sustainable Communities Regional Planning Grants*, [https://perma.cc/92LV-V4MQ].

Climate change, other environmental factors, and the need to generate economic growth seem to have strengthened the forces driving regionalism. These forces have caused all levels of governments to rethink past assumptions taken for granted. Both public and private sectors share concerns about sustainability and dialogue together about whether productive growth can be achieved and shared across a broader segment of society. See *American Planning Ass'n, Emerging Trends in Regional Planning PAS Report 586* (2017), https://perma.cc/7GM4-AVXR. Many believe that metropolitan areas hold the keys to national prosperity because they concentrate such assets as innovation, capital infrastructure, human capital, and quality places. See Katz, *What Comes Next for Our Metro Nation: The New Forces Driving Regionalism*

(Brookings Institution, 2009), available at https://www.brookings.edu/on-the-record/what-comes-next-for-our-metro-nation-the-new-forces-driving-regionalism/.

Consolidation and Federation

Although consolidations represent the epitome of metropolitan regionalism by bringing disparate local governments together under one governmental unit, they are generally disfavored by voters today. Mitchell-Weaver et al., *supra*, at 865. During the nineteenth century a number of smaller municipalities were either merged or annexed by cities, which would become metropolitan in nature. Boston, for example, between 1868 and 1874 expanded its reach by the annexation of Brighton, Charlestown, Dorchester, Roxbury, and West Roxbury. Present day New York City was created in 1898 when Manhattan merged with Brooklyn, Queens, the Bronx, and Staten Island. In a similar fashion, New Orleans, Baltimore, Philadelphia, St. Louis, and San Francisco expanded from their original territory. As seen in *Hunter v. City of Pittsburgh* [Ch. 1], some incorporated municipalities resisted such consolidation. In 1873, the Town of Brookline, a wealthy suburb of Boston, successfully rejected the City's attempted annexation, setting a turning point in the consolidation movement. At present and in the last century, most metropolitan areas have been unable to consolidate the ring of suburbs around them. Thus, metropolitan areas today are largely fragmented among a large number of smaller, incorporated municipalities. No governance structure exists to provide for the public good of the region as a whole.

Consolidation can occur as one-tier entity or as two-tier government in which area wide functions are separated from local ones. One-tier consolidation, typically established by state legislative authority, result in a new government. New York City and Boston above are examples. Two-tier governments are federated structures in which area-wide, regional, functions constitute one tier and local functions are performed at the local, second-tier level. One example of a two-tiered consolidation is Miami-Dade County, Florida (1957). Localities carry out functions prized by localities such as control over land uses and education. Mitchell-Weaver, et al., *supra*, at 865. The county, on the other hand, performs functions desired to be effectuated on a regional basis, such as transportation, sewers, solid waste disposal, and water resource management. *Id.* The region can thus benefit from operations best done on a large scale while giving localities neighborhood control in areas important to them. *Id.*

Consolidation and Federation Movement Stalls

Since World War II, only about 20 one-tier consolidations have occurred. *Id.* These include Baton Rouge, Louisiana (1949); Nashville, Tennessee (1962); Jacksonville, Florida (1968); and Indianapolis, Indiana (1970). *Id.* Most of the consolidations required voter approval and occurred in the South. *Id.* They were most likely to take place in a smaller metropolitan region where greater homogeneity could be found than in a large metropolis.

Although the Louisville-Jefferson County vote in November 2000 to merge effective January 1, 2003 received national attention, the consolidation and federation movement clearly is not healthy. See Bruck & Pinto, *Overruled by Home Rule: The Problems with New Jersey's Latest Effort to Consolidate Municipalities*, 32 Seton Hall Legis. J. 287 (2008) (describing the barriers to consolidation in New Jersey and failed efforts to consolidate small municipalities); Bucki, *Regionalism Revisited: The Effort to Streamline Governance in Buffalo and Erie County, New York*, 71 Alb. L. Rev. 117 (2008) (discussing the failed 2005 attempt to consolidate local governments in Erie County).

Very few consolidations, of very small governmental units, occurred in the thirty years between Indianapolis/Marion County and Louisville/Jefferson County. A 1997 study of the Jacksonville/Duval County, Florida consolidation in 1967 failed to find any significant link between consolidation and economic development (private sector manufacturing, retail, or service-sector growth). Feiock & Carr, *A Reassessment of City/County Consolidation: Economic Development Impacts*, 29 State & Local Gov't Rev., No. 3 (1997): 166–171. A move to dis-incorporate the City of Miami and abolish the two-tier Miami-Dade County governmental system was defeated at the polls in 1997. For an argument that it should have succeeded under Tieboutian public choice measures, see Steinacker, *Prospects for Regional Government: Lessons from the Miami Abolition Vote*, 37 Urb. Aff. Rev. No. 1 (2001): 100–118. For case studies of 13 of the more recent consolidations, see Case Studies of City-County Consolidation: Reshaping the Local Government Landscape (Leland & Thurmaier eds., 2004). Despite the faltering consolidation and federation movement, involuntary annexation continues to be an effective method of creating functional regional governments. See Tyson, *Localism and Involuntary Annexation: Reconsidering Approaches to New Regionalism*, 87 Tul. L. Rev. 297 (2012).

Legal Problems from Consolidation and Federation

Consolidation and federation can create complex legal problems. They may superimpose a new governmental authority on existing units, or add authority to an existing governmental unit which then becomes the consolidated or federated government for the area. Constitutional provisions eliminate or mitigate these legal problems in some states, but the courts must still determine the scope of the constitutional authority delegated to the consolidated government. A constitutional challenge is likely if the consolidation or federation is authorized by a statute. The following cases illustrate how the courts have handled these problems:

State v. Unified Gov't of Wyandotte County/Kansas City, 955 P.2d 1136 (Kan. 1998). The court upheld a consolidation form of government for Wyandotte County and Kansas City, Kansas. The new government became both a county and a city of the first class, except that its first class city powers could not be exercised within the territories of other existing incorporated cities and the unincorporated portion of the county. Emphasizing that the state constitution limits rather than confers power, see Chapter 1, the court upheld the consolidation against special legislation, delegation of power, and other challenges. The court found sufficient standards to guide the drafters of the plan in the requirements that efficiency and effectiveness as well as costs and benefits of consolidation be considered.

Holsclaw v. Stephens, 507 S.W.2d 462 (Ky. 1973). The court considered a challenge to a merger of the City of Lexington and Fayette County into an urban county form of government. The merger was carried out under statutory authority. The court held that the creation of the consolidated government did not violate the constitution. The legislature could create new forms of local government not limited to existing cities and counties, and could delegate the authority to alter the structure of affected governments.

Dortch v. Lugar, 266 N.E.2d 25 (Ind. 1971). The court rejected a series of constitutional challenges to the consolidation of Indianapolis and Marion County, which had been carried out by statute. One argument was that an unconstitutional evasion of the constitutional debt limitation had occurred because the consolidation transferred the control of special districts to the consolidated government. The court held that the independent status of the districts was not destroyed by the transfer. For discussion of the Indianapolis UNIGOV experiment, see C. Owen & Y. Willbern, Governing Metropolitan Indianapolis: The Politics of UNIGOV (1985).

Miami Shores Village v. Cowart, 108 So. 2d 468 (Fla. 1958). This case interpreted a set of ambiguous provisions in the charter defining the powers of the federated county government. A special constitutional provision authorized the charter. The court held that the charter authorized the county to carry out functions that were metropolitan in character. See Gustely, *The Allocational and Distributional Impacts of Governmental Consolidation: The Dade County Experience*, 12 Urb. Aff. Q., No. 1 (1977): 100–118.

The courts also have dismissed constitutional objections to the creation of metropolitan authorities and districts. In *Municipality of Metro. Seattle v. City of Seattle*, 357 P.2d 863 (Wash. 1960), the court rejected an argument that the creation of the metropolitan district violated local home rule powers. Contra, *Four-County Metro. Capital Improvement Dist. v. Board of County Comm'rs*, 369 P.2d 67 (Colo. 1962).

Most cases dealing with the creation of metropolitan special districts have avoided home rule and related objections by classifying the special district as a state "agency" serving a state purpose. This characterization is not difficult to apply when the district is dealing with environmental problems that transcend municipal boundaries. See *City of Dearborn v. Michigan Turnpike Auth.*, 73 N.W.2d 544 (Mich. 1955); *Omaha Parking Auth. v. City of Omaha*, 77 N.W.2d 862 (Neb. 1956); *Robertson v. Zimmermann*, 196 N.E. 740 (N.Y. 1935) (Buffalo sewage authority). See also *Jackson v. Vidalia Riverfront Development Dist.*, 982 So. 2d 346 (La. App. 2008) (district held political subdivision of state and subject to legislative control). These state or single-purpose authorities were limited to a single municipality.

Notes and Questions

1. *The "favored quarter."* An aspect of "metropolitan regionalism" that has receiving increasing attention is the phenomenon of the "favored quarter"—a term attributed to real estate consultants to describe the wealthy portion of a metropolitan area. The "favored quarter" is characterized by high concentrations of expensive housing, commercial and industrial property requiring little public service, and extensive public investment in parks, roads, and schools. Critics of the "favored quarter" advocate one or more of the metropolitan government reforms described *supra*. See, e.g., M. Orfield, Metropolitics, 5–6, 9 (1997); Cashin, *supra*, at 2033, 2033–2047 (2000) (advocating a "robust regionalism that better distributes benefits and burdens" through grassroots coalition building and the smart growth/sustainable development movement); Troutt, *Katrina's Window: Localism, Resegregation, and Equitable Regionalism*, 55 Buff. L. Rev. 1109 (2008) (discussing ways to effectuate equitable regionalism); Wilson, *Toward a Theory of Equitable Federated Regionalism in Public Education*, 61 U.C.L.A. L. Rev. 1416, 1423–24 (2014) (arguing that regionalism can combat educational disparities). But see Briffault, *Localism and Regionalism*, 48 Buff. L. Rev. 1, 29 (2000) ("the fate of regionalism will turn on whether regionalists will be able to persuade people that their interests are sufficiently tied in with those of the residents [of] other communities within the region").

2. *Per capita income in central cities v. suburbs.* Although poverty became increasingly concentrated in central cities (defined as the largest city in the metropolitan area) from 1970 to 1990, the overall per capita income gap between central cities and suburbs remained unchanged between 1990 and 2000 according to a Census 2000 study. See Swanstrom, Casey, Flack & Dreier, *Pulling Apart: Economic Segregation Among Suburbs and Central Cities in Major Metropolitan Areas* 1 (Brookings Institution 2004). Since the turn of the century, however, suburban poverty has grown rapidly. Between 2000 and 2015, large cities, as well as rural counties, experienced an increase in poor populations of roughly 20 percent, but residents living below the poverty level grew by 57 percent during that same time period in the suburbs surrounding the country's largest metropolitan areas. Elizabeth Kneebone, *The Changing Geography of US Poverty* (Testimony, Brookings Institution, Feb. 15, 2017), https://www.brookings.edu/testimonies/the-changing-geography-of-us-poverty/. Various factors have been given for the surge of suburban poverty: employment shifts away from city downtown areas, population growth, greater population diversity, shifting immigration patterns, regional housing market trends, rising inner city housing costs, foreclosures, and prevalence of low-wage work. *Id.* Based on these trends, what prospects for coalition building between central cities and suburban local governments might be expected? Do municipal boundary lines act to sort out economic classes? Should the "favored quarter" receive attention as a suburban as well as an inner city issue?

3. *Consolidation v. smaller sized local governments.* The Advisory Commission on Inter-governmental Relations (ACIR), an early critic of metropolitan fragmentation, revised its view and found merit in variety and diversity among metropolitan governance structures. The new wisdom relies heavily on political theories that emphasize the need for citizen choice and consent in local governance. ACIR applied its new theories to an analysis of local government in the St. Louis, Missouri metropolitan area, where it found intergovernmental agreements and other ad hoc arrangements that mitigated the effects of governmental fragmentation. ACIR, METROPOLITAN ORGANIZATION: THE ST. LOUIS CASE (1988). The study drew substantial local criticism. See *Metropolitan Governance Forum on the St. Louis Area*, 15 INTERGOVERNMENTAL PERSPECTIVE No. 1, at 9 (ACIR 1989). See also Reynolds, *Intergovernmental Cooperation, Metropolitan Equity, and the New Regionalism*, 78 WASH. L. REV. 93 (2003) (concluding that intergovernmental cooperative efforts fail to realize the New Regionalist's goal of a fairer allocation of resources).

The area at the time of the study was considering a charter revision for St. Louis County, an urban county providing a variety of services that would have incorporated the entire county and transformed the county government into a provider of designated services for incorporated governments. The plan was voided after the Supreme Court invalidated a property ownership requirement for membership on the Board of Freeholders, which was authorized by the Missouri Constitution to draft the charter revision proposal. *Quinn v. Millsap*, 491 U.S. 95 (1989). See Phares, *Bigger Is Better, or Is It Smaller?: Restructuring Local Government in the St. Louis Area*, 25 URB. AFF. Q., No. 1 (1989): 5–17. [Voting issues are discussed in Chapter 9.—Eds.]

For an argument supporting the ACIR position based on a review of the history of governmental reorganization efforts in St. Louis, see E. Jones, FRAGMENTED BY DESIGN (2000). See also Foster, *Exploring the Links Between Political Structure and Metropolitan Growth*, 12 POL. GEOGRAPHY, No. 6 (1993): 523–47 (preponderance of evidence from a study of 129 large U.S. metropolitan areas between 1962 and 1982 supports the view that integrated political structures will be associated with higher metropolitan growth rates than their politically fragmented counterparts); Gillette, *Regionalization and Interlocal Bargains*, 76 N.Y.U. L. REV. 190 (2001) (arguing for a decentralized approach to regional problems through informal "interlocal bargains"); Gordon, *Patchwork Metropolis: Fragmented Governance and Urban Decline in Greater St. Louis*, 34 ST. LOUIS. U. PUB. L. REV. 51 (2014) (favoring city and county consolidation in Greater St. Louis); Stansel, *Local Decentralization and Local Economic Growth: A Cross-Sectional Examination of U.S. Metropolitan Areas*, 57 J. URB. ECON. No. 1 (2005): 55–72 (finding that decentralization increases economic growth in a negative relationship between the central-city share of metropolitan area population and economic growth, and a positive relationship between both the number of municipalities per 100,000 residents and the number of counties per 100,000 residents and economic growth). If, as the economists say, we must make a second-best choice in solving problems of metropolitan governance, what should it be?

4. *Tax equity issues.* When local governments are consolidated over entire county areas, tax equity questions will arise if the entire area of the consolidated government is subjected to the property tax rate of the major city that becomes part of the consolidation. Undeveloped areas of the consolidated government will be subject to an urban tax rate that does not reflect the limited level of services they receive after consolidation. To remedy this problem, some consolidated governmental structures have provided for the creation of two or more service districts within the consolidated government within which the level of taxes reflects the level of services that is provided. For discussion, see White, *Differential Property Taxation in Consolidated City-Counties*, 63 NAT'L CIVIC REV. (1974): 301. The creation of these districts creates problems under constitutional uniformity clauses because they produce a tax rate that is not uniform for the entire area of the consolidated government.

In *Hart v. Columbus*, 188 S.E.2d 422 (Ga. App. 1972), the court upheld four differential taxing districts created by statute for the City of Columbus-Muscogee County consolidated government. A different level of services was provided in each service district, and tax rates in the service districts were based on the level of services rendered. The court applied a "reasonableness" test to uphold the districts by finding that the benefits conferred in each district were commensurate with the tax burden imposed. The court also rejected an equal protection attack, but the districts were not attacked under the uniformity of taxation clause of the state constitution. See also *Frazer v. Carr*, 360 S.W.2d 449 (Tenn. 1962) (upholding differential taxing districts created by constitution for Nashville's metropolitan government).

5. *Tax sharing.* Property tax inequities and disparities in metropolitan areas can be handled through tax sharing or tax pooling plans. Minnesota experimented with this approach in its Metropolitan Fiscal Disparities Act, MINN. STAT. ANN. § 473F.01 *et seq.*, upheld against a challenge based on uniformity of taxation grounds in *Village of Burnsville v. Onischuk*, 222 N.W.2d 523 (Minn. 1974). The Act is limited to the Minneapolis-St. Paul metropolitan area. The sharing formula is complicated but generally distributes a share of the increase in taxes on commercial and industrial property on an areawide basis. As the tax is redistributed under a formula that considers population and fiscal capacity, the formula provides a disincentive to zone property for commercial and industrial purposes. Some of the increased revenues from these properties are redistributed areawide based on the formula, and the formula may not return all of the revenue increase to the municipality in which the new commercial and industrial development is located. For discussion, see Orfield, *The Minnesota Fiscal Disparities Act of 1971: The Twin Cities' Struggle and Blueprint for Regional Cooperation*, 33 WM. MITCHELL L. REV. 591 (2007); Note, *The Minnesota Fiscal Disparities Act: A Model for Growth-Sharing in the 1980s*, 9 WM. MITCHELL L. REV. 410 (1983).

In the more than 30 years that tax sharing has been in effect, tax base disparities have been reduced from 10:1 to 4:1. One problem that has developed is that the act does not require municipalities to accept industrial and commercial uses. As a result, some wealthy bedroom suburbs have excluded these uses but still benefit from the tax redistribution under the tax sharing plan. For a case upholding a similar tax sharing plan adopted for the Hackensack Meadowlands redevelopment area in New Jersey, see *Meadowlands Reg'l Redevelopment Agency v. State*, 304 A.2d 545 (N.J. 1973). See generally Libonn, *From Cautionary Example to "City on a Hill": Revitalizing Saint Louis May Require an Innovative Regional Taxation Model*, 91 WASH. U. L. REV. 1035, 1038 (2014) (proposing a limited regional St. Louis revenue sharing arrangement modeled on the Twin Cities plan); Reschovsky, *An Evaluation of Metropolitan Area Tax Base Sharing*, 33 NAT'L TAX J. 55 (1980). For a discussion of the school finance problem raised by disparities in metropolitan fiscal capacity, and solutions to this problem, see Chapter 9.

6. For some of the literature on governmental consolidation and federation, see P. Calthorpe & W. Fulton, THE REGIONAL CITY (2001); D. Rusk, INSIDE GAME/OUTSIDE GAME (1999); M. Orfield, METROPOLITICS (1997); A. Downs, NEW VISIONS FOR METROPOLITAN AMERICA (1994); N. Peirce, CITISTATES: HOW URBAN AMERICA CAN PROSPER IN A COMPETITIVE WORLD (1993); Hendrick, Jimenez & Lal, *Does Local Government Fragmentation Reduce Local Spending*, 47 URB. AFF. REV., No. 4 (2011): 467–510; Mitchell-Weaver, et al., *supra*, at *Multilevel Governance and Metropolitan Regionalism in the USA*, 47 URB. STUD., No. 5/6 (2000): 851–876; Gage, *Leadership and Regional Councils: A Mismatch Between Leadership Styles Today and Future Roles*, 25 STATE & LOCAL GOV'T REV., No. 1 (1993): 9-18; DeHoog, Lowery & Lyons, *Metropolitan Fragmentation and Suburban Ghettos: Some Empirical Observations on Institutional Racism*, 13 J. URB. AFF. (1991): 479 (finds African-Americans do better in consolidated governments than in governments they dominate).

[2] Multi-Purpose Regional Agencies

Multi-purpose districts or public authorities are empowered to exercise several regional functions. By doing so they can coordinate such disparate tasks as land use planning or the operation of a regional transit system, an airport, a metropolitan convention center, or a region-wide system of parks and recreational areas. Portland's Metro and the Twin Cities Metropolitan Council are the best examples of multi-purpose regional agencies in the United States. These entities are the exception rather than the norm. Most of the country's metropolitan areas have not opted to consolidate several functions in one agency. The more typical state response to a crisis caused by political fragmentation has been the creation of a single-purpose regional agency, such as the Georgia Regional Transportation Authority (GRTA), to tackle problems necessitating regional coordination.

What functions do you believe are metropolitan in scale? Would you include transportation infrastructure, greenbelts, solid waste disposal, and air and water quality to be functions well suited for delegation to a multi-purpose regional entity? Note that the Portland and Twin Cities multi-purpose regional models leave general purpose local governments in place to perform functions not delegated for provision on a regional basis. What types of powers do you believe should remain vested in local governments irrespective of the creation of regional governance structures?

Portland's Metro

Considered the strongest form of regional governance in the United States, Portland's Metropolitan Service District (Metro), received voter approval of a constitutionally authorized (Or. Const., Art. XI, § 14) home rule charter in 1992. It is the only regional government in the United States with an elected council, consisting of a president elected at large and six councilors elected from districts. Metro: Metro Council, http://www.oregonmetro.gov/index.cfm/go/by.web/id=28 [https://perma.cc/WPK4-3VT8].

Metro's charter makes regional growth management its primary mission, but it performs other regional functions as well. Metro has been dubbed a "flexible governmental 'box' into which the voters of its three county jurisdictions or the legislature could assign service responsibilities that they selected," D. Rusk, Baltimore Unbound 51 (1996). In addition to its regional land use and transportation planning functions, Metro has also been given responsibilities for regional air and water quality (Or. Rev. Stat. § 268.390), operation of a solid waste disposal system, acquisition and management of open space and parks, natural disaster planning and response coordination, the development and marketing of data, and the administration of the area's local government boundary commission. It also operates regional facilities such as a zoo and the Oregon Convention Center. Metro Charter, http://www.oregonmetro.gov/metro-charter [https://perma.cc/44UT-DH2K]. Metro provides regional oversight and services, but it does not replace local governments.

In 1973, Oregon adopted a comprehensive state land use planning law. The legislation called for the creation of a number of state planning goals, which were adopted, and required localities to adopt comprehensive plans consistent with these state planning goals. Metro is closely linked to Oregon's land use programs and oversees compliance with state land use goals within its jurisdiction. Or. Rev. Stat. §§ 197.005–197.860, 199.420(3), 268.020.

Oregon's land use system further requires cities, counties, and regional governments to establish urban growth boundaries (UGBs). The UGBs, based upon 20-year population forecasts, separate urban land from rural areas. They are designed to curb urban sprawl by protecting rural land for rural uses such as farming and forestry. Land in the urban areas must be developed before growth can spread outside the UGB. The UGB boundary line must be drawn, however, to accommodate existing urban uses and to meet needs for urban development lands. Metro ensures compliance with the UGB requirements for the Portland area. Metro: Full Text of the Metro Charter, *supra*. For a discussion of Metro's success and role in managing urban growth, see Sullivan, *Urban Growth Management in Portland, Oregon*, 93 Or. L. Rev. 455 (2014).

Portland enjoys the reputation of a "city-region that works because it plans—and more than that, because it implements its plans." Abbott, *The Portland City-Region: Excavating the "Geopolitics of Success," in* Y. Dierwechter, Urban Growth Management and its Discontents: Promises, Practices, and Geopolitics in U.S. City-Regions 125 (2008). The centerpieces of the regional planning function may be described as a 50-year "Future Vision" (Portland 2040) and a "Regional Framework Plan." The Charter specifies that the following subjects must be covered in the regional framework plan:

> (1) regional transportation and mass transit systems; (2) management and amendment of the urban growth boundary; (3) protection of lands outside the urban growth boundary for natural resource, future urban or other uses; (4) housing densities; (5) urban design and settlement patterns; (6) parks, open spaces and recreational facilities; (7) water sources and storage; (8) coordination, to the extent feasible, of metro growth management and land use planning policies with those of Clark County, Washington; and (9) planning responsibilities mandated by state law. [Regional Framework Plan, http://www.oregonmetro.gov/regional-framework-plan [https://perma.cc/A2KU-Q657].]

The 2040 Regional Framework Plan relies upon mixed uses and transit- oriented development (TOD) to achieve greater densities, thereby increasing the feasibility of non-vehicular modes of transportation and concentrating development within the Urban Growth Boundary. The Plan also added a stronger open space element that preserves rural reserves and greenbelts in perpetuity. P. Calthorpe & W. Fulton, *supra*, at 119. The Metro Council has authority under the 1992 Charter to adopt ordinances requiring local governments to comply with the Regional Framework Plan in their comprehensive plans and zoning regulations, and to resolve inconsistencies between such plans. Rusk, *supra*, at 52–53.

Twin Cities Metropolitan Council

The classic example of a regional agency with comprehensive planning powers is the Metropolitan Council in the Twin Cities area in Minnesota. The Council is not a voluntary council of government (*see infra* at [4]). It was created by state legislation, and its members are appointed by the governor. The Metropolitan Council was formed in large part to provide direction for the development programs of metropolitan special districts. The statute accomplishes this objective by authorizing the Metropolitan Council to prepare a development guide, now designated under Metropolitan Council regulations as a Blueprint, which "shall consist of a compilation of policy statements, goals, standards, programs, and maps prescribing guides for an orderly and economic development, public and private, of the metropolitan area." Minn. Stat. Ann. § 473.145.

The Metropolitan Council is also directed to prepare a long-range comprehensive policy plan for transportation and wastewater treatment which "substantially conforms" to the development guide for the metropolitan special districts that are subject to Metropolitan Council supervision, as well as plans for regional recreation open space, solid waste, and water use and supply. *Id.* §§ 473.146–473.157. The Metropolitan Council also reviews the comprehensive plans of local government units "to determine their compatibility with each other and conformity with metropolitan system plans." *Id.* § 473.175. See *BBY Investors v. City of Maplewood*, 467 N.W.2d 631 (Minn. App. 1991) (applying consistency requirement to uphold a city's rejection of a conditional use permit).

If a local government unit fails to adopt a local comprehensive plan consistent with the system plans, the Metropolitan Council may take appropriate action in court. Minn. Stat. Ann. § 473.175. The statute only provides, however, that the Metropolitan Council "may require" local compliance with metropolitan plans. *Id.* Thus, enforcement remains discretionary, and the Metropolitan Council has been criticized for narrowly construing its enforcement powers. Note, *Putting the Use Back in Metropolitan Land-Use Planning: Private Enforcement of Urban Sprawl Control* Laws, 81 Minn. L. Rev. 1343, 1362–67 (1997). Further, a local government may contest a Metropolitan Council decision requesting modification of its plan and request a hearing before an administrative law judge. *Id.* § 473.866. See *City of Lake Elmo v. Metropolitan Council*, 685 N.W.2d 1 (Minn. 2004) (upholding the Council's action in requiring Lake Elmo to conform its land use plan to the Metropolitan Council's regional plans and describing the procedural steps for Metropolitan Council enforcement activity). The Metropolitan Council is also empowered to review any privately or publicly proposed "matters of metropolitan significance" for consistency, among other criteria, with the development guide, and may suspend action on the matter of metropolitan significance for twelve months. *Id.* § 473.173.

Legislation in 1994 strengthened the Metropolitan Council by eliminating the semi-independent metropolitan boards that were in charge of the regional wastewater collection and treatment system, the regional transit system, and the Metropolitan Housing and Redevelopment Authority and consolidating the activities with the Metropolitan Council. The legislation also strengthened the Governor's policy-making authority by making the terms of Metropolitan Council's members concurrent with the term of Governor, who can now replace them at any time. See Ballou, *A Future for the Met Council*, 12 U. St. Thomas L.J. 131 (2015) (discussing how Metro Council's powers expanded over five decades and proposing measures to make the Council more accountable); Haigh, *The Metropolitan Council*, 40 Wm. Mitchell L. Rev. 160 (2013) (providing an overview of the Metro Council and its new focus on transit-oriented development). For a discussion of the Council prior to the 1994 legislation, see Ohm, *Growth Management in Minnesota: The Metropolitan Land Planning Act*, 16 Hamline L. Rev. 359 (1993). For contrasting views of the Council's potential for responding to problems created by urban sprawl, compare Miara, *Council, My Council*, Urban Land 2001 60: 4, at 44 (optimistic), with Note,

Land Use Planning—The Twin Cities Metropolitan Council: Novel Initiative, Futile Effort, 27 WM. MITCHELL L. REV. 1941 (2001) (pessimistic).

Notes and Questions

1. *Elected versus appointed officials on metropolitan regional agencies.* Portland's Metro consists of a president and six council members who are elected from districts every four years on a nonpartisan basis. The president, who is elected region-wide, sets Metro's policy agenda. Metro Council, http://www.oregonmetro.gov/index.cfm/go/by.web/id=28 [https://perma.cc/447J-596N]. Minnesota's governor appoints the members of the Metropolitan Council causing a likely turnover of all members upon the election of a new governor. In devising a system of regional governance, consider the desirability of stability, consistency, innovation, accountability, and the implementation of measures that will effectuate the best interests of the region. Will both methods of representation accomplish these objectives? Is one form of representation more preferable than the other?

2. *Enforcement of state or regional growth management programs.* Studies have shown that the requirement of local plan consistency with state or regional comprehensive plans will not in itself prevent urban sprawl. Carruthers, *The Impacts of State Growth Management Programmes: A Comparative Analysis*, 29 URB. STUD., No. 11 (2002): 159, 1975–76. Land developers will avoid regulation by developing in areas where regulation is lax. *Id.* at 1976. When the jurisdictional boundary lines of metropolitan planning areas are narrowly drawn, development may increase in exurban areas beyond the regulated area. Should multi-purpose regional agencies be vested with discretion as to enforcement activities? Should enforcement of state growth management programs be enforced solely by regional or state agencies? See Note, *Putting the Use Back in Metropolitan Land-Use Planning: Private Enforcement of Urban Sprawl Control Laws*, 81 MINN. L. REV. 1343 (1997) (proposing a private right of action to enforce the Minnesota Metropolitan Land Planning Act).

3. *Multi-purpose regional agencies' responsibility for both regional planning and the operation of regional functions.* Portland's Metro and the Twin Cities Metropolitan Council both exercise land use controls throughout their respective regions and provide services in such areas as regional transit, solid waste disposal, and open space preservation. Should these two separate roles be vested in the same regional body? Does the provision of regional services detract from the ability of these regional entities to exercise land use enforcement powers? Does the power to exercise both functions enhance the viability of these regional entities?

[3] Single-Purpose Regional Agencies

1. *Task-specific governance.* In contrast to local governments that perform a comprehensive package of goods and services in limited, non-intersecting territorial jurisdictions, single-purpose entities fulfill distinct, task-specific functions in a potentially vast number of territorially scaled jurisdictions for flexible rather than

durable time periods. Hooghe & Marks, *Unraveling the Central State, But How? Types of Multi-level Governance*, 97 Am. Pol. Sci. Rev., No. 2 (2003): 233–243. In contrast to the lack of multi-purpose regional agencies, this type of governance is widespread at the local level. For example, the metropolitan area of Houston had 665 special districts. *Id.* at 237.

Most single districts deal with one of the following: power supply, natural resources, water supply, fire protection, sewerage, cemeteries, parks and recreation, libraries, highways, hospitals, and transportation systems, including airports and public transit. *Id.* Do you consider these functions to be better performed by a single district than a multi-purpose regional agency?

2. *Type of tasks performed by single-purpose agencies.* Single-purpose agencies, many of which are established by state law, usually provide mundane services such as transit, waste disposal, or water supply. They rarely intrude into areas that involve social equity issues such as education, housing, or land use. As such, their operations are less likely to create political controversy than would be generated by multi-purpose regional entities empowered to effectuate the regional health, welfare, and safety. Is task-specific governance preferable to general-purpose governance, or is a combination of both forms of governance desirable? How do you account for the increase in single-purpose entities in metropolitan areas during the last half of the 20th century? Does the nature of the functions performed by task-specific districts or public authorities suggest a reason why their performance has been delegated to different territorial scales?

3. *Effect of the proliferation of single-purpose agencies on regional governance?* Would the opponents of regional government favor special purpose governance? See Frug, *Beyond Regional Government*, 115 Harv. L. Rev. 1763, 1781–84 (2002) (arguing that governance by special purpose entities strengthens fractured local governance and is justified on grounds of efficiency rather than equity); Reynolds, *Local Governments and Regional Governance*, 39 Urb. Law. 483, 517–23 (2007) (pointing out that regional special districts cannot substitute for multi-purpose regional governments and operate so as to reduce regionalism).

4. *Criticism of special districts.* Special districts, while performing necessary functions in the context of fragmented local governments, have a number of imperfections. Due to their narrow focus, single-purpose districts do not coordinate the implementation of their function readily with other governmental entities, especially in a regional context. Reynolds, *supra*, at 511. Many operate without sufficient oversight and are detached from the citizenry. *Id.* at 513. They have been criticized as expanding their usually narrow, specific jurisdictions into the areas of general purpose governments and are susceptible to special interest capture. See Galvan, *Wrestling with MUDs to Pin Down the Truth About Special Districts*, 75 Fordham L. Rev. 3041, 3057–62 (2007); Zale, *Local Government Formation and Boundary Change in Texas: A Post-Harvey Assessment,* 8 HLRe 105, 115, 124 (2018). Further, special districts eviscerate home rule by operating with immunity from local regulations and by taking over functions that otherwise would be performed by local

governments). See Reynolds, *Home Rule, Extraterritorial Impact, and the Region*, 86 Denv. U. L. Rev. 1271, 1298–1302 (2009); Reynolds, *Local Governments and Regional Governance*, 39 Urb. Law. 483, 512–17 (2007).

5. *Regional transportation authorities*. A number of states have created regional transportation authorities to provide transit solutions on a metropolitan scale. In some jurisdictions, the creation of a number of separate public authorities with transportation functions have impeded coherent regional transit solutions. In Florida's Tampa Bay area, for example, seven different public bodies have been charged with developing transportation solutions. See Long, *One Bay Area, One Transit Voice*, Tampa Bay Times, May 8, 2016. Voters have sometimes balked at paying taxes to support regional transit. In 2012, voters rejected a proposed one percent transportation sales tax to fund transportation improvements in the 10-county Atlanta metro area, but recent trends suggest that population growth and traffic gridlock are causing the electorate to view the funding of regional mass transit systems more favorably. In addition, the connection between rail transit and a competitive economy has not been lost on local leaders such as Charlotte Nash, Chair of the Gwinnett County Commission. It was speculated that Gwinnett County was not competitive in Amazon's bidding process for a second headquarter because it had no possible sites served by rail transit. See Saporta, *Gwinnett's Charlotte Nash on MARTA: 'We Are Ready to Roll'*, Saporta Rep., Maria's Metro (Aug. 6, 2018), https://saportareport.com/gwinnett's-charlotte-nash-on-marta-we-are-ready-to-roll/.

Taxation powers granted to the Northern Virginia Transportation Authority were invalidated in *Marshall v. Northern Va. Transp. Auth.*, 657 S.E.2d 71 (Va. 2008). The Authority, comprised of various elected and appointed officials, was granted the power to impose regional taxes and fees at its own discretion. The Supreme Court of Virginia held that the state's constitution prohibited the delegation of taxing authority to the Authority because the General Assembly's taxing power could not reside in a non-elected body such as the Authority. *Id.* at 79. Thus, the court invalidated the taxes and fees that the Authority had imposed, thereby rendering it powerless to finance transportation projects in the manner contemplated by the General Assembly. Setting tolls to be collected for the use of roads, however, can be delegated to administrative bodies pursuant to specific legislative guidance, because they are not taxes. See *Elizabeth River Crossing OpCo, LLC v. Meeks*, 749 S.E.2d 176, 186–92 (Va. 2013).

[4] Councils of Government and Metropolitan Planning Agencies

Regional Councils of Governments and Regional Planning Agencies

Regional agencies are another alternative to the solution of metropolitan governmental problems. Voluntary regional councils of government (COG) and regional planning agencies are the best example, and they are now well established throughout the country. Regional planning agencies are usually organized under state enabling legislation and are usually authorized to adopt an advisory regional plan. Councils of government are organizations voluntarily formed by local governments in the region, although most of their funding has come from federal sources. COGs may be organized under state legislation or through intergovernmental agreements. They carry out regional planning responsibilities in many areas.

Metropolitan Planning Organizations

A metropolitan planning organization (MPO) is another type of regional planning agency, the creation of which is mandated by Congress for the receipt of federal transportation funding. See 23 U.S.C. § 134(d)(1). [The Federal-Aid Highway Act of 1962 first required the creation of MPOs.—Eds.] Congress desired that transportation funding be spent on the basis of metropolitan region-wide plans that involved intergovernmental collaboration. MPOs oversee this planning process. While a MPO can be a free-standing agency or a state agency, most MPOs became part of a COG or a regional planning agency. Today, joint regional council/MPO structures represent the majority of regional agency configurations, particularly in the nation's largest metropolitan areas. Bryan & Wolf, *Soft Regionalism in Action: Examining Voluntary Regional Councils' Structures, Processes and Programs*, 10 Pub. Org. Rev., No. 2 (2010): 99–115. Both the Portland Metro and the Twin Cities Metropolitan Council are designated as their region's MPO. For a history and critique of the structure and management of MPOs, see Sciara, *Metropolitan Transportation Planning: Lessons from the Past, Institutions for the Future,* 83 J. Am. Plan. Ass'n, No. 3 (2017): 262–276.

Evolution and Role of COGS and MPOs

The COG experiment, like the creation of MPOs, was an innovation in regional governance prompted by federal legislation beginning in the 1960s. Concerned about the fragmented delivery of its programs by many local governments, Congress began to use its power of the purse to encourage regional planning and collaboration. Federal planning legislation provided funding for the COGs, and a number of federal statutes gave them important planning responsibilities. A reduction in federal aid in the 1980s and 1990s led to a substantial drop in the number of regional councils.

Transportation planning funding from the Department of Transportation (DOT) has continued. See 23 U.S.C. § 134. Funds for transportation planning also are available under the Clean Air Act. 42 U.S.C. § 7504. Under the Partnership for Sustainable Communities, created in 2009, the DOT, the Department of Housing and Urban Development (HUD), and the U.S. Environmental Protection Agency (EPA) further support regional planning by making grants to help communities integrate transportation and land use, provide affordable housing, and enhance economic development. See Note 2.

Regional councils and planning agencies have become the most dominant form of organization used by local, state, and federal agencies to handle metropolitan level issues and challenges. Bryan & Wolf, *supra*, at 99–100. They reflect the political consensus that some form of regional cooperation is needed for the efficient delivery of certain public services. While the movement for consolidated regional governments and central city annexation has floundered, the public has been receptive to the more limited planning and advisory role played by regional councils.

Transportation Planning

The importance of transportation facilities, such as highways, to land use and development and the availability of federal funding has made transportation planning the most important planning function regional agencies like MPOs and COGs exercise today. Although the relationship is complex and not fully proved, studies tend to show that transportation facilities, such as new interstate highways, influence urban form and development. See Kelly, *The Transportation Land-Use Link*, 9 J. PLAN. LIT., No. 2 (1994): 128–145 (describing studies). The Intermodal Surface Transportation Efficiency Act of 1991 (ISTEA) and its successors, the Transportation Equity Act for the 21st Century (TEA-21) (1998), the Safe, Accountable, Flexible, Efficient Transportation Equity Act: A Legacy for Users (SAFETEA-LU) (2005), the Moving Ahead for Progress in the 21st Century (MAP-21) (2012), and the Fixing America's Surface Transportation Act (FAST Act) (2015) substantially strengthened the established regional transportation process. Congress requires MPOs to develop four-year transportation improvement programs with a priority list of projects and a financial plan for implementation. 23 U.S.C. § 134(i), (j), and (k).

In analyzing projects during the planning process, MPOs are required to consider a number of factors: metropolitan economic vitality; safety and security of transportation systems; accessibility and mobility of people and freight; environment, energy conservation, and quality of life; integration and connectivity across and between modes of transportation; efficient system management; preservation of existing transportation systems; improvement of transportation systems' resiliency and reliability; and travel and tourism enhancement. The environmental planning factor has been enhanced by the requirement to provide for consideration of projects that will "promote consistency between transportation improvements and State and local planned growth and economic development patterns." 23 U.S.C. § 134(h)(1)(J). Thus, the interrelationship between transportation policy and land use planning is formally recognized.

Notes and Questions

1. *Performance targets—new outcomes approach to transportation planning.* A 2009 study by U.S. Government Accountability Office (GAO) concluded that MPO transportation planning should become more performance based in lieu of an emphasis upon compliance with transportation planning rules. See U.S. Government Accountability Office, *Metropolitan Planning Organizations: Options Exist to*

Enhance Transportation Planning Capacity and Federal Oversight 28–29 (2009). In MAP-21, Congress responded by setting national transportation goals and requiring performance based measures to meet these goals. 23 U.S.C. § 134(h)(2)(A). MPOs must establish performance targets that track progress toward reaching the attainment of their critical regional outcomes. 23 U.S.C. § 134(h)(2)(B)(i)(I). A MPO's transportation plan must include a system performance report that assesses the ability of transportation systems to meet the performance targets. 23 U.S.C § 134(i)(2)(C) https://www. planning.dot.gov/documents/MPOStaffing_and_Org_Structures.pdf. [https://perma.cc/SXT-8-E9V6.] A 2017 DOT report indicated that nearly 90% of MPOs have incorporated performance measures for their long-range transportation plan and 34% of MPOs have established them for their Transportation Improvement Program. *U.S. Dep't of Transp., MPO Staffing and Organizational Structures 7.1.* (Oct. 2017), https://www.perma.cc/SXT8-E9V6.

The 2009 GAO study highlighted that most MPOs do not implement the transportation projects for which they planned. Because localities in most states make land use decisions, MPOs face the further challenge of integrating land use decisions into transportation planning. *Id.* at 19. Will MAP-21's performance measure framework strengthen MPO's planning functions? Will this framework enhance transportation planning on a regional basis?

2. *Sustainable communities regional planning grant program.* In 2009 HUD, DOT, and EPA formed an interagency partnership to coordinate and better align federal investments in communities throughout the country. The Partnership jointly develops programs and makes grants to meet multiple community goals relating to housing, transportation, environmental protection, and climate change. The Partnership is guided by six principles: (1) provide more transportation choices, (2) promote equitable, affordable housing, (3) increase economic competitiveness, (4) support existing communities, (5) leverage federal investment, and (6) value communities and neighborhoods. *HUD-DOT-EPA Partnership for Sustainable Communities*, available at https://www.brookings.edu/on-the-record/what-comes-next-for-our-metro-nation-the-new-forces-driving-regionalism/. For the Partnership's Fifth Anniversary Report, see [https://perma.cc/8XZE-UQL3].

3. *Role of COGs and MPOs in addressing urban sprawl and sustainability issues.* Councils of Government have been instrumental in addressing urban sprawl and sustainability issues by encouraging more compact developments and alternative transportation options. The Sacramento Region Blueprint Transportation/Land Use Study (2007) (available at [https://perma.cc/L5VW-ACX5]) has been viewed as instrumental in the adoption of California legislation known as SB 375 (Cal. Gov't Code § 65080 et seq.), which is designed to reduce greenhouse gases through improved land use practices that reduce vehicle miles traveled and curb sprawl. Comment, *Promise, Compromise and the New Urban Landscape*, 27 UCLA J. Envtl. L. & Pol'y 371, 383 (2009). To what extent should COGs and regional planning agencies play a role in engaging the public to influence new legislative developments to address regional issues involving economic development, social equity, or

environmental protection? For a discussion of SB 375, see INSTITUTE FOR LOCAL GOVERNMENT, *The Basics of SB 375*, available at [https://perma.cc/XNY8-4FH7], and CAL. GOV'T CODE § 14522.1 (Governor's Signing Message). For a discussion of the history and role of MPOs, see Note, *MPOS and the Integration of Transportation and Land Use Planning*, 27 VA. ENVTL. L. J. 275 (2009).

C. Neighborhood Government and Citizen Participation

Citizen participation in local government has a long history. It has varied from consultation and advice to the formation of citizen and neighborhood organizations with a formal role in the governmental decision making process. The reasons for developing neighborhood frameworks and the role of citizen participation have varied with changing governmental priorities and problems. In the 1960s, the federal government adopted programs for urban revitalization and the redistribution of income to lower income neighborhoods. Citizen participation was organized on the neighborhood level as an advocacy process in which lower income groups could participate in government decision making. Citizen participation as an advocacy movement declined with the weakening of participation requirements in federal programs and the weakening of citizen groups devoted to social change. As two noted observers point out, "[t]he election of Ronald Reagan in 1980 spelled an end to federal invocations of the 'neighborhood movement' and associated support for citizen participation." Fainstein & Fainstein, *Citizen Participation in Local Government, in* PUBLIC POLICY ACROSS STATES AND COMMUNITIES 223, 235 (1985).

The decline in federal incentives for neighborhood initiatives, however, has not diminished a movement towards more neighborhood level governance to improve the livability and character of neighborhoods. Dissatisfaction with local governance, especially in large urban areas, has led to a demand for institutionalizing neighborhood control over local environments. Calls for greater local governmental decentralization have been accompanied by the proliferation of community organizations, community associations, homeowners associations, downtown business improvement districts, and other districts to provide more localized services than traditional local governments undertake. Shragger, *The Limits of Localism*, 100 MICH. L. REV. 371, 380–81 (2001).

In response to the desire for greater neighborhood involvement in local government decision making, cities have institutionalized their own department-level agencies to focus solely on neighborhood empowerment. See, e.g., Los Angeles (Department of Neighborhood Empowerment); Seattle (Department of Neighborhood); Portland, Oregon, (Office of Community and Civic Life). It is the role of these departments to facilitate citizen participation, to preserve and enhance a diversity of neighborhoods, empower people to make contributions to their neighborhood and to improve communication among citizens, neighborhood associations, and city agencies.

Neighborhood Government in Los Angeles

In 1999, Los Angeles voters adopted a new charter that serves as a model for promoting citizen participation in government. See Fulton & Shigley, *Putting Los Angeles Together*, GOVERNING, at 20 (June 2000) (describing the charter reform movement and the new role created by the charter for neighborhood groups). The charter created a Department of Neighborhood Empowerment charged with the responsibility of preparing a plan for a "citywide system of neighborhood councils." LOS ANGELES CITY CHARTER, §§ 900, 901. It vests the Department with a number of duties, including the responsibility to establish the method by which neighborhood council boundary lines are drawn. *Id.* § 904. The charter grants a Board of Neighborhood Commissioners appointed by the Mayor with responsibility for policy setting and oversight. *Id.* § 902.

The City of Los Angeles provides official certification to neighborhood councils that petition for such certification and submit an organization plan and by-laws. *Id.* § 906. Certification requires that neighborhood council membership be open to everyone who lives, works or owns property in the neighborhood (stakeholders) and the development of a system for communication between the council and the stakeholders. *Id.* Councils must also show that their membership reflects the diverse interests within their area. *Id.* The Department provides assistance for neighborhoods seeking certification and arranges training for the neighborhood councils' officers and staff. *Id.* § 901. For an analysis of whether diversity within the community and dissimilarity between the community and the city increase the likelihood of early neighborhood council formation, see Jun, *Event History Analysis of the Formation of Los Angeles Neighborhood Councils*, 47 URB. AFF. REV., No. 1 (2007): 107–122.

The neighborhood empowerment charter provisions were designed to make government more responsive to local needs and to promote greater citizen participation in governance. *Id.* § 900. Although the councils play only an advisory role, *id.*, they provide input prior to City Council actions on matters of local concern. *Id.* § 907. They communicate with stakeholders on a regular basis and may hold public hearings prior to City Council decision making, if delegated this power by the City Council. *Id.* §§ 906, 908. Each neighborhood council may present an annual list of priorities for the city budget. *Id.* § 909. The councils also monitor city services delivered to their local jurisdictions. *Id.* § 910. For an analysis of the types of activities in which Los Angeles neighborhood councils engage, see Jun & Musso, *Participatory Governance and the Spatial Representation of Neighborhood Issues*, 49 URB. AFF. REV., No. 1 (2013): 71–110. See also Chemerinsky & Kleiner, *Federalism from the Neighborhood Up: Los Angeles's Neighborhood Councils, Minority Representation, and Democratic Legitimacy*, 32 YALE L. & POL'Y REV. 569 (2014) (crediting councils with serving as a check on city operations and bringing underrepresented groups into the political process).

Other Neighborhood Governmental Structures

Some cities have created additional layers of neighborhood governance between the city department level and neighborhood associations. In Portland, Oregon institutionalization of neighborhood control begins at the basic neighborhood association level. Neighborhood associations receive formal recognition upon meeting standards for neighborhood public involvement. Portland's neighborhood and business association system includes seven district coalitions that coordinate activities from the 95 neighborhood associations and the 45 business associations. For a review of legal mechanisms used to foster neighborhood collaborative planning, see Salsich, *Grassroots Consensus Building and Collaborative Planning*, 3 Wash. U. J. L. & Pol'y 709, 709–10 (2000).

Integrated Approach to Community Development

By focusing on entire neighborhoods, as opposed to a specific governmental function, a city-wide Department of Neighborhoods can bring an integrated approach to community development. Seattle's Department of Neighborhood, for example, operates neighborhood service centers that provide one-stop service delivery for the purchase of pet licenses, passport processing, or the payment of utility services, fines, or traffic tickets. Coordinators located at these service centers help citizens and organizations find the information they need to access city, county and state programs and services. They also serve as consultants to other city agencies and brief them on neighborhood aspirations and concerns. J. Diers, Neighborhood Power: Building Community the Seattle Way 44–48 (2004). Established in 2011, Houston's Department of Neighborhoods contains four subdivisions, covering such areas as gang prevention outreach and blighted residential property reduction, which assist its "super neighborhoods." See http://www.houstontx.gov/abouthouston/snc.

Neighborhood Participation Project Areas

In Portland, Oregon recognized neighborhood associations may make recommendations to any city agency on issues that affect the livability, safety or economic viability of the neighborhood. Areas of invited participation broadly include "land use, housing, community facilities, human resources, social and recreational programs, traffic and transportation, environmental quality and public safety." Portland City Code, § 3.96.030(B)(1).

Seattle's Neighborhood Matching Program has achieved recognition as one of the most innovative local government programs in the United States. It builds social relationships and connections in the process of making neighborhood-specific physical improvements. Communities match city funds with neighborhood resources, a large portion of which comes from volunteer labor. The funds have been used for a variety of purposes including a wheelchair accessible playground, a community school, mural paintings to combat graffiti, reforestation with native plants, wetland restoration, the conversion of asphalt to green space and the erection of the Fremont Troll sculpture to spark economic development. The nature of the program enables people to get involved in their neighborhoods without necessarily attending meetings and to make short term commitments in support of time-limited projects. J. Diers, *supra*, at 55–58 (2004). Since 1988, $49 million in city funds have been allocated to the matching program with a community match of nearly $72 million. Seattle Department of Neighborhoods, Neighborhood Matching Fund 2016 Guidelines, available at https://www.seattle.gov/Documents/Departments/Neighborhoods/NMF/2016%20NMF%20Guidelines_FINAL.pdf.

Citizen participation particularly thrives in the areas of zoning, planning, economic development, and capital improvements where the neighborhood citizenry desires to participate in decision making that directly impacts their neighborhoods. The City of Atlanta values its organized program of neighborhood development that provides for citizen involvement in land use planning and zoning. Neighborhood planning units that geographically encompass one or a few neighborhoods and include all areas of the city may recommend an action, policy or a comprehensive plan to the city that affects the livability of neighborhoods. Likewise, in New York City, 59 community boards (CBs) play an important advisory role in land use and zoning issues. These CBs also are empowered to make recommendations in the City's budget process and to address any issue that affects their community. N.Y.C. Mayor's Community Affairs Unit, About Community Boards, [https://perma.cc/DX3R-KEVT].

Five Models of Citizen Participation

An early analysis of five models of citizen participation, Schmandt, *Decentralization: A Structural Imperative, in* Neighborhood Control in the 1970s, at 17 (G. Frederickson ed., 1973), still provides a useful tool for analyzing how participation and control at the neighborhood governance level might be institutionalized or organized.

1. *The exchange model.*

> This model encompasses the decentralization devices for informing, advising, and interacting; in short, for communicating. Ideally, the process represents a two-way flow. Information about city plans, programs, and opportunities is made available to neighborhood residents through field offices, and feedback is passed upward to the relevant points in the bureaucratic structure. The same is true with respect to advice. . . . [*Id.* at 19.]

This method works well with groups and classes that identify with established agency goals, but it is not useful with lower class neighborhoods whose residents suspect manipulation by the bureaucratic structure.

2. *The bureaucratic model.*

> The bureaucratic model involves the delegation of authority to subordinate civil servants in the neighborhood. This delegation may take two forms: functional and territorial. In the first instance, power is vested in locality-based officials along functional lines. . . . In the second instance, authority over a mix of functions is placed in a district or neighborhood manager, with personnel administering the individual services or programs reporting to him. [*Id.* at 20–21.]

Several difficulties impede the effectiveness of this model. It interferes with the depersonalization demanded by bureaucratic system. It interferes with the depersonalization demanded by bureaucratic system. It gives the neighborhood managers to direct ties to the neighborhood. It leads these managers into protective and defensive positions when faced with a hostile lower class constituency.

3. *Modified bureaucratic model.* Under this model, the responsibilities of the neighborhood manager flow in two directions, to his superiors and to a neighborhood council representative of neighborhood residents. For example, the council might be given limited powers to pass on personnel appointments and to decide on the level of neighborhood services. Again, there are difficulties.

> One of the more evident and typical problems is the difficult position of the neighborhood manager under such an arrangement. An administrator invariably operates within a set of varying expectations. His superiors, his subordinates, and the organization's clientele all perceive his role in different ways. . . . In the case of the bureaucratic official assigned to a neighborhood, the divergent expectations of the resident council and the service personnel could lead to severe role conflict. [*Id.* at 23.]

4. *The development model.* Schmandt notes that minority group leaders, convinced

> that the poor cannot win over city hall and the established bureaucracy, . . . have turned to approaches that bypass the regular political and administrative institutions of the community and look at the neighborhood itself as a framework for control. One such approach is represented by the community development or neighborhood corporation chartered by the state, or federal government, and controlled by the residents. Incorporating physical and civic development, the new structural mechanism encompasses both economic activities and service delivery functions. [*Id.* at 24.]

The corporation may sponsor housing and development projects and contract with the city to administer public services. Federal legislation authorizes municipalities to make federal community development grants available to neighborhood corporations. The neighborhood corporation imposes new constraints. By taking on business and service functions, the residents become producers as well as consumers of public and private services. "The assumption of this responsibility necessarily places constraints on their freedom of action. For as board members and managers, they must relate not only inwardly to the constituents they serve but also outwardly to the established bureaucracies and funding agencies on which they are dependent for cooperation and resources." *Id.* at 24. See also Fainstein, *The Rationale for Neighborhood Planning*, 16 POL'Y STUD. J., No. 2 (1987): 384–392.

5. *Governmental model.* Under this model, legal powers are delegated to neighborhood subunits. Neighborhood government faces the same problems as a traditional bureaucracy and has the same needs for organizational maintenance, integration, adaptability, goal achievement, and stability and predictability in its operations. It must also set policy and develop program expertise.

Schmandt comments:

> [Over time] a neighborhood government will become more concerned with its survival and enhancement needs and more bureaucratic. . . . Similarly, whatever innovative potential the new structure may have, it is likely to be quickly submerged in the task of maintaining the enterprise. The inability of citizen self-help organizations of recent years to develop approaches to service needs and problems essentially different from the more traditional agencies attests to this likelihood. [*Id.* at 26.]

Schmandt does see some advantages in the governmental model, including the capacity to develop indigenous leadership and the provision of a governmental structure that is legitimate in neighborhood eyes.

Notes and Questions

1. *The role of neighborhoods in proposals to remake the city.* Would you suggest a form of neighborhood government for your city, and if so, what would you suggest? Before considering this question, review the proposals in the Notes that follow.

Professor Gerald Frug is a leading proponent of a movement to redefine cities by dissolving legal boundaries in favor of collaborations by people with similar interests throughout a region. Neighborhoods would elect representatives to serve on new regional legislatures in the "city as situated subject" model. These regional legislatures would promote inter-local collaboration in land use decisions and delivery of public services. In the "city as post-modern subject" model, neighborhoods identified by place would be de-emphasized in favor of coalitions of people uniting around common problems. G. Frug, CITY MAKING: BUILDING COMMUNITIES WITHOUT BUILDING WALLS 73–91, 111 (1999). See also Poindexter, *Legal Empowerment of the Neighborhood*, 33 URB. STUD. 1821, 1825 (1996) (proposing that the "legal concept of the city be dismantled (in favor of new political neighborhoods) to allow all residents to create the communities they desire"). Professor Poindexter would repeal local government secession laws, which generally require the consent of the municipality to be left behind, and permit residents to draw the boundaries of new "political neighborhoods."

For an argument that reform of local government should be combined with creation of "regionally bounded local governments" capable of deciding land use issues of "regional significance," collecting and distributing revenues "to promote greater equalization of local fiscal capacity and local service quality" and providing "region-wide physical infrastructure," see Briffault, *The Local Government Boundary Problem in Metropolitan Areas*, 48 STAN. L. REV. 1115 (1996). For a discussion of how neighborhood councils might be structured to achieve meaningful civic participation, see Parlow, *Civic Republicanism, Public Choice Theory, and Neighborhood Councils: A New Model for Civic Engagement*, 79 U. COLO. L. REV. 137, 166–83 (2008); Parlow, *Revolutions in Local Democracy? Neighborhood Councils and Broadening Inclusion in the Local Political Process*, 16 MICH. J. RACE & L. 81 (Fall 2010) (arguing that neighborhood councils provide civic engagement opportunities for marginalized groups).

2. *New York City's Community Boards.* Each Community Board (CB) may consist of up to 50 unsalaried members. City Council members nominate one half of the CB members within their district, and the Borough President of each borough selects and appoints the CB members who must reside in the community or have some active interest in it. NYC Mayor's Community Affairs Unit, *supra*. Where do the Boards fit in Schmandt's categories? See also Lowe, *Examination of Governmental Decentralization in New York City and a New Model for Implementation*, 27 HARV. J. LEGIS. 173 (1990) (proposing a decentralized government for New York City of 70–100 local unit councils with power to influence delivery of services, recommend capital improvements, and review proposed land use changes).

3. *District of Columbia.* The "home rule" act for the District of Columbia adopted by Congress in 1973 provides for the creation of Advisory Neighborhood Commissions ("ANC") whose written recommendations concerning proposed government action are to be given "great weight during the deliberations by the government entity," which "is required to articulate its decision in writing." D.C. CODE § 1-309.10 (d)(3)(A), (B). For a history of ANCs and their functions, including a cost/benefit analysis of ANC functions, see White, *Functions of Neighborhood Advisory Groups*, 10 NONPROFIT & VOLUNTARY Q., No. 2 (1981): 27–39.

Kopff v. District of Columbia Alcoholic Beverage Control Bd., 381 A.2d 1372 (D.C. 1977), held that the neighborhood commission's role was advisory and that the board did not have to give the same weight to a commission's recommendations that it gives to its construction of its own enabling statute. To hold otherwise would interfere with "the established pattern of governmental relationships" and would come "perilously close to, if not cross into, the realm of improper delegation of governmental authority to a private party." For more on this delegation problem, see Chapter 9. The court then interpreted the "great weight" requirement:

> It means . . . than an agency [governmental body] must elaborate, with precision, its response to the ANC [neighborhood commission] issues and concerns. It is a statutory method of forcing an agency to come to grips with the ANC view—to deal with it in detail, without slippage. An agency must focus particular attention not only on the issues and concerns as

> pressed by an ANC, but also on the fact that the ANC, as a representative body, is the group making the recommendation. That is, the agency must articulate why the particular ANC itself, given its vantage point, does—or does not—offer persuasive advice under the circumstances. [*Id.* at 1384.]

What must an agency do to meet this requirement? May an agency finding be reversed if it declines to follow an ANC recommendation? Does this interpretation fatally dilute the role of the commissions in agency decision making? For a case indicating that an agency need only articulate its response to a commission recommendation but need not follow it, see *Upper Georgia Ave. Planning Comm'n v. Alcoholic Beverage Control Bd.*, 500 A.2d 987 (D.C. App. 1985). Although the board of zoning adjustment (BZA) must make explicit reference to ANC issues and concerns in its written findings, the "great weight requirement" does not require it to treat the views of nearby property owners impacted by its decisions as material or make explicit reference to them in its findings. See *Lovendusky v. District of Columbia Bd. of Zoning Adjustment*, 852 A.2d 927 (D.C. App. 2004). See also *Quincy Park Condo. Unit Owners' Ass'n v. District of Columbia Bd. of Zoning Adjustment*, 4 A.3d 1283 (D.C. 2010) (BZA's denial of an ANC's request for rehearing on its grant of zoning relief to a developer was not a breach of its duty to give "great weight" to ANC's concerns, as D.C. Code § 1-309.10(d)(3)(A) required ANC's position to be considered as part of BZA's deliberative process, not after that process was complete).

See also *Metropole Condo. Ass'n v. District of Columbia Bd. of Zoning Adjustment*, 141 A.3d 1079, 1086–87 (2016) (BZA not required to give "great weight" to the recommendation of an ANC, but it is required to acknowledge the concerns raised by the ANC and articulate why those concerns were followed or rejected). But see *Kalorama Citizens Ass'n v. District of Columbia Bd. of Zoning Adjustment*, 934 A.2d 393 (D.C. 2007) (great weight test not met by BZA's failure to articulate with particularity and precision why it rejected ANC's position stated in a written report, but BZA was not required to give any weight to an ANC issue not addressed in its written report).

4. For additional literature on citizen participation and neighborhood government, see X. Briggs & E. Mueller, From Neighborhood to Community (1997); J. Diers, *supra*; W. Rohe & L. Gates, Planning with Neighborhoods (1985); Martz, *Neighborhood-Based Planning* (Am. Plan. Ass'n, Planning Advisory Serv. Rep. No. 455, 1995); McFarlane, *When Inclusion Leads to Exclusion: The Uncharted Terrain of Community Participation in Economic Development*, 66 Brook. L. Rev. 861 (2000); Miller, *Legal Neighborhoods*, 37 Harv. Envtl. L. Rev. 105 (2013); Rodriguez & Shoked, *Comparative Local Government Law in Motion: How Different Local Government Law Regimes Affect Global Cities' Bike Share Plans*, 42 Fordham Urb. L.J. 123, 161–65 (2014); Vidal, *Can Community Development Re-Invent Itself*, 6 J. Am. Plan. Ass'n, no. 4 (1997): 429–438; *Symposium, Paul Davidoff and Advocacy Planning in Retrospect*, 60 J. Am. Plan. Ass'n 139 (1994); Zhang, *Boundaries of Power: Politics of Urban Preservation in Two Chicago Neighborhoods*, 47 Urb. Aff. Rev., No. 4 (2011): 511–540.

Problem 3-2

You are an advisor to a recently elected mayor of a large urban city. During her campaign, the mayor stressed the need for more neighborhood input in economic development and community revitalization projects. At present, the city's charter authorizes neighborhood planning units (NPUs) that cover geographic areas defined by the city's Department of Planning. Generally, one or a few neighborhoods comprise a NPU, which is empowered to provide advice on comprehensive planning. In practice, however, NPUs review and make suggestions on zoning and land use matters that affect the livability of their neighborhoods. On a few occasions, when all of the NPUs have joined together to argue forcefully against certain city proposals, they have convinced the City Council to block mayoral economic development initiatives. The mayor expressed to you the concerns voiced by her chief operating officer to the effect that the NPU process is time-consuming and provides a forum for querulous complaining from a few misdirected community protagonists. The mayor also reported that other city mayors believe she will be unsuccessful in implementing her vision of a vibrant and revitalized city without strong neighborhood involvement and support. She expressed interest in some of the more expanded programs that Seattle and Portland have implemented that involve input from many forms of neighborhood associations, including non-profit organizations and local chambers of commerce. She has asked for your advice on the Schmandt models of citizen participation and the issues of inclusion, voting, and participation alternatives raised above. What would you recommend?

D. Privatization of Local Public Services and Government

The neighborhood government alternative discussed in the previous section features the delegation of one or more government activities to public or non-profit private entities smaller than municipalities. Still another alternative, which also features delegation, is the privatization movement through which government assets and/or activities are transferred to the private sector. While privatization tends to be linked to the administrations of former British Prime Minister Margaret Thatcher and former President Ronald Reagan, it has been a factor from the beginning of the American experience. DelFiandra, *The Growth of Prison Privatization and the Threat Posed by 42 U.S.C. § 1983*, 38 Duq. L. Rev. 591, 593 (2000); Morris, *The Impact of Constitutional Liability on the Privatization Movements After Richardson v. McKnight*, 52 Vand. L. Rev. 489, 490 (1999) (Christopher Columbus was a private contractor for the Spanish Monarchs).

The President's Commission on Privatization established by former President Ronald Reagan identified three standard techniques for privatizing the delivery of public services: (1) selling government assets, (2) contracting with private firms to provide goods and services for the public, and (3) distributing to eligible persons, vouchers that can be redeemed for goods and services such as food and housing. President's Commission of Privatization: Toward a More Effective Government 1–2 (1988), discussed in Salsich, *Solutions to the Affordable Housing Crisis: Perspectives on Privatization*, 28 John Mar. L. Rev. 263, 275–77 (1995). A survey under the auspices of the American State Administration Project (ASAP) showed that more than two-thirds of state agencies now use service contracts, and over one-fourth of those agencies allocate over 20 percent of their budgets to such form of privatization. *Continuity and Change in Executive Leadership*, 68 Pub. Admin. Rev. Supp. (2008): S29–S33. Further, a 2017 study showed that private companies increased their sales in 2017 to the federal government in comparison to 2016, with an expected increase coming in future years from the Department of Defense. See *2017 Government Contractor Survey*, Professional Services Council 6 (2018), available at [https://perma.cc/HG5P-J3TE].

Supporters of privatization of services seek "to increase economic efficiency at the level of individual firms and markets; to raise revenue for government activities; and to promote distributional and political ends." Linneman & Megbolugbe, *Privatization and Housing Policy*, 31 Urb. Stud., No. 4/5 (1994): 635, 639. About one-half of state agency executives in the ASAP survey reported an improvement in service delivery through outsourcing. See *Continuity and Change in Executive Leadership, supra*, at S33.

Despite the increased faith in markets and waning support for public institutions in recent years, public law scholars, who focus on the relationship between government and private citizens, express concerns that privatization will erode public law norms in the areas of accountability, due process, and rationality in decision making. See Freeman, *Extending Public Law Norms Through Privatization*, 116 Harv. L. Rev. 1285, 1290 (2003) (arguing that "privatization might extend public values to private actors to reassure public law scholars that mechanisms exist for structuring public-private partnerships in democracy-enhancing ways"). See also Lemos, *Patriotic Philanthropy? Financing the State with Gifts to the Government*, 106 Calif. L. Rev. 1130 (2018) (arguing that the increasing trend of reliance upon private money to finance particular governmental projects raises concerns about the democratic process, equality, and government capacity, because such gifts may entail private influence over the public sector).

Privatization raises concerns about political accountability, which has been defined as the "amenability of a government policy or activity to monitoring through the political process." Beermann, *Privatization and Political Accountability*, 28 Fordham Urb. L.J. 1507, 1507 (2001). When private actors become responsible for governmental activities that involve governmental discretion and power over individuals, serious questions about accountability arise. Some forms of privatization raise more accountability issues than others. Governmental functions or those deemed to be inherently public in nature pose the greatest accountability issues. Some functions may be found to be non-delegable. Taxation, the power of eminent domain and the exercise of the police power fall into this category. Judicial drawing of the line between public and private frequently has been unsuccessful, however. As public-private contracts have become more common with a blurring of public and private functions, courts have been faced with the necessity of making decisions based on precedents formed in the nineteenth century when a much sharper dichotomy existed between the public and private realms. See Cartee, *Behind Closed Doors: An Argument for State Constitutional Standing to Challenge Public-Private Development Corporations*, 76 Ohio St. L. J. 1423, 1428 (2015) (arguing in favor of state constitutional amendments to grant the citizenry standing to contest the constitutionality of public-private development corporations).

As privatization expands, the judiciary will have to lay out constitutional constraints to ensure political accountability. Some scholars are already engaged in exploring questions raised by this necessity. See Beermann, *supra*; Freeman, *supra*; Metzger, *Privatization as Delegation*, 103 Colum. L. Rev. 1367, 1376–77, 1388–94, 1400–01, 1430, 1456 (2003) (arguing that delegations of power to private actors must be structured to preserve constitutional accountability). See also Lee, *Rights at Risk in Privatized Public Housing*, 50 Tulsa L. Rev. 759, 762 (2015) (arguing that privatization of public housing erodes tenants' rights). Political accountability is often difficult to achieve, because commercial transactions differ from public sector arrangements, and public actors, facing public pressures, may be reluctant to enforce available contract remedies. See Epstein, *Contract Theory and the Failures of Public-Private Contracting*, 34 Cardozo L. Rev. 2211, 2215–19 (2013); Singer, *Competitive Public Contracts*, 102 Va. L. Rev. 1297, 1304–05 (2016).

Chicago's lease of 36,000 parking meters for 75 years to a private company to generate a payment of $1.157 billion has been sharply criticized. See Office of the Inspector General, City of Chicago, *An Analysis of the Lease of the City's Parking Meters* (2009), available at http://chicagoinspectorgeneral.org/wp-content/uploads/2011/03/Parking-Meter-Report.pdf [https://perma.cc/XDU7-LUAJ]; Hogan, *Protecting the Public in Public-Private Partnerships: Strategies for Ensuring Adaptability in Concession Contracts*, 2014 Colum. Bus. L. Rev. 420, 430–35, 441–44, 461(2014) (discussing the Chicago parking meter concession agreement and arguing that best practices and substantive limits governing contract terms should be put in place when municipalities lease infrastructure assets over a long term in exchange for upfront monies); Michaels, *Privatization Progeny*, 101 Geo. L.J. 1023, 1080–85 (2013) (pointing out that governments abdicate sovereignty when they lease public facilities for up to 99 years to raise cash for immediate needs); Roin, *Privatization and the Sale of Tax Revenues*, 95 Minn. L. Rev. 1965, 2028–2033 (2011) (arguing that large, up-front cash payments received from jurisdictions entering into privatization contracts, such as Chicago's receipt of $1.156 billion for a 75-year lease of its parking meters, should be placed in an escrow fund to generate an income stream equal to the net taxes or fees alienated).

Privatization of government regulation, particularly of local land use planning and zoning, has attracted support. The rise of the residential common interest ownership community, particularly in populous states such as California, Florida, Illinois, New York, Texas and the Washington, D.C. suburbs has spawned proposals to delegate local land use regulatory responsibility to the governing associations of such communities and to neighborhood associations in older neighborhoods. Nelson, *Privatizing the Neighborhood: A Proposal to Replace Zoning with Private Collective Property Rights to Existing Neighborhoods*, 7 Geo. Mason L. Rev. 827 (1999).

The following excerpt provides an additional perspective on privatization.

Metzger, *Privatization as Delegation*

103 Colum. L. Rev. 1367, 1376–77, 1388–94, 1400–01, 1403 (2003)*

[P]rivatization commonly entails not a "retraction" in government but rather a different form of government, one in which private actors wield substantial power over government programs and their participants . . . [A]s a result, government privatization often effectively serves to delegate government power to private entities.

. . . .

Privatization of Public Education.—Public education is a[n] . . . area characterized by recent moves to greater privatization, with an accompanying shift of core educational responsibilities to private hands. Charter schools, private management of public schools by educational management organizations (EMOs), and voucher programs provide the main examples.

Charter schools—the most significant of these initiatives to date are publicly-funded schools allowed to operate free from many of the rules governing traditional public schools. They are also least clearly an instance of privatization; in addition to being publicly funded, they are officially denominated public schools, come into existence as a result of government authorization (the grant of a charter), and are subject to the open admissions requirement applicable to traditional public schools. Yet charter schools also embody substantial private involvement: private individuals or groups initiate the creation of the school; the schools are headed by private boards; and a significant number are managed by EMOs, usually for-profit entities. EMOs also occasionally have won contracts to operate traditional public schools, in some cases managing all or many of a district's schools.

In . . . [the case of charter schools], private entities wield broad control over state-funded education. Charter school boards and EMOs operating charter schools possess considerable latitude over curriculum, discipline policies, and most aspects

---

* Metzger, *Privatization as Delegation*, 103 Colum. L. Rev. 1367, 1376–77, 1388–94, 1400–01, 1403 (2003).

of school operation—indeed, providing this autonomy is the underlying rationale of the charter school movement. EMOs often exercise similarly broad powers when they manage public schools. . . . Further enhancing the power of these private entities are the significant practical obstacles that limit students' ability to transfer schools, particularly during the school year. Moreover, here too exist concerns that the schools' interests may not align with those of students; for example, schools receive a set amount per student, thus creating incentives for them to avoid or expel students who require more expensive educational services. An additional danger, particularly with regard to charter schools . . . is that the schools' general freedom from oversight may lead to public funds being used to foster educational agendas that the public has refused to support.

Complicating the picture, however, is the factor of choice. Enrollment in charter and voucher schools is voluntary, and students have the option of remaining in their regular neighborhood or district school or perhaps attending public school in another district. Moreover, students usually are given the ability to transfer to another public school if their school becomes privately managed, as are teachers. The main effect of these privatization initiatives, from another perspective, is to empower parents and students, particularly given the prevalence of charter schools . . . in urban areas with perennially failing public schools. Interestingly, however, parental choice also represents yet a further way in which these measures privatize public education; decisions about educational content and quality become a personal rather than collective responsibility, thereby creating schools that, in essence, are private communities of like-minded families. [Charter schools are considered further in Chapter 9—Eds.].

. . . Private Prisons.—[Another] example, private prisons, is one of the most remarked-upon examples of government privatization. Extensive privatization characterized incarceration in the nineteenth century, with private entrepreneurs and companies managing prisons and indeed "leasing" convicts from the state. By 1940, however, this sort of private involvement had all but disappeared, largely in response to exposure of the extremely harsh conditions under which inmates were being held by their private jailors. Over the last two decades, pressures on governments to house expanding prison populations and improve prison conditions without substantially increasing costs kindled a rebirth of interest in private prisons. Governments turned to private entities not only to build prison facilities but to operate them. In 2001, 12.3% of all federal prisoners and 5.8% of all state prisoners, approximately 92,000 inmates, were housed in private prison facilities. Private prisons tend to be medium and low security facilities, and many community-based facilities (such as group juvenile homes and halfway houses) are also privately run.

Private prison operators exercise enormous coercive powers over the inmates in their custody. While their contracts with public prison authorities set out detailed requirements regarding prison conditions and operation, incarceration by its nature entails exercise of substantial discretion in closed environments with little public visibility. Given their extreme dependence and vulnerability, prisoners face a particularly acute potential for harm from abuse of these powers. Moreover, most private prisons are run or owned by for-profit corporations, which have a financial incentive to cut costs—for example, by hiring inexperienced and therefore cheaper personnel, understaffing, or failing to provide adequate medical care and other services. Such practices can lead to violation of inmates' rights. But the case against private prisons is easy to overstate, given the widespread problems and deficiencies in many public prisons. Indeed, factors such as private prisons' greater exposure to damage awards and contractual obligations arguably make them in some ways more accountable than public prisons. . . .

. . . .

Modern privatized government does not fit easily within the paradigms of U.S. constitutional law. A fundamental tenet of constitutional law posits an "essential dichotomy" between public and private, with only public or government actors being subject to constitutional restraints. With rare exception, the Constitution "erects no shield against merely private conduct, however discriminatory or wrongful." The reigning constitutional paradigm thus strictly compartmentalizes society into public and private spheres, and does not acknowledge any substantial blurring between the two.

As a result, the move to greater government privatization poses a serious threat to the principle of constitutional accountability. Although not often articulated, this principle also lies at the bedrock of U.S. constitutional law. To begin with, it embodies the core idea of constitutional supremacy and constitutional government, namely that the Constitution imposes restrictions on government that the political branches lack ability to alter. Crucially, these restrictions apply not only when the formal organs of government act, but also whenever government power is exercised. This broad scope of application reflects the proposition that the Constitution encompasses all "actions of the political body denominated a State, by whatever instruments or in whatever modes that action may be taken," coupled with the recognition that "the abstract thing denominated a State" can exert its powers only through the actions of persons. Restricting the Constitution's ambit to apply only when the government formally acts would avoid the difficulties in determining whether a private entity is wielding government power; doing so might also yield programmatic benefits, in that private entities and government could pursue the most efficient and effective forms of program operation unconcerned with constitutional requirements. But such an approach would significantly eviscerate the concept of a constitutionally constrained government. Adequately guarding against abuse of public power requires application of constitutional protections to every exercise of state authority, regardless of the formal public or private status of the actor involved: "It surely cannot be that government, state or federal, is able to evade the most solemn obligations imposed in the Constitution by simply resorting to the corporate form" and thereby transferring operation of government programs to private hands.

. . . .

The danger is that handing over government programs to private entities will operate to place these programs outside the ambit of constitutional constraints, given the Constitution's inapplicability to "private" actors.

One of the most active areas of current privatization efforts is local jails, which raises serious public accountability issues. The following case explores legal issues raised by the transfer of prisoners to privately operated prisons:

State ex rel. Curtis v. Litscher

256 Wis. 2d 787, 650 N.W.2d 43 (2002)

ROGGENSACK, J.

The seven inmate-petitioners (inmates) in this certiorari action were accused of participating in a riot/hostage situation at a private, contract prison facility located in Whiteville, Tennessee. The inmates claim, and the circuit court found, that a disciplinary hearing held at the Whiteville facility on December 9, 1999 was procedurally defective and that the Wisconsin Department of Corrections (DOC) improperly relied on the findings from that hearing in subsequent proceedings. We conclude that we have authority to review the December 9, 1999 disciplinary hearing by certiorari and that, even under DOC's version of events, the Whiteville facility violated its, and DOC's, procedures by selecting a hearing examiner who witnessed the relevant events. Therefore, we invalidate the December 9, 1999 disciplinary hearing and any subsequent hearings or changes in status that relied on the hearing examiner's findings as a basis for the decision. However, we also conclude that DOC may hold administrative confinement hearings and consider the inmates' alleged conduct to the extent that conduct is proved without relying on the findings of the hearing examiner at the December 9, 1999 hearing. Accordingly, we affirm in part and reverse in part the order of the circuit court. [The court's affirmation of the use of evidence outside of the scope of the findings of the hearing examiner is omitted.—Eds.]

BACKGROUND

The seven inmates were confined in a private correctional facility in Whiteville, Tennessee when they were charged with violations of facility rules, classified as major offenses, for allegedly participating in a riot/hostage situation that took place on November 30, 1999. An employee of the Whiteville facility conducted a disciplinary hearing on the charges on December 9, 1999. The staff member who served as the hearing examiner found all seven inmates guilty and penalized them with varying periods of disciplinary segregation.

Before the inmates could serve their time in disciplinary segregation at Whiteville, DOC approved a Program Review Committee (PRC) recommendation that the inmates should be transferred to Supermax Correctional Institution in Boscobel, Wisconsin. The inmates' involvement in the Whiteville uprising was a primary factor in the transfer decisions. After being transferred to Supermax, each of the inmates was placed in administrative confinement as a result of decisions by an Administrative Confinement Review Committee (ACRC). The ACRC decisions were premised, at least in part, on the findings from the December 9, 1999 hearing in Whiteville.

The Whiteville facility's internal disciplinary procedures provide that an inmate subjected to a disciplinary penalty may appeal the hearing examiner's decision to the warden of the facility. All seven inmates pursued this avenue of appeal, raising various claims of procedural error. The warden denied all appeals.

At the same time that the inmates were pursuing their appeals to Whiteville's warden, they were simultaneously seeking review of the Whiteville disciplinary decisions through the Inmate Complaint Review System (ICRS) in Wisconsin and by challenging the PRC and ACRC decisions that relied on the findings of the Whiteville disciplinary proceeding. DOC consistently took the position that the inmates could not obtain review of the Whiteville disciplinary decision by filing an inmate complaint in a Wisconsin prison. Similarly, DOC repeatedly asserted that the inmates could not collaterally challenge the Whiteville proceedings by raising the issues in PRC or ACRC proceedings.

Following the Whiteville warden's unfavorable decisions and the inmates' unsuccessful attempts to obtain administrative review of the Whiteville proceedings through DOC in Wisconsin, two of the seven inmates attempted to obtain review of the Whiteville disciplinary decisions by initiating actions in the Tennessee courts. *See* Wis. Stat. §§ 301.21(2m)(b)[1] and 302.02(3t). Those filings were dismissed with the following explanation: "Please be advised that since you are now a resident of the State of Wisconsin you will need to make your filings in the State of Wisconsin."

Apparently lacking any access to the Tennessee courts, the seven inmates jointly filed a petition for a writ of certiorari on June 13, 2000 in the circuit court for Dane County. The petition states that the inmates "are hereby asking the Court to review the disciplinary decisions and actions of the [Secretary of DOC] and disciplinary officer." The prayer for relief in the petition provides:

> Wherefore, the petitioners respectfully request that a writ of certiorari be granted to bring up for review and determination the proceedings in the matters set forth in this petition, and that upon review and return of that writ, the decision and actions of the [Secretary], the disciplinary committee and the administrative confinement review committee be reversed and adjudged to be null and void.

DOC argued that the circuit court's authority on certiorari does not extend to review of disciplinary decisions made by officials at an out-of-state, private prison.

---

1. Wisconsin Stat. § 301.21(2m)(b) provides:
While in an institution in another state covered by a contract under this subsection, Wisconsin prisoners are subject to all provisions of law and regulation concerning the confinement of persons in that institution under the laws of that state.

The circuit court disagreed, concluding that because the inmates were sentenced by Wisconsin courts, they had the right to seek certiorari review of major disciplinary proceedings in Wisconsin courts when no other avenue of judicial review was available.

On the merits, the circuit court held that the record established that the Whiteville hearing violated the inmates' rights because (1) the hearing examiner was directly involved in the events that gave rise to the charges, and (2) the hearing examiner's report failed to state adequate reasons for the decision. The court invalidated the disciplinary decisions and ordered DOC to conduct new PRC and ACRC hearings for each of the inmates at which DOC would not be permitted to consider the disciplinary charges that were adjudicated on December 9, 1999 or any information relating to the November 30, 1999 uprising at Whiteville.

DISCUSSION

Standard of Review.

We review the decision of the administrative agency, not the decision of the circuit court. Whether the scope of our review reaches the issues raised in a certiorari petition presents a question of law, and if we have authority to reach the issues, we decide *de novo* whether the administrative body acted within its jurisdiction, whether it acted according to applicable law, whether its action was arbitrary and unreasonable, and whether the evidence supported the determination in question.

Availability of Certiorari Review.

DOC first argues that Wisconsin courts do not have authority to review prison disciplinary decisions made at an out-of-state, private prison. Under the circumstances presented in this case, we disagree.

A decision may be reviewed by common law certiorari when no legislative provision establishes how review may be had. Certiorari is the well-established mode of judicial review for inmates of Wisconsin prisons who seek to challenge prison disciplinary decisions. And, although the legislature has provided that judicial review of disciplinary proceedings conducted by an out-of-state, contract prison may proceed in the county of the state where the prison is located. *See* Wis. Stat. § 302.02(3t),[2] unique circumstances in this case precluded this provision from affording the inmates judicial review in Tennessee.

Here, DOC transferred the inmates to a Wisconsin prison immediately after the disciplinary hearing. Once the inmates were returned to Wisconsin, the Tennessee court refused to review their cases. Because no statutory provision for judicial

2. Wisconsin Stat. § 302.02(3t) provides:
Institutions located in other states. For all purposes of discipline and for judicial proceedings, each institution that is located in another state and authorized for use under § 301.21 and the precincts of the institution shall be deemed to be in a county in which the institution is physically located, and the courts of that county shall have jurisdiction of any activity, wherever located, conducted by the institution.

review of a prison disciplinary decision applied to the inmates in this case, we conclude that Wisconsin courts may review the Whiteville disciplinary decision by certiorari.

DOC contends that, regardless of the availability or unavailability of judicial review in the Tennessee courts, our authority does not extend to a review of the disciplinary decisions of a private, out-of-state prison that houses Wisconsin inmates by contract. Again, we disagree. Although DOC has the statutory power to delegate some of its administrative functions to private prison facilities by contract, the contract facility performs those functions as agents of DOC and the State. *See* Wis. Stat. § 301.03(2) (mandating that DOC shall "supervise the custody and discipline of all prisoners"). [The court noted that disciplinary decisions made at and by an out-of-state, private facility become part of the prisoner's record, and may be relied on in later proceedings involving the prisoner.—Eds.] DOC's contract with the private facility in Whiteville neither absolves DOC from ultimate responsibility for the performance of its assigned administrative functions nor precludes Wisconsin courts from conducting certiorari review of the disciplinary hearings in this case. Accordingly, we conclude that we have authority to review the issues raised by the inmates' petition for a writ of certiorari. [The court further found that Wis. Stat. § 302.02(3t) demonstrated a legislative intent that inmates of contract facilities have access to judicial review.—Eds.]

Hearing Procedures.

A determination on certiorari review of whether a prison disciplinary hearing was conducted according to law includes a review of whether the hearing comported with the constitutional requirements of due process. *State ex rel. Meeks*, 289 N.W.2d at 361. However, even in the absence of a claim of constitutional dimension, an agency is required to follow its own procedural rules, and our certiorari inquiry encompasses the question of whether the agency has done so. *See id.* An agency acts beyond its authority when it abandons its own rules. *State ex rel. Riley v. DHSS*, 445 N.W.2d 693, 695 (Ct. App. 1989).

The inmates' petition alleges that the disciplinary hearing conducted by the hearing examiner at the Whiteville facility failed to conform to DOC's and Whiteville's procedures and also violated the inmates' due process rights. One of the inmates' primary contentions is that their December 9, 1999 disciplinary hearing was conducted by a hearing examiner who was directly involved in the riot/hostage situation that gave rise to the various charges. The inmates assert that under both DOC regulations and the internal disciplinary procedures of the Whiteville facility, the inmates have a basic procedural right to a hearing that is conducted by an impartial examiner.

Wisconsin Admin. Code § DOC 303.82 (1999) provides that due process disciplinary hearings shall be conducted by an adjustment committee and that "no person who has personally observed or been a part of an incident which is the subject of a hearing may serve on the committee for that hearing." We note that the Whiteville facility's internal disciplinary procedures contain a similar provision:

Selection of the Board or Hearing Officer

(a) The Disciplinary Board or Hearing Officer will be designated by the Warden/Administrator and will be impartial and fair.

. . . .

(d) Any staff will be disqualified in every case in which they have filed the complaint, participated or witnessed the incident; investigated the incident; is the person in charge of any subsequent review of the decision; or has any personal interest in the outcome.

[The court rejected DOC's argument that there was no evidence in the certiorari record concerning the status of the hearing examiner. The court found that the issue of the hearing examiner's bias was raised in at least some appeals to the warden.—Eds.]

The inmates' allegation of hearing examiner bias and DOC's admission that the hearing examiner was a witness raise significant concerns. First, neither Whiteville nor DOC has authority to conduct a disciplinary hearing that fails to comply with its own duly promulgated procedures. And, because the hearing examiner was a witness to the riot/hostage situation at the Whiteville facility, he should have been disqualified under both Wis. Admin. Code § DOC 303.82 and the Whiteville facility's internal disciplinary procedures. Second, the presence of a biased hearing examiner at a disciplinary hearing concerning a major rule violation raises due process concerns comparable to those addressed by the Wisconsin Supreme Court in *State ex rel. Anderson-El v. Cooke*, 610 N.W.2d 821 (holding that DOC's failure to provide a prisoner with a notice of hearing both violated DOC's procedures and denied the prisoner a fundamental procedural right). Prison hearing procedures that touch on basic procedural rights are enacted for the protection of prisoners, and as the supreme court instructed in *Anderson-El*, failure to follow those types of procedures cannot be considered harmless error. Accordingly, under the facts presented in this case, we decline to conclude that the inmates waived their claims by failing to clearly raise the issue of hearing examiner bias at the hearing itself.

[The court also rejected DOC's argument that the plaintiffs had no constitutional claims because they did not lose good time credits or suffer an extension of their mandatory release date. Again, the court concluded that disciplinary procedures that provide for a neutral and unbiased hearing examiner reach basic procedural rights.—Eds.]

Remedy.

In some past cases involving procedural issues, we have remanded disciplinary decisions and allowed prison officials to supplement a deficient certiorari record, provided that the remand did not involve the taking of new substantive evidence against the prisoner. However, as a matter of judicial economy, and considering the already lengthy history of these proceedings, we can see no benefit to be obtained from remanding this case for another round of disciplinary hearings. Accordingly, we affirm the circuit court's remedial order to the extent that it invalidated (1) the inmates' December 9, 1999 disciplinary hearing and (2) any subsequent hearing or change in status that relied on the findings from that hearing. DOC shall expunge any reference to such proceedings from the inmates' records. . . .

CONCLUSION

We conclude that we have authority to review the December 9, 1999 disciplinary hearings by certiorari and that, even under DOC's version of events, the Whiteville facility violated its, and DOC's, disciplinary procedures by selecting a hearing examiner who witnessed the relevant events. Therefore, we invalidate the December 9, 1999 disciplinary hearing and any subsequent hearing or change in status that relied on the findings from that hearing as a basis for the decision. . . .

Notes and Questions

1. *Certiorari review.* "Wisconsin courts have general subject matter jurisdiction that ordinarily permits them to review, by certiorari, disciplinary decisions regarding Wisconsin inmates." *State ex rel. Myers v. Swenson*, 691 N.W.2d 357, 360 (Wis. App. 2004). Can the courts of Wisconsin review by certiorari disciplinary decisions regarding inmates incarcerated in out-of-state prisons when, unlike in the principal case, inmates have access to the courts of the out-of-state private contractor? Because Wisconsin statutes [Wis. Stat. § 302.02(3t)] provide that Wisconsin prisoners are subject to the laws of the state where they are confined, Wisconsin courts lack competency to conduct certiorari review of out-of-state disciplinary proceedings. *Id.* at 360–61. Thus, unless an inmate can show that judicial review was unavailable in the courts of the out-of-state contractor, Wisconsin courts lack competency to entertain the prisoner's certiorari action. *Id.* at 361–62.

Would an inmate be successful in arguing that Wisconsin prisoners incarcerated in out-of-state prisons are denied the protection of the Equal Protection Clause because they are not subject to the Wisconsin statutes and regulations that govern Wisconsin prisoners incarcerated in-state? In *State ex rel. Myers*, the court found that the classification did not warrant heightened scrutiny and held that the classification need only bear a rational relationship to a legitimate government interest, which was found. *Id.* at 363. Certiorari review is discussed in Chapter 11.

2. *Accountability to the public.* The principal case demonstrates the tremendous impact that private actors performing governmental functions can have upon our society. The Wisconsin court held the private contractor must conform to the same constitutional standards imposed upon public officials. Can you think of situations in which it will be difficult to monitor private contractors' compliance with basic constitutional precepts?

3. *Accountability in the operation of private prisons.* What measures should be instituted to ensure that private prison operators follow constitutional norms? Should state statutes provide guidelines or should public officials have the flexibility

of incorporating safeguards in public/private contracts? What form of monitoring should the contracts provide? Should the disciplinary boards of privately operated prisons, for example, be comprised of representatives from state departments of corrections? Should public correctional officials be authorized to overrule the disciplinary decisions made by the employees of private prisons? See *Mandela v. Campbell*, 978 S.W.2d 531 (Tenn. 1998) (describing the appointment of a liaison between the Department of Corrections and the private contractor who observes certain disciplinary hearings and may modify recommendations of the private disciplinary board). See also O'Carroll, *Inherently Governmental: A Legal Argument for Ending Private Federal Prisons and Detention Centers*, 67 Emory L.J. 293, 295–96, 319–21, 332–34 (2017) (arguing that operating prisons is an "inherently governmental function" under the Federal Activities Inventory Reform (FAIR) Act of 1998, and therefore the function cannot be delegated to private actors).

The U.S. Department of Justice, Office of Justice Programs, Bureau of Justice Statistics provides prison statistics. A total of 128,300 inmates were in the custody of private prisons at year's end 2016, a 2% increase over the 126,200 inmates in private prisons at the end of 2015. In 2016, 8.5% of state and federal inmates were held in private prisons, an increase of 1.6% from 2015. See Carson, *Prisoners in 2016* at 22 (Jan. 2018), available at [https://perma.cc/4U9E-RTSG].

4. *Privatization as an expansion of governmental power.* Although privatization is commonly associated with less government, in practice it may broaden the reach of government by providing more tools to implement public policy. Private actors, as the principal case points out, must abide by constitutional norms. Because the government ultimately remains responsible for the incarceration of prisoners, it must devise structural mechanisms to ensure that private contractors accord prisoners constitutionally protected rights. These processes may very well expand more public control over private parties. See Freeman, *Extending Public Norms Through Privatization*, 116 Harv. L. Rev. 1285 (2003). What issues emerge when the federal government outsources military and national security functions? See Verstein, *The Corporate Governance of National Security*, 95 Wash. U. L. Rev. 775, 778–80, 806–11 (2018) (arguing that when private corporate boards become subject to the demands of national security, a loss of efficiency and accountability may occur).

5. *Delegation of power issues raised by privatization.* When the public entity delegates functions to private actors, it cannot delegate its policy making role to them. Delegation of power issues most commonly arise when a statute delegates authority to an administrative agency. This issue is discussed in Chapter 8 in the context of delegation to standard-setting agencies. Should this kind of delegation be treated differently than a delegation to a private entity? For a case involving statutory delegation of rule-making power to a private prison operator, see *Tulsa County Deputy Sheriff's Fraternal Order of Police, Lodge No. 188 v. Board of County Comm'rs*, 995 P.2d 1124 (Okla. 2000) (finding that the state legislature did not unlawfully delegate rule-making authority to counties by authorizing them to enter into contracts for

the private operation of prisons). See also Stevenson, *Privatization of State Administrative Services*, 68 La. L. Rev. 1285, 1307–10 (2008) (contrasting delegation of power to governmental administrative bodies from delegation to private parties through contracts).

6. *Public-private contracts: authorization and unlawfully binding contracts.* Notice that in the principal case, Wisconsin statutes authorized incarceration in out-of-state prisons. The lack of express statutory language authorizing privatization may raise legal problems. Local governments cannot enter into contracts with private parties without legal authorization, and the local officials who enter into the contracts must be authorized to act on behalf of the contracting local government. Contracts may also be invalidated if they bargain away police powers or unduly bind successive legislative bodies so as to prevent them from exercising essential powers. It is not always clear when a local governmental body has gone too far in binding itself by contract. Courts may turn to the governmental-proprietary test, the reserved powers doctrine, or public policy tests to resolve this issue. For proposed standards to determine whether a local government contract impairs the use of essential powers, see Griffith, *Local Government Contracts: Escaping from the Governmental/Proprietary Maze*, 75 Iowa L. Rev. 277 (1990).

E. Resolving Conflicts Among Local Governments

The proliferation of local governments in metropolitan areas creates a number of interlocal conflicts over major facilities, such as airports, that have to be resolved. Statutes seldom address these problems, and courts are not really equipped to resolve questions of interlocal authority. The following case illustrates how courts approach the problem in the absence of legislative direction.

Matter of County of Monroe

72 N.Y.2d 338, 533 N.Y.S.2d 702, 530 N.E.2d 202 (1988)

Bellacosa, Judge.

Should the expansion, with accessory uses, of the Greater Rochester International Airport by the County of Monroe be subject to the site plan approval requirements of the City of Rochester? Based on General Municipal Law § 350 and on the balancing of public interests, we agree with the result at the Appellate Division that it should not.

The facts before the Appellate Division, pursuant to CPLR 3222(b)(3), are that the airport is owned and operated by the County and is located substantially in the City. Between 1984 and 1986, the County proposed and approved amendments to its master plan for the airport, including expansion of the main terminal, improvement of the runway apron, and addition of an enclosed parking garage, an air freight facility, a hotel and a temporary parking facility for use during construction of the enclosed parking facility. All improvements were on property located wholly within the City.

The County initially submitted a site plan application to the City in February 1987, for all of the planned improvements except the temporary parking facility, the air freight facility, and the runways. The City requested additional information concerning the improvements and compliance with the State Environmental Quality Review Act. The County responded that the planned uses (with the exception of the hotel, which is not in issue in this case) were governmental and immune from City site plan oversight, and that its prior practice of keeping the City apprised of airport proposals had been only a courtesy, not an acquiescence to City review. The City asserted review jurisdiction based on the proprietary classification test.

The Appellate Division unanimously declared that the "ROCHESTER CITY CODE § 115-30D(7) and City permit requirements do not apply to the expansion" based on the traditional governmental versus proprietary categorization. Alternatively, it noted that since "the governmental versus proprietary distinction is of ancient vintage" and "may be unconvincing," the Rochester ordinances were nonetheless inapplicable because the State enabling legislation, General Municipal Law § 350, impliedly frees the County operation of the airport from City control. While the parties' arguments concentrate on the governmental-proprietary classification, both acknowledge that the test may have outlived its usefulness.

We conclude that the time has come for retiring this labeling device. In its place, a "balancing of public interests" analytic approach will be substituted. Talismanic application of the old test "beg[s] the critical question of which governmental interest should prevail when there is a conflict between the zoning ordinance of one political unit and the statutory authority of another unit to perform a designated public function." (Note, *Governmental Immunity from Local Zoning Ordinances*, 84 HARV. L. REV. 869 [1971].)

The governmental-proprietary function test, as traditionally applied in this State to land use, was borrowed from the field of tort liability as derived from the absolute sovereign immunity doctrine. Under the old test, a municipality is immune from zoning regulations if the uses qualify as governmental. However, a municipality has been subject to such prescriptions when it acts in a corporate or proprietary capacity.

The test has surely been on shaky ground for a long time. "Even during its heyday, the distinction between 'governmental' and 'proprietary' functions of government was subjected to a 'veritable landslide' of criticism and was labeled an 'enigma' and an 'absurdity' [citations omitted]. The abandonment of the rule of sovereign immunity has virtually destroyed the only real basis for the creation of the distinction." (*County of Nassau v. South Farmingdale Water Dist.*, 405 N.Y.S.2d 742 (App. Div.), *aff'd*, 386 N.E.2d 832 (N.Y.) [in affirming, this court added, "the demarcation between governmental or proprietary interests in property owned or operated by government or its subdivisions no longer is as clear as it was in the past"].

The Supreme Court itself noted in *Garcia v. San Antonio Metro. Transit Auth.*, 469 U.S. 528, 531, overruling *National League of Cities v. Usery*, 426 U.S. 833, that an "attempt to draw the boundaries of state regulatory immunity in terms of 'traditional governmental function' is not only unworkable but is also inconsistent with established principles of federalism." The court observed that the governmental function rationale of *National League of Cities v. Usery (id.)* had been construed as providing immunity from regulation in the governmental operation of a municipal airport (*Amersbach v. City of Cleveland*, 598 F.2d 1033, 1037–1038 [6th Cir.]), but not for the regulation of air transportation (*Hughes Air Corp. v. Public Utils. Commn.*, 644 F.2d 1334, 1340–1341 [9th Cir.]). Consistent with our own court's observation in *Nehrbas v. Incorporated Village of Lloyd Harbor*, 140 N.E.2d 241 (N.Y.), the Supreme Court in *Garcia (supra)* concluded that an organizing principle behind the test's application was not apparent and, thus, it discarded the governmental-proprietary function label in the field of regulatory immunity under the Commerce Clause.

Contradictions in governmental function designations have even cropped up within traditionally provided municipal services. In *O'Brien v. Town of Greenburgh* (268 N.Y.S. 173 (App. Div.), *aff'd without opn.* 195 N.E. 210 (N.Y.), for example, we affirmed an Appellate Division holding that the collection and disposal of garbage was a proprietary function. Twenty-two years later, we distinguished that holding, concluding that disposal of rubbish was a governmental function, and allowed the storage of garbage trucks in a residential area contrary to village zoning restrictions (*Nehrbas v. Incorporated Village of Lloyd Harbor, supra*). Such contradictions unmask the illusory benefit of the litmus governmental-proprietary distinction. "[T]he reasoned balancing of the competing public and private interests essential to an equitable resolution of such conflicts has been forsaken for a mechanical application of convenient labels." (Note, *Governmental Immunity from Local Zoning Ordinances*, 84 Harv. L. Rev. 869, 872 [1971].) One often cited denunciation of the imprecision of the governmental-proprietary function test contends that "no satisfactory basis for solving the problem whether the activity falls into one class or other has been evolved [and] [t]he rules sought to be established are as logical as those governing French irregular verbs." (Seasongood, *Municipal Corporations: Objections to the Governmental or Proprietary Test*, 22 Va. L. Rev. 910, 938.)

The American Law Institute and a great many States have adopted a balancing of public interests approach to resolve such land use disputes (see Model Land Dev. Code §§ 7-301, 7-304, 12-201). This balancing approach subjects the encroaching governmental unit in the first instance, in the absence of an expression of contrary legislative intent, to the zoning requirements of the host governmental unit where the extraterritorial land use would be employed. (*Rutgers State Univ. v. Piluso*, 286 A.2d 697, 702 [N.J.].) Then, among the sundry related factors to be weighed in the test are: "the nature and scope of the instrumentality seeking immunity, the kind of function or land use involved, the extent of the public interest to be served thereby, the effect local land use regulation would have upon the enterprise concerned and the impact upon legitimate local interests." (*Id.* at 702.) In *Orange County v. City of Apopka* (299 So. 2d 652, 655 [Fla. App.]), the catalogue of potential factors to be considered by the reviewing court was expanded to include the applicant's legislative grant of authority, alternative locations for the facility in less restrictive zoning areas, and alternative methods of providing the needed improvement. Another important factor is intergovernmental participation in the project development process and an opportunity to be heard. Realistically, one factor in the calculus could "be more influential than another or may be so significant as to completely overshadow all others," but no element should be "thought of as ritualistically required or controlling." (*Rutgers State Univ. v. Piluso*, 286 A.2d 697, 703, *supra.*)

Dealing first with the legislative intent factor in the instant case, our Legislature did not expressly provide that the operation of the airport should be immune from all land use oversight by the City of Rochester. General Municipal Law § 350(1) provides, in part, however, "[w]hen the airport or landing field is to be located in whole or in part *outside* the boundaries of the municipality seeking to establish or construct the facility, the approval of the local legislative body of the city, town or village within which the facility will be located shall be obtained." [Emphasis added.] Here, the airport is, of course, situated within the County and, also concentrically, within the boundaries of two separate townships and the City. Moreover, General Municipal Law § 350 is a provision dedicated to the establishment and operation "of a city, county, village or town" airport, and the restrictive portion previously quoted, by its terms, does not subject a "county" to the land use provision of lesser municipalities. Thus, the Legislature, by reasonable and natural interpretation of the entire section, exempted the County from the preapproval requirement of the City. Finally, competing land use restrictions and policy choices among these various municipalities could otherwise foil the fulfillment of the greater public purpose of promoting intra- and interstate air commerce.

Equally significant under the new test are these additional public interest factors in this case: the dispute involves a County plan which seeks to expand an existing use; given the existing land use, there is no other practical location for the proposed use; the expansion was subject to County land use oversight approval, including public hearings and a comment period in which the City could have participated; there is no express City oversight authority in the State enabling legislation; no detriment to adjoining landowners, as opposed to competing political interests, is alleged; and the nature of an international municipal airport, serving interstate and intrastate commerce goals, is in both the local and greater public interest.

That a portion of the planned improvements will be leased out for operation does not, in the context of this airport expansion case, affect the result. The Legislature expressly contemplated leases by a county for the operation or use of all or part of the county airport "for aviation purposes and for other purposes required for or necessary to the efficient and successful operation of an airport" (General Municipal Law § 352[5]).

Some 60 years ago, well before the congested, common air and space age of today, Chief Judge Cardozo presciently captured the public importance of municipal airports in *Hesse v. Rath*, 164 N.E. 342 (N.Y.): "A city acts for city purposes when it builds a dock or a bridge or a street or a subway. Its purpose is not different when it builds an airport. Aviation is today an established method of transportation. The future, even the near future, will make it still more general. The city that is without the foresight to build the ports for the new traffic may soon be left behind in the race of competition. Chalcedon was called the city of the blind, because its founders rejected the nobler site of Byzantium lying at their feet. The need for vision of the future in the governance of cities has not lessened with the years. The dweller within the gates, even more than the stranger from afar, will pay the price of blindness."

We thus hold that the expansion of the Monroe County Airport is free of land use oversight from the City of Rochester. The airport terminal, parking facilities, and air freight facility are embraced within the immunity from the requirements of the City's land use laws because they constitute accessory uses customarily incidental to an airport operation.

Notes and Questions

1. *Judicial tests.* The balancing test for resolving these conflicts is a recent judicial innovation, but a growing number of states have adopted it. *Native Village v. Alaska. R.R. Corp.*, 87 P.3d 41, 52–56 (Alaska 2004) (applying the balancing test to hold state railroad subject to local zoning laws and listing 14 states that have adopted the test). New York continues to apply the balancing test to resolve interlocal disputes. See *Incorporated Village of Munsey Park v. Manhasset-Lakeview Water District*, 57 N.Y.S.3d 154, 156–57 (2017) (water district held immune from Village zoning regulations). In New York, the balancing test has been extended to resolve state and local disputes. *In re Crown Communication N.Y., Inc. v. Department of Transp.*, 824 N.E.2d 934 (N.Y. 2005) (private installation and operation of two telecommunications towers on state-owned property held immune from local zoning regulations); *Town of Hempstead v. State*, 840 N.Y.S.2d 123 (N.Y.A.D. 2007) (placement of a state-owned telecommunications tower on state property immune from Town's zoning laws because state interests outweighed local interests). As the *Monroe* opinion indicates, the courts traditionally use more mechanical tests that require less exercise of judicial discretion once the test is applied. In addition to the governmental-proprietary rule discussed in the principal case, these rules are:

(a) *Eminent domain rule.* Under this rule, a governmental authority having the power of eminent domain is deemed superior in status and therefore immune from local zoning. *City of Washington v. Warren County*, 899 S.W.2d 863, 53 A.L.R.5th 1 (Mo. 1995). This rule is self-serving. The local government planning to build a facility almost always has the power of eminent domain. The zoning power is not an eminent domain power.

(b) *Superior policy rule.* The concurring judge applied this rule in *Township of Washington v. Village of Ridgewood*, 141 A.2d 308 (N.J. 1958), where the issue was whether Ridgewood's steel water tower had to comply with the zoning ordinance of the municipality in which it was erected. He would have found that the zoning power was superior. See also *Stopaquila Org. v. Aquila, Inc.*, 180 S.W.3d 24 (Mo. App. 2005) (rejecting eminent domain rule in favor of a public policy rule that harmonizes separate county and public utility police powers in lieu of absolute public utility immunity from county planning and zoning regulations).

(c) *Superior power rule.* The concurring judge in *Ridgewood* indicated that both zoning and the power to provide water facilities derived from legislative authorization. He implied that they were equal in stature, but must be reconciled whenever possible. If not, the court must determine which of the two powers is superior. See also *County of Venango v. Borough of Sugarcreek Zoning Hearing Bd.*, 626 A.2d 489 (Pa. 1993) (county's zoning power superior under court's legislative intent rule).

(d) *Legislative intent rule.* Some courts resolve interlocal conflicts by determining the legislative intent. Courts frequently view the determination of legislative intent as a threshold issue to be addressed prior to the application of other rules. See *Town of Fenton v. Town of Chenango*, 927 N.Y.S.2d 819 (2011), *aff'd*, 91 A.D.3d 1246 (App. Div. 2012) (application of the *Monroe* balancing test to resolve conflict between two towns in the absence of clear legislative intent as to whether one town could relocate a sewer pipe with state approval that discharged effluents in violation of another town's aquifer law); *Massachusetts Bay Transp. Auth. v. City of Somerville*, 883 N.E.2d 933 (Mass. 2008) (Massachusetts Bay Transportation Authority enabling statute expressed legislative intent to exempt MBTA's outdoor advertisements on its facilities from local zoning ordinances); *Herman v. Berrien County*, 750 N.W.2d 570 (Mich. 2008) (county outdoor-shooting ranges not exempt from local land use regulations because no legislative intent to grant such immunity to all of the ancillary land uses attendant to county's buildings); *Village of Logan v. Eastern New Mexico Water Util. Auth.*, 357 P.3d 433, 436–37 (N.M. 2015) (authority immune from village's zoning ordinance because a review of both entities' statutory powers revealed that the authority was more greatly empowered than the village); *Southeastern Pa. Transp. Auth. v. City of Philadelphia*, 101 A.3d 79, 87 (Pa. 2014) (superior entity rule rejected in favor of judicial examination of relevant statutes to ascertain which entity the legislature intended should have preeminent powers). For other decisions applying this rule, see Taylor & Wyckoff, *Intergovernmental Zoning Conflicts over Public Facilities Siting: A Model Framework for Standard State Acts*, 41 Urb. Law. 653, 670–73 (2009).

(e) *Superior entity rule.* Other courts decide interlocal conflict cases by giving priority to the superior governmental entity. This view has been adopted in cases in which the state was one of the governmental entities. The leading state case is *Kentucky Inst. for Educ. of the Blind v. City of Louisville*, 97 S.W. 402 (Ky. 1906). The court found an absolute immunity based on sovereign immunity principles. It held that the Institute did not have to comply with the city's fire safety code. More recent cases have not given state agencies a preferred status in intergovernmental conflict disputes. See *Southeastern Pa. Transp. Auth. v. City of Philadelphia*, 159 A.3d 443, 452–53 (Pa. 2017) (legislative intent, rather than hierarchical status of competing governmental entities, determines which entity should prevail). In addition to the *Rutgers* case discussed in *County of Monroe*, see *Town of Bourne v. Plante*, 708 N.E.2d 103 (Mass. 1999) (zoning not applicable to state-provided parking facility); *Senders v. Town of Columbia Falls*, 647 A.2d 93 (Me. 1994) (lessee from state agency immune from zoning). See also Taylor & Wyckoff, *supra*, at 661.

(f) *Most inclusive power rule.* Some courts give priority to the most inclusive power. In *Wilkinsburgh-Penn Joint Water Auth. v. Borough of Churchill*, 207 A.2d 905 (Pa. 1965), the authority planned to construct a water tower in an area where it was prohibited by the borough zoning ordinance. The court held that "the objectives of zoning regulation are more comprehensive than and, in fact, include the objectives of the Water Authority. . . . [T]he objectives of both statutes can be secured only if the Authority's land is subject to the Borough's zoning power." *Id.* at 910.

For a discussion of the above rules and cases citing them, see Taylor & Wyckoff, *supra*, at 660–75. The authors provide a framework for a new model law that would address public facility siting. *Id.* at 693–703. For additional decisions adopting the balancing test in interlocal zoning conflict cases, see *Hayward v. Gaston*, 542 A.2d 760 (Del. 1988); *Lake County Public Bldg. Comm'n v. City of Waukegan*, 652 N.E.2d 370 (Ill. App. 1995) (county public building commission must pay city building permit fee). For cases rejecting the balancing test, see *Township of West Orange v. Whitman*, 8 F. Supp. 2d 408 (D.N.J. 1998) (balancing test not applicable to group homes for disabled protected by federal Fair Housing Act); *Everett v. Snohomish County*, 772 P.2d 992 (Wash. 1989) (adopting legislative intent test); *Commonwealth, Dep't of Gen. Servs. v. Ogontz Area Neighbors Ass'n*, 483 A.2d 448, 454–55 (Pa. 1984) (legislative intent test favored over balancing test).

2. *Criticism of balancing test.* Reynolds, *The Judicial Role in Intergovernmental Land Use Disputes: The Case Against Balancing*, 71 Minn. L. Rev. 611 (1987), criticizes the balancing test. She points out that the test discourages compromise and increases litigation, involves the court in the original land use decision, does not sufficiently protect the host government and is an inadequate rule because "[i]t is not for courts . . . to pick and choose between valid public purposes." *Id.* at 641. Reynolds suggests decision rules for intergovernmental zoning conflicts that depend on the political relationship between the two competing governmental units and on the respective extrajudicial incentives each governmental unit has for compromise and rational decision making. *Id.* at 668.

3. *School districts.* School districts present special problems. Schools must locate where they can serve adjacent neighborhoods, but local residents may object, and the city may zone schools out of their optimum locations. The school district may

cover several municipalities, and may be subject to local political pressures in some of the municipalities it serves.

Most courts recognize this necessity and hold that school districts are immune from local zoning regulations. *Appeal of Radnor Township School Authority*, 252 A.2d 597 (Pa. 1969), is a typical case. The school authority planned an elementary school on land within an A-2 Zoning District in which the school use was not permitted by special exception or otherwise. The township refused to rezone or to grant a variance. The court compared the very general power of the township to enact zoning regulations with the specific power of the school authority to choose the location of schools, and held that the township had no authority to regulate the location of school buildings. The court noted additionally that a school district of the first class (at that time Philadelphia and Pittsburgh) had complete and plenary power over its physical plant, and that the ordinance in question did not involve school construction but location.

Some jurisdictions, however, have rejected the superior entity rule of treating a school district as a subordinate agent of the state that is immune from local zoning laws. Instead, they have examined legislative intent for such immunity and used a balancing of interests approach in the absence of such intent. *E.g., Charter Township of Northville v. Schulz*, 666 N.W.2d 213 (Mich. 2003) (legislative intent found to immunize school districts from local zoning ordinances); *Albany Preparatory Charter Sch. v. City of Albany*, 818 N.Y.S.2d 651 (N.Y. App. Div. 2006) (proposed education uses subject to city's special permit process that entails balancing of interests); *Independent Sch. Dist. No. 89 v. City of Oklahoma City*, 722 P.2d 1212 (Okla. 1986) (adopting balancing of interests test in the absence of expressed legislative intent for school district immunity from municipal zoning). While school districts may be immune from local zoning regulations regarding location of school buildings, they have been subject to local regulations that do not affect the location choice. *Hazleton Area Sch. Dist. v. Zoning Bd.*, 778 A.2d 1205 (Pa. 2001) (use of school athletic field for non-school related activities); *Robinson v. Indianola Mun. Separate Sch. Dist.*, 467 So. 2d 911 (Miss. 1985) (off street parking).

4. *Building code and zoning cases.* Municipalities may also apply their building code requirements to the construction of school buildings. In the absence of comprehensive regulation of school construction at the state level, courts may hold that the local building code applies. See *Edmonds Sch. Dist. No. 15 v. City of Mountlake Terrace*, 465 P.2d 177 (Wash. 1970). The courts may distinguish the local building code from the zoning ordinance. Compare *Port Arthur Indep. Sch. Dist. v. City of Groves*, 376 S.W.2d 330 (Tex. 1964) (school district compliance with city building ordinance required), *with Austin Indep. Sch. Dist. v. City of Sunset Valley*, 502 S.W.2d 670 (Tex. 1973) (city zoning ordinances cannot prevent location of school within city by school district).

Is this distinction between building code and zoning cases valid? Could it be attributable to the fact that all governmental entities should be interested in safe building construction whereas school facilities are difficult to locate as they generally adversely affect the residents of the area near them? See Levi, Gehring, & Groethe, *Application of Municipal Ordinances to Special Purpose Districts and Regulated Industries: A Home Rule Approach*, 12 URB. L. ANN. 77, 92, 97, 98 (1976).

5. *Publicly owned property.* Some state statutes provide that local zoning ordinances shall apply to publicly owned property, OR. REV. STAT. § 227.286, or contain a provision found in the Standard State Zoning Enabling Act, that other statutes and regulations shall prevail over the zoning ordinance when the zoning ordinance is less restrictive. E.g., N.C. GEN. STAT. § 160A-390. A California statute exempts counties and cities from each other's zoning ordinances, CAL. GOV'T CODE §§ 53090, 53091, see *Lawler v. City of Redding*, 9 Cal. Rptr. 2d 392 (Cal. App. 1992), and gives qualified exemptions to special districts, § 53,096, see *City of Lafayette v. East Bay Mun. Util. Dist.*, 20 Cal. Rptr. 2d 658 (Cal. App. 1993).

6. For discussion of intergovernmental immunity problems, see D. Mandelker, LAND USE LAW §§ 4.26–4.28 (5th ed. 2003); *Exempting Government from Zoning: Court Tests*, Rasso, LAND USE L. & ZONING DIG., Oct. 1986, at 3. For an argument that state legislation is necessary to avoid serious transaction costs concerning regulatory authority issues associated with the development of Intelligent Vehicle Highway Systems technology, see Libonati, *The Law of Intergovernmental Relations: IVHS Opportunities and Constraints*, 22 TRANSP. L.J. 225, 237–38 (1994).

A Note on the Condemnation of the Property of one Governmental Unit by Another

Intergovernmental conflicts also arise when one governmental unit seeks to condemn land for a public project when the land is owned by another governmental entity. In this situation, the courts are inclined to apply a method of analysis that differs somewhat from the doctrines they apply when a public project is blocked by the zoning ordinance or building code of another governmental unit, although there are similarities in the analytical devices applied.

Federal supremacy usually insulates federal agencies exercising the power of eminent domain from any limitations on that power that may be imposed at the state or local level. See, e.g., *United States v. Carmack*, 329 U.S. 230 (1946). The states also have a broad power of eminent domain; the state or one of its agencies, in general, can condemn successfully the property of a governmental subdivision of the state. See, e.g., *People v. City of Los Angeles*, 4 Cal. Rptr. 531 (Cal. App. 1960) (state condemnation of city park for construction of state highway), *appeal dismissed*, 364 U.S. 476 (1960); *State ex rel. State Highway Comm'n v. Hoester*, 362 S.W.2d 519 (Mo. 1962) (state condemnation of property of fire district).

As a general rule, one governmental unit or subdivision of a state does not have the power to condemn the public property of another unit or subdivision without either an express grant of power or a power that arises by necessary implication. See *Town of Parker v. Colorado Div. of Parks & Outdoor Recreation*, 860 P.2d 584 (Colo.

App. 1993) (no power to condemn state-owned land); *City of Worthington v. City of Columbus*, 796 N.E.2d 920 (Ohio 2003) (no power to condemn parkland owned by other city that was located within condemning city's borders). When the two governmental units are of comparable status and powers, there is a split of authority. Compare *Needham v. County Comm'rs*, 86 N.E.2d 63 (Mass. 1949) (unsuccessful county attempt to condemn city park land), with *Village of Richmond Heights v. Board of County Commr's*, 166 N.E.2d 143 (Ohio App. 1960) (successful county condemnation of municipal land when city had acquired land only to prevent construction of county airport).

Courts have developed exceptions to the general rule. The prior public use doctrine permits intergovernmental condemnation when the proposed use would not interfere with or be inconsistent with the public use to which the property is presently devoted. See, e.g., *Florida Water Servs. Corp. v. Utilities Comm'n*, 790 So. 2d 501 (Fla. App. 2001); *Montana Power Co. v. Burlington N.R.R.*, 900 P.2d 888, 49 A.L.R.5th 951 (Mont. 1995). Another exception has been recognized when the proposed use is a higher or more necessary use than the present one. See, e.g., *Montana Power Co. v. Burlington N.R.R., supra* (statute incorporating higher use standard inapplicable because two uses were compatible); *State v. Montgomery County*, 262 S.W.3d 439 (Tex. App. 2008) (finding no exception to the general rule unless the new use is of paramount importance to the public); *Village of Woodridge v. Board of Educ.*, 933 N.E.2d 392 (Ill. App. 2010) (holding of property for future use not an existing use).

Some courts refuse to make such determinations and rely exclusively upon the construction of relevant constitutional and statutory authority. See, e.g., *City of Northwood v. Wood County Reg'l Water & Sewer Dist.*, 711 N.E.2d 1003 (Ohio 1999); *City of Smithville v. St. Luke's Northland Hosp. Corp.*, 972 S.W.2d 416 (Mo. App. 1998). See generally Dau, *Problems in Condemnation of Property Devoted to Public Use*, 44 TEX. L. REV. 1517 (1966).

Most state constitutional provisions require that just compensation be paid only for the taking of private property. Courts generally acknowledge that there is no resulting constitutional right to compensation for a taking of public property. Invoking the familiar governmental-proprietary distinction, some courts will nevertheless award compensation for the taking of property held in a proprietary capacity, but deny it when the property is used for governmental purposes. In one of the early and leading decisions taking this approach, the city's "proprietary" property (a cemetery) was analogized to private property entitled to constitutional protection. *Proprietors of Mt. Hope Cem. v. City of Boston*, 33 N.E. 695 (Mass. 1893). The governmental-proprietary distinction continues to be invoked, but it appears less frequently as the basis for decision, and it seems also to have lost some of its constitutional character. For a discussion of how courts apply the governmental-proprietary rule and an analysis of the rule's deficiencies, see Griffith, *Local Government Contracts: Escaping from the Governmental/Proprietary Maze*, 75 IOWA L. REV. 277 (1990).

For an article disputing the prevailing view that compensation is not payable in intergovernmental condemnation cases and suggesting guidelines for the award of compensation in this situation, see Payne, *Intergovernmental Condemnation as a Problem in Public Finance*, 61 TEX. L. REV. 949 (1983).

Just as the governmental-proprietary standard does not serve well to resolve the issue of right to compensation, neither does the equally venerable theory that the state has absolute dominion over its creatures, the subunits of government. See, e.g., *People ex rel. Dixon v. Community Unit Sch. Dist.*, 118 N.E.2d 241 (Ill. 1954). As a result, some courts have read general eminent domain statutes, or a combination of statutory and constitutional provisions, to demonstrate a legislative intent that compensation be paid for a public taking of publicly held property. For example, in *State ex rel. State Hwy. Comm'n v. Board of County Comm'rs*, 380 P.2d 830 (N.M. 1963), the court found that the state statute establishing procedures for condemnation of public or private property for highway purposes contemplated payment whether the property taken was used for proprietary or governmental purposes.

When two governmental units have the power of eminent domain, who should prevail? Courts traditionally look to legislative intent, but what if there is no clear answer to be found in that inquiry? A student commentator documented the analysis some courts have engaged in to find the paramount public use of such property. See Naiman, Comment: *Judicial Balancing of Uses for Public Property: The Paramount Public Use Doctrine*, 17 B.C. ENVTL. AFF. L. REV. 893, 894–95, 913–20 (1990) (arguing in favor of the judicial balancing of uses when both governmental units possess the power of eminent domain and no clear legislative intent exists as to which use should prevail).

Another student commentator has argued that the courts should not adopt an absolute test that favors existing uses, nor should they apply a balancing test that weighs the more necessary use. Instead, the commentator proposes that the proposed use to prevail must be of paramount necessity and incapable of accomplishment in any other way. Arena, Comment, *The Accommodation of "Occupation" and "Social Utility" in Prior Public Use Jurisprudence*, 137 U. PA. L. REV. 233, 263 (1988). Would the proposed rule provide a better resolution of intergovernmental conflicts in the use of land? Which of these two tests is preferable: the balancing test or the paramount importance test?

F. Non-Structural Cooperative Arrangements

Zoning conflicts illustrated by *County of Monroe* illustrate the problems that can arise from fragmentation of governmental authority in metropolitan areas. A variety of approaches to realign governmental responsibilities, some voluntary and others mandatory, have been used to integrate governmental functions at the local level.

[1] Intergovernmental Cooperation

One or more local governments may contract for the provision of a service function, or to exercise regulatory powers. Governmental functions may also be transferred from a lower to a different or higher governmental level. This section reviews these voluntary governmental integration techniques. Intergovernmental cooperation is most common in the provision of governmental services. Intergovernmental service agreements can take several forms:

> (1) A contractual agreement—that is, one locality hires another local government to provide the service to its citizens, similar to the local government contracting with a private firm.
>
> (2) When two or more local governments jointly perform the service, provide support facilities or operate a public facility.
>
> (3) When a service is run by a jointly created separate organization which aids all jurisdictions party to the agreement.
>
> [ACIR, State and Local Roles in the Federal system 327 (1982)].

Intergovernmental cooperation has many advantages. It can improve services, lower service costs and promote service coordination. Cooperation also has disadvantages. It is voluntary, and can lead to intergovernmental conflict if the participating governments disagree. Cooperation may also create a patchwork provision of services because it is voluntary and ad hoc. One study also suggests that intergovernmental cooperation may not eliminate disparities in fiscal capacity in metropolitan areas. A study in the Philadelphia area found that "cooperation occurs among municipalities with similar social rank and tax resources, in that order." O. Williams, H. Herman, C. Liebman & T. Dye, Suburban Differences and Metropolitan Policies 264 (1965).

Inter-local contracts raise a number of issues. Local officials may be cautious about voluntarily ceding their control over service delivery or public policy by entering into a contract. What political factors can motivate a local government, or local politician, to voluntary abdicate power and enter into an intergovernmental agreement? See Zeemering, *Assessing Local Elected Officials' Concerns about Interlocal Agreements*, 53 Urb. Stud., No. 11 (2016): 2347 (discussing the roles of local officials in intergovernmental politics and the factors that influence their attitudes towards interlocal cooperation). See also Andrew, *Recent Developments in the Study of Interjurisdictional Agreements: An Overview and Assessment*, 41 State & Local Gov't Rev., No. 2 (2009): 133–142 (overview and assessment of inter-jurisdictional agreement usage); Bel & Warner, *Inter-Municipal Cooperation and Costs: Expectations and Evidence*, 93 Pub. Adm. no. 1 (2015): 59–62 (discussing factors deemed crucial to achieve cost savings from inter-municipal cooperation); Martin & Long, *Horizontal Intergovernmental Relations in the Portland Metropolitan Region: Challenges and Successes*, 50 Willamette L. Rev. 589 (2014) (documenting barriers to cooperation in a bi-state metropolitan area and the circumstances that facilitate the realization of benefits from collaboration); Reynolds, *Intergovernmental Cooperation, Metropolitan Equity, and the New Regionalism*, 78 WASH. L. REV. 93 (2003) (arguing that intergovernmental cooperation as currently structured does not advance the New Regionalists' goal for a fairer allocation of resources and opportunities in the nation's metropolitan areas).

Widespread intergovernmental cooperation has been stimulated by the adoption of constitutional provisions and enabling legislation based on models suggested by national organizations such as the ACIR. An ACIR survey showed that over half of the cities and counties provided services through intergovernmental contracts and that the proportion is much higher among the large jurisdictions. Economy of scale was the major reason for intergovernmental contracting. The services most frequently provided were library, police and fire communications, fire prevention and suppression and sewage disposal. ACIR, INTERGOVERNMENTAL SERVICE ARRANGEMENTS FOR DELIVERING LOCAL PUBLIC SERVICES: UPDATE 1983, at 92 (1985).

Counties, especially large counties facing the forces of urbanization and suburbanization, have been pressed into the role of providing municipal services. They are the primary deliverers of social services, such as welfare and health care, and their state-mandated duties include tax assessment, collection, and recording. Los Angeles County, according to a recent survey, provides services in the areas of law enforcement, fire protection, libraries, parks and recreation, planning and public works. More than half of the municipalities in Los Angeles County contract with it for service delivery. The county also provides services to residents of unincorporated areas and controls special districts that provide services to residents of both unincorporated areas and incorporated cities. Hoene, Baldassare & Shires, *The Development of Counties as Municipal Governments: A Case Study of Los Angeles County in the Twenty-first Century*, 37 URB. AFF. REV., No. 4 (2002) 575–591, 576–82. However, when the municipalities lie on the borders of states, some level of interlocal cooperation can be hindered. See Litwak, *State Border Towns and Resiliency: Barriers to Interstate Intergovernmental Cooperation*, 50 IDAHO L. REV. 193, 196 (2014) (documenting necessity of contractual agreements to ensure cooperation).

Practically all the states now have general enabling legislation authorizing intergovernmental cooperation, and they may also have legislation authorizing cooperation for designated governmental functions. A few states also have constitutional provisions authorizing intergovernmental cooperation. Adoption of a constitutional provision can eliminate some of the constitutional problems that an intergovernmental agreement can raise. Constitutional provisions are usually implemented through the adoption of statutory authorization.

The materials that follow review some of the legal problems that arise under intergovernmental agreements.

Constitutional and Statutory Authority for Interlocal Cooperation

New York Constitution. Art. IX, § 1(c):

Local governments shall have the power to agree, as authorized by act of the legislature, . . . to provide cooperatively, jointly or by contract any facility, service, activity or undertaking which each participating local government has the power to provide separately.

Illinois Constitution Art. VII, § 10(a):

Units of local government and school districts may contract or otherwise associate among themselves . . . to obtain or share services and to exercise, combine, or transfer any power or function, in any manner not prohibited by law or ordinance. . . . Participating units of government may use their credit, revenues, and other resources to pay costs and to service debt related to intergovernmental activities.

Advisory Commission on Intergovernmental Relations, State Legislative Program #2, Local Government Modernization: Interlocal Contracting and Joint Enterprise 2.204 (1975)

Section 4. Interlocal Agreements

(a) Any power or powers, privileges, or authority exercised or capable of exercise by a public agency of this state may be exercised and enjoyed jointly with any other public agency of this state [having the power or powers, privilege, or authority], and jointly with any public agency of any other state or of the United States to the extent that laws of such other state or of the United States permit such joint exercise or enjoyment. Any agency of the state government when acting jointly with any public agency may exercise and enjoy all of the powers, privileges, and authority conferred by this act upon a public agency.

(b) Any two or more public agencies may enter into agreements with one another for joint or cooperative action pursuant to the provisions of this act. Appropriate action by ordinance, resolution, or otherwise pursuant to law of the governing bodies of these participating public agencies shall be necessary before any such agreement may enter into force.

(c) Any such agreement shall specify the following:

(1) its duration;

(2) the precise organization, composition, and nature of any separate legal or administrative entity created thereby, together with the powers delegated thereto, which is hereby authorized to be created with its governing body composed solely of local elected officials *ex officio* unless otherwise provided by law;

(3) its purpose or purposes;

(4) the manner of financing the joint or cooperative undertaking, of establishing and maintaining a budget therefor, and of accounting and keeping records thereof;

(5) the permissible method or methods to be employed in accomplishing the partial or complete termination of the agreement and for disposing of property upon such partial or complete termination; and

(6) any other necessary and proper matters.

Notes and Questions

1. *Power of one unit vs. mutuality of powers.* The ACIR model act, *supra*, which a number of states have adopted, authorizes interlocal agreements providing for the joint exercise of "[a]ny power . . . exercised or capable of exercise by a public agency." E.g., OKLA. STAT. ANN. tit. 74, § 1004(A). Compare MINN. STAT. ANN. § 471.59(1), authorizing local governments to "cooperatively exercise any power common to the contracting parties." The ACIR model is known as a "power of one unit" provision and means that contracting governments can exercise a power even if only one of the contracting governments has the authority to exercise that power. The Minnesota provision is a "mutuality of powers" provision and limits contractual agreements to powers possessed by all of the contracting parties. See ACIR, INTERGOVERNMENTAL SERVICE ARRANGEMENTS, *supra*, at 9.

ACIR reported a decline in the number of states requiring mutuality of powers. *Id.* at 16. For discussion of the problems raised by the Minnesota provision, see Olson, *The Joint Exercise of Powers*, 42 BENCH & BAR, No. 7, at 25 (1985).

Another question is whether the entity created by an interlocal contract is a governmental public entity separate from the contracting parties. For provisions to this effect, see CAL. GOV'T CODE §§ 6507–6508.

The Illinois constitutional provision, *supra*, has been interpreted as a repeal of Dillon's Rule, see Chapter 2, and as removing "the necessity of obtaining statutory authority for cooperative ventures." See *Village of Sherman v. Village of Williamsville*, 435 N.E.2d 548 (Ill. App. 1982). On the Illinois experience, see Hall & Wallack, *Intergovernmental Cooperation and the Transfer of Powers*, 1981 U. ILL. L. REV. 775.

2. *Implementing cooperation.* Assume that Metro City is the only unit in the metropolitan area that has a modern sewage treatment plant. Because of a peculiar combination of three industrial wastes, sewage treatment in the area did not come up to State standards and the State ordered the surrounding communities to correct this problem. The six counties considered building their own plants, but subsequently five counties entered into forty-year contracts and one county a three-year contract with Metro City for sewage treatment service and water supply service. The Metro City plant was therefore established as a metropolitan area sewage plant. In view of the constitutional and statutory provisions quoted above, just how would

you implement this arrangement legally? Which provisions would be most helpful, and which might limit your efforts?

Goreham v. Des Moines Metropolitan Area Solid Waste Agency

179 N.W.2d 449 (Iowa 1970)

Larson, Justice.

This is a declaratory judgment action involving the validity of a contract and the constitutionality of chapter 28E, Code of Iowa 1966, and chapter 236, Acts of the Sixty-third General Assembly, submitted upon an agreed stipulation of facts.

Plaintiffs, who are residents, property owners, and taxpayers of the cities of Des Moines and West Des Moines, Iowa, brought this action at law against the Des Moines Metropolitan Area Solid Waste Agency (hereafter called the Agency) and its members asking an interpretation of chapter 28E, Code of Iowa 1966, and chapter 236, Acts of the Sixty-third General Assembly, First Session, with reference to the power and authority of the Agency under those laws. The vital question presented is whether under these statutes and the Iowa Constitution the Agency can issue bonds to finance the planned functions of the Agency in the collection and disposition of solid waste, and pay the interest and principal from fees legally collectible from its members for this service. The trial court held that the Agency was properly created, that due authority was properly delegated to it, that the submitted agreement between the members was valid, and that it could issue such revenue bonds and fix and collect fees from those using these services including interest and principal on the bonds.... Plaintiffs appeal as to the creation of the Agency, the propriety of the authority delegated, and the legality of the agreement....

Appellants further contend that the defendant Agency is invalid and has no legal character as a "public body corporate and politic" for the reason that chapter 28E of the 1966 Code of Iowa and Senate File 482 (also known as chapter 236, Acts of the 63rd General Assembly, First Session) under which said Agency was created is in violation of Article III, Section 1, of the Constitution of the State of Iowa, as an improper delegation of legislative authority, and that as a result the creation of said Agency by the "Intergovernmental Agreement, Exhibit A," is ultra vires and of no force and effect, and that as a consequence thereof said defendant Agency is without authority to issue revenue bonds pursuant to Senate File 482 enacted by the 63rd General Assembly of Iowa.

[The stipulation of facts recites the serious solid waste disposal problems that existed in the City of Des Moines. An application for federal funds and a study and report led to an intergovernmental agreement between the city and thirteen other governments in the metropolitan area creating the Metropolitan Area Solid Waste Agency.]

Pursuant to said agreement the Agency was duly organized, officers were elected and a director was hired to manage the affairs of the Agency under the direction of the Agency board which was composed of one representative from the governing body of each member of the Agency, each having one vote for every 50,000 or fraction thereof population in his area of representation.

....

I.

... Chapter 28E entitled "Joint Exercise of Governmental Powers" purports to authorize any political subdivision of the State of Iowa and certain agencies of the state or federal government to join together to perform certain public services and by agreement create a separate legal or administrative entity to render that service. Its worthy purpose is clearly expressed in section 28E.1. Section 28E.2 provides definitions, and section 28E.3 purports to define the limitations upon the participants as follows:

> 28E.3. Joint exercise of powers. [This section enacts §4(a) of the ACIR model act, *supra*.]

Sections 28E.4 and 28E.5 provide for the agreement and its contents as follows:

> 28E.4. Agreement with other agencies. Any public agency of this state may enter into an agreement with one or more public or private agencies for joint or co-operative action pursuant to the provisions of this chapter, *including* the creation of a separate entity to carry out the purpose of the agreement. Appropriate action by ordinance, resolution or otherwise pursuant to law of the governing bodies involved shall be necessary before any such agreement may enter into force. (Emphasis supplied.)
>
> 28E.5. Specifications. [This section enacts §4(c) of the ACIR model act.]

II.

Although appellants contend the creation of a separate legal entity or public body is solely a function of the legislature, we find no unconstitutional delegation of legislative power involved in this law providing for the creation of the Des Moines Metropolitan Area Solid Waste Agency. It is not the mere establishment or creation of such an agency or entity that causes trouble, but the functions to be performed by that agency in the legislative field which must be examined closely to determine whether there has been an unlawful delegation of legislative authority. See *Lausen v. Board of Supervisors*, 214 N.W. 682 (Iowa 1927).

In *Lausen*, in upholding the constitutionality of what is known as the "Bovine Tuberculosis Law," this court stated at page 685 of 214 N.W., "We think that the state has the power to select any reasonable means and methods it may choose, to establish these (area-eradication) districts, so long as they are in the interest of public health. ..."

In this connection it must also be noted that administrative agencies may be delegated certain legislative functions by the legislature when properly guidelined, and that when this is done, the distinction between such agencies and public bodies, corporate and politic, which have been delegated proper legislative functions, has largely disappeared. Ordinarily the latter body is created by an act of the legislature and the former by an already-established public body with legislative authority. However, the power and authority of each must be measured by the legality of the delegation thereof. If such power is derived from the State Legislature, is adequately guidelined, and does not violate the separation-of-powers provision of the State Constitution set forth in Article III, Section 1, the exercise thereof should be sustained.

Thus, our primary problem here is whether the authority provided in chapter 28E of the 1966 Code of Iowa and chapter 236, Acts of the Sixty-third General Assembly, constitutes a lawful delegation of legislative power.

III.

Regularly-enacted statutes are presumed to be constitutional, and courts exercise the power to declare such legislation unconstitutional with great caution. It is only when such conclusion is unavoidable that we do so.

Thus, while the provisions of section 28E of the 1966 Code leave much to be desired as to the extent of the authority granted to such a newly-created entity, the presumption of constitutionality operates strongly in its favor.

It is also well to remember that our function is not to pass upon the feasibility or wisdom of such legislation, but only to determine whether the power here exercised exceeds that which the legislature could or did delegate to the newly-created entity.

In this regard it is also well to note the importance of the expressed or recognized purpose or policy to be achieved by the legislation. Generally, when the legislature has adequately stated the object and purpose of the legislation and laid down reasonably clear guidelines in its application, it may then delegate to a properly-created entity the authority to exercise such legislative power as is necessary to carry into effect that general legislative purpose.

The purpose of this legislation, as recognized in chapter 28E, is to provide a solution to the growing problems of local government including the problem of collection and disposal of solid wastes by public bodies and to cooperate with the Office of Solid Waste of the United States Department of Health, Education and Welfare to accomplish that purpose by joint efforts. We further observe that this purpose may soon be made a legal requirement for all communities throughout the entire land under federal law. We are satisfied that this is health and general welfare legislation and that the legislative policy and purpose for chapter 28E is sufficiently stated. It amounts to this, that public agencies or governmental units may cooperate together to do anything jointly that they could do individually.

True, if chapter 28E is examined without reference to the powers granted the various governmental units by other legislation, the factors constituting sufficient guidelines might well be said to be insufficient. But this legislation must be interpreted with reference to the power or powers which the contracting governmental units already have. The pre-existing powers contain their own guidelines. The legal creation of a new body corporate and politic to jointly exercise and perform the powers and responsibilities of the cooperating governmental unit would not be unconstitutional so long as the new body politic is doing only what its cooperating members already have the power to do. This would be true under the above-recognized general rule that a statute is presumed to be constitutional until shown otherwise beyond a reasonable doubt.

Chapter 28E does not attempt to delineate the various governmental or proprietary functions which the individual governmental units may be implementing. While such a broad approach may be unwise, as appellants argue, it is not unconstitutional so long as the cooperating units are not exercising powers they do not already have.

With this in mind, it appears that chapter 28E supplies sufficient guidelines for the purposes necessary to the chapter. That is, the units are authorized to handle what might be called the mechanical details of implementing the joint project either by the creation of a separate entity or by using a joint administrator or board for the purpose of implementing the agreement reached. The agreement itself, of whatever nature, must have its specific contents delineated in section 28E.5 and specifically prohibits governmental units being involved in the new entity, except insofar as the new entity is in fact performing the same responsibilities as the units involved.

....

IV.

[The statute authorized revenue bonds to finance the construction of projects authorized by the act, the bonds to be paid off by revenues from the project. The court held that the bonds fell within the special fund doctrine and did not constitute debt of the contracting municipalities. Although the statute did not allow these municipalities to withdraw from the project, and although they were committed to the payment of the bonds, no financial obligation was imposed as charges for the use of project services to be passed on to the users. Any obligation on the part of the contracting municipalities to make up project revenues out of general taxation was contingent and speculative. The debt limitation problem is discussed in Chapter 4.]

....

IX.

Appellants further contend that the agreement creating the Agency is contrary to public policy to the extent that it permits elected officials of the member municipalities to serve on the governing board of the Agency. They argue that the integrity of representative government demands that the administrative officials should be able to exercise their judgment free from the objectionable pressure of conflicting interests. We agree with that proposition, but do not believe it appears here that these members of the Agency board are in such a position. It is conceded that here there is nothing to indicate a personal pecuniary interest of those representatives is involved such as appears in *Wilson v. Iowa City*, 165 N.W.2d 813, 820 (Iowa 1969).

Although the members of the board understandably will want to keep the rates their constituents must pay as low as possible, they are well aware that rates must be maintained sufficient to meet the Agency's cost for such services. This is not such a conflict of interest as to be contrary to public policy or fatal to the agreement.

In passing on this question the trial court said, "Inasmuch as each representative is on the board primarily to serve as spokesman for the particular municipality or political subdivision he represents, (it could) . . . see no conflict of interest such as would likely affect his individual judgment by virtue of his status as an elected official." It pointed out no compensation is provided for such service and the representative serves at the pleasure of his municipality or political subdivision. We agree with the trial court.

In the recent case of *Wilson v. Iowa City, supra* we discussed the issue of conflict of interest and held, where it appeared the official had a personal interest, either actual or implied, he would be disqualified to vote on a municipal project—in that case, urban renewal. No such interest would appear in connection with this project unless some litigation would occur between the municipality he represents and the Agency, in which event the contract itself provides for arbitration procedures. We conclude there is no merit in this assignment.

. . . .

All justices concur except Becker and LeGrand, who dissent.

Becker, Justice.

I respectfully dissent. [Omitted.]

Notes and Questions

1. *Judicial construction of cooperation statutes.* Is the court in the principal case concerned about the *vertical* delegation of power by the legislature to create the intergovernmental unit, with the *horizontal* delegation of power by the contracting municipalities to the intergovernmental unit, or with the *exercise* of powers through the interlocal contract that have not previously been delegated to the contracting units? Are these constitutional or statutory questions? For more on delegation, see Chapter 8.

The Iowa court appears to have construed its cooperation statute, which is based on the ACIR model act, as a "mutuality of powers" provision. Is this correct? In *Barnes v. Department of Hous. & Urb. Dev.*, 341 N.W.2d 766 (Iowa 1983), an interlocal cooperation agreement that created a regional housing authority under the statute construed in *Goreham* was at issue. The court held that the statute did not confer additional powers on the authority, which was still required to obtain approval of a housing project from the municipality in which the project was located even though the municipality had signed the interlocal contract. Approval was required by the state housing statute. Is this a correct reading of *Goreham*? Compare *Roberts v. City of Maryville*, 750 S.W.2d 69 (Mo. 1988) (holding under mutuality of powers interlocal cooperation law that project authorized by contract fell within powers of municipality); *Fischer v. City of Washington*, 55 S.W.3d 372, 379 (Mo. App. 2001) (interlocal cooperation law "does not limit governments to cooperation only on those projects that they could legitimately pursue alone"). See also *Foster Wheeler Energy v. Metropolitan Knox Solid Waste Auth., Inc.*, 970 F.2d 199, 204 (6th Cir. 1992) (Tennessee Interlocal Cooperation Act is a procedural statute, enabling local governments to jointly cooperate, but it does not impose additional substantive responsibilities or liabilities).

The courts have usually rejected delegation of power and similar objections to interlocal cooperation legislation. For cases rejecting a number of constitutional objections to joint agencies created by intergovernmental agreements, see *Durango Transp., Inc. v. City of Durango*, 824 P.2d 48 (Colo. App. 1991); *State ex rel. Grimes County Taxpayers Ass'n v. Texas Mun. Power Agency*, 565 S.W.2d 258 (Tex. Civ. App. 1978); *In re Quantification Settlement Agreement Cases*, 134 Cal. Rptr. 3d 244, 288–90 (2011). But see *AFSCME v. City of Detroit*, 704 N.W.2d 712 (Mich. App. 2005) (finding that a public entity created by statute to receive transportation funding was not empowered to transfer its functions to a regional transportation authority created pursuant to an interlocal agreement).

2. *Non-terminable contracts?* The Iowa statute in *Goreham* provided that the joint contract was non-terminable during the life of the joint project. A judicial disposition antagonistic to the termination of a joint contract is also evident in *Kansas City v. City of Raytown*, 421 S.W.2d 504 (Mo. 1967). The development of a joint sewer facility was contingent on the approval of a successful bond issue in one of the contracting municipalities by a certain date. Although the bond issue was not approved until the date had passed, the court was not troubled. It held that the cutoff date was inserted for the protection of the other contracting municipality that had raised no objection.

In a case in which one municipality sought to withdraw from a long-standing interlocal contract for the provision of sewage facilities, the court held that the contract would be allowed to run for a reasonable time but that governmental power to provide sewage services could not be surrendered indefinitely. *Borough of West Caldwell v. Borough of Caldwell*, 138 A.2d 402 (N.J. 1958). A fifty-year interlocal contract was upheld as reasonable in *Bair v. Layton City Corp.*, 307 P.2d 895 (Utah 1957).

Non-terminable interlocal contracts may create political problems if subsequent local administrations object to the bargain that was struck by their predecessors. *Village of Dennison v. Martin*, 210 N.E.2d 912 (Ohio 1964). The court found that the joint board created by contract to manage a joint waterworks system had sole management responsibility over the system, to the exclusion of the village board of one of the contracting municipalities. See also *Robinhood Plaza Inc. v. City Council of Jersey City*, 2017 WL 2535913 (N.J. Sup. 2017) (municipality entitled to enter into agreements to bind future municipalities or limit its own powers); *City of Sandpoint v. Independent Highway Dist.*, 384 P.3d 368 (Idaho 2016) (invalidating joint power agreement between highway district and city); *Town of Secaucus v. City of Jersey City*, 20 N.J. Tax. 562 (N.J. Tax. Ct. 2013) (municipal agreement to waive "forever" its right to sue with respect to certain property assessments held invalid as an agreement in perpetuity against public policy).

3. *Paying other governmental units.* When an interlocal contract requires one governmental unit to pay money over to another, problems may arise under the provision common to many constitutions that prevents one governmental unit from lending its credit to another. For the most part, this provision has not been an obstacle. See Antieau, *Some Legal Aspects of Municipal Finance*, 20 U. Kan. City L. Rev. 15, 42 (1951–1952). The court in *Johnson v. City of Louisville*, 261 S.W.2d 429 (Ky. 1953), held that the city could issue bonds to finance construction of a sewage disposal plant by a metropolitan sewer district. The district covered the city and some areas outside the city, although only 6% of the system's users resided outside the city limits. The court noted that the system would be a substantial benefit to city residents. In addition, the city had retained title to its portion of the system and had only turned over the management and operation of the system to the district. See also *Roberts v. City of Maryville*, *supra* Note 1 (benefits of recreation and flood control project to nonresidents of city held incidental); *Pease v. Board of County Comm'rs*, 550 P.2d 565 (Okla. 1976) (county contributions to a council of governments were for local purposes); *Urban Renewal Agency v. Hart*, 222 P.3d 467 (Idaho 2009) (Idaho's constitutional debt limit and prohibition against the loan of credit held not applicable to an urban renewal agency because it was not an alter ego of the city when it issued revenue allocation bonds to finance city projects.)

If the interlocal contract creates an independent authority to operate the facility, the constitutional provision prohibiting an appropriation of funds may not apply if appropriations to public authorities are not within the constitutional prohibition. *Opinion of the Justices*, 319 So. 2d 699 (Ala. 1975). For a case holding that an appropriation by a city to a school district covering most of the city's area was within the city's home rule powers, see *Madsen v. Oakland Unified Sch. Dist.*, 119 Cal. Rptr. 531 (Cal. App. 1975).

4. *Independent authorities resulting from cooperation agreements.* Interlocal agreements that establish independent authorities to carry out the cooperative activity add to the complexity of relationships between governments and people with whom they do business. Because each local government that is a party to an interlocal agreement may be bound by different procedural requirements had it exercised the powers now delegated to the independent, joint powers agency, a question arises as to which, if any, of these different laws bind the joint agency. The California Joint Exercise of Powers Act provides that the agency administering the joint powers agreement need comply only with the procedural restrictions binding upon one of the parties to the agreement and calls for the specification of that party in the joint agreement. Cal. Gov't Code § 6509. In *Zack v. Marin Emergency Radio Auth.*, 13 Cal. Rptr. 3d 323 (2004), the court upheld the designation of the county as the

party whose procedural restrictions were to be followed by the joint powers agency. Because the county was not subject to municipal building and zoning ordinances, the court, relying upon the statutory language, held that the joint agency likewise was exempt from their operation. *Id.* at 337–38. The court also held that the joint agency possessed the "common power" to construct and operate an emergency communications system upon finding that each of the parties to the agreement possessed at least an implied power to exercise this power. *Id.* at 337.

Revocation by one of the parties to the joint agreement presents another issue that may arise. What happens for example, if a city withdraws from a multi-government solid waste disposal project after bonds have been issued by the not-for-profit corporation created by the participating local governments? If the project then fails, can investors or suppliers recover losses from the governments that established the corporation, even though all contracts were with the corporation and not the participating governments? See *Foster Wheeler Energy v. Metro Knox Solid Waste Auth., Inc., supra* Note 1 (no additional substantive responsibilities or liabilities were created by cooperation act, and no basis was established for piercing corporate veil when governments were not members of the corporation and creditors were apprised of that fact at the time contractual relationships were established). See also *Burbank-Glendale-Pasadena Airport Auth. v. Hensler*, 99 Cal. Rptr. 2d 729 (Cal. App. 2000) (cooperating cities may delegate eminent domain power to joint powers authority).

5. *Infringement of local self-government?* Claims that an interlocal cooperation act infringed on the inherent right to local self-government were laid at rest in *City of Ecorse v. Peoples Community Hosp. Auth.*, 58 N.W.2d 159 (Mich. 1953). Interlocal agreements may also raise home rule objections. They were rejected in *City of Oakland v. Williams*, 103 P.2d 168 (Cal. 1940), holding that there was a state interest in regional cooperation for the purpose of studying sewage problems in the San Francisco Bay area. See also *Durango Transp., Inc. v. City of Durango*, 824 P.2d 48 (Colo. App. 1991) (upholding contract for operation of mass transit system). But note *Town of Plainfield v. Town of Avon*, 757 N.E.2d 705, 713 (Ind. App. 2001) (Indiana interlocal cooperation agreement statute does not authorize trial court to compel a municipality to enter into an interlocal cooperation agreement). For an argument that informal "interlocal bargains" can be an effective way of addressing regional interests by permitting "localities to realize the benefits of cooperative conduct and regional welfare while avoiding contracting difficulties," see Gillette, *Regionalization and Interlocal Bargains*, 76 N.Y.U. L. Rev. 190 (2001).

6. *Regulatory agreements.* Interlocal agreements are sometimes used for regulatory purposes. In *Vap v. City of McCook*, 136 N.W.2d 220 (Neb. 1965), the municipality and the state highway agency entered into a contract under which the city agreed to prohibit parking on a federal-aid highway that was being improved through the city. The contract was upheld against a contention that it was an improper bargaining away of the municipality's police power. A statute authorized contracts between municipalities and the highway department. The court appeared to rely on the

plenary power of the state to allocate state and local powers. It noted that the contract was necessary for the administration of the state highway system and to secure federal funds. See also *Local 22, Philadelphia Fire Fighters' Union v. Commonwealth*, 613 A.2d 522 (Pa. 1992) (intergovernmental agreement between state agency and city exchanging financial aid for adoption of financial plans and restraints upheld). For an argument that interlocal agreements can be effective in protecting natural resources and historic districts, see Mohnach, *Intermunicipal Agreements: The Metamorphosis of Home Rule*, 17 PACE ENVTL. L. REV. 161 (1999) (applying New York law). See also Nunn & Rosentraub, *Dimensions of Interjurisdictional Cooperation*, 62 J. AM. PLAN. ASS'N, NO. 2 (1997): 205-2019.

7. *Interstate compacts.* State and local governments in interstate areas have used the interstate compact to create transportation, water planning and other authorities with regional responsibilities. Newer uses for interstate compacts stem from the need to increase energy production, improve the nation's aging infrastructure, monitor prescription drugs, and regulate thoroughbred horse racing. Scott, *Interstate Compacts in 2009 and Beyond: Opportunities for an Increased Diversity of Use, in* Council of State Governments, 41 THE BOOK OF THE STATES, 35, 37 (2009). Most interlocal contracting enabling legislation authorizes interstate agreements, but the consent of Congress may be required under Art. I, § 10 of the federal Constitution. Where it is, Congress must either consent to each individual contract or provide consent in advance. Advance consent has been given in several federal laws, including the Clean Air Act and the Coastal Zone Management Act.

In the planning area, one important regional agency created by interstate compact is the Lake Tahoe Regional Planning Agency. See Comment, *Nationalizing Lake Tahoe*, 19 SANTA CLARA L. REV. 681 (1979). In *People ex rel. Younger v. County of El Dorado*, 487 P.2d 1193 (Cal. 1971), the court rejected home rule objections to the interstate compact. It held that the compact served important state and regional concerns in the protection of the environmental quality of the region.

For discussion of interstate, intergovernmental agreements to handle cross border issues, see Litwak, *State Border Towns and Resiliency: Barriers to Interstate Intergovernmental Cooperation*, 50 IDAHO L. REV. 193 (2014).

For discussion of the use of the interstate compact in the formation of interstate agencies, see ACIR, MULTISTATE REGIONALISM ch. 5 (1972); M. Ridgeway, INTERSTATE COMPACTS: A QUESTION OF FEDERALISM (1971). For cases upholding under the Compact Clause regional agencies created by Congress and authorized to develop and impose mandatory land use plans and conservation standards on local governments within their jurisdictions, see *Columbia River Gorge United v. Yeutter*, 960 F.2d 110 (9th Cir. 1992); *Seattle Master Bldrs. Ass'n v. Pacific Northwestern Elec. Power & Conserv. Planning Council*, 786 F.2d 1359 (9th Cir. 1986). See *Symposium, Seattle Master Builders and Creative Cooperative Federalism*, 17 ENVTL. L. 767 (1987).

Read literally, the Compact Clause prohibits any interstate compact or agreement unless Congress consents, but the Supreme Court has not adopted this interpretation. In *United States Steel Corp. v. Multistate Tax Comm'n*, 434 U.S. 452 (1978), the Court held that a multistate tax compact agreed to by a large number of states did not require congressional approval. The purpose of the compact was to resolve interstate taxation problems, including the taxation of multistate taxpayers. The Court reaffirmed the early holding in *Virginia v. Tennessee*, 148 U.S. 503 (1893), where the Court held that the application of the Compact Clause is limited to agreements that are "directed to the formation of any combination tending to the increase of political power in the States, which may encroach upon or interfere with the just supremacy of the United States." *Id.* at 519. For an argument that the Multistate Tax Commission's ability to set interstate transfer pricing violates the Compact Clause, see Pulver, *Interstate Transfer Pricing and the Provocation of the Compact Clause,* 46 Cumb. L. Rev. 103 (2016) (suggesting states enact a uniform law to avoid abusive transfer pricing activities).

The application of the *Tennessee* doctrine to interstate compacts providing for joint intergovernmental regulation is not clear. For example, what about an interstate compact providing for the joint administration of traffic laws in an interstate metropolitan area? See Engdahl, *Interstate Urban Areas and Interstate "Agreements" and "Compacts": Unclear Possibilities*, 58 Geo. L.J. 799 (1970). The Court in *United States Steel* did hold that congressional consent was not required just because the compact created an interstate administrative body. For studies of interstate compacts that include case studies of interstate compact organizations, see M. Ridgeway, *supra*; R. Leach & R. Sugg, The Administration of Interstate Compacts (1959). For a proposal to use the interstate compact as the foundation for an urban common market designed to help cities with significant black populations improve their economic status, see Hatcher, *Towards a New Form of Local Government: The Urban Common Market*, 7 DePaul Business L.J. 253 (1995).

[2] Transfer of Function

Eighteen states, through constitutional provision or statute or both, authorize the transfer of functions from one governmental unit to another. Kincaid, *Regulatory Regionalism in Metropolitan Areas: Voter Resistance and Reform Persistence*, 13 Pace L. Rev. 449 (1993). Transfer of function authority sometimes appears in the constitutional provision authorizing interlocal cooperation, as in the Pennsylvania constitutional provision, Art. 9, § 5. Most constitutions and statutes require voter approval of the transfer by both governmental units and may authorize permanent as well as temporary transfers. ACIR, Intergovernmental Service Arrangements, *supra*, at 18–22. Another survey indicated that 25 percent of the cities reporting had transferred some services. Public health, taxation and assessment, and solid waste collection and disposal were the services most frequently transferred. *Id.* at 69–71.

The Florida constitutional provision that follows illustrates a general grant of authority for a transfer of function. The New York provision illustrates a more detailed delegation of authority.

Florida Constitution Art. 8, § 4:

By law or resolution of the governing bodies of each of the governments affected, any function or power of a county, municipality or special district may be transferred to or contracted to be performed by another county, municipality or special district, after approval by vote of the electors of the transferor and approval by vote of the electors of the transferee, or as otherwise provided by law.

New York Constitution Art. 9, § 1(h)(1):

[Counties adopting alternative form of government] by act of the legislature or by local law, may transfer one or more functions or duties of the county or of the cities, towns, villages, districts or other units of government wholly contained in such county to each other or when authorized by the legislature to the state . . . provided, however, that [no such transfer] shall become effective unless approved on a referendum by a majority of the votes cast thereon in the area of the county outside of cities, and in the cities of the county, if any, considered as one unit.

Notes

The Florida courts have had to resolve conflicts between the constitutional transfer of function provision and a constitutional home rule provision that authorizes home rule counties to adopt ordinances that prevail over city ordinances within the county. In *Broward County v. City of Fort Lauderdale*, 480 So. 2d 631 (Fla. 1985), noted, 15 STETSON L. REV. 865 (1986), a home rule county adopted a handgun ordinance that prevailed over ordinances adopted by cities within the county. The court held that the ordinance did not require dual approval under the transfer of function constitutional provision because the ordinance was a regulatory ordinance and not an ordinance for the provision of services. Accord, *Seminole County v. City of Winter Springs*, 935 So. 2d 521 (Fla. App. 2006) (upholding county charter amendment requiring county approval of land use changes in rural area); *City of New Smyrna Beach v. County of Volusia*, 518 So. 2d 1379 (Fla. App. 1988) (uniform beach code adopted by home rule county).

A massive transfer of functions through intergovernmental agreement has occurred in Los Angeles County, California under the Lakewood Plan. To forestall annexations and incorporations that would impair the county's ability to provide services at economies of scale, the plan allows new municipalities that contract with the county for most of their services to incorporate. Although the Lakewood Plan has been hailed by government reformers, a study of the plan showed that it serves other purposes. "Minimal" cities have been incorporated by upper income homeowners who view the Lakewood Plan as an opportunity to protect themselves from higher taxes by financially pressed cities. A "Lakewood" incorporation also preserves local control over zoning while providing for municipal services without the need for a local bureaucracy. G. Miller, Cities by Contract (1981). See also M. Anderson, *The New Minimal Cities*, 123 Yale L.J. 1118 (2014); Kuyper, *Intergovernmental Cooperation: An Analysis of the Lakewood Plan*, 58 Geo. L.J. 777 (1970).

Chapter 4

State and Local Government Finance

Problem 4-1

You are an attorney in the corporate counsel's office of Big City, established in the early nineteenth century. Big City grew to prominence because of the development of labor-intensive "smokestack" industrial manufacturing and fabrication. The city attracted a diverse pool of labor—immigrants from southern and eastern Europe, African Americans from the south. As the city prospered in the twentieth century, outlying farmland was developed into suburban communities and shopping malls—populated primarily by white, middle-class families. In recent decades, the businesses that created wealth and employment in the city were acquired by global corporations that moved operations to "corporate parks" in the suburbs, or to states and other countries with lower taxes and government services costs. Over the years, Big City's population has become increasingly minority. Once proud manufacturing and fabrication plants now stand abandoned.

Big City's economy is dependent on government employment. It has been hard-hit by the opiod epidemic, and there is a substantial need for government support services, particularly given its increasingly rundown housing supply, significant crime rate and high levels of unemployment. City real property taxes and other revenues have not kept up with the costs of infrastructure maintenance and municipal services. The city has accumulated large budget deficits for the past seven years. The city has funded these budget deficits through borrowing and now has a staggering debt load. The city's employee pension fund is underfunded and will be entirely depleted in five years. To reverse these conditions, the city has solicited proposals from international project finance consultants to assist efforts to redevelop the city into a vibrant metropolis.

After considering proposals submitted, the City Council selected a proposal by D&D Development, Inc., now headquartered in London. D&D has developed large, mixed-use projects in urban settings throughout Europe and Asia. For Big City, D&D has proposed (i) annexing the adjacent suburban communities to the city to expand the city's tax and revenue base, (ii) demolishing 50 acres of structures in abandoned areas, (iii) developing a tech research and manufacturing center on the 50 acres, together with commercial and retail facilities, a variety of housing facilities, and a US campus for a major Chinese research university, (iv) installing sustainable wind and solar electric facilities, (v) building a light rail system from the central city to the outlying suburbs and the city's airport, (vi) developing a high-end resort and casino in the central city, (vii) developing an underground public parking garage, scenic park and gardens, and outdoor concert venue next to the casino, and (viii) developing world-class healthcare facilities specializing in treatment of and research into drug-related and sexually-transmitted illness.

D&D estimates the project will cost $2.7 billion to be raised as follows: (i) $1 billion from the federal government in the form of a grant for the light rail, (ii) $100 million from the state as annual budget appropriations for housing finance, (iii) $100 million for infrastructure and landscaping surrounding the casino to be funded by bonds issued by the city and repaid from the revenues generated from the garage and outdoor facilities, (iv) $350 million from bonds issued by the city for the casino payable from casino revenues, (v) $300 million from bonds for the wind and solar generating facilities payable through utility charges, (vi) $200 million in bonds payable from patents and licenses generated by the new tech research and manufacturing facilities, (vii) $150 million from bonds payable from healthcare facilities revenues, (viii) $150 million from bonds payable from lease payments by the Chinese university and retail and commercial tenants, and (ix) $350 million from bonds payable from a special assessment on all real property in the city and the annexed suburbs and a separate 1% sales tax on all goods and services sold within the 50 acre project area.

Consider the following questions: (a) Does the city have legal authority to undertake the purposes and activities contained in D&D's proposal? (b) Does the city have legal authority to enter into contracts required to undertake and finance the transactions in D&D's proposal? (c) What other legal and policy issues do you think might be raised by D&D's proposal?

Problem 4-2

The initial problem reflects realities prior to the impact of the COVID-19 pandemic that brought the United States and its citizens to their knees beginning in early 2020. Prior to the pandemic, many government officials, businesses, and citizens assumed that the future of public finance would stay on the course it had taken since the 2008–2009 Great Recession. In the face of the pandemic, all bets are off. Beginning in early 2020, Congress passed a series of stimulus and economic support packages that sought to address massive unemployment, stem stock market losses, and prop up businesses. State and local governments faced enormous losses and potential bankruptcy in the face of the virtual shut-down of most states in early 2020. Consider the materials that follow as a primer on the state of play prior to the pandemic, the constitutional constraints that have governed public finance options in the past as they will in the future, pre-pandemic strategies to foster economic growth, and prior federal strategies that affect economic development, state and local borrowing, protection against fraud, and interventions to deal with distressed governments. There are no ready answers to how the aftermath of the COVID-19 pandemic will affect state and local governments. As you explore the material that follows, think deeply about how existing understandings of legal requirements and available tools might be brought to bear in the post-pandemic world. If you were asked to advise the governor, state legislators, or local governments on strategies for rebuilding, what might you suggest?

A. Introduction

State and local government finance is an important part of the picture of governmental powers and functions. Most lay people lack experience or appreciation for the nuances of this complex field. Indeed, some attorneys specialize in the realm of public finance exclusively in order take on complex tasks relating to debt or other forms of sophisticated financing. This introduction in designed to provide a context for understanding the complex system of public finance that exists in the United States. It begins in this section with an overview of state and local revenue practices (sources, responsibilities and expenditures) and borrowing patterns, as a means of providing a context for the current system. Students will want to understand this overall context in order to navigate the future.

The public finance system that currently exists reflects the accretion of numerous policy choices made over past decades. As explained below, there are many storm warnings flying about resulting challenges facing the existing system as a result of changes in the economy, demographics, public attitudes, and shifting priorities. The global pandemic of 2020 raises the ante further. You should therefore consistently ask yourself: how do individual elements of the existing system work, why do they work that way, and should such elements or the overall system of intergovernmental finance including revenue sources, expenditure patterns, and borrowing practices be modified to face present and future challenges.

Following this introduction, the Chapter then considers issues related to public finance under state and federal constitutions. It then turns in more depth to the nuances of revenues, borrowing, and budgeting. Finally, it considers issues relating to federal law including those associated with bankruptcy and regulation of securities and associated activities.

[1] Roles, Revenue Sources, and Expenditures of States and Localities

[a] States

Role

States' roles in funding government have varied considerably over time. A 2009 study by the National Conference of State Legislatures framed state roles prior to the Great Depression as focusing primarily on highways, with 30% of general revenue coming from highway fuel and motor vehicle licensing taxes and 36% of their expenditure going toward road construction. They also contributed relatively small amounts to local government for elementary and secondary education, and modest funds to public higher education. Expenditures for health, hospitals, corrections, welfare and public assistance (including funds provided to local governments for those purposes) came to less than half of what was spent on highways. In 1927, property taxes contributed 82% of local revenues and 20% of state revenues. State and local governments' share of the gross domestic product at the start of the Great Depression in 1929 fell between 7 and 8%, while the federal share was less than 2%. By 1938, both the state/local government share and the federal share approached 9%, with the federal share continuing to increase to 14% into the World War II period, and state/local government declining to 7%. Snell, *State Finance in the Great Depression* 2–3 (March 2009), available at http://www.ncsl.org/Portals/1/documents/fiscal/STATEFINANCEGREATDEPRESSION.pdf.

During the Depression, both states and localities significantly increased payments for unemployment benefits, while the federal government contributed significantly to that end using a system of matching grants and competitive grants. Local property tax revenues fell significantly, and state property tax revenues fell to a somewhat lesser extent. By the 1930s, states introduced personal income taxes (often coupled with corporate income taxes), general sales tax, and taxes on alcohol and tobacco among others. *Id.* at 4–6. By 1940, states were spending much more on welfare (19% of their budgets) and unemployment compensation (9.9%), a good deal less on highways, and slightly less on education. *Id.* at 7. Ultimately, as explained in Chapter 9, many states have taken on a large share of the cost of public education in order to equalize the uneven funding available among localities reliant on property taxes. *A Very Brief History of Education Finance in the United States*, National Conference of State Legislatures (June 2019), available at http://www.ncsl.org/Portals/1/Documents/fiscal/Fiscal_meetings/Dan_Thatcher_Presentation_33403.pdf (reviewing data from National Center for Education Statistics for 2002–2016 showing that overall state expenditures on elementary and secondary education during the period generally equaled or slightly exceeded local expenditures, albeit differences in such patterns from state to state are also important).

Revenue Sources

Most states have increasingly relied upon personal income tax and general sales tax receipts as sources of revenue. Nationwide, pre-pandemic, personal income tax amounted to 38.1% of state revenue, while general sales tax amounted to 30.9%. Personal income taxes were the greatest source of revenue in 31 of the 41 states that imposed them. General sales tax was the largest source for 15 of the 45 states that imposed them. According to the Pew Charitable Trusts, revenue sources varied significantly from state to state. For example, Alaska, Florida, Nevada, South Dakota, Texas, Washington, and Wyoming did not impose any personal income tax, while Oregon was heavily reliant on such taxes (which made up more than 70% of its revenue). Alaska and New Hampshire had only a selective sales tax, while Florida and Nevada were very heavily reliant on that source (at 64.3% and 55.6% of state revenue respectively). Many others had a selective sales tax (typically on such items as alcohol and tobacco) as well as a general sales tax. A handful of states imposed a severance tax on extraction of natural resources, most significantly Alaska, Montana, New Mexico, North Dakota, Oklahoma, Texas, West Virginia, and Wyoming.

Some states tapped significant property tax revenues (for example, Vermont and New Hampshire). See Pew Charitable Trusts, *How States Raise Their Tax Dollars* (July 2019), available at https://www.pewtrusts.org/en/research-and-analysis/data-visualizations/2014/fiscal-50#ind0 (reporting on U.S. Census Bureau's 2018 Annual Survey of State Government Tax Collection). See also National Association of State Budget Officers, Summary, *Fall 2019 Fiscal Survey of States*, at 6 (Fall 2019), available at https://higherlogicdownload.s3.amazonaws.com/NASBO/9d2d2db1-c943-4f1b-b750-0fca152d64c2/UploadedImages/Issue%20Briefs%20/Summary_-_Fall_2019_Fiscal_Survey.pdf.

Two trends are particularly striking. There had been a significant growth in federal grants to the states, which was largely attributable to increased federal support for Medicaid expansion under the Affordable Care Act. See Pew Charitable Trusts, *Federal Grants Account for Newly a Third of State Revenues* (October 2019), available at https://www.pewtrusts.org/en/research-and-analysis/articles/2019/10/08/federal-funds-hover-at-a-third-of-state-revenue (using US Census Bureau, 2017 Annual Survey of State Government Finances); Pew Charitable Trusts, *Medicaid Makes Up Most Federal Grants to States* (March 2019), available at https://www.pewtrusts.org/en/research-and-analysis/fact-sheets/2019/03/medicaid-makes-up-most-federal-grants-to-states (Medicaid made up 65% of federal grants to states, but mix varies). There had also been a growing reliance on "sin taxes" such as those on gambling or marijuana. See Dadayan, Tax Policy Center, *Are States Betting on Sin? The Murky Future of State Taxation* (October 2019), available at https://www.urban.org/sites/default/files/publication/101132/are_states_betting_on_sin-the_murky_future_of_state_taxation.pdf.

State Expenditures

The National Association of State Budget Officers undertakes periodic surveys relating to state revenues and expenditure patterns.

Expenditures by Function (estimated fiscal year 2019)	Total State Expenditures	State Funds
Medicaid	28.9%	16.4%
K-12 Education	19.5%	24.9%
Higher Education	10.1%	13.1%
Transportation	8.1%	7.9%
Corrections	3.0%	4.4%
Public Assistance	1.2%	0.7%
All Other	29.1%	32.6%

NASBO, *Summary, State Expenditure Report* at 3 (November 2019), available at https://www.nasbo.org/reports-data/state-expenditure-report.

As with revenues, the mix of state expenditures varies from state to state. See NASBO, *State Expenditure Report* (November 2019), available at https://higherlogicdownload.s3.amazonaws.com/NASBO/9d2d2db1-c943-4f1b-b750-0fca152d64c2/UploadedImages/SER%20Archive/2019_State_Expenditure_Report-S.pdf.

[b] Localities

Roles

As discussed in Chapter 1, there are a variety of types of local government entities, including counties (that in many states perform functions as agents of the state, such as providing for public health, sheriffs, and court operations), various kinds of special purpose districts, and municipalities. Municipalities typically provide enhanced or more intensive services in areas that fall within their incorporated boundaries.

In some jurisdictions, municipalities may be coterminous with public school districts and may have authority over establishing tax rates to meet their budget requirements, while in others, counties may perform that requirement. Still elsewhere, town meetings may have responsibilities for ultimate action on recommendations from school boards (often based on recommendations from school boards to an elected town council or select board).

By way of introduction, it may be helpful to understand how municipal corporations differ from business corporations that also deliver goods and services. For example, business corporations may engage in any lawful activities to achieve a purpose set forth in law or in its articles of incorporation, while municipalities generally may not engage in profit-generating activities and may use their financial powers only as prescribed by state law and local legislation. Business corporations may raise revenues, spend money and borrow under general commercial law principles, while municipal corporations are typically much more legally constrained in such activities. Municipal revenue sources often include involuntary payments rather than voluntary sales transactions.

Business corporations are typically owned by shareholders who derive income through dividends and stock sales, but there is no stock ownership of municipal corporations and no dividends paid. Business corporations typically have as their goal making money and increasing value, while municipal corporations provide services such as infrastructure. Business corporations raise money by issuing debt and by selling stock, while municipalities do not issue stock and are managed by elected officials. Municipal corporations typically operate only within their geographic boundaries unless they receive requests and reach agreement to offer services more broadly. Municipal debt is typically more favorably treated for purposes of federal and state income taxation, compared to income derived from business corporations. Sale of stocks and bonds by publicly held business corporations must comply with review and reporting requirements managed by the states and by the federal Securities and Exchange Commission. Securities requirements applicable to municipal corporations differ in some important respects, as discussed later in this Chapter. Legal provisions governing bankruptcy protections likewise differ between business and municipal corporations as explained below.

Revenue Sources

Municipalities have long heavily relied upon property tax revenues, as previously discussed. That reliance made some considerable sense, since traditionally property ownership stood as a proxy for wealth, and property assessments could best be managed at a local level. Historically, at least in some states, municipalities experiencing development pressures just beyond their corporate boundaries engaged in annexation as a means of bolstering property tax revenue. As discussed in Chapter 1, annexation can be voluntary (by petition of a property owner) or involuntary (at the instance of a municipality if certain criteria are met). In North Carolina, among other states, rural hostility toward municipalities has led to greater constraints on involuntary annexation since the ascendency of Tea Party activism.

Some states have authorized municipalities (or counties) to receive some portion of general state-collected sales taxes (or may have authorized municipalities or counties to impose general sales taxes at their discretion). In some states, certain municipalities may be authorized to collect personal income taxes, particularly when urban workers may not live in the cities where they work but may contribute significantly to associated urban costs (such as road maintenance or public safety expenses).

Since the California tax revolt in the late 1970s, tax and expenditure limits have swept the country, as discussed below. Limitations have increasingly been imposed on tax increases at the state or local level or both, particularly when property taxes are concerned. As a result, localities have turned to other novel strategies, two of which warrant particular attention here. Increasingly, municipalities (and states) have imposed user charges or fees as a means of covering costs that may not otherwise be fundable through general revenue sources. Simple examples include charges for use of public parks or recreation activities, but other less common assessments or fees such as development impact fees, impervious surface fees, library fees or ambulance surcharges have been employed as discussed below. A related approach, discussed in Chapter 1 and again later in this Chapter, has been to increase the range and number of special purpose districts as a means of avoiding limitations on municipalities or counties to impose tax increases. Such districts are typically not covered by classic limitations and often are managed by appointed rather than elected officials. They often are organized to perform specific functions (such as improving downtown business districts, providing public transit, or providing water and sewer services) and can impose assessments or user charges associated with such activities directly on users to assure themselves of a dedicated revenue stream.

Expenditures

Local government spending priorities differ from those of the states. Local governments have typically spent a substantial portion of their budgets on K-12 education (40%), with lesser amounts on health and hospitals (10%), police and corrections (8%), highways and roads (4%), public welfare (4%) and higher education (3%). See https://www.urban.org/policy-centers/cross-center-initiatives/state-and-local-finance-initiative/state-and-local-backgrounders/state-and-local-expenditures#Question2 (reporting on fiscal year 2016 data from the Annual Survey of State and Local Government Finances). Such expenditures have varied significantly from state to state and locality to locality. *Id.* Updated information from the periodic national survey is available on the U.S. Census site at https://

www.census.gov/programs-surveys/gov-finances.html. The National League of Cities is another important source of periodic information on local spending practices. See https://www.nlc.org/resource/city-fiscal-conditions-2019-report. It is important to remember that significant differences are evident in expenditures depending on location, size, and circumstances of municipalities. See, e.g., Hendrick & Degnan, *In the Shadow of State Government: Changes in Municipal Spending After Two Recessions*, 50 Amer. Rev. of Pub. Admin. No. 2 (2019): 161–175.

[c] Anticipating the Future

This introductory section is designed to ground discussions of legal and policy issues throughout the rest of Chapter 4. Current realities are by no means static, particularly in light of the impact of the COVID pandemic, and it is therefore important also to offer some sense of what the future may hold.

The Significance of Intergovernmental Relations. Leading scholars attentive to policy issues affecting public finance have recommended that close attention should be given to the interplay of revenue sources and governmental responsibilities. For example, the Brookings Institution, among others, has emphasized the importance of thinking through the alignment of city tax structures with sound fiscal bases in order to create a "fiscal policy space" in which core city goals can be achieved. See Pagano & Hoene, *City Budgets in an Era of Increased Uncertainty*, Brookings Institution (July 2018), available at https://www.brookings.edu/research/city-budgets-in-an-era-of-increased-uncertainty/. For broader reflections on the implications of changing intergovernmental policy, see D. Berman, Local Government and the States: Autonomy, Politics, and Policy 31 (2d ed. 2020) (as part of discussion of federal, state and local relations generally, observing that federal government has moved since the 1970s from a cooperative pattern relationships to a more conflictual relationship characterized by less funding, more regulations and more mandates).

In thinking about intergovernmental relations in the future, it will be important to consider how federal and state governments might claim control of revenue sources traditionally reserved to state and local governments respectively. As federal deficits mount, it is very possible that the federal government might attempt to assert claims against traditional state revenue sources (such as sales or income taxes) and that state governments might assert claims against traditionally local sources of revenue (such as property taxes). Ebel, Petersen & Vu, *Introduction: State and Local Government Finance in The United States* at 3, *in* The Oxford Handbook of State and Local Government Finance (Robert D. Ebel & John E. Petersen, Eds.) (2012) (in light of major tax cuts and growing federal debt, the federal government is "on an unsustainable financial path [and] may try to address its financial mess in part by 'pushing the deficit down' to state and local budgets in the form of a more 'coercive federalism' of regulations, unfunded mandates, and preemptions of state revenues"). This risk has grown exponentially in view of massive federal debt and imperatives to address the financial consequences of the COVID pandemic.

Notwithstanding broad pressures for reallocation of revenue sources among different levels of government, other more specific factors affecting revenue sources and potential expenditures also need to be borne in mind.

- *TELs.* Many states and localities must now comply with taxation and expenditure limitations (TELs) instituted since the California property tax revolt that began in the 1970's. Substantial scholarly research suggests that such limitations (discussed later in this Chapter) have had a major impact on fiscal policies of states and localities and are likely to have a constraining influence going forward. See, e.g., McCubbins & McCubbins, *Cheating on Their Taxes: When are Tax Limitations Effective at Limiting State Taxes, Expenditures, and Budgets*, 67 Tax L. Rev. 507 (2014) (discussing tax and expenditure limitations); Sungho Park, *The Impact of State-Imposed Fiscal Rules on Municipal Government Fiscal Outcomes: Does Institutional Configuration Matter?* 50 State & Loc. Gov't Rev., No. 4 (2018): 230-43 (concluding that fiscal limitations' effects on local governments may vary depending on configuration of those limitations).
- *Health care.* Health care costs have continued to rise. The federal government has agreed to help subsidize state Medicaid programs, but such funding may be at risk if the Supreme Court strikes down other aspects of the federal Affordable Care Act. For a discussion of rising costs associated with Medicaid, see Kiewiet & McCubbins, *State and Local Government Finance: The New Fiscal Ice Age*, 17 Annual Rev. of Polit. Sci. (2014): 105–22, at 110–12 (citing growing Medicaid costs associated with growing number of elderly who cannot afford health costs associated with aging).
- *Pension costs.* Many states and localities have failed to provide sufficient funding to meet pension obligations to state and federal workers in coming years. Commitments to deliver such benefits have often been found to be protected under the federal (or state) constitutional Contracts Clause. Nonetheless, many states have failed to allocate sufficient funds to assure that their obligations to public employees are adequately funded from one year to the next and have instead opted to provide limited contributions from year to year to meet pension obligations. Many observers believe that pent-up obligations to provide pension funds for state and local government employees create significant risks to states and localities in meeting financial obligations going forward. See, e.g., Kiewiet & McCubbins, *supra*, at 110–112 (citing growing Medicaid costs associated with growing number of elderly who cannot afford health costs associated with aging).
- *Infrastructure needs.* It is well-documented that federal, state and local governments have failed to invest funds needed to maintain and update core infrastructure such as roads, bridges, dams and other public facilities. See McNichol, *It's Time for States to Invest in Infrastructure*, Center on Budget Policy and Priorities (March 19, 2019), available at https://www.cbpp.org/sites/default/files/atoms/files/2-23-16sfp.pdf. A crucial question will be how such costs can be addressed in the face of continuing deterioration when other pressing needs

have supplanted traditional funding for such expenditures at the state and local government level.

A Gloomy Picture. Even pre-pandemic, projections by the Government Accountability Office and others suggest that it is unlikely that state and local governments will be able to meet competing demands to fund Medicaid-related services and pensions while maintaining overall fiscal health unless they further shrink expenditures or increase revenues. See United States Government Accountability Office, GAO-20-269SP, *State and Local Governments' Fiscal Outlook* (December 2019 Update), available at https://www.gao.gov/assets/710/703475.pdf. When seen in the context of growing federal debt, antiquated revenue systems, significant caps on revenues and expenditures during a likely post-pandemic recession, times indeed look grim.

[2] Borrowing

The initial portion of this introduction has addressed government roles, revenues, and expenditures. This short section provides an overview on state and local borrowing, to help orient students about the issues addressed in later parts of this Chapter.

Limitations. The public has long sought to limit borrowing by state and local governments. You may want to consider why borrowing is not readily authorized, for example, because it creates obligations on future revenue streams, potentially benefits certain influential players, or competes with private sector providers in certain contexts. Not surprisingly, state constitutions have historically placed limitations on borrowing (types of borrowing, votes for approval, uses of funds raised), and state and local legislative provisions have constrained the circumstances when public borrowing is allowed. The Urban Institute has developed significant resources explaining such constraints. See Rueben & Randall, *Debt Limits: How States Restrict Borrowing,* Urban Institute (2017), available at https://www.urban.org/sites/default/files/publication/94906/debt-limits_9.pdf (40 states limited debt as of 2015); Rueben & Randall, *Balanced Budget Requirements: How States Restrict Borrowing,* Urban Institute (2017), available at https://www.urban.org/research/publication/balanced-budget-requirements (46 states and the District of Columbia have balanced budget requirements); Rueben & Randall, *Supermajority Tax and Budget Rules: How Voting Requirements Affect Budgets*, Urban Institute (2017), available at https://www.urban.org/sites/default/files/publication/94936/supermajority-budget-and-tax-rules_2.pdf (14 states impose supermajority requirements to pass budget or impose tax increases). Federal law has given favorable tax-benefited treatment to local borrowing, but has increasingly sought to target circumstances in which such benefits may arise.

Typology and Nuances. Many people are unfamiliar with some of the terminology and nuances employed in creating a range of local or state government debt/borrowing opportunities. It may therefore be helpful to review the spectrum of borrowing frameworks that are commonly used in the public sector.

- *General obligation bonds.* Such bonds are typically backed by the faith and credit of the government entity undertaking to borrow funds. The government typically pledges to repay the funds borrowed by employing its taxing power as necessary.
- *Revenue bonds.* Bonds reflecting borrowing of this type are typically designed to provide for repayment from a specific revenue source (such as transit revenues, student rents paid to on-campus housing facilities, and so forth). The point here is that the general taxing authority of the government is not committed as a source for repayment of associated borrowing, but instead, repayment is specified to come from a designated clear stream of revenue.
- *Moral obligation bonds.* Governments may at times try to bolster their borrowing power and secure favorable revenue streams by stating that they may in future agree to step in and contribute to repayment of funds borrowed because they believe that doing so is a non-binding "moral obligation." Typically, bonds of this sort are issued in conjunction with a governmental statement of intent potentially to step in and back up the borrowing with a supplemental stream of governmental funding. Bonds of this sort are not as clearly grounded in a clearly committed government funding source, but may be more desirable than borrowing that lacks any suggestion of government support in the future as necessary.
- *Innovative strategies and work arounds.*

  Engagement with the private sector. Increasingly, state and local governments have partnered with private sector individuals and entities to borrow funds and secure requisite infrastructure. One commonly used method is the issuance of "certificates of participation" that allow private parties to invest and glean investment revenue from public-private infrastructure projects. Other forms of public-private partnerships will be considered in depth later in the Chapter.

  Work arounds. A variety of strategies have been employed by state and local governments to avoid traditional constraints on governmental borrowing. For example, special purpose districts may be created and employed to deliver certain types of services or infrastructure without compliance with traditional constraints on borrowing and decision-making. As discussed below, state and local governments may employ lease-purchase agreements as a means of avoiding the application of more stringent borrowing rules.

B. Constitutional Limitations and Protections

[1] State Constitutions

Most state constitutions contain 19th century provisions that continue to shape public finance operations in the 21st century. Public finance law is primarily governed by state law, except to the extent that state policies or practices are constrained by federal constitutional provisions or federal statutes impose requirements that influence practices in state and local borrowing, influence the availability of federal funding, or influence matters such as bankruptcy protection. Important sources for understanding state constitutional provisions relating to public finance include Briffault, *Foreword: The Disfavored Constitution: State Fiscal Limits and State Constitutional Law*, 34 Rutgers L.J. 907 (2003) (discussing public purpose doctrine, limitations on debt and taxation); Shanske, *Interpreting State Fiscal Constitutions: A Modest Proposal*, 69 Rutgers U. L. Rev. 1331 (2017) (discussing distinctions between taxes and fees); Kinkaid, *The Constitutional Frameworks of State and Local Government Finance*, *in* The Oxford Handbook of State and Local Government Finance (ed. Ebel & Petersen, 2012) (discussing both state constitutional provisions and relevant federal provisions). Crucial clauses in state constitutions relating to public finance include those relating to taxation (uniformity, prohibition on double taxation, procedural requirements on imposition of taxes, tax limitations), requirements relating to public purposes (relating to expenditures and lending of credit), limitations on expenditures, and substantive fiscal obligations such as those relating to funding of public schools (as discussed in Chapter 9). This initial overview of some of the less familiar state constitutional provisions is intended to set the stage for more in-depth discussion of related points later in the Chapter.

[a] Taxation

[i] Uniformity

Constitutions of most states speak to the state taxing power and place limits on that power, including a requirement that taxation be "uniform" among classes of assets and persons. For example, Illinois expressly adopted the limitation theory: "The General Assembly has the exclusive power to raise revenue by law except as limited or otherwise provided in this Constitution." Ill. Const. art. IX, § 1. The Illinois Supreme Court gave this provision a broad interpretation along the intended lines in *Berry v. Costello*, 341 N.E.2d 709 (Ill. 1976), upholding a "privilege tax" on mobile homes. The Illinois Constitution also includes a series of limitations on the state's taxing power:

> Section 2. In any law classifying the subjects or objects of non-property taxes or fees, the classes shall be reasonable and the *subjects and objects within each class shall be taxed uniformly* [emphasis supplied]. Exemptions, deductions, credits, refunds and other allowances shall be reasonable. ["Uniformity Clause."]

The uniformity requirement found in Section 2 above is an example of "equal protection"—protection afforded taxpayers under state constitutional limits to tax, although it is not related to the Fourteenth Amendment other than its similarity of analysis to the "rational relationship" test in applying the federal constitutional requirement. Uniformity simply means that subjects of taxation (people and things) who are similar must be taxed in the same way.

Note that, as with many state constitutional provisions, nuances vary from state to state and may drive differences in judicial decisions. For example, in some states, the uniformity standard only applies to property taxes, while in others, it applies more broadly to additional types of taxes. See J. Hellerstein, W. Hellerstein & J. Swain, STATE TAXATION § 2.01 (3d ed. 2019) (comparing Maine Constitution's limits to property taxation with Georgia Constitution's requirement of uniformity in taxation as to the same class of subjects). Even if the state provisions apply to property taxation, additional lines may be drawn. In *2nd Roc-Jersey Assoc v. Town of Morristown*, 731 A.2d 1 (N.J. 1999), residential properties were excluded from assessments in an improvement district established to rehabilitate properties and attract new business (i.e., economic development). The court held that if the assessments were a tax, the assessment would violate the Uniformity Clause of the New Jersey Constitution because the assessment did not apply to residential properties, but concluded it was an assessment not a tax.

More detailed consideration will be given to the application of the uniformity requirement later in this Chapter in the section addressing property taxation more specifically. For a recent case addressing uniformity requirements outside the property tax context, see *Labell v. City of Chicago*, __ N.E.3d __, 2019 IL App (1st) 181379, 2019 WL 6258401 (Ill. App. 2019). In that case, plaintiffs challenged a City of Chicago amusement tax ordinance that applied to streaming services billed to accounts with city addresses. The court upheld the amusement tax as consistent with the state's home rule provisions, and then proceeded to review the effect of Article IX, section 2, of the Illinois Constitution that reads "In any law classifying the subjects or objects of non-property taxes or fees, the classes shall be reasonable and the subjects and objects within each class shall be taxed uniformly. Exemptions, deductions, credits, refunds and other allowances shall be reasonable." The court concluded that there was a real and substantial difference between residents and nonresidents that justified the application of the tax to those with city billing addresses, and found that there was also a "real and substantial difference" between streaming services and automatic amusement devices sufficient to justify the amusement tax's structure. For a detailed discussion of uniformity provisions and related caselaw see J. Hellerstein et al., STATE TAXATION §§ 2.01–2.06 (3d ed., 2019). For a classic study, see W. Newhouse, CONSTITUTIONAL UNIFORMITY AND EQUALITY IN STATE TAXATION (2d ed. 1984).

[ii] Double Taxation

In addition to uniformity, another common limitation on state taxing powers is a prohibition against double taxation. The prohibition is not absolute but is a matter of public policy that courts enforce unless legislative intent to the contrary is clear. In reversing an appellate court's approval of a decision to tax both the legal title to real property (tangible property) and the equitable right to dispose of the same real estate (intangible property) when the two interests were held by separate but related corporate taxpayers, the Supreme Court of Kentucky, in *Kentucky Power Co. v. Revenue Cabinet*, 705 S.W.2d 904 (Ky. 1985), stated:

> Double taxation is against public policy and will be permitted only where the legislature has clearly declared a contrary policy. Where the legislative intent is less than clear, a statute should be construed so as to avoid double taxation in any form.
>
> There is only one piece of property involved, the underlying real estate. Legal title and equitable title are vested in two different corporations. The separation of legal and equitable title does not in and of itself create another piece of tangible taxable property.
>
> Kentucky Power's equitable title is worth the purchase price or book value of the property. Franklin's [a real estate company organized to hold and dispose of property at Kentucky Power's direction] legal interest is virtually worthless because of itself it owns nothing and can exercise no control over the property. Together, their interests comprise the whole of the property: legal title plus equitable title, and these interests have a value equal to the purchase price of the property. We are not convinced by the Revenue Cabinet's arguments that the value of the right to dispose of the property is worth another $20 million to Kentucky Power.
>
> KRS 134.060 requires an *ad valorem* tax on the equitable owner of the tangible property. KRS 132.220(3) mandates the equitable owner to list the property for assessment. This Court has previously determined that the practical administration of *ad valorem* tax laws requires that in ordinary circumstances one person or entity be held responsible for the tax liability on each item of property.
>
> The power to dispose of property is an incident of ownership and not a taxable intangible.
>
> The fact that Kentucky Power was required to place the property for Federal Energy Regulatory Commission accounting purposes into an account known as "other investments," does not create a taxable intangible. The FERC regulates public utility interstate electric and natural gas rates. It is neither a taxing authority nor a prescriber of standards for taxing authorities.
>
> [*Kentucky Power Co. v. Revenue Cabinet*, 705 S.W.2d 904, 905–06 (Ky. 1985).]

[b] Spending and Borrowing: Public Purpose and Lending of Credit

Some specific constitutional limitations limit the taxing power and the borrowing power of states and local governments. One of these, the public purpose doctrine, is either expressly included in state constitutions or implied by judicial action. The public purpose doctrine limits the purposes for which public funds may be spent. This doctrine, and a related constitutional limitation prohibiting the lending of credit to private entities, also limits the purposes for which public debt may be incurred. These doctrines are straightforward: taxes and proceeds of borrowing can only be applied to facilities and services that serve the public at large. They cannot be applied to primarily benefit a private individual, corporation, or other entity.

The following case raises state and federal constitutional issues related to a determination of whether the proceeds of the bonds serve a public purpose. Can you identify those issues?

Idaho Water Resource Board v. Kramer

97 Idaho 535, 548 P.2d 35 (1976)

McQuade, Chief Justice

[This case challenged a state statute authorizing joint ventures between the Board and private companies for the construction of a dam and hydroelectric power generating facility in the Grandview-Guffey Reach of the Snake River. The statute is reproduced in full in the opinion. It authorized the Board to sell revenue bonds to finance the construction of the facility, and to enter into joint venture agreements with a privately-owned electric utility under which the facility is to be leased to the utility, all revenues from the lease to be pledged to the retirement of the bonds. Any surplus revenues from the facility were to be held in the custody of the Board in a special development fund and used by the Board "in the development of water and related land resources" in the state. Any agreements authorizing a joint venture were to be submitted to an interim committee, apparently in the legislature, if one was appointed, and, in any event, were subject to veto by the legislature at its next regular session.

The intervenor in this case, a private electric utility, proposed to enter into a joint venture with the Board pursuant to the statute. Under that joint venture, the utility would reconstruct a dam and power plant and construct a new dam and power plant in the Grandview-Guffey Reach, as part of a comprehensive water, land and related resources plan for southwestern Idaho that had been prepared prior to 1969 by the United States Bureau of Reclamation. This joint venture followed the terms of the statute. The dams were to be constructed by the state Board and leased to the utility, which would make payments to the Board to cover the cost of constructing the dams. Power generating facilities at the dam sites were to be constructed, owned, and operated by the utility. Any surplus payments made to the Board were to be applied by it for future irrigation development.—Eds.]

Appellant next argues that [the statute], and the agreement, constitute a violation of the due process clause provision of art. I, § 13 of the State Constitution because the proposed joint venture arrangement is not for a "public purpose." [Courts often assimilate the public purpose requirement to due process limitations.—Eds.]

Appellant contends that this provision of the Constitution requires that any activity engaged in by the state be for some public purpose. In appellant's view, the proposed undertaking does not effectuate a public purpose because the state is being placed in a position of constructing dams for the sole purpose of leasing them to a privately owned and operated company, with no showing that the state must construct the dams and lease them to the intervenor in order to adequately provide for its inhabitants. We do not agree with this argument.

It is a fundamental constitutional limitation upon the powers of government that activities engaged in by the state, funded by tax revenues, must have primarily a public rather than a private purpose. A public purpose is an activity that serves to benefit the community as a whole and which is directly related to the functions of government. The development and conservation of the state's water resources has long been recognized as constituting a necessary public purpose. Such a public purpose is evident in this case.

In addition, the Legislature in enacting chapter 265, as amended declared:

> SECTION 1. The legislature finds and declares that the development of the Grandview-Guffy Reach of the Snake River by the Idaho water resource board is in the public interest and that it is a public purpose that the Idaho water resource board exercise the powers authorized in sections 2, 3, 4, 5 and 6 of this act to: (a) maximize the recreational potential, development of fish and wildlife habitat, and uses of the water resources of Idaho; (b) facilitate irrigation of the arid lands of Idaho by providing means of utilizing the water resources of Idaho; and (c) by contributing to the development of necessary electrical energy for use in the Ada-Canyon County area of southwest Idaho, achieve economy in the generation of electricity through the use of water resources thereby meeting the future power needs of the state of Idaho and its inhabitants.

This declaration by the Legislature of public purpose is normally afforded great deference, although it is by no means binding or conclusive upon this Court. It will not be overturned, however, unless it is found to be arbitrary or unreasonable. We are not convinced that such is the situation in the present appeal.

Appellant next argues that the state in this proposed undertaking is loaning its "credit" to the intervenor, and that this is contrary to the prohibition contained in art. VIII, § 2 of the Idaho Constitution. Appellant places primary reliance upon this Court's decision in *Village of Moyie Springs, Idaho v. Aurora Mfg. Co.* [, 353 P.2d 767 (Idaho 1960)]. We believe appellant's reliance upon that case is misplaced.

Art. VIII, § 2 of the State Constitution provides in pertinent part:

> 2. *Loan of state's credit prohibited—Holding stock in corporation prohibited—Development of water power.*—The credit of the state shall not, in any manner, be given, or loaned to, or in aid of any individual, association, municipality or corporation;

In the case of *Engelking v. Investment Bd.*, [458 P.2d 213 (Idaho 1969),] this Court construed art. VIII, § 2 of the State Constitution as follows:

> The word "credit" as used in this provision (art. VIII, § 2) implies the imposition of some new financial liability upon the State which in effect results in the creation of State debt for the benefit of private enterprises. This was the evil intended to be remedied by Idaho Const. art. 8 § 2, and similar provisions in other state constitutions.

The Court later on in the opinion added:

> The credit clause of Idaho Const. art. VIII § 2 is intended to preclude only State action which principally aims to aid various private schemes.

We have previously decided that no state "debt" or "liability" for the benefit of a private enterprise will be created by respondent's proposed bond issuance. On the contrary, the bonds themselves clearly show that the state is *not* placing its faith or credit behind their payment. The bonds are to be retired out of revenues generated from the project only. Under no circumstances can a tax be levied or public property be encumbered to help pay any part of the bond issue. Prospective bond purchasers are put on notice that they have no payment recourse against any public entity. Furthermore, not only is the proposed issuance of revenue bonds by respondent not a loaning of the state's credit, as that term has been interpreted, but the contemplated bond issue is not ". . . in aid of any . . . corporation . . ." within the meaning of that prohibition contained in art. VIII, § 2. The principal benefits of the project inure to the public. Any benefit to the intervenor is secondary and incidental. We therefore hold that the joint venture arrangement does not contravene the prohibition on the loaning of state credit expressed in art. VIII, § 2.

We do not believe the *Moyie Springs* case compels us to reach a contrary conclusion. There are significant distinctions between the facts of that case and the circumstances of the present appeal which make the *Moyie Springs* decision inapposite.

In *Moyie Springs*, at issue was a state statute which authorized municipalities to issue revenue bonds for the purpose of financing the cost of acquiring land and constructing facilities which were to be sold or leased to private enterprises. The village of Moyie Springs acting pursuant to this statute, passed an ordinance providing for the issuance of revenue bonds to defray its cost of acquiring a site, and constructing an industrial plant which it planned to lease to the Aurora Manufacturing Company for a term of thirty years. When Aurora Manufacturing Company questioned the legality of the proposed arrangement and refused to perform its part of the agreement, the village brought an action for a declaratory judgment, to adjudicate both the rights of the parties, and the constitutionality of the statute and ordinance.

This Court found both the statute and ordinance to be invalid. It ruled that the proposed revenue bond issue was violative of the constitutional restriction against a municipality loaning its credit in aid of a private corporation. In addition, the proposed venture was found to have only an incidental or indirect benefit to the public.

In reaching its conclusion, the Court was particularly concerned with the specter of a state or one of its subdivisions promoting, sponsoring or regulating one private commercial or industrial enterprise to the detriment of others in the field, and the effect such a dangerous precedent would have upon the free enterprise system:

> It is obvious that private enterprise, not so favored, could not compete with industries operating thereunder. If the state-favored industries were successfully managed, private enterprise would of necessity be forced out, and the state, through its municipalities, would increasingly become involved in promoting, sponsoring, regulating and controlling private business, and our free private enterprise economy would be replaced by socialism. [*Village of Moyie Springs, Idaho v. Aurora Mfg. Co.*, 353 P.2d at 775.]

In the situation before us, there is no effort by the state to single out one private commercial or industrial enterprise in competition with several others in the field for preferential treatment or favored tax exemption status. Rather, what is involved is a joint cooperative effort between a state agency, and a public utility subject to state regulation, to enhance the production and availability of electrical power, essential to the welfare of all the citizenry of the state. The state is not proposing to engage in or sponsor a project traditionally left to the private domain, as was the situation in *Moyie Springs*, but instead is participating in an activity with a quasi-public entity, to produce a service necessary for the well being of the public. Unlike the *Moyie Springs* case, where the village sought to purchase the industrial land site and construct the entire facility for the private entity's commercial exploitation, here the state is only financing the cost of its part of the undertaking. The intervenor is responsible for financing the cost of the power generation facilities which it will use at the dam sites. In *Moyie Springs*, the state legislation pursuant to which the village was acting, authorized the municipalities to sell or otherwise dispose of any project upon such terms and conditions as it deemed advisable. There is no comparable provision in the enabling legislation providing for the Swan Falls-Guffey Project, nor is there any section in the agreement, as amended, which allows for the state's interest in the project to be sold or otherwise disposed of. For all of the above-mentioned reasons, we cannot agree with appellant's assertion that there is no real distinction between the present Swan Falls-Guffey Project and the project contemplated in *Moyie Springs*. We have carefully reviewed the additional authority cited by appellant from other jurisdictions and find them to be distinguishable.

Notes and Questions

1. *The public purpose limitation.* Virtually all states have a related clause in their constitutions that typically provides that the credit of the state and its political subdivisions "shall not in any manner be given or loaned to or in aid of any individual, association or corporation." This limitation applies both to taxing and spending. It arose out of the railroad scandals of the later nineteenth century. State legislatures authorized their municipalities to issue bonded debt in aid of railroad construction,

and massive defaults occurred when many of these enterprises failed. See, e.g., Wallwork & Wallwork, *Protecting Public Funds: A History of Enforcement of the Arizona Constitution's Prohibition Against Improper Private Benefit from Public Funds*, 23 Ariz. St. L.J. 249 (1991).

However, keep an open mind on what constitutes a "public purpose." As we will see later, the modern meaning of "public purpose" is much broader than the nineteenth century drafters had in mind. See *WDW Properties v. City of Sumter*, 535 S.E.2d 631 (S.C. 2000), where the court found that the use of tax-exempt revenue bonds for retail facilities in a blighted area serves a public purpose under state law. If legislation generally promotes the welfare of the state, public purpose is usually found. See *Wilson v. Connecticut Product Dev. Corp.*, 355 A.2d 72, 75 (Conn. 1974) (upholding state funding to private enterprises to develop new products). Should the public purpose test be satisfied if private interests benefit more directly from state action than the public? See *Wilson*, *supra* at 76:

> The presence of a direct benefit to the state from the expenditure of public funds is a useful factor in aiding the court's determination of whether a legislative act serves a public purpose. But other factors serve a similar function. This court has found that an act serves a public purpose . . . when it 'promote(s) the welfare' of the state; or when the 'principal reason' for the appropriation is to benefit the public. "The test of public use is not how the use is furnished but rather the right of the public to receive and enjoy its benefit."

Cutting edge issues have arisen in connection with the development of public-private partnerships and a variety of shared initiatives that blend public and private benefit. For a consideration of the evolution of "public purpose" requirements under Florida law, see Sale, *Free Enterprise vs. Economic Incentives: The Evolution of the "Public Purpose" Fulcrum*, 46 Stetson L. Rev. 481 (2017). One of the many areas in which the interpretation of "public purpose" requirements has been debated is the development of sports stadiums. See, e.g., Zavodnich, *If You (Pay to) Build It, They Will Come: Rethinking Publicly-Financed Professional Sports Stadiums after the Atlanta Braves Deal with Cobb County*, 53 Ga. L. Rev. 407 (2018). These and other issues will be explored in more detail later in the Chapter in connection with discussion of economic development and public-private partnerships.

At first blush, what lines do you think should be drawn in order to limit inappropriate participation of state and local government entities in the kinds of activities typically undertaken by the private sector? Your views will likely inform how you think the "public purpose" provisions in state constitutions should be interpreted. If you were drafting new provisions to address related concerns for a state constitution today, what focus would you believe should guide the drafting effort, and what language might be employed? As you consider this question, bear in mind that the federal Constitution and many state constitutions prohibit the "taking" of private property for "public use" without just compensation. How do "public use" and "public purpose" differ, and why are differences in language such as this important?

2. *Lending of credit.* Most state constitutions contain prohibitions against lending the credit of the state or local governments or making a gift to a private entity. The prohibition of lending credit or gifts is often confused with the public purpose doctrine, but the prohibition is a separate and distinct constitutional limitation. Even if a public purpose is found in the use of taxes or proceeds of lending, how those funds are spent can trigger the prohibition. See *Village of Moyie Springs v. Aurora Mfg. Co.*, 353 P.2d 767 (Idaho 1960) (revenue bonds used to acquire land for private commercial development were prohibited lending of credit for private benefit); *Casey v. South Carolina State Housing Auth.*, 215 S.E.2d 184 (S.C. 1975) (state housing bonds with state guaranty to provide mortgages to private parties violates the lending of credit prohibition). But consider *Frank v. City of Cody* 572 P.2d 1106, 1111 (Wyo. 1977) where the city and other municipalities formed an "agency" to provide electric power to their inhabitants. The agency entered into power purchase contracts with private power generating companies and issued bonds to finance the arrangement. Was there lending of credit government credit here? Said the state supreme court:

> While the section of the agreement in question does provide for making up deficiencies created by a defaulting participant, it also provides that a pro rate share of the portion of the system entitlement, owned by the defaulter [municipality], shall be accrue to the benefit of the other participants [other municipalities]. This neutralizes any concept of giving or lending credit to anyone since something is received in return. The [state] constitutional prohibition against a municipality lending its credit to a private corporation has no application when there is an exchange of consideration between parties.

For another example of an unsuccessful lending of credit challenge, see *Neuner v. City of St. Louis*, 536 S.W.3d 750 (Mo. App. 2017) (upholding St. Louis ordinance providing for reimbursement agreements designed to encourage employers to redevelop business sites and relocate their businesses and employees into city, against challenges based on uniformity of taxation and lending of credit provisions of state constitution).

Typical lending of credit prohibition constitutional provisions are found in New York and New Jersey:

> *New Jersey: Article VIII, Sec I, Pt. 2:* No county, city, borough, township or village shall hereafter give any money or property, or loan its money or credit, to or in aid of any individual, association or corporation, or become security for, or be directly or indirectly the owner of any stock or bonds of any association or corporation.

> *New York: Article VII, Sec 8(1)*: [The] money of the state shall not be given or loaned to or in aid of any private corporation or association, or private

> undertaking, nor shall the credit of the state be given or loaned to or in aid of any individual, or public or private corporation or association, or private undertaking.

Courts treat the prohibition of lending of credit as moot if a public purpose is achieved with the application of public funds. See, e.g., *Common Cause v. Maine*, 455 A.2d 1 (Me. 1983) (Maine Supreme Court articulates an early thesis of expanded public purpose for economic development as crafted by the legislature, and goes to some length to distance the facts from constitutional prohibitions against lending credit and voter requirements to authorize debt); *Hayes v. State Prop. & Bldgs. Comm'n*, 731 S.W.2d 797 (Ky. 1987) (upholding a state tax-increment financing program to induce businesses to relocate to Kentucky). As the *Hayes* court said:

> [A]s long as the expenditure of public money has as to its purpose, the effectuation of a valid public purpose, [the lending of credit prohibition] is not offended even in situations where the conveyance occurs without consideration. . . . Merely because the state incurs an indebtedness for its benefit and others may incidentally profit does not bring the action within the spirit of the prohibition of lending of state credit. [*Id.* at 799–800.]

3. *Broader perspective.* Both the public purpose limitation and the lending of credit provision were intended as restrictions on state and local borrowing powers, and as a method of limiting public debt. These restrictions are often used to challenge projects in which public borrowing powers are used to secure funding for privately owned and operated projects in which there is nevertheless a distinct public interest. In expending the public purpose doctrine and relegating the lending of credit prohibition to the archives, do states and local governments subject themselves to subjective standards as to the purposes for which they can spend public funds and bond proceeds? If so, how have the role of politics and the activities of lobbyists influenced government decisions to borrow and spend? In light of the fiscal challenges facing states and local governments and the seemingly strange nineteenth century state constitutional limitations on taxation and borrowing, should states and local governments consider overhauling their organic law in these areas?

4. *Other provisions: exclusive emoluments.* Another common provision in state constitutions that seeks to prohibit the bestowal of special personal benefits bars "exclusive" or "separate" emoluments or privileges. The federal Constitution also includes an Emoluments Clause that has given rise to litigation during the presidency of Donald Trump. "Emoluments" generally refer to profits or advantages, and some state constitutions provide that no exclusive or separate emoluments may be given except in consideration of public service or that no "hereditary emoluments" may be bestowed. For a discussion of associated history and legal principles, see Orth, *Unconstitutional Emoluments: The Emoluments Clauses of the North Carolina Constitution*, 97 N.C. L. Rev. 1727 (2019) (distinguishing the purposes of federal and state emoluments clauses, and explicating one state's experience in applying

a prohibition on exclusive emoluments as a means of furthering public purposes, uniform laws, and equal protection in state government).

[2] Federal Constitution

As we have seen, state constitutions are intended to limit the powers of state and local governments to tax, borrow, and spend to protect taxpayers and residents. In contrast, the federal constitution grants the people the right to object to the exercise of power by state and local governments in the protection of those rights. Major federal constitutional provisions relating to public finance include the equal protection, due process, and interstate commerce provisions as discussed below.

[a] Due Process

Most litigation against state and local governments (other than questions of authority to enact laws and exercise power under state constitutions), turns on broader limitations of state uniformity clauses, state or federal due process, equal protection and occasionally Commerce Clause, Contract Clause, First Amendment (in the case of borrowing) or supremacy issues. The following case indicates that federal due process challenges to state and local taxes have largely been set to rest. Bear in mind that the core question for federal substantive due process is whether the item (or event) taxed has a rational relationship to the state imposing the tax (since without such a relationship, a tax is imposed without any kind of return).

City of Pittsburgh v. Alco Parking Corp.

417 U.S. 369 (1974)

Mr. Justice White delivered the opinion of the Court.

The issue in this case is the validity under the Federal Constitution of Ordinance No. 704, which was enacted by the Pittsburgh, Pennsylvania, City Council in December 1969, and which placed a 20% tax on the gross receipts obtained from all transactions involving the parking or storing of a motor vehicle at a nonresidential parking place in return for a consideration. The ordinance superseded a 1968 ordinance imposing an identical tax, but at the rate of 15% which in turn followed a tax at the rate of 10% imposed by the city in 1962. Soon after its enactment, 12 operators of off street parking facilities located in the city sued to enjoin enforcement of the ordinance, alleging that it was invalid under the Equal Protection and Due Process Clauses of the Fourteenth Amendment, as well as Art. VIII, § 1, of the Pennsylvania Constitution, which requires that taxes shall be uniform upon the same class of subjects. It appears from the findings and the opinions in the state courts that, at the time of suit, there were approximately 24,300 parking spaces in the downtown area of the city, approximately 17,000 of which the respondents operated. Another 1,000 were in the hands of private operators not party to the suit. The balance of approximately 6,100 was owned by the Parking Authority of the city of Pittsburgh, an agency created pursuant to the Parking Authority Law of June 5, 1947, Pa. Stat. Ann., tit. 53, § 341 *et seq.* (1974). The trial court also found that there was then a deficiency of 4,100 spaces in the downtown area.

The Court of Common Pleas sustained the ordinance. Its judgment was affirmed by the Commonwealth Court by a four-to-three vote, on rehearing; but the Pennsylvania Supreme Court reversed, also four to three. 307 A.2d 841 (1973). That court rejected challenges to the ordinance under the Pennsylvania Constitution and the Equal Protection Clause, but invalidated the ordinance as an uncompensated taking of property contrary to the Due Process Clause of the Fourteenth Amendment. Because the decision appeared to be in conflict with the applicable decisions of this Court, we granted certiorari, 414 U.S. 1127 (1974), and we now reverse the judgment.

In the opinion of the Supreme Court of Pennsylvania, two aspects of the Pittsburgh ordinance combined to deprive the respondents of due process of law. First, the court thought the tax was "unreasonably high" and was responsible for the inability of nine of 14 different private parking lot operators to conduct their business at a profit and of the remainder to show more than marginal earnings. Second, private operators of parking lots faced competition from the Parking Authority, a public agency enjoying tax exemption (although not necessarily from this tax) and other advantages which enabled it to offer off street parking at lower rates than those charged by private operators. The average all-day rate for the public lots was $2 as compared with a $3 all-day rate for the private lots. The court's conclusion was that "[w]here such an unfair competitive advantage accrues, generated by the use of public funds, to a local government at the expense of private property owners, without just compensation, a clear constitutional violation has occurred. . . ." "[T]he unreasonably burdensome 20 percent gross receipts tax, causing the majority of private parking lot operators to operate their businesses at a loss, in the special competitive circumstances of this case constitutes an unconstitutional taking of private property without due process of law in violation of the Fourteenth Amendment of the United States Constitution."

We cannot agree that these two considerations, either alone or together, are sufficient to invalidate the parking tax ordinance involved in this case. The claim that a particular tax is so unreasonably high and unduly burdensome as to deny due process is both familiar and recurring, but the Court has consistently refused either to undertake the task of passing on the "reasonableness" of a tax that otherwise is within the power of Congress or of state legislative authorities, or to hold that a tax is unconstitutional because it renders a business unprofitable.

In *Magnano Co. v. Hamilton*, 292 U.S. 40 (1934), the Court sustained against due process attack a state excise tax of 1 cent per pound on all butter substitutes sold in the State. Conceding that the "tax is so excessive that it may or will result in destroying the intrastate business of appellant," *id.*, at 45, the Court held that "the due process of law clause contained in the Fifth Amendment is not a limitation upon the taxing power conferred upon Congress," that no different rule should be applied to the States, and that a tax within the lawful power of a State should not "be judicially stricken down under the due process clause simply because its enforcement may or will result in restricting or even destroying particular occupations or businesses." *Id.*, at 44. The premise that a tax is invalid if so excessive as to bring about the destruction of a particular business, the Court said, had been "uniformly rejected as furnishing no judicial ground for striking down a taxing act." *Id.* at 47. *Veazie Bank v. Fenno*, 8 Wall. 533, 548 (1869); *McCray v. United States*, 195 U.S. 27 (1904); and *Alaska Fish Salting & By-Products Co. v. Smith*, 255 U.S. 44 (1921), are to the same effect . . .

Neither the parties nor the Pennsylvania Supreme Court purports to differ with the foregoing principles. But the state court concluded that this was one of those "rare and special instances" recognized in *Magnano* and other cases where the Due Process Clause may be invoked because the taxing statute is "so arbitrary as to compel the conclusion that it does not involve an exertion of the taxing power, but constitutes, in substance and effect, the direct exertion of a different and forbidden power, as, for example, the confiscation of property." 292 U.S., at 44.

There are several difficulties with this position. The ordinance on its face recites that its purpose is "[t]o provide for the general revenue by imposing a tax," and in sustaining the ordinance against an equal protection challenge, the state court itself recognized that commercial parking lots are a proper subject for special taxation and that the city had decided, "not without reason, that commercial parking operations should be singled out for special taxation to *raise revenue* because of traffic related problems engendered by these operations." 307 A.2d at 858 (emphasis added).

It would have been difficult from any standpoint to have held that the ordinance was in no sense a revenue measure. The 20% tax concededly raised substantial sums of money; and even if the revenue collected had been insubstantial, *Sonzinsky v. United States*, 300 U.S. 506, 513–514 (1937), or the revenue purpose only secondary, *Hampton & Co. v. United States*, 276 U.S. 394, 411–413, Treas. Dec. 42706 (1928), we would not necessarily treat this exaction as anything but a tax entitled to the presumption of the validity accorded other taxes imposed by a State.

Rather than conclude that the 20% level was not a tax at all, the Pennsylvania court accepted it as such and merely concluded that it was so unreasonably high and burdensome that, in the context of competition by the city, the ordinance had the "effect" of an uncompensated taking of property. 307 A.2d, at 864. The court did not hold a parking tax, as such, to be beyond the power of the city but it appeared to hold that a bona fide tax, if sufficiently burdensome, could be held invalid under the Fourteenth Amendment. This approach is contrary to the cases already cited, particularly to the often-repeated principle that the judiciary should not infer a legislative attempt to exercise a forbidden power in the form of a seeming tax from the fact, alone, that the tax appears excessive or even so high as to threaten the existence of an occupation or business. . . .

Nor are we convinced that the ordinance loses its character as a tax and may be stricken down as too burdensome under the Due Process Clause if the taxing authority, directly or through an instrumentality enjoying various forms of tax exemption, competes with the taxpayer in a manner thought to be unfair by the judiciary. This approach would demand not only that the judiciary undertake to separate those taxes that are too burdensome from those that are not, but also would require judicial oversight of the terms and circumstances under which the government or its tax-exempt instrumentalities may undertake to compete with the private sector. The clear teaching of prior cases is that this is not a task that the Due Process Clause demands of or permits to the judiciary. We are not now inclined to chart a different course.

... More directly in point is *Puget Sound Power & Light Co. v. Seattle*, 291 U.S. 619 (1934), where the city imposed a gross receipts tax on a power and light company and at the same time actively competed with that company in the business of furnishing power to consumers. The company's contention was that "constitutional limitations are transgressed ... because the tax affects a business with which the taxing sovereign is actively competing." *Id.*, at 623. Calling on prior cases in support, the Court rejected the contention, holding that "the Fourteenth Amendment does not prevent a city from conducting a public waterworks in competition with private business or preclude taxation of the private business to help its rival to succeed." *Id.*, at 626. See also *Madera Water Works v. Madera*, 228 U.S. 454 (1913). The holding in *Puget Sound* remains good law and, together with the other authorities to which we have already referred, it is sufficient to require reversal of the decision of the Pennsylvania Supreme Court.

Even assuming that an uncompensated and hence forbidden "taking" could be inferred from an unreasonably high tax in the context of competition from the taxing authority, we could not conclude that the Due Process Clause was violated in the circumstances of this case. It was urged by the city that the private operators would not suffer because they could and would pass the tax on to their customers, who, as a class, should pay more for the services of the city that they directly or indirectly utilize in connection with the special problems incident to the twice daily movement of large number of cars on the streets of the city and in and out of parking garages. The response of the Pennsylvania Supreme Court was that competition from the city prevented the private operators from raising their prices and recouping their losses by collecting the tax from their customers. On the record before us, this is not a convincing basis for concluding that the parking tax effected an unconstitutional taking of respondents' property. There are undisturbed findings in the record that there were 24,300 parking places in the downtown area, that there was an overall shortage of parking facilities, and that the public authority supplied only 6,100 parking spaces. Because these latter spaces were priced substantially under the private lots it would be anticipated that they would be preferred by those seeking parking in the downtown area. Insofar as this record reveals, for the 20% tax to have a destructive effect on private operators as compared with the situation immediately preceding its enactment, the damage would have to flow chiefly, not from those who preferred the cheaper public parking lots, but from those who could no longer afford an increased price for downtown parking at all. If this is the case, we simply have another instance where the government enacts a tax at a "discouraging rate as the alternative to giving up a business," a policy to which there is no constitutional objection. *Alaska Fish Salting & By-Products Co. v. Smith*, 255 U.S., at 49; *Magnano Co. v. Hamilton*, 292 U.S., at 46.

The parking tax ordinance recited that "[n]on-residential parking places for motor vehicles, by reason of the frequency rate of their use, the changing intensity of their use at various hours of the day, their location, their relationship to traffic congestion and other characteristics, present problems requiring municipal services and affect the public interest, differently from parking places accessory to the use and occupancy of residences." By enacting the tax, the city insisted that those providing and utilizing nonresidential parking facilities should pay more taxes to compensate the city for the problems incident to off street parking. The city was constitutionally entitled to put the automobile parker to the choice of using other transportation or paying the increased tax.

The judgment of the Pennsylvania Supreme Court is reversed. . . .

MR. JUSTICE POWELL, concurring.

The opinion of the Court fully explicates the issue presented here, and I am in accord with its resolution. I write briefly only to emphasize my understanding that today's decision does not foreclose the possibility that some combination of unreasonably burdensome taxation and direct competition by the taxing authority might amount to a taking of property without just compensation in violation of the Fifth and Fourteenth Amendments.

To some extent, private business is inevitably handicapped by direct governmental competition, but the opinion of the Court makes plain that the legitimate exercise of the taxing power is not to be restrained on this account. It is conceivable, however, that punitive taxation of a private industry and direct economic competition through a governmental entity enjoying special competitive advantages would effectively expropriate a private business for public profit. Such a combination of unreasonably burdensome taxation and public competition would be the functional equivalent of a governmental taking of private property for public use and would be subject to the constitutional requirement of just compensation. As the opinion of the Court clearly reveals, no such circumstance has been shown to exist in the instant case.

Notes and Questions

1. *Constitutional issues.* While leaving open the possibility that the "special instances" rule might be applied to invalidate a tax on due process grounds, the *Alco* case nevertheless reflects the usual reluctance of the Supreme Court to examine the constitutional basis for the exercise of taxation powers. See Mazza & Kaye, *Restricting the Legislative Power to Tax in the United States*, 54 AM. J. COMP. L. 641,

641 (2006) ("[C]ourts in the United States almost invariably affirm the Government's power to tax in the face of constitutional challenges. This 'presumption of constitutionality' afforded most tax legislation is a long-standing and well-accepted proposition. As a result, constitutional law has played a relatively minor role in the development of tax laws in the United States."). See also *Route One Liquors, Inc. v. Secretary of Admin.*, 785 N.E.2d 1222, 1229–32 (Mass. 2003) (applying *Alco* and upholding excise tax on the "privilege of holding a license to operate a commercial parking lot within three miles of [Foxboro] stadium"); *Edwards v. County of Erie*, 932 A.2d 997, 1004 (Pa. Commw. 2007) (applying *Alco*, upholding state statute authorizing use of room tax revenues to support development of hotel connected to a new convention center, and concluding that "[p]laintiffs' general objection to a publicly funded competitor does not justify the relief they seek").

The Court's willingness in *Alco* to allow the use of taxing powers that accomplish a regulatory purpose should be contrasted with the care with which courts examine direct delegations of regulatory power to municipalities, both in home rule and statutory grant states. Of course, all taxes have an incidental regulatory effect. Should courts consider invalidating taxes that are clearly passed only for a regulatory purpose? What would be the basis for such a ruling? How should such a distinction be made, if at all? Several criteria are suggested in a student note, *Constitutional Limitations on the Power to Tax: Alco Parking Corp. v. Pittsburgh*, 26 HASTINGS L.J. 215 (1974). A tax should be considered regulatory, as the number of people subject to the tax increases; if the tax is not traditionally revenue-raising; if the tax is on businesses rather than people; if the revenue to be raised is excessive; and if the statement of purpose indicates that the tax is regulatory. *Id.* at 230. What kind of a tax would fit the regulatory mode?

Note that courts are also reluctant to review the excessiveness of a tax levy, at least in considering taxes other than special benefit taxes on property. This reluctance has been attributed to "the institutional inability of the judiciary to review the legislature's judgments on which the tax is based." *Id.* at 226. It will be of interest to consider why the judiciary considers itself more competent to review these questions in the special benefit taxation category.

2. *Tax invalidated.* With *Alco Parking*, compare *Continental Bank & Trust Co. v. Farmington City*, 599 P.2d 1242 (Utah 1979). The city levied a 2% license tax against Lagoon, a large, and the only, amusement park within the city limits. The court invalidated the tax. It noted that Lagoon provided a number of services usually provided by municipalities. It also noted that the contribution of Lagoon to city revenues from a number of city taxes was considerable, and that Lagoon's proportionate share of city revenues had nearly doubled in the past five years. The court's rationale for striking down the tax was as follows:

> Closely related is the question of the oppressiveness of the licensing tax imposed by Farmington upon Lagoon. Whenever a class is singled out for taxation, the amount of which is unduly burdensome, the question of abuse of taxing power is raised. Evidence is uncontradicted that Lagoon operates

> on a low margin of profit, traditionally pays no dividends, and has recently indebted itself in the installation of Pioneer Village on the east end of the park. Despite these facts, Farmington has seen fit to impose a tax on gross receipts, which makes no provision for high overhead. Moreover, the license tax adds to an already stiff tax burden imposed on Lagoon. Were the license tax permitted to stand, Lagoon would sustain a staggering ten-fold increase in taxation since 1975. In none of the cases to which Farmington directs us, where a tax of 2 percent or more of gross income has been sustained, was such a tax load already in existence.
>
> We are not unmindful of the fact that the action of Farmington in this matter is entitled to broad deference by a reviewing court, nor of the fact that any legislative enactment is entitled to a presumption of constitutionality. As was stated by this Court in the case of *Salt Lake City v. Christensen Co.*, [95 P. 523 (Utah 1908),] "[w]here neither the Constitution nor the statute imposes absolute restrictions, the courts may not arbitrarily impose any unless it clearly appears that the tax imposed is oppressive, or clearly and unreasonably discriminatory, and thus is an abuse of the [tax paying] power." The conclusion is inescapable that a situation such as the one at hand, where a municipality imposes a potentially crippling tax on a single business for the benefit of the community as a whole, coupled with vague promises of improved services which the business has not been guaranteed, and to a large extent, does not need, presents such a case of abuse of taxing power. We therefore hold the Farmington license tax invalid. [*Id.* at 1246.]

How does the opinion in *Continental Bank & Trust Co.* compare with the majority opinion in *Alco Parking*? How does *Continental Bank & Trust* compare with Justice Powell's concurring opinion? Note that a license tax may be levied in Utah solely for revenue-raising purposes. Since this is so, was the concurring and dissenting opinion in *Farmington* case (as to the invalidation of the license tax) justified when it commented that the tax does not "rise to any such level that it can properly be characterized as so oppressive and burdensome that the court can declare it to be confiscatory and therefore invalid"? *Id.* at 1248. As in *Alco Parking*, why did the Utah court simply not conclude that Lagoon could pass the license tax on to its customers? Note that the Lagoon amusement park had no competition. See also *Sands Bathworks Gaming LLC v. Pennsylvania Dep't of Revenue*, 932 A.2d 997 (Pa. 2019) (considering constitutionality under Due Process and Equal Protection Clauses of amendment to state Race Horse Development and Gaming Act, where licensees were required to pay supplemental assessment on slot machine revenue into casino marketing and capital development account; finding that distributions from account were made primarily to underperforming slot-machine facilities; concluding that notwithstanding presumption of constitutionality, the system violated due process and equal protection requirements due to creation of disproportionate burden compared to benefit; but determining that supplemental assessment provisions were severable from the remainder of the act).

3. *Notice problems.* Due process problems, particularly involving notice, may arise during the administration of state and local taxing programs. The most common setting for such problems is the tax foreclosure suit in which a taxing entity seeks court authority to sell property of a defaulting taxpayer and apply the proceeds to the delinquent tax. The general rule is that due process requires notice "reasonably calculated to reach the intended recipient when sent." *Jones v. Flowers*, 547 U.S. 220, 226 (2006). Due process notice requirements generally are satisfied by mailing service through first class mail without the necessity to prove that the notice actually was received. *Mennonite Bd. of Missions v. Adams*, 462 U.S. 791 (1983) (mortgagee); *Miner v. Clinton County*, 541 F.3d 464 (2d Cir. 2008) (property owner), but if mailed notice of a tax sale is returned unclaimed, "the State must take additional reasonable steps to attempt to provide notice to the property owner before selling his property, if it is practicable to do so." *Jones v. Flowers*, 547 U.S. at 225. In *Garden Homes Woodlands Co. v. Town of Dover*, 95 N.Y.2d 516 (2000), the court found posting and publishing a hearing was not in compliance with statutory notice under due process as to special assessments imposed on an out-of-state property owner who could not be expected to receive such notice. The court opined that actual notice should have been given. *Id.* at 596.

[b] Commerce Clause

There can be a good deal of overlap between due process doctrine relating to taxation and conceptually distinct Commerce Clause jurisprudence, at least in instances where challenges are brought concerning state taxation practices that affect those outside their physical limits. That is particularly the case where states seek to tax intangible property (rather than real and tangible personal property taxation that is more often addressed under due process doctrine alone). As the Court said in *Curry v. McCanlass*, 307 U.S. 357 (1939):

> When we speak of the jurisdiction to tax land or chattels as being exclusively in the state where they are physically located, we mean no more than that the benefit and protection of laws enabling the owner to enjoy the fruits of his ownership and the power to reach effectively the interests protected, for the purpose of subjecting them to payment of a tax, are so narrowly restricted to the state in whose territory the physical property is located as to set practical limits to taxation by others.

At the same time, it is worth remembering that interests relating to distant property can be taxed by a state in other ways, for example, through taxation of income derived by state residents from land or intangible properties located elsewhere. *People of State of New York ex rel. Cohn v. Graves*, 300 U.S. 308 (1937).

The Commerce Clause (Art. I, § 8, cl. 3) authorizes Congress "To regulate Commerce among the several states. . . ." This provision has become more important in recent years because of the growing desire of states to force nonresidents to contribute to state revenues through a variety of taxes. Severance taxes, general sales and use taxes, net income taxes and property taxes are examples of typical state efforts to export a portion of their tax burden to nonresidents. Most Commerce Clause challenges to taxation are brought under the auspices of the so-called dormant Commerce Clause. This concept provides that when Congress has not legislated to impose a tax or fee, the states generally are afforded leeway to tax as long as the particular tax does not affect interstate commerce.

In 1977, the Supreme Court attempted to resolve years of doctrinal uncertainty over the appropriate response to the conflicting principles that interstate commerce should be immune from state taxation when necessary to preserve free trade, but that interstate businesses may be required to pay their own way by ruling that such businesses may be subjected to taxes under a four-part test that requires taxes to be: 1) applied to an activity with a substantial nexus with the taxing state, 2) fairly apportioned, 3) non-discriminatory, and 4) fairly related to the services provided by the taxing state. *Complete Auto Transit, Inc. v. Brady*, 430 U.S. 274, 278–79 (1977). Since 1977, the Court has decided numerous cases under the *Complete Auto* formula, taking a generally permissive attitude toward state tax exportation.

For example, in *United Haulers Ass'n, Inc. v. Oneida-Herkimer Solid Waste Mgmt. Auth.*, 550 U.S. 330 (2007), the Supreme Court upheld county ordinances that required solid waste disposal businesses to dispose of their waste in facilities owned and operated by a public benefit corporation that charged higher fees than were charged by private entities. The Court held that there was not a dormant Commerce Clause violation, because the ordinances favored a public entity, rather than private businesses.

> Compelling reasons justify treating these laws differently from laws favoring particular private businesses over their competitors.... States and municipalities are not private businesses—far from it. Unlike private enterprise, government is vested with the responsibility of protecting the health, safety, and welfare of its citizens.... These important responsibilities set states and local government apart from a typical private business. [*Id.* 342.]

See also *American Trucking Associations, Inc. v. Michigan Public Service Comm'n*, 545 U.S. 429, 438 (2005), in which the Supreme Court upheld a flat fee imposed on trucks traveling intrastate, even though some of the same trucks were also being used in interstate business.

Kentucky's practice, similar to that of many other states, exempted interest income derived from bonds of the state and its political subdivisions but taxed the interest income derived from bonds of other states and political subdivisions. This approach survived a dormant Commerce Clause challenge in *Department of Revenue of Ky. v. Davis*, 553 U.S. 328 (2008). While the Court acknowledged that Kentucky was acting in the dual capacity of borrower (issuing bonds) and regulator (imposing taxes) and that "if looked at as a taxing authority [Kentucky] seems to invite dormant Commerce Clause scrutiny of its regulatory activity," the Court emphasized that Kentucky's status as a bond issuer is what makes a differential tax scheme reasonable. "[W]hen Kentucky exempts its bond interest, it is competing in the market for limited investment dollars, alongside private bond issuers and its sister States, and its tax structure is one of the tools of competition." 533 U.S. at 345. Separating the two roles and focusing solely on the regulatory aspect of the differential tax structure risks imposing a "federal rule to throw out the system of financing municipal improvements throughout most of the United States," *Id.* 356, something the Court was unwilling to do. Justice Kennedy, joined by Justice Alito, dissented, concluding that the differential tax scheme violated a long line of precedents invalidating discriminatory practices affecting interstate commerce. "Nothing in the Court's rationale justifying this scheme would stop Kentucky from taxing interest on out-of-state bonds at a high rate, say 80%, simply to give its own bonds further advantage." *Id.* 374. While agreeing with the Court's conclusion because "it preserved an important source of state funding in the midst of a severe economic downturn," one commentator criticized the majority's rationale as setting "a dangerous precedent for discriminatory legislation in the future, namely authorizing states to couple a discriminatory tax scheme with a traditional government function." Bennett-Ward, *Kentucky v. Davis: A Better Approach to Saving Differential Taxation of Municipal Bonds*, 62 TAX LAW. 503, 523 (2009). The case also is discussed in Comment, *Dormant Commerce Clause—State Taxation of Municipal Bonds*, 122 HARV. L. REV. 276 (2008).

On the other hand, the Supreme Court has been clear that taxes may not be imposed in ways that discriminate between income earned in-state and out-of-state. See *Comptroller of Treasury of Maryland v. Wynne*, 575 U.S. 542 (2015). In that case, Maryland taxpayers challenged the state's personal income tax system (made up of both a "state" and a "county" component). Residents who paid tax on income earned in other states received a credit against the "state" component but not the "county" component. Nonresidents who earned income from sources in Maryland had to pay "state" income tax, were not subject to the "county" tax, but had to pay a "special nonresident tax" instead of the county tax. In a 5-4 decision, the Court invalidated the Maryland system, concluding that the Commerce Clause mandated that double taxation of out-of-state income that discriminated in favor of in-state economic activity approximated a tariff against out-of-state income and was therefore invalid.

Application of core Commerce Clause requirements to state taxation schemes has become increasingly complicated given the evolution of electronic commerce. The Supreme Court's decision in *South Dakota v. Wayfair, Inc.* marks a landmark change in approaches to applying the Commerce Clause in such settings.

South Dakota v. Wayfair, Inc.

138 S. Ct. 2080 (2018)

[In *Quill Corp. v. North Dakota*, 504 U.S. 298 (1992), the Supreme Court had held that states could not collect sales tax on retail purchases made over the Internet or other e-commerce mechanisms unless the seller had a physical presence in the state. *Quill* was based on an interpretation of the dormant Commerce Clause that had been interpreted to prohibit states from interfering with interstate commerce unless authorized by Congress to do so. The *Quill* decision had come under increasing criticism as commerce had evolved over the last two decades to rely heavily on Internet-based sales. Following the *Quill* decision, many states had approached the problem of taxing Internet transactions by requiring purchasers to pay "use tax" on transactions even though sales tax might not be collected. However, consumer compliance with requirements to pay "use tax" were exceptionally low. *Wayfair* related to South Dakota's effort to require Internet sellers with no employees or real estate in the state to collect and remit sales tax. In *Wayfair*, the Supreme Court overruled *Quill* in an important but splintered decision. The decision was authored by Justice Kennedy with Justices Ginbsburg, Alito, Thomas and Gorsuch concurring; Chief Justice Roberts dissented with Justices Breyer, Sotomayor, and Kagan joining.]

Justice Kennedy delivered the opinion of the Court.

. . .

II

. . .

To understand the issue presented in this case, it is instructive first to survey the general development of this Court's Commerce Clause principles and then to review the application of those principles to state taxes. [The Court first reviewed its early Commerce Clause cases, then explained their bearing on analysis of state taxes] . . . .

B

These principles also animate the Court's Commerce Clause precedents addressing the validity of state taxes. The Court explained the now-accepted framework for state taxation in *Complete Auto Transit, Inc. v. Brady*, 430 U.S. 274 (1977). The Court held that a State "may tax exclusively interstate commerce so long as the tax does not create any effect forbidden by the Commerce Clause." The Court will sustain a tax so long as it (1) applies to an activity with a substantial nexus with the taxing State, (2) is fairly apportioned, (3) does not discriminate against interstate commerce, and (4) is fairly related to the services the State provides. [citations omitted] . . . .

The Court in *Quill* recognized that intervening precedents, specifically *Complete Auto*, "might not dictate the same result were the issue to arise for the first time today." But, nevertheless, the *Quill* majority concluded that the physical presence rule was necessary to prevent undue burdens on interstate commerce. [citations omitted] It grounded the physical presence rule in *Complete Auto*'s requirement that a tax have a "'substantial nexus'" with the activity being taxed. [citations omitted] . . . .

III

The physical presence rule has "been the target of criticism over many years from many quarters." [citations omitted]. And "while nexus rules are clearly necessary," the Court "should focus on rules that are appropriate to the twenty-first century, not the nineteenth." Hellerstein, *Deconstructing the Debate Over State Taxation of Electronic Commerce*, 13 HARV. J.L. & TECH. 549, 553 (2000). Each year, the physical presence rule becomes further removed from economic reality and results in significant revenue losses to the States. These critiques underscore that the physical presence rule, both as first formulated and as applied today, is an incorrect interpretation of the Commerce Clause.

[The Court then critiqued the analysis in *Quill*.] . . .

B

The *Quill* Court itself acknowledged that the physical presence rule is "artificial at its edges." [citations omitted] That was an understatement when *Quill* was decided; and when the day-to-day functions of marketing and distribution in the modern economy are considered, it is all the more evident that the physical presence rule is artificial in its entirety.

Modern e-commerce does not align analytically with a test that relies on the sort of physical presence defined in *Quill*. In a footnote, *Quill* rejected the argument that "title to 'a few floppy diskettes' present in a State" was sufficient to constitute a "substantial nexus." [citations omitted] But it is not clear why a single employee or a single warehouse should create a substantial nexus while "physical" aspects of pervasive modern technology should not. For example, a company with a website accessible in South Dakota may be said to have a physical presence in the State via the customers' computers. A website may leave cookies saved to the customers' hard drives, or customers may download the company's app onto their phones. Or a company may lease data storage that is permanently, or even occasionally, located in South Dakota. [citations omitted] What may have seemed like a "clear," "bright-line tes[t]" when *Quill* was written now threatens to compound the arbitrary consequences that should have been apparent from the outset. [citations omitted]

The "dramatic technological and social changes" of our "increasingly interconnected economy" mean that buyers are "closer to most major retailers" than ever before—"regardless of how close or far the nearest storefront." [citations omitted] Between targeted advertising and instant access to most consumers via any internet-enabled device, "a business may be present in a State in a meaningful way without" that presence "being physical in the traditional sense of the term." [citation omitted] A virtual showroom can show far more inventory, in far more detail, and with greater opportunities for consumer and seller interaction than might be possible for local stores. Yet the continuous and pervasive virtual presence of retailers today is, under *Quill,* simply irrelevant. This Court should not maintain a rule that ignores these substantial virtual connections to the State. . . .

IV

. . . If it becomes apparent that the Court's Commerce Clause decisions prohibit the States from exercising their lawful sovereign powers in our federal system, the Court should be vigilant in correcting the error. While it can be conceded that Congress has the authority to change the physical presence rule, Congress cannot change the constitutional default rule. It is inconsistent with the Court's proper role to ask Congress to address a false constitutional premise of this Court's own creation. Courts have acted as the front line of review in this limited sphere; and hence it is important that their principles be accurate and logical, whether or not Congress can or will act in response. It is currently the Court, and not Congress, that is limiting the lawful prerogatives of the States.

Further, the real world implementation of Commerce Clause doctrines now makes it manifest that the physical presence rule as defined by *Quill* must give way to the "far-reaching systemic and structural changes in the economy" and "many other societal dimensions" caused by the Cyber Age. [citations omitted] Though *Quill* was wrong on its own terms when it was decided in 1992, since then the Internet revolution has made its earlier error all the more egregious and harmful. . . .

The Internet's prevalence and power have changed the dynamics of the national economy. In 1992, mail-order sales in the United States totaled $180 billion. [citation omitted] Last year, e-commerce retail sales alone were estimated at $453.5 billion. Dept. of Commerce, U.S. Census Bureau News, Quarterly Retail E–Commerce Sales: 4th Quarter 2017 (CB18–21, Feb. 16, 2018). Combined with traditional remote sellers, the total exceeds half a trillion dollars. Sales Taxes Report, at 9. Since the Department of Commerce first began tracking e-commerce sales, those sales have increased tenfold from 0.8 percent to 8.9 percent of total retail sales in the United States. Compare Dept. of Commerce, U.S. Census Bureau, Retail E–Commerce Sales in Fourth Quarter 2000 (CB01–28, Feb. 16, 2001), https://www.census.gov/mrts/www/data/pdf/00Q4.pdf, with U.S. Census Bureau News, Quarterly Retail E–Commerce Sales: 4th Quarter 2017. And it is likely that this percentage will increase. Last year, e-commerce grew at four times the rate of traditional retail, and it shows no sign of any slower pace. See *ibid.*

This expansion has also increased the revenue shortfall faced by States seeking to collect their sales and use taxes. In 1992, it was estimated that the States were losing between $694 million and $3 billion per year in sales tax revenues as a result of the physical presence rule. Brief for Law Professors et al. as *Amici Curiae* 11, n. 7. Now estimates range from $8 to $33 billion. Sales Taxes Report, at 11–12; Brief for Petitioner 34–35. The South Dakota Legislature has declared an emergency, S.B. 106, § 9, which again demonstrates urgency of overturning the physical presence rule.

The argument, moreover, that the physical presence rule is clear and easy to apply is unsound. Attempts to apply the physical presence rule to online retail sales are proving unworkable. States are already confronting the complexities of defining physical presence in the Cyber Age. [citations omitted] . . .

In this case, however, South Dakota affords small merchants a reasonable degree of protection. The law at issue requires a merchant to collect the tax only if it does a considerable amount of business in the State; the law is not retroactive; and South Dakota is a party to the Streamlined Sales and Use Tax Agreement. . . .

Finally, other aspects of the Court's Commerce Clause doctrine can protect against any undue burden on interstate commerce, taking into consideration the small businesses, startups, or others who engage in commerce across state lines. . . .

For these reasons, the Court concludes that the physical presence rule of *Quill* is unsound and incorrect. . . .

Here, the nexus is clearly sufficient based on both the economic and virtual contacts respondents have with the State. The Act applies only to sellers that deliver more than $100,000 of goods or services into South Dakota or engage in 200 or more separate transactions for the delivery of goods and services into the State on an annual basis. S.B. 106, § 1. This quantity of business could not have occurred unless the seller availed itself of the substantial privilege of carrying on business in South Dakota. And respondents are large, national companies that undoubtedly maintain an extensive virtual presence. Thus, the substantial nexus requirement of *Complete Auto* is satisfied in this case. . . .

The judgment of the Supreme Court of South Dakota is vacated, and the case is remanded for further proceedings not inconsistent with this opinion.

It is so ordered.

[Concurring and dissenting opinions omitted.]

Notes and Questions

1. *Core Commerce Clause concerns.* Can you explain in your own words how concerns embodied in the Due Process Clause and in the Commerce Clause differ? Imagine what kinds of taxes states might impose (income, sales, excise, severance, amusement, service) and consider which are most likely to raise due process or Commerce Clause concerns.

2. *Narrowing Factors.* The statute in *Wayfair* limited the application of the South Dakota tax to remote sellers who annually have over $100,000 of sales of goods or services into the state or 200 or more transactions. See 138 S. Ct. at 2099. South Dakota also participated in the Streamlined Sales and Use Tax Agreement, that requires participating states to use uniform definitions and systems of state tax administration, as well as compliance software designed to facilitate audits. South Dakota's approach accordingly provided a baseline level of fairness to retailers

subject to the tax. The National Conference of State Legislatures provides information on how states have implemented similar tax systems. See https://www.ncsl.org/research/fiscal-policy/e-fairness-legislation-overview.aspx. For a thoughtful discussion of *Wayfair*, see Pomp, *Wayfair: Its Implications and Missed Opportunities*, 58 Wash. U. J.L. & Pol'y 1 (2019).

3. *Apportionment.* A significant consideration post-*Wayfair* will be how states draw lines as to the extent to which they can rightly tax economic activity in their states. For a discussion of related issues, including the role of multi-state agreements on taxation, see Johnson, *Wayfair, Inc.: Analysis from an Income Tax Perspective*, 28-Nov. J. Multistate Tax'n 22 (November-December 2018).

4. *Evolution of E-Commerce. Wayfair* opens the way for new approaches to taxation given changing patterns of e-commerce. If you were a member of Congress, what approaches might you think appropriate for adoption to guide state taxation of matters relating to e-commerce? See Internet Tax Freedom Act of 1998, https://www.govinfo.gov/content/pkg/PLAW-105publ277/pdf/PLAW-105publ277.pdf. For an insightful discussion of the future of taxation in the digital age, see Faulhaber, *Taxing Tech: The Future of Digital Taxation*, 39 Va. Tax Rev. 145 (2019).

[c] Equal Protection

Equal protection problems under both the federal and state constitutions arise frequently in state and local government finance. The inherent nature of the real property tax system, for example, raises equal protection questions, because decisions made concerning the type of property to be taxed, the rate of taxation, and the method of establishing value subject to taxation all involve subjective classification. Equal protection problems also arise in public finance in the context of state aid to education, as demonstrated in *Serrano v. Priest* discussed in Chapter 9. However, in applying the proceeds of borrowing, equal protection is rarely a basis for a claim. The court in the *Baker v. State* discussed in Chapter 1 gives the basic approach state courts have taken to equal protection challenges. The following case expresses the U.S. Supreme Court's agreement with a state court's equal protection analysis of a differential assessment scheme applied to sewer improvements.

Armour v. City of Indianapolis

566 U.S. 673 (2012)

Justice Breyer delivered the opinion of the Court.

For many years, an Indiana statute, the "Barrett Law," authorized Indiana's cities to impose upon benefited lot owners the cost of sewer improvement projects. The Law also permitted those lot owners to pay either immediately in the form of a lump sum or over time in installments. In 2005, the city of Indianapolis (City) adopted a new assessment and payment method, the "STEP" plan, and it forgave any Barrett Law installments that lot owners had not yet paid.

A group of lot owners who had already paid their entire Barrett Law assessment in a lump sum believe that the City should have provided them with equivalent refunds. And we must decide whether the City's refusal to do so unconstitutionally discriminates against them in violation of the Equal Protection Clause, Amdt. 14, § 1. We hold that the City had a rational basis for distinguishing between those lot owners who had already paid their share of project costs and those who had not. And we conclude that there is no equal protection violation.

I

A

Beginning in 1889 Indiana's Barrett Law permitted cities to pay for public improvements, such as sewage projects, by "apportion[ing]" the costs of a project "equally among all abutting lands or lots." Ind. Code § 36-9-39-15(b) (3) (2011). When a city built a Barrett Law project, the city's public works board would create an initial lot-owner assessment by "dividing the estimated total cost of the sewage works by the total number of lots." § 36-9-39-16(a). It might then adjust an individual assessment downward if the lot would benefit less than would others. § 36-9-39-17(b). Upon completion of the project, the board would issue a final lot-by-lot assessment.

The Law permitted lot owners to pay the assessment either in a single lump sum or over time in installment payments (with interest). The City would collect installment payments "in the same manner as other taxes." § 36-9-37-6. The Law authorized 10-, 20-, or 30-year installment plans. § 36-9-37-8.5(a). Until fully paid, an assessment would constitute a lien against the property, permitting the city to initiate foreclosure proceedings in case of a default. §§ 36-9-37-9(b), -22.

For several decades, Indianapolis used the Barrett Law system to fund sewer projects. But in 2005, the City adopted a new system, called the Septic Tank Elimination Program (STEP), which financed projects in part through bonds, thereby lowering individual lot owners' sewer-connection costs. By that time, the City had constructed more than 40 Barrett Law projects. We are told that installment-paying lot owners still owed money in respect to 24 of those projects. In respect to 21 of the 24, some installment payments had not yet fallen due; in respect to the other 3, those who owed money were in default.

B

This case concerns one of the 24 still-open Barrett Law projects, namely the Brisbane/Manning Sanitary Sewers Project. The Brisbane/Manning Project began in 2001. It connected about 180 homes to the City's sewage system. Construction was completed in 2003. The Indianapolis Board of Public Works held an assessment hearing in June 2004. And in July 2004 the Board sent the 180 affected homeowners a formal notice of their payment obligations.

The notice made clear that each homeowner could pay the entire assessment—$9,278 per property—in a lump sum or in installments, which would include interest at a 3.5% annual rate. Under an installment plan, payments would amount to $77.27 per month for 10 years; $38.66 per month for 20 years; or $25.77 per month for 30 years. In the event, 38 homeowners chose to pay up front; 47 chose the 10-year plan; 27 chose the 20-year plan; and 68 chose the 30-year plan. And in the first year each homeowner paid the amount due ($9,278 upfront; $927.80 under the 10-year plan; $463.90 under the 20-year plan, or $309.27 under the 30-year plan).

The next year, however, the City decided to abandon the Barrett Law method of financing. It thought that the Barrett Law's lot-by-lot payments had become too burdensome for many homeowners to pay, discouraging changes from less healthy septic tanks to healthier sewer systems. (For example, homes helped by the Brisbane/Manning Project, at a cost of more than $9,000 each, were then valued at $120,000 to $270,000). The City's new STEP method of financing would charge each connecting lot owner a flat $2,500 fee and make up the difference by floating bonds eventually paid for by all lot owners citywide.

On October 31, 2005, the City enacted an ordinance implementing its decision. In December, the City's Board of Public Works enacted a further resolution, Resolution 101, which, as part of the transition, would "*forgive all assessment amounts* . . . established pursuant to the Barrett Law Funding for Municipal Sewer programs *due and owing* from the date of November 1, 2005 forward." (emphasis added). In its preamble, the Resolution said that the Barrett Law "may present financial hardships on many middle to lower income participants who most need sanitary sewer service in lieu of failing septic systems"; it pointed out that the City was transitioning to the new STEP method of financing; and it said that the STEP method was based upon a financial model that had "considered the current assessments being made by participants in active Barrett Law projects" as well as future projects. *Id.* at 71–72. The upshot was that those who still owed Barrett Law assessments would not have to make further payments but those who had already paid their assessments would not receive refunds. This meant that homeowners who had paid the full $9,278 Brisbane/ Manning Project assessment in a lump sum the preceding year would receive no refund, while homeowners who had elected to pay the assessment in installments, and had paid a total of $309.27, $463.90, or $927.80, would be under no obligation to make further payments.

In February 2006, the 38 homeowners who had paid the full Brisbane/Manning Project assessment asked the City for a partial refund (in an amount equal to the smallest forgiven Brisbane/Manning installment debt, apparently $8,062). The City denied the request in part because "[r]efunding payments made in your project area, or any portion of the payments, would establish a precedent of unfair and inequitable treatment to all other property owners who have also paid Barrett Law assessments . . . and while [the November 1, 2005, cutoff date] might seem arbitrary to you, it is essential for the City to establish this date and move forward with the new funding approach." *Id.* at 50–51.

C

Thirty-one of the thirty-eight Brisbane/Manning Project lump-sum homeowners brought this lawsuit in Indiana state court seeking a refund of about $8,000 each. They claimed in relevant part that the City's refusal to provide them with refunds at the same time that the City forgave the outstanding Project debts of other Brisbane/Manning homeowners violated the Federal Constitution's Equal Protection Clause, Amdt. 14, § 1; *see also* Rev. Stat. § 1979, 42 U.S.C. § 1983. The trial court granted summary judgment in their favor. The State Court of Appeals affirmed that judgment. 918 N.E.2d 401 (2009). But the Indiana Supreme Court reversed. 946 N.E.2d 553 (2011). In its view, the City's distinction between those who had already paid their Barrett Law assessments and those who had not was "rationally related to its legitimate interests in reducing its administrative costs, providing relief for property owners experiencing financial hardship, establishing a clear transition from [the] Barrett Law to STEP, and preserving its limited resources." We granted certiorari to consider the equal protection question. And we now affirm the Indiana Supreme Court.

II

A

As long as the City's distinction has a rational basis, that distinction does not violate the Equal Protection Clause. This Court has long held that "a classification neither involving fundamental rights nor proceeding along suspect lines ... cannot run afoul of the Equal Protection Clause if there is a rational relationship between the disparity of treatment and some legitimate governmental purpose." *Heller v. Doe*, 509 U.S. 312 (1993). We have made clear in analogous contexts that, where "ordinary commercial transactions" are at issue, rational basis review requires deference to reasonable underlying legislative judgments. *United States v. Carolene Products Co.*, 304 U.S. 144 (1938). And we have repeatedly pointed out that "[l]egislatures have especially broad latitude in creating classifications and distinctions in tax statutes." *Regan v. Taxation With Representation of Wash.*, 461 U.S. 540 (1983).

Indianapolis' classification involves neither a "fundamental right" nor a "suspect" classification. Its subject matter is local, economic, social, and commercial. It is a tax classification. And no one here claims that Indianapolis has discriminated against out-of-state commerce or new residents. Hence, this case falls directly within the scope of our precedents holding such a law constitutionally valid if "there is a plausible policy reason for the classification, the legislative facts on which the classification is apparently based rationally may have been considered to be true by the governmental decisionmaker, and the relationship of the classification to its goal is not so attenuated as to render the distinction arbitrary or irrational." *Nordlinger v. Hahn*, 505 U.S. 1, 11 (1992). And it falls within the scope of our precedents holding that there is such a plausible reason if "there is any reasonably conceivable state of facts that could provide a rational basis for the classification." *FCC v. Beach Communications, Inc.*, 508 U.S. 307, 313 (1993) . . .

B

In our view, Indianapolis' classification has a rational basis. Ordinarily, administrative considerations can justify a tax-related distinction. *See, e.g., Carmichael v. Southern Coal & Coke Co.*, 301 U.S. 495, 511–512 (1937) (tax exemption for businesses with fewer than eight employees rational in light of the "[a]dministrative convenience and expense" involved). And the City's decision to stop collecting outstanding Barrett Law debts finds rational support in related administrative concerns . . .

The City had decided to switch to the STEP system. After that change, to continue Barrett Law unpaid-debt collection could have proved complex and expensive. It would have meant maintaining an administrative system that for years to come would have had to collect debts arising out of 20-plus different construction projects built over the course of a decade, involving monthly payments as low as $25 per household, with the possible need to maintain credibility by tracking down defaulting debtors and bringing legal action. The City, for example, would have had to maintain its Barrett Law operation within the City Controller's Office, keep files on old, small, installment-plan debts, and (a City official says) possibly spend hundreds of thousands of dollars keeping computerized debt-tracking systems current. Unlike the collection system prior to abandonment, the City would not have added any new Barrett Law installment-plan debtors. And that fact means that it would have had to spread the fixed administrative costs of collection over an ever-declining number of debtors, thereby continuously increasing the per-debtor cost of collection . . .

The rationality of the City's distinction draws further support from the nature of the line-drawing choices that confronted it. To have added refunds to forgiveness would have meant adding yet further administrative costs, namely the cost of processing refunds. At the same time, to have tried to limit the City's costs and lost revenues by limiting forgiveness (or refund) rules to Brisbane/Manning homeowners alone would have led those involved in other Barrett Law projects to have justifiably complained about unfairness. Yet to have granted refunds (as well as providing forgiveness) to all those involved in all Barrett Law projects (there were more than 40 projects) or in all open projects (there were more than 20) would have involved even greater administrative burden. The City could not just "cut . . . checks," (ROBERTS, C.J., dissenting), without taking funding from other programs or finding additional revenue. If, instead, the City had tried to keep the amount of revenue it lost constant (a rational goal) but spread it evenly among the apparently thousands of homeowners involved in any of the Barrett Laws projects, the result would have been yet smaller individual payments, even more likely to have been too small to justify the administrative expense.

Finally, the rationality of the distinction draws support from the fact that the line that the City drew—distinguishing past payments from future obligations—is a line well known to the law. Sometimes such a line takes the form of an amnesty program, involving, say, mortgage payments, taxes, or parking tickets. *E.g.*, 26 U.S.C. § 108(a)(1)(E) (2006 ed., Supp. IV) (federal income tax provision allowing homeowners to omit from gross income newly forgiven home mortgage debt); *United States v. Martin*, 523 F.3d 281, 284 (CA4 2008) (tax amnesty program whereby State newly forgave penalties and liabilities if taxpayer satisfied debt); *Horn v. Chicago*, 860 F.2d 700, 704, n. 9 (CA7 1988) (city parking ticket amnesty program whereby outstanding tickets could be newly settled for a fraction of amount specified). This kind of line is consistent with the distinction that the law often makes between actions previously taken and those yet to come.

C

... Petitioners go on to propose various other forgiveness systems that would have included refunds for at least some of those who had already paid in full. They argue that those systems are superior to the system that the City chose. We have discussed those, and other possible, systems earlier. *Supra*, at 2081–2082. Each has advantages and disadvantages. But even if petitioners have found a superior system, the Constitution does not require the City to draw the perfect line nor even to draw a line superior to some other line it might have drawn. It requires only that the line actually drawn be a rational line. And for the reasons we have set forth in Part II-B, *supra*, we believe that the line the City drew here is rational.

Petitioners further argue that administrative considerations alone should not justify a tax distinction, lest a city arbitrarily allocate taxes among a few citizens while forgiving many similarly situated citizens on the ground that it is cheaper and easier to collect taxes from a few people than from many. Petitioners are right that administrative considerations could not justify such an unfair system. But that is not because administrative considerations can *never* justify tax differences (any more than they can *always* do so). The question is whether reducing those expenses, in the particular circumstances, provides a rational basis justifying the tax difference in question.

In this case, "in the light of the facts made known or generally assumed," *Carolene Products Co.*, 304 U.S., at 152, it is reasonable to believe that to graft a refund system onto the City's forgiveness decision could have (for example) imposed an administrative burden of both collecting and paying out small sums (say, $25 per month) for years. As we have said, *supra*, at 2080–2082, it is rational for the City to draw a line that avoids that burden. Petitioners, who are the ones "attacking the legislative arrangement," have the burden of showing that the circumstances are otherwise, i.e., that the administrative burden is too insubstantial to justify the classification. That they have not done.

Finally, petitioners point to precedent that in their view makes it more difficult than we have said for the City to show a "rational basis." With but one exception, however, the cases to which they refer involve discrimination based on residence or length of residence. But those circumstances are not present here.

The exception consists of *Allegheny Pittsburgh Coal Co. v. Commission of Webster Cty.*, 488 U.S. 336 (1989). The Court there took into account a state constitution and related laws that required equal valuation of equally valuable property. *Id.*, at 345. It considered the constitutionality of a county tax assessor's practice (over a period of many years) of determining property values as of the time of the property's last sale; that practice meant highly unequal valuations for two identical properties that were sold years or decades apart. *Id.*, at 341. The Court first found that the assessors practice was not rationally related to the county's avowed purpose of assessing properties equally at true current value because of the intentional systemic discrepancies the practice created. *Id.*, at 343–344. The Court then noted that, in light of the state constitution and related laws requiring equal valuation, there could be no other rational basis for the practice. *Id.*, at 344–345. Therefore, the Court held, the assessor's discriminatory policy violated the Federal Constitution's insistence upon "equal protection of the law." *Id.*, at 346.

Petitioners argue that the City's refusal to add refunds to its forgiveness decision is similar, for it constitutes a refusal to apply "equally" an Indiana state law that says that the costs of a Barrett Law project shall be equally "apportioned." Ind.Code § 36-9-39-15(b)(3). In other words, petitioners say that even if the City's decision might otherwise be related to a rational purpose, state law (as in Allegheny) makes this the rare case where the facts preclude any rational basis for the City's decision other than to comply with the state mandate of equality.

Allegheny, however, involved a clear state law requirement clearly and dramatically violated. Indeed, we have described Allegheny as "the rare case where the facts precluded" any alternative reading of state law and thus any alternative rational basis. *Nordlinger*, 505 U.S., at 16. Here, the City followed state law by apportioning the cost of its Barrett Law projects equally. State law says nothing about forgiveness, how to design a forgiveness program, or whether or when rational distinctions in doing so are permitted. To adopt petitioners' view would risk transforming ordinary violations of ordinary state tax law into violations of the Federal Constitution.

. . . .

For these reasons, we conclude that the City has not violated the Federal Equal Protection Clause. And the Indiana Supreme Court's similar determination is Affirmed.

[Chief Justice Roberts, along with Justices Scalia and Alito, dissented. The dissenters were particularly biting in their critique about the City's justification for its decision, as indicated in the following excerpt.—Eds.]

. . . In seeking to justify [its decision], the City explained that it was presented with three choices: First, it could have continued to collect the installment plan payments of those who had not yet settled their debts under the old system. Second, it could have forgiven all those debts and given equivalent refunds to those who had made lump sum payments up front. Or third, it could have forgiven the future payments and not refunded payments that had already been made. The first two choices had the benefit of complying with state law, treating all of Indianapolis's citizens equally, and comporting with the Constitution. The City chose the third option.

And what did the City believe was sufficient to justify a system that would effectively charge petitioners *30 times more* than their neighbors for the same service—when state law promised equal treatment? Two things: the desire to avoid administrative hassle and the "fiscal[] challeng[e]" of giving back money it wanted to keep.

To the extent a ruling for petitioners would require issuing refunds to others who overpaid under the Barrett Law, I think the city workers are up to the task. The City has in fact already produced records showing exactly how much each lump-sum payer overpaid in every active Barrett Law Project—to the penny. . . . What the city employees would need to do, therefore, is cut the checks and mail them out.

Notes and Questions

1. *Standard of review.* Recall from Chapter 1 the several standards of review the Supreme Court applies to equal protection cases. What level of review did the Court employ in *Armour*? Do you see why the Court did not apply a heightened standard of review in this case? The Court traditionally grants extreme deference to the legislative will. So long as the facts "do not preclude" an inference supporting the legislative rationale, the Court will not second guess the legislature. See *Fitzgerald v. Racing Ass'n of Central Iowa*, 539 U.S. 103, 110 (2003). *Fitzgerald* upheld differential Iowa tax rates imposed on riverboat slot machines (20%) and racetrack slot machines (36%). Equal protection issues also are discussed in Chapter 9 on the role of the judiciary. Should "administrative convenience" cited in *Armour* become a judicially recognized factor for conferring deference or not applying a heightened standard of review?

2. *California's property tax limitation system and equal protection concerns.* California was at the forefront of state-based tax revolts beginning in the 1970s. Proposition 13 was a ballot initiative adopted in the face of significantly rising property values and associated tax burdens and reflected citizens' desire to impose property tax limits under the state constitution. The system adopted basically froze property values as they stood at the time of purchase, and imposed property taxes on that assessed value. The result was that those owning real property at the time the initiative was adopted were taxed at the value upon purchase, while those purchasing identical property at a later date in the same neighborhood were taxed at a much higher assessed value reflecting their purchase price at a later date. The core notion was to protect the interests of those purchasing property, and their expectations of property tax obligations at the time they purchased property in a rapidly rising

market. Related issues were addressed under state law in *Amador Valley Joint Union High School Dist. v. State Bd. of Equalization*, 583 P.2d 1281 (Cal. 1978). The United States Supreme Court reviewed challenges to this scheme in *Nordlinger v. Hahn*, 505 U.S. 1 (1992). Although there have been subsequent changes in California law that have meant that Proposition 13 is a less prominent model for tax policy than it was initially, it is nonetheless useful to understand how the Supreme Court grappled with associated equal protection issues in this important case.

In *Nordlinger*, the petitioner discovered she was paying about five times more in taxes than some of her neighbors who had owned comparable homes since 1975 within the same residential development. For example, one block away, a house of identical size on a lot slightly larger than petitioner's was subject to a general tax levy of only $358.20 (based on an assessed valuation of $35,820, which reflected the home's value in 1975 plus the up-to-2% per year inflation factor). According to petitioner, her total property taxes over the first 10 years in her home would approach $19,000, while any neighbor who bought a comparable home in 1975 stood to pay just $4,100. The general tax levied against her modest home was only a few dollars short of that paid by a pre-1976 owner of a $2.1 million Malibu beachfront home.

The Supreme Court concluded that the California scheme did not violate equal protection requirements, holding that the relevant standard of review should focus on whether the difference in treatment between older and newer property owners rationally furthered a legitimate state interest. The Court found that the California scheme applied the same standards relating to a tax rate ceiling and yearly assessment increases but differed only as to the initial value on which property is assessed. The Court concluded that the system was designed to facilitate neighborhood preservation and stability, and to take into account reliance interests. For a critique of *Nordlinger* and the California acquisition-based property tax system, asserting that this system raises questions of compliance with the federal Fair Housing Act, see Sarkar & Rosenthal, *Exclusionary Taxation*, 53 HARV. C.R.-C.L. L. REV. 619 (2018).

3. *Business taxes.* State courts may deal with equal protection issues in the context of business taxes. In *Helton v. City of Long Beach*, 127 Cal. Rptr. 737 (Cal. App. 1976), the court upheld a tax on businesses within a defined area that varied depending on the type of business and the business' distance from the center of the defined area. The purpose of the tax was to raise revenue for parking and other facilities in the area affected by the tax. What about an "occupancy fee" on attorneys practicing in a city? In *Moss v. City of Dunwoody*, 750 S.E.2d 326 (Ga. 2013), the Georgia Supreme Court upheld the charge as a license fee rather than a tax over plaintiff's objection that the fee violated equal protection because it was not charged outside the city limits, and established an unlawful precondition on the practice of law. The court reasoned that the purpose of the fee was to generate revenue for the city, not regulate lawyers. As to the equal protection claim, the court noted that the right to practice law was not a "fundamental right" so that the defendant city needed only to demonstrate a rational relationship to a legitimate public purpose (funding city operations). How does the "purpose" of these revenue-raising fees justify a

differential tax system? Has an "administrative convenience" doctrine announced in *Armour* supplanted the protection of rights of persons and small businesses in the name of fiscal stability for local governments? Would a court apply the "rational relationship" test if the facts demonstrated that the incidence of the fees was greater, not on attorneys and persons located next to a parking garage, but those in poor neighborhoods or predominantly minority neighborhoods?

4. *The utility of an equal protection claim on taxation.* Judicial deference to legislative tax regimes attacked on equal protection grounds means that such regimes are generally upheld even when the facts suggest that some deference is appropriate to accommodate the circumstances of the less fortunate plaintiff. In *Farneth v. Wal-Mart Stores, Inc.*, 2013 WL 6859013 (W.D. Pa. Dec. 30, 2013), the federal district court found no equal protection infirmity to a state tax law that applied the sales tax to the total cost of all items (here, shaving cream), before deducting the value of a buy-one-get-one free coupon. More recently, challenges have been mounted to application of sales tax on female hygiene products such as tampons. See Crawford & Spivack, *Tampon Taxes, Discrimination, and Human Rights*, 2017 Wis. L. Rev. 491 (2017) (reporting on legislative changes and litigation challenging taxation of female hygiene products as violating equal protection principles). See also Crawford & Waldman, *The Unconstitutional Tampon Tax*, 53 U. Rich. L. Rev. 439 (2019).

In a wide-ranging challenge to state sales tax practices that included numerous exemptions and caps, the Supreme Court of South Carolina in *Bodman v. State*, 742 S.E.2d 363 (S.C. 2013), dismissed the taxpayer's challenge that the sales tax was irrational on equal protection grounds, based on the following considerations: (i) "mere taxpayers" should not be accorded standing to bring an equal protection action in the absence of "concrete and particularized" injury and associated harm; (ii) legislative decisions regarding classifications should be given deference without regard to "motives"; and (iii) tax statues should be presumed constitutional. In your view, does the reasoning in *Bodman* limit any meaningful challenges to Balkanized sales tax regimes? Why or why not?

[d] Other Federal Constitutional Provisions

[i] Contract Clause

Article I, § 10, cl. 3 provides that "No State shall . . . pass any . . . Law impairing the Obligation of Contracts. . . ." The leading Contract Clause case in the area of state and local government finance is *U.S. Trust Co. v. New Jersey*, 431 U.S. 1 (1977), involving an attempt by the Port Authority of New York and New Jersey ("PANYNJ"), a bi-state agency established by the US Congress, to divert revenue pledged to outstanding bonds issued by PANYNJ to secure the payment of new bonds to be issued by PANYNJ to finance another transportation project. The bondholders whose bonds were affected by the diversion of revenues argued that the state impaired their contract with PANYNJ. The defense argued that such diversion was permitted so long as other adequate revenues remained available and the remedies of the plaintiff bondholders remained unimpaired. The defense further argued that its action to divert revenues was a legitimate exercise of the state's police power, which as an agency created by Congress, PANYNJ was empowered to exercise.

Faced with having to balance the police power against the power to contract, the US Supreme Court ruled that once exercised, the power to contract could not be impaired by exercising the police power unless such exercise was "reasonable and necessary to serve an important public purpose." *Id.* 25. The defense's reliance on the state-law bankruptcy decision in *Faitoute Iron & Steel v. City of Asbury Park*, 316 U.S. 502 (1942) in which the Court condoned the exercise of the police power to adjust defaulted municipal bonds was held to apply only in the case of financial emergencies such as conditions during the Great Depression of the 1930s and 1940s. Today, should similar facts in *Faitoute* face a federal bankruptcy court, the exercise of the court's bankruptcy powers to adjust debts would supersede, indeed preempt, the exercise of the state's police power to reform contracts. Municipal bankruptcy is considered in more detail later in this Chapter.

The Second Circuit took the opposite approach in deciding the Contract Clause claim of the City of Buffalo teachers' union in *Buffalo Teachers Federation v. Tobe*, 464 F.3d 362 (2d Cir. 2006). In *Buffalo Teachers*, plaintiffs argued that a state-imposed wage freeze on public school teachers as part of a fiscal stability program for the City violated the terms of teacher labor contracts, and therefore the state law imposing a wage freeze was unenforceable as a violation of the Contract Clause. The Second Circuit disagreed, concluding that the City's fiscal condition had deteriorated to such a point that a financial emergency existed thereby making the wage freeze a recognized exercise of the police power. The Contracts Clause is particularly relevant to discussions of public pension issues, considered later in this Chapter.

[ii] First Amendment

The First Amendment provides that "Congress shall make no law respecting an establishment of religion . . . or abridging the freedom of speech." State and local taxes occasionally are challenged as a violation of rights guaranteed by the First Amendment. Based on the notion that "the power to tax the exercise of a privilege is the power to control or suppress its enjoyment," the Supreme Court has invalidated license fees imposed on hand distributors or sellers of religious literature, *Murdock v. Pennsylvania*, 319 U.S. 105 (1943); *Follett v. McCormick*, 321 U.S. 573 (1944), as well as a discriminatory use tax on ink and paper products used in newspaper and magazine production, *Minneapolis Star & Tribune Co. v. Minnesota Comm'r of Revenue*, 460 U.S. 575 (1983). See also *Texas Monthly, Inc. v. Bullock*, 489 U.S. 1 (1989) (state sales tax exemption for religious publications violated Establishment Clause). However, the Court has approved of nondiscriminatory sales or use taxes on newspaper receipts, *Arkansas Writers' Project, Inc. v. Ragland*, 481 U.S. 221 (1987), and on receipts from the sale of religious merchandise such as Bibles, study manuals, printed sermons, religious books, pamphlets, and tapes, *Jimmy Swaggart Ministries v. Board of Equalization*, 493 U.S. 378 (1990).

The Supreme Court refused to hear an appeal of an Ohio court's decision concluding that an admissions tax imposed by municipalities on patrons of recreational facilities such as bowling alleys, concerts, and theaters did not violate the First Amendment. The Ohio court held that the tax was content neutral and focused on secondary effects of commercial entertainment such as crowd control, security and traffic. *Regal Cinemas, Inc. v. Mayfield Heights, Ohio,* 738 N.E.2d 42 (Ohio App. 2000). A variety of other cases have addressed First Amendment issues relating to taxation and expenditures in other settings. See, e.g., *Elster v. City of Seattle*, 444 P.3d 590 (Wash. 2019) (upholding "democracy voucher" program that allowed registered municipal voters and qualifying residents to give vouchers funded through property taxes to qualified municipal candidates for their use in electoral campaigns); *Deja Vu Showgirls of Las Vegas, LLC v. Nevada Department of Taxation*, 334 P.3d 392 (Nev. 2014) (upholding Nevada's Live Entertainment Tax, which imposed 10% excise tax on amounts paid for admission, food, refreshments, and merchandise at live-entertainment facilities with maximum occupancy of less than 7,500; finding that tax was not prior restraint, did not discriminate against exotic dancing establishments, target a small group of speakers, or threaten to suppress ideas or viewpoints so as to trigger strict scrutiny; and concluding that rational basis review applied).

Other First Amendment challenges have been brought based on assertions that taxing or spending practices impair the free exercise of religion. The Tenth Circuit struck down a decision by Colorado officials denying state scholarships to students attending a non-denominational evangelical Protestant university and a Buddhist university, while approving such scholarships for students at a Methodist university and a Roman Catholic university operated by the Jesuit order. *Colorado Christian Univ. v. Weaver*, 534 F.3d 1245 (10th Cir. 2008). The court distinguished *Locke v. Davey*, 540 U.S. 712 (2004) (which had held that a state may exclude students majoring in "devotional theology" from a state scholarship program), and held that the Colorado exclusion impermissibly "discriminates *among* religions . . . and it does so on the basis of criteria that entail intrusive governmental judgments regarding matters of religious belief and practice."

[iii] Tenth Amendment

The Tenth Amendment provides that "The powers not delegated to the United States . . . nor prohibited by it to the States, are reserved to the States . . . or to the people." The Tenth Amendment has faded as a defense to suits against state and local governments and no longer supports the now-historic Federalist concept of "intergovernmental immunity." But the Tenth Amendment is the bedrock for making the law of public finance primarily state law, not federal law. In *Hunter v. Pittsburgh*, 207 U.S. 161 (1907), discussed in Chapter 1, the Supreme Court ruled that the powers conferred on the municipalities of a state rest in the absolute discretion of the state, unrestrained by any provision of federal law or the U.S. Constitution. The *Hunter* decision may not be taken so seriously on its face today, as discussed earlier in this book, but in the areas of federal law that impact public finance (income tax, securities regulation, and bankruptcy), federal statutes and regulations are respectful of the reserved power in the states.

Notably, in *South Carolina v. Baker*, 485 U.S. 505 (1988), the Court upheld an Internal Revenue Code of 1986 mandate that long-term municipal bonds be issued in "registered" form to enjoy tax-exempt status. In *Blount v. U.S. Securities Exchange & Comm'n.*, 61 F.3d 938 (D.C. Cir. 1995) states sued the Securities Exchange Commission ("SEC") for promulgating regulations through the Municipal Securities Rulemaking Board ("MSRB," an arm of the SEC that regulates licensed broker/dealers who purchase and "underwrite" municipal bonds). The regulations prohibited participation by broker/dealers in purchasing or underwriting municipal bonds unless they ceased making political contributions (with a *de minimus* exception), reported the political contributions they made to the MSRB, and paid a fine. The regulation, Rule G-37, was found by the court to be "content neutral," not a direct regulation of the states or a rule to compel states to regulate private parties. The rule, said the court, fulfilled a federal purpose of protecting the investing public from broker/dealers who engage in bribery, coercion, fraud and deceit. Similarly, in *Wagner v. Federal Election Commission*, 793 F.3d. 1417 (D.C. Cir. 2015) (en banc), the D.C. Circuit upheld provisions of the Federal Elections Campaign Act that barred individuals and firms from making federal campaign contributions while negotiating or performing federal contracts, rejecting contentions that such limitations violated the First Amendment.

[iv] Supremacy Clause

Article VI, cl. 2 provides: "The Constitution, and the Laws of the United States . . . shall be the supreme Law of the Land . . ." This provision is clearly of concern when considering some new public purpose which the state or local government may wish to undertake. As a general rule, federal law cannot supersede the power of the states (including the police power, the power to tax, the power to borrow and spend, and the power of eminent domain) in the absence of a clear and manifest purpose of Congress. In *Shapp v. Sloan*, 391 A.2d 595 (Pa. 1978), the Pennsylvania Supreme Court determined that federal funds received by the Commonwealth belonged to the Commonwealth and therefore had to be appropriated through the legislature in the same way that state funds had to be appropriated pursuant to the state constitution. The court further determined that the Supremacy Clause did not interfere with the state constitutional mandate for the Commonwealth to appropriate all funds, so long as federal funds were not diverted from their intended purpose under federal law. Chapter 7 considers federal preemption in detail.

C. Revenues

Revenues are the money state and local governments receive to pay the expenses set forth in an annual budget as discussed later in this Chapter. Most of this money is paid involuntarily by persons and businesses located within the taxing jurisdiction in return for the government's provision of general services (i.e., police, fire protection, EMS), or special services like education, all of which serve the public generally, but no one taxpayer in particular. Because state and local government expense budgets pre-pandemic had have grown dramatically since the mid-twentieth century as the costs of services has increased, the financial management challenge has been not only to contain or reduce expenses but to increase revenues by (i) increasing existing taxes, assessments, and fee charges; (ii) enforcing collection of taxes, assessments and fees levied and charged; and (iii) creating new sources of revenues from economic activities that can be increased without public resistance and efficiently enforced. It is likely that such issues will be front and center as state and local governments attempt to address the impacts of the COVID pandemic.

[1] Real Property Taxes

[a] Design and Operation

Real property taxes are sometimes referred to as "*ad valorem*" taxes, meaning taxes determined "according to their value." Accordingly, the key to determining the property tax is the value of the "taxable real property." The tax is imposed on real property in the name of the person or entity that has "title" to the property as recorded with the local government (usually a county) in the custody of a government officer (usually the clerk or recorder of deeds). Title implies ownership but not necessarily use of the property. For example, a tenant who rents a residential apartment uses the property and may exclude the landlord (owner) under the terms of the lease but does not directly pay a real property tax.

The origins of the real property tax can be traced to the feudal land tenure system established in England following the Norman Conquest of 1066. Commentators have noted that the relationship to property ownership serves three basic purposes: (1) a means of measuring the tax liability, (2) a device for distributing tax burden, and (3) a rough approximation of public benefits received with the burden of paying for those benefits. J. Fordham, Local Government Law 510 (2d rev. ed. 1986). The property tax was once the staple of state and local government finance, but since World War II it has declined in relative importance as income taxes, sales taxes and user fees have gained importance, as explained in the introductory section of this Chapter.

The assessed value is generally determined by the "assessor," an appointed or elected local government official. The assessor prepares the annual "assessment roll" of all taxable property in the taxing jurisdiction. The roll is submitted to the governing body that adopts it as an item of revenue in approving the annual budget. Once adopted, the roll becomes the "tax levy," an amount each property owner is required to pay on a date certain to extinguish the lien of the tax. For an analysis of problems associated with the property tax and assessment practices, see Wease, *Averting the Next Property Tax Revolt: A Case for Changing the Tax Base of Residential Property*, 48 Real Est. L.J. 163 (2019).

Nonetheless, there are a range of complications regarding administration of the property tax that are worth noting. Consider, for example, that two properties of the same assessment classification (*i.e.*, residential, commercial), with similar structures, of similar quality, on similarly sized lots, and similar locations may have very different real property tax liabilities. While assessed values may reflect market realities at the time property is sold, in rapidly fluctuating markets, properties held for longer periods may not be as readily assessed at current values unless the local government engages in periodic re-evaluation. For example, a recently sold property may be assessed based on its sale price, while a property that has not been transferred for many years may bear an assessment which has not been adjusted to reflect current property values. Two components are used to determine the actual property tax due: (1) its assessed value, and (2) the millage rate, or percentage applied to the assessed value to calculate the tax. Thus, for example, property valued at $250,000 with a property tax (millage rate) of $.01 per dollar value, would have a property tax bill of $2,500. Note, however, that refinements are often employed, for example by exempting a certain property value as the value of a "homestead" or by providing reduced tax valuations for veterans or senior citizens. Often, when counties or municipalities engage in reassessment of property values, they will offset millage rates (reducing them) in the face of higher property assessment values in order to keep property tax bills from swinging wildly.

Nevertheless, the real property tax remains an important source of revenue for local governments, particularly for municipalities, counties, and single purpose special districts such as school districts. In some states, the property tax is the exclusive tax for local governments, and the state may not impose upon this form of taxation but must rely on other sources of revenue. Particular attention is paid to the property tax in this Chapter because of its historical standing, its continued importance as a source of revenue for local governments, and the controversial nature of its impact on individual property owners. Property taxes tend to trigger more litigation and other forms of protest than the income tax, sales tax, or user fees. For an important study on property tax policies across the individual states, see Lincoln Institute of Land Policy & Minnesota Center for Fiscal Excellence, *50 State Property Tax Comparison Study for Taxes Collected in 2017*, available at https://www.lincolninst.edu/publications/other/50-state-property-tax-comparison-study-2. The study reveals the extent to which cities with lower property valuations tend to charge higher property tax rates and demonstrates how some jurisdictions protect residential property owners by shifting tax burdens to commercial property. Some localities are beginning to address concerns that black homeowners pay higher property taxes as a result of intentional or inadvertent assessments of their property. See Wiltz, *Black Homeowners Pay More Than 'Fair Share' in Property Taxes*, STATELINE (an initiative of the Pew Charitable Trusts) (June 25, 2020), available at https://www.pewtrusts.org/en/research-and-analysis/blogs/stateline/2020/06/25/black-homeowners-pay-more-than-fair-share-in-property-taxes.

Why the protest and litigation? The real property tax is an easy tax to collect and enforce. Real property, unlike income and sales taxes, cannot move out of the taxing jurisdiction. If the tax is not paid it becomes a statutory lien against the property and accrues interest and penalties from its payment due date. If property taxes are not paid for several years, the property subject to the tax lien may be sold by the taxing jurisdiction, usually at public auction, at a minimum price (usually far below market value), to satisfy unpaid real property taxes (the tax lien is a "prior lien" with respect to the lien of a mortgage: all the taxes are paid before any of the mortgage is paid in foreclosure). To illustrate, the Oregon Supreme Court found that a charge cannot be considered a property tax unless the governmental unit has the statutory authority to place a lien upon the property in the event of nonpayment. *Knapp v. City of Jacksonville*, 151 P.3d 143, 147 (Or. 2007).

Keep in mind another issue in reviewing the evolution of property tax and associated challenges. It is not easy to find an appropriate remedy when state and local governments fail to maintain current assessments of property values, and a failure to do so can significantly disadvantage recent purchasers when compared to long-term property owners. State law generally provides an administrative appeal process reviewable by a court of general jurisdiction. The appeal is usually prospective only before the levy is effective (*i.e.*, before the annual budget is approved). In *Allegheny Pittsburgh Coal Co. v. County Comm'n of Webster County*, 488 U.S. 336 (1989), the Supreme Court held that revaluation of other property that may have been undervalued was not a sufficient response to a taxpayer who established that the assessment scheme as applied to its property violated the Equal Protection Clause. *Allegheny Pittsburgh Coal Co.* was followed by the Montana Supreme Court in *Roosevelt, IV v. Montana Dept. of Revenue*, 975 P.2d 295 (Mont. 1999), invalidating an annual 2% phase-in of property revaluation as unconstitutional when applied to a taxpayer whose property had suffered a substantial decline in value within one year.

[b] Classifications and Differential Assessments

In light of the uniformity provision in most state constitutions, one question is the validity of real property classifications when the rate of tax or assessment ratio is varied for each class. Differential assessments raise similar questions.

Associated Industries of Missouri v. State Tax Commission

722 S.W.2d 916 (Mo. 1987)

Blackmar, Judge.

Individual and corporate taxpayers filed a declaratory judgment action, challenging the constitutionality of § 137.016, RS Mo Supp. 1984 classifying as residential "all real property improved by a structure ... which contains not more than four dwelling units...." By reason of this classification, the involved property is assessed at 19% of its fair market value, whereas other rental property is classified in the general classification and assessed at 32% of its value. The trial court held that the statute violated the due process and equal protection clauses of the Fourteenth Amendment of the U.S. Constitution and the "uniformity" clause of the Missouri Constitution, art. X, because it was arbitrary and unreasonable, and that it established a prohibited subclass of real property, in violation of art. X, § 4(b) of the Missouri Constitution. We conclude that the statute is not shown to be arbitrary or capricious and that the challenges have failed to overcome the presumption of constitutionality. We therefore reverse and remand for the entry of a declaratory judgment sustaining the validity of the statute against the challenges made.

In 1982, art. X, § 4(b) of the Missouri Constitution was amended to permit the establishment of three subclasses of real property.... [The three subclasses are (1) residential, (2) agricultural and horticultural, and (3) utility, industrial, commercial railroad and other property. Pursuant to constitutional authority, the legislature then defined residential property to include structures that contained no more than four dwelling units. Structures containing more than four dwelling units were assessed as commercial property.]

The fact that our Constitution and statutes permit the establishment of subclasses of real property, and provide for different rates of assessment of property in different subclasses, does not demonstrate a constitutional violation under either the due process or equal protection clauses of the Fourteenth Amendment of the United States Constitution.

The plaintiffs do not make their case simply by showing that different classes of real property are assessed at different rates.

They argue, however, that the "rule of four" is wholly arbitrary and without reason....

> We do not agree. Statutes are presumed to be constitutional until the contrary is shown. Every indulgence must be made in favor of the legislature's handiwork. Classifications based on number have often been sustained.

Rental housing has both residential and commercial aspects. The legislature might appropriately conclude that the commercial aspect predominates for buildings containing numerous units, whereas those containing only a few units have a predominantly residential character. It might conclude that the selection of a definite figure, such as four, offered the most effective means of classifying rental property into residential and commercial categories. There might be reluctance to burden the owner of a small complex with commercial taxes, which necessarily will be passed on to the tenants. Larger units, however, might be expected to bear the commercial rate. We are unable to say that the legislature's choice lacked any rational basis. The cases relied on, then, are distinguishable.

Our conclusion is not changed because some elaborate "fourplexes" may bear all indicia of being commercial property. The legislature's judgment as to the overall picture must be respected. It should also be the function of the legislature to look for abuses and evasions of the governing principle and to take action if deemed appropriate. Perfect equity in the assessment of real property cannot be expected. The present constitutional and statutory provisions, coupled with state-wide reassessment, have the potential for relative equality of assessment of similarly classified property....

The statute does not create a prohibited additional subclass of real property. Its purpose, rather, is to allocate rental property between two of the constitutionally approved subclasses. This allocation is within the power of the legislature, unless shown to be arbitrary or unreasonable....

We do not disagree with Judge Welliver's assertion that real estate taxes on rental property may ultimately be borne by the tenants. By the same token, taxes on commercial property are ultimately borne by the general public. The problem he points to is inherent in the permissible classification of real property for tax purposes. It does not necessarily follow that the normal renter has a more severe tax burden than the normal homeowner. The classifying decision was made by the legislature, with its superior means of information about the effects of legislation on the public, and for the reasons stated we are not persuaded that it exceeded the authority conferred by the amended art. X, § 4(b) or that its choice was otherwise constitutionally infirm.

The judgment is reversed and the case remanded with directions to declare that the statute is not shown to be unconstitutional on any of the grounds assigned.

Robertson, Judge, concurring.

... Real property developed as apartments partakes of a dual nature. Like commercial property, it produces income; like residential property it provides shelter. Thus, apartments are both residential and commercial. In the presence of this dual nature, I am unwilling to say that the General Assembly violated the constitution by choosing to define the primary nature of larger apartment complexes as commercial....

... No one challenges the legitimacy of the State exercising its taxing power through the imposition of ad valorem taxes on real property. Thus, the constitutional challenge turns on whether the classifications created by the legislature are rationally related to the State's interests in taxation.

It is argued that apartments are purely residential. Yet, as has already been discussed, apartments have an undeniably commercial aspect. Thus, in my view, the legislature would have been justified in classifying all apartment property as commercial property.

The more thoughtful argument challenges the distinction drawn by the General Assembly between apartment property containing four or fewer units and apartment complexes containing five or more units. Does this distinction have a rational basis? As the principal opinion correctly holds, the distinction drawn by the legislature may have been based on the legislature's understanding that those "complexes" containing four or fewer units, because of their lack of size, are not truly commercial; such property may also have been developed for the purpose of providing housing for the extended family of the owner. Theses rationales are sufficient to ward off this constitutional challenge. As the principal opinion indicates, the cases upon which Judge Rendlen's dissent relies for the proposition that this statute is unconstitutional are distinguishable.

As I have already confessed, I disagree with the policy choice made by the General Assembly. The temptation we face as judges, when equal protection is invoked, is to assume that any policy choice with which we disagree is irrational and therefore in violation of the Constitution. To succumb to the temptation to substitute our chosen policy for that adopted by the elected representatives of the people is, however, to confuse power with authority. The fact that our system of government entrusts us with the power to declare an act of the legislature unconstitutional does not mean that we can exercise that power to effectuate our policy choices, absent a violation of the Constitution. The fact that the General Assembly's decision may be considered odd by us, does not, in my view, also render it unconstitutional. . . .

[The dissenters argued that the 1982 Amendment, art. X, § 4(b), had to be read together with § 4(a), which had existed since the inception of property tax classification in 1945, and which required property to be classified "solely on the nature and characteristics of the property, and not on the nature, residence or business of the owner, or the amount owned." According to the dissent, the legislative classification of apartments amounted to an impermissible classification based on the productive capability of the property. The dissenters found no rational basis for the apartment classification, and argued that the 1984 statute in question was an impermissible *division* rather than a permissible *definition* of property.]

Notes and Questions

1. *Property tax exemptions.* It is worth remembering that despite a political impulse to protect vulnerable populations like senior citizens and veterans, cities may lack the power to grant tax exemptions targeting such populations because of constitutional provisions relating to uniformity. See *City of Spokane v. Horton*, 406 P.3d 638 (Wash. 2017). Decisions like the one in *City of Spokane* put uniformity provisions to the test. In light of this decision, are you more or less convinced that uniformity requirements belong in state constitutions?

2. *Townhouse clusters.* The "rule of four" has continued to cause problems. Suppose a developer in Missouri builds 100 apartment units in townhouse clusters of 10

units each on one tract of land and another developer subdivides a tract of land into contiguous lots and then constructs 100 apartment units in groups of two or four on the separate lots ("duplexes" and "fourplexes"). Should both apartment developments be classified the same? Missouri courts said "yes" in subsequent cases, including *Rothschild v. State Tax Comm'n of Mo.*, 762 S.W.2d 35 (Mo. 1988) (duplexes and fourplexes on separate lots should be classified as residential property because the statute focuses on the number of units per structure rather than per taxpayer). But in *Westwood Partnership v. Gogarty*, 103 S.W.3d 152 (Mo. 2003), the court reversed a trial court decision invalidating the assessor's "residential" classification of several mixed-use developments (housing, and commercial) as containing equal protection infirmities. On appeal, the trial court decision was reversed, washing away *Rothschild* and its progeny leaning toward "residential" classification of multi-unit projects. The *Westwood Partnership* court reasoned:

> There is no longer an automatic [statutory] presumption regarding the correctness of an assessor's valuation . . . This statutory change from the previous situation in which the assessor's valuation was presumed to be correct does not mean that there is now a presumption in favor of the taxpayer. The taxpayer in a Commission tax appeal still bears the burden of proof by the preponderance of the evidence . . . [*Id.* at 8.]

The court concluded "Missouri courts have recognized that it is impossible to avoid all discriminatory impact in tax classifications, and that absolute uniformity of tax classifications and assessments is an unattainable ideal, while practical uniformity is the constitutional goal." *Id.* at 18.

3. *Decisions upholding assessment systems.* States have adopted different procedures for carrying out particular assessment plans. When such procedures are challenged, courts generally adopt a deferential view to the legislative schemes. In *Arizona Dep't of Revenue v. Trico Elec. Coop.*, 729 P.2d 898 (Ariz. 1986), the Supreme Court of Arizona upheld a statutory procedure for determining "full cash value" of electric and gas utility property by deducting annual depreciation amounts from the initial cash outlay for the property. Acknowledging that "discrepancies between property tax assessments on identical property (of cooperative electric utilities and investor-owned utilities) may result," the court held that such discrepancies did not violate constitutional uniformity requirements because they were the result of "discretionary depreciation practices permitted by law" (accelerated depreciation practices of profit-motivated companies) rather than a non-uniform rate of taxation. *Id.* at 901–02. Similarly, the Missouri Supreme Court has approved the use of "properly conducted ratio studies" to establish an average level of assessment and discrimination in individual cases. *Savage v. State Tax Comm'n*, 722 S.W.2d 72 (Mo. 1986) (en banc).

Ratio studies involve the appraisal of a selected number of parcels in a taxing district chosen at random by a computer program, rather than the appraisal of all parcels in the district. In upholding the use of ratio studies, the court stated: "Given the careful attention which the Commission and the legislative branch have given ratio studies as a means of discovering 'average true value ratios to be used, . . .' we cannot agree . . . that ratio studies are per se inadmissible for purposes of challenges to individual assessment." *Id.* at 76. The Missouri court also refused to order the State Tax Commission to increase assessments on agricultural property, which would have decreased the taxes on commercial property, concluding that the state legislature had given the commission discretion to take economic conditions into account in setting assessment rates. *Missouri Growth Ass'n v. State Tax Comm'n*, 998 S.W.2d 786 (Mo. 1999) (en banc). Missouri has very nuanced constitutional and statutory provisions relating to taxation. See *Armstrong-Trotwood, LLC v. State Tax Commission* 516 S.W.3d 830 (Mo. 2017) (en banc) (discussing state constitutional provisions regarding appellate judicial review as they related to multi-county taxing districts, inter-county equalization requirements, and application of uniformity provision of state constitution).

4. *Farmland: assessment and classification issues.* Differential assessments of land based on use are often attempted to encourage certain land uses. Urban planners and experts frequently allege that farmland adjacent to urbanized areas is assessed at high land values reflecting the higher values on nearby land, which is already in urban use. As a result, farmers unable to bear the increased tax burden are forced to sell their land for urbanization prior to the time when it is ready to be urbanized, or prior to the time a local plan indicates it should be urbanized, with negative effects on urban development patterns. In the absence of preferential assessment legislation or comparable assessment practices at the local level, agricultural land located near urbanized areas will be assessed at its market value and this value will reflect the possibility that the agricultural land may be put to urban use. See *Mohland v. State Bd. of Equalization*, 466 P.2d 582 (Mont. 1970) (market value was a proper assessment standard).

Practically all states and many municipalities have adopted tax abatement programs for agricultural land under which, primarily through lowered assessments, agricultural land is taxed at its value for agricultural, or current, use. This value is usually lower than the market value at which land is ordinarily assessed. While some states have now amended their constitutions to allow this kind of differential taxation, the acceptability of this kind of differential taxation under conventional uniformity clauses led to conflicting responses from the courts. Keene, *Differential Assessment and the Preservation of Open Space*, 14 Urb. L. Ann. 11 (1977); Wunderlich, *Land Taxes in Agriculture: Preferential Rate and Assessment Effects*, 56 Am. J. of Econ. & Soc. 215 (1997); Keene, *Differential Assessment and the Preservation of Open Space*, 14 Urb. L. Ann. 11 (1977). For example, a Florida law provided that "All lands being used for agricultural purposes shall be assessed as agricultural lands upon an acreage basis." The constitutionality of this law was upheld in *Lanier v. Overstreet*, 175 So. 2d 521 (Fla. 1965). The court dealt with the constitutional objections as follows:

> The appellants' contention that [this law] provides, in effect, for an unconstitutional partial exemption of this particular class of property, is without

> merit. The argument here is that property currently used for agricultural purposes may have a potential value far in excess of its value as agricultural land, attributable to other uses to which it is reasonably susceptible; that other classes of property—residential, commercial, recreational, etc.—have not been singled out by the Legislature and required to be assessed according to their current use without regard to their value for other reasonably susceptible uses, and that to sustain the legislative directive as to agricultural lands would, in effect, grant a partial exemption to such lands, commensurate with such additional potential value, and would also unjustly discriminate against all other classes of taxable property. The short answer to this contention is that there is nothing in the legislative regulations respecting the "just valuation" of taxable property to authorize the assessment of property in accordance with a potential use which might be made of the property at some future time. [*Id.* at 523.]

For cases construing preferential farm tax laws, see 98 A.L.R.3d 916 (1980). For a comprehensive review of legal issues relating to agricultural land preservation, see T. Daniels & J. Keene, The Law of Agricultural Land Preservation in the United States (American Bar Association 2018). For a report on the effect property taxes have had on farmers already reeling from floods, tariffs and low commodity prices, and the disparities in tax policy between states, see Simpson, *Property Taxes Sink Farmland Owners*, Stateline (January 16, 2020), available at https://www.pewtrusts.org/en/research-and-analysis/blogs/stateline/2020/01/16/property-taxes-sink-farmland-owners.

A Note on Property Tax Relief

Because the real property tax is a tax on non-liquid wealth, taxpayers with little or no liquid wealth are particularly vulnerable to real property tax increases. There are several methods of real property tax relief, including tax exemptions and abatements. For a study considering circuit breaker provisions in 2018, see https://itep.org/property-tax-circuit-breakers-in-2018/ (study by Institute for Taxation and Economic Policy, indicating that 18 states and the District of Columbia have circuit breaker provisions).

The primary beneficiaries of circuit breaker provisions are often elderly persons and low-income renters. Persons who qualify receive a rebate or income tax credit from the state if property tax liability (actual or imputed) exceeds a certain level of income. See, e.g., Ill. Comp. Stat. 320/§25 (Senior Citizens and Disabled Persons Property Tax Relief Act); N.C. Stat. Ann. §105-277.1, §3(a) (homestead exemption for disabled veterans); Vt. Stat. Ann. tit. 32, §6062 (Homestead Property Tax Income Sensitivity Adjustment). The term, "circuit breaker" is derived from a comparison of the ratio of property taxes to income with electric current flowing through a wire. Both are cut off if they get too high. Duncombe & Yinger, *Alternative Paths to Property Tax Relief*, Property Taxation and Local Government Finance 243, 253–55 (W. Oates, Ed., 2001). For a report arguing that circuit breakers have great potential for improving property tax fairness but that state programs are in need of reform, see Bowman, et al., *Property Tax Circuit Breakers: Fair and Cost Effective Relief for Taxpayers* (Lincoln Inst. of Land Policy Focus Report, 2009), available at www.lincolninst.edu. This report reviews eligibility requirements for circuit breakers, the main types of state programs, and contains a comprehensive appendix that summarizes the main features of circuit breakers in the thirty-three states that had such programs in 2008. The authors advise against certain pitfalls when designing a circuit breaker. For example, they identify eight states that exclude renters from circuit breaker provisions, which results in landlords passing property taxes on to renters in the form of higher rents. *Id.* at 32–33. How should a state design an effective program that includes renters? For a subsequent Lincoln Institute study, see Anderson, *Income-Based Property Tax Relief: Circuit Breaker Tax Expenditures*, Lincoln Land Institute 2012, available at https://www.lincolninst.edu/sites/default/files/pubfiles/2278_1617_Anderson_WP13JA3.pdf.

The homestead exemption, which began as an effort to assist farmers during the Great Depression provides direct relief from local property taxes. Another form of property tax relief is a "renters' deduction" that allows state income taxpayers to deduct a percentage (*e.g.*, one-half in Massachusetts) of the rent paid for the taxpayer's principal residence. Mass. Gen. Laws Ch. 62, § 3 B(a)(8). See *Massachusetts Teachers Ass'n v. Secretary of Commonwealth*, 424 N.E.2d 469, 486–90 (Mass. 1981) (deduction favoring renters over non-renters meets rational basis test as a means of offsetting federal and state tax advantages of homeowners, and the reasonable exemption requirement of uniformity provisions as a recognition of the untaxed economic benefit that a home owner receives in the use of her home). Would a "renters" deduction be vulnerable to an equal protection challenge or a state law tax uniformity requirement?

Mass. Gen. Laws Ch. 59 § 21 limits the maximum real property tax rate to 2.5% of a property's assessed value, the levy to 2.5% of a community's assessed value, and increases in the levy to 2.5% per year. Increases above 2.5% require a popular vote, except for increases brought about by "new growth." For a study of the impact of Proposition 2-1/2 and an argument that the "new growth" exception to its limits has encouraged sprawl in the Boston metropolitan area, see Alland, *Toward a Sustainable Tax Policy* (Metropolitan Area Plan. Council/McCormack Inst., 2001). For an analysis of Proposition 2-1/2, see Brown, *Strict Property Tax Caps: A Case Study of Massachusetts's Proposition 2-1/2, Its Shortcomings and the Path Forward, 16* U.N.H. L. Rev. 359 (2018). For a comparison of California's and Massachusetts' efforts to reduce real property taxes and limit future taxes, see Galles & Sexton, *A Tale of Two Tax Jurisdictions: The Surprising Effects of California's Proposition 13 and Massachusetts' Proposition 2 1/2*, 57 Am. J. Econ. & Soc. 123 (1998) (reporting initial success in reducing tax burdens, but recognizing that lost revenues were recouped within ten years through increases in non-tax fees and charges). In 2011, New York enacted its version of real property tax relief by limiting the budgeted tax levy to no more than 2% of the prior fiscal year's levy for school districts (NY EDUC. LAW, § 2023-a) and municipalities (NY GEN. MUN. LAW, § 3-c).

The Lincoln Institute of Land Policy has been particularly prominent in fostering research on property tax issues and reform. For a review of the "nature, development, extent, and effect of residential tax relief programs," with a special focus of circuit breakers, see Bowman, *Property Tax Circuit Breakers in 2007: Features, Use, and Policy Issues* (Lincoln Inst. of Land Policy Working Paper, January 2008), available at http://www.lincolninst.edu; Anderson, *Income Based Property Tax Relief: Circuit Breaker Tax Exemptions*, Lincoln Institute of Land Policy (2013), available at https://www.lincolninst.edu/sites/default/files/pubfiles/2278_1617_Anderson_WP13JA3.pdf; Langley, *How Do States Spell Relief? A National Study of Homestead Exemptions and Property Tax Credits*, Lincoln Institute of Land Policy (2015), available at https://www.lincolninst.edu/sites/default/files/pubfiles/2527_1866_How_Do_States_Spell_Relief_0415LL.pdf.

[2] Special Assessments and Special Benefit Taxation

State law recognizes that beyond basic municipal services available to all paid through a uniform regime of real property taxation, there may be additional services unique to a group of properties provided by the state or local government for which the benefitted members of the group—or their properties and only those members or properties—must pay an additional charge. These charges are known as special assessments and the administration of these charges sometimes referred to as special benefit taxation. Under state law these charges appear as a separate line item on the tax bill as additional real property taxes. They are collected and their payment enforced in the same manner and time as real property taxes. Should a taxpayer not pay the special assessments, they become a lien on the benefitted property just like real property taxes. But here the similarity between real property taxes and special assessments ends.

1. When collected, special assessments are not deposited or credited to the local government's general fund to provide general municipal services. They are deposited into a separate fund and segregated from the general fund and applied only to the purpose that confers the benefit to the unique group or its properties.

2. The entity that administers special assessments and the provision of special benefits may be the local government itself, a special district within the local government, or a separate agency or authority created by the governing body of the local government or the state legislature—all according to detailed statutory law. The local government's primary function in special benefit taxation may be simply to include the special assessments in the annual tax levy.

3. The assessor, that mystic arbiter of real property values to determine real property taxes, is nowhere to be found in determining special assessments. Rather, accountants, engineers, and architects design the project that provides the special

benefit and determines the cost of the project to be spread among the members of the benefitted group or their properties. Here a classic cost/benefit analysis is applied to determine who pays what using, among other criteria, the already established assessed values of the benefitted properties.

4. The determination of the allocation of costs to benefitted persons or properties is left by the courts to the wide discretion of local government officials (just as in determining assessed value for real property taxes) so long as the factors taken into account are rational (i.e., amount of front footage, assessed value, area, and use of the special benefit service) in relation to the benefitted person or property. Unlike real property taxes, legal uniformity requirements do not apply—some persons and properties will pay more in proportion to their respective benefits.

5. The service or purpose provided and paid for on a special assessment basis must be susceptible to objective measurements and there must be, instead of uniformity, rational proportionality among all members or properties within the benefitted group between cost and benefit. For example, access to water supply services and to sewer disposal services for individual homeowners works well under special assessment analysis—it is not hard to figure out what you get for what you pay. However, social infrastructure such as police, fire protection, and emergency services are difficult to evaluate under a special assessment analysis.

6. Local governments that provide general municipal services are most often enabled by statute to employ special benefit taxation. It is rarely used by states, other than by state agencies, or by specialized units of local government, such as school districts.

7. In enacting a special assessment regime, local governments need to exercise care to avoid unintentionally enacting a "tax" that most likely will be found by a court to be void and unenforceable.

The difference between a special assessment and a tax was described in *City of Boca Raton v. State of Florida*, 595 So. 2d 25 (Fla. 1992) as follows:

> A tax is an enforced burden of contribution imposed by sovereign right for the support of the government, the administration of the law, and to execute the various functions the sovereign is called on to perform. A special assessment is like a tax in that it is an enforced contribution from the property owner, it may possess other points of similarity to a tax but it is inherently different and governed by entirely different principles. It is imposed upon the theory that that portion of the community which is required to bear it receives some special or peculiar benefit in the enhancement of value of the property against which it is imposed as a result of the improvement made with the proceeds of the special assessment. It is limited to the property benefitted, is not governed by uniformity and may be determined legislatively or judicially. [*Id.* at 3.]

Use of special assessment financing was more prevalent in the first half of the twentieth century than in the 40 years following World War II. During that post-war period of rapid suburban growth and urban renewal efforts, public funds raised through general taxation became the favored method of financing major capital improvements. Public works projects such as parks, roads, schools, and water and sewer systems were funded through a combination of federal, state and local tax dollars. Special assessment financing declined in the post-war period because of experience with defaults in special assessment collections during the Great Depression and the rapid growth of private sector businesses, personal and corporate incomes, retail sales and property values, all of which generated abundant tax revenues—including state and federal grants and low-cost loans to local governments, to fund infrastructure and support state and local government debt that finances capital improvements for public facilities.

Special assessments gained new popularity as a result of the tax revolts in the late 1970s and 1980s, discussed elsewhere in this Chapter, coupled with the privatization movement discussed in Chapter 3, *supra*. Strong local opposition to tax increases and the sharp decline in federal funding for infrastructure led state and local governments to search for alternative revenues beyond the real property tax, especially special benefit taxation.

The following case illustrates the principles, and some of the issues of contention, of special assessments and special benefit taxation. In particular the case highlights a nagging issue in special benefit taxation: should nonprofit entities exempt from real property taxation also be exempt from special benefit taxation even though they receive the same benefits as others in the community who are paying for those benefits through special assessments?

Sarasota County v. Sarasota Church of Christ, Inc.

667 So. 2d 180 (Fla. 1995)

Overton, Justice

... We have for review *Sarasota County v. Sarasota Church of Christ, Inc.*, 641 So. 2d 900 (Fla. 2d DCA 1994), in which the district court invalidated the special assessment at issue in this case.... In summary, we conclude that the special assessment for stormwater services at issue in this case is a valid special assessment that is expressly authorized by the legislature because: (1) the assessment applies to the two classes of developed real property that contribute most of the stormwater runoff requiring treatment; (2) the assessment does *not* apply to undeveloped real property given that the undeveloped real property actually contributes to the absorption of stormwater runoff; (3) the properties assessed receive a special benefit from the funded stormwater services through the treatment of polluted stormwater contributed by those properties and (4) the cost of those services has been properly apportioned. To require that the stormwater utility services be funded thorough a general ad valorem tax, as requested by the religious organizations who filed this action, would shift part of the cost of managing the stormwater drainage problems, which are created by developed real property, to undeveloped property owners who neither significantly contributed to nor caused the stormwater drainage problems. We quash the district court's decision.

The facts of this case are as follows. In 1989, Sarasota County (the County) adopted Ordinance No. 89-117, which created a stormwater environmental utility and imposed special assessments to fund the stormwater improvements and services. The ordinance was enacted in accordance with the policy directives of the Federal Clean Water Act and the Florida Air and Water Pollution Control Act (chapter 403, Florida Statutes (1987)). This stormwater ordinance imposed special assessments on all *developed* property but *not* on undeveloped property or property without physical improvements. After the County levied the assessment, a class action suit was filed against the County seeking to have the assessment declared to be an invalid tax. The class consisted of religious organizations or entities owning developed real property in Sarasota County (the Churches) that are exempt from ad valorem taxes but not from special assessments.

[According to the trial transcript, the amount of the special assessment on the Sarasota Church of Christ was $1,365.53 for 1990, while other churches affected by the requirement were charged less. This amount was based on the following calculations. First, the actual amount of horizontal impervious area was calculated in terms of the number of "equivalent residential units" ("ERUs"). For example, if the total horizontal impervious area were 25,820 sq. ft., this number would then be divided by the average impervious area of an ERU (*e.g.*, 2,582 sq. ft.). The quotient would be the number of ERUs that are represented by the nonresidential developed property (in this instance, 10 ERU's). This quotient would then be multiplied by the flat rate per ERU (*e.g.* 10 × 38.25 = $382.50). This formula would thus create a direct relationship between the method of assessing a non-residential unit and the average residential unit.—Eds.]

After a non-jury trial, the trial judge determined that stormwater services benefitted the community as a whole and that no evidence had been presented to show the services provided any direct or special benefit to the Churches. The trial judge then indicated that stormwater services should be funded through a tax rather than an assessment. Because the Churches are exempt from taxation, the trial judge found that the assessment could not be applied to them. As such, the trial judge invalidated the assessment as to the Churches and ordered a refund....

Although a special assessment is typically imposed for a specific purpose designed to benefit a specific area or class of property owners, this does not mean that the costs of services can never be levied throughout a community as a whole. Rather, the validity of a special assessment turns on the benefits received by the recipients of the services and the appropriate apportionment of the cost thereof. This is true regardless of whether the recipients of the benefits are spread throughout an entire community or are merely located in a limited, specified area within the community....

From the above analysis, we know that a valid special assessment must meet two requirements: (1) the property assessed must derive a special benefit from the service provided; and (2) the assessment must be fairly and reasonably apportioned accordingly to the benefits received. These two prongs both constitute questions of fact for a legislative body rather than the judiciary. . . .

We recognize, however, that cases addressing these issues sometimes blur the standard that is to be applied in determining whether the legislative conclusions regarding benefits and apportionment should be sustained. . . .

To eliminate any confusion regarding what standard is to be applied, we hold that the standard is the same for both prongs; that is, the legislative determination as to the existence of special benefits and as to the apportionment of the costs of those benefits should be upheld unless the determination is arbitrary.

The Instant Special Assessment

The County argues that the trial court substituted its judgment for that of the state and local legislative entities in determining that the stormwater utility services do not provide special benefits to the Churches and that those services cannot be funded by non-ad valorem assessments. Additionally, the County points out that, in this case, the Sarasota County Commission made specific findings regarding the benefits the stormwater services would provide. Further, the County stresses that the type of assessment at issue complies with the requirements of and is expressly authorized by the legislature in chapter 403 in addressing the problems of stormwater drainage and the contamination of Florida's fresh water supply.

The Churches, on the other hand, argue that we should uphold the trial court's ruling because "[n]o evidence was presented of any direct or special benefit to any of the church properties involved in this lawsuit" from the stormwater utility services. The Churches maintain that the trial court did not substitute its judgment for that of the government; it merely considered the declarations of the county and chapter 403 and found no evidence to support them as to this assessment. Additionally, the Churches point out that, even if the services do provide a special benefit to the church properties, chapter 403 anticipates that the fees for the services are to be assessed based on a reasonable relationship to the benefits received. The Churches assert that the method of apportionment used by the County is not reasonable. We disagree. As the following discussion indicates, we find that: (1) developed property, such as that owned by the Churches, receives the special benefit of the treatment of contaminated stormwater runoff caused primarily by the improvements on such property, and (2) the method of apportionment used by the County is proper because it requires the properties that create the contaminated stormwater runoff to pay for the treatment of that runoff.

The Question of a Special Benefit

As previously indicated, the Sarasota County Commission implemented this special assessment pursuant to the Federal Clean Water Act and chapter 403, which encompasses Florida's Air and Water Pollution Control Act (the "Act"). In adopting the Act, the Florida legislature specifically set forth the public policy behind this legislation.... To achieve these goals, chapter 403 specifically provides for, among other things, the construction of stormwater management systems, stating: "In addition to any other funding mechanism legally available to local government to contruct, operate, or maintain stormwater systems, a county or municipality may:... (2) Create a stormwater facility benefit area. *All property owners within said area may be assessed* a per acreage fee to fund the construction, operation, maintenance, and administration of a public stormwater facility which serves the benefitted area. *Any facility benefit area containing different land uses which receive substantially different levels of stormwater benefits shall include facility benefit sub-areas which shall be assessed different per acreage fees from sub-area to sub-area based upon a reasonable relationship to benefits received.* [§403.0893, Fla. Stat. (1987) (emphasis added).]

Through the adoption of the Act and related provisions, the legislature determined that the creation, maintenance, and operation of stormwater facilities are necessary to prevent the pollution of the state's waters....

To comply with the directives of chapter 403, the County promulgated ordinance 89-117 and made the following findings in relation to the need for the stormwater services at issue. First, the County determined that stormwater services would be beneficial to the County. Second, the County concluded that the assessment was necessary for the funding of stormwater management in Sarasota County. Third, the County found that the costs of the services should be allocated in relationship to the respective stormwater contributions of individual parcels of property. To further this goal, the County determined that only developed properties were to be assessed because those are the properties with impervious surfaces that contribute the polluted stormwater to be treated by the system. Testimony at trial indicated that undeveloped properties were not assessed because undeveloped properties actually provide a benefit to the stormwater management system itself by assisting in the absorption of runoff created by developed properties.

As the above discussion indicates, both the legislature and the County have determined that the creation, maintenance, and operation of stormwater facilities benefit the individual properties that contribute to the stormwater problem caused by developed properties, particularly those with impervious surfaces, by assisting in the control, collection, and disposition and treatment of the stormwater within the areas for which the facilities provide service. We do not find that the declarations of the legislature and County regarding the benefit of stormwater facilities are arbitrary or unreasonable in any respect.

In reaching this conclusion, we emphasize two important factors. First, stormwater drainage services and the treatment of stormwater runoff from developed property are not special, locally initiated projects. Rather, they are, as discussed above, designed to implement national and state policies. Second, developed property, which is the only property assessed under the County's ordinance, contributes almost all of the contaminated stormwater runoff that is to be treated by the stormwater facilities. Because this stormwater must be controlled and treated, developed properties are receiving the special benefit of control and treatment of their polluted runoff. This special benefit to developed property is similar to the special benefit received from the collection and disposal of solid waste. . . .

Given the legislative declarations discussed above, it is clear that the Church properties receive a special benefit from the stormwater services at issue because a special benefit is received by all properties with impervious surfaces. Having determined that the Church properties receive a special benefit from the stormwater services, we turn to the issue of whether the costs of the stormwater services have been properly apportioned among the properties within the County.

The Question of Proper Apportionment

Under the ordinance at issue, the County has attempted to apportion the costs of the services based on the relative stormwater contributions of different types of developed property. Developed properties are classified for purposes of assessment into two major classes, residential and non-residential. Additionally, a subcategory of residential properties exists for smaller dwelling units such as condominium units and mobile homes. As indicated previously, undeveloped property is not assessed for stormwater services. Residential property owners pay a flat fee for the services based on the number of individual dwelling units on the property; non-residential developed property owners pay a fee based on a formula that is designed to create a direct relationship between the method of assessing a non-residential unit and the average residential unit.

This method for apportionment focuses on the projected stormwater discharge from developed parcels based on the amount of "horizontal impervious area" assumed for each parcel and divides the contributions based on varying property usage. In developing this method of apportionment, the County has followed the statutory directives set forth in section 403.0893(2). As noted earlier, that statute provides that all property owners within a stormwater facility benefit area may be assessed fees to support stormwater facilities. It further states that areas containing different *land uses* are to be assessed fees according to the benefits received. In summary, under the County's plan, developed properties are assessed fees differently depending on whether the property is residential or commercial. Undeveloped properties are not assessed for the services because, in general, they actually assist in the absorption of runoff. We conclude that this method of apportioning the costs of the stormwater services is not arbitrary and bears a reasonable relationship to the benefits received by the individual developed properties in the treatment and control of polluted stormwater runoff.

Notably, under the County's special assessment, the Churches and other owners of developed property are now required to contribute to the costs of the stormwater management facility based on their relative contribution of polluted stormwater runoff. Previously, the costs of stormwater services in the County were funded through a flat tax. Owners of both developed and undeveloped property paid for stormwater services without regard to the property's relative contribution of polluted runoff. Moreover, given that the Churches are exempt from taxation, they paid no money whatsoever towards the cost of the specific benefits received by these services. Although we do not find that the previous funding of stormwater services through taxation was inappropriate, we do find that the stormwater funding through the special assessment at issue complies with the dictates of chapter 403 and is a more appropriate funding mechanism under the intent of that statute....

[Grimes, Chief Justice, dissented, stating that he saw no benefit for developed properties that was larger than the benefits received by undeveloped properties. Wells and Harding, Justices, dissenting, viewed the assessment levied as the equivalent of a tax, which would not otherwise be applicable to the church as a religious entity.]

Notes and Questions

1. *Tax or special assessment?* The trial court in the principal case had decided that no "special benefit" was received by those burdened by the stormwater assessment. In the absence of a special benefit, there could be no special assessment, and instead the charges were deemed an illegal tax from which the churches would have been exempt. What is the conceptual difference between a tax and a special assessment? Should the assessment here have been deemed a tax as dissenting judges believed? Remember that if charges are regarded as "taxes," they may be subject to more stringent review pursuant to state constitutional requirements. The issue of "taxes" or "something else" is a recurring one, as states and localities have tried to supplement revenues and moved to user charges of various sorts rather than traditional forms of taxation. For a discussion of these challenging questions, see Scharff, *Green Fees: The Challenge of Pricing Externalities Under State Laws*, 97 Neb. L. Rev. 168 (2018). Note, in particular, that some entities (such as churches) with charitable status may be exempt from property taxation but not from payment of special assessments. See, e.g., *Bryant Avenue Baptist Church v. City of Minneapolis*, 892 N.W.2d 852 (Minn. App. 2017) (holding that church was not exempt from special assessment for street resurfacing).

2. *Calculation of special assessments.* Do you understand how and why the local government's formula for the special assessment was calculated? Special assessments are often used as a tool for paying for sidewalk improvements or paving gravel roads. How should special assessments in such circumstances be calculated? What is the "benefit" associated with paving a sidewalk? Is such a benefit conferred only to property owners whose property is crossed by the sidewalk? What are the implications? What approach to calculating special benefits might be appropriately used primarily for parks?

3. *Assessments levied over large geographical areas.* Traditionally, special assessments financed public infrastructure in close proximity to the assessed property

owner's land. Special assessment financing has been expanded, however, to cover large geographical areas such as the county-wide assessments upheld in *Sarasota County.* Another example is the use of special assessments to finance open space improvements or greenways; individual properties will be benefitted by green space in proximity, but the community as a whole will also benefit from open space enhancements. The preservation of open space shares another similarity with *Sarasota County.* The assessments produce a benefit by preventing harm (stormwater runoff). See Griffith, *Green Infrastructure: The Imperative of Open Space Preservation*, 42/43 URB. LAW. 259, 297–302 (2011) (discussing the use of special assessments to finance open space acquisitions). How would you judge the legality of special assessment districts in residential areas designed to provide more extensive services than a city can provide based on its core available funding? See Sawyer, *Special Assessment Districts: Neighborhood-Driven Improvements in Distressed Cities*, 63 WAYNE L. REV. 705 (2018) (discussing residential special assessment districts in Detroit, modeled on business improvement districts).

4. *Benefitted property v. benefitted persons.* Special assessments can be useful mechanisms for financing local government infrastructure, but, as their name implies, the property subject to an assessment must receive a special benefit different from general benefits received by all property within the jurisdiction imposing the assessment. What about the persons on the property—is it material that they are benefitted? Yes and no. If the benefit is primarily for the persons rather than the property itself, then the costs takes on characteristics of a general population tax and the special assessment will fail. In *City of North Lauderdale v. SMM Properties, Inc*, 825 So. 2d 343 (Fla. 2002), the court invalidated that part of a special assessment program earmarked for "emergency medical services" while upholding the partial funding of an integrated fire rescue program. Noting that the test for conferring a special benefit is "whether there is a 'logical relationship' between the services provided and the benefit to real property," the court concluded that emergency medical services "provide a personal benefit to individuals" rather than a special benefit to property. The court acknowledged that a person's "use and enjoyment" of property may be enhanced by the availability of emergency medical services but concluded that the "sense of security" emergency medical services may offer is provided to individuals not property. *Id.* at 349–50. For a subsequent Florida decision relating to special assessments for police protection, see *Indian Creek Country Club, Inc. v. Indian Creek Village*, 211 So. 3d 230 (Fl. App. 2017) (concluding that village's special assessments on country club land to support police services was not supported by sufficient evidence of special benefit to land or fair apportionment). Is it justifiable to provide enhanced police protection based on special assessments? See Kazis, *Special Districts, Sovereignty, and the Structure of Local Police Services*, 48 URB. LAW. 417 (2016) (defining special police districts; exploring why this approach to funding police services is not commonly used; considering its possible viability in Connecticut, New York and Illinois; and comparing such an approach with more commonly employed private police service strategies).

Similarly, in *Heavens v. King County Rural Library Dist.*, 404 P.2d 453 (Wash. 1965), a special assessment to fund a library was invalidated on the basis that "assessments . . . are for the construction of local improvements that are appurtenant to specific land and bring a benefit substantially more intense than is yielded to the rest of the municipality. The benefit to the land must be actual, physical and material and not merely speculative or conjectural." *Id.* at 456. Likewise, in *Ruel v. Rapid City*, 167 N.W.2d 541 (S.D. 1969), the city attempted to levy a special assessment throughout the city for a convention center. Only residential property was exempted from the special assessment. Holding that a special assessment could not be levied for this purpose, the court reasoned that a convention center might help the city's economy generally but could not be "translated into a specific benefit" to commercial or other nonexempt real estate. *Id.* at 545. Do you agree with these rulings? How would you formulate a rule regarding when special assessments might or might not be used?

5. *Incidental community benefit.* Where some community benefit results from the object of a special assessment, so long as specific property is primarily benefited, incidental general benefits may not cause the special assessment to be set aside. In *Citizens Advocating Responsible Environmental Solutions, Inc. v. City of Marco Island*, 959 So. 2d 203 (Fla. 2007), the Supreme Court of Florida upheld the use of special assessments to retire bonds issued to fund expansion of wastewater collection and treatment facilities to provide services to new users not previously connected to the system. Special assessments were to be imposed only on new users, even though all users would receive some benefits from the upgrades. In upholding the special assessments, the court stated: "The fact that an entire community might receive a collateral or incidental benefit from new users being connected to a sanitary sewer system does not negate the evidence presented below that new users will specially benefit by virtue of their inclusion in the extended and expanded central wastewater system." *Id.* at 209; See also *Quietwater Entertainment, Inc. v. Escambia County*, 890 So. 2d 525, 527 (Fla. App. 2005) (upholding special assessment against leasehold property located on an island "which . . . has unique tourist and crowd control needs requiring specialized law enforcement services . . . and is subject to mosquito infestation requiring mosquito control services enhancing the habitation of the island and the value of the leaseholds").

6. *Judicial restraint.* As with state law tax regimes, the requirement of a special benefit by the governing body is statutory or constitutional. Accordingly, courts exercise judicial restraint when reviewing a special assessment to determine whether a special benefit has been conferred. See, e.g., *Western Amusement Co. v. City of Springfield*, 545 P.2d 592 (Or. 1976) (in which court expresses policy of restraint when reviewing special assessments that have aspects of legislative function).

7. *Assessments for future use and development.* Assessments for facilities serving large areas, such as sewer systems, may sometimes be saved if the court is willing to treat benefits accruing to the future use of the property as justifying the assessment. Note that the special assessment is against the land and not the improvements, and

to this extent differs from the general real property tax. Thus, the rule, generally, is that future uses of the land may be taken into account in justifying the assessment. Cf. *Baglivi v. Town of Highlands*, 537 N.Y.S.2d 552 (App. Div. 1989). See also Griffith, *supra*, at 301 (discussing future open space acquisitions funded by special assessments). If a lot receives no present benefit and future enhancement in value is uncertain, courts may not approve a special assessment. *Village of Bloomingdale v. LaSalle Nat'l Bank*, 387 N.E.2d 416 (Ill. 1979) (there must be either a present or assured future use of the improvement which can be enforced).

8. *Discriminatory assessments: remedying past problems.* The use of special assessments to finance public improvements can raise troublesome problems when the area to be benefited is populated by persons with low or moderate incomes. What should the local government do if affected citizens cannot afford to pay the special assessments? In *Williams v. City of Dothan,* 818 F.2d 755 (11th Cir. 1987), the court was faced with an equal protection challenge to a special assessment for street paving and sewer improvements. Residents of a predominantly black area of the city contended that they were required to pay a disproportionately higher percentage of the project cost than had residents of predominantly white areas of the city for previous projects. The project in question was initiated in response to a court finding that the city had illegally discriminated against black citizens in the provision of government services, and provided for the paving of streets that had remained unpaved since their inclusion in the city street system in the early 1900s. Residents were assessed $24 per linear foot of paving and $8 per linear foot of new sewer service, a substantial increase over average per linear foot assessments for previous projects in white areas.

The court applied a discriminatory effect test rather than the stricter discriminatory intent test applicable under the federal Constitution because the suit was analyzed as an enforcement action of a previous court order barring discrimination under federal statutes. The court found that the tax was illegally discriminatory because, even though more than 50% of the property owners assessed for the project were whites, over 70% of the property assessed was occupied by African American tenants and the costs of the assessment could be expected to be passed on to those renters. In addition, the court found that the actual number of white property owners affected by the sharply higher assessments was small in comparison to the number of white residents who had benefitted from previous projects with significantly lower assessments.

[3] User Charges — The Cousin of Special Assessments

User charges are the equivalent of utility charges. When you pay your electric and gas bill each month to an investor-owned utility (a business corporation owned widely by shareholders and regulated by a state public utility commission), you are paying a user fee. If you live in a community with a "municipal utility" that may provide electricity, heating by electricity or natural gas, water supply and sewerage disposal, the bill you pay each month is a user fee. A "municipal utility" is either an administrative division of a local government or a separate political subdivision created by the state legislature. Administrative divisions are usually created by referendum with a separate budget; borrowing for the utility's capital improvements is through the local government and its assets owned by the local government. Separate political subdivision (often called "authorities"), are created to provide a utility service within the local government or a broader geographic region. The authority's governing body is distinct from that of the local government and it maintains a separate budget and borrows on its own credit based on the strength of its revenues. The electric rates, gas rates, water rates, and sewer rates you pay the municipality are user charges.

Municipal utilities and investor-owned utilities are subject to regulation by a state public utility commission ("PUC"), a division of the executive branch of state government whose members are usually appointed by the governor and approved by the state legislature. Unlike special assessments set by a local government's governing board pursuant to state law, rates and rate increases of investor-owned utilities are determined by the PUC. The local government can participate in a rate hearing before a PUC, but it has no authority to set the rates.

Utility user fees are similar to special assessments because the rates and service benefits bear a proportionality determined by considering a number of factors (usually increases in personnel wage and benefits, increases in the cost of producing energy including capital facilities and improvements) through a public hearing process coordinated by a governmental body. But the similarities end at that. Special assessments, although not a real property tax, are levied and enforced just like real property taxes. User charges essentially a contractual agreement between the utility and the consumer to pay a per-unit fee for the quantity of the service consumed. Because sewer disposal is a function of the water utility, sewer service cannot be shut off (nor would that promote sanitary building conditions). Under most state laws, sewer user charges are enforced as a real property tax lien against the property served. When a seller goes to the closing to collect the price paid for the seller's property, the tax and sewer utility liens, if any, are deducted from the price and paid to government and sewer utility.

User charges vary in regional popularity; states in the southeast rely most heavily on them, followed by the far west and southwest. New England states rely least on user charges. ACIR, *Local Revenue Diversification—User Charges* 10–11 (1987). The ACIR report defines user charges as follows:

> [I]mportant characteristics of user-based charges and fees which help to differentiate them from general taxes. . . .
>
> [U]tility charges and user fees [are] sources which are viewed as public sector counterparts to prices in the private sector. These charges have the distinguishing characteristics of being voluntary payments based on direct, measurable consumption of publicly provided goods and services. . . .

> [T]he total cost to users varies with the quantity of goods and services consumed. Individuals who do not use the services or consume the outputs of government programs financed by charges and fees generally do not have to contribute to their funding. In effect, user charges establish a direct link between the expenditure and revenue sides of the budget for specific government services. Examples of utility charges and user fees include water, sewer and electricity charges; garbage collection fees; and fees for recreational facilities, such as municipal golf courses and parks.... [*Id.* at 3. *See also* ICMA, Management Policies in Local Government Finance (6th ed. 2012).]

How service and user charges should be set is another matter. Since municipal service suppliers have a monopolistic hold on the market, these suppliers will not be constrained by market pressures to set prices at a level that will maximize demand for the service. Charges for municipal services are set instead by public decision or regulation. What limits the courts place on municipal pricing of services are indicated by the following case:

Platt v. Town of Torrey

949 P.2d 325 (Utah 1997)

Howe, Justice:

Plaintiffs appeal from the trial court's judgment that the rate schedule imposed by defendant Town of Torrey charging different rates to resident and nonresident water users is valid and enforceable and denying plaintiffs' request for an injunction and damages.

Facts

[The Town of Torrey operates a municipal water system that provides water to residents and nonresidents of the town, imposing connection fees and monthly user charges. In June 1989, the town adopted a moratorium on nonresidential commercial hookups. Plaintiffs, who reside just outside the Torrey limits, purchased a water connection for $1000 and in early 1990 began developing an RV park on their property. They sought but were denied permission to install a commercial one-inch water pipe because of the moratorium. Over the next four years, plaintiffs negotiated off and on with town officials for a commercial hookup and finally were told they could obtain one but under a new rate structure that imposed higher connection fees and service charges for nonresidents. Plaintiffs objected to the higher charges for nonresidents and opened their RV park without the commercial hook up permit, using their existing residential hookup as a source for water. The park was then shut down and this suit followed. The trial court approved the town's rate schedule.—Eds.]

Analysis

Plaintiffs first contend that Torrey's disparate rate schedule is unlawfully discriminatory. They acknowledge that Torrey is under no obligation to provide water to nonresidents but assert that having elected to provide that service, Torrey cannot discriminate and is therefore required to treat all users within its service the same. Whether a municipality must charge the same rate for water to residents and to nonresidents is an issue of first impression in this court. . . .

The requirement that a municipality supplying public services to its own residents must act reasonably is stated more explicitly throughout Utah law. Article XI, section 6 of the Utah Constitution mandates that a municipal corporation supply water owned by it to its inhabitants "at reasonable charges." Utah Code Ann. § 10-8-38 authorizes municipalities to construct and operate sewer systems and to "make a reasonable charge for the use thereof." This court has also held that water and sewer connection fees must be reasonable. . . .

We turn now to the furnishing of services by a municipality to nonresidents. We begin by observing that Utah Code Ann. § 10-8-14 (1996) authorizes municipalities to construct and operate "waterworks, sewer collection, sewer treatment systems, gas works, electric light works, telephone lines or public transportation systems" and to "deliver the surplus product or service capacity of any such works, not required by the city or its inhabitants, to others beyond the limits of the city." The statute is silent on whether the charges to nonresidents must be reasonable, as charges to residents are required to be. Nevertheless, upon reflection we find no reason why the requirement of reasonableness that protects municipal residents should not also be extended to nonresidents who subscribe to municipal services. In fact, several reasons dictate that municipalities should act reasonably with their nonresident customers when furnishing necessary services, which many times are not available to them elsewhere.

. . . [T]he requirement of reasonableness, which attends all actions by municipalities, should not cease at the city limits. This is especially so because nonresident customers have less political recourse to combat unreasonable rates than do residents. If politically empowered residents have recourse to the courts when their municipal government acts unreasonably, even more so should nonresidents enjoy the protection of the judiciary against similar conduct. Indeed, judicial review for unreasonableness may be the nonresidents' sole remedy.

Requiring that nonresident rates be reasonable strikes the proper balance between competing issues in this area—affording nonresidents protection while allowing a municipality to recoup some return on its investment in the utility and maintain considerable autonomy. . . . Requiring a reasonable basis for higher nonresident rates accords with the overwhelming majority of cases from other jurisdictions. . . . In the instant case, because we are specifically concerned with water rates, additional concerns enter into our analysis. The most fundamental principle of water law in this arid state is found in Utah Code Ann. § 73-1-1 (1989):

> All waters in this state, whether above or under the ground are hereby declared to be the property of the public, subject to all existing rights to the use thereof.

The extent of anyone's right to use water (including municipalities) is limited to that amount which can be put to beneficial use. *See* UTAH CODE ANN. § 73-1-3 ("Beneficial use shall be the basis, the measure, and the limit of all rights to use the water in this state."). Thus, the nonuse of water for five years by an appropriator works a loss of the right to the unused water, and it reverts to the public for appropriation and use by someone else. *Id.* § 73-1-4(1)(a), (4)(a)-(b). Even the water rights owned by municipalities are subject to forfeiture for nonuse. *Nephi City v. Hansen*, 779 P.2d 673 (Utah 1989). Thus, it appears that the legislature, in authorizing municipalities to sell their surplus water to nonresidents, accorded them a measure of protection against the loss of the right to such surplus water. In availing themselves of that protection, municipalities ought to deal reasonably with those who purchase the surplus water and who might otherwise be able to appropriate it for their own use.

Arguably, some nonresidents may be able to annex and take advantage of the constitutional protection of "reasonable rates" accorded to residents. However, for a nonresident to be annexed, certain rigorous requirements must be met: The property must be contiguous to the municipal limits; the municipality must consent; and a majority of the real property owners and the owners of at least one-third in value of the real property must petition for annexation. UTAH CODE ANN. § 10-2-416. Therefore, the opportunity for annexation offers insufficient protection for nonresidents against unreasonable water rates.

On the basis of these considerations, we conclude that in the sale of this scarce resource in which the public has an interest, municipalities must deal reasonably with nonresidents, as they do with their own residents. Thus, a showing by nonresident plaintiffs, when contesting a rate schedule that rate discrimination rests solely on the nonresident status of the user, without some other legitimate justification, will invalidate the schedule. . . .

Higher rates may be justified by a variety of circumstances, some of which may exist in this case. Although testimony and evidence were adduced that alluded to the possible existence of some of these circumstances, the trial court made no findings of fact concerning them. We will therefore address the justifications that might exist in this case on which other appellate courts have relied and remand this case to the trial court for a determination of whether sufficient justification for the higher nonresident rate exists here.

At the threshold, plaintiffs must prove that the cost of servicing nonresidents who are charged the higher rate does not justify the price differential. It has been widely held in other jurisdictions and appears to be well settled, that greater costs associated with nonresidents in and of themselves justify a higher rate to nonresidents that reflects those cost differences. We agree. In this regard, we note that plaintiffs bore the expense of extending a six-inch line to their property. However, if on remand the trial court finds that there are other increased costs in servicing nonresidents which justify the higher rate that Torrey charged nonresidents, it should uphold the rate schedule without additional inquiry into other possible justifications. Simply put, "if the difference in rates is reasonably related to a difference in the costs of providing the service, there is no unreasonable discrimination." *Austin View Civic Ass'n v. City of Palos Heights*, 405 N.E.2d 1256, 1265 (Ill. App. 1980).

However, even if no cost justification exists, other justifications could exist.... One might be that residents of Torrey bear risks that nonresidents do not bear. For example, it is unclear from the record who would be responsible for financing a major repair in the event of a catastrophe or breakdown. It is pertinent whether residents alone bear this risk.... In addition, Torrey argued, although once again no findings were made regarding the issue, that the citizens of Torrey would be responsible for paying the bond if the revenues from the connection and water fees became insufficient. It also seems that only Torrey bears the risk of tort liability. If residents of Torrey alone bear these risks and the risks are tangible and proportional to the difference in rates, the schedule should be validated.

Another justification might be that residents of Torrey as a class have made or are making contributions to the system that nonresidents have not made or are not making. Torrey asserts in its statement of facts that the water system was constructed with contributions of money and volunteer labor from early residents of Torrey, but the trial court made no finding in this regard. If residents have contributed money, be it tax dollars or other funds, or labor to create the water system from which nonresidents now seek to benefit, the residents are entitled to a lower water price that reasonably reflects those contributions. It may also be that monies from the general fund have been or are currently being used to pay personnel who manage and operate the system. The record indicates that engineers oversee the system along with the mayor and a town clerk, and other people may be involved. However, there are no indications whether these persons are paid for performing these functions and, if so, whether their salaries are paid from the general fund or water revenues. If employees who operate the water system are paid with general funds, this may justify a lower rate for residents.... Thus, if the trial court should find on remand that residents have subsidized or are currently subsidizing, directly or indirectly, the construction, maintenance, or supervision of the water system in a way that nonresidents are not, in an amount sufficient to justify the higher rates, the rate schedule should be upheld.

Finally regarding this issue, we note: "Reasonable discretion must abide in the officers whose duty it is to fix rates. Rate making ... is an inexact science and their determination should not be disturbed if there is any reasonable basis for that determination ..." *McQuillan*, § 35.37.05 (footnotes omitted). Rate making is a legislative function to which courts owe a degree of deference.... Courts are not the equivalent of a utilities commission, but rather serve as a protection against arbitrary, capricious, or unreasonable behavior. Therefore, the trial court should not require that the higher rate for nonresidents be justified dollar for dollar. Instead, courts should seek to determine whether the rate is unreasonable in light of the factors addressed in this opinion....

BRAITHWAITE, DISTRICT JUDGE, dissenting:

I respectfully dissent. I will not attempt to respond to all of the extended analysis of the majority. Stripped to its essentials, the issue in this case is whether district courts should be installed as profit referees in water sale contracts between municipalities and nonresidents. My view is that the majority opinion reverses present Utah case law and mandates unneeded and unworkable guidelines that are not required by the Utah Constitution, Utah statutes, or sound public policy. . . .

This case represents a financial decision to be made by a nonresident. It is a situation played out frequently across the state. The decision the nonresident faces is this: Is it better for me financially to stay outside town limits, paying lower taxes but higher service rates (either town nonresident rates or the extra expense of installing a well), or is it better for me to join the town, paying lower service rates but higher taxes?

Residents located just beyond town limits may make frequent use of a town's streets, police and fire protection, parks, playgrounds, recreational programs, libraries, and other services, incurring no expenses through the town's real property taxes to pay for the facilities, the maintenance and operating costs, and the salaries of employees required to provide and operate such governmental amenities. Towns such as Torrey may in reality be using nonresident water rates to make up some of this difference. Doing so, if they are, would be neither illegal nor unconscionable.

There has been no showing that the Town of Torrey in this case, or towns generally, pursue disadvantaged nonresidents to coerce them into agreements charging unreasonable rates. This case represents the more typical situation: A nonresident purchases land outside a town yet approaches the town requesting town services. The parties dicker and may or may not reach an agreement. If no agreement is reached, the nonresident may pursue annexation to the town and obtain all the rights (voting, resident rates, etc.) and all the responsibilities (town taxes, zoning, etc.) of residency. Both statutes and case law favor annexation to municipalities where municipal services are needed outside the municipal limits.

This court should continue to allow parties to negotiate freely and should not begin to regulate the agreements they reach in an effort to "even" rates out for non-taxpaying nonresidents.

As a practical matter, it may be that as a result of this case, both the majority's belief that the strict contract guidelines adopted will be beneficial and my belief that they will not may very well be moot. The reaction of municipalities may very well be simply not to enter into such contingent, voidable contracts. This will benefit neither the nonresidents nor municipalities with surplus water.

I would affirm the district court.

Notes and Questions

1. *Limits on user fees.* The principal case appears to state the usual rule. However, there is authority indicating that profits from utility charges must be "modest," and that an unreasonable reliance on utility revenues for general government purposes imposes unfair burdens on ratepayers. See *Contractors & Bldrs. Ass'n v. City of Dunedin*, 329 So. 2d 314, 318–19 n.5 (Fla. 1976). See also *State of Florida v. Port Orange*, 650 So. 2d 1, 4 (Fla. 1994) (transportation utility fee struck down as illegal tax that would "convert the roads [in] the municipality into a toll road system, with only owners of developed property in the city required to pay the tolls"). Utility commissions in many states do not regulate the rates of publicly owned utilities. The problem also arises in connection with building permits and similar licensing charges. Compare *Weber Basin Home Bldrs. Ass'n v. Roy City*, 487 P.2d 866 (Utah 1971), in which the court struck down on equal protection grounds an increase in building permit fees concededly made to obtain additional revenues for the city's general fund. This increase was found to weigh unequally on new residents and was not justified even though each new resident increased the cost of city government. An increase in service charges falls equally on new and old residents and was suggested as a method of meeting increased service costs without violating equal protection restrictions.

2. *User fees v. taxes.* In *Antosh v. City of College Park*, 341 F. Supp. 2d 565 (D. Md. 2004), the court held that a charge for trash collection assessed against rental units, but not owner-occupied units was a tax rather than a fee. Applying a three prong test under the federal Tax Injunction Act (28 U.S.C. § 1341) that prohibits federal courts from hearing cases involving state or local taxes when suitable remedies exist in state courts, the court concluded that the charge was a tax because (1) the charge was imposed by the elected city council and placed in the city's general fund, rather than by an administrative agency and deposited in a special fund, (2) the charge was imposed on a "considerable segment of the population (all renters)," rather than on a specific and relatively small group, and (3) the money raised was to help cover the increased cost of "collecting everyone's garbage." No data was presented to establish that renters produce more or bulkier trash than homeowners, the court noted. *Id.* at 568–69.

Courts have used a variety of approaches to distinguishing user fees from taxes. User fees were distinguished from taxes by the Indiana Supreme Court in *City of Gary v. Indiana Bell Telephone Co.*, 732 N.E.2d 149 (Ind. 2000). At issue was a "requirements-based fee" imposed on telecommunications providers for use of city rights-of-way for their cable lines. In upholding Gary, Indiana's home rule authority to impose the fee, the court held that the fee is "not a tax but instead is compensation, representing a specific charge assessed . . . for . . . commercial use of Gary-owned rights-of-way to generate private profit." *Id.* at 156. The court concluded that the fee was a "user fee or service charge" designed to compensate the city for the services it provides and not an unauthorized attempt to generate revenue in excess of costs. *Id.* at 158. The Court also noted that the legislature had narrowed the scope of city authority by prohibiting municipalities from receiving any form of "payment" other than "the direct, actual, and reasonably incurred management costs" for a utility's occupation or use of a public right-of-way. INDIANA CODE § 8-1-2-101(b). 732 N.E.2d at 159.

In *Bolt v. City of Lansing*, 587 N.W.2d 264 (Mich. 1998), the court held that a storm water service charge imposed by ordinance was a tax requiring voter approval and not a user fee. Applying a three-prong test for user fees: (1) was the charge regulatory rather than tied to revenue-raising purpose, (2) proportionate to costs of the services provided, and (3) voluntary in that property owners could refuse or limit the service and thus the charge. The court concluded that the storm water service charge failed all three prongs of the test. In a subsequent Michigan case, the court of appeals considered whether water and sewer fees were valid user charges or invalid taxes. See *Shaw v. City of Dearborn*, — N.W.2d — 329 Mich.App. 640 (Mich. App. 2019) (upholding water and sewer rates as consistent with state constitution, where rates served regulatory purpose of providing water and sewer service, residents paid proportionate share of expenses, residents decided amount and frequency of their use of city water and sewer, and complainant failed to demonstrate inequity in rates).

In *Missouri Growth Ass'n v. Metro St. Louis Sewer Dist.*, 941 S.W.2d 615 (Mo. App. 1997), the court applied a multi-factor test developed in *Keller v. Marion County Ambulance Dist.*, 820 S.W.2d 301 (Mo. 1991), to conclude that a revised schedule of wastewater charges was a user fee and not a tax.

Note the three-prong tests used by the Federal District Court in *Antosh* and the Michigan Supreme Court in *Bolt*. Are they the same? What is the significance of the decision being made by elected rather than administrative officials? How does one determine that the purpose is regulatory rather than revenue raising? Are multi-factor tests such as these helpful analytical tools? For an examination of the state of Washington's handling of the user fee-tax distinction, see Spitzer, *Taxes vs. Fees: A Curious Confusion*, 38 GONZ. L. REV. 335 (2002); Erin Adele Schaff, *Powerful Cities? Limits on Municipal Taxing Authority and What to Do About Them*, 91 N.Y.U. L. REV. 282 (2016).

3. *Multi-unit buildings.* One problem that frequently arises is whether apartments, motels, hotels, and mobile home parks are to be charged for services such as water services on the basis of the number of units in the structure or whether a single charge must be made for the entire building. If each dwelling unit is charged separately the rate in the aggregate is likely to be higher. Since these users generally have only one meter for each building, and are billed only once, and since service charges are based to some extent on the cost of providing the service, it can be argued that only one charge should be made to the building as a single customer. For discussion, see *Kliks v. Dalles City*, 335 P.2d 366 (Or. 1959) (separate dwelling

unit charges may not be made for apartments when units are not separately charged in hotels and rooming houses).

Some courts, however, use an "ultimate consumer" theory to justify separate dwelling unit charges for apartments and hotels, which has the effect of treating them like single-family residences and differentiating them from other commercial users. These are charged bulk rates based on the use by the business as a whole. See *Oklahoma City Hotel & Motor Hotel Ass'n v. Oklahoma City*, 531 P.2d 316 (Okla. 1974). The separate dwelling unit charge was sustained for apartment houses and mobile home parks; the court noted that apartments were an "aggregation of dwellings" comparable to single-family homes. However, the separate units charge was struck down for hotels and motels, because, according to the court, "[t]he mere fact that people sleep in motels and hotels does not place them in the same class as single-family dwellings." *Id.* at 320. The court justified its reliance on the ultimate consumer theory by noting that the increased rate would be passed on to the tenant.

4. *Equal protection.* As the principal case notes, user charge classifications raise an equal protection problem. The equal protection standard applicable is the relaxed "rational relationship" standard. Applying this standard, the Supreme Court upheld a state statute giving local public-school districts that had not reorganized into large systems the option of charging user fees for bus service without obtaining voter approval for the charges. Reorganized school districts had instituted free bus transportation as part of their reorganization and could adopt user fees only with voter approval. The Court found a rational basis for the distinction between reorganized and non-reorganized school districts in the desire to encourage districts to reorganize and to alleviate parental concern about continued availability of free transportation that had been established as part of the reorganization process, and the determination that, in non-reorganized school districts, school boards should have the ability to charge persons who take advantage of the service being offered. *Kadrmas v. Dickinson Pub. Schools*, 487 U.S. 450 (1988). See also *Alamo Rent-A-Car, Inc. v. Sarasota-Manatee Airport Auth.*, 825 F.2d 367 (11th Cir. 1987) (upholding user charge differential between off-airport car rental companies' courtesy vehicles and hotel and motel courtesy vehicles).

[4] Other Taxes

As the cost and services of state and local governments has grown since the 1950s, continued reliance on the real property tax would have driven those taxes to levels few could pay and driven down the prices and values of real property. There has developed in most states a "three legged stool" to support the costs of state and local government. Real property taxes are largely directed to local government costs, the sales tax imposed primarily by the state and sometimes counties and large units of local government, and the income tax imposed primarily by the state and major urban centers. Today, the sales and income taxes comprise a larger share of state and local revenues that the real property tax.

With respect to real property taxes, special assessments and, to an extent, user charges, we speak of taxes "levied" on property that is "assessed." These taxes relate directly to the property and persons on the property served by the government unit providing the service. These taxes are measured by the value of the property served or the service provided on the property. Sales taxes and income taxes are disconnected from the property served and the amount of tax imposed measured by things other than real property. Sales taxes and income taxes are authorized only by the state legislature; state law can authorize a local government to impose the tax by local legislation. Enacting a state law imposing these taxes requires opportunity for public input. The process to assess real property and levying taxes must be transparent. In addition, there must be a process that enables challenges for property taxes, special assessments, and user charges to go to administrative bodies and the courts. The same is not true of sales taxes and income taxes.

[a] Sales and Use Taxes

Sales and use taxes generally. The sales tax has become a popular tax for policy makers, both at the state and local level. Originating in Mississippi in 1932, the sales tax spread rapidly to over half the states during the Great Depression. Following a 10-year hiatus during and after World War II, adoptions of the sales tax resumed. J. Due & J. Mikesell, SALES TAXATION: STATE AND LOCAL STRUCTURE AND ADMINISTRATION 1 (1994). Sales tax applies to the "final" sale of a product or service, usually in a retail transaction. Components that are used in the manufacture of products may be exempt from sales tax depending on state tax law. In 2009, 38 states authorized local governments to impose a local sales tax, D. Berman, *State-Local Relations: Authority and Finances* 60–61, in ICMA, MUNICIPAL YEAR BOOK (2009), and the sales tax had grown to be the second largest locally generated source of city tax revenue, THE PRACTICE OF LOCAL GOVERNMENT PLANNING 405 (C. Hoch, L. Dalton & F. So, 3d ed. 2000). Sales taxes are easy to calculate—they are a percentage of the sale price. Enforcement of payment is at the point of sale and is included in the total sale price. When the vendor deposits its sales receipts with a bank, the bank calculates the amount that is sales tax and pays to the state or local government. Sales tax rates may be changed (usually increased) only by state law. Public input to any sales tax rate increase is limited to testifying at legislative hearings upon published notice. An appeal of a sales tax rate increase requires finding standing to sue the state—a difficult hurdle to surmount.

Closely related to the sales tax is the "use" tax, imposed generally on an "initial use of goods purchased from outside the state and brought into the state for use." J. Due & J. Mikesell, SALES TAXATION 245 (2d ed. 1994). The concept of a use tax was approved by the Supreme Court "on the basis that the tax was imposed not upon interstate commerce, as such, but upon the privilege of use after interstate commerce was completed . . . so long as it did not discriminate against interstate commerce." *Id.*, citing *Henneford v. Silas Mason, Inc.*, 300 U.S. 577 (1937). Use taxes are designed to prevent a potential loss of revenue from sales taxes by out-of-state purchasing that would be exempt from such taxes, and must meet the four-part test to be valid under the Commerce Clause imposed by *Complete Auto Transit, Inc. v. Brady*, 430 U.S. 274 (1977), discussed *supra*. See, e.g., *Kirkwood Glass Co. v. Director of Revenue*, 166 S.W.3d 583 (Mo. 2005) (local use tax that does not exceed the locality's sales tax meets Commerce Clause standards, even though it might be higher than the use tax in some other local jurisdiction).

Tax on services. Although traditionally sales tax was levied on physical goods, in the last few decades a number of states have extended sales tax to cover certain types of services. See Federation of Tax Administrators, *Number of Services Taxed by Category and State* (January 2017), available at https://www.taxadmin.org/index.php?option=com_content&view=article&id=768:services-category-2017&catid=20:site-content (reviewing taxes by category including utilities, personal services, business services, computer services, online services, admissions/amusement, professional services, fabrication/repair/installation, and other services; some states did not report so 2007 data was used in those instances). Professor Hellerstein has attributed the reluctance to tax services as rooted in history and politics. See J. Hellerstein, et al., State Taxation ¶ 12.05 (3d ed. 2019). According to Hellerstein, in the 1930s, sales taxes on services initially covered only utilities and admissions fees. *Id.* Subsequently such taxes were expanded to include entertainment and amusements, hotel and motel services, as well as in some instances repairs of real property, data processing, information services and cleaning services. *Id.* While taxes on construction, professional services, and health care would generate more substantial revenues, such expansion has typically been unsuccessful. *Id.* Notably, both Florida and Massachusetts enacted broader sales taxes to cover most services, but those taxes were repealed shortly after being adopted. See Bruskin & Parker, *State Sales Taxes on Services: Massachusetts as a Case Study*, 45 Tax Law 49 (1991); W. Hellerstein, *Florida's Sales Tax on Services,* 41 Nat'l Tax J. 1 (1988). For more extensive consideration of sales taxes on services, see J. Hellerstein, et al., State Taxation ¶¶ 15.01–15.16 (3d ed. 2019).

Gross receipts tax. Gross receipts taxes are close kin to sales taxes. Scholars have suggested that "gross receipts taxes," understood broadly, includes sales taxes that can be imposed on sellers or buyers, measured in a variety of ways (weight, volume, quantity), and imposed either on individual sales or on an annual or other periodic basics. See C. Trost, Federal Limitations on State and Local Tax § 9:1 (2d ed. 2019). A narrower definition would treat "gross receipts taxes" as those that are designated as such and paid on an a periodic (annual or other) basis. *Id.* Gross receipts taxes may be imposed on receipts from sales or services, and may be subject to exemptions. *Id.*

[b] State and Local Income Tax

As discussed in the introduction to this chapter, many states impose an income tax on individuals. A Pew Charitable Trusts report in July 2019 indicated that only a handful of states (Alaska, Florida, Nevada, South Dakota, Texas, Washington and

Wyoming) have not taxed income, while two more (New Hampshire and Tennessee) have limited such taxes to dividend and interest income. See Pew Charitable Trusts, *How States Raise Their Tax Dollars: FY 2018* (July 2019), available at https://www.pewtrusts.org/en/research-and-analysis/data-visualizations/2019/how-states-raise-their-tax-dollars. New pressures are emerging on state income tax levels as a result of changes in federal tax legislation. See Huffer, Iselin, Sammartino & Weiner, *Effects of the Tax Cuts and Jobs Act on State Individual Income Taxes,* 58 WASH. U. J.L. & POL'Y 205 (2019) (discussing implicates that limit tax deductions for certain state and local taxes).

Local income taxes have been imposed in nearly 5,000 local jurisdictions in 17 states, most significantly in Ohio and Pennsylvania. See Walczak, *Local Income Taxes in 2019* (Tax Foundation 2019), available at https://taxfoundation.org/local-income-taxes-2019/. Other states that have had substantial local income tax requirements in some of their jurisdictions include New York and Kentucky. *Id.* County income taxes are particularly prominent in Indiana and Maryland. *Id.*

Commuter taxes are somewhat related. Some cities apply taxes to those living in the suburbs who commute into the city to work, while others tax city residents who commute to work in the suburbs. Both of these approaches are designed to capture costs and burdens associated with demands for services in urban centers. See Shaforth, *The Always Tricky Reverse-Commuter Tax*, GOVERNING (November 2015), available at https://www.governing.com/columns/public-money/gov-reverse-commuter-tax.htm.

[c] Severance Taxes

Several states have imposed severance taxes on mineral extraction such as extraction of natural gas, oil and coal. Only states with significant natural resources likely to be extracted are likely to pursue this alternative (often in lieu of income taxes). For further discussion of this source, see the introductory section to this Chapter.

[d] Excise Taxes

An excise tax is an early form of taxation in which each state administers its own tax on the production or sales of certain goods which the state considers to be regulated as to its quality and consumption on account of public safety and general welfare concerns. Excise taxes are usually taxes on events, such as the purchase of a quantity of a particular item like gasoline, diesel fuel, liquor, wine, cigarettes, airline tickets, tires, trucks, guns, etc. These taxes are usually included in the price of the item—not listed separately like sales taxes. To minimize tax accounting complications, the excise tax is usually imposed on quantities like gallons of fuel, gallons of wine or drinking alcohol, packets of cigarettes, etc. and are usually paid initially by the manufacturer or retailer directly to the state tax department. All of these non-property taxes are not subject to state legal uniformity requirements, because they came into existence long after the real property tax. But they may raise legal questions relating to equal protection, and policy questions relating to the regressive nature of tax rates, which fall disproportionately on low-and middle-income persons and families.

[5] Additional Revenue Sources

[a] Lotteries

A growing number of jurisdictions have opted for state-sponsored lotteries, some of which designate resulting funds for particular purposes such as education. For a discussion of state lotteries, see Miller, *State Lotteries and Their Customers,* 9 UNLV Gaming L. J 177 (2019) (discussing characteristics and beneficiaries of lotteries).

[b] Sports Betting

In *Murphy v. National Collegiate Athletic Ass'n,* 138 S. Ct. 1461 (2018), the Supreme Court struck down a New Jersey statute prohibiting betting on amateur sports, based on its judgment that the federal Professional and Amateur Sports Protection Act "commandeered" state legislative determinations about the legitimacy of betting on amateur sports. Following this decision, the way has been opened for states to allow betting on sports and to collect associated revenue. See Holden, *Prohibitive Failure: The Demise of the Ban on Sports Betting,* 35 Ga. St. U. L. Rev. 329 (2019).

[c] Broader Overview

For a broader overview of tax trends as of early 2020, see J. Walczak, Tax Foundation, *Tax Trends at the Dawn of 2020* (January 2020), available at https://taxfoundation.org/2020-tax-trends/.

[D] Expenditures and the Annual Budget

Local government budgeting is a complex matter, perhaps best understood by exploring budgets of nearby jurisdictions. The spending of public funds begins with adopting a budget. With certain exceptions, no money can be spent without first adopting an annual budget. Key elements are summarized in the short discussion provided below.

[1] The Annual Budget

[a] Introduction to the Annual Budget

A budget is an estimate of future revenues and expenses. The goal in every case is to ensure that the items of expense do not exceed the revenues during an accounting period. Variations in budget outcomes over accounting periods significantly affect the status of persons and businesses. State and local governments primarily provide services and are not designed to make profits like businesses. In some ways, therefore, their budgets differ.

State statutes and some state constitutions require that every state and local government (plus a host of "conduits" like state and local government agencies and authorities) adopt an annual budget before its next "fiscal year" to manage its "government accounting." A *fiscal year* is a 12-month accounting period to which an annual budget applies. Fiscal years vary among states and among units of government within a state. If a fiscal year begins on January 1, it is sometimes referred to as a "calendar fiscal year." Fiscal years are often designed to begin at the beginning of the real property tax payment period (so that government has money to pay its budgeted expenses in the new fiscal year). Different fiscal years impact intergovernmental funding—the payment of one government's revenues to another. For example, if school taxes are payable in July, a school fiscal year may begin on July 1. If state income taxes are paid in April and the state has an April 1 fiscal year, state funding of school aid will occur for the school's fiscal year ending the following July 1. Thus, the school manages its government accounting by relying on real property taxes at the beginning of its fiscal year and state aid at the end of its fiscal year. "Government accounting" refers to the methodology by which a state or local government accounts for its revenues and expenses during a fiscal year pursuant to the annual budget.

Although state law is important in government accounting (i.e., requiring that the annual budget be balanced or that taxes be paid in full and in cash), it is more broadly governed by nationally recognized accounting principles promulgated by the Government Accounting Standards Board ("GASB"), an industry-supported non-profit organization. The principles that are referred to as the Generally Accepted Accounting Principles ("GAAP"). Compliance with GAAP is often required by state law for local governments if local governments are required to report their annual government accounting results to a state fiscal oversight entity. Similarly, compliance with GAAP may be required if a local government produces annual "certified financial statements" prepared by a "certified public accountant" or firm thereof. Under federal securities laws discussed in Section E, for a state or local government to borrow money from a federally regulated financial institution (i.e., most commercial banks and investment banks), it must submit current certified financial statements to potential purchasers of its debt and to investors who own the debt thereafter. A state or local government needs to undertake its budget process with the foregoing requirements in mind.

[b] The Budget Process

Regulatory and market factors require that an annual budget upon its adoption be in balance. The budget is initially submitted for adoption. It is then generally subject to at least one public hearing following notice. The budget is then adopted. Adoption of a budget generally is considered a legislative power not subject to normal judicial review. But the power is not unlimited. For example, suppose that a city council in a home rule city adopts a budget that includes the deletion of all the investigator positions in the city attorney's office. The city charter provides that the city attorney has the duty to represent the city in legal matters and to prosecute certain violations of state law. Can the city attorney block the budget decision? See *Scott v. Common Council*, 52 Cal. Rptr. 2d 161 (Cal. App. 1996) (in the absence of charter provisions for reduction or elimination of personnel, Council lacked authority to use budgetary process to eliminate functions otherwise prescribed by the city charter before eliminating functions not mandated by the charter).

[2] Categories of Expenditures

The categories of expenditures contained in an annual general fund budget typically include the following:

(a) Operations and personnel;

(b) Capital improvements;

(c) Utility accounts;

(d) Intergovernmental transfers;

(e) Debt service;

(f) Mandated expenses;

(g) Reserves.

Some of these categories are clear on their face, but the category for "reserves" may not be. State governments fund reserves for various purposes, and state law typically authorizes local governments (including school districts) to establish and fund reserves from the general fund in the annual budget. A reserve is a segregated account established for a specific public purpose that may be funded on an annual or periodic basis. The reserve usually specifies the maximum dollar amount to which it can grow. If state law requires a reserve to be established by voter approval, voter approval is usually required to withdraw money from the reserve. Capital reserves and tax reserves are typically subject to voter approval. Funding reserves through annual payments in the annual budget are a prudent method to have cash on hand when tax revenues fall short of anticipated receipts or to reduce the amount and cost of debt financing for infrastructure projects.

[3] Appropriations

The actual expenditure of public funds is subject to specific state control. The basic control, found in many state constitutions, prohibits any withdrawal of funds from the treasury except by appropriations made by the legislative body. In *Leonardson v. Moon*, 451 P.2d 542 (Idaho 1969), the Idaho Supreme Court, after reviewing the cases, defined an appropriation as "(1) authority from the legislature, (2) expressly given, (3) in legal form, (4) to proper officers, (5) to pay from public monies, (6) a specified sum, and no more, and (7) for a specified purpose, and no other." *Id.* at 550. Cf. Ky Const. § 230; *Fletcher v. Commonwealth of Ky.*, 163 S.W.3d 852, 864 (Ky. 2005) (governor may not withdraw funds from the state treasury "in the absence of a specific appropriation, or a statutory, constitutional, or federal mandate"); *N.Y. State Ass'n of Retarded Children v. Carey*, 631 F.2d 162 (2d Cir. 1980) (governor may not pay judgment per court order unless appropriated by the legislature, nor draw on other appropriations to pay).

The appropriations process is linked to the budget process, with exceptions made for emergencies declared by the governor, as noted in the following provision from the Mo. Const., art. 4, § 25:

> Until it acts on all the appropriations recommended in the budget, neither house of the general assembly shall pass any appropriation other than emergency appropriations recommended by the governor.

Most states typically restrict appropriations by requiring a balanced budget. The New Jersey Constitution provides:

> [n]o general appropriation law or other law appropriating money for any State purpose shall be enacted if the appropriation contained therein, together with all prior appropriations made for the same fiscal period, shall exceed the total amount of revenue on hand and anticipated which will be available to meet such appropriations during such fiscal period, as certified by the Governor. [N.J. Const. art. VIII, § II, par. 2.]

In addition, statutes restrict the power of state officials to incur indebtedness or otherwise bind the state without an appropriation.

> No state officer, employee, board, department or commission shall contract indebtedness on behalf of the state, nor assume to bind the state, in an amount in excess of money appropriated or otherwise lawfully available. [N.Y. State Finance Law § 41.]

Similarly, state constitutional provisions and statutes apply to local governments, agencies and authorities as to their power to appropriate funds. Just as the in the adopted annual budget is to the levy on of real property taxes in determining revenues, it is also to appropriations to determine expenses.

One of the questions that often arises is the degree of flexibility such provisions give to public officials. The following case examines that issue in the context of a home rule provision requiring the adoption of an annual operating budget and adherence to rules affecting appropriations:

Krahmer v. McClafferty

288 A.2d 678 (Del. 1972)

O'Hara, Judge.

Plaintiff, a taxpayer of the City of Wilmington, has initiated this suit seeking a Writ of Mandamus to compel the defendants, members of The Council of the City of Wilmington ("Council"), to enact an annual operating budget ordinance in compliance with the Home Rule Charter of the City of Wilmington ("Charter"). Defendants have moved for judgment on the pleadings. For purposes of this motion the Court assumes, as it must, that all of the allegations of plaintiff's complaint are true.

The Charter, § 2-300, requires defendants to adopt, on or before May 31 of each year, an annual operating budget for the fiscal year beginning July 1 thereafter. § 2-300(2) specifically provides:

> ... shall make appropriations to [specified branches of city government] ... and for all other items which are to be met out of the revenue of the city. All appropriations shall be made in lump sum amounts and according to the following classes of expenditures for each office, department, board or commission: (a) personal services, (b) materials, supplies and equipment, (c) debt service, (d) such additional classes as the mayor shall recommend in his proposed annual budget ordinance.

In 1971 prior to the deadline Council passed an annual operating budget ordinance which, in addition to other items, provided for an appropriation of $310,564.00 for "materials, supplies and equipment." The complaint alleges that in actual fact defendants intended to spend only about $49,510.00 for materials, supplies and equipment and the balance was intended for other purposes.

The complaint further contends that the defendants, members of the majority party, proposed by this device to, in effect, hold back an appropriated fund which Council could from time to time during the fiscal year appropriate to other uses for the purposes of gaining partisan political advantage.

Prior to the passage of the budget ordinance, Council was advised by the City Solicitor that it was not empowered to create such a "contingency fund," it not having been recommended by the Mayor. Disregarding such advice, defendants proceeded to the enactment of the ordinance including within it the questioned appropriation as indicated. Subsequent thereto the Mayor vetoed the appropriation allotted for materials, supplies and equipment and returned the ordinance to Council with a message pointing out what the Mayor designated as the illegality of the action of Council. The message of the Mayor was accompanied by a written opinion of the City Solicitor supporting the Mayor's conclusion. Thereafter the defendants overrode the Mayor's veto and passed the ordinance, including the questioned item, by a two-thirds vote. It is the contention of the complaint that in view of the circumstances of the passage of this ordinance that it was a knowing and deliberate falsehood on the part of Council.

The provisions of § 2-300(2) would seem to be a clear and unequivocal direction and authorization that Council had to make *all* its appropriations at once in the annual operating budget ordinance. This conclusion is einforced by examination of § 2-301 which provides that "the Council may not make any operating appropriations in addition to those included in the annual operating budget ordinance [with specified exceptions not here applicable]."

The obligations imposed by § 2-300 are, generally speaking, mandatory and when violated may be enforced by mandamus. 15 McQuillin, Municipal Corporations (3d ed. 1970); 55 C.J.S. Mandamus § 139. The defendants herein rely, however, upon the general rule that a court may not inquire into the legislative motives of a legislative body. Defendants, applying this general rule, contend that the ordinance provision itself is valid on its face and that plaintiff does not dispute this but simply contends that the motives behind the passage of the ordinance, which do not appear on its face, were invalid. Defendants rely heavily upon the decision in *Klaw v. Pau-Mar Construction Company*, 135 A.2d 123 (Del. 1957) and *McQuail v. Shell Oil Company*, 183 A.2d 581 (Del. Ch. 1962). In both of these decisions, involving zoning questions, our Delaware Courts have indicated that they "will not inquire into the motives of members of a municipal legislative body in order to determine the validity of an ordinance enacted by them within the scope of their admitted powers."

Balanced against these decisions is that of *Piekarski v. Smith*, 153 A.2d 587 (Del. Ch. 1959). In the *Piekarski* case the Wilmington City Council had passed a resolution which was attacked on grounds of fraud and bad faith and the Court had the following to say with regard to both the general rule of law referred to hereinabove and the problem raised by allegations of fraud and bad faith:

> The legal basis for the contention that the resolution was adopted "in bad faith" is found in an exception to the general rule that courts will not inquire into the motives of or inducements to legislators that may influence them in the passage of acts or resolutions....
>
> The exception is that the validity of municipal ordinances or resolutions may be attacked if fraud or bad faith is proved. This rule is recognized in Delaware, although in none of the decided cases was any fraud or bad faith found.

The Court must here assume to be true plaintiff's contention that defendants were fully informed of the limitation of their Charter powers and deliberately set out to evade them and that in carrying out that evasion they deliberately enacted an ordinance that was not the truth. If either of these facts can be proved "fraud or bad faith" would be established....

The final argument of defendants is to the effect that plaintiff mistakenly relies upon the isolated language of § 2-300(2) requiring that Council must make all of its appropriations at once in the annual operating budget ordinance. Defendants argue that this narrow a restriction of Council's powers is not required by the language of subsection (2) and, in fact, is in conflict with the provisions of § 2-300(6) which reads as follows:

> The annual operating budget ordinance may be amended after its passage to authorize the transfer of items but the aggregate of the appropriations made by it may not be increased and transfer of budget items may not be made during the last four months of any fiscal year, except upon the recommendation of the mayor.

Defendants argue that subsection (6), by limiting Council's power to transfer budgetary items during the last four months of any fiscal year except upon the recommendation of the Mayor, is implicit recognition that Council has the power to make such transfers during the first eight months without such recommendation. The Court believes that defendants strain the language of subsection (6) to reach this conclusion. At most, subsection (6) merely *authorizes* a transfer of funds originally recommended by the executive. The purpose of subsection (6) is not to give broad powers to Council to manipulate the budget for improper purposes.

The Wilmington Charter is substantially copied from the Philadelphia Home Rule Charter, and the key provision of § 2-300 is identical in all material respects with the corresponding provision of the Philadelphia Charter. It is significant that in the annotations to the Philadelphia Home Rule Charter the following language is found with regard to the purpose of subsection (6):

> Subsection (6) is intended to serve as a check on the present practice of transferring items of the budget at the end of the fiscal year. Some agencies, finding at the end of the fiscal year that they have surplus funds left under certain items, have from time to time requested and received authorization from the Council for spending those surpluses for other purposes. This sub-section prohibits such transfers during the last four months of any fiscal year except upon the recommendation of the Mayor.

This Court believes that such definition of the purposes of subsection (6) is correct and that defendants' attempt to rely upon it to expand its otherwise restricted powers is incorrect.

The point of all this is that in subsection (2) Council is granted its specific powers with regard to the annual operating budget and, in fact, has clearly enunciated for it categories within which it may appropriate moneys. This subsection requires not only that money be appropriated for specific valid purposes but that the overall budget shall consist of all of the appropriations to be made. The only category within subsection (2) which would permit of something in the nature of an emergency or a contingency fund is found in sub-paragraph (d) of subsection (2) wherein appropriations may be made for "additional classes" not otherwise specifically mentioned, if the Mayor shall so recommend in his proposed annual budget ordinance. Subsection (6) merely recognizes that within this overall budget there are times and occasions when moneys allotted for a particular class and for a valid purpose therein may within the budget year be transferred to another class named in the budget. This can be done if Council should determine this is appropriate, within the first eight months of the fiscal year and if Council and the Mayor together deem it appropriate within the last four months of the fiscal year. In this effort to control budgetary juggling but at the same time permitting some leeway, this Charter provision is hardly intended as a contradiction of the mandatory requirements of subsection (2).

For the reasons herein stated this Court concludes that the plaintiff has alleged a sufficient factual basis which, if established, would form the basis for the issuance of the Writ of Mandamus requested. Having reached this conclusion it follows that defendants' motion for a judgment on the pleadings must be denied.

It is so ordered.

Notes and Questions

1. *Home rule.* The effect and extent of home rule authority is discussed in Chapter 2. Note how local charters act to confine the flexibility of local officials to spend money. See also *Roddey v. County Council*, 841 A.2d 1087, 1092 (Pa. Commw. 2004) ("[T]he [Allegheny County] Charter grants the chief Executive only the power to strike certain items entirely, and not the power to reduce the amounts appropriated for individual line items in a budget resolution"). Accord, *Jubelirer v. Rendell*, 953 A.2d 514, 537–538 (Pa. 2008) (holding that the governor could not change the language of an appropriations bill even when the amount appropriated remained the same. But the governor was authorized to veto a specific earmark of $1.5 million for widening pavement markings). The veto power is discussed in Chapter 10 *infra.*

2. *Required spending.* The principal case demonstrates that the courts will enforce limitations on local government spending powers. Mandamus is the judicial writ used to enforce a governmental duty, such as the duty to appropriate. A writ of mandamus was used in the principal case. Mandamus is discussed in Chapter 11. The principal case for that discussion, *State ex rel. Parks v. The Council of the City of Omaha*, 766 N.W.2d 134 (Neb. 2009), involved an attempt by citizens to persuade the court to mandamus a city appropriation. A court may also find within its authority the power to order appropriations when it establishes that a city has a contractual obligation to provide benefits. In *Tate v. Antosh*, 281 A.2d 192 (Pa. Commw. 1971), city employees challenged the city's decision to discontinue their disability benefits. The city personnel director had advised employees that the city would make no further payments after the present fund was exhausted. After finding that the city had an obligation to the employees, the court concluded:

> [S]imply because City Council refuses to appropriate sufficient funds to effectuate payment, the City as a public employer is not relieved of its duty to follow the mandate of the arbitration panel. The appropriation of funds does not involve the performance of any illegal act on the part of the City. Unquestionably the City has the power to make appropriations for all lawful purposes as defined in its Home Rule Charter. The City can lawfully

> make the necessary appropriation and, where it has a mandatory duty to do so pursuant to a valid arbitration award, a court may order that duty to be performed....

See also *Jorgensen v. Blagojevich*, 811 N.E.2d 652 (Ill. 2004) (holding that the legislature and executive violated the state constitution by refusing to appropriate and pay statutorily granted cost of living increases for judicial salaries); *Oneida v. Berle*, 49 N.Y.2d 515 (1980) (holding that governor may not refuse to spend money appropriated by legislature; no discretion to adjust appropriations to "balance the budget").

3. *Programs as contracts?* Does a legislative decision to establish a program of public assistance constitute a contractual obligation to appropriate a specific amount of money for that program? See *Davidson v. Sherman*, 848 P.2d 1341 (Wyo. 1993) (state is not obligated to appropriate a particular amount for Aid to Families with Dependent Children recipients, but it must employ an accurate standard of need in administering this cooperative federalism program). But see *Knoll v. White*, 595 A.2d 665 (Pa. Commw. 1991) (Supremacy Clause requires state to continue to make federally funded public assistance payments even though state has failed to appropriate funds to do so because of a budget impasse).

4. *Balanced budgets and court orders?* Can a public official ignore requirements for operating within a balanced budget or refuse to comply with court orders to disburse funds on the grounds that the funds were not "appropriated"? See *Delaware Valley Citizens Council v. Commonwealth of Pa.*, 678 F.2d 470 (3d Cir. 1982) (civil contempt sanction approved for failure to spend funds in compliance with consent decree); *Duran v. Lamm*, 701 P.2d 609 (Colo. App. 1984) (court order constitutes authorization by law to pay judgment).

A Note on State Control of Federal Grant Funds

Many federal grant programs historically employed a "carrot and stick" approach of dangling federal assistance and then threatening to withdraw it if states do not comply with the wishes of Congress. The Affordable Health Act and No Child Left Behind are two examples that have spurred a number of states to seek better control of federal funds by requiring legislative appropriation of federal funds before they can be expended. Questions of federalism (discussed in Chapter 7) and separation of powers are raised by these efforts.

In *Shapp v. Sloan*, 391 A.2d 595 (Pa. 1979), the Pennsylvania Court held that federal funds coming into a state become subject to the state legislative power, and that the state constitutional requirement for legislative appropriation applies to federal as well as state funds. The problem arises, in part, because federal grants are made to a particular state agency in the executive branch, thus bypassing the state legislature. But Congress, of course, cannot control the limitations on state appropriations. A strong dissent argued that the state statutes requiring state legislative appropriation before federal grant funds could be spent violated the Supremacy

Clause of the United States Constitution and the separation of powers doctrine (the funds in controversy were for an investigation by a special prosecutor into allegations of political and official corruption).

The courts are divided on the issues raised in *Shapp.* About half of the court decisions to date have agreed with the Pennsylvania court. See, e.g., *Legislative Research Comm'n v. Brown*, 664 S.W.2d 907 (Ky. 1984) (state legislature has power to appropriate federal block grant funds); *Anderson v. Regan*, 53 N.Y.2d 356 (1981); *Cooper v. Berger*, 837 S.E.2d 7 (N.C. App. 2019) (state legislature could constitutionally modify allocation of federal block funds as proposed by the Governor). For contrary decisions see, e.g., *Application of State ex rel. Dep't of Transp.*, 646 P.2d 605, 609 (Okla. 1982) (federal money is held in trust for a specific purpose); *MacManus v. Love*, 499 P.2d 609 (Colo. 1972); *Anderson v. Regan*, 425 N.E.2d 792 (N.Y. 1981) (federal funds must be appropriated through the budget adopted by legislature; federal funds are deemed in the state treasury or under its management).

The use of block grants since 1981 as the mechanism for dispensing federal aid has intensified the efforts of state legislatures to control the allocation of federal funds. Unlike categorical grants, most of the newer block grants go to the states directly, not to local governments, and they are dispensed with relatively few restrictions. Can an argument be made that block grants should be appropriated even in states like Colorado, which rejected earlier attempts at legislative appropriation of federal funds? See *Colorado General Assembly v. Lamm*, 738 P.2d 1156 (Colo. 1987) (only those federal block grants that require state matching funds or that allow block grant funds to be transferred to other block grants are subject to legislative appropriation).

Legislative reassertion of appropriation authority over federal grants raises both political and constitutional problems. Because the separation of powers doctrine as it applies to executive power is sufficiently pliable, the political considerations affecting this appropriation issue may well influence judicial determination of the constitutional issue. These issues are discussed in Brown, *Federal Funds and National Supremacy: The Role of State Legislatures in Federal Grant Programs*, 28 Am. U. L. Rev. 279 (1979). Brown points out that most federal assistance legislation does not specify a role for state legislatures, some require use of the applicable state procedure for state funds, and some specify an executive role in program administration without necessarily foreclosing legislative appropriation. An example of this last category is a federal assistance statute requiring administration of the federal program by a "single state agency." This kind of limitation is common and reflects a federal preference to avoid complexities in program administration. For an argument that the federal grant system should be modified to encourage state legislative participation in an oversight capacity see Comptroller General of the United States, Federal Assistance System Should Be Changed to Permit Greater Involvement by State Legislatures (1980). The report stresses that improvements in state legislatures (annual sessions, improved staff, use of post-audit, and evaluation procedures by legislative committees) and the enormous impact of federal grants on state budgets are substantial reasons for increasing the role of state legislatures in the federal grant-in-aid system. See also Schleef, *Comment, Federal Funds and Separation of Powers: Who Controls the Purse?* 53 U. Cin. L. Rev. 611 (1984), for a similar conclusion.

Legislative appropriation of federal assistance funds also raises a federal supremacy question. In the *Shapp* case, the court found no conflict with the federal legislation. If there is a direct conflict, welfare cases such as *King v. Smith*, 392 U.S. 309 (1968), indicate that state legislation inconsistent with federal grant legislation is invalid. That case invalidated a state welfare regulation inconsistent with the federal law. See also *Davidson v. Sherman*, 848 P.2d 1341 (Wyo. 1993). Differing views on immigration policy have also raised questions of federal supremacy and statutory interpretation. Under President Trump, the Department of Homeland Security (particularly Immigration and Customs Enforcement) has sought to tap local government law enforcement personnel to enforce immigration requirements, while many cities have declared themselves "sanctuaries" that are not willing to comply with federal preferences that they devote law enforcement resources to enforcing immigration requirements (particularly since they believe such practices will make it more difficult to serve and protect immigrants). See Margulies, *Deconstructing "Sanctuary Cities": The Legality of Federal Grant Conditions that Require State and Local Cooperation on Immigration Enforcement*, 75 Wash. & Lee L. Rev. 1507 (2018) (discussing Byrne Justice Assistance Grant Program and efforts to curb eligibility for funding to "sanctuary cities"). A federal appellate courts have epressed disparate views about federal efforts to apply limiting conditions on grants to sanctuary cities. Compare *City of Chicago v. Barr*, __ F.3d __, 2020 WL 3037242 (7th Cir. June 4, 2020) (striking down requirements) with State of New York v. Dept. of Justice, 951 F.3d 84 (2d Cir. 2020) (upholding requirements).

Shifting from entitlement programs to block grants, as has increasingly been proposed, can be criticized on policy grounds. For example, block grants (unlike entitlement programs) do not automatically respond to community vulnerabilities, often result in failure to keep up with needs (resulting in waiting lists or constraints on eligibility), and can be redeployed to meet alternative priorities. See Center on Budget and Policy Priorities, *The Problems with Block-Granting Entitlement Programs*, (2017), available at https://www.cbpp.org/the-problems-with-block-granting-entitlement-programs; Schott et al., *How States Use Funds Under the TANF Block Grant* (2019), Center on Budget and Policy Priorities (2019), https://www.cbpp.org/research/family-income-support/policy-brief-how-states-use-funds-under-the-tanf-block-grant (discussing Temporary Assistance for Needy Families, and explaining that only half of funds distributed are used to address core needs).

[4] Tax and Expenditure Limitations

State and local government tax and expenditure limitations ("TELs") began in the nineteenth century as reactions to borrowing excesses in the railroad expansion era. Restrictions on real estate tax rates and assessment practices, discussed in Part D, were the first type of limit, and occurred in two waves, first during the late 1800s and later during the Depression Era 1930s. A second type of restriction, the revenue (levy) limit, which restricts the amount of revenue that can be generated by property taxes, was popularized by California's Proposition 13 (the Jarvis-Gann initiative) in 1978. During the 1990s, a stronger version was enacted in Colorado, popularly known as the Taxpayer Bill of Rights ("TABOR"). In addition, states have imposed direct restrictions on spending levels such as prohibitions on annual governmental budget increases above a set percentage. For a history of the development of TELs, see ACIR, Tax and Expenditure Limits on Local Governments, No. M-194 (1995). A report for the National Conference of State Legislatures (NCSL) noted that in 2009, thirty states imposed TELs, 23 of which were spending limits, four were tax limits and three states had both types, with about an even split between constitutional and statutory limitations. For ongoing work on TELS by the NCSL, see https://www.ncsl.org/research/fiscal-policy/state-tax-and-expenditure-limits-2010.aspx Modern-day TELs were primarily enacted in three waves, 1977–1982, 1991–1996, and 2000–2006. For a summary of tax limitations, see Kearns, Todorov & Stone, *Ladders Out of Chaos: State Constitutional Limitations on State and Local Taxes,* 29-JUL J. of Multistate Taxation and Incentives at 1 (July 2019) (discussing tax limitations in particular).

Excerpts from several representative constitutional limitations follow.

1. California

Constitution Art. XIII A (1978, with amendments, 1986 and 2000 [Proposition 13])

> Sec 1(a). The maximum amount of any ad valorem tax on real property shall not exceed one percent (1%) of the full cash value of such property. The one percent (1%) tax to be collected by the counties and apportioned according to law to the districts within the counties.
>
> Sec 2(a)(1). The "full cash value" means the county assessor's valuation of real property as shown on the 1975–76 tax bill under "full cash value" or, thereafter, the appraised value of real property when purchased, newly constructed, or a change in ownership has occurred after the 1975 assessment. All real property not already assessed up to the 1975–76 full cash value may be reassessed to reflect that valuation. . . .
>
> (b) The full cash value base may reflect from year to year the inflationary rate not to exceed 2 percent for any given year or reduction as shown in the consumer price index or comparable data for the area under taxing

jurisdiction, or may be reduced to reflect substantial damage, destruction or other factors causing a decline in value.

Constitution Art. XIII B (1979)

Sec. 1. The total annual appropriations subject to limitation of the state and of each local government shall not exceed the appropriations limit of the entity of government for the prior year adjusted for the change in the cost of living and the change in population, except as provided in this article [provisions for emergencies—Eds.].

Sec 2(a) [Fifty percent of any excess over allowable revenues is to be transferred to the state school fund and fifty percent is to be "returned by a revision of tax rates or fee schedules within the next two subsequent fiscal years."]

(b) [All excess revenues received by local governmental entities are to be returned by revision of tax rates or fee schedules.]

2. Missouri

Constitution, Art. X, § 18 (1980) (Hancock Amendment)

(a) There is hereby established a limit on the total amount of taxes which may be imposed by the general assembly in any fiscal year on the taxpayers of this state. Effective with fiscal year 1981–1982, and for each fiscal year thereafter, the general assembly shall not impose taxes of any kind which, together with all other revenues of the state, federal funds excluded, exceed the revenue limit established in this section. The revenue limit shall be calculated for each fiscal year and shall be equal to the product of the ratio of total state revenues in fiscal year 1980–1981 divided by the personal income of Missouri in calendar year 1979 multiplied by the personal income of Missouri in either the calendar year prior to the calendar year in which appropriations for the fiscal year for which the calculation is being made, or the average of personal income of Missouri in the previous three calendar years, whichever is greater.

(b) For any fiscal year in the event that total state revenues exceed the revenue limit established in this section by one percent or more, the excess revenues shall be refunded pro rata based on the liability reported on the Missouri state income tax (or its successor tax or taxes) annual returns filed following the close of such fiscal year. If the excess is less than one percent, this excess shall be transferred to the general revenue fund. . . .

3. Colorado

Constitution Art. X, § 20 (Taxpayers Bill of Rights)

(4) Starting November 4, 1992, districts [including local governments—Eds.] must have voter approval in advance for:

(a) . . . any new tax, tax rate increase, mill levy above that for the prior year, valuation for assessment ratio increase for a property class, or extension of an expiring tax, or a tax policy change directly causing a net tax revenue gain to any district.

(b) Except for refinancing district bonded debt at a lower interest rate or adding new employees to existing district pension plans, creation of any multiple-fiscal year direct or indirect district debt or other financial obligation whatsoever without adequate present cash reserves pledged irrevocably and held for payments in all future fiscal years. . . .

(7) (a) The maximum annual percentage change in state fiscal year spending equals inflation plus the percentage change in state population in the prior calendar year, adjusted for revenue changes approved by voters after 1991. . . .

(b) The maximum annual percentage change in each local district's fiscal year spending equals inflation in the prior calendar year plus annual local growth, adjusted for revenue changes approved by voters after 1991 and (8)(b) and (9) reductions.

(c) The maximum annual percentage change in each district's property tax revenue equals inflation in the prior calendar year plus annual local growth, adjusted for property tax revenue changes approved by voters after 1991. . . .

(d) If revenue from sources not excluded from fiscal year spending exceeds these limits in dollars for that fiscal year, the excess shall be refunded in the next fiscal year unless voters approve a revenue change as an offset. . . . Voter-approved revenue changes do not require a tax rate change.

Notes and Questions

1. *Property tax limits.* California's constitutional limitation on property taxes was adopted in 1978, at the start of the "tax revolt" that spread across the country. Proposition XIII is discussed in the *Nordlinger* case, addressed in an earlier note following *Armour v. City of Indianapolis.* State property tax limitations have been adopted through constitutional referenda and legislation in a number of states, such as Massachusetts, Michigan, and Oregon. An analysis of the experiences in these states indicated that drops in local property tax resulting from such initiatives were not made up from other state or federal sources. As a result, localities have been unable to provide requisite financial support for public education, infrastructure upkeep, affordable housing, and similar initiatives. More regressive forms of taxation (such as sales taxes) have been adopted that exacerbate inequality. See Lav & Leachman, *State Limits on Property Taxes Hamstring Local Services and Should be Relaxed or Repealed*, 46 Real Est. Tax'n. 13 (2018).

It will be worth following developments in California in the future. For a discussion of the complex dynamics of reform that may affect Proposition XIII, see James Brasuell, *Prop 13 on the Ballot in California, Just Not the Prop 13 Everyone is Worried About,* PLANETIZEN (Feb. 19, 2020), available at https://www.planetizen.com/features/108406-prop-13-ballot-california-just-not-prop-13-everyones-worried-about. The author explains the confusing state of affairs created by California's ballot initiative numbering system and multiple potential initiative propositions that may touch on funding affecting public schools. A proposition (numbered 13) on the March 2020 primary ballot that would have authorized bonds for school facilities was defeated. Another proposal (the "California Schools and Local Communities Funding Act of 2019"), may be placed on the ballot, and if so, would limit local governments from imposing development fees (used in lieu of residential property tax levies that are substantially capped) and instead create a "split roll" that mandates higher taxes on commercial and industrial property.

2. *Spending limits.* While California's Proposition 13 received the most publicity, its Article XIII B, adopted by the voters one year later, imposed spending limits that have become the most popular form of limitation across the country. For background on Article XIII B, see California Assembly, https://arev.assembly.ca.gov/sites/arev.assembly.ca.gov/files/publications/CHAPTER5.pdf. Colorado's constitutional provision, called TABOR, triggered a bitter debate in Colorado and nationally about the wisdom of rigid restrictions on the ability of state and local governments to fund public programs and services. See, e.g., Lav, A FORMULA FOR DECLINE: LESSONS FROM COLORADO FOR STATES CONSIDERING TABOR (Center on Budget and Policy Priorities, October 9, 2009). A critical aspect of TABOR and like-minded spending limitations is the so-called "ratchet" effect. When state tax revenues fall during an economic downturn, TABOR's spending limits also fall. When the economy recovers, the spending limits remain low. Because of serious declines in services, a five-year suspension of TABOR, Referendum C, was adopted by Colorado voters in 2005. Referendum C retained the spending limits for FY 2010–11 and beyond, but eliminates the "ratchet" effect by pegging annual spending limits to the "prior year's limit, 'regardless of actual revenues collected.'"

Subsequently, in 2019, local governments challenged TABOR in federal court. See *Kerr v. Polis*, 930 F.3d 1190 (10th Cir. 2019). The federal appellate court considered assertions that TABOR denied a "republican form of government" and concluded that the district court had erred in dismissing the litigation based on its conclusion that local government subdivisions lacked standing. Colorado's TABOR provision is the most extreme in the country. For a discussion and critique of TABOR, see Center on Budget and Policy Priorities, *Policy Basics: Taxpayer Bill of Rights (TABOR)*, (2019), available at https://www.cbpp.org/research/state-budget-and-tax/policy-basics-taxpayer-bill-of-rights-tabor (concluding that TABOR limits state revenues and budget choices; contending that as a result of TABOR, the economic climate in Colorado has worsened and that Colorado has accordingly failed to meet education and public health obligations). For a more positive view, see Hoover, *TABOR at*

Twenty, National Conference of State Legislatures (2013), available at https://www.ncsl.org/Portals/1/Documents/magazine/articles/2013/SL_0313-Tax.pdf.

3. *Statutory TELs.* Approximately 28 states had adopted tax and expenditure limitations as of 2015. See Rueben & Randall, *Tax and Expenditure Limits: How States Restrict Revenues and Spending,* Urban Institute (2017), available at https://www.urban.org/sites/default/files/publication/94926/tax-and-expenditure-limits_5.pdf. The Urban Institute concluded that early studies on TELs had shown that they had little effect on state taxes and spending; such studies failed to explore nuanced differences among the states sufficiently. They concluded that more recent and more methodologically sound research had demonstrated that TELs could effectively constrain government growth under certain circumstances.

4. *TELs versus state mandates.* The Hancock Amendment in Missouri limits state revenues and expenditures and local government taxes, licenses, or fees, in addition to protecting local governments from bearing increased expenditures placed upon them by the state, either by reducing state financial assistance for required local activities or requiring new local activities without providing state funding for those activities. Mo. Const., Art. X, § 21. The Missouri Supreme Court, in *Boone County v. State*, 631 S.W.2d 321 (Mo. 1982), held that a state-mandated salary increase for tax collectors of second-class counties must be funded by the state. The court found that the payment of a county tax collector's salary was an activity conducted by the county pursuant to a state mandate. The term "activity" was broadly construed to include the general functions of the county government. Accordingly, a required increase in salary was an increased level of activity, i.e., government operations. Therefore, any state-mandated increase in expenditures for that activity beyond pre-Hancock Amendment levels must be paid by the state. A complicating factor was a separate, long-standing constitutional requirement that the state set salaries for county officials. Mo. Const., Art. VI, § 11. A strong dissent argued that § 21 did not apply because no new activity was required of the tax collectors. More recently, the Missouri Supreme Court concluded that the state constitutional provision was not violated and should not be invalidated as a result of a claimed "unfunded mandate" that school districts cover transportation costs for districts that had lost accreditation. See *Breitenfeld v. School Dist. of Clayton*, 399 S.W.3d 816 (Mo. 2013) (en banc).

5. *Evaluating TELs.* An early study examining the effect of TELs and debt limitations on the structure of state revenue and indebtedness concluded that, while TELs have resulted in reduced tax burdens, they also have generated increased non-tax revenue and debt issues. States with TELs have had to resort to less-constrained ways of generating revenue to make up for the reduction in tax revenue. Hur, *Fiscal Limits and State Fiscal Structure: An Analysis of State Revenue Structure and Indebtedness*, 28 Municipal Fin. J. 19 (Fall 2007). See also Deller & Stillman, *Tax and Expenditure Limitations and Economic Growth*, 90 Marq. L. Rev. 497 (2007) (outlining the range of TELs in place across the United States and providing an overview of the literature on the impacts of TELs on state and local governments). Morgaape recent studies have questioned the efficacy of TELs. See Gamage & Shanske, *The*

Trouble with Tax Increase Limitations, 6 ALB. GOV'T L. REV. 50 (2013); McCubbins & McCubbins, *Cheating on Their Taxes: When are Tax Limitations Effective at Limiting State Taxes, Expenditures, and Budgets?* 67 TAX L. REV. 507 (2014); Lav & Leachman, *State Limits on Property Taxes Hamstring Local Services and Should be Relaxed or Repealed*, 46 REAL EST. TAX'N 13 (2018); Benedict S. Jimenez, *Fiscal Institutional Externalities: The Negative Effects of Local Tax and Expenditure Limits on Municipal Budgetary Solvency*, 3 PUB. BUDG & FIN., No. 3 (2018): 3–31.

6. *Federal tax reform*. Ordinarily, limitations on state taxes rely upon state constitutional or legislative provisions to constrain state and local decisions. Recent political developments have changed that calculus. The 2017 Tax Cuts and Jobs Act sharply limited the deductions allowed for state and local tax payments, imposing exceptional pressure on states to limit historically higher state and local taxes that could in turn be deducted on federal income tax returns. See Barker, *The Tax Cuts and Jobs Act of 2017: The SALT Deduction, Tax Competition, and Double Taxation*, 56 SAN DIEGO L. REV. 73 (2019); Campisano, *SALT in the Wounds: Issues and Solutions Surrounding the TCJA SALT Deduction Cap*, 50 SETON HALL L. REV. 525 (2019) (discussing state efforts to challenge provisions capping deductions). It remains to be seen how such pressures will be addressed by state legislatures in coming years.

E. Borrowing

[1] Introduction to Borrowing

Borrowing for states and local governments is a contract undertaken by legal and valid official action or authorization by a governmental officer or governing body to pay money over a period of more than one fiscal year to a creditor for consideration received (usually, money), and to pay a fee for the right to pay the obligation over more than one fiscal year. A contract to borrow money and repay it over more than one fiscal year is "debt" or "indebtedness." The amount of the debt is called "principal." The fee is, of course, "interest" calculated as a percentage of the amount of the unpaid principal on the date the interest is calculated. The principal unpaid at any point in time is referred to as "outstanding." In this context, "outstanding" is synonymous with "unpaid." Interest that is due in the future computed from an earlier date to a later date is referred to as "accrued." Putting it all together, if Big City issued $10 million bonds on January 1, 2020, payable in the *principal* amount of $1 million on January 1 in each of the years 2021 through 2030, with interest payable on January 1 and July 1 in each year the principal is *outstanding*, and the City was current on its payments of principal and interest on the bonds. On July 1, 2024, we would say that the *principal outstanding* is $6 million with *accrued* interest thereon due today. Within the aforementioned plumbing of borrowing is some of the law explored in the remaining parts of this Chapter.

Here are some additional basics. An obligation to repay money in one fiscal year or less is a "note." A cash-flow note is not debt, but a "bond anticipation note" ("BAN") is debt. A BAN is like a construction loan, which will be taken out (i.e., "renewed" or "refunded") by long-term debt (i.e. a "bond"). In either case, a note or a bond is a contract. The contract contains the name of the state or local government borrower (known as the "issuer"); the name of the creditor or institution to which debt service payment must be made (called the "paying agent'); the date the debt is incurred (i.e., the date from which interest accrues); the principal amount of the debt; the rate computed each year ("per annum") to determine how much interest is payable; the dates principal and interest are to be paid; a statement of the authority under which the note or bond is sold by the issuer (i.e., "issued"); a statement of the how the debt is to be paid (i.e., from real estate states, certain revenues, or sale of assets), and what assets, if any, are set aside exclusively for payment of debt service (i.e., principal and interest) and secured (i.e., "pledged") for the payment of the debt; a statement that the issuer has done everything it should to authorize and issue the note or bond (known as "recitals," discussed *infra*); the signature of the authorized officer of the issuer which binds the issuer to the contract; and, in a nod to nineteenth century methods of assuring authenticity, the official seal of the issuer (the idea being that anyone could forge a signature, but it would take a smart crook to unlock the safe in the clerk's office and drag out the "official seal" which often weighed 20–30 pounds). Some statutes have eliminated the requirement of the seal, and its inadvertent absence today does not usually cause the bond or note to be invalid or raise a claim for repudiation of the obligation by the issuer.

Before bonds or notes are issued they must first be authorized by the issuer. The process of authorization requires attention to detailed formalities unknown in personal or corporate borrowing. This is because the earliest (nineteenth century) debt for which authorization laws were written was paid from real property taxes, and the taxpayers insisted on transparency and full disclosure from their government officials when the taxpayers were at risk. Hence, voting requirements and debt limits incorporated into state constitutions and statutes as discussed in Part C. Although today most bonds and notes (i.e., "municipal securities") are no longer paid from or secured by real estate taxes, the formalities for authorization are universally applied in the authorization of all municipal securities.

Once any voter authorization is completed, and debt limits calculated to make sure the principal amount of the new debt issue will fall within the limit, the issuer adopts a bond or note resolution. In the case of a state agency or authority, the statute may prescribe the form of the resolution. In the case of local governments, the statute usually lists specific items which must be included in the bond resolution (i.e., name of issue, amount to be issued, purpose of the issue, source of payment of the debt, maximum period the bonds may be outstanding (their "maturity"), etc.). The bond resolution must be adopted usually by a super-majority of all those members of the governing body who are entitled to vote (not of a quorum of members present at the meeting), and the adoption must take place at a physical meeting with notice under applicable "sunshine laws." In some cases the bond resolution must be adopted like an ordinance: first subjected to a hearing, then adopted at a following meeting. Unlike corporate and business meetings, bond resolutions cannot be adopted by votes through telephone calls or emails.

[a] Authority to Borrow

A critical provision of the bond resolution is its statement of public purpose. Purposes such as water and sewer projects, street paving and parks are common. But what of a contract to pay to build nuclear power plants in cooperation with other states and local governments in order to receive less expensive electric power in the future power? Is it a public purpose to be required to make payments for debt service on the bonds whether the plants are built or any power is produced? The lawyers concluded that the answer was yes. But the Washington Supreme Court, in the following case, said they were wrong, cutting against the grain of judicial restraint in reviewing legislative enactments. Thus, the contracts were not valid, no payments had to be made thereunder, and the bonds, already issued and outstanding, went into default.

Chemical Bank v. Washington Public Power Supply System

99 Wash. 2d 772, 666 P.2d 329 (1983)

Brachtenbach, J.

The Washington Public Power Supply System (WPPSS) issued revenue bonds to obtain funds to construct two nuclear generating plants known as WNP-4 and WNP-5. Bonds in the face amount of approximately $2.25 billion have been issued; repayment with interest will cost approximately $7.2 billion. Chemical Bank is the trustee for the bondholders.

Construction of the two plants was undertaken. On January 22, 1982 WPPSS terminated construction of both plants. At that time WNP-4 was approximately 24 percent completed and WNP-5 approximately 16 percent completed. Costs to date had almost reached the original estimated total cost for complete construction of both plants. WPPSS alleges that termination was necessary due to its inability to obtain adequate financing to complete the projects.

Chemical Bank brought a declaratory judgment action against WPPSS and the participants (defined hereafter) seeking a determination that the participants owe to WPPSS sufficient funds to pay the bonds, with interest. In general WPPSS has responded to the suit by substantially agreeing with Chemical Bank as to the rights and obligations of the various parties. Most of the participants, however, have interposed numerous defenses to any payment obligation.

To understand the complex issues, a recital of facts is necessary. WPPSS is a "joint operating agency" established in 1957 under RCW 43.52. [This is a statutory citation.—Eds.] It is a municipal corporation. Its members are 19 public utility districts and four cities, Ellensburg, Richland, Seattle and Tacoma. It has authority to acquire, build, operate, and own power plants and systems for the generation and transmission of electricity. WPPSS also has authority to issue revenue bonds payable from the revenues of the utility properties operated by it. It may not levy taxes or issue general obligation bonds. . . .

A 117-page "Bond Resolution" was adopted by WPPSS on February 23, 1977 providing a plan for the construction of both plants and providing for the issuance of revenue bonds.

Each Participants' Agreement provided that "[s]upply System hereby sells, and the Participant hereby purchases, its Participant's Share of Project Capability.

"Project Capability" is defined in section 1(v) of the agreement as:

> the amounts of electric power and energy, if any, which the Projects are capable of generating at any particular time (including times when either or both of the Plants are not operable or operating or the operation thereof is suspended, interrupted, interfered with, reduced or curtailed, in each case in whole or in part for any reason whatsoever), less Project station use and losses.

The Participants' Agreement requires each participant to pay monthly its proportionate share of a "Billing Statement" issued annually by WPPSS and based upon an "Annual Budget." The "Annual Budget" is to be adopted by WPPSS commencing with the "Date of Continuous Operation" (defined in effect as when the plant is ready to be operated and the output scheduled on a commercial basis) or the date 1 year after the termination of a project. The Bond Resolution in turn similarly requires WPPSS to collect and set aside funds sufficient to make payments on the bonds. Termination thus established a trigger date for various payments, and gave rise to this lawsuit.

The Participants' Agreement purports to require payment to WPPSS whether or not the projects are ever completed, operable or operating. . . . [known as "take or pay" contracts—Eds.]

Thus, if the agreements are valid, and subject to interpreting the contract, the participants collectively could pay approximately $7 billion for nuclear plants which will never generate any electricity. Ultimately the ratepaying consumers of the participants would pay for the nonexistent electricity. . . .

I. Purchase of Electricity

The Washington participants have explicit statutory authority to buy electricity on behalf of citizens. . . . .Initially, we must decide whether this agreement is authorized as a purchase of electricity by the participants. As discussed in greater detail *infra*, the purchase of "project capability" under this agreement is essentially an unconditional guaranty of payments on the revenue bonds, secured by a pledge of the participants' utility revenues, in exchange for a share of any power generated by these projects. The agreement expressly provides for the possibility that no electricity will be generated and that participant payments will be due even if the project is not completed. The unconditional obligation to pay for no electricity is hardly the purchase of electricity. We hold that an agreement to purchase project capability does not qualify as a purchase of electricity.

II. Acquisition of Electric Generating Facilities

Another type of express authority granted to cities and towns is the power to construct, acquire, and operate electric generating facilities. . . .

In construing these provisions, however, this court has never found authority for a project in which the participants did not have an ownership interest. Under this agreement, section 1.1(o) of the Bond Resolution expressly provides that only WPPSS and Pacific Power & Light Company retain any ownership interest in the projects. In comparison, the participants do not retain an ownership share in this project but only contracted to buy from WPPSS a share of project capability. Section 1(v) of the Participants' Agreement defines "project capability" as:

> "Project capability" means the amounts of electric power and energy, if any, which the Projects are capable of generating at any particular time (including times when either or both of the Plants are not operable or operating or the operation thereof is suspended, interrupted, interfered with, reduced or curtailed, in each case in whole or in part for any reason whatsoever), less Project station use and losses.

The "electric power and energy, if any" language indicates that the parties anticipated a possible share of no power. This impression is reinforced by section 6(d) of the Participants' Agreement which purportedly mandates payment by the participants irrespective of project completion. This so-called "dry hole" provision states:

> The Participant shall make the payments to be made to the Supply System under this Agreement whether or not any of the Projects are completed, operable or operating and notwithstanding the suspension, interruption, interference, reduction or curtailment of the output of either Project for any reason whatsoever in whole or in part. Such payments shall not be subject to any reduction, whether by offset or otherwise, and shall not be conditioned upon the performance or nonperformance by Supply System or any other Participant or entity under this or any other agreement or instrument, the remedy for any nonperformance being limited to mandamus, specific performance or other legal or equitable remedy.

In effect, the participants unconditionally guaranteed WPPSS bonds with no guaranty of electricity in return.

Some states have provided statutory authority for such unconditional guaranties and courts have recognized the validity of projects developed under those provisions. *Johnson v. Piedmont Mun. Power Agency*, 287 S.E.2d 476 (S.C. 1982). That recognition, however, is based upon very explicit statutory authority. . . .

Nonetheless, rather than ruling that an ownership interest is an absolute requirement when acquiring or constructing generating facilities, we will examine the present agreement to determine whether the participants retained sufficient control over the project to constitute the equivalent of an ownership interest. In the present case, several provisions of the agreement limit the participants' role in management to an extent inconsistent with control of any facilities acquired or constructed. . . . . It appears to this court that such limited involvement in project management does not satisfy the type of ownership control envisioned in the statutes.

It should be noted that we recognize the necessity and propriety of establishing representative committees to manage and oversee joint development projects. Our concern is not with the use of such committees in general; it is with the structuring of such committee procedures in a way that does not allow sufficient participant involvement in project management to control their risk. Thus, although this court recognizes the need for delegating duties in the context of joint development agreements, we are not prepared to sanction a virtual abdication of all management functions and policy decisions to an operating agency such as WPPSS. Here, the participant's committee apparently served as a rubber stamp for WPPSS' decisions, resulting in two terminated projects, less than 25 percent complete, at a cost of $2.25 billion, or almost $7 billion over the 30-year repayment period. As a matter of public policy, the enormous risk to ratepayers must be balanced by either the benefit of ownership or substantial management control.

Also, there is language common to each set of statutes indicating the Legislature intended that cities and PUD's [Public Utility District—Eds.] should retain significant control over the use of any facilities acquired. . . .

Applying the language of the acquisition or construction statutes and the principles derived from the cases construing that language, we do not believe the participants retained sufficient ownership interests or management responsibilities under this agreement to constitute acquisition or construction of an electric generating facility.

III. Implied Powers

On separate grounds, respondents urge, and the trial court ruled, that the express authority to acquire or construct generating facilities and provide electricity carries with it an implied power to pay for that service. *Municipality of Metro Seattle v. Seattle*, 357 P.2d 863 (Wash. 1960). In *Metro* this court upheld the City of Seattle's power to pledge city revenues to a countywide agency in order to pay for sewage disposal service. Since the statutes authorized the cities to provide sewage services and systems, we held: "[i]t must follow that with the power to provide a sewer system there is implied the power to pay for it, unless otherwise prohibited by the charter or statute." In the present case, the trial court extended this reasoning and concluded that the implied power to pay also included the power to make financing arrangements such as the present agreement. We disagree.

The services the city contracted for in *Metro* were to be paid as the services were provided, which is significantly different from the type of unconditional pledge of revenues contained in this agreement. Also, the countywide agency agreed to process and dispose of the sewage in part through the use of the city's existing sewage treatment plants. Since the city continued to own the sewage treatment facilities, the revenues pledged were actually paid back to the city for the use of its facilities and these funds helped pay for those plants. That arrangement is distinguishable from the present agreement because here the pledges of revenues are not conditioned upon the receipt of services and in *Metro* the city owned the facility used to provide the services.

This court subsequently adopted a more stringent test for a municipality seeking to incur indebtedness based upon general grants of authority to provide services. In *Edwards v. Renton*, 409 P.2d 153 (Wash. 1965), we held that the power to borrow money: "should not and will not be inferred or implied from a general statutory authority permitting municipalities to enter into contracts or to incur indebtedness." Moreover, a municipal corporation's powers are limited to those conferred in express terms or those necessarily implied. If there is any doubt about a claimed grant of power it must be denied. The test for necessary or implied municipal powers is legal necessity rather than practical necessity. *Hillis Homes, Inc. v. Snohomish County*, 650 P.2d 193 (Wash. 1982). As we stated in *Hillis:* "[i]f the Legislature has not authorized the action in question, it is invalid no matter how necessary it might be." . . .

The holding in *Hillis* vitiates the arguments that this type of bond guaranty was a necessity to sell the bonds in the investment market. That may well be true, but necessity does not provide authority. Accordingly, we do not believe that this agreement is authorized as an implied power to pay for an admittedly proper municipal service. . . .

VI. Conclusion

. . . .

In the present case, the participants lacked substantive authority to enter into this type of contract because they constructed an elaborate financing arrangement that required the participants to guarantee bond payments irrespective of whether the plant was ever completed; to surrender ownership interest and considerable control to WPPSS; and to assume the obligations of defaulting participants. As such, these contracts failed to protect unsuspecting individuals, the ratepayers, represented by the participants. By choosing such an alternative arrangement in lieu of a statutory scheme that incorporated protections against those very liabilities, the participants exceeded their statutory authority, rendering the contracts ultra vires. . . .

The trial court ruling that the Washington PUDs, cities and towns had authority to enter into this agreement is reversed.

Dore, Justice (concurring). [Omitted.]

UTTER, JUSTICE (dissenting). [Most of the dissent is omitted, but the following excerpts indicate the views of the dissenting Justice:]

I dissent. The majority, by its narrow reading of municipal authority to provide electric power, places constraints on municipalities not intended by the Legislature. Municipal authority in this area must be read broadly to provide the flexibility which is absolutely crucial in furnishing such a capital-intensive service. The contractual arrangement in the present case is a form of purchase which, viewed at the time the contract was made, may well have been the most economically advantageous for all concerned. While the result has been tragic, the decision here today may not free municipalities of all potential costs in even the present case, will bar them from potentially advantageous contracts in the future, and may well make financing of future projects more costly. . . .

Other courts which have considered the validity of contracts containing comparable "dry hole" provisions have reached conclusions similar to mine. While most of those cases are factually distinguishable, they are unanimous in upholding such provisions. *State ex rel. Mitchell v. Sikeston*, [555 S.W.2d 281 (Mo. 1977)] actually involved a fact situation almost identical to that in the present case. There, four cities entered into contracts with a neighboring city whereby they agreed to pay for a specified quantity of electric power whether or not actually needed and whether or not actually available. Despite this "dry hole" provision and a complete lack of any ownership interest at all, the court did not even question the authority of the purchaser cities. . . .

Notes and Questions

1. *Dillon's rule.* The principal case indicates that Dillon's Rule is alive and well in some states. This is how the Washington Supreme Court stated the Rule:

> A state or local government's powers are limited to those conferred in express terms or those necessarily inferred or implied. If any doubt exists about a claimed power it must be denied. The test for necessary or implied powers is that they must derive from an express power for a legal necessity rather than a practical necessity. Mere convenience is not enough.

Was the court deciding whether the legally necessary powers (guaranty debt service on WPPSS bonds) could be implied? Or was it ruling on the advisability of the agreement? Keeping in mind that Dillon's Rule was enunciated at a time when property taxes were the principal source of repayment of municipal bonds, is the court suggesting that the contract is an implied pledge of the taxing power and, as such, it should have been approved by voters or subject to constitutional debt limits? Would "ownership" of the project be an important factor if the case came before a court today? For an analysis of Dillon's Rule and its role in local government law, see Williams, *The Constitutional Vulnerability of American Local Government: The Politics of City Status in American Law*, 1986 WIS. L. REV. 83 (1986). Professor Williams discusses an opinion by Judge Dillon in which the judge held that a statute authorizing railroad bonds was unconstitutional because the bonds served a private purpose. *Id.* at 95. How is such an opinion consistent with the decisions of cases relating to economic development discussed later in this Chapter? For an additional assessment of Dillon's Rule in Washington State, see Spitzer, *"Home Rule" vs. "Dillon's Rule" for Washington Cities*, 38 SEATTLE U. L. REV. 809 (2015).

2. *Other decisions on WPPSS.* A similar conclusion on the WPPSS default was reached by the Supreme Court of Idaho in *Asson v. City of Burley*, 670 P.2d 839 (Idaho 1983), on the basis that the agreements constituted long-term debt issuable only after authorization by a two-thirds vote of the people. See also *Barnhart v. City of Fayetteville*, 900 S.W.2d 539 (Ark. 1995) (follows *Chemical Bank* and invalidates dry hole provision); *Department of Pub. Serv. v. Massachusetts Mun. Wholesale Elec. Co.*, 558 A.2d 215 (Vt. 1988) (power sale agreements for the purchase of "project capability" whether or not power is supplied invalidated as unauthorized). However, the Supreme Court of Oregon upheld the WPPSS agreements under a broad construction of local home rule authority. *DeFazio v. WPPSS*, 679 P.2d 1316 (Or. 1984). In his opinion, Justice Linde made the following comments which would echo many years later in decisions by the New York Court of Appeals giving deference to legislative enactments of complex financing schemes unless "patently illegal":

> The decision to join in the agreement was one of policy for responsible public officials to make. It was under conditions and on terms largely created by BPA, the federal agency on whom local public entities have been dependent for supplies of electric power. Officials responsible for electric utilities without generating capacity were led to believe that they had little alternative to the proposal offered them. Their policy decision to commit themselves to a share of the power WPPSS would undertake to produce at projects [involved in this case], including the risk of high costs and little or no power, may have been wise or unwise when it was made. But it was a policy choice, not one for this court to undo by devising new law for the purpose. [*Id.* at 1345.]

For a discussion of the *WPPSS* case, see 2 Gelfand, STATE & LOCAL GOVERNMENT DEBT FINANCING §§ 12.6, 13:12 (2d ed. 2019). What if the contract in *WPPSS* was subject to annual appropriation?

3. *Transaction parties and their lawyers. WPPSS* precedes federal securities regulations and enforcement actions against investment banks, issuers and attorneys, which have grown out of the New York City bond default of 1975, the Orange County investment scandal of 1995 (discussed in Part E), and the enactments of the Municipal Securities Rulemaking Board ("MSRB") and the Dodd-Frank legislation discussed below. However, the massive default of billions of dollars of municipal bonds arising from *WPPSS* raised the question whether financial advisers, attorneys, accountants, engineers and investment bankers who put the deal together should be held accountable for the loss. In *Haberman v. Washington Pub. Power Supply Sys.*, 744 P.2d 1032 (Wash. 1987), the court held that, while the project guarantees that

had been declared unenforceable were exempt from federal securities laws because they were issued by public bodies, they were not exempt from state securities law, and persons "whose participation in the sale was a substantial factor in causing the transaction to take place" could be held liable for state securities law violations. For further discussion see 2 Gelfand, STATE & LOCAL GOVERNMENT DEBT FINANCING § 13:22 (2d ed. 2019).

One by-product of defaults such as WPPSS and Orange County is increased scrutiny by professional advisors, such as accountants and lawyers. To what extent are attorneys who help public agencies devise elaborate financing schemes vulnerable to claims by investors when things go wrong? See also, *Mehaffy, Rider, Windholz & Wilson v. Central Bank Denver, N.A.*, 892 P.2d 230 (Colo. 1995) (where issuer's counsel gave a "no merit" opinion as to pending litigation on the validity of an urban renewal project to be financed with proceeds of the bonds; ultimately, the litigation resulted in a decision that the plan was invalid; opining attorneys were found liable to non-clients [bond purchasers] for negligence but not for malpractice since no attorney-client relationship existed between the attorneys and the bond purchasers). Should bond attorneys be subject to financial adviser rules promulgated by the MSRB? These issues are discussed later in the Chapter.

4. *Aftermath of the WPPSS Default.* Writing in 2008, Daniel Pope of the *Seattle Times* traced the history following the Washington Supreme Court's decision. Bondholders (some 80,000 of them) sued WPPSS, the 88 public utilities who had contracted to buy portions of the plants' projected capability, and others associated with the project. Hundreds of attorneys filed thousands of motions. Trial proceedings opened in September 1988, but many defendants settled out of court. Pope, *A Northwest Distaste for Nuclear Power*, SEATTLE TIMES (July 31, 2008), available at http://seattletimes.nwsource.com. The article points out that WPPSS assured buyers its bonds were low-risk investments. Wall Street paid little attention to the massive projects themselves or to the disconnect between Bonneville [Power Authority]'s faulty projections of soaring demand and the region's actual experience. The call today is for financial transparency, so buyers and sellers can evaluate potential risks and rewards "clearly." *Id.* When you study Part J, consider whether current rules requiring "primary" and "secondary" disclosure to protect investors would have stopped the WPPSS deal from being done at all, or would the financial risks of constructing and operating the project had been apportioned more evenly among the parties with the ratepayers having a bigger role in negotiating the deal?

[b] Issuing Bonds and Notes

Once authorized, municipal securities must be issued, *e.g.*, sold for consideration, which is usually money. Issuing municipal securities under state law requires undertaking several tasks each with unfortunate consequences if not executed correctly according to legal requirements and accepted standards in the municipal securities market. Federal securities and tax law are also critical to the issuance process, but we look at them in Part I and Part J, respectively. Precision in legal analysis and execution of documentation is a hallmark in public finance law practice. In corporate and real estate finance it is common to amend and rewrite documents following the transfer of debt for consideration (referred to as the "closing"), and for lawyers to issue legal opinions on the validity and legality of the transaction with detailed disclaimers and reasoning as to conclusions of law. In public finance, lawyers opining on the legality and validity of municipal securities (referred to as "bond counsel") are required to issue "unqualified approving legal opinions." The market will not countenance equivocation, and for a good reason: repudiation. Notwithstanding the dicta in cases that issuers would never consider defaulting on bonds issued for essential purposes, repudiation of municipal indebtedness was common in the nineteenth century. See *Cagwin v. Town of Hanock*, 84 N.Y. 532 (1881), which permitted repudiation of debt: "But there can be no *bona fide* holders of bonds, within the meaning of the law applicable to negotiable paper, which have been issued without authority . . . all persons taking the bonds are chargeable with knowledge of the statute, and they must see to it that the statute has been complied with . . ." *Id.* at 532. Modern public finance issuance practice, as noted below, has eradicated the bondholder's risk of repudiation. Several important legal processes and principals govern issuance of municipal securities:

1. *Preliminary Proceedings*: Municipal bonds are not issued in a vacuum. Preceding the financing of a purpose, other legal matters concerning the purpose must be resolved before investors will buy. For example, if the issuer is at risk of losing a major claim in litigation for damages that would adversely affect its ability to pay its bills, the litigation should be settled before bonds are issued. The same holds true for the resolution of zoning and other land use issues, environmental mitigation issues on the project site, administrative hearings, and substantial completion of the underlying bond authorization proceedings prescribed by state constitutions and statutes. Indeed, many of the cases discussed below were brought on the complaint that preliminary proceedings (i.e., voter approval) were not undertaken.

2. *Validation, Estoppel and Recitals:* Many states authorize issuers to "validate" bond issues through court proceedings or publication notices. These proceedings are undertaken at the discretion of the issuer, but because they enhance investor protection against default, investors insist on them whenever available. Validation/estoppel is intended to (i) protect the issuer against suits for failure to authorize and issue bonds in strict compliance with legal proceedings (i.e., failed to give notice of a hearing and other administrative and procedural defects), and (ii) protect investors against issuer repudiation of debt on account of the alleged administrative or procedural defect. In states with validation procedures (as prescribed by statute), a "friend of the issuer" files an action in court to "test" the validity of the bonds. At a hearing, if the issuer describes the bond issue, urges its validity to the judge and, if the friendly petitioner is silent, the court validates the bonds. Estoppel thereafter applies to all parties, to the extent of the judgment, to seek to declare the bonds

invalid or repudiate the debt. Recall *Escambia County, supra*, where the court first invalidated a TIF bond financing, then reversed it, "receding" from precedent and validated the bonds. See, e.g., VA. CODE §§ 15.2-2650 to 15.2-2658, applying a validation proceeding in *Virginia Coll. Bldg. Auth. v. Lynn*, 538 S.E.2d 682 (Va. 2000). In some jurisdictions, a judgment in favor of the validity of the bonds is conclusive on all questions which might have been raised and decided in the proceeding. In other jurisdictions, however, the judgment may be binding only as to issues actually litigated in the proceeding, or not apply to constitutional defects (i.e., debt limits and debt incurring procedures).

Alternatively, state laws may provide that the bond authorization proceedings include an "estoppel clause," which must be published with the bond resolution following adoption. Such publication tolls the statute of limitations to a very short period (i.e, 20–30 days) so that the closing may occur following the publication period and assure investors that the bonds are free from any validity attacks or repudiation, save constitutional defects (i.e., debt limits and debt incurring procedures). The protection afforded investors is similar to that of a validation proceeding without the hassle of going to court.

Whether required by law or not, the municipal securities market requires that all bonds and notes conclude with a recitals clause similar to the following:

> It is hereby certified and recited that all conditions, acts and things required by the constitution and statutes of the State of ________ to exist, to have happened and to have been performed precedent to and in the issuance of these bonds/notes, exist, have happened and have been performed, and that these bonds/notes, together with all other indebtedness of the Issuer, is within every debt and other limit prescribed by the constitution and laws of such state.

These are the "recitals" which are intended to defeat any claim of fraud by the issuer after validation and estoppel in further protection of investors. The recitals are made by the issuer's chief financial officer ("CFO") who executes and delivers the bonds. It reverses the nineteenth century *caveat emptor* risk of a *bona fide* purchaser for value against issuer repudiation, because the investor is not obligated to investigate whether the bonds were duly authorized and issued; the issuer certifies to the investor that it is so. If the recitals are false and fraud is present, the investor may still face a financial risk of default, but the CFO and the issuer are now under the klieg lights of federal securities law prosecutors, as well as the attorneys who opined that the bonds were legal, valid and binding.

3. *Sale of Bonds*: The prospectus for a municipal bond sale (referred to as an "official statement") and how the official statement is distributed to potential and eventual investors is a matter of federal securities law. State law prescribed how bonds and notes must be sold. Statutes often provide that bonds may be "sold at public or private sale." Public sales are competitive, with the issuer benefiting from the competition by obtaining the lower interest rate in the market on the sale for bonds with

similar credit ratings. A public sale is an auction requiring written sealed bids be submitted to the issuer or its agent by hand or electronically and opened "in public view" on a date and time certain. The bonds or notes are awarded to the "bidder" (financial institution which resells the bonds or holds them for investment) offering the lowest interest rate. In a private sale, the auction is eliminated, and the issuer may sell directly to a financial institution or engage an underwriter to sell the nods or notes to the public.

In a public sale, only unconditional offers that adhere to the terms of a "notice of sale" can be considered. See *Mercer v. North Little Rock Special School Dist.*, 6 S.W.2d 16, 19 (Ark. 1928). Most public sales involve government obligation full faith and credit bonds that pledge real property taxes and are issued for bread and butter public purposes. These conditions do not require the bidder to know more about the issuer or the bonds other than what the bidder provides in the notice of sale and official statement to solicit bids. For a discussion of the bond issue process, see D. Gelfand, State & Local Debt Financing §§ 3:1–3.15 (2d ed. 2019). By contrast, revenue bonds are almost always sold by negotiation, because the underwriter conducts an extensive examination into the structure and feasibility of the bond issue and the nature and financial condition of the issuer (a process called "diligence") before it offers to buy the bonds. Before the diligence process begins, the issuer selects the underwriter it invites to buy the bonds. If the underwriter is satisfied after diligence is complete, the underwriter estimates a maturity schedule and interest rate schedule for the bonds, then offers the bonds to its investors. If enough investors decide to buy the bonds, the underwriter offers the issuer terms previously estimated, and if agreed to by the issuer, the parties sign a "bond purchase agreement" and close the deal. Several changes in MSRB rules required by the federal Dodd-Frank Act now impact private bond sales.

[2] Types of Issues

There are two major types of municipal bonds: (i) general obligation bonds ("GOs"), and (ii) revenue bonds. A GO is always payable from and secured by the pledge of the "full faith and credit" of the issuer. Such pledge must be expressed in a constitutional or statutory provision, and the issuer must be authorized or required to exercise the pledge in the bond resolution as a contract term of the bonds. All other municipal bonds, however characterized, are revenue bonds. The hallmark of a GO is that real estate taxes are pledged to its payment. GOs are the types of bonds the drafters of state constitutional and statutory provisions had in mind when they enacted voter approval requirements, debt limits and strict limits on what constitutes a public purpose. Revenue bonds range from bonds indistinguishable from GOs but for the absence of the full faith and credit pledge substituted with a pledge of utility revenues, to bonds payable from and secured by the mere promises of the well-intended who have no resources to repay the bonds when issued, but convince investors, everything notwithstanding to the contrary, that after the application of bond proceeds, prosperity is just around the corner.

[a] General Obligation Bonds

The following case arose from the New York City financial crisis in 1975, when the City defaulted on $2 billion of revenue anticipation notes ("RANs")—cash-flow notes issued several times during a succession of fiscal years to sustain an annual budget perpetually in deficit. The RANs were sold pursuant to a 4-page "Notice of Sale" that featured the City seal, a picture of the Brooklyn Bridge, an annual budget resembling Table D-1, and a brief description of the RANs including a statement that they were "full faith and credit" obligations of the City. In fact, the City had no revenues to pay the RANS and relied on major commercial banks to buy renewals of the RANs. One day, all the banks refused to renew the RANs at any price (*i.e.*, a very high interest rate) and the notes defaulted. The banks had lost confidence in the City's financial management. To cure the default, the state legislature enacted a new state authority, the Municipal Assistance Corporation for the City of New York ("MACC"), to issue bonds to be paid from state appropriations. The proceeds of MACC bonds were to be applied to pay the defaulted RANS and other City GOs—at a few cents on the dollar. There was precedent for this approach in *Faitoute Iron & Steel Co. v. City of Asbury Park*, 316 U.S. 502 (1942) where the U.S. Supreme Court had held that "full faith and credit" was simply a good faith promise to pay a general creditor in bankruptcy—i.e., a few cents on the dollar. The City's GO holders sued claiming the state constitution guaranteed them 100 cents on the dollar.

Flushing National Bank v. Municipal Assistance Corp.

40 N.Y.2d 731, 358 N.E.2d 848 (1976)

Breitel, Chief Judge.

This is an action by a holder of New York City short-term anticipation notes to declare unconstitutional the New York State Emergency Moratorium Act for the City of New York (L. 1975, ch. 874, as amd. by ch. 875). Special Term and the Appellate Division held the act constitutional under both the Federal and State Constitutions.

A pledge of the city's faith and credit is both a commitment to pay and a commitment of the city's revenue generating powers to produce the funds to pay. Hence, an obligation containing a pledge of the city's "faith and credit" is secured by a promise both to pay and to use in good faith the city's general revenue powers to produce sufficient funds to pay the principal and interest of the obligation as it becomes due. That is why both words, "faith" and "credit" are used and they are not tautological. That is what the words say and that is what courts have held they mean when rare occasion has suggested comment. . . .

A "faith and credit" obligation is, therefore, entirely different from a "revenue" obligation, which is limited to a pledge of revenues from a designated source or fund.... It is also in contrast to a "moral" obligation, which is backed not by a legally enforceable promise to pay but only by a "moral" commitment....

The constitutional requirement of a pledge of the city's faith and credit is not satisfied merely by engraving a statement of the pledge in the text of the obligation. The last is a strange argument made by respondents. It is difficult to understand the financial value of such a commitment as contrasted with a "moral" obligation, wisely prohibited by the Constitution for municipalities (N.Y. Const. art. VIII, § 2). Instead, by any test, whether based on realism or sensibility, the city is constitutionally obliged to pay and to use in good faith its revenue powers to produce funds to pay the principal of the notes when due. The effect of the Moratorium Act is, however, to permit the city, having given it, to ignore its pledge of faith and credit to "pay" and to "pay punctually" the notes when due. Thus, the act would enable the city to proceed as if the pledge of faith and credit had never been.

It is argued that the city has insufficient funds to pay the notes and cannot in good faith use its revenue powers to pay the notes. The city has an enormous debt and one that in its entirety, if honored as portions become due, undoubtedly exceeds the city's present capacity to maintain an effective cash flow. But it is not true that any particular indebtedness of the city, let alone the outstanding temporary notes, is responsible for any allocable insufficiency. In short, what has happened is those responsible have made an expedient selection of the temporary noteholders to bear an extraordinary burden. The invidious consequence may not be justified by fugitive recourse to the police power of the State or to any other constitutional power to displace inconvenient but intentionally protective constitutional limitations.

The constitutional prescription of a pledge of faith and credit is designed, among other things, to protect rights vulnerable in the event of difficult economic circumstances. Thus, it is destructive of the constitutional purpose for the Legislature to enact a measure aimed at denying that very protection on the ground that government confronts the difficulties which, in the first instance, were envisioned....

It is not only the faith and credit clause of the State Constitution which marks out the constitutional plan for performance of municipal financial obligations. Other parts of article VIII control the debt-incurring or spending power of municipalities and yet also provide exception in order that outstanding debt obligations may be paid (§§ 2-a-6, 7, 7-a, applicable to New York City). Thus, for example, real estate taxes which the city may levy are limited, with certain exceptions, to 2 1/2% of the average full valuation of taxable real estate (§§ 10, 11). The limit, however, may be exceeded to provide for all debt service (§ 10). So, too, although the Legislature is given the duty to restrict municipalities in order to prevent abuses in taxation, assessment, and in contracting of indebtedness, it may not constrict the city's power to levy taxes on real estate for the payment of interest on or principal of indebtedness previously contracted (§ 12)....

While phrased in permissive language, these provisions, when read together with the requirement of the pledge of faith and credit, express a constitutional imperative: debt obligations must be paid, even if tax limits be exceeded. A Constitution is no less violated because one would undermine only its prevailing spirit, and, arguably, not its letter. . . . However, in this case there is no split; spirit and letter speak in unison.

Thus, it is disingenuous to contend that, since the constitutional language allowing the city to exceed tax limits to pay its indebtedness is in form permissive, it may be disregarded. Similarly disingenuous is the argument that the Legislature has not unconstitutionally restricted the power of the city to levy taxes to pay its indebtedness because the city is "free" under the Moratorium Act to pay the notes if it wishes. The problem is not that, but that the city is free under the questioned legislation not to pay them. . . .

The point is that the Moratorium Act, if it were valid, would bar all remedies for a period of three years. For this there is no warrant. And the city's position on the appeal and the discussions publicized in connection with the exchange offers of MAC bonds for the temporary notes make quite clear that the noteholders would have to have a life expectancy of longer than three years if they expect the city voluntarily to redeem the notes. In short, if a three-year moratorium be valid, then one for a longer period should be valid, and perhaps too, one so long until all the noteholders take MAC bonds "voluntarily" in exchange for their notes.

It is not without significance that although Special Term and the Appellate Division treated the many Federal constitutional issues, neither offered any analysis to overcome the crux of the case—the faith and credit clause and its implications. As for the respondents they offer only a chimera.

In sum, to hold, as respondents would have the court do, that the operative effect of the faith and credit clause is exhausted when the indebtedness has been incurred would result in an economic and legal chimera. The only practical significance of a pledge of faith and credit with respect to an indebtedness must be in relation to its payment here on earth and on its due day. To interpret the constitutional provision otherwise would be to honor it as a form of window-dressing but to deny it substantive significance. . . .

Emergencies and the police power, although they may modify their applications, do not suspend constitutional principles. It is not merely a matter of application to interpret the words of the Constitution and obligations issued subject to the Constitution to mean exactly the opposite of what they say. The notes in suit provided that the city pledged its faith and credit to pay the notes and to pay them punctually when due. The clause and the constitutional mandate have no office except when their enforcement is inconvenient. A neutral court worthy of its status cannot do less than hold what is so evident. . . .

Accordingly, the order of the Appellate Division should be reversed, with costs, the moratorium statute declared unconstitutional, and the proposed remittitur settled on 30 days' notice. . . .

Cooke, Judge (dissenting).

The New York City Emergency Moratorium Act of 1975, is, I submit, constitutional.

[In Judge Cooke's opinion, the Act was a valid exercise of the state's police power and one that had been explicitly authorized by a 1963 constitutional amendment requiring the legislature to provide for continuity of government during periods of emergency.—Eds.]

A faith and credit pledge simply means that the issuing government agrees to be generally obligated to pay the indebtedness out of all the government's revenues, rather than restrictively obligated only from specific revenues; it expresses an undertaking by the government to be irrevocably obligated in good faith to use such of its resources and taxing power as may be authorized or required by law for the full and prompt payment of the obligation according to its terms. . . .

The faith and credit pledge, as the words imply, requires no more than that the city make a good faith effort to use its resources, credit and powers to pay its indebtedness. This effort must be measured in the light of the city's over-all financial condition and its over-all obligations to its citizens and others. . . .

[The dissent concluded that a good faith effort had been made as evidenced by the imposition of hiring and wage freezes, adoption of a crisis budget, increases in numerous city taxes, establishment of the Municipal Assistance Corporation, approval of a three-year financing plan calling for a balanced budget and the closing of numerous public facilities including fire stations and schools.—Eds.]

Notes and Questions

1. *Flushing and the New York constitution.* Had the New York Constitution simply said that the City's full faith and credit will be pledged to real estate tax-supported indebtedness, the view of Judge Cooke might have prevailed. But the language of Article VIII, § 2 of that document is unique and its mandate is unequivocal:

> . . . Provisions shall be made annually by appropriation by every county, city, town, village and school district for the payment of interest on all indebtedness and for the amounts required for (a) the amortization and redemption of term bonds, sinking fund bonds and serial bonds, . . . If at any time the respective appropriating authorities shall fail to make such appropriations, a sufficient sum shall be set apart from the first revenues thereafter received and shall be applied to such purposes. The fiscal officer of any county, city, town, village or school district may be required to set apart and apply such revenues as aforesaid at the suit of any holder of obligations issued for any such indebtedness.

A mere good faith effort in applying available resources is not enough, said the majority. Indeed, bondholders are to receive 100 cents on the dollar before anyone else is paid—including police and fire fighters, pension funds or the city attorney.

If *Flushing* was before a court today would the decision be the same? Would public policy support the decision? It is likely that such questions will be raised in the wake of the COVID pandemic. Shortly after the *Flushing* decision the state legislature adopted Title 6-A of the Local Finance Law to authorize the state's local governments (but not likely its school districts) to seek protection from creditors under Chapter 9 of the U.S. Bankruptcy Code (see Part J). In bankruptcy, would the "first revenues" language in Art. VIII, § 2 be viewed as a "pledged revenue" to remove the bondholders from classification as general creditors? Does the lien of "first revenues" mean that all revenues need to be set aside to pay bondholders first after *Flushing*? The same court answered "no" in *Quirk v. Municipal Assistance Corp. for the City of New York*, 363 N.E.2d 549 (N.Y. 1977), holding that a diversion of City sales tax and stock transfer tax for debt service on other bonds did not violate the constitutional full faith and credit pledge, because the constitution does not require that a particular tax be maintained or a new one imposed to produce the "first revenues." Further, Art. VIII, § 12 of the constitution prohibits the legislature from restricting the power of local governments from levying real estate taxes without limit to pay debt service on its bonds. In enacting the tax levy limit (§ 3-c of the General Municipal Law) discussed in Part E, did the legislature violate Art. VIII, § 12?

2. *Saving New York City.* Despite the holding in *Flushing*, MACC was able to carry out its mandate because of an agreement reached with trustees of the city's retirement systems to invest about $2.5 billion from the pension funds in city for MACC obligations. With substantial assistance from the federal government, the New York City fiscal crisis was eased. By 1979, New York City was able to reenter the municipal securities markets (successfully marketing $125 million in short-term notes). Although the financial problems of New York City were far from resolved, the experience demonstrated to one group of analysts that "the untapped and largely disguised resources inherent in the structure of the nation's public finance systems have the resiliency to turn a likely mammoth fiscal disaster into a much more stable financial situation within a relatively short time." R. Lam & S. Rappaport, MUNICIPAL BONDS 253 (2d ed. 1987).

Federal assistance for the City came in two stages. The New York City Seasonal Financing Act, 31 U.S.C. § 1501, authorized the Secretary of the Treasury to lend the city up to $2.3 billion annually for three years. This was replaced in 1978 by the New York City Loan Guarantee Act of 1978, 31 U.S.C. § 1521, which authorized federal loan guarantees for up to $1.65 billion in city securities, which would be sold only to city or state agency employee pension funds.

Budget shortfalls and reductions in state and federal aid in the mid-1990s created a new financial crisis in New York City that prompted the state legislature to enact legislation in May 2003, over the governor's veto of the entire state budget bill, creating a complicated mechanism to assist the city in paying the debt service on the final $2.5 billion principal of the original 30-year MACCNY bonds, which were payable in five annual installments of $500 million each. Municipal Assistance Corporation Refinancing Act (L. 2003, ch. 62, part A4; ch. 63, part V), codified at

Public Authorities Law §§ 3238-A & 3240 and State Finance Law § 92-r. Over the years, the MACCNY debt service requirements had been met by diverting a portion of state sales tax revenues from the city to MACCNY.

The 2003 statute permitted the city to receive the sales tax revenues previously diverted to MACCNY bond debt service, and required the state to make 30 annual payments of $170 million each ($5.1 million total) to the city through the Local Government Assistance Corporation ("LGAC"), a state authority created in 1990 to issue tax and revenue anticipation notes to fund state aid to school districts in anticipation of the receipt of state taxes and revenues (see discussion of Annual Budget, Part E). The city planned to use the state payments to finance a new bond to be issued by a not-for-profit corporation created by the city, the Sales Tax Asset Receivable Corporation ("STARC"). In a declaratory judgment action brought by LGAC to test the constitutionality of the refinancing scheme, the New York Court of Appeals upheld the constitutionality of the Act against allegations of illegal debt and impairment of bondholders' contractual rights. *Local Gov't Assistance Corp. v. Sales Tax Asset Receivable Corp.*, 813 N.E.2d 587 (N.Y. 2004). Are such complicated schemes necessary? Desirable? Should the state and/or the courts supervise local government debt more closely? The debt limitation materials, *infra*, consider these questions.

3. *Tax and revenue limitations versus debt obligations.* The interplay of tax limitation provisions and municipal debt obligations is illustrated by *Kurrus v. Priest*, 29 S.W.3d 669 (Ark. 2000). A proposed constitutional amendment to abolish the sales and use tax on used goods was invalidated by the Arkansas Supreme Court as an unconstitutional impairment of contracts. The City of Brinkley had issued bonds secured by collections of the sales and use taxes levied by the city. Some of the bonds would not mature until 2017. The bond covenants stipulated that the bonds were payable from and secured by a pledge of sales and use taxes on all goods. The Arkansas court held that the proposal constituted an impermissible impairment of contract because the proposed abolition of the tax on used goods was designed to become effective immediately upon securing voter approval, and the proposal did not contain an alternative source of revenue to replace the tax. For related discussion, see the section on the Contracts Clause, earlier in this chapter, discussing *U.S. Trust Co. of New York v. New Jersey*, 431 U.S. 1 (1977)

A Note on Debt Limits

Statutory and constitutional limitations on municipal borrowing apply only to general obligation bonds. They are controversial because (i) they apply to socio-economic conditions and policy and political views, which are over 150 years out of date; and (ii) they raise such politically difficult barriers to authorization that the municipal securities industry has for decades devoted its resources to characterizing most bond issues as some type of revenue bond. All states have either constitutional or statutory limitations on municipal debt for either some or all of their local government units. ACIR, *Federal—State—Local Finances: Significant Features of Fiscal*

Federalism 143–52 (1974). In addition, almost all states have constitutional or statutory provisions requiring referendum approval for general obligation long-term debt. *Id.* at 153–54. Practically all states also have constitutional or statutory restrictions on local taxes. See generally R. Amdursky et al., Municipal Debt Finance Law, Ch. 4 (2d ed. 2013).

The discussion that follows concentrates on the debt limitation provisions, although it is clear that the referendum provisions also create problems of compliance for municipalities seeking to embark on local borrowing programs. Unless the debt obligation issued by the local government is found to fall outside the debt limitation or referendum requirement, it will be found to violate the applicable constitutional or statutory restriction unless (1) the amount of that obligation together with all other outstanding obligations does not exceed the debt limit and (2) voter approval has been obtained. Both conditions may often be difficult to satisfy. Debt limitations are being pressured as municipal debt increases and voter approval for new obligations is increasingly harder to obtain. The debt limitation problem also arises at the state level because many states also have debt limitation requirements, although these are often expressed as monetary ceilings rather than related to the property tax base.

The structure and character of debt limitations is explained in Briffault, *Foreword: The Disfavored Constitution: State Fiscal Limits and State Constitutional Law,* 34 Rutgers L.J. 907, 915–17 (2003). Professor Briffault explains that state constitutions impose a variety of limitations on incurring debt, as been explained previously. Such limitations include barring state debt, imposing limits on amount of debt, tying debt to a proportion of revenues, or other approaches to tie debt to "carrying capacity." Professor Briffault observes that

> Most commonly, state constitutions rely on a procedural restriction: Debt may not be incurred without the approval of a supermajority in the legislature, of voters in a referendum, or both. This legislative supermajority or voter approval requirement may stand on its own or may be combined with a substantive cap on the amount of state or local debt. For the states, the procedural requirements are often the real restrictions on debt. As state constitutions can be relatively easily amended, an absolute prohibition on debt or a low dollar limit on debt can be circumvented by a constitutional amendment authorizing a specific bond issue.... [T]he legal requirements for a constitutional amendment typically, a combination of a legislative supermajority and voter approval—also become the requirements for issuance of debt. Thus, although the Alabama Constitution flatly bars state debt, as of the early 1900s, it contained thirty-three amendments authorizing specific bond issues.

See also Sterk & Goldman, *Controlling Legislative Shortsightedness: The Effectiveness of Constitutional Debt Limitations*, 1991 Wis. L. Rev. 1301 (tracing the history of debt limitations and concluding that they provide a limited check on legislative power to incur debt). More details about current debt limitations and supermajority requirements are included above.

Election requirements. As discussed *supra*, voter approval is required in many states before state or local debt can be incurred. Voter approval requirements are part of the effort that began in the nineteenth century to limit the borrowing power of state and local governments. What does a voter approval requirement add to the protection afforded by detailed state authorization requirements? In studying the following cases, do you think the financial assistance governments agree to pay each year should be subject to voter approval?

Reforms. A variety of reforms of the constitutional debt limit approach to local government finance have been urged for decades, ranging all the way from repeal of the constitutional debt limit, to state technical assistance on financial matters to local governments, to state supervision and approval of local government debt. See Bastress, *Constitutional Consideration for Local Government Reform in West Virginia*, 108 W. VA. L. REV. 125 (Fall, 2005); Elias, *A Simple Suggestion for Substantial Protection: Amending the New Jersey Constitution to Create Contractual Rights for Public Employees to Their Pension Benefits*, 44 RUTGERS L. J. 89 (2013) for general approaches to reform state constitutions in including finance provisions. See also Roin, *Privatization and the Sale of Tax Revenues*, 95 MINN. L. REV. 1965, 1977 (2011), in which the author discusses state and local government debt reform including the complete repeal of constitutional debt limits. For a more recent analysis of the implications of local debt limitations, see Shoked, *Debt Limits' End*, 102 IOWA L. REV. 1239 (2017) (challenging traditional assumptions regarding justifications for local debt limitations based on intergenerational equity, arguing that the real basis for such limits is to assure equitable terms in borrowing as between local governments, and arguing that debt limits should be significantly modified or abolished).

[b] Revenue Bonds

Revenue bonds in their original form are municipal bonds not paid from real property taxes or any resource of the state or local government issuer. However, they are issued to fulfill a legal purpose of the issuer—such as water supply. How can that be? The U.S. Supreme Court took up that issue in *Walla Walla v. Walla Walla Water Company*, 172 U.S. 7 (1898). In the early 1890s the city, under direction of an ordinance from the Territory of Washington to provide a supply of water for its inhabitants, contracted with a private company to construct a water works financed by city bonds payable from "water rents," i.e., the revenues the company received from supplying water. After the contract and "water bonds" were in place, the city repudiated the contract and bonds on the basis that the bonds exceeded a debt limit in its charter. The court struggled with the issue, but finally said Justice Brown:

> There is a considerable conflict of authority respecting the proper construction of such limitations in municipal charters. There can be no doubt that if the city proposed to purchase outright, or establish a system of water

> works of its own, the section would apply, though bonds were issued therefor, made payable in the future.... There are also a number of respectable authorities to the effect that the limitation covers a case where the city agrees to pay a certain sum per annum, if the aggregate amount payable under such agreement exceeds the amount limited by the charter.... But we think the weight of authority, as well as of reason, favors the more liberal construction, that a municipal corporation may contract for a supply of water or gas, or a like necessary, and may stipulate for the payment of an annual rental for the gas or water furnished each year, notwithstanding the aggregate of its rentals during the life of the contract may exceed the amount of the indebtedness limited by the charter. There is a distinction between a debt and a contract for a future indebtedness to be incurred, provided the contracting party perform the agreement out of which the debt may arise. There is also a distinction between the latter case and one where an absolute debt is created at once, as by the issue of railway bonds, or for the erection of a public improvement, though such debt be payable in the future by installments. In the one case the indebtedness is not created until the consideration has been furnished; in the other, the debt is created at once, the time of payment being only postponed. In the case under consideration the annual rental did not become an indebtedness, within the meaning of the charter, until the water appropriate to that year had been furnished. If the company had failed to furnish it, the rental would not have been payable at all; and, while the original contract provided for the creation of an indebtedness, it was only upon condition that the company performed its own obligation. [*Id.* at 19–20.]

The Court reasoned that no debt arises until the contract is performed. Yet the debt is valid under state (or territorial law in this case) because it fulfills a public purpose. Not mentioned by the court, but equally important, while "absolute debt" (i.e., full faith and credit debt) is payable from taxes or other government recourses, placing the risk of default on the issuer, debt payable on "condition of performance" by a third party (i.e., revenue bonds) places the risk of default on the bondholder (i.e., the creditor). As revenue bonds gained acceptance in the municipal securities markets, there developed a Special Fund Doctrine that provides that bonds payable from utility rents or other non-tax revenues received from an enterprise serving a public purpose are valid governmental obligations even though legal debt limits do not apply to them. Revenue bonds initiated the need for credit ratings (since the viability of the enterprise, not the government's taxing power, is liable on the debt) and a way to measure the creditworthiness of a revenue bond, called "coverage." If a water works was expected to produce $1 million per year, and its costs were $400,000 per year, leaving $600,000 available for debt service, and its debt service on bonds is $200,000, we would say the coverage is 3:1—a very secure investment, indeed. The following case discusses the Special Fund Doctrine and illustrates its limitations.

Winkler v. West Virginia School Building Authority

434 S.E.2d 420 (W. Va. 1993)

Miller, Justice:

The question that we are asked to decide on this appeal is whether the Circuit Court of Kanawha County was in error when it held in its July 9, 1993 order that the Capital Improvement and Revenue and Refunding Bonds, Series 1993, issued by the appellant, State of West Virginia School Building Authority (SBA) in the amount of $338,145,000, were invalid as violating Sections 4 and 6 of Article X of the Constitution of West Virginia. These constitutional provisions restrict the ability of the State to issue bonds that draw upon the State's general revenue funds.

I.

The appellants are the SBA and the United National Bank (Bank). The Bank is the Trustee under a certain Trust Indenture between it and the SBA dated January 1, 1990, which is part of the bond financing arrangements. The appellees are two citizens and taxpayers who sought a declaratory judgment with attendant injunctive relief against the SBA on June 16, 1993, in the Circuit Court of Kanawha County. Their claim was that the 1993 Series revenue bonds about to be issued pursuant to W. Va. Code, 18-9D-1, *et seq*., were unconstitutional because issuance of the bonds violated the provisions of Sections 4 and 6 of Article X of the West Virginia Constitution prohibiting state debt.

... After several hearings were held, the circuit court, by order entered July 9, 1993, held that issuance of the bonds was unconstitutional, and therefore enjoined the SBA from issuing the bonds. The basis for the circuit court's holding was that the bonds commit the State Legislature to fund the bonds' retirement and that this commitment constitutes an impermissible debt against the State. We granted this appeal on July 13, 1993, on an expedited basis because of the urgent need for a decision on the issues involved in this case ...

There is no question that the challenged bonds were authorized by the SBA under the provisions of W. Va. Code, 18-9D-1, *et seq*. The general outline of that article, with regard to the bond arrangement, is as follows. Under Section 4, the SBA may issue revenue bonds under the guidelines set out in that section. Pursuant to Section 6, a building capital improvement fund is "created in the state treasury." This same section authorizes the SBA to pledge this fund to liquidate the revenue bonds. Section 8 provides further directions as to the issuance of the bonds, the trust indenture agreement, and the pledge of funds to liquidate the bonds. Section 12 spells out in more detail the trust agreement for the benefit of the bondholders. Section 13 mandates that a sinking fund be created in the State Treasurer's office in order to liquidate the bonds. Finally, under Section 14, this statement is made:

> "No provisions of this article shall be construed to authorize the school building authority at any time or in any manner to pledge the credit or taxing power of the state, nor shall any of the obligations or debts created

> by the school building authority under the authority herein granted be deemed to be obligations of the state."

It is Section 14, together with the disclaimer on the face of the bonds and language in the trust agreement, that causes the appellants to claim that the bonds are neither legal obligations of the State nor of the SBA, and therefore, that the bonds do not constitute a debt obligation of the State under Sections 4 and 6 of Article X of the West Virginia Constitution. The relevant proposed bond language is as follows:

> "The Series 1993 Bonds are limited obligations of the Authority payable solely from the Trust Estate pledged under the Indenture. The Authority may not at any time or in any manner pledge the credit or taxing power of the State, nor shall any of the obligations or debts created by the Authority under the Indenture be deemed to be obligations of the State . . . AMOUNTS AVAILABLE TO BE TRANSFERRED TO THE TRUSTEE FOR DEPOSIT IN THE REVENUE FUND ARE SUBJECT TO ANNUAL APPROPRIATION BY THE STATE LEGISLATURE. THE STATE LEGISLATURE IS NOT LEGALLY OBLIGATED TO MAKE APPROPRIATIONS IN AMOUNTS SUFFICIENT TO PAY DEBT SERVICE ON THE BONDS."

The applicable language in the trust agreement relied upon by the appellants is:

> "All Bonds issued under the Indenture, including the Series 1993 Bonds, are secured by a pledge of Revenues. 'Revenues' means (i) any moneys appropriated by the State Legislature, deposited in the Building Fund and transferred to the Trustee in conformance with the Constitution and laws of the state and (ii) any other moneys, income or property pledged by the Authority to the payment of Bonds. . . .

Before addressing the merits of the particular bond issue in this case, it is useful to review some of our prior cases analyzing Sections 4 and 6 of Article X of the West Virginia Constitution.

II

A

We wish to say at the outset that we are fully aware of the gravity of the bond issue in this case, particularly since it relates to our public educational system . . . Almost fifteen years ago in *Pauley v. Kelly*, 255 S.E.2d 859 (W. Va. 1979), we spoke forcefully to these needs, stating that the Thorough and Efficient Education Clause in Section 1 of Article XII of the West Virginia Constitution was not an empty vessel . . .

Pauley did not address the question of the issuance of bonds to fund school building construction and capital improvements. The appellees appear to suggest that the Thorough and Efficient Education Clause can validate revenue bonds that are authorized by the Legislature, but are found to be unconstitutional under Sections 4 and 6 of Article X of our Constitution. We cannot agree with such an assertion because the generality of the Thorough and Efficient Education Clause in Section 1 of Article XII of our Constitution cannot override the more specific provisions on state debt limitation contained in Sections 4 and 6 of Article X . . . "The general rule of statutory construction requires that a specific statute be given precedence over a general statute relating to the same subject matter where the two cannot be reconciled."

Finally, we acknowledge that when we are called upon to determine the constitutionality of a legislative enactment, we are guided by various restraints that we have imposed upon our judicial powers . . . "In considering the constitutionality of a legislative enactment, courts must exercise due restraint, in recognition of the principle of the separation of powers in government among the judicial, legislative and executive branches." [W. Va. Const. art. V, § 1.] . . .

B

We begin our legal discussion regarding the validity of these school revenue bonds by noting that there is a category of bonds that override the specific limitations contained in Sections 4 and 6 of Article X. They are bonds that the Legislature issues after following the procedures contained in Section 2 of Article XIV of our Constitution relating to constitutional amendments. Under the amendment procedure, a majority of qualified voters voting on the issue must approve the issuance of the bonds. Bonds issued pursuant to a constitutional amendment override the more general bond limit restrictions because they were approved by the voters for the specific purposes contained in the amendment. Thus, under our traditional rules of constitutional construction, these bonds supersede the general bond limitations. . . . The bonds in this case do not fall into the category of bonds approved by constitutional amendment.

C

The two constitutional provisions at issue in this case, Sections 4 and 6 of Article X, have been interpreted by this Court to serve the common purpose of restricting the Legislature's ability to create long-term debt. These provisions are often cited together in the same case; however, each provision serves a separate purpose. The restrictions contained in Section 4 of Article X deal with the creation of long-term debt by the State or its agencies through revenue bonds or other similar obligations by way of legislative enactments. . . . [W]e compared the purpose of Section 6 of Article X with Section 4, noting: " Section 4 of Article X of the Constitution imposes upon the state limitations with respect to indebtedness similar to those imposed upon counties and cities by Article X, Section 6 of the Constitution[.]" Indeed, the plain language of Section 6 is designed to restrict the State from granting credit to subordinate political subdivisions such as municipalities and counties, as well as to forbid the State from granting credit or assuming liabilities for debts of private persons or other entities.

Thus, we believe our cases make clear the substantive distinction between the provisions of Sections 4 and 6 of Article X of our Constitution. In this case, we deal only with Section 4: "Under Section 4, Article X, of the Constitution of this State, the Legislature is without power to create an obligation to appropriate funds, for a purpose not mentioned in said section, by future Legislatures. Such legislation, if otherwise valid, would be void under said section, as creating a debt inhibited thereby."

... [I]t seems clear that the Court did not literally mean that any contract entered into by a state agency that extended over more than one year was constitutionally infirm. *Dyer* [*State ex rel. Dyer v. Sims*, 58 S.E.2d 766, 773 (W. Va. 1950)] recognized that by creating state agencies, the Legislature was obligating itself, in a constitutionally permissible manner, to pay funds necessary for those agencies' operational expenses from future general revenue funds:

> "Ordinarily, the creation of a State board or commission which requires an appropriation of public funds to carry out its purposes is not treated as the creation of a debt, although its generally contemplated continuation from year to year, and for an indefinite period, must necessarily involve future appropriations. Practically all agencies created by the Legislature require appropriations from time to time, and that was necessarily contemplated at the time they were created." 58 S.E.2d at 773.

Much of this same type of reasoning also was recognized in *State ex rel. Hall v. Taylor*, 178 S.E.2d 48, 56 (W. Va. 1971), where we said: "[A]dmittedly it is contemplated by the statute that the rent will be paid from general revenue funds to be appropriated by the Legislature to the various agencies and departments of the state government from year to year." Moreover, in *State ex rel. Board of Governors v. Sims*, 55 S.E.2d 505, 508 (W. Va. 1949), we specifically recognized that the Legislature's creation of a pension system, which required periodic funding from general revenues, did not constitute "the creation of a debt inhibited by Section 4 of Article X of the Constitution."

It is the fact that state agencies have recurring needs for services, such as rental space and utility services that form the basis for our cases approve the State's lease-financing arrangements. In such a situation, the lease payments are used to retire revenue bonds that were issued to construct the building. We stated ... "Bonds of a state or political subdivision payable solely out of revenue derived from a utility of a public nature acquired by the money derived from the bonds do not create debts within the constitutional inhibition against the contraction of public debt." *State ex rel. West Virginia Resource Recovery—Solid Waste Disposal Authority v. Gill*, 323 S.E.2d 590 (W. Va. 1984).

Moreover, the foregoing rationale also was behind our approval of the issuance of industrial and commercial revenue bonds under W.Va.Code, 13-2C-1 ... [citations omitted] All these various types of lease arrangements have been generally accepted elsewhere as valid against a claim of constitutional debt infirmity.

In addition, we have given our approval to the payment of revenue bonds that are liquidated out of a special fund. This concept is related to the lease-financing arrangement, but differs because the special fund is ordinarily a tax or a fee generated from the facility itself, such as tolls for the use of a bridge or road, or parking-garage fees. In *State ex rel. Hall v. Taylor*, 178 S.E.2d at 56, we stated the general basis for the special fund concept:

> "It is difficult to state the 'separate fund doctrine' precisely. Its application varies somewhat among appellate courts of various states. It is applied uniformly in relation to projects or facilities which are self-liquidating, such as the toll bridge cases. Some courts hold that the doctrine applies in any case of a fund created by a special excise tax as distinguished from property taxes."

The special fund doctrine provided the basis for both our approval of the State Road Commission's special fund to generate revenues to construct the building for the Department of Highways in *State ex rel. Building Commission v. Moore*, 184 S.E.2d 94 (W.Va. 1971), and the use of the Alcoholic Beverage Control Commission's profits in the same case to fund the construction of its warehouse. The same rationale supports our toll-bridge cases and our cases dealing with the construction of student dormitories at West Virginia University out of special student fees. The special fund doctrine is generally recognized in other jurisdictions as not being violative of constitutional debt limitations. The appellants argue that both the special fund doctrine and the service contract or lease agreement concept still involve funds that ultimately can be said to come from potential general revenue sources. Thus, they assert that these principles, which we have acknowledged to be acceptable as not violating Section 4 of Article X, are really no different than the more direct payments from general revenue funds used in this case.

We disagree because appellants overlook several significant differences. First, the special fund doctrine is based on the fact that a specific source of revenue is required to be identified and committed to the repayment of the bonds beyond mere annual appropriations from the general revenue fund. Second, by identifying and dedicating this specific source of funds, the process automatically limits the total value of bonds that can be used. The Legislature will have to quantify initially the amount it is willing to commit in order to avail itself of the special fund doctrine.

Much the same process occurs in the case of a service contract or lease arrangement. There, the revenue source is the rental payments or the amounts paid under the service contract. These amounts are ultimately controlled by the cost of the building, which determines the total value of bonds to be issued. The cost of the proposed building, in turn, will be governed by economic and market considerations which limit the cost of the project and the total value of bonds to be issued.

In other words, these funding sources, which we have approved in earlier cases, have built-in restraints that must be considered by the Legislature when it authorizes legislation for the issuance of the bonds. In this case, the bonds have no such identifiable controls because their payment is directly from the general revenue fund. There is no statutory restriction on the total value of SBA bonds that may be issued and, unlike special-fund or lease-payment bonding, there is no identifiable source that controls the total value of bonds to be issued.

From the foregoing law, the general principle emerges that Section 4 of Article X is not designed to prohibit the State or the State's agencies from issuing revenue bonds that are payable from contracts that require rental payments of another state agency or require other necessary recurring contractual expenses such as utilities; nor does this constitutional provision preclude the issuance of revenue bonds which are to be redeemed from a special fund.

D

The appellants place primary reliance on *State ex rel. West Virginia Resource Recovery—Solid Waste Disposal Authority v. Gill*, 323 S.E.2d 590 (W. Va. 1984), and in particular: . . .

> "The ultimate issue in determining whether bond financing creates a state debt in violation of Article X, Section 4 [of the West Virginia Constitution] is not whether the bonds may be paid from future legislative appropriations, but whether successive legislatures are obligated to make such appropriations."

We do not find *Gill* persuasive simply because in *Gill* there was a revenue source for liquidation of the bonds that was independent of a direct grant from the State's general revenue fund. In *Gill*, the West Virginia Resource Recovery–Solid Waste Disposal Authority (Authority) was authorized to issue revenue bonds to construct a power generating facility in Morgantown. West Virginia University had contracted to purchase a substantial amount of its energy use from the Authority and the University's payment for this service was to be used to liquidate the bonds issued by the Authority.

In the instant case, the appellants argue that although future legislative appropriations may be used to pay for the bonds, it is clear from the language of the bonds themselves that there is no legal obligation requiring the Legislature to make such appropriations . . . Under such an interpretation, the Legislature could authorize the State or its agencies to issue bonds in any amount so long as the bonds are used for a public purpose, and so long as the terms of the bonds make clear that the bonds are not state obligations and that the Legislature is under no obligation to fund the bonds. . . .

While we may admire the legal sophistry of this argument, it defies our practical judgment. If the bonds are not paid, it is obvious that the State's credit will be impaired. The default on a bond issue of this size hardly can be expected to draw cheers from the bondholders or their brokerage houses or the bond financial rating services.

In considering the validity of revenue bonds, *Hall v. Taylor*, supra, admonishes us that "[i]t is the duty of this Court . . . to consider the substance of the plan envisioned by the statute in determining the question of constitutionality." 178 S.E.2d at 57. Moreover, *Hall* espoused the concept that a "mere legislative declaration that a state debt is not created . . . is not conclusive or binding on a court." 178 S.E.2d at

57. Following other jurisdictions, *Hall* held that it is a judicial and not a legislative question "[w]hether a state debt is created by [a] statute[.]" 178 S.E.2d at 57 . . .

When we analyze the School Building Authority Act, W. Va. Code, 18-9D-1, *et seq.*, we find . . . W. Va. Code, 18-9D-6, creates in the "state treasury a school building capital improvements fund to be expended by the authority for the purposes of this article." This same section authorizes the SBA "to pledge all or such part of the revenues paid into the school building capital improvements fund as may be needed to meet the requirements of any revenue bond issue or issues authorized by this article . . . and in any trust agreement made in connection therewith[.]"

W. Va.Code, 18-9D-8, relates to the issuance of the bonds and requires them to be signed by the governor and by the president or vice-president of the SBA "under the great seal of the state, attested by the secretary of state[.]" It goes on to require:

> "Any pledge of revenues for such revenue bonds made by the school building authority shall be valid and binding between the parties from the time the pledge is made; and the revenues so pledged shall immediately be subject to the lien of such pledge without any further physical delivery thereof or further act." . . .

From the foregoing provisions, it would be difficult to conclude that the revenue bonds issued by the SBA are not obligations of the State. Certainly, the requirement of maintaining the sinking fund in order to service the bonds and provide for their redemption indicates a financial commitment by the Legislature. The same is true with respect to the pledge of the fund for the benefit of the bondholders.

Finally, unless we are to abandon our logic and common sense, we cannot help but conclude that the statutory scheme surrounding these bonds bespeaks a legislative requirement that they be funded. . . . Even if we were to close our eyes to this statutory language, we could not close our minds to the practical consequences of this revenue arrangement. To accept the premise that the Legislature is not bound to fund the bonds and would allow a default, thereby impairing the credit rating of the State, assumes a naivete on our part that we simply do not possess.

Accordingly, we hold that the revenue bonds authorized under the School Building Authority Act constitute an indebtedness of the State in violation of Section 4 of Article X of the West Virginia Constitution . . .

Affirmed.

Notes and Questions

1. *Special fund doctrine. Winkler* represents the high-water mark in maintaining the "purity" of the Special Fund Doctrine: a separate and discrete source of revenue, like water rents, sewer rents, and utility fees not associated with the general funds of the issuer are the sole "revenues," which may distinguish revenue bonds from general obligation bonds with their full faith and credit pledge and power to levy unlimited real property taxes to pay debt service. The court rejects the claim

that the absence of a requirement to appropriate by successive legislatures is all that is needed to remove the debt from constitutional limits on indebtedness. But it is exactly this view that courts adopted after *Winkler.* In *Local Government Assistance Corp. v. Sales Tax Receivable Corp.*, 813 N.E.2d 587 (N.Y. 2004), the complaint was that New York City was incurring unconstitutional debt by appropriating the $170,000 per year from the State to the debt service of Sales Tax Asset Receivable Corporation, an "on-behalf-of" entity created by the city (see below and Part I). What saved the payments from the city to STARC was that they were "subject to annual appropriation" by the City Council even though, as the court points out in *Winkler,* the city would, as a practical matter, not appropriate for fear of disappointing investors and impairing the city's credit.

2. *Spectrum of debt obligations.* As was suggested in the introductory section of this Chapter, it is often helpful to think about various types of borrowing and debt as existing along a spectrum. The best type of debt (most valued by debtors and likely to have the lowest interest rate for governments), is debt backed by general obligation bonds (that is, backed by the obligation to pay using tax revenues). Second best is debt backed by clear "revenue" streams that can be evaluated for ongoing viability with a definite source of anticipated repayment. It might seem as though these types of debt would exhaust the possibilities. But in modern times, that has not been the case. Another form of debt called "appropriations-backed debt" is created if there is a legislative commitment to assuring repayment through a commitment to make appropriations to repay debt. Shading down a bit further is "moral obligation" debt, in which a legislative body may say it will "consider" future payments to repay the debt through future appropriations (with no commitments made at the outset). A crucial question is whether "appropriations-backed debt" is debt that should be treated as falling within well-established state constitutional requirements regarding standards and processes constraining decisions by states and local governments in taking on debt. Likewise, as noted below, a significant legal question exists as to whether "moral obligation bonds" should be considered as "debt" (and subjected to procedural protections and debt limits). Then, again, as considered subsequently in this Chapter, there are questions whether "work arounds" (such as "lease-purchase" agreements or creation of special districts or authorities that can take on their own debt) are available.

3. *Lease revenue bonds.* Bonds for constructing government facilities that are leased to the government form another extension of the Special Fund Doctrine. In *Bulman v. McCrane,* 312 A.2d 857 (N.J. 1973), the New Jersey Supreme Court treated bonds payable from rents by the state to a private developer to be annually appropriated by the legislature as outside the constitutional limitations on debt on the theory that the annual lease payments are not debt of the state—even though (i) the rent matched the debt service on the so-called "lease revenue bonds" and (ii) the facility leased to the state was essential for carrying out its governmental operations making it highly unlikely that the legislature would not appropriate in future years.

4. *Appropriations-backed debt.* A lesson on appropriations-backed bonds can be gleaned from New Jersey. In *Lonegan v. State*, 819 A2d 395 (N.J. 2003), the New Jersey Supreme Court rejected the state's use of contract- and appropriations-backed debt as a funding mechanism for education facility bonds. The court relied upon the language of the New Jersey constitution regarding debt limitations, notwithstanding the state's argument that school-related bonds could be authorized without limitation under provisions of the state constitution relating to school finance. The court reasoned that "only debt that is legally enforceable against the State is subject to the Debt Limitation Clause," and thus subject to voter approval. The court's majority then embraced the majority view that appropriations-backed debt was not subject to state constitutional limitations and urged the state legislature to address related issues as appropriate.

Subsequently, in *Burgos v. State*, 188 A.3d 270 (N.J. 2015), the New Jersey court revisited its analysis in *Lonegan*. In *Burgos*, the issue related to state practices in addressing public pension obligations. The state had adopted legislation that created an expectation that the state would contribute funds annually to address unfunded pension obligations and associated existing liabilities for past underfunding. State employees sued, alleging contract violations, when the state legislature failed to carry through on appropriating funds in keeping with stated obligations. At issue, in particular, was a provision of the New Jersey Constitution that stated:

> The Legislature shall not, in any manner, create in any fiscal year a debt or debts, liability or liabilities of the State, which together with any previous debts or liabilities shall exceed at any time one per centum of the total amount appropriated by the general appropriation law for that fiscal year, unless the same shall be authorized by a law for some single object or work distinctly specified therein.... [N]o such law shall take effect until it shall have been submitted to the people at a general election and approved by a majority of the legally qualified voters of the State voting thereon. [N.J. Const. art. VIII, § 2, ¶ 3.]

The New Jersey court ultimately concluded that the Legislature and Governor lacked authority to enact an enforceable and legally binding financial agreement by statute, in contravention of the limitations imposed by the Debt Limitation Clause of the state constitution.

5. *"Tax-exempt" leasing:* Similar issues arise when a state or local government acquires equipment to be used and paid for over an extended period. In *Allstate Leasing Corp. v. Board of County Comm'rs*, 450 F.2d 26 (10th Cir. 1971), the court upheld county leases of heavy road equipment for periods of 34 and 60 months; the lease contract did not constitute a debt. The court, however, distinguished an earlier New Mexico case, *Shoup Voting Mach. Corp. v. Board of County Comm'rs*, 256 P.2d 1068 (N.M. 1953), in which the county had contracted to purchase voting machines and to pay for them over a 10-year period. Because the purchase contract constituted an unconditional obligation to pay, it was held to constitute a debt. Similarly, in *Marine Midland Trust Company of Southern New York v. Village of*

Waverly, 248 N.Y.S.2d 729 (Sup. Ct. 1963), *affd.*, 251 N.Y.S.2d 937 (App. Div. 1964), in an action against the village for money due under an agreement designated as a lease of real property for 20 years for the purpose of public parking with an option to purchase at lease termination, the court ruled the agreement was void as being unconstitutional debt.

6. *Special assessment bonds:* The classic revenue bond reflecting the special fund doctrine is a municipal bond funded by a special assessment on real property. Street paving, road improvements, and sidewalks have traditionally been financed by special assessments levied against benefitted, and in some cases, abutting real property owners. The assessment is not considered a tax as it is based on a benefit that has been received by the adjoining landowner. Because assessments are ordinarily collected over a period of time, funds to construct the improvements have to be obtained presently by issuing municipal bonds. These bonds in turn are funded by the special assessments, which may be included in the real property tax levy. See *Wagner v. Salt Lake City*, 504 P.2d 1007 (Utah 1972) (upholding the use of the special assessment to finance bonds used to bury overhead utility lines). Special assessment bonds are also used to finance infrastructure through a special district where a special benefit is provided to benefitted real property, or persons on real property, which pays through special assessments. The improvement district may or may not be a political subdivision with power to borrow or tax, but will always be tied to a geographic area in which the special assessment is levied and the benefit conferred.

7. *TIF bonds as revenue bonds.* Tax increment financing ("TIF") is an economic development revenue raising technique discussed in more detail below. The basic concept underlying TIF bonds is that it is possible and desirable to disaggregate increased property value increases associated with property improvements, and repay investments giving rise to such improvements by diverting associated property tax increases to the specific purpose or repaying borrowing used to create the improvements (rather than to general purpose uses). However, when the revenue takes on the characteristic of the general real property levy (i.e., real property taxes are "available" or "pledged" to the revenue bonds), the bonds may be considered invalidly issued general obligation bonds for failure to meet state constitution debt incurring limitations. See *Bay County v. Town of Cedar Grove*, 992 So. 2d 164, 168–170 (Fla. 2008) (proposed TIF bonds were not debt because, by express language in the bond resolutions, "bondholders would have no right, if the trust funds were insufficient to meet the bond obligations, to compel the levy of ad valorem taxation"). See also *Oklahoma City Urban Renewal Auth. v. Medical Technology and Research Auth. of Oklahoma*, 4 P.3d 677 (Okla. 2000) (noting split of authority and agreeing with the Wisconsin Court that TIF debt-servicing instruments may constitute debt within meaning of the state constitution).

8. *Are non-real estate taxes as the source of payment enough to invoke the special fund doctrine?* The answer is usually yes, particularly if a state agency, or conduit, is the bond issuer and the state expressly disclaims liability in a constitutional or statutory provision that the agency's debt is not that of the state. For example, see

In re Application of Oklahoma Dept. of Transp., 82 P.3d 1000 (Okla. 2003) (state debt implicating debt limitation provisions is not created when anticipated future receipts of federal aid are pledged to repay promissory notes); *Long v. Napolitano*, 53 P.3d 172 (Ariz. App. 2002) (pledge of income taxes to be paid by professional football team and its employees along with transaction privilege taxes paid by stadium contractors and vendors to retire bonds issued to finance new stadium did not constitute debt); *Directors of La. Recovery Dist. v. Taxpayers*, 529 So. 2d 384, 392 (La. 1988) (bonds to be retired from the proceeds of a sales and use tax are not general obligation bonds requiring an election). But in a contrary view, the court in *Winkler* would approve, in a consolidation the several state agencies in, and the assumption of their outstanding revenue bonds by an administrative department of the state, the court held that the assumption by the state of state agency debt constituted a violation of the constitutional limit on incurring state debt, even though the debt assumed was payable exclusively from project revenues. In *American Nat'l Bank & Trust Co. v. Indiana Dep't of Hwys.*, 439 N.E.2d 1129 (Ind. 1982), the court held that

> Although the special fund is present in the case before us, the separate entity that was originally the Toll Road Commission is not. The state of Indiana, through its Highway Department, is responsible for the maintenance and operation of the Toll Road and it is the one obligated on and issuing the bonds of indebtedness as to the $259,500,000 now extant and the completion bonds needed for further work. For this Court to provide that the legislation involved here is constitutional merely upon the existence of a special fund doctrine, would be to provide that any and every agency of the state could issue bonds of indebtedness so long as that authorization provided for special funds from which to pay that indebtedness. This would be nothing short of once again opening the floodgates of authorizing unlimited state indebtedness. [*Id.* at 1135.]

A Note on Certificates of Participation (COPS)

1. *COPS defined:* Certificates of participation ("COPS") are a form of long-term financing similar to lease revenue bonds discussed *infra*. But the investors do not receive bonds; they receive a "certificate of participation" indicating the right to receive payment of a portion of the rent on the lease (*e.g.*, the principal and interest on the COPS). A COPS regime can only be used where expressly authorized in statutes, which make clear that the rent payments are not in violation of the state's debt incurring restrictions and are payable only on a "subject to appropriation" basis. The lessee is always a government that "rents" the facility (i.e., a school, jail, office building). The lessor is usually a "straw man," an entity established by the issuer (i.e., a not-for-profit corporation) to act "on-behalf of" the issuer to finance the project (*see* discussion of Conduits, *infra*). The COPS takes the place of GO debt and relieves the issuer of referenda, debt limits, and the like in complying with debt incurring restrictions. Unlike GOs, no full faith and credit pledge attaches to the COPS, nor does the real property tax levy need to include the debt service on

COPS as is the case with GOs. Yet, the investor risk of non-appropriation in a COPS for purposes like schools, court houses, jails, etc. is extremely low on account of the purpose's essentiality. Discretionary facilities (ice rink, football field, etc.) are riskier candidates for COPS financing because the issuer may decide to terminate the purpose before the COPS mature.

2. *COPS as debt:* Is a COPS transaction debt? The Securities and Exchange Commission and other regulatory agencies consider COPS to be "municipal securities" within the provisions of federal securities law applicable to state and local government debt (*see* Part I). See Gelfand, *supra*, § 3:26. Most courts that have considered this question have held that a COPS transaction is not unconstitutional debt. *Bauerband v. Jackson County*, 598 S.E.2d 444 (Ga. 2004) (COPS-funded lease/purchase agreement to finance construction of new county courthouse not debt); *Employers Ins. Co. v. State Bd. of Examiners*, 21 P.3d 628 (Nev. 2001) (lease/purchase agreement to fund state office building not debt); *State Dept. of Ecology v. State Finance Comm.*, 804 P.2d 1241 (Wash. 1991) (COPS used to finance state building not debt).

But in *Montano v. Gabaldon*, 766 P.2d 1328 (N.M. 1989), the court held that a lease transaction featuring the sale of COPS to finance construction of a jail constituted debt requiring an election. While under the lease agreement the county held no legal obligation to continue the lease from year to year or to purchase the facility, the court concluded that "once the County accepted this lease, it would be obligated to continue making rental payments in order to protect a growing equitable interest in the facility, as well as to protect the County's interest in the title to County land." *Id.* at 1330. If you were legal counsel to a municipality considering similar projects, what opinion would you give your client? Would the holdings in *Flushing* and *WPPSS* provide guidance on how you would advise your client on the adequacy of the law to authorize COPS? Would judicial treatment of appropriation-backed debt and "moral obligation bonds," discussed *infra*, be relevant? See Bisk, *State and Municipal Lease-Purchase Agreements: A Reassessment*, 7 HARV. J.L. & PUB. POL'Y 521 (1984) (concluding that a non-appropriation mechanism making rent payment obligations contingent upon future appropriations to protect the public from "fiscal extravagance" should resolve the debt question). See generally Goldner, *State and Local Government Fiscal Responsibility: An Integrated Approach*, 26 WAKE FOREST L. REV. 925 (1991).

3. *Who owns the facility?* Since the government entity is leasing the facility, who owns it and does it matter? It matters if the fee owner is an entity for which real property tax exemptions and other state fee exclusions would not apply. The owner is always the "straw man" who sells the COPS to investors. The straw man should be a quasi-governmental entity under state law, so that the availability of exemptions and exclusions the government entity would take or be granted are not challenged. In a strange decision, *Board of Educ. v. Department. of Rev.*, 825 N.E.2d 746 (Ill. App. 2005), the court concluded that the COPS transaction at issue was both a financing transaction designed to benefit the Glen Ellyn, Illinois school district, and a "business transaction" designed to provide a "profit" for the LaSalle Bank

and its investors. Because the school board did not establish that it had "sufficient control" over the facility to qualify as owner, and because the lease was designed to secure profit for investors, the board was not eligible for a statutory real property tax exemption on a facility it was occupying through a 99-year lease with the bank. The adverse result for the school in this Illinois case is easily avoided by stipulating in the financing documents that (i) the government entity has ownership and control of the facility through a long-term lease, and (ii) the investors' profit is not a contract term: investors receive principal and interest as if the COPS were municipal bonds. Whether investors make a profit on their investment is of no concern to any transaction party except the investors.

[c] Moral Obligation Bonds

A hybrid form of bond is the moral obligation bond. These bonds have been extensively used at the state level to finance a variety of state programs, especially housing assistance programs undertaken by state agencies. They first came to prominence in New York State after a series of defeats of public housing bond issues in public referenda. The theory of the moral obligation bond is that the state legislature will be called upon to make an appropriation to pay any deficiency that may occur, should the reserve fund maintained to make principal and interest payments fall below the maximum amount of principal and interest that could become due in any one year.

When a moral obligation is included in legislation authorizing revenue bonds, the question arises whether the moral obligation converts the revenue bond into debt because of the implied obligation to make up any deficits in project revenues. This issue is considered in *Fults v. City of Coralville*, 666 N.W.2d 548 (Iowa 2003). This case considered a challenge to a hotel/conference center project in an urban renewal area that was to be financed by the issuance of $33 million in TIF notes and bonds, discussed below. The notes and bonds contained a statement that they were subject to repayment only if the city annually appropriated sufficient funds to make debt service payments. The Iowa Supreme Court, in holding that the TIF bonds and notes did not violate the state constitutional requirements for incurring debt, characterized the city's obligation to make debt service payments as only a "moral obligation":

> There is nothing in the agreements [loan agreement and indenture of trust] creating the notes and bonds that binds the city to any particular future course of action. Each year, it is the option of the city council to appropriate the necessary money for repayment. If the city council does not appropriate money for this purpose, the city is not bound to repay the remaining amount on the notes and bonds. These notes and bonds are debts only if each year the city council says they are debts. This is the very essence of debt that does not constitute constitutional debt. The repayment of a debt that is not certain to take place regardless of future events is not subject to the constitutional debt limitation....

Property owners argue the practical effect of the language creating the notes and bonds is that the city has "pledged" to repay the money. Specifically, property owners assert "[w]hen a future city council faces the decision of whether to cause [a nonappropriation] to happen, it will both morally and practically be in a position where it must continue to appropriate general tax revenues." Property owners predict a certain disastrous result of nonappropriation; the city's inability "to borrow money for even essential city services or of having that money at higher interest rates." Given these claimed consequences of a nonappropriation, the property owners, in essence, argue the city has morally bound itself to repay the notes and bonds. Because of the likelihood of repayment, the property owners urge us to expand the definition of constitutional debt to include appropriations-backed debt. We are not persuaded by their contention.

"A moral obligation . . . is not in and of itself 'debt.'" *Schulz v. State*, 639 N.E.2d 1140, 1148 (N.Y. 1994). "That is, the constitutional debt limitation provision of our constitution applies to legally enforceable obligations, not to moral obligations. . . . . Though the consequences that could follow from the city's nonappropriation may serve to assure creditors of repayment, this assurance does not constitute a legal obligation. Even if the practical effect of these agreements is that the city will repay the notes and bonds, this does not affect our analysis as long as the city cannot be held legally responsible for the debt for a year other than one in which funds have been appropriated. . . . The claimed expectations of the notes and bonds holders do not create cognizable debt because these beliefs do not impose an enforceable duty or liability upon the city. . . .

Finally, property owners' argument that the city is attempting to do indirectly what it may not do directly is similarly unavailing. If the express terms of the city's agreement do not offend the constitution, then the purpose alone will not render the agreement unconstitutional . . . [*Id.* at 557–559.]

Notes and Questions

1. *What is "moral"?* If moral obligation bonds are not legally enforceable, why do the parties bother to include the provision? Is it pabulum for investors who believe that the issuer would not risk the reputational risk of a bond default? What was it about the purpose of the project in *Fults* that made the moral obligation necessary? The answer lies in the nature of the debt—a revenue bond where hotel revenues were expected to pay debt service (remember the Special Fund Doctrine?). But would hotel revenues be sufficient? What if the hotel was a commercial failure? It is the "financial assistance" that may be "morally" provided by the local government "subject to annual appropriation" should project revenues fall short that gives moral obligation or appropriation-backed bonds the appearance of *de facto* constitutional debt. Why? Because politics and policy abhor a project failure and a bond default.

As a practical matter, petitioners in these cases are right: the moral obligation or "subject to appropriation" language is meaningless if the object or purpose financed is a purpose that serves the public interest. Do you think the city would ever fail to make an appropriation?

In *State ex rel. Warren v. Nusbaum*, 208 N.W.2d 780 (Wis. 1973), the court observed that such provisions have been construed as intending "only to express to succeeding legislatures an expectation and aspiration that the project might be found worthy of financial assistance, if later needed." *Id.* at 803. See generally Griffith, *"Moral Obligation" Bonds: Illusion or Security?* 8 URB. LAW. 54, 70–93 (1976). Contra, *Gibson v. Smith*, 531 P.2d 724 (Or. App. 1975). The court noted that the constitutional provision limiting state debt applied as well to liabilities of the state, and that the moral obligation provision attempted to do indirectly what was prohibited directly and "so would bear characteristics of misrepresentation which could eventually result in an indirect legal defeat of the positive direct proscription." *Id.* at 728.

2. *Debt limit avoidance—the morality of bonds payable from rents:* A number of debt avoidance structures have been adopted for state and local government financing and have been accepted by some courts as not creating debt that comes within debt incurring limitations. For example, lease financing or sale-leasebacks, where the government conveys title to its land asset to a conduit (see item 3 below) for use of a new facility to be built with proceeds of the conduit's bonds, with repayment of the bonds by the government "leasing" the facility from the conduit, is a debt-avoidance structure. At the end of the lease term, the title to the facility goes back to the government for nominal consideration (i.e., $1.00). If the "rent" is in excess of commercial rent for occupancy and happens to equal debt service on the conduit's bonds, is the state's lease not unconstitutional debt? Why do courts excuse these arrangements from constitutional debt restraint when the essentiality of the facility to a public purpose (i.e., a school, jail, courthouse, government office building) financed with lease revenue bonds makes the legislative discretion to not appropriate "rent" a highly unlikely event?

Yet, as *Bulman v. McCrane*, discussed *supra*, suggests, conduit bonds secured by lease payments (which are no more than annual appropriations) are the funding scheme least offensive to the Special Fund Doctrine, although conduit bonds have led to judicial acceptance of more widespread use of appropriate-backed and moral obligation debt. Obviously, sale-leaseback structures can be challenged as a subterfuge. Nevertheless, many courts have been willing to ignore all of these objections and hold that the municipality or school district has merely leased the building. See *Protsman v. Jefferson-Craig Consol. School Corp.*, 109 N.E.2d 889 (Ind. 1953). Contra, *City of Phoenix v. Phoenix Civic Auditorium & Convention Center Ass'n*, 408 P.2d 818 (Ariz. 1965) (excellent review of the cases). The result is that the only debt incurred by the governmental entity is the annual rent, payable out of the annual budget, which becomes a succession of renewable annual obligation in each year of the lease term. This technique has also been used extensively to build state office buildings and other state facilities. See Morris, *Evading Debt Limitations with Public Building Authorities: The Costly Subversion of State Constitutions*, 68 YALE L.J. 234 (1958). What if the state or local government tires of the "leased" facility? Could it terminate the "lease" with impunity and move its functions to another facility? How would you expect conduit bond investors to react? Would a court equate the government's terminating the lease and vacating the facility as repudiation of a government obligation? What argument would the government make that there is no repudiation but that is simply upgrading its facilities?

In *Enourato v. New Jersey Bldg. Auth.*, 440 A.2d 42 (N.J. App. Div. 1981), following the precedent *Bulman, supra*, the court held that the statute establishing the New Jersey Building Authority did not violate the debt limitation provision because of the leasing arrangement. The court held that the only appropriations contemplated were for the rent payments (not bond payments), and even those future appropriations were subject to the express reservation that they might not be made. See also *St. Charles City-County Library Dist. v. St. Charles Library Corp.*, 627 S.W.2d 64 (Mo. App. 1981) (upholding one-year lease-purchase agreement with 24 successive options to renew between the library district and not-for-profit corporation to finance new library building, after voters defeated two separate proposals to finance the building through general obligation bond and tax increases). How secure would investors feel about buying long-term bonds where the lease would expire automatically each year unless the library corporation took affirmative action to renew the lease? Is there more risk in reviewing the entire lease before renewing versus merely appropriating funds annually for an existing lease?

3. *New forms: social impact and "green" bonds.* New forms of investment and associated bonds continue to emerge. It is worth tracking emerging frameworks and imagining new forms that may emerge in the future.

(a) *Social impact bonds.* Social impact bonds (SIB) initially emerged in the United Kingdom in 2010, with the first example in the United States associated with efforts to reduce recidivism at Rikers Island, New York. See Humphries, *Not Your Older Brother's Bonds: The Use and Regulation of Social Impact Bonds in the United States*, 76 LAW & CONTEMP. PROBS. 433, 436-38 (2013). Despite their name, SIBs typically involve investment contracts (rather than issuance of securities), that establish partnerships between investors, governments, and others to achieve social goals such as reducing juvenile recidivism or improving early childhood education. *Id.* at 439. Returns on investment are based on independent evaluation of benchmarks of success. Social impact bonds have become more well-established since their introduction in the last decade. For a further critique of SIBs, see Toussaint, *The New Gospel of Wealth: On Social Impact Bonds and the Privatization of the Public Good*, 56 HOUS. L. REV. 153 (2018). Note that there are important questions about how SIBs should be treated in terms of registration requirements that might otherwise apply to purveyors of government bonds. Also note that individual states have been exploring models similar to social impact bonds. See National Conference of State Legislatures,

Funding Social Programs with Social Impact Bonds, available at https://www.ncsl.org/research/fiscal-policy/funding-social-programs-with-social-impact-bonds.

(b) *Green bonds.* "Green bonds" are more closely aligned with typical bonds and borrowing. See Municipal Securities Rulemaking Board (MSRB), *About Green Bonds,* available at http://www.msrb.org/~/media/files/resources/about-green-bonds.ashx? MRSB defines "green bonds" as bonds issued by municipalities or others to finance projects with an environmental or climate impact. While there is no universally accepted standard for designating a bond issuance as "green," "green bond principles" have been developed as "best practices principles." Evolving practices regarding "green bonds" deserve continuing attention going forward. See, e.g., Park, *Investors as Regulators: Green Bonds and the Governance Challenges of the Sustainable Finance Revolution,* 54 Stan. J. Int'l L. 1 (2018). See also Trompeter, *Green Greed is Good: How Green Bonds Cultivated into Wall Street's Environmental Paradox,* 17 Sustainable Dev. L. & Pol'y 4 (2017).

[3] Conduit Structure and Finance

In all the principal cases presented here, none of the parties have been a state or local government. *WPPSS* involved an interstate power agency; *Flushing* involved a public benefit corporation; *Winkler* and *Lonegan* each involved state education construction agencies. These entities are referred to generally as "conduits," meaning that a public purpose of a state or local government is accomplished through an entity that is not the state or local government. The knee jerk rationale for conduits is that they are established to avoid constitutional debt incurring restrictions, and that the restraints embedded in state organic law are defeated to the detriment of taxpayers. Indeed, the use of conduits can be abusive, for example, by financing a project with a conduit after the proposition to finance the project with constitutional debt is defeated.

But the use of conduits serves purposes which did not exist in the nineteenth century when constitutional debt restraint provisions were first enacted. First, conduits can finance projects that overlap local government and state boundaries. The accepted widespread use of the automobile in the early twentieth century required public road and bridge projects to be financed and managed by regional public agencies; hence, the Port Authority of New York and New Jersey established in 1923 by an act of Congress to regulate water and surface transportation on and across the Hudson River, and later air transportation in the New York City area. Second, the projects undertaken by conduits involve administration, financial management, and professional and technical expertise that basic state and local government functions would be strained to provide. Imagine sending the clerk to fill in for the air traffic controller at the airport? Third, these large, technical and regional purposes are not attractive to private service providers or investors. They tend to operate at a loss, requiring supplemental appropriations from the state and local governments.

An exception to this point is "public-private partnerships" (P3), discussed later in the Chapter. The assumption of P3 is that the private sector as owner/operator can make money for equity investors, and provide a better service more efficiently, a proposition stemming from the high and increasing cost of public labor and benefits. Accordingly, state and local governments may be empowered to fulfill a purpose but not empowered to finance the power. Residential housing is a case in point. State and local governments do not provide housing at the taxpayers' expense (i.e., GO bonds), but they are empowered, and in some cases, mandated to provide safe, decent, and affordable housing within their jurisdictions. Conduits enable the public purpose to be financed.

State and local agencies: State agencies (also called authorities) are public corporations established by the state legislature as independent public entities—and independent of the state itself—to fulfill a state purpose. This may seem an oxymoron, but the separation of the entity from the state has been upheld as beyond judicial judgment when the agency is fulfilling a state purpose (i.e., education, housing, transportation, healthcare facilities) under "complicated financing schemes." Thus, enabling legislation for state agencies expressly disclaims any liability of the state itself with respect to the agency's debt, and most challenges to collapse an agency's debt into unauthorized state constitutional debt have failed. The same holds true for local agencies that are established through special state legislation or under a general state statute that prescribes procedures for a local government to undertake (resolutions, hearings, referenda, etc.) to establish the local agency. Again, enabling legislation always disclaims that the local agency's debt is not that of the sponsoring local government or the state. The taxing power is never granted to state or local agencies, although taxes collected by the taxing jurisdiction may be assigned or appropriated from the general fund once commingled with other revenue, to pay debt service on the agency's debt. As we have seen in the principal cases in Part F, it is this annual bleeding of public money into conduit debt which offends constitutional restrictions on incurring state or local government debt.

Special districts with their own borrowing power. Special districts, or improvement districts, are also conduits if they are authorized under state law to borrow in their own name, separate and apart from the local government. Their borrowing is supported by revenues consistent with the Special Fund doctrine: special assessments for public purposes (water, sewer. roads, parks and recreation, lighting, etc.) specifically benefiting property or persons on property as discussed above. Special districts are generally established by the properties or persons to be benefitted and burdened through petitions, hearings, resolutions and referenda. Special districts are never established on motion of the governing body of the local government without right to appeal by those to be affected. If the special district is independently organized, it may escape the constitutional debt limitation altogether if it is found not to be among the governmental units to which the constitutional provision applies. *Albuquerque Metro. Arroyo Flood Control Auth. v. Swinburne*, 394 P.2d 998 (N.M. 1964). Even if the constitutional debt limitation applies, the special district will be entitled to its own debt limit or its debt excluded from calculation of the debt limit of the local government. The creation of overlapping special districts may be challenged in court, however. For a case taking the position that the creation of additional special districts overlaying existing units of government is not reviewable, see *Carlisle v. Bangor Recreation Center*, 103 A.2d 339 (Me. 1954). See also *Directors of La. Recovery Dist. v. Taxpayers*, 529 So. 2d 384 (La. 1988) (statewide special district with separate tax and debt limitations upheld).

The same result as to the validity of a special district's revenue bonds occurs when user fees are charged based on a measure tied to real property factors. Where a special district is established to perform a service function for which a user charge may be assessed, courts are often willing to extend the revenue bond theory applicable to special assessments—no unconstitutional debt.

On-behalf-of issuers. The term "on-behalf-of" to describe a conduit issuer is borrowed from federal tax law, in which the interest on this type of issue is exempt from federal income tax (see Part H). The issuer may be a governmental entity but is often a not-for-profit corporation that under state law may assist government through its power to borrow "on-behalf-of" a local government. An example of an on-behalf-of issuer is the Sales Tax Receivables Corporation, a not-for-profit which issued debt on behalf of New York City to refund MACC bonds discussed in *LGAC v. STARC, supra*. Local agencies that finance housing projects are also, for tax purposes, on-behalf-of issuers because they finance a purpose of local government for which local governments lack the power to finance.

Documenting the financing. The documentation of conduit financings involves more parties than full faith and credit GOs, issued directly by a state or local government. In the case of GOs the transaction parties are the issuer and the bond or note purchaser. The bonds are authorized by the governing body, and if sold by public sale, simply delivered to the purchaser with appropriate closing certificates and opinions. If GO bonds are sold at private sale, the issuer and purchaser also enter an agreement stipulating the terms under which purchaser will pay for and take delivery of the bonds. As real property taxes are collected, the issuer's CFO funds the debt service account in the annual budget before the dates payment of principal and interest is due. Similar documentation applies if revenue bonds are issued—special assessments, water rents, electricity charges, and other utility-type payments are segregated by the issuer's CFO applied to debt service on the bonds—this is the Special Fund Doctrine working as intended.

A conduit is often not much more than a paper entity without a full-time sophisticated financial management staff. Even where the conduit is a large state agency, the protection afford investors in GO issues—real property tax levy, enforcement of liens and resort to mandamus to compel the issuer to honor the full faith and credit pledge—is not available. Accordingly, conduit issuers interpose an independent trustee, usually a commercial bank with trust powers, to collect revenues and pay them over to investors. This arrangement requires that the issuer enter into an "indenture of trust" with the trustee in which revenues are assigned by the issuer to the trustee as collected. The trustee works for the investors. It is, for the bond issuer, the issuer's debt manager, making sure sufficient revenues are collected, including legislative appropriations, held for investment until needed, then paid to investors. In *Chemical v. WPPSS*, *supra*, Chemical Bank was the trustee, and the lawsuit was about the trustee's exercising its powers on behalf of investors to recover funds from the issuer to pay investors who held defaulted bonds. The default, you will recall, was the result of the State of Washington's failure to pay WPPSS under its "take or pay" contracts on the basis that they were invalid as unconstitutional debt.

The role of the trustee. A trustee in a conduit financing must have trust powers conferred by state law. It is highly unusual that an individual or an entity that is not a financial institution would act of trustee in a bond issuer. As such, the trustee is liable to the issuer and the investor if it does not follow the precise instructions contained in the trust indenture as to the deposit and application of revenues, the payment of bonds and interest thereon, and the enforcement of investors' rights to payment of their bonds. One of the key features of the trust indenture is the "flow of funds," i.e., the order of priority in which revenues as received are applied to accounts established in the trust indenture. We have a glimpse of the "flow of funds" process in the court's opinion in *Massy I*, *infra*, where the decision recites: ". . . [t]hey [meaning the county, city and other political subdivisions] agree to pay that amount by which the 'operating expenses' exceed the revenues from the transit system *after provision is first made for debt service and reserve requirements for the revenue bonds issued by the Authority* . . ." (emphasis supplied). Here the court acknowledges the flow of funds established in the indenture, where the transit system revenues as received must be applied first to the debt service account and the debt service reserve account (so investors' risk of default is minimized) before applying revenues to the operating account and lower tier accounts. If the trustee is requested to take action under the indenture by the issuer or investors, which it believes is not expressly stated in the duties of the trustee, the trustee may seek an opinion of legal counsel that it is empowered to so act.

Notes and Questions

Guaranty of conduit obligations as constitutional debt. Conduit financing invokes an examination of issuing unconstitutional GO debt when the GO issue contracts with a conduit to make up shortfalls in its revenues to pay its debt service. Investors and underwriters are eager for a guarantee in a conduit financing where operating revenues, not the largesse of government appropriations, is the only revenue supporting debt service. It is a valuable technique to fudge the economics of a revenue bond issue to the Special Fund Doctrine with back-door government funding to eliminate risk of default and make the conduit bonds more attractive to investors.

But the courts are wise to this approach. In *Board of Supervisors v. Massey*, 169 S.E.2d 556 (Va. 1969) ("*Massey I*"), the governing bodies of Fairfax County and the City of Falls Church sought mandamus to compel their respective CFOs to enter into a "Transit Service Agreement" (the "Agreement") with the Washington Metropolitan Area Transit Authority (the "Authority") a body corporate and politic and an agency and instrumentality of each of the signatory parties thereto, established under an interstate agreement between Virginia, Maryland, and the District of Columbia, to plan, develop, finance, and provide improved transit facilities and service for the Washington metropolitan area. Under the terms of the Agreement, notwithstanding that the Authority's engineers estimated that fare box receipts would be sufficient to pay operating costs and debt service Authority bonds, just in case they were not, the county and city and other political subdivisions who were parties to the Agreement agreed to make payments for transportation services to the Authority in order for the Authority to pay its obligations, including debt service on its bonds.

The obvious question in the case is: Do the terms of the Agreement constitute unconstitutional debt of the county, city and other political subdivision signatories? Petitioners argued the principle that a local government may lawfully contract for necessary services such as water, electricity, or sewerage, over a period of years and agree to pay therefore in periodic installments as the services are furnished; such contracts do not give rise to a present indebtedness and such contracts are not rendered invalid by the fact that the aggregate of the installments exceeds their debt limitation as the U.S. Supreme Court held in the *Walla Walla Water Company*, discussed *supra*. But, said the Virginia Supreme Court after an examination of the Virginia constitution's debt incurrence limits:

> We do not think, however, that the principle relied on is applicable in the present cases. Our examination of the authorities cited by the petitioners did not reveal a single case in which the local governments underwrote or guaranteed the deficit incurred in the operation of the facilities furnishing the services under their contracts.... Although the County's and City's contract is designated a "Transit Service Agreement," the label placed upon it does not necessarily make it such. The obligations of the County and City under the Agreement are for more than just payments for transit service. They agree to pay that amount by which the "operating expenses" exceed the revenues from the transit system after provision is first made for debt service and reserve requirements for the revenue bonds issued by the Authority ... Thus we hold that the obligations of the County and City under the Agreement constitute debt or indebtedness within the meaning of the constitutional prohibitions of §§ 115(a) and 127 and under the charter provisions of the City of Falls Church.... [*Id.* at 19–22.]

Following *Massey I*, the parties went back to their desks and law libraries and drafted new agreements providing for Fairfax County and the City of Falls Church to make payments to the Authority for transit services based on the number of train miles operated within the county and the city and the number of their residents using the system. In *Board of Supvrs. v. Massey*, 173 S.E.2d 869 (Va. 1970) ("*Massey II*"), the court approved the arrangement as a valid service contract. Did the change in the method of calculating the charge really justify the reversal in the court's opinion? Yes, because in the first *Massey* case, the obligations of the county and city were open ended guaranties not measured by any consideration: patrons of the Authority's transit system could have ridden for free and the taxpayers of the county and city and other political subdivision signatories would have had to pay for the Authority's operating expenses and debt service. For the Special Fund Doctrine to work properly there must be consideration for the debt obligation: revenues.

That point is made in *Utah Power & Light Co. v. Campbell*, 703 P.2d 714 (Idaho 1985), where the Idaho Supreme Court upheld a ground lease and power sale contract in which the city leased land from a private utility upon which the city agreed to construct a hydroelectric project, and agreed to sell a portion of the energy produced by the project to the utility for a period in excess of the proposed term of general obligation bonds approved for the project by the electorate. Rejecting arguments that the arrangement constituted an illegal extension of credit to a private corporation, the court held that the agreement was not a loan "in which the public credit is under the control of private interests," but rather "an arms-length contract, based on the exchange of adequate consideration," which "insures a source of revenue to assist in paying the bonds. . . ." *Id.* at 718.

By contrast, the Supreme Court of Georgia struck down an agreement between the City of Atlanta and the Downtown Development Authority (DDA), a public agency, in which the city agreed to make up 90% of any shortfall in revenue from a leasing scheme to finance the redevelopment of a "festival marketplace" known as Underground Atlanta. *Nations v. Downtown Dev. Auth.*, 338 S.E.2d 240 (Ga. 1985) (*Nations I*). Under the agreement, the city would lease the property to the DDA, who would sublease the commercial portion to a private developer who would in turn sublease to commercial tenants. The court held that the city's guarantee constituted an illegal debt, and not an exception to the debt clause authorized by the intergovernmental contracts clause of the state constitution, because the guarantee was "not a contract for services . . . facilities or equipment" nor was it "an activity, service or facility which the city [was] authorized by law to undertake or provide." *Id.* One year later, the same court upheld as a valid intergovernmental contract an agreement in which the city would acquire the project property, convey it to DDA, then lease it back from DDA and sublease it to a private developer who in turn would sublease it to commercial tenants. The city also pledged to make up any deficits in the rents the city would be obligated to pay. *Nations v. Downtown Dev. Auth.*, 345 S.E.2d 581 (Ga. 1986) (*Nations II*). Are the cases distinguishable? Is the fact that the contracting party was a private company in the Idaho case and a public entity in the Georgia case important? Hint: Intergovernmental lending between the state and its political subdivisions and agencies, or among its political subdivisions or agencies is not "lending of credit." The prohibition applies to lending money or credit to corporations and persons who are not part of the government. For additional discussion of intergovernmental cooperation see Chapter 3, *supra*.

F. Economic Development Finance

[1] Introduction to Economic Development

Economic development encompasses a state's policies and state and local government practices of using governmental entities, and sometimes public funds, to provide financial assistance to private sector entities for the public purpose of providing public facilities or economically improving the local or regional economy. The policies and practices are applied in three categories: (i) borrowing money to finance economic development projects with a view of lowering the cost of financing through the federal income exemption on interest, (ii) providing state tax incentives with a view of reducing the cost of operating a business, and (iii) recouping the cost of providing government services for new development. The consideration for borrowing and state tax incentives is the elimination of blight, creation of employment, the strengthening of the real property and other tax basis by developing facilities which increase economic activity.

Economic development began in the Great Depression. A town in Mississippi attempted to issue general obligation bonds to make a loan to a hosiery company to build a factory to increase employment. In *Albritton v. City of Winona*, 178 So. 799 (Miss. 1938) the Mississippi Supreme Court analyzed the statute authorizing municipalities to levy a tax for the purpose of purchasing land and constructing buildings thereon to be leased to individuals or private corporations to operate manufacturing establishments in order to relieve unemployment and promote agricultural and industrial welfare of the state and to issue its general obligation bonds therefor. The court held that the statute (i) did not violate the due process clauses of State and Federal Constitutions; (ii) retained power in the municipality by requiring the lease to be of such character as will insure the continued operation of the proposed industry, under supervision of the state Industrial Commission, to enforce the continued operation, to best promote and protect the public interest, and to constitute the lessee as the municipality's agent for operating the industry without liability on the municipality or others arising therefrom, (iii) did not violate the Constitution prohibiting appropriation of property to private individuals or corporations where the lease must contain provisions giving the municipality power to enforce use of property for such purposes, and (iv) did not violate the Constitution prohibiting the state from pledging or loaning its credit in aid of any person, association, or corporation.

Albritton is a radical departure from financing facilities used by the general public with either GOs or revenue bonds, issued either directly by the state or local government under state constitutional debt incurring restraints or by a conduit state or local agency (often referred to as "traditional finance"). First, it expands the definition of public purpose beyond a thing financed for public use to the improvement of the economic condition of the community as a whole. Second, it violates prohibitions on lending or gift of credit clauses because bond proceeds were paid directly to a private sector entity in the form of a loan or lease. Third, notions of tax uniformity and proportionality between cost and benefits are of no concern because debt service was paid by a private business. Fourth, there was no gift of public property in conveying land or loaning funds to a private business because the private sector borrower/lessee acted as the agent of the issuer. Fifth, there was no pledge of the issuer's faith and credit because it was, by agreement, not liable on the bonds.

Mississippi's pioneering decision initiating economic development finance was not shared by all states. As late as the 1960s, courts in Idaho, one of the last states to embrace economic development finance, invalidated a statute that authorized a municipality to issue bonds for the acquisition of manufacturing, industrial or commercial enterprises and a village ordinance providing for acquisition by the village of a site and the construction of an industrial plant thereon to be leased to a corporation which would occupy and use the plant in a private manufacturing enterprise because it was in violation of state constitutional prohibition against any municipality lending its credit in aid of a corporation, notwithstanding that the bonds were revenue bonds and that there would be only an incidental benefit to the corporation. See *Village of Moyie Springs v. Aurora Manufacturing Company*, 353 P.2d 767 (Idaho 1960).

Beginning in the 1960s, economic development became an important state program to attract business and industry. By 1967 industrial development bonds ("IDBs") were issued in 40 states totaling over $1 billion. (See Memorandum accompanying letter, 23 January 1968 from Stanley S. Surrey, Asst. Sec'y of the Treasury, to Representative Wilbur D. Mills, Chairman of House Ways and Means Committee. CCH Standard Fed. Tax Reporter (1968) at 71,136–37.) The financing aspect, if state law would cooperate, was attractive because federal income tax laws at the time did not distinguish between bonds issued for traditional finance and economic development finance, meaning the private sector borrower could obtain funds at lower interest rates than through bank loans or corporate finance. The cases that tested the legality of economic development finance in the 1955–1980s period struggled with the issues raised in *Albritton* and *Moyie Springs*. Courts were not favorably disposed to permit general obligation bonds to be used for economic development financing even if the state and local government liability was disclaimed. See, e.g., *State ex rel. Beck v. City of York*, 82 N.W.2d 269 (Neb. 1957).

It became customary for state legislatures to establish new conduits for economic development finance to overcome the friction with existing state constitutional and statutory debt restraints and limitations. As we have seen, conduits go to great length to stress their independence from the state or local government, primarily for this reason. Housing authorities and urban renewal agencies were already familiar conduits for affordable residential rental housing and downtown redevelopment to capture federal funds for these programs starting in the 1950s. Many state legislatures continued the pattern, establishing "economic development authorities" ("EDAs") as independent political subdivisions of the state to issue this type of revenue bond and administer economic development incentives, primarily tax abatements. These types of bonds are referred to generically as "industrial development bonds," a term to describe them adopted in the Internal Revenue Code, as well.

Today, if a private company seeks state financial assistance for an economic development project, it looks for a "package of economic benefits" to reduce its borrowing and operating costs: (i) low interest tax-exempt bonds, (ii) abatement of taxes and fees, including a payment-in-lieu-of-taxes agreement (referred to as a "PILOT"), (iii) tax increment financing ("TIF"), if available, and (iv) the least cost from exactions or impact fees as a condition to land use permits. Are these cost reductions more than an incidental benefit? Where is the compelling public purpose and by what standards is it determined?

Economic development initiatives accordingly raise a variety of legal and policy issues. A threshold question is whether a local government entity has the authority to engage in economic development activities, either in its own right, in partnership with private parties, or as a facilitator of private activities designed to address certain public purposes. Authority of different local government entities may vary, and increasingly special authorities have been created to facilitate economic development rather than relying on general purpose local governments to undertake related tasks. In addition, a variety of constitutional questions may be raised. At times business interests ask government entities to condemn private property to facilitate "assemblage" of land desired for development (raising questions under the "eminent domain" provisions of federal and state constitutions requiring condemnation to be used only for "public use" upon payment of "just compensation"). If public funds are to be expended, then "public purpose" requirements (a distinct notion that should be considered apart from "public use" for "takings" purposes) must be satisfied. Many states have "lending of credit" limitations that have historically been incorporated into state constitutions to protect the public against steps legislatures might take to subsidize private ventures leaving the public at risk. Questions may also be raised regarding debt, whether various forms of finance should be regarded as "debt," what entity is responsible for debt service and on what terms, and whether debt limits apply. A variety of issues are also raised under state and local laws regarding borrowing that may be associated with such ventures, including whether the participating public entity is eligible to foster projects using tax-preferred debt. For a discussion of tax-exempt bonds, see Congressional Research Service, RL30638, *Tax Exempt Bonds: A Description of State and Local Debt*, https://crsreports.congress.gov/product/pdf/RL/RL30638 (2018). https://crsreports.congress.gov/product/pdf/RL/RL30638.

Legal and policy issues are also often intertwined. Many local governments have employed "tax increment financing" (TIF) as a means to facilitate economic development in particular areas, using the anticipated stream of increased property tax revenues as a means to repay associated debt, as discussed more fully below. Such strategies have been challenged on a number of grounds including whether this tactic should be treated as "debt" subject to debt limitations, and whether it is advisable to segregate increased property value in certain areas as a means of repaying costs of improvement rather than allocating incremental value increases and associated tax revenue for general purposes.

Another area that has given rise to significant debates is whether the increasing tendency of state and local governments to try to lure corporate entities to their jurisdictions in the hopes of fostering job creation actually give rise to employment opportunities that would not otherwise exist. Moreover, there are questions about whether associated practices help the "haves" rather than "have nots" (that is, whether such programs amount to "corporate welfare"), whether corporate entities would relocate quite apart from such incentives and are simply receiving subsidies for decisions that they might have reached without the incentives offered, and whether promises made by relocating corporations are actually being honored. Both of the policy issues just highlighted—the legitimacy of TIF financing, and the value of economic relocation incentives—are explored in more depth below.

[2] Industrial Development Bonds

Industrial development bonds ("IDBs") start with the basic elements of traditional finance found in GOs and revenue bonds: the bond issuer and the bond purchaser. As noted elsewhere in this Chapter, where a conduit issuer is involved, a trustee is required to administer the receipt of revenues and the payment of debt service on behalf of bondholders through an indenture of trust. The revenues are always paid by users of a public facility (water, sewer, etc.) or the issuer itself through annual appropriations or a moral pledge. The only involvement of a private sector entity is as a contract vendor: pipe and value manufacturer, water tank contractor, road paving contractor, etc. The contract vendor has no interest in the financing of the project other than to perform its duties under a contract and be paid from bond proceeds for what is owed under the contract.

In economic development finance, the private sector entity becomes a party to the transaction because it, not the state or local government, is obliged to fulfill the public purpose of the state and local government as agent for the economic development agency ("EDA")—create jobs, eliminate blight, improve general welfare, etc. Alternatively, the private sector entity is obliged to construct a facility for public use: solid waste treatment facility, hospital, fiber optic cable network, etc. In an IDB, we have a three-party transaction: the issuer, the bond purchaser, and the private sector borrower (as well as the trustee administering the trust indenture). How these parties are obligated contractually should be viewed as a commercial transaction between the private sector entity and the bond purchaser. The EDA is in the transaction solely to provide financial assistance: a low-interest rate loan to the borrower and tax incentive for the borrower arising from the EDA's ownership of the project. Yet the EDA needs to be a transaction party to confer these benefits to the borrower. In our three-party transaction, the EDA owns the project and leases it to the private sector borrower. The rent on the lease equals or exceeds the debt service on the bonds. The EDA assigns the rents to the trustee to pay the bondholders. As owner of the project, the indenture may require that bondholders hold a mortgage on the project so the project can be foreclosed and liquidated if the project fails to generate revenue or the borrower defaults in rent payments. This basic structure of an IDB can, of course, take on many variations and permutations. But keep it in mind when reading the following case. Can you identify the issuer of the bonds? How about the private sector borrower? This case discusses many issues on the validity of IDBs under state law, particularly whether the borrowing fulfills a public purpose.

WDW Properties v. City of Sumter

342 S.C. 6, 535 S.E.2d 631 (2000)

WALLER, JUSTICE:

WDW Properties (WDW) brought a declaratory judgment action challenging the legitimacy of a program in which the proceeds of tax-exempt bonds issued by a state agency would be loaned to a developer renovating retail and commercial properties in a blighted area of the city of Sumter (City). A master-in-equity rejected WDW's claims after a bench trial and WDW appeals.

The parties have stipulated to the following facts. The Internal Revenue Code authorizes the use of federally tax-exempt local government bonds that finance business enterprises in designated urban "empowerment zones." The secretary of the United States Department of Housing and Urban Development (HUD), at the request of local government officials, in 1998 declared about 18 square miles located in Richland and Sumter counties as an urban empowerment zone. The governing body of City in 1999 declared its downtown to be a "slum and blight area" and designated it as a "redevelopment project area" located in the empowerment zone.

An area is eligible for designation as an "empowerment zone" only if it meets criteria that relate to population, economic distress, geographic area, and poverty rates. Such areas are nominated by local governments in a competitive process. Designations are effective for ten years unless revoked earlier by HUD. A commercial, retail, or service business in an empowerment zone qualifies for tax-exempt financing if at least thirty-five percent of its employees live in the empowerment zone, and most of its income and property are generated by or engaged in the business in the empowerment zone.

Uptown Synergy plans to develop the Hampton at Main Project, located in the redevelopment project area. The $4.3 million project consists of interior and exterior renovations of three adjoining historic buildings, which would be leased for commercial office and retail space. The project is expected to create twenty full-time jobs, and the developer hopes to target low- and moderate-income persons for employment at the various offices and retail businesses. In its application for financing to the South Carolina Jobs-Economic Development Authority (JEDA), Uptown Synergy stated the project would "serve as the cornerstone for the revitalization of downtown Sumter and the surrounding communities."

JEDA's governing board adopted a resolution in which it pledged to seek authorization from the state Budget and Control Board to issue $2.5 million in economic development revenue bonds that would be exempt from state and federal income taxation. Under loan documents executed in 1999, JEDA would loan the bond proceeds to Uptown Synergy to finance about 58 percent of the project's cost. Uptown Synergy would repay the loan with revenue from the project. No tax money is involved or pledged with regard to the project. However, the tax-exempt nature of the bonds would result in lower interest costs to Uptown Synergy than it would pay if it had to obtain conventional financing.

WDW, a general partnership, owns and leases Liberty Square, which includes mini-warehouse units, retail businesses, and commercial office space. Liberty Square is not located in the empowerment zone and is not eligible for government-sponsored financing. Uptown Synergy's project would compete with Liberty Square for tenants and patrons. The apparent reason for WDW's lawsuit is its belief that government-sponsored financing gives Uptown Synergy an unfair economic advantage in the competition for tenants and patrons.

Did the master err in holding that the JEDA loan program serves a public purpose through the redevelopment of blighted urban areas? . . .

WDW contends the master erred in ruling that the JEDA loan program at issue in this case serves a public purpose through the redevelopment of blighted urban areas. The master erred by reading *Carll v. South Carolina Jobs-Economic Development Authority*, 327 S.E.2d 331 (S.C. 1985), to mean that so long as the issuance of a given series of bonds is authorized by the JEDA Act, then the issuance of such bonds necessarily serves a required public purpose. *Carll* should be interpreted only to hold that the issuance of revenue bonds to finance industrial facilities serves a public purpose, a principle previously established by this Court, WDW argues.

WDW bases its argument on the fact that, when *Carll* was decided in 1985, JEDA regulations prohibited loans to retail or food establishments. Current JEDA regulations allow economic development bond loans to commercial businesses in certain situations, including downtown redevelopment and in economically distressed areas. WDW believes those regulatory changes mean *Carll* is not dispositive. . . .

JEDA regulations were first promulgated in 1984. The regulation at issue initially stated, as it did when *Carll* was decided, that: A. [JEDA] will make loans only to manufacturing, industrial, or service businesses which: (1) Operate as private "for profit" enterprises; and (2) Have a net worth not exceeding three million dollars; and (3) Have a net profit after taxes averaging 20% or less of net worth for the previous three years. B. No loans will be made to: (1) Retail establishments; (2) Food establishments. The regulation was amended in 1985 after *Carll* was decided to provide: A. [JEDA] will make loans to manufacturing, industrial, service, and other commercial businesses which: (1) Operate as private "for profit" enterprises. B. No loans will be made to: (1) Retail establishments except where downtown redevelopment is involved; (2) Food establishments. The regulation was last amended in

1987 and has since remained unchanged. It presently provides: A. [JEDA] will make Community Development Block Grant loans, economic development bond loans, on either a tax-exempt or taxable basis, and loans from any other program funds which become available, to manufacturing, industrial, research, service, commercial and other businesses which: (1) Are located in South Carolina; and (2) Create or maintain jobs in South Carolina. B. No economic development bond loans or Community Development Block Grant loans will be made to: (1) Commercial establishments, including hotels, shopping malls, office buildings, and mercantile establishments, except where downtown redevelopment is involved or where located in an economically distressed area or where it will result in increased employment; provided, however, that in the case of hotels, loans may also be made regardless of location for projects which will have a higher than usual promotional impact upon the tourism industry in the State; and provided further that, in the case of medical facilities, loans may also be made regardless of location where there has been a showing that the assistance will help relieve a shortage of doctors, specialists or medical services in the area where the project is located; (2) Restaurant establishments except where such establishments are located on the premises of a hotel and for which economic development bonds are being issued.

WDW urges us to follow the views expressed in *State ex rel. McLeod v. Riley*, 278 S.E.2d 612 (S.C. 1981), and *Anderson v. Baehr*, 217 S.E.2d 43 (S.C. 1975). In *McLeod*, this Court considered amendments to the Industrial Revenue Bond Act that allowed the issuance of revenue bonds for the benefit of commercial and retail facilities. The Court also considered a statute allowing the State to issue general obligation bonds to finance an alcohol fuel development program. The Court struck down both the amendments and the statute as unconstitutional, ruling, among other things, that neither primarily served a public purpose. The *McLeod* Court stated that revenue bonds for retail and commercial businesses would provide only a "remote or indirect public benefit." Such businesses would not alleviate the pervasive problems of lack of industry and employment, would provide a minuscule number of jobs compared to industrial projects, and would merely result either in the relocation of existing businesses or importation of national chains to compete with existing businesses. Approving the issuance of revenue bonds for retail and commercial businesses would "permit local governments to effectually promote undertakings to compete in free enterprise with other businesses which do not have the advantage which the Act would give."

In *Anderson, supra*, the city of Spartanburg intended to issue revenue bonds in order to purchase property in blighted areas (through condemnation if necessary), find an interested developer, and lease or sell the property to the developer in the hope that such payments would cover repayment of the city-issued bonds. The Court held that the act, which it described as allowing the city to "join hands" with unknown private developers, did not serve a public purpose because the benefit to the developer would be substantial, while the benefit to the public would be negligible and speculative. The Court also noted the Legislature had not made any findings of public purpose in the act. . . . In response, City argues that *Carll*, supra, is dispositive. City further asserts that the views expressed in *McLeod* and *Anderson* have been implicitly rejected by later cases in which this Court has taken a broader view of public purpose and exhibited greater deference to the legislative determinations regarding public purpose. The public purpose doctrine "is an evolving concept that reflects the changing needs of society." Even if *Carll* is not dispositive, the JEDA loan program in this case serves a public purpose, City asserts.

Revenue bonds such as those that JEDA would issue in this case are payable solely from the revenues of the particular project or enterprise, not from taxpayer funds. . . . Revenue bond debt, as well as general obligation debt incurred by the government and repaid by government funds, may be incurred only for a public purpose. S.C. Const. art. X, § 13(9); *Elliott*, (holding that Industrial Revenue Bond Act serves a public purpose as required by state constitution); *Feldman & Co. v. City Council of Charleston*, 23 S.C. 57, 62–63 (1885) (holding that a law authorizing taxation for any purpose other than a public purpose is void).

In *Carll*, we rejected several constitutional challenges to the 1983 act creating JEDA. In discussing whether the Act served a public purpose, we explained that "[a]ll legislative action must serve a public rather than a private purpose. In general, a public purpose has for its objective the promotion of the public health, morals, general welfare, security, prosperity, and contentment of all the inhabitants or residents within a given political division. . . . It is a fluid concept which changes with time, place, population, economy, and countless other circumstances. It is a reflection of the changing needs of society. . . . We held that the JEDA Act served a public purpose because its provisions were reasonably related to the legitimate public goals of economic development and job creation. We observed the Legislature's findings regarding the State's economic development problems were "detailed and comprehensive."

We agree with WDW that *Carll* is not dispositive. *Carll* did not involve any particular bond issue or loan, but was an attack on the facial validity of the act creating JEDA. More importantly, regulations then in existence prohibited JEDA from making government-sponsored loans to retail or commercial businesses. JEDA regulations were amended in 1987 to allow such loans in certain situations. A statutory or regulatory change could transform a previously constitutional loan program into one that violates the public purpose doctrine. Therefore, *Carll* should not be read to foreclose challenges to JEDA programs simply because a given loan does not violate JEDA's statutory or regulatory framework as it exists when the loan is proposed or made.

However, we hold that the JEDA loan program in this case serves a public purpose as required by the constitution. We adhere to the views espoused in *Carll* and *Nichols v. South Carolina Research Authority*, 351 S.E.2d 155 (S.C. 1986). In *Nichols*, we upheld a statute authorizing a state agency to issue revenue bonds in order to provide financial assistance to advanced technology businesses. We overruled *Byrd v. County of Florence*, 315 S.E.2d 804 (S.C. 1984), in which we had struck down on public purpose grounds Florence County's proposal to issue general obligation bonds to acquire and develop an industrial park to be used to attract industrial investment. In *Nichols*, we extensively discussed the public purpose doctrine and its inconsistent application in various cases over the years. We explained that "[t]imes change. The wants and necessities of the people change.... On the one hand, what could not be deemed a public use a century ago may, because of changed economic and industrial conditions, be such today."

The consensus of modern legislative and judicial thinking is to broaden the scope of activities which may be classed as involving a public purpose. It reaches perhaps its broadest extent under the view: that economic welfare is one of the main concerns of the city, state and the federal governments. The views we express here reflect the decisions of multiple other jurisdictions which recognize industrial development as a public purpose.

Finally, legislation may subserve a public purpose even though it (1) benefits some more than others and, (2) results in profit to individuals. Legislation does not have to benefit all of the people in order to serve a public purpose. At the same time legislation is not for a private purpose merely because some individual makes a profit as a result of the enactment. We emphasized anew that "[i]t is uniformly held by courts throughout the land that the determination of public purpose is one for the legislative branch.... The question of whether an Act is for a public purpose is primarily one for the Legislature."

We reached a similar conclusion in *Wolper*, decided the year before *Nichols*. In *Wolper*, we upheld the constitutionality of a statute that allows cities to incur debt to revitalize deteriorating areas, with the debt service to be provided from the increased increments of property tax revenue resulting from the redevelopment project. We concluded that elimination of decaying and unhealthy areas within a city directly benefits the public, although private parties within the area also may benefit incidentally.

Although we overruled *Byrd*, *supra*, in *Nichols*, we adopted the four-part test from *Byrd* to use in determining whether the public purpose doctrine is violated. "The Court should first determine the ultimate goal or benefit to the public intended by the project. Second, the Court should analyze whether public or private parties will be the primary beneficiaries. Third, the speculative nature of the project must be considered. Fourth, the Court must analyze and balance the probability that the public interest will be ultimately served and to what degree."

Accordingly, we apply the *Nichols* test in this case. First, the ultimate benefits to the public are to increase the number of jobs available, improve the appearance of rundown buildings in Sumter's downtown, attract new businesses, and reinvigorate a downtown area that has been classified by the local and federal governments as economically distressed. Second, deferring to the Legislature's determination in establishing the JEDA program-the public will be the primary beneficiary, although the developers certainly will benefit from a more favorable loan rate. Third, the project is speculative, as is any redevelopment effort, but it is not so speculative that it violates the public purpose doctrine. And fourth, the public interest is likely to be served to a substantial degree through the creation of jobs, the reinvigoration of the downtown area, and benefits, both tangible and intangible that should result from that reinvigoration.

We conclude that our opinion in *Nichols* implicitly overruled *McLeod*'s holding that revenue bonds may not be issued on behalf of retail or commercial businesses. We now take a broader view of the public purpose doctrine and give substantial weight to legislative determinations of the issue.... [T]he role of City and JEDA in this case is more limited in that neither is actively promoting business undertakings to compete in free enterprise with other local businesses.

We affirm the master's ruling that the JEDA loan program serves a public purpose as required by the state constitution.

AFFIRMED.

Notes and Questions

1. *Public purpose.* Following the Panic of 1837 and the defaults on railroad and canal bonds, state legislatures began imposing state constitutional restraints on the "public purpose" reviewed earlier in this Chapter to protect taxpayers and ratepayers against the pressures of private businesses to obtain funding for their projects from the states, even if those projects serve the public. For the remainder of the nineteenth century courts honored the divide between public purpose and private benefit set forth in state constitutions. During this period, the public purpose requirement operated to constrain the scope of state and local governments, resulting in the invalidation of a host of economic development and social welfare programs that state courts found benefitted private, not public, interests. A century later, conduit financing had been firmly imbedded in public finance jurisprudence. Nearly every state supreme court had upheld economic development programs that involve direct assistance—including cash grants, low-interest loans, loan guaranties, and tax abatements—to private sector sponsored projects.

Significant cases expanding the definition of public purpose include *Common Cause v. State,* 455 A.2d 1 (Me. 1983), in which the Maine Supreme Court upheld the state's plan to commit $15 million in taxpayer funds to improve the facilities of the Bath Iron Works in order to persuade the company to remain in the state, and *Hayes v. State Property & Buildings Commission,* 731 S.W.2d 797 (Ky. 1987) in which the Kentucky Supreme Court upheld a package of inducements worth over $125 and $268 million to induce Toyota Motor Corporation to open a plant in the state. Although courts have tried to supervise the expansion of "public purpose," they have taken a posture of extreme deference to state legislatures, finding that a broad range of goals fall under the rubric of public purpose, and that legislative determinations that a spending, loan, or tax incentive program will promote the public purpose are to be accepted as long as they are "not ... irrational" and rejected "only if it is 'clear and palpable' that there can be no benefit to the public." Because the states are split on the law—whether state financial incentives are a public purpose, or lending of credit, or invalid constitutional debt—given similar facts, no uniform measurement test is recognized.

2. *Competing projects.* Economic development programs raise concerns that they create a zero-sum game. That was the point of plaintiff in *WDW Properties*, i.e., that assisting one business would give it a competitive advantage that would act to the detriment of another business. This problem has been raised in anti-pirating statutes, which forbid EDAs within a state to cause businesses to move around looking for the best financial assistance package. In *Matter of Main Seneca Corporation v. Town of Amherst Industrial Development Agency*, 792 N.E.2d 1067 (N.Y. 2003), the Court of Appeals found that an EDA's approval of a project that caused a business to move "from one area of the state to another area of the state" where it also received financial assistance from an EDA violated the IDB statute, causing the business that moved to reimburse real property taxes avoided in the jurisdiction it moved from.

3. *Retail facilities.* Many courts do not view lending financial assistance for expansion of retail operations to be a public purpose under EDA statutes. For example, in *McDonald's Corp. v. De Venney*, 415 So. 2d 1075 (Ala. 1982), the Alabama Supreme Court held an expansion of McDonald's fast-food facilities not to be an industrial or commercial facility under the EDA statute. Likewise, in *Orange County Indus. Development Authority v. State*, 427 So. 2d 174 (Fla. 1983), the court held that financing the expansion of a commercial television station was an invalid purpose, because there was little or no new employment or other public benefit stemming from the project. But in *Allen v. City of Minot*, 363 N.W.2d 553 (N.D. 1985), the court held that if the recitals in the IDBs say the bonds have been properly authorized, the court need not look further to determine whether IDBs issued to renovate an existing shopping center was a public purpose.

4. *New prototypes: athletics facilities.* In recent days, the development of athletics stadiums has provided a new prototype for urban economic development initiatives. Often professional teams seek support from local governments to build expanded stadium facilities, and governments may in turn develop partnerships that secure funding streams for such improvements based on hotel taxes, meal taxes, sales or excise taxes, property tax increases that can be redeployed to repay TIF bonds, and a variety of other tools. Consider what legal questions may be raised by such arrangements. For example, do they serve a "public purpose"? If land is condemned for facility improvements, are eminent domain requirements regarding "public use" satisfied? Are associated borrowings to be treated as "debt" and subject to debt limitations? What legal issues may be raised by diverting increased property tax revenues to repay associated debt? What processes may be required to guide association municipal decisions? How do public meetings and public records requirements apply? Numerous articles have been written on related issues. See, e.g., Baker, *Playing a Man Down: Professional Sports and Stadium Finance—How Leagues and*

Franchises Extract Favorable Terms from American Cities, 59 B.C. L. Rev. 281 (2018). TIFs are considered in more detail *infra*.

5. *Mortgages securing IDBs*. Because the source of debt service payments in an IDB is the revenues from the project financed with the proceeds thereof or the general obligation of private sector entity itself, bondholders and lenders attempt to secure their investment with a lien on the financed assets—i.e., a mortgage. Granting a mortgage on property owned by an EDA and leased or conveyed to the private sector borrower has been upheld against claims of violations of gift and loan clauses, granting private emoluments, and invalid takings (eminent domain). See *State v. Volusia County Industrial Development Agency*, 400 So. 2d 1222 (Fla. 1981) (proposed use of a mortgage lien on nursing home as security for county IDBs was not unconstitutional on the basis that it involved a pledge of public credit where the nursing home project involved a private institution and each bond contained a statement [part of the recitals—Ed.] that it did not constitute debt of the local agency and that neither faith and credit nor taxing power of State or its subdivisions was pledged). However, attempts by local governments to secure mortgage payments with general fund appropriations have been uniformly viewed as invalid constitutional debt: there is no concept of "appropriation-backed bonds" in economic development financing. See *West Virginia Housing Development Fund v. Waterhouse*, 212 S.E.2d 724 (W.Va. 1974), where a statute mandating that appropriated funds shall be transferred to the state sinking fund commission for deposit in the mortgage finance bond insurance fund to make up any deficiency in that fund for IDBs was unconstitutional as invalid debt; *Maryland Industrial Development Financing Authority v. Helfrich*, 243 A.2d 869 (Md. 1968) (accord).

6. *Equal protection claims:* The relationship between the taxes foregone through economic development incentives and the economic benefit produced (increased employment, higher real property tax revenues, etc.) is not only difficult to measure but usually not recorded and analyzed by the issuer. In *State ex re. Tomasic v. Kansas City*, 962 P.2d 543 (Kan. 1998), the Kansas Supreme Court considered the constitutionality of a statute under which General Motors (GM) sought a package of tax incentives to build a manufacturing plant in Kansas City. In addressing the equal protection claim that the real property tax exemption established an unlawful preference as against other taxpayers, the court proffered four elements to consider: (i) whether exemptions further public welfare; (ii) whether exemptions provide substantial, peculiar benefits; (iii) whether exemptions provide for large accumulations of tax-exempt property; and (iv) whether exemptions are improper or preferential classifications of property. The court found that a 10-year real property tax exemption for property used or owned by the state and leased to GM had a public benefit and purpose and complied with "uniform and equal assessment and taxation" requirements. In applying equal protection, the court noted that "flexibility and variety appropriate to reasonable taxation schemes are permitted . . ." and that the state taxation scheme must have a rational basis for classification based on differences having fair and substantial relation to the object of legislation. The court

found that the real property tax exemption for property acquired and improved with proceeds of IDBs bears a rational relationship to the purpose of promoting economic growth in the state through the attraction of new industries and retention of existing business, and therefore the statute did not violate the Equal Protection Clause of the United States Constitution or equal protection under the state constitution. Are there any rights of the owners who pay real property taxes protected by equal protection against distributing tax exemptions in the name of economic development?

[3] Tax Increment Financing

The origins of tax increment financing ("TIF") lie in the development of urban renewal financing. Urban renewal was the state and local government's response to the federal government's policy of funding affordable inner-city housing and clearing blighted areas of cities in anticipation of future private sector development. Like IDBs, urban renewal arose from the Great Depression of the 1930s. TIF began in the 1950s in a few states, in particular California, as a means to provide matching funds for federal urban renewal projects. Statutes in nearly all states provide authority for some form of TIF.

Although TIF originated to promote urban renewal development projects, TIF programs have expanded to become an important local government economic development tool. Put simply, TIF creates economic development funding by borrowing against future tax revenues that are expected to be generated by the redevelopment of blighted or underused land. In studying TIF, critical legal issues include: (i) whether TIF bonds constitute unconstitutional debt; (ii) whether TIF bonds require voter approval to be authorized; (iii) whether the incremental revenue needed to be raised to pay debt service on TIF bonds violates constitutional provisions requiring uniform levy and assessment of taxes; (iv) whether the incremental revenue needed to be raised to pay debt service on TIF bonds violates state constitutional provisions requiring voter approval for an increase in government revenues and expenditures; (v) whether payments in lieu of taxes paid into a special fund securing TIF bonds for a redevelopment project constitute taxes; (vi) whether the issuer's eminent domain powers extended to condemnation of land within a TIF area; and (vii) whether the condemnation of land for redevelopment purposes constituted condemnation for a public purpose, whether school financing provisions are violated, and whether there is a tax exemption, see *Tax Increment Financing Commission of Kansas City v. J.E. Dunn Construction Co., Inc.*, 781 S.W.2d 70 (Mo. 1989). For discussion of the use of TIFs generally, see Briffault, *The Most Popular Tool: Tax Increment Financing and the Political Economy of Local Government*, 77 U. Chi. L. Rev. 65 (2010) (observing that TIF development was originally intended to facilitate urban renewal efforts, and is widely adopted, but that there is little evidence that it helps municipalities that use this tool). For a more recent study of TIF practices since the recession with examples from several cities, see Peterson, *Tax*

Increment Financing: *Tweaking for the 21st Century*, Urban Land, May/June 2014, at 102, https://urbanland.uli.org/economy-markets-trends/tax-increment-financing-tweaking-tif-21st-century/.

TIF is referred to by developers as "wedge financing." The term comes from the concept that a large redevelopment project, such as a shopping center, requires several sources of capital to finance the project. These sources collectively are referred to as the "capital stack." Within the stack may be a large mortgage-back construction loan from a commercial bank, low-interest tax-exempt for a specific function of the project, the tax abatements provided by the EDA, developer's equity in cash, state grant funds for economic development purposes, and TIF bonds. Usually the TIF bonds are a small, but critical portion of the capital stack to raise all the funds required. Further, the TIF bonds can only be used for particular purposes as providing the infrastructure the issuer could provide with the proceeds of its GOs plus the costs of urban renewal-type purposes: assemblage (that is, purchasing, including through eminent domain proceedings), site clearance, and, perhaps environmental remediation to the assembled and cleared parcels, and installation of utility connections (water, sewer, gas, electrical, etc.). State law does not usually permit use of TIF bond proceeds for financing the private developers' project "above the ground" and if so, the interest on TIF bonds would not be tax-exempt. For an example of state law constraints on use of TIF financing, see *Concerned Citizens of Southeast Polk School District. v. City of Pleasant Hill, Iowa*, 878 N.W.2d 252 (2016) (city lacked authority to extend renewal area and TIF financing to a broader area after consolidating urban renewal areas, and could not use TIF revenue from the original urban renewal area to find economic development such as street improvements outside the originally designated area).

The TIF process begins with either the local government or a developer identifying an area in the issuer that is blighted or economically underutilized. The developer or local government submits a project redevelopment plan (the "plan") to the statutorily empowered agency (usually a planning or other land use approval board) reciting how the project qualifies for TIF bonds and the project redevelopment plan. The project redevelopment plan may include (i) the boundaries of the TIF area or district subject to the imposition of the incremental revenue, (ii) costs to complete redevelopment, (iii) proposed property assemblage and clearance (including using the issuer's eminent domain powers), (iv) proposed principal amount of TIF bonds and incremental revenues required therefore, and (v) feasibility of the project and projected taxes, new employment and other economic benefits that will derive form the project when placed in service. The plan is then subjected to hearings and ultimately the approval of the governing body of the issuer.

One of the tests the plan undergoes is whether "but for" the TIF bonds (that wedge in the capital stack) the project would go forward. Not all states require this. To "go forward" means whether the other participants in the capital stack would commit to fund without the TIF bonds. If the plan is approved, the TIF area or district ("TIF area") is established and the issuer can adopt a resolution to issue TIF bonds. Either the issuer (local government), or a conduit agency thereof, will issue TIF bonds to support the debt service with the incremental revenues. The TIF area should specify boundaries that encompass persons, businesses, and real property that will be benefitted from the project. Determining the TIF area is not unlike establishing an area in which special assessments will be used to make improvements. As to real property in the TIF area, upon plan approval for the following fiscal year and thereafter until the final maturity of the TIF bonds, the issuer will freeze the real property tax assessment, referred to as the "base assessed value" ("BAV"), and taxing jurisdictions within the TIF area will share thereafter only tax revenues generated by the BAV. All taxes collected above BAV (the "tax increments") will be deposited into a segregated fund (as the Special Fund Doctrine requires) and pledged to the payment of TIF bonds. The TIF enabling statute may also, depending on state law, (i) pledge increments above a base amount as to sales and use tax generated in the TIF area, and (ii) authorize a contingent special assessment on the parcels in the TIF area (having no relation to a benefit) to generate sufficient revenues to pay debt service on the TIF bonds if the incremental taxes prove insufficient.

It is important to recognize that nuanced TIF requirements differ from state to state depending on applicable statutes. A growing number of studies have closely reviewed regional use of TIFS or individual state TIF requirements and suggested ways in which they might be reformed. See, e.g., Eagon, *TIF-for-Tax: Upholding TIF's Original Purpose and Maximizing its Use as a Catalyst for Community Economic Development*, 2017 WIS. L. REV. 179 (2017) (discussing Wisconsin); Walker, *Tax Increment Financing in Maine*, 70 ME. L. REV. 115 (2017); Mahone, *Redeveloping Redevelopment in Indiana*, 46 REAL EST. L.J. 128 (2017); Venteicher, *TIF in Nebraska: Is the Community Development Law Broken or Art Proponents of Reform Merely Playing a Broken Record on Repeat*, 49 CREIGHTON L. REV. 651 (2016); Coffin, *The Promises and Pitfalls of TIF in the St. Louis Metropolitan Region: A Look at Neighborhood Disparities*, 33 ST. LOUIS U. PUB. L. REV. 57 (2013).

The following case illustrates the legal and constitutional issues that can arise in financing redevelopment when TIF is present as part of the capital stack.

Meierhenry v. City of Huron

354 N.W.2d 171 (S.D. 1984)

WOLLMAN, JUSTICE

This is an original proceeding in which the Attorney General, joined by a resident and taxpayer of the city of Huron, and a resident and taxpayer of the city of Rapid City, seeks a declaratory judgment declaring SDCL ch. 11-9 (hereinafter referred to as "the Act") unconstitutional and a writ of prohibition restraining the cities of Huron and Rapid City from proceeding with the establishment of tax incremental districts and the issuance of bonds pursuant to the Act. We deny the relief requested.

In 1978, the South Dakota Legislature authorized municipalities to create tax incremental districts, prepare and implement project plans, issue tax incremental bonds and notes, deposit money in a special fund, and enter into contracts and agreements to implement the provisions and effectuate the purposes of the project plans.

The basic purpose of statutes authorizing the creation of tax incremental districts is to enable the increased tax revenues generated by community redevelopment projects to be placed in a special fund for the purpose of repaying the public costs of the projects.

After the planning commission or committee of a municipality provides notice and a hearing regarding the creation of a tax incremental district, it submits to the governing body a recommendation regarding the creation of such district. SDCL 11-9-3, 11-9-4. The aggregate assessed value of the taxable property in the district plus all other existing districts must not exceed a specific percentage of the taxable property of a municipality. SDCL 11-9-7. It must be found that at least twenty-five percent of the area of the real property qualifies as a blighted area and that the improvement of the area is likely to significantly enhance the value of substantially all the other realty in the district. SDCL 11-9-8. When these and other statutory requirements have been met, the governing body of a municipality may pass a resolution creating a tax incremental district. SDCL 11-9-5.

Once a tax incremental district is created, the State Department of Revenue (Department) must determine its tax incremental base. SDCL 11-9-20. The tax incremental base is the aggregate assessed value of all taxable property located within a tax incremental district on the date of its creation. SDCL 11-9-19. Department thereafter gives annual notice of both the assessed value of property within a district and the assessed value of the tax increment base, as well as an explanation that the tax increment will be paid to the municipality. SDCL 11-9-24.

The tax increment is computed in accordance with the following formula set forth in SDCL 11-9-26:

$$\text{Total taxes levied on all taxable property within the tax incremental district} \times \text{Current Assessed Value Less Tax Incremental Base} \div \text{Current Assessed Value}$$

The positive tax increments are paid to the municipality and deposited in a special fund, SDCL 11-9-31, until all project costs are paid or until fifteen years after making the last expenditure in the project plan. SDCL 11-9-25.

Once determined, the tax incremental base constitutes a cap on the assessed valuation of property within the tax incremental district for school and local governmental purposes by virtue of SDCL 11-9-27, which provides:

> With respect to the county, school districts, and any other local governmental body having the power to levy taxes on property located within

> a tax increment district, the calculation of the assessed valuation of taxable property in a tax incremental district may not exceed the tax incremental base of the district until the district is terminated. Payment by the municipality of project costs may be made from the special fund of the tax incremental district, the municipality's general fund, proceeds of sale of municipal improvement bonds under SDCL ch. 9-44, proceeds of the sale of revenue bonds issued under SDCL ch. 9-54, proceeds of the sale of tax incremental bonds or notes issued pursuant to the Act, or any combination of the above. SDCL 11-9-30.

The city of Huron created a tax incremental district by resolution dated March 7, 1983. Both the city of Huron and the city of Rapid City have indicated an intention to issue bonds pursuant to the Act.

In addressing the many constitutional claims raised by plaintiffs, we begin with the premise that legislative action is accorded a presumption in favor of validity and propriety and should not be held unconstitutional by the judiciary unless its infringement of constitutional restrictions is so plain and palpable as to admit of no reasonable doubt. . . .

I

[The court found a valid public purpose for the expenditure of public funds. — Eds.]

II

Plaintiffs contend that by providing for a non-uniform tax, the Act violates Art. VI, §§ 17 and 18, and Art. XI, §§ 2 and 10 of the South Dakota Constitution and the state and federal constitutional guarantees of due process and equal protection. We disagree. . . .

Plaintiffs contend that taxpayers within a taxing jurisdiction levying property taxes within a tax incremental district pay higher property taxes than they otherwise would were the assessed valuation of taxable property within the district not frozen at the tax incremental base for the purposes of taxation for general municipal purposes. As a result, those property owners are required to carry more than their fair share of the general costs of government, which has the effect of constituting a non-uniform scheme of taxation in violation of the above-quoted constitutional provisions.

Although it is true that under the Act the additional tax revenues derived from the increase in the assessed valuation of the property within the tax incremental district is earmarked for the repayment of the project costs, SDCL 11-9-31, and thus is not available to defray the costs of school and local governmental operations this fact does not necessarily render the Act unconstitutional. Constitutional requirements of equality and uniformity relate to the levy of taxes, and neither the requirement of uniformity nor of equal protection of the law limit the legislature's authority to allocate or distribute public funds. . . . The findings that the governing body of the municipality must make as a prerequisite to establishing a tax incremental district, SDCL 11-9-8, presuppose that in the absence of the creation of the district the assessed valuation of the property within the area of the proposed district will not increase and, indeed, will likely decline. . . .

Other courts which have addressed this issue have found that the tax incremental financing statutes in their respective jurisdictions do not violate constitutional prohibitions against non-uniform taxation either under their respective state constitutions or under the United States Constitution. Likewise, we reject plaintiffs' efforts to challenge the Act on similar grounds. . . .

[The court concluded that TIF bonds constituted debt but held that an election was not required to issue TIF bonds so long as the constitutional debt limitation of five percent is not exceeded.—Eds.]

VI

Article VI, § 12 of the South Dakota Constitution provides that "[n]o ex post facto law, or law impairing the obligation of contracts or making any irrevocable grant of privilege, franchise or immunity, shall be passed."

Plaintiffs maintain that by temporarily freezing the assessed value of taxable property in the tax incremental districts, the Act impairs contracts entered into between the taxing jurisdictions and holders of general obligation bonds. We do not agree. Although it is true that Art. VI, § 12, forbids the passage of a law impairing the obligation of contracts entered into by municipalities with holders of instruments representing municipal indebtedness . . . we do not view the operation of the Act as in any way limiting the taxes that municipalities may levy to service debts previously incurred. The holders of general obligation bonds lose no security to which they are entitled. The tax incremental base is fully available to meet the obligations previously incurred, and thus the holders of those obligations are no worse off than they were prior to the creation of the tax incremental district. Nor can such holders of general obligations complain because the increased assessed valuation brought about by the redevelopment activities undertaken in the tax incremental district is not available as a source of tax revenue to repay those obligations. . . .

X

Plaintiffs contend that the Act violates [the constitution] because a tax incremental district created thereunder constitutes a separate classification of taxable property by diverting a portion of the tax revenue derived therefrom (the positive tax increments) to the payment of the cost of redevelopment activity within the district. Also, plaintiffs seem to suggest that because the Act exempts the value of the taxable property in the district in excess of the tax incremental base from taxation for general municipal purposes, the Act violates [the constitutional prohibition against non-enumerated tax exemptions]. Neither contention has merit. Article XI, § 2 requires only a uniform classification with respect to the assessment, levy, and collection of taxes, none of which requirements is violated by the Act. Likewise, the Act does not create an exemption within the meaning of Art. XI, § 7. As the Supreme

Court of Iowa held with respect to § 403.19 of the Iowa statute: "§ 403.19 can hardly be said to create a partial exemption for the urban renewal developer. He will pay taxes at the same rate as everyone else; § 403.19 only affects the use of taxes after collection." *Richards v. City of Muscatine*, 237 N.W.2d 48 60 (Iowa 1975). We agree with defendant cities' contention that because taxable property in a tax incremental district is subject to assessment and levy of property taxes in the same manner and to the extent as all taxable property within a taxing jurisdiction, the property within the tax increment district cannot be deemed to be rendered exempt from taxation within the meaning of Art. XI, § 7 of the South Dakota Constitution. . . .

Notes and Questions

1. *Tax increment financing: is debt involved?* A crucial threshold issue is raised by TIF financing: does this system of financing implicate local government debt limits? The principal case held that TIF bonds were debt but that an election to approve the TIF borrowing was not required because the amount did not exceed the applicable 5% threshold. A number of other courts have also held that TIF borrowing constitutes debt subject to debt limitations of the sort discussed earlier in this Chapter. See, e.g., *Oklahoma City Urb. Renewal Auth. v. Medical Tech. and Res. Auth. of Okla.*, 4 P.3d 677 (Okla. 2000); *City of Hartford v. Kirley*, 493 N.W.2d 45 (Wis. 1992). The Wisconsin court in *City of Hartford* gave a particularly clear explanation of its rationale, in an opinion by Chief Justice Shirley Abramson. The court first explained that the judicial branch was obliged to determine whether constitutional debt was created, notwithstanding legislative views that TIF financing did not give rise to such debt. It then considered the text of Wisconsin's constitutional provisions, which limited local debt to no more than 5% of taxable property value. The court referenced prior authority that indicated that "debt" included "all absolute obligations to pay money, or its equivalent, from funds to be provided, as distinguished from money presently available or in the process of collection and so treatable as in hand." *Id.* at 51. The court reviewed several factors associated with debt (an undertaking to pay money or its equivalent; a voluntary undertaking; a set amount; an absolute undertaking; and an undertaking that is enforceable) and concluded that debt was in fact created. Do you agree with the court's conclusion? For further discussion, see Geheb, *Tax Increment Financing Bonds as "Debt" Under State Constitutional Debt Limitations*, 41 URB. LAW. 725 (2009) (reviewing split in jurisdictions; discussing rationales in some jurisdictions for finding TIF financing does not give rise to debt and noting that in the midst of recession courts may find other ways to deal with debt default and project failures). For an exceptionally thoughtful review of a range of financing tools that seek to avoid constitutional debt constraints and the associated risks created, see Roind, *Privatization and the Sale of Tax Revenues*, 95 MINN. L. REV. 1965 (2011).

2. *Equal protection and tax uniformity.* Constitutional issues in addition to eminent domain seem attracted to TIF bonds because the process converts a real property tax into an "incremental revenue" that continues to be (mistakenly) analyzed

as a tax. Thus, TIF bonds for urban renewal projects and improvements in *Tribe v. Salt Lake City Corp.*, 540 P.2d 499 (Utah 1975), were challenged on equal protection grounds. An argument was made that equal protection was violated because diversion of increased taxes in the TIF area to payment of debt service on TIF bonds would lead to the shifting of a disproportionate share of the tax burden onto other taxpayers. This argument was answered in the concurring opinion as follows:

> But in looking at the overall picture, any such inequity may be minimized or perhaps eliminated if it is the taxation on *the assessed valuation of the property in the project area*, which is pegged down as of 1970, and if the total fair assessed evaluation is subject to taxation, including any increased mill rate of taxes levied in subsequent years, and it is *only the extra taxes generated from the amount of increased valuation over the base year, 1970*, that is diverted into a special fund and used to pay on the bonds. [*Id.* at 506 (emphasis in original).]

Likewise, TIF legislation has been upheld by most courts against uniformity of taxation objections. See, e.g., *Tax Increment Fin. Comm'n v. Dunn Constr. Co.*, 781 S.W.2d 70 (Mo. 1989) (rejecting a variety of challenges to TIF, including lack of public purpose, improper pledging of credit, and illegal tax arguments).

3. *TIF and eminent domain.* TIF, as an economic development technique, contemplates development, operation and financing by the private sector. How can economic development justify the use of eminent domain (taking for a public purpose)? The answer lies in *Kelo v. City of New London*, 545 U.S. 469 (2005): economic development is a public purpose for Fifth Amendment purposes, and in deferring to legislative determinations of what public purpose means, the courts will not interfere.

Not all state courts buy the economic development analysis in *Kelo*. See *City of Norwood v. Horney*, 853 N.E.2d 1115 (Ohio 2006) (redevelopment of problematic area not a public use). Nonetheless, in *Goldstein v. Pataki*, 516 F.3d 50 (2d Cir. 2008), the Second Circuit applied *Kelo* and held that condemnation of property for a sports arena and related development in the Atlantic Yards area of Brooklyn was rationally related to a public purpose. In so holding, the court rejected the "mere pretext" basis for the property owners' challenge: "We do not read *Kelo*'s reference to 'pretext' as demanding . . . a full judicial inquiry into the subjective motivation of every official who supported the Project, an exercise as fraught with conceptual and practical difficulties as with state-sovereignty and separation-of-power concerns." *Id.* at 63. In the state court challenge to the same development, the New York Court of Appeals came to the same conclusion. *Goldstein v. New York State Urban Development Corp.*, 921 N.E.2d 164 (N.Y. 2009). A comprehensive review of the law of TIF and TIF bonds, including detailed discussions of the law of several states, is contained in TAX INCREMENT FINANCING (D. Callies & W. Gowder eds., 2012). For additional reading on *Kelo* and related developments, see Berger, *Kelo and the Constitutional Revolution that Wasn't*, 48 CONN. L. REV. 1429 (2016); Eagle & Perotti, *Coping with Kelo: A Potpourri of Legislative and Judicial Responses*, 42 REAL PROPERTY, PROBATE & TRUST J. 800 (2008).

4. *The lament of public schools.* School districts have been among the most vocal of TIF critics. If schools participate in a real property tax-based TIF program, they are giving up tax dollars sorely needed to fund wages, pensions and benefits in the face of declining state aid for public primary education and limits on real property tax levies and rates. TIF may generate sufficient new revenue to pay for improved public facilities such as streets and sidewalks within the TIF district, but such improvements may not be ones that public schools value or need most. See *Leonard v. City of Spokane*, 897 P.2d 358 (Wash. 1995) (statute authorizing establishment of incremental financing program in "redevelopment apportionment districts" unconstitutionally diverted tax dollars from public schools to public improvements). For a statistical analysis of the negative impact of TIF on school districts, see Weber, *Equity and Entrepreneurialism: The Impact of Tax Increment Financing on School Finance*, 38 Urb. Aff. Rev. No. 5 (2003): 619–644.

5. *Broader critiques of TIF financing.* Although TIFs were in their prime a favored form of financing urban renewal projects, they have increasingly been subject to close scrutiny to determine the extent to which their promise yielded results. One particularly important critique is offered by Merriam, *Improving Tax Increment Financing (TIF) for Economic Development* (Lincoln Institute of Land Policy, 2018), available at https://www.lincolninst.edu/gateway/download/42106/1581901371. Professor Merriam provides very useful case studies on a number of TIF projects that demonstrate how they work. He notes the benefits of TIF financing, including galvanizing partnerships between public and private actors and facilitating public support for needed project development. He also describes pitfalls, including capturing of revenues that would otherwise go to overlying governments (including school districts); reduced transparency and risk that public funds are used to foster private gains; and encouragement of competition between nearby governments. Merriam concludes that TIF can be a useful tool, but notes that such financing can be manipulated by cities to the detriment of school districts; is unevenly used around the country and tends to benefit areas that are already moderately successful; often results in lack of transparency; may not offer benefits beyond those that would have been realized without employing TIF; and may lead to underfunding of schools and financial volatility during economic downturns. Moreover, reasons for TIF successes and failures are not well understood. The study offered a number of recommendations relating to TIF financing, including providing local governments with an option to opt out of TIF participation, assuring that there is more transparency regarding TIF revenues and resources, and checking the extent to which TIF arrangements may capture revenues that should go to some local government entities rather than others.

A growing number of jurisdictions are taking concerns relating to transparency and equity seriously. See, e.g., Illinois TIF Reform Task Force, Final Report (June 1, 2018), available at https://www2.illinois.gov/rev/research/taxresearch/Documents/TIF_Reform_Task_Force_Report.pdf. Illinois now requires that tax bills include references to all TIFs in which property is located. 35 ILCS 200/20-15(b-5). For recent Chicago proposals for change, see Press Release, Mayor Lightfoot Announces Major Reforms to The City's Approach to Allocating Tax Increment Financing (TIF) Funds (February 5, 2020), available at https://www.chicago.gov/city/en/depts/mayor/press_room/press_releases/2020/february/TIFReforms.html.

[4] State Incentives for Economic Development

States have increasingly crafted strategies through which to keep or lure corporate employers to their jurisdictions in order to bolster state and local economies, and replace jobs lost as the result of declines in agriculture and manufacturing or moves off-shore. At times, state strategies may rely upon cuts in corporate taxes or taxes on manufacturing inventory in order to make the state a more appealing locale for businesses. Other strategies may give priority to state support for economic development initiatives targeting particular types of economic ventures (for example, filmmaking or computer manufacturing) or particular locales within a state that have lost jobs or have especially imperiled workforces.

Typically, states and localities create composite packages designed to make retention or relocation appealing. Such packages can include a number of different benefits including special debt opportunities (for example use of revenue bonds or TIFs), tax incentives (delayed or reduced application of standard property, sales, corporate or other tax obligations if legally viable, sometimes in the form of tax abatements and sometimes in the form of tax credits), infrastructure assistance (use of eminent domain powers or construction of roads or other needed improvements), and job training or other workforce development opportunities. In return, well-structured statutory provisions or memoranda of understanding will often require the corporate entity to create a given number of jobs at a certain income level within a specified period, payment of taxes to commence on a particular date, and repayment of inducements in the event that the project does not meet stated objectives or the business chooses to withdraw without meeting state obligations.

Before turning to evaluations of state economic incentive strategies, it is worth discussing the nature of public-private partnerships and highlighting some features commonly included as part of economic development partnerships that have not yet been discussed here.

[a] Public-Private Partnerships

Government entities can engage in economic development undertakings on their own accord, but typically find it worth partnering with private parties in order to tap development expertise and additional capital. Since World War II, it has become increasingly accepted that harnessing private sector actors to achieve government goals is consistent with an expanded view of "public purpose." The concept of "public-private-partnerships" (P3) has accordingly emerged and flourished.

A key element in many public/private partnerships is the use of public funds as a "lever" to attract private funds to a public redevelopment program or to enable a development project that would be beneficial to the community to be financed primarily by private resources. Used in this manner, the impact of public funds may be increased substantially. But that leveraging feature depends on investments by persons and institutions that have discretionary funds to invest and may accordingly be structured to give significant tax benefits to persons in higher income tax brackets.

The hallmarks of P3 are (i) introducing private sector equity capital (as opposed to solely public sector debt) to finance the project, often referred to as a "concession payment," (ii) establishing the costs of the facility not only in terms of the cost to acquire and construct, but also the costs of operation and maintenance over the useful life of the project (referred to as "life cycle financing"), (iii) streamlining of "procurement" (i.e., the process of buying items used in the acquisition, construction, operation, and maintenance of the facility), (iv) ownership of the facility by a "consortium" of the involved parties through a separate entity (referred to as a "special purpose vehicle"), (v) shift in financial risks from the government (i.e., taxpayers and ratepayers required to pay debt) to private sector "equity" owners, (vi) different risk levels of "profit" or "return on investment" for equity owners, and (vii) government oversight at project inception and throughout the facility's lifecycle.

P3 projects currently take (or could take) a number of forms, ranging from development of sports stadiums, to airport improvements, to affordable housing initiatives. See Irizarry, *If You Build It, They Will Relocate: Public Private Partnerships in Sport Stadium Financing*, 46 Pub. Cont. L.J. 853 (2017) (discussing P3 in the context of sports stadiums); Santini, *Fixing Our Aging Infrastructure: How to Pay for Airport Improvements*, 46 Hofstra L. Rev. 1031 (2018) (discussing airport financing); Brown, *Public Private Partnerships: HUD's Lost Opportunities to Further Fair Housing*, 21 Lewis & Clark L. Rev. 735 (2017) (arguing that public-private partnerships could be better employed to foster fair housing). The underlying concept can also be applied even more broadly. For general discussion of related matters, see Napoleon, Vilmenay & Newton, *The Use of Public-Private Partnerships as a Model for the Delivery of Goods and Services to the Government—Is This a New Concept in Government Contracting?* 35 J.L. & Com. 119 (2017) (discussing P3s in the context of federal contracting, exploring the historical development of P3s and current practices, and exploring financial models); Shultz, *Public-Private Partnerships: Structuring the Revival of Fiscally Distressed Municipalities*, 15 N.Y.U. J.L. & Bus. 189 (2018) (providing comprehensive review of P3s, state legislative authorization, financial risks, and possible responses to fiscal distress); Matthews, *Blueprint for Modernizing Built Environment Law: A View from the Budget*, 6 Alb. Gov't L. Rev. 148 (2013); McFarlane, *Putting the "Public" Bank into Public-Private Partnerships for Economic Development*, 30 W. New Eng. L. Rev. 39 (2007).

[b] Additional Elements of PPPs

Payment-in-lieu of taxes agreements (PILOTS). One way to reduce corporate property taxes is to have certain property interests owned by a "conduit" entity that is exempt from paying property taxes (for example certain types of public authorities).

The private sector entity seeking to benefit from the development would typically enter into a long-term lease with the conduit as a way to avoid direct property tax liability and may instead offer other benefits in lieu of real property taxes to the pertinent government as part of an incentive package. Associated taxing jurisdictions may be parties to relevant contracts to facilitate their enforcement of private sector entities' obligations. See also, *Board of Assessors v. City of New Orleans*, 829 So. 2d 501 (La. App. 2002) (upholding statute allowing for payment-in-lieu-of-taxes agreement between city and private developer as permissible when challenged under state lending of credit provisions). Challenges against PILOTS as violating state uniformity of taxation requirements have also been unsuccessful. See *Powers v. City of Cheyenne*, 435 P.2d 448 (Wyo. 1967) (tax uniformity requirement not violated where PILOT based on tax-exempt real property).

Tax abatements. In addition to property tax relief provisions, state and local governments have made significant use of tax exemptions as part of incentive packages designed to encourage business expansion and economic development. In return for the tax concessions, jurisdictions hope to receive new investment that produces jobs and additional sales and/or income tax revenues. It is well established that real property conveyed to a conduit to perform the public purpose of economic development or any traditional public purpose is exempt from real property tax. For example, in *Land Clearance for Redevelopment Authority of Kansas City v. Missouri*, 790 S.W.2d 454 (Mo. 1990), the Missouri Supreme Court held that a redevelopment authority's ownership interest in real property, leased to private owners for land clearance, was exempt from assessment and collection of taxes because it was part of the municipal economic development plan to rehabilitate property. The Missouri constitution authorizes tax abatements. For discussion of the Missouri experience, see D. Mandelker et al., Reviving Cities with Tax Abatement (1980).

Some commentators have begun to warn against localities relying too heavily on these so-called "economic development incentives" ("EDIs") because of concern over increased competition among states and localities to either lure or keep businesses within their jurisdiction. These concerns are discussed in greater depth below.

Tax credits. Tax credits have also become popular forms of public assistance to private development. Tax credits differ from direct public funding of community development and social welfare programs in that they depend on the willingness of private sector individuals and organizations to invest in those programs in return for receipt of the tax credits. A tax credit is subtracted dollar for dollar from a taxpayer's tax liability. While no public money is expended as a result of the awarding of tax credits, tax credits can have a significant impact on the budgets of government entities granting the credits. Tax credits are tax "expenditures," which are defined as "revenue losses attributable to provisions of the Federal [or state] tax laws which allow a special exclusion, exemption, or deduction from gross income or which provide a special credit, a preferential rate of tax, or a deferral of liability."

Office of Management and Budget, Analytical Perspectives, Budget of the U.S. Government, Fiscal Year 2011, at 207, quoting the Congressional Budget Act of 1974 (P.L. 93-344). The popularity of tax credits is due in large part to their leveraging feature. Through the use of tax credits, governments can attract private investment to community development and social welfare programs in two ways: (1) agreeing to match a *contribution* from a private donor, or (2) persuading private individuals and entities to *invest* in a particular program. Tax credits have at times been challenged as hidden expenditures that are not readily apparent to voters.

Defenders of tax credits argue that, when applied properly, tax credits do not represent state expenditures. Applying a "but for" standard that requires a showing that a particular private investment would not have occurred "'but for' the availability of the [credit] subsidy," a study of the impact of the Missouri historic preservation tax credit program concluded that "the private investment, which by the program's design is always many times the amount of the project, never would have occurred without the credits. Therefore, while the state does forgo a certain amount of revenue, it is offset many times by the economic activity that otherwise would not have been generated." S. Coffin et al., An Evaluation of the Missouri Historic Tax Credit Program's Impact on Job Creation and Economic Activity Across the State 3 (2010). The study, prepared for the Missouri Growth Association, examined two or three projects from each of the six clusters in Missouri: 1) small town/urban, 2) big city central business district, 3) historic urban neighborhood, 4) rural and small town landmarks, 5) revitalized neighborhood, and 6) suburban landmarks. *Id.* at 14–26. Persons surveyed emphasized that the tax credits provided developers with early access to capital because "[b]anks view the tax credits as equity allowing the developers to leverage them and qualify for a more favorable risk rating when borrowing funds." *Id.* at 26.

Other tax benefits under federal law. Federal tax law provisions often drive investment decisions, and Congress shapes crucial legislation with related goals in mind. For example, the federal Tax Cuts and Jobs Act of 2017 created a system designed to help taxpayers defer tax on capital gains or receive tax exemptions in return for investments in "opportunity funds" used to foster development areas of low-income communities designated as "opportunity zones." See Layser, *A Typology of Place-Based Investment Tax Incentives*, 25 Wash. & Lee J. Civil Rts. & Soc. Just. 403 (2019) (discussing opportunity zones legislation, comparing it to other approaches to place-based investment, and offering critiques); Lee, *Opportunity Without Reach: The Problems with the Opportunity Zone Program and the Need for Clarification, Oversight, and Regulation*, 47 Fordham Urb. L.J. 117 (2019) (providing in-depth discussion of legislation and associated issues). The Internal Revenue Service's website provides detailed information on the nuances and requirements of opportunity zone investment. See https://www.irs.gov/newsroom/opportunity-zones-frequently-asked-questions.

[c] Critiques of State Economic Development Incentive Practices

While state and local government practices to recruit corporate entities and associated jobs had been praised and embraced in their early years, more recent analysis has brought more stringent scrutiny to bear and challenged the benefits associated with initiatives to recruit corporate employers to states and localities. Some have critiqued such practices as giving rise to bidding wars in which governments unwisely compete to land desired employers. See, e.g., McGee, *The Modern Day Border War: How Kansas Can End Its Economic Development Battle with Missouri in the Kansas City Metropolitan Area*, 25-FALL KAN. J.L. & PUB. POL'Y 111 (2015) (discussing competition between nearby localities using economic incentives policies); Pollard, *"Cut—and That's a Wrap"—The Film Industry's Fleecing of State Tax Incentive Programs*, 50 AKRON L. REV. 425 (2016) (arguing that many states are wasting tax revenue on tax incentives to the film industry that do not result in net economic growth, and suggesting reforms).

Others have questioned whether, even if state and local governments impose controlling standards for creation of well-paid jobs and local benefits, corporate interests will actually achieve requisite standards. See Pollard, *"Was the Deal Worth It?": The Dilemma of States with Ineffective Economic Incentives Programs*, 11 HASTINGS BUS. L.J. 1 (2015) (calling for better information on the cost of incentives, means to limit or cap incentives, and hold businesses accountable for performing under incentive agreements). For a discussion of more effective ways to design and implement tax incentive programs, see *What Factors Influence Effectiveness of Business Incentives*, The Pew Charitable Trusts, April 2019, available at https://www.pewtrusts.org/en/research-and-analysis/issue-briefs/2019/04/what-factors-influence-the-effectiveness-of-business-incentives (emphasizing need to consider four factors, including costs, targets, design and economic conditions); *How States Can Consider and Design Effective Tax Credits*, The Pew Charitable Trusts, March 2019), available at https://www.pewtrusts.org/en/research-and-analysis/articles/2019/03/06/how-states-can-consider-and-design-effective-tax-incentives (establish principles up front, use deliberative process, conduct up front analysis to assess effectiveness). Others have stressed the need to examine assumptions in the context of local realities. See Bartik, *Who Benefits from Economic Development Incentives? How Incentive Effects on Local Incomes and Income Distribution Vary with Different Assumptions about Incentive Policy and the Local Economy*, The W.E. Upjohn Institute (March 2018), available at https://research.upjohn.org/up_technicalreports/34/.

Other critiques have focused on documenting the extent of economic development subsidy packages. See Mattera & Tarczynska, *Megadeals: The Largest Economic Development Subsidy Packages Ever Awarded by State and Local Governments*, Good Jobs Now (2013), available at https://www.goodjobsfirst.org/megadeals (documenting large subsidy packages). Questions can also be raised as to whether it is worth local expenditures paid for by those with limited means to foster job creation for positions they are unlikely to gain, and whether corporate relocation decisions are actually based on government incentives or are instead simply giveaways that simply add costs for localities where corporate interests are likely to relocate anyway. For a broad critique of economic incentive practices, illustrated through four case studies, see Parilla & Liu, *Examining the Local Value of Economic Development Incentives*, The Brookings Institution (March 2018), available at https://www.brookings.edu/wp-content/uploads/2018/02/report_examining-the-local-value-of-economic-development-incentives_brookings-metro_march-2018.pdf.

For an example of related debates, consider the rabid competition evident when Amazon.com announced a contest to seek incentives to locate a second major headquarters outside Seattle. See Casselman, *Promising Billions to Amazon: Is it a Good Deal for Cities?* New York Times (Jan. 26, 2018) (citing economists who questioned benefits of incentives spent to lure an already very wealthy company and the associated costs relating to housing and education that successful recruitment of Amazon would bring). See also Wilson, *States, cities rethink tax incentives after Amazon HQ2 backlash*, The Hill (February 17, 2020), available at https://thehill.com/homenews/state-watch/483127-states-cities-rethink-tax-incentives-after-amazon-hq2-backlash (reporting on legislative proposals to rethink tax incentives, add transparency, and reduce competition between local governments). A careful analysis critiquing state and local business tax incentives in the aftermath of Amazon's HQ2 initiative confirmed many of the concerns raised above. See Slattery & Zidar, *Evaluating State and Local Business Tax Incentives*, 34 J. of Econ. Perspectives No. 2 (2020): 90–118.

Slattery and Zidar found that business tax incentives had tripled since the 1990's, amounted to approximately $30 billion a year in state and local funding, and in 2014 were targeted to less than .01% of firms (often individual, specifically identified firms) opening in new locations. They found little evidence that incentives bolstered state economies. Indeed, their data indicated that top spenders like Michigan, West Virginia, New York, Vermont and New Hampshire had 2014 per capita incentive spending that amounted to 56% of public safety expenditures, 40% of spending on health and hospitals, 30% of spending on transportation and 12% of spending on education. While business tax breaks varied from state to state, they amounted on average to 40% of corporate tax revenues, or even more. Average costs per job for firm-specific subsidies had increased, amounting to about $12,000 per year. However, payments often continue over a span of years, so that the authors concluded that the mean cost per job is $120,000 (using a ten-year horizon). Poorer areas provide larger incentives and spend more per job, so that, for example, counties with an average wage of less than $40,000 may be spending over $400,000 per job on average. Firms benefiting from firm-specific subsidies tend to be larger in size. Automobile manufacturing firms were among those that received subsidies during the period studied, with the average manufacturer promising to create 2,700 jobs and receiving $290 million (more than $100,000 per job).

What are your views about the methods and extent to which state and local governments should offer incentives to corporate employers to relocate within their jurisdictions? Are your views based on legal or policy considerations? If you believe that relocation incentives are desirable, how do you think they should be framed in order to protect the public interest as well as foster desirable economic development? How should remedies be crafted to provide relief if initial hopes for economic development success are not realized?

G. The Role of Federal Law in State and Local Government Finance

[1] Tax-Exempt Financing

[a] Basics

The single distinguishing feature of state and local government debt, whether issued directly by a state or political subdivision, state or local conduit, or any other entity acting on behalf of a state or local government, is that the interest on the debt is exempt from federal income taxation. This provision in the Internal Revenue Code of 1986 (the "Code") is contained in §§ 103 and 144. Although the technical rules of the Code relating to tax-exempt municipal securities take up volumes, the basic rules emanate from a fundamental principal of fiscal federalism: "intergovernmental immunity"—to wit, the states do not tax the federal government and vice versa—enunciated in *Pollock v. Farmers' Loan and Trust Co.*, 157 U.S. 429 (1895), where the Supreme Court held an early attempt by Congress to impose a tax on income of states and local governments was unconstitutional as a tax on their power to borrow. The holding in *Pollack* has eroded as Congress has attempted to stem the rise of tax-exempt bonds, particularly since the 1960s, when industrial development bond volume soared as states increasingly validated economic development as a public purpose and businesses and developers sought to borrow at lower tax-exempt rates through conduits.

In *South Carolina v. Baker*, 485 U.S 505 (1988), the Supreme Court held that there is no Tenth Amendment violation by requiring state and local government bonds maturing over 13 months to be in registered form (as prescribed in the Tax Equity and Fiscal Responsibility Act of 1982 [TEFRA]) in order for the tax-exemption to apply. This overruled *Pollack* and made clear that whatever sovereignty remains with the states, the immunity of their obligations and those of their political subdivisions from federal income taxation has no safe harbor in the federal Constitution.

[b] Specifics

The Code, U.S. Treasury regulations, revenue rulings, technical advice memoranda and cases decided in the U.S. Tax Court and federal courts set forth the principles that must be observed and the prohibitions that must be avoided for interest on municipal bonds to be tax-exempt. The policy reasons for exempting interest payments from income tax are to encourage investment in governmental projects and to reduce the costs of government borrowing (by providing an exemption for interest earned from qualifying bonds, thereby making them marketable at lower interest rates than if investors had to pay tax on associated interest). For a careful review of the reasons and costs associated with federal policies relating to tax-exempt bonds, see Driessen, *Tax-Exempt Bonds: A Description of State and Local Government Debt*, Congressional Research Service, RL30638 (February 2018), available at https://fas.org/sgp/crs/misc/RL30638.pdf (estimating that foregone federal tax revenue from exclusion of interest income on public-purpose tax-exempt bonds as $20.5 billion in 2016, and $422.8 billion from 2017 to 2026).

Not surprisingly, government entities and private investors might wish that such benefits were broadly available. However, federal policy makers must also consider countervailing concerns, such as the extent to which income tax revenues would be lost if these important tax benefits were too widely available.

Three major constraints have historically applied to state and local government borrowing that seeks to qualify for associated federal tax benefits.

(1) The issuer must be a state or local government, political subdivision or conduit or other entity authorized to act on behalf of the state or local government to fulfill an "essential governmental function" under state law. This policy is designed to help assure that the tax-exempt borrowing is to be used for a public purpose. See Driessen, *supra*. The IRS explained its interpretation of this requirement in PLR 201735020 (IRS PLR), 2017 WL 3839726 (May 30, 2017):

> The Internal Revenue Code does not define the term "political subdivision." Section 1.103-1(b) provides that the term "political subdivision" denotes any division of any state or local governmental unit that is a municipal corporation or that has been delegated the right to exercise part of the sovereign power of the unit. As thus defined, a political subdivision of any state or local governmental unit may or may not, for purposes of this section, include special assessment districts such as road, water, sewer, gas, light, reclamation, drainage, irrigation, levee, school, harbor, port improvement, and similar districts and divisions of these units.
>
> The three generally acknowledged sovereign powers of states are the power to tax, the power of eminent domain, and the police power. *Commissioner v. Estate of Alexander V. Shamberg*, 3 T.C. 131 (1944), acq. 1945 C.B. 6, aff'd, 144 F.2d 998 (2d Cir. 1944), *cert. denied*, 323 U.S. 792, 65 S. Ct. 433, 89 L. Ed. 631 (1945). It is not necessary that all three of these powers be delegated in order to treat an entity as a political subdivision for purposes of the Code. However, possession of only an insubstantial amount of any or all of the sovereign powers is not sufficient. All of the facts and circumstances must be taken into consideration, including the public purposes of the entity and its control by a government. Rev. Rul. 77-164, 1977-1 C.B. 20.

The IRS concluded that the metro transportation authority in question qualified as a "political subdivision" based on its responsibilities, after a fact-intensive inquiry. See also PLR 201816007 (IRS PLR), 2018 WL 1900639 (April 20, 2018) (concluding that a public authority formed under state law to provide county-wide health care services and promote health qualified as a political subdivision where it was a division of state or local government unit delegated to exercise part of the unit's sovereign power to exercise eminent domain, governing board was controlled by county, and authority was required to report on its activities, budget and financial matters).

(2) The "interest" on the obligation must be incurred pursuant to the government's borrowing power. For an introduction to this issue, see 1 Gelfand, State and Local Government Debt Financing § 6:3 (2d ed. 2019). "Interest" is widely understood to refer to money paid or deemed paid for borrowed funds. It is not enough to designate payments as "interest," however, since the IRS will engage in much more thorough-going review.

(3) The borrowing must be compliant with state law. For a discussion of compliance with state law, see *Newlin Machinery Corp. v. Commissioner of Internal Revenue*, 28 T.C. 837, 843 (1957) (discussion of compliance with Kansas law). See also *Power Equipment Company v. United States*, 748 F.2d 1130 (6th Cir. 1984) (denying tax-exemption for installment sales contract as not authorized under state law).

[c] Tripwires: When Tax Exemption Does Not Apply

[i] Private Activity Bonds

The tax exemption does not apply in the same way if the municipal bonds are "private activity bonds" ("PABs"), that is, bonds that are not primarily for a public purpose. Bonds are considered to serve a public purpose if they meet either of the following requirements: less than 10% the proceeds are used directly or indirectly for a non-governmental entity, or less than 10% of the bond proceeds are secured directly or indirectly by property used in a trade or business. Driessen, *supra*, at 7. Bonds that fail both of these tests are deemed "private activity bonds" and are not eligible for tax-exempt financing unless they have "qualified" status that entitles them to limited privileges under the tax laws.

While these standards might seem clear, there is uncertainty around the edges. Consider, for example, situations in which a shopping center or sports stadium is leased to a private entity, but industrial development bonds are repaid with payments in lieu of taxes, special assessments, user fees, or real property taxes. A Tax Advisory Memorandum issued in 2013 provides some guidance. See IRS TAM 201334038 (IRS TAM), 2013 WL 4496050 (Aug. 23, 2013). There, a family-owned developer created a retirement community with various amenities located in town and a nearby unincorporated area. Once the retirement community was established, the developer acquired more land and successfully petitioned the town to designate it as a "community development district." After purchasing yet more land, the developer successfully petitioned for additional areas to be designated as "community development districts." The community development districts were controlled by a board of supervisors drawn from property owners based on acreage owned, and despite more than twenty years of existence, there had never been an election of the board by qualified electors. The Internal Revenue Service challenged the issuance of bonds by the Issuer (community development districts), rejecting the eligibility of the borrowing for tax-exempt status. The decision concluded that the issuer and affiliated community development districts were not "divisions" of state or local government because they were perpetually controlled by private interests rather than by the local government or the public electorate, given the facts at hand. For a discussion of this decision, see *Comments on the Definition of Political Subdivision for Tax-Exempt Bonds and Other Tax-Advantaged Bonds*, 69 Tax Law. 313 (2016).

[ii] Arbitrage Bonds

Arbitrage bonds can also be a problem. "Arbitrage" basically entails borrowing at a low rate and then lending the money borrowed to others at a higher rate to make a profit. Local governments were tempted into such arrangements during rising markets, and paid the price when markets fell. The Tax Code was ultimately revised to state that if governments invested a substantial portion of borrowing proceeds "to acquire higher yielding investments, or to replace funds which were used directly or indirectly to acquire higher yielding investments" such borrowings would not be tax exempt. See 26 U.S.C. § 148(a); Driessen, *supra,* at 12. For further discussion of arbitrage bonds, see the *Ira Weiss* case, *infra.*

Tax law changes with some frequency, so it is important to review current regulations and rulings.

[d] Additional Nuances

[i] Tax-Exempt Status of TIF Bonds

For purposes of the Internal Revenue Code, § 144(c), TIF bonds are exempt-facility bonds referred to as "qualified redevelopment bonds." Thus, at least 95% of the proceeds of a TIF bond must be applied to redevelopment purposes in a locally designated blighted area and must be secured by incremental or general tax revenues of the issuing governmental unit. Tax rates and assessment methods for TIF district property must be the same as applied to comparable property elsewhere in the jurisdiction. TIF bond proceeds may be used to acquire property in a designated blighted area if the acquiring governmental unit has eminent domain power to clear land for redevelopment, to rehabilitate real property and to relocate occupants of the acquired property. TIF bonds may be issued only pursuant to state enabling legislation and locally adopted redevelopment plans that define blighted areas based on state statutory criteria "which take into account all relevant factors" and contain affirmative findings of a "substantial presence of these factors." In general, no more than 20% of the assessed value of all real property in the jurisdiction may be declared blighted. Individual blighted areas must be at least "100 compact and contiguous acres" or between 10 and 100 compact acres with no more than 25% of the bond-financed land provided by any one person or related persons. How do the

Congressional restrictions on tax-exempt financing affect local TIF schemes? Is this an appropriate congressional response to a serious federal revenue loss, or an inappropriate federal intrusion into local and state prerogatives? See Chapter 7, *infra*.

It should be noted that TIF bonds have no special statutory basis or limitations, but typically qualify as tax-exempt because no private loans are created or repaid from private sources. Since interest on such bonds is generally paid from public funds, TIF bonds typically are not treated as private activity bonds. However, the IRS continues to look closely at the details of related transactions, and it is important to stay up to date on federal agency rulings.

[ii] "On Behalf of" Issues

A separate category of entities that may issue tax-exempt bonds are referred to as "on behalf of" issuers that issue bonds on behalf of a state or local government. See Treas. Reg. 1.103-1(b). The IRS has provided guidance as to the facts that must exist for an on-behalf-of issuer to issue tax-exempt debt. In Rev. Rul. 57-187, 1957-1 C.B. 65, 1957 WL 11962, where state law permits an entity to file a certificate of incorporation with the express approval of the local government for whose benefit the entity is being created, the following facts will qualify the issuer as a "constituted authority" of the local government: (i) the state statute which authorizes the incorporation should characterize the entity as a public corporation or public body and specify the governmental purpose it may fulfill, (ii) the entity should be under substantial control of the local government for which it is created (i.e., the local government appoints the entity's board of directors), (iii) the entity and interest on its obligations should be exempt from state taxation, acknowledging that its purpose is public in nature, (iv) no part of the earnings of the entity may inure to benefit a private person (except for fair value pay for services performed for the entity), and (v) on dissolution of the entity, all its assets vest in the local government for which it was created.

In Rev. Rul. 63-20 (IRS RRU), 1963-1 C.B. 24, 1963 WL 13305, the IRS recognized not-for-profit corporations ("NFPC") authorized under state statute to perform public purposes for the benefit of local governments and issuers of tax-exempt bonds if the following criteria are met: (i) the activities of the NFPC are essentially public in nature as specified in state law, (ii) the NFPC cannot be organized for profit except to pay debt service on its obligations and operating and maintenance expenses, (iii) the local government for whose benefit the NFPC is created must approve each issue of its bonds, (iv) no corporate income may inure to a private person (except reasonable compensation for goods and services received), and (v) the local government for whose benefit the NFPC was created must have a beneficial interest in it while bonds are outstanding and receive legal title and exclusive possession of the property financed when the bonds are paid in full.

"On behalf of" entities are employed infrequently at the state level because legislatively created conduits (agencies and authorities) provide adequate revenue bond issuers. On the other hand, they are frequently used at the local level in two situations: (i) where the local government is expressly authorized with a power it cannot perform without financing, but the financing is not authorized under the state finance law, and (ii) where the local government is expressly authorized with the power to finance a purpose, but does not wish to directly incur the liability with full faith and credit debt. The first situation is illustrated by a statute that authorizes a local government to provide energy efficiency and alternative energy facilities or safe and affordable residential housing, but those purposes are not recognized in law as public purposes for which general obligations can be financed and/or the bonds could be PABs, discussed, *supra*. The second situation is illustrated by a statute that authorizes the construction and financing of water, sewer, and park facilities. However, the project to be developed, while public in nature, is primarily for the benefit of a mixed-use commercial and/or residential development. The governing body of the local government would require that the liability on the bonds be limited to the properties benefited in the development rather than the entire local government. Special utility districts, if not possessing the powers required to be political subdivisions in their own right, may need to qualify as constituted authorities in order to issue tax-exempt bonds. See also *In re Allstate Life Insurance Company Litigation*, 971 F. Supp. 2d 930 (D. Ariz. 2013) (town named as defendant in securities litigation did not play a central and specialized role in securities transactions where it received no bond proceeds, investors did not rely on town's credit, and industrial development authority acted as on-behalf-of conduit issuer which, along with developers, was primarily responsible for bond default).

[2] Securities Law and Disclosure Requirements

Securities law is a complex field typically addressed in semester-long courses that explore the obligations of those involved in selling interests in financial interests with money value that can be traded. As has been discussed previously, local and state governments are unlike corporate entities that operate in the marketplace with the principal goal of making money. Governments do not have "shareholders" but instead are accountable to voters. Nonetheless, as has been explained previously, state and local government entities issue debt, in the form of bonds and notes, and private investors purchase such debt. In order to protect the interests of investors, state and local government borrowing, the conduct of intermediaries assisting them, and associated "securities" have to varying degrees been subject to regulatory oversight. This section is organized as follows. It provides an initial overview of relevant securities law requirements and the extent to which they are applicable to state and local government entities or associated players. It then presents an important case that illustrates the issues that can arise when local governments or their lawyers fail to comply with securities law. After considering provisions relating to securities fraud that apply to municipal and state issuers of securities, it concludes with a discussion of the role of the Municipal Securities Rulemaking Board.

[a] Overview

Two major federal statutes adopted during the Great Depression are central to the federal system to oversee sale of stocks and bonds ("securities") to investors. The Securities Act of 1933 (the "1933 Act"), 15 U.S.C. § 77a et seq., mandates that investors receive financial and other significant information concerning securities being offered for public sale (typically through "registration" of securities to be offered for sale), and prohibits deceit, misrepresentation, and other fraud in the sale of securities. The Securities Exchange Act of 1934 (the "1934 Act"), 15 U.S.C. § 78a et seq., created the Securities and Exchange Commission ("SEC") with authority over many aspects of the securities industry, including power to register and regulate securities exchanges and brokerage firms among others. The SEC also has power to prohibit certain kinds of conduct in the market, discipline regulated entities and associated persons, and require reports of information from companies with publicly traded securities. For an overview of these acts and other federal laws relating to the securities industry, see https://www.sec.gov/answers/about-lawsshtml.html#secexact1934.

Note, however, that there are exemptions to the registration requirements of the 1933 Act for several classes of securities including: "private offerings" (involving a limited number of persons or institutions); offerings of limited size; and intrastate offerings. Congress explicitly provided that securities of municipal and state governments need not be registered. See Section 3(a)(2) of the 1933 Act, 15 U.S.C. § 77c(a)(2); section 3(a)(12) of the 1934 Act, 15 U.S.C. § 78c(a)(12).

As discussed in more detail below, municipalities are nevertheless subject to the anti-fraud provisions of the federal securities laws, including section 10 of the 1934 Act, with applies to "persons" without exempting municipalities. See 15 U.S.C. § 78j(b) (which prohibits: "us[ing] or employ[ing], in connection with the purchase or sale of any security registered on a national securities exchange or any security not so registered, any manipulative or deceptive device or contrivance in contravention of such rules and regulations as the Commission (i.e., the Securities and Exchange Commission) may prescribe as necessary or appropriate in the public interest or for the protection of investors."). The SEC has acted under this authority to promulgate Rule 10b-5, 17 C.F.R. § 240.10b-5. That Rule states that

> It shall be unlawful for any person, directly or indirectly, by the use of any means or instrumentality of interstate commerce, or of the mails or of any facility of any national securities exchange,
>
> (a) To employ any device, scheme, or artifice to defraud,
>
> (b) To make any untrue statement of a material fact or to omit to state a material fact necessary in order to make the statements made, in the light of the circumstances under which they were made, not misleading, or
>
> (c) To engage in any act, practice, or course of business which operates or would operate as a fraud or deceit upon any person,

in connection with the purchase or sale of any security.

Additional provisions of federal securities law may also come into play, including section 12(2) of the 1933 Act (prohibiting fraud by parties engaged in the sale of securities) and section 17 of the 1933 Act (covering use of interstate commerce for fraudulent or deceptive purposes and imposing disclosure requirements on any person that publishes or circulates information about a security in exchange for consideration). For detailed discussion of these and other aspects of federal securities law bearing on municipalities and their agents, see 1 Gelfand, State and Local Government Debt Financing §§ 9:1-9.4 (2d ed. 2019).

Congress and federal agencies have also taken additional steps to curb potential misconduct by municipalities and associated actors, a matter of concern particularly in the wake of the WPPSS debacle and New York City developments recounted in connection with the *Flushing* case, above. Two important steps were taken in 1975. Congress at that time amended the 1934 Act to require that firms transacting business in municipal securities and banks dealing with such securities register with the SEC, and subsequently imposed more stringent requirements on "municipal advisers" involved in the securities trade pursuant to the Dodd-Frank Act of 2010. See 15 U.S.C. § 78o-4(d)(1). Congress also created the Municipal Securities Rulemaking Board ("MSRB") to promulgate rules for broker-dealers, municipal securities dealers, and others subject to regulation in the municipal securities arena. See http://www.msrb.org/. The MSRB is discussed in more detail below.

[b] An Example: The Ira Weiss *Case*

The *Ira Weiss* case, discussed below, was decided some years ago, but still offers valuable lessons about what can go wrong in a municipal securities offering. Since the time of this decision, more stringent rules have been adopted pursuant to the 2010 Dodd-Frank Act, which expanded oversight of municipal advisers and imposed an explicit fiduciary duty regarding their representation of clients.

In the Matter of Ira Weiss

Release No. 8641 (S.E.C. Release No.),
Release No. 52875,
Release No. 33-8641,
Release No. 34-52875,
86 S.E.C. Docket 2009,
2005 WL 3273381
Administrative Proceeding File No. 3-11462
December 2, 2005

[Ira Weiss served as bond counsel for a school district, and offered an unqualified opinion that interest on notes issued by the school district would be exempt from federal income tax. The SEC ordered Weiss to cease and desist from committing or causing violations under the Securities act, and ordered him to pay disgorgement in the amount of $9,509.63 plus prejudgment interest. The SEC determined that Weiss had violated antifraud provisions by negligently rendering an unqualified opinion that interest on notes would be exempt from federal income taxation and representing that funds raised by the bonds would be used for school renovation and construction projects.]

[The school district is located in New Castle, Pennsylvania. It sought to repair physical and mechanical deficiencies in an elementary school. At the same time, it was considering adopting a "middle school concept" and constructing related middle school facilities. A registered broker-dealer (Shupe) learned of the possible construction projects and contacted Weiss as potential counsel.]

[At the time, Treasury Regulations provided that a school district could issue up to $10 million in tax-exempt securities, including notes, and invest the proceeds in higher yielding investments for up to a three-year period, without the notes being considered arbitrage notes, if, and only if, the issuer reasonably expected to satisfy requirements regarding expenditures, time, and due diligence. Satisfaction of these requirements must be based on reasonable expectations as of the date notes are issued. Discussions with school officials suggested they intended to proceed with the elementary school project but that they did not have consensus on the middle school project but had identified an architect. Based on these conversations, Weiss contacted the registered broker-dealer and agreed to serve as bond counsel and write a bond opinion indicating that bonds would be exempt from federal taxes.]

[Subsequently, the school superintendent (Mento) contacted the school district's solicitor (Flannery) who had previously served as bond counsel and who stated that the concept presented was not consistent with the school district's past experience regarding the timing of bond issuance. The solicitor also expressed concern that the underwriting work was not being put out to bid as had been the prior practice.]

[Weiss subsequently contacted the school district's solicitor and asserted his expertise, even though he had not previously given an opinion on a note structured like the one at issue. Weiss also stated that proceeds of notes would be tax exempt, without qualifying those observations to take into account requirements about objectively reasonable plans to use the proceeds in a timely manner. At a subsequent meeting, Shupe, the broker-dealer, argued that revenues from bonds could be invested for profit on an interim basis [arbitrage] but Weiss did not raise questions about the legality of such a venture and continued to support Shupe's position in meetings with the school board, notwithstanding clear issues relating to compliance with applicable legal standards.]

[Subsequently, the school board approved the financing proposal. Weiss failed to advise the school board that tying up bond proceeds for three years as proposed would result in their being declared to be taxable. Weiss prepared a non-arbitrage certificate even though the school district had not confirmed the priority or costs associated with various projects. Subsequently, Weiss reviewed and approved the official disclosure document for the proposed borrowing (including a statement that the notes issued were "not arbitrage notes"). He then prepared legal opinions stating that note proceeds would not be subject to federal income taxation and were not arbitrage bonds. At closing, Weiss delivered his legal opinions, and the school board president signed the official statement in reliance on Weiss's representations.]

[Subsequently, in May 2000, the school district issued $9.6 million in three-year general obligation bonds. Proceeds were invested in Federal Home Loan Bank securities. Weiss received payment in the amount of $9,509.63 for his work, paid out of note proceeds. In November 2000, the IRS notified the school district that it had commenced an examination of the notes. In response to this notification, Weiss asserted that he had not known that the school board had placed the net note proceeds in a three-year investment. In 2001, the school district redeemed the notes. None of the note proceeds had been spent on construction projects, and the school district had received approximately $150,000 in arbitrage profits after calling the notes.]

[In September 2001, the IRS issued a preliminary determination that the interest on the notes was taxable, based on their view that the school district issued the notes with no reasonable expectation of using the proceeds on capital projects. No work was performed on any construction project for over a year after the notes were issued. The Board did not authorize the elementary school repairs, which were supposed to start at the end of the 2000 school year, until June 2001. The total cost of those repairs was around $350,000, significantly less than $480,000, or 5% of the $9.6 million the Board was obligated to commit to spending in the first six months under the Treasury regulations.]

....

III.

Securities Act Sections 17(a)(2) and 17(a)(3) make it unlawful for any person in the offer or sale of any securities to obtain money or property by means of any material misrepresentations or omissions, or to engage in any transaction, practice, or course of business which operates as a fraud or deceit on the purchaser. Proof of scienter is not required to establish violations of those provisions; negligence alone is sufficient. Negligence is the failure to exercise reasonable care.

Weiss is primarily liable for his role in the Note issue. Weiss reviewed and approved the Official Statement, which misrepresented that Note proceeds would be used to fund school construction projects. Weiss also rendered an unqualified bond opinion, reinforced by a second, supplemental opinion, that misrepresented the risk that interest on the Notes would be taxable. The Official Statement referred to Weiss's unqualified opinion that interest on the Notes would be tax-exempt. Weiss knew the statements in the Official Statement and in his legal opinions were communicated to, and relied on, by prospective investors in deciding whether to purchase the Notes. As the Division's expert testified, the Notes were sold to investors, and priced, based on Weiss's unqualified opinion that interest on the Notes would be tax-exempt. Weiss also knew that information about the Notes' tax-exempt character was material to investors because they would have wanted to know that their interest earnings might be taxable, at a minimum reducing the return from the Notes.

A. Weiss's Conduct

Before rendering an unqualified opinion, Weiss was obligated to determine, based on all the objective facts and circumstances, whether the School District had reasonable expectations to satisfy the expenditure, time, and due diligence tests as of June 28, 2000, the issuance date of the Notes. Weiss acknowledged that he also was obligated to conduct a reasonable investigation of the facts to establish the objective reasonableness of the School District's expectations. The evidence adduced at the hearing indicates that Weiss knew or should have known that the Note transaction was intended to earn arbitrage profits, and that the School District lacked sufficiently concrete plans for the use of the proceeds to justify the Notes' tax-exempt status. The evidence also indicates that Weiss did not make adequate inquiry to determine the level of certainty of the School District's construction plans, objectively viewed, before reviewing and approving the Official Statement and issuing his legal opinions. Weiss's failure to look for even minimal objective indicia of the School District's reasonable expectations to spend Note proceeds on projects was at least negligent. From the outset of the transaction, Weiss understood that the Board had gone "back and forth" on the elementary school project, and that the Board had not committed to the middle school project. He also understood that Solicitor Flannery had concerns about the financing because the Board had not determined which projects it was going to undertake.

After being advised of Solicitor Flannery's concerns, Weiss wrote the June 2 letter in which he misstated the Treasury regulation requirements by indicating it was sufficient for the tax-exempt status of the Notes that the School District merely "contemplate" projects on which the Note proceeds would be spent "should the projects be undertaken." In a follow-up conversation with Solicitor Flannery, Weiss told Solicitor Flannery of the requirement that the School District spend 85% of the net proceeds in three years. However, as he acknowledged, Weiss did not mention the potential risk to the Notes' tax-exempt status if the School District did not spend that amount during the three-year period. Nor did Weiss describe the time and due diligence tests.

At the May 8 meeting, Shupe articulated to the Board the arbitrage opportunity presented by the Note transaction. Weiss understood that Shupe proposed that the School District issue the Notes solely to invest the net proceeds and to earn $225,000 in arbitrage profits. Weiss admitted that he knew at the time that Shupe's proposal was contrary to the Treasury regulations. Weiss also admitted that he knew Shupe's $225,000 figure was based on the School District investing all the net Note proceeds for the full three years, and not spending any of those proceeds, much less 5% in six months or 85% in three years.

Board members asked Weiss if Shupe's proposal was "too good to be true." They also asked whether the Note issue committed the School District to proceed with the projects, or whether it was sufficient that there were projects to be done. Weiss did not advise the Board that Shupe's proposal was illegal. Nor did Weiss explain what the Board had to do in order to comply with the Treasury regulations. While Weiss informed the Board that it had to have projects, he did not advise the Board about the time or due diligence tests. Those two requirements were critical. The Board did not comprehend that it had to commit 5% of the net proceeds on projects within six months of the issue date of the Notes, or that it had to proceed with due diligence to complete the projects. At best, the Board was left with the impression that it had three years in which to undertake projects. At worst, the Board believed that it merely had to identify some projects that could be funded by the Notes.

Following the May 8 meeting, Shupe presented Weiss with a document showing Shupe's intention to tie up the Note proceeds for three years in an illiquid investment. Weiss told Shupe to take the provision out of the final Note proposal. Weiss did not mention to the Board when it approved the Note issue that tying up the proceeds for a full three-year period could result in the interest on the Notes being taxable.

Weiss also asked Mento for a list of projects that the Board "contemplated undertaking" with associated costs. In response, Weiss received an unapproved list of potential projects, without costs. At no time prior to the Notes' issuance did Weiss review a single cost estimate for any of the projects. Despite the requirement that the Non-Arbitrage Certificate set forth the facts and estimates underlying the issuer's expectations, Weiss prepared a Non-Arbitrage Certificate that did not contain any estimates and was short on facts. Weiss himself recognized that he should have obtained a list of costs.

Thereafter, Weiss failed to ascertain whether there was a time schedule for spending Note proceeds, failed to confirm the nature and scope of any engagement with the architect, and failed to determine whether a majority of Board members wished to proceed with the projects, despite acknowledging that he viewed all of these considerations as important in issuing an unqualified opinion. Indeed, the Treasury Regulations required, among other things, that the School Board "incur[] within 6 months of the issue date a substantial binding obligation to a third party to expend at least 5 percent of the net sale proceeds of the issue on the capital projects." Had Weiss exercised even minimal care, he would have learned that there was no time schedule for spending Note proceeds, no written contract with Eckles, and no agreement on proceeding with any of the projects. At the time, Weiss was aware that the School District had not yet advertised for bids. Nonetheless, Weiss reviewed and approved the offering documents, and signed and reiterated an unqualified opinion that the Notes were tax-exempt, when he knew or should have known that the School District's primary purpose in issuing the Notes was to earn arbitrage profits, and that it did not have any objectively reasonable expectation of satisfying the Treasury regulations. His conduct departed from the standard of reasonable prudence and was at least negligent. Weiss violated Securities Act Sections 17(a)(2) and 17(a)(3).

B. Weiss's Contentions

1. Weiss notes that the Order Instituting Proceedings ("OIP") alleged that he "violated Section 17(a) of the Securities Act" without specifying a particular subsection. Weiss argues that the Division "made no allegations in the OIP supporting a violation of Section 17(a)(2) or 17(a)(3)," [these provisions related to fraud conducted in the course of interstate commerce—Eds.] and did not assert before its final brief to the law judge that he was negligent. Weiss concedes that the law judge considered whether he acted intentionally, recklessly, or negligently.

We believe that the OIP fairly placed Weiss on notice that all subsections of Securities Act Section 17(a) would be at issue [including (a)(1) that makes it illegal to employ any device, scheme, or artifice to defraud—Eds.]. While the Division's primary focus was violation of Section 17(a)(1), the OIP alleged misconduct that sounded in negligence. For example, the OIP charged that Weiss drafted an "inaccurate" certificate and "made untrue statements of material fact and omitted to state material facts" in connection with the note offering. Weiss's answer to the OIP reflected his awareness that the allegations therein could provide a basis for negligence liability. Weiss asserted in his answer that he acted with "due care" and performed his professional duties in compliance with NABL standards, which he indicated were the applicable industry standards. At the hearing, Weiss introduced expert testimony on the issue of whether his conduct conformed to NABL standards, and was given full opportunity to defend himself. The OIP gave Weiss sufficient notice of the charges against him.

2. Weiss contends that, for the purposes of his unqualified opinion, he was entitled to rely on the representations from School District officials and Board members that the School District had projects it intended to undertake and plans to proceed with them. As bond counsel, Weiss was obligated to determine whether all the objective facts and circumstances, established, for example, by Board minutes and resolutions, contracts, and estimates, justified an unqualified opinion that the Board's intention to undertake projects satisfied the objective standard under the Treasury regulations. Weiss's reliance on vague, subjective expressions of intent to undertake projects, without independent inquiry, was unreasonable and an abdication of his responsibilities as bond counsel. Moreover, even assuming that the School District had projects it was planning to do in the future, the Notes were issued prematurely. Treasury regulations provide that issuers may not issue bonds any sooner than necessary.

3. Weiss contends that he was entitled to rely on the Non-Arbitrage Certificate. Weiss concedes, however, that he could not base an unqualified opinion on the Non-Arbitrage Certificate if he was aware of facts indicating that it was inaccurate. The Non-Arbitrage Certificate contained no cost estimates and was devoid of information supporting the School District's expectations to spend Note proceeds

on projects. Weiss offered no explanation for his preparation of a Non-Arbitrage Certificate with insufficient facts and no estimates, which therefore failed to comply with Treasury regulations. Although Weiss twice asked for cost estimates from Mento, none were provided to him. Mento's failure or refusal to provide cost estimates for the projects should have prompted Weiss to question whether the School District was ready to proceed with its projects and comply with the Treasury regulations. In the absence of the requisite facts and estimates, the list of projects from Mento was merely a "wish" list and could not be used as a basis for rendering an unqualified opinion.

4. Weiss accuses the Division of taking a "fraud by hindsight" approach, and seeking to hold him liable for not being able to foresee that the IRS would declare interest on the Notes to be taxable. In order that interest on the Notes be tax-exempt, Weiss was required to evaluate the objective reasonableness of the School District's expectations to meet the expenditure, time, and due diligence tests as of the issue date. Weiss's liability under antifraud provisions arises from his negligence in his role of bond counsel, and not as a result of actions taken by the IRS after the Notes were issued.

IV.

Under Securities Act Section 8A(a), the Commission may order any person who is violating, has violated, or is about to violate any Securities Act provisions to cease and desist from committing or causing any violation or future violation of those provisions. In determining the appropriateness of a cease-and-desist order, we look to the risk of future violations and other factors, including the seriousness of the violation, the isolated or recurrent nature of the violation, whether the violation is recent, the degree of harm to investors or the marketplace resulting from the violation, the respondent's state of mind, the sincerity of assurances against future violations, the respondent's recognition of the wrongful nature of the conduct, the respondent's opportunity to commit future violations, and the remedial function to be served by the cease-and-desist order in the context of other sanctions sought in the proceeding. We impose a cease-and-desist order only when we have determined that there is some risk of future violation.

Weiss was responsible for misrepresentations and omissions in the Official Statement and in his legal opinions which were made available to investors. Weiss's conduct caused harm to investors who purchased the Notes because they were without full information concerning the substantial risk that the IRS would find the Notes to be taxable. Weiss's conduct also caused harm to the marketplace by eroding confidence in bond counsels' unqualified opinions. The importance that investors place on such opinions cannot be overestimated. We have stated that "[t]he smooth functioning of the securities markets will be subject to serious disruption if the public cannot safely rely on the expertise proffered by lawyers rendering their opinions." As we have found, Weiss was at least negligent. He appears not to acknowledge any wrongdoing. Weiss, moreover, continues to practice in the area of municipal finance, and could give another unqualified opinion in the future. We believe there is a sufficiently high level of risk of future violations that would endanger the public. A cease-and-desist order is therefore warranted against Weiss to protect the public.

Under Securities Act Section 8A(e), the Commission may enter an order requiring disgorgement, including reasonable interest. The remedy of disgorgement seeks to deprive the wrongdoer of his ill-gotten gains. It returns the violator to where he would have been absent the violative activity. An order to disgorge a certain amount need only be a reasonable approximation of the profits causally connected to the violations. Once the Division shows that its disgorgement figure reasonably approximates the amount of unjust enrichment, the burden shifts to the respondent to demonstrate that the Division's figure is not a reasonable approximation. Any risk of uncertainty as to that amount falls on the wrongdoer whose illegal conduct created the uncertainty.

The Division has established that Weiss received $9,509.63 for his work relating to the transaction. The Division also has established that this figure was causally connected to Weiss's wrongdoing because it represented his fee for his negligently rendered services as bond counsel.

The Division's showing has presumptively satisfied its burden of proof. Weiss has not argued or shown that the $9,509.63 figure is an unreasonable approximation of his unjust enrichment. We will order Weiss to disgorge $9,509.63, plus prejudgment interest.

An appropriate order will issue.

By the Commission (Chairman Cox and Commissioners Atkins, Campos, and Nazareth); Commissioner Glassman dissenting.

Notes and Questions

1. *Subsequent history.* The SEC's decision was later sustained by the federal court of appeals. See *Weiss v. S.E.C.*, 468 F.3d 849 (D.C. Cir. 2006). For further discussion of the *Weiss* case, see 5 Bromberg & Lowenfels on Securities Fraud § 7:395.70 (2d ed. 2019).

2. *Basis for findings and standard of review.*

(a) *General rationale.* What did Weiss do wrong? What is the basis for finding him at fault? What standard of review was applied?

(b) *Negligence or more.* The discussion in Bromberg & Lowenfels, *supra*, provides more details about the history in *Weiss.* In their recounting, there was some uncertainty within the SEC staff about the standard under which Weiss was charged and how and when that standard evolved during the course of litigation. Weiss was criticized for relying on representations of the school district and financial advisors without conducting his own independent due diligence. If Weiss knew the projects were not likely to proceed in a timely fashion, did he have a duty to disclose this information? To whom? Why? Compare *SEC v. City of Miami*, 988 F. Supp. 2d 1343 (S.D. Fla. 2013) (action by SEC alleging securities fraud based on allegations that city misstated material information about its general fund, when CFO transferred money from capital improvement fund to general fund to bolster reserves, considering whether "scienter" could be shown based on "severe recklessness" relating to highly unreasonable omissions or misrepresentations, or inexcusable negligence with extreme departure from standards of ordinary care, causing a present danger of misleading buyers or sellers; court denied motion to dismiss). Considering the facts in *In re Weiss*, would you hold that the bond counsel's conduct amounted to "severe recklessness"? See Patrick, *The Liability of Lawyers for Fraud Under the Federal and State Securities Laws,* 34 St. Mary's L.J. 915 (2003), for a discussion of liability that can attach to lawyers whose clients are accused of violations of the federal and state securities laws.

(c) *Due diligence defense.* What is the standard for due diligence? How can the attorney opining on the validity and legality of the bonds avoid responsibility for misstatements and omissions in the official statement? A claim for securities fraud can be defended on the basis that the person alleged to have committed fraud undertook a reasonable investigation and exercised reasonable care, i.e., "due diligence"—built a record of the transaction prior to the closing—to collect information in preparing a bond issue and was reasonable in relying on the misstatements and omissions. Due diligence must be sufficient so that the person is entitled to rely on the misstatements and omissions. If an attorney has been recently retained, major effort is required to investigate the facts in sustaining a due diligence defense. Given the facts in *In re Weiss,* was there any due diligence? What investigation should have been made to demonstrate bond counsel's due diligence?

3. *Obligations to others.* As discussed in the introductory overview, municipal advisors have obligations to their municipal clients, but different rules may affect liability to investors. Should, for example, investors be able to bring private lawsuits against a trustee of a municipal securities issue for aiding and abetting fraud under the federal securities laws? The Supreme Court, in a 5-4 decision, said "no" in a case involving an allegation that a decision to delay an independent review of an appraisal of property—securing a bond issue for public improvements in a planned residential development—until after the closing of a second bond issue was fraudulent because the trustee allegedly knew land values were dropping. *Central Bank of Denver v. First Interstate Bank of Denver,* 511 U.S. 164 (1994) (because the trustee did not commit a manipulative or deceptive act within the meaning of § 10(b) of the 1934 Act, it was not liable as a secondary party for aiding and abetting).

[c] Anti-Fraud Requirements

As the overview to this section explains, municipalities as well as advisers and intermediaries are subject to federal prohibitions on fraud and fraudulent activities that satisfy "scienter" requirements. "Scienter" generally refers to intent or wrongness in state of mind. Negligence may be sufficient to give rise to liability for experts (such as bond counsel Weiss in the principal case above). However, state and local government liability for fraud under § 10(b)-5 of the 1934 Act is limited by "scienter" requirements. The following case illustrates issues raised regarding municipal liability in the context of allegations of securities fraud.

In the Matter of West Clark Community Schools

Rel. No. 9435 / July 29. 2013 (Securities Act of 1933)
Rel. No. 70057 / July 29. 2013 (Securities Exchange Act of 1934)
Securities and Exchange Commission, Washington, D.C.
Fed. Sec. L. Rep. P 80335 (C.C.H.), 2013 WL 12309911 (July 29, 2013)

[The case was brought as a cease and desist proceeding against the school district under section 8A of the 1933 Act and section 21C of the 1934 Act. The school district submitted an offer of settlement that the SEC determined to accept. Based on its order and the school district's offer, the SEC made the following findings.]

[The West Clark Community Schools is a corporate entity and political subdivision, located in Clark County, Indiana. It employs approximately 400 staff at eight different schools to teach approximately 4,500 students. An elected, five-member Board of School Trustees ("School Board") governs the School District. The school district used City Securities Corporation as a broker-dealer and underwriter for a public offering of $52 million in municipal bonds in 2005. In connection with that offering, the school district executed a continuing disclosure agreement requiring it to submit annual financial information and operating data.]

[Subsequently, in December 2007, the school district in connection with a $31 million municipal bond offering stated in public bond offering documents that it had not failed in the previous five years to comply in all material respects with any prior disclosure undertakings. This statement was materially false, since between 2005 and 2010, the school district had never submitted required disclosures. The school district either knew or was reckless in not knowing that its statements were false. As a result, the school district violated Section 17(a)(2) of the 1933 Act and section 10(b) of the 1934 Act.]

16. Legal Discussion—Municipal securities issuers, or obligated persons such as the School District, are subject to the antifraud provisions of the federal securities laws. Section 17(a)(2) of the Securities Act [the 1933 Act—Eds.] prohibits any person from, directly or indirectly, "obtain[ing] money or property by means of any untrue statement of a material fact" or misleading omissions. Section 10(b) and Rule 10b-5(b) of the Exchange Act [the 1934 Act—Eds.] prohibit the making of (1) a false statement or omission; (2) of material fact; (3) with scienter; (4) in connection with the purchase or sale of any security. See *SEC v. McConville*, 465 F.3d 780, 786 (7th Cir. 2006). A fact is material if there is a substantial likelihood that a reasonable investor would consider it important in making an investment decision. See *Basic Inc. v. Levinson*, 485 U.S. 224, 231 (1988). The Supreme Court has previously defined scienter as "a mental state embracing intent to deceive, manipulate or defraud." Recklessness is sufficient to establish scienter under Section 10(b)

and Rule 10b-5. *Miller v. Champion Enter., Inc.*, 346 F.3d 660, 672 (6th Cir. 2003). "Recklessness" has been defined for purposes of liability under Section 10(b) of the Exchange Act as an "extreme departure from the standards of ordinary care, which presents a danger of misleading buyers or sellers that is either known to the defendant or is so obvious that the actor must have been aware of it."). Section 17(a)(2) violations do not require proof of scienter. *Aaron v. SEC*, 446 U.S. 680, 697 (1980). There is a substantial likelihood that a reasonable investor determining whether to purchase the municipal securities would attach importance to the School District's failure to comply with its prior continuing disclosure undertakings.

17. Rule 15c2-12 was adopted in an effort to improve the quality and timeliness of disclosures to investors in municipal securities. Disclosure of sound financial information is critical to the integrity of not just the primary market, but also the secondary markets for municipal securities. Therefore, the Rule requires an underwriter to obtain a written agreement, for the benefit of the holders of the securities, in which the issuer undertakes (among other things) to annually submit certain financial information. Failure to provide such annual financial information is the type of information required to be disclosed to a customer by a broker-dealer and is a significant factor to be taken into account by a dealer in determining whether or not to recommend a security.

18. In addition, it is important for investors and the market to know the scope of any ongoing disclosure undertakings, and the type of information to be provided. The Rule therefore requires that the undertakings provided pursuant to the Rule be described in the final Official Statement. This allows investors to ascertain whether the undertakings have been satisfied.

19. Moreover, critical to any evaluation of an undertaking to make disclosures, is the likelihood that the issuer or obligated person will abide by the undertaking. Therefore, the Rule requires disclosure in the final Official Statement of all instances in the previous five years in which any person providing an undertaking failed to comply in all material respects with any previous undertakings. This provides an incentive for issuers, or obligated persons, to comply with their undertakings, allowing underwriters, investors and others to assess the reliability of the disclosure representations. . . .

IV. In view of the foregoing, the Commission deems it appropriate to impose the sanctions agreed to in the School District's Offer.

Accordingly, it is hereby ORDERED that:

A. Pursuant to Section 8A of the Securities Act and Section 21C of the Exchange Act, the School District shall cease and desist from committing or causing any violations and any future violations of Section 17(a) of the Securities Act and Section 10(b) of the Exchange Act and Rule 10b-5 thereunder.

By the Commission.

Elizabeth M. Murphy Secretary

Notes and Questions

1. *Sanctions.* West Clark Community Schools is important because it is the first time the SEC imposed sanctions against an issuer. It is just one of several cease-and-desist orders the SEC issued during 2013 relating to disclosure failures by local governments; others of note include *In the Matter of City of South Miami*, Release No. 9404 / May 22, 2013 [1933 Act] (issuer omitted to disclose misapplication of bond proceeds which jeopardized the tax-exempt status of bonds); *In the Matter of the Greater Wenatchee Regional Events Center Public Facilities District*, Release No. 9471/November 5, 2013 [33 Act]) (after bonds defaulted, discovered that issuer had omitted key financial projections from official statement; the issuer was fined by the SEC [first time SEC fined issuer] on theory that fine was to be paid by project revenues rather than by taxpayers); *In the Matter of the City of Harrisburg, PA*, Release No. 69515 / May 6, 2013 [34 Act] (since 2008 city had not submitted annual information to EMMA (the on-line data system for the Municipal Securities Rulemaking Board) and no material events filing under Rules 15c2-12; mayor failed to mention city's financial distress in "state of the city address" [first time SEC imposed sanction on public information not in official statement]). Does the SEC have a duty to protect investors against the acts of state and local governments? Is the federal government seeking to protect its wealthiest citizens while burdening local governments in fiscal stress without the resources to ward off intrusive federal investigation?

2. *Precedents for applying liability to state and local government finance officers.* In *SEC v. McConville*, cited in *West Clark Community Schools*, the facts involved allegations by the SEC that a pharmaceutical manufacturer's CFO failed to disclose billing disputes with its customers and drafted financial statements that overestimated the corporation's profits, causing the corporation to make material misstatements to investors in SEC filings. This action, said the court, was reckless. Likewise, in *Miller v. Champion Enter., Inc.*, cited in *West Clark Community Schools*, the facts involved a corporation that produced manufactured housing and the adequacy of a cautionary "forward-looking statement" from the CFO to shareholders, which disclosed investor risks regarding inventory and outstanding loans. Here the court said the statement was not actionable under § 10(b) and Rule 10b-5; the warning to investors was adequate and nothing "reckless" occurred in disclosing the material information. What do the facts in these cases applying securities fraud liability to publicly held for-profit corporations have in common with a school district that failed to comply with continuing disclosure filings under Rules 15c2-12? In *McConville* and *Miller*, the cases arose because investors lost money on their investments allegedly because of fraudulent CFO actions. In *West Clark Community Schools*, the only fault was a failure to file forms with EMMA. Can a school business official operating a school district operating with a balanced budget be compared with a business corporation in financial difficulty under the 34 Act or the 33 Act? In *West Clark Community Schools*, the SEC said "yes." What training and advice do public finance officials need to avoid becoming deer in the headlights for federal regulators?

3. *State of mind requirements.* "Scienter" exists when fraud is committed with intent or knowledge, and scienter requires more than negligence as a basis for liability. The principal case suggests that negligence under § 17(a) of the 1933 Act may represent a form of "recklessness" that could give rise to liability on the part of public officials and broker/dealers. In *SEC v. Dain Rauscher*, 254 F.3d 852 (9th Cir. 2001), the appellate court held that the standard of care for an underwriter of municipal offerings was one of "reasonable prudence." More recently, in a case involving an investment banker who had allegedly committed securities fraud by emailing potential investors while omitting relevant information about devaluation of the client's assets, the United States Supreme Court held that a person or entity who disseminates false or misleading statements with intent to defraud can be found to violate the anti-fraud provisions of federal securities law, even if the person or entity could not be found liable for securities fraud as a maker of an untrue statement of material fact. See *Lorenzo v. SEC*, 139 S. Ct. 1094 (2019).

4. *Additional example.* An SEC complaint against the town of Ramapo, New York in connection with development of a baseball stadium provides another cautionary tale. See https://www.sec.gov/news/pressrelease/2016-68.html. The SEC alleged that the town, a local development corporation and four town officials had hidden a deteriorating financial situation from municipal bond investors. More particularly, the town had committed to a $60 million investment to build a baseball stadium at a time when it was also experiencing declining sales and property tax revenues. The SEC claimed that those involved "cooked the books" of the town's primary operating fund in order to falsely to portray positive balances notwithstanding substantial deficits. Inflated general fund balances were allegedly used in supporting materials for 16 municipal bond offerings. Ultimately, criminal charges were also brought against a town supervisor and finance director of the local development authority, who were found liable for civil penalties and further enjoined from participating in municipal securities offerings. See https://www.chapman.com/insights-publications-SEC_Enforcement_Action_Ramapo_Officials.html. An assistant town attorney was also charged. What lessons should be learned from this example?

[d] The Role of the Municipal Securities Rulemaking Board

As noted earlier, the MSRB was established in 1975, in the aftermath of WPPSS and other financial debacles relating to municipal debt. Following the Great Recession, Congress adopted the Dodd-Frank Wall Street Reform and Consumer Protection Act ("Dodd-Frank") (Pub. Law No. 111-203, 124 Stat. 1376 [2010]), which, among other things, amended §15B of the 1934 Act, to provide for the regulation by the SEC and the MSRB of "municipal advisors" as well as broker/dealers and financial institutions that underwrite and purchase municipal securities. In interpreting Dodd-Frank's expansion of the MSRB's role, the SEC also took the view that it should "protect municipalities and obligated persons" from other actors (such as broker/dealers, financial institutions and financial advisors) who might not act in the best interests of those they sought to serve. Dodd-Frank granted the MSRB broad rulemaking authority over financial advisors (subsequently referred to as "municipal advisors") and their activities with state and local governments. For insights about all aspects of the MSRB and its rulemaking authority, see http://www.msrb.org/. It is worth noting that the MSRB provides substantial "plain English" explanations of all aspects of municipal finance, bonds, and securities regulation that can be helpful to laypeople and lawyers alike. The MSRB website provides information on the agency's multiple regulations and rules. See, e.g., MSRB Rule 42 (relating to fiduciary duties owed by municipal advisors to municipality clients); MSRB Rule 23 (relating to registration requirements for broker/dealers). The MSRB also supports the EMMA reporting website that provides the public with information relating to municipal securities offerings.

The MRSB is an independent agency within the SEC. Historically, the SEC rarely brought enforcement actions against issuers or underwriters for violations of Rule 15c2-12. However, in 2012, pursuant to the Dodd-Frank Wall Street Reform and Consumer Protection Act, the SEC established the Office of Municipal Securities and intensified its focus on the municipal securities market. For information on SEC activities relating to municipal securities oversight, see https://www.sec.gov/municipal.

H. Fiscal Stress, State Oversight, and Bankruptcy

[1] The Elements of Fiscal Stress

Attention to "fiscal stress" facing state and local governments came to the fore in connection with the 2008 "Great Recession" and will surely come into play again in the aftermath of the COVID-19 pandemic. As a result of the economic contraction, both states and local governments were significantly constrained by shortfalls in projected revenue while at the same time being expected to continue to meet basic financial obligations such as those associated with public pensions and core services. In 2010, the Congressional Budget Office published an issues brief describing the economic conditions and budgeting practices that tended to lead to significant budgetary challenges (which the CBO described as "fiscal stress" at the local level). See Congressional Budget Office, *Fiscal Stress Faced by Local Governments* (December 2010), available at https://www.cbo.gov/sites/default/files/111th-congress-2009-2010/reports/12-09-municipalitiesbrief.pdf (describing short-term transitory shocks and longer-term fiscal structural imbalances). The CBO analysis also outlined options for states to intervene or exercise further oversight, and highlighted issues associated with municipal bankruptcy. For more recent analyses of fiscal stress, see Anderson, *Dissolving Cities*, 21 Yale L.J. 1364 (2012); Anderson, *The New Minimal Cities*, 123 Yale L.J. 1118 (2014).

Fiscal stress has at least two principal causes: fiscal mismanagement and economic decline, or a combination of the two. Examples of fiscal mismanagement included New York City during the 1970's (as discussed in the notes following the *Flushing* case), and the City of Long Beach, California in the latter part of the first decade of the twenty-first century.

Fiscal stress caused by economic decline is more serious and its remedy, if any, is often multi-faceted and long-term in application. The remedy may be enforced by higher levels of government or by a bankruptcy court. The City of Detroit, Michigan provides a prime example of fiscal stress caused by economic decline. See *In re City of Detroit, Mich.,* 504 B.R. 97 (Bankr. E.D. Mich. 2013). The city had lost 63% of its population since 1950, was liable for over $18 billion in various forms of debt, had depleted its public pension fund and had funded none of its accrued liability for employee benefits. It had realized operating deficits in its annual budget for seven consecutive years, lost 80% of its jobs between 1972 and 2007, and had an unemployment rate of 18% in 2012. It experienced high rates of crime and blight. The economic decline of the city over a protracted period of time swamped the ability of city or state officials to either eliminate structural deficits or fund adequate essential municipal services through legal proceedings relating to budgets and financing.

Fiscal stress can have a third cause that may be present any time expenses exceed revenues during a fiscal year: public corruption. A leading example of fraud, bribery and coercion in public finance causing fiscal stress is apparent in the 2002 financing of the Cahaba River Wastewater Treatment Plant in Jefferson County, Alabama (where Birmingham, AL is located) at an estimated cost of $1.5 billion. Ultimately, $3 billion in bonds were issued, sewer rates quadrupled, the bonds defaulted, and eventually, the county filed a petition for adjustment of debt in Chapter 9 (relating to government bankruptcy, as discussed below). Over the course of several years, underwriters, county officials, and others allegedly collaborated in using bond proceeds to pay bribes, coerce unnecessary financings to generate fees, and defraud investors. JPMorgan, the lead underwriter, was charged by the SEC with securities fraud and paid a $50 million fine. The FBI intervened, and eventually over 20 contractors and county officials were convicted of crimes under state law and went to jail. Through bankruptcy Chapter 9 proceedings, investors lost over 60% of their investment in the county's sewer bonds, and the cost of sewer services increased. For a summary of the scandal before the county filed for bankruptcy, see Floyd, *A Brief History of the Jefferson County, Alabama Sewer Financing Crisis*, 40 Cumb. L. Rev. 691 (2009–2010). For further developments, see discussion at 2 Gelfand, State and Local Government Debt Financing § 14:35 (2d ed. 2019) (discussing the tortured history of the Jefferson County bankruptcy litigation).

[2] State Oversight of Fiscal Stress

With fiscal stress widespread since the Great Recession that are likely to worsen in the wake the pandemic, and many years before in northeast and mid-western states that lost "smokestack" industries and related jobs to southern states and Asian nations, states have used several approaches to shore up fiscally failing communities. See Pew Charitable Trusts, *State Strategies to Detect Local Distress* (August 2017), available at https://www.pewtrusts.org/-/media/assets/2019/10/state_strategies_fiscal_distress_v4.pdf (highlighting 23 states with monitoring systems). For an analysis of associated issues, see Shanske, *The (Now Urgent) Case for State-Level Monitoring of Local Government Finances: Protecting Localities from Trump's "Potemkin Village of Nothing,"* 20 N.Y.U. J. Legis. & Pub. Pol'y 773 (2017) (arguing for state-level supervision). Some examples of state oversight include the following:

New Jersey. The Local Finance Board ("LFB"), N.J. Stat. Ann. § 52:27D-18, a division of the Department of Community Affairs ("DCA"), approves all local government bond issues and approves the establishment of local revenue bond authorities. The LFB has not had an announced fiscal stress program for local governments as do New York and Pennsylvania. However, the DCA administers federal funds received for disaster aid, such as Hurricane Sandy relief. Along with New York and North Carolina, New Jersey's LFB has its origins in the 1930s as a response to the Great Depression. These three states set the model for requiring annual financial reports to be submitted to a state agency and general supervision of local government finance activities.

New York. The Legislature has created several "interim finance agencies" to operate distressed communities (i.e., Nassau County Interim Finance Agency, N.Y. Pub. Auth. Law, Art 10-D, Title 1; Buffalo Interim Finance Agency, N.Y. Pub. Auth. Law Art 10-D, Title 2). The agency's director advises municipal officials and supervises multi-year budgeting and financial planning, but does not operate the local government, except that the agency may approve (or reject) and revise labor contracts. For the rest of the state's municipalities and school districts, the Office of State Comptroller ("OSC") has audit power under Art. V of the state constitution to engage in "supervision of the accounts of any political subdivision of the state." That power is used to cajole local entities into greater fiscal discipline. In the New York 2014–15 fiscal year budget, the Legislature appropriated nearly $715 million in aid for communities listed by OSC as most severely distressed based on annual financial reports. Because of the diversity of New York's local governments (New York City to New Berlin) and degrees of urbanization (8 million to 150 million), managing relief for state-wide fiscal stress is challenging.

North Carolina. The Local Government Commission ("LGC"), established by N.C. Gen. Stat. § 159-3, provides assistance to local governments and public authorities in North Carolina. The LGC is staffed by the Department of State Treasurer and approves the issuance of debt for all local governments and assists those units with fiscal management. The primary mission of the LGC is focused in three areas of responsibility and authority. First, a unit of government must seek LGC approval before it can borrow money. Second, once a borrowing is approved, the LGC is responsible for selling the debt (or bonds) on the unit's behalf. While state agencies in some other states are charged with approving local government debt, it is the combination of the power of approval with the power of sale that makes the

LGC approach to oversight unique. Third, the LGC staff regulates annual financial reporting by oversight of the annual independent auditing of local governments, by monitoring the fiscal health of local governments and by offering broad assistance in financial administration to local governments. Partly on account of the state's oversight mechanism, widespread little local government stress has in the past been present.

Pennsylvania. Pennsylvania addressed related problems through the Municipal Financial Recovery Act of 1987, Pa. Stat. Ann. tit. 53, § 11701 ("Public Act 47"). The Local Government Commission, created in 1985, initially established a task force to examine municipalities experiencing economic and fiscal distress as a result of structural changes in their local economies or managerial deficiencies. The task force's report resulted in the enactment of Public Act 47. In its 25 years of existence, 27 municipalities have entered Public Act 47 seeking recovery but only six have left the program, putting its effectiveness in doubt. New proposed legislation to enhance Public Act 47 would permit a state agency to appoint a "coordinator" to advise the local government on fiscal recovery and provide state grants for fiscal stability. The coordinator could require non-profit entities to enter into PILOTs with the local government and recommend dissolution of the community if it is deemed "nonviable." The current law encourages local governments to restructure debt, consolidate for efficiency and consider Chapter 9 bankruptcy protection (state permission for which is unclear). Public Act 47 has been criticized as merely a device to permit raising taxes above statutory limits and issuing cash-flow notes to staunch budget deficits indefinitely without a deadline for when fiscal stability must be restored. There has been provision for a state agency or manager to take over running the local government, as in Michigan or New York.

Michigan. The Local Financial Stability and Choice Act, Mich. Comp. Laws §§ 141.1541 *et. seq.*, is the fiscal stress statute under which Detroit was managed prior to entering bankruptcy under Chapter 9 of the Bankruptcy Act. The statute calls for a financial review by the state treasurer and other officials when a "local financial emergency" ("LFE") may be present. A structural deficit qualifies as a LFE. The review is forwarded to the governor who may declare a LFE. If so, the local government may file for Chapter 9 bankruptcy protection, enter mediation, enter into a consent decree with the state, or accept an emergency manager ("EM") (as was true in the case of Detroit). The EM may hire and fire municipal employees, terminate or negotiate labor contracts, dispose of municipal assets with state approval, change the annual budget, revise contracts generally, and file for protection under Chapter 9 with the governor's approval. The EM may not raise taxes and may be removed by the governing body of the community after 18 months unless the LFE is resolved earlier. Of all the various state fiscal stress regimes, Michigan's provides the broadest general law for the state to control a local government's finances with minimal power for local elected officials to object. For further discussion of the Michigan experience, see note on Flint, Michigan and sources cited, *infra*.

Note and Questions

Opinions vary on the roles of state government in financial oversight of political subdivisions. Professor Gillette in *Dictatorships for Democracy: Takeovers of Financially Failed Cities*, 114 COLUM. L. REV. 1373 (2014), argues that "takeover boards" may be more capable of satisfying the interests of residents for public goods, and the creditors and investors involved with municipal bonds, than locally elected officials. In such a case, would home rule powers have any meaningful role? How would the powers of the community's CFO be curtailed? Other scholars disagree on the merits of state takeovers. See Anderson, *Democratic Dissolution: Radical Experimentation in State Takeovers of Local Governments*, 39 FORDHAM URB. L.J. 577 (2012). Professor Anderson argues that state financial oversight and receivership do little to cure the underlying causes of fiscal stress while removing the vitality of democratic processes in local government. State receivership is discussed in Kossis, *Examining the Conflict Between Municipal Receivership and Local Autonomy*, 98 VA. L. REV. 1109 (2012). The application of state finance and control boards is discussed in Kimhi, *A Tale of Four Cities—Models of State Intervention in Distressed Localities Fiscal Affairs*, 80 U. CIN. L. REV. 881 (2012). If states provide funding or authorize long-term borrowing to staunch a structural deficit, what corresponding responsibilities should the local government assume to assure balanced budget operations in future years?

Flint, Michigan, provides a cautionary tale relating to state oversight of distressed local governments. There, the state appointed an emergency manager who switched the source of public water from Lake Huron to the Flint River. Roughly 18 months later, the source of water was switched back, but only after many of Flint's children had been subjected to high levels of lead in their drinking water resulting in adverse health effects. See *Mays v. Snyder*, 916 N.W.2d 227 (Mich. App. 2018), *appeal granted sub nom. Mays v. Governor of Michigan*, 926 N.W.2d 803 (Mich. 2019). See also Lora Krusulich, *Polluted Politics*, 105 CALIF. L. REV. 501 (2017) (discussing problems with emergency manager systems); Massaro & Brooks, *Flint of Outrage*, 93 NOTRE DAME L. REV. 155 (2017) (discussing constitutional issues and *Mays* litigation); Berliner, *Environmental Injustice/Racism in Flint, Michigan: An Analysis of the Bodily Integrity Claim in Mays v. Synder as Compared to Other Environmental Justice Cases*, 35 PACE ENVTL. L. REV. 108 (2017) (discussing litigation in depth). The litigation about Flint and liability for its emergency management practices is ongoing.

[3] Municipal Bankruptcy

Chapter 9 of the U.S. Bankruptcy Code provides for municipal bankruptcies. See 11 U.S.C. § 901 et seq. This portion of the Bankruptcy Code is designed to allow qualified municipalities to restructure debt, under a plan approved by creditors and approved by the bankruptcy court. Chapter 9 is modeled after Chapter 11 of the Bankruptcy Code that allows a business to enter bankruptcy to adjust its debts while continuing in operation and emerging as viable. Before reviewing a bankruptcy court decision involving a municipality, it is worth reviewing some basic aspects of the statutory framework governing municipal bankruptcies. For a clear and well-organized overview of municipal bankruptcy, see 2 Gelfand, STATE AND LOCAL GOVERNMENT DEBT FINANCING Ch. 14 (2d ed. 2019).

To summarize:

(a) *Municipality.* Section 109(c) of the Bankruptcy Code requires that a debtor must be a municipality. "Municipality" for these purposes is not as narrow as one might suppose. The term is defined in the Bankruptcy Code to mean a "political subdivision or public agency or instrumentality of a State," 11 U.S.C. § 101(40). Even that definition is relatively unclear and has been subject to judicial interpretation. See, e.g., *In re County of Orange,* 183 B.R. 594 (C.D. Cal. 1995) (concluding that county treasurer's "investment fund" was not a "public agency" where "public agency was defined under § 81(6) of the Code as 'incorporated authorities, commissions, or similar public agencies organized for the purpose of constructing, maintaining and operating revenue producing enterprises'").

(b) *Authorized by state law.* This requirement stems from deference to states pursuant to the Tenth Amendment. States may authorize municipalities generally, or by name, or by decisions of a designated oversight authority to pursue bankruptcy. Not all states do so, and some states only authorize municipalities to pursue bankruptcy relief under certain circumstances (for example, if overwhelming debt arises involuntarily as a result of litigation).

(c) *"Insolvency" requirement.* The meaning of "insolvency" is complicated when it comes to municipalities. Municipalities are obligated to provide certain services to residents within their boundaries and that can limit their options in bankruptcy. In light of Tenth Amendment concerns, the Bankruptcy Code does not allow for court-ordered liquidation of municipal assets. Accordingly, the key test is whether the municipality is paying or is able to pay its debts as they become due.

(d) *Willingness to implement a plan.* Bankruptcy filings may not be used simply to buy time or evade creditors.

(e) *Negotiation with creditors.* Municipalities seeking relief must also satisfy statutory tests regarding negotiation in good faith with creditors.

There are many nuances of municipal bankruptcy practice that are beyond the scope of discussion here. Instead, the emphasis is on introducing key concepts regarding elementary aspects of qualifying for Chapter 9 bankruptcy protection and basic questions likely to arise in such litigation.

At the outset, however, it is worth asking: in your opinion, does the Bankruptcy Code framework for municipal bankruptcies take into account all relevant concerns? What competing policy considerations would you anticipate arise in municipal bankruptcy litigation? For consideration of related legal and policy issues, see Buccola, *The Logic and Limits of Municipal Bankruptcy Law*, 86 U. Chi. L. Rev. 817 (2019) (critiquing municipal bankruptcy law as ad hoc and arguing for earlier forms of intervention); Coordes, *Gatekeepers Gone Wrong: Reforming the Chapter 9 Eligibility Rules*, 94 Wash. U. L. Rev. 1191 (2017) (arguing that bankruptcy eligibility rules overemphasize deterrence and are insufficiency tied to the goals of the Chapter 9 bankruptcy system); Moringiello, *Decision-Making and the Shaky Property Foundations of Municipal Bankruptcy Law*, 12 Brook. J. Corp. Fin. & Com. L. 5 (2017) (offering suggestions regarding Chapter 9 decision-making). See also Watkins, *In Defense of the Chapter 9 Option: Exploring the Promise of a Municipal Bankruptcy as a Mechanism for Structural Reform*, 39 J. Legis. 89 (2012–2013); Skeel, *Is Bankruptcy the Answer for Troubled Cities and States?* 50 Hous. L. Rev. 1063 (2013). Are there other solutions to municipal insolvency that should be considered? See, e.g., Tatum, *To Disappear a City*, 69 Syracuse L. Rev. 105 (2019) (suggesting combination of Chapter 9 bankruptcy and disincorporation, and using Hamtramck, Michigan as an example).

In the following case, the petitioner's fiscal stress is not particularly severe—a single, unfunded judgment. However, Judge Myers instructed the petitioner on the requirements for "eligibility" to become a debtor under Chapter 9 of the Bankruptcy Code before rejecting the petition. The decision provides a useful bookend to this Chapter, since it demonstrates the overall interplay of various aspects of public finance law.

In re Boise County

465 B.R. 156 (Bankr. D. Idaho 2011)

Terry L. Myers, Chief Judge.

FACTS

A. Alamar Judgment

Alamar and YTC are Idaho limited liability companies. Boise County (the "County") is a rural mountain county in the state of Idaho with a population of approximately 7,000. The County's seat, Idaho City, is located roughly 40 miles northeast of the City of Boise.

On January 8, 2009, Alamar and YTC (hereinafter referred to collectively as "Alamar") filed a complaint in the United States District Court for the District of Idaho against the County ("District Court Case"). The complaint stemmed from conditions the County had imposed on a Conditional Use Permit requested by Alamar in April 2007 in order to operate a residential treatment facility and private school for at-risk youth on a piece of property located within the County. Alamar alleged that the conditions imposed by the County were illegal and discriminatory under the Fair Housing Act, 42 U.S.C. §§ 3601–3619 . . . .

On December 16, 2010, following a nine-day trial, a jury rendered a verdict in Alamar's favor and against the County for $4,000,000, finding the County had violated the Fair Housing Act. The following day, the District Court entered a Judgment against the County for "the sum of $4,000,000, with interest to accrue at the applicable federal rate." On December 30, 2010, Alamar filed a "Bill of Costs" and a "Motion for Attorney Fees and Nontaxable Expenses." Between the Cost Bill and the Fee Motion, Alamar requested an award of $1,236,557.50 for attorney's fees, $21,692.06 for taxable costs, and $139,864.01 for nontaxable costs. The County objected, asserting that Alamar's claim for attorney's fees was excessive and unreasonable, that the claim for nontaxable costs should either be disallowed in total or substantially reduced, and that the taxable costs should also be reduced. The District Court has yet to rule on Alamar's request for fees and costs.

B. Post-Judgment, Pre-Bankruptcy Events

... On February 22 the parties met and the County presented Alamar with a settlement offer [$3.2 million]. The County represented that its offer reflected a "good faith effort" to identify all funds available to pay the judgment given certain limitations placed on it by the Idaho Constitution and Idaho Code. Attached to the settlement [offer] as support for the County's position were several pages of financial documents detailing the County's actual and projected revenues and expenses for fiscal years 2010 through 2015. After consulting with legal counsel Alamar rejected the offer.... Alamar filed, on February 28, 2011, an "Application and Declaration for Writ of Execution" with the District Court.

C. Bankruptcy

Believing Alamar intended to use the Writ to execute on the County's accounts, and fearing that such execution would significantly interfere with County operations, the County Board of Commissioners ... voted on the record and passed a resolution to have the County file for bankruptcy protection under Chapter 9. On March 1, 2011, the County filed a petition for relief under Chapter 9, commencing this case. In its schedules, the County listed total assets of $27,765,617.34, and total liabilities of $7,377,343.79, including the $4 million District Court Judgment and a $1.5 million debt to [Alamar's attorneys]. The debt for Alamar's legal fees was designated as contingent, unliquidated, and disputed; the judgment debt was not. The County also listed on Schedule F claims for medical indigency payments held by several health care providers reaching back as far as two years that the County had discovered in preparing its bankruptcy schedules. Although the exact amount of each claim was undetermined, the County estimated the total amount to be approximately $550,000. The County designated these claims as contingent and unliquidated.

D. County Finances

The County accounts for and reports its receipts and expenditures in various, separate "funds." The County's financial reporting is made pursuant to standards promulgated by the governmental accounting standards board ("GASB") ... (requiring counties to use a system for accounting of receipts, expenditures and reporting that meets the criteria of generally accepted accounting principles ("GAAP") .... Accounting for its financial activities in this manner facilitates greater transparency in the reporting process and is intended to allow the County to ensure that its financial activities comply with the restrictions placed on its revenue receipts and the funds into which those receipts are allocated. The County's budget for fiscal year 2011 (October 1, 2010 through September 30, 2011) contemplates total expenditures of $9,352,734, allocated amongst various, separate "funds." ... To meet the anticipated expenditures in each of these funds, the budget lists cash to be carried forward in each fund from the previous year's budget, projects revenue from sources other than property taxes (*e.g.*, federal and state grants and programs, payments in lieu of taxes [PILOTS], revenue sharing, fees), and states the remaining amounts that would need to be levied as property taxes to meet the expected expenditures in each fund. As of March 1, 2011, the County had collected revenues of $6,007,950 and made expenditures of $3,040,595 for fiscal year 2011. With these revenues, less expenditures, and the moneys the County had accumulated over previous years, the County had the following cash balances in its various funds on the date of the bankruptcy filing ... giving the County a total cash balance of $9,945,787 at the time of filing. ...

E. Postpetition Filings

On June 14, 2011, the County filed a Plan of Reorganization and accompanying Disclosure Statement. The County's Plan proposes to pay Alamar $500,000 on its claim, relying on the limitation on damages contained in the Idaho Tort Claims Act, Idaho Code §§ 6-901 to -929. It also proposes to pay $550,000 to unidentified medical providers for medical indigency claims, the amount of claims the County estimates should have been paid prepetition but were not.

DISCUSSION AND DISPOSITION

To be a debtor under Chapter 9, an entity must meet the eligibility requirements of § 109(c). That section provides: An entity may be a debtor under Chapter 9 of this title if and only if such entity—

(1) is a municipality;

(2) is specifically authorized, in its capacity as a municipality or by name, to be a debtor under such chapter by State law, or by a governmental officer or organization empowered by State law to authorize such entity to be a debtor under such chapter;

(3) is insolvent;

(4) desires to effect a plan to adjust such debts; and

(5)

(A) has obtained the agreement of creditors holding at least a majority in amount of the claims of each class that such entity intends to impair under a plan in a case under such chapter;

(B) has negotiated in good faith with creditors and has failed to obtain the agreement of creditors holding at least a majority in amount of the claims of each class that such entity intends to impair under a plan in a case under such chapter;

(C) is unable to negotiate with creditors because such negotiation is impracticable; or

(D) reasonably believes that a creditor may attempt to obtain a transfer that is avoidable under section 547 of this title.

A Chapter 9 petitioner must satisfy each of the mandatory provisions of § 109(c)(1)-(4), and one of the requirements under § 109(c)(5) to be eligible for relief under the Code. If a petitioner fails to meet the eligibility requirements of § 109(c), the bankruptcy court must dismiss the petition under § 921(c) . . .

The burden of establishing eligibility under § 109(c) rests on the debtor. In determining whether the debtor has met its burden, the bankruptcy court is to "construe broadly § 109(c)'s eligibility requirements 'to provide access to relief in furtherance of the Code's underlying policies.'" Although Alamar has not objected to the County's eligibility on all aspects of § 109(c), the Court will, for purposes of completeness, address each of the requirements. In doing so, however, the Court takes the question of the County's insolvency out of turn, considering it last.

A. Boise County is a municipality

"Municipality" is defined by § 101(40) of the Code as a "political subdivision or public agency or instrumentality of a State." Under Idaho law, the County is a body politic of the state of Idaho. As a political subdivision of the state, the County qualifies as a municipality for purposes of § 109(c)(1).

B. Boise County is authorized to be a debtor under Chapter 9

Idaho Code § 67-3903 authorizes any "taxing district" in the state of Idaho to file a petition under the Bankruptcy Code. "Taxing district" is defined, for purposes of Idaho Code § 67-3903, . . . to be . . . any "municipality or other political subdivision of any State, including (but not hereby limiting the generality of the foregoing) any county, city, borough, village, parish, town, or township, unincorporated tax or special assessment district, and any school, drainage, irrigation, reclamation, levee, sewer, or paving, sanitary, port, improvement, or other districts." Bankruptcy Act of 1898, ch. 9, sec. 80(a) . . .

Idaho Code § 67-3904 also requires that, before filing the petition, a taxing district adopt a resolution authorizing the filing. Here, the County adopted such a resolution following a public vote by the Board of Commissioners at the February 28, 2011, County Commissioners' meeting. The Court concludes that the County was specifically authorized by Idaho law to be a Chapter 9 debtor and § 109(c)(2) is satisfied.

C. Boise County has demonstrated the requisite desire to effect a plan to adjust its debts

An entity may be a debtor under Chapter 9 only if it "desires to effect a plan to adjust [its] debts." Section 109(c)(4). No bright-line test exists for determining whether a debtor desires to effect a plan. The inquiry under § 109(c) (4) is a highly subjective one that may be satisfied with direct and circumstantial evidence. A debtor may prove its desire by attempting to resolve claims, submitting a draft plan of adjustment, or by other evidence customarily offered to demonstrate intent. "The evidence needs to show that the 'purpose of filing of the Chapter 9 petition not simply be to buy time or evade creditors.'"

The County has shown a desire to effect a plan to adjust its debts. County officials worked at negotiating a settlement with Alamar before filing the petition. The assertions of [the] Commissioners that they view adjustment of Alamar's claim through bankruptcy as the only viable alternative given Alamar's escalating collection tactics and their obligation to keep the County operating were credible. Each of the Commissioners testified that they believed the Alamar Judgment was a valid debt that should be paid. The purpose of filing the petition was not to evade Alamar but to find a way to pay the Judgment in a manner that County officials believed would comply with Idaho law and not cripple County operations.

Based on the evidence of record, the Court finds that the County has met its burden under § 109(c)(4) of demonstrating a desire to effect a plan to adjust its debts.

D. For Boise County, further negotiation with Alamar had become impracticable

The next step is to determine whether the County satisfies at least one of the requirements of § 109(c)(5). The County argues that by the time of filing further negotiation with Alamar had become impracticable. Section 109(c)(5)(C) requires the County demonstrate that it "is unable to negotiate with creditors because such negotiation is impracticable." Whether negotiation with creditors is impracticable is dependent upon the circumstances of the case. In the context of § 109(c)(5)(C), negotiation is impracticable where "(though possible) it would cause extreme and unreasonable difficulty." A petitioner may demonstrate impracticability by the sheer number of its creditors or by its need to file a petition quickly to preserve assets. The need to act quickly to protect the public from harm may also show the impracticability of negotiation. . . .

The evidence demonstrates the parties had effectively reached an impasse in their negotiations, and that Alamar, through . . . its application for the Writ, had demonstrated a sincere intent to promptly execute on its Judgment. The County's need to preserve its cash assets in order to maintain County operations uninterrupted for the benefit of its residents made further negotiations with Alamar impracticable.

The Court finds that the County has met its burden under § 109(c)(5)(C).

E. Boise County had a reasonable belief that Alamar might attempt to obtain a transfer avoidable under § 547

Alternatively, the County contends that it has satisfied § 109(c)(5)(D). Section 109(c)(5)(D) provides that an entity may be a debtor under Chapter 9 if it "reasonably believes that a creditor may attempt to obtain a transfer that is avoidable under section 547 of [title 11]." The Court agrees that the County has demonstrated that at the time of filing it reasonably believed Alamar may attempt to obtain a preferential transfer avoidable under § 547.15.

... § 109(c)(5)(D) is intended to allow a "municipality to file its petition and obtain the benefits of the automatic stay while it negotiates its plan with creditors, when aggressive creditor action may result in a preferential payment, which by its nature is unfair to other creditors." Such was the case here. Alamar's increasingly aggressive attempts to collect on its Judgment ... created a reasonable belief in the County that Alamar would obtain a payment that would prevent the County from fulfilling its other financial obligations. Had Alamar successfully utilized its Writ to execute on the County's accounts, it would have received a transfer of the County's property on account of the Judgment, an antecedent debt.

The Court finds the County's concern that it would be unable to withstand execution on the Alamar Judgment and effectively continue operations, and that such execution could constitute a potentially avoidable preference, was reasonable. It is thus sufficient that the County reasonably believed it was insolvent, though it may not have in fact been so. The Court therefore concludes that the County satisfies § 109(c)(5)(D).

F. Boise County has not established that it was insolvent on the date of filing

Finally, the Court addresses what has developed, in its view, into the major issue dividing the parties—whether at the time of filing the County was insolvent as required by § 109(c)(3). A municipality is insolvent if it is "(i) generally not paying its debts as they become due unless such debts are the subject of a bona fide dispute; or (ii) unable to pay its debts as they become due." Section 101(32)(C)(i). The test under § 101(32)(C)(i) involves current, general nonpayment, while the test under § 101(32)(C)(ii) looks to future inability to pay. The reference point for the insolvency analysis under both prongs is the petition date. As with other eligibility requirements, the petitioner bears the burden of proving one of the § 101(32)(C) insolvency tests is met.

1. Section 101(32)(C)(i)

The County concedes that at the time of filing it was paying its debts as they came due, with the exception of the estimated $550,000 in medical indigency claims it had neglected to process.... It argues that these unpaid medical indigency claims represent a debt not paid when due, thus rendering the County insolvent under § 101(32)(C)(i). The Court disagrees.

Section 101(32)(C)(i) requires *general* nonpayment of debts as they become due. The County's failure to process and pay a single category of claims, which represents only a small portion of its budgeted expenditures, from what appear to be adequate funds does not rise to the level of the general nonpayment contemplated by § 101(32)(C)(i) . . . .

The evidence presented shows that the County Indigent Fund contained more than sufficient funds to pay the estimated outstanding medical indigency claims and still cover the projected claims for the remainder of fiscal year 2011 . . . .

In addition, the Court is not persuaded that the purported $550,000 in medical indigency payments is in fact "due" for purposes of § 101(32)(C)(i). "Due" in this context has been defined as "presently, unconditionally owing and presently enforceable." Accordingly, evidence of when debts arose and amounts owed by a debtor without evidence of when the amounts are actually payable is insufficient to prove the petitioner is not meeting its debts.

Here, the County offered no evidence concerning when the medical indigency payment claims became, or would become, payable. . . . The Court is thus left with evidence that a debt for medical indigency payments exists, equivocal evidence as to the amount of that debt, and no evidence concerning when the debt was or will be actually payable. Based on this showing, the Court cannot find that the debt is "due" under § 101(32)(C)(i).

2. Section 101(32)(C)(ii)

The County also alleges insolvency under the second prong of § 101(32)(C), claiming it will be unable to pay the Alamar judgment and meet its other expenses for supporting county operations.

The test under § 101(32)(C)(ii) is a prospective one, which requires the petitioner to prove as of the petition date an inability to pay its debts as they become due in its current fiscal year or, based on an adopted budget, in its next fiscal year. This analysis is made on a cash flow, rather than a budget deficit, basis.

Alamar contends that the County's own financial records show that it has sufficient cash on hand in its various investments and accounts to pay the Judgment and meet the County's other expenses for the upcoming fiscal year. The County counters that, although it had close to $10 million in cash and investments on the petition date, most of the cash in its accounts are "restricted" by federal and state law to certain uses, which do not include payment of the Alamar judgment. The Court finds the County's arguments unpersuasive.

The County presented no . . . evidence of restrictions or limitations on these [trust] funds [which it had contended were "restricted"]. . . .

Second, the County has also failed to convince this Court that it would be unable to utilize the reserves it has accumulated. . . .

Generally, counties in Idaho are prohibited from making expenditures in excess of their budget appropriations. . . .

There are exceptions, however, to the prohibition of expenditures in excess of a county's adopted budget. One is for expenditures made upon an order of a court of competent jurisdiction. Another is for certain emergencies enumerated in the Idaho Code. . . . These exceptions allow a county to meet emergency expenses not anticipated by its annual budget.

All expenditures made under Idaho Code § 31-1608 are to be paid from moneys on hand in the county treasury in the fund properly chargeable with such expenditures. If there are insufficient moneys available in the treasury to pay warrants [a term synonymous with cash-flow notes—*see* Part D—Eds.] for any such expenditures, then those warrants must be registered and bear interest. Until a warrant redemption levy is established, the county treasurer is to identify ways of redeeming warrants, including short term borrowing from other county funds at market interest rates and interim financing from local financial institutions. Idaho Code § 31-1507. The total amount of emergency warrants issued, registered and unpaid, during the current fiscal year are included in the annual budget submitted to the board of county commissioners by the county clerk and the board must include in their appropriations for the ensuing fiscal year an amount equal to the total of such registered and unpaid warrants. . . .

These provisions of the Idaho Code, among others, are part of a well-planned county financial program, enacted by the Legislature "to give the several counties of the state a balanced budget, in order that expenditures shall not exceed revenues." . . . To further assure a balanced budget, ample provisions are made for expeditiously satisfying any residual indebtedness accrued in making such expenditures through the use of a county's levy authority and the transfer of funds not needed to meet current expenses.

The Court is not persuaded the County is unable to pay the Alamar judgment under this system. The County admits the Judgment is "a mandatory expenditure required by law. . . ." Yet it asserts . . . that Idaho Code § 31-1608 does not authorize the Commissioners to incur indebtedness or make expenditures in excess of the County's income for the year in order to satisfy the Alamar judgment because such authorization would violate Idaho Constitution, article VIII, § 3, which places limitations on a county's expenditures.

[However, the Idaho Supreme Court has held] . . . that the expenditures in excess of the county's budget made to meet emergent circumstances under Idaho Code § 30-1208 were not prohibited by the Idaho Constitution given those expenditures qualified as "ordinary and necessary expenses authorized by the general laws of the state."

In summary, the Court reads [the Idaho Supreme Court cases] as standing for three propositions of importance here, which when combined refute the County's contention that the Idaho Constitution prohibits it from using registered warrants to satisfy the Alamar judgment. First, merely changing the form of evidence of an already existing indebtedness or liability does not run afoul of Idaho Constitution [i.e., cash-flow notes which fund a judgment—Eds.]. Second, a county may issue registered warrants to meet expenditures, exceeding the county's revenue for the year, occasioned by emergencies.... And third, an expenditure to satisfy a tort judgment qualifies as an ordinary and necessary expense....

In short, the County has not convinced the Court of legal impediments to the issuance of registered warrants, the creation of a warrant redemption fund, and the transfer, at the appropriate time under the statute, of the surplus moneys ... as a means to pay the Alamar judgment. Nor has the County established a factual impediment to such an approach.

The evidence establishes that the County has sufficient surplus moneys to satisfy the Alamar Judgment and continue operations ...

When added together, these excess funds total $3,112,661. Based on the County's own projections, these moneys would not be needed to meet expenses for the remainder of the current fiscal year or for fiscal year 2012. The County has not carried its burden of establishing that it is prohibited from accessing these various funds to satisfy warrants that could be used to pay the Alamar judgment. Combining the $2,045,383 immediately available in the County's "trust accounts" with these excess moneys in [various funds] yields $5,158,044, more than enough to pay Alamar's judgment.

For the reasons stated above, the Court finds that the County has not established it was insolvent under § 101(32)(C)(ii).

CONCLUSION

The Court finds Alamar's objection to be well taken. The County did not meet its burden of proving it was insolvent under § 109(c)(3) and, therefore, is ineligible to be a debtor under Chapter 9. Alamar's Motion, Doc. No. 69, will be granted and the County's Chapter 9 case will be dismissed pursuant to § 921(c) ...

Notes

1. *Analyzing the Boise decision and its lessons.* The introduction to this section outlines some of the differences between Chapter 9 and bankruptcy provisions applicable to private sector entities. How does *In re Boise County* demonstrate such differences? Why should admission to bankruptcy protection be difficult for units of local government? Federal bankruptcy law permits all local units of government to file for bankruptcy, but only if the local government's state allows it, as discussed above. In addition, some states have different thresholds or procedures to file bankruptcy for special districts as opposed to general purpose governments. Why would this be so?

2. *Public employee pensions and benefits.* Once a unit of local government gains admission to Chapter 9 bankruptcy, a federal bankruptcy court has the authority to impair local government contracts, including pension obligations, notwithstanding the constraints of the Contracts Clause. See *In re City of Detroit*, 504 B.R. 97, 154

(Bankr. E.D. Mich. 2013) (court had authority to impair pensions but would not lightly do so). Even though general obligation bonds are backed with a pledge of tax revenues, they are not secured against particular assets, so bondholders are treated the same as other creditors. See Dick, *Bondholders vs. Retirees in Municipal Bankruptcies: The Political Economy of Chapter 9*, 92 Am. Bankr. L.J. 73, 83-86 (2018). As a result, major debt owed for underfunded government pensions and debt on government borrowing often represent the two largest classes of claims in municipal bankruptcy and must both be addressed as part of resulting "work out" plans. *Id.* at 91–110 (providing several case studies that show the complexity of such decisions). Should one or the other of these types of claims be privileged over the other? For a further discussion of the risk that municipalities might decline to raise tax revenues to a level needed to meet pension obligations, and might then file for bankruptcy protection in order to "shed" pension debt, see Hunt, *Taxes and Ability to Pay in Municipal Bankruptcy*, 91 Wash. L. Rev. 515 (2016) (arguing that bankruptcy courts should only provide relief from pension obligations when municipalities are reasonably unable to meet their obligations).

3. *Bankruptcy standards and procedures.* For a comprehensive discussion of procedures in Chapter 9 bankruptcy proceedings involving municipalities, see 2 Gelfand, State and Local Government Debt Financing §§ 14.8 et seq. (2d ed. 2019). Step back from current practices and consider, based on first principles, the following questions: (a) is the standard of eligibility for municipal bankruptcy tied to actual insolvency appropriate? (b) how should actual insolvency be determined? (c) how should the "good faith" of municipalities seeking bankruptcy protection be assessed? (d) what sorts of stays should apply during the pendency of bankruptcy proceedings? (note that, currently, the automatic stay imposed by a bankruptcy court will generally not apply to obligations paid from pledged non-tax revenues such as revenue bonds paid from "special revenues" or those protected by "statutory liens"); (e) what mechanisms should be provided to facilitate municipalities' negotiation with creditors to develop a proposed plan to move forward? (f) what other factors in your opinion should be considered as part of a "new and improved" bankruptcy law governing municipalities in the wake of the pandemic?

4. *Case studies.* Detailed review of specific municipalities' bankruptcy experiences can be illuminating. See generally Congressional Research Service, R41738, *Chapter 9 of the U.S. Bankruptcy Code: "Municipal Bankruptcy,"* (March 31, 2011), available at https://www.everycrsreport.com/reports/R41738.html (including discussion of Orange County, California; Vallejo, California; Jefferson County, Alabama; Harrisburg, Pennsylvania; Boise, Idaho). For a detailed review of the Detroit bankruptcy, see Chung, *Zombieland/The Detroit Bankruptcy: Why Debts Associated with Pensions, Benefits and Municipal Securities Never Die . . . and How They are Killing Cities Like Detroit,* 41 Fordham Urb. L.J. 771 (2014). For a study endeavoring to predict municipal bankruptcies, see Coordes & Reilly, *Predictors of Municipal Bankruptcies and State Intervention Programs: An Exploratory Study,* 105 Ky. L.J. 493

(2016-17) (identifying factors associated with municipal bankruptcy and identifying driving factors including union density, unfunded pension liability, and financial mismanagement).

5. *The global economic shock of COVID-19 and fiscal stress.* As this book goes to print, cities and counties across the country are looking for budget cutting measures. Under state and local governments' stay-at-home orders, economic activity and tax revenues are spiraling downward, and medical, public safety, and public health costs are soaring. While it is impossible to predict how federal, state, and local government responses and responsibilities will change as the country adjusts and recovers from the pandemic, those changes will come at a heavy financial cost. As a result, the country's familiarity with fiscal stress, on an individual and institutional level, will undoubtedly increase. Moving forward, the legal profession will be called upon to help every aspect of society regain footing; a basic understanding of public finance will be required to do so. An approach to dealing with fiscal stress of the future is discussed in Chung, *Government Budgets as the Hunger Games: The Brutal Competition for State and Local Government Resources Given Municipal Securities Debt, Pension and OPEB Obligations, and Taxpayer Needs,* 33 Rev. Banking & Fin. L. 663 (2014) (discussing municipal obligations relating to pay pensions, benefits, and complex forms of debt; suggesting changes in federal securities law and associated reporting; arguing for more transparency in financial decision-making; and urging compliance with uniform accounting standards, better data collection and oversight and expanded application of fiduciary standards). What changes in municipal bankruptcy law might be warranted under the present circumstances?

Note: Looking Ahead

Revisit the questions posed in Problem 4-2. How viable is the current system of public finance likely to be in the post-pandemic era? Think tanks that have proposed major changes have generally faced inertia, since changing fundamental assumptions and tools that are tried and true is a difficult task. Current law students will be guiding the future of federal, state and local governments as they navigate related challenges in the future. What changes in policy and law relating to public finance should in your opinion be considered to address issues arising from the COVID-19 pandemic and its aftermath? What fundamental issues regarding equity and social justice, economic viability, and local businesses and populations are of greatest concern to you? It is often said that crisis provides opportunity. In your opinion, what opportunities for constructive change in the wake of the COVID-19 pandemic should be at the heart of upcoming debates about pandemic recovery?

Chapter 5

Serving the Public Sector: Officers and Employees

Introduction

Public officers and employees play a crucial role in developing policy and delivering the services state and local governments provide to their citizens. Consequently, the legal structure governing public employment provides a fascinating template for examining the historical and philosophical development of the compact of governance between the people and their representatives. Conceptions of government employment have evolved over time from an early patrician model to the political vision of Andrew Jackson's presidency and the merit-oriented civil service model that prevailed throughout the latter part of the twentieth century. More recently, increasing attention has been devoted to the possibilities for "privatization," as a variety of functions are outsourced by all levels of government.

Data from the 2017 Annual Survey of Public Employment and Payroll, reported by the U.S. Census Bureau, indicated that in March 2017, there were a total of 14,617,399 full-time and 4,926,514 part-time employees in state and local governments combined (for an overall total of 19,543,913 state and local government employees). The bulk of these employees worked for local governments (14,144,066 full- and part-time employees, compared to 5,399,847 total state employees). The 2017 combined total was slightly more than the total reported in the 2012 Annual Survey (when there were 14.4 million full-time and 4.9 million part-time employees in state and local governments combined). The greatest proportion of these workers are involved in education, hospitals, police, and corrections.

The Congressional Research Service estimated that for FY 2019, there were approximately 4.2 million federal employees (including Postal Service workers and members of the uniformed military), while for FY 2020, 4.3 million were projected. Congressional Research Service, Federal Workforce Statistics Sources: OPM and OMB, Report R43590 at 6 (Oct. 24, 2019), available at https://fas.org/sgp/crs/misc/R43590.pdf.

Paul Light, a scholar formerly affiliated with the Brookings Institution, has engaged in extensive study of the federal government and has tracked emerging trends relating to its size and effectiveness. His major study, A Government Ill-Executed (2008), discussed the growth in the "hidden workforce," including contractors and grantees, and related methodological challenges. *Id.* at 189–211. He attributed recent growth in the "hidden" federal workforce to employment caps and freezes designed to make the size of the federal government look smaller and to reduce the level of accountability. His more recent book, THE GOVERNMENT-INDUSTRIAL COMPLEX: THE TRUE SIZE OF THE FEDERAL GOVERNMENT, 1984–2018 (2019), brings an historical perspective to bear, demonstrating how different administrations struck differing balances between employees and contractors or grantees.

While the dynamics influencing state and local government staffing patterns differ in important respects (for example, due to the differences in crucial functions and budgeting practices), "outsourcing," "privatization," and accountability are questions in those sectors as well. Issues relating to the changing patterns of government staffing and employee responsibilities will be discussed as pertinent below.

In managing their substantial and varied workforce, state and local government employers must attend to the wide array of human resources and personnel issues facing any business, as well as other specialized challenges associated with their public sector role. Appointment and discharge of public employees is generally controlled by statute, rules or regulations. Employees' civil liberties may be implicated by how they are treated by their employers and their failure to perform their duties carefully and conscientiously may implicate the constitutional rights of citizens. In addition, elected officials and the public have an active interest in the ongoing employer-employee relationship, creating distinctive and complex forms of oversight and special obligations for government employees charged with conducting the public's business in an ethical and responsible fashion. For a thoughtful article identifying the several ways in which public employment and municipal labor relations matter to the public as well as academia, see Kapoor, *Public Sector Labor Relations: Why It Should Matter to the Public and to Academia*, 5 U. PA. J. LAB. & EMP. L. 401 (2003).

This Chapter is designed to accomplish several important objectives. It uses selected topics relating to government employment to illuminate more fully the critical characteristics of state and local governments, including those introduced in other chapters. In order to do so, it highlights the differences between private and public sector employment relating to hiring and retention, operational practices, and collective bargaining as points of departure. It also provides a specific context in which close attention can be paid to the complex interplay of state and federal statutes, constitutional provisions, and local ordinances. Finally, it illustrates important issues of policy development, statutory and regulatory drafting, and the ethical obligations and distinctive roles of policymakers and government attorneys.

The Chapter proceeds in four sections. The first section provides a brief overview of the legal framework in which government employment occurs as a prelude to considering the legitimacy of neutral criteria (residency requirements) and partisan criteria (political affiliation) for public employment. The second section focuses on requirements designed to ensure integrity in government service, including those intended to prevent conflicts of interest. The third section considers issues relating to public records and open meetings that apply to the work of public employees and officials and then uses that context to explore the ethical responsibilities of government attorneys as counselors. The Chapter concludes with a fourth section that briefly introduces public sector collective bargaining and related topics.

Problem 5-1

Amy Smith has served as Personnel Administrator of the District Attorney's Office of Agricola County for 20 years under successive Democratic administrations. As a state employee, she is paid through the state Administrative Office of the Courts and is covered by state civil service laws and a state-wide collective bargaining agreement. She is based in Hillsborough, the county seat, but lives 25 miles away in the adjacent county (Suburbia County) in one of the older neighborhoods in Metro City.

Last year, a Republican District Attorney was elected for Agricola County. Six months after taking office, he adopted an office policy that requires all employees to reside within the county, based on his reading of a state statute that authorizes district attorneys to manage their local offices. Amy spoke to the new DA, telling him that she thought the policy was wrong, then talked to her co-workers and wrote a letter to the local newspaper in which she explained why she thought the new requirement was unfair and inappropriate. The DA called Amy in and asked her when she was going to move. When she said she wasn't going to, the District Attorney discharged her.

Amy is considering her options for redress. She has heard from friends that she might be able to sue Agricola County in federal court for reinstatement. She also wonders whether she can request the appointment of a review committee under state civil service law in order to review her grievance, but knows that Agricola County's new senior deputy DA is currently chair of the standing review committee at the state level and thinks she would not get a fair hearing unless he could be disqualified. She contacted top people in the union that represents public employees and they recently filed a request with the state personnel agency to bargain collectively to ensure that no state-funded office imposes a residency policy, but that request has been rebuffed on the ground that state agencies are not required to bargain collectively on matters of "management." Amy's letter-writing campaign has had some success in raising the local consciousness. She knows the new mayor of Metro City, and he has promised to propose a new ordinance to the city council giving a preference for city jobs to candidates who agree to live in Metro City or in any adjacent county that affords Metro City residents a similar preference for public employment within its jurisdiction.

How likely is it that Amy could prevail in federal court? Could she have the deputy DA disqualified from the grievance panel, and could the union prevail if it insists on pursuing the issue of residency requirements as part of the next collective bargaining agreement? How might the Metro City Attorney advise the mayor about drafting an ordinance that would make his proposal most likely to withstand legal challenge?

A. The Civil Service System, the Legal Landscape, and Political Considerations

Appointment and continued service as a public employee affords important benefits: the prestige of public service, the opportunity to influence government policymaking, generally competitive pay and benefits, and the possibility of stable long-term employment. An important threshold question therefore concerns the basis on which government employees are selected and retained.

Exploration of this question provides a dramatic example of the competing ideals of discretion and constraint that have influenced the development of this area of the law. On the one hand, the corps of public employees may be seen as adjunct to a system of governance with deep roots in the political process. Under this view, wide discretion concerning allocation of employment opportunities can be justified as an appropriate means of dividing spoils in order to grease the wheels of the political system and as a method of ensuring loyal and responsive public servants who reflect the will of elected officials and the voters who choose them. On the other hand, constraint may be justified as a way of ensuring a public work force that serves the public good in an efficient and nonpartisan manner, and of guaranteeing public employees that their individual rights are protected from abusive political whims.

The Emergence of Civil Service Systems

A major turning point in this debate occurred with the enactment of the Pendleton Act of 1883, ch. 27, 22 Stat. 403, creating a federal "civil service" system in the wake of President James Garfield's assassination by a disappointed office-seeker. The term "civil service laws" is currently defined under federal regulations as:

> a personnel system established by law which is designed to protect employees from arbitrary action, personal favoritism, and political coercion, and which uses a competitive or merit examination process for selection and placement. It must provide covered employees with continued tenure of employment except for cause.

29 C.F.R. § 553.11(c). For an extensive discussion of the evolution and characteristics of the federal civil service system see *Developments in the Law—Public Employment*, 97 Harv. L. Rev. 1611, 1619–76 (1984).

Although the federal Civil Service System is long-standing, proposals for reform continue to be offered. See P. Light, A Government Ill-Executed (2008) (providing a powerful critique of the current civil service system, discussing the characteristics of public sector employment, and urging reforms to draw better candidates into public service). Similar civil service systems were subsequently adopted in the states. A complex mosaic of legal provisions controls government employment at the state and local level. In some instances, state constitutions include provisions for the use of "merit principles" or mandate the creation of a "civil service system." See, e.g., La. Const. Art. X, § 1 (establishing the state and the local civil service systems). Detailed requirements are generally imposed by civil service statutes and related regulations; by local charters, ordinances, or policies; and in some places by collective bargaining agreements. See generally, Markowitz, *A Practical Guide to Hiring and Firing Public Employees*, 29 URB. LAW. 293 (1997).

Three significant trends that have transformed the characteristics, scope, and dynamics of civil service systems at state and federal levels: limitations on the traditional job security of public employees, the role of the private sector in performing traditional "government work," and the implications of government shut-downs that have significantly burdened government employees and undercut their expectations of security of employment.

State Reforms and Re-Emergence of At Will Employment in the Public Sector

In recent decades, several states have experimented with civil service reform involving a reintroduction of "at will" employment and reduction in the extent to which civil service systems apply. Georgia, in particular, adopted legislation in 1996 under the leadership of Governor Zell Miller that placed new hires in unclassified (rather than classified) service, modified options for pay increases to emphasize "pay for performance," and changed procedural protections. See GA. CODE ANN. §45-20-1 *et seq.* Legal challenges to the new system were unsuccessful. See *Service Employees Intern. Union v. Perdue*, 628 S.E.2d 589 (Ga. 2006) (in 4-3 decision, upholding Georgia legislation that removed new state employees from the rules of the merit system and substituted "at will" employment system without equivalent protections of tenure and due process, in face of union's argument that legislation violated state constitutional provision providing for a "State Merit System of Personnel Administration" and specifying that "State personnel shall be selected on the basis of merit as provided by law"). Florida and Texas have also adopted substantial changes in their civil service systems. For analysis of the implications of these changes, see E. Kellough & L. Nigro (Eds.), CIVIL SERVICE REFORM IN THE STATES: PERSONNEL POLICY AND POLITICS AT THE SUBNATIONAL LEVEL (2006) (discussing experiences of Georgia, Florida, Texas, South Carolina, California, Wisconsin, and New York). See also Brewer & Kellough, *Administrative Values and Public Personnel Management: Reflections on Civil Service Reform*, 45 PUB. PERSONNEL MANAGEMENT, No. 2 (2016): 171–189 (reviewing civil service reforms over the past 35 years in many countries, and suggesting that they have relaxed traditional merit system rules, decentralized the personnel function, and augmented agency and managerial discretion); West, *Re-Balancing the Pendulum: A Recommendation for Civil Service Reform*, 68 ADMIN. L. REV. 359 (2016) (suggesting ways to address performance issues regarding employees and fostering accountability).

Privatization and Its Implications

The notion of privatization as an alternative model for delivery of governmental services was introduced in Chapter 3. In recent years, there has been a growing interest in reconsidering the extent to which jobs should remain within government civil service systems or instead be "privatized" by contracting with private firms. Proposals to "privatize" key functions continue to be explored at both the state and federal level. On a policy level, proponents often argue that privatization can lead to less expensive and more efficient delivery of services by more highly motivated and responsive personnel. Opponents typically raise concerns about potential cronyism, inadequate accountability, and inconsistent quality of service delivery. Some reject this dichotomy. See Sagers, *The Myth of "Privatization,"* 59 ADMIN. L. REV. 37 (2007) (employing a sociological lens to understand "privatization," challenging recent literature as conceptually flawed, and arguing that "the basic choice in the organization of society is not between organization by government bureaucracy on one hand, and markets on the other," but instead between "two kinds of bureaucracy, which really do not differ much at all" except that "one of them lacks even a nominal obligation toward the public interest"). For thoughtful views on the implications and possible future of privatization, see Michaels, *Privatization's Progeny*, 101 GEO. L.J. 1023 (2013) (reviewing traditional justifications for privatization, tracing its evolution through marketization and reduction of public employee rights, and suggesting its possible future implications for policy processes and judicial review); J. Michaels, CONSTITUTIONAL COUP: PRIVATIZATION'S THREAT TO THE AMERICAN REPUBLIC (2017). See also Epstein, *Contract Theory and the Failures of Public-Private Contracting*, 34 CARDOZO L. REV. 2211 (2013) (arguing that contracts for services such as prisons and welfare administration tend to result in low quality services because limited competition costs of poor services are not internalized by the parties; and suggesting that such public-private contracts should be interpreted to include a mandatory obligation to act in furtherance of the public interest); Epstein, *Public-Private Contracting and the Reciprocity Norm*, 64 AM. U. L. REV. 1 (2014) (drawing on literature relating to behavioral economics, contending that more open-ended contracts would lead to better service from private providers and urging reconsideration of typical public-private contract strategies that have tended to incorporate extremely detailed technical requirements).

Provisions of state civil service laws have been seen to control the means by which personnel services can be secured and thus may preclude privatization of standard functions such as the operation of public landfills. *Konno v. County of Hawai'i*, 937 P.2d 397 (Hawai'i 1997) (holding the county violated state statutes and constitutional provisions in attempting to privatize the operation of landfills); *Salera v. Caldwell*, 375 P.3d 188 (Hawai'i 2016) (holding that it was impermissible to discontinue front-loader refuse collection and disposal services where positions associated with such services were covered by civil service requirements). For a collection of cases involving privatization of various functions, see *Privatization of Governmental Services by State or Local Governmental Agency*, 65 A.L.R.5th 1 (1999). City charter provisions may also have a bearing. See, e.g., *Giles v. Horn*, 123 Cal. Rptr. 2d 735 (Cal. App. 2002) (challenge to San Diego County decision to contract out certain functions relating to welfare-to-work program on grounds that such action violated county charter's provisions regarding civil service, remanded for consideration of mootness). In *Civil Service Comm'n v. City of New Orleans*, 854 So. 2d 322 (La. 2003), the Civil Service Commission challenged a decision of the City of New Orleans to contract out for management of the city's municipal auditorium and performing arts center, which had employed 19 staff and run a substantial deficit. The court held that the Commission did not have constitutional power to block such privatization, but allowed a challenge to the contract to determine whether the contracts had been entered into for good faith, rather than political reasons.

Privatization may raise a variety of policy questions. Consider, for example, which types of governmental services can best be privatized, using the examples of engineering services, services relating to welfare for the poor, and privatization of prisons.

(a) *Engineering services.* For changing views in California regarding engineering of highway projects, compare *Professional Engineers v. Dep't of Transportation*, 936 P.2d 473 (Cal. 1997) (finding no authority to contract out highway design work), with *Consulting Engineers and Land Surveyors of California v. California Dept. of Transp.*, 84 Cal. Rptr. 3d 900 (Cal. App. 2008) (declaring state statute that provided for use of public Caltran personnel in development of high occupancy vehicle lanes to be unconstitutional following public initiative that amended Article XXII section 1 of the state constitution to specify that the "State of California and all other governmental entities . . . shall be allowed to contract with qualified private entities for architectural and engineering services for all public works of improvement . . . without regard to funding source . . .").

(b) *Services to the poor.* For discussion of services to the poor, see Super, *Privatization, Policy Paralysis and the Poor*, 96 CAL. L. REV. 393 (2008) (discussing privatization of delivery of subsistence benefits programs); Bach, *Welfare Reform, Privatization and Power*, 74 BROOK. L. REV. 275 (2009) (considering privatization of New York City welfare function, arguing that a shift to contracts and monitoring of contracts has imposed punitive welfare policies that fail to meet the needs of the poor, and proposing that community-controlled monitoring bodies are needed to address accountability problems).

(c) *Prisons and immigration enforcement.* The privatization of prisons and immigration enforcement services have grown increasingly controversial. See Appleman, *Cashing in on Convicts: Privatization, Punishment, and the People*, 2018 UTAH L. REV. 579 (2018) (arguing that private prisons create risks of death and dereliction of duty); Chacon, *Privatized Immigration Enforcement*, 52 HARV. C.R.-C.L. L. REV. 1 (2017) (providing a description of different facets of immigration enforcement that have been privatized, and critiquing the resulting effects on detention conditions and core values). For a discussion of possible privatization of air traffic control functions, see Heher, *ATC Privatization: A Solution in Search of a Problem*, 83 J. AIR L. & COM. 521 (2018) (arguing against privatization on grounds that it would reduce equity, increase costs, and compromise safety).

Other discussions of privatization or "contracting out" include the following important books: J. Freeman & M. Minnow (Eds.), GOVERNMENT BY CONTRACT: OUTSOURCING AND AMERICAN DEMOCRACY (2008) (discussing history of outsourcing; reasons for changes in government work; contracting in a variety of sectors including environmental regulation, military, and prisons, and related constitutional issues); P. Verkuil, OUTSOURCING SOVEREIGNTY: WHY PRIVATIZATION OF GOVERNMENT FUNCTIONS THREATENS DEMOCRACY AND WHAT WE CAN DO ABOUT IT (2007) (discussing outsourcing of sovereignty, exploring outsourcing of transportation security services, considering issues of delegation and contract theory, and examining structural reforms).

The Implications of Government Shutdowns.

The late 2018–early 2019 shutdown of the federal government caused many federal employees to reconsider the security of their employment status, often seen as a factor offsetting lower pay typical of government positions. While it is too soon to expect data and analysis about the implications of the extended federal government shutdown (which affected government employees who were subsequently paid but also federal contractors who were not), it is worth considering the implications of insecurity that may affect government recruitment and workforces in the future. See Piatak, *Weathering the Storm: The Impact of Cutbacks on Public Employees,* 48 PUB. PERSONNEL MANAGEMENT, NO. 1 (2019): 97–119 (discussing implications of cutbacks from 2008–2009 recession).

Public employers may not only be regulated by differing statutory schemes, but they may be influenced by distinctive policy considerations in defining relevant criteria for selection and retention of their employees. As the following materials illustrate, special hiring and retention requirements may be neutral and nonpartisan in character (for example, local government policies requiring employees to reside within the employing jurisdiction), or may reflect concerns for the political and policy environment in which public employees serve (for example, hiring or retention decisions that take into account employees' political affiliation, speech or conduct). State and federal constitutional requirements may provide special protection for public employees under these circumstances, as the cases and notes that follow demonstrate.

[1] Nonpartisan Eligibility Requirements

State and local governments may limit entry into governmental service by imposing a variety of eligibility criteria concerning education, experience, and skills. Some criteria may be less plainly neutral, however. For example, United States citizenship or residence within the hiring jurisdiction may be required to qualify for employment, or members of particular groups may be given preference over other applicants (preferences have at times been afforded to military veterans). Both exclusionary criteria and preferences may reflect nonpartisan political influence.

Cases challenging requirements that employees reside within the jurisdiction in which they work serve as a useful example of neutral criteria such as these. Sometimes such requirements pose issues of local government power. See *City & County of Denver v. State*, 788 P.2d 764 (Colo. 1990) (upholding local home rule power as a basis for establishing residency requirement). On other occasions, they pose questions of policy. Some years ago, a survey by the International Personnel Management Association found that 39% of public employers responding required that employees, in some or all positions, reside within specified locales. See *Recruiting: Survey Shows Internal Vacancy Posting Drop, Sharp Increase in Electronic Applications*, 39 Gov'T Empl. Rel. Rep. (BNA) 645 (2001). As gentrification has increased costs in urban housing markets, parents shopped for desirable schools, and competition for talented employees increased, however, residency requirements were called into question in some areas. See Ehrenhalt, *The Residency Rebellion*, Governing, May 2000, at 6–7. Periodically, policymakers revisit related questions, and it appears that residency requirements may be on the upswing once again. See Kerigan, *Wisconsin Reignites the Residency Debate*, Governing, March 2013, available at http://www.governing.com/columns/col-wisconsin-reignites-residency-requirement-debate.html.

Most commonly, residency requirements have been applied to public safety personnel and schoolteachers, where justification for their use is most evident because of special benefits to the public of having such personnel actively involved in community life. At times, however, residency requirements are applied more broadly as illustrated by the following case, where residency requirements were applied to all non-uniformed employees in New York City's mayoral agencies. The case also illustrates additional issues commonly faced in connection with the discharge of public employees, including the applicability of constitutional and statutory due process requirements.

Felix v. New York City Department of Citywide Administrative Services

3 N.Y.3d 498, 788 N.Y.S.2d 631, 821 N.E.2d 935 (2004)

G.B. Smith, J.

The issue before this Court is whether a person employed by the municipality of New York City, with permanent, civil service status, can be deemed to have forfeited his employment after failing to establish his city residency following notice of and an opportunity to contest the claimed nonresidency. We conclude that failure to establish residency is a violation of the City's residency requirement, which results in forfeiture of employment, and is not misconduct that would entitle the employee to a preremoval hearing.

On July 30, 1986, Edward I. Koch, then Mayor of the City of New York, signed into law a bill, sponsored at his request by members of the City Council of New York City, that required all nonuniformed employees in mayoral agencies, hired on or after September 1, 1986, to establish and maintain residence within the five boroughs of New York City as a condition of employment. [According to Mayor Koch, the residency requirement was meant to: (1) increase employment opportunities for New York City residents; (2) bolster the local economy; and (3) increase accountability of city employees and the level of concern and pride in the delivery of services to the City.] Prior to signing the bill into law, Mayor Koch specifically stated that "[f]ailure to establish or maintain City residence will constitute forfeiture of employment."

Local Law No. 40 (1986) of the City of New York, the law in question, amended sections . . . the Administrative Code of the City of New York [which in pertinent part] provides:

> "Except as otherwise provided in section 12-121, any person who enters city service on or after September first nineteen hundred eighty-six (i) shall be a resident of the city on the date that he or she enters city service or shall establish city residence within ninety days after such date and (ii) shall thereafter maintain city residence as a condition of employment. Failure to establish or maintain city residence as required by this section shall constitute a forfeiture of employment; provided, however, that prior to dismissal for failure to establish or maintain city residence an employee shall be given notice of and the opportunity to contest the charge that his or her residence is outside the city."

. . . [New York City Administrative Code § 12-119 provides that "residence" means domicile, "resident" means domiciliary and the term "city service" means "service as an employee of the city or of any agency thereof other than service in a position which is exempted from municipal residence requirements pursuant to the public officers law or any other state law."

[Felix did not contend that he fell within any relevant exceptions, and the Court noted that even employees who come within the provisions of the state civil service law are subject to New York City's residency requirement.]

In August 1993, respondent Felix was hired by appellant New York City Department of Citywide Administrative Services (DCAS) and permanently appointed to the competitive class position of high pressure plant tender [a position that was subject to both the New York City Administrative Code and the state civil service laws]. At the time he was hired he completed, sign, swore to and had notarized a residency form in which he acknowledged that his employment was conditioned on maintaining residence in New York City and that if he failed to remain a New York City resident, he could forfeit his employment. The residency form stated in pertinent part:

> "I, Francisco Felix, am or expect to be employed by the above agency or department on the date of appointment and in the position indicated above. I hereby certify that I reside at the above address which is in The City of New York. . . .

> "I hereby agree that I will notify the head of the above agency and the Department of Personnel of The City of New York prior to any change of residence by me or my spouse during such time as I remain employed by The City of New York. I understand that if I fail to remain a resident during the period of my employment with The City of New York I may forfeit my employment unless I have been granted an exemption from the residency requirements in accordance with the Mayoral Directive on Residence or Section 12-119 et seq. of the Administrative Code."

Approximately nine years after Felix's appointment, DCAS began to suspect that Felix resided in Nassau County, in violation of New York City's residency requirement. In a memorandum, DCAS informed Felix of its suspicion, and directed Felix to attend a meeting on January 23, 2002, at which time he would have an opportunity to contest the allegation. The memorandum stated that if Felix planned to contest the allegation, he should bring documentation demonstrating his New York City residency including deeds and leases for real property, utility bills, his driver's license and vehicle registration, voter registration cards and federal and state tax returns. The memorandum further stated that "*[t]ax returns are necessary documentation.*" Felix was advised that he could bring an attorney or union representative to the meeting.

Felix appeared at the January 23 meeting with a union representative and, in accordance with DCAS procedures, was asked to produce two forms of identification. He produced a New York State driver's license with a Corona (Queens County), New York address and an expiration date of June 3, 2004. DCAS requested additional documents regarding his residency, but Felix said that he did not bring any additional documentation with him. Felix further stated that he was not aware that he was required to be a New York City resident. DCAS then showed Felix the residency form he had completed and sworn to. In order to afford Felix the opportunity to produce additional documentation, DCAS adjourned the meeting for two days.

On January 25, 2002, the meeting reconvened and Felix again appeared with a union representative. This time, however, when asked to produce documentation to establish his place of residence, Felix submitted the following documents:

(1) a letter from his sister, dated January 23, 2002, stating that he lived with her in Flushing (Queens County), New York;

(2) voter registration card, dated January 23, 2002;

(3) an interim driver's license, issued on January 23, 2002;

(4) a vehicle registration card, issued on January 24, 2002;

(5) a New York State insurance identification card pertaining to an insurance policy with an effective date of January 23, 2002;[4]

4. Documents (2)-(5) indicated that Felix's address was in Flushing, New York.

(6) a letter from Felix's union, dated January 24, 2002, stating that according to its records, Felix resided in Kew Gardens (Queens County), New York;

(7) a delinquency notice from an out-of-state dentist's office, dated January 24, 2002, reflecting that Felix's address was in Flushing, New York; and

(8) a W-2 form and federal income tax return for the tax year 2000 which both indicated that Felix resided in Valley Stream (Nassau County), New York.

In a letter dated January 28, 2002, DCAS advised Felix that, based on its review of the submitted documentation, it had determined that the evidence submitted by Felix did not credibly establish that he maintained residence in New York City as required by New York City Administrative Code § 12-120. DCAS concluded that all of the documentation reflecting Felix's residence in New York City was created after the January 23, 2002 meeting had adjourned for the sole purpose of establishing a New York City residence. Accordingly, DCAS found that Felix violated the residency requirement for his job and was deemed to have forfeited his position. He was immediately dismissed from his employment.

Felix filed a CPLR article 78 proceeding to challenge his dismissal, arguing that he was entitled to reinstatement with back pay because he was discharged without a preremoval hearing under Civil Service Law § 75(1).[5] Supreme Court granted Felix's petition. The Appellate Division affirmed, and this Court granted leave to appeal.

A municipal employee must be afforded procedural due process before he or she is dismissed from employment for violating New York City's residency requirement. Accordingly, this Court must determine two questions: first, whether Felix's non-residency was a forfeiture of employment or misconduct for which he was entitled to a preremoval hearing and second, did the "notice of and the opportunity to contest the charge" procedure set forth under New York City Administrative Code § 12-120 satisfy due process.

We note at the outset that the act of failing to maintain one's residence within the municipality is separate and distinct from an act of misconduct by a municipal employee in the performance of his or her work. Failure to maintain residence renders an individual ineligible for continued municipal employment under New York City Administrative Code § 12-120, while an act of misconduct invokes Civil Service Law § 75 disciplinary procedures, including a preremoval hearing if removal of the municipal employee is contemplated (*see e.g., Mandelkern v. City of Buffalo*, 409 N.Y.S.2d 881 [4th Dept.1978]). In *Mandelkern*, the Appellate Division, Fourth

---

5. Civil Service Law § 75 sets forth a procedure under which certain employees, including those with permanent, civil service status, may be removed or subjected to other disciplinary action for misconduct or incompetency. Civil Service Law § 75(1) provides, in pertinent part:

> "A person [holding a position by permanent appointment in the competitive class of the classified civil service] shall not be removed or otherwise subjected to any disciplinary penalty provided in this section except for incompetency or misconduct shown after a hearing upon stated charges pursuant to this section."

Department held that a City of Buffalo ordinance setting forth residency requirements for city employees did not violate Civil Service Law § 75(1). In so holding, the Court noted that residency requirements define eligibility for employment, not misconduct to which civil service protections would apply. The Court stated as follows:

> "[t]he local legislation and the Civil Service Law have different purposes. The [local legislation] is designed with the legitimate purpose of encouraging city employees to maintain a commitment and involvement with the government which employs them by living within the city [citations omitted]. When so viewed, it is clear that residence is a consideration unrelated to job performance, misconduct or competency. It is a qualification of employment, . . . and a qualification which the city may impose if it chooses to do so without running afoul of the Constitution or general laws of the State. The Civil Service Law, on the other hand, prescribes the procedures for removal of a protected employee charged with delinquencies in the performance of his job. It has nothing to do with eligibility for employment" (*Mandelkern*, 409 N.Y.S.2d 881).

Similarly, the instant residency requirement has a different purpose than Civil Service Law § 75(1) . . . for purpose of New York City's residency requirement. Accordingly, the procedural due process afforded under Civil Service Law § 75(1), i.e., a preremoval hearing, is not necessarily required for dismissals pursuant to New York City Administrative Code § 12-120. . . .

We next address the question whether the procedure itself comported with state and federal due process requirements. The instant residency requirement provides that a municipal employee "shall be given notice of and the opportunity to contest the charge that his or her residence is outside the city" (New York City Administrative Code § 12-120). To determine whether this procedure satisfied due process here, we necessarily take into account that Felix was required and/or requested to produce various documents, e.g., tax documents, driver's license and voter registration card, in order to establish a New York City residence. Documents such as these need not be subjected to the adversarial testing of a hearing in order for the municipality to determine whether a municipal employee has established that he or she resides in New York City. The municipality need only review each document to make that determination. As such, we conclude that the "notice of and the opportunity to contest the charge" procedure set forth in New York City's residency requirement satisfies due process.

Here, Felix was afforded the requisite due process; however, the documents he submitted did not establish that his current residence was in New York City. To the contrary, Felix submitted a driver's license with a New York City address he later admitted was no longer current, seven documents that were clearly created after the January 23 meeting for the sole purpose of establishing that Felix's residence was in New York City, and most significantly, two tax documents which established that Felix's residence was outside of New York City. Thus, DCAS correctly determined that Felix forfeited his position and that dismissal was warranted.

Accordingly, the order of the Appellate Division should be reversed, with costs, and the petition dismissed.

CHIEF JUDGE KAYE and JUDGES CIPARICK, ROSENBLATT, GRAFFEO, READ and R.S. SMITH concur.

Order reversed, etc.

Notes and Questions

1. *Durational and continuing residency requirements.* Two types of residency requirements are sometimes imposed: those that require that those affected have maintained residency for a prior period in order to qualify ("durational") and those that mandate that those affected employees commence and maintain residence in the future ("continuing"). The United States Supreme Court has considered related issues in connection with various forms of welfare benefits, striking down a durational requirement in *Shapiro v. Thompson*, 394 U.S. 618 (1969) (invalidating a requirement that a recipient of welfare assistance be a resident of the state for one year in order to qualify to receive benefits), and more recently in *Saenz v. Roe*, 526 U.S. 489 (1999) (invalidating under the Privileges and Immunities Clause a California requirement that capped welfare payments at a lower level for new state residents who had relocated from another country or from states that paid lower levels of welfare benefits, notwithstanding the state's concern for fiscal management, disavowal of any intent to deter migration, and authority under federal welfare reform legislation to develop tailored state policies). State and local efforts to target other types of benefits based on duration of residence have also been rebuffed. See, e.g., *Attorney General of N.Y. v. Soto-Lopez*, 476 U.S. 898 (1986) (invalidating veterans preference system that benefited only those veterans who had lived in state at time they entered military service). The Supreme Court upheld a continuing residence requirement in *McCarthy v. Philadelphia Civil Service Comm'n*, 424 U.S. 645 (1976), where in a brief per curiam opinion, the Court stated that

> [We have not] questioned the validity of a condition placed upon municipal employment that a person be a resident *at the time* of his application. In this case appellant claims a constitutional right to be employed by the city of Philadelphia *while* he is living elsewhere. There is no support in our cases for such a claim. [*Id.* at 646–47 (emphasis in original).]

What type of residency requirement was involved in the principal case? Is the distinction between durational and continuing residency requirements a persuasive one?

2. *Legal challenges to residency requirements.* The court in the principal case spent little time considering the legitimacy of the residency requirement, moving instead to the procedural issues associated with the employee's discharge. In other cases, courts have considered a number of different types of legal challenges to such requirements, including the following.

(a) *Equal protection and right to travel.* Federal challenges have been successful where the right to interstate travel is implicated. See *Walsh v. City and County of Honolulu*, 460 F. Supp. 2d 1207 (D. Hawai'i 2006) (concluding that requirement that applicants for public employment be current legal residents of the state at the time of application violated non-residents' fundamental right to interstate travel where state failed to show that such individuals were more likely to leave positions soon after employment and claim of government necessity was undercut by state's demonstration that residency could be gained readily upon arrival to the state). Other courts have generally applied limited scrutiny in instances in which the right to travel across state lines is not implicated (the right to travel interstate is deemed a fundamental right under the federal Constitution and "compelling" governmental interests must exist when it is substantially infringed).

Analysis may vary, however, since some state courts apply more rigorous standards than the United States Supreme Court or address specific provisions in state constitutions that differ from those in the United States Constitution. See *Bruno v. Civil Service Comm'n of City of Bridgeport*, 472 A.2d 328, 334 (Conn. 1984) (in case involving appointment of recreation superintendent, durational residence requirement implicated right to intrastate travel under state constitution; more searching scrutiny was found appropriate, and city requirement was invalidated where alternative means could be identified to test candidates' familiarity with the city and to ensure that employees were available during their tenure in office). See also *Barrow v. City of Detroit Election Comm'n*, 836 N.W.2d 498 (Mich. App. 2013) (in case brought by mayoral candidate against second candidate based on second candidate's alleged failure to comply with charter provision requiring one-year residency, concluding that charter had minimal effect on intrastate travel and did not violate the equal protection clause since it did not implicate rights to move in and out of city, did not deny fundamental rights, and assured candidates were familiar with constituency).

(b) *Residency requirements and state civil service legislation.* The principal case cited earlier New York case law finding no conflict between local residency requirements and state statutes governing civil service employees. The *Mandelkern* decision, quoted in the principal case rejected a challenge of city attorneys who wished to move outside the city of Buffalo and asserted that enforcement of continuing residency requirements would conflict with state civil service law that provided for removal only for "misconduct or incompetence." The principal case elaborates on the New York civil service statutes' purpose, explaining that procedural protections provided in instances of "misconduct" or "incompetence" did not apply when an employee failed to comply with a "condition of employment" such as the residency requirement. How would you define "misconduct" and "incompetence"? Is the distinction between a failure to meet the residency requirements and "misconduct" a meaningful and clear one? Why wasn't the employee's violation of the residency requirement "misconduct" for purposes of the civil service law? If his supervisor had asked him where he lived, and he had lied, would that constitute "misconduct" that would have assured him of a hearing? For a New York case finding that no due process hearing was required when a bridge repair mechanic lost his commercial driver's license after a DUI conviction, see *Stolzman v. New York State Dep't of Transportation*, 890 N.Y.S.2d 181 (N.Y. 2009). For another New York decision upholding municipal residency requirements, see *Beck-Nichols v. Bianco*, 987 N.E.2d 233 (N.Y. 2013) (citing *Felix* and *Mandelkern*, upholding residency requirement, and concluding that due process requirements were met).

(c) *Residency requirements and job characteristics.* The nature of the jobs performed by employees covered by residency requirements may make a difference in either constitutional or statutory interpretation. See *Seabrook Police Ass'n v. Town of Seabrook*, 635 A.2d 1371 (N.H. 1993) (upholding residency requirement as applicable to police given need to respond to emergencies); *Airport Taxi Cab Advisory Comm'n v. City of Atlanta*, 584 F. Supp. 961 (N.D. Ga. 1983) (upholding one-year residency requirement for licensure of taxicab drivers, after applying minimal scrutiny standard and considering city's concern that drivers be familiar with city streets and be screened to check for past criminal records). See also *Southern Wine and Spirits of America, Inc. v. Division of Alcohol and Tobacco Control,* 731 F.3d 799 (8th Cir. 2013) (upholding Missouri residency requirement applicable to licensees who wished to sell liquor at wholesale, based on the Twenty-First Amendment, and a determination that the state legislature could have legitimately believed that wholesalers governed predominantly by Missouri residents would be more apt to be socially responsible and promote temperance).

(d) *Legislation limiting residency restrictions.* Litigation in states that have legislatively limited municipal residency requirements raise interesting questions. See, e.g., *Lash v. City of Travers City*, 735 N.W.2d 628 (Mich. 2007) (finding that city's residency requirement violated state statute, interpreting 20-mile distance requirement, and rejecting asserted private cause of action for damages in connection with refusal to employ candidate for police position); *Ass'n of Cleveland Firefighters v. City of Cleveland*, 5 N.E.3d 676 (Ohio App. 2013) (striking down system that allocated points toward promotion as violating state statutory provision). Ohio and New Jersey have both limited the power of municipalities to impose residency requirements. For discussion, see Mulligan, *Not in Your Backyard: Ohio's Prohibition on Residency Requirements for Police, Firefighters, and Other Municipal Employees*, 37 U. Dayton L. Rev. 351 (2012) (discussing Ohio municipalities' experience with charter provisions relating to employment, nearby states' experience, Ohio litigation, resulting legislation, and Ohio Supreme Court decision upholding statutory constraints against challenge based on home rule powers); Rindosh, *Continuing Residency Requirements: Questioning Burdens on Public Employment in New Jersey*, 42 Seton Hall L. Rev. 1635 (2012) (discussing "New Jersey First" legislation that required public employees, and officers, with some exceptions, to live within the state). Wisconsin, too, has imposed limitations on the rights of cities like Milwaukee to retain long-standing residency requirements, allowing only a requirement that police, fire, and emergency personnel live within 15 miles of city boundaries.

Following state litigation in which the city unsuccessfully challenged the legislation as violating its home rule prerogatives, *Black v. City of Milwaukee*, 882 N.W.2d 333 (Wis. 2016), the federal court of appeals upheld the application of the new 15-mile residency requirement against a substantive due process claim by a police officer. See *Milwaukee Police Ass'n v. City of Milwaukee*, 856 F.3d 480 (7th Cir. 2017).

3. *Uniform application of policies.* Must local governments enforce residency requirements for all covered employees in order to do so in particular cases? See *Newark Council No. 21, NJCSA, IFPTE, AFLCIO v. James*, 723 A.2d 127 (N.J. App. Div. 1999) (lax application of requirements that did not amount to studied policy of non-enforcement would not be enjoined). See also *Crowley v. Board of Educ. of City of Chicago*, 8 N.E.3d 1101 (Ill. App. 2014) (upholding tenured teacher's discharge despite inconsistent and lax application). The principal case did not discuss the reasons for the employee's decision to relocate his residence. Would inclusion of provisions authorizing waiver of requirements in cases of "hardship" render ordinances more or less supportable? See *Gusewelle v. City of Wood River*, 374 F.3d 569 (7th Cir. 2004) (holding that city employee, who admittedly resided within city limits only two days per week and lived with his wife outside the city limits the remainder of the time for period of 20 years, violated city residency ordinance, requiring city employees to have primary residence within the city limits, even though employee paid taxes, registered his car, voted, and obtained his driver's license using his city address). How should an ordinance be drafted to deal with situations such as these?

4. *Residency requirements and elective office.* Residency restrictions on elective office raise additional questions because they also affect fundamental rights to vote or to hold public office. See, e.g., *Bullock v. Carter*, 405 U.S. 134 (1972) (striking down excessive filing fee for candidates as an impairment of the right to vote); *Johnson v. Hamilton*, 541 P.2d 881 (Cal. 1975) (invalidating durational residency requirement for candidates for city office).

What are the reasons for applying durational residency requirements to candidates for public office? The justification usually asserted is that the candidate must be familiar with the issues likely to arise in the election, and the voters must be familiar with the candidate. The residency requirement is claimed to serve these objectives. The California court decisively rejected this reasoning, concluding that duration of residency was as a poor proxy for the knowledge and comprehension which a candidate needed to develop based on motivation, intelligence, and experience. The court also took notice of increasing voter apathy, and suggested that this danger "suggests the wisdom of widening rather than narrowing the candidate options available to the public." Other courts uphold durational residency requirements, especially when applied to state offices, if carefully tailored to the circumstances. Compare *Mobley v. Armstrong*, 978 S.W.2d 307 (Ky. 1998) (upholding two-year residency requirement for district judge as permissible under federal Equal Protection Clause), with *Antonio v. Kirkpatrick*, 579 F.2d 1147 (8th Cir. 1978) (ten-year residency requirement for elected state auditor invalid under rational relationship test). Would the residency requirement in *Antonio v. Kirkpatrick*, *supra*, be invalid if it applied to the governor? See *Hankins v. State of Hawaii*, 639 F. Supp. 1552 (D. Haw. 1986) (upholding five-year durational residency requirement for governorship). See also Dow, *Mr. Emanuel Returns from Washington: Durational Residence Requirements and Election Litigation*, 90 WASH. U. L. REV. 1515 (2013) (discussing 2011 Chicago mayoral race and related litigation).

5. *Procedural protections in instances of employee discharge.* The *Felix* case focused in substantial part on the plaintiff's assertion that he should have been afforded a pre-termination hearing. What is the source of his procedural claim? Do all government employees have rights to such hearings? Procedural protections can stem from several sources. In the *Felix* case, the plaintiff sought to invoke procedures provided to government employees under the state civil service law. In other instances, procedural protections can be afforded by the terms of contracts (for example, those of tenured university professors), or collective bargaining agreements as discussed later in this chapter. In the absence of such provisions, government employees may be able to assert that they are entitled to procedural protections as a matter of constitutional doctrine.

The United States Constitution provides that "No person shall . . . be deprived of life, liberty, or property, without due process of law" (Fifth Amendment) and further specifies that "nor shall any State deprive any person of life, liberty, or property without due process of law" (Fourteenth Amendment). In *Perry v. Sindermann*, 408 U.S. 593 (1972), the United States Supreme Court considered the case of a college professor who had been employed on a series of short-term contracts before publicly disagreeing with members of the college Board of Regents and subsequently no longer being renewed. He was not tenured but argued that he had an expectation of continuing employment, sufficient to constitute a right to property which had been denied by government action without procedural due process. The Court held that the lack of tenure or a contractual obligation to renew Sindermann's contract did not defeat his claim that he had been denied employment without procedural due process in violation of a possible property interest in employment implied by the continuing series of appointments.

Appellate decisions have also addressed whether employees fired for publicly announced reasons (such as dishonesty) that may implicate their reputation relating to moral character have "liberty" interests that require an opportunity for a hearing to clear their names. See *Lawson v. Sheriff of Tippecanoe County*, 725 F.2d 1136 (7th Cir. 1984) (liberty interest implicated when radio dispatcher was discharged and character impugned, remanded for determination whether alternative employment offered negated adverse effect on reputation); *Cotton v. Jackson*, 216 F.3d 1328 (11th Cir. 2000) (six-part test required in "stigma-plus" cases implicating liberty interest, including showing that there had been a false statement of a stigmatizing nature attending a governmental employee's discharge, which statement was made public by the government employer without affording the employee a hearing to clear his or her name); *Blantz v. California Dept. of Corrections and Rehabilitation*,

727 F.3d 917 (9th Cir. 2013) (upholding dismissal of nurse on temporary limited contract, finding liberty interests implicated only if government statements foreclosed individual altogether from her chosen area of employment; concluding that no due process violation had occurred).

The situations in which rights in employment are created and the nature of the process to be afforded government employees in termination cases were elucidated in *Cleveland Bd. of Education v. Loudermill*, 470 U.S. 532 (1985). For a subsequent case addressing procedural protections owed an employee in connection with a layoff, see *Levine v. City of Alameda*, 525 F.3d 903 (9th Cir. 2008) (property manager was entitled to a pre-termination hearing pursuant to union contract; informal conversation with human resources director about due process rights was not sufficient to provide due process protection of property interest in continued employment).

Consider once again the potential for state civil service reforms as outlined earlier in this Chapter, including changes from systems requiring just cause for dismissal to "at will" employment. Is it likely that such changes would alter dismissal patterns? See Elling & Thompson, *Dissin' the Deadwood or Coddling the Incompetents? Patterns and Issues in Employee Discipline and Dismissal in the States*, 31 Int'l J. Pub. Admin. No. 5 (2008): 552–573 (reviewing survey of state employee dismissal patterns; considering implications of procedures, collective bargaining patterns and views of managers; finding relatively low levels of formal dismissals but more frequent use of informal means to force employees to quit; finding little correlation between manager views and proportion of civil service employees supervised; finding little correlation between simplification of appeals processes and proportion of dismissals; finding that collective bargaining correlated with higher public salaries and lower dismissal rates that can be explained by multiple hypotheses; noting implications of turnover rates and difficulties in hiring top employees where salaries are low).

6. *Other "neutral" criteria for hiring, and adverse employment actions.* Governments use other facially neutral criteria for hiring that may raise legal questions. See, e.g., *Lanier v. City of Woodburn*, 518 F.3d 1147 (9th Cir. 2008) (pre-appointment suspicionless drug test requirement that applied to job applicants as condition of employment was unconstitutional as applied to applicant for position of page in library in absence of showing of "special need" such as demonstrable risk to public safety in absence of test); *Seegmiller v. Laverkin City*, 528 F.3d 762 (10th Cir. 2008) (police officer estranged from her husband engaged in affair with officer not within her department while at off-site training; husband falsely alleged that she had had affair with police chief; officer and chief were suspended and press coverage ensued before facts were clarified; officer received private reprimand pursuant to official policy that officers "keep [their] private life unsullied as an example to all and [to] behave in a manner that does not bring discredit to the [officer] or [the] agency"; court found no fundamental right to personal sexual conduct and concluded that

city only needed to show rational basis for its policies which were designed to foster internal discipline and public respect for the police).

[2] Patronage and Political Activity

The principle of political neutrality that characterizes civil service systems may seem simple and straightforward, but that is not necessarily the case. Because civil service systems typically exist side-by-side with systems of elected and appointed officials chosen through the political process, it may be difficult to determine which positions may properly be filled by political appointment and which are off-limits from the patronage system. Moreover, questions can arise concerning the rights of government employees to express political views or to engage in partisan political activity. The materials that follow explore these questions.

Branti v. Finkel

445 U.S. 507 (1980)

Mr. Justice Stevens delivered the opinion of the Court.

The question presented is whether the First and Fourteenth Amendments to the Constitution protect an assistant public defender who is satisfactorily performing his job from discharge solely because of his political beliefs.

Respondents, Aaron Finkel and Alan Tabakman, commenced this action in the United States District Court for the Southern District of New York in order to preserve their positions as assistant public defenders in Rockland County, New York. On January 4, 1978, on the basis of a showing that the petitioner public defender was about to discharge them solely because they were Republicans, the District Court entered a temporary restraining order preserving the status quo. After hearing evidence for eight days, the District Court entered detailed findings of fact and permanently enjoined petitioner from terminating or attempting to terminate respondents' employment "upon the sole grounds of their political beliefs." 457 F. Supp. 1284, 1285 (1978). The Court of Appeals affirmed in an unpublished memorandum opinion, judgment order reported at 598 F.2d 609 (CA2 1979) (table).

The critical facts can be summarized briefly. The Rockland County Public Defender is appointed by the County Legislature for a term of six years. He in turn appoints nine assistants who serve at his pleasure. The two respondents have served as assistants since their respective appointments in March 1971 and September 1975; they are both Republicans.

Petitioner Branti's predecessor, a Republican, was appointed in 1972 by a Republican-dominated County Legislature. By 1977, control of the legislature had shifted to the Democrats and petitioner, also a Democrat, was appointed to replace the incumbent when his term expired. As soon as petitioner was formally appointed on January 3, 1978, he began executing termination notices for six of the nine assistants then in office. Respondents were among those who were to be terminated. With one possible exception, the nine who were to be appointed or retained were all Democrats and were all selected by Democratic legislators or Democratic town chairmen on a basis that had been determined by the Democratic caucus.

The District Court found that Finkel and Tabakman had been selected for termination solely because they were Republicans and thus did not have the necessary Democratic sponsors. . . . The court rejected petitioner's belated attempt to justify the dismissals on nonpolitical grounds. Noting that both Branti and his predecessor had described respondents as "competent attorneys," the District Court expressly found that both had been "satisfactorily performing their duties as Assistant Public Defenders." *Id.*, at 1292.

Having concluded that respondents had been discharged solely because of their political beliefs, the District Court held that those discharges would be permissible under this Court' s decision in *Elrod v. Burns*, 427 U.S. 347, only if assistant public defenders are the type of policymaking, confidential employees who may be discharged solely on the basis of their political affiliations. He concluded that respondents clearly did not fall within that category. . . .

In light of these factual findings, the District Court concluded that petitioner could not terminate respondents' employment as assistant public defenders consistent with the First and Fourteenth Amendments. On appeal, a panel of the Second Circuit affirmed. . . . We granted certiorari, 443 U.S. 904, and now affirm.

Petitioner advances two principal arguments for reversal:[6] First, that the holding in *Elrod v. Burns* is limited to situations in which government employees are coerced into pledging allegiance to a political party that they would not voluntarily support and does not apply to a simple requirement that an employee be sponsored by the party in power; and, second, that even if party sponsorship is an unconstitutional condition of continued public employment for clerks, deputies, and janitors, it is an acceptable requirement for an assistant public defender.

---

6. Petitioner also makes two other arguments. First, he contends that the action should have been dismissed because the evidence showed that he would have discharged respondents in any event due to their lack of competence as public defenders. *See Mt. Healthy City Board of Education v. Doyle*, 429 U.S. 274. The Court of Appeals correctly held this contention foreclosed by the District Court's findings of fact, which it found to be adequately supported by the record. In view of our settled practice of accepting, absent the most exceptional circumstances, factual determinations in which the district court and the court of appeals have concurred, we decline to review these and other findings of fact petitioner argues were clearly erroneous. Second, relying on testimony that an assistant's term in office automatically expires when the public defender's term expires, petitioner argues that we should treat this case as involving a "failure to reappoint" rather than as a dismissal and, as a result, should apply a less stringent standard. Petitioner argues that because respondents knew the system was a patronage system when they were hired, they did not have a reasonable expectation of being rehired when control of the office shifted to the Democratic Party. A similar waiver argument was rejected in *Elrod v. Burns*. After *Elrod*, it is clear that the lack of a reasonable expectation of continued employment is not sufficient to justify a dismissal based solely on an employee's private political beliefs. . . .

I

In *Elrod v. Burns* the Court held that the newly elected Democratic Sheriff of Cook County, Ill., had violated the constitutional rights of certain non-civil-service employees by discharging them "because they did not support and were not members of the Democratic Party and had failed to obtain the sponsorship of one of its leaders." 427 U.S., at 351. That holding was supported by two separate opinions.

Writing for the plurality, Mr. Justice Brennan identified two separate but interrelated reasons supporting the conclusion that the discharges were prohibited by the First and Fourteenth Amendments. First, he analyzed the impact of a political patronage system[7] on freedom of belief and association. Noting that in order to retain their jobs, the Sheriff's employees were required to pledge their allegiance to the Democratic Party, work for or contribute to the party's candidates, or obtain a Democratic sponsor, he concluded that the inevitable tendency of such a system was to coerce employees into compromising their true beliefs.[8] That conclusion, in his opinion, brought the practice within the rule of cases like *Board of Education v. Barnette*, 319 U.S. 624, condemning the use of governmental power to prescribe what the citizenry must accept as orthodox opinion.[9]

---

7. Mr. Justice Brennan noted that many other practices are included within the definition of a patronage system, including placing supporters in government jobs not made available by political discharges, granting supporters lucrative government contracts, and giving favored wards improved public services. In that case, as in this, however, the only practice at issue was the dismissal of public employees for partisan reasons. In light of the limited nature of the question presented, we have no occasion to address petitioner's argument that there is a compelling governmental interest in maintaining a political sponsorship system for filling vacancies in the public defender's office.

8. An individual who is a member of the out-party maintains affiliation with his own party at the risk of losing his job. He works for the election of his party's candidates and espouses its politics at the same risk. The financial and campaign assistance that he is induced to provide to another party furthers the advancement of that party's policies to the detriment of his party's views and ultimately his own beliefs, and any assessment of his salary is tantamount to coerced belief. *See Buckley v. Valeo*, 424 U.S. 1, 19 (1976). Even a pledge of allegiance to another party, however ostensible, only serves to compromise the individual's true beliefs. Since the average public employee is hardly in the financial position to support his party and another, or to lend his time to two parties, the individual's ability to act according to his beliefs and to associate with others of his political persuasion is constrained, and support for his party is diminished. [427 U.S.] 355–36.

Mr. Justice Brennan also indicated that a patronage system may affect freedom of belief more indirectly, by distorting the electoral process. Given the increasingly pervasive character of government employment, he concluded that the power to starve political opposition by commanding partisan support, financial and otherwise, may have a significant impact on the formation and expression of political beliefs.

9. Regardless of the nature of the inducement, whether it be by the denial of public employment or, as in *Board of Education v. Barnette*, 319 U.S. 624 (1943), by the influence of a teacher over students, "[i]f there is any fixed star in our constitutional constellation, it is that no official, high or petty, can prescribe what shall be orthodox in politics, nationalism, religion, or other matters of opinion or force citizens to confess by word or act their faith therein." *Id.*, at 642.

Second, apart from the potential impact of patronage dismissals on the formation and expression of opinion, MR. JUSTICE BRENNAN also stated that the practice had the effect of imposing an unconstitutional condition on the receipt of a public benefit and therefore came within the rule of cases like *Perry v. Sindermann*, 408 U.S. 593. In support of the holding in *Perry* that even an employee with no contractual right to retain his job cannot be dismissed for engaging in constitutionally protected speech, the Court had stated:

> For at least a quarter-century, this Court has made clear that even though a person has no "right" to a valuable governmental benefit and even though the government may deny him the benefit for any number of reasons, there are some reasons upon which the government may not rely. It may not deny a benefit to a person on a basis that infringes his constitutionally protected interests—especially, his interest in freedom of speech. For if the government could deny a benefit to a person because of his constitutionally protected speech or associations, his exercise of those freedoms would in effect be penalized and inhibited. This would allow the government to "produce a result which [it] could not command directly." *Speiser v. Randall*, 357 U.S. 513, 526. Such interference with constitutional rights is impermissible....
>
> Thus, the respondent's lack of a contractual or tenure "right" to re-employment for the 1969–70 academic year is immaterial to his free speech claim. Indeed, twice before, this Court has specifically held that the non-renewal of a nontenured public school teacher's one-year contract may not be predicated on his exercise of First and Fourteenth Amendment rights. *Shelton v. Tucker*, [364 U.S. 479]; *Keyishian v. Board of Regents*, [385 U.S. 589]. We reaffirm those holdings here. *Id.*, at 597–598.

If the First Amendment protects a public employee from discharge based on what he has said, it must also protect him from discharge based on what he believes. Under this line of analysis, unless the government can demonstrate "an overriding interest," 427 U.S., at 368, "of vital importance," *id.*, at 362, requiring that a person's private beliefs conform to those of the hiring authority, his beliefs cannot be the sole basis for depriving him of continued public employment.

MR. JUSTICE STEWART's opinion concurring in the judgment avoided comment on the first branch of MR. JUSTICE BRENNAN's analysis, but expressly relied on the same passage from *Perry v. Sindermann* that is quoted above.

Petitioner argues that *Elrod v. Burns* should be read to prohibit only dismissals resulting from an employee's failure to capitulate to political coercion. Thus, he argues that, so long as an employee is not asked to change his political affiliation or to contribute to or work for the party's candidates, he may be dismissed with impunity—even though he would not have been dismissed if he had the proper political sponsorship and even though the sole reason for dismissing him was to replace him with a person who did have such sponsorship. Such an interpretation would surely emasculate the principles set forth in *Elrod*. While it would perhaps eliminate the more blatant forms of coercion described in *Elrod*, it would not eliminate the coercion of belief that necessarily flow from the knowledge that one must have a sponsor in the dominant party to retain one's job.[11]

More importantly, petitioner's interpretation would require the Court to repudiate entirely the conclusion of both Mr. Justice Brennan and Mr. Justice Stewart that the First Amendment prohibits the dismissal of a public employee solely because of his private political beliefs.

In sum, there is no requirement that dismissed employees prove that they, or other employees, have been coerced into changing, either actually or ostensibly, their political allegiance. To prevail in this type of an action, it was sufficient, as *Elrod* holds, for respondents to prove that they were discharged "solely for the reason that they were not affiliated with or sponsored by the Democratic Party." 427 U.S., at 350.

II

Both opinions in *Elrod* recognize that party affiliation may be an acceptable requirement for some types of government employment. Thus, if an employee's private political beliefs would interfere with the discharge of his public duties, his First Amendment rights may be required to yield to the State's vital interest in maintaining governmental effectiveness and efficiency. *Id.*, at 366. In *Elrod*, it was clear that the duties of the employees—the chief deputy of the process division of the sheriff's office, a process server and another employee in that office, and a bailiff and security guard at the Juvenile Court of Cook County—were not of that character, for they were, as Mr. Justice Stewart stated, "nonpolicymaking, nonconfidential" employees. *Id.*, at 375.

As Mr. Justice Brennan noted in *Elrod*, it is not always easy to determine whether a position is one in which political affiliation is a legitimate factor to be considered. *Id.*, at 367. Under some circumstances, a position may be appropriately considered political even though it is neither confidential nor policymaking in character. As one obvious example, if a State's election laws require that precincts be supervised by two election judges of different parties, a Republican judge could be legitimately discharged solely for changing his party registration. That conclusion would not depend on any finding that the job involved participation in policy decisions or access to confidential information. Rather, it would simply rest on the fact that party membership was essential to the discharge of the employee's governmental responsibilities.

---

11. As Mr. Justice Brennan pointed out in *Elrod*, political sponsorship is often purchased at the price of political contributions or campaign work in addition to a simple declaration of allegiance to the party. *Id.*, at 355. Thus, an employee's realization that he must obtain a sponsor in order to retain his job is very likely to lead to the same type of coercion as that described by the plurality in *Elrod*. While there was apparently no overt political pressure exerted on respondents in this case, the potential coercive effect of requiring sponsorship was demonstrated by Mr. Finkel's change of party registration in a futile attempt to retain his position....

It is equally clear that party affiliation is not necessarily relevant to every policymaking or confidential position. The coach of a state university's football team formulates policy, but no one could seriously claim that Republicans make better coaches than Democrats, or vice versa, no matter which party is in control of the state government. On the other hand, it is equally clear that the Governor of a State may appropriately believe that the official duties of various assistants who help him write speeches, explain his views to the press, or communicate with the legislature cannot be performed effectively unless those persons share his political beliefs and party commitments. In sum, the ultimate inquiry is not whether the label "policymaker" or "confidential" fits a particular position; rather, the question is whether the hiring authority can demonstrate that party affiliation is an appropriate requirement for the effective performance of the public office involved.

Having thus framed the issue, it is manifest that the continued employment of an assistant public defender cannot properly be conditioned upon his allegiance to the political party in control of the county government. The primary, if not the only, responsibility of an assistant public defender is to represent individual citizens in controversy with the State.[13]

As we recently observed in commenting on the duties of counsel appointed to represent indigent defendants in federal criminal proceedings:

> [T]he primary office performed by appointed counsel parallels the office of privately retained counsel. Although it is true that appointed counsel serves pursuant to statutory authorization and in furtherance of the federal interest in insuring effective representation of criminal defendants, his duty is not to the public at large, except in that general way. His principal responsibility is to serve the undivided interests of his client. Indeed, an indispensable element of the effective performance of his responsibilities is the ability to act independently of the government and to oppose it in adversary litigation. [*Ferri v. Ackerman*, 444 U.S. 193, 204.]

Thus, whatever policymaking occurs in the public defender's office must relate to the needs of individual clients and not to any partisan political interests. Similarly, although an assistant is bound to obtain access to confidential information arising out of various attorney-client relationships, that information has no bearing whatsoever on partisan political concerns. Under these circumstances, it would undermine, rather than promote, the effective performance of an assistant public defender's office to make his tenure dependent on his allegiance to the dominant political party.[14]

---

13. This is in contrast to the broader public responsibilities of an official such as a prosecutor. We express no opinion as to whether the deputy of such an official could be dismissed on grounds of political party affiliation or loyalty. Cf. *Newcomb v. Brennan*, 558 F.2d 825 (CA7 1977) (dismissal of deputy city attorney).

14. As the District Court observed at the end of its opinion, it is difficult to formulate any justification for tying either the selection or retention of an assistant public defender to his party affiliation:

Accordingly, the entry of an injunction against termination of respondents' employment on purely political grounds was appropriate and the judgment of the Court of Appeals is

Affirmed.

[Three justices dissented. Justice Stewart filed a separate dissent in which he stated that "nonpolicymaking, nonconfidential" government employees could not be discharged for their political beliefs, but that assistant public defenders were in fact involved in a confidential relationship with the appointing public defender. Because that confidential relationship resembled the professional association created by private sector law firms, in which mutual trust and confidence is essential, in his view the public defender should have wide discretion in making appointments of his deputies.

[Justice Powell, Chief Justice Rehnquist and Justice Stewart joined in a second dissenting opinion. Justice Powell criticized the majority's opinion as involving a vague standard that would have uncertain application, and as representing an inappropriate judicial usurpation of legislative and executive decisionmaking. The dissent also argued that more serious attention should have been given to the significant interests served by patronage practices before concluding that a balance should be struck in favor of employees' First Amendment rights. The dissenters reasoned that patronage appointments help build stable political parties by offering rewards to those who perform tasks necessary to the continued functioning of political organizations. Political parties, in their view, serve a variety of substantial governmental interests: they allow candidates to marshal campaign workers to benefit candidates who lack substantial personal resources or financial contributions; assist in effective governance once campaigns end by providing loyal employees who will assist in efforts to implement publicly supported policies; facilitate cooperation among the executive and legislative branches; and help voters choose wisely among candidates. The dissenters concluded that the benefits of political patronage

---

> Perhaps not squarely presented in this action, but deeply disturbing nonetheless, is the question of the propriety of political considerations entering into the selection of attorneys to serve in the sensitive positions of Assistant Public Defenders. By what rationale can it even be suggested that it is legitimate to consider, in the selection process, the politics of one who is to represent indigent defendants accused of crime? No "compelling state interest" can be served by insisting that those who represent such defendants publicly profess to be Democrats (or Republicans). [457 F. Supp. at 1293, n.13.]

In his brief petitioner attempts to justify the discharges in this case on the ground that he needs to have absolute confidence in the loyalty of his subordinates. In his dissenting opinion, Mr. Justice Stewart makes the same point, relying on an "analogy to a firm of lawyers in the private sector."

... We cannot accept the proposition, however, that there cannot be "mutual confidence and trust" between attorneys, whether public defenders or private practitioners, unless they are both of the same political party. To the extent that petitioner lacks confidence in the assistants he has inherited from the prior administration for some reason other than their political affiliations, he is, of course, free to discharge them.

in strengthening the effectiveness of political parties justified the continued application of the patronage system to the positions in question.]

Notes and Questions

1. *The role of patronage.* The major focus of debate between the majority and the dissent in *Branti* concerned the relative weight to be accorded First Amendment rights and the public interests arguably served by the patronage system. *Elrod v. Burns* articulated the standard of review to be applied in First Amendment cases:

> It is firmly established that a significant impairment of First Amendment rights must survive exacting scrutiny. "This type of scrutiny is necessary even if any deterrent effect on the exercise of First Amendment rights arises, not through direct governmental action, but indirectly as an unintended but inevitable result of the government's conduct. . . ." Thus encroachment "cannot be justified upon a mere showing of a legitimate state interest." The interest advanced must be paramount, one of vital importance, and the burden is on the government to show the existence of such interest. [427 U.S. at 362.]

Did the majority adequately weigh the state interests that can be advanced in support of the patronage system? One interest advanced for patronage discharge in *Elrod* was "the need to insure effective government and the efficiency of public employees." The Court rejected this argument. "The inefficiency resulting from wholesale replacement of large numbers of public employees every time political office changes hands belies this justification." *Id.* at 364. Do you agree? For a thoughtful argument that judicial decisions curtailing political patronage have contributed to making bureaucracy more autonomous, but also less accountable and flexible, see Johnson & Libecap, *Courts, A Protected Bureaucracy, and Reinventing Government*, 37 Ariz. L. Rev. 791 (1995).

"Preservation of the democratic process" was also advanced as a paramount interest. The Court answered that "the elimination of patronage practice . . . will [not] bring about the demise of party politics. . . . Patronage dismissals thus are not the least-restrictive alternative to achieving the contribution they may make to the democratic process." *Id.* at 369. Is Justice Powell's dissent in *Branti* a convincing answer to this argument? As the traditional political patronage system has been curtailed through judicial action, there has been a marked growth in large campaign contributions by special interests which seek to curry favor with elected officials. For discussions of how changes in approaches to campaign finance and staffing have effected government and politics, see Hasen, *An Enriched Economic Model of Political Patronage and Campaign Contributions: Reformulating Supreme Court Jurisprudence*, 14 Cardozo L. Rev. 1311 (1993) (proposing an integrated jurisprudence covering both political patronage and campaign contributions); Yablond, *Campaigns, Inc.*, 103 Minn. L. Rev. 151 (2018) (suggesting that campaigns are now run as businesses and their emergence and power reflects changes in legal rules).

The Supreme Court in *Elrod* expressed the view that "[c]onditioning public employment on partisan support prevents support of competing political interests. Existing employees are deterred from such support, as well as the multitude seeking jobs. . . . Patronage thus tips the electoral process in favor of the incumbent party. . . ." 427 U.S. at 356. Assuming this observation to be true, are there any downsides to sharply curtailing systems of patronage? Some have noted that while machine politics were problematic insofar as they were often characterized by corruption, inefficiency and concentration of political power, they also functioned to resolve conflicts. See Sandalow, *Distrust of Politics*, 56 N.Y.U. L. REV. 446, 456 (1981). Others have argued that the decline of the patronage system in big cities has deprived minorities and the poor of the opportunities for advancement and political participation it provided. See Piven, *Federal Policy and Urban Fiscal Strain*, 2 YALE L. & POL'Y REV. 291, 302–11 (1984). Should the Court have given greater weight to this consideration?

After four decades marked by remarkable changes in political campaigning, fundraising, and party fragmentation, does *Branti* seem more or less well-grounded in retrospect? For scholarly insight on this point, see El-Haj, *Networking the Party: First Amendment Rights and the Pursuit of Responsive Party Government*, 118 COLUM. L. REV. 1225 (2018) (arguing that the Court has historically employed a theory of democratic accountability referred to as "responsible party government" which "views political parties primarily as speakers and presumes that electoral accountability emerges from the choice between ideologically distinct political parties during competitive elections," but that theory needs to be revised in light of drastic changes in party functioning); Issacharoff, *Outsourcing Politics: The Hostile Takeover of our Hollowed-Out Political Parties*, 54 HOUS. L. REV. 845 (2017) (referencing the 2016 Presidential election and suggesting that contemporary political parties are "less able to control their internal party selection processes" thereby hampering their ability to govern effectively).

2. *Protected parties.* In the aftermath of *Branti*, questions have arisen concerning the types of government-worker relations that are encompassed by First Amendment protections. One area of particular interest has been the protections afforded independent contractors, particularly in the wake of the increasing tendency of governments to "contract out" or "privatize" provision of public services. In two cases handed down on the same day, *Board of Comm'rs v. Umbehr*, 518 U.S. 668 (1996), and *O'Hare Truck Service, Inc. v. City of Northlake*, 518 U.S. 712 (1996), the Supreme Court held that the existing framework for government employee cases should apply to independent contractors, since

> [t]here is ample reason to believe that such a nuanced approach, which recognizes the variety of interests that may arise in independent contractor cases, is superior to a brightline rule distinguishing independent contractors from employees. [A] brightline rule . . . would give the government carte blanche to terminate independent contractors for exercising First Amendment rights. And that brightline rule would leave First Amendment

> rights unduly dependent on whether state law labels a government service provider's contract as a contract of employment or a contract for services, a distinction which is at best a very poor proxy for the interests at stake. Determining constitutional claims on the basis of such formal distinctions, which can be manipulated largely at the will of the government agencies concerned, is an enterprise that we have consistently eschewed. [*Board of County Comm'rs v. Umbehr*, 518 U.S. at 678–79.]

For a critique of the Court's decision in *Umbehr* and a call for more nuanced approach to analysis of how contractors should be treated, see Parker, *Two Steps Forward, One Step Back: A Critique of the Supreme Court's Extension of the Pickering Balancing Test to Government Contractors*, 28 FED. CIRCUIT B.J. 41 (2018) (arguing that with the expansion of government contracting into such areas as information technology, auditing support and homeland security, there is need to consider factors regarding the interrelation of the government entity and the contractor, using an "economic realities" test).

Are other types of personnel with work-related connections to government protected under the Court's reasoning? Should it matter what duties they perform, how long they have done so, how they are paid, and whether their business relationship is permanent or temporary? On the rights of contingent workers and analogies to the independent contractor cases, see Berger, *Unjust Dismissal and the Contingent Worker: Restructuring Doctrine for the Restructured Employee*, 16 YALE L. & POL. REV. 1 (1997); Hensel, *The First Amendment and Independent Contractors Lacking Pre-existing Commercial Relationships with the Government: Entering a Zone of Uncertainty*, 32 PUB. CONT. L.J. 635 (2003). Should a grantee of federal funds be covered by related protections? The federal courts of appeal are divided on the treatment of Planned Parenthood as a government grantee. Compare *Planned Parenthood Ass'n of Utah v. Herbert*, 828 F.3d 1245 (10th Cir. 2016) (finding viable claim of unconstitutional conditions on grant contract), with *Planned Parenthood of Greater Ohio v. Hodges*, 917 F.3d 908 (6th Cir. 2019) (on rehearing en banc, finding no First Amendment violation).

3. *The meaning of "political" patronage.* Must adverse actions be based on partisan political ties? What happens if "political" patronage is linked to affiliation with one wing of the party or a commitment to individuals or groups in non-partisan settings? In *Galli v. New Jersey Meadowlands Comm'n*, 490 F.3d 265 (3d Cir. 2007), an employee hired under an earlier Republican administration challenged her discharge from a position with the Commission (an agency charged with environmental protection, economic development, and solid waste management) following the election of a Democratic administration. Assuming that the district court had properly accepted the employee's showing that her duties did not involve meaningful input into policymaking (a matter of continuing dispute), the Third Circuit ruled that the employee's action in remaining "apolitical" rather than affiliating with a party or actively supporting candidates of either major political party, was protected to the same degree as would have been true had she actively supported the losing

Republican candidate. The dissenting judge disagreed, saying that prior precedent did not justify such a holding where one "who chooses to remain non-political, or apolitical, or silent, has, by definition, not 'exercised' political rights and therefore cannot claim the same constitutional protection from adverse employment decisions." What if a firing is based on perceived lack of "personal loyalty"? See *Nichols v. Dancer*, 567 F.3d 423 (9th Cir. 2009) (finding that patronage dismissal doctrine did not justify termination of administrative assistant of former school district general counsel after she sat next to counsel to provide moral support during his dismissal hearing, and remanding for First Amendment analysis to determine whether she could be dismissed based on school district's concern that her "personal loyalty" to him reflected a lack of loyalty to the district). What if retaliation against an employee results from a government employer's mistaken view as to an employee's activities in a political campaign? See *Hefferman v. City of Paterson, N.J.*, 136 S. Ct. 1412 (2016) (holding that the fact that the employee's supervisors were mistaken in their beliefs about his activities did not bar the suit under federal civil rights law).

4. *Positions subject to patronage dismissals.* While it is clear that decisions to discharge government employees because of political affiliation trigger application of the Court's analysis in *Branti*, it is not always clear how that analysis is to be applied. The Court articulated the following test for determining which positions may continue to be subject to patronage dismissals: "The ultimate inquiry is not whether the label 'policymaker' or 'confidential' fits a particular position; rather, the question is whether the hiring authority can demonstrate that party affiliation is an appropriate requirement for the effective performance of the public office involved." 445 U.S. at 518. How would you apply this test to the position of city treasurer? See *Snyder v. City of Moab*, 354 F.3d 1179 (10th Cir. 2003) (city treasurer could be discharged by incoming mayor notwithstanding years of service and expectation of role within classified service, since treasurer was expected to carry out policy using discretion; no pre-termination hearing required). To a deputy sheriff? See *Ezell v. Wynn*, 802 F.3d 1217 (11th Cir. 2015) (holding that office of deputy sheriff in Georgia could be filled on a patronage basis, notwithstanding its treatment as a city civil service position, where the deputy served as the agent of the sheriff). To an administrative hearing officer? See *Walsh v. Heilmann*, 472 F.3d 504 (7th Cir. 2006) (holding that such a village administrative hearing officer held a policymaking position since he had discretion in setting fines for non-vehicular offenses)? To a solid waste enforcement officer? See *Griggs v. Chickasaw County, Mississippi*, 930 F.3d 696 (5th Cir. 2019) (finding position was not "policymaking," and concluding county had illegally retaliated against employee by eliminating his position after he ran unsuccessfully for county sheriff).

5. *Types of personnel actions covered. Branti* involved discharge of a government employee. What other sorts of personnel actions are covered by the *Branti* rationale? In 1990, the Supreme Court extended the protections created by *Elrod* and *Branti* to other government personnel actions, namely hiring, promotions, transfers, and recalls. *Rutan v. Republican Party of Illinois*, 497 U.S. 62 (1990). The Court held

that political conviction or partisan affiliation could not be considered in employment decisions, except for the highest offices, without violating the First Amendment guarantees of freedom of speech and association. For additional discussion of the *Rutan* decision, see Bowman, *Public Policy: "We Don't Want Anybody Sent": The Death of Patronage Hiring in Chicago*, 86 Nw. U. L. Rev. 57 (1991) (concluding that "the most common objections to the prohibition of patronage hiring are, by and large, unfounded").

6. *Discharge for cause.* In many situations, private-sector employees serve "at will," and can be discharged if the employer sees fit. The courts may temper this doctrine by creating a common law "public policy exception" that allows employees to bring claims for retaliatory discharge if they were discharged because they failed to commit an illegal or unethical act, performed a legal duty, exercised legal rights or disclosed employer misconduct. Civil service legislation, on the other hand, usually authorizes discharge only for "just cause." The cases hold that a "cause" discharge must be based on a substantial fault or shortcoming of the dismissed employee which is substantially related to his employment. See, e.g., *Turnley v. Town of Vernon,* 71 A.3d 1246 (Vt. 2013) (false statements by police chief at public meeting regarding when he learned about presence of low-level sex offender did not support finding of deliberate misconduct unbecoming a police officer and did not justify termination of chief). Is the *Elrod-Branti* patronage rule the equivalent of a discharge for cause test in view of the *Mt. Healthy* causation test discussed in Note 7 below? Would it make any difference in the *Paulson* case that the chief of police and mayor belonged to different political parties, and that the discharge was partly based on political motives? Consider the discussion of "radical" state civil reforms earlier in the Chapter.

7. *Mixed motives.* What if an employee is dismissed for political reasons and also because she was found to be incompetent? This problem is handled by the causation rule of *Mt. Healthy School Dist. Bd. of Education v. Doyle*, 429 U.S. 274 (1977), which is discussed in footnote 6 of the *Branti* decision. In *Mt. Healthy*, an untenured school teacher who had engaged in misconduct on his job sent to a radio station a memorandum on teacher dress and appearance which had been circulated by his principal. The communication to the radio station was arguably protected as free speech. The Court adopted a "rule of causation" to avoid placing an employee "in a better position as a result of the exercise of constitutionally protected conduct than he would have occupied had he done nothing," requiring the employee to show that his conduct was constitutionally protected and that the conduct was a "substantial" "motivating" factor in the Board's decision not to rehire him. The School Board was then obliged to show by a preponderance of the evidence that "it would have reached the same decision . . . even in the absence of the protected conduct." *Id.* at 287. The factual analysis required in assessing motivation and alternative grounds for discharge is complex. See, e.g., *Coogan v. Smyers*, 134 F.3d 479 (2d Cir. 1998) (in order to determine whether purpose of legislative body was retaliatory, it is necessary to evaluate motives of the majority of individuals who voted not to reappoint individual whose First Amendment rights were implicated).

8. *Statutory solutions.* Congress and many state legislatures have adopted statutory strategies designed to protect government employees from pressures to support those in power. The federal "Hatch Act" (5 U.S.C. § 7323) originally included a variety of protections limiting political activity by federal employees (as well as state and local government employees who work in programs funded with federal financial assistance), but has been modified over the years to reduce constraints for all employees. See Hatch Act Modernization Act, Pub. Law 112-230 (2012) (allowing employees to run for office unless salaries are fully funded by federal government). See Azzaro, *The Hatch Act Modernization Act: Putting the Government Back in Politics*, 42 FORDHAM URB. L.J. 781 (2016) (discussing that legislation).

For further consideration of the implications of Hatch Act revisions for federal contractors, see Bell, *Procuring Votes: The Hatch Act in the Modern Age of Government Contracting*, 43 PUB. CONT. L.J. 373 (2014); Schwartzman, *Giving Contractors the Hatch, Not the Axe: Extending Political Activity Speech Rights to Personal Service Contractors Under the Hatch Act*, 48 PUB. CONT. L.J. 189 (2018). Many states have also adopted "Little Hatch Acts" that limit state and local government employee involvement in political activities.

A Note on Government Employee Speech and Activities

How are the rights of government employees to engage in personal or political speech and other activities affected by their public employment? This recurring question has led to extensive litigation in a range of settings, as well as frequent academic commentary. See, e.g., Kozel, *Reconceptualizing Public Employee Speech*, 99 NW. U. L. REV. 1007 (2005) (arguing that doctrinal focus on workplace "disruption" is dysfunctional and noting the confounding overlap of patronage and speech case law); Kim, *Market Norms and Constitutional Values in the Government Workplace*, 94 N.C. L. REV. 601 (2016) (challenging the assumption that public and private employment are analogous, particularly since government employers with obligations to achieve publicly defined purposes do not have the kind of wide discretion allowed private employers, are not subject to the same market pressures applicable in the private sector, and need their employees to observe improper government conduct and serve as whistleblowers for the public good).

Framework for Analyzing Government Employee Speech that May Implicate the First Amendment

The Supreme Court has developed a distinct body of case law regarding the free speech rights of government employees. In *Pickering v. Board of Educ.*, 391 U.S. 563 (1968), the Court held that a school board had impermissibly dismissed a public school teacher for writing a letter to the local newspaper criticizing the school board and school superintendent for funding athletic programs in preference to expenditures to further academic goals. The Court stated that the relevant test in analyzing such cases required "arriv[ing] at a balance between the interests of the teacher, as a citizen, in commenting on matters of public concern and the interest of the State, as an employer, in promoting the efficiency of the public services it performs through its employees." *Id.* at 568. The Court also cited key factors relevant to this balance: the parties' working relationship; the detrimental effect of the speech on the employer; and the nature of the issue upon which the employee spoke and the employee's relationship to that issue. *Id.* at 569. The Supreme Court later clarified that comments made in private could nonetheless relate to a public concern and thus be subject to First Amendment protection under *Pickering*. See *Givhan v. Western Line Consolidated School Dist.*, 439 U.S. 410 (1979) (involving office conversation between principal and teacher about desegregation).

Subsequently, in *Connick v. Myers*, 461 U.S. 138 (1983), the Court upheld the discharge of an assistant district attorney after she had distributed an intra-office questionnaire raising questions concerning transfer policy, office morale, level of confidence in supervisors, and pressure to work in political campaigns. The Court concluded that only the latter of these issues presented a matter of public concern, the questionnaire primarily related to an internal grievance, and the *Pickering* balance therefore justified upholding the employee's discharge.

In essence, *Pickering/Connick* analysis requires courts to determine, first, whether the employee's speech or action address a matter of "public concern" (taking into account its content, form, and context), and then to balance the employee's interest in commenting against the public employee's interest in promoting operational efficiency, before determining whether the employee's speech or action is the cause of the adverse employment action. If the speech is found to be protected under *Pickering/Connick*, the employee must then show that the speech was a substantial or motivating factor in the employer's adverse action, leaving it to the employer to present rebuttal evidence that the adverse action was justified on other grounds.

Exception: Public Employee Speech Pursuant to Official Duties

The United States Supreme Court created a significant exception to the *Pickering/Connick* line of analysis in *Garcetti v. Ceballos*, 547 U.S. 410 (2006), involving an action under 42 U.S.C. § 1983 by a California deputy district attorney who had been subject to adverse employment actions after writing a disposition memorandum in which he recommended dismissal of a criminal case on the basis of what he believed to be governmental misconduct. Ceballos had concerns about the truth of statements in an affidavit used to justify a search warrant, wrote a memorandum to his supervisor to that effect, participated in a "heated" meeting with members of the sheriff's department, was called to testify by the defense and reported his concerns, and later gave a speech about related matters. He was denied a promotion and transferred. In a split decision, the Supreme Court concluded that Ceballos' speech was not protected where "made pursuant to [his] official duties."

Writing for a five-person majority, Justice Kennedy reviewed prior precedent, noting that government employees are only protected if speaking on a matter of public concern, within limitations involving the government's right to assure the efficient provision of public services without constitutionalizing every employee grievance. In effect, their expression of views may also undermine the government's official policy judgments and confuse the public. The majority concluded that the fact that Ceballos' comments were made within the office was not dispositive. His role as a calendar deputy within the district attorney's office was the controlling factor since he spoke pursuant to his official duties rather than as a citizen. The majority gave particular emphasis to the importance of affording supervisors the discretion to control employee speech made in an official capacity and to engage in disciplinary action as the supervisor believed warranted without intrusive judicial oversight. Justice Kennedy also stated that the result was warranted in light of concerns for federalism and separation of powers and rejected the Ninth Circuit's view that failure to apply the *Pickering/Connick* balancing test would result in a doctrinal anomaly. Justice Kennedy concluded the majority opinion by stating that the Court reserved the question of how employees' duties should be defined and noted that the Court did not intend to reach questions relating to academic freedom when academic scholarship or classroom instruction was implicated.

Subsequently, in *Lane v. Franks*, 573 U.S. 228 (2014), the Court unanimously concluded that not every action by a public employee in relation to his duties fell within the *Garcetti* rule. Lane served as director of a federally funded program at a community college. In the course of reviewing expenditures, he discovered that a state legislator who worked for the program had not been reporting for work and terminated her. She was subsequently indicted for mail fraud and theft and Lane testified against her, under subpoena, at trial. Lane was subsequently discharged by the community college president. The Supreme Court concluded that Lane's judicial testimony was speech outside his job duties, that it related to a matter of public concern, and that it was thus protected under the First Amendment, citing *Pickering* and *Connick*. For a discussion of *Lane*, see Diaz, *Truthful Testimony as the "Quintessential Example of Speech as a Citizen": Why Lane v. Franks Lays the Groundwork for Protecting Public Employee Truthful Testimony*, 46 Seton Hall L. Rev. (2016) (discussing *Lane*).

There are a myriad of cases applying *Garcetti*, many of which have denied protection to affected employees. For an academic critique, see Zenor, *This Is Just Not Working for Us: Why After Ten Years on the Job It is Time to Fire Garcetti*, 19 Rich. J.L. & Pub. Int. 101 (2016) (reviewing lower court case law applying *Garcetti*, explaining that lower courts have extended that case to cover any speech that is a product of job duties even if the speech would serve the public interest, and arguing that *Garcetti* should be refocused with an emphasis on the public trust, rather than the employee-employer relationship). Other scholars have contended that speech by lawyers (as was the case in *Garcetti*) and other professionals should be given special consideration. See Knake, *Lawyer Speech in the Regulatory State*, 84 Fordham L. Rev. 2099 (2016) (discussing lawyer speech); Zick, *Professional Rights Speech*, 47 Ariz. St. L.J. 1289 (2015) (discussing other professionals including physicians who have recently been directed to make disclosures about abortion and constrained in discussing gun violence); Schutzman, *We Need Professional Help: Advocating for a Consistent Standard of Review When Regulations of Professional Speech Implicate the First Amendment*, 56 B.C. L. REV. 2019 (2015) (reviewing conflicting court of appeals decisions). One area of emerging significance is the conduct of public employees on social media. See Olaya, *Public Employees' First Amendment Speech Rights in the Social Media World: #Fire or #Fire-d?* 36 HOFSTRA LAB. & EMP. L.J. 431 (2019) (discussing application of "public concern" test in context of social media and emerging technology, and suggesting restructured analysis given such trends as the use of emojis).

B. Integrity in Government Service: Conflicts of Interest

Government service provides opportunities for profit and self-advantage. Apart from the obvious possibilities for corruption, kickbacks, self-dealing and the like, government service raises problems of conflict of interest that often are difficult to resolve. Especially at the local level, government officials have a personal and financial interest in the community which may be difficult to separate from their official roles. This section looks at the conflict of interest problem as one of the important issues affecting the integrity of government service.

Citizens for Des Moines, Inc. v. Petersen

125 Wash. App. 760, 106 P.3d 290 (2005)

KENNEDY, J.

A month after Gary W. Petersen was sworn in as a member of the Des Moines City Council, a [sic] for-profit corporation named Citizens for Des Moines, Inc., and its president Allan Furney filed this lawsuit seeking to have Petersen removed from office based on a conflict of interest under RCW 42.23.030. [These are statutory citations.—Eds.]

Ch. 42.23 RCW contains the Code of Ethics for Municipal Officers. Petersen is the president, majority shareholder, and a salaried employee of Petersen Northwest Corporation. That company has six divisions, one of which is Pete's Towing. For several decades before Petersen's election, city police and authorized staff persons from the marina, parks, and public works departments of the city routinely called Pete's Towing when vehicles needed to be towed from city property. The city had no express or implied contract with Pete's Towing, and no written policies regarding towing requests. Pete's Towing was simply preferred by police and other city staff, to the exclusion or near exclusion of other providers, because it was the only conveniently located full-service operator with sufficient trucks and related facilities and equipment to meet the needs of the city, and it had a 40-year history of consistently providing quality service in a professional manner.

The record indicates that police and other authorized staff ask Pete's Towing to remove vehicles from public property and rights-of-way approximately 500 times a year. Pete's Towing shows some $250,000 in accounts receivable on its books for any given year based on these requests, though its actual collections amount to some $100,000 of annual gross revenue. Petersen is paid an annual salary of $60,000 by Petersen Northwest Corporation.

[On cross-motions for summary judgment, the trial court held as a matter of law that a "contract" was created between Pete's Towing and the city each time the towing company towed a vehicle at the request of a police officer or other authorized staff member; Peterson had a "beneficial interest" in such contracts based on his ownership interest in the company; and each such "contract" constituted a separate violation of the state statute. It found that all such individual "contracts" created from the time Petersen took office were void and ordered Peterson not to accept additional contracts while he remained in office.]

Because the individual towing transactions that are at issue in this case do not constitute "contracts" between the City of Des Moines and Pete's Towing that are "made by through or under the supervision of" Petersen or the city council "in whole or in part," RCW 42.23.030 does not extend to them. On this record, Petersen is entitled to judgment as a matter of law. Accordingly, we reverse and remand for dismissal of the lawsuit. . . .

II

Ch. 42.32 RCW contains the Code of Ethics for Municipal Officials. RCW 42.23.030 provides:

> *No municipal officer shall be beneficially interested, directly or indirectly, in any contract which may be made by, through or under the supervision of such officer, in whole or in part*, or which may be made for the benefit of his or her office, or accept, directly or indirectly, any compensation, gratuity or reward in connection with such contract from any other person beneficially interested therein. (Emphasis added).

Contracts made in violation of the statute are void, and any municipal officer who violates the statute is liable to the municipality for a fine of $500, and may also be removed from office. RCW 42.23.050.

The Code of Ethics defines "contract" to be "any contract, sale, lease or purchase." RCW 42.23.020(3). Thus, somewhat unhelpfully for our purposes, a "contract" is a "contract." More helpfully, the Code "is directed at *self-dealing* where a public official would otherwise have the discretion to use his public office to favor his private interests over the interests of others." *City of Seattle v. State*, 668 P.2d 1266 (Wash. 1983).

In that case, the City of Seattle enacted a campaign finance ordinance under which both incumbents and challengers could use public funds to partially finance their campaigns by contracting to comply with various mandatory provisions regarding campaign contributions and to limit their campaign expenditures. The ordinance created a Campaign Fair Practices Commission to make rules and hear complaints arising under the ordinance. The ordinance was designed to encourage wide participation of the public in the electoral process, and to reduce the dependence of candidates on special interest contributions. . . .

[The court upheld the ordinance as constitutional then considered whether any incumbent who decided to participate in public financing would thereby violate RCW 42.23.030, and concluded that there would be no such violation.] The court reasoned that any such contract by an incumbent was not made "under the supervision" of any elected official within the meaning of RCW 42.23.030 because no elected official had the power to control or direct the work of the Fair Campaign Practices Commission. Moreover, the term "supervision" as used in RCW 42.23.030 contemplates a degree of direction and control, in that standard dictionary definitions of "supervise" include "to oversee for direction; to superintend; to inspect with authority"; "to oversee (a process, work, workers, etc.) during execution or performance"; and to "oversee, have the oversight of, superintend the execution or performance of (a thing), the movement or work of (a person)." . . . The court also observed that the campaign finance ordinance did not compel action by an elected official despite a conflict of interest, for the official could always disqualify himself, and only if he or she failed to do so would there be any conflict of interest.

There is no evidence in this record that Councilman Peterson self-dealt with respect to any individual towing transaction or with respect to towing transactions generally. Instead, after Petersen took office, towing transactions were handled as they had been for decades previously—police officers and other authorized city staff decided which towing company to call, and not because Petersen took office but because they had always done it that way, they almost always called Pete's Towing. Thus, the trial court's ruling is tantamount to a ruling that, given the preference among city police and other authorized officials to use Pete's Towing, due to the superior service it provided, Petersen was simply disqualified from serving as a city council person for so long as he held any interest in Pete's Towing.

III

We first consider whether the individual towing transactions initiated by police and other authorized officials of the City of Des Moines constitute "contracts" between the city and Pete's Towing within the meaning of RCW 42.23.030. We conclude that they do not. For a contract to exist, there must be an offer, acceptance, and consideration. . . . To be enforceable, every contract must be supported by consideration. "Consideration is any act, forbearance, creation, modification or destruction of a legal relationship, or return promise given in exchange."

The trial court apparently reasoned that consideration flowed to Pete's Towing each time it towed or impounded a vehicle at the request of a city police officer or other authorized city official because a state statute provides Pete's Towing with statutory authority to recover fees from the registered owner of the vehicle when the vehicle has been towed or impounded at the direction of an authorized official such as a police officer—and because, without that direction from an authorized official, Pete's Towing could not legally tow or impound the vehicle. *See generally*, RCW 46.55.105(1), RCW 46.55.120(1)(e), and RCW 46.55.140. And the court apparently reasoned that consideration flowed from Pete's Towing back to the city, even though the city was not obligated to pay towing fees, because by towing away the vehicle, Pete's Towing either cleared city streets of a safety hazard, or removed an abandoned vehicle from a city right-of-way, or freed up a publicly-owned parking space after the expiration of the permitted time for parking, or in the case of certain traffic violations justifying impoundment of vehicles, removed an offending driver's vehicle from the streets as permitted by law.

But "[b]efore an act or promise can constitute consideration, it must be bargained for and given in exchange for the promise." ... Such economic benefit as may flow to Pete's Towing by virtue of a request by a Des Moines police officer that a vehicle belonging to a third party be towed or towed and impounded flows by operation of Ch. 46.55 RCW, and not in exchange for any promise made by the police officer. Municipal authority to authorize towing and impoundment derives from state statute, specifically, Ch. 46.55 RCW. Towing companies and the impounding of vehicles are heavily regulated by the state. The fee rights and lien rights of towing companies derive from statute, not from any business arrangement between a city and the company.

Towing companies must be licensed by the state; their tow trucks must be physically inspected by the Washington State Patrol before permits to operate them may be issued; and their storage facilities are subject to annual inspection by the State Patrol.... Tow trucks must be rated by towing capabilities.... Fee schedules must be approved by the Department of Licensing, towing fees must be charged on an hourly basis, and after the first hour must be charged to the nearest quarter hour; and storage fees must be charged on a 24-hour basis, and to the nearest half day from the time the vehicle arrived at the storage area.

Police officers may but are not required to impound vehicles in certain circumstances specified by statute, and to cause them to be removed to a place of safekeeping. RCW 46.55.113. Because impoundment is a seizure for purposes of the Fourth Amendment, impoundment must be reasonable—and impoundment is not reasonable when a reasonable alternative exists.... An agency that attempts to limit police officer discretion regarding when to impound a vehicle exceeds its statutory authority.

Municipalities may pass ordinances concerning unauthorized, abandoned, or impounded vehicles, so long as the ordinances include applicable portions of Ch. 46.55 RCW. RCW 46.55.240(1). Municipalities may enter into contracts with registered towing companies for the impounding of vehicles. RCW 46.55.240(4). However, such municipalities remain subject to Fourth Amendment requirements regarding the seizure of property, and they may not limit police officers' statutory discretion regarding when to impound and not to impound a vehicle.

The City of Des Moines has not made any such contract, express or implied, with Pete's Towing. Not only has Councilman Petersen engaged in no self-dealing, but even if inclined to do so, his ability, and that of the city council as a whole to affect the exercise of discretion by police is limited, both by statute and the Fourth Amendment.

IV

As a practical matter, Petersen would have no reason to try to influence an officer's choice of which towing company to call—Pete's Towing became the near-unanimous choice of officers not based on Petersen's recent election to the city council but based on 40 years of reliable service by the company. Moreover, Petersen would be barred by law from supervising or overseeing an individual officer's discretion—or that of the police chief for that matter—regarding which towing company to call on any given occasion. Des Moines is a non-charter code city with a council-manager form of government. The seven-member city council appoints the city manager, who in turns appoints the chief of police and other department heads. RCW 35A.13.010. Although the manager reports to the city council, the city manager is the sole person vested with authority to supervise the administrative affairs of the city. RCW 35A.13.080. And RCW 35A.13.120 expressly provides that "*neither the council nor any committee or member thereof shall give orders to any subordinate of the city manager, either publicly or privately.*" Thus, we reject the premise that Councilman Petersen could, if he wanted, supervise the decision of an officer on the beat with respect to which towing company to call on any given occasion.

A city can enter into a contract with a towing company for the impounding of vehicles, and in that event, the towing company must comply with administrative regulations adopted by the city on the handling and disposing of vehicles. *See* RCW 46.55.240(4). Arguably, under the council-manager form of government, the city manager would select the towing company or companies with which to contract, and would adopt the administrative regulations—these would seem to be executive functions. But as we have noted, RCW 46.55.240 also gives cities the authority to adopt ordinances governing towing and impoundment—which clearly is a legislative act. In that context, then, depending upon the nature of the proposed ordinance, and to the extent that it might include "making" a contract with Pete's Towing, Councilman Petersen could find himself facing a conflict of interest.... [H]owever, nothing would compel him to act on behalf of the city with respect to making any contract involving Pete's Towing, and his remedy would be to disqualify himself.

This case is not like *City of Raymond v. Runyon*, 967 P.2d 19 (Wash. App. 1998).

... There, the city was a non-charter code city governed by the commission form of government as provided by Ch. 35.17 RCW. Under that form of government, executive and administrative powers were distributed among three commissioners. One of them served as the mayor, the second served as the financial officer, and the third, Runyan, served as the superintendent of public works. Runyon owned a gravel pit that sold gravel to certain contractors who in turn did business with the city....

When Runyon realized that by acting on behalf of the city with respect to public works contracts involving the particular contractors with whom he did business at the gravel pit he could be in a conflict of interest situation, he attempted to insulate himself by delegating to his subordinate, the city engineer, his responsibility to sign work contracts with those contractors. . . . Eventually, the city brought an action for declaratory judgment, asking the court to determine whether Runyon had successfully insulated himself, or whether he had violated RCW 42.23.030.

The appellate court concluded that notwithstanding his good faith effort to insulate himself from the conflict of interest, Runyon had violated the statute, in that he was directly responsible by law for all contracts that came into his office—whether or not responsibility for any particular contract had been delegated to his subordinate—in that by law, Runyon could not delegate his ultimate authority as the public works commissioner. . . . Thus, the court held any contracts signed by the commissioner's subordinate after he took public office that financially benefited the commissioner through sales at his quarry to builders who had contracts with the city necessarily violated the terms of RCW 42.23.030. In contrast, contracts made before the commissioner took office were "made through or under the supervision of the previous commissioner" and did not violate the statute.

The form of city government and the nature of the public office at issue could be dispositive with respect to whether a given official "makes" a contract, and with respect to whether any such contract is made "through or under the supervision" of the official as provided by the ethics code. Each case must rest on its own facts. In *Runyon*, the public works commissioner had the ultimate responsibility for public works contracts and could not insulate himself from conflicts of interest by delegating responsibility to an underling. In *City of Seattle*, a different entity from elected officials had ultimate responsibility for enforcing the campaign financing ordinance, and in the event that an elected official somehow found himself auditing his or her own contract, that official was not compelled to act, and could avoid the conflict of interest by disqualifying himself. This case is nothing like *Runyon*. It has similarities to the campaign finance case in that an entity other than Petersen individually and the council as a whole has responsibility to supervise police officers and other city staff. Indeed, a statute forbids the city council from supervising police and other staff people.

And to the extent that the city council might consider adopting an ordinance with respect to towing and impoundments that would, if adopted, operate to Petersen's economic benefit to the detriment of others, like in the campaign finance case, Petersen could disqualify himself from participating in the decision of whether to adopt the ordinance.

Finally, to the extent that the trial court's ruling implies that because the city council might have the authority to grant an exclusive contract for towing services to—for example—Pete's Towing, Peterson, by serving on the council, was in violation of RCW 42.32.030 as a matter of law, such was error. The fact that an act would, if performed, violate RCW 42.32.030 does not, by itself, violate the statute. The act would actually have to be performed before there would be a violation.

Nothing in the language of the statute or the case law provides to the contrary. It would be an oddity for an elected official automatically to be placed in violation of the ethics code merely by being sworn into office. Even in *Runyon*, it is likely that a means could have been found to avoid the conflict of interest. The appellate court suggested one such means in the opinion itself: an ordinance could have been passed modifying the ordinance setting forth the responsibilities of each of the commissioners, to enable them to act for each other when necessary to avoid conflicts of interest.

Were no such remedy available, soon it would be difficult to find capable people willing to run for public office, particularly in small towns where virtually every proprietor in the village may at least occasionally do business with the town. In sum, on this record, Petersen was entitled to judgment as a matter of law and his cross-motion for summary judgment ought to have been granted. Accordingly, we reverse and remand for dismissal of the plaintiffs' lawsuit.

WE CONCUR: SCHINDLER and AGID, JJ.

Notes and Questions

1. *"Conflicts of interest" and specific forms of self-dealing.* The principal case arose under a statute that specifically focused on contracts involving self-dealing (one type of decision-making that involves a conflict between the government official's responsibilities to the public to make the best decision possible as a steward of public funds, and a personal financial interest in the outcome of such decisions). At times, specific legislation of this sort may be adopted to respond to prior wrongdoing, while in other states contracting is assumed to be covered by broader "codes of ethics" that may address "conflicts of interest," gifts, honoraria, lobbying, nepotism, and disclosure of financial interests or campaign contributions. The National Conference of State Legislatures maintains a comprehensive database of such statutory restrictions. See www.ncsl.org. State legislation may also be complemented by local ordinance or charter requirements. For a website devoted to ethics issues arising in the municipal context, see http://www.cityethics.org. Prohibitions on contracting are one of the clearer types of prohibition but raise questions of interpretation as is evident in the *Petersen* case. Are specific prohibitions on "contracting" needed or are more general proscriptions on participating in any action involving a personal financial interest to be preferred? Many governments require financial disclosures by candidates as a means of assuring transparency and providing public oversight of public officials' decisions where self-dealing might be involved. See, e.g., *Coyne v. Edwards*, 395 S.W.3d 509 (Mo. 2013) (upholding disqualification of candidate for board of community fire district where candidate had failed to make mandatory financial disclosures, applying rational basis test). For an analysis of bribery and public corruption from the perspective of lawyers involved in white collar crime

representation, see Tompkins, *Public Corruption*, 56 AM. CRIM. L. REV. 1269 (2019). For a thoughtful examination of the deep tensions that underlie conflict of interest analysis, see Stark, THE DEEP STRUCTURE OF CONFLICTS OF INTEREST: CONFLICT OF INTEREST IN AMERICAN PUBLIC LIFE (2000).

2. *Self-dealing involving contracts.* The *Peterson* case involved a claim that contracts for removal of cars by Pete's Towing were invalid and should prospectively be prohibited following Peterson's election to the town's governing board, and that Peterson had violated state law by allowing his company to engage in such contracts. Common law plays a crucial role in fleshing out statutory provisions. The appellate court focused on the statutory language relating to "contracts." What contract or contracts were being challenged? Why did the court conclude that the towing transactions did not constitute "contracts" within the meaning of the statute? Do you agree with that conclusion or with the reasoning of the trial court?

Note that the statutory text includes several other elements including references to any contract "which may be made" "by, through or under" the "supervision" of a municipal officer "in whole or in part." Did these other parts of the statute have a bearing? The statute is drafted to prohibit a municipal officer from "being" beneficially interested. Other parts of the Washington statute are framed more directly. See RCW 42.23.070 (stating that "no municipal officer may" use his or her position to secure special privileges, directly or indirectly receive compensation or a gift connected to his or her services, accept employment that would induce him or her to disclose confidential information).

Could the statute under consideration in *Petersen* have been drafted more clearly? If so, how? The court also distinguishes the earlier decision in *Runyon*. Are you persuaded by the distinctions? In *Petersen*, the town had a history of using Pete's Towing well before Peterson's election. What analysis would be appropriate if they had not previously used that service provider, or if Pete's Towing were more expensive or had a poorer record of performance than others? For a case involving a different kind of "contractual" benefit to a mayor who negotiated a settlement on behalf of the city in a case that he himself had brought prior to assuming public office, see *Thompson v. City of Atlantic City*, 921 A.2d 427 (N.J. 2007) (finding actual and inherent conflict of interest and requiring disgorgement of settlement proceeds).

3. *Land use.* Contracting is not the only arena in which particularized legislation is employed and important case law has developed. Decisions regarding zoning and land use permits often have significant financial implications for real estate developers and nearby land owners, as well as social implications for citizens at large. There may also be constitutional or substantive statutory requirements of "fairness" in quasi-judicial proceedings involving the regulation of land, resulting in high stakes and potential liability for the governments involved. Some states, such as Connecticut, have adopted statutes specially tailored to address the obligations of planning commission members, in this case by prohibiting their participation in hearings or decisions. See CONN. GEN. STAT. § 8-21 ("No member of any planning commission . . . shall appear for or represent any person, firm or corporation or

other entity in any matter pending before the planning or zoning commission . . . [nor] shall participate in the hearing or decision of the commission of which he is a member upon any matter in which he is directly or indirectly interested in a personal or or financial sense"). For a case interpreting this provision, see *MJM Self Storage of Clinton, LLC v. Town of Clinton Planning & Zoning Comm'n*, 68 Conn. L. Rptr. 519, 2019 WL 2442288 (Conn. Super. 2019) (striking down town planning commission action in amending local zoning requirements where proponent of change was daughter and business associate of alternate commissioner who sat at commission table and participated actively in deliberations in support of the proponent's recommendation). Even clear financial conflicts may raise interesting wrinkles. See, e.g., *Sivick v. State Ethics Commission*, 202 A.3d 814 (Pa. 2019) (holding that chair of board of supervisors who also served as roadmaster and public works supervisor had violated ethics law in awarding major contract to his son's benefit), *appeal granted*, 2019 WL 3561826 (Pa. 2019) (to consider whether father could be ordered to reimburse the town for funds).

4. *Direct and indirect financial interests.* Courts will find a disqualifying interest when the conflict is direct. What is the difference between benefits that are "direct" as opposed to those that are "indirect"? "Indirect" benefits sometimes arise in instances in which there is a derivative or attenuated relationship between a government official and an entity which contracts with a local government (for example, if someone holds stock or if a family member is employed with the contractor). See, e.g., *Drake v. City of Elizabeth, N.J.*, 54 A. 248 (N.J. 1903) (councilmember's wife's ownership of stock in publishing company awarded city printing contract was sufficient to invalidate resolution, notwithstanding the fact that there were sufficient votes to pass the resolution had councilmember abstained); *Randolph v. City of Brigantine Planning Bd.*, 963 A.2d. 1224 (N.J. Super. A.D. 2009) (invalidating planning board's approval of site plan where owner of engineering firm that reviewed site plan lived with the planning board chair). The Washington statute in the principal case includes an additional provision delineating "remote interests" that, if disclosed and officially noted, would not invalidate good faith council action without counting the vote of the person concerned so long as the officer does not influence or attempt to influence any other officer to enter into the contract. See Wash. Rev. Code § 42.23.040 (defining "remote interest" to include that of a nonsalaried officer of a nonprofit corporation; an employee or agent of a contracting party who is compensated entirely by fixed wages or salary, a landlord or tenant of the contracting party, and a holder of less than one percent of the shares of the contracting party).

5. *Relationships and conflicts.* Complex questions can arise when relationships are at stake, rather than direct financial interests. Consider the following decisions: *Brooks v. Planning and Zoning Comm'n of the Town of Haddam*, 26 Conn. L. Rptr. 397 (Conn. Super. 2000) (planning commission members not disqualified from involvement in decision to grant permit for construction of municipal outdoor recreational facility including ballfields notwithstanding active participation

in local little league and work to support construction of new ballfields); *Lincoln Heights Ass'n v. Township of Cranford Planning Bd.*, 714 A.2d 995 (N.J. Super. Ct. Law Div. 1998), *aff'd*, 729 A.2d 50 (1999) (board member not disqualified from decision regarding approval of grocery store when his parents lived within a block of proposed store and would arguably benefit); *Piscitelli v. City of Garfield Zoning Bd. of Adjustment*, 205 A.3d 183 (N.J. 2019) (concluding that a meaningful doctor-patient relationship between zoning board member or family and doctor with interests connected to site plan approval application would amount to disqualifying conflict of interest). For a compilation of cases raising similar thorny issues, see Salkin, Brown & Scholes, *Relationships and Ethics in the Land Use Game*, 42 No. 5 ZONING & PLANNING L. REPT. NL 1 (May 2019). For discussion of other assorted developments, see Salkin & Stakey, *Further Developments in Land Use Ethics*, 47 URB. LAW. 739 (2015).

6. *Benefited parties and coverage considerations.* Many states prohibit governmental contracts not only with decision-makers themselves, but also with their "relatives" in order to bar "nepotism" that provides unfair advantage to relatives and corrupts public decision-making. States that have not updated their statutes may run into difficulties as families and personal relationships have changed in recent years. See, e.g., *Mississippi Ethics Com'n v. Grisham*, 957 So. 2d 997 (Miss. 2007) (in action by state Ethics Commission against county supervisor after county board of supervisors accepted bid for asphalt from supervisor's step-son, holding that state statute regarding nepotism was unambiguous and did not cover step-relations). Can a member of the public violate ethical requirements? For a case finding an ethics violation by a member of the public, see *Parkhouse v. Stringer*, 912 N.E.2d 48 (N.Y. 2009) (subpoena could be issued in connection with alleged misrepresentation by a member of the public in reading statement of borough president that had been modified without permission).

7. *Remedies: invalidation, recusal and more.* Washington's statutes specify that

> Any contract made in violation of the provisions of this chapter is void and the performance thereof, in full or in part, by a contracting party shall not be the basis of any claim against the municipality. Any officer violating the provisions of this chapter is liable to the municipality of which he or she is an officer for a penalty in the amount of five hundred dollars, in addition to such other civil or criminal liability or penalty as may otherwise be imposed upon the officer by law. [RCW 42.23.050.]

The statute further provides that "In addition to all other penalties, civil or criminal, the violation by any officer of the provisions of this chapter may be grounds for forfeiture of his or her office." *Id.* How can local officials keep from running afoul of such serious penalties? In most cases, statutes or municipal codes require officials who have a conflict of interest to refrain from participating in the government decision. The breadth of such prohibitions may be unclear in practice. Can an affected official contact the town planner or town attorney to ask questions about interpretation of relevant ordinance provisions? Attend hearings and speak from the audience? Submit letters indicating point of view? Compare *Phillips v. Town of Salem Planning*

& Zoning Comm'n, 1998 WL 258332 (Sup. Conn., 1998) (member of commission did not act inappropriately in discussing questions with town planner and town attorney, presenting views through personal attorney, and discussing clarifying amendment regarding meaning of "concrete" within ordinance, where she owned campsite across road from proposed facility to manufacture bituminous concrete), with *South Brunswick Associates v. Township Council of the Township of Monroe*, 667 A.2d 1 (N.J. Super. 1994) (township council president could not represent other citizens before zoning board in quasi-judicial proceeding nor in subsequent review of agency's action). Recession of a contract may also be an option, and may be triggered by a lawsuit brought by a private party, at least in some jurisdictions. See *Leder v. Superintendent of Schools of Concord*, 988 N.E.2d 851 (Mass. 2013) (discussing procedural requirements for lawsuit challenging policy on rental band instruments).

8. *Special issues: judges and ethical constraints.* Special ethical issues may arise in connection with state regulation of judicial candidates' speech during an election. See *Williams-Yulee v. Florida Bar*, 135 S. Ct 1656 (2015) (upholding Florida's ban on direct financial solicitation by judicial candidates in the face of First Amendment challenge); see Wright, *Williams-Yulee v. Florida Bar: Judicial Elections, Impartiality, and the Threat to Free Speech*, 93 Denv. L. Rev. 551 (2016) (discussing case).

C. Serving in the Sunshine: Public Records, Open Meetings, and Related Legal and Ethical Obligations of Public Officials and Employees

This Chapter has so far explored ways in which the qualifications and obligations of public officials and employees may differ from those applicable to their private sector counterparts. Another important difference relates to the role of the public and the press in the day-to-day life of those in the public sector. Rights to public and press access to both governmental records and government agency meetings have become the norm at least since 1966, when the federal Freedom of Information Act (FOIA), 5 U.S.C. § 522, was enacted, to be followed in 1976 with adoption of the federal "Government in the Sunshine Act," 5 U.S.C. § 522b, as well as adoption of the Federal Advisory Committee Act, 5 U.S.C. App. 2. For a history of the evolution of the Federal Freedom of Information Act, see Eckart, *The Freedom of Information Act—The Historical and Current Status of Walking the Tight Rope Between Public Access to Government Records and Protecting National Security Interests*, 41 Seton Hall Legis. J. 241 (2017). For a critique suggesting potential theoretical flaws in federal FOIA, see Pozen, *Freedom of Information Beyond the Freedom of Information Act*, 165 U. Pa. L. Rev. 1097 (2017). The federal FOIA was amended in 2016. See Public Law No: 114-185, https://www.congress.gov/bill/114th-congress/senate-bill/337.

Most states have also passed public records and open meeting laws. For a comprehensive survey of state freedom of information acts ("state FOIAs"), see *50 State*

Statutory Surveys: Government: Privacy, 0095 SURVEYS 8 (Westlaw March 2019). There are also free on-line sources for similar information. See, e.g., National Freedom of Information Coalition, https://www.nfoic.org/coalitions/state-foi-resources/state-freedom-of-information-laws. Provisions in state constitutions and statutes in some instances predated these federal actions, while in many other instances they were amended or added thereafter using the federal provisions as models. Still other states have approached the area in their own ways, using differing structures and terminology. State legislation typically covers both state and local governmental entities, although there may be differences between levels and branches of government and types of agencies covered. State statutes have also been amended with some regularity as new issues have surfaced (for example, the need to deal with electronic communication and concerns about public security in the wake of the September 11, 2001 terrorist attacks). The thrust of the legislation remains the same, however: using "sunshine" to spotlight the operation of government so that the public has information about the public's business, and reminding government officials that the public may be watching so that their activities should be above board in all cases.

Because each state's governing statutes differ in detail, it is essential to examine statutory texts very closely when dealing with public records and open meetings questions. For some broader perspectives on open meetings and public records laws, see, e.g., Johnson, *Open Meetings and Closed Minds: Another Road to the Mountaintop*, 53 Drake L. Rev. 11 (2004); Solove, *Access and Aggregation: Public Records, Privacy and the Constitution*, 86 Minn. L. Rev. 1327 (2002); Nowadzky, *A Comparative Analysis of Public Records Statutes*, 28 Urb. Law. 65 (1996).

As a general proposition, however, four classic questions are central to both public records and open meetings statutes and case law: (a) is the governmental entity in question an entity covered by the statute? (b) is the record or meeting in question within the scope of "record" or "meeting" as statutorily defined? (c) is there an exemption or exception that takes the situation in question out from under the general definition? (d) have procedural requirements been followed and if not, what remedy might apply? The following case focuses on the third of these questions, while the Notes explore the full range of questions in greater detail.

New York Times Company v. City of New York Fire Dep't

4 N.Y.3d 477, 796 N.Y.S.2d 302, 829 N.E.2d 266 (2005)

R.S. Smith, J.

The issue here is whether the New York City Fire Department is required by the Freedom of Information Law (FOIL) to disclose tapes and transcripts of certain conversations that occurred on and shortly after September 11, 2001. Supreme Court and the Appellate Division held that FOIL requires disclosure of some, but not all, of the materials in dispute. We affirm most of the rulings below, but we modify the Appellate Division's order in two respects.

Facts and Procedural History

Some four months after the September 11 attacks on the World Trade Center, Jim Dwyer, a New York Times reporter, requested "various records" from the Fire Department [including transcripts of interviews conducted by the Fire Department with its employees and all tapes and transcripts of radio communications involving Fire Department personnel. The Fire Department denied these requests in large part.] As a result, three categories of tapes and transcripts are now at issue. They contain: (1) calls made on September 11 to the Department's 911 emergency service; (2) calls made on the same day on the Fire Department's internal communications system, involving Department dispatchers and other employees, which are referred to as "dispatch calls"; and (3) "oral histories," consisting of interviews with firefighters in the days following September 11. [The Times and Dwyer sought to compel disclosure, and family members of eight men who died in the World Trade Commission intervened in support of those seeking disclosure.]

[The lower court ordered disclosure of tapes and transcripts to the extent that they recorded the words of public employees and those whose families had intervened; the dispatch calls redacted to delete opinions and recommendations of Fire Department personnel, and the oral histories redacted to delete the personal expressions of feelings of those interviewed. The Appellate Division affirmed the lower court in large part but ordered the release of the remainder of the oral histories. On appeal the Times, Dwyer, and intervenors sought disclosure of all materials.]

Discussion

FOIL requires state and municipal agencies to "make available for public inspection and copying all records," subject to 10 exceptions (Public Officers Law § 87[2]). Here, the Fire Department relies on three of those exceptions—the "privacy," "law enforcement" and "intra-agency" exceptions. To the extent they are relevant here, these exceptions permit agencies to "deny access to records or portions thereof that:

> "(b) if disclosed would constitute an unwarranted invasion of personal privacy under the provisions of subdivision two of section eighty-nine of this article;
>
> ....
>
> "(e) are compiled for law enforcement purposes and which, if disclosed, would:
>
> > "i. interfere with law enforcement investigations or judicial proceedings; [or]
> >
> > "ii. deprive a person of a right to a fair trial or impartial adjudication;
>
> ....
>
> "(g) are inter-agency or intra-agency materials which are not:

"i. statistical or factual tabulations or data; [or]

"ii. instructions to staff that affect the public." (*Id.*)

The Fire Department contends that the privacy exception applies to the portions of the 911 calls that are in dispute; that the intra-agency exception applies to the disputed portions of the dispatch calls; and that both these exceptions apply to portions of the oral histories. [The Department also sought to protect certain potential exhibits relevant to the trial of one of the hijackers, and in a section of the opinion not included here the court allowed in camera review by the trial court.] Thus, we . . . consider the application of the privacy and intra-agency exceptions to each category of materials. . . .

A. The 911 Calls

The Fire Department does not now oppose disclosure of the words spoken in the 911 calls by 911 operators, or by the eight men whose families are seeking disclosure. Thus, the only issue before us is whether the disclosure of words spoken by other callers would constitute an "unwarranted invasion of personal privacy." . . .

We first reject the argument . . . that no privacy interest exists in the feelings and experiences of people no longer living. The privacy exception, it is argued, does not protect the dead, and their survivors cannot claim "privacy" for experiences and feelings that are not their own. We think this argument contradicts the common understanding of the word "privacy."

Almost everyone, surely, wants to keep from public view some aspects not only of his or her own life, but of the lives of loved ones who have died. It is normal to be appalled if intimate moments in the life of one's deceased child, wife, husband or other close relative become publicly known, and an object of idle curiosity or a source of titillation. The desire to preserve the dignity of human existence even when life has passed is the sort of interest to which legal protection is given under the name of privacy. We thus hold that surviving relatives have an interest protected by FOIL in keeping private the affairs of the dead. . . .

The recognition that surviving relatives have a legally protected privacy interest, however, is only the beginning of the inquiry. We must decide whether disclosure of the tapes and transcripts of the 911 calls would injure that interest, or the comparable interest of people who called 911 and survived, and whether the injury to privacy would be "unwarranted" within the meaning of FOIL's privacy exception. [The Court concluded that none of the non-exclusive list of unwarranted forms of invasion of personal privacy were applicable in the current cases. Accordingly] we must decide whether any invasion of privacy here is "unwarranted" by balancing the privacy interests at stake against the public interest in disclosure of the information.

The privacy interests in this case are compelling. The 911 calls at issue undoubtedly contain, in many cases, the words of people confronted, without warning, with the prospect of imminent death. Those words are likely to include expressions of the terror and agony the callers felt and of their deepest feelings about what their lives and their families meant to them. The grieving family of such a caller—or the caller, if he or she survived—might reasonably be deeply offended at the idea that these words could be heard on television or read in the New York Times.

We do not imply that there is a privacy interest of comparable strength in all tapes and transcripts of calls made to 911. Two factors make the September 11 911 calls different. First, while some other 911 callers may be in as desperate straits as those who called on September 11, many are not. Secondly, the September 11 callers were part of an event that has received and will continue to receive enormous—perhaps literally unequalled—public attention. Many millions of people have reacted, and will react, to the callers' fate with horrified fascination. Thus it is highly likely in this case—more than in almost any other imaginable—that, if the tapes and transcripts are made public, they will be replayed and republished endlessly, and that in some cases they will be exploited by media seeking to deliver sensational fare to their audience. This is the sort of invasion that the privacy exception exists to prevent.

We acknowledge that not everyone will have the same reaction to disclosure of the 911 tapes. The intervenors in this case, whose husbands and sons died at the World Trade Center, favor disclosure. They may feel, as other survivors may also, that to make their loved ones' last words public is a fitting way to allow the world to share the callers' sufferings, to admire their courage, and to be justly enraged by the crime that killed them. This normal human emotion is no less entitled to respect than a desire for privacy.... Surviving callers who want disclosure are also entitled to it.... But the privacy interests of those family members and surviving callers who do not want disclosure nevertheless remain powerful.

On the other hand, there is a legitimate public interest in the disclosure of these 911 calls. In general, it is desirable that the public know as much as possible about the terrible events of September 11. And more specifically, as the Times and Dwyer point out, the public has a legitimate interest in knowing how well or poorly the 911 system performed on that day. The National Commission on Terrorist Attacks Upon the United States, which had access to the tapes and transcripts at issue here, identified significant flaws in the system's performance, and more public scrutiny might make these problems better understood. But the parties seeking disclosure here do not request only particular calls that may be relevant to this subject; they seek complete disclosure of all the 911 calls.

We are not persuaded that such disclosure is required by the public interest. Those requesting it have not shown that the information that will be disclosed under our ruling—including the words of the 911 operators, and of callers whose survivors seek, or who themselves seek, disclosure—will be insufficient to meet the public's need to be informed. We conclude that the public interest in the words of the 911 callers is outweighed by the interest in privacy of those family members and callers who prefer that those words remain private.

B. The Dispatch Calls

The dispatch calls are communications within the Fire Department; the only participants in the calls were Department dispatchers and other Department employees. The tapes and transcripts of these calls are therefore "intra-agency materials," and are protected from disclosure by Public Officers Law § 87(2)(g) unless they fit within one of two exclusions from the intra-agency exception: the exclusions for "statistical or factual tabulations or data" (§ 87[2][g][i]) and for "instructions to staff that affect the public" (§ 87[2][g][ii]). [The court explained that it had earlier interpreted these exclusions to mean that "[f]actual data . . . simply means objective information, in contrast to opinions, ideas, or advice exchanged as part of the consultative or deliberative process of government decision making." The court also concluded that the lower courts had applied this standard appropriately in redacting nonfactual material in the form of opinions and recommendations.]

The parties seeking disclosure argue otherwise, relying on cases in which we have characterized the intra-agency exception as being applicable to "'deliberative material,' i.e., communications exchanged for discussion purposes not constituting final policy decisions." [The court distinguished earlier cases that involved films shown by a public college to its students, and a report prepared for a public agency by an outside consultant, explaining that the films were not used in internal decision-making while the report was used for that purpose.] Neither case implies that materials that fit squarely within the plain meaning of "intra-agency"—in this case, tapes and transcripts of internal conversations about the agency's work—are not within the scope of the intra-agency exception to FOIL. . . .

The point of the intra-agency exception is to permit people within an agency to exchange opinions, advice and criticism freely and frankly, without the chilling prospect of public disclosure. . . . This purpose applies not only to comments made in official policy meetings and well-considered memorandums, but also to suggestions and criticisms offered with little chance for reflection in moments of crisis. A Fire Department dispatcher who believes that a rescue operation is being badly handled should feel free to say so without the concern that a tape of his or her remarks will be made public.

C. The Oral Histories

The record here leads us to conclude, subject to the qualification discussed below, that the oral histories are not protected from disclosure by either the privacy or the intra-agency exception. We infer from the record that the oral histories were exactly what their name implies—spoken words recorded for the benefit of posterity—and that the Department intended, and the people interviewed for these histories understood or reasonably should have understood, that the words spoken were destined for public disclosure. If this inference is correct, the privacy exception obviously has no application here. Nor does the intra-agency exception apply where, though agency employees are speaking to each other, the agency and the employees understand and intend that a tape of the conversation will be made public. The point of the intra-agency exception, as we explained above, is to permit the internal exchange of candid advice and opinions between agency employees. The exception is not applicable to words that are intended to be passed on verbatim to the world at large.

[The court cited affidavits that indicated that the oral histories were collected for two purposes: "to be an invaluable historical record, in addition to assisting in any investigations or assessments of the incident."] . . . While the record is less clear than it might be, it establishes that the interviews were intended as an "historical record"—which implies that the interviews would be disclosed to the public. If that is the case, they should not be protected from disclosure merely because they also were, as the Fire Department says, intended to be used in "investigations or assessments." The record does not show that any interviewee was given a promise of confidentiality or led to believe that his or her words would be kept secret. Thus, the best inference is that the Department intended, and the interviewees knew or should have known, that the words spoken in the interviews would become a public record. . . . [The Court concluded that all the oral histories were subject to disclosure, but gave the Fire Department an opportunity to present evidence in individual instances suggesting that there were expectations of privacy.] . . .

Conclusion

Accordingly, the order of the Appellate Division should be modified to the extent described in this opinion, and, as modified, affirmed, without costs.

Rosenblatt, J. (dissenting in part). [The dissent concluded that the public interest supported broader disclosure of the 911 calls and would have required release of a written transcript of the callers' side of the 911 conversations, redacted so as exclude anything that would identify nonofficial callers in calls that have some unusually personal component, such as an expression of dying wishes to be relayed to family members, as opposed to the ordinary reporting of crime scene facts.]

Judges G.B. Smith, Graffeo and Read concur with Judge R.S. Smith.

Judge Rosenblatt dissents in part in a separate opinion in which Chief Judge Kaye and Judge Ciparick concur.

Notes and Questions

1. *Defining "public records."* The court in the principal case had no need to consider whether the "911" tapes were "records" for purposes of the New York statute. Sometimes the meaning of "records" is less clear. Consider, for example, the extent to which e-mail of public employees constitutes a "record" for statutory disclosure purposes. When electronic mail was first introduced many statutory definitions of "records" did not explicitly address the question. Many attorneys general, and in some cases, courts have ruled that definitions of "records" that reference "computerized records" include e-mail within their scope. See, e.g., 81 Op. Att'y Gen. Md. 140 (1996) (finding that e-mail is a covered record). Many state statutes now explicitly address this issue. See, e.g., Washington State's provisions, RCWA 42.56.010(3)

(2017) (defining "public record" as including "any writing containing information relating to the conduct of government or the performance of any governmental or proprietary function prepared, owned, used, or retained by any state or local agency regardless of physical form or characteristics.").

Are personal e-mails of government employees on government computers "public records"? Depending on the language of controlling statutes, most courts have concluded that such emails are subject to public records disclosure only if related to the transaction of public business. See., e.g., *Pennsylvania Office of Attorney General v. The Philadelphia Inquirer*, 127 A.3d 57 (Pa. 2015) (rejecting disclosure request for pornographic emails sent from office computers contrary to government policy); *Griffis v. Pinal County*, 156 P.3d 418 (Ariz. 2007) (en banc) (holding that e-mails created or maintained on government-owned computer system were not automatically public records, but that when withheld on the grounds that they were personal, requesting party may request in camera inspection by court to determine whether disclosure is required under public records law). What about work-related e-mail on an employee's home computer? See *City of Champaign v. Madigan*, 992 N.E.2d 629 (Ill. App. 2013) (use of personally owned electronic devices during city council meetings to engage in communications public business were subject to state FOIA).

The definition of "public records" may also apply in less obvious settings. For example, it may cover information accessed by public employees and officials that are kept on premises not controlled by the government itself. For a fascinating case involving alleged misconduct by college athletes investigated by the National Collegiate Athletic Association (NCAA), see *National Collegiate Athletic Ass'n v. Associated Press*, 18 So. 3d 1201 (Fla. App. 1st Dist. 2009) (holding that documents in digital form fell within the Florida public records act, and that placement of such documents by the NCAA on a secure website accessed by member institutions in connection with disciplinary proceedings were "public records" even though prepared by a private organization since they were "received" by agents of a public entity and used in connection with public business, notwithstanding promises that a document would be kept confidential; and rejecting NCAA contentions that treating such documents as public records impeded interstate commerce and freedom of association). "Public records" may also include "metadata" (data associated with documents, reflecting date of creation, date of access, who accessed, when printed). See *Lake v. City of Phoenix*, 218 P.3d 1004 (Ariz. 2009) (in employment discrimination case, employee sought notes made by police supervisor, including embedded metadata; court ruled that such information was available as a public record).

2. *Exemptions: privacy.*

(a) *"911" calls.* The principal case focused on a statutory provision authorizing nondisclosure where disclosure would constitute an "unwarranted" invasion of "personal privacy" (covering such matters as employment references, medical and credit histories, lists that could be used for fundraising purposes, and information that could cause personal hardship if not relevant to the agency requesting or maintaining it). N.Y. Public Officers Law § 87.2(b), § 89. There was no explicit reference to "911" information. It further specifies that disclosure does not constitute an unwarranted invasion of personal privacy "when identifying details are deleted." Should the absence of any explicit reference to "911" information have influenced the court's decision? If the public record demand had been targeted to a "911" call involving the death of a single individual, would the court have reached the same conclusion?

In an earlier decision concerning access to "911" information, the Supreme Court of Virginia had concluded that tapes of "911" calls were public records but could be withheld under an exception for "noncriminal incidents records" that sheriffs must maintain (defined at the time to include "compilations of noncriminal occurrences of general interest to law-enforcement agencies, such as missing persons, lost and found property, suicides and accidental deaths."). *See Tull v. Brown*, 494 S.E.2d 855 (Va. 1998). *Tull* involved the request of news media for tapes of a "911" call from parents of a child who had stopped breathing, and interaction with rescue and police personnel. The child later died in the hospital. The matter was initially treated as potentially involving criminal activity until that possibility was ruled out by an autopsy. The sheriff had contended that private individuals using the "911" service did not expect that their communications would be treated as public records accessible to the media, but the Virginia court rejected that view. *See also A.H. Belo Corp. v. Mesa Police Dep't*, 42 P.3d 615 (Ariz. 2002) (concluding that audio tape of "911" call involving injured child was not subject to disclosure, when transcript had been provided and balancing test weighing "privacy, confidentiality, and the best interests of the state" was applied). Is the balancing test a suitable way of resolving such matters, or should more explicit statutory provisions be employed? Not all state public information statutes have privacy exceptions. For an analysis of ongoing developments, see Coyle & Whitenack, *Access to 911 Recordings: Balancing Privacy Interests and the Public's Right to Know about Deaths*, 24 Comm. L. & Pol'y 307 (2019) (recommending in general that in camera reviews be employed to reach balancing decisions).

(b) *Sensitivity of information.* The principal case involved requests for particularly sensitive personal information. Are government employees' home addresses, phone numbers, and similarly sensitive information entitled to protection as private? Does it matter if such information is compiled and made available to employees for work-related use? See *Michigan Federation of Teachers and School Related Personnel, AFT-CIO v. University of Michigan*, 753 N.W.2d 28 (Mich. 2008) (University released home addresses and phone numbers of university personnel who had authorized publication of such information in campus directory but declined to provide such information for employees who had opted out of publication of such information; state supreme court held that Michigan FOIA privacy exemption covered the requested information since the information was personal in nature and release would result in a clearly unwarranted invasion of privacy that was unjustified in absence of justification linking release to core purpose of public records law designed to provide information on whether government agency was being operated properly and consistently with legal requirements). Compare *Bitterman v. Village of Oakley*, 868 N.W.2d 642 (Mich. App. 2015) (names of donors to village police fund not protected from disclosure under privacy provision). For a helpful analysis of theoretical issues relating to sunshine laws and privacy, see Ohm, *Sensitive Information*, 88 S. Cal. L. Rev. 1125 (2015) (proposing a multi-factor test for sensitive information).

(c) *Deaths, criminal charges, and police activity.* How should public records laws treat "death records" such as death certificates and autopsy reports? See Boles, *Documenting Death: Public Access to Government Death Records and Attendant Privacy Concerns*, 22 Cornell J.L. & Pub. Pol'y 237 (2012) (discussing need for balance between privacy and public information). How should "mug shots" be treated, when they can be "monetized" for sale by on-line database providers? See Lee, *Monetizing Shame: Mugshots, Privacy, and the Right of Access*, 70 Rutgers U. L. Rev. 557 (2018) (explaining that many states treat mug shots as public records and arguing that the presumption that such records are public should be reconsidered). One of the most highly contested current issues regarding public records relates to access to body cam videos made by police in connection with their law enforcement activities. See, e.g., Wenner, *Policing the Police*, 2016 U. Chi. Legal F. 873 (2016); Maury, *Who Watches the Watchmen's Tape? FOIA's Categorical Exemptions and Police Body-Worn Cameras*, 92 Notre Dame L. Rev. 479 (2016).

(d) *Changing technology.* Public employees are not always sensitive to how their privacy rights may be affected by use of advanced communication equipment and the claims their employers, as well as members of the public, may have to what they believe to be private information. See, e.g., *City of Ontario v. Quon*, 560 U.S. 746 (2010) (police officer used government-issued pager for both official business and for private romantic communications, and government subsequently sought to audit his used; holding that search by government was permissible under the Fourth Amendment, where question existed about expectations of privacy and search was reasonable). For discussion, see Dammeier, *Fading Privacy Rights of Public Employees*, 6 Harv. L. & Pol'y Rev. 297 (2012). Text messaging has supplanted email for many users. How should text messages be addressed under state FOIA law? See Vera, *"Regardless of Physical Form": Legal and Practical Considerations Regarding the Application of State Open-Records Laws to Public Business Conducted by Text Message*, 32-SPR Comm. Law. 24 (2017) (reviewing state law including attorney generals' opinions and litigation, and identifying emerging issues).

3. *Covered entities and covered records.* Although it was clear in the principal case that the Fire Department was covered by the state public records statute, questions have increasingly arisen concerning coverage of quasi-public entities or private entities under contract with public agencies, as well as certain records that are in the possession of a public entity where those records would otherwise be private. See, e.g., *State ex rel. Cincinnati Enquirer v. Krings, Cty. Admr.*, 758 N.E.2d 1135 (Ohio 2001) (records of private contractor relating to possible cost overruns in construction of public football stadium were subject to Ohio Public Records Act when the

private party was obligated to prepare the records in order to carry out a public office's responsibilities; the public office needed to monitor the private entity's performance; and the public office had to have access to the records for this purpose); *State v. Beaver Dam Area Development Corp.*, 752 N.W.2d 295 (Wis. 2008) (holding that corporation was a quasi-governmental corporation subject to open meetings and public records law because under the totality of the circumstances it resembled a governmental corporation in function, effect and status, given the facts that the corporation was funded exclusively with public tax dollars and interest, was located in a municipal building, was listed on the city website, was provided with clerical support and office supplies by the city, had two city officials on its board, had no clients other than the city, functioned exclusively to promote economic development in and around the city, and had assets that would revert to the city if dissolved).

Some states address such issues explicitly by statute. See, e.g., GA. CODE ANN. § 50-18-70(a) (stating that "public record" means documents "prepared and maintained or received in the course of the operation of a public office or agency"; specifying that the statute should be construed "to disallow an agency's placing or causing such items to be placed in the hands of a private person or entity for the purpose of avoiding disclosure" and directing that records "received or maintained by a private person, firm, corporation, or other private entity in the performance of a service or function for or on behalf of an agency, a public agency, or a public office shall be subject to disclosure to the same extent that such records would be subject to disclosure if received or maintained by such agency, public agency, or public office."). Most state statutes are not so explicit, however. For a review of related litigation over the past 15 years, see Capeloto, *Transparency on Trial: A Legal Review of Public Information Access in the Face of Privatization*, 13 CONN. PUB. INT. L.J. 19 (2013). For discussion of ongoing demands for access to records maintained by foundations associated with universities, although those entities are typically incorporated and distinct nonprofit entities, see Capeloto, *Private Status, Public Ties: University Foundations and Freedom of Information Laws*, 33 QUINNIPIAC L. REV. 339 (2015) (arguing for access to related records). Another currently contested area concerns the extent to which private prisons are subject to state public information legislation. See Parker, *Private Prisons Behind Bars: Why Corrections Corporations Must Abide by Public Information Laws*, 48 TEX. TECH L. REV. ONLINE EDITION 39 (2016).

4. *Procedures and remedies.* Often public records and public meetings legislation includes definitions and exemptions that may seem clear in theory, but become murky when applied due to changing times and complex facts. Should there be a means for governmental entities to secure a judicial interpretation in situations such as these more promptly and simply than through extended litigation? Governmental agencies may seek advice from state attorneys general by requesting advisory opinions when legal issues of this sort are in doubt, and attorneys general opinions are an important source of law in this arena. Public records and open meetings statutes often include "cost shifting" provisions that may afford courts discretion or mandate that plaintiffs' costs of litigation and attorneys' fees be borne by the

government agency if the agency incorrectly withholds records or does so without reasonable grounds (although the agency typically is not awarded costs or fees if it prevails). How might such considerations play into judgments regarding disclosure of records or opening of meetings? See, e.g., Hull, *Disappearing Fee Awards and Civil Enforcement of Public Records Laws*, 52 U. Kan. L. Rev. 721 (2004); Engstrom, *Defining North Carolina's Public Records and Open Meetings Fee-Shifting Provisions in the Larger National Context*, 96 N.C. L. Rev. 1725 (2018) (considering specifics of North Carolina as well as federal FOIA and other states' FOIA provisions). Another important question concerns the cost of searching for and copying public records when they are requested by citizens. Statutes may specify per page copying costs, but if there is a substantial volume of requests the governmental entity may need to develop very efficient file and document management systems and employ additional personnel. These systems may be particularly important when requests are made for e-mail correspondence.

A Note on Government Lawyers' Ethical Responsibilities

Government attorneys who advise local and state government officials often face particular challenges in interpreting public records and open meetings acts, as well as in helping their clients understand applicable legal requirements. Such situations may also raise important questions of professional responsibility for the government lawyer. Consider the following fact pattern in light of the preceding sections on integrity in government and sunshine laws in order to see how legal ethics issues may arise.

Problem 5-2

Assume you are the city attorney for the city of Middletown (a hypothetical municipality with a population of 100,000 and a council-manager form of government). The city manager has asked for your advice in dealing with the situation described below. Middletown has for the last ten years enjoyed the presence of a minor league baseball team (the Middletown Marauders). The team plays in City Center Stadium, an outdoor facility located in the heart of downtown dedicated wholly to the team's use. The presence of the team has benefited the community by providing a source of entertainment; revenues from property, sales and amusement taxes; and part-time jobs for some city residents. During its early years, the team drew a great deal of support from the community and turned a significant profit. In each of the last three years, however, the team has lost more games than it won.

Matt Means, a former mayor of Middletown, organized a private investment group to build and operate City Center Stadium and own the Marauders' franchise since the team's inception. During the last year he's let it be known that he and the investment group would like to sell the team rights and the stadium. Although he's had some tentative inquiries, nothing serious developed once potential buyers became aware of what he and the investment group believe is a fair price. Recently, a newly elected city council member (Cathy Cashman), Means' daughter-in-law, has spoken to City Manager Albert Arnold about her idea that the City should purchase the stadium and all rights to the Marauders. Arnold heard her out, but said he wasn't sure that the City could come up with the money needed or that it would be advisable to take on that kind of operation. Arnold has been contacted by Tom Truax, another member of the Council, who thinks it's a terrible idea even to talk about such a proposal. Truax has objected on a number of grounds, questioning the legality of such an undertaking, its wisdom as a policy matter, and the appearance of undue influence associated with involvement by the former mayor (who he's long opposed).

According to Arnold, Truax reported that Cashman has been pushing the idea pretty strongly over the Council's private e-mail listserv (which is operated through city government computer facilities but is not accessible to anyone on the town staff or to members of the public). Apparently, she contends that the City needs the team to keep civic pride alive (she cites the long-standing success of the Green Bay Packers). She also claims that the investors and her father-in-law are likely to sell the team or declare bankruptcy (shutting the stadium down and leaving an unsightly, unoccupied facility in the downtown) if they don't get a break soon. In addition, she's argued that the City could turn a profit if it operated the Marauders in the evenings, while renovating the facility as a community recreational center that could be used for other purposes when the Marauders aren't playing (are out of town or in their off-season). Truax advised Arnold that he'd told Cashman he strongly opposed the whole notion, but warned that Cashman seems to be picking up growing support among other members of the City Council.

Arnold has asked for your advice. Assume that you've already explained whether the City could legally borrow funds to purchase the stadium and team franchise (or create any other sort of quasi-public entity that could); and how any operating deficit could be covered if the City proceeded with such a strategy, as you've come to understand these matters after studying Chapter 4. Assume, too, that you've already explained the operation of the state's public records and open meetings act, as well as the provisions relating to conflicts of interest, after studying the materials earlier in this Chapter. Focus instead on how your obligations under the Rules of Professional Responsibility might influence your actions, and on the possible actions you might take. In thinking through these issues, consider the following critical part of the American Bar Association's Model Rules of Professional Conduct (2003) (which has been adopted in many states with some local variations). Certain aspects of the Rules were modified as a result of the ABA's Ethics 20/20 initiative; and many states are making changes as a result.

Notes and Questions

1. *Who is the client?* A threshold question concerns who is the government attorney's client. Consider the possibilities. Is it the city manager? Individual members of the council? A faction among the council? The council itself? The city as an entity? Members of the public? The "public good" as the attorney conceives it?

RULE 1.13. Organization as Client*

(a) A lawyer employed or retained by an organization represents the organization acting through its duly authorized constituents.

(b) If a lawyer for an organization knows that an officer, employee or other person associated with the organization is engaged in action, intends to act or refuses to act in a matter related to the representation that is a violation of a legal obligation to the organization, or a violation of law that reasonably might be imputed to the organization, and that is likely to result in substantial injury to the organization, then the lawyer shall proceed as is reasonably necessary in the best interest of the organization. Unless the lawyer reasonably believes that it is not necessary in the best interest of the organization to do so, the lawyer shall refer the matter to higher authority in the organization, including, if warranted by the circumstances, to the highest authority that can act on behalf of the organization as determined by applicable law.

. . . .

(f) In dealing with an organization's directors, officers, employees, members, shareholders or other constituents, a lawyer shall explain the identity of the client when the lawyer knows or reasonably should know that the organization's interests are adverse to those of the constituents with whom the lawyer is dealing.

Comment: . . . [3] When constituents of the organization make decisions for it, the decisions ordinarily must be accepted by the lawyer even if their utility or prudence is doubtful. Decisions concerning policy and operations, including ones entailing serious risk, are not as such in the lawyer's province. Paragraph (b) makes clear, however, that when the lawyer knows that the organization is likely to be substantially injured by action of an officer or other constituent that violates a legal obligation to the organization or is in violation of law that might be imputed to the organization, the lawyer must proceed as is reasonably necessary in the best interest of the organization. As defined in Rule 1.0(f), knowledge can be inferred from circumstances, and a lawyer cannot ignore the obvious.

See, e.g., *Salt Lake County Comm'n v. Short*, 985 P.2d 899 (Utah 1999) (elected county attorney served in dual role as attorney and as elected official and had attorney-client relationship with county as entity rather than with individual county commissioners or with the commission as a group of individuals; under Utah law, commission could not hire an outside attorney in place of elected county attorney simply because they disagreed with the advice provided by the elected county attorney). For a helpful overview of government attorney ethics generally under Utah requirements, see Call, *Ethics for the State and Local Government Attorney*, 31-JUN Utah B.J. 38 (2018). For additional perspective on the public records issues raised by the principal problem, see *Baker v. Jones*, 199 S.W.3d 749 (Ky. App. 2006) (holding that e-mail between mayor and city council should be treated as preliminary recommendations and memorandum that were not subject to disclosure, despite ordinance provision saying that all messages were subject to open records act and disclosure of e-mail to local newspaper). For a discussion of the identity of government clients, see Edris, *Issues of Client Identification for Municipal Attorney: An Agency and Public Interest Approach*, 24 Geo. J. Legal Ethics 517 (2011); Seipel, *Discord and Distortion: Organizational Psychology and the Public Interest Approach to Government Lawyering*, 42 Law & Psychol. Rev. 35 (2017–2018) (discussing role ambiguity and role conflict that can arise in government lawyering). For in-depth consideration of the obligation to organizational clients, including governments, see Simon, *Duties to Organizational Clients*, 29 Geo. J. Legal Ethics 489 (2016).

2. *Obligations of confidentiality.* What is the extent of the City Attorney's obligation or option to maintain the confidences shared by the Manager in subsequent discussions with individual members of the Council (if such discussions later occur)? Can or must the attorney keep confidences shared by individual Council members? Can or must the attorney keep such information confidential should he or she decide to discuss concerns with the Council in closed session? Can the attorney disclose related information in the face of inquiries from the press or members of the public, and under what circumstances? How should the attorney take notes (or not) in working through this issue? What if one of the members of the Council itself goes public with allegations of misconduct? Would it matter if conduct by one or more of the Council may or may not clearly fall within state law prohibitions or city charter prohibitions on self-dealing such as those discussed in the section of the Chapter on integrity in government? What are the attorney's obligations should he or she choose to resign or is discharged by the Council because of the way this situation is handled? Consider the following excerpt from the ABA's Model Rules:

RULE 1.6 Confidentiality of Information*

(a) A lawyer shall not reveal information relating to the representation of a client unless the client gives informed consent, the disclosure is impliedly authorized in order to carry out the representation or the disclosure is permitted by paragraph (b).

> *Comment* [3] . . . The principle of client-lawyer confidentiality is given effect by related bodies of law: the attorney-client privilege, the work product doctrine and the rule of confidentiality established in professional ethics. The attorney-client privilege and work product doctrine apply in judicial and other proceedings in which a lawyer may be called as a witness or otherwise required to produce evidence concerning a client. . . . The rule of client-lawyer confidentiality applies in situations other than those where evidence is sought from the lawyer through compulsion of law.

For an important case upholding the attorney-client privilege in the public sector, see *Suffolk Construction Co., Inc. v. Division of Capital Asset Management*, 870 N.E.2d 33 (Mass. 2007) (in case involving a dispute regarding construction costs between a construction company and the governmental division charged with overseeing the construction of a courthouse in Boston, upholding application of attorney-client privilege despite absence of specific statement in public records act acknowledging its application, and linking existence of privilege to provisions of Rules of Professional Conduct relating to competence and confidentiality of information). For an extensive discussion of the attorney-client privilege in the public sector, see Clark, *Government Lawyers and Confidentiality Norms*, 85 WASH. U. L. REV. 1033 (2008) (analyzing who is the client of the government lawyer, the implications of public information laws on confidentiality obligations, and the possible need to revise confidentiality rules to address situations in which government lawyers may have special disclosure obligations).

3. *Conflicting interests.* In considering this problem, it appears that the City Attorney is likely to be pulled in many directions. Does that mean that he or she has a "conflict of interest" that triggers relevant provisions of the Model Rules? If not, why not? If so, how should the possible conflicts be handled? Consider the relevant ethical provisions and commentary including the following excerpt:

RULE 1.7. CONFLICT OF INTEREST: CURRENT CLIENTS*

(a) Except as provided in paragraph (b), a lawyer shall not represent a client if the representation involves a concurrent conflict of interest. A concurrent conflict of interest exists if:

* ABA Model Rules of Professional Conduct, 2014 Edition. Copyright © 2014 by the American Bar Association. Reprinted with permission. Copies of ABA Model Rules of Professional Conduct, 2014 Edition are available from Service Center, American Bar Association, 321 North Clark Street, Chicago, IL 60654, 1-800-285-2221. This information or any or portion thereof may not be copied or disseminated in any form or by any means or stored in an electronic database or retrieval system without the express written consent of the American Bar Association.

(1) the representation of one client will be directly adverse to another client; or

(2) there is a significant risk that the representation of one or more clients will be materially limited by the lawyer's responsibilities to another client, a former client or a third person or by a personal interest of the lawyer.

Comment: Organizational Clients [34] A lawyer who represents a corporation or other organization does not, by virtue of that representation, necessarily represent any constituent or affiliated organization, such as a parent or subsidiary. *See* Rule 1.13(a). Thus, the lawyer for an organization is not barred from accepting representation adverse to an affiliate in an unrelated matter, unless the circumstances are such that the affiliate should also be considered a client of the lawyer, there is an understanding between the lawyer and the organizational client that the lawyer will avoid representation adverse to the client's affiliates, or the lawyer's obligations to either the organizational client or the new client are likely to limit materially the lawyer's representation of the other client.

See also Hazard, *Conflicts of Interest in Representation of Public Agencies in Civil Matters*, 9 Widener J. Pub. L. 211 (2000); *Note, Rethinking the Professional Responsibilities of Federal Agency Lawyers*, 115 Harv. L. Rev. 1170 (2002).

4. *Attorney as advisor.* Often, law students (and sometimes attorneys) lack full appreciation for the nuances of the ethical obligations of counsel who are acting in the role of advisers rather than litigators. In this Problem, the City Attorney must function first and foremost as an advisor in dealing with the immediate situation, but must also bear in mind that litigation might arise (in connection with public records or open meetings requirements, but also in connection with possible purchase of assets or challenges to such purchases). What is the scope of the attorney's obligation to function as an advisor? Is the advice limited to an assessment of the legal issues, or can (or should) it extend to questions of policy, ethics, and judgment? Can the attorney bring to bear his or her own judgments concerning the "public good"? How is the "public good" to be understood and defined, and by whom? Is the stance, obligations, or constraints of a government attorney different from those applicable to an attorney functioning as an adviser in the private sector with private clients? Consider the following excerpt from the ABA's Model Rules:

RULE 2.1. Advisor*

In representing a client, a lawyer shall exercise independent professional judgment and render candid advice. In rendering advice, a lawyer may refer not only to law but to other considerations such as moral, economic, social and political factors that may be relevant to the client's situation.

> *Comment*: Scope of Advice [1] A client is entitled to straightforward advice expressing the lawyer's honest assessment. Legal advice often involves unpleasant facts and alternatives that a client may be disinclined to confront. In presenting advice, a lawyer endeavors to sustain the client's morale and may put advice in as acceptable a form as honesty permits. However, a lawyer should not be deterred from giving candid advice by the prospect that the advice will be unpalatable to the client.

5. *Prevention as the best practice.* The City Attorney in the Problem presented should probably look back with deep, deep regret if he or she did not anticipate possible problems such as those posed here. The best practice would surely have been to provide an effective orientation for all City Council members (and all new staff) at the time they took office. Coverage should have included clear guidance on who is the client (the City, not individual members of the Council); the ground rules for confidentiality if individual members of the Council have questions; the applicability of state law and municipal codes relating to ethics, conflicts of interest, and self-dealing; and the operation of public records and open meetings law. It is often very challenging to explain these issues in plain English to non-lawyers, but it is crucially important in heading off difficulties before they arise. In the case presented, it might be possible for the City Attorney to provide such a "training" session as part of a Council work session (covered by open meetings requirements, but typically employing less formal procedures).

6. *Additional perspectives: government attorneys at the state level.* Important new insights about the role of government attorneys continue to be documented, not only as to local government attorneys but also as to state agency attorneys. See Chambliss & Remus, *Nothing Could be Finer? The Role of Agency General Counsel in North and South Carolina*, 84 Fordham L. Rev. 2039 (2016) (providing in-depth comparative analysis of agency counseling functions). The roles of state attorney generals have also evolved. See Lemos & Quinn, *Litigating State Interests: Attorneys General as Amici*, 90 N.Y.U. L. Rev. 1229 (2015) (reviewing state attorney general amicus participation in cases before the U.S. Supreme Court, finding that before 2000 that there was relatively little partisanship in merits-stage briefs, but that after 2000, Attorney General coalitions were decided more partisan); Grumet, *Hidden Nondefense: Partisanship in State Attorneys General Amicus Briefs and the Need for Transparency*, 87 Fordham L. Rev. 1859 (2019) (tracing growing partisanship and its implications).

D. Unions, Collective Bargaining, and Strikes

Historic Context for Public Unions

The role of unions, collective bargaining, and strikes in the public sector are worth considering for a number of reasons. See Kapoor, *Public Sector Labor Relations: Why It Should Matter to the Public and to Academia*, 5 U. PA. J. LAB. & EMP. L. 401 (2003). Kapoor argues that public sector labor relations have had an important personal impact on citizens affected by public sector employees' delivery of services relating to public safety, fire protection, sanitation, transit, corrections, and courts. He also cites the important fiscal impact of public employees on city budgets, estimating that labor costs may constitute 70 percent of total costs since cities are primarily producers of public services rather than commercial goods.

In subsequent years, much has changed in this arena, however. See Slater, *The Strangely Unsettled State of Public-Sector Labor in the Past Thirty Years*, 30 HOFSTRA LAB. & EMP. L.J. 511 (2013) (discussing trends). Several states long seen as committed to public collective bargaining have modified their statutes so as to sharply undercut long-standing protections for public employees. Wisconsin's gutting of traditional public employee protections was perhaps the most notable. See Malin, *Life after Act 10? Is There a Future for Collective Representation of Wisconsin Public Employees?* 96 MARQ. L. REV. 623 (2012) (describing history of legislation and suggesting possible alternative approaches). Many states and localities have also faced difficulties in paying public employees' pensions, as discussed in Chapter 4. See also Beerman, *The Public Pension Crisis*, 70 WASH. & LEE L. REV. 3 (2013). As employee rights have been reduced in the private sector, it appears that a significant backlash has fueled decisions to curb public employee protections as well. For a broader overview of developments, see Clark, *Public Sector Collective Bargaining at the Crossroads*, 44 URB. LAW. 185 (2012) (summarizing data comparing private and public sector wages and benefits; reviewing states with public collective bargaining legislation, and steps being taken by states to limit public employee rights and benefits including reduction in collective bargaining rights, shifts in pension plans, creation of multiple tiers of benefit programs, reducing frequency of cost of living adjustments for retirees, and requiring increased public employee contributions toward benefit programs).

Like private employees, government employees associate together in labor unions, bargain through their unions over the terms and conditions of their employment, and may even strike against their government employers. The federal Department of Labor reported that, in 2019, overall union membership was 10.3% (with a total of 14.3 million workers belonging to unions). Public sector workers had a membership rate of 33.6% (more than five times the rate of the private sectors, which stood at 6.2%). Nonunion workers had wages that stood at 81% of wages for workers who were members of unions. Union membership was particularly high in Hawaii and New York, and particularly low in North and South Carolina. See https://www.bls.gov/news.release/pdf/union2.pdf. Because of the high incidence of unionization in the public sector, it is important to appreciate the basics of collective bargaining and related issues concerning the balance of responsibility and power between governments, unions, and employees. Reflection on this subject also provides another window through which the fundamental characteristics of state and local governments, state courts, administrative agencies, and legislatures can be observed.

In the private sector, labor relations are governed by the provisions of the National Labor Relations Act (NLRA) and comparable state legislation, but the national act exempts state and local governments. 29 U.S.C. § 152(2). This exemption means that labor relations in the public sector are governed by state legislation and state decisional law. Most state courts hold that government employees may not be prohibited from joining labor unions, but do not require state and local governments to bargain with them. A prohibition on joining labor unions is usually held to violate the freedom of association protected by the First Amendment.

The 2018 Janus Decision and its Implications for Financing Public Union Collective Bargaining

A major United States Supreme Court decision in 2018 has also put public unions under increasing pressure. In *Janus v. American Federation of State, County, and Mun. Employees, Council 31*, 138 S. Ct. 2448 (2018), the Governor of Illinois challenged the state statute that authorized public sector unions to charge non-union public employees an "agency fee" amounting to a proportionate share of union dues associated with the union's service as a collective bargaining representatives. In a 5-4 decision by Justice Alito, the Court's majority concluded that the Illinois "agency fee" system violated the free speech rights of non-members by subsidizing private speech on matters of substantial public concern, and could not be sustained based on arguments that the system fostered labor peace or prevented non-members from becoming free-riders. In reaching this decision, the Court overrode substantial earlier precedent and effectively undercut the commonly used financial structure that had historically supported public unions in financing their collective bargaining efforts. It remains to be seen how public sector employees and their unions will respond to the resulting dislocation.

Scholars have begun to suggest new strategies for supporting public union activities, very likely through revised statutory frameworks. See, e.g., Roser-Jones, *Reconciling Agency Fee Doctrine, The First Amendment, and the Public Sector Union*, 112 Nw. U. L. Rev. 597 (2018) (in article written before the *Janus* decision, suggesting the creation of structures more comparable to those governing political contributions and campaign finance); Tang, *Life After Janus*, 119 Colum. L. Rev. 677 (2019) (arguing that public unions may still be able to craft legislative responses in pro-labor states, for example, by requiring public employers to reimburse unions for bargaining costs and suggesting model legislation); Pierson, *After Janus What Comes Next? Possible Solutions to the Free-Rider Problem*, 43(4) Labor Studies J. 269 (2018) (suggesting variety of statutory and non-statutory responses). Even before *Janus*, however, some state legislatures were undercutting traditional forms of financial support for collective bargaining. See, e.g., *AFSCME Iowa Council 61 v.*

State of Iowa, 928 N.W.2d 21 (Iowa 2019) (upholding against constitutional challenge recent statutory amendments to the state public employees relations act discussed in the principal case that follows, including curtailment of traditional fee system and the subject of collective bargaining for public unions not composed of at least 30 percent public safety personnel).

State Public Employee Relations Acts

The law of government employee labor relations has been modified in most states by the adoption of "public employee relations acts" (PERA) modeled on the federal act. The PERAs comprehensively regulate labor relations in government employment. Like the federal Act, the PERAs grant government employees the right to join or to refrain from joining a labor union. Employees are also granted the right to bargain collectively with their government employers over the terms and conditions of their employment.

The PERAs provide procedures to be followed in the exercise of these rights, and these procedures also are modeled on the federal Act. PERAs indicate which government employees and employers are covered by the Act, and may be limited to local employees or to certain types of employees, such as teachers. Procedures are provided to determine the appropriate government employee unit which may organize as a labor union. Election procedures also are provided to determine which union shall act as a bargaining representative. The statute also prohibits employer and union practices which interfere with an employee's exercise of his statutory rights. These practices are known as unfair labor practices.

A PERA usually creates a new state agency or designates an existing agency to administer the statute. These agencies, although they have different names, are referred to here as public employee relations boards (PERBs). Their equivalent at the national level is the National Labor Relations Board. Decisions by the PERBs are subject to limited judicial review.

The state PERAs differ in some respects from the National Labor Relations Act. Government employee strikes are usually prohibited. As an alternative to the strike, a PERA may provide other means for the settlement of disputes arising out of collective bargaining, such as fact finding, mediation or binding arbitration. As is true with regard to other legal questions relating to public employees, state attorney general opinions can also be an important source of legal authority. See, e.g., Ark. Att'y Gen. Op. No. 2002-179, 2002 WL 2005933 (addressing the questions regarding the right of state employees to communicate with representatives of labor organizations during breaks, the right to choose to join or not join labor organizations and to be free from coercion, and the rights of labor organizers to have access to public areas to the same extent as other members of the public).

Many of the labor relations problems that arise under the PERAs are similar to those that arise in the private sector under the National Labor Relations Act. Government employee labor relations present some issues that do not arise in the private sector, however, and these issues are considered in this section.

One important issue concerns the scope of collective bargaining in the public sector. Some conditions of government employment require policy decisions by government entities and are not subject to collective bargaining. Collective bargaining may also conflict with the requirements of civil service laws. Whether a collective bargaining agreement can alter civil service tenure requirements is one example.

Strikes also present a special problem in the public sector. Government employee strikes have been considered to be against the public interest and are prohibited in most states. Government employee strikes occur despite these prohibitions, and government agencies may then seek judicial relief. Whether courts may enjoin government employee strikes requires a balancing of the employee's interest in improving his working conditions with the public's interest in preventing the disruption of government services.

[1] The Scope of Collective Bargaining

Waterloo Education Ass'n v. Iowa Public Employment Relations

740 N.W.2d 418 (Iowa 2007)

Appel, Justice.

In this case, we must decide whether an overload pay proposal submitted by the Waterloo Education Association (Association) to the Waterloo Community School District (District) is a mandatory or permissive subject of collective bargaining under section 20.9 of the Iowa Public Employment Relations Act (PERA). The Public Employment Relations Board (PERB) ruled that the proposal was a permissive subject of bargaining. The district court affirmed. We find the specific proposal in this case to be a mandatory subject of collective bargaining. We therefore reverse the district court and remand the matter for further proceedings.

[The court summarized prior proceedings. The overload pay proposal provided that elementary teachers who teach more than three hundred minutes per day as part of regular work assignments "shall receive additional compensation." "Secondary and middle school teachers who are assigned to teach six (6) classes per day" were also entitled to additional compensation. The overload pay proposal provided that additional teaching assignments would be compensated at "the employee's hourly proportionate per diem rate."]

[Section 20.9 of the Iowa Code, relating to scope of negotiations, provided as follows:

> The public employer and the employee organization shall meet at reasonable times, including meetings reasonably in advance of the public employer's budget-making process, to negotiate in good faith with respect to wages, hours, vacations, insurance, holidays, leaves of absence, shift differentials, overtime compensation, supplemental pay, seniority, transfer procedures, job classifications, health and safety matters, evaluation procedures,

procedures for staff reduction, in-service training and other matters mutually agreed upon. . . ."]

[Section 20.7 of the Iowa Code, relating to public employer rights, provided as follows:

Public employers shall have, in addition to all powers, duties, and rights established by constitutional provision, statute, ordinance, charter, or special act, the exclusive power, duty, and the right to:

1. Direct the work of its public employees.

2. Hire, promote, demote, transfer, assign and retain public employees in positions within the public agency.

3. Suspend or discharge public employees for proper cause.

4. Maintain the efficiency of governmental operations.

5. Relieve public employees from duties because of lack of work or for other legitimate reasons.

6. Determine and implement methods, means, assignments and personnel by which the public employer's operations are to be conducted.

7. Take such actions as may be necessary to carry out the mission of the public employer.

8. Initiate, prepare, certify and administer its budget.

9. Exercise all powers and duties granted to the public employer by law.]

[To a substantial degree, the case turned on the court's efforts to reconcile these two statutory provisions.]

PERB issued a preliminary ruling finding that the proposal constituted a permissive subject of bargaining . . . [and] stated that it believed that the precedents of this court required the result.

[The court then considered the standard of review and stated that it needed to determine whether deference to the PERB was warranted or whether its review should focus on errors at law. It concluded that state statutes did not vest the issue whether a matter was a mandatory subject of collective bargaining in the PERB's discretion and then proceeded to focus on whether there was need to correct errors at law.]

III. Discussion

A. Introduction to Scope of Bargaining Issues

With the enactment at the height of the Great Depression of the National Labor Relations Act (NLRA), 29 U.S.C. sections 151–69 (2005), the prevailing view was that mandatory collective bargaining was an appropriate mechanism to adjust the conflicting relationship between economically powerful employers and comparatively weak employees. While the power of employees would obviously be strengthened by collective bargaining, it was generally believed that market forces would prevent employees from gaining too much at the expense of an employer. If wages became too high, the price of goods or services offered by the employer could become uncompetitive, thereby forcing moderation in employee demands.

In contrast, it was almost unanimously assumed that the collective bargaining model had no application to the public sector. Even President Franklin D. Roosevelt advised public employee leaders that "the process of collective bargaining, as usually understood, cannot be translated into the public service" because the employer was "the whole people" speaking through their public representatives. . . . In short, it was feared that collective bargaining would intrude too deeply upon public policy matters that should be decided by responsible public officials.

Over time, the presumption that the collective bargaining model had no application to the public sector came under challenge. . . . Beginning with Wisconsin in 1959, state legislatures began to enact legislation authorizing collective bargaining in the public sector. By 1974, forty states had adopted some kind of collective bargaining for public employees, while twenty-eight states enacted comprehensive statutes of general applicability.

Most of these state public collective bargaining statutes adopted language similar to the NLRA model, which expansively authorized mandatory collective bargaining over wages, hours, and "other terms and conditions of employment." Many state public collective bargaining statutes, however, also included management rights provisions designed to reserve certain managerial and policy decisions. The goal seems to have been to allow public employees to collectively bargain to improve their economic well-being without unduly sacrificing the ability of politically responsible officials to manage public bodies and establish the broad contours of public policy.

Iowa lagged behind in the enactment of public employment collective bargaining legislation. At first, public employees pursued collective bargaining through exclusive employee representatives without express legislative authorization. . . . Four years later in 1974, the Iowa legislature enacted PERA. . . .

In PERA, the legislature declined to adopt the NLRA model on the question of what subject matters are mandatory subjects of collective bargaining. Instead of incorporating the expansive NLRA language mandating collective bargaining over wages, hours and "other terms and conditions of employment," the Iowa legislature instead specifically enumerated seventeen topics subject to collective bargaining. Iowa Code § 20.9.

These seventeen topics are sometimes referred to as the "laundry list" of mandatory subjects of collective bargaining. Specifically, section 20.9 provides that the public employer and the employee organization "shall" negotiate in good faith with respect to "wages, hours, vacations, insurance, holidays, leaves of absence, shift differentials, overtime compensation, supplemental pay, seniority, transfer procedures, job classifications, health and safety matters, evaluation procedures, procedures for staff reduction, in-service training, and other matters mutually agreed upon." *Id.*

Like many other states, the Iowa legislature also included a management rights provision in the statute. Section 20.7 of PERA states that public employers shall have "the exclusive power, duty, and right to," among other things, "[d]irect the work of its public employees," "[m]aintain the efficiency of governmental operations," and "[d]etermine and implement methods, means, assignments and personnel by which the public employer's operations are to be conducted." *Id.* § 20.7. Thus, Iowa's PERA contains both a provision establishing mandatory collective bargaining on specified matters and a contrapuntal management rights clause preserving exclusive, public management powers in traditional areas.

This court has recognized that section 20.9 establishes two classes of collective bargaining proposals: mandatory and permissive. . . . Mandatory subjects are those matters upon which the public employer is required to engage in bargaining. . . . Permissive subjects are those that the legislature did not specifically list in section 20.9, but are matters upon which both the public employer and the employee organization simply agree to bargain. . . .

Whether a proposal is a mandatory or permissive subject of bargaining under section 20.9 is a critical issue. If a subject is within the scope of mandatory bargaining, the parties are required to bargain over the issue, and if agreement is not reached, the statutory impasse procedures, which ultimately lead to binding arbitration, are available. . . . If, on the other hand, the proposal is a permissive subject of bargaining under section 20.9, the public employer may reserve the right to decide the issue unilaterally by declining to participate in bargaining. When the employer declines to bargain over a permissive subject, the impasse procedures in PERA are not available and decisions related to the subject remain within the exclusive power of the public employer.

The central issue presented in this case is whether the Association's overload wage proposal is a mandatory or permissive subject of collective bargaining.

B. Methods of Resolving Scope of Bargaining Disputes

1. *Scope of bargaining in the state and federal courts.* From the beginning of collective bargaining, the question of what subject matters are mandatory subjects of collective bargaining sparked considerable litigation as employers and employee organizations jockeyed for position. In general, the United States Supreme Court has construed the NLRA to provide a relatively broad scope of mandatory bargaining under the phrase "wages, hours, and other terms and conditions of employment."

In the context of state public bargaining statutes that use the expansive NLRA phrase "other terms and conditions of employment" to describe mandatory bargaining subjects, the analysis becomes even more complicated with the inclusion of a management rights provision. Employment terms and conditions are often intertwined or entangled with public policy issues that have traditionally been within the purview of public employers. In order to accommodate the special needs of public employers, state courts with NLRA-type scope-of-bargaining provisions have developed a wide variety of "balancing tests" to be applied at the threshold stage of the scope-of-bargaining analysis. See, e.g., *Central City Educ. Ass'n, IEA/NEA v. Illinois Educ. Labor Relations Bd.*, 599 N.E.2d 892, 904–05 (Ill. 1992) (holding that test includes whether benefits of bargaining for employee outweighs burden on employer)....

The rationale of state courts adopting the threshold balancing approach is that the "terms and conditions of employment" that constitute mandatory subjects of collective bargaining are also invariably connected with some functions arguably within the purview of management, either through a management rights provision or through traditional analysis....

Thus, in cases involving statutes with expansive NLRA-type scope-of-bargaining provisions, there is a conflict between the expansive concepts of employee rights and traditional public employer prerogatives. These are two highly territorial pikes at large in the legal pond of collective bargaining, each with the capacity of devouring the other. In order to avoid the predominance of either management or employee rights, state courts have concluded that they have no other choice but to engage in balancing of some kind....

The judgment of these courts that they must somehow accommodate employee and management rights through a balancing process is certainly understandable. Without clear legislative standards as to the scope of bargaining, the courts in these states have been left to their own devices to fill in the statutory gap....

While a judicially created balancing test has the potential of preserving the rough contours of the grand legislative compromise between management and employee rights over time, any balancing test is extraordinarily difficult to apply in individual cases. This difficulty is not surprising in light of the fact that it is impossible to objectively measure or quantify the weight of employer and employee interests.

Further, even if there was some kind of objective measurement of each interest, the balancing test requires courts to balance the apples of employee rights against the oranges of employer rights. No court has been able to successfully advance a convincing formula for determining how many employee rights apples it takes to equal an employer rights orange. Finally, the ill-defined nature of balancing tests in general gives rise to the possibility that invisible, unconscious, but perhaps inevitable judicial bias could creep into the decision-making process. See *Developments in the Law—Public Employment*, 87 Harv. L. Rev. 1676, 1689 (1984) (noting that with no clear standards in balancing tests, judges invariably fall back on their own political visions of the ideal power relationship between government and its employees). As noted by Harry H. Wellington and Ralph K. Winter in their classic essay, courts are badly suited to make judgments about which issues should be bargainable. Harry H. Wellington & Ralph K. Winter, *The Limits of Collective Bargaining*, 78 Yale L.J. 1107, 1126 (1968).

In light of these challenges, it is not surprising that the state court application of threshold balancing tests in the scope-of-bargaining context has yielded a riot of fact-specific results that defy orderly characterization. While a balancing test for determining scope-of-bargaining issues may be necessary when legislatures have delegated open-ended authority to the courts, it is an imperfect approach for courts that favor principled decision-making over ill-defined discretionary exercises. Balancing tests are a product of raw legal necessity, not judicial preference. . . .

Where a legislature elects not to use the expansive NLRA phrase "other terms and conditions of employment" and chooses instead to list a finite number of enumerated topics, the case for a balancing test becomes even less compelling. For example, in Kansas, the legislature originally adopted an NLRA-type mandatory bargaining provision in a statute regarding public teacher collective bargaining. In response, the Kansas Supreme Court developed an impact test that involved balancing the impact of an issue on the well-being of the individual against the overall effect on the operation of the school system. . . .

While the Kansas legislature at first embraced the approach [used by the Kansas court] . . . it later amended its statute to delete the NLRA-type scope-of-bargaining language. . . . Instead the legislature provided a closed, finite list of topics that would be mandatory subjects of collective bargaining for teaching professionals. In light of the legislative action, the Kansas Supreme Court, following the lead of the responsible administrative agency, sanctioned the adoption of a topics test to replace its prior impact balancing test to determine scope-of-bargaining issues.

Under the topics test, the scope of bargaining is determined by whether the topic of a proposal is within the scope of one of the specifically enumerated subjects of collective bargaining. If a proposal was definitionally within the scope of one of the enumerated topics, it is a mandatory subject of collective bargaining. If it fell outside the definition of any mandatory topic, the proposal was not negotiable. . . . A threshold balancing determination is not required under the topic test because the legislature has already performed the balancing by including each specific topic as a subject of mandatory bargaining.

Thus, instead of dealing with two pikes in a pond, legislatures that have adopted a "laundry list" have gone to dry land and established a legal shooting range with a series of legislatively established targets of mandatory bargaining. Proponents of mandatory bargaining must hit one of the targets, or come close enough to one, in order to avoid characterization of the proposal as permissive. The role of the courts in this setting is not to balance the pikes, but to judge the accuracy of the proponent's legal shot.

2. *Iowa approach to scope of bargaining issues.* In determining whether a proposal is within the scope of section 20.9, this court noted early on that the Iowa House of Representatives approved an amendment to the original bill deleting the expansive NLRA phrase "or other terms and conditions of employment" from the list of mandatory subjects. . . . The final version of the bill did not contain the expansive NLRA

language. Instead, the final version of the Iowa PERA contained a finite, or laundry list, of mandatory subjects of collective bargaining.... Because the Iowa PERA does not include the phrase "other terms and conditions of employment," this court has held that if a proposal does not fall within one of the laundry list of terms contained in section 20.9, it is not a subject of mandatory bargaining.... In other words, this court has held that the legislature's laundry list in section 20.9 is exclusive and not merely descriptive or suggestive....

In [an earlier case] the court announced a two-pronged test to determine negotiability questions.... The first prong was a topics test—whether a particular proposal fell within the scope of any of the specifically delineated terms in section 20.9. If a proposal was not within the scope of one of the specifically delineated terms, it was not subject to mandatory bargaining. If, however, the proposal was within the scope of one of the delineated terms, the court moved on to the second prong, specifically, whether collective bargaining over the proposal would be illegal....

Even though the early PERA cases articulated this straightforward two-pronged scope-of-bargaining test, the court nonetheless struggled with the relationship between section 20.7, which contains the exclusive rights of management, and section 20.9, which contains the mandatory bargaining provisions.

C. Application of Scope-of-Bargaining Principles

... In this case, ... the proposal now advanced by the Association does not allow teachers to opt out of overload assignments. As a result, ... management retains the unfettered right to assign overload work to any teacher of its choosing. In addition, PERB has taken the unusual posture of participating actively in this litigation.

At the outset, we must determine the proper test for determining whether a proposal is subject to mandatory bargaining under section 20.9. The determination of whether a proposal is a mandatory subject of collective bargaining is an issue of law based upon a facial review of the proposal....

In resolving scope-of-bargaining issues, we reject the approach that any proposal which "infringes" upon management rights is not subject to mandatory bargaining. As was stated [earlier cases] all mandatory subjects of bargaining infringe in some way on management rights. If the test of negotiability were truly a simple infringement test, literally nothing would be subject to mandatory collective bargaining.... Certainly any wage proposal "infringes" on management rights by allocating resources that might be otherwise available for programming or other educational expenditures....

We also reject the notion that the issue of negotiability should ordinarily be resolved at the outset by balancing the employer's interest in management rights against the interest of employees in mandatory bargaining. As noted above, while many states adopt such threshold balancing tests, the states which employ this method are generally operating under NLRA-type statutes which couple the expansive "other terms and conditions of employment" language with management rights provisions. The balancing test is necessary, in these jurisdictions, to prevent management rights from being totally eviscerated by unfettered collective bargaining.

Because Iowa's PERA does not contain this expansive language, the subjects of mandatory bargaining delineated in section 20.9 should be viewed as exceptions to management rights reserved in section 20.7. By creating the section 20.9 laundry list of exceptions to management prerogatives, the legislature has already done the balancing. There is no occasion for this court to judicially rebalance what the legislature has already balanced.

As a result, we reject the "infringement" or threshold balancing test approach and instead reaffirm the two-pronged approach to negotiability described in [earlier cases]. The first prong for determining whether a proposal is subject to collective bargaining, the threshold topics test, is ordinarily a definitional exercise, namely, a determination of whether a proposal fits within the scope of a specific term or terms listed by the legislature in section 20.9. Once that threshold test has been met, the next inquiry is whether the proposal is preempted or inconsistent with any provision of law. Ordinarily, this two-step process is the end of the matter. Only in unusual cases where the predominant topic of a proposal cannot be determined should a balancing-type analysis be employed to resolve the negotiability issue.

. . . Having determined that the two-pronged approach . . . is the proper test of negotiability, we now must apply the test to the overload pay proposal presented here. In order to apply the threshold topics test, however, we must first determine the meaning of the term "wages" in section 20.9. Then, we must determine if the proposal falls within the scope of that definition.

In determining the meaning of the term "wages," our prior cases embrace several guides to interpretation. These cases hold that because the legislature has listed the term "wages" in section 20.9 as a topic separate and apart from other tangible employee benefits, such as vacation and insurance, the term "wages" is subject to a relatively narrow construction in order to avoid an interpretation that renders subsequent items in the laundry list redundant and meaningless. Under these cases, the term "wages" cannot be interpreted to include a broad package of fringe benefits because the legislature has specifically included some fringe benefits in this section's laundry list. We see no reason to depart from the approach of these prior cases.

On the other hand, the legislature's use of a laundry list of negotiable subjects does not mean that the listed terms are subject to the narrowest possible interpretation, but only that the listed terms cannot be interpreted in a fashion so expansive that the other specifically identified subjects of mandatory bargaining become redundant. The approach most consistent with legislative intent thus is to give the term "wages" its common and ordinary meaning within the structural parameters imposed by section 20.9.

In order to determine the common or ordinary meaning of words, we have often consulted widely used dictionaries. *Black's Law Dictionary* defines "wages" as "[p]ayment for labor or services, usually based on time worked or quantity produced." *Black's Law Dictionary* 1573 (7th ed. 1999). *Merriam-Webster's Collegiate Dictionary* defines wages as payment for labor or services on an "hourly, daily, piecework basis." *Merriam-Webster's Collegiate Dictionary* 1322 (10th ed. 2002).

Applying the threshold topics test . . . , we conclude that the proposal falls within the definition of the term "wages." At its core, the proposal simply seeks to introduce an element of piecework pay into the school district's wage structure. The proposal, moreover, calls for the payment of money and not some other kind of fringe benefit. The proposal if implemented would provide an economic reward based upon services rendered. As noted by one state public employee relations board when considering the bargainability of an overload pay proposal, "It is only possible to rationally bargain for 'an honest day's pay' if one can also negotiate the boundaries and the contents of 'an honest day's work.'" . . .

The employee's economic interest in more pay for more work is precisely the kind of employee interest that leading commentators for decades have suggested should be subject to collective bargaining. . . . The interest of the employees in more pay for less work is generally opposed by the majority of voters and taxpayers who are interested in obtaining more services at less cost. The inclusion of the term "wages" in the laundry list is designed to provide employees with a degree of protection on economic issues from potentially powerful low-wage political influences.

The overload pay proposal in this case is distinct from the proposal involved in [prior cases]. In [prior cases] the proposal sought to prohibit management from assigning overload work to an employee who did not wish to undertake it. As a result, . . . the proposal involved a hybrid of "wages" and "management rights." Although not articulated in this fashion, there was at least an issue as to which topic dominated the proposal. In contrast, the proposal here does not seek to limit management's discretion to assign work, but relates solely to payment for an amount of services rendered by an individual teacher. The proposal does not handcuff management prerogatives in any way other than to require increased payment for certain services.

Of course, whenever management is required to pay more for teacher services, the resultant increase in costs impinges on other management choices by diverting available resources from other potential uses. This impingement happens, in all cases involving wages and simply cannot be the basis for excluding a proposal from mandatory collective bargaining. Otherwise, the term "wages" would be entirely written out of the statute.

We recognize the possibility that artful negotiators may attempt to craft proposals that incidentally involve payment of increased wages to teachers, but which are really designed to influence educational policy or limit management discretion. [Our test] however, requires that a proposal relate predominantly to a bargainable issue. It further allows a balancing of interests in those unusual hybrid cases where mandatory and permissive elements are inextricably intertwined in a proposal.

Having concluded that the Association's overload pay proposal meets . . . [the] threshold topics test, we now turn to the second prong of the [relevant] test—whether collective bargaining over the proposal would be illegal. Neither the District nor PERB has suggested that the overload pay proposal violates or is preempted by Iowa law. As a result, we find that the overload pay proposal presented here is a mandatory subject of collective bargaining.

In closing, we note that, as was consistently emphasized in our prior cases, we do not pass in any way on the merits of the overload pay proposal. We hold only that the question of whether the overload pay proposal made in this case should be adopted in whole or in part by the district must be determined, if possible, by the parties themselves through good faith negotiations and in the event of impasse, through binding arbitration as provided in PERA. The finding of this court that the overload pay proposal is subject to mandatory bargaining is an endorsement only of the legislature's chosen process of resolving employer-employee disputes involving "wages," not the merits of the proposal.

IV. CONCLUSION

We hold that the overload wage proposal in this case presents a mandatory subject of collective bargaining under section 20.9 of PERA. As a result, the decision of the district court is reversed and the case remanded for further proceedings.

REVERSED AND REMANDED.

Notes and Questions

1. *Scope of collective bargaining*: Decisions regarding the scope of collective bargaining in the public sector are influenced by some of the significant differences between the private and public sectors. A leading scholar of public labor relations law, Professor Claude Summers, offered important insights about these differences. Summers noted that a public sector collective bargaining agreement "is more than a contract but is instead an instrument of government and the product of government decision making," which reflects the desires of the electorate regarding the services desired and the levels of taxation needed as a result. It therefore differs from private sector collective bargaining that is done in private, relates to costs and benefits to those involved (rather than the welfare of the public), and reflects market considerations. The structure of bargaining on the management side differs because the negotiators for the public may have no authority to commit public funds and ultimately proposals must be approved by those with these powers in a political context. Summers stated that balancing tests provide little clarity or guidance, since public sector collective bargaining about issues like teacher salaries or class sizes constitutes governmental decision making which, in the absence of collective bargaining, would take place in the open with opportunities for public comment and

disagreement rather than behind closed doors. He suggested that the competing interests of employees, taxpayer/residents, and elected officials should be taken into account in structuring bargaining processes and the subjects of mandatory bargaining, and recommended that

> Where the two opposing political interests—taxpayer/residents and employees—are grossly unbalanced, collective bargaining serves to adjust the imbalance. Where public management and the employees have opposing interests, but taxpayers or other groups have no substantial interests, the two interest groups can be allowed to work out their differences collectively. However, if bargaining by the two parties shuts out other groups that have substantial interests, depriving them of effective voice in the decision, then collective bargaining is inappropriate. Finally, if the employees have strongly opposing interests among themselves, then the union ought not be able to shut out from public discussion those who have different views.

See Summers, *Public Sector Collective Bargaining: A Different Animal?* 5 U. Pa. J. Lab. & Emp. L. 441, 442–49, 450 (2003). How would you apply this analysis in the principal case?

2. *Laundry list approach.* The Iowa court employed a "laundry list" approach to determine the scope of mandatory collective bargaining topics, and in doing so rejected a "balancing test" employed by some other jurisdictions. The court contended that the "laundry list" approach provided greater clarity and concluded that the question of overload wages fell within the reference to "wages" included in the list of mandatory bargaining subjects. Under the court's two-part test, if the overload pay constituted "wages," mandatory bargaining would ensue unless such bargaining was otherwise illegal. Do you agree that the "laundry list" approach adds clarity to determinations of subjects of mandatory bargaining?

The principal case, decided by the Iowa court in 2007, may be contrasted to a case decided in 2002 in which the court considered an overload pay proposal that allowed teachers to "opt out" of overload responsibilities if they chose (the 2007 proposal had no such opt-out provision). See *Waterloo Community School Dist. v. Public Employment Relations Bd.*, 650 N.W.2d 627 (Iowa 2002). In the 2007 decision, the court explicitly rejected the notion that any proposal that infringes upon management rights should be exempt from mandatory bargaining, stating that if that notion governed, virtually nothing would fall within the mandatory bargaining arena. Are these proposals really distinguishable?

Subsequently, the Iowa Supreme Court reviewed a decision by the Iowa PERB that had considered whether a proposal to outsource work performed by public employees constituted "staff reduction" and was therefore a mandatory subject of collective bargaining. See *AFSCME Iowa Council 61 v. Iowa Public Employment Relations Board*, 846 N.W.2d 873 (Iowa 2014). The state supreme court concluded that, insofar as the purpose of the proposal regarding outsourcing was to preclude the state from reducing staff, it was a permissive rather than mandatory subject of bargaining. Do you agree with that conclusion?

3. *Balancing tests.* A number of states, including Illinois, have adopted a "balancing test" rather than a laundry list approach. The *Central City Education Association* decision referenced in the principal case, sets out the rationale for adopting this alternative. The *Central City Education Association* case involved issues relating to elimination of educational staff positions and teacher evaluations. The Illinois court had to reconcile competing statutory positions, including one that required employee unions and employers to "meet at reasonable times and confer in good faith with respect to wages, hours and other terms and conditions of employment" and another that provided that employers

> shall not be required to bargain over matters of inherent managerial policy, which shall include such areas of discretion or policy as the functions of the employer, standards of services, its overall budget, the organizational structure and selection of new employees and direction of employees. Employers however shall be required to bargain collectively with regard to policy matters directly affecting wages, hours and terms and conditions of employment as well as the impact thereon upon request by employee representatives.

The Illinois court adopted a three-step approach that required the state PERB to determine (a) whether the matter concerns wages, hours and terms and conditions of employment (in which case the subject was subject to a mandatory duty to bargain); (b) whether the matter was also one of "inherent managerial policy"; and, if so (c) how a balance should be struck between these competing considerations. 599 N.E.2d 892 at 509–10. Is this approach more consistent with the relevant statutes? How would it be applied to such issues as overload pay, reductions in force, and teacher evaluations? What about parking places for campus police? See *Board of Trustees of University of Illinois v. Illinois Educational Labor Relations Bd.*, 862 N.E.2d 944 (Ill. 2007) (proposal for parking spaces in proximity to members' work station did not concern matters that affected university's inherent managerial rights). What about a variety of issues affecting personnel in a sheriff's office, including requirement to disclose any and all memberships and associations with gangs, and social media policies? See *International Brotherhood of Teamsters, Local 700 v. Illinois Labor Relations Board*, 373 N.E.3d 108 (Ill. App. 2017) (order re gang membership was within inherent managerial authority, and social media policy was not unfair labor policy). How would you assess this test as developed in Illinois?

4. *Budget concerns.* Reductions in force have often been found to be mandatory subjects of bargaining since substantial benefits would be gleaned from involving union representatives who possess requisite knowledge and could provide alternatives that could alleviate economic conditions and avoid employee layoffs, and since burdens on management were "illusory at best." See *AFSCME v. Illinois State Labor Relations Board*, 653 N.E.2d 1357 (Ill. App. 1995). When state employees work

during a budget impasse, they are assured of full salary for work performed once funds are appropriated under the terms of the state constitution's impairment of contracts clause. See *White v. Davis*, 133 Cal. Rptr. 2d 648 (Cal. 2003). See also *Beerman, supra*.

Other types of budget issues are not so readily resolved, as has become clear during recent economic downturns. A collective bargaining agreement usually is signed by a state or local executive or state agency, but the legislative body must appropriate the funds to carry out the agreement. What if the agreement calls for an 8% percent pay increase but the legislature, believing it too high, appropriates only 5% percent? What are the executive's or agency's options? At times such cutbacks have been challenged as an unconstitutional "impairment of contract." See, e.g., *United Automobile, Aerospace, Agricultural Implement Workers of America International Union v. Fortuno*, 677 F. Supp. 2d 530 (D.P.R. 2009) (finding no violation of the Contracts Clause when government declared state of fiscal emergency, asked some state employees to accept reduced hours, and proposed significant numbers of employee layoffs); Buck, *The Legal Ramifications of Public Pension Reform*, 17 Tex. Rev. L. & Pol. 25 (2012) (discussing public pension issues).

5. *Civil service*. Statutory provisions other than those defining the scope of collective bargaining may also need to be taken into account. A common question has concerned the interplay of state PERAs and civil service legislation which incorporate provisions mandating the use of merit principles in recruitment and selection of employees, the classification of employment positions, promotion, and discipline. Conflicts with collective bargaining arise because the employee union may seek to make the issues subject to the bargaining process. See, e.g., *California State Personnel Bd. v. California State Employees Ass'n*, 31 Cal. Rptr. 3d 201 (Cal. 2005) (concluding that pilot programs negotiated by public employee unions and approved by state legislature violated state constitutional provision mandating merit principle in civil service system insofar as "post and bid" system based appointments and promotions in certain job classifications on seniority without providing for comparative merit evaluations of employees seeking positions); *Patrolmen's Benev. Ass'n of City of New York, Inc. v. New York State Public Employment Relations Bd.*, 786 N.Y.S.2d 269 (App. Div. 2004) (PERB did not abuse discretion when determined that discipline of police officers was prohibited subject of bargaining where city charter and administrative code allocated police officer discipline to city police commissioner); *Matter of City of New York v. Patrolmen's Benevolent Assn. of the City of New York, Inc.*, 924 N.E.2d 336 (N.Y. 2009) (change in drug testing from urine-based to radioimmune assay test of hair, and testing triggers used, fell within police commissioner's disciplinary authority as a matter of policy; these specific aspects of drug testing did not require mandatory collective bargaining as a "material change").

[2] A Note on Strikes and Strike Injunctions

If bargaining fails, the strike is the tactic of last resort. Although the right to strike is conferred by statute in the private sector, there is generally not a similar right available to employees in the public sector. The United States Department of Labor reported that there were 25 work stoppages in 2019 involving 1,000 or more workers, the highest rate in the decade 2000–2019. See https://www.bls.gov/news.release/wkstp.nr0.htm. Of these work stoppages, 13 were in the educational services industry. For the decade 2000–2019, the Department of Labor reported that there were a total of 93 work stoppages in private industry, 37 in local government, and 24 in state government. The three largest work stoppages (in terms of number of workers affected) involved disputes between the North Carolina State Legislature and North Carolina Association of Educators (in 2018 and 2019), and between the Arizona State Legislature and Arizona Education Association (in 2018).

Public employees do not have a constitutional right to strike. *Anchorage Education Ass'n v. Anchorage School Dist.*, 648 P.2d 993 (Alaska 1982). Neither are public employee strikes legal at common law. In the absence of a statutory right to strike (permissible in some states after the mandatory negotiation process has been exhausted), enforcement of the common law strike ban is comparatively simple, at least on the surface, in most states. Strikes are enjoinable, and strikers are subject to civil and criminal contempt for violating strike injunctions. Some states allow public employee strikes under limited circumstances, however. See Marin, *The Motive Power in Public Sector Collective Bargaining*, 36 Hofstra Lab. & Emp. L.J. 123 (2018) (comparing structures for dealing with situations that might otherwise give rise to strikes in New York, Pennsylvania, Illinois, Ohio, Florida and Michigan).

The California Supreme Court granted nonessential public employees a qualified right to strike in *County Sanitation Dist. No. 2 v. Los Angeles County Emps. Ass'n, Local 660*, 699 P.2d 835 (Cal. 1985), *noted*, 17 Pac. L.J. 5334 (1985); 64 Wash. U. L.Q. 263 (1986). The court rejected arguments that strikes would undermine government authority, government employers would be unable to respond to strike pressures because statutes set employment terms, and government employers would make excessive concessions to avoid a strike. The court held that government employers could prohibit strikes by employees providing truly essential services but not by employees providing nonessential services unless the strike created "a substantial and imminent threat to the health or safety of the public." *Id.* at 850. See also Hanslowe & Acierno, The Law and Theory of Strikes By Government Employees (1982). Other courts have been reluctant to recognize a right to strike in the absence of a statutory scheme for collective bargaining by public employees. See *Jefferson County Board of Education v. Jefferson County Educ. Ass'n*, 393 S.E.2d 653 (W. Va. 1990). California subsequently modified legislation governing its PERB, and there is pending litigation regarding the extent to which the PERB rather than the courts has exclusive jurisdiction with regard to rights related to work stoppages.

See *County of Sacramento v. AFSCME Local 146*, 80 Cal. Rptr. 3d 911 (Cal. App. 3 Dist. 2008) (discussing legislative developments).

Most states have ratified the common law ban on government employee strikes by adopting legislation denying the right to strike. Some of this legislation carries penalties. See Nev. Rev. Stat. §§288.230–288.360, authorizing injunctions, union fines, union official fines and prison sentences, and dismissal or suspension of union members. Other state legislation simply adopts the common law ban without specifying remedies or penalties. This legislation raises a remedial problem, especially in connection with an injunction, which is the most effective remedy for ending a strike.

Whether the illegality of a public employee strike under the statutory ban is enough to trigger an injunction is one of the principal questions raised. In *Timberlane Regional School District v. Timberlane Regional Education Association*, 317 A.2d 555 (N.H. 1974), the New Hampshire Supreme Court held that it would not automatically issue an injunction requiring illegally striking school teachers to return to work. The court reasoned that judicial intervention should occur only when it was evident that the parties were unable to settle their disputes, in order to avoid the risk of becoming "an unwitting third party at the bargaining table and a potential coercive force in the collective bargaining processes."

More explicit policy reasons have been suggested for prohibiting public employee strikes. Some have argued for a strike ban because market restraints are weak in the public sector where services are essential. The public may also impose pressure for a quick settlement. Other public interest groups have no comparable weapon. Strikes may also distort the political process. See Malin, *Public Employees' Right to Strike: Law and Experience*, 26 U. Mich. J.L. Reform 313 (1993). The arguments against public employee strikes are similar to the arguments for limiting the scope of the bargaining process in the public sector. Is the likelihood of a strike affected by the scope of the bargaining process? Are public employees more likely to strike if the issues which can be considered in the bargaining process are extensive? For a discussion of the historical development of rights to strike in the private and public sectors, see McCartin, *Unexpected Convergence: Values, Assumptions, and the Right to Strike in Public and Private Sectors, 1945–2005*, 57 Buff. L. Rev. 727 (2009).

Some courts have held that a failure on the part of a school district to bargain in good faith weighed against the issuance of an injunction. "It has long been a basic maxim of equity that one who seeks equitable relief must enter the court with clean hands." *School Dist. No. 351, Oneida County v. Oneida Education Ass'n*, 567 P.2d 830 (Idaho 1977). The court also held that it was error for the trial court to issue an ex parte preliminary injunction. Testimony introduced in a hearing might have led to an injunction barring the strike but conditioned on good faith bargaining by the school district. Is this a good remedy? Are other more draconian measures ever warranted? In a well-publicized case involving a teacher work-stoppage in New Jersey, the court ordered that striking teachers be incarcerated to enforce an injunction, rather than imposing financial penalties or ordering forfeiture of jobs. See *Board of Educ. Tp. of Middletown v. Middletown Tp. Educ. Ass'n*, 800 A.2d 286 (N.J. Ch. 2001).

For insights on the interplay of collective bargaining, the right to strike, and arbitration, see Malin, *Two Models of Interest Arbitration*, 28 Ohio St. J. on Disp. Resol. 145 (2013); Gely, *Collective Bargaining and Dispute System Design,* 13 U. St. Thomas L.J. 218 (2017).

Chapter 6

Governmental Liability

Scope of Chapter

"Of course, it is not a tort for government to govern." *Dalehite v. United States*, 346 U.S. 15, 57 (1953) (Jackson, J.). Justice Jackson made this assertion while dissenting to a decision denying liability for an explosion by application of the discretionary function exemption in the Federal Tort Claims Act. In doing so he captured the spirit of a long-standing approach to the question of whether ordinary citizens should have access to traditional tort remedies for injuries caused by government activity. Based on the common law maxim, "The king can do no wrong," the doctrine of governmental immunity developed as a liability shield that enabled government at all levels to avoid responsibility in tort for harm done to private individuals.

Early notions of governmental tort immunity were buttressed by nineteenth century attempts to distinguish "public" from "private" corporations, and quasi-corporations (counties, towns, school districts and most special districts) from municipal corporations (cities, boroughs and villages). Influential scholarly work in the 1920s and 1930s paved the way for path-breaking decisions in state courts during the 1950s and 1960s and in the Supreme Court in the 1970s and 1980s. These developments opened the courthouse doors by dismantling the judicially-created immunity doctrine.

Following the lead of California, Florida and Illinois, state courts concluded that, whatever historical basis that may have existed for governmental immunity under state common law, the doctrine had long since outlived its usefulness. At about the time these state court developments reached their climax, the Supreme Court in 1978 concluded that local governments were subject to suit under the Civil Rights Act of 1866, 42 U.S.C. § 1983, as "persons" and were not automatically entitled to the "state action" exemption from the Sherman Anti-Trust Act, 15 U.S.C. § 1 *et seq.*

As the doctrine of governmental immunity broke down, confusion developed between the concept of immunity and the different bases for municipal liability under state and federal law. The fact that governmental immunity was abrogated did not mean that governments automatically became liable in tort for injuries caused by public officials or employees. Important policy considerations centering around the need to encourage public officials to exercise necessary discretion and judgment, as well as concern about separation of powers and federalism questions, led to the development of exceptions to governmental liability for discretionary activities (federal and state), activities based on general duties to the public (state), and activities based on state policies to displace competition (federal anti-trust). However, because the discretionary activity exemption from liability might make it impossible for an injured person to obtain relief, the Supreme Court concluded that the Federal Civil Rights Act, 42 U.S.C. § 1983, would be meaningless unless municipalities could be held responsible for deprivation of constitutional and statutory rights resulting from acts taken under official governmental policy. Section 1983 can thus be viewed as a statutory remedy for a constitutional tort.

The following years saw considerable state legislative activity in response to the judicial abrogation of governmental immunity, and extensive federal court activity to define the extent of municipal responsibility under the anti-trust and civil rights statutes. Courts and legislatures have struggled to strike a proper balance between protecting decisions made by government agencies as well as elected and appointed government officials and providing redress for injuries caused by those decisions. At the close of the second decade of the twenty-first century, it is possible to draw some general conclusions concerning the development of the law of state and local governmental liability to private citizens:

(1) local municipal governments are subject to tort liability under state law, except for discretionary acts or more narrow policy-related decisions of public officials in connection with governmental actions, subject to statutory modifications to reflect local conditions;

(2) local governments are subject to liability under federal civil rights statutes when governmental policies or customs cause injury to recognized property or liberty interests;

(3) local government officials, as individuals, are afforded absolute or limited immunity, depending on their positions, for discretionary actions taken in the discharge of their public responsibilities.

The parallel expansion of potential government liability under both federal and state law raises numerous common questions, such as standards for determining liability in particular instances, the role of discretion and what constitutes the exercise of discretion, and the extent and application of the doctrine of "official immunity." This Chapter will explore these matters, as well as others such as appropriate remedies, including attorneys' fees and punitive damages, standards of proof, and techniques of risk management such as liability insurance. While federal anti-trust liability issues might also be considered in depth in this Chapter, that topic is instead considered in Chapter 8 as part of the discussion of licensing (an arena in which anti-trust issues involving government tend to arise).

A. State Law

Problem 6-1

The East Ridge Police Department was contacted by the Hillside Police Department, informing them that an individual named Harry Smith, who was recently released from a state mental institution, had attacked a woman in their jurisdiction, telling her that he intended to kill his former girlfriend who lived in East Ridge. The Hillside police said that Harry Smith was armed and had shot out the windows in a diner in their city before leaving and heading in a direction toward East Ridge. They were able to give the East Ridge police a description of the car he was driving. The East Ridge police knew that Harry Smith had previously threatened, harassed, and assaulted one of their residents, Elizabeth Connors, because they had been called to her home in the past. They immediately called and warned Ms. Connors, advising her to avoid the windows, keep the lights out and avoid opening the door. They also told her that they would have additional police patrols in her neighborhood, and should she see or hear anything unusual to call them immediately.

Ms. Connors knew how dangerous Mr. Smith was and that he probably would try to carry out his pronounced intentions to harm her. However, when her parents tried to persuade her to leave her home and stay with them in a nearby city, she refused because, as she told them, "With all the police cars driving through my neighborhood, I am safer if I stay put." In addition, a college friend, Nancy Mack, had unexpectedly stopped to see her as she traveled through town. When Ms. Mack learned of the threat against Ms. Connors, she insisted on staying with her friend until the police had apprehended Mr. Smith.

The East Ridge police checked the neighborhood regularly the following day. However, when the shifts changed, the instructions left for the officers coming on duty did not include the information that Mr. Smith had threatened to kill Ms. Connors, or stress the severity of the situation. In addition, fewer officers were on duty because a contagious influenza had been quickly spreading among the police force and two had called in sick. As a result, although there was surveillance, it was less frequent. Unfortunately, when the officers drove through the neighborhood around 11:00 p.m., they spotted Mr. Smith's abandoned car. When they went to Ms. Connors' door, they discovered that both Ms. Connors and Ms. Mack had been shot and were lying dead in the living room.

Lawsuits have been filed by the estates of both women against East Ridge.

As you begin a discussion of potential municipal and state tort liability, consider the wide range of potential injuries that might arise when private parties intersect with local and state governments or when government inaction gives rise to potential risks. Before moving to a litigator's thought processes, consider assuming a different role—that of "risk manager" responsible for helping state and local governments to limit risks relating to potential liability. The Problem posed above relates to police conduct. What kind of training or protocols might have avoided the injuries described? What other situations involving police conduct might raise potential claims in tort? As you are aware there have been many recent calls for reform of police practices in the face of the "Black Lives Matter" movement.

Often governments would be better served to avoid problems and costly litigation, and instead do their best to manage risk before it arises. What kinds of issues might occur, for example, as a result of the conduct of building inspectors, parks and recreation personnel, public works staff, fire fighters, school teachers, and others? For some novel scenarios, consider possible liability risks associated with cyberbullying, Fenn, *A Web of Liability: Does New Cyberbullying Legislation Put Public Schools in a Sticky Situation?* 81 Fordham L. Rev. 2729 (2013); climate change, Ruppert & Grimm, *Drowning in Place: Local Government Costs and Liabilities for Flooding Due to Sea Level Rise*, Fla. B.J., Nov. 2013, at 29; involvement of companion animals in prisons, Huss, *Canines (and Cats!) in Correctional Institutions: Legal and Ethical Issues Relating to Companion Animal Programs*, 14 Nev. L.J. 25 (2013); and vacant buildings that have become derelict during the economic downturn that began in 2008, Kroha, *Potholes in the Motor City: How Vacant Properties and Neighborhood Stabilization Can Subject Detroit and Similarly Situated Municipalities to Liability*, 47 New Eng. L. Rev. 715 (2013).

In what other areas can you imagine that challenging issues about tort liability and immunity might arise? Tort liability is not the only type of liability that may be relevant. For example, challenges under the United States Constitution's "Taking Clause" or state constitutional "taking or damaging" clauses are likely to emerge as governments try to address challenges to public safety and property values arising from climate change. See Patashnik, *The Trolley Problem of Climate Change: Should Governments Face Takings Liability if Adaptive Strategies Cause Property Damage?* 119 Colum. L. Rev. 1273 (2019).

You will note that the discussion of state torts that follows focuses in particular on potential government defenses, including those relating to sovereign immunity, governmental immunity, and public duty immunity. Why do you think that these questions have dominated the attention of the courts for so many decades? In part, the answer has to do with history, since sovereign immunity and governmental immunity were widely accepted common law doctrines until the middle of the twentieth century. At that point, courts began to reconsider common law doctrine that they realized was antiquated, and state legislatures began to adopt state and local torts claims acts and to waive or limit immunity by statute, as recounted below.

You should also note that much of the discussion that follows addresses liability and immunity of local municipal governments. State agencies (including those that function under state auspices such as counties and school districts in some jurisdictions) may retain greater immunity from tort liability than municipal governments, depending on state court analysis and interpretations of state statutes relating to government tort immunity and liability. See 18 McQuillin Mun. Corp. § 53:25 (3d ed. 2018) ("Some jurisdictions distinguish between municipal corporations proper and quasi-municipal corporations, such as school districts, hospitals, and counties, concerning liability for torts. Although the law has changed in several jurisdictions, the general rule has been that the quasi-municipal corporations are not liable for torts unless so provided by statute.").

[1] The General Demise of Municipal Tort Immunity

During the many years that municipal tort immunity was a recognized doctrine of American law, it was subjected to severe criticism. Two of the most influential critics were Professor Edwin M. Burchard and Professor James D. Barnett. See generally Borchard, *Governmental Liability in Tort*, 34 YALE L.J. 1, 129, 229 (1924–1925), 36 YALE L.J. 1, 757, 1039 (1926–1927), 28 COLUM. L. REV. 577, 734 (1928); Barnett, *The Foundations of the Distinction Between Public and Private Functions in Respect to the Common-Law Tort Liability of Municipal Corporations (The Antecedents of Bailey v. City of New York)*, 16 OR. L. REV. 250 (1937). The chief target of Professor Borchard's scholarship was tort immunity, and his articles helped to lay the foundation for the subsequent demise of the doctrine. Professor Barnett found that there was no good authority for the distinction between "public" and "private" corporations that American courts developed in the 19th century when considering corporate tort liability. For a review of the history of federal and state immunity, see Kramer, *The Governmental Tort Immunity Doctrine in the United States 1790–1955*, 1966 U. ILL. L.F. 795, 796–810 (1966). At the same time, evolving views among courts and state legislatures paved the way for change. Particularly when municipal or state employees injured members of the public in the same ways that corporate employees might (for example in auto accidents), it seemed unfair to prevent those injured from receiving comparable remedies in both settings.

A number of dilemmas were evident, however. Sovereign immunity doctrine was in many states the product of judge-made law. Should the courts abrogate earlier precedent, or leave it to the legislature to restructure the liability regime applicable to public entities? How might separation of powers principles play out in situations such as these?

Moreover, what approach should replace the doctrine of sovereign immunity as it had developed in the courts? There remained certain functions that were quintessentially "governmental" in character, and which by their nature created risks that might give rise to inevitable private injuries for which governments very likely could not afford to pay. For example, certain types of public service activities (provision of police and fire protection services) seek to protect the citizenry from the acts of third-party wrong-doers or from the impact of natural forces. Should governments be made to pay private parties damages for injuries that arose incidentally in protecting the community as a whole?

Another wrinkle concerns the types of governmental entities that should receive protection under applicable immunity doctrine. The state and agencies of the state (including in many jurisdictions counties and school districts) were protected by immunity under early doctrine. Since municipalities were viewed as having a dual character (governmental and "proprietary" given their status as municipal "corporations"), different types of governmental entities were treated differently, starting with assumptions that "proprietary" activities should be treated in the same way that private businesses were treated.

Courts and ultimately legislatures struggled with drawing lines between those types of activities conducted by state and local governments that should not give rise to compensation for damages and those that should. As a matter of common law, the struggles of courts (and later legislatures) evolved through several stages.

(a) *Governmental versus proprietary distinctions.* In some jurisdictions courts, in particular, sought to distinguish between "governmental" functions (those historically or commonly performed only or primarily by government entities) and those regarded as "proprietary" in nature (either because they were historically performed by business entities or resulted in financial profits against which liabilities could be charged). In effect, this approach focused on institutional characteristics and moved beyond the original distinction (between "government" entities and "business" entities) to distinctions between essentially "governmental" and essentially "business" functions.

While the governmental-proprietary distinction has declined in importance in determining local government tort liability in many jurisdictions, it continues to drive analysis in some. North Carolina case law illustrates some of the associated difficulties. *Estate of Williams ex rel. Overton v. Pasquotank County Parks & Rec. Dep't*, 732 S.E.2d 137 (N.C. 2012), involved the death of a patron in a swimming pool located in a county park. The court first considered whether the matter involved a "governmental" function that is "discretionary, political, legislative, or public in nature and performed for the public good in behalf of the State rather than for itself," or rather a "proprietary" function that is "commercial or chiefly for the private advantage of the compact community." In evaluating how to classify the function, it considered several factors, including (a) whether "the undertaking is one in which only a governmental agency could engage," (b) whether the service is traditionally a service provided by a governmental entity; (c) whether a substantial fee is charged for the service provided; and (d) whether that fee does more than "simply cover the operating costs of the service provider." *Id.* at 142–43. The court added additional caveats, however. It noted that "although an activity may be classified in general as a governmental function, liability in tort may exist as to certain of its phases; and conversely, although classified in general as proprietary, certain phases may be considered exempt from liability." *Id.* at 143. It also observed that "it does not follow that a particular activity will be denoted a governmental function even though previous cases have held the identical activity to be of such a public necessity that the expenditure of funds in connection with it was for a public purpose." *Id.* The case was remanded for further consideration in light of the stated principles. How would you expect it to be resolved given the facts described? See also *Meinck v. City of Gastonia*, 819 S.E.2d 353 (N.C. 2018) (applying governmental/proprietary distinction; concluding that local government's lease of property to nonprofit art guild was governmental rather than proprietary; finding no liability for fall by subtenant on exterior stairs).

How should the work of city-owned emergency medical services be classified? Does the fact that fees are charged for the services matter? In a matter of first impression in Missouri, a Missouri court held that such service, "whether considered a part of the services offered by the city's fire department or as a provider of medical services to the 'consuming public,'" is "clearly a governmental function." The fact that the city charges a fee is "not determinative." *Richardson v. City of St. Louis*, 293 S.W.3d 133, 137–38 (Mo. Ct. App. 2009). Accord *Smyser v. City of Peoria*, 160 P.3d 1186, 1193–94 (Ariz. Ct. App. 2007) (citing cases).

For an important discussion of governmental versus proprietary distinctions, see Spitzer, *Realigning the Governmental/Proprietary Distinction in Municipal Law*, 40 Seattle U. L. Rev. 173 (2016). Professor Spitzer argues that much of the difficulty with the governmental/proprietary distinction arises because of that dichotomy's use in a number of different contexts (including tort law, contracts, tax exemption, municipal authority, eminent domain and adverse possession), with a wide-ranging set of divergent rationales. He then proposes that rather than abolishing the governmental/proprietary distinction, a three-part set of distinctions be employed. He would retain the "proprietary category," but divide the "governmental" category into a "governmental sovereign powers" subset that would continue to be treated as "governmental" (including coercive powers such as the police power, law enforcement, taxation, and eminent domain) and a "governmental service activities" subset that would be treated as "proprietary" (relating to schools, parks, roads, and other matters paid by taxes). As you review the material later in this chapter, consider whether you agree with Professor Spitzer.

(b) *Discretionary versus ministerial distinctions.* Subsequently, courts focused on the nature of decisionmaking in determining when liability might be assigned to governmental entities, to some degree out of an appreciation for separation of powers principles. Those following this approach often interpreted state legislation modeled after the Federal Tort Claims Act, which provides an exemption from liability for certain discretionary decisions. See 28 U.S.C. § 2680 ("The provisions of this chapter and section 1346(b) of this title shall not apply to—(a) Any claim based upon an act or omission of an employee of the Government, exercising due care, in the execution of a statute or regulation, whether or not such statute or regulation be valid, or based upon the exercise or performance or the failure to exercise or perform a discretionary function or duty on the part of a federal agency or an employee of the Government, whether or not the discretion involved be abused."). In the view of many courts in jurisdictions adopting this model, "discretionary" judgments were not to be penalized, while "ministerial" decisions applying policies developed by others were fair game for liability. The core concern was preserving executive branch decisionmaking authority without the courts' intervening in ways that would stifle core decisions. For a discussion of the discretionary exemption under the Federal Torts Claim Act, see Cohen, *Not Fully Discretionary: Incorporating a Factor-Based Standard into the FTCA's Discretionary Function Exception*, 112 Nw. U. L. Rev. 879 (2018) (recommending consideration of five factors in interpreting "discretionary function" exception, including the following: (1) whether the government employee exercised a choice, (2) whether the choice related to policy considerations, (3) whether the government employee's conduct, if performed by a private person, would violate state law, (4) what practical concerns might inhibit essential government functioning, and (5) whether sovereign immunity should be minimized in order to allow private citizens to sue the government for wrongful or negligent conduct). As you consider the material that follows, reflect on whether refinements in understanding immunity for "discretionary" functions would be more satisfactory if such a five-factor standard were incorporated into state law.

(c) *Policy-making versus implementation decisions.* In due course, a number of state courts further refined and narrowed their standards regarding sovereign immunity so that an ever more limited array of decisions would be deemed to be immune and not give rise to liability. Once again, this dichotomy was designed to preserve the freedom of executive branch agencies to make important, necessary decisions without having the courts second guess them and without paralyzing decisionmakers by fear of potential liability. Note the courts' efforts to respect underlying separation of powers concerns. The principal case that follows embodies this approach. How would you evaluate the facts presented and determine immunity or possible liability under the three approaches just outlined (governmental/proprietary; discretionary/ministerial; and policy-making/implementation standards)?

[2] Legislative Responses to Judicial Abrogation of Tort Immunity

The judicial developments just summarized reflected important initiatives by the courts. At the same time, however, legislatures sought to develop rational policies concerning tort liability of local and state government entities. Such legislative initiatives in turn resulted in further interpretations by the courts as briefly summarized below.

During the period when immunity was being successfully challenged in the courts, state legislatures continued to act, in some cases to carve out additional selected areas of liability, in other cases to enact virtually unconditional waivers of immunity, and in still others to develop a framework combining appropriate areas of liability and immunity after the courts had judicially abolished immunity.

Georgia provides one example. In *Mixon v. City of Warner Robins*, 444 S.E.2d 761 (Ga. 1994), the state supreme court interpreted a statute that provided that a police officer pursuing a suspect "shall not [be] relieve[d] . . . from the duty to drive with due regard for the safety of all persons" and held that a municipality could be liable for injuries to an innocent third party caused by a suspect who was fleeing police. The state legislature then revised the statute so that, in its amended version, it provided that an officer's pursuit of a suspect "shall not be the proximate cause or a contributing proximate cause of the damage, injury or death caused by the fleeing suspect unless the law enforcement officer acted with reckless disregard for proper law enforcement procedures." See GA. CODE § 40-6-6(d)(2). Interpreting the amended statute, the court, in *City of Winder v. McDougald*, 583 S.E.2d 879 (Ga. 2003), held that local governments are immune from liability for injuries to suspects pursued in police chases unless there is an actual intent to cause injury. In the *City of Winder* case, the court ruled that a city was not liable for the death of a 14-year-old girl who was pursued at high speeds by law enforcement officers while she was driving her father's car without permission. The court said that making local governments liable for injuries to fleeing suspects would be inconsistent with public policy. The court observed that the law enacted to deal with high speed chases was only intended to provide for liability of local governments in cases where an innocent bystander was injured rather than someone who was themselves a suspect. For a different jurisdiction's approach, see *Smith v. City of Stillwater*, 328 P.3d 1192 (Okla. 2014) (statutory provision that granted exemptions to the traffic laws for authorized emergency vehicles did not provide that law enforcement officers of a state or political subdivision engaged in a police pursuit owed a duty of care to a fleeing suspect).

Legislative responses to judicial abrogation of tort immunity are varied. Broadly, they have generally either abolished tort liability for local governments, provided a statutory listing of instances in which governmental immunity continues to apply, provided a listing of instances in which local governments may face liability, or left matters for the courts to address as a matter of common law. Where state agencies and employees are concerned, most states have developed state tort claims statutes. Many states have modeled their legislation on the Federal Tort Claims Act, 28 U.S.C. § 1346(b). For a very brief summary of state legislation as of 2007, see Rosenthal, *A Theory of Governmental Damages Liability: Torts, Constitutional Torts, and Takings*, 9 U. PA. J. CONST. L. 797, 804–813 (2007) and associated footnotes.

Before moving on to consider how common law and legislative reforms have come together, we should stop to consider the following significant questions about legislative reforms.

Notes and Questions

1. *Constitutional limits on legislative authority.* A majority of courts, including, of course, those that judicially abolished the doctrine of immunity, have taken the position that because the doctrine was judicially created, the courts were free to abandon it when they found the doctrine caused injustice and served no useful social purpose. Many of the courts used very strong language in condemning and then abrogating the doctrine. That result raises the question whether there are any limitations on what the legislature may do in reacting to a court's action.

Ways in which such questions might arise are exemplified in Illinois. There, the state supreme court abolished school district immunity specifically and all local government immunity. See *Molitor v. Kaneland Cmty. Unit Dist.*, 163 N.E.2d 89 (Ill. 1959). The legislature's first response was to pass a series of bills which had the effect of restoring immunity to some local governments, authorizing the purchase of insurance by some, placing dollar limitations on the liability of others, requiring indemnification of employees by some and allowing liability to stand with respect to others. In *Harvey v. Clyde Park Dist.*, 203 N.E.2d 573 (Ill. 1964), the court was faced with one of these statutes that reinstated total immunity for park districts. The plaintiff had been injured in a park district playground accident, and his complaint had been dismissed. The Supreme Court reversed, holding that the statute barring recovery against a park district, in conjunction with others, violated the Illinois constitutional prohibition against special legislation. The problem of special legislation is discussed in Chapter 8. The state tort immunity act was subsequently revised in 1965. 745 Ill. Comp. Stat. § 10/1-101 *et seq*. The Illinois state constitution was subsequently revised in 1970 to include the following text: "Sovereign Immunity Abolished. Except as the General Assembly may provide by law, sovereign immunity in this State is abolished." Ill. Const. Art. 13, § 4 (1970). Litigation has continued. See *Monson v. City of Danville*, 115 N.E.3d 81 (Ill. 2018) (provisions of state torts claim statute that established duty on part of local government to maintain property in reasonably safe condition did not override other provisions creating immunity for discretionary actions by municipality including those relating to sidewalk repair). Should limitations on governmental tort liability appear in state constitutions? Why or why not? Are statutory solutions better than common law approaches to immunity? Why or why not?

2. *More nuanced options through legislation?* As noted earlier, courts in some jurisdictions have distinguished between liability and immunity determinations affecting municipal governments and state agencies or government entities acting on behalf of the state (in some instances counties and school boards). To some extent, the distinction between "proprietary" functions and "governmental" functions has reflected this divide, since municipalities are a "corporate" form. Might it not be better to step back and consider first principles as to liability and immunity of state and local government entities, rather than to rely on common law proxies? How would you frame a legislative scheme addressing state agencies? Municipal governments?

Consider, for example, Minnesota's approach. Compare Minn. Stat. § 3.736 (including limits on liability and list of exclusions from liability including exclusion for discretionary action, certain losses relating to operation of outdoor recreational system, losses relating to lack of care in state hospitals or correctional system facilities, if reasonable use had been made of available appropriations to provide care) with Minn. Stat. §§ 466.02 to 466.04 (as general rule, municipalities liable for actions whether governmental or proprietary, subject to numerous listed exceptions including one for acting or failing to exercise or perform a discretionary function or duty, whether or not the discretion is abused and others relating to operation of pools, certain 911 operations, and GIS data; and setting maximum liability limits).

[3] Continued Immunity and Other Protection for Discretionary Activities

Despite the declarations concerning the demise of governmental tort immunity, the continued life of the discretionary-ministerial distinction applied to acts of public officials suggests that governmental immunity has been modified rather than abolished.

Courts from the beginning of the period of judicial abrogation of governmental immunity recognized a policy-based exception for discretionary activity, with different standards for applying the exception to government officials and government agencies. In part, this approach reflects an appreciation for separation of powers between judicial and executive branches. Statutory and judicial recognition of a discretionary function exception requires consideration of how specific acts should be analyzed to determine whether such acts were discretionary or not. The *Peavler* decision, below, discusses this problem.

Many jurisdictions have also grappled with a second approach to finessing immunity questions, by evaluating claims of negligence carefully with an eye to whether duties created by state legislation are owed to the public at large or to a narrower group. The resulting "public duty" doctrine has been used to shield state agencies, and municipal entities in some states, from liability on the theory that a duty to the public at large does not give rise to an actionable duty to individuals. The *Kolbe* case, below, illustrates this approach to limiting liability and sets the stage for related doctrine concerning special duties and special relationships.

Peavler v. Board of Commissioners of Monroe County

528 N.E.2d 40 (Ind. 1988)

Shepard, Chief Justice.

Two cases before us on petitions for transfer require that we construe the provision in the Indiana Tort Claims Act which provides governmental immunity for discretionary acts.

Richey Wayne Peavler filed suit against the Monroe County Board of Commissioners, alleging "negligence in the failure to place or maintain a curve warning sign, and/or reduced speed limit sign or advisory speed limit sign on a portion of a county road." The jury returned a verdict for the county. The Court of Appeals found that the trial court erred in instructing the jury that any duty on the part of the county to post warning signs was discretionary. The Court of Appeals concluded that the county was not immune as a matter of law and held the jury should decide the question of immunity. The court remanded the case for a new trial.

In a separate action, Ronald and Pamela Hout sued the Board of Commissioners of Steuben County, alleging that it negligently failed to place a warning sign for motorists approaching a "T" intersection. The county moved for summary judgment on the basis of governmental immunity for discretionary functions. The trial court denied the motion. In an interlocutory appeal, the Court of Appeals determined that such a decision was discretionary and directed entry of summary judgment for the county. We grant transfer to resolve the conflict between districts. . . .

II. Indiana Tort Claims Act

The Indiana Torts Claims Act (ITCA) provides that governmental entities may be liable for torts committed by [their] agencies and [their] employees. Ind. Code §§ 34-4-16.5-1 to 20 (Burns 1986 Repl.). The ITCA protects governments from liability in certain circumstances. Among other more specific exceptions, "[a] government entity or an employee acting within the scope of his employment is not liable if a loss results from: (6) The performance of a discretionary function." Ind. Code § 34-4-16.5-3(6). Each of the cases at bar turns on the meaning of discretionary function.

III. Approaches to Discretionary Function

Governmental immunity has generated a great deal of discussion in state and federal jurisdictions. Out of this debate, several approaches have emerged to determine whether an act is discretionary and thus entitled to immunity. While these approaches are instructive, the purpose and policy underlying governmental immunity must be the cornerstone for evaluating any claim of governmental immunity.

A. *The Ministerial/Discretionary Distinction.* Courts have attempted to distinguish immune governmental functions from those which expose the government to liability by describing activities as ministerial or discretionary.

> A duty is discretionary when it involves on the part of the officer to determine whether or not he should perform a certain act, and if so in what particular way, and in the absence of corrupt motives, in the exercise of such discretion, he is not liable. His duties, however, in the performance of the act, after he has once determined that it shall be done, are ministerial, and for negligence in such performance, which results in injury, he may be liable in damages. [*Adams v. Schneider*, 124 N.E. 718, 720 (Ind. App. 1919).]

This common law distinction has found favor within our Court of Appeals since the ITCA passed. A duty is discretionary when the officer must determine whether he should perform a certain act, and, if so, in what manner. Performance of a discretionary function requires judgment and choice and involves what is proper and just under the circumstances. A ministerial act is performed in a prescribed manner, in obedience to the mandate of legal authority, without the exercise of judgment upon the propriety of the act. Ministerial acts "are those done by officers and employees who are required to carry out the orders of others or to administer the law with little choice as to when, where, how or under what circumstances their acts are to be done." Restatement (Second) of Torts, § 895D comment h. Under this dichotomy any governmental act involving choice, judgment or decision-making is discretionary and immune from tort liability. Only those acts which require no judgment are ministerial and subject to tort liability.

This Court has recognized that the application of this standard is unclear. This difficulty has also been noted by scholars and commentators.

> It seems almost impossible to draw any clear and definite line, since the distinction, if one exists, can be at most one of degree. "It would be difficult to conceive of any official act, no matter how directly ministerial, that did not admit of some discretion in the manner of its performance, even if it involved only the driving of a nail." [W. Prosser, THE LAW OF TORTS, *supra* § 132 at 990 (*quoting Ham v. City of Los Angeles County*, 46 Cal. App. 148, 162, 189 P. 462, 468 (1920)).]

If discretionary functions included every act which involves any element of choice, judgment or ability to make responsible decisions, every act would fall within the exception.

B. *Planning vs. Operation.* Another method of analysis has emerged primarily from interpretation of federal statutory immunity. In 1946, the United States gave consent to be sued in tort when it enacted the Federal Tort Claims Act, 28 U.S.C. § 1346(b) (1982) (FTCA). The FTCA generally exposes the government to tort liability but provides immunity for certain enumerated acts and for any claim based on the exercise of a "discretionary function or duty." 28 U.S.C. § 2680(a) (1982).

In interpreting discretionary functions, the U.S. Supreme Court has rejected the distinction between governmental and proprietary functions:

> Furthermore, the Government in effect reads the statute as imposing liability in the same manner as if it were a municipal corporation and not as if it were a private person, and it would thus push the courts into the "non-governmental"-"governmental" quagmire that has long plagued the law of municipal corporations. A comparative study of the cases in the forty-eight States will disclose an irreconcilable conflict. More than that, the decisions in each of the States are disharmonious and disclose the inevitable chaos when courts try to apply a rule of law that is inherently unsound. [*Indian Towing Co. v. United States*, 350 U.S. 61, 65 (1955).]

Rather, the Supreme Court has determined which acts are entitled to immunity by distinguishing acts performed at the planning level from acts performed at the operational level. The federal government is not subject to liability when the alleged negligence arises from decisions which are "responsibly made at a planning rather than operational level and involved considerations more or less important to the practicability" of the government's program.

Thus, immunity for discretionary functions under this analysis does not extend to all acts involving choice or judgment. The FTCA protects the discretion of the executive or the administrator to act according to his or her judgment of the best course, a concept of substantial historical ancestry in American law. The discretionary function or duty "includes more than the initiation of programs and activities. It also includes determinations made by executives or administrators in establishing plans, specifications or schedules of operations."

C. *Separation of Power and Purposes of Governmental Immunity.* Ultimately, the determination of whether a governmental action is immune as a discretionary function must be based on the purposes and policy underlying governmental immunity. The early purposes of governmental immunity largely have been eliminated. While the historical reasons supporting the doctrine of sovereign immunity are no longer vital, governmental immunity under some circumstances still serves valid purposes. Common law forms of immunity, such as immunity for legislative and judicial functions, remain even absent statutory immunity. Even as it abandoned the governmental/proprietary distinction, this Court acknowledged the continuing vitality of such forms of governmental immunity.

The policy underlying governmental immunity is the fundamental idea that certain kinds of executive branch decisions should not be subject to judicial review. The separation of powers doctrine forecloses the courts from reviewing political, social and economic actions within the province of coordinate branches of government. In this way, the discretionary function exception articulates "a policy of preventing tort actions from becoming a vehicle for judicial interference with decision-making that is properly exercised by other branches of the government. . . ." *Blessing v. United States*, 447 F. Supp. 1160, 1170 (E.D. Pa. 1978) (interpreting FTCA discretionary function exception).

Governmental immunity for discretionary functions also avoids inhibiting the effective and efficient performance of governmental duties. Policy-making activities lie at the heart of governance and such essential acts should not be subject to judicial second-guessing or harassment by the actual or potential threat of liability litigation. Tort immunity for basic planning and policy-making functions is necessary to avoid the chilling effect on the ability of the government to deal effectively with difficult policy issues which it confronts daily.

Moreover, the traditional tort standard of negligence does not provide an adequate basis for evaluating certain governmental decisions. As the district court in *Blessing* said:

> [T]he judiciary confines itself . . . to adjudication of facts based on discernible objective standards of law. In the context of tort actions . . . these objective standards are notably lacking when the question is not negligence but social wisdom, not due care but political practicability, not unreasonableness but economic expediency. Tort law simply furnishes an inadequate crucible for testing the merits of social, political, or economic decisions. [*Blessing*, 447 F. Supp. at 1170–72.]

Immunity for discretionary functions, however, does not protect all mistakes of judgment. The discretionary function exception insulates only those significant policy and political decisions which cannot be assessed by customary tort standards.

In this sense, the word discretionary does not mean mere judgment or discernment. Rather, it refers to the exercise of political power which is held accountable only to the Constitution or the political process.

This interpretation of the discretionary function exception also comports with the Restatement (Second) of Torts:

> Even when a State is subject to tort liability, it and its governmental agencies are immune to liability for acts and omissions constituting
>
> (a) the exercise of a judicial or legislative function, or
>
> (b) the exercise of an administrative function involving the determination of fundamental government policy. [Restatement, *supra* § 895B(3).]

The distinction between planning and operational functions relates well to the purposes of governmental immunity. It requires an inquiry into the nature of the governmental act and the decision-making process involved. Merely labeling an action as planning or operational, without more, cannot pass for analysis. The critical inquiry is "not merely whether judgment was exercised but whether the nature of the judgment called for policy considerations." *Blessing*, 447 F. Supp. at 1178 (quoting *Griffin v. United States*, 500 F.2d 1059, 1064 (3d Cir. 1974)). In many cases, courts have looked to the purposes of immunity in determining whether an act is planning or operational.

Under the planning/operational dichotomy, the type of discretion which may be immunized from tort liability is generally that attributable to the essence of governing. Planning activities include acts or omissions in the exercise of a legislative, judicial, executive or planning function which involves formulation of basic policy decisions characterized by official judgment or discretion in weighing alternatives and choosing public policy. Government decisions about policy formation which involve assessment of competing priorities and a weighing of budgetary considerations or the allocation of scarce resources are also planning activities.

The distinction between planning and operational functions is a standard, rather than a precise rule. The focus must remain on the policy underlying governmental immunity. If the act is one committed to coordinate branches of the government involving policy decisions not reviewable under traditional tort standards of reasonableness, the government is immune from liability even if the act was performed negligently.

IV. Policy-Based Analysis of Immunity

The ministerial/discretionary test does not advance the public policy of government immunity because it does not consider the type of decision protected by immunity. Rather, it considers only the resulting conduct and attempts to label that conduct. The ministerial/discretionary test defines "discretionary" in the negative: anything which is non-ministerial is discretionary. The test does not require an affirmative finding that the governmental action arose from the type of policy-making decision protected by governmental immunity. It operates by process of elimination, removing ministerial acts from the more general category of discretionary, immune acts.

The discretionary function exception of the ITCA removes discretionary acts from the broader spectrum of liability. This requires an affirmative finding that the governmental act is of the type intended to be protected by immunity. The planning/operational test provides a better framework for such an analysis. This test advances the policy underlying governmental immunity and allows consideration of the nature of the challenged decisions. In defining discretionary acts immune under the ITCA, we reject the ministerial/discretionary test in favor of the planning/operational test, to be applied in light of the policy and [rationale] supporting governmental immunity.

The issue of whether an act is discretionary and therefore immune is a question of law for the court's determination. The question may require an extended factual development, but the essential inquiry is whether the challenged act is the type of function which the legislature intended to protect with immunity. This determination should be made by the court.

Discretionary immunity must be narrowly construed because it is an exception to the general rule of liability. The governmental entity seeking to establish immunity bears the burden of proving that the challenged act or omission was a policy decision made by consciously balancing risks and benefits.

In deciding whether the function is the type intended to benefit from immunity, the court should look to the purposes of immunity to determine whether those purposes would be furthered by extending immunity to the act in question. Factors which would, under most circumstances, point toward immunity, include:

1. The nature of the conduct—

a) Whether the conduct has a regulatory objective;

b) Whether the conduct involved the balancing of factors without reliance on a readily ascertainable rule or standard;

c) Whether the conduct requires a judgment based on policy decisions;

d) Whether the decision involved adopting general principles or only applying them.;

e) Whether the conduct involved establishment of plans, specifications and schedule; and

f) Whether the decision involved assessing priorities, weighing of budgetary considerations or allocation of resources.

2. The effect on governmental operations—

a) Whether the decision affects the feasibility or practicability of a government program; and

b) Whether liability will affect the effective administration of the function in question.

3. The capacity of the court to evaluate the propriety of the government's action—Whether tort standards offer an insufficient evaluation of the plaintiff's claim.

Immunity assumes negligence but denies liability. Thus, the issues of duty, breach and causation are not before the court in deciding whether the government entity is immune. If the court finds the government is not immune, the case may yet be decided on the basis of failure of any element of negligence. This should not be confused with the threshold determination of immunity.

V. Resolution of the Cases

Both Peavler and Hout allege that the respective defendant counties were negligent for failing to place traffic control devices warning motorists of dangerous sections of county roads. Both counties answer that such a decision is a discretionary function and that each county is therefore immune from any liability arising from a failure to place a warning sign.

The counties argue that, while failure to maintain a previously posted traffic sign is non-discretionary, the original decision to install one is discretionary. Clearly, there are cases on either end of the spectrum which will fall automatically into the category of discretionary or non-discretionary functions. Such is the case of the failure to properly maintain a warning sign. It does not follow, however, that the decision to post such a sign is automatically discretionary.

While warning signs are posted to further the safety of the community, they are also regulatory devices, and they may have a penal effect on violators. While the Indiana Manual on Uniform Traffic Control Devices offers guidelines for warning signs, the Manual does not "mandate the use of any control devices or procedures at a particular location." The decision may involve gathering data regarding traffic flow, average speed, and other factors. It may also involve weighing priorities to determine if safety considerations outweigh inconveniences to individual motorists, and determining whether uniformly marking all similar sites can be accommodated within a given budget.

While potential liability may have some effect on this government function, the government is still shielded by immunity for actual policy-making decisions regarding warning signs. Thus, the government is exposed to liability only when no policy oriented decision-making process has been undertaken.

Tort standards of reasonableness do not provide an adequate basis for evaluating the failure to erect a warning sign if that failure arises from an actual, affirmative policy decision. If the decision is based on professional judgment, however, rather than policy oriented decision-making, traditional tort standards for professional negligence afford a basis for evaluation. Thus, a county's considered decision to entrust placement of traffic control devices to a traffic engineer is not reviewable under tort standards, while the engineer's subsequent decisions as to warning signs are reviewable under tort standards of professional negligence.

Considering the nature of the conduct, the effect on government operations, and the capacity of the courts to evaluate the propriety of the government's actions, we cannot say that governmental policy is so clearly implicated by decisions regarding placement of warning signs that all such decisions are discretionary under the ITCA as a matter of law. Had the legislature intended for such an act to be immune outside the parameters of the discretionary functions exception, it could have provided specific immunity.

The discretionary nature of a decision to place a warning sign must be determined case by case. Immunity may be established by government defendants who can show that the challenged decision was discretionary because it resulted from a policy oriented decision-making process. If the counties engaged in this decision-making process, the courts may not judge the wisdom of their decisions. That judgment is left to the political process.

The defendants here seek to establish the defense of immunity. Each bears the burden to show that a policy decision, consciously balancing risks and benefits, took place. Neither defendant county presented evidence to show that its decision regarding the warning signs was the result of such a process. . . .

Failure to engage in this decision-making process does not automatically result in liability. The county simply is not shielded by immunity if the failure to erect a warning sign did not result from a policy decision consciously balancing risks and advantages.

If the county in either case can present evidence that the commissioners engaged in a policy oriented decision-making process and determined, for whatever reason, that a warning sign should not be posted, the courts will not second-guess their judgment. On remand, the counties bear the burden to demonstrate the discretionary nature of the decision in order to prevail on a claim of immunity. . . .

Notes and Questions

1. *Applying the distinctions: planning versus operational.* As the principal case indicates, courts have become wary of the use of labels when specific cases require them to decide whether particular governmental action is entitled to immunity. Considering the generally unsatisfactory results of uncritical application of the governmental-proprietary distinction, it should come as no surprise that a similar lack of analysis in the use of a discretionary-ministerial distinction should produce equally unsatisfactory results. Does the planning-operational distinction discussed in the case help resolve the question of what constitutes discretion, or does it simply substitute another set of labels? How did the Indiana court apply the planning-operational distinction in reaching its conclusion in *Peavler*? Would a decision by a sheriff's office dispatcher to search for the owner of cattle reported to be loose on a state road, rather than sending someone to the scene, be entitled to discretionary function immunity as a planning activity? See *Greathouse v. Armstrong*, 616 N.E.2d 364, 368 (Ind. 1993) (he was merely implementing a pre-determined policy, not the

formulation of policy so it is "operational" and not "planning" and no immunity based on an exercise of discretion). See also *City of Beech Grove v. Beloat*, 50 N.E.3d 135 (Ind. 2016) (in case involving pedestrian's fall into pot hole while crossing major street near crosswalk resulting in broken leg, finding that discretionary immunity did not apply since evidence was insufficient to demonstrate that city had engaged in financial and policy judgment needed to adopt policy of wholesale reconstruction of street rather than piecemeal repairs).

Can you explain in your own words the differences between planning and operational decisions? Do some contexts lend themselves better to application of the planning v. operational distinction than others? Compare *Cutler v. Kodiak Island Borough*, 290 P.3d 415 (Alaska 2012) (borough sought to foreclose on recorded outstanding tax and garbage-service liens, and property owner asserted lien was invalid and sought damages; court concluded that liens had been illegally recorded, but found municipality was immune under statute finding no liability for discretionary functions because the municipal decisions underlying the action of recording the liens involved basic planning or policy rather than being operational in the sense of implementing plans or carrying out policy), with *City of Hooper Bay v. Bunyan*, 359 P.3d 972 (Alaska 2015) (holding that city did not have qualified immunity in case where drunken prisoner committed suicide, where implementation of protocols relating to incarceration of intoxicated individuals had required search of records and inspection every five minutes and risk to prisoner was reasonably foreseeable).

2. *Quintessential cases.* Based on your initial thinking about how to distinguish planning and operational decisions, consider the following situations, which present particularly hard decisions.

(a) *Allocating scarce resources.* Budget decisions seem to entail core policy judgments that should not be second-guessed by the courts. Does the "planning v. operational" framework in *Peavler* really explain how such issues should be resolved and where and when immunity might apply? Compare *Hagan v. Georgia DOT*, 739 S.E.2d 123 (Ga. App. 2013) (in case involving pedestrian's fall on sidewalk adjacent to state road, concluding that state transportation department's decision to deploy funds and personnel toward highway safety and efficiency, rather than toward sidewalk maintenance and repair, fell within discretionary function exception to waiver of sovereign immunity, where state personnel were called to exercise policy judgment based on considering alternative options and relevant factors; stressing that the "key" to relevant analysis was the difference between design and operational decisions and policy decisions), with *Steward v. State*, 322 P.3d 860 (Alaska 2014) (in negligence action on behalf of motorist who had died after leaving road where guardrail had been removed and not replaced, court observed that "discretionary function immunity" is intended to ensure that private citizens do not interfere with government processes by bringing tort suits challenging policy judgments; court concluded that immunity applied, stating that the decision regarding replacement of guardrail was discretionary in character). The *Steward* court stated that:

> [w]hen determining whether discretionary immunity applies to a specific act, [courts distinguish] between decisions that involve basic planning or policy and those that are merely operational in the sense that they implement plans or carry out policy; planning decisions fall under the exception because they involve formulation of basic policy including consideration of financial, political, economic, or social effects of the policy, while normal day-by-day operations of the government are not planning decisions and are not entitled to immunity under the discretionary function exception.

Are these courts' decisions and their reasoning contradictory?

(b) *Rules and application.* Diverse activities occur in school settings, and courts can find it challenging to determine when liability may attach, particularly when rules and their applications are involved. See *Yanero v. Davis*, 65 S.W.3d 510 (Ky. 2001), the court held that a state athletic association's failure to promulgate a rule requiring student athletes to wear batting helmets during baseball practice, although such a rule was in force for varsity games, was entitled to official immunity because such rule-making is a discretionary function and there was no evidence that the association acted in bad faith. The court, however, refused to grant immunity to two coaches of the junior varsity team who failed to enforce an unwritten school rule to wear batting helmets in practice as well as during games because they were acting in a ministerial capacity. The Kentucky court applied *Yanero* in a very different context in *Lamb v. Holmes*, 162 S.W.3d 902, 911 (KY. 2005) (finding that teachers' and administrators' actions in performing a search of female middle school students were protected by qualified immunity as to both federal § 1983 claims and state tort claims because the acts "were made in good faith, were discretionary in nature and within the scope of their authority"). Compare *Ritchie v. Turner*, 559 S.W.3d 822 (Ky. 2018) (in case involving allegations of sexual abuse of student by teacher, concluding that supervision of students was discretionary, not ministerial, and did not give rise to liability); *Palosz v. Town of Greenwich*, 194 A.3d 885 (Conn. App. 2018) (holding that school board was not entitled to sovereign immunity in face of allegations that student who committed suicide following ongoing bullying when school district allegedly failed to comply with safe school climate plan mandated by state statute). See also Bittner, *A Hazy Shade of Winter: The Chilling Issues Surrounding Hazing in School Sports and the Litigation that Follows,* 23 Jeffrey S. Moorad Sports L.J. 211 (2016) (discussing potential state and federal liability).

3. *Transportation activities: what kind of tests?* It is worth considering the range of government activities in a given area and how immunity standards might apply. Consider the following cases, and think about whether the courts' approaches are cohesive and well-justified. See if you can develop a rule statement that encompasses all the holdings summarized below.

(a) *Road signs.* In another case involving road signs, the Minnesota Supreme Court canvassed judicial opinion on the question and concluded that "The critical inquiry that emerges . . . is whether the challenged governmental conduct involved a balancing of policy objectives." *Nusbaum v. County of Blue Earth*, 422 N.W.2d 713, 722–24 (Minn. 1988). Under this test, not all exercises of judgment qualify for discretionary function immunity, particularly where the exercise of professional or scientific judgment that does not involve a balancing of policy objectives. Government conduct becomes protected "only where the state produces evidence that the conduct was of a policy-making nature involving social, political, or economical considerations." Applying this approach, the court denied discretionary function status to decisions regarding the placement of speed signs on a highway. While a decision not to recommend the placement of warning signs along a sharp curve was an exercise in professional judgment, there was no evidence that the decision was mandated or influenced by any policy considerations, the court concluded. See also *Bibler v. Stevenson*, 80 N.E.3d 424 (Ohio 2016) (finding liability for accident arising when stop sign was obscured by foliage, pursuant to statute requiring municipalities to keep roads in repair).

(b) *Timing of traffic lights and posting signs.* For cases concluding that setting the timing of signal lights or posting traffic signs required judgment which constituted discretion and was thus entitled to immunity, see *Aguehounde v. District of Columbia*, 666 A.2d 443, 448 (D.C. 1995) (construing Federal Tort Claims Act); *Kolitch v. Lindedahl*, 497 A.2d 183 (N.J. 1985) (state not liable for failure to warn of hazardous nature of curve where automobile accident occurred). An analysis of highway signage cases prepared for the National Cooperative Highway Research Program (NCHRP) concluded that "courts are beginning rather uniformly to hold that decision-making with respect to the installation of signing and signaling takes place at the planning level and hence is discretionary in nature, whereas the maintenance of signs and signals once erected is an activity conducted at the operational level and hence is unprotected; . . . [however] discretion is exhausted when the State has actual or is charged with constructive notice of 'dangerous conditions.'" Vance, *Supplement to Liability of State and Local Governments for Negligence Arising out of the Installation and Maintenance of Warning Signs, Traffic Lights, and Pavement Markings*, NCHRP, LEGAL RESEARCH DIG. 1, 9 (Dec. 1988). Which approach, the case-by-case approach of the Indiana and Minnesota courts, or the installation-maintenance distinction discussed in the NCHRP report, appears sounder?

(c) *Ice storms and power outages.* See *Ford v. N.H. Dep't of Transp.*, 37 A.3d 436 (N.H. 2012) (in negligence action against state agency brought by motorist who had been struck by another car in intersection during power outage caused by ice storm, concluding that town had no duty to warn motorist of outage and that state transportation department's decisions on how to plan and allocate limited state resources in face of ice storms and related power outages was a discretionary function). A growing number of states have addressed ice/snow removal liability in state/municipal tort claims statutes. Case law suggests that there may be a general duty to remove ice and snow but that such a duty is not actionable by individual motorists. See, e.g., *MacPage v. City of Philadelphia*, 25 A.3d 471 (Pa. 2011) (no duty to individual motorists regarding black ice) (related issues are addressed in connection with the public duty doctrine discussed below). See also *Graham v. Comm'r of Transp.*, 195 A.3d 664 (Conn. 2018) (considering terms of state highway defect statute, and concluding that insufficient nexus had been shown been notification of state police regarding black ice conditions and obligations of state Transportation Commissioner).

4. *Oversight responsibilities and failure to act?* As you will see in the following section relating to federal civil rights liability, claims can at times be asserted for a failure by government employees or agencies to act. See, e.g., *Ga. Dep't of Human Servs. v. Spruill*, 751 S.E.2d 315 (Ga. 2013), where the Georgia Supreme Court found that a case manager's decisions about how to investigate reports from a pediatrician about the malnourishment, neglect and abuse of prematurely-born infant twin boys required a balancing of policy considerations and were therefore covered under the discretionary function exception of the Georgia Tort Claims Act.

5. *Applying the discretionary function exception in other contexts.* Courts have applied various standards in evaluating conduct in determining the applicability of the discretionary function exception. Some courts apply a strict standard with outcomes similar to the planning-operational test. See, e.g., *Olson v. City of Garrison*, 539 N.W.2d 663 (N.D. 1995). These courts generally adopt an approach similar to the federal test for determining the scope of discretionary conduct that is used for analyses related to the Federal Tort Claims Act. They look to the conduct in question, determine if it involved an exercise of judgment, and then further evaluate if the judgment involved governmental policy. If it did not, it is not granted discretionary immunity.

Another approach merely focuses on whether the activity involved an exercise in personal judgment and deliberation, which is granted discretionary immunity, or if it involved only the execution of an absolute duty, which is not granted immunity. See, e.g., *Jasa v. Douglas County*, 510 N.W.2d 281 (Neb. 1994) (strong dissent), criticized in Note, *The Discretionary Function Exemption Returns Sovereign Immunity to the Throne of Douglas County—Once Again the King Can Do No Wrong: Jasa v. Douglas County*, 28 Creighton L. Rev. 247 (1994); see also *Holloway v. State*, 875 N.W.2d 435 (Neb. 2016) (concluding that discretionary exception to sovereign immunity doctrine applied to contractor in case involving shooting of former inmate in state correctional facility; no liability found in absence of special duty relationship).

Does the conclusion that a particular activity involves a discretionary function insulate a governmental entity from liability for abuses in the exercise of such discretion? See *Snyder v. Minneapolis*, 441 N.W.2d 781, 787 (Minn. 1989) (discretionary function is proper standard to apply, but municipal officials have no discretion to approve permits in clear violation of the law). In *Sletten v. Ramsey County*, 675 N.W.2d 291 (Minn. 2004), the court reviewed the question of discretionary immunity in a nuisance action brought against a county for harm caused to neighbors near its public compost site. Because of the ministerial nature of the duties of the staff operating the facility, neither the employees nor the county were entitled to immunity for their actions. However, the county was entitled to immunity on the claim of negligent failure to warn the neighbors of potential harm.

Kolbe v. State

625 N.W.2d 721 (Iowa 2001)

Lavorato, Chief Justice.

The issue here is whether the State is liable to an injured party for the State's negligence in issuing a driver's license to the person who caused the injury with his vehicle. The district court sustained the State's motion for summary judgment, concluding the State owed no duty to the injured party. We agree and affirm.

I. Background Facts and Proceedings

On June 28, 1997, Justin Allen Schulte, while driving a motor vehicle, struck Charles Leon Kolbe, who was riding a bicycle at the time. The accident occurred on Sac County road D-54 in Sac County, Iowa. As a result of the accident, Kolbe suffered severe injuries.

Schulte was driving with a restricted license, which required him to wear corrective lenses. Additionally, he was not to operate a motor vehicle in excess of forty-five miles per hour.

Schulte has a vision condition known as Stargardt's disease. Stargardt's disease results in loss of central vision and decrease in sharpness of peripheral vision. The disease is inherited and begins between the ages of 8 to 20. 2 J.E. Schmidt, M.D., *Attorney's Dictionary of Medicine and Word Finder* S-198 (1991). At the time of the accident, Schulte was eighteen.

One of Schulte's physicians, Dr. Alan Kimura, reported to the Iowa Department of Transportation (IDOT) that Schulte had Stargardt's disease and that the disease caused difficulty with central vision. At the time of this report, Dr. Kimura was an associate professor in the Department of Ophthalmology at University of Iowa Hospitals and Clinics. Dr. Kimura had diagnosed Schulte as having Stargardt's disease while Schulte was in the sixth grade.

The Stargardt's disease did not prevent Schulte from leading an active life. For example, he participated in high school athletics, did family farm chores, and worked for a construction company as a skid loader operator. He also completed a driver's education course in high school and received a "B plus" grade.

The IDOT first issued Schulte a driver's license in 1995. To receive the license, Schulte underwent a process that permitted the IDOT to issue him a license on a "discretionary basis." As part of this process, Schulte obtained recommendations from eye specialists, who performed eye examinations before recommending he receive a driver's license. The IDOT forwarded information from the eye specialists to a medical advisory board. The board is a group of doctors selected by the Iowa

Medical Society to serve anonymously as an independent source of medical review for the IDOT. The doctors all recommended issuance of a driver's license to Schulte.

As part of the process, the IDOT subjected Schulte to testing. One test consisted of an oral knowledge exam. The other was a driver's test in which Schulte had to ride with an IDOT officer in town and in the country. During that ride, Schulte had to identify road signs and vehicles on the road.

The IDOT tested Schulte again in June 1996 and on June 23, 1997—five days before the accident in question. In both instances, Schulte successfully completed a driving test with an IDOT officer. Each time Schulte had to drive during daylight, dusk, and at night in rural areas upon the highway and in the city.

In May 1998, Charles Kolbe and his wife Karen Sue filed suit against the State of Iowa and the IDOT. They alleged, among other things, that the defendants "negligently and without adequate investigation issued driving privileges" to Schulte, which negligence was a proximate cause of the accident and injuries. Karen Sue asked for loss of spousal consortium. The Kolbes later dropped the IDOT as a defendant.

Later, the district court sustained the State's motion for summary judgment. The court ruled that the State was immune from suit under the discretionary function exception of the State Tort Claims Act, *see* Iowa Code § 669.14(1) (1997). The court also ruled that the State owed no duty to the Kolbes.

On appeal, the Kolbes contend that the State has no such statutory immunity. They also contend that the State has a statutory and regulatory duty not to issue a driver's license to a person it knows or should know is, by reason of mental or physical disability, incapable of operating a motor vehicle safely. They further contend that the State breached this duty. In the alternative, the Kolbes contended the State has a common law duty to exercise ordinary care when it issues a driver's license. In this case, they contend the State breached that duty. Because we conclude there was no such duty, we need not address the immunity issue. *See Engstrom v. State*, 461 N.W.2d 309, 314 (Iowa 1990) (holding that State Tort Claims Act creates no new cause of action but merely recognizes and provides remedy for those already existing).

II. Scope of Review

....

III. Duty

To prove their negligence claim, the Kolbes must establish (1) the State owed them a duty; (2) the State breached or violated that duty; (3) this breach or violation was a proximate cause of their injuries; and (4) damages. *See Sanford v. Manternach*, 601 N.W.2d 360, 370 (Iowa 1999). When determining the existence of a duty, we are guided by "legislative enactments, prior judicial decisions, and general legal principles." *Id.*

In their petition, the Kolbes raised a variety of allegations that essentially accuse the State of (1) failing to suspend or revoke Schulte's driving privileges, (2) failing to require additional testing, (3) issuing a license when Schulte allegedly could not complete minimum testing requirements, (4) relying upon the advice of "unqualified" persons in determining whether to issue a license, and (5) issuing a license to Schulte when the State knew or should have known that Schulte could not safely operate an automobile.

These allegations involve a combination of asserted claims of negligence by the State in *failing* to perform statutory duties and *performing* such duties with lack of due care.

The Kolbes first assert the State has a statutory and regulatory duty not to issue a driver's license to an applicant who, by reason of mental or physical disability, is incapable of operating a vehicle safely. They contend the State breached this duty, which they assert is derived from Iowa Code § 321.177(7) and Iowa Administrative Code rule 761-600.4(2).

In the alternative, the Kolbes contend that common law imposes on the State a duty to exercise ordinary care when it issues a driver's license, and that in this case the State failed to exercise such care.

We begin with the Kolbes' contention that the State had a statutory and regulatory duty which it breached, and which breach gave rise to an actionable claim of negligence.

A. Statutory and Regulatory Duty

. . . .

We conclude Iowa Code section 321.177(7) and rule 761-600.4(2) provide the Kolbes with no right of action against the State. This still leaves for our consideration, however, their contention that they have a common law claim against the State.

B. Common Law Duty

The Kolbes contend that common law imposes on the State an affirmative duty to exercise ordinary care to avoid injury to persons in carrying out the functions it undertakes, whether or not those functions are mandated by statute or regulation.

Applying this reasoning here, the Kolbes argue that the statutory and administrative mandates that govern the licensing of motor vehicle operators in Iowa are for the benefit of a particularized class—rightful users of the Iowa roads. The Kolbes assert that they were members of this class at the time of the accident and for that reason the State owed them a legal duty to act with due care in carrying out such statutory and administrative mandates. They further assert that failure of the IDOT to adhere to those statutory and administrative mandates, and to otherwise act with care, creates a legal duty owed to them by the State.

The issue boils down to whether the State owed a legal duty to the Kolbes to exercise due care when it issued a driver's license to Schulte. In determining whether a defendant owes a legal duty to the plaintiff, three factors usually govern our analysis: (1) the relationship between the parties, (2) reasonable foreseeability of harm to the person who is injured, and (3) public policy considerations. *See J.A.H. v. Wadle & Assocs., P.C.*, 589 N.W.2d 256, 258 (Iowa 1999).

We use these factors under a balancing approach and not as three distinct and necessary elements. In the end, whether a duty exists is a policy decision based upon all relevant considerations that guide us to conclude a particular person is entitled to be protected from a particular type of harm. *Id.*

A linkage of a legal duty to a particular relationship between the parties is not always a requirement for actionable negligence. *See Keller v. State*, 475 N.W.2d 174, 179 (Iowa 1991). For example, such a linkage is not required when the direct consequences of a negligent act cause harm to another. *Id.* Such linkage, however, is required "for most claims based on an alleged failure of a [defendant] to aid or protect another person or to control the conduct of a third party." *Id.; see also Restatement, supra; see also* RESTATEMENT (SECOND) OF TORTS § 314 cmt. c (1965) (explaining the origin of the requirement).

Restatement (Second) Torts of section 315 is the general rule pertaining to an alleged failure of a defendant to aid or protect another person or to control the conduct of a third party. The rule provides:

> There is no duty so to control the conduct of a third person as to prevent him from causing physical harm to another unless—
>
> (a) a special relation exists between the actor and the third person which imposes a duty upon the actor to control the third person's conduct, or
>
> (b) a special relation exists between the actor and the other which gives to the other a right to protection.

RESTATEMENT (SECOND) OF TORTS § 315. We have applied the rule on several occasions. . . .

Here, the Kolbes are asserting a legal duty by virtue of an asserted special relationship between the State and them that gives them the right of protection. They do not claim a specific individualized relationship between the State and them, but rather claim membership in a specific group or class—the traveling public, or as they phrase it, the "rightful users of the roads." We note that the Kolbes do not claim a special relationship arising out of the unique or particularized facts of this case, but rather claim such a relationship is created or conferred by Iowa Code chapter 321, and in particular Iowa Code section 321.177(7).

The State disputes the assertion that these motor vehicle statutes create or confer such a special relationship. The State further contends that what we have here is nothing more than a duty owed to the general public and that by virtue of the "public duty doctrine," breach of such duty is not actionable. The Kolbes respond that even if the statutes do not confer or create a special relationship, the public duty doctrine has been eliminated in this state, and therefore they are not precluded from pursuing an action for breach of a general duty.

The public duty doctrine provides that "if a duty is owed to the public generally, there is no liability to an individual member of that group." *Wilson v. Nepstad*, 282 N.W.2d 664, 667 (Iowa 1979). The Kolbes contend that this court discarded this doctrine in *Wilson* and in *Adam v. State*, 380 N.W.2d 716 (Iowa 1986). . . .

Since *Wilson* and *Adam*, we have not expressly abolished the public duty doctrine, although we have narrowed its application. We have routinely held that a breach of duty *owed to the public at large* is not actionable *unless the plaintiff can establish, based on the unique or particular facts of the case, a special relationship between the State and the injured plaintiff* consistent with the rules of Restatement (Second) of Torts section 315. *See Sankey [v. Richenberger]*, 456 N.W.2d [206] at 209 [(Iowa 1990)]. Our holdings have been "consistent with the principle that public employees share the same—but not greater—liability to injured parties as other defendants under like circumstances." *Id.* The duty to the public can either arise from a statute or from the State's obligation to protect the public at large. *See Fitzpatrick v. State*, 439 N.W.2d 663, 667 (Iowa 1989) (holding that although State had duty to keep felons in custody which obligation flowed to the public at large, State had no legal duty to police officer injured by parolee given lack of special relationship between State and victim).

We agree with the State that the licensing provisions in Iowa Code chapter 321, and more specifically Iowa Code section 321.177(7), are for the benefit of the public at large. Accordingly, we reject the Kolbes' contention that they can avoid the preclusive effect of the public duty doctrine by claiming membership to a special, identifiable group for whose benefit the statutes were enacted. Furthermore, as mentioned, the Kolbes do not claim a special relationship arising out of the particular facts of this case. For these reasons, we conclude that there are no facts establishing a special relationship upon which the Kolbes' claims of liability may be premised.

Additionally, we think public policy considerations support our determination that the State is not liable for negligently issuing a driver's license when there is no special relationship existing between the State and the victim. We reach this conclusion even though it is reasonably foreseeable such negligent action might result in harm to a highway user.

One such policy consideration is that our rule is consistent with the principle that the State "shares the same—but not greater—liability to injured parties as other defendants under like circumstances." *Sankey*, 456 N.W.2d at 209; *see also* Iowa Code § 669.2(3)(a) (providing that under the State Tort Claims Act, the State's exposure in tort does not go beyond that of a private person).

A recognition of the tort for "negligent issuance of a driver's license" would likely chill the State's licensing determinations, making it unreasonably difficult for certain segments of our society to secure a driver's license. Senior citizens with declining vision and visually impaired citizens, both of whom would ordinarily pass existing stringent state requirements, would face the possibility of not driving at all.

A similar policy consideration prompted one court to refuse to recognize the tort of negligent issuance of a driver's license. *See Ryan v. State*, 420 A.2d 841, 843 (R.I. 1980). At issue in that case was a statute that allowed the State to reinstate revoked licenses of those drivers whom it considered safe. *Id.* In refusing to recognize a duty running from the State to individual members of the public for negligently reinstating a driver, the court said:

> In enacting [the statute] the Legislature intended to empower the [State] to withhold reinstatement after examining the applicant's driving record. Thus, the statute clearly has as its purpose the protection of the public at large. We are unable to conclude, however, that the Legislature intended to create a duty running to individual members of the public. We are not convinced that the Legislature intended such a drastic result when it enacted [the statute]. *Furthermore, such a drastic remedy would likely deter the [State] from reinstating any drivers under [the statute].* [*Id.* (citations omitted) (emphasis added).]

In *Johnson v. Indian River School District*, the court noted that allowing the tort of negligent issuance of a driver's license "would generate a drastic expansion of liability" and "[s]ince the [m]otor vehicle field is highly regulated by state statute, such a significant policy change, if warranted, should be made by the General Assembly, not the courts." 723 A.2d 1200, 1203 (Del. Super. 1998). Here, the motor vehicle field is similarly highly regulated. We too think the policy decision to impose liability should be the legislature's choice, not ours.

IV. Disposition

In sum, we conclude that neither statutory nor common law gives rise to an actionable claim for negligent issuance of a driver's license. Accordingly, the district court was correct in sustaining the State's motion for summary judgment.

AFFIRMED.

Notes and Questions

1. *Rationale for public duty rule.* As discussed in the principal case, the public duty rule generally has been applied to deny municipal or state tort liability for harm resulting from the provision of public services, particularly as to public safety and emergency personnel. The public duty rule has also been applied to protect governments from suits for negligence involving the enforcement of regulatory provisions (such as licensing requirements and land use regulation). Compare *McDowell v. Sapienza*, 906 N.W.2d 399 (S.D. 2018) (public duty rule barring liability for negligence in building inspections applied and special duty doctrine did not apply in suit involving allegations of negligent building code inspection to property subject to

historic preservation requirement), with *Maher v. City of Box Elder*, 925 N.W.2d 482 (S.D. 2019) (city owed duty to owner of mobile home park to use reasonable care in operating city's water system). The "public duty doctrine" is a judicially-created doctrine that protects governmental units from liability unless an injured person can show that the duty breached was a duty owed to the individual himself, and not merely to the public at large. In your view, is this exception to liability sound? Under what circumstances should it apply (to public safety services, building inspections, or both)?

2. *Interplay of public duty doctrine and immunity doctrine.* It is important initially to understand the interplay of governmental immunity and public duty doctrine, since in important respects, the public duty doctrine steps in to limit liability in situations in which the potential for liability might arise given the application of the government immunity doctrine. There is a significant risk of confusion relating to the overlapping application of these doctrines. For example, the public duty doctrine may protect government entities from liability in instances in which there is willful misconduct, even though willful misconduct would not give rise to immunity under traditional governmental immunity doctrine. Do you see distinctive rationales for these two doctrinal concepts? Is the "public duty doctrine" simply a special exception to the government immunity doctrine, or is it something else going on?

3. *Competing viewpoints in other states.* In the years since the *Kolbe* decision, the Iowa Supreme Court has repeatedly confirmed its commitment to the viability of the public duty doctrine. *Johnson v. Humboldt County*, 913 N.W.2d 256 (Iowa 2018) (reaffirming public duty doctrine in case in which vehicular passenger went off road and into ditch, striking concrete embankment). There remains a significant split among the states, however. Even as Iowa has continued to maintain the doctrine, Illinois has rejected both the public duty doctrine and the related special duty doctrine. See *Coleman v. E. Joliet Fire Prot. Dist.* (*In re Estate of Coleman*), 46 N.E.3d 741 (Ill. 2016). *Coleman* concerned a claim by the decedent's estate, based on alleged willful and wanton conduct by the fire protection district, ambulance personnel, a "911" operator and dispatcher, and local county in connection with an emergency call for medical assistance where the initial operator and the dispatcher failed to give and receive relevant information. The Illinois Supreme Court conducted an extensive review of case law and legislation affecting the vitality of the doctrine, *id.* at 754, before concluding that it was appropriate to overrule it in that state. It cited three principal reasons for this outcome: prior caselaw was inconsistent and muddled, the legislature had granted only limited immunity in cases of willful and wanton conduct, and the legislature's adoption of statutory immunities had rendered the doctrine obsolete. *Id.* at 756. Can a principled and intelligible body of governmental tort liability law be developed to deal with situations when the public duty rule might be applied, or should such concepts as the "public duty" rule be abandoned as unworkable? Do you agree with the Iowa or Illinois viewpoint?

4. *Special duty.* What is the basis for the "special duty" exception to the "public duty" rule? In Massachusetts, the special duty exception was applied to find a municipality liable for a police officer's negligence in failing to prohibit an intoxicated motorist from continuing to drive on a highway. The court stated that "[t]he statutes which establish police responsibilities . . . evidence a legislative intent to protect both intoxicated persons and other users of the highway." *Irwin v. Town of Ware*, 467 N.E.2d 1292 (Mass. 1984). Several years later the Massachusetts court announced its intention to do away with the public duty rule as inconsistent with the State Tort Claims Act. See *Jean W. v. Commonwealth*, 610 N.E.2d 305 (Mass. 1993). In response, the Massachusetts legislature adopted amendments to the Tort Claims Act that codified the public duty rule and the special duty exception. MASS GEN. L. c. 258, § 10(j); *Brum v. Town of Dartmouth*, 704 N.E.2d 1147, 1155 (Mass. 1999) ("principal purpose of § 10(j) is to preclude liability for failures to prevent or diminish harm, including harm brought about by the wrongful act of a third party"). Subsequently, the Massachusetts Supreme Judicial Court concluded that school districts were not liable for school bullying. See *Cormier v. City of Lynn*, 91 N.E.3d 662 (Mass. 2018) (no special duty arising from failure to act). Do you think allowing drunken drivers to use the highway is different from giving someone disabled a license to operate a car, as was true in the principal case?

As noted in connection with the *Coleman* case discussed in a prior Note, injuries in the aftermath of calls to "911" lines can raise questions under the public duty doctrine, but have frequently raised issues about the special duty exception (and sometimes the special relationship doctrine) as well. Compare *De Long v. County of Erie*, 455 N.Y.S.2d 887 (App. Div. 1982) (local governments assumed a special duty of care toward person calling 911), with *Grieshaber v. City of Albany*, 720 N.Y.S.2d 214 (App. Div. 2001) (no special relationship unless justifiable reliance by individual who called "911"), and *Kinsey v. City of New York*, 36 N.Y.S.3d 8 (App. Div. 2016) (no special duty on part of EMT and police personnel who answered "911" call and moved mentally ill individual into ambulance before the individual escaped and ultimately died in fall from roof). Note that the second case (along with others addressing "911" calls) applied the "special relationship" doctrine, considered below. Can you see why? Other courts have reached similar conclusions. See *Munich v. Skagit Emergency Communication Center*, 288 P.3d 328 (Wash. 2012) (en banc) (in suit by decedent's estate alleging negligence in handling 911 emergency call concerning threats by neighbor who subsequently shot decedent, explaining that duty under special relationship exception to public duty doctrine arose without regard to whether representations by "911" operator were true or false, and further observing that no liability for a public actor will arise unless plaintiff establishes elements of tort, including breach of duty, proximate cause, and damages).

Does the test defining the existence of a special duty matter? See *Tipton v. Town of Tabor*, 538 N.W.2d 783, 787 (S.D. 1995) (*Tipton I*) (adopting four-part analytical approach requiring (1) actual knowledge by the government of a dangerous condition, (2) reasonable reliance on the government's representations and conduct, (3) an ordinance or statute establishing mandatory procedures "clearly for the protection of a particular class of persons rather than the public as a whole," and (4) failure of the government to use due care to avoid increasing the risk of harm; but refusing to find a special duty in a case involving an attack by a dog because none of the four factors was present); *Sabia v. State*, 669 A.2d 1187, 1191–92 (Vt. 1995) (applying four-part test grounded in statutory language mandating specific acts to protect a particular class of persons and finding a special duty to assist children seeking protection from child abuse). For an argument that recognition of a "special duty" as a basis for governmental tort liability is a "just compromise" see Comment, *The Special Duty Doctrine: A Just Compromise*, 31 St. Louis U. L.J. 409 (1987). See also Markowitz, *Municipal Liability for Negligent Inspection and Failure to Enforce Safety Codes*, 15 Hamline J. Pub. L. & Pol'y 181 (1994) (finding that reported cases, in which the special duty exception actually is applied to hold a municipality liable for failure to enforce safety codes or for negligent inspections, are rare).

5. *Special relationship.* Many courts have held that a special relationship between the local government and a claimant creates an exception to the public duty rule of non-liability. The court in the principal case rejected the argument that the motor vehicle laws of Iowa created a special relationship between the state and the "rightful users of the roads." The New York Court of Appeals similarly refused to find a special relationship in a case involving a failure of a family day care center to register as required by state law where there was no contractual or other obligation arising between the litigant and the city. See *McLean v. City of New York*, 905 N.E.2d 1167 (N.Y. 2009).

How would you describe the differences between the "special duty" and "special relationship" exceptions to the public duty rule? Typically, "special relationships" arise in situations such as when explicit understandings are reached that protection will be provided to police informants, and an informant justifiably relies on the affirmative representations given by a government actor. Consider the views expressed by the court in *Francis v. State*, 321 P.3d 1089 (Utah 2013) (in negligence suit alleging failure to warn of danger, parents of camper who was killed by black bear while camping sued state; court determined that bear was not a "natural condition" on publicly-owned or controlled land for purposes of state tort claims act, and concluded that there was a "special relationship" between camper and state agency that gave rise to "special duty," since state employees had tried to track bear and were aware of its dangerousness). Was the court's resolution correct? Compare *Francis* with *Simmons v. Sanpete County*, 321 P.3d 1089 (Utah App. 2018) (holding that public duty rule applied and special relationship doctrine did not apply, where third party called to alert authorities to remove a deer carcass from a state road, and subsequent motorist hit carcass and careened across the highway killing an oncoming driver, based on conclusion that situation reflected inaction by the county and no "special relationship" in the absence of detrimental reliance by decedent who had no contact with authorities).

In another New York case, *Valdez v. City of New York*, 936 N.Y.S.2d 587 (N.Y. 2011), the court articulated a four-part test for finding municipal liability based upon a special relationship, including proof that (1) the municipality had assumed an affirmative duty, through its promises or action, to act on behalf of the party who was injured, (2) there was knowledge on the part of the municipality's agents that inaction could lead to harm, (3) some form of direct contact between the municipality's agents and the injured party had occurred, and (4) there had been justifiable reliance on the municipality's affirmative undertaking. How do these factors compare with the factors adopted in the *Tipton* case, *supra*? In *Valdez*, the plaintiff asserted that she had told police that her former boyfriend had threatened to shoot her. She was advised by police that the boyfriend would be arrested immediately and that she could return to her apartment. The court found no special relationship with the police when the complainant was shot 28 hours after talking with them. In the court's view, it was not reasonable for the complainant to relax her vigilance indefinitely and exit her apartment at that time with no further contact with police. Moreover, there was no indication that the complainant knew where her former boyfriend was calling from or that she had provided information about his whereabouts to the police. What do you think of the court's test? Was the court's application of that test well-grounded? Return to the Problem at the start of this Chapter. How should it be resolved?

6. *Other exceptions to the public duty rule.* In addition to the "special relationship" and "special duty" exceptions, courts have recognized exceptions to the public duty rule in cases where legislation extends a governmental duty to a specific group of persons (the "legislative intent" exception), responsible government officials fail to respond in cases where they have a duty to do so (the "failure to enforce" exception), or governments or their agents undertake to warn or rescue and fail to exercise reasonable care (the "rescue doctrine" exception). For a review of these exceptions, see *Vergeson v. Kitsap County*, 186 P.3d 1140, 1146–47 (Wash. App. 2008).

7. *Punitive damages.* Punitive or exemplary damages will not be awarded against a state or municipality unless authorized by statute. Punitive damages are intended to inflict punishment for wrongdoing and deter similar conduct. Who would actually bear the burden if punitive damages were assessed against a state or local government? See *Chappell v. Springfield*, 423 S.W.2d 810 (Mo. 1968). See also *City of Newport v. Fact Concerts, Inc.*, 453 U.S. 247 (1981), discussed *infra*. Statutes adding interest to judgments from the day on which the verdict was rendered have been held applicable to judgments against political subdivisions. *Lucius v. City of Memphis*, 925 S.W.2d 522 (Tenn. 1996).

8. *Insurance as a means of limiting liability.* Local governments have sought to contain their exposure to liability in a number of ways, including agreeing to be sued but only insofar as they have waived immunity to the extent of their insurance coverage, see, e.g., Ark. Code Ann. § 21-9-303 (only applies to motor vehicle insurance); S.D. Code Ann. § 21-32A-1 (monetary limitations on damages). Some have been successful; others have not. For example, in *Smith v. Philadelphia*, 516 A.2d

306 (Pa. 1986), the Supreme Court of Pennsylvania upheld a statute imposing a $500,000 aggregate limitation on recovery of damages against political subdivisions. In rejecting an equal protection challenge based on the fact that there is no similar limitation against private parties, the court applied a "heightened" standard of review and concluded that "preservation of the public treasury as against the possibility of unusually large recoveries in tort cases is . . . an important governmental interest" that was closely related to the classification in question. *Id.* at 311. While the personal right to receive a full recovery in a tort suit against a political subdivision was an "important interest," it was not a "fundamental right" requiring strict scrutiny because it had already been limited by a state constitutional provision construed by the court as authorizing the state legislature to limit recovery against governmental units. The Pennsylvania Commonwealth Court also upheld a statute requiring persons to sue governmental tortfeasors within six months, while allowing two years for the commencement of suits against non-governmental tortfeasors. *James v. Southeastern Pa. Transp. Auth.*, 477 A.2d 1302 (Pa. 1984). Important scholarship has addressed issues concerning insurance, including insurance relating to police liability that may arise under state or federal law. See, e.g., Rappaport, *How Private Insurers Regulate Public Police,* 130 Harv. L. Rev. 1539 (2017).

On the other hand, the Supreme Court of Iowa, applying a rational basis standard, struck down a statute requiring suit to be filed against a governmental unit within six months, unless a notice of intent to sue is filed within 60 days. The court found the resultant classification to be arbitrary, in part because "local governments 'rarely budget for claims but carry liability insurance as the statutes permit. . . .'" *Miller v. Boone County Hospital*, 394 N.W.2d 776 (Iowa 1986). Which approach is more persuasive?

For a proposal that states should fund a municipal tort insurance program through state income taxes and impose a state regulatory scheme mandating standards for education and training of municipal officials see Hackney, *A Proposal for State Funding of Municipal Tort Liability*, 98 Yale L.J. 389 (1988). The author argues that decentralized systems of municipal insurance coverage funded by regressive local property and sales taxes are inadequate and are threatened by sharp increases in liability insurance premiums. See also Rynard, *The Local Government as Insured or Insurer: Some New Risk Management Alternatives*, 20 Urb. Law. 103 (1988). Another approach would be for states to set caps on tort awards. See Findley, *Statutory Tort Caps: What States Should Do When Available Funds Seem Inadequate*, 46 Ind. L. Rev. 849 (2013). In the event that local governments may face liability for regulatory takings arising in connection with climate change, new insurance strategies to address such risks are likely to become more widespread. See Serkin, *Strategic Land Use Litigation: Pleading Around Municipal Insurance*, 43 B.C. Envtl. Aff. L. Rev. 463 (2016).

Of course, reliance on insurance contracts requires careful attention to be paid to the specific language of the policies. See, e.g., *Cowell v. Gaston County*, 660 S.E.2d 915, 920 (N.C. App. 2008), holding that Gaston County waived immunity from suit because of alleged negligence of its building inspectors through its purchase of an insurance policy. The court concluded that there were "multiple ambiguities in the . . . policy endorsement, and based upon established rules of contract interpretation, these ambiguities must be construed against [the insurance company] (and therefore against defendant's arguments), and in favor of liability coverage."

A Note on the Immunity of Public Officials

The discussion to date has focused on the potential liability of local governments and state agencies for tortious acts committed by their associated public officials and employees. Remember that, where sovereign immunity has been abolished, specific legislation or common law reforms have modified the extent to which government entities or agencies are themselves liable (or have immunity or public duty defenses that remain). In such litigation, governmental officials may be included as defendants who are joined "in their official capacity" perhaps if declaratory or injunctive relief is sought, with or without damages.

Organizational versus personal liability. This Note considers a somewhat different question: when may government officials or employees themselves be *sued personally*, asserting *personal* liability stemming from allegedly tortious conduct? Can you think of any reasons why a plaintiff might take this approach? Perhaps an official or employee was acting outside the scope of public employment (a police officer moonlighting as a private security guard or taking official equipment for personal use that results in an injury). Perhaps an officer or employee might be covered by a different insurance policy with different limitations than the policy covering the government itself (for example an individual's policy might have different limits than the town's institutional insurance policy). Perhaps the plaintiff wants vindication because they feel personally wronged by a particular government officer or employee ("the mayor personally interfered with the approval of my development project").

Official immunity: a complex calculus for executive branch personnel? Consider, to begin, whether the defenses (including immunities) available to public officers and employees in their personal capacity should be different from those covering the government they serve. In your view, what policy factors should influence common law or legislative frameworks for determining liability for government officials and employees sued in their personal capacity? Should the type of alleged tort (intentional torts such as false imprisonment versus negligence, for example) or the nature of the job (police officers versus teachers) affect how such personnel are treated? Bear in mind that this Note considers that question as a matter of state tort law, whereas "A Note on Legislative and Official Immunity" later in the Chapter considers similar questions relating to federal law, particularly with regard to liability under 42 U.S.C. § 1983, a federal civil rights statute enacted after the Civil War.

Then consider the use of terminology. When the term "official immunity" is used, it can give rise to a fair degree of confusion, particularly if care is not taken to distinguish nuances of state and federal law and differences among the three branches of government. As used with specificity in this Note, the phrase refers to a defense that may be asserted by government officers and employees in the executive branch if they are sued in their personal capacity by a plaintiff asserting tort liability under state law. Although this area of the law is very complex and varies significantly from state to state, framing key trends in terms of four basic approaches should prove helpful.

(a) *Immunity based on principles similar to immunity for government entities, with twists.* Some states recognize "official immunity" when an employee who is sued in a personal capacity acts within the scope of his official duties, particularly when those duties are without doubt governmental in character. For example, in *Brown v. Town of Chapel Hill*, 756 S.E.2d 749 (N.C. App. 2014), the Court of Appeals reversed a denial of summary judgment sought by a police officer sued in his personal capacity allegedly for making a false arrest after an outstanding warrant had been canceled without the officer's knowledge. The court noted that the police officer had acted based on the judgment and discretion with which he was invested by virtue of his office, kept within the scope of his official authority, and acted without malice or corruption. Other courts may simply treat the employee and the town as deserving of similar immunity, without clearly distinguishing whether the employee was sued in an official or personal capacity. See, e.g., *Hermer v. Dover*, 215 A.2d 693 (N.H. 1965) (in suit for declaratory relief and damages, concluding that both city and building inspector were immune from tort damages following the wrongful closing of a retail store by order of the building inspector, when the building inspector was performing a governmental function at the time, even though building inspector not listed as individual defendant).

In many states, the courts focus on whether the official or employee's decisions or actions were "discretionary," but "discretionary" is at times an ambiguous concept as you have seen earlier in this Chapter. Consider an example from Minnesota. In *Nusbaum v. Blue Earth County*, 422 N.W.2d 713 (Minn. 1988), the court found in a negligence suit against the county and state that placement of speed signs at the end of a speed zone did not involve a discretionary function that would have given rise to immunity for the governmental entities. The court took considerable pains to state in dicta that "[t]he tort immunity of a governmental unit provided by the discretionary function exception of the state and municipal tort claims acts should be distinguished from common law immunity of a government employee" because "[i]mmunity of an employee honestly exercising discretion under common law was based in the notion that imposition of liability for an erroneous decision would inhibit decisionmaking." *Id.* at 718 n.4.

Considering types of cases by subject matter can also provide useful insights. Take, for example, the conduct of public safety personnel. You will remember from your earlier reading that courts have recognized the "public duty doctrine" as a means to block state tort liability for asserted failures of such personnel to protect plaintiffs injured by third parties when public safety personnel have not intervened to prevent injuries. Similar or broader protection against liability is typically available under the "official immunity" doctrine to protect public safety personnel from individual liability. *Everitt v. GE*, 932 A.2d 831 (N.H. 2007), provides a good example. There, the New Hampshire court applied the official immunity doctrine to protect police officers who were sued for negligence after releasing an individual to whom they had administered a field sobriety test. The person released was subsequently involved in a car accident. The court was particularly helpful in setting out relevant policy considerations, stating that "encouraging independent police judgment for the protection and welfare of the citizenry at large must prevail over ensuring common law civil recourse for individuals who may be injured by errant police decisions. . . . Municipal police officers are immune from personal liability for decisions, acts or omissions that: (1) are made within the scope of their official duties while in the course of their employment; (2) discretionary, rather than ministerial; and (3) not made in a wanton or reckless manner." *Id.* at 938. For a suit involving fire personnel, see *Chirieleison v. Lucas*, 72 A.3d 1218 (Conn. App. 2013) (in suit against town fire truck driver, where driver had parked fire truck in center lane and set out flares on interstate highway to reduce hazards when responding to an earlier traffic incident, court concluded that decision about how to proceed was "discretionary activity" drawing on fire truck driver's experience and judgment; estate of decedent who had crossed line of warning flares and hit fire truck parked in center lane therefore could not prevail).

Note that the courts routinely emphasize that there is no official immunity for public officers and employees who have acted outside the scope of their duties or who have acted with malice. A good example is provided by *Medeiros v. Kondo*, 522 P.2d 1269 (Hawai'i 1974). There, a civil service employee alleged that the director of the state department of taxation had maliciously harassed and humiliated him. The court concluded that the director was not immune from tort liability if he had acted maliciously, but held the plaintiff to a higher than normal standard of proof (of malice) in order to afford some protection to innocent public officers.

(b) *Good faith immunity similar to "qualified immunity" under federal law.* Some states apply an approach to official immunity that mirrors that referred to as "qualified immunity" for officers and employees under federal civil rights law. Texas is one such jurisdiction. See *City of Lancaster v. Chambers*, 883 S.W.2d 650, 653 (Tex. 1994) (in case involving high-speed police chase, explaining that "Government employees are entitled to official immunity from suit arising from the performance of their (1) discretionary duties in (2) good faith as long as they are (3) acting within the scope of their authority"). Defining "good faith" is not always easy. In the case of police engaged in a high-speed pursuit, the court concluded that "an officer acts in good faith in a pursuit case if a reasonably prudent officer, under the same or similar circumstances, could have believed that the need to immediately apprehend the suspect outweighed a clear risk of harm to the public in continuing the pursuit"). *Id.* at 656. The test "is derived substantially from the test that has emerged under federal immunity law for claims of qualified immunity in § 1983 cases" and is one of "objective legal reasonableness, without regard to whether the government official involved acted with subjective good faith." It protects "all but the plainly incompetent or those who knowingly violate the law." *Id.* See also *Bachner Co. v. Weed*, 315 P.3d 1184 (Alaska 2013) (applying good faith qualified immunity standard for purposes of official immunity determination in case involving discretionary action by bidding committee alleged to have tortuously interfered with economic advantage of prospective contractor).

(c) *Immunity based on nature of position.* In Pennsylvania, "high public officials" enjoy absolute immunity when acting officially within the scope of their authority, while lesser officials have a conditional immunity which is available when they are acting both within the scope of their authority and without malice or recklessness. *DuBree v. Commonwealth*, 303 A.2d 530 (Pa. 1973). The test of whether one is a "high" public official depends on the nature of the official duties, particularly whether they involve policymaking. In *DuBree*, the Secretary of Highways and possibly several subordinates, including the district engineer and superintendent of maintenance, were found to be high public officials. The Michigan court followed a similar approach in *Petipren v. Jaskowski*, 833 N.W.2d 247 (Mich. 2013) (in case against village police chief for negligence and intentional infliction of emotional distress, concluding that police chief was "highest appointive executive official" who was entitled to absolute immunity even when performing low-level duties typically carried about by subordinate; in reaching this conclusion, court interpreted state tort claims act, MICH. COMP. LAWS § 691.1407(5) which reads: "A judge, a legislator, and the elective or highest appointive executive official of all levels of government are immune from tort liability for injuries to persons or damages to property if he or she is acting within the scope of his or her judicial, legislative, or executive authority.").

(d) *Statutory solutions.* Sometimes express statutory provisions modify common law standards. Some directly address the personal liability of government officers and employees. See Annotation, 163 A.L.R. 1435 (1946). Others very specifically address areas of potential personal liability and set specific standards for personal liability. For example, a number of states set statutory rules for high-speed police chases or other dangerous situations which may create potential liability but only in the event of a higher standard of neglect, in effect acknowledging that such actions are outside the scope of responsible conduct while on duty and should be deterred. See, e.g., N.C. GEN. STAT. § 166A-46 (applying "good faith" standard for officers rendering aid pursuant to emergency management compact, but excepting actions that reflect gross negligence). For another useful example, see GA. CODE § 46-5-131 (immunity for emergency telephone number "9-1-1 System").

[4] Inverse Condemnation

Courts wishing to impose liability for injurious damages arising out of governmental conduct have also developed another doctrine from the "taking" clauses of state constitutions, which require compensation to be paid when private property is taken or damaged by public entities. The doctrine was first articulated with regard to the federal Constitution's "takings" clause by Justice Douglas in *United States v. Causby*, 328 U.S. 256 (1946). There the Court held that a "taking" equivalent to the imposition of a servitude had occurred based on the continuous nuisance-light flights by military aircraft engaged in taking off and landing from a nearby airport, when these activities adversely affected a privately-owned dwelling and chicken farm. Justice Douglas explained the Court's reasoning as follows:

> We have said that the airspace is a public highway. Yet it is obvious that if the landowner is to have full enjoyment of the land, he must have exclusive control of the immediate reaches of the enveloping atmosphere. Otherwise buildings could not be erected, trees could not be planted, and even fences could not be run. The principle is recognized when the law gives a remedy in case overhanging structures are erected on adjoining land. The landowner owns at least as much of the space above the ground as he can occupy or use in connection with the land.... The fact that he does not occupy it in a physical sense—by the erection of buildings and the like—is not material. As we have said, the flight of airplanes, which skim the surface but do not touch it, is as much an appropriation of the use of the land as a more conventional entry upon it. We would not doubt that, if the United States erected an elevated railway over respondents' land at the precise altitude where its planes now fly, there would be a partial taking, even though none of the supports of the structure rested on the land. The reason is that there would be an intrusion so immediate and direct as to subtract from the owner's full enjoyment of the property and to limit his exploitation of it. While the owner does not in any physical manner occupy that stratum of airspace or make use of it in the conventional sense, he does use it in somewhat the same sense that space left between buildings for the purpose of light and air is used. The super adjacent airspace at this low altitude is so close to the land that continuous invasions of it affect the use of the surface of the land itself. We think that the landowner, as an incident to his ownership, has a claim to it and that invasions of it are in the same category as invasions of the surface. [*Id.* at 264–265.]

As the following case and notes indicate, the taking and damaging clauses have given rise to so-called actions in reverse eminent domain or inverse condemnation, in which compensation for the taking or damaging of property can be awarded after the fact. *Inverse* condemnation refers to court actions brought by the adversely affected private party against the government for actions that result in limiting use of private property and thus are to be contrasted with "eminent domain" proceedings through which the government itself acts to condemn property or an interest in property for "public use."

V.T.C. Lines, Inc. v. City of Harlan

313 S.W.2d 573 (Ky. App. 1957)

Moreman, Chief Justice.

Appellant, V. T. C. Lines, Inc., a common carrier of passengers for hire, has its bus station and garage located across the street from a swimming pool owned and operated as a recreational facility by the city of Harlan. Appellant filed complaint in the Harlan Circuit Court and alleged that for several days in the spring of 1953, the city cleaned its swimming pool by sand-blasting it with the result that the emery dust used, settled in great quantities in and on the bus station and garage and caused damage to the working parts of the diesel engines which were used in the buses. It was explained that diesel engines do not have electrically operated ignition systems, that the motors are started by forcing air into the cylinders in large quantities so that the temperature of the air, because of the compression, becomes very hot and causes the fuel to ignite and the cylinders to fire. It was averred that the polluted air caused great wear and tear in the metal and moving parts of the automobile engines and destroyed their usefulness and life.

Appellee filed answer which set up, among other defense, that the damages, if any, resulted from the exercise of a governmental function.

The city filed a motion for summary judgment and the court, being of the opinion that

> [t]he ground for sustaining the motion for summary judgment is based on the proposition that the City being an arm of the state government and the acts complained of being in the nature of a governmental function and that the property claimed to have been injured being personal property and not such property that may have been condemned pursuant to section 242 of the Kentucky Constitution, the plaintiff has no cause of action against the City. *Davis v. The City of Lebanon*, 108 Ky. 688 [57 S.W. 471], dismissed appellant's complaint.

Appellant has based its right to recover upon § 242 of the Kentucky Constitution which reads:

> Municipal and other corporations, and individuals invested with the privilege of taking private property for public use, shall make just compensation for property taken, injured or destroyed by them; which compensation shall be paid before such taking, or paid or secured, at the election of such corporation or individual, before such injury or destruction. . . .

This section, which did not appear in the Constitution of 1850, is an extension to municipalities, and others, of the limitations placed on a sovereign. It extends also to "injuring or destroying," while section 13 is confined solely to "taking." The constitutional protection against a "taking" by the sovereign state is found in section 13 of the Constitution and reads, "nor shall any man's property be taken or applied to public use without the consent of his representatives, and without just compensation being previously made to him."

We have found these sections to be self-executing and in cases where property has been appropriated, the owner, despite a lack of statutory authority, has been permitted to recover damages. A suit, which seeks to recover damages after land has been taken, has been termed "a retroactive condemnation of land." . . . And, "a condemnation [suit] in reverse." . . .

The seriousness of the question here involved arises from the fact that there are several rights which stem from the principle that private rights must yield to the general public welfare.

To understand the various rights, we must remember that in the beginning the power of a sovereign was absolute and each ruler had complete ownership of all land and complete domination over the lives and property of his subjects to the extent that he could capriciously take either. The right of eminent domain is a vestige of that despotism and was attributed to the sovereign long before this commonwealth existed.

The constitutional provisions which we have quoted are in the nature of limitations rather than grants of right because they restrict the sovereign to taking only where reimbursement is made. We have also retained recognition of the ancient sovereign immunity which denied to citizens the right to recover for deliberate or negligent acts of the sovereign.

At the same time we have recognized that which we call police power is a separate and valid authority of the state, the only difference being that eminent domain authorizes or permits taking without the consent of the owner upon compensation being paid to him, while police power authorizes regulation and destruction of property without compensation if it promotes the general welfare of the citizens. . . . This police power is harsh in execution and permits the destruction of private property in event of necessity, such as war. It is under this power that the government exercises its right of taxation.

The third theory, which our cases seem to entwine with the eminent domain and the police power theories, is that which relates to the immunity of a sovereign to answer for negligent acts committed by it, unless that immunity has been waived.

This immunity arises not in connection with eminent domain or police power, but from the primitive right, which absolute sovereigns had, to be free from the consequences of any act, and exists separate and apart from the other two theories.

All three of these subjects are based upon a primitive conception of sovereign immunity and each one, under our present development and softening of the law, should be considered distinctly. We should not borrow from the eminent domain theory of compensation for injury or damage and apply it to either of the other two premises.

It would then seem to be a simple thing, to conclude that under § 242 a recovery may be had only when property is taken for a public use and then only in cases where the property itself is of the character which may be devoted to public use. This distinction was pointed out in *T. B. Jones & Co. v. Ferro Concrete Construction Co.*, 154 Ky. 47, 156 S.W. 1060, 1062, where, in connection with § 242, it was said:

> In other words, the provision has reference to property taken under the power of eminent domain; it has no reference to property which was not taken and could not be taken under the power of eminent domain. It is not the purpose of the constitutional provision to make municipal corporations liable for all injuries to property inflicted by the negligence of their servants, irrespective of the fact that the corporation was in this work acting as an arm of the state government and discharging a governmental function.

In subsequent cases this distinction is not too clear. In *City of Louisville v. Hehemann*, 161 Ky. 523, 171 S.W. 165, L.R.A. 1915C, 747 it was held that a city, in maintaining a garbage dump in such condition that it was annoying and dangerous to the residents in the vicinity, was, under § 242, liable for injury to the property rights of a neighboring resident. In *Jefferson County v. Bischoff*, 238 Ky. 176, 37 S.W.2d 24, a recovery was allowed for damages to a neighboring home for injury to the property and for interference with its occupancy as a home by reason of the operation of a rock quarry by the county in connection with the construction and maintenance of its roads. Each of these cases apparently involves the maintenance of a nuisance, and a nuisance and an act of negligence are not always the same. But neither of these cases is predicated on the theory that private property was deliberately taken for public use and that the damage was incidental to the taking.

In *Commonwealth v. Moore*, Ky., 267 S.W.2d 531, 532, owners of property which adjoined a highway right-of-way sought damages from the commonwealth allegedly caused by the construction of a highway which destroyed appellees' tobacco crop by reason of the fact that large quantities of dust settled on the tobacco. The actual taking of land was involved from the outset because plaintiffs had voluntarily conveyed a portion of their property for a right-of-way. The court held that when property is appropriated for public use, the compensation to which a landowner is entitled embraces consequential damage to his remaining land and includes damage from the debris that was tossed upon it. The court concluded:

> It is our opinion that the damage caused to appellees was of a consequential nature incident to the prudent and proper exercise of the Commonwealth's right to use the property it acquired for highway purposes. It did not constitute a new taking of their property and consequently they should not have been permitted to recover compensation in these actions.

While this case does not recognize that the damage may have been the result of a negligent act or, for that matter, may have been the result of a nuisance created by the Department of Highways, still recovery was denied even though the act which caused the damage was a positive one which had occurred after the acquisition of the right-of-way was consummated.

It is somewhat difficult to reconcile the theory of this case with that previously announced in *Commonwealth v. Kelley*, 314 Ky. 581, 236 S.W.2d 695, 697, in which case Kelley bought a house on the south side of Highway 460. On the north side of the highway opposite Kelley's house was a ditch into which water drained from a hillside. A culvert lay under the road and emptied at the corner of Kelley's property. When there were heavy rains the water overflowed onto Kelley's property. Kelley sued for damages. There was evidence that the commonwealth had permitted the culvert to become choked with stones, branches and other materials. Even though Kelley had purchased the house after the culverts, ditches, et cetera, had been constructed, we authorized recovery and, after a discussion of sovereign immunity, said:

> The appellants argue that to show a "taking" of property, the petition must state facts from which the court may infer a total ouster from possession, or at least a substantial deprivation of all beneficial use of the land affected. It seems to us, however, that an interference with the legally protected use to which land has been dedicated, which destroys that use or places a substantial and additional burden on the landowner to maintain that use, is a "taking" of his property.

In *Department of Highways v. Corey*, Ky., 247 S.W.2d 389, 390, a case similar in fact to the *Kelley* case, we reaffirmed our position and stated:

> Unless the physical damage detailed in the testimony is of such a nature as to amount to a "taking" of property for a public purpose without just compensation, for which the State's sovereign immunity from suit is waived by Sections 13 and 242 of the Constitution, Mrs. Corey was not entitled to a judgment in her favor, and her petition should have been dismissed because the State is immune to such a suit for negligence.

The petition was based on negligent construction of culverts.

In *Commonwealth v. Geary*, Ky., 254 S.W.2d 477, it was again stated that such an action which is in the nature of a trespass could be maintained although we observed that the court had traveled a somewhat circuitous route in order to justify recovery on the theory that the property had been taken without just compensation.

The distinction made in the last quotation above seems to lack a foundation because whenever property is physically damaged, it is taken to that extent and the circuitous route which we have traveled seems to lead us inevitably to the rule that whenever any property is damaged by a sovereign, whether it is the result of common acts of negligence or is related to the exercise of eminent domain or of police power, damages must be paid by the sovereign.

We have discussed at length a few of the great number of decided cases on this point because we believe the whole group discloses that this court, in most instances, has, with reluctance, enforced the rule of sovereign immunity and, at times, has seemed to accept any excuse, however sophisticated, in order to grant relief to a person who has been harmed. This indicates that we should either abandon the original premise and recede from our prior decision concerning governmental immunity or should cease to contrive artificial distinctions and decide the cases by judicial fiat.

The courts of Florida have taken a giant step in *Hargrove v. Town of Cocoa Beach*, Florida, Fla., 96 So. 2d 130. This case contains a remarkable and courageous opinion and we will quote at some length from the opinion in our discussion of the case. [In this case, discussed *supra*, the Florida court abolished the immunity doctrine.]

It was concluded and the opinion affirmatively stated that a municipal corporation may be held liable for the torts of police officers under the doctrine of respondeat superior. However, the court specifically excepted, and did not impose liability on, a municipality in the exercise of legislative or judicial, or quasi legislative or quasi judicial, functions.

Regardless of how the majority of the personnel of this court may feel at the present time concerning whether we should follow the path marked by the Florida Court, we must recognize that we are faced with a judicial problem which results from the fact that the immunity rule (although never clearly defined) has become so imbedded in the common law of this state over the years that it has become a definite part of our mores. We must make a choice as to whether the change in such a rule should be made by the legislature or by us. The majority of the court believes that the change addresses itself to legislative discretion and that we must content ourselves only with criticism of the rule which we have created.

When we return to the facts of the instant case, we are faced with the problem of placing it in its proper category. We believe that it is not an action where our rule of "reverse eminent domain" should apply. It falls more properly into the group of cases which concern the responsibility of a city for its negligent act. We have held that maintenance of parks and recreational facilities may be classified as a governmental function and we find that the acts complained of here were the result of the negligent acts of a servant of the city while performing that function.... We further believe that the property destroyed was not of the type which ordinarily may be devoted to public use.

Judgment affirmed.

Notes and Questions

1. *Distinction between tort and inverse condemnation claims.* Can you explain the difference between a negligence claim in tort as opposed to an inverse condemnation claim that results in strict liability in the form of "just compensation"? A "takings" claim is based on government action under the Fifth Amendment (or a comparable state constitutional provision) and does not depend on a showing of duty. Note that the point of "inverse condemnation" is that private parties can claim that government actors have *de facto* "taken" private property even though

the government has not launched an actual condemnation action. Why is a taking claim (framed in terms of "inverse condemnation" in which a party's property is not overtly condemned) different from an action in tort? The Kentucky court later abandoned sovereign immunity in tort. *Haney v. City of Lexington*, 386 S.W.2d 738 (Ky. 1964). Since this is so, why may it still be necessary or desirable for injured plaintiffs to resort to inverse condemnation actions in that state? Consider the possibility that the measure of damages in the inverse condemnation suit may be different, and that a different statute of limitations may apply. Moreover, as inverse condemnation suits are not tortious, they may not permit the assertion of defenses based on the absence of negligent conduct on the defendant's part. See *Snyder v. City of Minneapolis*, 441 N.W.2d 781, 786 (Minn. 1989) (zoning cases asserting governmental liability should be analyzed as inverse condemnation cases rather than tort cases).

2. *The inverse condemnation remedy and negligence.* The *V.T.C.* case indicates that the principles covering compensation in inverse condemnation (reverse eminent domain) lawsuits can rather easily be extended to situations in which the injury occurs because of the negligent acts of the local government unit. Nevertheless, most courts do not allow inverse condemnation for what they consider to be acts of negligence. Mandelker, *Inverse Condemnation: The Constitutional Limits of Public Responsibility*, 1966 Wis. L. Rev. 3, 24–28. There is no satisfactory judicial rationale for this position. "Sometimes the decisions simply say that no liability can be imposed under the constitution for single tortious acts which fall under the immunity rule. In other cases no real explanation may be given, the court may fall back on the suggestion that the injury is incidental and consequential, or it may rely on a variety of related concepts which suggest that liability cannot be imposed for acts unconnected with the construction of a government improvement." *Id.* at 25.

3. *Inverse condemnation and nuisance.* Is the interplay between nuisance and takings doctrine any different? Early precedent has allowed such overlap in some instances. For example, consider *Richards v. Washington Terminal Co.*, 233 U.S. 546 (1914). There, the plaintiff landowner claimed his property had been damaged as a result of the operation of nearby railroad tracks and an associated tunnel. The operation of the tunnel's vent resulted in gases and smoke affecting plaintiff's property. The Court considered his claims of public and private nuisance, as well as the implications of the Fifth Amendment. Ultimately the Court held that the impact of the smoke from the tunnel vent constituted a private nuisance for which compensation could be awarded in light of the diminution of property value, so long as the landowner had suffered "special and peculiar" damage.

For a more modern case finding both a taking and a nuisance, see *Varjabedian v. Madera*, 572 P.2d 43 (Cal. 1977) (suit by vineyard owners against city whose nearby waste water treatment facility emitted noxious odors; finding that state statute authorizing construction of waste water treatment plants did not negate claim for nuisance, upholding damages for nuisance, and reversing dismissal of inverse condemnation claim so that plaintiffs could demonstrate that they had suffered direct, special and peculiar damage, using the *Richards* standard). For a more comprehensive review of case law, see Ball, *The Curious Intersection of Nuisance and Takings Law*, 86 B.U. L. Rev. 819 (2006). Courts that are willing to extend inverse condemnation liability to tortuous activity or inactivity amounting to a nuisance require that the elements of nuisance, "injury, damage, and causation," be established. *Christ v. Metropolitan St. Louis Sewer Dist.*, 287 S.W.3d 709, 711–712 (Mo. App. 2009), quoting *Basham v. City of Cuba*, 257 S.W.3d 650, 653 (Mo. App. 2008) (no inverse condemnation liability for sewer system blockage because sewer district did not have notice of, and thus no duty to correct, the defect).

4. *Nuisance, "taking" and the federal Constitution.* In recent years, the Supreme Court has displayed a strong and recurring interest in "takings" doctrine. Consider, for example, its 2012 decision in *Arkansas Game and Fish Comm'n v. United States*, 568 U.S. 23 (2012). In an 8-0 decision by Justice Ginsburg (Justice Kagan recused), the Court held that intermittent "temporary" flooding resulting from the government's periodic release of water from a retaining dam over a period of seven years could give rise to a "taking." Note that the *Arkansas Game* decision was based on the Fifth Amendment of the United States Constitution (prohibiting "taking" for public use without just compensation, in contrast to the provisions of the Kentucky Constitution addressing both "taking" and "damaging." If this Supreme Court decision had been decided before the principal case, would it have affected the result? Why or why not? For a decision finding that sewage flooding did not involve taking for "public use," see *Henderson v. City of Columbus*, 827 N.W.2d. 486 (Neb. 2013). See also *St. Bernard Parish Government v. United States*, 887 F.3d 1354 (Fed. Cir. 2018) (concluding that government's alleged failure properly to maintain Mississippi River-Gulf Outlet channel did not constituted a taking, where owner failed to establish that government's construction and operation of channel was cause of property damage). For a scholarly exploration of state constitutional provisions that link "taking" and "damaging" of property, see Brady, *The Damagings Clauses*, 104 Va. L. Rev. 341 (2018).

5. *More examples.* Consider the following cases and see if you can derive a general rule about the availability of inverse condemnation in flooding and similar cases: *Biron v. City of Redding*, 170 Cal. Rptr. 3d 848 (Cal. App. 2014) (in inverse condemnation action by apartment building owners based on failure of city storm drains to protect their property during two storms, concluding that inverse condemnation claim required application of reasonableness standard rather than strict liability; finding that city had reasonably provided service to citizens generally, and that apartment area was a lower priority for upgraded storm drains than other areas, particularly since the property owners could themselves have mitigated damages by installing flood gates and purchasing flood insurance); *Livingston v. Virginia Dept. of Transp.*, 726 S.E.2d 264 (Va. 2012) (finding that single occurrence of flooding could be sufficient to state inverse condemnation action by homeowners and renters in residential subdivision that was subject to severe flooding, where plaintiffs claimed that flooding resulted from inadequate maintenance of river tributary after it had been

relocated in connection with freeway construction); *Henderson v. City of Columbus*, 827 N.W.2d 486 (Neb. 2013) (in action for inverse condemnation against city following flooding of basement with raw sewage during rainstorm, concluding that homeowners had not demonstrated that property was "taken or damaged" "for public use"); *Edwards v. Hallsdale-Powell Utility* Dist., 115 S.W.3d 461 (Tenn. 2003) (in suit for nuisance and inverse condemnation after basement was flooded with raw sewage on two occasions, finding that flooding did not constitute a taking since it was not caused by purposeful or intentional act); *Lorman v. City of Rutland*, 193 A.3d 1174 (Vt. 2018) (in suit alleging negligent design, construction, and maintenance of city sewer lines, homeowners unsuccessful in claims that sewage backups amounted to nuisance, trespass, and unconstitutional takings; court held city was immune from negligence and trespass claims, immune due to discretionary-function from nuisance claim, and plaintiffs had suffered no unconstitutional taking).

6. *Consequential damages.* The original position in eminent domain law was that compensation was payable only when property was physically taken and title appropriated by the public agency for public use. If property not physically taken was in some way injured or damaged by an adjacent public facility there was no compensation. Compensation began to be awarded in cases like this as soon as courts were willing to recognize that an interference with the use of land was compensable as a taking of a property right in that land. See, e.g., *Eaton v. Boston, C. & M.R.R.*, 51 N.H. 504 (N.H. 1872).

Nevertheless, as the Kentucky nuisance-based inverse condemnation cases demonstrate, the courts are divided on how far inverse condemnation recovery in this situation can be extended. Obviously, a broad extension of liability for compensation in these cases would make public agencies responsible in a wide variety of situations for indirect impacts on adjacent property. For example, suppose a school district builds an elementary school across the street from my house. The noise and congestion that the school brings reduce the value of my property. Is the school district liable? See *Willis v. Univ. of N. Ala.*, 826 So. 2d 118 (Ala. 2002) (denying inverse liability for damages alleged to have occurred when university built parking lot across from plaintiff's residence). The following cases indicate the different approaches that courts have taken to this and similar problems:

(a) *Roadway traffic noise. Felts v. Harris County*, 915 S.W.2d 482 (Tex. 1996). Landowners sought damages in inverse condemnation resulting from roadway traffic noise. Nine years after plaintiffs built a home on a half-acre lot, planned construction of a four-lane "major thoroughfare" to run adjacent to plaintiff's property was announced. Plaintiffs then put their home on the market for $165,000, but sold it for only $119,000 three years later, during construction of the roadway. Recovery for the cost of erecting a noise barrier was denied because the court concluded that roadway noise had a "similar impact on the community as a whole," and thus any damages suffered by the plaintiffs were community damages "not connected with the landowner's use and enjoyment."

(b) *Airplane noise. Jackson v. Metropolitan Knoxville Airport Auth.*, 922 S.W.2d 860 (Tenn. 1996). Plaintiffs brought an inverse condemnation action alleging interference in the use of their property caused by noise, vibration and pollutants from airplanes that fly near, but not directly over, their property. The Supreme Court of Tennessee held that plaintiffs stated a cause of action, even though there was no physical invasion or direct interference with plaintiffs' use of their property. The court reviewed the cases, agreed with the Supreme Court of Oregon that the "better reasoned rule" did not require direct overflights, *Thornburg v. Port of Portland*, 376 P.2d 100, 106 (Or. 1962). It adopted the test of the Supreme Court of Minnesota in *Alevizos v. Metropolitan Airports Comm'n of Minneapolis and St. Paul*, 216 N.W.2d 651, 662 (Minn. 1974), providing compensation for a showing of "direct and substantial invasion" of property rights that deprived the owner of the "practical enjoyment" of the property resulting in "a definite and measurable diminution" of the property's value. For discussion of the airport noise problem, see Stoebuck, *Condemnation by Nuisance: The Airport Cases in Retrospect and Prospect*, 71 Dick L. Rev. 207 (1967). See also Lesser, *The Aircraft Noise Problem: The Past Decade and, at Least for a While Longer, Local Liability*, 13 Urb. Law. 285 (1981); Pilsk, *Airport Noise Litigation in the 21st Century: A Survey of Current Issues*, 11 Issues Aviation L. & Pol'y 371 (2012).

(c) *Municipal zoo. City of Louisville v. Munro*, 475 S.W.2d 479 (Ky. 1971). Plaintiffs brought an action in inverse condemnation alleging that the "mere establishment" of a municipal zoo adjacent to their residence had depreciated its value. Recovery was denied, the court noting that in no case had it allowed recovery in inverse condemnation "where the alleged taking, injury or interference did not have *physical* aspects." *Id.* at 482 (emphasis in original). Accord *Evans v. JOG*, 251 S.E.2d 546 (Ga. 1979) (prison). But cf. *Edwards v. Bridgeport Hydraulic Co.*, 211 A.2d 679 (Conn. 1965), construing a statute authorizing damages against a private utility company for the erection of utility structures to include the depreciation in nearby property values resulting from the construction of a water tower.

B. Section 1983 of the Federal Civil Rights Act

Problem 6-2

Smith is a police officer for the Town of Doonesbury and was on duty the night of October 31, which was Halloween. Toward midnight, Smith observed an automobile on the Western Expressway weaving from side to side and traveling at over 90 miles per hour. Smith pursued and stopped the automobile and took its driver and passenger, Jones and Green, into custody at the nearest police station because they appeared intoxicated.

Jones became aggressive on arrival at the station and the police took him to a back room, where he claims he was beaten. Assume there had been a series of abusive incidents at this station, and that supervisors in the police department knew about them. After about an hour, the supervising officer at the station decided to keep Jones in custody but released Green after testing for alcohol content in his blood but finding none. He began traveling down a local street, but after a few blocks, his car jumped a curb, crashed into, and demolished a small florist shop owned by Johnson.

A state statute provides that police officers "may" take drivers into police custody who "appear intoxicated." It also provides that "any appointed supervisor at a police precinct station may release from custody any driver detained for apparent intoxication if, in the opinion of the supervisor, the driver is not a threat to the general public."

Does Jones have a cause of action against the Town of Doonesbury in federal court? If the town is liable, are the officers who beat Jones liable? What causes of action, if any, does Johnson have against the town in state court?

The legal picture changes substantially when questions of municipal liability move from the state to the federal level. Tort liability is clearly a matter of state law, although federal maritime law also can impose liability on municipalities. See, e.g., *In re City of N.Y.*, 522 F.3d 279, 283 (2d Cir. 2008) (New York City, as owner of the Staten Island Ferry, held liable for Director of Ferry Operations' negligence that was "causally connected" to crash killing several persons). Federal statutes, such as the Robert T. Stafford Disaster Relief and Emergency Assistance Act ("Stafford Act"), § 305, 42 U.S.C. § 5148 (discretionary function immunity) also can extend "derivative federal immunity" to states and cities. *In re World Trade Center Disaster Site Litigation*, 521 F.3d 169, 193–198 (2d Cir. 2008). In addition, federal courts have an opportunity under § 1983 of the Federal Civil Rights Act to make municipal torts actionable under the federal Constitution.

Section 1983 reads as follows:

> Every person who, under color of any statute, ordinance, regulation, custom, or usage, of any state or territory or the District of Columbia, subjects, or causes to be subjected, any citizen of the United States or other person within the jurisdiction thereof to the deprivation of any rights, privileges, or immunities secured by the Constitution and laws, shall be liable to the party injured in an action at law, suit in equity, or other proper proceeding for redress. . . . [42 U.S.C. § 1983.]

Section 1983 is remedial. It does not create rights but rather creates a cause of action to redress violations of the federal Constitution and statutes where those violations infringe individual rights. For example, a property tax assessment claimed to violate the Equal Protection Clause or the discharge of a municipal employee claimed to violate procedural due process both could be challenged in a § 1983 action. However, though § 1983 is a remedy for violations of the federal Constitution and statutes, a § 1983 action can also be brought in state court.

Whether a § 1983 suit is brought in federal or state court, it cannot be brought directly against a state, because the Supreme Court held that states are not "persons" that can be sued for purpose of applying § 1983. *Will v. Michigan Dep't of State Police*, 491 U.S. 58 (1989). However, litigants can use § 1983 to sue state officials for prospective relief, thus preventing future violations. See also Jeffries, *In Praise of the Eleventh Amendment and Section 1983*, 84 Va. L. Rev. 47 (1998).

The Supreme Court also held initially that local governments could not be sued as persons under § 1983. *Monroe v. Pape*, 365 U.S. 167 (1961). The Court reversed that decision in *Monell v. New York City Dep't of Soc. Servs.*, 436 U.S. 658 (1978), and in so doing, opened the federal courts to suits against local governments under § 1983:

> Local governing bodies, therefore, can be sued directly under § 1983 for monetary, declaratory, or injunctive relief where, as here, the action that is alleged to be unconstitutional implements or executes a policy statement, ordinance, regulation, or decision officially adopted and promulgated by that body's officers. Moreover, although the touchstone of the § 1983 action against a government body is an allegation that official policy is responsible for a deprivation of rights protected by the Constitutions, local governments, like every other § 1983 "person," by the very terms of the statute, may be sued for constitutional deprivations visited pursuant to governmental "custom" even though such a custom has not received formal approval through the body's official decisionmaking channels. . . .
>
> On the other hand, . . . a municipality cannot be held liable *solely* because it employs a tortfeasor or, in other words, a municipality cannot be held liable under § 1983 on a *respondeat superior* theory. [*Id.* at 690–91.]

The *Monell* case illustrates an important attribute of local government liability under § 1983. It is not enough for § 1983 liability that a court finds a violation of the federal Constitution or a federal statute. The court must also find that the local government is liable under § 1983, and the Supreme Court has adopted a number of doctrines, as *Monell* indicates, that determine when § 1983 liability attaches. This section reviews some of the more important of these doctrines. The first case considers the immunity of municipal corporations from § 1983 liability. The second case considers the standard of municipal liability under § 1983. Remember, however, that direct injunctive relief is always available under *Ex parte Young*, 209 U.S. 123 (1908), without recourse to § 1983.

Owen v. City of Independence

445 U.S. 622 (1980)

Mr. Justice Brennan delivered the opinion of the Court....

I

[The police chief and the city manager became involved in a controversy over the chief's administration of his department. After an investigation of the department, the city manager asked the chief to resign but he refused. He then demanded written notice of the charges against him and an opportunity for a public hearing with reasonable opportunity to respond to those charges. There was no action on the request. The city manager discharged the chief after a city council hearing, which heard a report on the investigation, and the council passed a motion at the manager's request ordering the investigative report to be turned over to a grand jury. The city manager gave no reasons for the discharge and the grand jury, after considering the charges, returned a "no true bill."]

II

Petitioner named the city of Independence, City Manager Alberg, and the present members of the City Council in their official capacities as defendants in this suit. Alleging that he was discharged without notice of reasons and without a hearing in violation of his constitutional rights to procedural and substantive due process, petitioner sought declaratory and injunctive relief, including a hearing on his discharge, backpay from the date of discharge, and attorney's fees. The District Court, after a bench trial, entered judgment for respondents....

[The Court of Appeals initially reversed the District Court. Respondents appealed, certiorari was granted, and the case was remanded for further consideration in light of *Monell.* The Court of Appeals on remand reaffirmed its original decision that the city had violated petitioner's constitutional rights, but held that all respondents, including the city, had a qualified immunity from liability because Supreme Court cases establishing employee due process rights were decided two months after the discharge.] ...

We turn now to the reasons for our disagreement with this holding.

III

Because the question of the scope of a municipality's immunity from liability under § 1983 is essentially one of statutory construction, the starting point in our analysis must be the language of the statute itself. By its terms, § 1983 "creates a species of tort liability that on its face admits of no immunities." *Imbler v. Pachtman*, 424 U.S. 409, 417 (1976). Its language is absolute and unqualified; no mention is made of any privileges, immunities, or defenses that may be asserted....

Moreover, the congressional debates surrounding the passage of § 1 of the Civil Rights Act of 1871 — the forerunner of § 1983 — confirm the expansive sweep of the statutory language....

However, notwithstanding § 1983's expansive language and the absence of any express incorporation of common-law immunities, we have, on several occasions, found that a tradition of immunity was so firmly rooted in the common law and was supported by such strong policy reasons that "Congress would have specifically so provided had it wished to abolish the doctrine." *Pierson v. Ray*, 386 U.S. 547, 555 (1967). Thus in *Tenney v. Brandhove*, 341 U.S. 367 (1951), after tracing the development of an absolute legislative privilege from its source in 16th-century England to its inclusion in the Federal and State Constitutions, we concluded that Congress "would [not] impinge on a tradition so well grounded in history and reason by covert inclusion in the general language" of § 1983. *Id.*, at 376.

Subsequent cases have required that we consider the personal liability of various other types of government officials. . . .

In each of these cases, our finding of § 1983 immunity "was predicated upon a considered inquiry into the immunity historically accorded the relevant official at common law and the interests behind it." *Imbler v. Pachtman, supra*, at 421. Where the immunity claimed by the defendant was well-established at common law at the time § 1983 was enacted, and where its rationale was compatible with the purposes of the Civil Rights Act, we have construed the statute to incorporate that immunity. But there is no tradition of immunity for municipal corporations, and neither history nor policy support a construction of § 1983 that would justify the qualified immunity accorded the city of Independence by the Court of Appeals. We hold, therefore, that the municipality may not assert the good faith of its officers or agents as a defense to liability under § 1983.

A

Since colonial times, a distinct feature of our Nation's system of governance has been the conferral of political power upon public and municipal corporations for the management of matters of local concern. As *Monell* recounted, by 1871, municipalities—like private corporations—were treated as natural persons for virtually all purposes of constitutional and statutory analysis. In particular, they were routinely sued in both federal and state courts. Local governmental units were regularly held to answer in damages for a wide range of statutory and constitutional violations, as well as for common-law actions for breach of contract. And although, as we discuss below, a municipality was not subject to suit for all manner of tortious conduct, it is clear that at the time § 1983 was enacted, local governmental bodies did not enjoy the sort of "good-faith" qualified immunity extended to them by the Court of Appeals.

As a general rule, it was understood that a municipality's tort liability in damages was identical to that of private corporations and individuals. . . .

Under this general theory of liability, a municipality was deemed responsible for any private losses generated through a wide variety of its operations and functions, from personal injuries due to its defective sewers, thoroughfares, and public utilities, to property damage caused by its trespasses and uncompensated takings.

Yet in the hundreds of cases from that era awarding damages against municipal governments for wrongs committed by them, one searches in vain for much mention of a qualified immunity based on the good-faith of municipal officers. . . . [The Court noted that nothing in the legislative debates over § 1983 recognized a good faith immunity for local governments. The Court next recognized the doctrines holding local governments immune for the exercise of governmental and discretionary functions and noted:]

. . . A brief examination of the application and the rationale underlying each of these doctrines demonstrates that Congress could not have intended them to limit a municipality's liability under § 1983.

The governmental-proprietary distinction owed its existence to the dual nature of the municipal corporation. . . . But the principle of sovereign immunity—itself a somewhat arid fountainhead for municipal immunity—is necessarily nullified when the State expressly or impliedly allows itself, or its creation, to be sued. Municipalities were therefore liable not only for their "proprietary" acts, but also for those "governmental" functions as to which the State had withdrawn their immunity. And, by the end of the 19th century, courts regularly held that in imposing a specific duty on the municipality either in its character or by statute, the State had impliedly withdrawn the city's immunity from liability for the nonperformance or misperformance of its obligation. Thus, despite the nominal existence of an immunity for "governmental" functions, municipalities were found liable in damages in a multitude of cases involving such activities.

That the municipality's common-law immunity for "governmental" functions derives from the principle of sovereign immunity also explains why that doctrine could not have served as the basis for the qualified privilege respondent claims under § 1983. First, because sovereign immunity insulates the municipality from unconsented suits altogether, the presence or absence of good faith is simply irrelevant. The critical issue is whether injury occurred while the city was exercising governmental, as opposed to proprietary, powers or obligations—not whether its agents reasonably believed they were acting lawfully in so conducting themselves. More fundamentally, however, the municipality's "governmental" immunity is obviously abrogated by the sovereign's enactment of a statute making it amenable to suit. Section 1983 was just such a statute. By including municipalities within the class of "persons" subject to liability for violations of the Federal Constitution and laws, Congress—the supreme sovereign on matters of federal law—abolished whatever vestige of the State's sovereign immunity the municipality possessed.

The second common-law distinction between municipal functions—that protecting the city from suits challenging "discretionary" decisions—was grounded not on the principle of sovereign immunity, but on a concern for separation of powers. . . . For a court or jury, in the guise of a tort suit, to review the reasonableness of the city's judgment on these matters would be an infringement upon the powers properly vested in a coordinate and coequal branch of government. . . .

[H]ere, too, a distinction was made that had the effect of subjecting the city to liability for much of its tortious conduct. While the city retained its immunity for decisions as to whether the public interest required acting in one manner or another, once any particular decision was made, the city was fully liable for any injuries incurred in the execution of its judgment. Thus municipalities remained liable in damages for a broad range of conduct implementing their discretionary decisions.

Once again, an understanding of the rationale underlying the common-law immunity for "discretionary" functions explains why that doctrine cannot serve as the foundation for a good-faith immunity under § 1983. That common-law doctrine merely prevented courts from substituting their own judgment on matters within the lawful discretion of the municipality. But a municipality has no "discretion" to violate the Federal Constitution; its dictates are absolute and imperative. And when a court passes judgment on the municipality's conduct in a § 1983 action, it does not seek to second-guess the "reasonableness" of the city's decision nor to interfere with the local government's resolution of competing policy considerations. Rather, it looks only to whether the municipality has conformed to the requirements of the Federal Constitution and statutes. . . .

B

Our rejection of a construction of § 1983 that would accord municipalities a qualified immunity for their good-faith constitutional violations is compelled both by the legislative purpose in enacting the statute and by considerations of public policy. The central aim of the Civil Rights Act was to provide protection to those persons wronged by the "'[m]isuse of power, possessed by virtue of state law and made possible only because the wrongdoer is clothed with the authority of state law.'" *Monroe v. Pape*, 365 U.S. 167, 184 (1961) (quoting *United States v. Classic*, 313 U.S. 299, 326 (1941)). By creating an express federal remedy, Congress sought to "enforce provisions of the Fourteenth Amendment against those who carry a badge of authority of a State and represent it in some capacity, whether they act in accordance with their authority or misuse it." Monroe v. Pape, supra, at 172.

How "uniquely amiss" it would be, therefore, if the government itself—"the social organ to which all in our society look for the promotion of liberty, justice, fair and equal treatment, and the setting of worthy norms and goals for social conduct"—were permitted to disavow liability for the injury it has begotten. A damages remedy against the offending party is a vital component of any scheme for vindicating cherished constitutional guarantees, and the importance of assuring its efficacy is only accentuated when the wrongdoer is the institution that has been established to protect the very rights it has transgressed. Yet owing to the qualified immunity enjoyed by most government officials, see *Scheuer v. Rhodes*, 416 U.S. 232

(1974), many victims of municipal malfeasance would be left remediless if the city were also allowed to assert a good-faith defense. Unless countervailing considerations counsel otherwise, the injustice of such a result should not be tolerated.

Moreover, § 1983 was intended not only to provide compensation to the victims of past abuses, but to serve as a deterrent against future constitutional deprivations, as well. See *Carey v. Piphus*, 435 U.S. 247, 256–257 (1978). The knowledge that a municipality will be liable for all of its injurious conduct, whether committed in good faith or not, should create an incentive for officials who may harbor doubts about the lawfulness of their intended actions to err on the side of protecting citizens' constitutional rights. Furthermore, the threat that damages might be levied against the city may encourage those in a policy making position to institute internal rules and programs designed to minimize the likelihood of unintentional infringements on constitutional rights. Such procedures are particularly beneficial in preventing those "systemic" injuries that result not so much from the conduct of any single individual, but from the interactive behavior of several government officials, each of whom may be acting in good faith.

Our previous decisions conferring qualified immunities on various government officials are not to be read as derogating the significance of the societal interest in compensating the innocent victims of governmental misconduct. Rather, in each case we concluded that overriding considerations of public policy nonetheless demanded that the official be given a measure of protection from personal liability. The concerns that justified those decisions, however, are less compelling, if not wholly inapplicable, when the liability of the municipal entity is at issue. [The Court based official immunity on the belief that subjecting to liability an officer compelled to exercise his discretion was unjust, and that the threat of liability would deter a willingness to execute an office with the required decisiveness and judgment.] . . .

The first consideration is simply not implicated when the damage award comes not from the official's pocket, but from the public treasury. It hardly seems unjust to require a municipal defendant which has violated a citizen's constitutional rights to compensate him for the injury suffered thereby. Indeed, Congress enacted § 1983 precisely to provide a remedy for such abuses of official power. Elemental notions of fairness dictate that one who causes a loss should bear the loss.

It has been argued, however, that revenue raised by taxation for public use should not be diverted to the benefit of a single or discrete group of taxpayers, particularly where the municipality has at all times acted in good faith. On the contrary, the accepted view is that stated in *Thayer v. Boston, supra*, 19 Pick. 511—"that the city, in its corporate capacity, should be liable to make good the damages sustained by an [unlucky] individual, in consequence of the acts thus done." 19 Pick., at 516. After all, it is the public at large which enjoys the benefits of the government's activities, and it is the public at large which is ultimately responsible for its administration. Thus, even where some constitutional development could not have been foreseen by municipal officials, it is fairer to allocate any resulting financial loss to the inevitable costs of government borne by all the taxpayers, than to allow its impact to be felt solely by those whose rights, albeit newly recognized, have been violated. . . .

[The second reason for official immunity did not apply because "consideration of the *municipality's* liability for constitutional violations is quite properly the concern of its elected or appointed officials. Indeed, a decisionmaker would be derelict in his duties if, at some point, he did not consider whether his decision comports with constitutional mandates and did not weigh the risk that a violation might result in an award of damages from the public treasury. . . ."]

IV

In sum, our decision holding that municipalities have no immunity from damages liability flowing from their constitutional violations harmonizes well with developments in the common law and our own pronouncements on official immunities under § 1983. Doctrines of tort law have changed significantly over the past century, and our notions of governmental responsibility should properly reflect that evolution. No longer is individual "blameworthiness" the acid test of liability; the principle of equitable loss-spreading has joined fault as a factor in distributing the costs of official misconduct.

We believe that today's decision, together with prior precedents in this area, properly allocates these costs among the three principals in the scenario of the § 1983 cause of action: the victim of the constitutional deprivation; the officer whose conduct caused the injury; and the public, as represented by the municipal entity. The innocent individual who is harmed by an abuse of governmental authority is assured that he will be compensated for his injury. The offending official, so long as he conducts himself in good faith, may go about his business secure in the knowledge that a qualified immunity will protect him from personal liability for damages that are more appropriately chargeable to the populace as a whole. And the public will be forced to bear only the costs of injury inflicted by the "execution of a government's policy or custom, whether made by its lawmakers or by those whose edicts or acts may fairly be said to represent official policy." *Monell v. New York City Dept. of Social Services*, 436 U.S., at 694.

Reversed.

MR. JUSTICE POWELL, with whom THE CHIEF JUSTICE, MR. JUSTICE STEWART, and MR. JUSTICE REHNQUIST join, dissenting. . . .

[The dissent disagreed with the majority's holding on municipal immunity under § 1983. It also argued that "basic fairness" required a qualified immunity for local governments and that many did not have the resources to meet the demands of strict liability. The dissent's argument based on the separation of powers doctrine is especially of interest:]

Important public policies support the extension of qualified immunity to local governments. First, as recognized by the doctrine of separation of powers, some governmental decisions should be at least presumptively insulated from judicial review.... The allocation of public resources and the operational policies of the government itself are activities that lie peculiarly within the competence of executive and legislative bodies. When charting those policies, a local official should not have to gauge his employer's possible liability under § 1983 if he incorrectly—though reasonably and in good faith—forecasts the course of constitutional law. Excessive judicial intrusion into such decisions can only distort municipal decision-making and discredit the courts. Qualified immunity would provide presumptive protection for discretionary acts, while still leaving the municipality liable for bad faith or unreasonable constitutional deprivations.

Notes and Questions

1. *Understanding immunities.* The issues of immunity and liability that arise under § 1983 are similar to those that arise under state tort law, with the difference that § 1983 is a federal statute imposing liability for violations of the federal Constitution. Did that factor influence the *Owen* decision? Immunities under § 1983 are based on an historic analysis of immunity law at the time the statute was passed, thus the historic analysis of local government immunity in *Owen*. Notice how the adoption of § 1983 trumped state immunity doctrine. Another aspect of the decision is Justice Brennan's views on the allocation of responsibility for governmental damage. He favored governmental assumption of liability. How does that compare with the way in which state courts view this issue?

Nevertheless, the Court's view of local government liability at the time § 1983 was adopted is the basis for its conclusion on the § 1983 liability of local governments. There is an argument that Justice Brennan misinterpreted or at least mischaracterized local government liability in tort under state law at that time. An even deeper question is whether local government immunity at state law is even relevant if, as Justice Brennan suggests, it is trumped by the federal statute. In any event, there is no good faith immunity for municipalities under § 1983.

Owen held only that municipalities do not have good faith immunity under § 1983. The case *does not* mean that municipalities are *automatically* liable under § 1983. As one basis for liability, a plaintiff must successfully prove a federal constitutional violation. What kinds of cases previously studied in this course can raise potential federal constitutional liability? A municipal annexation? A special assessment? A patronage discharge? What else?

Some scholars have in recent years suggested that the core judgments reflected in the line of cases leading to *Owen* and *Owen* itself be revisited. See Dawson, *Replacing Modell Liability with Qualified Immunity for Municipal Defendants in 42 U.S.C. § 1983 Litigation*, 86 U. Cin. L. Rev. 483 (2018) (arguing that statutory text and relevant history would support applying respondeat superior doctrine to make municipalities liable for the conduct of employees, but allowing them to assert employees' qualified immunity protections from liability); Cover, *Revisionist Municipal Liability*, 52 Ga. L. Rev. 375 (2018) (challenging the historical explanation for federal municipal liability doctrine, arguing that the difficulties in proving "custom or policy" undercut the importance of holding local governments accountable, observing that particular problems arise in cases involving suits against local governments for police brutality, and suggesting a change in standards for damage relief).

2. *Suits for violation of a federal "law."* Section 1983 also imposes liability for the violation of "any law." In *Maine v. Thiboutot*, 448 U.S. 1 (1980), the Court held this phrase means what it says and that any federal law, not just civil rights laws, can provide a basis for liability. This was a radical holding, as previously the Court allowed private actions to enforce federal laws only when they expressly granted the cause of action or the Court could imply one.

In *Gonzaga Univ. v. Doe*, 536 U.S. 273 (2002), the Court limited the "open door" implications of *Thiboutot* while addressing the availability of § 1983 to enforce federal statutes. It held a student could not sue a private university for damages under § 1983 to enforce the Family Educational Rights and Privacy Act of 1974, which prohibits federal funding of educational institutions if they have a policy or practice of releasing education records to unauthorized persons. It held this statute did not create personal rights that are enforceable under § 1983. The Court explained the basis on which it would find a federal right enforceable through a § 1983 action:

> We now reject the notion that our cases permit anything short of an unambiguously conferred right to support a cause of action brought under § 1983. Section 1983 provides a remedy only for the deprivation of "rights, privileges, or immunities secured by the Constitution and laws" of the United States. Accordingly, it is rights, not the broader or vaguer "benefits" or "interests," that may be enforced under the authority of that section. This being so, we further reject the notion that our implied right of action cases are separate and distinct from our § 1983 cases. To the contrary, our implied right of action cases should guide the determination of whether a statute confers rights enforceable under § 1983. [*Id.* at 383.]

The Court's language substantially curtails the availability of § 1983 to enforce federal statutory rights by placing a heavier burden of proof on plaintiffs. It also changed the Court's practice of applying different and more liberal tests to § 1983 actions than it did to actions based on an implied right of action under a federal statute. However, the Court did not expressly repudiate its three-part test for enforcing § 1983 actions it had adopted in *Blessing v. Freestone*, 520 U.S. 329 (1997):

> First, Congress must have intended that the provision in question benefit the plaintiff. Second, the plaintiff must demonstrate that the right assertedly protected by the statute is not so "vague and amorphous" that its enforcement would strain judicial competence. Third, the statute must

> unambiguously impose a binding obligation on the States. In other words, the provision giving rise to the asserted right must be couched in mandatory rather than precatory terms. [*Id.* at 340–41.]

Critics nevertheless claim that *Gonzaga* changed existing law without admitting it, and that the test adopted by the Court is ambiguous. See Mank, *Suing Under § 1983: The Future After Gonzaga v. Doe*, 39 Hous. L. Rev. 1417 (2003); Note, *How to Read Gonzaga: Laying the Seeds of a Coherent Section 1983 Jurisprudence*, 103 Colum. L. Rev. 1838 (2003). See also *City of Rancho Palos Verdes v. Abrams*, 544 U.S. 113 (2005), applying *Gonzaga* to the Telecommunications Act and refusing to allow a § 1983 remedy. As applied to federal spending statutes, the limitations on § 1983 suits adopted in *Gonzaga* may curtail their enforcement. For a discussion of the federal Adoption Assistance and Child Welfare Act's provisions for foster care maintenance payments and whether the Act creates a private right of action under § 1983, see Eudy, *Enforcement of the Right to Foster Care Maintenance Payments Under the Child Welfare Act*, 85 U. Chi. L. Rev. 1719 (2018) (reviewing circuit split and arguing that a private right of action should be recognized).

3. *Damages under § 1983.* The language of § 1983, stating that the party sued shall be liable in "an action at law," authorizes an award of damages to successful plaintiffs. *Carey v. Piphus*, 435 U.S. 247 (1978), held that common law tort damages provide a helpful analogy in § 1983 cases but must be carefully applied when a constitutional right protected under § 1983 does not have a tort analogy. In *Carey*, high school students who were suspended without procedural due process sued under § 1983. There was no proof that a different decision would have been reached even if procedural due process requirements were observed. The Court held that under these circumstances the students were entitled only to nominal and not compensatory damages. See also *Memphis Community School Dist. v. Stachura*, 477 U.S. 299 (1986) (*Carey* rule also applies to substantive due process claims).

In *City of Newport v. Fact Concerts, Inc.*, 453 U.S. 247 (1981), the Court overturned a lower court's award of punitive damages in a case involving an unsuccessful, last-minute attempt by various city officials to cancel an entertainment license for a rock concert. The Court concluded that common law municipal immunity from punitive damages was well-established when the Civil Rights Act of 1871 (the predecessor to § 1983) was enacted, and thus, if Congress had intended to abolish that particular immunity, it would have done so at the time. In addition, the Court reasoned that public policy considerations cut against an award of punitive damages. Innocent taxpayers would be hurt through increased taxes or decreased public services and fully compensated plaintiffs would receive windfalls if punitive damages were awarded. *Id.* at 267. For a criticism of absolute immunity from punitive damages because of a concern that voter apathy and inadequate internal municipal controls will prevent effective control of official misconduct, see Note, *Municipal Corporations Are Immune from Exemplary Damages Under 42 U.S.C. § 1983*, 13 Tex. Tech. L. Rev. 156 (1982). However, in *Smith v. Wade*, 461 U.S. 30 (1983), individual prison guards allegedly involved in grossly negligent conduct, without proof of actual malicious intent, could be held liable for punitive damages. Does this holding undercut the Note's criticism?

4. *Attorneys' fees.* Courts may award attorneys' fees to prevailing parties in § 1983 actions under 42 U.S.C. § 1988, the Civil Rights Attorneys' Fees Award Act of 1976. Potential liability for attorneys' fees is an important strategic consideration in § 1983 actions. The provisions of this act are not limited to civil rights claims, but apply to any claim brought under federal statutes or the federal Constitution.

In order to recover attorneys' fees under the statute, a plaintiff must be a "prevailing" party. The Court limited the reach of this term in *Buckhannon Board & Care Home, Incorporated v. West Virginia Department of Health and Human Resources,* 532 U.S. 598 (2001). It rejected a "catalyst" theory that would allow a fee award "where there is no judicially sanctioned change in the legal relationship of the parties," but the plaintiff achieves the result of the lawsuit because the defendant voluntarily changes its conduct. The Court added that a court might award attorneys' fees only when there has been a "corresponding alteration in the legal relationship of the parties" including a settlement agreement enforced through a consent decree, citing *Maher v. Gagne*, 448 U.S. 122 (1980). Congress subsequently amended the Freedom of Information Act to reintroduce the catalyst theory that had been at issue in *Buckhannon*, at least in that context. See 5 U.S.C. § 552(E)(ii). Claims for attorneys' fees may well exceed liability on the merits. For this reason, defendants often felt pressured to settle claims that may not have had merit in order to avoid excessive fee awards. The effect may also be to drive up litigation costs for plaintiffs. Why is this so? Will this defeat the purpose of the fee award act?

A Note on Legislative, Judicial, and Official Immunity

Immunity is a key issue in § 1983 litigation, as it is under state tort law. Although there is no immunity for local governments, their liability under the statute may be limited because there is no respondeat superior liability. If the local government is not liable then the only recourse is against a local official, but they may also be immune, as the *Owen* case noted. As that case pointed out, questions of immunity for municipal officials have been resolved in two ways. Absolute immunity under § 1983 has been granted to judges, legislators and prosecutors, while a qualified immunity has been accorded government officials when acting "in good faith," though this term may be misleading because immunity is based on objective, not subjective, standards.

Legislative immunity. In *Bogan v. Scott-Harris*, 523 U.S. 44 (1998), the Court held that legislative actions of city's mayor and city council's vice president in enacting an ordinance that eliminated the position of city administrator was protected by absolute immunity from liability under § 1983. The Court held that legislative immunity has long been recognized in Anglo-American law, and noted it had granted immunity to state legislators in *Tenney v. Brandhove*, 341 U.S. 367 (1951), where it held that Congress did not intend in § 1983 to alter a tradition "well-grounded in history and reason." The same reasons that required immunity for state legislators applied at the local government level. The Court held that "the exercise of legislative discretion should not be inhibited by judicial interference or distorted by the fear of personal liability," and that the "time and energy required to defend against a lawsuit are of particular concern at the local level, where the part-time citizen-legislator remains commonplace." In addition, the "ultimate check" on legislative abuse through the electoral process also applied at the local level.

Legislative immunity applies to all actions in the legitimate sphere of legislative activity. The actions in this case were legislative, even though directed at a specific individual, because whether an act is legislative turns on its nature rather than its motive or intent. The Court had "little trouble" finding the actions in this case legislative because the acts of voting for and signing an ordinance were "formally" legislative. See *Leapheart v. Williamson*, 705 F.3d 310 (8th Cir. 2013) (firing of specific individual would be administrative, but wholesale elimination of position would be legislative); *Arabbo v. City of Burton*, 680 Fed. Appx. 418 (6th Cir. 2017) (in case involving allegations of real estate developer that city council had rejected a proposal to refinance his mortgage due to anti-Arab sentiments, concluding that council members had absolute legislative immunity and city attorney had qualified immunity).

Judicial immunity. The Supreme Court early on recognized absolute immunity for judicial decisionmakers. See *Pierson v. Ray*, 386 U.S. 547 (1967) (recognizing historical immunity of judges and concluding they could not be held liable under § 1983 for an unconstitutional conviction). Subsequently, in *Stump v. Sparkman*, 435 U.S. 349 (1978), the Court had to grapple with an egregious case in which a state court judge ordered a woman to be sterilized based on an action instigated by her mother, without a guardian ad litem, ex parte, but the divided Court granted the judge absolute immunity nonetheless. Given the Court's strong commitment to protect judicial immunity, subsequent cases have inevitably had to explore what amounts to "judicial" action and what exceptions might apply. The Supreme Court adopted an exception to good faith immunity in *Butz v. Economou*, 438 U.S. 478 (1978), by conferring an absolute immunity on federal officials who initiated an adjudicatory proceeding against the plaintiff. The Court held there might be "exceptional situations where it is demonstrated that absolute [executive] immunity is essential for the conduct of the public business." Adjudication by agencies is "functionally equivalent" to adjudication by judges and should enjoy the absolute immunity judges enjoy. *Butz* required a functional approach to immunity, as illustrated by *Forrester v. White*, 484 U.S. 219 (1988) (immunity denied to state judge charged with unconstitutional employee discharge because conduct was administrative, not judicial). How does absolute adjudicatory immunity apply at the local level? What about a board of appeals that hears appeals on variances from the building code? What would you have to know about the board's procedures to determine whether absolute immunity applies? See *Akins v. Deptford Township*, 813 F. Supp. 1098 (D.N.J. 1993) (board of construction appeals and board clerk granted absolute judicial immunity), *aff'd without opinion*, 17 F.3d 1428 (3d Cir. 1994). Accord, *Buckles v. King County*, 191 F.3d 1127 (9th Cir. 1999) (state Growth Management Hearings Board that hears land use appeals was immune).

Official immunity. Official immunity for executive branch personnel is important because litigants may sue an official rather than a municipality to avoid problems with establishing municipal liability without the benefit of a respondeat superior doctrine. Local employees and officials will not be personally liable because most municipalities indemnify them for their non-willful actions. The Court first adopted a two-part test for official immunity that required a subjective and objective test in *Scheuer v. Rhodes*, discussed in the *Owen* case. It dropped the subjective part of *Harlow v. Fitzgerald*, 457 U.S. 800 (1982), and substituted an objective good faith test that is protective of public officials:

> [G]overnment officials performing discretionary functions generally are shielded from liability insofar as their conduct does not violate clearly established constitutional rights of which a reasonable person would have known. [*Id.* at 818.]

See also *Davis v. Scherer*, 468 U.S. 183 (1984) (violation of law or regulation not enough, standing alone, to defeat good faith immunity).

Anderson v. Creighton, 483 U.S. 635 (1987), extended *Harlow* to hold that a police officer who conducted an unconstitutional search could be immune from liability even though the constitutional right he allegedly violated was clearly established. Immunity attached unless the constitutional rules governing official conduct were specific enough to allow the official to understand whether he was violating them. The police officer was immune from liability even if he mistakenly believed his conduct was lawful if this belief was reasonable in light of the facts he considered at the time. *Hope v. Pelzer*, 536 U.S. 730 (2002), held, however, that law can be clearly established even in novel factual circumstances if officials have "fair warning" that their conduct is unconstitutional. Fair warning does not require cases to be fundamentally similar, as even cases with "notable factual distinctions" can put an official on notice that his actions are unconstitutional.

However, the Supreme Court has granted qualified immunity in certain cases. In *Ziglar v. Abbasi*, 137 S. Ct. 1843 (2017), the Court addressed claims by alien detainees held on immigration violations after the September 11, 2001 attacks that they had been subject to illegal physical and verbal abuse, and were entitled to relief under *Bivens* and § 1983. In an opinion written by Justice Kennedy, the Court held that plaintiffs were not entitled to relief against individual officers under § 1983, where legal principles were not clearly established at the time of the official conduct. For a discussion of related issues, see Wells, *Qualified Immunity After Ziglar v. Abbasi: The Case for a Categorical Approach*, 68 Am. U. L. Rev. 379 (2018). Two decisions in 2018 appear to have further expanded government employees' protection from suit pursuant to the qualified immunity doctrine, at least in the context of police use of force and criminal arrests. See *Kisela v. Hughes*, 138 S. Ct. 1148, 1152–53 (2018) (in case alleging excessive use of force by police officer, extending qualified immunity to officer, stating that "clearly established law" doctrine requires that "existing precedent must have placed the statutory or constitutional question beyond debate" and that the qualified immunity doctrine is intended to protect "all but the plainly incompetent or those who knowingly violate the law"); *District of Columbia v. Wesby*, 138 S. Ct. 577 (2018) (even if police officers lacked probable cause to arrest, they were protected by qualified immunity; cautioning lower courts that they "should think hard, and then think hard again, before addressing both qualified immunity and the merits of an underlying constitutional claim"). On the facts in the *Owen* case, would the mayor and police chief have good faith/official immunity?

Emerging issues. A great deal has been written in recent years concerning issues raised by excessive use of force by police, particularly insofar as such use of force has disproportionately resulted in death or injury to people of color. Why might litigation challenging police conduct in specific cases or more generally be brought under federal law rather than state law? For related insights, see Duckett, *Unreasonably Immune: Rethinking Qualified Immunity in Fourth Amendment Excessive Force Cases*, 53 Am. Crim. L. Rev. 409 (2016) (discussing issues raised in excessive force cases including need to show that force used was objectively unreasonable and that the relevant law was clearly established at the time of police conduct); Lawrence Rosenthal, *Good and Bad Ways to Address Police Violence*, 48 Urb. Law. 675 (2016) (outlining reform agenda and assessing policy recommendations to reduce police misconduct); Ravenell & Brigandi, *The Blurred Blue Line: Municipal Liability, Police Indemnification, and Financial Accountability in Section 1983 Litigation*, 62 Vill. L. Rev. 839 (2017) (discussing role of indemnification practices on police conduct). For other articles challenging the overall framework of qualified immunity, see Preisa, *Qualified Immunity and Fault*, 93 Notre Dame L. Rev. 1969 (2018) (discussing related doctrine, with focus on federal law, but also providing insights on state law of qualified immunity); Schwartz, *The Case Against Qualified Immunity*, 93 Notre Dame L. Rev. 1797 (2018) (challenging qualified immunity doctrine generally based on analysis of historical precedent and policy concerns). Professor Schwartz also conducted an empirical study of cases involving qualified immunity claims against state and local law enforcement officials in five federal district courts over a two-year period, and found that very few such cases were dismissed without requiring defendants to undergo at least initial stages of litigation and discovery. *See* Schwartz, *How Qualified Immunity Fails*, 127 Yale L.J. 2 (2017). For a contrasting view, see Baude, *Is Qualified Immunity Unlawful?*, 106 Calif. L. Rev. 45 (2018) (arguing Supreme Court doctrine on qualified immunity is inconsistent with rules of statutory construction and that justifications for expansion of qualified immunity protections is not justified given cited rationales).

A denial of municipal immunity does not mean that municipalities are necessarily liable under § 1983 for constitutional violations. One important question is the extent to which the § 1983 remedy constitutionalizes state torts. The following case considers this problem:

Collins v. City of Harker Heights

503 U.S. 115 (1992)

JUSTICE STEVENS delivered the opinion of the Court.

The question presented is whether § 1 of the Civil Rights Act of 1871, 42 U.S.C. § 1983, provides a remedy for a municipal employee who is fatally injured in the course of his employment because the city customarily failed to train or warn its employees about known hazards in the workplace. Even though the city's conduct may be actionable under state law, we hold that § 1983 does not apply because such conduct does not violate the Due Process Clause.

On October 21, 1988, Larry Michael Collins, an employee in the sanitation department of the city of Harker Heights, Texas, died of asphyxia after entering a manhole to unstop a sewer line. Petitioner, his widow, brought this action alleging that Collins "had a constitutional right to be free from unreasonable risks of harm to his body, mind and emotions and a constitutional right to be protected from the city of Harker Heights' custom and policy of deliberate indifference toward the safety of its employees." Her complaint alleged that the city violated that right by following a custom and policy of not training its employees about the dangers of working in sewer lines and manholes, not providing safety equipment at job sites, and not providing safety warnings. The complaint also alleged that a prior incident had given the city notice of the risks of entering the sewer lines[1] and that the city had systematically and intentionally failed to provide the equipment and training required by a Texas statute. The District Court dismissed the complaint on the ground that a constitutional violation had not been alleged. No. W-89-CA-168 (W.D. Tex., Oct. 30, 1988). The Court of Appeals for the Fifth Circuit affirmed on a different theory. 916 F.2d 284 (CA5 1990). It did not reach the question whether the city had violated Collins' constitutional rights because it denied recovery on the ground that there had been no abuse of governmental power, which the Fifth Circuit had found to be a necessary element of a § 1983 action.

The contrary decision in *Ruge v. City of Bellevue*, 892 F.2d 738 (CA8 1989), together with our concern about the Court of Appeals' interpretation of the statute, prompted our grant of certiorari.

I

Our cases do not support the Court of Appeals' reading of § 1983 as requiring proof of an abuse of governmental power separate and apart from the proof of a

1. In particular, the complaint alleged that "prior to October, 1988, the City of Harker Heights was on notice of the dangers to which the employees were exposed because Larry Michael Collins' supervisor had been rendered unconscious in a manhole several months prior to October, 1988, in fact, several months before Larry Michael Collins began work at the City of Harker Heights."

constitutional violation. Although the statute provides the citizen with an effective remedy against those abuses of state power that violate federal law, it does not provide a remedy for abuses that do not violate federal law, *see, e.g., DeShaney v. Winnebago County Department of Social Services*, 489 U.S. 189 (1989). More importantly, the statute does not draw any distinction between abusive and nonabusive federal violations. . . .

Nevertheless, proper analysis requires us to separate two different issues when a § 1983 claim is asserted against a municipality: (1) whether plaintiff's harm was caused by a constitutional violation, and (2) if so, whether the city is responsible for that violation. *See Oklahoma City v. Tuttle*, 471 U.S. 808, 817 (1985). Because most of our opinions discussing municipal policy have involved the latter issue, it is appropriate to discuss it before considering the question whether petitioner's complaint has alleged a constitutional violation.

II

Section 1983 provides a remedy against "any person" who, under color of state law, deprives another of rights protected by the Constitution. In *Monell*, the Court held that Congress intended municipalities and other local government entities to be included among those persons to whom § 1983 applies. At the same time, the Court made it clear that municipalities may not be held liable "unless action pursuant to official municipal policy of some nature caused a constitutional tort." *Id.*, at 691. [The Court also noted *Monell* held municipalities could not be held liable on a respondeat superior theory.] . . .

In a series of later cases, the Court has considered whether an alleged injury caused by municipal employees acting under color of state law provided a proper basis for imposing liability on a city. In each of those cases the Court assumed that a constitutional violation had been adequately alleged or proved and focused its attention on the separate issue of municipal liability. Thus, for example, in *Oklahoma City v. Tuttle, supra*, it was assumed that the police officer had violated the decedent's constitutional rights, but we held that the wrongful conduct of a single officer without any policy-making authority did not establish municipal policy. And in *St. Louis v. Praprotnik*, without reaching the question whether the adverse employment action taken against the plaintiff violated his First Amendment rights, the Court concluded that decisions by subordinate employees did not necessarily reflect official policy. On the other hand, in *Pembaur v. Cincinnati*, the Court held that the County was responsible for unconstitutional actions taken pursuant to decisions made by the County Prosecutor and the County Sheriff because they were the "officials responsible for establishing final policy with respect to the subject matter in question," [475 U.S. 469] at 483–484 [(1986)].

Our purpose in citing these cases is to emphasize the separate character of the inquiry into the question of municipal responsibility and the question whether a constitutional violation occurred. It was necessary to analyze whether execution of a municipal policy inflicted the injury in these cases because, unlike ordinary tort litigation, the doctrine of respondeat superior was inapplicable. The city is not vicariously liable under § 1983 for the constitutional torts of its agents: It is only liable when it can be fairly said that the city itself is the wrongdoer. Because petitioner in this case relies so heavily on our reasoning in *Canton v. Harris*, 489 U.S. 378 (1989)—and in doing so, seems to assume that the case dealt with the constitutional issue—it is appropriate to comment specifically on that case.

In *Canton* we held that a municipality can, in some circumstances, be held liable under § 1983 "for constitutional violations resulting from its failure to train municipal employees." *Id.*, at 380. Among the claims advanced by the plaintiff in that case was a violation of the "right, under the Due Process Clause of the Fourteenth Amendment, to receive necessary medical attention while in police custody." *Id.*, at 381. Because we assumed arguendo that the plaintiff's constitutional right to receive medical care had been denied, *id.*, at 388–389, n. 8, our opinion addressed only the question whether the constitutional deprivation was attributable to a municipal policy or custom.

We began our analysis by plainly indicating that we were not deciding the constitutional issue.

> "In *Monell*, we decided that a municipality can be found liable under § 1983 only where the municipality itself causes the constitutional violation at issue. . . .
>
> "Thus, our first inquiry in any case alleging municipal liability under § 1983 is the question whether there is a direct causal link between a municipal policy or custom and the alleged constitutional deprivation." *Id.*, at 385.

We did not suggest that all harm-causing municipal policies are actionable under § 1983 or that all such policies are unconstitutional. Moreover, we rejected the city's argument that only unconstitutional policies can create municipal liability under the statute. Instead, we concluded that if a city employee violates another's constitutional rights, the city may be liable if it had a policy or custom of failing to train its employees and that failure to train caused the constitutional violation. In particular, we held that the inadequate training of police officers could be characterized as the cause of the constitutional tort if—and only if—the failure to train amounted to "deliberate indifference" to the rights of persons with whom the police come into contact. *Id.*, at 388.

Although the term "deliberate indifference" has been used in other contexts to define the threshold for finding a violation of the Eighth Amendment, *see Estelle v. Gamble*, 429 U.S. 97, 104 (1976), as we have explained, that term was used in the *Canton* case for the quite different purpose of identifying the threshold for holding a city responsible for the constitutional torts committed by its inadequately trained agents.[7] In this case, petitioner has used that term to characterize the city's failure to train the employees in its sanitation department. We assume for the purpose of decision that the allegations in the complaint are sufficient to provide a substitute for the doctrine of respondeat superior as a basis for imposing liability on the city for the tortious conduct of its agents, but that assumption does not confront the question whether the complaint has alleged a constitutional violation. To that question we now turn.

III

Petitioner's constitutional claim rests entirely on the Due Process Clause of the Fourteenth Amendment. The most familiar office of that Clause is to provide a guarantee of fair procedure in connection with any deprivation of life, liberty, or property by a State. Petitioner, however, does not advance a procedural due process claim in this case. Instead, she relies on the substantive component of the Clause that protects individual liberty against "certain government actions regardless of the fairness of the procedures used to implement them." *Daniels v. Williams*, 474 U.S. 327, 331 (1986).

As a general matter, the Court has always been reluctant to expand the concept of substantive due process because guideposts for responsible decisionmaking in this unchartered area are scarce and open-ended. The doctrine of judicial self-restraint requires us to exercise the utmost care whenever we are asked to break new ground in this field. It is important, therefore, to focus on the allegations in the complaint to determine how petitioner describes the constitutional right at stake and what the city allegedly did to deprive her husband of that right.

A fair reading of petitioner's complaint does not charge the city with a willful violation of Collins' rights. Petitioner does not claim that the city or any of its agents deliberately harmed her husband. In fact, she does not even allege that his supervisor instructed him to go into the sewer when the supervisor knew or should have known that there was a significant risk that he would be injured. Instead, she makes the more general allegation that the city deprived him of life and liberty by failing to provide a reasonably safe work environment.[9] Fairly analyzed, her claim advances two theories: that the Federal Constitution imposes a duty on the city to provide its employees with minimal levels of safety and security in the workplace, or that the city's "deliberate indifference" to Collins' safety was arbitrary Government action that must "shock the conscience" of federal judges.

---

7 Indeed, we expressly stated: "The 'deliberate indifference' standard we adopt for § 1983 'failure to train' claims does not turn upon the degree of fault (if any) that a plaintiff must show to make out an underlying claim of a constitutional violation." 489 U.S., at 388, n. 8.

9. Petitioner alleges that her husband had "a constitutional right to be free from unreasonable risks of harm to his body, mind and emotions and a constitutional right to be protected from the City of Harker Heights' custom and policy of deliberate indifference toward the safety of its employees." The city's policy and custom of not training its employees and not warning them of the danger allegedly caused Collins' death and thus deprived him of those rights.

Neither the text nor the history of the Due Process Clause supports petitioner's claim that the governmental employer's duty to provide its employees with a safe working environment is a substantive component of the Due Process Clause. "The Due Process Clause of the Fourteenth Amendment was intended to prevent government from abusing [its] power, or employing it as an instrument of oppression." *DeShaney v. Winnebago County Department of Social Services*, 489 U.S., at 196 (quoting *Davidson v. Cannon*, 474 U.S. 344, 348 (1986)). As we recognized in *DeShaney*,

> "The Clause is phrased as a limitation on the State's power to act, not as a guarantee of certain minimal levels of safety and security. It forbids the State itself to deprive individuals of life, liberty, or property without due process of law, but its language cannot fairly be extended to impose an affirmative obligation on the State to ensure that those interests do not come to harm through other means. Nor does history support such an expansive reading of the constitutional text." 489 U.S. at 195.

Petitioner's submission that the city violated a federal constitutional obligation to provide its employees with certain minimal levels of safety and security is unprecedented. It is quite different from the constitutional claim advanced by plaintiffs in several of our prior cases who argued that the State owes a duty to take care of those who have already been deprived of their liberty. We have held, for example, that apart from the protection against cruel and unusual punishment provided by the Eighth Amendment, the Due Process Clause of its own force requires that conditions of confinement satisfy certain minimal standards for pretrial detainees, for persons in mental institutions, for convicted felons, and for persons under arrest. The "process" that the Constitution guarantees in connection with any deprivation of liberty thus includes a continuing obligation to satisfy certain minimal custodial standards. Petitioner cannot maintain, however, that the city deprived Collins of his liberty when it made, and he voluntarily accepted, an offer of employment.

We also are not persuaded that the city's alleged failure to train its employees, or to warn them about known risks of harm, was an omission that can properly be characterized as arbitrary, or conscience-shocking, in a constitutional sense. Petitioner's claim is analogous to a fairly typical state law tort claim: The city breached its duty of care to her husband by failing to provide a safe work environment. Because the Due Process Clause "does not purport to supplant traditional tort law in laying down rules of conduct to regulate liability for injuries that attend living together in society," *Daniels v. Williams*, 474 U.S., at 332, we have previously rejected claims that the Due Process Clause should be interpreted to impose federal duties that are analogous to those traditionally imposed by state tort law. The reasoning in those cases applies with special force to claims asserted against public employers because state law, rather than the Federal Constitution, generally governs the substance of the employment relationship.

Our refusal to characterize the city's alleged omission in this case as arbitrary in a constitutional sense rests on the presumption that the administration of

Government programs is based on a rational decisionmaking process that takes account of competing social, political, and economic forces. Decisions concerning the allocation of resources to individual programs, such as sewer maintenance, and to particular aspects of those programs, such as the training and compensation of employees, involve a host of policy choices that must be made by locally elected representatives, rather than by federal judges interpreting the basic charter of Government for the entire country. The Due Process Clause "is not a guarantee against incorrect or ill-advised personnel decisions." *Bishop v. Wood*, 426 U.S. [341], at 350 [1976]. Nor does it guarantee municipal employees a workplace that is free of unreasonable risks of harm. . . .

In sum, we conclude that the Due Process Clause does not impose an independent federal obligation upon municipalities to provide certain minimal levels of safety and security in the workplace and the city's alleged failure to train or to warn its sanitation department employees was not arbitrary in a constitutional sense. The judgment of the Court of Appeals is therefore affirmed.

Notes and Questions

1. *Constitutional torts.* It has been clear since *Paul v. Davis*, 424 U.S. 693 (1976), that not every tort actionable at state law is a violation of § 1983. Would the municipality be liable under state law in this case? Reconsider the application of the discretionary function exception in *Peavler*, reproduced earlier in this Chapter, *supra.* Note the two-step inquiry into liability required by § 1983. A court must first determine whether there is a constitutional violation. It must then determine whether the municipality is responsible for the constitutional violation. What was the issue in *Collins*? Note that the "state created danger" rule, referenced in *Collins,* can apply in the context of workplace injuries, so *Collins* should not be read as always precluding relief. See, e.g., *Kedra v. Schroeter,* 876 F.3d 424 (3d Cir. 2017) (finding that substantive due process claim had been stated when state trooper was killed by instructor during firearms training drill in which instructor failed to comply with applicable, clearly known safety protocols).

2. *Affirmative vs. negative.* One question in *Collins* was whether substantive due process places a duty on a governmental employer "to provide its employees with a safe working environment." The Court answered this question by applying the distinction between affirmative and negative governmental duties in the constitutional context, and reinforced the formalistic view that government is liable for active but not passive misconduct. Commentators have been fascinated with the affirmative duty problem because of the perplexing questions it raises about moral and legal responsibility. Why is this problem analyzed differently under § 1983 than it is under state law governing municipal liability? Which view of the problem do you prefer?

Collins cited decisions where the Court found an affirmative duty to act in cases where an individual was in protective custody. The *Harris* case, which it discusses, is an example. Why should these cases be treated differently? Would a state court treat them differently? For discussion of the precedent, see Armacost, *Affirmative Duties, Systemic Claims, and the Due Process Clause*, 94 MICH. L. REV. 982 (1996); Wells, *Constitutional Torts, Common Law Torts, and Due Process of Law*, 72 CHI-KENT L. REV. 617 (1997).

3. *The private actor problem.* The affirmative-negative and duty to protect issues also arise in cases where harm is inflicted by a private actor because of a government failure to act. *DeShaney v. Winnebago County Dept. of Social Services*, 489 U.S. 189 (1989), discussed in the principal case, is the leading decision. An action was brought on behalf of a four-year-old who had been repeatedly and savagely beaten by his natural father, and who suffered violence when a social service agency put him back in his father's custody. The Court held the Due Process Clause did not require the state to protect its citizens against harm by private actors because the Clause is a limitation on state power, not a guarantee of minimal levels of safety and security. It also held the Due Process Clause did not impose an affirmative duty to protect the child, even though state authorities were aware of the beatings for more than two years. One exception to this rule arises when the state limited a person's freedom to act by taking him into custody, an exception recognized in *Collins. DeShaney* attracted substantial criticism. See Soifer, *Moral Ambition, Formalism, and the "Free World" of DeShaney*, 57 GEO. WASH. L. REV. 1513 (1989), arguing that "Chief Justice Rehnquist's opinion for the majority in *DeShaney* is an abomination. It is illogical and extremely mechanistic; it also abuses history, fails to consider practical impact, and demonstrates moral insensitivity. Not only that, it is wrong. The decision holds that the state has no constitutional duty to protect a child not in custody." *Id.* at 1514. Do you agree with Dean Soifer?

4. *The "state-created danger" exception. DeShaney* recognized an exception that has come to be known as the "state-created danger" exception. This exception is based on a statement in *DeShaney* that "[w]hile the State may have been aware of the dangers that Joshua faced in the free world, it played no part in their creation, nor did it do anything to render him any more vulnerable to them." *Id.* at 201. The state-created danger rule provides potential liability for such cases under § 1983 and in cases like *DeShaney.* Professor Oren has reviewed the treatment of this doctrine in the courts of appeal. Oren, *Safari into the Snake Pit: The State-Created Danger Doctrine*, 13 WM. & MARY BILL RTS. J. 1165 (2005). She observes:

> Since 1989, the search for (non-"custodial") constitutional liability for the State's failure to protect someone from injury by third parties has been a safari into this "snake pit." Liability under the Due Process Clause of the Fourteenth Amendment will attach only if the State can be said to have crossed the putative line between action and inaction by creating the danger or substantially increasing it. Moreover, taking their cues from subsequent Supreme Court decisions on other related points, the circuits have held that the journey into the snake pit also requires an extremely high level of culpability to be actionable. No matter how it is defined, "deliberate

> indifference" is the minimum standard required. It is a degree of responsibility that assumes different content in different contexts, and which, therefore, may or may not, equate with conscience-shocking conduct. [*Id.* at 1168.]

Some courts have therefore stressed that the "state-created danger" exception applicable to substantive due process claims requires that the plaintiff not only show that the state (rather than a third party) has created the danger, but also that state actions must "shock the conscience of the court," that is, must be "so egregious, so outrageous, that it may fairly be said to shock the contemporary conscience." *Irish v. Maine,* 849 F.3d 521, 526 (1st Cir. 2017). The *Irish* court also observed that "where actors have an opportunity to reflect and make reasoned and rational decisions, deliberately indifferent behavior may suffice," and that it may be appropriate to consider the "conscience shocking" test before considering the "state-created danger" aspect. *Id.* Others have added additional requirements to provide a fuller picture of all elements that must be pled. See *Sauers v. Borough of Nesquehoning,* 905 F.3d 711 (3d Cir. 2018) (citing four elements: (1) the harm ultimately caused was foreseeable and fairly direct; (2) a state actor acted with a degree of culpability that shocks the conscience; (3) a relationship between the state and the plaintiff existed such that the plaintiff was a foreseeable victim of the defendant's acts, or a member of a discrete class of persons subjected to the potential harm brought about by the state's actions, as opposed to a member of the public in general; and (4) a state actor affirmatively used his or her authority in a way that created a danger to the citizen or that rendered the citizen more vulnerable to danger than had the state not acted at all).

For a case similar to *DeShaney* that found a constitutional violation for purposes of § 1983, see *T.D. v. Patton,* 868 F.3d 1209 (10th Cir. 2017) (holding that child's substantive due process rights were violated when social worker placed child with father, a registered sex offender, who abused the child, where social worker did not investigate whether father was abusing child or disclose to court the father's status as a registered sex offender). In a case similar to the situation presented in the Problem, *supra,* a court applied the state-created danger exception where an accident caused by an intoxicated driver released by police caused a fatality and serious injuries. *Reed v. Gardner,* 986 F.2d 1122 (7th Cir. 1993). The court pointed out that "*DeShaney,* however, leaves the door open for liability in situations where the state creates a dangerous situation or renders citizens more vulnerable to danger." *Id.* at 1125. For a similar case involving state tort law, consider the *Kolbe* case, reproduced earlier in this Chapter, where the court rejected a tort claim brought when a disabled person who was given a driver's license injured a bicyclist. Would a court impose liability under the state-created danger test? For a discussion of the application of the "state-created danger" exception in the context of psychiatric confinement, see Hagan, *Sheltering Psychiatric Patients from the DeShaney Storm: A Proposed Analysis for Determining Affirmative Duties to Voluntary Patients,* 70 Wash. & Lee L. Rev. 725 (2013).

5. *Failure to train.* The Court reconsidered "failure to train" as the basis for § 1983 liability in *Connick v. Thompson*, 563 U.S. 51 (2011). Plaintiff was improperly convicted because the prosecutor's office failed to reveal exculpatory evidence. He claimed § 1983 liability based on a failure to train prosecutors about their duty to produce such evidence, which was why the nondisclosure occurred. Citing *Canton*, discussed in the principal case, the Court held a failure to train must amount to "deliberate indifference" to constitutional rights to be a § 1983 violation. Plaintiff had not shown deliberate indifference through "a pattern of similar constitutional violations by untrained employees." The Court rejected "single incident" liability as hypothesized in *Canton*. The single incident of nondisclosure in this case was not enough, and prosecutors did not need training on disclosure requirements. *The Supreme Court 2010 Term: Leading Cases*, 125 Harv. L. Rev. 331 (2011), criticizes *Connick* for narrowing *Canton* and the basis for § 1983 liability. *Connick* "weakens the deterrence power of municipal liability by confining liability to those rare cases where the victim can prove" a pattern of violations. *Id.* at 338. For a discussion of supervisory liability under § 1983, see Nahmod, *Constitutional Torts, Over Supervisory Liability After Iqbal*, 14 Lewis & Clark L. Rev. 279 (2010) (arguing the Supreme Court has made it more difficult to find such liability). Failure to train claims may arise in a number of contexts, including schools, and can be tied to constitutional claims other than substantive due process. See, e.g., *Littell v. Houston Independent School District*, 894 F.3d 616 (5th Cir. 2018) (holding that school's action in authorizing employees to strip search girls to their underwear constituted a "policy," and violated clear principles regarding search and seizure; school's failure to provide any training at all, while providing wide authorization for employees to conduct such searches, caused reasonably foreseeable harm, constituted "deliberate indifference," and violated students' substantive due process rights).

6. *Custom and policy.* Under the *Monell* holding, a municipality is not automatically liable under § 1983 for every constitutional deprivation inflicted by its employees. This is a rejection of respondeat superior liability. A municipality is liable under *Monell* only when constitutional injury is inflicted by a government's "lawmakers or by those whose edicts and acts may fairly be said to represent government policy." 436 U.S. at 694. This requirement is easily met when a municipality adopts an unconstitutional ordinance, enforces an unconstitutional formal policy or persists in an unconstitutional practice. Proof of custom or policy is more difficult when based on the decision or act of a municipal official or employee. Unfortunately, a majority of the Court has not been able to agree on what is necessary to show a policy or custom in this situation. In *City of St. Louis v. Praprotnik*, 485 U.S. 112 (1988), a majority of the Justices reaffirmed the holding in *Pembaur v. City of Cincinnati*, 475 U.S. 469 (1986), that a municipality is liable for an isolated single action by a final policymaker in the area of responsibility in question. A majority of the Court again confirmed these rules in *Board of County Comm'rs v. Brown*, 520 U.S. 397 (1997). The Justices could not agree in *Pembaur*, however, on the rules for identifying final policymakers. Justice O'Connor's plurality opinion asserted a municipality

is liable for an isolated act of an actor designated by state law as the "final policymaking authority" in the area of business in question. Justice Brennan's concurring opinion elevated function over form, and contended that state law is only a starting point for a decision on whether final policymaking authority is conferred. Justice Stevens' dissent repeated his argument that § 1983 imposes respondeat superior liability. Note that difficulties in making municipalities liable for acts of officers means that officers will be the only persons responsible in many § 1983 actions. However, immunity rules may shield them from liability, as discussed *supra*.

Chapter 7

Federalism

Scope of Chapter

For the better part of the twentieth century, the case for studying federalism as a separate topic within a casebook about American state and local government law was weaker than it is today. The supremacy of federal mandates was so well-established, and the scope of federal power so broadly encompassing, that the principal lesson for those concerned with state and local government was simply to recognize the superior authority of a rapidly-evolving national power.

This post-New Deal, nationalist vision of the state-federal relationship has eroded considerably. The so-called "New Federalism," which describes a more central role for the states, has been both a political reality and an increasingly prominent feature of the United States Supreme Court's constitutional doctrine since the 1980s. The assertion of a state-centered vision of American government in the late 20th and early 21st centuries is associated with, and perhaps prompted by, a political shift rightward, skepticism about the role of government generally, a turn to legal formalism and frustration with the lack of "quick fixes" to fundamental structural problems affecting the economy and individual aspirations.

The Chapter proceeds in three parts. It first clarifies what courts and commentators mean by "federalism" and provides historical context for different visions of this concept. It then turns to "regulatory federalism," addressing both federal preemption and Tenth Amendment issues. Finally, it considers "fiscal federalism," focusing on the federal spending power and its limitations. For a treatment of the federalism-related clauses of the United States Constitution informed by their historical background, see L. Strang, FEDERAL CONSTITUTIONAL LAW, VOL. 4: FEDERALISM LIMITATIONS ON STATE AND FEDERAL POWER (2011).

A. Framing the Debate: The Meaning of "Federalism" in Historical and Present Context

Federalism can be described as a political concept, a statement of binding legal principles, the specific arrangement of the American federal-state relationship, or a particular set of normative commitments. Each of these conceptions of federalism is discussed briefly below.

Federalism as a political concept. Federalism can describe a political system in which political power is divided between central and subordinate authorities, and where officials of the subordinate units do not derive their power from, and cannot be removed by, officials of the central government. Moreover, most theories of federalism assume that the subordinate units possess some areas of authority that cannot be invaded by the central government. See Kramer, *Understanding Federalism*, 47 Vand. L. Rev. 1485, 1488 n.5 (1994). This definition is broad enough to include not only the political structure of the United States, but also the quite different federal systems in Canada, Switzerland, Australia and India, among others. What makes federalism in the United States unique is its particular allocation of authority among different governmental units, a division that arises from the structure of the United States Constitution and the Supreme Court opinions interpreting it and political pressure applied by both state and federal actors.

Federalism as constitutional law. The term "federalism" appears nowhere in the United States Constitution. Rather, its existence and contours can be inferred, albeit roughly, from specific provisions of the Constitution and their relationship with one another. A few provisions explicitly address the relative powers of the states and federal government, like the Supremacy Clause and the Tenth Amendment. Some other provisions affirmatively grant powers to Congress, most saliently the spending power, the power to regulate commerce, and the power to enforce the Fourteenth and Fifteenth Amendments. Other provisions explicitly prohibit powers to the states, like the prohibition on state laws that violate obligations of contract. Still other provisions expand or contract the jurisdiction of the federal courts over cases involving states, most notably the Eleventh Amendment and the portions of Art. III that it modifies. Together, these provisions, and the cases that interpret them, set the relationship between the states and the federal government and make up the contours of "our federalism."

As many scholars have argued, however, "our federalism" is more than simply a series of constitutional provisions and occasional Supreme Court cases interpreting them. In order to be considered a principle of constitutional weight, a principle of federalism must, at least, also comport with the historical record that fleshes out these provisions. The resort to historical materials can be enlightening, but also frustrating; as Professor Fallon described, the historical record is "messy":

> [S]ome of the relevant provisions resulted from hard bargaining and compromise at the Constitutional Convention. More particularly, some reflect the views or preferences of those who generally favored a strong federal government, while others reflect the views or preferences of those who were most concerned to preserve state powers and influence. We also know that the Civil War Amendments were designed to alter the preexisting balance of state and federal authorities but that the Fourteenth Amendment, in particular, reflected compromises. In important respects, vagueness and ambiguity appear to reflect the drafters' design, rather than their oversights.

[Fallon, *Federalism as a Constitutional Concept*, 41 Ariz. St. L.J. 961, 965 (2017).]

Despite the messiness of the historical record, both judges and scholars have gained great insights about the historical understanding of the distribution of power between the state and federal governments from the essays collected as The Federalist Papers. In a pair of essays comparing the relative power of the state and federal governments under the proposed Constitution, James Madison wrote that the:

> [s]tate governments will have the advantage of the Federal government, whether we compare them in respect to the immediate dependence of the one on the other; to the weight of personal influence which each side will possess; to the powers respectively vested in them; to the predilection and probable support of the people; to the disposition and faculty of resisting and frustrating the measures of each other. [No. 45, The Federalist Papers (C. Rossiter ed.).]

Madison expanded on each of these attributes. With respect to the size of the federal government, he predicted that the "number of individuals employed under the Constitution of the United States would be much smaller than the number employed under the particular States. There would consequently be less of personal influence on the side of the former than of the latter." With respect to the powers of the respective governments, he characterized the powers delegated to the federal government as "few and defined," limited to such "external" matters like war and peace, as opposed to the powers of the state governments, which are "numerous and indefinite." Moreover, the states would have power over those matters which are of greater concern to the people, those powers affecting the "lives, liberties, and properties of the people, and the internal order, improvement, and prosperity of the State." *Id.*

Madison further predicted that the loyalties of the people would lie with the states; but in an important passage, he recognized the possibility that the federal government might be better administered than the state governments, changing this balance of loyalty. Even then, however, Madison argued, the Constitution places limits on federal influence:

> If . . . the people should in future become more partial to the federal than to the State governments, the change can only result from such manifest and irresistible proofs of a better administration, as will overcome all their antecedent propensities. And in that case, the people ought not surely to be precluded from giving most of their confidence where they may discover it to be most due; but even in that case the State governments could have little to apprehend, because it is only within a certain sphere that the federal power can, in the nature of things, be advantageously administered. [No. 46, The Federalist Papers (C. Rossiter ed.).]

Are Madison's assessments of the relative importance of state and federal governments an accurate reflection of the state-federal relationship today? Is Madison's description of the state-federal relationship required (or permitted) by the text and structure of the Constitution? When the text and the historical background conflict, which should control? See Pettys, *Competing for the People's Affection: Federalism's Forgotten Marketplace*, 56 VAND. L. REV. 329 (2003) (urging renewed attention to Madison's notion of competition between state and federal government, urging an effort to combine substantive and process federalism, and exploring the extent to which the judiciary is well-positioned to help or hinder healthy competition of this sort).

Describing the changing vision of federalism over the centuries, Professor Greve posits a distinction between two types of federalism. "Competitive" federalism, which he believes was embodied in the Constitution originally, focuses upon citizens' vantage points, requires states to compete for people and businesses and assumes that the point of federalism is to discipline governments at all levels. "Cartel" federalism, in contrast, focuses on the states and their preferences, and assumes that states and local elites wish to claim greater power, and expect the federal government to enhance their surplus capacity to tax citizens in excess of the cost of providing services. M. Greve, THE UPSIDE-DOWN CONSTITUTION 4–5 (2012). Greve further contends that the original constitutional understanding embodied "competitive" federalism, but that in the face of industrialization, the Great Depression, and the 1936 election, "cartel" federalism became the norm. *Id.* at 12–13. Greve argues that the current approach to federalism creates nonsensical results in terms of what level of government can control what decisions. *Id.* at 328. Do you understand and agree with Professor Greve's distinctions between "competitive" and "cartel" federalism? How should critical historical events such as the Great Depression or the Great Recession affect federalism analysis, if at all?

Federalism as a dynamic relationship. Rather than thinking about federalism as a static statement of the state-federal relationship, some scholars have described it as the lived experience—both cooperative and uncooperative—of state, local, and federal officials jointly implementing policy. See Gerken, *Forward: Federalism All the Way Down*, 124 HARV. L. REV. 4, 7–12 (2010). Professor Gerken uses the term "federalism-all-the-way-down" to describe the "institutional arrangements that our constitutional account too often misses—where minorities rule without sovereignty." *Id.* In Gerken's view, overlap and interdependence between the authority of the states and the federal government "are the rule, not the exception." As a result, neither the states nor the federal government are wholly independent of one another in any field. The federal government depends on the states' administrative apparatus to enforce federal law; and the states regulate their traditional fields only in light of extensive federal regulation. Gerken, *Federalism 3.0*, 105 CAL. L. REV. 1695 (2017).

In their project assessing the implementation of the Affordable Care Act (ACA), Professors Gluck and Huberfeld detail the complicated relationship between the federal government and the states engendered by the implementation of federal policy. As they describe, the federalism dynamic found in the ACA "is defined not by separation between state and federal, but rather by a national structure that invites state-led implementation." The result can be fairly described neither as state- nor federal-controlled. On one hand, by inviting states to participate in the implementation the ACA, Congress strengthened state control. On the other hand, by permitting the states to define key terms under the ACA, the ACA masked the federal directive underlying the decision while allowing the states to take credit for popular federal programs. Gluck & Huberfeld, *What Is Federalism in Healthcare for?*, 70 Stan. L. Rev. 1689 (2018).

Professor Bulman-Pozen describes how congressional dysfunction augments the relative power of states in determining national policy. Early in the Trump Administration, the federal government made it clear that restricting illegal immigration is a federal priority. However, in the absence of congressional action, the enforcement of immigration laws has remained highly location-specific. Some states have passed laws explicitly requiring cooperation with federal officials for immigration enforcement; by contrast, other states have explicitly passed laws *prohibiting* cooperation with federal officials for immigration enforcement. The result is that states, rather than the federal government, have taken the primary role in setting the scope of immigration enforcement. Bulman-Pozen, *Preemption and Commandeering Without Congress*, 70 Stan. L. Rev. 2029 (2018). The federal executive branch has tried to bring states into line by conditioning significant federal spending on the states' greater compliance with federal immigration initiatives. Challenges to these measures are working their way through the courts, with splits between the Courts of Appeals already appearing. Compare *City of Providence v. Barr*, 954 F.3d 23 (1st Cir. 2020) (holding that United States DOJ lacks authority to impose immigration-related conditions on receipt of grants for law-enforcement activities), *with New York v. Department of Justice*, 951 F.3d 84 (2d Cir. 2020) (upholding federal authority to impose immigration-related conditions on receipt of these grants).

Perhaps no event has made the dynamic relationship between state and federal authority more visible to the public than the COVID-19 pandemic. Both the federal government and individual states possess tools and justifications for addressing this crisis: on one hand, it is the states that traditionally exercise the police power, including the power to protect the health of its citizens. On the other hand, a highly infectious disease that crosses state lines and international borders with impunity implicates the federal government's power to regulate interstate and foreign commerce. Under these circumstances, the relative powers of the states and federal government to address the pandemic will depend largely on their response to this crisis rather than on well-defined spheres of authority. The early stages of the COVID-19 pandemic saw the states take the lead over the federal government in responding to the crisis. In the absence of a coordinated federal response, a number of states attempted to stem the spread of the virus through stay-at-home orders and declarations of emergencies. And without strong and consistent federal guidance, many citizens have relied on governors as a primary source of information about COVID-19.

Federalism as political philosophy. The above accounts of federalism describe the actual or perceived relationship between the federal government and state and local governments. However, the term "federalism" can also refer to a normative view, that is, it can refer to a vision about how government ought to be structured. Some commentators have noted that federalism is sometimes seen to promote values like increased political participation, intergovernmental competition, representation of diverse interests, and keeping government close to the people. Briffault, *"What About the 'Ism'?" Normative and Formal Concerns in Contemporary Federalism*, 47 VAND. L. REV. 1303, 1305 (1994). Others scholars have added autonomy, cooperation, experimentation and variation to the list of values that federalism is supposed to produce, while noting that these values can flourish under an assortment of state-federal relationships. Gluck & Huberfeld, *What Is Federalism in Healthcare for?*, 70 STAN. L. REV. 1689 (2018). Some commenters use the term "federalism" to refer bluntly to a decentralized system of governance, although other scholars have been critical of that view. See Rubin & Feeley, *Federalism: Some Notes on a National Neurosis*, 41 U.C.L.A. L. REV. 903 (1994). Still other scholars have contributed important perspectives on the values underlying federalism at the time of the nation's founding and today. See McConnell, *Federalism: Evaluating the Founders' Design*, 54 U. CHI. L. REV. 1484 (1987); D. Shapiro, FEDERALISM: A DIALOGUE (1995). Perhaps most significantly, the use of the term "federalism" by many "new Federalists" often reflects what historically might be described as an "anti-Federalist" view—one that favors strong state autonomy and power and a limitation on the authority of the federal government. This new federalist view, as you will read below, has taken hold in the Supreme Court in recent decades.

Consider again Madison's description of the state-federal relationship, noted above: should Madison's predictions have normative weight—that is, should his predictions about future events determine how we should structure our governments? What events that took place subsequent to the original structuring of the United States, both legal and historical, might affect your analysis?

Problem 7-1

The regulation of cigarette smoking and advertising has been a matter of great interest to federal, state and local governments in recent years. Congress has limited the role of states and local governments and has both constrained and empowered federal agencies to act in this area. The states, in turn, have employed a number of strategies to limit sales of cigarettes to young people and to reduce the contexts in which cigarettes can be sold. State and local governments have also prohibited certain advertising strategies, for example, by constraining how close to schools cigarettes can be displayed and sold. The newest phase of the "tobacco wars" concerns the marketing of "e-cigarettes." E-cigarettes are typically battery powered devices that use a heating element to vaporize a nicotine-bearing liquid solution in order to simulate the experience of smoking. Some have argued that e-cigarettes should be allowed, and their use encouraged, because damaging health effects from their use are thought to be less severe than the damage associated with cigarettes. Others, relying on data about the addictive nature of nicotine, argue that e-cigarette use is not associated with smoking cessation; and, in addition, e-cigarette users may graduate to traditional cigarettes, with all of the health hazards associated with them. After an alarming spike in the number of middle school and high school-aged students reportedly using e-cigarettes, the Federal Food and Drug Administration (FDA) deemed e-cigarettes to be tobacco products in 2016 and proposed restrictions on e-cigarette products in 2018. Although the proposed restrictions do not ban e-cigarettes, they would restrict the locations where flavored e-cigarettes could be sold, effectively eliminating their sale in convenience stores and other places where they are easily purchased by minors.

If the FDA's proposed regulations are ultimately promulgated, will states remain free to regulate e-cigarettes as part of their traditional powers to regulate for public health and safety? What if a state believes that the federal regulations do not go far enough; can it regulate more stringently than did the FDA? What if a new tobacco product is invented? Does the existence of the FDA's e-cigarette rules have an impact on the power of the states to regulate this new product? Could the federal government condition awards of federal funding for public health initiatives on actions by states to prohibit e-cigarettes? Does the amount of funding matter?

B. Regulatory Federalism

This section addresses the problems of regulatory federalism. Such problems can arise in several different contexts: when the federal government regulates in a field in which the states could, but have not, regulated; when the federal government and the states each seek to regulate similar conduct; and when a federal statutory scheme requires or invites state implementation. It examines federal preemption doctrine, which has its roots in the Constitution's Supremacy Clause, and the Tenth Amendment, whose import has waxed and waned dramatically over the last century.

[1] Federal Preemption

The Constitution prescribes the basic powers of the federal government. Most saliently, it grants Congress certain enumerated powers (such as the powers to declare war, regulate interstate and foreign commerce, and enforce the Fourteenth and Fifteenth Amendments) and the power to "make all laws which shall be necessary and proper for carrying into execution" not only these enumerated powers, but also "all other powers vested by this Constitution in the government of the United States." U.S. Const. art. I, § 8. Reflecting the failures of the Articles of Confederation, and the bitter disagreements between federalists and anti-federalists during the debate over the proposed Constitution, the Constitution also provides that laws made under the authority of the United States are to be "the Supreme Law of the Land, . . . anything in the Constitution or laws of any State to the contrary notwithstanding." U.S. CONST. art. VI. Because federal law is supreme, state and local regulatory efforts to the contrary are invalid, that is, *preempted* by federal law.

Although a valid federal law's supremacy over state law is beyond question, preemption analysis can be challenging, because discerning the meaning of federal and state statutory language often poses difficult questions of interpretation. As a result, whether, in fact, a federal statute controls the conduct at issue can be far from obvious. Preemption questions tend to fall into the following categories. In some straightforward cases, federal statutes expressly preempt state law by stating something to the effect of "No state or political subdivision of a state shall have any authority to establish" a standard that is not identical to the federal standard.

When federal law does not *expressly* preempt state law, preemption can still be *implied* by the statutory scheme. When a court holds that federal preemption is implied, it is because Congress either has occupied the field that is subject to regulation (field preemption) or because the state law conflicts with federal law (conflict preemption). As the *Lorillard* case, below, demonstrates, even express preemption cases can involve difficult exercises in statutory interpretation. As you read the Court's preemption analysis, identify what methods of statutory interpretation the Court used to reach its result. Could the result have come out differently using different interpretive methods? Should the method of interpretation matter?

Lorillard Tobacco Company v. Reilly

533 U.S. 525 (2001)

JUSTICE O'CONNOR delivered the opinion of the Court.

In January 1999, the Attorney General of Massachusetts promulgated comprehensive regulations governing the advertising and sale of cigarettes, smokeless tobacco, and cigars. 940 Code of Mass. Regs. §§ 21.01–21.07, 22.01–22.09 (2000). Petitioners, a group of cigarette, smokeless tobacco, and cigar manufacturers and retailers, filed suit in Federal District Court claiming that the regulations violate federal law and the United States Constitution. [The District Court largely upheld the regulations. On appeal, the First Circuit held that the regulations were not preempted by federal law and did not violate the First Amendment.] The first question presented for our review is whether certain cigarette advertising regulations are preempted by the Federal Cigarette Labeling and Advertising Act (FCLAA), 79 Stat. 282, as amended, 15 U.S.C. § 1331 et seq. The second question presented is whether certain regulations governing the advertising and sale of tobacco products violate the First Amendment.

I

[The regulations in question were adopted following the 1998 settlement of law suits by 40 states against cigarette manufacturers. While signing on to the settlement, the Massachusetts Attorney General announced his intention to "close holes" in the settlement and to take measures designed to provide additional protection for children. Under state law authorizing the attorney general to proscribe unfair and deceptive trade practices, new regulations were promulgated to "address the incidence" of use of cigarettes, smokeless tobacco and cigars, and to prevent access to such products by underage consumers. The regulations prohibited use of self-service displays of tobacco products; required such products to be placed out of reach of all consumers; banned outdoor advertising, including advertising within retail establishments that were visible from outside; and barred promotional sampling or "give-aways" of cigars or "little cigar" products].

The term "advertisement" is defined as"

> any oral, written, graphic, or pictorial statement or representation, made by, or on behalf of, any person who manufactures, packages, imports for sale, distributes or sells within Massachusetts [tobacco products], the purpose or effect of which is to promote the use or sale of the product. Advertisement includes, without limitation, any picture, logo, symbol, motto, selling message, graphic display, visual image, recognizable color or pattern of colors, or any other indicia of product identification identical or similar to, or identifiable with, those used for any brand of [tobacco product]. This includes, without limitation, utilitarian items and permanent or semi-permanent fixtures with such indicia of product identification such as lighting fixtures, awnings, display cases, clocks and door mats, but does not include utilitarian items with a volume of 200 cubic inches or less. . . .

[Cigarette, smokeless tobacco and cigar manufacturers challenged the regulations under the Commerce Clause, Supremacy Clause, First and Fourteenth Amendments and 42 U.S.C. § 1983.]

II

Before reaching the First Amendment issues, we must decide to what extent federal law pre-empts the Attorney General's regulations. The cigarette petitioners contend that the FCLAA, 15 U.S.C. § 1331 et seq., pre-empts the Attorney General's cigarette advertising regulations.

A

Article VI of the United States Constitution commands that the laws of the United States "shall be the supreme Law of the Land; . . . any Thing in the Constitution or Laws of any State to the Contrary notwithstanding." Art. VI, cl. 2. See also *McCulloch v. Maryland*, 17 U.S. (4 Wheat.) 316 (1819) ("It is of the very essence of supremacy, to remove all obstacles to its action within its own sphere, and so to modify every power vested in subordinate governments"). This relatively clear and simple mandate has generated considerable discussion in cases where we have had to discern whether Congress has pre-empted state action in a particular area. State action may be foreclosed by express language in a congressional enactment, *see, e.g., Cipollone v. Liggett Group, Inc.*, 505 U.S. 504, 517 (1992), by implication from the depth and breadth of a congressional scheme that occupies the legislative field, *see, e.g., Fidelity Fed. Sav. & Loan Assn. v. De la Cuesta*, 458 U.S. 141, 153 (1982), or by implication because of a conflict with a congressional enactment, *see, e.g., Geier v. American Honda Motor Co.*, 529 U.S. 861, 869–874 (2000).

In the FCLAA, Congress has crafted a comprehensive federal scheme governing the advertising and promotion of cigarettes. The FCLAA's pre-emption provision provides:

(a) Additional statements

> "No statement relating to smoking and health, other than the statement required by section 1333 of this title, shall be required on any cigarette package."

(b) State regulations

> "No requirement or prohibition based on smoking and health shall be imposed under State law with respect to the advertising or promotion of any cigarettes the packages of which are labeled in conformity with the provisions of this chapter." 15 U.S.C. § 1334.

The FCLAA's pre-emption provision does not cover smokeless tobacco or cigars.

In this case, our task is to identify the domain expressly pre-empted, because "an express definition of the pre-emptive reach of a statute . . . supports a reasonable inference . . . that Congress did not intend to pre-empt other matters." Congressional purpose is the "ultimate touchstone" of our inquiry. Because "federal law is said to bar state action in [a] field of traditional state regulation," namely, advertising, we "work on the assumption that the historic police powers of the States are not to be superseded by the Federal Act unless that [is] the clear and manifest purpose of Congress."

Our analysis begins with the language of the statute. In the pre-emption provision, Congress unequivocally precludes the requirement of any additional statements on cigarette packages beyond those provided in § 1333. 15 U.S.C. § 1334(a). Congress further precludes States or localities from imposing any requirement or prohibition based on smoking and health with respect to the advertising and promotion of cigarettes. § 1334(b). Without question, the second clause is more expansive than the first; it employs far more sweeping language to describe the state action that is pre-empted. We must give meaning to each element of the pre-emption provision. We are aided in our interpretation by considering the predecessor pre-emption provision and the circumstances in which the current language was adopted.

In 1964, the groundbreaking Report of the Surgeon General's Advisory Committee on Smoking and Health concluded that "cigarette smoking is a health hazard of sufficient importance in the United States to warrant appropriate remedial action." Department of Health, Education, and Welfare, U.S. Surgeon General's Advisory Committee, Smoking and Health 33. In 1965, Congress enacted the FCLAA as a proactive measure in the face of impending regulation by federal agencies and the States. The purpose of the FCLAA was twofold: to inform the public adequately about the hazards of cigarette smoking, and to protect the national economy from interference due to diverse, nonuniform, and confusing cigarette labeling and advertising regulations with respect to the relationship between smoking and health. The FCLAA prescribed a label for cigarette packages: "Caution: Cigarette Smoking May Be Hazardous to Your Health." § 4. The FCLAA also required the Secretary of Health, Education, and Welfare (HEW) and the Federal Trade Commission (FTC) to report annually to Congress about the health consequences of smoking and the advertising and promotion of cigarettes. § 5.

Section 5 of the FCLAA included a pre-emption provision in which "Congress spoke precisely and narrowly." Subsection 5(a) prohibited any requirement of additional statements on cigarette packaging. Subsection 5(b) provided that "no statement relating to smoking and health shall be required in the advertising of any cigarettes the packages of which are labeled in conformity with the provisions of this Act." Section 10 of the FCLAA set a termination date of July 1, 1969 for these provisions....

The FCLAA was enacted with the expectation that Congress would reexamine it in 1969 in light of the developing information about cigarette smoking and health. [After further hearings, legislation passed in 1969 included new stronger labeling requirements, and prohibited cigarette advertising in electronic media. Congress also] enacted the current pre-emption provision, which proscribes any "requirement or prohibition based on smoking and health ... imposed under State law with respect to the advertising or promotion" of cigarettes. The new [preemption provision] did not pre-empt regulation by federal agencies, freeing the FTC to impose warning requirements in cigarette advertising. [Congress amended the FCLAA again in 1984, with the purpose of alerting Americans to health hazards associated with smoking and allowing them to make informed decisions. The FTC continued to monitor trade practices in the cigarette industry.].

The scope and meaning of the current pre-emption provision become clearer once we consider the original pre-emption language and the amendments to the FCLAA. Without question, "the plain language of the pre-emption provision in the 1969 Act is much broader." Rather than preventing only "statements," the amended provision reaches all "requirements or prohibitions ... imposed under State law." And, although the former statute reached only statements "in the advertising," the current provision governs "with respect to the advertising or promotion" of cigarettes. Congress expanded the pre-emption provision with respect to the States, and at the same time, it allowed the FTC to regulate cigarette advertising. Congress also prohibited cigarette advertising in electronic media altogether. Viewed in light of the context in which the current pre-emption provision was adopted, we must determine whether the FCLAA pre-empts Massachusetts' regulations governing outdoor and point-of-sale advertising of cigarettes.

B

The Court of Appeals acknowledged that the FCLAA pre-empts any "requirement or prohibition based on smoking and health . . . with respect to the advertising or promotion of . . . cigarettes," 15 U.S.C. § 1334(b), but concluded that the FCLAA does not nullify Massachusetts' cigarette advertising regulations. The court concentrated its analysis on whether the regulations are "with respect to" advertising and promotion, relying on two of its sister Circuits to conclude that the FCLAA only pre-empts regulations of the content of cigarette advertising. The Court of Appeals also reasoned that the Attorney General's regulations are a form of zoning, a traditional area of state power; therefore the presumption against pre-emption applied. . . .

Turning first to the language in the pre-emption provision relied upon by the Court of Appeals, we reject the notion that the Attorney General's cigarette advertising regulations are not "with respect to" advertising and promotion. We disagree with the Court of Appeals' analogy to the Employee Retirement Income Security Act of 1974 (ERISA). In some cases concerning ERISA's pre-emption of state law, the Court has had to decide whether a particular state law "relates to" an employee benefit plan covered by ERISA even though the state law makes no express reference to such a plan. Here, however, there is no question about an indirect relationship between the regulations and cigarette advertising because the regulations expressly target cigarette advertising.

Before this Court, the Attorney General focuses on a different phrase in the pre-emption provision: "based on smoking and health." The Attorney General argues that the cigarette advertising regulations are not "based on smoking and health," because they do not involve health-related content in cigarette advertising but instead target youth exposure to cigarette advertising. . . .

As Congress enacted the current pre-emption provision, Congress did not concern itself solely with health warnings for cigarettes. In the 1969 amendments, Congress not only enhanced its scheme to warn the public about the hazards of cigarette smoking, but also sought to protect the public, including youth, from being inundated with images of cigarette smoking in advertising. In pursuit of the latter goal, Congress banned electronic media advertising of cigarettes. And to the extent that Congress contemplated additional targeted regulation of cigarette advertising, it vested that authority in the FTC.

The context in which Congress crafted the current pre-emption provision leads us to conclude that Congress prohibited state cigarette advertising regulations motivated by concerns about smoking and health. Massachusetts has attempted to address the incidence of underage cigarette smoking by regulating advertising, much like Congress' ban on cigarette advertising in electronic media. At bottom, the concern about youth exposure to cigarette advertising is intertwined with the concern about cigarette smoking and health. Thus the Attorney General's attempt to distinguish one concern from the other must be rejected.

The Attorney General next claims that the State's outdoor and point-of-sale advertising regulations for cigarettes are not pre-empted because they govern the location, and not the content, of advertising.

The content versus location distinction has some surface appeal. The pre-emption provision immediately follows the section of the FCLAA that prescribes warnings. *See* 15 U.S.C. §§ 1333, 1334. The pre-emption provision itself refers to cigarettes "labeled in conformity with" the statute. But the content/location distinction cannot be squared with the language of the pre-emption provision, which reaches all "requirements" and "prohibitions" "imposed under State law." A distinction between the content of advertising and the location of advertising in the FCLAA also cannot be reconciled with Congress' own location-based restriction, which bans advertising in electronic media, but not elsewhere. . . .

Moreover, any distinction between the content and location of cigarette advertising collapses once the implications of that approach are fully considered. At oral argument, the Attorney General was pressed to explain what types of state regulations of cigarette advertising, in his view, are pre-empted by the FCLAA. The Attorney General maintained that a state law that required cigarette retailers to remove the word "tobacco" from advertisements, or required cigarette billboards to be blank, would be pre-empted if it were a regulation of "health-related content." The Attorney General also maintained, however, that a complete ban on all cigarette advertising would not be pre-empted because Congress did not intend to invade local control over zoning. The latter position clearly follows from the factual distinction between content and location, but it finds no support in the text of the FCLAA's pre-emption provision. We believe that Congress wished to ensure that "a State could not do through negative mandate (*e.g.*, banning all cigarette advertising) that which it already was forbidden to do through positive mandate (*e.g.*, mandating particular cautionary statements)." . . .

Our holding is not as broad as the dissent states; we hold only that the FCLAA pre-empts state regulations targeting cigarette advertising. States remain free to enact generally applicable zoning regulations, and to regulate conduct with respect to cigarette use and sales. The reference to *Lopez* is also inapposite. [The dissent had tartly inquired whether any regulation was possible to protect school children's health and safety, since the Court's decision in *Lopez* foreclosed federal regulation of handguns in proximity to schools, and the case at bar foreclosed state regulation of cigarette advertising in similar settings]. In *Lopez*, we held that Congress exceeded the limits of its Commerce Clause power in the Gun-Free School Zones Act of 1990, which made it a federal crime to possess a firearm in a school zone. This case, by contrast, concerns the Supremacy Clause and the doctrine of pre-emption as applied in a case where Congress expressly precluded certain state regulations of cigarette advertising. Massachusetts did not raise a constitutional challenge to the FCLAA, and we are not confronted with whether Congress exceeded its constitutionally delegated authority in enacting the FCLAA.

In sum, we fail to see how the FCLAA and its pre-emption provision permit a distinction between the specific concern about minors and cigarette advertising and the more general concern about smoking and health in cigarette advertising, especially in light of the fact that Congress crafted a legislative solution for those very concerns. We also conclude that a distinction between state regulation of the location as opposed to the content of cigarette advertising has no foundation in the text of the pre-emption provision. Congress pre-empted state cigarette advertising regulations like the Attorney General's because they would upset federal legislative choices to require specific warnings and to impose the ban on cigarette advertising in electronic media in order to address concerns about smoking and health. Accordingly, we hold that the Attorney General's outdoor and point-of-sale advertising regulations targeting cigarettes are pre-empted by the FCLAA.

C

Although the FCLAA prevents States and localities from imposing special requirements or prohibitions "based on smoking and health" "with respect to the advertising or promotion" of cigarettes, that language still leaves significant power in the hands of States to impose generally applicable zoning regulations and to regulate conduct. . . .

For instance, the FCLAA does not restrict a State or locality's ability to enact generally applicable zoning restrictions. We have recognized that state interests in traffic safety and esthetics may justify zoning regulations for advertising. Although Congress has taken into account the unique concerns about cigarette smoking and health in advertising, there is no indication that Congress intended to displace local community interests in general regulations of the location of billboards or large marquee advertising, or that Congress intended cigarette advertisers to be afforded special treatment in that regard. Restrictions on the location and size of advertisements that apply to cigarettes on equal terms with other products appear to be outside the ambit of the pre-emption provision. Such restrictions are not "based on smoking and health."

The FCLAA also does not foreclose all state regulation of conduct as it relates to the sale or use of cigarettes. The FCLAA's pre-emption provision explicitly governs state regulations of "advertising or promotion." [The Senate Report explained that the pre-emption provision "would in no way affect the power of any State or political subdivision of any State with respect to the taxation or the sale of cigarettes to minors, or the prohibition of smoking in public buildings, or similar police regulations. It is limited entirely to State or local requirements or prohibitions in the advertising of cigarettes.] Accordingly, the FCLAA does not pre-empt state laws prohibiting cigarette sales to minors. To the contrary, there is an established congressional policy that supports such laws; Congress has required States to prohibit tobacco sales to minors as a condition of receiving federal block grant funding for substance abuse treatment activities.

In Massachusetts, it is illegal to sell or distribute tobacco products to persons under the age of 18. Having prohibited the sale and distribution of tobacco products to minors, the State may prohibit common inchoate offenses that attach to criminal conduct, such as solicitation, conspiracy, and attempt. States and localities also have at their disposal other means of regulating conduct to ensure that minors do not obtain cigarettes. . . .

IV

We have observed that "tobacco use, particularly among children and adolescents, poses perhaps the single most significant threat to public health in the United States." From a policy perspective, it is understandable for the States to attempt to prevent minors from using tobacco products before they reach an age where they are capable of weighing for themselves the risks and potential benefits of tobacco use, and other adult activities. Federal law, however, places limits on policy choices available to the States. . . .

JUSTICE STEVENS, with whom JUSTICE GINSBURG and JUSTICE BREYER join, and with whom JUSTICE SOUTER joins as to Part I, concurring in part, concurring in the judgment in part, and dissenting in part. . . .

As the majority acknowledges, under prevailing principles, any examination of the scope of a preemption provision must "'start with the assumption that the historic police powers of the States [are] not to be superseded by . . . [the] Federal Act unless that [is] the clear and manifest purpose of Congress.'" As the regulations at issue in this suit implicate two powers that lie at the heart of the States' traditional police power—the power to regulate land usage and the power to protect the health and safety of minors—our precedents require that the Court construe the preemption provision "narrowly." If Congress' intent to preempt a particular category of regulation is ambiguous, such regulations are not preempted.

The text of the preemption provision must be viewed in context, with proper attention paid to the history, structure, and purpose of the regulatory scheme in which it appears. . . . [In 1969, Congress had sought to avoid inconsistencies in labeling requirements concerning cigarette packages and advertisements and to reduce the waste of regulatory resources attendant to competing regulatory systems].

There was, however, no need to interfere with state or local zoning laws or other regulations prescribing limitations on the location of signs or billboards. Laws prohibiting a cigarette company from hanging a billboard near a school in Boston in no way conflict with laws permitting the hanging of such a billboard in other jurisdictions. Nor would such laws even impose a significant administrative burden on would-be advertisers, as the great majority of localities impose general restrictions on signage, thus requiring advertisers to examine local law before posting signs whether or not cigarette-specific laws are preempted. Hence, it is unsurprising that Congress did not include any provision in the 1965 Act preempting location restrictions.

The Public Health Cigarette Smoking Act of 1969 (1969 Act), made two important changes in the preemption provision. First, it limited the applicability of the advertising prong to States and localities, paving the way for further federal regulation of cigarette advertising. FCLAA., § 4. Second, it expanded the scope of the advertising preemption provision. Where previously States were prohibited from requiring particular statements in cigarette advertising based on health concerns, they would henceforth be prohibited from imposing any "requirement or prohibition based on smoking and health . . . with respect to the advertising or promotion" of cigarettes.

Ripped from its context, this provision could theoretically be read as a breathtaking expansion of the limitations imposed by the 1965 Act. However, both our precedents and common sense require us to read statutory provisions—and, in particular, preemption clauses—in the context of both their neighboring provisions and of the history and purpose of the statutory scheme. When so viewed, it is quite clear that the 1969 amendments were intended to expand the provision to capture a narrow set of content regulations that would have escaped preemption under the prior provision, not to fundamentally reorder the division of regulatory authority between the Federal and State Governments. . . . All signs point inescapably to the conclusion that Congress only intended to preempt content regulations in the 1969 Act. . . . The legislative history of the provision also supports such a reading. . . .

I am firmly convinced that, when Congress amended the preemption provision in 1969, it did not intend to expand the application of the provision beyond content regulations. . . . Even if I were not so convinced, however, I would still dissent from the Court's conclusion with regard to preemption, because the provision is, at the very least, ambiguous. The historical record simply does not reflect that it was Congress' "clear and manifest purpose," to preempt attempts by States to utilize their traditional zoning authority to protect the health and welfare of minors. Absent such a manifest purpose, Massachusetts and its sister States retain their traditional police powers.

[Justices Kennedy and Thomas also filed concurring opinions, while Justice Souter filed a separate opinion concurring in part and dissenting in part.]

Notes and Questions

1. *Express preemption.* The Court treated *Lorillard* as an "express preemption" case, focusing on the following statutory language: "No requirement or prohibition based on smoking and health shall be imposed under State law with respect to the

advertising or promotion of any cigarettes the packages of which are labeled in conformity with the provisions of this chapter." What interpretive tools do the Court and Justice Stevens use to interpret the preemptive effect of this language? Consider how the Court used statutory language, structure, and legislative history; does the interpreter's choice of interpretive tools affect the outcome? Should it?

The majority and the dissent agree that, for preemption to arise, the intent of Congress must be "clear and manifest." What lies at the heart of the disagreement between the majority and Justice Stevens? Should there be a "presumption" against preemption when express preemption provisions are ambiguous? What is the origin of this presumption against preemption? Because Congress can override court decisions—even decisions of the Supreme Court—on matters of statutory interpretation, Congress can always correct a judicial misinterpretation of a statute to alter its preemptive effect. If Congress lets a judicial decision resting on a presumption against preemption stand, does that imply that Congress agrees with that decision? For statistics on Congress's reaction to judicial use of the presumption against preemption, see Note, *New Evidence on the Presumption Against Preemption: An Empirical Study of Congressional Responses to Supreme Court Preemption Decisions*, 120 Harv. L. Rev. 1604, 1626 (2007) (noting that Congress has rarely overridden the Court's interpretation on preemption issues, occasionally has enacted additional legislation inadvertently affecting prior case law, but primarily acts pragmatically by allowing decisions to remain in effect).

As was true in *Lorillard*, express preemption provisions do not always clearly answer questions about the conduct that they cover. In *Bruesewitz v. Wyeth LLC*, 562 U.S. 223 (2011), the federal statute provided that "[n]o vaccine manufacturer shall be liable in a civil action for damages arising from a vaccine-related injury or death . . . if the injury or death resulted from side effects that were unavoidable even though the vaccine was properly prepared and was accompanied by proper directions and warnings." The Court held that this language preempted state tort law that would otherwise have permitted recovery for defects in the design of the vaccine. The dissent would have read the preemption clause to preempt design-defect claims only when a manufacturer shows, on a case-by-case basis, "that the vaccine was properly manufactured and labeled, and that the side effects stemming from the vaccine's design could not have been prevented by a feasible alternative design that would have eliminated the adverse side effects without compromising the vaccine's cost and utility." *Id.* Does the language of the statute resolve the issue about preemption of design defects?

Sometimes, the same statutory language in different statutes can take on different import. In *Gobeille v. Liberty Mut. Ins. Co.*, 136 S. Ct. 936 (2016), the Court interpreted statutory language that preempted state laws that "relate to" any employee benefit plan. The Court was careful to note that if the "relate to" language was "taken to extend to the furthest stretch of its indeterminacy, then for all practical purposes pre-emption would never run its course." *Id.* at 943. The Court noted that "no sensible person could have intended" an "uncritical literalism" in applying these terms. *Id.* As a result, the Court limited the meaning of "relate to" to state laws that "act immediately and exclusively" on insurance plans governed by federal law or state laws that "interfere with nationally uniform" administration of the federal law. *Id.* The Court took a different tone in *Coventry Health Care of Missouri, Inc. v. Nevils*, 137 S. Ct. 1190 (2017). In that case, the Court interpreted the preemptive effect of statutory language that purported to supersede state law governing contract terms that "relate to" health insurance coverage. *Id.* at 1194. The Court noted that "relate to" should be interpreted expansively. The Court noted that it has "repeatedly recognized that the phrase 'relate to' in a preemption clause express[es] a broad pre-emptive purpose." *Coventry Health Care of Missouri, Inc. v. Nevils*, 137 S. Ct. 1190, 1197 (2017) (citations omitted). If you were drafting statutory language, would these cases provide guidance about how to achieve your desired scope of preemption?

For discussion of "presumptions" regarding preemption, see Clark, *Process Based Preemption*, *in* W. Buzbee (ed.), PREEMPTION CHOICE: THE THEORY, LAW, AND REALITY OF FEDERALISM'S CORE QUESTION 192–213 (2009) (discussing the presumption against preemption and "clear statement" rule); Hills, *Against Preemption: How Federalism Can Improve the National Legislative Process*, 82 N.Y.U. L. REV. 1 (2007) (arguing that a presumption against preemption would lead to more robust debate and sounder lawmaking). See also Sharpe, *Legislating Preemption*, 53 WM. & MARY L. REV. 163 (2011) (arguing that the Supreme Court has tended to favor preemption if Congress fails to provide adequate explicit direction and legislative history and urging that Congress should be more attentive to providing express directions on preemption). For a discussion of textualism and preemption, see Meltzer, *Preemption and Textualism*, 112 MICH. L. REV. 1 (2013). For an innovative argument against a wholesale presumption against preemption in the context of health law, see McCuskey, *Body of Preemption: Health Law Traditions and the Presumption Against Preemption*, 89 TEMPLE L. REV. 95 (2017).

2. *Implied preemption*. Even in the absence of an express preemption provision, courts will sometimes find that preemption is implied by statutory language and structure. Within the category of implied preemption, there are two subcategories: "field" preemption and "conflict" preemption. A federal statute preempts a "field" when federal law occupies an entire legislative field, or subject matter, of law. State law is subject to "conflict" preemption when a federal statute does not occupy an entire field, but instead preempts state law to the extent that it conflicts with the federal law. Conflict preemption can occur either if it is impossible to comply both with state and federal law or if the state law stands as an obstacle to the accomplishment of the purpose of the federal law. In all of these cases, whether federal law preempts state law is a matter of statutory interpretation. Although the results of preemption cases can be somewhat unpredictable, some patterns emerge across statutes based on subject matter.

(a) *Foreign affairs*. Where congressional or presidential power relating to foreign affairs is implicated, a court is very likely to hold that state law is preempted.

Consider the following cases: in *Crosby v. National Foreign Trade Council*, 530 U.S. 363 (2000), the Supreme Court struck down the Massachusetts "Burma law," which had prohibited state agencies from purchasing goods or services from companies doing business with Burma, now Myanmar. The Court reasoned that Congress intended to give the President considerable flexibility in imposing or lifting sanctions against Myanmar, and that the state law undermined the "congressional calibration of force" by penalizing conduct Congress permitted, employing a "conflict" preemption theory.

In *American Insurance Ass'n v. Garamendi*, 539 U.S. 396 (2003), the Court struck down a California statute that required insurers licensed in that state to provide information to Holocaust survivors about insurance policies that the insurers had issued in Europe from 1925 to 1945. Those that failed to comply ran the risk of losing their state insurance licenses. The Court reasoned that the California law was inconsistent with national policy as reflected in Presidential Executive Orders and the conduct of diplomacy. In reaching this conclusion in the absence of a clear conflict between state and federal law, the Court also put aside the historical role of states in regulating insurance, taking the position that an individual state had a limited interest and limited authority to regulate with regard to insurance policies issued in Europe prior to World War II. See Crace, *Gara-Mending the Doctrine of Foreign Affairs Preemption*, 90 CORNELL L. REV. 203 (2004) (arguing that the latter case embodies a statutory preemption standard applicable in instances relating to foreign affairs).

In *Arizona v. United States*, 567 U.S. 387 (2012), the Court struck down part of a statute that criminalized both the failure to complete or carry an alien registration document and also working while an unauthorized alien. It also invalidated authority given to state officers to arrest a person without a warrant where there was probable cause to believe that person had committed any public offense that made him removable from the United States. Notably, the majority found the state's action in authorizing state officers to arrest those suspected of being unauthorized aliens created an "obstacle" to the "full purposes and objectives of Congress" which had established a scheme in which trained federal immigration officers were to address such situations. The *Arizona* decision is particularly interesting in light of a decision just one year prior, *Chamber of Commerce of U.S. v. Whiting*, 563 U.S. 582 (2011). In that case, the Court upheld an Arizona law requiring employers in that state to verify the immigration status of employees at the risk of losing pertinent licenses. The Court found no express preemption under the Immigration Reform and Control Act. What accounts for the differences in these cases? Do all immigration cases equally implicate "foreign affairs" concerns?

Scholars do not uniformly see foreign affairs as exclusively a federal prerogative. For an argument that the realm of foreign affairs is not, and should not be, exclusively federal, see M. Glennon & R. Sloane, FOREIGN AFFAIRS FEDERALISM (2017). See also Abebe & Huq, *Foreign Affairs Federalism: A Revisionist Approach*, 66

VAND. L. REV. 723 (2013) (arguing that neither states nor federal government should have exclusive domain over foreign affairs).

(b) *Environmental regulation.* Preemption concerns run throughout environmental law. Perhaps because land use and public health are both traditionally governed by state law, courts are more reluctant to find that federal law preempts state restrictions and remedies, even in the broad language of comprehensive federal environmental statutes like the Clean Air Act and Clean Water Act. One issue that is currently working its way through the federal courts of appeals is whether the Clean Air Act preempts common law nuisance actions based on air pollutant emissions standards that are more stringent than federal standards. In *Merrick v. Diageo Americas Supply, Inc.*, 805 F.3d 685 (6th Cir. 2015), the Sixth Circuit held that the Clean Air Act does not preempt state common law claims brought against a polluter when those claims are based on the law of the state in which the polluter operates. Compare *North Carolina ex rel. Cooper v. Tennessee Valley Auth.*, 615 F.3d 291 (4th Cir. 2010) (holding that North Carolina could not proceed on a public nuisance theory based on state law against the TVA in light of the Clean Air Act).

For some of the many fine articles about preemption and environmental law, see Glicksman, *The Firm Constitutional Foundation and Shaky Political Future of Environmental Cooperative Federalism, in* CONTROVERSIES IN AMERICAN FEDERALISM AND PUBLIC POLICY (Banks, ed. 2018) (arguing that the environmental cooperative federalism venture that has served the nation so well is threatened by executive action); Kalen, *Policing Federal Supremacy: Preemption and Common Law Damage Claims as a Ceiling to the Clean Air Act Regulatory Floor*, 68 FLA. L. REV. 1697 (2016) (arguing that Congress intended to preserve state law damages claims in the Clean Air Act); Learner, *Restraining Federal Preemption When There Is an "Emerging Consensus" of State Environmental Laws and Policies*, 102 NW. U. L. REV. 649 (2008) (arguing that courts should weigh the evidence of emerging state approaches in reaching preemption decisions); Adler, *When Is Two a Crowd? The Impact of Federal Action on State Environmental Regulation*, 31 HARV. ENVTL. L. REV. 67 (2007) (exploring the interplay of federal and state regulatory choices); Farber, *Climate Change, Federalism, and the Constitution*, 50 ARIZ. L. REV. 879 (2008) (discussing preemption and its relation to climate change); Resnick, Civin & Frueh, *Ratifying Kyoto at the Local Level: Sovereigntism, Federalism, and Translocal Organizations of Government Actors (TOGAS)*, 50 ARIZ. L. REV. 709 (2008) (discussing relationship between local governmental efforts on climate change, the international dimensions of climate change, and related federalism issues); Cuskelly, *Factors to Consider in Applying a Presumption Against Preemption to State Environmental Regulations*, 39 ECOLOGY L.Q. 283 (2012).

(c) *Nutritional information.* Like environmental regulation, courts often find that nutritional labeling requirements, like other state health and safety regulations, are not preempted by federal law. See *N.Y. State Rest. Ass'n v. N.Y. City Bd. of Health*, 556 F.3d 114 (2d Cir. 2009). In this case, the portions of the New York City Health Code requiring chain restaurants to post calorie content information on menus were challenged on the ground that they were preempted by the federal Nutrition Labeling and Education Act of 1990 (NLEA). The court concluded that the City's requirement was not preempted by the NLEA's requirement for mandatory labeling of nutritional content on packaged foods, restaurants were not exempt from requirements that they conform with federal requirements regarding nutritional claims, the NLEA does not regulate nutritional labeling on restaurant foods and the NLEA allows states to adopt non-identical labeling rules for restaurants. See Rutkov, Vernick, Hodge & Teret, *Preemption and the Obesity Epidemic: State and Local Menu Labeling Laws and the Nutrition Labeling and Education Act*, 36 J.L. MED. & ETHICS 2008 36.1: 772. For a discussion of the newest frontier in the nutrition-preemption debate, see Craig, *Labeling Genetically-Engineered Foods: An Update from One of the Front Lines of Federalism*, 47 ENV. L. 609 (2017) (exploring federal statutes and regulations preempting state labeling requirements for genetically engineered foods); Murphy et al., *More than Curiosity: The Constitutionality of State Labeling Requirements for Genetically Engineered Foods*, 38 VT. L. REV. 477 (2013).

3. *The preemptive power of federal agencies: general principles and their application.* How should the existence of federal regulations affect preemption analysis? In *New York v. FERC*, 535 U.S. 1 (2002), the Supreme Court reviewed a challenge by New York State to orders by the Federal Energy Regulatory Commission requiring owners of electric transmission lines to provide open access to unbundled retail transmissions of electricity. The Court concluded that a federal agency may preempt state action only if it is acting within the scope of congressionally delegated authority (a threshold issue to be addressed before considering a presumption against preemption by the agency). The Court also said that agency action rooted in a clear and specific grant of jurisdiction was sufficient to ground preemptive action notwithstanding prefatory statutory language reserving state authority of certain sorts. For a review of agency procedures and their implications for federalism, see Sharkey, *Inside Agency Preemption*, 110 MICH. L. REV. 521 (2012) (arguing that federal agencies now play a role more dominant than Congress in the realm of statutory interpretation and preemption, and calling for reforms). See also Engstrom, *Agencies as Litigation Gatekeepers*, 123 YALE L.J. 616 (2013) (discussing the role of agencies as "gatekeepers" affecting potential litigation).

Related issues have arisen in a number of different contexts including the following:

(a) *Marijuana.* Marijuana is illegal under federal law. Nevertheless, after the United States Department of Justice, under President Obama, discouraged federal prosecutors from pursuing marijuana-related cases in states that legalized the drug, a number of states have permitted marijuana for medical or recreational use. Even though the Department of Justice reversed course under President Trump, states continue to legalize marijuana. Is this situation, in which states treat the drug as legal while the federal government continues to regard it as a controlled substance, stable? Is the treatment of marijuana anomalous or is it a leading indicator of a change in the federal-state relationship? For discussions of the significant federalism issues raised by these developments, see Nickles, *Federalism and State Marijuana Legislation*, 91 Notre Dame L. Rev. 1253 (2016) (tracking trends in state marijuana laws); Chemerinsky, Forman, Hopper & Kamin, *Cooperative Federalism and Marijuana Regulation*, 62 U.C.L.A. L. Rev. 74 (2015) (arguing that federal government should adopt a cooperative federalism approach that allows states to opt out of provisions of Controlled Substances Act); Schwartz, *High Federalism: Marijuana Legalization and the Limits of Federal Power to Regulate States*, 35 Cardozo L. Rev. 567 (2013) (considering both preemption and Tenth Amendment issues).

(b) *Lending.* Banking federalism is complicated by the fact that the United States has a dual banking system, in which banks can be chartered either by a state or by a federal agency. Either way, a bank is subject both to state and federal law. For example, state banks are subject to federal tax, consumer protection, and anti-discrimination laws. Similarly, federally chartered banks are subject to state laws concerning contracts, property and debt collection. The 2010 passage of the Dodd-Frank Wall Street Reform and Consumer Protection Act (Dodd-Frank), Pub L. No. 111-203, has important implications for preemption in the areas of banking and consumer protection. Dodd-Frank limited federal preemption with respect to the operating subsidiaries of national banks and thrifts, in effect overturning the result in *Watters v. Wachovia Bank*, 550 U.S. 1 (2007), which had found state efforts to regulate banks operating subsidiaries to be preempted based on regulations issued by the federal Office of the Comptroller of the Currency. State authorities were given expanded "visitorial" authority as recognized in *Cuomo v. Clearing House Ass'n*, 557 U.S. 519 (2009), and state attorneys general may sue banks to require compliance with rules to be issued by the Bureau of Consumer Financial Protection. Dodd-Frank preempts "state consumer finance law" (that is, state law that "directly and specifically regulates . . . any financial transaction [or] account"), but only if that law is preempted by another federal law, discriminates against federal banks or significantly interferes with the exercise of a national bank's powers (to be determined by the Comptroller of the Currency on a case-by-case basis).

Dodd-Frank also substitutes a regime of "conflict preemption" for the earlier "occupation of the field" preemption that had been in effect prior to the new statute. The *Watters* case turned on the proposition that the federal Comptroller could assert wide-ranging authority to preempt state action not only where there was a conflict between state and federal law, but also more generally wherever federal regulatory power might be found. The new legislation's preemption provision requires preemption to be based on another specific federal statute, findings of discrimination, or substantial interference with a national bank's powers. Such situations need to be analyzed on a case-by-case basis before preemption will be found (rather than asserting that federal authority precludes state action across the wider field of banking or finance). For more on preemption and Dodd-Frank, see Bailey, *Preemption Principles: Weighing the Impact of Dodd-Frank*, 34 No. 7 Bank. and Fin. Serv's Pol'y Repo. 1 (2015); Hovatter, *Preemption Analysis Under the National Bank Act:*

Then and Now, 67 CONSUMER FIN. L.Q. REP. 5 (2013) (comparing the state of the law in 2010 with more recent developments).

(c) *Medical devices.* In *Riegel v. Medtronic, Inc.*, 552 U.S. 312 (2008), the United States Supreme Court concluded that "pre-market clearance" of a specific medical device by the Food and Drug Administration preempted state law claims based on negligence, strict liability and implied warranty theories. The Food, Drug, and Cosmetics Act, in relevant part, includes the following preemption provision: "no State or political subdivision of a State may establish or continue in effect with respect to a device intended for human use any requirement—(1) that is different from, or in addition to, any requirement applicable under this chapter to the device, and (2) which relates to the safety or effectiveness of the device or to any other matter included in a requirement applicable to the device under this chapter." 21 U.S.C. § 360k(a). Because the FDA's pre-market clearance system was specific to particular devices, state claims were preempted, although in some other instances, a state damage remedy premised upon violation of federal regulations might be allowed. Not all state law medical device claims, however, are preempted by the Medical Device Amendments. See, e.g., *Mink v. Smith & Nephew, Inc.*, 860 F.3d 1319 (11th Cir. 2017) (holding that negligence claim is not preempted by federal law to the extent that it is premised on a manufacturing defect theory in violation of federal law). For a discussion about preemption in the context of medical devices, see Horvath, *Recovery and Preemption: The Collison of the Medicare Secondary Payer Act and the Medical Device Amendments*, 103 CAL. L. REV. 1353 (2015).

(d) *Drugs.* Regulation of drugs by the federal Food and Drug Administration (FDA) has raised a number of preemption questions. In *Wyeth v. Levine*, 555 U.S. 555 (2009), the United States Supreme Court considered several issues related to preemption by federal agencies, including agencies' use of "preemption by preamble" in federal regulations as a means of limiting state prerogatives. *Wyeth* involve a state tort action by a professional violinist who sued a drug manufacturer for failure to warn about risks associated with intravenous "push" injection of anti-nausea medication that, when injected, resulted in gangrene and amputation of her arm. She asserted that there had been at least 20 incidents since 1967, prior to her own experience, in which injection of the drug had resulted in gangrene and amputation. The Court held that her claim was not preempted by federal law, rejecting theories that a manufacturer could not have modified its warning label after FDA approval, as well as assertions that it was impossible for the manufacturer to comply with federal and state labeling requirements and that federal law would have been obstructed had the manufacturer provided stronger warnings about risks.

In *PLIVA, Inc. v. Mensing*, 564 U.S. 604 (2011), the Court held that patients who developed a neurological disease after taking a generic drug could not bring suit under state law against the drug manufacturers because federal law preempted state claims that the drug's label should have been changed to reflect growing awareness of adverse side effects. The majority concluded that, if such suits were allowed, then generic manufacturers would have had to get approval both from federal authorities and from brand manufacturers prior to changing their labels, a process that would be difficult if not impossible. The dissenters viewed the situation differently, contending that the generic manufacturers could have done more to advise doctors of associated risks or seek FDA assistance. In the dissenters' view, the mere "possibility of impossibility" should not have been grounds for preemption. Subsequently, in *Mutual Pharmaceutical Co, Inc. v. Bartlett*, 133 S. Ct. 2466 (2013), the Court concluded that a design defect claim could not be asserted under state law based on a generic drug manufacturer's failure to strengthen warnings in light of provisions of federal law that expressly prohibited manufacturers of generic drugs from making any unilateral changes to a drug's label. Considering these two cases, at least one commentator sees the potential death of drug design litigation by federal preemption. Twerski, *The Demise of Drug Design Litigation: Death by Federal Preemption*, 68 AM. U. L. REV. 281 (2018). See also Zettler, *Pharmaceutical Federalism*, 92 IND. L.J. 845 (2017) (considering preemption and the consequences of state interest in regulating drugs).

(e) *Government contracts.* Federal agencies act not only through the promulgation of rules, but in other ways, too, including by entering into contracts with private entities. Can the terms of a contract entered into by a federal agency with a private party preempt state contract law to the contrary? In *Coventry Health Care of Missouri, Inc. v. Nevils*, 137 S. Ct. 1190 (2017), the Court considered the preemptive effect of the Federal Employees Health Benefit Act (FEHBA). The Act provided that the Office of Personnel Management (OPM) could contract with private insurance carriers for federal employees' health insurance coverage. The statute further provided that the "terms of any contract . . . which relate to the nature, provision, or extent of coverage or benefits . . . shall supersede and preempt any State or local law . . . which relates to health insurance." *Id.* at 1194. Missouri's state contract law conflicted with contract terms that OPM often included in its contracts under the statute. The Court interpreted the statutory language broadly, holding that the phrase "relate to" in a preemption clause demonstrates Congress's purpose to preempt broadly. *Id.* As a result, the Court held, state contract law was preempted by the statute's provisions.

4. *Comparison of federal and state preemption.* How closely does federal preemption analysis parallel the analysis of state-local preemption problems discussed in Chapter 3? Are there differences in policy, history or analytical method that might influence the approaches taken by the courts in these different contexts? Consider, for example, the following: Congress, unlike state legislatures, possesses constitutionally enumerated powers; federal legislation is often introduced to address matters already regulated by the states; federal legislation is often implemented by powerful federal regulatory agencies; and federal legislation is often enacted following the development of extensive legislative history.

A Note on Next Steps in Tobacco Regulation

Consider the following post-*Lorillard* events for an idea of the ways in which judicial decisions and legislation often intersect in federal preemption matters.

More litigation challenging state regulatory efforts after Lorillard. Litigation continued following *Lorillard*, with states attempting to limit the sale of tobacco products to children. In *Rowe v. New Hampshire Motor Transport Ass'n*, 552 U.S. 364 (2008), Maine's Tobacco Delivery Law prohibited a person from delivering tobacco products to any Maine consumer if the products had been bought from unlicensed retailers, providing that a person delivering packages was "deemed to know" that they contained tobacco products if the packages showed that there were tobacco products inside or a list maintained by the state attorney general indicated that the shipper was an unlicensed tobacco retailer. The Supreme Court concluded that provisions of Maine's Tobacco Delivery Law had been preempted.

Subsequently, challenges relating to "light" cigarettes were pursued under the Maine Unfair Trade Practices Act. In *Altria Group, Inc. v. Good*, 555 U.S. 70 (2008), the federal statute provided that "[n]o requirement or prohibition based on smoking and health shall be imposed under State law with respect to the advertising or promotion of any cigarettes the packages of which are labeled in conformity with the provisions of this chapter." A state law action was brought by smokers of "light" cigarettes against tobacco manufacturers based on manufacturers' statements that such cigarettes had "lowered tar and nicotine." The Court held that the federal statute neither expressly or impliedly preempted the historic police powers of the state in the absence of the "clear and manifest purpose of Congress."

New legislation and new preemption provisions. In 2009, Congress adopted the Family Smoking Prevention and Tobacco Control Act. See Pub. L. No. 111-131, §§ 2(3), 2(5), 2(31) and 2(49), 123 Stat. 1776, 1777–1781 (2009). This legislation gave the Food and Drug Administration (FDA) substantial control over many aspects of tobacco product design, production, marketing and advertising. The new statute contained extensive congressional findings, additional definitions, stronger restrictions on misbranding and additives, additional recordkeeping and reporting requirements and further limitations on advertising. For general discussion of the new statute, see Carvajal, Clissold & Shapiro, *The Family Smoking Prevention and Tobacco Control Act: An Overview*, 64 Food & Drug L.J. 717 (2009).

The 2009 statute included new preemption language. Consider how the following preemption provisions affected the power of states and localities to adopt regulations of the sort at issue in *Lorillard*. If the following provisions had been in effect at the time *Lorillard* was litigated, would the result in that case have differed?

One preemption provision in the 2009 statute was included in title 15 (relating to trade and commerce), and specifically modified provisions at issue in *Lorillard*, 15 U.S.C. § 1334, part of the Federal Cigarette Labeling and Advertising Act:

> (a) Additional statements. Except to the extent the Secretary requires additional or different statements on any cigarette package by a regulation, by an order, by a standard, by an authorization to market a product, or by a condition of marketing a product, . . . no statement relating to smoking and health, other than the statement required by section 1333 of this title [e.g., "Warning: Cigarettes are addictive"], shall be required on any cigarette package.
>
> (b) State regulations. No requirement or prohibition based on smoking and health shall be imposed under State law with respect to the advertising or promotion of any cigarettes the packages of which are labeled in conformity with the provisions of this chapter.
>
> (c) Exception. Notwithstanding subsection (b), a State or locality may enact statutes and promulgate regulations, based on smoking and health, that take effect after the effective date of the Family Smoking Prevention and Tobacco Control Act, imposing specific bans or restrictions on the time, place, and manner, but not content, of the advertising or promotion of any cigarettes.

The 2009 legislation included a second preemption provision in title 21 of the U.S. Code (dealing with food and drug matters). 21 U.S.C. § 387p(a) provides:

> (1) [N]othing in this subchapter . . . shall be construed to limit the authority of . . . a State or political subdivision of a State . . . to enact, adopt, promulgate, and enforce any law, rule, regulation, or other measure with respect to tobacco products that is in addition to, or more stringent than, requirements established under this subchapter, including a law, rule, regulation, or other measure relating to or prohibiting the sale, distribution, possession, exposure to, access to, advertising and promotion of, or use of tobacco products by individuals of any age. . . .
>
> (2) Preemption of certain State and local requirements
>
> (A) In general. No State or political subdivision of a State may establish or continue in effect with respect to a tobacco product any requirement which is different from, or in addition to, any requirement under the provisions of this subchapter relating to tobacco product standards, premarket review, adulteration, misbranding, labeling, registration, good manufacturing standards, or modified risk tobacco products.
>
> (B) Exception. Subparagraph (A) does not apply to requirements relating to the sale, distribution, possession, information reporting to the State, exposure to, access to, the advertising and promotion of, or use of, tobacco products by individuals of any age, or relating to fire safety standards for tobacco products.

21 U.S.C. § 387p(b) reads as follows:

> Rule of construction regarding product liability. No provision of this subchapter relating to a tobacco product shall be construed to modify or otherwise affect any action or the liability of any person under the product liability law of any State.

Why was this second statutory provision needed? Are its provisions clear or overly complicated? Why were they drafted as they were? For a discussion of preemption under the Act, see Halabi, *The Scope of Preemption under the 2009 Family Smoking Prevention and Tobacco Control Act*, 71 Food & Drug L.J. 300 (2016) (analyzing the statute's preemption provision in light of Supreme Court authority interpreting analogous preemption provisions).

Litigation in the aftermath of the new legislation. In *U.S. Smokeless Tobacco Mfg. Co. LLC v. City of New York*, 708 F.3d 428 (2d Cir. 2013), plaintiffs involved in the manufacture and distribution of smokeless tobacco products challenged New York City ordinances that limited sale of "flavored tobacco products," other than cigarettes, to tobacco bars. "Flavored tobacco products" include chewing tobacco, dip, and snuff. Only eight tobacco bars existed in New York City, all of them in Manhattan. The plaintiffs challenged the city ordinances on grounds that the United States Secretary of Health and Human Services had been expressly prohibited from issuing regulations "(A) banning all cigarettes, all smokeless tobacco products, all little cigars, all cigars other than little cigars, all pipe tobacco, or all roll-your-own tobacco products; or (B) requiring the reduction of nicotine yields of a tobacco product to zero." The court concluded, however, that the ordinance fell within a statutory exception to preemption for local laws that establish "requirements relating to the sale . . . of . . . tobacco products." See also *National Ass'n of Tobacco Outlets, Inc. v. City of Providence*, 731 F.3d 71 (1st Cir. 2013) (upholding local ordinances that limited sales of specified "flavored" tobacco products other than cigarettes to smoking bars, and prohibiting retailers from using coupons or multi-pack discounts to reduce prices of tobacco products in order to appeal to young people in light of clear terms of 15 U.S.C. § 1334(c) (quoted above). More recently, in *Graham v. R.J. Reynolds Tobacco Co.*, 857 F.3d 1169 (11th Cir. 2017), the Court of Appeals for the Eleventh Circuit held that federal law does not preempt claims for money damages arising under state law premised on the theory that all cigarettes are inherently dangerous. Could a state ban cigarettes altogether, even if the FDA may not?

FDA Regulations. In 2016, the FDA issued a final rule interpreting the scope of its authority in light of the 2009 Act. The FDA determined that its authority to regulate tobacco products extends to all "tobacco products" as defined in the Food, Drug, and Cosmetic Act. Among the new regulations, the FDA clarified that all electronic nicotine delivery systems, including e-cigarettes, are covered by the FDA's authority. As a result, e-cigarettes (along with other tobacco products) are subject to FDA packaging, labeling, and other requirements. In its final rulemaking, the FDA expressed the view that these new regulations did not preempt any state or local laws in effect at the time of the promulgation of the new rule, although the statutory provisions described above continue to have preemptive effect.

Final questions. Is it ever possible to eliminate the ambiguity of preemption by statute? How much of a role do presumptions against preemption play? How responsive is Congress to the Court; and conversely, how responsive is the Court to the work of Congress (that is, the legislative process)? How would you draft a preemption provision to minimize ambiguity?

[2] Reserving Rights to the States: The Tenth Amendment

As seen in the previous section, the Supremacy Clause provides that federal law is supreme to state law. But the Supremacy Clause itself does not set out the permissible scope or subjects of federal law. Rather, other parts of the Constitution must be consulted to determine the scope of federal authority. Most saliently, Congress possesses certain enumerated powers as well as the power to "make all laws which shall be necessary and proper for carrying into execution" both these enumerated powers and "all other powers vested by this Constitution in the government of the United States." U.S. Const. art. I, § 8. This constitutional language is broad; and, indeed, the Supreme Court has interpreted it broadly. But, as the Constitution itself also strongly suggests, not all conceivable government power is vested in the United States. In particular, the Constitution's Tenth Amendment provides: "The powers not delegated to the United States by the Constitution, nor prohibited by it to the States, are reserved to the States respectively, or to the people."

By its express terms, the Tenth Amendment does not make any law. That is, by declaring that any power not given to the United States belongs elsewhere, the Tenth Amendment does not add or subtract from the power of either the federal government or the states. This was, at least, the Supreme Court's view for nearly two centuries; and it is for this reason that the Supreme Court, during the New Deal period, called the Tenth Amendment a "truism." *United States v. F. W. Darby Lumber Co.*, 312 U.S. 100 (1941). However, as the New Deal sentiment started to give way in the 1970s, the Supreme Court began to entertain the idea that the Tenth Amendment has some substantive content to it, affirmatively limiting federal power even when that power falls within the scope of authority granted elsewhere in the Constitution. In *National League of Cities v. Usery*, 426 U.S. 833, 842 (1976), the Court held that the Tenth Amendment establishes "limits upon the power of Congress to override state sovereignty, even when exercising its otherwise plenary powers," a conclusion that the dissent, perhaps justifiably, found astounding. Specifically, the Court held that some "traditional governmental functions" could not be displaced by authority granted to Congress by the Constitution. But *National League of Cities*' resurrection of the Tenth Amendment was brief; just ten years later, in *Garcia v. San Antonio Metropolitan Transit Auth.*, 469 U.S. 528 (1985), the Court expressly overruled *National League of Cities*, holding that the "traditional governmental function" test was unworkable and inconsistent with established principles of federalism.

But, if ever a doctrine had nine-lives, it is surely the doctrine surrounding the Tenth Amendment. Despite the seeming finality of *Garcia*, just a few years later, the Supreme Court once again imbued the Tenth Amendment with substantive content, albeit in a novel way. As you read *New York v. United States*, below, consider the following questions: how is the reasoning of this case different from both *National League of Cities* and *Garcia*?; what became of the concept of "traditional state functions"?; should precedent trump the plain language of the Tenth Amendment?; if precedent matters, which precedent should the Supreme Court follow in its next case about the Tenth Amendment: *National League of Cities*, *Garcia*, or *New York v. United States*?

New York v. United States

505 U.S. 144 (1992)

Justice O'Connor delivered the opinion of the Court.

This case implicates one of our Nation's newest problems of public policy and perhaps our oldest question of constitutional law. The public policy issue involves the disposal of radioactive waste. In this case, we address the constitutionality of three provisions of the Low-Level Radioactive Waste Policy Amendments Act of 1985, Pub. L. 99-240, 99 Stat. 1842, 42 U.S.C. §2021b et seq. The constitutional question is as old as the Constitution: It consists of discerning the proper division of authority between the Federal Government and the States. We conclude that while Congress has substantial power under the Constitution to encourage the States to provide for the disposal of the radioactive waste generated within their borders, the Constitution does not confer upon Congress the ability simply to compel the States to do so. We therefore find that only two of the Act's three provisions at issue are consistent with the Constitution's allocation of power to the Federal Government.

[The Act includes three types of incentives to encourage the states to comply with their statutory obligation to provide for the disposal of low-level radioactive waste generated within their borders. One type of incentive was a monetary incentive through which states with low-level radioactive waste sites collect surcharges from waste depositors. A portion of the surcharges is held by the United States Secretary of Energy in escrow and states which had taken appropriate steps to dispose of low-level radioactive waste within their borders qualify to receive a rebate from the fund. A second type of incentive is the imposition of substantial surcharges or denial of access to disposal sites for states that had not met relevant deadlines for developing disposal facilities or belonging to interstate compacts for disposal of low-level radioactive waste. A third incentive involves a "take title" requirement. If a state or compact region in which low-level radioactive waste was generated is unable to provide for the disposal of all waste generated by a future date, the state in which the waste was generated is obliged to take title and possession of the waste. It is also liable for all damages directly or indirectly incurred by the generator or owner as a consequence of the failure to take possession after the relevant deadline. The state of New York and two of its counties challenged these three aspects of the federal legislation under the Tenth Amendment.]

These questions can be viewed in either of two ways [as described by *National League of Cities* and *Garcia*.]. In some cases the Court has inquired whether an Act of Congress is authorized by one of the powers delegated to Congress in Article I of the Constitution. In other cases, the Court has sought to determine whether an Act of Congress invades the province of state sovereignty reserved by the Tenth Amendment. . . .

Petitioners do not contend that Congress lacks the power to regulate the disposal of low level radioactive waste. . . . [They] contend only that the Tenth Amendment limits the power of Congress to regulate in the way it has chosen. Rather than addressing the problem of waste disposal by directly regulating the generators and disposers of waste, petitioners argue, Congress has impermissibly directed the States to regulate in this field.

Most of our recent cases interpreting the Tenth Amendment have concerned the authority of Congress to subject state governments to generally applicable laws. . . . This case instead concerns the circumstances under which Congress may use the States as implementers of regulation; that is, whether Congress may direct or otherwise motivate the States to regulate in a particular field or a particular way. Our cases have established a few principles that guide our resolution of the issue.

As an initial matter, Congress may not simply "commandee[r] the legislative processes of the States by directly compelling them to enact and enforce a federal regulatory program." . . . While Congress has substantial powers to govern the Nation directly, including in areas of intimate concern to the States, the Constitution has never been understood to confer upon Congress the ability to require the States to govern according to Congress' instruction. . . . [T]he [Philadelphia] Convention opted for a Constitution in which Congress would exercise its legislative authority directly over individuals rather than over States; for a variety of reasons, it rejected the New Jersey Plan in favor of the Virginia Plan. . . .

This is not to say that Congress lacks the ability to encourage a State to regulate in a particular way, or that Congress may not hold out incentives to the States as a method of influencing a State's policy choices. Our cases have identified a variety of methods, short of outright coercion, by which Congress may urge a State to adopt a legislative program consistent with federal interests. Two of these methods are of particular relevance here.

First, under Congress' spending power, "Congress may attach conditions on the receipt of federal funds." . . . Second, where Congress has the authority to regulate private activity under the Commerce Clause, we have recognized Congress' power to offer States the choice of regulating that activity according to federal standards or having state law pre-empted by federal regulation. . . . By either of these two methods, as by any other permissible method of encouraging a State to conform to federal policy choices, the residents of the State retain the ultimate decision as to whether or not the State will comply. If a State's citizens view federal policy as sufficiently contrary to local interests, they may elect to decline a federal grant. If state residents would prefer their government to devote its attention and resources to problems other than those deemed important by Congress, they may choose to have the Federal Government rather than the State bear the expense of a federally mandated regulatory program, and they may continue to supplement that program to the extent state law is not preempted. Where Congress encourages state regulation rather than compelling it, state governments remain responsive to the local electorate's preferences; state officials remain accountable to the people.

By contrast, where the Federal Government compels States to regulate, the accountability of both state and federal officials is diminished.... [W]here the Federal Government directs the States to regulate, it may be state officials who will bear the brunt of public disapproval, while the federal officials who devised the regulatory program may remain insulated from the electoral ramifications of their decision.

[The first two types of incentives described above do not run afoul of the Tenth Amendment. The creation of a monetary incentive is an arrangement that coupled an exercise of Congress' power to authorize the states to burden interstate commerce with its power to impose the equivalent of a federal tax on interstate commerce, and a conditional exercise of its authority under the Spending Clause. Limiting access to disposal sites by gradually increasing the cost of access to the sites and then denying it altogether likewise falls within Congress' Commerce Clause power to allow discrimination against interstate commerce.]

The take title provision is of a different character. This third so-called "incentive" offers States, as an alternative to regulating pursuant to Congress' direction, the option of taking title to and possession of the lower level radioactive waste generated within their borders and becoming liable for all damages waste generators suffer as a result of the States' failure to do so promptly. In this provision, Congress has crossed the line distinguishing encouragement from coercion.

... [T]he Constitution would not permit Congress simply to transfer radioactive waste from generators to state governments. Such a forced transfer, standing alone, would in principle be no different than a congressionally compelled subsidy from state governments to radioactive waste producers. The same is true of the provision requiring the States to become liable for the generators' damages. Standing alone, this provision would be indistinguishable from an Act of Congress directing the States to assume the liabilities of certain state residents. Either type of federal action would "commandeer" state governments into the service of federal regulatory purposes, and would for this reason be inconsistent with the Constitution's division of authority between federal and state governments. On the other hand, the second alternative held out to state governments—regulating pursuant to Congress' direction—would, standing alone, present a simple command to state governments to implement legislation enacted by Congress. As we have seen, the Constitution does not empower Congress to subject state governments to this type of instruction.

Because an instruction to state governments to take title to waste, standing alone, would be beyond the authority of Congress, and because a direct order to regulate, standing alone, would also be beyond the authority of Congress, it follows that Congress lacks the power to offer the States a choice between the two.

[Justices White, Blackmun and Stevens concurred in part and dissented in part.]

Notes and Questions

1. *The expanding anti-commandeering principle.* The principal case stands for the proposition that Congress is precluded from "commandeering" the states as a means of implementing federal policy; that is, Congress may not require the states to regulate. At the very least, the principal case suggests that Congress may not require a state legislature to pass a statute to implement federal policy. Other questions raised but not answered by the principal case include the following: can federal action result in a state's executive or judicial officers being unconstitutionally commandeered?; can a federal law prohibit a state legislature from passing a new law or from repealing an old one?; how is a principle against commandeering consistent with the proposition that federal law is supreme over state law?; is it unconstitutional commandeering to *encourage* a state to pass a law?; what if the encouragement appears to be an offer the state can't refuse?

In subsequent years, the Court has partially answered these questions as it extended the concept of commandeering. In *Printz v. United States*, 521 U.S. 898 (1997), the Court invalidated provisions of the Brady Handgun Control Act as an unconstitutional "commandeering" of state and local *executive* officials. The Court held that Congress could not require state and local executive officials to enforce federal background checks, suggesting that it would violate the Tenth Amendment. The Court distinguished, however, commandeering of state executive officials and state legislatures from judges. State judges, the Court reiterated, are not commandeered when, because of the Supremacy Clause, they apply federal law. Is there a difference between, on one hand, commandeering a legislature or executive officials and, on the other hand, expecting state judges to apply federal law? In the principal case, the Court suggested that the difference might be political accountability, noting that when "Congress encourages state regulation rather than compelling it, state governments remain responsive to the local electorate's preferences; state officials remain accountable to the people." *Id.* What are the limits of a principle of political accountability? If commandeering is problematic whenever a politically accountable state or local official implements federal law, does it matter that most state judges are elected rather than appointed? Compare U.S. Const. art. VI ("the Judges in every State shall be bound" by federal law). For more on *Printz* and commandeering, see Jackson, *Federalism and the Uses and Limits of Law: Printz and Principle?* 111 Harv. L. Rev. 2180 (1998).

In *Murphy v. National Collegiate Athletic Ass'n*, 138 S. Ct. 1461 (2018), the Court addressed whether the anti-commandeering principle prohibits Congress from preventing state legislatures from repealing statutes that comport with federal law. In that case, the federal Professional and Amateur Sports Protection Act (PASPA) prohibited states from "authorizing" sports gambling. The Court held that PASPA violated the anti-commandeering principle because it would have prevented states from repealing old state laws prohibiting sports gambling. The Court characterized PASPA as follows: "It is as if federal officers were installed in state legislative chambers and were armed with the authority to stop legislators from voting on any offending proposals. A more direct affront to state sovereignty is not easy to imagine." *Id.* at 1478. Under the logic of *Murphy*, would a federal statute violate the anti-commandeering principle if it read: "no state may enact any statute inconsistent with federal law"? If such a law is unconstitutional commandeering, can the commandeering principle be reconciled with the Supremacy Clause?

What if the federal statute encourages the state to change its law by making the state an offer that it can't refuse? See THE GODFATHER (Paramount 1972). In *National Federation of Independent Business (NFIB) v. Sebelius*, 132 S. Ct. 2566 (2012), the Court held that the anti-commandeering principle prevents Congress not only from ordering the state to enact a law, but also from conditioning federal spending on the implementation of federal policy when the offer of federal spending is so enticing as to be *coercive*. *Id.* at 2659. How does coercion differ from commandeering? What otherwise lawful federal action may be "coercive." For a discussion of coercion, see Posner, *The Politics of Coercive Federalism in the Bush Era*, PUBLIUS 2007 37.3: 390 (proposing a taxonomy of coercion that ranges from direct mandates for action to various forms of preemption to tax provisions, regulatory requirements and exposure of state and local governments to law suits). More on coercion and the spending power in Part C, below.

2. *Justifications for the anti-commandeering principle.* As commentators have noted, it is debatable whether an anti-commandeering principle was contemplated at the time the Constitution was framed. See Campbell, *Commandeering and Constitutional Change*, 122 YALE L.J. 1104 (2013) (arguing that antifederalists *favored* commandeering of state and local officials to collect certain taxes in order to avoid a bloated federal bureaucracy and that shifting political priorities moved the country away from viewing commandeering as constitutional). Historical arguments aside, there are a number of justifications for an anti-commandeering principle. The Supreme Court articulated three of them in *Murphy*:

> First, the rule serves as one of the Constitution's structural protections of liberty. The Constitution does not protect the sovereignty of States for the benefit of the States or state governments as abstract political entities. To the contrary, the Constitution divides authority between federal and state governments for the protection of individuals. A healthy balance of

> power between the States and the Federal Government [reduces] the risk of tyranny and abuse from either front.
>
> Second, the anticommandeering rule promotes political accountability. When Congress itself regulates, the responsibility for the benefits and burdens of the regulation is apparent. Voters who like or dislike the effects of the regulation know who to credit or blame. By contrast, if a State imposes regulations only because it has been commanded to do so by Congress, responsibility is blurred.
>
> Third, the anticommandeering principle prevents Congress from shifting the costs of regulation to the States. If Congress enacts a law and requires enforcement by the Executive Branch, it must appropriate the funds needed to administer the program. It is pressured to weigh the expected benefits of the program against its costs. But if Congress can compel the States to enact and enforce its program, Congress need not engage in any such analysis. *See, e.g.,* E. Young, Two Cheers for Process Federalism, 46 Vill. L. Rev. 1349, 1360–1361 (2001). [*Murphy v. National Collegiate Athletic Ass'n*, 138 S. Ct. 1461, 1477 (2018).]

Do these justifications support the Court's pre-anti-commandeering Tenth Amendment decisions in *National League of Cities*? Do the anti-commandeering decisions overrule *Garcia*? If *Garcia* is still good law, is the basis of the anti-commandeering principle the Tenth Amendment or something else? There have been many excellent articles about the commandeering principle. For articles about the past, present and possible future of commandeering, see Coan, *Commandeering, Coercion, and the Deep Structure of American Federalism*, 95 B.U. L. Rev. 1 (2015); Greve, *Coercision, Conditions, and Commandeering: A Brief Note on the Medicaid Holding of NFIB v. Sebelius*, 37 Harv. J. L. Pub. Pol'y 83 (2014); McGreal, *Unconstitutional Politics*, 76 Notre Dame L. Rev. 519 (2001); Adler, *State Sovereignty and the Anti-Commandeering Cases*, 574 Ann. Amer. Acad. Pol. and Soc. Sci. 158 (2001); Caminker, *State Sovereignty and Subordinacy: May Congress Commandeer State Officers to Implement Federal Law?*, 95 Colum. L. Rev. 1001 (1995).

3. *Costs of the anti-commandeering principle.* In *Murphy*, the Supreme Court laid out the major normative arguments for the anti-commandeering principle. But there are some costs imposed by adhering to this principle as well. One cost may be revealed when a natural disaster or other emergency situation calls for the deployment of federal resources. Does the principle prohibit the federal government from heading up a joint federal-state response to, say, a hurricane? For arguments about the implications of the anti-commandeering principle for emergencies like terrorist attacks and hurricanes, see E. Ryan, Federalism and the Tug of War Within 257 (2011) (arguing that the Court's approach to federalism, including the anti-commandeering principle, can lead to abdication in a variety of areas, including the government's response to threats of terrorism and natural disasters); Siegel, *Commandeering and Its Alternatives: A Federalism Perspective*, 59 Vand. L. Rev. 1629

(2006) (arguing that anti-commandeering principle should be reexamined in light of the potential need to require state and local personnel to assist federal personnel in the event of a future terrorist attack); Mazzone, *The Commandeerer in Chief*, 83 NOTRE DAME L. REV. 265 (2007) (arguing that it should be permissible for the federal government to call state emergency personnel into service in certain circumstances); Giuliano, *Emergency Federalism: Calling on States in Perilous Times*, 40 U. MICH. J.L. REFORM 341 (2007) (discussing emergency responses in the wake of 9/11 and Hurricane Katrina). See also Kent, *"Where's the Cavalry?" Federal Response to 21st Century Disasters*, 40 SUFFOLK U. L. REV. 181 (2006); Winston, *Federalism after Hurricane Katrina: How Can Social Programs Respond to a Major Disaster*, 81 TUL. L. REV. 1219 (2007); Ryan, *Federalism and the Tug of War Within: Seeking Checks and Balance in the Interjurisdictional Gray Area*, 66 MD. L. REV. 503 (2007).

Consider how the anti-commandeering principle might prevent a more coordinated national response to the COVID-19 pandemic. If Congress formulated a comprehensive plan to prevent the spread of disease—say, requiring schools and businesses to remain closed or operate at lower capacity—would the anti-commandeering principle prevent Congress from requiring state executive officials to enforce federal law? Consider, also, the opposite situation: if state law requires schools and businesses to remain closed, does the anti-commandeering doctrine prevent the federal government from *forcing* the states to allow them to reopen? Should these two scenarios be treated differently under the anti-commandeering principle? If so, why?

Another cost of the anti-commandeering principle, counter-intuitively perhaps, may be the increased size of the federal government and pervasiveness of federal regulation. Recall the various state-federal arrangements created by complex federal statutory schemes discussed at the beginning of the chapter. The arrangements resulting from the give-and-take of negotiation between state and federal entities can, at times, gives states a strong voice in the implementation of federal policy. Such has been true with the implementation of the ACA. Gluck & Huberfeld, *What Is Federalism in Healthcare for?*, 70 STAN. L. REV. 1689 (2018). But a strong anti-commandeering principle can have the effect of disrupting these collaborative relationships. If a strong anti-commandeering rule prevents Congress from involving the states in a collaborative process, the result may be, instead, an expanded federal government and more direct federal control over citizens without the moderating influence of the states.

4. *Regulating states "as" states.* At times, Congress regulates state or local governments themselves rather than regulating their citizens. Does this kind of regulation offend Tenth Amendment principles or the principles of anti-commandeering or coercion discussed above? Consider the following situations:

(a) *Drivers' Privacy Protection Act.* Consider the Drivers' Privacy Protection Act, which prohibits state departments of motor vehicles from knowingly disclosing "personal information" about any individual contained in databases maintained by the states and requires states to change their methods of maintaining driver record databases. In *Reno v. Condon*, 528 U.S. 141 (2000), the Court upheld provisions of this Act against an anti-commandeering challenge where its requirements were also applicable to private parties who maintained drivers' license information databases. For a thoughtful discussion, see Cosgrove, *Reno v. Condon: The Supreme Court Takes a Right Turn in Its Tenth Amendment Jurisprudence by Upholding the Constitutionality of the Driver's Privacy Protection Act*, 68 Fordham L. Rev. 2543 (2000).

(b) *Tax Equity and Fiscal Responsibility Act.* Consider also the Tax Equity and Fiscal Responsibility Act, which removes a federal income tax exemption for non-registered state and municipal bonds in an effort to limit tax evasion associated with bearer bonds, notwithstanding the impact on states' decisions regarding the types of bonds to be issued. In *South Carolina v. Baker*, 485 U.S. 505 (1988), the Court upheld the Act, finding no coercion of state decisions or commandeering of their personnel, based on the states' ability to gain recourse to the national political process.

(c) *REAL ID Act.* Finally, consider the REAL ID Act of 2005, P.L. 109-13, § 201 *et seq.*, 49 U.S.C. § 30301. The Act obligates states to modify drivers' license issuance procedures in order to comply with federal verification standards, digital imaging standards, reporting, database creation, management and retention standards, all of which were estimated to substantially exceed the costs estimated by the federal Department of Homeland Security. The main provision of the Act prohibits state driver's licenses and ID cards from being accepted for federal identification purposes unless a state complies with national standards relating to name, address and photograph technology, and requiring presentation of birth certificates and documentation of legal residence for verification through a national database prior to issuance. The Act is still being phased in. See http://www.ncsl.org/research/transportation/count-down-to-real-id.aspx. For a look at the implications of the Act, see Miller, *Constitutional Law—The Real ID Act: Violating Massachusetts Residents' Right to Travel and the Tenth Amendment*, 38 W. New Eng. L. Rev. 127 (2016); see also Thiessen, *The REAL ID Act and Biometric Technology: A Nightmare for Citizens and the States that Have to Implement It*, 6 J. Telecomm. & High Tech. L. 483 (2008).

5. *The political process.* How does the Tenth Amendment bear on term limits, voting procedures, and elections? In *United States Term Limits, Inc. v. Thornton*, 514 U.S. 779 (1995), the Supreme Court considered a challenge to an amendment to the Arkansas state constitution which precluded those who had served three terms in the House of Representatives or two terms in the Senate from seeking re-election to those offices. The Court concluded that the power to add qualifications for federal offices was not within the states' original powers and thus was not reserved pursuant to the Tenth Amendment. Even had such power existed prior to the adoption of the Constitution, the Constitution's own terms specify the qualifications for these federal offices and therefore cannot be contradicted by the states. Is the decision in *U.S. Term Limits* restricted to its facts, or does it have broader implications? How

does its reasoning comport with that in *New York*? To what extent can Congress dictate details of voting procedures (such as voting machine standards, voting hours, training of voter registrars) for federal elections when such requirements inevitably also affect election practices applicable in state elections?

The Supreme Court altered the state-federal balance of power in the area of voting when, invoking the Tenth Amendment, it struck down provisions of the federal Voting Rights Act (VRA). In *Shelby County v. Holder*, 133 S. Ct. 2612 (2013), the Court considered provisions of the VRA that suspended state election law changes until these changes were precleared by federal authorities. The preclearance requirements applied to nine states, and a few other counties, with a history of election practices that discriminated based on race. The jurisdictions subject to the preclearance requirement were selected based on the application of a statutory formula that took into account historical evidence of low voter registration coupled with the presence of tests or devices required for voter registration. Congress enacted the VRA pursuant to its power under the Fifteenth Amendment, which provides that the "right of citizens of the United States to vote shall not be denied or abridged by the United States or by any State on account of race, color, or previous condition of servitude" and gives Congress the power to enforce this provision. U.S. CONST. amend. XV. The Court held that the formula used to determine which states were subject to the preclearance requirements was unconstitutional because it treated the states differently in violation of a principle of "equal sovereignty." The Court outlined this principle in the language below:

> Not only do States retain sovereignty under the Constitution, there is also a "fundamental principle of equal sovereignty" among the States. Over a hundred years ago, this Court explained that our Nation was and is a union of States, equal in power, dignity and authority. Indeed, the constitutional equality of the States is essential to the harmonious operation of the scheme upon which the Republic was organized. . . . [T]he fundamental principle of equal sovereignty remains highly pertinent in assessing subsequent disparate treatment of States. The Voting Rights Act sharply departs from these basic principles. [*Shelby County*, 133 S. Ct. at 2623–24].

Some observers have questioned the basis for the Court's assertion that the Constitution contains a "fundamental principal of equal sovereignty among the States." See Litman, *Inventing Equal Sovereignty*, 114 MICH. L. REV. 1207 (2016). Others have acknowledged that the majority in *Shelby County* did a poor job explaining the "equal sovereignty" concept but conclude that a more narrow principle might be justified to guarantee the states an equal capacity for self-government. Colby, *In Defense of the Equal Sovereignty Principle*, 65 DUKE L.J. 1087 (2016). For a defense of *Shelby County* on historical grounds, see Schmitt, *In Defense of* Shelby County*'s Principle of Equal State Sovereignty*, 68 OKLA. L. REV. 209 (2016). Even if there was an "equal sovereignty" principle embodied in the original Constitution, did this principle survive the adoption of the Fourteenth and Fifteenth Amendments?

For more on the relative powers of Congress and the states over voting and elections, see Tolson, *Election Law "Federalism" and the Limits of the Antidiscrimination Framework*, 59 Wm. & Mary L. Rev. 2211, 2216 (2018) (arguing that "Congress and the courts can disregard state sovereignty in enacting, enforcing, and resolving the constitutionality of legislation passed pursuant to the Elections Clause"); Weinstein-Tull, *Election Law Federalism*, 114 Mich. L. Rev. 747 (2016) (proposing a framework for considering federal, state and local involvement in election law); Siegal, *Congressional Power Over Presidential Elections: The Constitutionality of the Help America Vote Act Under Article II, Section 1*, 28 Vt. L. Rev. 373 (2004) (discussing constitutional issues); Post, *Uniform Voting Machines Protect the Principle of "One-Person, One-Vote"*, 47 Ariz. L. Rev. 551 (2005) (discussing voting machine systems in detail). Could Congress enact legislation prohibiting gerrymandering of congressional districts by state legislatures? See Note, *A New Map: Partisan Gerrymandering as a Federalism Injury*, 117 Harv. L. Rev. 1196 (2004) (arguing that gerrymandering should be addressed under the federal Elections Clause rather than the Equal Protection Clause and should be informed by federalism concerns); O'Neill, *The Case for Federal Anti-Gerrymandering Legislation*, 38 U. Mich. J. L. Reform 683 (2005) (arguing that Congress should adopt legislation incorporating standards to be applied by the states).

6. *Standing.* Who is the Tenth Amendment intended to protect and who can assert claims under its provisions? In *Bond v. United States*, 131 S. Ct. 2355 (2011), the Supreme Court offered some guidance on these questions, holding that private citizens may have prudential standing to assert Tenth Amendment claims. The case involved federal charges brought against Ms. Bond, a woman who sought to injure a romantic rival by putting a caustic chemical substance on her mailbox, car door handle and front doorknob. Bond was initially convicted on minor state criminal law grounds but, after continued attempts to injure her rival, she was charged under a federal statute adopted to implement an international treaty prohibiting the use of chemical weapons. The statute prohibited knowing possession or use of any chemical that "can cause death, temporary incapacitation or permanent harm to humans or animals" where not intended for a "peaceful purpose." The Court explained that, although the Tenth Amendment does relate to the rights of states, Bond was seeking to vindicate her own rights in light of her alleged injury "from governmental action taken in excess of the authority that federalism defines. Her rights in this regard do not belong to a State." 131 S. Ct. at 2363.

The Court continued: the "federal system rests on what might at first seem a counterintuitive insight, that freedom is enhanced by the creation of two governments, not one. . . . The Framers concluded that allocation of powers between the National Government and the States enhances freedom, first by protecting the integrity of the governments themselves, and second by protecting the people." It emphasized that "federalism secures to citizens the liberties that derive from the diffusion of sovereign power," and observed that the "limitations that federalism entails are not therefore a matter of rights belonging only to the States." The Court stressed the prudential dimensions of the Court's standing doctrine in the case at hand and cautioned that plaintiffs seeking to assert rights under the Tenth Amendment must show "actual or imminent harm that is concrete and particular, fairly traceable to the conduct complained of, and likely to be redressed by a favorable decision." It noted, however, that "in some instances, the result may be that a State is the only entity capable of demonstrating the requisite injury." *Id.* at 2366–2367. The Supreme Court subsequently concluded that the federal treaty in question did not apply to the rather mundane events involved in *Bond*. For an analysis of *Bond*, see Gerken, *Slipping the Bonds of Federalism*, 128 Harv. L. Rev. 85 (2014).

The Supreme Court has also recognized the right of states to bring suit against federal agencies when state sovereign prerogatives have been implicated and statutory provisions permit. In *Massachusetts v. EPA*, 549 U.S. 497 (2007), the Court allowed Massachusetts to challenge the Environmental Protection Agency's failure to adopt regulations governing greenhouse gas emissions, including carbon dioxide, under the Clean Air Act. Although the decision rested on analysis of the Clean Air Act's provisions, the Court had first to consider the question of justiciability and standing. In concluding that Massachusetts had standing, the majority observed that states were not normal litigants for purposes of invoking federal jurisdiction and referenced Eleventh Amendment case law in reaching its decision that Massachusetts could proceed with its suit. Explaining that sovereign prerogatives to protect its sovereign territory are now lodged in the federal government, and that Congress has ordered the EPA to protect Massachusetts among others, the Court noted that Congress has "recognized a concomitant procedural right to challenge the rejection of its rulemaking petition as arbitrary and capricious . . . and that [g]iven this procedural right and Massachusetts' stake in protecting its quasi-sovereign interests, the Commonwealth is entitled to special solicitude in our standing analysis." *Id.*

A related issue arose in *United States v. Texas*, 136 S. Ct. 2271 (2016), in which Texas challenged the establishment of the Deferred Action for Parents of Americans and Lawful Permanent Residents (DAPA) program. This program was intended to grant lawful immigration status to what could be millions of undocumented immigrants. In a 4-4 split decision, the Supreme Court affirmed the lower court's determination that the state of Texas had standing to challenge this executive action. For an analysis of the standing issues involved in *Texas*, see Mank, *State Standing in United States v. Texas: Opening the Floodgates to States Challenging the Federal Government, or Proper Federalism?*, 2018 U. Ill. L. Rev. 211, 213 (2018) (considering the costs and benefits of state standing and favoring state standing in certain circumstances); Nash, *Sovereign Preemption State Standing*, 112 Nw. U. L. Rev. 201, 230 (2017) (introducing the concept of state sovereign preemption standing to sue the federal government).

States have challenged federal government authority through lawsuits with increasing frequency. As the Trump Administration has delayed or rolled back a number of Obama-era administrative rules, state attorneys general have sued the federal government to block these changes. In a wide variety of policy areas, including pollution control standards, vehicle emissions, and immigration, among others, the federal courts have been called on to interpret the boundary between state and federal authority. Rose & Goelzhauser, *The State of American Federalism 2017–2018: Unilateral Executive Action, Regulatory Rollback, and State Resistance*, PUBLIUS 2018 48.3:319. Is the federal judiciary the right institution to set the balance between state and federal authority? Could clearer preemption provisions reduce the role of the courts?

7. *The Contract Clause.* The Tenth Amendment is not the only constitutional clause affecting the state-federal relationship that has undergone significant doctrinal changes over the last two centuries. The Constitution provides that "No State shall . . . pass any . . . Law impairing the Obligations of Contract." U.S. CONST. art. I, § 10. The inclusion of this clause in the Constitution reflected, in large part, a reaction to the social and economic unrest caused by debtor relief laws enacted by the newly independent states during the confederation period. During the early days under the Constitution, the Contract Clause was enforced strongly, preventing the states from impairing contractual obligations; indeed, before the enactment of the Fourteenth Amendment, the Contract Clause was the "principle vehicle by which the Supreme Court asserted federal constitutional control over state governments." Merrill, *Public Contracts, Private Contract, and the Transformation of the Constitutional Order*, 37 CASE W. RES. L. REV. 597 (1986). Early Supreme Court cases confirmed that the primary focus of the Contract Clause was the protection of contract rights among private parties. Because of the expanding scope of the Fourteenth Amendment, the Court's reliance on the Contract Clause slowly diminished in the late nineteenth century; and its vitality came to an abrupt end during the New Deal. In *Home Bldg. & Loan Ass'n v. Blaisdell*, 290 U.S. 398 (1934), the Supreme Court subjected the once-robust clause to a rational basis-type review, upholding a state law placing a moratorium on the repayment of mortgage obligations because it was a reasonable response to a legitimate end, that is, the protection of homes and lands that provided shelter and subsistence to members of the public. After *Blaisdell*, the Supreme Court did not strike down another state law under the Contract Clause for more than 40 years, and lower courts followed suit.

It surprised many commenters, therefore, when the Supreme Court partially resurrected the Contract Clause. The Court still accords great deference to state legislatures when they impair *private* obligations. However, the Court now views with heightened scrutiny state attempts to impair *public* contracts, that is, contracts to which the state itself is a party. *United States Trust Co. of New York v. New Jersey*, 431 U.S. 1 (1977). In *United States Trust*, the Court invalidated state laws of New York and New Jersey that breached the states' obligations to bondholders. Limiting *Blaisdell*, the Court held that there was a distinction between contracts among private parties alone and contracts to which the state is itself a party. As the Court described, routine deference to a state's decision to impair contractual obligations is based on the premise that the state is acting for a public purpose. There will be winners and losers as a result of the state's decision to breach a generally applicable set of contractual obligations, to be sure; but the legislature, rather than a court, is best situated to weigh the costs and benefits created by the impairment. By contrast, when the state itself is a party to a contract, deference to legislative judgment about whether to breach that obligation is not appropriate. Unlike in the case of a purely private obligation, when the state has the ability to breach its own contractual obligation, it has the power to pick itself as a winner. *Id.*

Courts continue to maintain this distinction between public and private contracts. When a state impairs purely private obligations, its action will be upheld so long as the state can articulate a "legitimate public purpose" and the impairment "reasonably" furthers that interest. *Energy Reserve Group, Inc. v. Kansas Power & Light Co.*, 459 U.S. 400 (1983). By contrast, when a state breaches a contract to which it is itself a party, the test is different and the scrutiny more exacting: a state's breach will be held unconstitutional unless the state can demonstrate that its breach was meant to achieve an "important public purpose" and that the statute's approach was "reasonable" and "necessary" to achieve the state's purpose. *United States Trust*, 431 U.S. at 25.

Is it surprising that the Court resurrected the Contract Clause, which restricts state action, around the same time that it expanded the scope of the Tenth Amendment, which provides more autonomy for the states? Does the text or history of either of these provisions account for the result? If not, what is driving the Court's change of heart in each circumstance? What is the result of a robustly enforced Contracts Clause for the state-federal relationship? For commentary on the public contract/private contract distinction that now marks Contract Clause doctrine, see Fissell, *The Dual Standard of Review in Contracts Clause Jurisprudence*, 101 Geo. L.J. 1089 (2013); Zoldan, *The Permanent Seat of Government: An Unintended Consequence of Heightened Scrutiny Under the Contract Clause*, 14 N.Y.U. J. Legis. 163 (2011).

C. Fiscal Federalism

Not only does the federal government have power to regulate conduct directly, but it also has the power to spend federal funds to achieve its desired objectives. It can achieve these objectives by developing federal programs operated by federal personnel, of course. However, it also can seek to induce state and local governments to work cooperatively to achieve its goals. When federal resources are plentiful, policy judgments are well-aligned between federal and state levels, and the political compromises are readily achieved, such partnerships might proceed smoothly. However, when budgets are constrained, state and federal policymakers see the world differently, and political and philosophical schisms abound, it becomes more difficult for the federal government to induce the states to cooperate with federal designs.

Some scholars have argued that the fiscal aspects of federalism—including taxing and spending powers—should be viewed separately from regulatory federalism because of the differences between them. Professor Super suggests that fiscal federalism comes with a number of issues that "lack a significant parallel in regulatory federalism." Super, *Rethinking Fiscal Federalism*, 118 Harv. L. Rev. 2544, 2560–61 (2005). With respect to regulatory federalism, the locus on responsibility is on the courts, which interpret provisions of the Constitution and statutes that set the state-federal relationship. By contrast, with respect to spending, the political branches, rather than the courts, set the state-federal relationship. Super sets out three differences between fiscal and regulatory federalism: "First, federal policymakers wishing to enhance states' fiscal positions have a wider array of tools at their disposal than they (or the courts) do in enhancing states' regulatory authority." *Id.* For example, the federal government may give states money directly or ease restrictions on states' ability to raise revenue. "Second, because money is fungible, the amount of relief provided is far more important than the specific subject matter of the intervention." That is, if the federal government gives the states money for one purpose, this grant has the effect of allowing the state to reallocate other money to other priorities. *Id.* "By contrast, . . . regulatory power has little fungibility. Third, because states have broad revenue-raising powers on their own and large, diversified budgets, a failure to provide fiscal assistance—a disinterest in federalism—does not necessarily prevent states from acting unilaterally." *Id.* Has this distinction between regulatory and fiscal federalism become more blurry after *NFIB v. Sebelius*, discussed at length below?

This Part first describes the major types of federal financial assistance that have been used over the last half century, tracing the evolution of such assistance over a period marked by changing political philosophies, a shifting balance of power between federal and state governments and variations in the social agenda. Second, it looks more closely at the "strings" that Congress and federal agencies may attach to federal funds, exploring the degree to which the federal government can condition spending on state assistance implementing federal programs. These issues have become increasingly important as the Supreme Court has constrained congressional action under the Tenth and Eleventh Amendments and narrowed interpretations of the Interstate Commerce Clause and the Fourteenth and Fifteenth Amendments.

[1] Benefits and Burdens: An Overview of the Fiscal Relations Between the Federal Government and the States

Before plunging into controversies over the extent to which the federal government can trade financial aid for state acquiescence in federal policy decisions, it is important to understand the terminology used, the long history of federal financial assistance to the states and the diverse funding systems that have developed over time.

Early federal financial assistance sometimes took the form of land grants, such as those authorized under the Morrill Act of 1862, as a means of encouraging states to create land grant colleges. Once a federal income tax was authorized by constitutional amendment, more federal funds became available. During the Great Depression, Congress passed a number of statutes providing emergency grants in order to create programs that would be administered by the states in response to broadly applicable national initiatives. Beginning in the 1960s, Congress authorized many "categorical grant" programs, ones that targeted funds for specific projects and purposes. Funds provided under these programs could be used only for specific programs and usually were limited to narrowly defined activities. Legislation of this type generally detailed the parameters of the program, specified the types of activities that could be funded and employed a variety of methods for allocating funding (by formula, grant or reimbursement). Categorical grants were generally designed to close the fiscal gap between governmental levels by allocating productive revenue sources available at the national level to address the heavy service burdens placed on states and localities, addressing the differences in fiscal capacities at the state and local level and responding to interest group pressures.

In the 1970s and 1980s, the use of categorical aid programs diminished in favor of other types of financial assistance. From 1972 until 1986, states and localities received a share of federal revenues with virtually no restrictions on its use. This approach, called "revenue sharing," proved popular because of its low administrative cost and greater freedom for recipients, but was ultimately discontinued because of concerns about its overall financial toll (in the fourteen years of its existence, revenue sharing cost approximately $85 billion). Later, under President Reagan, efforts were made to sort out federal versus state or local responsibilities, with attendant "swaps" of responsibilities. In 1982, the federal government began to assume responsibility for Medicaid (a health care program for the poor), while states became more central to the support of welfare and food stamp programs. Many categorical aid programs were subsequently eliminated, consolidated into block grants, or sharply reduced during the fiscal austerity of the late 1980s and 1990s. This process of reducing expenditure restrictions and shifting responsibilities to the states became known as "devolution." Grant programs continue to be employed in critical areas, however. For example, controversy arose about the allocation of grants for homeland security, with small states receiving more homeland security grant money per capita than large states with substantial population concentrations. See Roberts, *Shifting Priorities: Congressional Incentives and the Homeland Security Granting Process*, 22 Rev. of Pol'y Research 437 (2005).

"Block grants" became an increasingly important form of federal financial assistance in the past several decades, particularly during times of Republican control. Block grants differ from categorical grants in that recipients have more discretion in deciding what project or purposes will be funded within a broad program or functional area. Planning, auditing and reporting requirements are reduced in order to reduce federal supervision and control. Funds are dispensed on a formula basis, little matching financial aid is required and eligibility provisions are fairly precise. Block grants are favored by the states as a form of aid because of their simplicity and lower administrative costs. They also afford flexibility to state and local governments and have paved the way for phasing out or curbing programs that were perceived as burdening the federal budget.

Block grants became an especially important part of federal "welfare reform" legislation. Reform replaced the Aid to Families with Dependent Children (AFDC) program (providing benefits with few restrictions) with the Temporary Assistance for Needy Families (TANF) program (providing block grants to the states with significant eligibility requirements) and the Personal Responsibility and Work Opportunity Reconciliation Act. See 42 U.S.C. §603. Scholars and major policy organizations have closely tracked the implementation of the TANF program, yielding insights that are important to the national and state commitment to aid those in need, as well as broader lessons that may bear on the design of future federal financial assistance programs.

Research by the Brookings Institution noted some implications of these changes. See Finegold, Wherry & Scharin, Block Grants: Historical Overview and Lessons Learned (Brookings Institution 2004). For example, block grants eliminate any individual entitlement to benefits and do not guarantee that the same level of funding (adjusted for costs and inflation) will be available from one year to the next. In addition, notwithstanding initial flexibility, there has been a tendency for Congress to add restrictions over time. Block grant programs also tend to work best when state administrative capacities already exist. The Brookings authors recommend that attention be given to several crucial problems. The federal government has a flagging institutional capacity to monitor relationships with other levels of government in the federal system. Its ability to execute important economic policy reforms is limited during times of stress when state funds are constrained. Medicaid's growth appears to be unsustainable, imposing difficult burdens on states and distorting their fiscal relationships with the federal government. Finally, the fiscal partnership between the federal government and the states is outdated and needs to be reformed, particularly in the areas of education and infrastructure funding. *Id.*

The amount of federal money granted to state and local governments has risen dramatically in the last twenty years. In the year 2000, the total federal outlay for grants to state and local governments was $285 billion. For fiscal year 2018, this amount rose to $728 billion, an increase of more than 250% in nominal dollars as well as an increase as a percentage of total federal spending. Of the 2018 expenditure, more than half ($433 billion) was allocated for health spending, $111 billion for income security, $64 billion for transportation, $64 billion for education training, employment and social services, $31 billion for community and regional development, and $28 billion for other expenditures. This amount represents a significant increase over fiscal year 2017, the largest increases accruing to spending on healthcare and community and regional development. Perhaps the single most notable change in spending patterns over the last few decades is the change in who receives federal spending. In the 1960s and 1970s, only one-third of the outlays for federal grants to state and local governments went to individuals. The rest went to places, that is, state and local governments that used the funds for infrastructure improvement, economic development, or other local matters. Today, more than 75% of federal funds allocated to state and local governments go to individuals directly. Dilger, Congressional Research Service, *Federal Grants to State and Local Governments: A Historical Perspective on Contemporary Issues* (2018), available at https://crsreports.congress.gov/product/pdf/R/R40638.

Because most states are required to balance their budgets, they are particularly dependent on federal funds in times of economic decline. The COVID-19 pandemic, which has led to skyrocketing expenses and greatly reduced revenues, precipitated a severe and unexpected decline in state and local government financial stability. In anticipation, in part, of the economic shock that is expected as a result of these changes, Congress enacted the Coronavirus Aid, Relief, and Economic Security (CARES) Act, which included about $150 billion in grants for state and local governments. Even this significant sum is not expected to meet the shortfall that state and local governments will face.

In this discussion about "federal funds," the point should not be lost that federal grants are not costless, but rather redistributive. That is, the money granted to states comes from somewhere; and that somewhere is in large part taxpayers. Crucially, however, the amount of federal funds received by a state or its citizens is not linked to the amount that is paid in federal taxes by citizens of that state. To the contrary, the citizens of some states pay far more in federal taxes than the amount of federal funds spent in their state; conversely, the citizens of some states pay far less in federal taxes than the value of federal funds spent in their state. In recent years, the biggest net recipients have been South Carolina, North Dakota and Florida, receiving between $4 and $8 for every dollar they spend on federal taxes. The biggest net payors are Delaware, Minnesota and Illinois, each of which pay more than they receive in federal spending. Given the distributive nature of federal funds, do you think that federal grants distort state regulatory incentives? How would state and federal policy look if federal spending were drastically reduced? For more on federal grants to state and local government and the implications for federalism, see Galson & Davis, 21st Century Federalism: Proposals for Reform (Brookings Institution 2014); *Federal Investment, 1962–2018* at https://www.cbo.gov/publication/55375. For a more in-depth discussion of state and local government revenues, including the role of federal revenue sources, tax benefits and oversight, see Chapter 4.

[2] Conditional Spending

Conditioning federal largesse on compliance with federal policy objectives is not a new phenomenon. Nevertheless, the impetus for the federal government to induce cooperation from state and local authorities through conditional spending has become stronger as the Supreme Court has limited Congress' ability to set policy directly. As noted, the Court has restricted Congress' ability to regulate directly under, for example, the Commerce Clause and the Fourteenth and Fifteenth Amendments. Moreover, it has restricted the recourse of private parties against the states under federal remedial legislation on Tenth and Eleventh Amendment grounds. As a result, Congress has fewer regulatory alternatives and must increasingly rely on financial incentives with associated conditions as a means of accomplishing desired policy objectives. But, although the Constitution grants Congress the power to "provide for the common Defense and General Welfare of the United States," the Court has read limitations into this grant of authority. U.S. CONST. art. I, § 8.

The following case remains a leading authority on conditional spending, setting out key principles. More recent decisions, including *National Federation of Independent Business v. Sebelius*, have added some critical limitations discussed in the Notes that follow.

South Dakota v. Dole

483 U.S. 203 (1987)

CHIEF JUSTICE REHNQUIST delivered the opinion of the Court.

Petitioner South Dakota permits persons 19 years of age or older to purchase beer containing up to 3.2% alcohol. S.D. Codified Laws § 35-6-27. In 1984, Congress enacted 23 U.S.C. § 158 ("§ 158"), which directs the Secretary of Transportation to withhold a percentage of federal highway funds otherwise allocable from States "in which the purchase or public possession of any alcoholic beverage by a person who is less than twenty-one years of age is lawful." The State sued in United States District Court seeking a declaratory judgment that § 158 violates the constitutional limitations on congressional exercise of the spending power and violates the Twenty-first Amendment to the United States Constitution. The District Court rejected the State's claims, and the Court of Appeals for the Eighth Circuit affirmed. 791 F.2d 628 (1986).

In this Court, the parties direct most of their efforts to defining the proper scope of the Twenty-first Amendment. Relying on our statement in *California Retail Liquor Dealers Ass'n v. Midcal Aluminum, Inc.*, 445 U.S. 97, 110 (1980), that the "Twenty-first Amendment grants the States virtually complete control over whether to permit importation or sale of liquor and how to structure the liquor distribution system," South Dakota asserts that the setting of minimum drinking ages is clearly within the "core powers" reserved to the States under § 2 of the Amendment.[1]

1. Section 2 of the Twenty-first Amendment provides: "The transportation or importation into any State, Territory, or possession of the United States for delivery or use therein of intoxicating liquors, in violation of the laws thereof, is hereby prohibited."

Section 158, petitioner claims, usurps that core power. The Secretary in response asserts that the Twenty-first Amendment is simply not implicated by § 158; the plain language of § 2 confirms the States' broad power to impose restrictions on the sale and distribution of alcoholic beverages but does not confer on them any power to permit sales that Congress seeks to prohibit. That Amendment, under this reasoning, would not prevent Congress from affirmatively enacting a national minimum drinking age more restrictive than that provided by the various state laws; and it would follow a fortiori that the indirect inducement involved here is compatible with the Twenty-first Amendment.

These arguments present questions of the meaning of the Twenty-first Amendment, the bounds of which have escaped precise definition. Despite the extended treatment of the question by the parties, however, we need not decide in this case whether that Amendment would prohibit an attempt by Congress to legislate directly a national minimum drinking age. Here, Congress has acted indirectly under its spending power to encourage uniformity in the States' drinking ages. As we explain below, we find this legislative effort within constitutional bounds even if Congress may not regulate drinking ages directly.

The Constitution empowers Congress to "lay and collect Taxes, Duties, Imposts, and Excises, to pay the Debts and provide for the common Defense and general Welfare of the United States." Art. I, § 8, cl. 1. Incident to this power, Congress may attach conditions on the receipt of federal funds, and has repeatedly employed the power "to further broad policy objectives by conditioning receipt of federal moneys upon compliance by the recipient with federal statutory and administrative directives." The breadth of this power was made clear in *United States v. Butler*, 297 U.S. 1, 66 (1936), where the Court, resolving a longstanding debate over the scope of the Spending Clause, determined that "the power of Congress to authorize expenditure of public moneys for public purposes is not limited by the direct grants of legislative power found in the Constitution." Thus, objectives not thought to be within Article I's "enumerated legislative fields," *id.*, at 65, may nevertheless be attained through the use of the spending power and the conditional grant of federal funds.

The spending power is of course not unlimited, but is instead subject to several general restrictions articulated in our cases. The first of these limitations is derived from the language of the Constitution itself: the exercise of the spending power must be in pursuit of "the general welfare." In considering whether a particular expenditure is intended to serve general public purposes, courts should defer substantially to the judgment of Congress. Second, we have required that if Congress desires to condition that States' receipt of federal funds, it "must do so unambiguously . . . , enabl[ing] the States to exercise their choice knowingly, cognizant of the consequences of their participation." Third, our cases have suggested (without significant elaboration) that conditions on federal grants might be illegitimate if they are unrelated "to the federal interest in particular national projects or programs." Finally, we have noted that other constitutional provisions may provide an independent bar to the conditional grant of federal funds.

South Dakota does not seriously claim that § 158 is inconsistent with any of the first three restrictions mentioned above. We can readily conclude that the provision is designed to serve the general welfare, especially in light of the fact that "the concept of welfare or the opposite is shaped by Congress. . . ." Congress found that the differing drinking ages in the States created particular incentives for young persons to combine their desire to drink with their ability to drive, and that this interstate problem required a national solution. The means it chose to address this dangerous situation were reasonably calculated to advance the general welfare. The conditions upon which States receive the funds, moreover, could not be more clearly stated by Congress. *See* 23 U.S.C. § 158. And the State itself, rather than challenging the germaneness of the condition to federal purposes, admits that it "has never contended that the congressional action was . . . unrelated to a national concern in the absence of the Twenty-first Amendment." Indeed, the condition imposed by Congress is directly related to one of the main purposes for which highway funds are expended—safe interstate travel. This goal of the interstate highway system had been frustrated by varying drinking ages among the States. A presidential commission appointed to study alcohol-related accidents and fatalities on the Nation's highways concluded that the lack of uniformity in the States' drinking ages created "an incentive to drink and drive" because "young persons commut[e] to border States where the drinking age is lower." Presidential Commission on Drunk Driving, Final Report 11 (1983). By enacting § 158, Congress conditioned the receipt of federal funds in a way reasonably calculated to address this particular impediment to a purpose for which the funds are expended.

The remaining question about the validity of § 158—and the basic point of disagreement between the parties—is whether the Twenty-first Amendment constitutes an "independent constitutional bar" to the conditional grant of federal funds. . . . Petitioner, relying on its view that the Twenty-first Amendment prohibits direct regulation of drinking ages by Congress, asserts that "Congress may not use the spending power to regulate that which it is prohibited from regulating directly under the Twenty-first Amendment." But our cases show that this "independent constitutional bar" limitation on the spending power is not of the kind petitioner suggests. *United States v. Butler*, 297 U.S., at 66, for example, established that the constitutional limitations on Congress when exercising its spending power are less exacting than those on its authority to regulate directly.

We have also held that a perceived Tenth Amendment limitation on congressional regulation of state affairs did not concomitantly limit the range of conditions legitimately placed on federal grants. In *Oklahoma v. Civil Service Comm'n*, 330 US. 127 (1947), the Court considered the validity of the Hatch Act insofar as it was applied to political activities of state officials whose employment was financed in whole or in part with federal funds. The State contended that an order under this provision to withhold certain federal funds unless a state official was removed invades its sovereignty in violation of the Tenth Amendment. Though finding that "the United States is not concerned with, and has no power to regulate, local political activities as such of state officials," the Court nevertheless held that the Federal Government "does have power to fix the terms upon which its money allotments to state shall be disbursed." *Id.*, at 143. The Court found no violation of the State's sovereignty because the State could, and did, adopt "the 'simple expedient' of not yielding to what she urges is federal coercion. The offer of benefits to a state by the United States dependent upon cooperation by the state with federal plans, assumedly for the general welfare, is not unusual." *Id.* at 143–44 (citation omitted). *See also Steward Machine Co. v. Davis*, 301 U.S. 548, 595 (1937) ("There is only a condition which the state is free at pleasure to disregard or to fulfill"); *Massachusetts v. Mellon*, 262 U.S. 447, 482 (1923).

These cases establish that the "independent constitutional bar" limitation on the spending power is not, as petitioner suggests, a prohibition on the indirect achievement of objectives which Congress is not empowered to achieve directly. Instead, we think that the language in our earlier opinions stands for the unexceptionable proposition that the power may not be used to induce the States to engage in activities that would themselves be unconstitutional. Thus, for example, a grant of federal funds conditioned on invidiously discriminatory state action or the infliction of cruel and unusual punishment would be an illegitimate exercise of the Congress' broad spending power. But no such claim can be or is made here. Were South Dakota to succumb to the blandishments offered by Congress and raise its drinking age to 21, the State's action in so doing would not violate the constitutional rights of anyone.

Our decisions have recognized that in some circumstances the financial inducement offered by Congress might be so coercive as to pass the point at which "pressure turns into compulsion." *Steward Machine Co. v. Davis, supra*, 301 U.S., at 590. Here, however, Congress has directed only that a State desiring to establish a minimum drinking age lower than 21 lose a relatively small percentage of certain federal highway funds. Petitioner contends that the coercive nature of this program is evident from the degree of success it has achieved. We cannot conclude, however, that a conditional grant of federal money of this sort is unconstitutional simply by reasons of its success in achieving the congressional objective.

When we consider, for a moment, that all South Dakota would lose if she adheres to her chosen course as to a suitable minimum drinking age is 5% of the funds otherwise obtainable under specified highway grant programs, the argument as to coercion is shown to be more rhetoric than fact. As we said a half century ago in *Steward Machine Co. v. Davis*:

> "[E]very rebate from a tax when conditioned upon conduct is in some measure a temptation. But to hold that motive or temptation is equivalent to coercion is to plunge the law in endless difficulties. The outcome of such a doctrine is the acceptance of a philosophical determinism by which choice becomes impossible. Till now the law has been guided by a robust common

> sense which assumes the freedom of the will as a working hypothesis in the solution of its problems." *Id.*, at 589–590.

Here Congress has offered relatively mild encouragement to the States to enact higher minimum drinking ages than they would otherwise choose. But the enactment of such laws remains the prerogative of the States not merely in theory but in fact. Even if Congress might lack the power to impose a national minimum drinking age directly, we conclude that encouragement to state action found in § 158 is a valid use of the spending power.

Accordingly, the judgment of the Court of Appeals is

Affirmed.

[Justices O'Connor and Brennan dissented. Justice O'Connor agreed with the majority's articulation of the constitutional principles governing conditional spending, but disagreed with the application of those principles to the case at hand. Justice O'Connor concluded that the drinking age condition could not be sustained as an exercise of the spending power since, in her view, the condition bore only an attenuated relationship to highway use or safety and represented an undue intrusion into the state's social, political and economic life. Justice O'Connor also reasoned that the condition could not be imposed under the Commerce Clause where the authority to regulate liquor sales is reserved to the states under the Twenty-First Amendment. Justice Brennan likewise concluded that federal funds could not be conditioned in a manner that abridged the rights reserved to the states under that Amendment.]

Notes and Questions

1. *The federal interest and relatedness.* The Court in *Dole* noted that conditions on federal grants will be unlawful if unrelated (or not "germane") to the federal interest in the particular national project or program. Is this requirement linked to the Constitution's language providing power for federal spending? Is the drinking age condition in *Dole* sufficiently related to highway safety or is Justice O'Connor correct that only more closely related conditions, such as those specifying how federal funds might be spent, meet this test? Justice O'Connor posed an extreme hypothetical in her dissent: could federal highway funds be conditioned upon moving a state capital in order to avoid excessive traffic or to facilitate access to government offices in places easily accessible to interstate highways? One value that the relatedness prong protects is political accountability; that is, it prevents Congress from requiring the state to adopt one policy on the pretext of complying with grant conditions encouraging a different policy. This relatedness requirement, then, to the extent it is enforced, helps state citizens know why their state government adopted its chosen policy. See Howard, *Breaking Down the Supreme Court's Spending Clause Ruling in* NFIB v. Sebelius*: A Huge Blow to the Federal Government or a Mere Bump in the Road?*, 35 U. Ark. L. Rev. 609 (2013); Sullivan, *Unconstitutional Conditions*, 102 Harv. L. Rev. 1413, 1456–58, 1461–62 (1989) (arguing that "germaneness" standard

seems intended to prevent legislative corruption by triggering an enhanced level of judicial scrutiny in situations likely to involve manipulation or extortion). When seen through the lens of political accountability, how does *Dole*'s relatedness requirement connect with the values advanced by the anti-commandeering principle, described above?

2. *Clear statement.* In *Dole*, the Court also reaffirmed that Congress must clearly state the conditions on which the states are entitled to receive federal funds. In *Pennhurst State School Hosp. v. Halderman*, 451 U.S. 1 (1981), the Court previously fleshed out the requirement that conditions be clearly stated. In *Pennhurst*, the Court held that the Developmentally Disabled Assistance and Bill of Rights Act, 42 U.S.C. § 6000 *et seq.* (1982), articulated a federal policy to provide better care and treatment for people who are disabled, but did not impose binding requirements on the states to do so. The Court offered the following explanation:

> [L]egislation enacted pursuant to the spending power is much in the nature of a contract: in return for federal funds, the States agree to comply with federally imposed conditions. The legitimacy of Congress' power to legislate under the spending power thus rests on whether the State voluntarily and knowingly accepts the terms of the "contract." . . . There can, of course, be no knowing acceptance if a State is unaware of the conditions or is unable to ascertain what is expected of it. Accordingly, if Congress intends to impose a condition on the grant of federal moneys, it must do so unambiguously. . . . By insisting that Congress speak with a clear voice, we enable the States to exercise their choice knowingly, cognizant of the consequences of their participation. [451 U.S. at 17.]

Is the contract analogy a sound one? See Galle, *Getting Spending: How to Replace Clear Statement Rules with Clear Thinking About Conditional Grants of Federal Funds*, 37 Conn. L. Rev. 155 (2004) (rejecting the analogy as formalistic, insufficiently grounded in core values of federalism or an appreciation for underlying congressional powers). Does the effectiveness of this approach rely on assumptions about the effectiveness of states and localities in the national political process? See Rosenthal, *Conditional Federal Spending and the Constitution*, 39 Stan. L. Rev. 1103, 1141 (1987) (contending that governments that must rely on federal financial assistance are unlikely to lobby effectively against objectionable conditions). Does the "clear statement" rule articulated by the Court provide a meaningful approach to limiting the potentially intrusive effects of federally-imposed conditions? For discussions about the ambiguity of the clear statement prong of the spending power test, see Huberfeld, *Clear Notice for Conditions on Spending, Unclear Implications for States in Federal Healthcare Programs*, 86 N.C. L. Rev. 441 (2008) (discussing the implications of Spending Clause jurisprudence in the context of the pharmaceutical benefits under Medicare and Medicaid and related "clawback" provision); Caffrey, *No Ambiguity Left Behind: A Discussion of the Clear Statement Rule and the Unfunded Mandates Clause of No Child Left Behind*, 18 Wm. & Mary Bill of Rts. J. 1129 (2010) (discussing the application of the clear statement rule with regard to No

Child Left Behind); Seligmann, *Muddy Waters: The Supreme Court and the Clear Statement Rule for Spending Clause Legislation*, 84 Tul. L. Rev. 1067 (2010).

The *Pennhurst* prong of the conditional spending test played a prominent role in the Court's opinions in *National Federation of Independent Business (NFIB) v. Sebelius*, 132 S. Ct. 2566, one of a series of cases that considered the constitutionality of portions of the Affordable Care Act (ACA). In *NFIB*, Congress considered the ACA's provision conditioning future grants to the states for Medicaid on the states' agreement to expand Medicaid eligibility. Chief Justice Roberts, in an opinion joined by Justices Breyer and Kagan, reiterated *Pennhurst*'s contract analogy, but read it in a novel way, giving it far more potency. Under *Pennhurst*, the grant conditions must be clear so that the states know, at the time they accept the grant, what they are promising to do in the future. Under this definition, the statutory condition at issue in *NFIB* would qualify as clearly stated: the states knew what they had to do in order to qualify for Medicaid funds in the future. However, the Chief Justice's opinion read the clear statement prong to mean that the states must have understood "at the time they agreed to participate in the *original* Medicaid plan that those funds might later be at risk unless additional conditions—to be disclosed at some unknown point in the future—were met." Baker, *The Spending Power after* NFIB v. Sebelius, 37 Harv. J. L. & Pub. Pol'y 71 (2015). Is this expansion of the *Pennhurst* prong a one-off misapplication of *Pennhurst* or a new limitation on the spending power? If this is a new limitation on the spending power, what do you think of the viability of *Pennhurst*'s contract analogy?

3. *Independent constitutional bar.* The principal case also reasserted and reinterpreted previous doctrine holding that federal spending cannot be conditioned on an activity that is itself unconstitutional, called the "independent constitutional bar" prong. In its most basic form, as the Court in *Dole* noted, this prong stands for the proposition that the power "may not be used to induce the States to engage in activities that would themselves be unconstitutional. Thus, for example, a grant of federal funds conditioned on invidiously discriminatory state action or the infliction of cruel and unusual punishment would be an illegitimate exercise of Congress' broad spending power." *Dole*, 483 U.S. at 2010.

In subsequent cases, the Court has wrestled with the implications of grant programs that condition funds to *nongovernmental* organizations on the restriction of rights. In *Agency for International Development (AID) v. Alliance for Open Society International, Inc.*, 570 U.S. 205 (2013), the Supreme Court expanded on its statement in *Dole* that certain conditions might be prohibited because they were barred independently by other parts of the Constitution. The *AID* case concerned a challenge to provisions of the United States Leadership Against HIV/AIDS, Tuberculosis, and Malaria Act requiring organizations that received funding under Act to have policy statements expressly opposing prostitution. The Court distinguished between conditions that define the limits of Government spending programs and the activities they are intended to subsidize, and those that seek to use funding as a means of leverage that in effect regulate speech outside the program being funded. The Court found that the legislation in question went further than simply prohibiting the use of government funds to "promote or advocate the legalization or practice of prostitution or sex trafficking," or banning use of private funds to undercut federal objectives. Instead, the legislation would have required fund recipients to pledge support for the government's stated policy of eradicating prostitution, thereby violating the First Amendment. Under what other circumstances might the independent constitutional bar doctrine apply? Can you reconcile this decision with *Dole*?

Conditions imposed by the Executive Branch may be unconstitutional for different reasons than conditions imposed by Congress. In recent cases, the federal government has clashed over funding with cities that adopt "sanctuary" policies. By Executive Order, President Trump directed the Attorney General and the Secretary of the Department of Homeland Security to withhold federal grants from jurisdictions that "willfully refuse" to comply with a federal law requiring states and local governments to share immigration status information with the federal government. So-called "sanctuary cities," including major cities like San Francisco and Chicago, have challenged the implementation of this order on the ground that it violates the principle of separation of powers. These cases are still working their way through the federal courts of appeals. See, e.g., *City and County of San Francisco v. Trump*, 897 F.3d 1225 (9th Cir. 2018) (holding that, in the absence of congressional direction, the "Administration may not redistribute or withhold properly appropriated funds in order to effectuate its own policy goals"). Imagine that Congress enacts the substance of the Executive Order described above; would it survive an unconstitutional conditions analysis under *Dole*?

For commentary on the independent constitutional bar doctrine, see Hamburger, *Unconstitutional Conditions: The Irrelevance of Consent*, 98 VA. L. REV. 479 (2012) (arguing that the issue of consent to unconstitutional conditions is irrelevant when the government exceeds its power); Wick, *Rethinking Conditional Federal Grants and the Constitutional Bar Test*, 83 S. CAL. L. REV. 1359 (2010) (discussing the National Minimum Drinking Age Act and proposing that rather than limit the "independent constitutional bar" doctrine to facially unconstitutional conditions, that doctrine should be viewed as invalidating any condition that could not be pursued directly by the federal government).

4. *Coercion*. In the principal case, the Court reiterated that some financial inducements offered by Congress might be so coercive that they transform encouragement into compulsion. In that case, the financial inducement did not coerce the states because the states would lose only a small percentage of funds otherwise obtainable under highway grant programs—in the case of South Dakota, only 5%. The Court breathed new life into the coercion prong of the *Dole* test in the *NFIB* case, described above. In *NFIB*, seven members of the United States Supreme Court (in multiple opinions) determined that Congress had engaged in unconstitutional "coercion" under the spending power by requiring states either to expand Medicaid programs to cover more uninsured individuals or lose both existing federal

allocations of funds and additional potential federal funds. Five members of the Court concluded that the remedy for this problem was to interpret the provisions of the ACA so as to allow states to "opt out" of the Medicaid expansion effort without forfeiting funds they had previously received in support of their existing Medicaid programs. Important questions are raised by this conclusion in *Sebelius*, including how to interpret the scope of the Court's "coercion" conclusion (made more difficult because of the fragmented opinions in that case).

What is the basis, in *NFIB*, for a finding that "coercion" existed if states could lose preexisting Medicaid funds for failing to expand their programs under revised Medicaid requirements? The amount of money at risk? The long-standing dedication of prior funds to needed programming? The fact that the loss of funds of the sort envisioned had not been evident at the time Medicaid programs were initially started? The risk that members of the public would view the states, rather than the federal government, as responsible? The fact that more than half the states protested related requirements? What difference did it make that Congress did not include a "backup" provision, as emphasized by the joint dissent? What does the opinion bode for the future? The resolution of these questions will determine whether *NFIB* heralds a new era for spending power federalism or whether its spending power limitation was a "ticket good for one day only."

There have been numerous excellent analyses of *NFIB v. Sebelius*, including the following: Baker, *The Spending Power After NFIB v. Sebelius*, 37 Harv. J.L. & Pub. Pol'y 71 (2014) (interpreting *Sebelius* as imposing the following standards: expecting Congress at the outset to advise states participating in the original Medicaid plan that future changes might be imposed; imposing a "germaneness" or "relatedness" requirement that links the availability of federal funds to the federal interest in particular programs; and adopting a new view of the "anti-coercion" element of *Dole* as prohibiting pressure that "turns into compulsion"); Huberfeld, Leonard & Outterson, *Plunging into Endless Difficulties: Medicaid and Coercion in National Federation of Independent Business v. Sebelius*, 93 B.U. L. Rev. 1 (2013) (discussing the *Sebelius* decision and its relationship to *Dole*, with a particular emphasis on clear notice requirements and germaneness); Pasachoff, *Conditional Spending After NFIB v. Sebelius: The Example of Federation Education Law*, 62 Am. U. L. Rev. 577 (2013) (concluding that the *Sebelius* decision will be unlikely to result in finding federal education law provisions dependent upon congressional spending powers to be unconstitutional).

Part Two

Intra-Governmental Distribution of Power

Chapter 8

The State Legislature

Scope of Chapter

On the surface, state legislatures closely resemble the United States Congress. All but one state has a bicameral legislature, consisting of an upper house (a Senate) and a lower house (usually a House of Representatives). All state legislatures exercise lawmaking authority and, in addition, most state senates have certain non-lawmaking powers, like the power to confirm executive officers and the power to try impeachments. State legislatures, like Congress, operate through committees that consider and make recommendations on bills before they are submitted to the full legislature for a vote. But, despite these similarities, there are fundamental differences between state legislatures and Congress. Most saliently, unlike Congress, which exercises powers enumerated by the United States Constitution, state legislatures have plenary authority to make law. In other words, unless affirmatively limited by its constitution, a state's legislature has complete lawmaking authority. T. Cooley, A TREATISE ON THE CONSTITUTIONAL LIMITATIONS WHICH REST UPON THE LEGISLATIVE POWER OF THE STATES OF THE AMERICAN UNION 87 (1868).

The centralization of state authority in the legislature is part of a long Anglo-American tradition. Even before independence from Great Britain, colonial Americans viewed their legislatures as the protectors of their liberties against royal governors and judges, who were representatives of the British monarchy and seen to represent royal interests. After independence, then, it was natural that early state constitutions elevated the authority of their legislatures to the detriment of the other branches of government. The result, perhaps predictable in hindsight, was large-scale abuse by state legislatures of their lawmaking power. Among the worst excesses, confederation-era legislatures set aside court judgments, prohibited courts from hearing certain cases, granted pardons, transferred property between private parties, condemned individuals through bills of attainder, and expropriated property for the state. When considering this pattern of legislative abuses, both state lawmakers and the framers of the United States Constitution drew the same conclusion: liberty requires the separation of the powers of government—legislative, executive, and judicial—from one another. See *Address of the Council of Censors* (Feb. 14, 1786) *in* RECORDS OF THE COUNCIL OF CENSORS OF THE STATE OF VERMONT 60–72 (1991).

The principle of separation of powers, although deeply important to the generation that framed the United States Constitution and early state constitutions, was never implemented as absolutely as the rhetoric about the principle sometimes suggests. Indeed, although the framing generation was acutely aware that, unrestrained, the legislature was capable of "drawing all power into its impetuous vortex," the United States Constitution neither separates the powers of the federal government absolutely nor requires the states to separate their own powers. No. 48, The Federalist Papers (C. Rossiter ed.). As the United States Supreme Court has recognized, the powers of the federal government have always been shared among the three branches:

> James Madison, writing in the Federalist No. 47, defended the work of the Framers against the charge that these three governmental powers were not *entirely* separate from one another in the proposed Constitution. He asserted that while there was some admixture, the Constitution was nonetheless true to Montesquieu's well-known maxim that the legislative, executive, and judicial departments ought to be separate and distinct:
>
> > "The reasons on which Montesquieu grounds his maxim are a further demonstration of his meaning. 'When the legislative and executive powers are united in the same person or body,' says he, 'there can be no liberty, because apprehensions may arise lest *the same* Monarch or senate should *enact* tyrannical laws to execute them in a tyrannical manner.' Again: 'Were the power of judging joined with the legislative, the life and liberty of the subject would be exposed to arbitrary control, for *the judge* would then be *the legislator.* Were it joined to the executive power, *the judge* might behave with all the violence of *an oppressor.*' Some of these reasons are more fully explained in other passages; but briefly stated as they are here, they sufficiently establish the meaning which we have put on this celebrated maxim of this celebrated author."
>
> Yet it is also clear from the provisions of the Constitution itself and from the Federalist Papers, that the Constitution by no means contemplates total separation of each of these three essential branches of Government. The President is a participant in the lawmaking process by virtue of his authority to veto bills enacted by Congress. The Senate is a participant in the appointive process by virtue of its authority to refuse to confirm persons nominated to office by the President. The men who met in Philadelphia in the summer of 1787 were practical statesmen, experienced in politics, who viewed the principle of separation of powers as a vital check against tyranny. But they likewise saw that a hermetic sealing off of the three branches of Government from one another would preclude the establishment of a Nation capable of governing itself effectively. [*Buckley v. Valeo*, 424 U.S. 1, 120–21 (1976) (emphasis in original).]

Similarly, state constitutional versions of the separation of powers principle do not, and perhaps cannot, totally separate the powers of government from one another. Moreover, there is not a single state model of separation of powers. Instead, the particular historical development of each state's constitution accounts for the way it implements the separation of powers principle. Tarr, *Interpreting the Separation of Powers in State Constitutions*, 59 N.Y.U. Annual Survey Am. L. 329 (2003). Despite this variation, the principle of separation of powers is almost universally reflected in state constitutional law through two complementary prohibitions on state legislatures. First, if the legislature enacts a law that is so specific that it affects only a single individual, entity, or location, it impinges on the principle of separation of powers because it leaves no work for the judicial or executive branches to do. Legislation that is impermissibly specific violates state constitutional provisions prohibiting special legislation. Conversely, if the legislature enacts a statute that is so general that it fails to guide officials responsible for the statute's implementation, the legislature impinges on the principle of separation of powers by abdicating its policymaking obligation. Legislation that is impermissibly general violates state constitutional principles against delegation of legislative authority. These two manifestations of the principle of separation of powers—the prohibition on special legislation and the nondelegation doctrine—are the subjects of this Chapter.

Problem 8-1

College Town is a non-home rule municipality located in the State of South Minnesota. Among other provisions, the South Minnesota Constitution prohibits special legislation. In addition, its constitutional caselaw prohibits the legislature from vesting legislative authority in agencies without providing standards or guidelines for the agency to follow.

The Town Council of College Town has recently been receiving complaints from citizens and area visitors about downtown parking. Many local restaurants and shops have put up signs stating that only those people patronizing their establishments are allowed to park in nearby private parking lots and that those without merchant-approved parking permits will be treated as trespassers and towed by private towing companies. When those people who have parked without permission return to the lots where they have parked, they often find their cars missing. And when they call the phone numbers posted in the private lots, they learn that they face very high towing charges, which the towing companies require them to pay in cash. The Town Council has recently passed an ordinance under its "general welfare" powers to require private lot-owners to post larger signs and towing companies to comply with town anti-price gouging policies limiting towing fees and requiring towing companies to accept credit and debit cards.

After the towing companies threatened the Town Council with litigation, the Council worked with their local legislative delegation to persuade the South Minnesota General Assembly to adopt legislation authorizing College Town, but no other jurisdiction, to "regulate the operation of private towing companies within the town limits." The Town Council immediately reenacted its previously enacted towing and signage ordinance. No other town in the state has sought or received authorization to regulate towing companies.

During the same session, the South Minnesota General Assembly enacted legislation creating a new Department of Consumer Protection. The new department was authorized to "adopt regulations that address problems facing consumers, including those relating to unfair trade practices, deceptive advertising, and abuse of vulnerable populations." The new department quickly issued regulations prohibiting excessive charges by towing companies and requiring all towing companies to allow consumers to use credit and debit cards.

What constitutional challenges might be raised by a towing company that objects to the College Town ordinances capping prices and requiring use of credit and debit cards? What constitutional challenges might it raise in response to the Department of Consumer Protection's regulation of towing companies?

A. Special Legislation

A special law is a statute that targets an individual or small, identifiable group for treatment that is not imposed on the population in general. Although a statute may affect a single individual fortuitously, most often, a legislature enacts special legislation for the purpose of providing a benefit for, or imposing a burden on, a particular person, location, corporation, or industry. Special legislative benefits often include transferring public wealth to a particular individual or exempting a named individual from some restriction found in the generally applicable laws. Special burdens can include the confiscation of property or abrogation of specific government contracts. Some special laws benefit one person while simultaneously imposing a burden on another; for example, a statute that directs a court to rule in favor of a particular party in a pending case at once benefits the winning party while burdening the losing party.

Because it has the ability to benefit or burden known or identifiable individuals, special legislation has long been abused by legislatures. During the confederation period, individuals suspected of disloyalty, but neither indicted nor convicted of a crime, were punished with bills of attainder or subjected to the confiscation of their property. During this same period, legislatures often granted favored individuals monopoly rights, exempted them from some burden imposed by the generally applicable laws, or transferred state property to them. Because of the economic and social dislocations caused by special legislation, early Americans denounced their legislatures for enacting all types of special laws, including laws punishing individuals by name, amending titles to land, granting individuals extraordinary state benefits, and intervening in lawsuits. Zoldan, *Reviving Legislative Generality*, 98 Marq. L. Rev. 625, 660–79 (2014).

Despite their experiences during the framing period, confederation-era Americans did not explicitly prohibit special legislation either in the federal Constitution or in early state constitutions. Not surprisingly, then, the problems associated with special legislation resurfaced and intensified in the following decades. By the middle of the nineteenth century, most laws enacted by legislatures were special; in many states, special legislation accounted for 90% or more of the statutes enacted. Judges, legislators, and commentators again described the significant costs associated with special legislation, including the following: many state legislators took bribes in exchange for promoting special laws; the massive number of special bills that clogged the legislative docket made it impossible for legislatures to enact laws of general applicability; special laws benefitted the rich and powerful at the expense of the public welfare; and special laws interfered with the autonomy of local governments. Zoldan, *Legislative Design and the Controllable Costs of Special Legislation*, 78 Md. L. Rev. 415 (2019). For an excellent historical account of special and local legislation in the nineteenth century, see Ireland, *The Problem of Local, Private, and Special Legislation in the Nineteenth-Century United States*, 46 Am. J. L. Hist. 271 (2004).

In order to curb the legislative abuses associated with special legislation, nineteenth century state constitutional conventions adopted explicit prohibitions on special legislation. Although there are a number of different types of special legislation clauses, almost all state constitutional prohibitions on special legislation take one or more of the following forms. First, most state constitutions prohibit special legislation related to enumerated subject matters. The most common clauses prohibit special laws granting divorces, changing names, altering rules of evidence, and locating or altering county seats, among other subject matters. Second, fewer than half of the states prohibit special legislation without enumerating specific subject-matters that may not be addressed by special legislation. These states' constitutions provide, more generally, that their legislatures "shall pass no special or local law." Third, approximately half the states' constitutions prohibit special legislation when "a general law can be made applicable." Fourth, a few state legislatures permit special legislation, but only if the state legislature follows certain specified procedures, like providing public notice that special legislation is being contemplated and giving the public a chance to object. For a description of types of special legislation restrictions, see O. Reynolds, Local Government Law 89–94 (4th ed. 2015). For treatments of state constitutional prohibitions on special legislation, see Van Kley, *Article V, Section 12 of the Montana Constitution: Restoring Meaning to a Forgotten Provision*, 79 Mont. L. Rev. 115 (2018); Long, *State Constitutional Prohibitions on Special Laws*, 60 Clev. St. L. Rev. 719 (2012); Shaman, *The Evolution of Equality in State Constitutional Law*, 34 Rutgers L.J. 1013, 1043–51 (2003).

Although explicit special legislation provisions have been present in state constitutions for more than one hundred years, the scope of these clauses is far from settled, and their interpretation is frequently litigated in state courts. As you read the following cases interpreting special legislation provisions, consider the following questions: why do legislatures continue to enact special laws despite state constitutional prohibitions on special legislation?; why might courts have a difficult time enforcing the types of constitutional provisions described above?; what other provisions of state constitutions or the United States Constitution address concerns similar to those addressed by special legislation provisions?

Anderson v. Board of Commissioners of Cloud County

77 Kan. 721, 95 P. 583 (1908)

Porter, J.

In April, 1907, the board of county commissioners of Cloud county appropriated the sum of $8,000, for the purpose of removing and rebuilding a bridge across the Republican river, and afterwards proceeded to let the work by contract to the Western Bridge & Construction Company. The plaintiff, who is the owner of a 640-acre farm in Cloud county, brought suit to enjoin the proceedings. The court refused to grant a temporary injunction, and plaintiff brings the case here for review.

The facts are not disputed. The bridge in question is located upon a regularly established road, which leads north from the city of Concordia across the Republican river. The road is known as "McCrary Road," and crosses the plaintiff's farm. That portion of plaintiff's land where his buildings are located is an island, by reason of there being a branch of the Republican river south of his improvements, which has its upper opening in the river above the bridge, and connects again with the river below. The bridge therefore furnishes the only means of getting to and from that portion of his farm on which his improvements are located. It is alleged that its removal would cause irreparable injury to the plaintiff. The bridge was built in 1903, at a cost of $10,000. In the opinion of the board there is a necessity for its removal, on account of a change in the channel of the river, which has left it practically useless.... [I]t is the intention of the board to remove the bridge to another road across the river a mile west of its present location.... The sole contention is that the act of the Legislation under which the board is proceeding is unconstitutional.... The first section [of the Act] provides:

> That the board of county commissioners of Cloud county, Kansas, be and are hereby authorized and empowered, in their discretion, to erect and maintain such bridge or bridges for the use of the public across the Republican river and its various channels and cutoffs in the vicinity of the city of Concordia, Cloud county, Kansas, at such points as may be by said board of county commissioners selected; and to remove and relocate any bridge heretofore or hereafter erected by said county and which, by reason of changes in the channel of said river, has, in the opinion of said board, become useless to the general public.

The ground upon which its validity is assailed is that it is a special act, and for that reason repugnant to the second clause of section 17 of article 2 of the Constitution. By its express terms the act is special, and applies to Cloud county alone.... [At the time of the Act], the language of section 17 of article 2 read as follows: "All laws of a general nature shall have a uniform operation throughout the state; and in all cases where a general law can be made applicable, no special law shall be enacted."... This constitutional limitation is based upon the theory that the state is a unit, to be governed, throughout its length and breadth, on all subjects of common interest, by the same laws, and that these laws should be general in their application and uniform in their operation. When it was adopted the evil effects of special legislation, enacted at the behest of private individuals or local communities, were well understood and appreciated. The makers of the Constitution were confronted with the experience of the older states, which had demonstrated that Legislatures were wholly unable to withstand the constant demands for private grants of power and special privilege. The same year that our Constitution was adopted the conditions in Illinois had reached such a stage that, in the language of the Supreme Court, the mischief of special legislation were "beyond recovery or remedy." . . .

The inherent vice of special laws is that they create preferences and establish irregularities. As an inevitable consequence, their enactment leads to improvident and ill-considered legislation. The members whose particular constituents are not affected by a proposed special law become indifferent to its passage. It is customary, on the plea of legislative courtesy, not to interfere with the local bill of another member; and members are elected, and re-elected, on account of their proficiency in procuring for their respective districts special privileges in the way of local or special laws. The time which the Legislature would otherwise devote to the consideration of measures of public importance is frittered away in the granting of special favors to private or corporate interests or to local communities. Meanwhile, in place of a symmetrical body of statutory law on subjects of general and common interest to the whole people, we have a wilderness of special provisions, whose operation extends no further than the boundaries of the particular school district or township or county to which they were made to apply. For performing the same services the sheriff or register of deeds or probate judge of one county receives an entirely different compensation from that received by the same officer of another county. The people of one community of the state are governed, as to many subjects, by laws wholly different from those which apply to other localities. Worse still, rights and privileges, which should only result from the decree of a court of competent jurisdiction after a full hearing and notice to all parties in interest, are conferred upon individuals and private corporations by special acts of the Legislature, without any pretense of investigation as to merits, or of notice to adverse parties.

Commenting upon the evils of special legislation, Mr. Samuel P. Orth, in the *Atlantic Monthly* for January, 1906 (volume 97, p. 69), uses this language: "The Romans recognized the distinction between private bills and laws. To them special laws were privilegia or constitutionis privilegia. In England they used to say, when a public bill was passed: 'Le roi le veut'—it is the king's wish; and of a private measure: 'Soit fait comme il est désire'—let it be granted as prayed for. Here is the gist of the matter: A public law is a measure that affects the welfare of the state as a unit; a private law is one that provides an exception to the public rule. The one is an answer to a public need, the other an answer to a private prayer. When it acts upon a public bill, a Legislature legislates; when it acts upon a private bill, it adjudicates. It passes from the function of a lawmaker to that of a judge. It is transformed from a tribune of the people into a justice shop for the seeker after special privilege."

It has been estimated that fully one-half of the laws enacted by the state Legislatures in recent years have been special laws. . . . The Legislature of 1905, which differed in this respect but little from its predecessors, passed no less than 25 special acts relating to bridges, and 35 fixing the fees of officers in various counties and cities. Out of a total of 527 chapters more than half are special acts. This does not include appropriation laws which, from their nature, are inherently special. The first act passed by this Legislature declared a certain young woman the adopted child and heir at law of certain persons. Others changed the names of individuals. Many granted valuable rights and privileges to private corporations. Hundreds granted special favors to municipal corporations, and many others conferred special privileges upon individuals. Such were the conditions which induced the people, at the general election in 1906, to change the Constitution, by adopting the amendment to section 17 of article 2. . . . The only change [made by the amendment] is to require the courts to determine, as a judicial question, whether in a given case this provision has been complied with by the Legislature. . . .

The first clause of this section of the Constitution involves the question of classification, which it is apparent does not enter into the present case. Here there will doubtless remain in the future an ample field, upon which lawyers may contend and courts and judges differ. It may be said in passing, however, that it will be the duty of the courts, when that question arises, to apply the established tests to determine whether an attempted classification of the Legislature is a proper one, based upon some apparently natural reason, suggested by necessity and occasioned by a real difference in the situation and circumstances of the class to which it applies, or whether it is arbitrary or capricious, and excludes from its provisions some persons, localities, or things to which it would naturally apply except for its own limitations. It may be said, however, that it will not become the duty of the courts to invent reasons for upholding a law which is repugnant to either clause of this provision.

It requires no argument or discussion to demonstrate that the special act in question violates the Constitution. To enact a general law on the subject, giving to boards of county commissioners in every county in the state authority to build or remove bridges, appropriate funds, and issue bonds to meet the expense thereof, under such restrictions and limitations, upon their authority in the premises as the Legislature may deem wise and salutary, would not require more than ordinary skill in the science of legislation.

We are not concluded either way by the fact that a general law on the subject was in existence when a special act was passed. That fact, however, serves as an apt illustration of the adaptability of a general law upon the subject, and as an argument against the necessity for a special law. It is argued that the local conditions in Cloud county are such as to authorize an exception to be made, and to require this special act. It appears that the bridge which the board were intending to remove was built, in the first place, by authority of a special law enacted in 1903; that the claims for a special law at that time were that the river had abandoned its channel and left a former bridge useless. Everybody knows that the rivers of the Missouri valley frequently change their course, and create conditions similar to those which existed in Cloud county in 1906. The experience of Cloud county in this respect differs from that of many other counties in the state, if at all, only in the extent to which that county has suffered. From 25 to 30 special laws of this nature have been passed by almost every Legislature for years, and practically the same reasons urged for their enactment. No reason can be suggested why a general law upon the subject could not be made to apply with a uniform operation throughout the state wherever similar conditions are likely to arise. In fact, the only suggestion made as to why the general law, already in existence, authorizing the erection of bridges, is not sufficient to meet the conditions is that, in the opinion of the members of the board, the voters would defeat any proposition submitted. This amounts to a confession that in the act in question there inhere the vices which the amendment was designed to prevent. To hold that the reasons suggested are sufficient to warrant a special law would raise again the lid of Pandora's box only to permit its evils to escape. It follows, therefore, that the act must be declared void.

The judgment will be reversed, and the cause remanded for further proceedings.

Notes and Questions

1. *Judicial review.* In the principal case, the constitutional provision stated that the legislature may not pass a special law when a general law "can be made applicable." A court reviewing a challenge to a special law under this language must determine, as a threshold matter, who decides—the court or the legislature—whether a general law can be made applicable. Some constitutional provisions expressly state that whether a general law can be made applicable is a judicial question, while others provide that the legislature shall make this determination. Compare ALA. CONST. art. IV, § 105 (justiciable), *with* VA. CONST. art. IV, § 15 (*contra*). In the absence of an express constitutional statement about which institution should decide, courts vary in their level of deference to the legislature's judgment. Some courts read "can be made applicable" language to mean that a special law is prohibited only when a general law on the subject actually has been enacted. Other courts will uphold a special law even if there is a general law, but the general law is incomplete or not exhaustive. See *Hedrick v. County Court*, 172 S.E.2d 312 (W. Va. 1970). Still other courts read the provision to mean that a special law is invalid if the subject could have been dealt with by a general law. Courts apply the usual presumption of constitutionality to laws claimed to be special, but the presumption is not absolute. In order to save a special law, a court may also try to harmonize it with a general statute. See *Richardson v. Phillips*, 711 S.E.2d 358 (Ga. App. 2011) (construing special legislation regarding county commissioners' ethics requirements in conjunction with remedies provided in generally applicable statutes).

2. *Closed classes.* Irrespective of the language of the particular constitutional provision involved, courts often hold that a challenged law is special when it creates a "closed class." A class is closed rather than open if it is impossible, or extremely unlikely, that another person or entity will fall within the statutory classification in

the future. In *Teigen v. State*, 749 N.W.2d 505, 508 (N.D. 2008), a statute required a state agency to enter into a contract with "no more than two" trade associations for the representation of wheat producers. Although the statute did not name any particular trade association, the statute defined the qualifications so narrowly that it could only have applied to two particular organizations. The court held that the statute was prohibited as a special law because, although it did not name a particular entity, it did not "permit future entry" into the class. See also *In re Cesar R.*, 4 P.3d 980, 983 (Ariz. App. 1999) (invalidating a statute applying to counties with a population of 500,000 that effectively limited its prohibition to two counties, making "improbable entry and exit by other counties"); *Department of Bus. Regulation v. Classic Mile, Inc.*, 541 So. 2d 1155 (Fla. 1989) (invalidating statute that provided for licensing wagering facilities when only one county would ever fall within its terms).

Conversely, courts tend to uphold classifications that are narrowly drawn if the class is "open," that is, if other people or entities may fall into the class in the future. In *Hotel Dorset Co. v. Trust for Cultural Resources of City of New York*, 385 N.E.2d 1284 (N.Y. 1978), a statute provided financial assistance to cultural institutions for the construction of combined-use facilities with the expectation that the commercial portion of the facility would generate income to support the cultural purpose. Because the statute established eligibility criteria relating to the population of the city in which the cultural institution was located, the institution's annual admissions, and the size of the property it owned contiguous to the proposed building site, its applicability was limited to the Museum of Modern Art in New York City. However, because no showing was made that other institutions in the future would not be able to meet the criteria, the court refused to invalidate the statute as special legislation. *Id.* at 1288. See also *Arkansas Health Services v. Regional Care Facilities*, 93 S.W.3d 672, 681 (Ark. 2002) (upholding a statute applying to one county because it was likely that, in near future, it would apply to future counties).

Courts are often deferential to the legislature's determination about whether a class is open or closed. In *Bopp v. Spainhower*, 519 S.W.2d 281 (Mo. 1975), the court upheld a law authorizing a county to impose a sales tax provided that, within the following six months, the county did not contain a city or part of a city with more than 400,000 inhabitants. St. Louis County was the only county to which the statute applied; nevertheless, the court held that the class was open because Jackson County, which had more than 500,000 inhabitants, could have had a city that fell below the 400,000 population ceiling "by reason of war or an extensive fire or an epidemic of serious proportions or other unforeseen disaster." *Id.* at 285. See also *Houston v. Governor*, 810 N.W.2d 255, 257 (Mich. 2012) (upholding a population-based statute that applied only to a single county, the court held that the "probability or improbability" that other localities will fall within the statutory criteria "is not the test of a general law.... It must be assumed" that other localities will fit within the classification in the future); *Gallardo v. State*, 336 P.3d 717 (Ariz. 2014) (upholding a statute classifying counties by population although no other county likely would enter or leave the class "in the near future").

The open class/closed class distinction does not always drive a court's decision: even if a statute does create a closed class, courts sometimes uphold it if there is sufficient justification for the statutory classification. See *Steven Bank v. Heineman*, 837 N.W.2d 70 (Neb. 2013) (concluding that exemption from nameplate capacity tax on wind-generation did not violate a provision against special laws where the exemption relieved a single entity from double taxation); *Lamasco Realty Co. v. City of Milwaukee*, 8 N.W.2d 372, 377 (Wisc. 1943) (upholding statute that applied only to Milwaukee because "the requirements of a metropolitan city like Milwaukee as against the smaller municipal corporations of the state are so obvious that any other result would be opposed to the public welfare"); *Foster v. Jefferson County Bd. of Election Comm'rs*, 944 S.W.2d 93 (Ark. 1997) (upholding a statute applying to counties with a population between 76,000 and 76,100, although it applied to only one county, because the statute was motivated by the non-discriminatory purpose of giving all voters an opportunity to vote on municipal judges). Some courts explicitly reject the open class/closed class distinction. *City of Aurora v. Spectra Communications Group, LLC*, 592 S.W.3d 764, 779 (Mo. 2019) (en banc) (rejecting open class/closed class distinction in favor of rational basis test).

3. *Narrow classes.* Although the paradigmatic case of a special law is a statute that affects a single individual, statutes sometimes affect a small class rather than an individual. Courts often invalidate these narrowly drawn statutes as special laws. In *People v. Canister*, 110 P.3d 380, 384 (Colo. 2005), a statute created a class of two people that could not be augmented in the future. The court invalidated the law as special, holding that "a class that is drawn so that it will never have any members other than those targeted by the legislation is illusory, and the legislation creating such a class is unconstitutional special legislation." But see *Mahwah Township v. Bergen County*, 486 A.2d 818 (N.J. 1985) (upholding statute creating tax rebate for two large counties that housed nontaxable state institutions because it was rational to conclude that "an institution in a county with a larger population will be utilized by more people than a similar institution in a smaller county").

By contrast, courts are more likely to uphold legislation that singles out a large class rather than a narrow class. This has come up frequently in challenges to statutes limiting tort liability for medical professionals. *Kirkland v. Blaine County Medical Ctr.*, 4 P.3d 1115 (Idaho 2000) (upholding legislation imposing a $400,000 damages cap for medical malpractice because it was part of a legislative plan to solve the problem of large civil jury awards driving up the cost of insurance); *Miller v. Rosenberg*, 749 N.E.2d 946 (Ill. 2001) (upholding a statute making it easier for health professionals to bring malicious prosecution claims, noting that the legislation was adopted to remedy a crisis in medical malpractice litigation). Contra *Best v. Taylor Machine Works*, 689 N.E.2d 1057 (Ill. 1997) (invalidating a statute placing a half-million dollar cap on the recovery of compensatory damages for noneconomic injuries, noting that the limitation undermined the goal of providing consistency and rationality in the civil justice system).

4. *Equal protection distinguished.* The concerns addressed by special legislation clauses—including favoring the politically well-connected with special legislative privileges—resonate with the protection provided by state and federal equal protection guarantees. For this reason, some courts apply, either explicitly or implicitly, a special legislation test that closely resembles an equal protection rational basis test. In *Blaske v. Smith & Entzeroth, Inc.*, 821 S.W.2d 822, 832 (Mo. 1991), a statute created a special limitations period for architects, engineers and providers of construction services. In upholding the statute against a special legislation challenge, the court noted that the test for special legislation under the Missouri Constitution "involves the same principles and considerations that are involved in determining whether the statute violates equal protection in a situation where neither a fundamental right nor a suspect class is involved, *i.e.*, where a rational basis test applies." See also *Harrisburg School District v. Zogby*, 828 A.2d 1079 (Pa. 2003) ("Indeed, it is now generally accepted that the meaning and purpose of the Equal Protection Clause of the United States Constitution . . . and the state Constitution's prohibition against special laws . . . are sufficiently similar to warrant like treatment, and that contentions concerning the two provisions may be reviewed simultaneously.").

By contrast, some courts have explicitly held that the special legislation prohibition is not subsumed within equal protection. In *Benderson Dev. Co., Inc. v. Sciortino*, 372 S.E.2d 751, 756 (Va. 1988), the court held a Sunday Closing Law that erratically exempted a number of businesses from its effect and allowed cities and counties to adopt a referendum exempting themselves from the law did not violate equal protection but did violate the prohibition on special legislation. It noted that the limitation imposed by the special legislation prohibition was not the same as that imposed by the equal protection clause: "[T]he special-laws prohibitions contained in the Virginia Constitution are aimed squarely at economic favoritism, and have been so since their inception." See *Petitioners for Deannexation v. City of Good Year*, 773 P.2d 1026, 1031–32 (Ariz. 1989) (special legislation prohibition was designed to eliminate legislative favoritism through population, geography, or time classifications, an inquiry beyond an equal protection/rational basis investigation). For arguments that state special legislation clauses and equal protection should not be treated as coextensive, see Schutz, *State Constitutional Restrictions on Special Legislation as Structural Constraints*, 40 J. Legis. 39 (2014); Long, *State Constitutional Prohibitions on Special Laws*, 60 Clev. St. L. Rev. 719 (2012).

Even when courts assert that their special legislation doctrine differs from equal protection, it can be challenging to determine how different these doctrines really are. See *Gourley v. Methodist Health Sys.*, 663 N.W.2d 43 (Neb. 2003) ("The analysis under a special legislation inquiry focuses on the Legislature's purpose in creating the class and asks if there is a substantial difference of circumstances to suggest the expediency of diverse legislation. This is different from an equal protection analysis under which the state interest in legislation is compared to the statutory means selected by the Legislature to accomplish that purpose. Under an equal protection analysis, differing levels of scrutiny are applied depending on if the legislation involves a suspect class."). Accord *Hug v. City of Omaha*, 749 N.W.2d 884, 890 (Neb. 2008) (adopting *Gourley* test). Compare *Illinois Polygraph Soc'y v. Pellicano*, 414 N.E.2d 458, 462–463 (Ill. 1980) ("Special legislation confers a special benefit or exclusive privilege on a person or a group of persons to the exclusion of others similarly situated. . . . It arbitrarily, and without a sound, reasonable basis, discriminates in favor of a select group. . . . [E]qual protection . . . consists of arbitrary and invidious discrimination against a person or a class of persons.").

Equal protection doctrine, following the concept of formal equality, does not disallow treating two things differently if they are not "similarly situated"; that is, two things may be treated differently if they are different in a relevant way. Tussman & tenBroek, *The Equal Protection of the Laws*, 37 Cal. L. Rev. 341, 343–44 (1949). And if something is different in a relevant way from everything else, then formal equality suggests that it should not be treated the same as anything else. In other words, if a thing is unique, formal equality suggests that the law should accord it unique legal treatment. Does formal equality justify special legislation if the target of the legislation is unique, that is, different in a relevant way from everything else? Aren't all things unique in at least some sense? How can a court or legislature determine whether a difference between two things is relevant or irrelevant? For an argument that equal protection doctrine is not up to the task of dealing coherently and meaningfully with the imposition on equality caused by special legislation, see Zoldan, *The Equal Protection Component of Legislative Generality*, 51 U. Rich. L. Rev. 489, 518–542 (2017).

5. *Special legislation in states without explicit constitutional prohibitions.* A few states have no constitutional clauses that explicitly prohibit special legislation. It would be a mistake to conclude, however, that these constitutions place no restrictions on special legislation. Indeed, the states that chose not to add explicit special legislation provisions in the nineteenth century were among the earliest to include provisions in their constitutions prohibiting individualized legislative privileges and punishments. The Vermont Constitution's Common Benefits Clause provides that the "government is, or ought to be, instituted for the common benefit, protection, and security of the people, nation, or community, and not for the particular emolument or advantage of any single person, family, or set of persons." Vt. Const. art. I, § 7. In similar language, Massachusetts and New Hampshire's constitutions provide that no individual is entitled to exclusive privileges other than those available to the community in general. Mass Const. Part I, art. VI; N.H. Const. Part I, art. X. Not only do these states' constitutions prohibit special privileges, they also prohibit some special punishments, like bills of attainder. Are these general provisions sufficient to address the types of special laws described above?

6. *Special legislation enacted by municipalities.* Courts have held that municipalities also fall within the purview of prohibitions on special legislation. See, e.g., *Hunter Ave. Property, L.P. v. Union Elec. Co.*, 895 S.W.2d 146 (Mo. App. 1995) ("It is a well established rule of law that this proscription applies with equal force to municipalities and their ordinances as it does to the general assembly."). For a more recent case holding that special legislation provisions apply to municipal regulation, see *Dowd Grain Co., Inc. v. County of Sarpy*, 867 N.W.2d 599 (Neb. 2015) (holding that a municipal zoning ordinance is subject to restrictions on special legislation but ultimately upholding the ordinance).

Some of the cases discussed above apply to particular geographic locations while others apply to individuals, corporations or even entire industries. The following case draws a distinction between legislation that affects a particular area—local legislation—and other particularized legislation.

Clean Water Coalition v. The M Resort, LLC

127 Nev. 301, 255 P.3d 247 (2011)

Hardesty, Justice.

Confronting a statewide budget crisis, the Nevada Legislature, during the 2010 special session, undertook several revenue-adjustment and cost-cutting measures in an effort to balance the State's budget, which resulted in the enactment of Assembly Bill 6 (A.B. 6), 26th Special Session (Nev. 2010). Section 18 of A.B. 6 mandates the transfer of $62 million in securities and cash from a political subdivision of the State created by interlocal agreement into the State's general fund for the State's unrestricted, general use.

In this appeal, we are asked to consider whether A.B. 6, section 18 violates the fundamental law of the state—the Nevada Constitution. We recognize that the Legislature is endowed with considerable lawmaking authority under Article 4, Section 1 of the Nevada Constitution. But that authority is not without some restraints. Two such restrictions are contained in Article 4, Section 20, which prohibits, among other things, local and special laws for the "assessment and collection of taxes for state . . . purposes," and Article 4, Section 21, which requires laws to be "general and of uniform operation throughout the State" in all cases "where a general law can be made applicable."

We conclude that A.B. 6, section 18 violates both. . . .

FACTS AND PROCEDURAL HISTORY . . .

Litigation over A.B. 6, section 18

A.B. 6 was adopted and approved as part of the Legislature's effort to balance the state's budget during its 2010 special session. Section 18 of that bill requires the Clean Water Coalition [CWC], an entity created pursuant to interlocal agreement by the Clark County Water Reclamation District and the Cities of Henderson, Las Vegas, and North Las Vegas, to "transfer to the State of Nevada securities and cash which together total $62,000,000, for deposit in the State General Fund for unrestricted State General Fund use." In adopting A.B. 6, section 18(1), the Legislature found and declared that:

> (a) The transfer of money from the Clean Water Coalition to the State General Fund is necessary to ensure that the government of this State is able to continue to operate effectively and to serve the residents, businesses and governmental entities of this State;
>
> (b) The transfer of money from the Clean Water Coalition to the State General Fund will promote the general welfare of this State; and
>
> (c) A general law cannot be made applicable to the provisions of [Section 18] because of special circumstances. . . .

DISCUSSION

The CWC and The M Resort and other Clark County business cross-appellants (hereinafter The M Resort) challenge A.B. 6, section 18 on two grounds: that it impermissibly converts funds assessed as user fees and exacted on a local basis into a tax for distribution on a statewide basis in violation of Nevada Constitution Article 4, Section 20; and that it is a local or special law that operates over a particular locality, and is directed at funds obtained from wastewater treatment users in Clark County, in violation of Nevada Constitution Article 4, Section 21, which requires laws to be general and to operate uniformly throughout the state. . . .

In determining whether A.B. 6, section 18's mandate requiring the CWC to turn over $62 million to the State for its unrestricted general use is permissible under the Nevada Constitution's local and special law proscriptions, we first analyze whether section 18 is local or special legislation. In so doing, we examine the origin of the Nevada Constitution's proscriptions on local and special laws, as that history provides a framework for our analysis. Since, as explained below, we conclude that A.B. 6, section 18 is both a local and special law, we next analyze whether it violates Nevada Constitution Article 4, Section 20, which prohibits local or special laws that assess and collect taxes for state purposes, and Article 4, Section 21, which otherwise prohibits local or special laws in cases where a general law could apply. As discussed below, we determine that A.B. 6, section 18 violates both Article 4, Sections 20 and 21, and it therefore fails under the Nevada Constitution.

Nevada constitutional provisions proscribing local and special laws

The Nevada Constitution provides that "[t]he legislature shall not pass local or special laws . . . [f]or the assessment and collection of taxes for state, county, and township purposes," Nev. Const. art. 4, § 20, and it further requires that "[i]n all cases enumerated in [Section 20], and in all other cases where a general law can be made applicable, all laws shall be general and of uniform operation throughout the State." Nev. Const. art. 4, § 21. This court has explained the prohibition against local and special laws under Article 4, Sections 20 and 21 as follows:

> [I]f a statute be either a special or local law, or both, and comes within any one or more of the cases enumerated in section 20, such statute is unconstitutional; if the statute be special or local, or both, but does not come within any of the cases enumerated in section 20, then its constitutionality depends upon whether a general law can be made applicable.

Conservation District v. Beemer, 56 Nev. 104, 116, 45 P.2d 779, 782 (1935).

Because history instructs the analysis that follows, we first explain the origins of the Nevada Constitution's proscriptions on such laws and the constitutional framers' purpose in adopting provisions limiting the Legislature's authority to enact local and special laws before delving into why A.B. 6, section 18 fits within the proscribed local and special laws set forth under Nevada Constitution Article 4, Sections 20 and 21.

History leading to the adoption of Nevada Constitution Article 4, Sections 20 and 21

During Nevada's Constitutional Convention in 1864, the delegates, in structuring Article 4, Section 20 for adoption into the Nevada Constitution, used as a guide Indiana's constitutional provisions prohibiting special legislation. *See Debates & Proceedings of the Nevada State Constitutional Convention of 1864*, at 466 (Andrew J. Marsh off. rep. 1866). The Nevada constitutional framers' purpose in adopting mandates proscribing local and special legislation was to "remedy an evil into which it was supposed the territorial legislature had fallen in the practice of passing local and special laws for the benefit of individuals instead of enacting laws of a general nature for the benefit of the public welfare." *Evans v. Job*, 8 Nev. 322, 333 (1873). The framers of the Indiana Constitution had similar concerns with local and special legislation, deeming the practice of legislators agreeing to vote for the local bills of other legislators in return for comparable cooperation for passing their own local bills a "growing evil." *See Municipal City of South Bend v. Kimsey*, 781 N.E.2d 683, 686 (Ind. 2003). The problem with such lawmaking is that when "a law affects only one small area of the state, voters in most areas will be ignorant of and indifferent to it." *Id.* Likewise, early in Nevada's jurisprudence, this court explained that the purpose behind requiring statutes to be general in nature is that when a statute affects the entire state, it is more likely to have been adequately considered by all members of the Legislature, whereas a localized statute is not apt to be considered seriously by those who are not affected by it. At their core, local and special law proscriptions "reflect a concern for equal treatment under the law," Robert F. Williams, *Equality Guarantees in State Constitutional Law*, 63 Tex. L. Rev. 1195, 1209 (1985), and seek to fix inequities in the areas of "economics and social welfare." *See* Donald Marritz, *Making Equality Matter (Again): The Prohibition Against Special Laws in the Pennsylvania Constitution*, 3 Widener J. Pub.L. 161, 184–85 (1993) (explaining the origins of Pennsylvania's constitutional prohibition against special laws).

Although the Nevada Constitution expresses a preference for generally applicable laws, local or special laws are not *ipso facto* unconstitutional. Nev. Const. art. 4,

§§ 20, 21. A local or special law may be upheld so long as (1) it does not come within any of the cases enumerated in Nevada Constitution Article 4, Section 20; and (2) a general law could not have been made applicable. Nev. Const. art. 4, § 21. For the reasons explained below, A.B. 6, section 18 fails on both counts.

A.B. 6, section 18 is a local and special law

The CWC and The M Resort argue that because A.B. 6, section 18 applies in only a single Nevada county, and only to users of the municipal or county sewer systems in that county, it is a local law, and because it applies specifically and directly to a single entity in the state to the exclusion of all others similarly situated, it is a special law. The CWC also points out that the assembly bill's text admits that it is being used in lieu of a general law. The State responds that even though, on its face, A.B. 6, section 18 operates selectively in a few political subdivisions and in only a limited geographical area, it is not a local or special law because it advances supervening statewide budget concerns that transcend purely local interests. The State also urges this court to disregard the legislative admission that section 18 is being used in lieu of a general law.

A law is local if it operates over "a particular locality instead of over the whole territory of the State." *Damus v. County of Clark*, 93 Nev. 512, 516, 569 P.2d 933, 935 (1977). A law is special if it "pertain[s] to a part of a class as opposed to all of a class." *Id.*; *see State of Nevada v. Cal. M. Co.*, 15 Nev. 234, 249 (1880) (describing a special law as one that "imposes special burdens, or confers peculiar privileges upon one or more persons in no wise distinguished [way] from others of the same category"). On the other hand, a general law is one that is applied uniformly. Nev. Const. art. 4, § 21; *see Black's Law Dictionary* 963 (9th ed. 2009) (defining a general law as one that is "neither local nor confined in application to particular persons").

In drafting A.B. 6, section 18, the Legislature found and declared that "[a] general law cannot be made applicable to the provisions of this section because of special circumstances." A.B. 6, § 18(*l*)(c), 26th Spec. Sess. (Nev. 2010). The State acknowledges that when legislative findings are expressly included within a statute, those findings should be accorded great weight in interpreting the statute, but it points out that such findings are not binding and this court may, nevertheless, properly conclude that section 18 is a general law despite the Legislature's declaration to the contrary. The Legislature's express finding and declaration that section 18 is not a general law, however, is consistent with the bill section's text, which, as the district court found, is directed specifically at the CWC and funds collected from wastewater treatment users within specified areas of Clark County. The law applies only to the CWC. The State argues that a law need not be operative in every part of the state to be general, but the determination of whether a law is local or special is based on how it is applied, not on how it actually operates. . . .

Since section 18 on its face advances statewide objectives, but burdens only the CWC by appropriating funds collected from certain residents and businesses within a particular locality for the state's general use, it is special (pertaining to only the CWC) and local (applying to only a particular locality).

By requiring the CWC to turn over fees it assessed against its members for capital improvement projects and services for the benefit of Las Vegas Valley sewer service users, A.B. 6, section 18 imposes an unconstitutional local and special tax against the CWC in violation of Nevada Constitution Article 4, Section 20

The Legislature is not permitted to pass local or special laws "[f]or the assessment and collection of taxes for state, county, and township purposes." Nev. Const. art. 4, § 20. An exaction of money for the purpose of generating revenue is a tax.... Accordingly, looking at A.B. 6, section 18's true purpose, which is to raise the State's revenue base through an assessment against one political subdivision of the state that operates in only a specific locality in the state, we conclude that section 18 is an impermissible local and special tax under Article 4, Section 20 of the Nevada Constitution [rather than merely a "fee," as the State argues].

A.B. 6, section 18 is contrary to Article 4, Section 21 because a general law could apply to address the State's budget shortfall

Even if this court were to credit the State's argument that A.B. 6, section 18 involves only fees, not a tax, taking it outside Article 4, Section 20, the measure still fails because it violates Article 4, Section 21, which mandates general laws in all cases where they "can be made applicable." While A.B. 6, section 18 declares that a general law could not apply "because of special circumstances," and the Legislature's decision on whether a general law can be made applicable in a given case is presumed correct, a law's compliance with Article 4, Section 21 nevertheless is subject to judicial review.

When determining whether a local or special law is permissible because a general law could not be made "applicable" for purposes of Nevada Constitution Article 4, Section 21, we look to whether the challenged law "best subserve[s] the interests of the people of the state, or such class or portion as the particular legislation is intended to affect." [*State of Nevada v.*] *Irwin*, 5 Nev. at 122. In upholding local or special legislation in the past, this court has focused on whether "the general legislation existing was insufficient to meet the peculiar needs of a particular situation," or whether a particular emergency situation existed, requiring more speedy action and relief than could be had by proceeding under the existing general law. With those precepts in mind, local or special laws have been upheld in situations where an emergency situation existed within a certain county or locality and a general law could not apply to address the situation because only that county or locality was affected. In all of those cases, the challenged local or special laws addressed immediate concerns within a locality and directly burdened and benefited those who were subject to the laws. This court has also upheld local or special laws on the basis that the general legislation existing was insufficient to meet the peculiar needs of a particular local or special situation and a general law could not be made applicable....

Although we agree with the State that the statewide budget crisis presents exigent circumstances that must be addressed, those circumstances are of statewide concern and cannot be addressed through legislation that does not comport with Article 4, Section 21's local and special law proscription. Political differences that might make it difficult to agree on a generally applicable law to address the State's budget crisis do not create "special circumstances" that would permit a local or special law to address a concern that affects the entire state. The State's position in this appeal fails to recognize that the common thread in this court's jurisprudence from the beginning of Nevada's statehood is that permissible local or special laws address particular concerns that pertain only to the locality or to the part of the class affected by the laws, and not to statewide concerns. No Nevada case has upheld a challenged local or special law that addressed a statewide concern, and the State points to no other jurisdiction that has permitted such a law. Indeed, just shortly after the Nevada Constitution was forged, this court explained that in determining the validity of any local or special law, "a general law should always be construed . . . to be applicable in all cases where the subject is one in which from its very nature the entire people of the State have an interest." *Evans v. Job*, 8 Nev. 322, 336 (1873). . . .

A.B. 6, section 18 requires one political subdivision to turn over money collected in a local area to the State's general fund coffers for statewide benefit. It affects the people of the entire state of Nevada, and the State's budget crisis is, by its very nature, a subject of interest to all people of the state. For that reason, it cannot be addressed by a local or special law that applies to burden only one entity of the state that operates in one locality of the state. The State offers special circumstances but does not indicate why a general law, uniformly applied to all political subdivisions or based on some other qualifying criteria was not used to address the budget shortfall. . . .

Accordingly, since A.B. 6, section 18 is a local and special law that addresses a statewide concern to which a general law could have applied, it is not permissible under Article 4, Section 21. We thus conclude that the district court erred by declaring it constitutional.

Notes and Questions

1. *Local versus special laws.* The principal case draws a distinction between local and special laws, holding that the statute was special because it pertained only to a particular entity (the Clean Water Coalition) and it was local because it applied only to a particular locality. If a state constitutional provision prohibits both local and special laws, is anything gained by categorizing local laws separately from special laws? The terminology surrounding special laws and local laws is notoriously confused. Some courts and commentators explain that local laws are a subset of special laws; others maintain that not all local laws are special. Cloe & Marcus, *Special and Local Legislation*, 24 Ky. L.J. 351, 364–66 (1936). Some states explicitly define special laws to include local laws. Fla. Const. art. X, § 12. For more on this confusing terminology, and for a comprehensive description of special and local legislation in

its heyday, see C. Binney, Restrictions upon Local and Special Legislation in State Constitutions 21–26 (1894).

Both the principal case and the *Anderson* case, above, allude to the role that logrolling plays in the enactment of local legislation. Consider hypothetical Legislator X, who introduces a local bill that will bring economic benefits to her district alone. Legislator X has an interest in returning legislative favors to her constituents because, she expects, her constituents will reward her with reelection for benefitting them. Legislators Y and Z are not similarly motivated because they will see no electoral benefits from benefitting Legislator X's constituents. However, Legislators Y and Z also know that, someday soon, they too may want a special favor for their constituents. This knowledge motivates them, although disinterested in Legislator X's bill, to vote for it; they know that, in the future, Legislator X will return the favor by voting for legislation they support. This informal exchange of votes is known as logrolling. In the aggregate, logrolling allows the passage of legislation, including local legislation, that inures to the benefit of private interests rather than the public's interest. For a discussion of logrolling and special legislation, including a proposal for defining special legislation to include "legislation that emerges from a trade among representatives that returns net losses to the state as a whole," see Gillette, *Expropriation and Institutional Design in State and Local Government Law*, 80 Va. L. Rev. 625, 642–57 (1994).

2. *Special conditions justifying special laws.* The court in the principal case invalidated the statute despite the fact that it was intended to address an emergency situation, in that case a budget crisis. Courts are sometimes more sympathetic to legislative findings of emergency conditions, holding that targeted statutes are not special, or excused even though they are special, because of an emergency. In *Colman v. Utah State Land Bd.*, 795 P.2d 622 (Utah 1990), rising water levels in the Great Salt Lake threatened to flood adjacent land. The Great Salt Lake Causeway, which divided the lake into separate arms, exacerbated the danger of flooding by preventing the water levels in the separate arms from equalizing. In order to induce the Causeway's owner, a private railway company, to breach the Causeway, the state enacted a special indemnification provision, shielding the company from liability resulting from its decision to breach it. Although the indemnification provision applied only to one structure and provided the benefit of indemnification to one entity alone, the court held that it was not prohibited as special, because it had the purpose of "preventing widespread flood damage to public lands, major transportation routes, and other public facilities." *Id.* at 636.

Similarly, courts sometimes excuse targeted statutes from the restrictions of special legislation provisions when they deem the statutes "curative," that is, if they are intended to fix a mistake or oversight in the generally applicable law. *State ex rel. Tomasic v. Kansas City, Kansas Port Auth.*, 636 P.2d 760 (1981) ("Curative legislation has long been recognized as a valid exercise of legislative power which is not special legislation in contravention" of state special legislation provision); *City of Muscatine v. Waters*, 251 N.W.2d 544, 548 (Iowa 1977) (opining that curative statutes "cure or validate errors or irregularities in legal or administrative proceedings" and are "of necessity special, and can not be made general"). Is there a coherent way to distinguish an "emergency" from any other public policy choice that the legislature makes? Aren't special laws always intended to cure some defect in the generally applicable law? Do the "emergency" and "curative" exceptions threaten to render special legislation provisions meaningless? Do these exceptions help explain why state legislatures continue to enact special laws despite constitutional restrictions?

Consider the reverse situation: what if a law is targeted to reach a particular party, but it is designed to eliminate a special privilege or special benefit? Some state constitutions specifically permit special laws enacted for the purpose of repealing other special laws. Even in the absence of a written provision, some courts have held that a targeted law is not "special" within the meaning of its state's constitutional prohibition if it repeals another special law or mitigates the disuniformity caused by a previously enacted special law.

3. *Special legislation and the United States Constitution.* Given how important special legislation is to state constitutional law, it might come as some surprise that courts do not find a prohibition on special legislation in the United States Constitution. This was not always the case. At the end of the nineteenth century, at the same time that states were explicitly adopting special legislation provisions in their constitutions, the United States Supreme Court strongly suggested that special legislation was antithetical to federal constitutional values. In *Hurtado v. California*, 110 U.S. 516, 536 (1884), the Supreme Court held that a "special rule for a particular person or a particular case," including "acts of confiscation, acts reversing judgments, and acts directly transferring one man's estate to another," is prohibited. Although the Supreme Court has continued to hold that a limited set of special laws violate the United States Constitution, see *United States v. Brown*, 381 U.S. 437 (1965), the modern Supreme Court is less receptive to the idea that special legislation is problematic simply because it is targeted. *Bank Markazi v. Peterson*, 136 S. Ct. 1310, 1327 (2012) (noting that "the assumption that legislation must be generally applicable" is "flawed"). For an argument that the history, text, and philosophical underpinnings of the United States Constitution all suggest that special legislation ought to considered unconstitutional, see Zoldan, *Reviving Legislative Generality*, 98 MARQ. L. REV. 625, 650–660 (2014).

4. *First and second cities.* Legislation is often drafted to apply only to the largest city in the state to address its legislative needs without affecting the rest of the state. Courts tend to uphold these laws, because they perceive that large cities have special problems. Consider, for example, the Illinois legislature's approach to the city of Chicago. In *City of Chicago v. Boulevard Bank Nat'l Ass'n*, 688 N.E.2d 844 (Ill. App. 1997), a statute authorizing streamlined eminent domain procedures in cities having a population of more than 500,000 was held not to violate the special legislation prohibition. The city sought a "quick take" of the Oliver Building to assist in the redevelopment of the Oriental Theater in accord with its North Loop Tax Increment Financing project. The court found a rational basis for the population classification

due to the need to redevelop more quickly in dense commercially blighted areas to offset the longer time periods for demolition and renovation of large buildings and the relocation of numerous tenants.

Courts are less likely to uphold legislative classifications when they are drafted to apply only to the second-largest city or county in the state, or to the second tier of cities and counties, and exclude the largest city. In *Elias v. City of Tulsa*, 408 P.2d 517 (Okla. 1965), the court invalidated a statute conferring extraterritorial zoning power applied only to Tulsa, the second-largest city in the state, excluding Oklahoma City, the largest city. The court noted that urban problems within the purview of zoning increase rather than decrease with city size. See also *Kinney v. Bd. of County Comm'rs*, 894 P.2d 444 (Okla. App. 1995) (invalidating statute limiting home rule option to Tulsa); *Frost v. City of Chattanooga*, 488 S.W.2d 370 (Tenn. 1972) (invalidating an annexation statute applicable only to that city and excluding larger cities in the state).

5. *Special legislation and sports.* Among the most high-profile examples of special legislation are statutes providing financial support for individual professional sports teams, including subsidizing expensive new stadiums. In *CLEAN v. State*, 928 P.2d 1054 (Wash. 1996), the court upheld the state's Stadium Act, which permitted the construction of baseball stadiums only in counties with one million people or more when only one county met this criterion. The court held that the Stadium Act was not special although it applied to one county alone; rather, it was general, because locating a new stadium in the most populous county in the state was a rational way to increase ticket sales. *Id.* at 1064. See also *Libertarian Party of Wisconsin v. State*, 546 N.W.2d 424 (Wis. 1996) (upholding Stadium Act that applied only to districts exceeding 500,000 people when only Milwaukee fit that description). For an argument for applying state constitutional provisions on special legislation to limit public aid to professional sports teams, see Rubin, *Public Aid to Professional Sports Teams—A Constitutional Disgrace: The Battle to Revive Judicial Rulings and State Constitutional Enactments Prohibiting Public Subsidies to Private Corporations*, 30 U. Tol. L. Rev. 393 (1999).

6. *Political issues.* Many of the above-described cases suggest the political controversies that underlie the enactment of special legislation. Legislators from outlying areas of the state may resist enabling legislation applicable statewide that provides the authority for a controversial governmental program even though its adoption is not mandated. The existence of legislative authority for the program provides the legal basis for local mobilization of support to get the program adopted at the local level. Attempts to limit the legislation authorizing urban renewal projects in Kansas to Kansas City, the second-largest city in the state, illustrate this tendency. See *Redevelopment Auth. v. State Corp. Comm'n*, 236 P.2d 782 (Kan. 1951) (invalidating law when limited to cities with populations between 125,000 and 150,000); *State ex rel. Fatzer v. Redevelopment Auth.*, 269 P.2d 484 (Kan. 1954) (invalidating law applicable to cities with population in excess of 125,000 with townsites more than ninety years old). In both of these cases, the effect of the classification was

to limit the law to Kansas City. The law was finally upheld when it was amended to apply to all cities with a population of more than 75,000 and covered the three largest cities in the state, although some cities with old townsites were excluded. See also *Illinois Hotel and Lodging Ass'n v. Ludwig*, 869 N.E.2d 846 (Ill. App. 2007) (upholding legislation applicable only to hotel workers in Cook County because the legislation, if applied statewide, as it was initially introduced, would impose economic burdens on small hotels in areas of the state less competitive than the Chicago metropolitan area).

Statewide enabling legislation for controversial programs can be made more palatable when a local referendum is required. Legislation excluding only the largest cities from the referendum requirement have been upheld. *City of Kansas City v. Robb*, 332 P.2d 520 (Kan. 1958). The Kansas City referendum exclusion case came after the law had been extended to the two largest cities. The court noted that urban renewal was more urgent in the larger cities, which could not afford the expense and delay of a referendum. It also pointed out that more controversy over the selection of urban renewal areas might be expected in smaller communities.

B. Delegation of Power

As described in Part A, state constitutions implement the principle of separation of powers by preventing their legislatures from enacting laws so specific that they do the work of the other branches of government. Conversely, constitutional prohibitions also enforce the principle of separation of powers by limiting the legislature's power to give away legislative authority to other bodies, including coordinate branches of government, local governments, private entities and even the voters. The principle that legislatures may not transfer legislative authority to another body is enforced by courts through the nondelegation doctrine.

In order to understand what the nondelegation doctrine protects—and impedes—it is important to understand what delegation is, why legislatures delegate, and what types of authority they delegate.

What is delegation? The practice of legislatures in the United States has been, since at least the time of the framing of the United States Constitution, to vest other bodies, including courts and administrative agencies, with the power to make binding rules. When upholding a federal statute empowering the courts to regulate their own procedures, the early Supreme Court distinguished between "powers which are strictly and exclusively legislative" (which cannot be delegated), and other powers, which Congress may choose to exercise itself or to vest in other bodies. *Wayman v. Southard*, 23 U.S. 1, 43–44 (1825). The Court also hinted at the difficulty in distinguishing between permissible and impermissible grants of authority:

> The line has not been exactly drawn which separates those important subjects, which must be entirely regulated by the legislature itself, from those of less interest, in which a general provision may be made, and power

> given to those who are to act under such general provisions to fill up the details. [*Id.*]

In the Court's formulation, when the legislature has empowered another body, like a court or administrative agency, to "fill up the details" of a general provision, it is a lawful grant of authority; when the legislature has transferred legislative authority itself, it is an unlawful delegation. As Chief Justice Marshall suggested, however, the line between permissible grants of authority and impermissible delegations is indistinct at best.

Why do legislatures delegate? When a legislature delegates authority to make binding rules, it gives up some of its power. Although it may seem counterintuitive, it is entirely rational for a legislature to relinquish authority to another entity voluntarily. One reason is expertise: the body to which power is delegated is often better equipped than the legislature to develop expertise in the area that is subject to delegation. For example, if a legislature requires the government to ensure that drinking water is "safe," a department of environmental quality staffed with scientists can bring their expertise in biology and water chemistry to bear when formulating specific criteria for what makes water "safe" to drink. Another reason is efficiency. Agencies employ not only makers of rules, but also rule enforcers and dispute adjudicators. When controversies about the implementation of policy inevitably arise, an agency is better-equipped than a legislature to resolve them quickly and with little cost. Finally, and more cynically, a legislature may want to relinquish authority in order to avoid the political backlash of making difficult policy decisions. When a legislature delegates broad rulemaking authority for an agency to exercise, it lets the agency test the political waters. If the agency makes a rule that is unpopular, the legislature can always "take credit" for taking some action, "but then shift blame to the agency for imposing regulatory costs." See Rao, *Administrative Collusion: How Delegation Diminishes the Collective Congress*, 90 N.Y.U. L. Rev. 1463 (2015).

What authorities do legislatures delegate? At both the state and federal level, legislatures delegate a wide variety of authorities to other bodies. Most saliently, legislatures grant administrative agencies the power to regulate private activities, like gambling, waste disposal and land use. State legislatures also vest courts, local governments and private organizations with a variety of powers, including the authority to set taxation rates, make expenditures from the public fisc, set conditions for permitting, set professional licensing standards and many other functions. See Iuliano & Whittington, *The Nondelegation Doctrine: Alive and Well*, 93 Notre Dame L. Rev. 619 (2017).

The nondelegation doctrine. The origins of a doctrine prohibiting the delegation of legislative authority are somewhat obscure. The common law maxim *delegata potestas non potest delegari*—a power that is delegated cannot be redelegated—was invoked to challenge delegations of authority in American courts as early as the eighteenth century, albeit not always successfully. The United States Constitution makes no explicit reference to the delegation of legislative power. And, although most state constitutions contain stronger separation of powers language than the

United States Constitution, few state constitutions specifically prohibit the delegation of legislative power. Even those states that do prohibit legislative delegation explicitly do so only in a limited way. Pennsylvania's Constitution, for example, provides that: "The General Assembly shall not delegate to any special commission, private corporation or association, any power to make, supervise or interfere with any municipal improvement, money, property or effects, whether held in trust or otherwise, or to levy taxes or perform any municipal function whatever." PA. CONST. art. III, § 31.

Despite the absence of a strong textual basis, the principle that legislatures may not delegate legislative authority to other bodies is well-entrenched in constitutional law. The nondelegation doctrine is widely thought to protect liberty and enhance political accountability. By ensuring that the agencies that enforce policy do not also get to set that policy, nondelegation doctrine is thought to limit the possibility of oppression by the executive branch. Nondelegation doctrine also is seen to assist with political accountability by ensuring that the legislature—an elected body—is responsible for making policy. As a result, the electorate can reward their elected officials for making popular policy decisions and punish them for making unpopular ones. As Alexander Bickel wrote when assessing the dangers of delegation in the arena of making war, the nondelegation doctrine "is concerned with the sources of policy, with the crucial joinder between power and broadly based democratic responsibility, bestowed and discharged after the fashion of representative government. Delegation without standards short-circuits the lines of responsibility that make the political process meaningful." Bickel, *The Constitution and the War*, COMMENTARY, July 1972, at 52. For a historical account of the *delegata potestas* maxim and its curious integration into American legal thought, see Duff & Whiteside, *Delegata Potestas Non Potest Delegari: A Maxim of American Constitutional Law*, 14 CORNELL L. REV. 168 (1929).

There are two basic approaches that courts and scholars have taken to the nondelegation doctrine: first, standards or guidelines; and second, procedural safeguards. In the first model, the legislature may vest authority in another body as long as it provides standards or guidelines for the other body to follow. This model is employed by courts interpreting the United States Constitution as well as many state constitutions. As stated by the Supreme Court, Congress may vest decision-making authority in another body so long as Congress has provided an "intelligible principle" to guide the exercise of discretionary authority. *Industrial Union Dept. v. American Petroleum Inst.*, 448 U.S. 607 (1980). An "intelligible principle" requires Congress to delineate a general policy, identify the agency that must apply the policy and set the boundaries of the authority vested. *Mistretta v. United States*, 488 U.S. 361, 372–73 (1989). Although the Supreme Court has struck down only two statutes under this standard (and not since 1935), many state courts following a standards or guidelines approach more strongly enforce nondelegation principles. *Bush v. Schiavo*, 885 So. 2d 321, 332 (Fla. 2004) (holding that the nondelegation doctrine requires that "statutes granting power to the executive branch must clearly announce adequate standards to guide . . . in the execution of the powers delegated"). See Iuliano & Whittington, *The Nondelegation Doctrine: Alive and Well*, 93 Notre Dame L. Rev. 619 (2017).

In the second model, the legislature may vest authority as long as the body exercising that authority is constrained by procedural safeguards. Kenneth Culp Davis, a noted administrative law scholar, argued persuasively that the nondelegation doctrine's focus on standards was a failure: despite the doctrine, legislatures continue to delegate legislative power and courts continue to uphold these delegations despite a lack of meaningful standards. Instead of focusing on standards, he argued, courts should use the nondelegation doctrine to focus on "protecting private parties against injustice on account of unnecessary and uncontrolled discretionary power." He suggested that agency action is more deserving of judicial support when agency action is checked by procedural safeguards, like holding hearings, abiding by precedent and providing written findings and reasons. Davis, *A New Approach to Delegation*, 36 U. Chi. L. Rev. 713, 725–27 (1969). A minority of states follow the Davis approach. See *Panzer v. Doyle*, 680 N.W.2d 666 (Wis. 2004) ("the nondelegation doctrine with respect to subordinate agencies is now primarily concerned with the presence of procedural safeguards that will adequately assure that discretionary power is not exercised unnecessarily or indiscriminately"). Some states require both adequate standards and safeguards. See *Wyoming Coalition v. Wyoming Game & Fish Comm'n*, 875 P.2d 729 (Wyo. 1994) (upholding a statute against nondelegation challenge when "general standards together with adequate procedural safeguards are present").

Scholars have categorized delegations in a number of other ways, as well. Thomas Merrill classified them based on the way in which standards are written. Professor Merrill divided legislative standards as follows: (1) Standards containing specific prescriptions, such as a provision that a licensee may be disciplined "who has been convicted in a court of competent jurisdiction"; (2) standards providing a "reasonably detailed portraiture of legislative purpose," which leave the administrator a substantial degree of freedom but whose intent may be ascertained from the purpose of the act, such as a provision authorizing uniform standards of purity in food; (3) imprecise standards that gain clarity from being confined to a limited subject matter, such as a provision requiring professional competence as the basis for the issuance of an occupational license; and (4) imprecise words that acquire legal significance through usage, like a "reasonableness" standard. Merrill also notes that imprecise words can be aided by analogous statutes and can be made specific through administrative action. Merrill, *Standards—A Safeguard for the Exercise of Delegated Power*, 47 Neb. L. Rev. 469, 479–89 (1968). Jim Rossi categorized state nondelegation cases as either weak (mostly following Davis's approach); strong (applying a more muscular version of the standards approach); or moderate (in which both procedural safeguards and some minimal set of standards are required). Rossi, *Institutional Design and the Lingering Legacy of Antifederalist Separation of Powers Ideals in the States*, 52 Vand. L. Rev. 1167, 1191–99 (1999).

Although courts uphold most grants of authority against nondelegation challenges under any of the models described above, delegation cases are common; and, contrary to their federal counterparts, many nondelegation challenges are successful in the states.

[1] Delegation to Administrative Agencies and Officials

When state legislatures vest authority in other bodies, they normally do so in administrative agencies. Whether courts will uphold these grants of authority, or strike them down as unconstitutional delegations, can appear unprincipled at times. Nevertheless, some patterns exist. As you read the following cases, identify which of the two basic approaches to nondelegation each court takes and consider whether the court's approach can be applied to other cases in a principled way.

Stofer v. Motor Vehicle Casualty Co.

68 Ill. 2d 361, 369 N.E.2d 875 (1977)

Clark, Justice

This is a consolidated, direct, interlocutory appeal pursuant to our Rules 302(b) and 308 from decisions of the circuit court of Cook County holding sections 397 and 401 of the Insurance Code of 1937 invalid on the grounds that the power thereby granted the Director of Insurance to prescribe uniform insurance contracts (including contractual limitations on the time within which suits may be brought against the insurer by the insured) violated the separation of governmental branches and powers mandated by section 1 of article II of our constitution (Ill. Const. 1970, art. II, sec.1). We reverse, because we conclude that the powers thus exercised by the Director of Insurance are of the type which the legislature could (and did) properly lodge in an executive officer.

Section 397 of the Insurance Code of 1937 provides:

"The Director of Insurance shall promulgate such rules and regulations as may be necessary to effect uniformity in all basic policies of fire and lightning insurance issued in this State, to the end that there be concurrency of contract where two or more companies insure the same risk."

Section 401 further provides:

> "The Director . . . shall have the power
>
> (a) to make reasonable rules and regulations as may be necessary for making effective such laws."

Pursuant to that authority, the Director had promulgated Rule 23.01, which prescribed "the Standard Policy for fire and lightning insurance of the State of Illinois" and prohibited the making, issuance, and delivery of insurance contracts and policies which did not conform to the standard policy.

The standard policy includes the following clause:

"No suit or action on this policy for the recovery of any claim shall be sustainable in any court of law or equity unless all of the requirements of this policy shall have been complied with, and unless commenced within twelve months next after inception of the loss."

The plaintiffs in these two actions, Robert Stofer and Joseph Fox, and the defendant insurance companies entered into temporary contracts of fire insurance ("binders") which incorporated the above-quoted standard clause. [Fox and Stofer both suffered insured losses and the insurance companies raised the statute of limitations as a defense. The trial court held that the statute under which the Director of Insurance adopted the regulation was an unconstitutional delegation of power.] ...

We now address the constitutional question. The separation of powers and branches of government raises extremely complex and subtle questions about the nature and function of government itself. ...

Fox and Stofer argue that, while it may be clear that the Director can promulgate reasonable regulations to effectuate the legislature's desire to provide "concurrency of contract" and while the legislature itself could have enacted a uniform one-year limit on the time for actions against the insurer under the contract, the legislature could not give the Director the power to prescribe such a limit. They reason that limiting a person's access to judicial remedies is a "legislative act" which only can be done by statute and not by regulation, and that, even if it could be done by regulation, the enabling statute does not set forth sufficient standards to cabin the administrator's discretion in promulgating such a regulation.

We hold that the legislature may delegate to the Director the power to prescribe a uniform insurance contract containing a clause limiting the time during which actions may be brought by the insured against his insurer. This term is but another provision of the standard policy, one of many that may effectively bar relief to the insured.

We no longer find the legislative-act administrative-act distinction helpful to a reasoned analysis of the separation of powers and branches of government mandated by our constitution in the context of statutes enabling administrators to promulgate regulations prescribing rights and duties under a comprehensive regulatory statute. Rather, we think this case may be more appropriately analyzed under the second issue presented by Fox and Stofer, i.e., whether the legislature provided sufficient guidance to limit the powers granted the Director.

Many of our early cases adhere to the notion that administrative rule making basically is interstitial, interpolating among the standards set by the legislature to fill in details and create a comprehensive regulatory scheme. Subsequent experience, however, with the administrative regulation of highly complex and technical subjects leads us to conclude that the administrative task necessarily differs substantially from the traditional model. In determining to regulate a particularly complex subject, the legislature frequently intends only to eliminate a particular class of abuse from an otherwise lawful and valuable activity. In many cases, it simply is impractical for legislators to become and remain thoroughly apprised of the facts necessary to determine which aspects of that activity are harmful and how they might be modified. In most cases, therefore, the administrator's task is not merely to interpolate among broadly stated legislative prohibitions, but, rather, to extrapolate from the broad language of his enabling statute, and, using the regulatory tools given him by the legislature, to deal with the problems which the legislature sought to address.

To require the legislature continually to determine the specific actions which ought to be prohibited and those which ought to be required would be to render the regulation of many matters hopelessly inefficient. Yet the demands of administrative efficiency are not dispositive of the mandate of our constitution. A structure which enables government to serve its citizens more efficiently also may enable it to oppress them more efficiently. The separation of powers and branches of government mandates a distribution of authority which may, on occasion, impede one of the branches in attempting to address a particular problem. This impediment is necessary, however, to impede the abuse of power by any one particular branch acting alone.

At least one commentator thus views the question of separation of powers as being limited to preventing the oppression of one branch of government by another. (See 1 F. Cooper, State Administrative Law 16 (1965).) We find that analysis inadequate. It is not enough that the other branches of government remain unimpeded in their ability to remedy an abuse of power by the offending branch. Rather, the requirement of affirmative authority from more than one branch of government is itself an important protection against the misguided acts of a particular bureaucracy. It is for this reason that our earlier cases emphasized the need for intelligible legislative standards to guide administrative rule making.

Without sufficient statutory directions against which to compare administrative regulations, the mere existence of judicial review is not a meaningful safeguard against administrative abuses. "The law is not a 'brooding omnipresence in the sky,' . . . and it cannot be drawn from there like nitrogen from the air." (*Textile Workers Union v. Lincoln Mills* (1957), 353 U.S. 448, 465 (Frankfurter, J., dissenting, and quoting Justice Holmes' dissent in *Southern Pacific Co. v. Jensen* (1917), 244 U.S. 205, 222).) Thus, unless found in the statute, the restraints which the judiciary is to apply to safeguard against the abuse of discretion in administrative rule making simply do not exist.

Accordingly, we find that the view which has developed through the decisions of this court in recent years requires that the legislature, in delegating its authority provide sufficient identification of the following:

(1) The *persons* and *activities* potentially subject to regulation;

(2) The *harm* sought to be prevented; and

(3) The general *means* intended to be available to the administrator to prevent the identified harm.

We recognize that the term "sufficient identification" itself is not free from ambiguity and will have to receive additional content from its application to particular facts and circumstances. The following principles should guide such applications: (1) The legislature must do all that is practical to define the scope of the legislation, i.e., the persons and activities which may be subject to the administrator's authority. This effort is necessary to put interested persons on notice of the possibility of administrative actions affecting them. Of course, the complexity of the subject sought to be regulated may put practical limitations upon the legislature's ability to identify all of the forms the activity may take. (2) With regard to identifying the harm sought to be prevented, the legislature may use somewhat broader, more generic language than in the first element. It is sufficient if, from the language of the statute, it is apparent what types of evil the statute is intended to prevent. (3) Finally, with regard to the means intended to be available, the legislature must specifically enumerate the administrative tools (*e.g.*, regulations, licenses, enforcement proceedings) and the particular sanctions, if any, intended to be available. If sanctions are provided, the legislature also must provide adequate standards and safeguards such as judicial review of the imposition of those sanctions. In the instant case, we find that the rule-making authority provided in sections 397 and 401 of the Insurance Code meets the test which we have today articulated, because the legislature has adequately identified both the harm sought to be remedied and the means intended to be available to prevent such harm. (The scope of the regulation is not at issue.)

First, the legislature has indicated that it intended to prevent a chaotic proliferation of disparate fire insurance policies. But that is not all. Indeed, had the legislature left the Director completely free to promulgate a "reasonable" uniform fire insurance policy, we would have serious doubts as to the constitutionality of such uncabined discretion. We find, however, that the legislature has provided substantial additional standards defining the harm sought to be prevented and thereby limiting the Director's discretion. Section 143(2) of the Insurance Code provided in part:

> The Director shall require the filing of all policy forms issued by any company transacting the kind or kinds of business enumerated in Classes 2 and 3 [fire insurance] of section 4. He may require, in addition thereto, the filing of any generally used riders, endorsements, application blanks and other matter incorporated by reference in any such policy or contract of insurance. Companies that are members of an organization, bureau or association may have the same filed for them by organization, bureau or association. If the Director shall find from an examination of any such policy form, rider, endorsement, application blank or other matter incorporated by reference in any such policy so filed that *it violates any provision of this Code, contains inconsistent, ambiguous or misleading clauses, or contains exceptions and conditions that will unreasonably or deceptively affect the risks that are purported to be assumed by the policy*, he shall order the company or

companies issuing such forms to discontinue the use of the same. (Emphasis added.)

The policies governed by section 143 inevitably incorporate the underlying contract. The Director's discretion under sections 397 and 401 in promulgating that contract thus is limited by the terms of section 143. The requirements that the terms be consistent, unambiguous, and not contain "exceptions or conditions that will unreasonably or deceptively affect the risks that are purported to be assumed by the policy" are affirmative requirements of fairness to and protection of the persons who purchase insurance. These standards identify the harm sought to be prevented in terms not unlike those which we have found adequate on several previous occasions. We therefore hold that the legislature has sufficiently identified both the harm sought to be prevented by the Director's rule-making power and the means (standard terms which comply with section 143) intended to be available to remedy that harm. . . .

Reversed and remanded.

The distinction between making and applying policy often is far from clear. The following case, from a state court that frequently invalidates legislation as an unconstitutional delegation of power, provides an example of a statute found to have delegated policymaking responsibilities:

Department of Business Regulation v. National Manufactured Housing Federation, Inc.

370 So. 2d 1132 (Fla. 1979)

Boyd, Justice

This appeal is from a judgment of the Circuit Court of the Second Judicial Circuit, in and for Leon County. It comes directly to us because the trial court, in announcing its judgment, declared a state law invalid. Art. V, § 3(b)(1), Fla. Const. The proceeding was begun when the appellees sought declaratory and injunctive relief from the effect of chapter 77-49, Laws of Florida. The action was defended by the governor, the attorney general, and the Department of Business Regulation. The plaintiffs based their claim for relief upon three grounds: that the statute unlawfully delegates legislative authority; that it deprives mobile home park owners of property without due process of law; and that it constitutes a denial of equal protection of the laws. In its order enjoining implementation of the statute, the court declared it unconstitutional on the first two grounds stated. The court did not address the equal protection argument.

Section 1 of the act contains a recitation of legislative findings and a statement of the purposes of the enactment: "The Legislature finds that there exists an emergency in rental accommodations in mobile home parks. The Legislature further finds that this condition, coupled with the inordinate expense of relocating a mobile home causes tenants in such parks to be placed in an unequal bargaining position with respect to increases in charges imposed by the owners or managers of such parks. The Legislature further finds that this inequality can only be alleviated by the enactment of reasonable legislative restraints which provide both a reasonable return [on] a park owner's investment and a safeguard to tenants against exorbitant rental or service charges."

To accomplish this purpose, section 4 of the act creates the State Mobile Home Tenant-Landlord Commission to regulate rental increases in mobile home parks. The commission is placed within the Department of Business Regulation.

Section 8 sets out the essence of the regulatory scheme. Subsection (1) provides that if a park owner proposes a charge increase, in the form of an increase in rent or service charges or a decrease in service, "in any calendar year in excess of the net United States Department of Labor Consumer Price Index increases since the last rental increase," then, upon petition of fifty-one percent of the park tenants the commission is required to act. It is to hold a hearing to determine whether the charge increase is "unconscionable or not justified under the facts and circumstances of the particular situation." Subsection (2) provides a list of certain costs that may be passed on to the tenants if they are reasonable and justified. Subsection (3) provides that by November 1 of the year preceding a charge increase, the park owner must notify the tenants of the proposed amount of any increase. Without notice no increase is to be allowed.

Section 9, subsection (1), requires that the hearings be held in accordance with chapter 120, Florida Statutes (1977), the Administrative Procedure Act, and gives the commission the power to rule on a contested charge increase in one of four ways. It shall require the owner "to either reduce the rental or service charges to a rate set by the commission, to continue rental or service charges as they existed under the former lease or agreement, to increase the rental or service charges to a rate set by the commission or to increase the rental or service charges" to the rate proposed by the owner.

Section 9, subsection (2), gives the commission power to adopt rules governing its proceedings and directs the commission to adopt rules providing that increases collected but subsequently held to be unauthorized "shall be either returned to the tenants or credited toward future rental charges."

Section 11 permits appeal of the decisions of the commission to circuit court. . . .

The commission, under the legislative plan, is to be composed of seven members, including two mobile home park owners or operators, two mobile home park tenants, and three members of the general public.

For the following two reasons, we hold that the circuit court was correct in ruling that chapter 77-49 is unconstitutional.

The court held that subsections (1)(a) and (2)(a) of section 83.784, Florida Statutes (1977), unlawfully delegate legislative power to an administrative body. As was made abundantly clear by our decision in *Askew v. Cross Key Waterways*, 372 So. 2d 913 (Fla. 1978), announced in an opinion by Justice Sundberg, the doctrine against delegation of legislative power is of continuing vitality in Florida. We held that the legislature must take heed of article II, section 3, Florida Constitution, which provides: "The powers of the state government shall be divided into legislative, executive and judicial branches. No person belonging to one branch shall exercise any powers appertaining to either of the other two branches unless expressly provided herein." The opinion explained why strict adherence to the above constitutional admonition is imperative:

> A corollary of the doctrine of unlawful delegation is the availability of judicial review. In the final analysis it is the courts, upon a challenge to the exercise or nonexercise of administrative action, which must determine whether the administrative agency has performed consistently with the mandate of the legislature. When legislation is so lacking in guidelines that neither the agency nor the courts can determine whether the agency is carrying out the intent of the legislature in its conduct, then, in fact, the agency becomes the lawgiver rather than the administrator of the law.

The interests of a mobile home park owner and a mobile home park tenant necessarily compete. Similar to the posture of a buyer and seller in the commercial arena, a mobile home park tenant has as his goal affordable living accommodations, while a park owner endeavors to maximize his profits. Rent control legislation seeks a balance between these competing interests by stabilizing rentals under emergency conditions in order to prevent extortionate increases in rent resulting from housing shortages, while at the same time allowing landlords a fair and equitable return upon their investments. Because of the fundamental nature of these concerns and the pervasiveness of mobile home living in Florida, the point where rent control legislation strikes this balance is undoubtedly of great public moment.

The criteria for determining the validity of rental or service charge increases in subsections (1)(a) and (2)(a) of section 83.784 are constitutionally defective because they charge the commission with the fundamental legislative task of striking this balance between mobile home park owner and mobile home park tenant, without any meaningful guidance. The subsections provide:

> (1)(a) Upon petition of 51 percent of the tenants of any dwelling units in a mobile home park who will be subject to a rental or service charge increase or a decrease in services in any calendar year in excess of the net United States Department of Labor Consumer Price Index increases since the last rental increase, the commission shall hold a hearing at the mobile home park or at such other facility selected by the commission, so long as it is reasonably accessible to all parties, at a date to be set by the commission, to determine whether or not the rental or service charge increase or a decrease in services is so great as to be unconscionable or not justified under the facts and circumstances of the particular situation.

(2)(a) The increased costs to the owner of a mobile home park attributable to:

1. Increases in utility rates;

2. Property taxes;

3. Fluctuation in property value;

4. Governmental assessments;

5. Cost of living increases attributable to and relevant to incidental services, normal repair, and maintenance; and

6. Capital improvements not otherwise promised or contracted for may be passed on to the tenants or prospective tenants in the form of increased rental or service charges if such increases are reasonable and justified under the facts and circumstances of the particular case.

The terms "unconscionable or not justified under the facts and circumstances" in (1)(a), and the terms "reasonable and justified under the facts and circumstances of the particular case" in (2)(a), are not accompanied by any standards or guidelines to aid a court or administrative agency in ascertaining the true legislative intent underlying the act. The legislature may have wanted to afford the word "unconscionable" in (1)(a) a liberal construction, so as to circumscribe narrowly a park owner's ability to pass on costs to tenants beset by inflation. As written, the act gives no hint whether this is a correct interpretation. It is thus left to the "unbridled discretion or whim" of the commission to formulate basic legislative policy.

Moreover, "unconscionability" is a term which has meaning in the context of an equitable proceeding in our courts between two adverse parties. A chancellor sitting in equity is guided in the exercise of his discretion in this regard by sound principles of law which have been articulated and applied on a case-by-case basis over a long period of time during the development of our rich common law heritage. No such guiding principles are supplied by the legislature here. Furthermore, the joining of that term with the phrase "or not justified under the facts and circumstances of the particular situation" makes the legislative standard even more nebulous.

In *Sarasota County v. Barg*, 302 So. 2d 737 (Fla. 1974), this Court invalidated portions of the act creating the Manasota Key Conservation District. Employing language similar to that contained in section 83.784, the act prohibited "undue or unreasonable dredging, filling or disturbance of submerged bottoms," as well as "unreasonable destruction of natural vegetation." In finding the above provisions violative of article II, section 3, Florida Constitution, the Court stated:

> The Act does not contain any standards or guidelines to aid any court or administrative body in interpreting these terms. The determination of what conduct falls within the proscription of these ambiguous provisions is left to the unbridled discretion of those responsible for applying and enforcing the Act. This amounts to an unrestricted delegation of legislative authority. . . .

The judgment of the circuit court is affirmed.

Notes and Questions

1. *Unequal bargaining power and agency regulation.* Both the Illinois and Florida cases consider regulations that govern contractual relationships in which one of the contracting parties has a bargaining disadvantage. Insurance policyholders cannot easily bargain over the terms of an insurance contract. Mobile home park spaces are in short supply, giving park owners a bargaining advantage. The Florida court decided that the adjustment of this bargaining relationship required a clear expression of legislative policy. The Illinois court allowed the state agency to adjust the bargaining relationship without a clear expression of legislative policy. If there is a principled way to reconcile these cases, what would the rule be? Would that same rule also explain *East St. Louis Fed'n of Teachers, Local 1220 v. East St. Louis Sch. Dist. No. 189 Fin. Oversight Panel*, 687 N.E.2d 1050 (Ill. 1997)? In that case, applying *Stofer*, the court upheld a statute authorizing the takeover of school districts by a state oversight panel in order to return them to financial health. The parties affected were identified, the purpose was clear, and the statute "specifically" delineated the means to carry out the statutory purpose.

The Florida legislation authorized an adjustment in rental charges if they were "unconscionable." Although the ordinary meaning of this word is vague, it is a legal term of art that has acquired a more specific meaning through judicial interpretation. If "unconscionable," as a term of art, has a specific meaning, shouldn't the court be more willing find that the legislature provided sufficient statutory guidance to the agency? Consult Professor Merrill's delegation categories, as explained *supra*. Does this delegation of power fall within one of his categories?

2. *Rent control and rate making.* The Florida court noted that rent-setting is a critical policy decision requiring detailed standards; not all courts agree. In *Chelmsford Trailer Park, Inc. v. Town of Chelmsford*, 469 N.E.2d 1259 (Mass. 1984), the court upheld a statute allowing the town to control rents and evictions in mobile home parks. It held that a statutory provision requiring that any rent adjustments must assure mobile home park owners a "fair net operating income" was not an unconstitutional delegation of legislative power. The court noted it had interpreted identical language as requiring rent to be set to assure a "reasonable return on the fair value of the landlord's investment." Would this statutory standard satisfy the Florida court?

Carson Mobilehome Park Owners Ass'n v. City of Carson, 672 P.2d 1297 (Cal. 1983), also upheld an ordinance regulating rent increases and evictions in mobile home parks. The ordinance stated that its purpose was to counteract the effects of a shortage of mobile home spaces that had resulted in rapidly rising space rents. It authorized a local board to grant rent increases if they were "just, fair and reasonable." In making this determination, the board was directed by the ordinance to consider twelve specified but nonexclusive factors included in the ordinance. The court held that the ordinance provided sufficient standards by stating its purpose and by providing a nonexclusive list of relevant factors. "That the ordinance does not articulate a formula for determining just what constitutes a just and reasonable return does not make it unconstitutional." *Id.* at 1300. The court pointed out that mobile home rent control was a "rational curative measure" designed to counteract a shortage of mobile home spaces that had led to a low vacancy rate and rapidly rising space costs. See also *Cottrell v. City & County of Denver*, 636 P.2d 703 (Colo. 1981), applying Davis's "safeguards not standards" rule to uphold a charter amendment that authorized the water board to set water rates, taking into account the usual utility costs, "including those reasonably required for the anticipated growth of the Denver metropolitan area." *Id.* at 705. Do the standards in these cases fall within one of Professor Merrill's categories?

3. *Public health concerns and separation of powers principles.* Statutory purpose may play an important role in the outcome of delegation of power cases. Promoting public health, for example, is an important statutory purpose that can lead a court to uphold a delegation of power. See *Eagle Envtl. II, LP v. Commonwealth of Pennsylvania Dept. of Envtl. Protection*, 884 A.2d 867 (Pa. 2005) (upholding delegation of authority to Department of Environmental Protection to establish regulations to mitigate public health hazards, environmental pollution, and economic loss that might result from improper and inadequate solid waste disposal). Some courts even have permitted delegations to agencies to make rules with criminal consequences when public health is at stake. In *Tiplick v. Indiana*, 43 N.E.3d 1259 (Ind. 2015), the legislature delegated the Board of Pharmacy the authority to classify newly discovered compounds as "synthetics," which are minor variants, or look-alikes, of unlawful drugs. The legislature granted this power to the Board because the legislature could not, in a timely fashion, evaluate new substances synthesized and introduced into the market illegally. Although possessing and dealing a look-alike drug carried criminal penalties, and although the court held that "the creation of criminal statutes is an inherently legislative function," the court held that the power was properly vested in the Board.

Consider also a case challenging the power of the New York City Board of Health to adopt regulations in support of Mayor Michael Bloomberg's efforts to reduce obesity by capping the size of soft drinks with substantial sugar content ("Sugary Drinks Portion Cap Rule"). See *In the Matter of New York Statewide Coalition of Hispanic Chambers of Commerce v. New York City Dept. of Health and Mental Hygiene*, 10 N.E.3d 1152 (N.Y. 2014). The New York court concluded that the Board of Health did not itself have "legislative authority." Moreover, the Board had exceeded its statutory authority to engage in regulation (it was charged to "add to and alter, amend or repeal any part of the health code, . . . [to] publish additional provisions for security of life and health in the city and [to] confer additional powers on the [Department of Health and Mental Hygiene] not inconsistent with the constitution, laws of this state or this charter" (N.Y.C. Charter § 558[b]). In reaching that conclusion, the court considered the following factors to determine whether the Board's soft drink regulations had crossed the line into legislative territory: whether the Board had (a) balanced competing concerns of public health and economic cost, (b) acted in the

952 S.W.2d 454, 469 (Tex. 1997), the court was sensitive to the fact that "the private delegate may have a personal or pecuniary interest which is inconsistent with or repugnant to the public interest to be served." See also *Krierlow v. Louisiana Dept. of Agriculture & Forestry*, 125 So. 3d 384 (La. 2013) (striking down state system that required rice producers to pay an assessment on rice grown in Louisiana, then delegated the power to impose and set the relevant assessment levels or to repeal the provisions for refunds to a group of "private voters" who could impose their wishes through private elections). But see *Sims v. Besaw's Café*, 997 P.2d 201 (Or. 2000) (finding anti-discrimination ordinance did not unlawfully delegate power to private persons to bring a cause of action to enforce it).

6. *Adoption by reference to federal law.* Delegation questions also arise when federal statutes or administrative regulations are incorporated by reference. *Lee v. State*, 635 P.2d 1282 (Mont. 1981), struck down a statute mandating the state attorney general to adopt a speed limit "not less than that required by federal law." *Id.* at 1283. The court held that "[a] more blatant handover of the sovereign power of this state to the federal jurisdiction is beyond our ken." *Id.* at 1286. In *State v. Rodriguez*, 379 So. 2d 1084 (La. 1980), the state agency was required to list a substance as a "controlled dangerous substance" if it was so classified by the United States Drug Enforcement Administration. The court held that the legislature could not surrender its legislative power to a federal agency to determine the state's law. Accord *Oklahoma City v. State ex rel. Dept. of Labor*, 918 P.2d 26 (Okla. 1995) (invalidating minimum wage statute that required the state Labor Commissioner "to adopt the prevailing wage as determined by the federal Department of Labor"). Other courts have been more willing to permit the adoption of federal standards. *Taylor v. Smithkline Beecham Corp.*, 658 N.W.2d 127 (Mich. 2003) (upholding statute that limited the liability of drug manufacturers and sellers if the drug was approved by United States Food and Drug Administration and labeled in accordance with federal regulations); *State v. All Pro Paint & Body Shop, Inc.*, 639 So. 2d 707 (La. 1994) (upholding statute prohibiting transportation or discharge of "hazardous waste" as defined through administrative interpretations taking into account provisions of federal hazardous waste law). For a discussion of subject areas in which states historically have incorporated federal law, see Boyd, *Looking Glass Law: Legislation by Reference in the States*, 68 La. L. Rev. 1201, 1261–74 (2008).

It is common for state statutes enacted to comply with federal grant-in-aid legislation or federally enacted mandates to provide that the state administrative agency shall do everything necessary to comply with the federal law. Some courts uphold these delegations under state law based on the policies and requirements stated in the federal statute. See *Orsinger Outdoor Adver., Inc. v. Department of Highways*, 752 P.2d 55 (Colo. 1988) (upholding state outdoor advertising act adopted to comply with regulatory program mandated by federal-aid highway act); *Department of Transp. v. Armacost*, 532 A.2d 1056 (Md. 1987) (upholding vehicle emissions inspection program mandated by federal Clean Air Act). Are these cases consistent with cases finding an improper delegation of power when state statutes reference federal legislation?

For a discussion of state appellate court applications of the nondelegation doctrine in the context of state implementation of federal law, see Rossi, *Dual Constitutions and Constitutional Duels: Separation of Powers and State Implementation of Federally Inspired Regulatory Programs and Standards*, 46 Wm. & Mary L. Rev. 1343, 1370–84 (2005) (arguing that state courts should view state constitutions as part of an institutional design in which authority is shared between the states and federal government rather than treating them as the source of independent sovereign power).

7. *Delegation to the voters.* State legislatures sometimes delegate authority to the voters themselves by making legislation contingent on a future popular referendum. When they do, courts often invalidate these statutes as impermissible delegations. In *Akin v. Director of Revenue*, 934 S.W.2d 295, 297 (Mo. 1996), the legislature enacted a statute providing that it would become effective only if it was "submitted to a statewide vote and a majority of the qualified voters voting on the issue approve such question, and not otherwise." The court invalidated this statute, holding that it was an improper "delegation of a power to make law, which involves a discretion as to what the general law will be." Similarly, in *Amalgamated Transit Union Local 587 v. Washington*, 11 P.3d 762, 797 (Wash. 2000), the court held that "when a legislature conditions legislation solely on a vote of the people, it relinquishes the decision to pass a law to the voters, thus delegating its legislative authority to make law to the voters." Accord *Joytime Distributors and Amusement Co. v. South Carolina*, 528 S.E.2d 647 (S.C. 1999) (invalidating statute made contingent on subsequent voter approval).

But, if delegations are problematic because they interfere with political accountability, wouldn't decision-making by the voters themselves ameliorate this concern? Other courts have permitted delegations of lawmaking authority to the voters provided that the legislature provides "specific rules and conditions." *Rogers v. Desiderio*, 655 N.E. 930 (Ill. App. 1995). If a legislature may provide "specific rules and conditions" to constrain the voters, who is sovereign: the people or the legislature?

8. *Differences between state and federal nondelegation doctrines.* As suggested above, state high courts are far more willing to strike down statutory delegations as unconstitutional than has been the United States Supreme Court. Although most scholars considered the federal nondelegation doctrine a dead letter for decades, the Supreme Court recently has expressed willingness to imbue it with life. *Gundy v. United States*, 139 S. Ct. 2116 (2019). But, although the fate and contours of the federal nondelegation doctrine remain uncertain, as we have seen, the nondelegation doctrine is alive and well in the states. Considering that the United States Congress is a legislature of enumerated powers and that state legislatures have plenary legislative power, isn't it surprising that the nondelegation doctrine is stronger in the states? That is, shouldn't the power of Congress, which is already more limited than the states, be more tightly constrained by the nondelegation doctrine? One reason for the distinction between federal and state constitutional law may be textual. Although the federal Constitution has no express separation of powers provision,

most state constitutions have specific provisions separating state legislative, executive and judicial powers. To take just one example, the Kentucky Constitution provides that:

> The powers of the government of the Commonwealth of Kentucky shall be divided into three distinct departments, and each of them be confined to a separate body of magistracy, to wit: Those which are legislative, to one; those which are executive, to another; and those which are judicial, to another. No person or collection of persons, being of one of those departments, shall exercise any power properly belonging to either of the others. [Ky. Const. §§ 27–28.]

Text aside, consider three other differences between state agencies and federal agencies that may explain stricter enforcement of nondelegation principles at the state level: expertise; independence; and regulatory scope. First, although they deal with many complex economic and social issues, most state administrative agencies are not the equal of their federal counterparts in terms of staffing and professionalization. As a result, state courts may be less willing to defer to agency delegations than are the federal courts. Consistent with this justification, state courts appear to be more willing to uphold an agency delegation if the agency has longstanding experience in a specialized subject matter. See, e.g., *Southern Alliance for Clean Energy v. Graham*, 113 So. 3d 742, 750 (Fla. 2013). In *Graham*, the court upheld a delegation to the state Public Service Commission to determine a cost recovery structure for nuclear power plant construction, in part, because of the "arcane complexities of utility rate-making." The court continued: the "specificity with which the legislature must set out statutory standards and guidelines may depend on the subject matter dealt with and the degree of difficulty involved in articulating finite standards." Conversely, state courts tend to look askance at delegations to newly created agencies without a long history of regulating experience or known safeguards. In *Miller v. Covington Dev. Authority*, 539 S.W.2d 1 (Ky. 1976), the court struck down the creation of new local agencies, in part, because they were not "a long-established administrative agency such as the highway department or department of education, with a track record of experience and expertise in a well-recognized field."

Second, political distance may also be a factor. Federal administrative agencies are certainly not immune from pressure, but the closer contacts that state and local agencies have with those they regulate provide the opportunity for more insidious kinds of personal pressures. These pressures, in turn, can lead to the arbitrary actions that courts seek to control through more rigorous nondelegation requirements. For an argument that the possibility of capture of the state legislative process by factions requires the nondelegation doctrine, see Rossi, *Institutional Design and the Lingering Legacy of Antifederalist Separation of Powers Ideals in the States*, 52 Vand. L. Rev. 1167, 1224–25 (1999).

Third, and in some tension with the first point, the massive scope of regulation at the federal level makes detailed policymaking by the legislature less realistic than detailed regulation through legislation at the state level. Based on this perception, some state courts hold their legislatures to a more stringent standard than they would Congress. *Miller v. Covington Dev. Authority*, 539 S.W.2d 1 (Ky. 1976) (holding that while it is "understandable that the federal Congress cannot survey the boundaries for national parks or choose the sites of federal buildings," "[w]ithin the much smaller bounds of a city or county, however, the problem is not so formidable." *Id.* For an argument that the federal nondelegation doctrine has not died, but merely relocated to interpretive presumptions, see Sunstein, *The American Nondelegation Doctrine*, 86 GEO. WASH. L. REV. 1181 (2018).

9. *Separation of powers and state agency efforts to address political disagreements.* State courts sometimes identify delegation problems when agencies take policy positions that are contrary to the legislature's intention or if the legislature appears to have reserved the topic for later legislative resolution. See, e.g., *Hampton v. Hailey*, 743 S.E.2d 258 (S.C. 2013) (state budget agency violated separation of powers and delegation doctrines when it split yearly health plan premium increases between state and public employees in contravention of legislature's decision to use appropriated funds to cover such costs). In *In the Matter of NYC C.L.A.S.H., Inc. v. New York State Office of Parks, Recreation & Historic Preservation*, 975 N.Y.S.2d 593 (Sup. Ct. 2013), the state parks agency adopted regulations designating certain outdoor landmarks and parks as "no-smoking" areas, applying a four-part test to determine the line between administrative rule-making and legislative policymaking. The test required the court to consider whether (1) the regulation is based solely upon economic and social concerns; (2) the regulation created a comprehensive set of rules in the absence of legislative guidance; (3) the agency was acting in an area in which the legislature has repeatedly tried, but failed, to reach agreement; and (4) the regulation involved issues which required no special expertise or technical competence in the agency's field. The court concluded that the agency had violated the separation of powers doctrine in the absence of any legislatively declared policy in a socially "messy" area. See also *Beason v. N.C. Sec'y of State*, 742 S.E.2d 209 (N.C. App. 2013) (holding that agency lacked authority to interpret "lobbying" to include indirect communications of lobbyist, acting with others to achieve lobbying efforts).

[2] Delegation to the Judiciary

When the legislature vests policymaking functions in the judiciary, courts may strike them down as impermissible delegations of legislative power. In *In re Dailey*, 465 S.E.2d 601 (W. Va. 1995), the court invalidated a statute granting state courts the authority to issue licenses to carry concealed, deadly weapons in accordance with certain criteria. Specifically, the statute in question required the court to grant the license when the applicant certified:

> that she was a citizen of the United States, a resident of Cabell County, and was at least eighteen (18) years of age; that she was not addicted to alcohol or a controlled substance, had not been convicted of a felony or any act of violence involving a deadly weapon, and desired to carry a concealed,

> deadly weapon for a lawful purpose; that she was physically and mentally competent to carry a deadly weapon, and had satisfied the minimum requirements for handling and firing such firearms[; and] . . . that she had successfully completed a course in Firearms Training and Safety sponsored by the Cabell County Sheriff's Department. [*Id.* at 602–03.]

Despite the specific standards delineated by the statute, the court held that the statute impermissibly vested the judiciary with a legislative function, holding that the "regulation of the right to carry a concealed, deadly weapon is exclusively a legislative function." Conversely, it is not a judicial function, because an application for a license involves no "claim of legal right asserted by one party and denied by the other."

The line between the legislative power and the judicial power is a fine one. In another case involving the regulation of firearms, *Kasler v. Lockyer*, 2 P.3d 581 (Cal. 2000), the court upheld a statute against a nondelegation challenge. In *Kasler*, the statute authorized a procedure in which, on application of the Attorney General, the state courts could declare a particular type of weapon an "assault weapon," prohibited under state law, because of its similarity to an already prohibited weapon. The courts were required to determine, under the applicable statute, whether the new weapon was "identical" to a prohibited weapon, "except for slight modifications or enhancements." The court held that these determinations were "essentially adjudicatory" and therefore, consistent with nondelegation principles.

Why would the legislature in each case vest authority in the courts rather than an administrative agency? Would this same transfer of authority have violated the nondelegation doctrine if it had been vested in an administrative agency? Are there particular concerns with blurring the line between the legislature and judiciary that do not arise when policing the line between the legislature and the executive? Chapter 9 considers the related issue of the use of judicial power to resolve difficult issues such as those relating to school finance, when the courts must often make policy choices without the benefit of legislation.

[3] Delegation to Local Governments

State ex rel. City of Charleston v. Coghill

156 W. Va. 877, 207 S.E.2d 113 (1973)

NEELY, JUSTICE

This is an original action in mandamus in which the City of Charleston, a municipal corporation of the State of West Virginia, seeks to require its clerk, Kenneth L. Coghill, to publish a certain notice inviting proposals from all persons interested in purchasing or leasing space included in a proposed off-street parking facility in Charleston. Respondent Coghill was authorized and directed to perform this duty by resolution No. 228-73 which was adopted by the Charleston City Council on April 2, 1973.

The respondent clerk has refused to publish the notice upon the ground that Chapter 8, Article 16, Section 4a of the Code of West Virginia, 1931, which gives authority to municipal corporations to construct motor vehicle parking facilities, is unconstitutional. If Code 8-16-4a is constitutional, then the City Clerk has a non-discretionary legal duty to publish the notice as directed by the council. The purpose of this litigation is to test the validity under the State and Federal Constitutions of the enabling legislation, Code 8-16-4a, in order to facilitate the preparation of plans and orderly financing for a project in Charleston. . . .

The respondent clerk first maintains that the Legislature's delegation of authority to a municipal corporation to determine the amount of space in a public parking facility which will be leased or sold for private business, commercial, or charitable uses is an unconstitutional delegation of legislative power. While noticing that respondent's position finds its source in the well known constitutional principle that a legislature may not abdicate its legislative power, it has also long been established law that a legislature may delegate legislative powers to municipal corporations as to matters of purely local concern. This Court said in Syllabus pt. 1 of *West Virginia Water Service Company v. Cunningham*, 98 S.E.2d 891 (W. Va. 1957):

> Under the police power of the State, the Legislature has power to provide for the protection of the safety, health, morals, and general welfare of the public, and may delegate such powers to municipalities created by it. [citing cases.]

This Court, therefore, holds that the Legislature is entitled to delegate power to a municipal corporation to determine the appropriate mix of public and private uses of a public parking facility, subject to the constitutional limits on the municipality's discretion which will be further discussed in this opinion.

Notes and Questions

1. *Distinguishing local governments.* The court went on to discuss the constitutional limits to which it alluded in the portion excerpted above, implying that the delegation of power objection in this context was not serious. While the law as stated by the principal case appears to be well established, why does the delegation of legislative power to a local government stand on a different footing than the delegation of that power to an administrative agency or to the judiciary? Consider the following analysis in *Territory of Hawaii ex rel. County of Oahu v. Whitney*, 17 Hawaii 174, 177 (1905), in which the court upheld a delegation of legislative power to a county:

> This brings us to the question of the principles upon which the question should be solved. It is a fundamental rule that delegated power cannot be delegated. This applies to legislatures as well as to other bodies. Legislative power delegated to legislatures cannot be delegated to other persons or bodies. There is, however, an exception to this maxim as well established as the maxim itself. This exception arises by implication from the immemorial practice which has recognized the propriety of vesting in municipal

> organizations certain powers of local regulation over matters in which the persons within such organizations are especially interested and in regard to which they are supposed to be especially competent to judge.... The implication is that in delegating to legislatures the legislative power the people could not have intended to prevent the further delegation by the legislatures of certain police and other powers of a local nature which had always been exercised by municipal corporations and the exercise of which by the local communities acting through such corporations has been regarded as one of the fundamental features of the American and English systems of government. [*Id.* at 177–78.]

For other cases upholding delegations of power to local governments, see *Chicagoland Chamber of Commerce v. Pappas*, 880 N.E.2d 1105 (Ill. App. 2007) (upholding authority to opt into an alternative homestead exemption program); *Webster v. Town of Candia*, 778 A.2d 402 (N.H. 2001) (upholding authority to prohibit tree cutting and stone wall removal along designated scenic roads).

Does the court's analysis in the Hawaii case provide a satisfactory explanation for the exception? Could it be that the reason lies in the inapplicability of separation of powers doctrine to state-local relationships? Or does the explanation lie somewhere in accepted notions of plenary state power over local governments? Consult Chapter 1.

2. *Local governments versus local agencies.* In the principal case, the legislature delegated authority directly to a municipality. In other cases, the legislature delegates authority to a local agency instead. In *Tri-Nel Mgmt., Inc. v. Board of Health*, 741 N.E.2d 37 (Mass. 2001), the court upheld a statute giving local boards of health the authority to adopt "reasonable" health regulations. The board had adopted a ban on smoking in food service establishments, bars and lounges. The court noted that "in view of the long-standing tradition of municipal regulation of local health matters, the Legislature has provided appropriate guidance for the implementation of regulations by requiring that they address the 'health' of the community and that they be 'reasonable.'" *Id.* at 45.

Contrast this case with *MCT Transportation, Inc. v. Philadelphia Parking Auth.*, 60 A.3d 899 (Pa. Commw. 2013). There, taxicab and limousine companies challenged the city's parking authority's power to set yearly medallion and licensing fees at the level it believed "necessary to advance" statutory purposes. The authority was required to provide legislative committees with advance information about its proposed budget and supporting documentation. The taxicab companies argued that the authority to propose fees lacked legislatively imposed standards; the parking authority contended that, because the legislature reviewed the proposed fees, it effectively adopted standards through the state budget process. The court ultimately concluded that the statutory scheme comingled the traditional duties of the various branches. Even though legislative review was contemplated, insufficient standards existed to control the parking authority's discretion. What was the problem with this arrangement? Are delegation issues more likely to arise with regard to local government agencies than with cities themselves? Was the parking authority in effect functioning as a state agency because it was established pursuant to state legislation? Is the delegation in the case more like the delegation in *Tri-Nel* or the principal case?

Finally, consider *Indiana Univ. v. Hartwell*, 367 N.E.2d 1090 (Ind. App. 1977). A delegation of power challenge was brought to state legislation authorizing local civil rights commissions. The statute authorized the local legislative council, by ordinance, to delegate to the commission "such powers . . . as may be deemed necessary or appropriate to implement its purpose and objective." The delegation of power was held unconstitutional. The court noted that

> the legislature has, unwittingly or not, arrayed the full panorama of powers of the State and has given any city, town, or county uncontrolled discretion to select in smorgasbord fashion those powers "deemed necessary and appropriate" to implement the purpose and objective of the Civil Rights Act and to vest a local commission agency with such selected powers. [*Id.* at 1093.]

It concluded that "[s]o long as there exists residual statutory authority to usurp powers constitutionally reserved to the three departments of the State, the statute is constitutionally defective." *Id.* at 1094. The court did not believe that the expertise of the agency constituted "an acceptable substitute for the imposition of express standards where there is a delegation of discretionary powers." *Id.*

3. *Invalidating delegations to municipalities.* Some states hold implicitly that a delegation of authority to a municipality raises a delegation of power question by finding that the statute contains adequate standards. See *Opinion of the Justices*, 696 N.E.2d 502 (Mass. 1998) (authorizing city of Boston to extend insurance coverage to "domestic partners"); *Howard v. City of Lincoln*, 497 N.W.2d 53 (Neb. 1993) (upholding power of city to require removal of weeds). These decisions carry the implicit warning that the court will invalidate a delegation of authority to a municipality if it does not limit the municipality's discretion. See *Metals Recycling Co. v. Maccarone*, 527 A.2d 1127 (R.I. 1987) (invalidating statute authorizing council to renew or revoke auto salvage license).

Delegations to municipalities may be subject to constitutional restraint even if the delegation of power doctrine does not apply. In *Bottone v. Town of Westport*, 553 A.2d 576 (Conn. 1989), a statute authorized municipalities to establish waterway setback lines and to prohibit encroachments beyond those lines. A property owner who was prohibited from developing beyond a setback established by the town brought an action challenging the statute as an unconstitutional delegation of power. The court held that the nondelegation rule as applied to delegations from the legislative to the executive branch of government, including its administrative departments, was based on the separation of powers doctrine. This doctrine does not apply to legislative delegations to municipalities, because municipalities are not one of the three departments of government named in the state constitution. The court then turned to the due process clause as another form of limitation upon the legislature's delegation of power and held that this clause applied to statutes delegating power to municipalities as it does to all statutes. The court found that the statute in this case was not unconstitutionally vague under due process analysis, because an ordinary person was capable of knowing what conduct was permitted or prohibited under it. Should relying on a constitution's due process clause result in different outcomes than relying on the nondelegation doctrine?

4. *Concurrent authority.* Even courts that do not apply the nondelegation doctrine to delegations to local governments sometimes adopt other rules that limit these delegations, like a due process clause, as described above. Another rule is that two local governments may not exercise the same powers over the same territory at the same time. The rule has been applied to prohibit the organization of a special district within the limits of an incorporated municipality or another special district. See *Town of Merrillville v. Merrillville Conservancy Dist.*, 649 N.E.2d 645 (Ind. App. 1995).

When local governments attempt to exercise competing powers over the same territory, the courts apply a variety of rules to avoid conflict. The powers may be found not to conflict. See *Sandia Conservancy Dist. v. Middle Rio Grande Conservancy Dist.*, 259 P.2d 577 (N.M. 1953) (upholding organization of a conservancy district to operate in an area already under the jurisdiction of another conservancy district, because the new entity was to serve a different purpose). Municipalities may preempt districts operating within their jurisdiction. See *Windham First Taxing Dist. v. Town of Windham*, 546 A.2d 226 (Conn. 1988) (primary responsibility for overall government rests with the town, and special purpose district cannot preempt the town from providing competing services). Priority may also be given to the local government that first exercises jurisdiction. *Edwards v. Hous. Auth.*, 19 N.E.2d 741 (Ind. 1939). Nor may the rule apply when one of the local governments is exercising proprietary functions. *Public Util. Dist. No. 1 v. Town of Newport*, 228 P.2d 766 (Wash. 1951).

5. *Delegation and legislative oversight.* When a legislature delegates authority, it may want to retain authority to reverse any decision made by the delegate in the future. Of course, a legislature can (almost) always pass a law to reverse the delegate's decision, but the lawmaking process can be cumbersome. May the legislature exercise oversight of delegated authority other than by legislating?

For decades, Congress employed a tactic known as the "one-house veto," in which a statute delegated authority with the proviso that either chamber of Congress, by resolution, could rescind a particular application of the delegate's decision. The one-house veto was held unconstitutional in *Immigration & Naturalization Service v. Chadha*, 462 U.S. 919 (1983). *Chadha* is often read to resonate with nondelegation principles, because it prevents Congress from delegating the authority to reverse an administrative decision to some subset of the legislature, like a single legislative chamber. By preventing the legislative rescission of the particular application of a generally applicable law, does it also resonate with concerns about special legislation?

Similarly, many state legislatures have enacted statutes that permit legislative disapproval of regulations, both through a one-house veto and also through other types of oversight that raise nondelegation concerns. In many states, "a rules review committee within the legislature has the power to veto, suspend, or delay rules or the power to allow proposed rules to lapse absent approval, making legislative committee approval of rules a mandatory requirement in the rulemaking process." Rossi, *Institutional Design and the Lingering Legacy of Antifederalist Separation of Powers Ideals in the States*, 52 Vand. L. Rev. 1167 (1999). Following *Chadha*, some state courts have struck down these types of statutory provisions as unconstitutional. See, e.g., *Gilliam County v. Department of Envtl. Quality*, 849 P.2d 500 (Or. 1993) (invalidating legislative committee's power to veto agency rules). Contra *North Carolina State Board of Education v. State*, 814 S.E.2d 54 (N.C. 2018). In this latter case, the court upheld a statutory scheme that permits a Rules Review Commission, composed of members appointed by the General Assembly, to review rules proposed by state administrative agencies. If the Rules Review Commission objects to the agency's adoption of the rule, then the rule does not become effective. The Rules Review Commission, in turn, is subject to oversight by a Joint Legislative Administrative Procedure Oversight Committee, a committee made up of members of the General Assembly, which is responsible for reviewing every rule that the Rules Review Commission disapproves. The court upheld the scheme, in part, because the Rules Review Commission was provided with adequate procedural safeguards by the legislature. Does this double layer of delegation (first review by the Rules Review Commission and then review by the legislative committee) mitigate or exacerbate delegation concerns?

Chapter 9

The Role of the Judiciary

Scope of Chapter

The role of the judiciary as a participant in state and local government decision making is an important theme in this book. This Chapter selects three areas of substantive concern and examines the extent to which the judiciary has intervened to modify and revise governmental decisions and decision making. The progression is from occupational and professional licensing, where judicial intervention is minimal, to voting rights and school finance, where judicial intervention is more aggressive. As you read how the courts deal with these issues, consider whether or not the judicial process is the best way to handle them.

A. In Ordinary State and Local Government Issues: Occupational and Professional Licensing

Problem 9-1

Members of the Association of Professional Social Workers, a private organization in a Midwest state, are concerned that large numbers of "non-professionals" are being hired by public and private agencies to perform social work responsibilities. They have approached the state legislature to seek licensing for their profession. As counsel and lobbyist for the Association, what provisions would you seek to include in the legislation, and what arguments would you present to the legislature? If you were counsel and lobbyist for the Public Welfare Association, whose members train and employ some of those non-professionals, what position would you take before the legislature?

[1] Licensing Under State Law

State and local governments engage in an extensive array of business and economic regulation, the most prominent being occupational and business licensing. Numerous occupations and professions are regulated by the states through licensure, certification, or registration.[1] The vast majority are subject to regulation in

1. A helpful source of information on state licensing is the Council on Licensure Enforcement and Regulation (CLEAR). See http://www.clearhq.org/. CLEAR provides a collection of

some but not all of the states. Standards differ from state to state, and licensing reciprocity is limited. Nonetheless, licensing is pervasive and touches virtually every aspect of our daily lives, from the way in which our hair is cut to the way in which our teeth are cleaned. It also affects every business, indirectly if not directly. For a brief history of occupational and professional licensing in the U.S., see Hogan, *The Effectiveness of Licensing*, 7 LAW & HUMAN BEHAVIOR, No. 2–3 (1983): 117, 118–21 [Volume 7, No. 2/3 is a special issue devoted to professional regulation]; Law & Kim, *Specialization and Regulation: The Rise of Professionals and the Emergence of Occupational Licensing Regulation*, 65 J. ECON. HIST. No. 3 (2005): 723–756. The Council of State Governments' BOOK OF THE STATES periodically reviews the status of state occupational licensing.

Those who have studied occupational licensing have usually been critical. Professor Walter Gellhorn, a long-time leading critic, summed up the case against occupational licensing:

> [O]ccupational licensing has typically brought higher status for the producer of services at the price of higher costs to the consumer; it has reduced competition; it has narrowed opportunity for aspiring youth by increasing the costs of entry into a desired occupational career; it has artificially segmented skills so that needed services, like health care, are increasingly difficult to supply economically; it has fostered the cynical view that unethical practices will prevail unless those entrenched in a profession are assured of high incomes; and it has caused a proliferation of official administrative bodies, most of them staffed by persons drawn from and devoted to furthering the interests of the licensed occupations themselves.
>
> Moreover—and this is a point largely unnoticed—members of ethnic minorities are systematically discouraged from becoming licensees by irrelevant requirements. [Gellhorn, *The Abuse of Occupational Licensing*, 44 U. CHI. L. REV. 6, 16–18 (1976).]

See also Kleiner & Kudrle, *Does Regulation Affect Economic Outcomes? The Case of Dentistry*, 43 J.L. & ECON. 547 (2000) (analyzing empirical analysis of data on dental health of incoming Air Force personnel in order to determine effects of differing stringency in licensing regimes among the states, and concluding that tougher licensing does not improve outcomes but does raise prices for consumers and earnings for practitioners).

Professor Gellhorn's critique provides a starting point for judicial review of the constitutionality of licensing law. At an earlier period, the Supreme Court regularly called upon substantive due process to strike down state legislation regulating for social and economic purposes. One of the leading cases of that era, *New State Ice Co.*

occupational regulation statutes. See http://www.clearhq.org/Default.aspx?pageId=481836. For a database that allows identification of licensure requirements by state and by occupation, see http://www.careerinfonet.org/licensedoccupations/lois_keyword.asp?nodeid=16&by=occ.

v. Liebmann, 285 U.S. 262 (1932), for example, held invalid on Fourteenth Amendment due process grounds a state statute that required a license based on public need to engage in the business of distributing ice. But, as is well known, the Court's attitude to the Fourteenth Amendment shifted, and by 1955 the shift was complete. In *Williamson v. Lee Optical Co.*, 348 U.S. 483 (1955), the Court upheld an Oklahoma statute which, among other restrictions, prohibited opticians from duplicating or fitting lenses without a prescription from an optometrist or ophthalmologist and from advertising the sale of eyeglasses:

> The Oklahoma law may exact a needless, wasteful requirement in many cases. But it is for the legislature, not the courts, to balance the advantages and disadvantages of the new requirement.... But the law need not be in every respect logically consistent with its aims to be constitutional. It is enough that there is an evil at hand for correction, and that it might be thought that the particular legislative measure was a rational way to correct it.
>
> The day is gone when this Court uses the Due Process Clause of the Fourteenth Amendment to strike down state laws, regulatory of business and industrial conditions, because they may be unwise, improvident, or out of harmony with a particular school of thought. [*Id.* at 487–88.]

Equal protection challenges proved equally ineffective. In *Friedman v. Rogers*, 440 U.S. 1 (1979), the Court rejected an equal protection challenge to the Texas Optometry Act which required four of six members of the state licensing board to be members of an association whose membership excluded the plaintiff, a licensed optometrist.

> We stated the applicable constitutional rule for reviewing equal protection challenges to local economic regulations ... in *New Orleans v. Dukes*, 427 U.S. 297, 303 (1976).
>
> When local economic regulation is challenged solely as violating the Equal Protection Clause, this Court consistently defers to legislative determinations as to the desirability of particular statutory discriminations. Unless a classification trammels fundamental personal rights or is drawn upon inherently suspect distinctions such as race, religion, or alienage, our decisions presume the constitutionality of the statutory discriminations and require only that the classification challenged be rationally related to a legitimate state interest. [440 U.S. at 17.]

Despite its reluctance to invoke the Fourteenth Amendment against restrictive licensing, the Court has struck down limitations on the practice of trades and professions on other grounds. Increasing numbers of challenges to regulatory restrictions in recent years have invoked commercial free speech; and the Supreme Court has relied on the First Amendment to invalidate state-sanctioned prohibitions on business advertising and communication. *Virginia State Bd. of Pharmacy v. Virginia Citizens Consumer Council*, 425 U.S. 748 (1976) (Virginia statute prohibiting licensed pharmacists from advertising prescription drug prices); *Bates v. State Bar*, 433 U.S. 350 (1977) (court-imposed restraint on advertising by lawyers).

Relying primarily on the First Amendment law applicable to commercial free speech, a federal district court held that the Pennsylvania Board of Funeral Directors had gone too far in totally prohibiting employees of a funeral home to solicit preneed funeral services. *Walker v. Flitton*, 364 F. Supp. 2d 503 (M.D. Pa. 2005). "We fail to see, on the record before us, what substantial government interest exists relating to allowing only licensed funeral directors, rather than non-licensed insurance salespeople who are employed by, or agents of those funeral directors, to interact with customers and disseminate price and other information regarding preneed services. . . ." *Id.* at 519–20.

The Court has also enforced procedural due process. In *Gibson v. Berryhill*, 411 U.S. 564 (1973), the Court agreed that members of an optometry licensing board were so tainted with personal pecuniary interest that they could not constitutionally conduct hearings in the pending license revocation proceedings.

In the state courts, as Chapter 1 indicated, the judicial attitude to substantive due process and equal protection oversight of licensing and regulation is more aggressive, although the picture is mixed. The justification for the difference between federal and state court oversight is discussed in Chapter 1. This tendency is also reflected in state court decisions on licensing. It is by now relatively rare for a court to deny to a state altogether the police power right to license and regulate a particular occupation. See Note, *Due Process Limitations on Occupational Licensing*, 59 Va. L. Rev. 1097, 1099 n.14 (1973), and the cases following in this section. But even where the power to license and regulate is upheld, that result may follow a closer scrutiny than the Supreme Court would deem appropriate; and it is not infrequent that particular aspects of a licensing scheme are invalidated in the state courts. For scholarly perspective on recent developments, see Larkin, *Public Choice Theory and Occupational Licensing*, 39 Harv. J.L. & Pub. Pol'y 209 (2016) (discussing occupational licensing characteristics and resulting problems; arguing that legislatures regulate too many occupations for weak reasons unrelated to public health and safety; suggesting two new challenges that can be raised against occupational licensing regimes using public choice theory).

It can be argued that it is appropriate for state courts to be more assertive than the federal judiciary in subjecting licensing legislation to substantive due process and equal protection. One author who has taken that position pointed out that much of this legislation results from the activities of economic pressure groups which are in a position to focus their efforts on state legislatures to bring about the enactment of laws which further their own rather than the public interest.

> In such a situation the only remedy of those whose interests are adversely affected and who for one reason or another are unable to assert sufficient political pressure to protect their interests before the legislature, is in the courts and in the constitutional doctrines of substantive due process and

> equal protection. Judicial invalidation of such legislation may be technically anti-democratic, but it can hardly be called frustration of the popular will in any meaningful sense. [Hetherington, *State Economic Regulation and Substantive Due Process of Law*, 53 Nw. U. L. Rev. 13, 226, 249 (1958).]

He then noted that "[s]tate courts, since their precedents are not of national authority, may better adapt their decisions to local economic conditions and needs.... Local variations in economic conditions thus may justify varying local standards of economic due process...." *Id.* at 250.

There is a growing policy literature regarding the increase in occupational licensing in the last several decades. See Kleiner & Vorotnikov, *Analyzing Occupation Licensing Among the States*, 52 J. Regul. Econ. No. 2 (2017): 132–158 (using economic analysis of representative samples at the state level, concluding that there is considerable variation in percentage of workforce with a license, finding no regional patterns in the distribution of occupational licensing, finding considerable variation in the influence of earnings and demonstrating the influence of occupational regulation on wage inequality); Mercatus Center, George Mason University, *Quantifying Regulation in the United States* (November 13, 2019), available at https://www.mercatus.org/publications/regulation/quantifying-regulation-us-states (endeavoring to quantify level of licensing regulations in the states, and concluding that the most regulations exist in California and New York, followed by Illinois, Ohio, and Florida); Obama White House, *Occupational Licensing: A Framework for Policymakers*, available at https://obamawhitehouse.archives.gov/sites/default/files/docs/licensing_report_final_nonembargo.pdf

---

The two decisions that follow illustrate opposing state court views to the licensing of watchmaking, an occupation for which licensing requirements might be thought to be unnecessary. They also reflect a different perception of the relative role of the courts and the legislature.

Watchmaking Examining Board v. Husar

49 Wis. 2d 526, 182 N.W.2d 257 (1971)

This is an appeal from a judgment of the circuit court for Waukesha county which declared that ch. 125, Stats., regulating the watchmaking trade is unconstitutional. The Watchmaking Examining Board (hereafter the Board) commenced an action for declaratory judgment against Lyle C. Husar, alleging that the defendant held himself out as a watchmaker in Brookfield, Wisconsin, that he engaged in watch repairing for profit, and that he had never obtained a certificate of registration. The complaint asked for a declaration that the defendant was engaged in watchmaking and asked that the defendant be restrained from such further activity.

The defendant admitted all allegations of the complaint. He contended, however, that ch. 125, Stats., was unconstitutional in that it was an improper exercise of the state's police power.

Subsequent to the joining of issue, the parties stipulated that the only question to be tried was the constitutionality of ch. 125, Stats. It was agreed that, in the event the statute were found constitutional, further trial might be necessary in regard to certain provisions of the Administrative Code, particularly sec. Watch 1.08, which regulates the terms of apprenticeship.

Following a stipulation of facts, the cause was submitted to the trial court on briefs. The trial judge, in an extensive memorandum decision, concluded that ch. 125, Stats., was an unconstitutional exercise of the police power, which deprived the defendant of property without due process of law. He also held that the chapter unconstitutionally delegated legislative power to the administrative board. Judgment was thereupon entered dismissing the complaint of the Board. The Board has appealed from the judgment.

HEFFERNAN, JUSTICE.

It is well established in this state that the police power may be properly exercised to limit certain substantial rights of citizens if, in the reasonable legislative judgment, the conduct of individuals must be controlled to protect the general welfare of the community. In the case of *State ex rel. Saveland Park Holding Corp. v. Wieland* (Wis. 1955), 69 N.W.2d 217, we quoted with approval the following statement of the New York Court of Appeals in *Wulfsohn v. Burden* (N.Y. 1925), 150 N.E. 120, 122:

> The [police] power is not limited to regulations designed to promote public health, public morals, or public safety, or to the suppression of what is offensive, disorderly, or unsanitary, but extends to so dealing with conditions which exist as to bring out of them the greatest welfare of the people by promoting public convenience or general prosperity.
>
> In a series of opinions since *Saveland*, we have explained the scope of the state's police power and the nature of the public interest that may invoke its exercise.

In *Chicago & North Western Ry. Co. v. La Follette* (Wis. 1969), 169 N.W.2d 441, we reviewed some of the criteria which are to be used in determining whether the exercise of police power is unconstitutional. Therein, we pointed out that a statute is presumed to be constitutional and that a heavy burden is placed upon one challenging the constitutionality of a police-power statute. The court's function in such a challenge is not to weigh evidence in the traditional sense, but only to determine whether there is any reasonable basis for the legislative enactment. Nor will this court strike down legislation on the basis of its belief that the statute is good or bad or wise or unwise. If there is any reasonable basis for the exercise of police power by the legislature, the court must uphold the right of the legislature to act.

Chapter 125, Stats., regulates the rights of citizens to engage in a legitimate phase of private enterprise. Statutory enactments and administrative rules have been established to implement these regulations.

Section 125.04, Stats., provides that applicants shall be examined for certification by the Board. Applicants are to be "of good moral character, at least 20 years of age and possess such training and experience as the board shall by rule determine."

Section 125.05, Stats., provides that the examination: ". . . shall be confined to such knowledge, practical ability and skill as is essential in the proper repairing of watches, and shall include an examination of theoretical knowledge of watch construction and repair, and also a practical demonstration of the applicant's skill in manipulation of watchmaker's tools."

Section 125.07, Stats., provides for the registration of apprentice watchmakers. Pursuant to the statutes, the Board has adopted certain rules. One of them is Watch 1.10 Examination (1), which provides that the examinee will be furnished a 17-jewel watch in need of repair, and he will then be obliged to fit a balance staff, true the hairspring, adjust the escapement, and make all needed repairs. Certain other skills are also required to be demonstrated. In addition, he is required to submit to an examination consisting of 50 questions pertaining to the theory of construction and repair of the modern watch.

Watch 1.08 Applicant's affidavit provides that an applicant for certification file certain affidavits, including evidence of the completion of an apprenticeship of four years or its equivalent in school training and practical experience.

These enactments are presumptively constitutional, and the burden of showing that they are unreasonable and bear no relationship to the public interest rests upon the defendant in this case. If there is any reasonable basis for the exercise of the legislative power, we are obliged to uphold the enactment.

The statutes provide that the applicant must be of good moral character, be twenty years of age, and possess the training and experience required to perform watchmaking skills in the manner prescribed by the Board. A certificate showing the attainment of these standards is required to be placed in the watchmaker's place of business.

From the face of the statute, it is obvious that the legislature sought to protect the public from fraud and incompetence in the field of watchmaking and watch repair. The legislature could reasonably have reached that conclusion and decided that the statute provided a method of protecting the public welfare. The legislature may well have believed that, because of the complexity of watch repair and watchmaking, the average citizen would be at the mercy of the watchmaker when he takes his timepiece in for repair. It would not be difficult for a watchmaker, either by design or by negligent omission, to replace parts which were not in need of repair, to use defective or substandard parts in his repair work, to create latent defects in the watch mechanism, or even to charge for repairs that were, in fact, never made. It is impossible for the average customer to determine whether he has been dealt with fairly and whether the watchmaker has conformed with minimum standards.

The legislature might well have concluded that, in view of these facts, the public could be protected only by the examination of watchmakers and the establishment of standards calculated to insure that workmanlike standards were lived up to. It could well have concluded that it was in the interest of the public to take steps to insure that only men of professional training, of high skills and competence, and of suitable moral character enter and remain in the trade. The legislature could reasonably have assumed that the ordinary contractual obligations which the customer and the watchmaker enter into were insufficient to assure protection of the general welfare. In *State ex rel. Hickey v. Levitan* (Wis. 1926), 210 N.W. 111, 114, we said, "The prevention of fraud is a subject in which the public at large is vitally interested." The protection of the consumer from abuses that might occur as a result of incompetent or unethical practices by watchmakers falls within the scope of the police power which the legislature could employ to regulate the watchmaker trade for the general welfare. . . .

In oral argument, it was pointed out that there was no showing that there were widespread abuses that required the enactment of an all-pervasive system of state regulation. This, of course, goes to the burden of proof, which is not upon the state but upon the party seeking to upset the constitutionality of the statute. The defendant has failed to assume that burden.

In oral argument, it was also pointed out that [there] were other areas of free enterprise which were obviously of much more concern to the general welfare than watchmaking. The licensing of automobile repairmen was cited as an area in which state regulation, in regard to competence and ethical practices, would serve a far greater need than the licensing of watchmakers. This court, however, has frequently taken the position that the police power need not be exercised to eliminate all abuses, and that the legislature may selectively exercise its power. The fact that the legislature has failed to enact regulations in an area where they are arguably required does not vitiate the exercise of such power in another field where it reasonably considers regulation necessary. Inasmuch as the record is devoid of a showing that no public interest is served by the watchmaker's code and the legislature could reasonably have concluded that the public interest was served, we declare ch. 125, Stats. a constitutional enactment. . . .

[The court then held that the statute did not unconstitutionally delegate legislative power to the Board. Delegation is discussed in Chapter 8, *supra.*]

State ex rel. Whetsel v. Wood

207 Okla. 193, 248 P.2d 612 (1952)

HALLEY, VICE CHIEF JUSTICE.

This action involves the constitutionality of the Watchmaking Act of 1945, being Secs. 771–782, inclusive, Title 59, O.S. 1951.

The State of Oklahoma, ex rel. the County Attorney of Pittsburg County, seeks a permanent injunction restraining Thomas S. Wood, Jr., from practicing watchmaking in Oklahoma without first having obtained a license or certificate of registration as a watchmaker from the Oklahoma Board of Examiners in Watchmaking. . . .

It was alleged that the defendant never had been licensed by the Board to practice watchmaking in this State, nor had he applied for or obtained a certificate of registration as an apprentice, but that he had publicly represented himself as being a qualified watchmaker and had practiced watchmaking for compensation in Pittsburg County, and would continue to do so unless restrained, all in violation of the above law and to the irreparable damage and injury of the public, and especially of persons who patronize him, and to the damage and injury of persons lawfully engaged in watchmaking, rendering them insecure in their property and thus constituting a public nuisance; that the conduct of the defendant would endanger the health and safety of others, and that the plaintiff was without adequate remedy at law.

Defendant demurred to the petition generally, and also upon the ground that . . . the Watchmaking Act is void in that it deprives defendant of inherent rights, privileges and immunities guaranteed by the State and Federal Constitutions in numerous particulars. . . .

The court sustained the demurrer upon the ground that the Act sought to be enforced by this action is unconstitutional and void. The plaintiff declined to plead further and judgment was entered for the defendant. . . .

Plaintiff alleges that the first question to be determined is whether the State has the right to regulate watchmaking under what is termed the "police power" of the sovereign state. The defendant contends that the principal question involved is whether or not the manner of regulation provided by the Act invades the constitutional rights of the defendant. The term "police power" was aptly defined by this court in *Ex parte Tindall* (Okl.), 229 P. 125, 126, as follows:

> The police power is an attribute of sovereignty, inherent in every sovereign state, and not derived from any written Constitution nor vested by grant of any superior power.
>
> The term "police power" comprehends the power to make and enforce all wholesome and reasonable laws and regulations necessary to the maintenance, upbuilding, and advancement of the public weal and protection of the public interests.

The Watchmaking Act provides that in the future, an applicant must have served an apprenticeship of four years or its equivalent, as determined by the Board, before he is eligible for a license. This apprenticeship must be served under a licensed watchmaker and with his consent. This provision has the effect of placing in the hands of those holding a license the power to limit the number of those allowed to engage in watchmaking in Oklahoma, and clearly tends to create a monopoly.

Sec. 2 of the Act provides that no one shall engage in watchmaking for profit or compensation without first obtaining a license in the manner therein provided. In *State ex rel. Short v. Riedell* (Okl.), 233 P. 684, 691, this court held the Accountancy

Act of 1917 unconstitutional because of a similar provision as to accountants. In the body of that opinion it was said:

> The effect of the act is that in a growing, expanding, and lucrative field of usefulness of accountants, power is given a board in which accountants have control, to restrict their number, and tends to a monopoly. It deprives those desiring an audit the right of contract in matters purely a private concern, and deprives accountants not certified of the enjoyment of the gains of their own industry guaranteed to them by the Bill of Rights, in that it denies to them the right to follow the occupation for which they have qualified themselves by the expenditure of time and toil. . . .

The holding in the *Riedell* case, *supra*, has been approved by this court in several later cases, including *Cornell v. McAllister* (Okl.), 249 P. 959. A review of our decisions upholding laws regulating certain classes of business shows that they are based generally upon a finding that the business or calling is affected with a public interest. . . . While watchmaking is an important calling, it is not such a business as affects the public health, safety and welfare.

The Watchmaking Act clearly prohibits one who may be fully qualified by years of training and experience from following his chosen craft and forces him to seek some other work or trade, thus depriving him of the fruits of his own industry, as guaranteed by Art. II, Sec. 2 of the Oklahoma Constitution. The provisions of the Act are unreasonable, arbitrary, and discriminatory, and are not designed to promote the general welfare or contribute to the public morals, health, or safety. The Act vests in the Board powers to make rules and regulations which may deny some citizens their inherent right to earn their livelihood in a private field of work, thus depriving them of a valuable property right without due process of law.

We have been cited to no case involving the regulation of watchmakers; but we have read with considerable interest the case of *State v. Ballance* (N.C.), 51 S.E.2d 731, 7 A.L.R.2d 407, where the Supreme Court of North Carolina had under consideration a statute regulating the occupation of photography.

That court . . . held that the Act was unconstitutional. We quote from that opinion [51 S.E.2d 735]:

> It is undoubtedly true that the photographer must possess skill. But so must the actor, the baker, the bookbinder, the bookkeeper, the carpenter, the cook, the editor, the farmer, the goldsmith, the horseshoer, the horticulturist, the jeweler, the machinist, the mechanic, the musician, the painter, the paper-hanger, the plasterer, the printer, the reporter, the silversmith, the stonecutter, the storekeeper, the tailor, the watchmaker, the wheelwright, the woodcarver, and every other person successfully engaged in a definitely specialized occupation, be it called a trade, a business, an art, or a profession. Yet, who would maintain that the legislature would promote the general welfare by requiring a mental and moral examination preliminary

> to permitting individuals to engage in these vocations merely because they involve knowledge and skill? . . .

This [ALR] note shows that the supreme courts of Arizona, Florida, Georgia, Hawaii, North Dakota, Tennessee, and Virginia have passed on this question as to photographers. There is no more excuse for requiring a watchmaker to pass a test as to his technical qualifications than for requiring a photographer to pass such a test.

The judgment of the trial court is affirmed.

Arnold, C.J., and Corn, Davison, Johnson and O'Neal, JJ., concur.

Gibson and Bingaman, JJ., dissent.

Notes and Questions

1. *Rationales and analysis.* What were the principal rationales for upholding the constitutionality of the regulatory regime for watchmakers in *Husar* but invalidating it in *Wood*? How should the challenge of drawing lines about which occupations may be licensed weigh in driving a court's analysis? Consider, for example, the statements by the Tennessee and North Carolina courts in the following cases. In *Livesay v. Tennessee Bd. of Examiners in Watchmaking*, 322 S.W.2d 209 (Tenn. 1959) the court invalidated the state's watchmaking licensing act, rejecting the contention that licensing was needed to prevent incompetence and fraud, and observing that such a view would result in expecting the legislature to regulate "every conceivable business." In *Poor Richard's, Inc. v. Stone*, 366 S.E.2d 697 (N.C. 1988), the court upheld a statute licensing businesses that buy and sell military property. The court concluded that an occupation may be licensed if it has a feature that distinguishes it from other occupations. The photographers' licensing case, cited in *Whetsel, supra*, was listed as a case which lacked such a distinguishing feature. The state argued that licensing of this business was necessary to stem the tide of thefts of military property, and the court agreed that the business had a distinguishing feature because this property was never intended for sale at retail. Why is this a distinguishing feature? For a thoughtful exploration of rationales for occupational licensing beyond economic protectionism, see Robinson, *The Multiple Justifications of Occupational Licensing*, 93 Wash. L. Rev. 1903 (2018) (noting that resistance to occupational licensing may be fueled by economic libertarianism and antagonism toward professional self-regulation; providing insightful observations about the range of justifications for occupational licensing, including the need to foster communities of knowledge and competence, development of relationships of trust, and buffering producers from the market; suggesting that if there is to be federal intervention with regard to occupational licensing, Congress and the executive branch are better situated to undertake that effort than the federal judiciary).

2. *Rational relationship test.* Even when it is fairly clear that the structure of a licensing law effectively denies an applicant the opportunity to practice an occupation, the courts are likely to apply a rational relation test on the theory that the right

to pursue a profession is not a fundamental right. The non-traditional forms of healing arts give especially frequent rise to litigation. The Illinois Medical Practice Act requires a physician licensee to be a graduate either of a medical or osteopathic college (for a full license) or of a chiropractic college (for a limited license). In *Potts v. Illinois Dep't of Registration & Educ.*, 538 N.E.2d 1140 (Ill. 1989), the court upheld denial of a license to practitioners of naprapathy. As the court saw it, nothing in the act prohibited the practice of naprapathy so long as the practitioner was properly licensed as a graduate of one of the three categories of colleges. A similar holding confronted acupuncturists: anyone holding a full or limited medical license can practice acupuncture, which is the practice of medicine, but those trained at professional acupuncture schools who do not also possess a medical license can't practice acupuncture. There is no denial of constitutional rights. *Mitchell v. Clayton*, 995 F.2d 772 (7th Cir. 1993). Illinois now licenses those engaged in acupuncture and naprapathy. See 225 ILL. COMP. STAT § 2/1 (acupuncturists); 225 ILL. COMP. STAT. § 63/1 (those engaged in naprapathy).

Although most state courts have continued to apply rational basis review, at least Texas courts have begun to apply a higher standard of scrutiny. See *Patel v. Texas Department of Licensing and Regulation*, 469 S.W.3d 69 (Tex. 2015). *Patel* involved a challenge by practitioners of "eyebrow threading" (use of cotton thread to shape eyebrows) against requirements that they be licensed as cosmetologists or estheticians in order to pursue their preferred line of work. The Texas Supreme Court first reviewed three different formulations of the relevant standard of review under the Texas Constitution's due process clause (requiring no denial of property or liberty but for "due course of the law of the land"). The threaders asserted that three distinct standards had emerged under the courts' interpretation of the Texas Constitution. The first ("real and substantial") required that the legislature have a proper purpose for a particular statute, that there be a real and substantial connection between that purpose and the language of the statute as applied in practice, and that the statute works an excessive or undue burden on the person challenging the relation of the statute to its purposed purpose. *Id.* at 80–81. The second approach ("rational basis including consideration of evidence") was similar to the federal due process standard. *Id.* at 81–82. The third approach ("no evidence rational basis") would not require review of evidence but only conceivable justification for the government regulation, not necessarily demonstrably relied upon or proven by evidence) and whether the action was arbitrary. *Id* at 82. In the 5-3 decision, the court concluded that the first standard was the one that should apply, and determined that the training required for cosmeticians and estheticians was more comprehensive and costly than needed for threaders to safely perform the functions they sought to deliver. For more detailed discussion of the case, see Smith, *Unspooling the Furrowed Brow: How Eyebrow Threaders Will Protect Economic Freedom in Texas*, 48 TEX. TECH L. REV. ONLINE EDITION 71 (2016).

For further discussion of the rational relationship test, see Allensworth, *The (Limited) Constitutional Right to Compete in an Occupation*, 60 WM. & MARY L.

Rev. 1111 (2019) (arguing against robust "right to earn a living" claims; contending that courts should chart a middle path in considering due process and free speech challenges to licensing laws rather than imposing enhanced scrutiny; noting that claims of a "right to earn a living" raise concerns about whether naked economic protectionism is a legitimate state interest but viewing cases challenging licensing in general as falling at the margins; explaining concerns with reviving pre-*Lochner* substantive due process doctrine; recommending that meaningful solutions be found elsewhere by requiring states to take a more meaningful role in regulating occupations). See also Bernstein, *The Due Process Right to Pursue a Lawful Occupation: A Brighter Future Ahead?*, 126 Yale L.J. 287 (2016) (considering decisions finding that economic protectionism is not a rational basis for regulation of occupational licensing and arguing that changes in Supreme Court's approach to fundamental rights may provide opening for litigation about restrictions on entry to occupations); Klein, *The Freedom to Pursue a Common Calling: Applying Intermediate Scrutiny to Occupational Licensing Statutes*, 73 Wash. & Lee L. Rev. 411 (2016) (calling for enhanced scrutiny). In your view, is more stringent state court review warranted in the current context? Why or why not? Might more stringent review be appropriate with regard to some types of requirements or in certain contexts? How might appropriate lines be drawn?

3. *Licensing health care occupations: traditional and non-traditional.* Apprenticeship-type requirements are not uncommon in licensing statutes. As noted above, where they are patently exclusionary or "monopolistic," they may be invalidated. Similar forms of exclusion or monopolization are common in the health care licensing laws. For example:

> Another form of monopolization exists when the regulatory scheme creates a hierarchy of persons within a particular profession and requires anyone below the highest level to practice only through a person who is the "first-class citizen." For example, in the dental field, in addition to dentists there are dental hygienists, dental assistants, and dental technicians. However, only the licensed dentists may deal directly with the public. Regardless of the competence of dental hygienists or dental technicians to perform certain services, they are not permitted to deal directly with the public and must offer their services through the dentist. Such requirements deny the public a choice between different types of services and deprive the public of the benefits of competition that would occur from the increased number of persons offering particular services. Moreover, it gives the "first-class" professional the right to control the price at which the other persons' services are sold. [Rose, *Occupational Licensing: A Framework for Analysis*, 1979 Ariz. St. L.J. 189, 197.]

The courts have usually upheld these restrictions as applied to the practice of dentistry. For example, in *Wrzesinski v. State*, 522 S.E.2d 461 (Ga. 1999), the defendant, who operated a dental lab and took impressions for a plate, was convicted of practicing dentistry without a license. The court upheld the licensing statute against equal protection, due process and anti-monopoly challenges. *Sutker v. Illinois State Dental Soc'y*, 808 F.2d 632 (7th Cir. 1986), upheld under the usual rational relationship test a statute that, while allowing denturists to manufacture dentures, permitted only licensed dentists to fit the appliances to the patient. The court noted that the dentists' argument should be made to the Illinois legislature, not the federal courts. See also *People ex rel. Illinois State Dental Soc'y v. Sutker*, 395 N.E.2d 14 (Ill. App. 1979) (Illinois dental licensing act held to apply to dental technician whose entire business was repair and duplication of dentures for out-of-state customers by mail order).

Midwifery has given rise to a number of legal challenges involving hierarchies or exclusions, many of them related to the differential treatment of nurse midwives and lay midwives. Compare *Watson v. Kentucky Bd. of Nursing*, 37 S.W.3d 788 (Ky. App. 2000) (recognizing that the practical effect of the state regulation was to render it impossible to practice lay midwifery, the court held the requirement that only a nurse could be licensed as a midwife was rationally related to promoting the health of the woman and infant), with *Albini v. Connecticut Medical Examining Bd.*, 72 A.3d 1208 (Conn. App. 2013) (board exceeded its statutory authority, and improperly purported to regulate midwifery as the unauthorized practice of medicine, when it interpreted statutory provision that defined the practice of medicine and who could practice it to include the diagnosis or assessment of "conditions"). For a review of states' licensing of alternative medical professions, including proposals for "health freedom legislation" to facilitate the practice of these professions, see Lescure, *Health Freedom: The Practice of Complementary and Alternative Medicine*, 42-DEC Md. B.J. 38 (2009).

4. *Licensing funeral homes and embalming services.* How should funeral homes and embalming services be regulated? Should licensing requirements for such services be upheld? This topic is one that has divided courts around the country. Compare *St. Joseph Abbey v. Castille*, 712 F.3d 215 (5th Cir. 2013) (in § 1983 action by abbey that sought to sell hand-made caskets, holding that state embalming and funeral directors act was not rationally related to legitimate governmental interests in consumer protection or promotion of public health and safety), and *Craigmiles v. Giles*, 312 F.3d 220 (6th Cir. 2002) (enjoining application of Tennessee requirement that those who sold caskets at retail but engaged in none of the other activities of funeral directors be licensed), with *Heffner v. Murphy*, 745 F.3d 56 (3d Cir. 2014) (rejecting Commerce Clause challenges; concluding that no substantive due process problems were created by requirements that limited funeral directors to one principal place of business and one branch, limiting funeral establishments from serving food and intoxicating beverages, and requiring funeral directors who entered into pre-need contracts to deposit 100% of proceeds into escrow account), and *Powers v. Harris*, 379 F.3d 1208 (10th Cir. 2004) (upholding Oklahoma funeral licensing statute and observing that "intra-state economic protectionism, absent a violation of a specific federal statutory or constitutional provision, is a legitimate state interest [and] we have little difficulty determining that the [funeral licensing statute]

satisfies rational-basis review"). For a further twist on associated issues, see *Porter v. State of Wisconsin*, 913 N.W.2d 842 (Wisc. 2018) (upholding state law provisions prohibiting joint ownership or operation of cemetery and funeral home against equal protection and due process challenges).

5. *Licensing tour operators: tour guides and the First Amendment.* Another interesting development concerns challenges to licensing standards involving tour guides in Washington, D.C., and New Orleans, Louisiana. *Edwards v. District of Columbia*, 755 F.3d 996 (D.C. Cir. 2014), concerned a District of Columbia ordinance that required those seeking to serve as paid tour guides to pass a written examination covering knowledge of history and buildings in the District and pay a $200 registration fee. *Kagan v. City of New Orleans, La.*, 753 F.3d 560 (5th Cir. 2014), involved a constitutional challenge to similar testing requirements as well as a drug testing requirement and a requirement not to have been convicted of a felony in the past two years applicable to tour guides in New Orleans. The cases reached opposite conclusions. The Court of Appeals for the District of Columbia Circuit applied an intermediate level of scrutiny to strike down the licensing requirement as unjustified by the District's interest in protecting its tourism industry and assuring visitors that guides had a minimum level of competence, asserting that the general test did not particularly advance government objectives when applied to specialty tour guides and asserting that the market for tour guides would take care of itself. The Fifth Circuit regarded the regulations as unrelated to any content-based viewpoint and thus supportable under the city's rationales of informing and protecting visitors. See also *Billups v. City of Charleston, S.C.*, 331 F. Supp. 3d 500 (D.S.C. 2018) (in action by tour guide license applicants, concluding that city's tour guide licensing law created impermissible burden on First Amendment speech and finding the licensing law was not narrowly tailored to serve the significant government interest, and thus violated the First Amendment under intermediate scrutiny).

For discussion of these decisions, see Post & Shanor, *Adam Smith's First Amendment*, 128 HARV. L. REV. 165 (2015) (critiquing the *Edwards* decision and similar developments in which the First Amendment is being used to attack commercial regulation as potentially ushering in a return to the pre-*Lochner* era); Deyo, *A Tale of Two Cities: The Constitutionality of Tour Guide Licensing Requirements*, 90 TUL. L. REV. 671 (2016) (discussing both decisions and contending that testing requirement was unwarranted given other alternatives such as self-regulation within the tourism industry or certification as opposed to licensing options).

6. *Remedies: validation, invalidation, or something in between?* Courts continue to uphold regulatory laws and licensing statutes applicable to occupations which are of doubtful harm to the public health and safety. See, e.g., *North Dixie Theatre, Inc. v. McCullion*, 613 F. Supp. 1339 (S.D. Ohio 1985) (upholding requirement that flea market operators who wish to rent space to sellers of used cars obtain motor vehicle license); *C & H Enters. v. Commissioner of Motor Vehicles*, 355 A.2d 247 (Conn. 1974) (upholding licensing of business of operating auto wrecker for hire). Despite the general trend to uphold licensing statutes, courts occasionally invalidate one,

particularly when the anticompetitive purpose is clear. For example, the court in *Schroeder v. Binks*, 113 N.E.2d 169 (Ill. 1953), although conceding the general power of the state to license and regulate plumbers, struck down the "economic hierarchy" which required apprentices and journeymen plumbers to work under the supervision of a master plumber, relying on substantive due process, equal protection, and "special legislation" grounds. The court held that the statute gave too much control over access to the profession to master plumbers, and took judicial notice that the skills necessary to carry on the plumbing trade could as easily be learned in an educational institution. A court that is hostile to and wishes to invalidate a licensing law may also hold that the licensing standards contained in the law are an unconstitutional delegation of power to the licensing board. See *supra*, Chapter 8. A decision invalidating licensing standards will at least force the legislature to constrain the discretion of the licensing board by adopting more specific licensing criteria.

Even where courts uphold the state's right to license and regulate a business or occupation, they may be willing to invalidate a particular provision in the regulatory scheme that they deem unduly restrictive or unfair. What principles should guide such determinations? In *Church v. State*, 646 N.E.2d 572 (Ill. 1995), the court was faced with a challenge to the Act licensing private alarm contractors. "The fact that the legislature has invoked its police power to regulate a particular trade . . . is not conclusive that such power was lawfully exercised." *Id.* at 579. The court went on to invalidate the part of the Act that required a license applicant to have worked full-time within the industry for three years. "This portion of the Act confers upon members of a regulated industry a monopolistic right to instruct and control entry into the private alarm contracting trade." *Id.* at 582.

Examples of partial invalidation abound in the beauty care field. In *Cornwell v. California Bd. of Barbering and Cosmetology*, 962 F. Supp. 1260 (S.D. Cal. 1997), the court conceded that the California legislature clearly can require a license and a licensing exam for African American hair stylists, but it invalidated a requirement that hairbraiders receive 1600 hours of instruction in specific techniques that they would never use. Finding no rational connection between the required curriculum and a legitimate government interest, the court concluded that "it acts as an [*sic*] barrier to the entry of African American hairstylists into their chosen profession." (*Id.* at 1273). Contra *Diwara v. State Bd. of Cosmetology*, 852 A.2d 1279 (Pa. Commw. 2004). For further consideration of regulation of hair braiding, see *Niang v. Carroll*, 879 F3d 870 (8th Cir. 2018) (upholding regulation of hair braiders against equal protection challenge); *Niang v. Tomblinson*, 139 S. Ct. 319 (2018) (*cert granted*, directed to dismiss as moot); Note, *Rational Basis Review—Substantive Due Process—Eighth Circuit Upholds Licensing Requirements for African-American Hair Braiders—Niang v. Carol, 879 F3d 870 (8th Cir. 2018)*, 131 Harv. L. Rev. 2453 (2018) (analyzing *Niang* decision).

7. *Grandfather clauses.* When can a legislature legitimately implement a licensing scheme that applies to those who will engage in an occupation in the future but

not "reach back" to those already engaged in a particular field? Consider *Independent Electricians & Electrical Contractors' Ass'n v. New Jersey Board of Examiners of Electrical Contractors*, 256 A.2d 33 (N.J. 1969). That case examined the application of statutory provisions governing the licensure of electrical contractors. A newer system, established by statute, required prospective licensees to gain five years of practice experience in the electrical trade, satisfy the board of requisite practice and educational experience, and pass a state licensing exam. This new system took the place of an older regimen in which the state licensing board could approve candidates who had been allowed licensure based on experience alone. The statute implementing the new examination requirement had grandfathered candidates who had six years of experience in electrical contracting and had operated their "principal business" as electrical contractors for the two years prior to the statutory change. The licensing board had received 4,000 applications for licensure under the grandfather provision and had granted licenses to 3,000 such candidates after individual review, but had denied the plaintiffs who had only operated as an electrical contractors in the prior two years on a part-time basis. The court upheld the arrangement, noting that it accorded considerable deference to the state legislature. For a similar result, see *City of New Orleans v. Dukes*, 427 U.S. 297 (1976) (upholding city ordinance prohibiting pushcart vendors in the French Quarter but exempting vendors who had operated their businesses in that area for at least the eight prior years). Grandfather clauses may, however, violate state constitutional provisions relating to due process and equal protection. See, e.g., *Cities Service Co. v. Governor, State of Md.*, 431 A.2d 663 (Md. 1981) (prohibition of refinery-operated retail gas stations with grandfather exemption violates equal protection component of state due process clause).

Although grandfather clauses are typically included and almost always upheld, isn't there a fundamental contradiction in their inclusion? In enacting restricted entry regulatory schemes, states and cities are acting pursuant to their police power. The premise is that the licensing standards—educational requirements, experience, examination, good moral character—are necessary to protect the public health or safety. If the police power justification is valid, why isn't it equally necessary to apply the same standards to those already engaged? Could a legislature forego a grandfather clause, or is it constitutionally required? See *City of Louisville v. Coulter*, 197 S.W. 819 (Ky. 1917) (upholding the absence of a grandfather clause in the plumbers licensing act).

A Note on Licensing Boards and Administration

The administration of licensing laws has also presented constitutional problems. Most licensing statutes establish a board to administer the act, and these boards have a dual role.

> The dual role of most licensing boards is a matter of the utmost importance. On the one hand boards serve as gatekeepers to determine the qualifications and competence of applicants. On the other, they must see that

> standards are adhered to by practitioners and, when necessary, adjudicate disputes between the public and members of the regulated occupation [or, in some cases, between warring factions of the regulated occupations—Eds.]. Given the composition of the boards [typically, all or a substantial majority are licensed members of the occupation they preside over—Eds.], it is almost impossible for them to function effectively as both licensing and enforcement agencies. [B. Shimberg, B. Esser & D. Kruger, Occupational Licensing: Practices and Policies 14–15 (1973).]

Recognition of these problems, combined with the frequent complaint that we are over-licensed in the first place, has led courts to review the administration of the licensing statutes more carefully and in some cases require higher standards of fairness. See Note, *Due Process Limitations on Occupational Licensing*, 59 Va. L. Rev. 1097, 1118–29 (1973). This development has been assisted by the demise of the right-privilege distinction in United States Supreme Court jurisprudence. Historically, occupational licenses were treated as privileges, and for this reason subject to the state's plenary regulatory power. See, e.g., *Barsky v. Board of Regents*, 347 U.S. 442 (1954) (upholding suspension of physician's license when physician convicted of contempt of Congress). The right-privilege distinction appears to have been abandoned in cases like *Schware v. Board of Bar Exam'rs*, 353 U.S. 232, 239 n.5 (1957), striking down a refusal of a state to allow a law graduate to take a bar examination because he lacked good moral character. See *Due Process Limitations, supra*, at 1100–03. Comment, *Expert Testimony and Professional Licensing Boards: What Is Good, What Is Necessary and the Myth of the Majority-Minority Split*, 53 Me. L. Rev. 139 (2001), is a detailed analysis of the practices of state professional licensing boards with respect to the use of expert testimony in disciplinary proceedings involving health care professionals. For a decision finding a state statute regulating interior designers to be overbroad, see *State v. Lupo*, 984 So. 2d 395 (Ala. 2007) (definition of interior design to include selection of decorative accessories and paint was overbroad and not substantially related to the public health, safety or morals or to the general welfare and public convenience).

With respect to the makeup of licensing boards, the Supreme Court has rejected due process and equal protection challenges based on membership from the regulated profession. See *Friedman v. Rogers*, discussed *supra*. Compare *Abramson v. Gonzalez*, 949 F.2d 1567 (11th Cir. 1992) (objection that "interested" persons, specifically the American Psychological Association, controlled much of the licensing procedure rejected, relying on *Friedman v. Rogers*), with *Stivers v. Pierce*, 71 F.3d 732 (9th Cir. 1995) (while noting that industry representation on governing boards is accepted practice throughout the U.S., court found triable claims of due process unfairness in this case). In *Watkins v. North Carolina State Bd. of Dental Exam'rs*, 593 S.E.2d 764 (N.C. 2004), a disciplinary order was upheld against an orthodontist despite his objection that the Dental Board lacked the requisite expertise to determine the standard of care required of orthodontists because there were no orthodontists on the Board. The court rejected his arguments, concluding that "in the statutory scheme adopted by the legislature, orthodontists are regulated as dentists, by dentists." *Id.* at 768.

In two earlier cases, the Court did address the issue of fairness in disciplinary proceedings before a licensing board. In *Gibson v. Berryhill*, 411 U.S. 564 (1973) the Court found that members of the Alabama optometric board had such a possible personal pecuniary interest in the outcome of proceedings against the plaintiff optometrists (apparently commercial optometrists, as in *Friedman v. Rogers*) that the board could not constitutionally conduct hearings on the revocation of their licenses. Personal interest was claimed because the disciplinary action was aimed at revoking the licenses of optometrists who were employed by business corporations, nearly half of all those in the state. The board members were all in private practice and would presumably pick up the business abandoned by plaintiffs if their licenses were revoked. The Court specifically did not pass on the question of the "extent to which an administrative agency may investigate and act upon the material facts of a case and then, consistent with due process, sit as an adjudicative body to determine those facts finally" (*id.* at 579 n.17) an issue which, the Court noted, "has occasioned some divergence of views among federal courts." Subsequently, the Court addressed that issue in a case in which a doctor objected that the combination of investigative and adjudicatory functions in the Wisconsin Medical Examining Board violated his due process rights. *Withrow v. Larkin*, 421 U.S. 35 (1975). Although acknowledging that "special facts and circumstances" may dictate a contrary finding, the Court concluded that the investigative-adjudicative combination did not constitute a due process violation in this case.

The membership or method of selection of licensing boards has been successfully challenged in some state court actions, although not necessarily on equal protection grounds. See, e.g., *Rogers v. Medical Ass'n*, 259 S.E.2d 85 (Ga. 1979) (holding that the requirement that appointees to the state Board of Medical Examiners must come from a list of nominees submitted by the Medical Association was an unconstitutional delegation of the appointing power to a private organization); but cf. *Humane Soc'y of the U.S. v. New Jersey State Fish & Game Council*, 362 A.2d 20 (N.J. 1976) (upholding against various constitutional challenges the requirement that nine of eleven members of the Fish and Game Council be recommended by designated private associations). See also *State ex. rel. State Bd. of Healing Arts v. Beyrle*, 7 P.3d 1194 (Kan. 2000) (court determined that the legislature had not authorized a private organization to set future standards, and accordingly had not engaged in unconstitutional delegation).

A Note on Legislation to Reform Licensing

Just as criticisms of occupational licensing have run the gamut from inadequate enforcement to due process nightmares to unjustified proliferation, so also have proposals for reforming the system. Consider the following possible reforms. To what aspect of the criticism is each directed? Which are most likely to alleviate the concerns about licensing?

(a) *Eliminate some of the confusion, inconsistency and inefficiency caused by the presence of separate bureaucracies by centralizing administration of all licensing in one agency or board.* The licensing statutes would be made uniform with respect to structure and procedures—with appropriate allowance for any special requirements of a particular occupation. See *A Model Professional and Occupational Licensing Act*, 5 HARV. J. ON LEGIS. 67 (1967). Centralization would also facilitate codification of procedures and the development of a body of written decisions to provide precedents in disciplinary proceedings. Would it make sense to invest all of the adjudicatory authority in a single board?

(b) *In the enforcement (disciplinary) component of licensing, separate the investigative and adjudicative functions.* This might be done by placing the adjudicative role in a single agency (as suggested above), although given the number of occupations licensed, all of them with disciplinary proceedings, the caseload could be staggering. Another way would be to assign disciplinary cases to hearing officers appointed by the state attorney general, perhaps followed by administrative appeal to a professional appeal board. One disadvantage of this approach might be the absence of technical knowledge if the hearing officers and board were predominantly lawyers. How might that problem be overcome?

(c) *Reduce educational requirements and reliance on written exams, which are major entry barriers set up in almost all licensing acts.* See S. DORSEY, THE OCCUPATIONAL LICENSING QUEUE (Center for Study of American Business, Work Paper No. 34, 1978), a study showing that written exams work against entry into licensed occupations by the less educated, the less formally trained, and minorities. Dorsey shows that in a nonprofessional trade, at least, there is no particular correlation between written scores and ability to pass a practical examination. He suggests, at the least, improving the quality of the written exam and, preferably, requiring only a practical examination. *Id.* at 26. Is the current movement to require continuing education in the professions and some occupations consistent or inconsistent with Dorsey's findings?

(d) *Require public members on all licensing boards in order to provide adequate representation of the "public interest."* California was an early leader in adding public members to licensing boards, and a significant number have a majority of public members. H. Schutz, L. MUSOLF & L. SHEPARD, REGULATING OCCUPATIONS IN CALIFORNIA: THE ROLE OF PUBLIC MEMBERS ON STATE BOARDS 5 (1980). By now, most states have one or more public members on some or all of their boards, although the debate continues as to their effectiveness.

(e) *"Sunset" review.* In light of the typical judicial deference to state legislatures in matters of licensing, many states have enacted sunset and sunrise laws, intended to instill more deliberation into the legislative decision to license. Colorado pioneered sunset legislation in 1976. Since then a majority of states have adopted some form of sunset law, not all of which have survived. Under "sunset" review the licensing regulatory acts are automatically repealed unless the legislature, usually following review by a special committee or independent study group, affirmatively acts to continue or modify the affected licensing statute. The sunset cycle can range from a one-time review to a periodic review. As the reform fervor diminished, some states extended the cycle, suspended the process, or even allowed their sunset law to sunset. For the most part sunset review has not resulted in large-scale elimination of many licensed occupations, particularly the larger, more influential groups.

Perhaps responding to the difficulty of sunsetting regulatory legislation, a number of states, adopted "sunrise" review, by which the legislature attempts to restrain itself by institutionalizing procedures to be followed before it enacts any new licensing scheme. The purpose is to require the legislature to confront a series of standards which will help it evaluate the need for licensing and the relative merits and demerits of restricting practice of the occupation. In some cases, the legislature is aided, as in sunset, by an independent review committee.

(f) *Replace licensing with a less restrictive system such as registration or certification.* In registration, all practitioners of the trade must register with a state agency that has supervisory authority over them, but registrants are not required to meet any preconditions of education, experience, or ability. In certification, the applicants must meet predetermined minimum standards and they are then entitled to practice as, for example, a certified public accountant. Noncertified practitioners are equally free to offer their services, and very likely at a lower price, but without the special designation. See Gellhorn, *The Abuse of Occupational Licensing, supra*, at 26–27. Another less restrictive alternative would be enactment of a statute, without licensing, which prohibited designated unprofessional practices and provided civil penalties for violation. In some cases, the public can be protected by regulating the business establishment—a restaurant or grocery store—without licensing the workers. Consider, for example, the case of paralegals. Should they be licensed (requiring passage of a licensure exam), certified (requiring documentation of education and experience), or registered (requiring that they notify state agencies of their roles and employment)? For a discussion advocating for certification of paralegals, see Jones, *Why Indiana Lawyers Should be in Favor of Paralegal Registration*, 57-SEP Res Gestae 12 (2013) (discussing Indiana proposal and comparing other states' practices).

Reforms within the existing structure of licensing are largely dependent on the will of state legislatures, which have been slow to respond. Does that suggest that the courts should play a more vigorous role in policing regulatory licensing, whether the inquiry be equal protection, delegation, antitrust, or substantive or procedural due process? See generally K. Meir, Regulation (1985).

[2] Licensing and Federal Antitrust Law

Problem 9-2

The State of West Carolina has established a regulatory board responsible for the licensure, disciplinary oversight and regulation of dentists (the "Dental Board"). The State's action is predicated on the state legislature's judgment that the practice of dentistry implicates the public health, safety, and welfare. The Dental Board has eight members, six of whom are licensed dentists selected through an election in which all licensed dentists may vote. The Dental Board also has one dental hygienist (selected by election in which all dental hygienists may vote), and one public member appointed by the Governor.

State law provides that it is unlawful for an individual to practice dentistry without a license from the Dental Board. State statutes specify that a person "shall be deemed to be practicing dentistry" if that person, "[r]emoves stains, accretions or deposits from the human teeth." State statutes also provide that, if the Dental Board suspects an individual of engaging in the unlicensed practice of dentistry, it may bring an action to enjoin the practice in superior court or refer the matter for criminal prosecution.

Historically, teeth-whitening has been performed by dentists in their offices using procedures that are fast, effective, but comparatively expensive. Recently, others have begun to enter the marketplace by using alternative strategies for whitening teeth, for example through offering over-the-counter products for sale or providing services by non-dentists in beauty salons and shopping mall kiosks. Generally, these new strategies rely on applying peroxide to the teeth repeatedly using gels or strips. Such practices do not whiten teeth as quickly as might be done through procedures performed by dentists, but they are less expensive.

Recently the Dental Board has issued a number of "cease-and-desist" orders to those involved in teeth-whitening activities who are not dentists, asserting that such activities involve the "practice of dentistry" and may be conducted only by licensed dentists. The Federal Trade Commission has recently brought an action against the Dental Board under the federal antitrust laws. As discussed below, the "state action" doctrine provides that the antitrust laws "not apply to anticompetitive restraints imposed by the States 'as an act of government.'" Can the Dental Board's enforcement efforts be enjoined?

An Introduction to Federal Antitrust Law

Federal statutory provisions. Several federal statutes prohibit different forms of anticompetitive conduct. The Sherman Act addresses conspiracies in restraint of trade and monopolies.[2] The Clayton Act prohibits activities that may ultimately

---

2. Section 1 of the Sherman Antitrust Act, 15 U.S.C. § 1, provides:

"Every . . . conspiracy, in restraint of trade or commerce among the several States, . . . [is] hereby declared to be illegal." Section 2 of the Sherman Act, 15 U.S.C. § 2, provides:

tend to create a monopoly, including acquisition of stock and other share capital.[3] The Fair Trade Commission Act gives that Federal Trade Commission authority to address unfair methods of competition.[4]

State action exemption: action by the state. The courts have recognized an exemption from the antitrust laws referenced above, based on the assumption that Congress did not intend to cover state policy judgments in certain circumstances. In *Parker v. Brown*, 317 U.S. 341 (1943), the Court construed the Sherman Act to contain a "state action" exemption that excused, on principles of intergovernmental comity, *state*-approved anticompetitive behavior. *Parker* itself concerned the action of the California state legislature in establishing a raisin marketing program, administered by a state commission, which controlled marketing of the state's raisin crop through a "prorate program" so as to maintain or enhance prices. The Court upheld the program against a Sherman Act challenge, stating that

> [i]t is the state which has created the machinery for establishing the prorate program. Although the organization of a prorate zone is proposed by producers, and a prorate program, approved by the Commission, must also be approved by referendum of producers, it is the state, acting through the Commission, which adopts the program and which enforces it with penal sanctions, in the execution of a governmental policy.

It is thus clear that actions by state legislatures themselves fall within the state action exemption. The United States Supreme Court has also confirmed that actions by state supreme courts are exempt. See *Hoover v. Ronwin*, 466 U.S. 558 (1984) (finding no antitrust liability for state bar examiners in setting cut scores on the bar examination where state supreme court reserved right to review licensure decisions).

"Every person who shall monopolize, or attempt to monopolize, or combine or conspire with any other person or persons, to monopolize any part of the trade or commerce among the several States . . . shall be deemed guilty of a felony."

3. Section 7 of the Clayton Act, 15 U.S.C. § 18 provides:

No person engaged in commerce or in any activity affecting commerce shall acquire, directly or indirectly, the whole or any part of the stock or other share capital . . . , where in any line of commerce or in any activity affecting commerce in any section of the country, the effect of such acquisition may be substantially to lessen competition, or to tend to create a monopoly.

No person shall acquire, directly or indirectly, the whole or any part of the stock or other share capital . . . , where in any line of commerce or in any activity affecting commerce in any section of the country, the effect of such acquisition, of such stocks or assets, or of the use of such stock by the voting or granting of proxies or otherwise, may be substantially to lessen competition, or to tend to create a monopoly.

4. Section 5 of the Fair Trade Commission Act, 15 U.S.C. § 45, provides:

(1) Unfair methods of competition in or affecting commerce, and unfair or deceptive acts or practices in or affecting commerce, are hereby declared unlawful.

(2) The Commission is hereby empowered and directed to prevent persons, partnerships, or corporations, . . . from using unfair methods of competition in or affecting commerce and unfair or deceptive acts or practices in or affecting commerce.

In certain instances involving significant involvement by private parties, state authorization of anticompetitive behavior may not satisfy state action doctrine requirements, however. For example, in *California Retail Liquor Dealers Ass'n v. Midcal Aluminum, Inc.*, 445 U.S. 97 (1980), California statutes authorized price setting and enforced prices established by private parties, but the state itself did not establish prices, review the reasonableness of price schedules, regulate the terms of contracts, monitor market conditions, or engage in close reexamination of the program. The Court concluded that the state action doctrine did not apply because the state had not clearly articulated and affirmatively expressed a judgment favoring anticompetitive activities as state policy, nor had it actively supervised the private parties involved in establishing the wine prices.

State action exemption: application to local governments. It was initially assumed that the *Parker v. Brown* exemption also applied to local governments. However, local governments have not been accorded categorical state action immunity of the sort recognized for state legislatures and state supreme courts. In *City of Lafayette v. Louisiana Power & Light Co.*, 435 U.S. 389 (1978), the Supreme Court considered the applicability of the Sherman and Clayton Acts where cities that owned and operated electric utility systems brought an antitrust action against a privately-owned utility and the private utility counterclaimed. The Court concluded that cities were "persons" covered by the antitrust laws. The Court further held that the state action doctrine did not automatically exempt all governmental entities by reason of their status, particularly since local governments are themselves not "sovereign." However, in the Court's view, "the actions of municipalities may reflect state policy ... [but] the *Parker* doctrine exempts only anticompetitive conduct engaged in as an act of government by the State as sovereign, or, by its subdivisions, pursuant to state policy to displace competition with regulation or monopoly public service." *Id.* at 413. The Court subsequently reiterated its views in *Community Communications Co. v. City of Boulder*, 455 U.S. 40 (1982) (in case challenging a city's moratorium on new cable television licenses, concluding that city's home rule status did not afford it immunity under the state action doctrine, absent a clearly and affirmatively expressed state policy to displace competition). Following this decision, Congress enacted the Local Government Antitrust Act of 1984, 15 U.S.C. §§ 34–36, which prohibits awards of damages and attorney's fees against local governments in antitrust actions.

Notwithstanding the diminished incentives for litigation that resulted from this legislation, antitrust claims have continued to be asserted against local governments, particularly in the context of land use regulation. In *Town of Hallie v. City of Eau Claire*, 471 U.S. 34 (1985), four adjacent unincorporated townships brought an antitrust action against Eau Claire, Wisconsin, claiming that the city had used its monopoly power over sewage treatment to gain an unlawful monopoly over the provision of sewage collection and transportation services, services that the nearby townships also wished to provide. The Court upheld the district court's dismissal of the complaint, reasoning that applicable Wisconsin statutes gave cities the authority to construct sewerage systems and to determine the area to be served. The statutes evidenced "a 'clearly articulated and affirmatively expressed' state policy to displace competition with regulation in the area of municipal provision of sewerage services." The Court held it was enough if these statutes contemplated that the city might engage in anticompetitive conduct, and that such conduct was "a foreseeable result of empowering the City to refuse to serve unannexed areas." It was not necessary for the state legislature to state explicitly that it expected the City to engage in anticompetitive conduct. *Lafayette* means it is enough if "the statutes authorized the City to provide sewage services and also to determine the areas to be served. We think it is clear that anticompetitive effects logically would result from this broad authority to regulate." *Id.* at 42. The Court also held it was not necessary that the state "compelled" the city to act.

In *City of Columbia v. Omni Outdoor Advertising Co.*, 499 U.S. 365 (1991), the Court held that state action immunity protected a municipality from antitrust liability claimed to arise from an ordinance restricting the size, location and spacing of billboards. These restrictions, especially those on spacing, benefitted an existing billboard company that controlled 95% of the local market, because they already had billboards in place, and severely hindered a potential competitor that was trying to enter the market. The Court held that state action immunity was conferred by the city's "unquestioned zoning power over the size, location and spacing of billboards" that the state zoning act, which was based on the Standard Act, authorized. The Court rejected a defense that state action immunity did not apply if a municipality exercises its delegated authority in a substantively or procedurally defective manner. This defense would undercut the "very interests of federalism" the state action doctrine was designed to protect. This holding means immunity is available even if a state court holds a zoning regulation invalid because it is an improper control of competition. The Court next held the "clear articulation" rule was "amply met here" because "[t]he very purpose of zoning regulation is to displace unfettered business freedom in a manner that regularly has the effect of preventing normal acts of competition, particularly on the part of new entrants." An ordinance restricting the size, location and spacing of billboards, which the Court characterized as "a common form of zoning," necessarily protects existing billboards from new competition. The Court also rejected a conspiracy exception to state action immunity and held that bribery and misconduct would not make state action immunity unavailable.

Novel antitrust problems continue to arise in the context of local land use regulation. Consider, for example, the antitrust implications that might arise when municipalities adopt "green" building standards such as the LEED standards recommended by the United States Green Building Council (USGBC). Other organizations have also entered the marketplace and are recommending their own standards. See Prum, Aalberts & Del Percio, *In Third Parties We Trust? The Growing Antitrust Impact of Third-Party Green Building Certification Systems for State and Local Governments*, 27 J. Envtl. L. & Litig. 191, 194–201 (2012) (describing competing systems). If a local government creates financial incentives for developers to employ LEED standards to engage in green building practices, or adopts LEED standards as part of an innovative uniform development ordinance, does it run the risk of antitrust litigation?

State action exemption: actions by other local governmental entities. In a decision involving challenges under the Clayton Act and Federal Trade Commission Act, the Supreme Court considered the application of the state action doctrine to activities of a hospital created by a local special-purpose "hospital authority." See *F.T.C. v. Phoebe Putney Health System, Inc.*, 133 S. Ct. 1003 (2013). The hospital authority owned the Phoebe Putney Memorial Hospital (Memorial), and decided to purchase the second hospital located in the county in order to lease it to a nonprofit entity involved in managing Memorial. The FTC contended that the proposed action would reduce competition for acute care medical services. The Court concluded that the state action doctrine did not apply because Georgia had not clearly articulated and affirmatively expressed a policy allowing hospital authorities to make acquisitions that substantially lessened competition. Citing the *City of Boulder* case, the Court emphasized that there must be a "clearly articulated and affirmatively expressed" state policy to displace competition before the state action doctrine would apply. Citing *Hallie*, the Court opined that a state legislature need not "expressly state" its intent to displace competition, but the anticompetitive effect must have been the "foreseeable result" of what the state had authorized. In the case at hand, the Court found that there was no clearly articulated and affirmatively expressed state policy since the hospital authority's powers mirrored general powers conferred on private corporations and could be used in ways that were not anticompetitive. The state legislation authorizing the creation of hospital authorities also failed the "foreseeability" prong of the state action analysis. Although state legislatures are not expected to "catalog all the anticipated effects" of statutes delegating authority to sub-state governmental entities, the displacement of competition must be "the inherent, logical or ordinary result of the exercise of authority delegated by the state legislature." The Court rejected the view that the state had foreseen and implicitly endorsed the anticompetitive effects of its policy where the policy in effect granted only a general power to act that was situated against the backdrop of federal antitrust law. For a discussion of the *Phoebe Putney* case, see Amezcua & Marx, Jr., *Implications of the Supreme Court's Ruling in FTC v. Phoebe Putney Health System for Healthcare Providers and Payers*, 7 J. Health & Life Sci. L. 1 (2013).

An additional exemption: the Noerr-Pennington doctrine. The Supreme Court has recognized another exemption from antitrust liability that arises when private parties engage in speech protected under the First Amendment when seeking redress from government decisionmakers. This exemption is referred to as the *Noerr-Pennington* doctrine, and it provides a free speech defense for competitors who petition to influence a local government to take an action that may violate the antitrust laws. See *United Mine Workers v. Pennington*, 381 U.S. 657 (1965); *Eastern R.R. Presidents' Conference v. Noerr Motor Freight Co.*, 365 U.S. 127 (1961). The doctrine is important in land use cases, like *Omni*, where private entities can use their political influence to pressure municipalities to adopt a land use regulation that harms a competitor. The Court held in *Omni* that there is no exception to the *Noerr-Pennington* doctrine based on a claim that parties attempting to influence a noncompetitive action were engaged in a conspiracy. Another exception to this doctrine makes it unavailable when petitioning activities are a "sham." The Supreme Court has substantially restricted opportunities to prove a sham exception, holding in *Professional Real Estate Investors, Inc. v. Columbia Pictures Indus., Inc.*, 508 U.S. 49 (1993), that the sham exception requires objective proof and cannot be based on the subjective intent of the parties.

North Carolina Dental Board and its significance. Responding to facts similar to those set out in the introductory Problem 9-2, the United States Supreme Court struck down the North Carolina dental board's actions in issuing cease and desist orders to non-dentists offering teeth whitening services in *North Carolina State Bd. of Dental Examiners v. FTC*, 574 U.S. 494 (2015). The North Carolina Dental Board was constituted as described in Problem 9-2. It was shown to have acted against the non-dentists based upon complaints from fellow dentists. The Supreme Court, in a 6-3 decision by Justice Kennedy, provided significant guidance concerning the future application of the *Parker* state action immunity doctrine as to occupational licensing going forward, focusing on the operation of the *Midcal* case discussed earlier in the casebook, *California Retail Liquor Dealers Ass'n v. Midcal Aluminum, Inc.*, 445 U.S. 97 (1980), and adding further depth to its analysis. *Midcal* had employed a two-prong test that allowed state immunity to apply to the actions of private parties only if there was a "clearly articulated and affirmatively expressed" judgment that favored anti-competitive activities as a matter of state policy, and if there was "active state supervision" of the private parties involved. The Dental Board decision put more teeth into the "active state supervision" requirement by rejecting the claim that mere designation of a regulatory board as a "state agency" was sufficient to meet the "active supervision" requirement for purposes of the federal antitrust laws (albeit, a regulatory board may be a state agency for other purposes). Instead, where a state has "delegated regulatory power" to "active market participants," there is too great a risk that anti-competitive motives will influence resulting policies and practices. To satisfy the "active supervision" requirement in instances where "market participants" play such an active role, it is essential that there be substantive (not just procedural) review of the regulatory board's decisions, the supervisor must have power to modify or veto such decisions, and the supervisor itself may not be an active market participant.

States have scrambled to review their regulatory board structures since the *North Carolina Dental Board* decision and have considered a variety of responses. One particularly convincing approach to the decision was offered in an opinion by the California Attorney General. See 98 Ops. Cal. Atty. Gen. 12 (Sept. 10, 2015). That opinion emphasized that all types of regulatory board decisions are not necessarily equally affected by the Supreme Court decision. For example, decisions that place boundaries around certain types of occupational practice and thus shape competitive markets are more clearly within the *Dental Board* area of concern than those involving discipline of licensed practitioners (where court proceedings or other forms of appeal provide due process protections and risks of anti-competitive behavior are not as high). The Federal Trade Commission has also offered guidance on its intended interpretation of the decision. https://www.ftc.gov/policy/advocacy/advocacy-filings/2019/11/ftc-staff-comment-north-carolina-state-board-dental.

For scholarly analysis of the *North Carolina Dental Board* decision, see Allensworth, *Foxes at the Henhouse: Occupational Licensing Boards Up Close*, 105 Calif. L. Rev. 1567 (2017) (considering the dynamics of occupational licensing boards and the implications of occupational licensing in raising consumer prices, potentially adversely affecting service quality, and curtailing worker access; exploring the significance of *North Carolina State Board of Dental Examiners v. FTC*, and recommending board reforms to address antitrust and occupational licensing concerns); Walker, *Cavity Filling or Root Canal? How Courts Should Apply North Carolina State Board of Dental Examiners v. FTC*, 66 Emory L.J. 443 (2017) (calling for narrow construction of the decision); Roea, *Licensing Liability: Responding to Judicial Expansion of Antitrust Enforcement in North Carolina Dental*, 103 Minn. L. Rev. 425 (2018) (considering personal liability risk for members of occupational licensing boards in wake of *North Carolina Dental,* and related need for legislative responses). See also Edlin & Haw [Allensworth], *Cartels by Another Name: Should Licensed Occupations Face Antitrust Scrutiny?,* 162 U. Pa. L. Rev. 1093 (2014) (demonstrating how licensing boards can raise prices and arguing, prior to *North Carolina Dental Board* decision, than occupational licensing should be subject to antitrust review).

In the meantime, there have been a number of legal challenges against licensing regulations brought on antitrust grounds. See, e.g., *Teladoc, Inc. v. Texas Medical Board*, 112 F. Supp. 3d 529 (W.D. Tex. 2015). This decision involved a challenge to Texas regulations requiring doctors to first undertake an in-person ("face-to-face") examination before providing other medical services such as prescribing drugs, and thus limiting the scope of "telemedicine." The challengers to the regulation wanted to allow licensed physicians in Texas and elsewhere to provide prescriptions after reviewing medical records and talking with the patient by phone, and based their challenge to the rules on antitrust grounds and Commerce Clause claims. The trial court held that the Medical Board had the burden of showing that it could sustain a claim of immunity based on the *Parker* doctrine. The Medical Board was largely composed of "market participants." While its actions could be reviewed by the state office of administrative hearings, in the courts, and by the state legislature through a "sunset" review, none of these forms of review satisfied the "active supervision" requirements. For subsequent developments, see Wortham, *2017 Legislation Expands Telemedicine Opportunities in Texas and Ends Teladoc Dispute*, 10 Health Care Compliance No. 4 (2018): 59–62 (discussing Texas legislation allowing virtual telemedicine relationship relevant standard of care).

B. In Major Policy Decisions

[1] Reapportionment and Voting Rights

Problem 9-3

Metro City is the largest municipality in and the capital of State of Western Carolina (a large southern state). Metro City is surrounded by four suburbs of varying size. Urban County (which includes the City and its suburbs as well as more rural surrounding areas) has therefore grown significantly since the last decennial census. The metropolitan area as a whole is now among the top 20 fastest growing metropolitan areas in the country. There are several reasons for this substantial growth. Metro City's economy has remained solid notwithstanding the recent recession because it is the home of a substantial federal military base, the state capital, two large universities, and many businesses that have located there to tap the area's highly educated workforce. In addition, Urban County's favorable climate, high quality health care, and growing number of retirement communities have drawn retirees from other parts of the country.

Metro City is governed by a strong mayor, elected at large, and eight council members elected by districts. Its suburbs each have seven-member city councils, operating within council-manager forms of government, with the mayor and all council members elected at large. Urban County is governed by five elected County Commissioners, each elected from a designated district. The Urban County School District includes all parts of the County (Metro City, its suburbs, and more rural surrounding areas) and is governed by a seven-member School Board elected in districts. Currently those districts are composed so that Metro City constitutes one district (with two School Board members elected by its electorate from candidates who reside within the city limits). Each of the four suburbs constitutes a separate district (with one member of the Board residing in and elected by that suburb's voters). The rural area surrounding Metro City and its suburbs elects one school board member residing therein.

Metro City, its suburbs, Urban County and the Urban County School Board have each received data from the most recent decennial census. It is apparent that there have been shifts in population such that the districts previously used by Metro City, Urban County, and the Urban County School Board are out of balance within their respective districts. Moreover, some of the suburbs have grown substantially while others have stayed relatively the same since they were fully-developed some time ago.

(a) Will the governments that have previously relied on districts to apportion seats on their governing boards need to engage in redistricting? What legal principles will guide them?

(b) Some constituents living in the suburbs have been arguing that those governments should also adopt districting schemes, rather than continuing to elect their council members at large. What legal considerations, if any, might affect such decisions?

(c) The School Board has recognized that the schools are bursting at the seams and that significant and expensive new construction will be needed to provide adequate facilities. If the Urban County Board of Commissioners agrees that there is such a need, how might a bond referendum to raise construction funds be structured? Must non-resident property owners be given a vote along with property owners and non-property owning residents in the County?

(d) The state annexation law presently requires an affirmative vote for annexation only in the annexing city. Are there any constitutional problems with the statute?

(e) There are several special districts in the county providing water, fire, and sewer services. How should voting opportunities in these districts be provided?

No area of the law in recent history has brought the courts into a more direct supervisory role over states and local governments than that of voting rights. At least since the Supreme Court's reapportionment decisions in the early 1960s, there has been an explosion of litigation challenging not only the validity of representative districts but also the voting patterns established by states and local governments for a wide array of other activities in which they engage. The developments in this area are by no means settled or complete. The materials that follow will, however, illustrate how the courts have been drawn into the voting rights issues and how they have responded.

We begin with the principles laid down in the reapportionment[5] cases and then trace the courts' attempts to apply them to the local level of government where the tremendous variety in form and function makes those principles not easily applicable. We then examine the question of who is entitled to vote on uniquely local issues such as annexation and conclude with a note on the federal Voting Rights Act.

The voting rights issue arises in a number of very important contexts in state and local government. Elections called to secure voter approval of bond issues or tax increases are an important example. The issue here is who is entitled to vote. The voting rights issue also affects the composition of government bodies, including

---

5. "*Apportionment* is the distribution of legislative seats among previously defined territorial or other units entitled to representation while *districting* establishes the precise geographical boundaries of a territorial constituency." Silva, *The Population Base for Apportionment of the New York Legislature*, 32 FORDHAM L. REV. 1, 3 (1963). The term "reapportionment" has, since *Baker v. Carr*, 369 U.S. 186 (1962), become widely used to embrace either or both parts of the process, and will be so used here.

which bodies, in addition to the legislative body must be elected, whether voting for these bodies can be weighted, and if so, how. Voting rights issues also arise in annexations, consolidations and other governmental organization proceedings. These are only some of the most obvious examples. As you study these materials, contrast the degree to which courts are willing or unwilling to review substantive issues arising in these situations with their willingness to ensure that these issues are decided in a constitutionally fair electoral process.

[a] The One Person-One Vote Principle in Legislative Apportionment

Legislative apportionment

When the Supreme Court decided *Baker v. Carr* in 1962 (369 U.S. 186), it authorized federal court intervention in matters of legislative apportionment for the first time. *Baker v. Carr* was the culmination of a long and tortuous history of attempts in federal and state courts to obtain judicial review of malapportioned congressional and state legislative districts. The Court itself had slammed the door on such attempts sixteen years earlier when Justice Frankfurter, in refusing review of unequal congressional districts in Illinois, had admonished that "[c]ourts ought not to enter this political thicket." *Colegrove v. Green*, 328 U.S. 549, 556 (1946). But in *Baker v. Carr* the Court put aside Justice Frankfurter's warning and marched full speed ahead into the political thicket, holding that a Fourteenth Amendment equal protection challenge to state legislative districting was clearly within the subject matter jurisdiction of the federal courts, and that it was not a nonjusticiable political question. For a symposium reflecting on *Baker* 50 years after the decision, see Entin, *Introduction*, 62 Case W. Res. L. Rev. 941 (2012), Lund, *From Baker v. Carr to Bush v. Gore*, 62 Case W. Res. L. Rev. 947 (2012), and Brunell, *The One Person, One Vote Standard in Redistricting: The Uses and Abuses of Population Deviations in Legislative Redistricting*, 62 Case W. Res. L. Rev. 1057 (2012). For articles discussing the history of the one person-one vote principal and offering interesting perspectives on older cases, see Charles & Fuentes-Rohwer, *Reynolds Reconsidered*, 87 Ala. L. Rev. 485 (2015) (discussing historical context for early decisions); Muller, *Perpetuating "One Person, One Vote" Errors*, 39 Harv. J.L. & Pub. Pol'y 371 (2016) (using archival information to trace evolution of Supreme Court doctrine from sweeping propositions toward greater restraint); Sachia, *Excising Federalism: The Consequences of Baker v. Carr Beyond the Electoral Arena*, 101 Va. L. Rev. 2263 (2015) (discussing political question doctrine and related issues).

Two years after the Supreme Court opened the door to federal court supervision, it announced the standards by which state legislative districting would be tested. In *Reynolds v. Sims*, 377 U.S. 533 (1964), the Court stated:

> We hold that, as a basic constitutional standard, the Equal Protection Clause requires that the seats in both houses of a bicameral state legislature must be apportioned on a population basis. Simply stated, an individual's right

> to vote for state legislators is unconstitutionally impaired when its weight is in a substantial fashion diluted when compared with votes of citizens living in other parts of the State. [*Id.* at 568.]

This was the one man (subsequently, person) one vote standard. In explaining how it arrived there, the Court said:

> The right to vote freely for the candidate of one's choice is of the essence of a democratic society, and any restrictions on that right strike at the heart of representative government. And the right of suffrage can be denied by a debasement or dilution of the weight of a citizen's vote just as effectively as by wholly prohibiting the free exercise of the franchise. [*Id.* at 555.]
>
> ... [T]he fundamental principle of representative government in this country is one of equal representation for equal numbers of people, without regard to race, sex, economic status, or place of residence within a State. [*Id.* at 560–61.]
>
> Legislators represent people, not trees or acres. Legislators are elected by voters, not farms or cities or economic interests. As long as ours is a representative form of government, and our legislatures are those instruments of government elected directly by and directly representative of the people, the right to elect legislators in a free and unimpaired fashion is bedrock of our political system. It could hardly be gainsaid that a constitutional claim had been asserted by an allegation that certain otherwise qualified voters had been entirely prohibited from voting for members of their state legislature. And, if a State should provide that the votes of citizens in one part of the State should be given two times, or five times, or 10 times the weight of votes of citizens in another part of the State, it could hardly be contended that the right to vote of those residing in the disfavored areas had not been effectively diluted. [*Id.* at 562.]

The one person-one vote mandate did thrust courts into the political thicket which has grown denser in the intervening years.

At an early stage, the Supreme Court identified a different standard for congressional as distinguished from state or local legislative districts. Congressional districting is governed by Article I, § 2 of the Constitution, which requires that representatives in Congress be chosen "by the People of the several States," and that means that "as nearly as is practicable one man's vote in a congressional election is to be worth as much as another's." *Wesberry v. Sanders*, 376 U.S. 1, 7–8 (1964). The Court has imposed a strict standard of mathematical equality to congressional districts. *Karcher v. Daggett*, 462 U.S. 725 (1983), in which the Court invalidated a deviation of 0.7 percent. The states apparently got the Court's message.

With respect to state legislative districts, the Court has been more flexible in applying the Fourteenth Amendment requirement of one person-one vote. In *Reynolds v.*

Sims it had acknowledged that "[m]athematical exactness or precision is hardly a workable constitutional requirement" (377 U.S. at 577); and it vowed an intent to permit consideration of additional factors, especially the integrity of political subdivisions, so long as the population disparities "are based on legitimate considerations incident to the effectuation of a rational state policy." 377 U.S. at 579. The Court reaffirmed that position in *Voinovich v. Quilter*, 507 U.S. 146 (1993). A series of Supreme Court decisions had established a three-step guideline for state legislative districts. A maximum population deviation of under 10% is prima facie valid, and the states strive, usually successfully, to stay within that yardstick. A deviation between 10% and 16.4% creates a prima facie case of discrimination and must be justified by the state—but can be justified by the objective of preserving the integrity of political subdivision lines. A deviation in excess of 16.4% is virtually indefensible. See, e.g., *Mahan v. Howell*, 410 U.S. 315 (1973); *Brown v. Thomson*, 462 U.S. 835 (1983). Some doubt was cast on the "safe harbor" of below 10% deviation in a decision invalidating the Georgia Senate and House state districts which had population deviations of 9.98%. The district court invalidated the districts, *Larios v. Cox*, 300 F. Supp. 2d 1320 (N.D. Ga. 2004), and the Supreme Court affirmed without opinion, *Cox v. Larios*, 542 U.S. 947 (2004). In a concurring opinion, Justice Stevens noted that the disparities were not motivated by the desire to observe compactness or contiguity or to maintain county boundaries but rather by impermissible partisan gerrymandering. In this light Justice Stevens believed that the districting plan failed to meet the prima facie test. Justice Scalia dissented. Senate districts which strayed slightly over the 10% guideline were upheld on the ground that the legislature had done a good job of balancing competing goals, *Deem v. Manchin*, 188 F. Supp. 2d 651 (N.D.W. Va. 2002), *aff'd sub nom. Unger v. Manchin*, 536 U.S. 935 (2002).

Because one person-one vote has been the law of the land for some decades now, it is easy to forget the dramatic impact it had. Legally, it thrust courts, federal and state, into the political thicket of passing on and in some cases even drawing legislative maps. Politically, it resulted in a shift in power in almost every state legislative body from rural to urban and suburban. That, in turn, has affected the work product of state legislatures, although that effect is not easily measured. See, e.g., Hanson & Crew, *The Policy Impact of Reapportionment*, 8 L. & Soc'y Rev. 69 (1973). For an analysis of shifts from rural to urban power and beyond, see Altman & McDonald, *A Half-Century of Virginia Redistricting Battles: Shifting from Rural Malapportionment to Voting Rights to Public Participation*, 47 U. Rich. L. Rev. 771 (2013) (discussing Virginia's experience and possible implications of use of redistricting commissions). Subsequent commentators on developments since *Baker* have also stressed other underappreciated but fundamental changes that have resulted. See, e.g., Manheim, *Redistricting Litigation and the Delegation of Democratic Design*, 93 B.U. L. Rev. 563 (2013) (considering the role and power of litigants who bring redistricting suits, and suggesting the need for institutional adjustments that would give more power to nonlitigants).

Political gerrymandering

In the last quarter-century, waves of litigation have challenged Congressional and state legislative districting on grounds of political gerrymandering. In *Davis v. Bandemer,* 478 U.S. 109 (1986), the Supreme Court considered Indiana redistricting that sought to preserve legislative majorities by employing a mix of single-member, double-member, and triple-member districts. A plurality of the divided Court found justiciable equal protection questions, but stated that establishing a claim for relief would require proof of both intent to engage in political gerrymandering and impact that resulted in essentially shutting out the opposing party.

The Court considered additional cases but found difficulty in developing a feasible standard for review. See *Vieth v. Jubelirer,* 541 U.S. 267 (2004) (upholding in split decision conclusion that congressional redistricting did not violate Constitution in absence of judicially discernible and manageable standard to review political gerrymandering, with Justice Kennedy concurring only in the judgment); *League of United Latin American Citizens v. Perry,* 548 U.S. 399 (2006) (in highly fractured decision, holding that mid-decade redistricting by Texas legislature did not give rise to reliable standard to govern constitutionally suspect political gerrymanders, but did constitute violation of § 2 of the Voting Rights Act).

Opponents of alleged gerrymandering developed novel strategies to challenge resulting "cracking" (dividing minority party voters among districts rather than allowing them to reside in districts where they might successfully elect representatives of their party) and "packing" (concentrating minority party voters within particular districts so that they had a strong majority rather than distributing them among a number of other districts in which they might influence outcomes). They also asserted First Amendment rights to association and free speech, rather than only relying on equal protection grounds. For a discussion of analysis tied to the right of association, see Tokaji, *Gerrymandering and Association*, 59 Wm. & Mary L. Rev. 2159 (2018).

Among the strategies used was the development of sophisticated social science analysis that considered such issues as demonstrating that highly partisan gerrymandering of districts was marked by demonstrable "efficiency gaps" (that is, the difference between parties' respected wasted votes in an election, divided by the total number of votes cast). For a discussion of the "efficiency gap," see Finneran & Luther, *Filling the Gap in the Efficiency Gap: Measuring Partisan Gerrymandering on a Per-District Basis,* 46 Hastings Const. L.Q. 385 (2019) (discussing efficiency gap in connection with *Gill* litigation including the Supreme Court's decision in *Gill*).

The Supreme Court then issued two important decisions that put challengers' hopes to rest. In *Gill v. Whitford,* 138 S. Ct. 1916 (2018), the Court further narrowed the door on political gerrymandering challenges by limiting those with standing. Plaintiffs alleged that Wisconsin's Republican legislature had engaged in "packing" and "cracking," claiming resulting violations in First Amendment rights of association and speech as well as equal protection. Plaintiffs also introduced social science evidence showing significant "efficiency gaps" had resulted from the redistricting plan. The Supreme Court rejected plaintiffs' claims of standing based on their allegation of statewide impairment of their representation in the state legislature, and concluded that such claims did not give rise to Article III standing. The Court then remanded for further proceedings to determine whether standing could be demonstrated by plaintiffs assigned to particular districts.

Subsequently, in a case arising from North Carolina, the Court in a 5-4 decision, concluded that partisan gerrymandering claims were not justiciable and instead raised political questions. See *Rucho v. Common Cause,* 139 S. Ct. 2484 (2019). The Court rejected the proposition that groups with a particular level of political support should enjoy a commensurate level of political power and influence, and found no basis in the Constitution for the view that proportional representation at the state level based on state-wide support should be guaranteed in the composition of the legislature. See Note, *Article III—Justiciability—Political Question Doctrine—Rucho v. Common Cause,* 133 HARV. L. REV. 252 (2019). A three-judge state court subsequently applied state law to rule the challenged districts unconstitutional as a matter of state law. See *Common Cause v. Lewis,* No 18CVS 014001, 2019 WL 4569584 (N.C. Super. Sept. 03, 2019).

The Pennsylvania Supreme Court in a 2018 decision relied on the state's "free and equal elections clause" in upholding a challenge to a congressional redistricting plan (concluding that the state's "free and equal elections" and "equal protection" clauses and federal Equal Protection Clause did not require use of the same standard of review, political gerrymandering violated state constitutional provisions, and legislature's inability or choice not to remediate congressional redistrict plan made it the judiciary's role to determinate an appropriate plan).

Independent Redistricting Commissions

A number of states have moved toward bi-partisan or non-partisan redistricting commissions as a means of moving beyond intensifying partisanship and incumbent protection dynamics. For a discussion of the benefits of independent redistricting commissions, see Lowenthal, *The Ills of Gerrymandering and Independent Redistricting Commissions as the Solution,* 56 HARV. J. ON LEGIS. 1 (2019). The National Conference of States Legislatures retains background information on redistricting commissions. See http://www.ncsl.org/research/redistricting.aspx. The United States Supreme Court upheld Arizona's use of an independent congressional redistricting commission created by ballot initiative in the face of a challenge by state legislators, finding that the legislature had standing, state statutes creating redistricting procedures for the commission were permissible, and no violation of the federal Elections Clause occurred. See *Arizona State Legislature v. Arizona Independent Redistricting Commission,* 135 S. Ct. 2652 (2015). See also *Harris v. Arizona Independent Redistricting Commission*, 136 S. Ct. 1301 (2016) (upholding independent redistricting commission's design of state legislative districts where population disparities reflected good faith efforts to comply with federal Voting Rights Act and preclearance requirements).

The Implications of the Decennial Census

Challenges relating to the 2020 Census are already emerging. See *Department of Commerce v. New York*, 139 S. Ct. 2551 (2019) (challenge against use of a citizenship question on 2020 Census, concluding that Enumeration Clause permitted use of citizenship question but that Secretary of Commerce's explanation for including citizenship question did not permit judicial review, resulting in remand). For a broader discussion of issues relating to the 2020 Census, see Levitt, *Citizenship and the Census*, 119 COLUM. L. REV. 1355 (2019).

Population base. In 2016, the Supreme Court resolved a lingering question about what population should be counted for purposes of federal one person-one vote analysis. See *Evenwel v. Abbott*, 136 S. Ct. 1120 (2016) (concluding that state and local jurisdictions could draw legislative districts based on total population, in light of history, precedent and practice; reserving question whether drawing districts based on voter-eligible population rather than total population is permissible). See Persily, *Who Counts for One Person, One Vote?* 50 U.C. DAVIS L. REV. 1395 (2017) (discussing *Evenwel*, observing that no accurate, accepted list enumerating citizens, voters, or eligible voters exists, and arguing that failure to use census data would result in significant problems). See also *Davidson v. City of Cranston, R.I.*, 837 F.3d 135 (1st Cir. 2016) (upholding city's use of US Census data in apportionment of population to municipal ward districts). Ongoing debates relate to how prison populations should be handled, particularly since treating such populations within the rural, conservative locations where many prisons are found means that prison residents cannot be counted toward the population of their home communities that are often situated in urban areas with substantial minority populations, which can therefore lose population for purposes of one person-one vote analysis. See, e.g., Skocpol, *The Emerging Constitutional Law of Prison Gerrymandering*, 69 STAN. L. REV. 1474 (2017); Stachulski, *Prison Gerrymandering: Locking Up Elections and Diluting Representational Equality*, 2019 U. ILL. L. REV. 401 (2019).

The cases that follow consider two major areas of litigation arising from these one person-one vote developments. Subsection (b) addresses the extent to which one person-one vote principles apply to local governments and special districts of various subsection, while subsection (c) probes judicial decisions that have limited the application of the one person-one vote requirement by ruling that it does not apply to one-time local referenda and does not require local jurisdictions to extend the franchise to those within their extraterritorial jurisdictions.

[b] Application of "One Person-One Vote" to Local Governments

While the courts were struggling with the many issues that grew out of one person-one vote, the question arose whether its dictates would apply to local units of government. The answer came in the following case.

Avery v. Midland County

390 U.S. 474 (1968)

MR. JUSTICE WHITE delivered the opinion of the Court.

Petitioner, a taxpayer and voter in Midland County, Texas, sought a determination by this Court that the Texas Supreme Court erred in concluding that selection of the Midland County Commissioners Court from single-member districts of substantially unequal population did not necessarily violate the Fourteenth Amendment. . . . We hold that petitioner, as a resident of Midland County, has a right to a vote for the Commissioners Court of substantially equal weight to the vote of every other resident.

Midland County has a population of about 70,000. The Commissioners Court is composed of five members. One, the County Judge, is elected at large from the entire county, and in practice casts a vote only to break a tie. The other four are Commissioners chosen from districts. The population of those districts, according to the 1963 estimates that were relied upon when this case was tried, was respectively 67,906; 852; 414; and 828. This vast imbalance resulted from placing in a single district virtually the entire city of Midland, Midland County's only urban center, in which 95% of the county's population resides.

The Commissioners Court is assigned by the Texas Constitution and by various statutory enactments with a variety of functions. According to the commentary to Vernon's Texas Statutes, the court:

> is the general governing body of the county. It establishes a courthouse and jail, appoints numerous minor officials such as the county health officer, fills vacancies in the county offices, lets contracts in the name of the county, builds roads and bridges, administers the county's public welfare services, performs numerous duties in regard to elections, sets the county tax rate, issues bonds, adopts the county budget, and serves as a board of equalization for tax assessments.

The court is also authorized, among other responsibilities, to build and run a hospital, an airport, and libraries. It fixes boundaries of school districts within the county, may establish a regional public housing authority, and determines the districts for election of its own members, Tex. Const., Art. V, § 18. . . .

[The Midland County District Court held the apportionment plan unconstitutional, the Texas Court of Civil Appeals reversed the District Court, but the Texas Supreme Court reversed the Court of Civil Appeals. — Eds.]

In *Reynolds v. Sims* [377 U.S. 533 (1964)], the Equal Protection Clause was applied to the apportionment of state legislatures. Every qualified resident, *Reynolds* determined, has the right to a ballot for election of state legislators of equal weight to the vote of every other resident, and that right is infringed when legislators are elected from districts of substantially unequal population. The question now before us is whether the Fourteenth Amendment likewise forbids the election of local government officials from districts of disparate population. As has almost every court which has addressed itself to this question, we hold that it does. . . .

Although the forms and functions of local government and the relationships among the various units are matters of state concern, it is now beyond question that a state's political subdivisions must comply with the Fourteenth Amendment. The actions of local government *are* the actions of the State. . . .

When the State apportions its legislature, it must have due regard for the Equal Protection Clause. Similarly, when the State delegates lawmaking power to local government and provides for the election of local officials from districts specified by statute, ordinance, or local charter, it must insure that those qualified to vote have the right to an equally effective voice in the election process. If voters residing in oversize districts are denied their constitutional right to participate in the election of state legislators, precisely the same kind of deprivation occurs when the members of a city council, school board, or county governing board are elected from districts of substantially unequal population. If the five senators representing a city in the state legislature may not be elected from districts ranging in size from 50,000 to 500,000, neither is it permissible to elect the members of the city council from those same districts. In either case, the votes of some residents have greater weight than those of others; in both cases the equal protection of the laws has been denied.

That the state legislature may itself be properly apportioned does not exempt subdivisions from the Fourteenth Amendment. While state legislatures exercise extensive power over their constituents and over the various units of local government, the States universally leave much policy and decision making to their governmental subdivisions. Legislators enact many laws but do not attempt to reach those countless matters of local concern necessarily left wholly or partly to those who govern at the local level. What is more, in providing for the governments of their cities, counties, towns, and districts, the States characteristically provide for representative government—for decision making at the local level by representatives elected by the people. And, not infrequently, the delegation of power to local units is contained in constitutional provisions for local home rule which are immune from legislative interference. In a word, institutions of local government have always been a major aspect of our system, and their responsible and responsive operation is today of increasing importance to the quality of life of more and more of our citizens. We therefore see little difference, in terms of the application of the Equal Protection Clause and of the principles of *Reynolds v. Sims*, between the exercise of state power through legislatures and its exercise by elected officials in the cities, towns, and counties.

We are urged to permit unequal districts for the Midland County Commissioners Court on the ground that the court's functions are not sufficiently "legislative." The parties have devoted much effort to urging that alternative labels—"administrative" versus "legislative"—be applied to the Commissioners Court. As the brief description of the court's functions above amply demonstrates, this unit of local government cannot easily be classified in the neat categories favored by civics texts.

The Texas commissioners courts are assigned some tasks which would normally be thought of as "legislative," others typically assigned to "executive" or "administrative" departments, and still others which are "judicial." In this regard Midland County's Commissioners Court is representative of most of the general governing bodies of American cities, counties, towns, and villages.[7]

One knowledgeable commentator has written of "the states' varied, pragmatic approach in establishing governments." (R. Wood, In Politics and Government in the United States) 891–892 (A. Westin ed. 1965). That approach has produced a staggering number of governmental units—the preliminary calculation by the Bureau of the Census for 1967 is that there are 81,304 "units of government" in the United States—and an even more staggering diversity. Nonetheless, while special-purpose organizations abound and in many States the allocation of functions among units results in instances of overlap and vacuum, virtually every American lives within what he and his neighbors regard as a unit of local government with general responsibility and power for local affairs. In many cases citizens reside within and are subject to two such governments, a city and a county.

The Midland County Commissioners Court is such a unit. While the Texas Supreme Court found that the Commissioners Court's legislative functions are "negligible," the court does have power to make a large number of decisions having a broad range of impacts on all the citizens of the county. It sets a tax rate, equalizes assessments, and issues bonds. It then prepares and adopts a budget for allocating the county's funds, and is given by statute a wide range of discretion in choosing the subjects on which to spend. In adopting the budget the court makes both long-term judgments about the way Midland County should develop—whether industry should be solicited, roads improved, recreation facilities built, and land set aside for schools—and immediate choices among competing needs.

The Texas Supreme Court concluded that the work actually done by the Commissioners Court "disproportionately concern[s] the rural areas." Were the Commissioners Court a special-purpose unit of government assigned the performance of functions affecting definable groups of constituents more than other constituents, we would have to confront the question whether such a body may be apportioned in ways which give greater influence to the citizens most affected by the organization's functions. That question, however, is not presented by this case, for while Midland County authorities may concentrate their attention on rural roads, the relevant fact is that the powers of the Commissioners Court include the authority to make a

7. Midland County is apparently untypical in choosing the members of its local governing body from districts. "On the basis of available figures, coupled with rough estimates from samplings made of the situations in various States, it appears that only about 25 percent of . . . local government governing boards are elected, in whole or in part, from districts or, while at large, under schemes including district residence requirements." Brief for the United States as Amicus Curiae 22, n. 31, filed in *Sailors v. Board of Education*, 387 U.S. 105 (1967), and the other 1966 Term local reapportionment cases.

substantial number of decisions that affect all citizens, whether they reside inside or outside the city limits of Midland. The Commissioners maintain buildings, administer welfare services, and determine school districts both inside and outside the city. The taxes imposed by the court fall equally on all property in the county. Indeed, it may not be mere coincidence that a body apportioned with three of its four voting members chosen by residents of the rural area surrounding the city devotes most of its attention to the problems of that area, while paying for its expenditures with a tax imposed equally on city residents and those who live outside the city. And we might point out that a decision not to exercise a function within the court's power—a decision, for example, not to build an airport or a library, or not to participate in the federal food stamp program—is just as much a decision affecting all citizens of the county as an affirmative decision.

The Equal Protection Clause does not, of course, require that the State never distinguish between citizens, but only that the distinctions that are made not be arbitrary or invidious. The conclusion of *Reynolds v. Sims* was that bases other than population were not acceptable grounds for distinguishing among citizens when determining the size of districts used to elect members of state legislatures. We hold today only that the Constitution permits no substantial variation from equal population in drawing districts for units of local government having general governmental powers over the entire geographic area served by the body.

This Court is aware of the immense pressures facing units of local government, and of the greatly varying problems with which they must deal. The Constitution does not require that a uniform straitjacket bind citizens in devising mechanisms of local government suitable for local needs and efficient in solving local problems. Last Term, for example, the Court upheld a procedure for choosing a school board that placed the selection with school boards of component districts even though the component boards had equal votes and served unequal populations. *Sailors v. Board of Education*, 387 U.S. 105 (1967). The Court rested on the administrative nature of the area school board's functions and the essentially appointive form of the scheme employed. In *Dusch v. Davis*, 387 U.S. 112 (1967), the Court permitted Virginia Beach to choose its legislative body by a scheme that included at-large voting for candidates, some of whom had to be residents of particular districts, even though the residence districts varied widely in population.

The *Sailors* and *Dusch* cases demonstrate that the Constitution and this Court are not roadblocks in the path of innovation, experiment, and development among units of local government. We will not bar what Professor Wood has called "the emergence of a new ideology and structure of public bodies, equipped with new capacities and motivations. . . ." R. Wood, 1400 Governments, at 175 (1961). Our decision today is only that the Constitution imposes one ground rule for the development of arrangements of local government: a requirement that units with general governmental powers over an entire geographic area not be apportioned among single-member districts of substantially unequal population.

The judgment below is vacated and the case is remanded for disposition not inconsistent with this opinion.

[The Court's decision was 5-3. Of the dissenting justices, only Justice Harlan would decline to extend one person-one vote to local governments at all. Among other things, his concern was that the majority decision would inhibit the formation of metropolitan governments.—Eds.]

Notes and Questions

1. *Key principles.* In *Avery*, the Court concluded that the one person-one vote principle applies not only to state and federal governments, but also to at least some local governmental entities such as the county commissioners court in Midland County. What was the basis for the Court's conclusion? The Court emphasized that its conclusion was rooted in the characteristics of the commissioners court, including the selection process for commissioners (election) and their specific responsibilities (general governmental responsibilities over an entire area, including important legislative and policy-making roles). Why are these characteristics important to the Court's conclusion?

2. *School boards.* Local school boards are often elected but are sometimes appointed. They have responsibility for educational oversight, a function that is important to a broad local community, but their responsibilities are not as broad-ranging as those of the county commissioners in *Avery.* Should school boards be subject to one-person-one-vote requirements? Two leading Supreme Court decisions give guidance on this point.

In *Sailors v. Board of Education*, 387 U.S. 105 (1967), a case that arose prior to *Avery*, the Court addressed the analysis appropriate when a local government board is appointed rather than elected. *Sailors* involved a claim that a county board of education was unconstitutionally constituted. The members of the county board were not elected by popular vote, but by delegates from local school boards, who were popularly elected. The Court found no constitutional violation:

> We find no constitutional reason why state or local officers of the nonlegislative character involved here may not be chosen by the governor, by the legislature, or by some other appointive means rather than by an election. [*Id.* at 108.]

The Court reserved the question whether a State might appoint rather than elect a local legislative body with more wide-ranging responsibilities. *Id.* at 109.

Shortly after *Avery*, the Court confronted a second case involving a governing board elected to oversee a local junior college district. See *Hadley v. Junior College Dist.*, 397 U.S. 50 (1970). The metropolitan Kansas City junior college district was formed by the consolidation of eight separate school districts following referendum approval. One of the districts, Kansas City, contained approximately 60% of the school age population but under the statutory formula was entitled to elect only three of the six trustees (50%). Residents of the Kansas City school district claimed that the apportionment violated their Fourteenth Amendment rights under *Avery.* The Court concluded that the board's powers included "important governmental functions" which were general enough and had "sufficient impact" to justify application of the *Avery* principle. The purpose of the election was not controlling since, in the Court's view, "[i]f one person's vote is given less weight through unequal apportionment, his right to equal voting participation is impaired just as much when he votes for a school board member as when he votes for a state legislator." 397 U.S. at 55. Finally, the Court rejected the argument that apportionment should turn on the distinction between elections for legislative officials and administrative officers. Such a distinction was not judicially manageable. *Id.* at 56.

Do you think the distinctions drawn between appointed and elected boards in these two cases are appropriate? Do the Court's decisions create an incentive to establish local boards by appointment rather than election? Is that a good or bad result? Consider, for example, *Mixon v. Ohio*, 193 F.3d 389 (6th Cir. 1999), which considered a state statute restructuring the Cleveland school board, which covered Cleveland and four suburban areas. The new board was appointed by the mayor of the largest municipality within the district, and replaced a previously elected board. The statute authorized the mayor of the largest municipality within the school district (Cleveland) to appoint all nine members of the board from a list of eighteen nominees. In response to the equal protection challenge, the court held that an appointive system is acceptable for non-legislative offices, and, relying on *Sailors*, said there is no fundamental right to an elected school board. The advantages of an appointed school board in a troubled school district satisfied the rational relation test. The court also rejected a separate contention by residents of the suburban areas that they were denied one person-one vote because they could not vote for the mayor who appointed their school board.

Voters have also challenged the composition of the Chicago school board in federal court, claiming that under the Voting Rights Act, discussed below, the board should have been elected rather than appointed by the mayor. The Seventh Circuit concluded that the board could be appointed, and upheld the mayor's appointment authority as authorized under state legislation and consistent with the Equal Protection Clause. See *Quinn v. State of Illinois,* 887 F.3d 322 (7th Cir. 2018). City residents including parents, grandparents, property owners and current and former members of city school councils also sought relief in state court. See *Quinn v. Board of Education of City of Chicago*, 105 N.E.3d 106 (Ill. App. 2018). There, plaintiffs contended that the system by which the mayor appointed school board members violated the state constitution by denying them the right to vote, denying them due process, and subjecting them to taxation to support the schools without approval of elected representatives. The state appellate court found that the rational basis standard should apply, since no fundamental right was implicated, the statute allowing appointment to school board positions was rationally related to legitimate legislative purposes, did not violate the state constitution's guarantee of free and equal elections, and did not violate due process by the taxing power accorded the board.

An Ohio state court subsequently extended *Sailors*, applying a rational relation standard to hold that "the fundamental right to vote is not implicated by statutes that create an appointed commission to oversee an elected board of education's finances in a fiscally distressed district." *Barnesville Education Assn. v. Barnesville Exempted Village Sch. Dist. Bd. of Education*, 2007-Ohio-1109, 2007 WL 745095 (Ohio App. March 6, 2007). Similar questions have been raised in connection with litigation relating to the state's appointment of an emergency manager and the interrelated Flint, Michigan water crisis. See *Phillips v. Snyder*, 836 F.3d 707 (6th Cir. 2016) (rejecting claims by voters and local elected officials where local voters did not have a substantive due process right to vote for those exercising legislative power at the local level, Equal Protection Clause had not been violated, and § 2 of the Voting Rights Act did not provide relief).

3. *Judicial selection.* Should elections of state judges be subject to the one person-one vote principle? See *Wells v. Edwards*, 409 U.S. 1095 (1973), in which the Court affirmed, without opinion but with three dissents, a district court decision holding that one person-one vote does not apply to the elections of state supreme court judges. This position was reaffirmed in a later decision which nevertheless held that § 2 of the Voting Rights Act does apply to judicial elections. *Chisom v. Roemer*, 501 U.S. 380 (1991). See also *Alabama State Conference of NAACP v. State* (M.D. Ala. 2017) (in Voting Rights Act challenge to Alabama's at-large appellate judge election system, refusing to dismiss in face of plausible standing and need to develop record); *Terrebone Parish Branch NAACP v. Jindal*, 274 F. Supp. 3d 395 (M.D. La. 2017) (in suit claiming Louisiana's at-large voting system for election of state court judges in one district diluted voting rights of black voters violated the Voting Rights Act, Fourteenth and Fifteen Amendments, finding violations of the Voting Rights Act and racial discriminatory purpose in violation of the Voting Rights Act and constitutional provisions). Adopting a different approach to the election of judges, the North Carolina Supreme Court set aside its usual "lockstep" interpretation of equal protection and held that the state constitution's equal protection clause requires "population proportionality in the districts drawn for the election of superior court judges." *Blankenship v. Bartlett*, 681 S.E.2d 759 (N.C. 2009). The court determined, however, that the role of judges is not the same as that of legislative or executive officers and that it was more appropriate to apply intermediate scrutiny than strict scrutiny.

What is the appropriate analysis when merit selection panels used to screen and designate preferred judicial candidates are composed of and elected only by members of the bar? See *Carlson v. Wiggins*, 675 F.3d 1134 (8th Cir. 2012) (upholding Iowa's judicial merit selection system using rational basis standard where election of selection board was an election of special interest and where merit selection process was rationally related to state's legitimate interests); *Dool v. Burke*, 497 Fed. Appx.

782 (10th Cir. 2012) (upholding Kansas judicial selection system, applying rational basis not strict scrutiny analysis, and concluding that one person-one vote analysis did not apply); Lund, *May Lawyers Be Given the Power to Elect Those Who Choose Our Judges? "Merit Selection" and Constitutional Law*, 34 Harv. J.L. & Pub. Pol'y 1043 (2011) (discussing issues raised by *Dool* case). See also Gaylord, *Section 2 Challenges to Appellate Court Elections: Federalism, Linkage, and Judicial Independence*, 69 Case W. Res. L. Rev. 117 (2018) (focusing on implications of the Voting Rights Act on judicial elections).

4. *Population disparity in local districts.* How precisely must apportionment decisions track the calculation of one-person-one-vote under *Reynolds* when establishing apportionment strategies for state and local government districts? In the leading case of *Abate v. Mundt*, 403 U.S. 182 (1971), the Court upheld a county board apportionment with a deviation of 11.9%, in part because of an absence of built-in bias, in part because of the longstanding interrelationship between the New York county involved and its constituent towns. Reaffirming the principles established by *Abate*, a court later invalidated another New York county's weighted voting system which resulted in a deviation of 156%. *Jackson v. Nassau County Bd. of Supervisors*, 818 F. Supp. 509 (E.D.N.Y. 1993). See also *Navajo Nation v. San Juan County*, 929 F.3d 1270 (10th Cir. 2019) (in challenge by Native American tribe and tribal members who alleged that county commission and school board districts within the county violated Equal Protection Clause, finding that community commission districts were invalidly based on race, deviation of 38% among school districts violated one person-one vote equal protection requirements, and race-based boundaries were not adequately tailored to a compelling interest and thus violated the Voting Rights Act).

Courts reviewing local government apportionment plans most often invoke the 10% prima facie guideline applied by the Supreme Court to state legislative districts—although *Abate* would seem to allow a little more leeway for local government population disparities. See, e.g., *Braun v. Borough*, 193 P.3d 719 (Alaska 2008). However, a state can apply a stricter one person-one vote standard than the Fourteenth Amendment requires if it elects to do so. In Minnesota, for example, a maximum 10% population deviation was included in the state statute governing redistricting of counties; but the court invalidated a county redistricting which was under 10% because the board had not adequately explained why it had not chosen a plan with "more nearly equal" districts. *Fay v. St. Louis County Bd. of Comm'rs*, 674 N.W.2d 433 (Minn. App. 2004).

In *Avery* the Court left open the question of whether one person-one vote would apply to a special purpose unit of government with functions "affecting definable groups of constituents more than other constituents" (390 U.S. at 484). That question was addressed in the following case.

Salyer Land Co. v. Tulare Lake Basin Water Storage District

410 U.S. 719 (1973)

Mr. Justice Rehnquist delivered the opinion of the Court. . . .

[The Court considered the constitutionality of voting qualifications for the board of directors of a California water storage district. The Court first described the importance to California, as well as other western states, of obtaining and controlling an adequate water supply for agriculture and other uses. To respond to this need, state and federal resources were utilized to construct major dams; but for less costly projects, the California legislature authorized the creation of a number of local instrumentalities, including water storage districts.]

Appellee district consists of 193,000 acres of intensively cultivated, highly fertile farm land located in the Tulare Lake Basin. Its population consists of 77 persons, including 18 children, most of whom are employees of one or another of the four corporations that farm 85% of the land in the district.

Such districts are authorized to plan projects and execute approved projects "for the acquisition, appropriation, diversion, storage, conservation, and distribution of water. . . ." Calif. Water Code § 42200 et seq. Incidental to this general power, districts may "acquire, improve, and operate" any necessary works for the storage and distribution of water as well as any drainage or reclamation works connected therewith, and the generation and distribution of hydroelectric power may be provided for.[4]

They may fix tolls and charges for the use of water and collect them from all persons receiving the benefit of the water or other services in proportion to the services rendered. The costs of the projects are assessed against district land in accordance with the benefits accruing to each tract held in separate ownership. And land that is not benefited may be withdrawn from the district on petition.

Governance of the districts is undertaken by a board of directors. Each director is elected from one of the divisions within the district. General elections for the directors are to be held in odd-numbered years.

It is the voter qualification for such elections that appellants claim invidiously discriminates against them and persons similarly situated. Appellants are landowners, a landowner-lessee, and residents within the area included in the appellee's water storage district. They brought this action under 42 U.S.C. § 1983, seeking declaratory and injunctive relief in an effort to prevent appellee from giving effect to certain provisions of the California Water Code. They allege that §§ 41000 and 41001 unconstitutionally deny to them the equal protection of the laws guaranteed by the Fourteenth Amendment, in that only landowners are permitted to vote in

---

4. There is no evidence that the appellee district engages in the generation, sale, or distribution of hydroelectric power.

water storage district general elections, and votes in those elections are apportioned according to the assessed valuation of the land. [A majority of a three-judge district court upheld the statute.] . . .

I

It is first argued that § 41000, limiting the vote to district landowners, is unconstitutional since nonlandowning residents have as much interest in the operations of a district as landowners who may or may not be residents. Particularly, it is pointed out that the homes of residents may be damaged by floods within the district's boundaries, and that floods may, as with appellant Ellison, cause them to lose their jobs. Support for this position is said to come from the recent decisions of this Court striking down various state laws that limited voting to landowners, *Phoenix v. Kolodziejski*, 399 U.S. 204 (1970), *Cipriano v. City of Houma*, 395 U.S. 701 (1969), and *Kramer v. Union School District*, 395 U.S. 621 (1969).

In *Kramer*, the Court was confronted with a voter qualification statute for school district elections that limited the vote to otherwise qualified district residents who were either (1) the owners or lessees of taxable real property located within the district, (2) spouses of persons owning qualifying property, or (3) parents or guardians of children enrolled for a specified time during the preceding year in a local district school.*

Without reaching the issue of whether or not a State may in some circumstances limit the exercise of the franchise to those primarily interested or primarily affected by a given governmental unit, it was held that the above classifications did not meet that state-articulated goal since they excluded many persons who had distinct and direct interests in school meeting decisions and included many persons who had, at best, remote and indirect interests.

Similarly, in *Cipriano v. City of Houma, supra*, decided the same day, provisions of Louisiana law which gave only property taxpayers the right to vote in elections called to approve the issuance of revenue bonds by a municipal utility were declared violative of the Equal Protection Clause since the operation of the utility systems affected virtually every resident of the city, not just the 40% of the registered voters who were also property taxpayers, and since the bonds were not in any way financed by property tax revenue. And the rationale of *Cipriano* was expanded to include general obligation bonds of municipalities in *Phoenix v. Kolodziejski, supra*. It was there noted that not only did those persons excluded from voting have a great interest in approving or disapproving municipal improvements, but they also contributed both directly through local taxes and indirectly through increased rents and costs to the servicing of the bonds.

---

* [Plaintiff was a bachelor living with his parents. Although he paid state and federal taxes, he had no vote. On the other hand, as the Court noted, an unemployed uninterested young man who paid no taxes but rented an apartment was entitled to vote. *See* 395 U.S. at 632 n.15.—Eds.]

Cipriano and *Phoenix* involved application of the "one person, one vote" principle to residents of units of local governments exercising general governmental power, as that term was defined in *Avery v. Midland County. Kramer* and *Hadley v. Junior College District* extended the "one person, one vote" principle to school districts exercising powers which,

> while not fully as broad as those of the Midland County Commissioners, certainly show that the trustees perform important governmental functions within the districts.

But the Court was also careful to state that:

> It is of course possible that there might be some case in which a State elects certain functionaries whose duties are so far removed from normal governmental activities and so disproportionately affect different groups that a popular election in compliance with *Reynolds, supra*, might not be required.

We conclude that the appellee water storage district, by reason of its special limited purpose and of the disproportionate effect of its activities on landowners as a group, is the sort of exception to the rule laid down in *Reynolds* which the quoted language from *Hadley* and the decision in *Avery* contemplated.

The appellee district in this case, although vested with some typical governmental powers, has relatively limited authority. Its primary purpose, indeed the reason for its existence, is to provide for the acquisition, storage, and distribution of water for farming in the Tulare Lake Basin.[8] It provides no other general public services such as schools, housing, transportation, utilities, roads, or anything else of the type ordinarily financed by a municipal body. There are no towns, shops, hospitals, or other facilities designed to improve the quality of life within the district boundaries, and it does not have a fire department, police, buses, or trains.

Not only does the district not exercise what might be thought of as "normal governmental" authority, but its actions disproportionately affect landowners. All of the costs of district projects are assessed against land by assessors in proportion to the benefits received. Likewise, charges for services rendered are collectible from persons receiving their benefit in proportion to the services. When such persons are delinquent in payment, just as in the case of delinquency in payments of assessments, such charges become a lien on the land. In short, there is no way that the economic burdens of district operations can fall on residents *qua* residents, and the operations of the districts primarily affect the land within their boundaries.

Under these circumstances, it is quite understandable that the statutory framework for election of directors of the appellee focuses on the land benefited, rather

---

8. Appellants strongly urge that districts have the power to, and do, engage in flood control activities. The interest of such activities to residents is said to be obvious since houses may be destroyed and, as in the case of appellant Ellison, jobs may disappear. But . . . any flood control activities are incident to the exercise of the district's primary functions of water storage and distribution.

than on people as such. California has not opened the franchise to all residents, as Missouri had in *Hadley*, nor to all residents with some exceptions, as New York had in *Kramer*. The franchise is extended to landowners, whether they reside in the district or out of it, and indeed whether or not they are natural persons who would be entitled to vote in a more traditional political election. Appellants do not challenge the enfranchisement of nonresident landowners or of corporate landowners for purposes of election of the directors of appellee. Thus, to sustain their contention that all residents of the district must be accorded a vote would not result merely in the striking down of an exclusion from what was otherwise a delineated class, but would instead engraft onto the statutory scheme a wholly new class of voters in addition to those enfranchised by the statute. . . .

II

Even though appellants derive no benefit from the *Reynolds* and *Kramer* lines of cases, they are, of course, entitled to have their equal protection claim assessed to determine whether the State's decision to deny the franchise to residents of the district while granting it to landowners was "wholly irrelevant to achievement of the regulation's objectives," *Kotch v. Board of River Port Pilot Comm'rs*, 330 U.S. 552, 556 (1947). No doubt residents within the district may be affected by its activities. But this argument proves too much. Since assessments imposed by the district become a cost of doing business for those who farm within it, and that cost must ultimately be passed along to the consumers of the produce, food shoppers in far away metropolitan areas are to some extent likewise "affected" by the activities of the district. Constitutional adjudication cannot rest on any such "house that Jack built" foundation, however. The California Legislature could quite reasonably have concluded that the number of landowners and owners of sufficient amounts of acreage whose consent was necessary to organize the district would not have subjected their land to the lien of its possibly very substantial assessments unless they had a dominant voice in its control. Since the subjection of the owners' lands to such liens was the basis by which the district was to obtain financing, the proposed district had as a practical matter to attract landowner support. Nor, since assessments against landowners were to be the sole means by which the expenses of the district were to be paid, could it be said to be unfair or inequitable to repose the franchise in landowners but not residents. Landowners as a class were to bear the entire burden of the district's costs, and the State could rationally conclude that they, to the exclusion of residents, should be charged with responsibility for its operation. We conclude, therefore, that nothing in the Equal Protection Clause precluded California from limiting the voting for directors of appellee district by totally excluding those who merely reside within the district. . . .

IV

The last claim by appellants is that § 41001, which weights the vote according to assessed valuation of the land, is unconstitutional. They point to the fact that several of the smaller landowners have only one vote per person whereas the J. G.

Boswell Company has 37,825 votes, and they place reliance on the various decisions of this Court holding that wealth has no relation to resident-voter qualifications and that equality of voting power may not be evaded.

Appellants' argument ignores the realities of water storage district operation. Since its formation in 1926, appellee district has put into operation four multi-million-dollar projects. The last project involved the construction of two laterals from the Basin to the California State Aqueduct at a capital cost of about $2,500,000. Three small landowners having land aggregating somewhat under four acres with an assessed valuation of under $100 were given one vote each in the special election held for the approval of the project. The J. G. Boswell Company, which owns 61,665.54 acres with an assessed valuation of $3,782,220 was entitled to cast 37,825 votes in the election. By the same token, however, the assessment commissioners determined that the benefits of the project would be uniform as to all of the acres affected, and assessed the project equally as to all acreage. Each acre has to bear $13.26 of cost and the three small landowners, therefore, must pay a total of $46, whereas the company must pay $817,685 for its part.[10]

Thus, as the District Court found, "the benefits and burdens to each landowner . . . are in proportion to the assessed value of the land." We cannot say that the California legislative decision to permit voting in the same proportion is not rationally based.

Mr. Justice Douglas, with whom Mr. Justice Brennan and Mr. Justice Marshall concur, dissenting. [Omitted.]

Notes and Questions

1. *The exception and its limits.* The *Salyer* case is not the only one in which the Supreme Court has confirmed that limiting the franchise for certain types of special districts is constitutionally permissible In *Associated Enterprises v. Toltec Watershed Improvement Dist.*, 410 U.S. 743 (1973) (per curiam), decided the same day as *Salyer*, the Court similarly rejected an equal protection challenge to the referendum by which a watershed district was created, where voting was limited to landowners, and votes allocated and weighted according to acreage. Subsequently in *Ball v. James*, 451 U.S. 355 (1981), the Court upheld a system by which directors of the Salt River Project Agricultural Improvement and Power District were elected. The franchise was limited to otherwise qualified voters who owned land within the District in proportion to the number of acres owned. The Court applied the two-pronged test of *Salyer*, which was "whether the purpose of the District is sufficiently specialized and narrow and whether its activities bear on landowners so disproportionately as

10. . . . [S]mall landowners are protected from crippling assessments resulting from district projects by the dual vote which must be taken in order to approve a project. Not only must a majority of the votes be cast for approval, but also a majority of the voters must approve. In this case, about 189 landowners constitute a majority and 189 of the smallest landowners in the district have only 2.34% of the land.

to distinguish the district from those public entities whose more general governmental functions demand application of the *Reynolds* principle." *Id.* at 362. Since the district's voting scheme met those tests, the Court needed only to satisfy the rational relationship rather than the more stringent compelling state interest standard. *Id.* at 371 and 364–65 n.8.

The special district in *Ball* was quite different from that in *Salyer* or *Toltec*, however, since the Salt River Project covered half the population of Arizona, including large parts of Phoenix, was a major supplier of electric power, derived 98% of its revenues from sales of electricity, serviced its bonds from electric power revenue, and delivered 40% of its water for urban or other nonagricultural uses. The Court nonetheless concluded that the district did not exercise broad governmental powers of the sort that triggered *Reynolds*' s one person-one vote standard. The Court viewed the district's creation for purposes of delivering water as controlling, and concluded that its substantial involvement in the electric power enterprise did not transform its relationship with nonvoting residents who purchased electricity.

Professor Briffault describes the *Salyer-Toltec-Ball* line of cases as recognizing a proprietary model of local government that contrasted with the democratic model of local government reflected in earlier decisions such as *Hadley* and the *Kramer* case discussed in *Salyer* itself. He notes that the Supreme Court was "markedly more deferential to state determinations concerning local arrangements and much less protective of the interest of local residents in voting in local elections than it had been previously." Briffault, *Who Rules at Home?: One Person/One Vote and Local Governments*, 60 U. Chi. L. Rev. 339, 361 (1993). Should the significant evolution of special districts and their growing popularity affect current application of the one person-one vote principle? See Shoked, *Quasi-Cities*, 93 B.U. L. Rev. 1971 (2013) (discussing the legal dichotomy between "cities" and "special districts" and arguing that a third category—the "quasi-city" should be recognized in instances in which governments designated as "special districts" functions like a city yet are not subject to federal and state laws relating to citizen participation, equality and more).

An important decision by the Fifth Circuit considered the intersection of leading United States Supreme Court cases including *Avery* and *Salyer* in the context of a governmental entity typically seen as a special purpose district. See *League of United Latin American Citizens (LULAC) v. Edwards Aquifer Authority (EAA)*, 937 F3d 457 (5th Cir. 2019). The case was brought by individuals, advocacy organizations and the San Antonio Regional Water Authority, who challenged the method used to elect directors in single member districts representing subregional water districts responsible for managing groundwater reserves in a substantial portion of Texas. Plaintiffs asserted that residents of the San Antonio covered nearly 75% of the costs of the Authority, but had a much lower capacity to guide policy given the vast disproportion of voters in that area compared to those in outlying very rural areas. They also asserted that the Authority had significant powers including borrowing, settings fees (comparable to taxation), conservation and other duties. Defendants conceded that the electoral districts were malapportioned but claimed that they were exempt from complying with one person-one vote requirements because they were a special-purpose district that did not provide an array of general services and affected particular geographic areas in different ways. In ruling for defendants, the court discussed *Avery*, *Salyer*, and other cases considered in this section, concluding that a bright-line test should be used in continuing to exempt special districts from one person-one vote requirements. A growing body of literature has increasingly challenged systems for operation and governance of various types of water districts. See, e.g., Dyble, *Aquifers and Democracy: Enforcing Voter Equal Protection to Save California's Imperiled Groundwater and Redeem Local Government*, 105 CALIF. L. REV. 1471 (2017) (arguing that evolving roles of water districts justify a fresh approach to voting systems). Do you agree that, in light of the growing importance of such districts and increased conflicts arising in the face of water scarcity and climate change, relevant case law should be revisited? Why or why not?

2. *Business improvement districts.* Business improvement districts (BIDs) have proliferated, as discussed in Chapter 4. How might the one person-one vote principle apply to BIDs? Consider *Kessler v. Grand Central Dist. Mgmt. Assn.*, 158 F.3d 92 (2d Cir. 1998), in which the court addressed an Equal Protection one person-one vote challenge to the system used for electing board members of the Grand Central Business District Board which used weighted votes to guarantee majority representation to property owners. Under New York law, municipalities were authorized to establish business improvement districts to promote commercial development in urban areas. When established, owners of non-exempt real property paid an assessment beyond their regular municipal taxes to help fund capital improvements in the BID. The court concluded that while the matter is not free from doubt, the Grand Central BID fell within the *Salyer-Ball* exception because it existed for the special limited purpose of business promotion, the management association's activities have a disproportionate effect on property owners, and its operating board does not have typical governmental powers. For a discussion of related issues see Briffault, *A Government for Our Time? Business Improvement Districts and Urban Governance*, 99 COLUM. L. REV. 365, 431 (1999) (discussing constitutional issues involved affecting BIDS); Comment, *What's the BID Deal? Can the Grand Central Business Improvement District Serve a Special Limited Purpose?*, 148 U. PA. L. REV. 1733 (2000) (discussing the Grand Central Business District); Batchis, *Business Improvement Districts and the Constitution: The Troubling Necessity of Privatized Government for Urban Revitalization*, 38 HASTINGS CONST. L.Q. 91 (2010) (discussing *Kessler*).

3. *Public transit systems and "special benefit districts."* If a separate unit of government operates the mass transit system for a large metropolitan area, is the election of its governing board subject to one person-one vote? See *Southern Cal. Rapid Transit Dist. v. Bolen*, 822 P.2d 875 (Cal. 1992). The Transit District was created by the state legislature to construct, finance and operate a mass transit system for the Los Angeles area. To help in the financing, the Transit District was authorized to

establish "special benefit assessment districts" around subway stations on the rapid transit line. They would operate much like traditional special assessments: property within the district would be assessed according to the special benefit received from the improvement. The Transit District had approved two such districts for submission to referendum approval. By statute the vote in the referendum election was limited to property owners on the basis of their assessed valuation. In this case the vote was even more limited because residential property was exempted from assessment, as the statute permitted.

The court majority framed the issue in terms of whether the *Reynolds v. Sims* one person-one vote principle applies to such a property-based assessment district voting scheme, or whether the *Salyer-Ball* exception would permit this kind of flexibility and experimentation at the local government level. Concluding that the special assessment districts lacked anything approaching general governmental powers and that there were genuine differences in the interests of those enfranchised and those denied the vote, the court found a reasonable basis for the legislature's exclusion, in this case of residents and commercial lessees. The dissenting judges found the reliance on *Salyer* misplaced: the local unit at issue was the Transit District, not the benefit assessment districts, which, in fact, were not districts at all, have no employees or powers and cannot be compared to the water districts in *Salyer* and *Ball*.

4. *The role of property ownership in other settings.* Note that in the *Sailors* and *Hadley* cases (relating to school boards) the Fourteenth Amendment issue was unrelated to property ownership and was presented in a form akin to that of the more "traditional" one person-one vote cases—equality of voting power in the selection of their governing authority. In *Salyer* and its circle of cases, the one person-one vote issue is posed in a different form—ownership of property forms the basis for defining eligible voters and effectively diluting or enhancing voting rights based on the extent of land that is owned. When is it legitimate to accord voting rights based on land ownership? Consider *Quinn v. Millsap*, 491 U.S. 95 (1989), in which the Court invalidated on equal protection grounds a provision of the Missouri Constitution authorizing reorganization of the governments of the city of St. Louis and St. Louis County pursuant to a voter approved plan drafted by a "board of freeholders" (that is, property owners). Note that the board was appointed and no voting rights as such were involved; in fact, the board's proposal was required to be submitted to the electorate. Applying a rational review standard, the Court held that "it is a form of invidious discrimination to require land ownership of all appointees to a body authorized to propose reorganization of local government." *Id.* at 107. According to the Court, the board of freeholders is "unlike any of the governmental bodies at issue in the three water-district cases." *Id.* at 109. How so?

The South Carolina Supreme Court also considered the issue of land ownership as a prerequisite to voting rights, striking down a state law that required, before a town could sell utility assets, that the issue be placed on the municipal ballot by petition signed by 25 percent of freeholders in the town. The court applied heightened scrutiny and held that because utilities are of "general interest" to the entire community, the statute was not justified by a compelling state interest. *Sojourner v. Town of St. George*, 679 S.E.2d 182 (S.C. 2009). Is this decision consistent with *Salyer* and related cases? Why or why not?

[c] Voting Rights in Local Elections

In most of the cases previously considered there was a continuing electoral relationship involving, broadly defined, the selection of government representatives, for example, the election of county commissioners in *Avery*, and of school board members in *Hadley* and *Kramer.* In *Associated Enterprises v. Toltec* the challenged voting restriction occurred in the election creating the district, although the Supreme Court applied the same analysis as it had to the election of directors in *Salyer*, decided the same day. For this reason, all of the voting rights cases previously considered should be treated as part of a spectrum, however blurred it may be at times.

Nevertheless, the issues are not identical, nor are the results, when the right to vote is claimed in a peculiarly local government setting involving "single shot" referenda or elections such as those that arise with regard to consolidation of local governments, incorporation or annexation. Recall the discussion in Chapter 1 of the *Hunter* case in which the consolidation of Allegheny with Pittsburgh was approved over the negative vote of the residents of Allegheny. In *Hunter* the Court rejected two federal constitutional claims made by the plaintiff-citizens of Allegheny: impairment of obligation of contract between the city and the plaintiffs that they were to be taxed only for the purposes of that city, and denial of due process by subjecting the residents of Allegheny to the burden of additional taxation resulting from the consolidation. The plaintiffs did not fashion an equal protection dilution challenge to the voting scheme, and the Court did not directly pass on its validity. The Court did note, however, the plaintiffs' argument that "[t]he manner in which the right of due process of law has been violated . . . is that the method of voting on the consolidation prescribed in the act has permitted the voters of the larger city to overpower the voters of the smaller city, and compel the union without their consent and against their protest." 207 U.S. at 177.

In the following case the Court considered the validity of a dual or concurrent vote majority in a local government election.

Town of Lockport v. Citizens for Community Action at the Local Level, Inc.

430 U.S. 259 (1977)

Mr. Justice Stewart delivered the opinion of the Court.

New York law provides that a new county charter will go into effect only if it is approved in a referendum election by separate majorities of the voters who live in the cities within the county, and of those who live outside the cities.... [A three-judge federal district court held that these requirements violate equal protection and the Court noted probable jurisdiction.]

I

County government in New York has traditionally taken the form of a single-branch legislature, exercising general governmental powers. General governmental powers are also exercised by the county's constituent cities, villages, and towns. The allocation of powers among these subdivisions can be changed, and a new form of county government adopted, pursuant to referendum procedures specified in Art. IX of the New York Constitution and implemented by § 33 of the Municipal Home Rule Law. Under those procedures a county board of supervisors may submit a proposed charter to the voters for approval. If a majority of the voting city dwellers and a majority of the voting noncity dwellers both approve, the charter is adopted.

In November 1972, a proposed charter for the county of Niagara was put to referendum. The charter created the new offices of County Executive and County Comptroller, and continued the county's existing power to establish tax rates, equalize assessments, issue bonds, maintain roads, and administer health and public welfare services. No explicit provision for redistribution of governmental powers from the cities or towns to the county government was made. The city voters approved the charter by a vote of 18,220 to 14,914. The noncity voters disapproved the charter by a vote of 11,594 to 10,665. A majority of those voting in the entire county thus favored the charter....

[The prior proceedings resulted in a district court holding that the concurrent majority requirement violated equal protection. The Court began its opinion by discussing *Reynolds v. Sims* and continued:]

The equal protection principles applicable in gauging the fairness of an election involving the choice of legislative representatives are of limited relevance, however, in analyzing the propriety of recognizing distinctive voter interests in a "single-shot" referendum. In a referendum, the expression of voter will is direct, and there is no need to assure that the voters' views will be adequately represented through their representatives in the legislature. The policy impact of a referendum is also different in kind from the impact of choosing representatives—instead of sending legislators off to the state capitol to vote on a multitude of issues, the referendum puts one discrete issue to the voters. That issue is capable, at least, of being analyzed to determine whether its adoption or rejection will have a disproportionate impact on an identifiable group of voters. If it is found to have such a disproportionate impact, the question then is whether a State can recognize that impact either by limiting the franchise to those voters specially affected or by giving their votes a special weight. This question has been confronted by the Court in two types of cases: those dealing with elections involving "special-interest" governmental bodies of limited jurisdiction, and those dealing with bond referenda.

[The Court then discussed the *Salyer, Kramer, Cipriano* and *Hill v. Stone* cases.]

These decisions do not resolve the issues in the present case. Taken together, however, they can be said to focus attention on two inquiries: whether there is a genuine difference in the relevant interests of the groups that the state electoral classification has created; and, if so, whether any resulting enhancement of minority voting strength nonetheless amounts to invidious discrimination in violation of the Equal Protection Clause.

III

The argument that the provisions of New York law in question here are unconstitutional rests primarily on the premise that all voters in a New York county have identical interests in the adoption or rejection of a new charter, and that any distinction, therefore, between voters drawn on the basis of residence and working to the detriment of an identifiable class is an invidious discrimination. If the major premise were demonstrably correct—if it were clear that all voters in Niagara County have substantially identical interests in the adoption of a new county charter, regardless of where they reside within the county—the District Court's judgment would have to be affirmed under our prior cases. That major premise, however, simply cannot be accepted. To the contrary, it appears that the challenged provisions of New York law rest on the State's identification of the distinctive interests of the residents of the cities and towns within a county rather than their interests as residents of the county as a homogeneous unit. This identification is based in the realities of the distribution of governmental powers in New York, and is consistent with our cases that recognize both the wide discretion the States have in forming and allocating governmental tasks to local subdivisions, and the discrete interests that such local governmental units may have *qua* units.

General-purpose local government in New York is entrusted to four different units: counties, cities, towns, and villages. The State is divided into 62 counties; each of the 57 counties outside of New York City is divided into towns, or towns and one or more cities. Villages, once formed, are still part of the towns in which they are located. The New York Legislature has conferred home rule and general governmental powers on all of these subdivisions, and their governmental activities may on occasion substantially overlap. The cities often perform functions within their jurisdiction that the county may perform for noncity residents; similarly villages perform some functions for their residents that the town provides for the rest of the town's inhabitants. Historically towns provided their areas with major social services that more recently have been transferred to counties; towns exercise more regulatory power than counties; and both towns and counties can create special taxing and improvement districts to administer services.

Acting within a fairly loose state apportionment of political power, the relative energy and organization of these various subdivisions will often determine which one of them in a given area carries out the major tasks of local government. Since the cities have the greatest autonomy within this scheme, changes serving to strengthen the county structure may have the most immediate impact on the functions of the towns as deliverers of government services.

The provisions of New York law here in question clearly contemplate that a new or amended county charter will frequently operate to transfer "functions or duties" from the towns or cities to the county, or even to "abolish one or more offices, departments, agencies or units of government." Although the 1974 Charter does not explicitly transfer governmental functions or duties from the towns to Niagara County, the executive-legislative form of government it provides would significantly enhance the county's organizational and service delivery capacity, for the purpose of "greater efficiency and responsibility in county government." The creation of the offices of County Executive and Commissioner of Finance clearly reflects this purpose. Such anticipated organizational changes, no less than explicit transfers of functions, could effectively shift any pre-existing balance of power between town and county governments to county predominance. In terms of efficient delivery of government services, such a shift might be all to the good, but it may still be viewed as carrying a cost quite different for town voters and their existing town governments from that incurred by city voters and their existing city governments.

The ultimate question then is whether, given the differing interests of city and noncity voters in the adoption of a new county charter in New York, those differences are sufficient under the Equal Protection Clause to justify the classifications made by New York law. If that question were posed in the context of annexation proceedings, the fact that the residents of the annexing city and the residents of the area to be annexed formed sufficiently different constituencies with sufficiently different interests could be readily perceived. The fact of impending union alone would not so merge them into one community of interest as constitutionally to require that their votes be aggregated in any referendum to approve annexation. *Cf. Hunter v. City of Pittsburgh.* Similarly a proposal that several school districts join to form a consolidated unit could surely be subject to voter approval in each constituent school district.

Yet in terms of recognizing constituencies with separate and potentially opposing interests, the structural decision to annex or consolidate is similar in impact to the decision to restructure county government in New York. In each case, separate voter approval requirements are based on the perception that the real and long-term impact of a restructuring of local government is felt quite differently by the different county constituent units that in a sense compete to provide similar governmental services. Voters in these constituent units are directly and differentially affected by the restructuring of county government, which may make the provider of public services more remote and less subject to the voters' individual influence.

The provisions of New York law here in question no more than recognize the realities of these substantially differing electoral interests. Granting to these provisions the presumption of constitutionality to which every duly enacted state and federal law is entitled, we are unable to conclude that they violate the Equal Protection Clause of the Fourteenth Amendment.

For the reasons stated in this opinion the judgment is reversed.

It is so ordered.

The Chief Justice concurs in the judgment.

Notes and Questions

1. *Recollecting Hunter.* Note the Court's oblique reference to *Hunter.* Does Justice Stewart mean to say that Pennsylvania could have required separate majorities in Allegheny and in Pittsburgh for approval of the consolidation? Could the state have permitted annexation of Allegheny without any vote at all among residents of Allegheny, (a) following adoption of a resolution by the Pittsburgh city council, or (b) following a successful referendum in Pittsburgh? Could it have required concurrent majorities consisting of (a) majority approval in both cities aggregated, plus (b) majority approval either in Allegheny, or in Pittsburgh? If the New York statute in *Lockport* failed to provide for concurrent majorities, would the Court invalidate it? What are the differences among these various combinations? For a discussion of the interplay of *Hunter* and one person-one vote principles, see Note, *Local Government Law—Municipal Boundaries—Georgia Authorizes the Creation of the City of Eagle's Landing—S.B. 263, 154 Gen. Assemb., Reg. Sess. (Ga. 2018),* 132 Harv. L. Rev. 2410 (2019) (discussing state legislation allowing wealthy segment of Atlanta suburb to secede from their existing municipality and form their own city).

2. *Interests and parties.* Almost every local government organization also involves several sets of interests or interested parties, as the Court seemed to recognize in *Lockport.* Do the courts clearly identify those interests and give them adequate recognition? Or is that the role of the courts? See Briffault, *Who Rules at Home?: One Person/One Vote and Local Governments,* 60 U. Chi. L. Rev. 339 (1993); Note, *Interest Exceptions to One-Resident, One-Vote: Better Results from the Voting Rights Act?,* 74 Tex. L. Rev. 1153 (1996); Note, *State Restrictions on Municipal Elections: An Equal Protection Analysis,* 93 Harv. L. Rev. 1491 (1980).

Consider, for example, *Board of Supervisors v. Local Agency Formation Comm'n,* 838 P.2d 1198 (Cal. 1992), a state court opinion addressing the issue of whose interests are entitled to a vote in a local government organization dispute. Residents of an unincorporated community of 69,000 population in Sacramento County received approval to incorporate in accordance with California's Cortese-Knox Local Government Reorganization Act, which includes "elaborate safeguards designed to protect the political and economic interests of affected local governments." Under the act a confirming election was to be held only in the territory of the proposed city. County officials challenged that limitation on equal protection grounds, and the court acknowledged the "tension between California's financially beleaguered counties and the desire of residents of unincorporated areas to form cities and draw local government closer to home." *Id.* at 1200. Conceding that the state is not required to provide any vote for changes in municipal organization, the court said that nonetheless, when it has provided for voter input, "the equal protection clause requires that those similarly situated not be treated differently unless the disparity is justified." *Id.* at 1204. The court relied heavily on *Hunter v. Pittsburgh* and the reasoning in *Lockport* to conclude that "the essence of this case is not the fundamental right to vote, but the state's plenary power to set the conditions under which its political subdivisions are created." *Id.* at 1206. Applying the rational relation rather than strict scrutiny standard, the court accepted as reasonable the legislature's decision to deny a vote to the county residents with a "lesser degree" of interest in the proposed incorporation. A similar result obtained in a Michigan appeals court, where a state statute was construed to properly bar residents of a township from which land was proposed to be annexed from voting in the annexation election, unless they resided on the actual site to be annexed. *Charter Township of Meridian v. Ingham County Clerk*, 777 N.W.2d 452 (Mich. App. 2009). See *infra* for an extended discussion of voting rights in boundary changes.

3. *Memphis and Shelby County.* Although *Lockport* seems to have established clear precedent relating to consolidation of local governments, similar issues continue to arise and result in heated litigation. An example concerned a proposal to consolidate Memphis, Tennessee with surrounding Shelby County in order to form a metropolitan government. After development of a proposal for consolidation, an election was held in which a majority of county voters rejected the consolidation proposal, while a majority of city residents supported it. As a result, the consolidation could not proceed. Both city and county residents challenged related state constitutional and statutory provisions that provided for "dual voting" (that is, requiring a majority favorable vote of both city and non-city county residents for the proposed consolidation to take effect), contending that there were not meaningful differences between the two groups each of whom had to approve the consolidation. See *Tigrett v. Cooper*, 7 F. Supp. 3d 792 (W.D. Tenn. 2014). The federal district court applied the two-prong *Lockport* test, asking whether there was a genuine difference in relevant interests in the two groups, and whether invidious discrimination resulted from enhancement of minority voting strength. The court applied a rational basis test (rather than a strict scrutiny test) and upheld the consolidation requirements against the plaintiff's Equal Protection challenge. It also rejected plaintiffs' claim under § 2 of the federal Voting Rights Act. For a discussion of the context in which the litigation arose and associated legal contentions, see Setterlund, *Two Claims, Two Keys—Overcoming Tennessee's Dual-Majority Voting Mechanism to Facilitate Consolidation Between Memphis City and Shelby County*, 41 U. Mem. L. Rev. 933 (2011).

4. *More discretion for local governments to expand the franchise?* Some local governments have opted to expand, rather than constrain, voting rights in local elections, for example by allowing non-citizens who are lawful permanent residents,

felons, non-residents who are taxpayers, or younger people to vote. What kind of justifications might apply and what legal questions might be raised by such proposals? See Douglas, *The Right to Vote Under Local Law*, 85 Geo. Wash. L. Rev. 1039 (2017). Professor Douglas contends that courts should defer to local laws of this sort but not defer to restrictions on the right to vote. He recognizes, however, that there may be legal impediments to such reforms, for example if state constitutions or legislation specify voter qualifications in terms of restrictions, local governments lack power over local elections, state preemption rules apply, or practical difficulties create problems in allowing votes for local races but not state or national elections. *Id.* at 1081. He explores relevant state and federal constitutional doctrine, *id.* at 1088–97, and enumerates details of state law, *id.* at 1101.

Nonresidents of a municipality may also have an interest in the governmental affairs of their neighboring city. How can this be accommodated? The following case considers this question.

Holt Civic Club v. City of Tuscaloosa

439 U.S. 60 (1978)

Mr. Justice Rehnquist delivered the opinion of the Court.

Holt is a small, largely rural, unincorporated community located on the northeastern outskirts of Tuscaloosa, the fifth largest city in Alabama. Because the community is within the three-mile police jurisdiction circumscribing Tuscaloosa's corporate limits, its residents are subject to the city's "police [and] sanitary regulations." Ala. Code § 11-40-10 (1975). Holt residents are also subject to the criminal jurisdiction of the city's court, Ala. Code § 12-14-1 (1975), and to the city's power to license businesses, trades, and professions, Ala. Code § 11-51-91 (1975). Tuscaloosa, however, may collect from businesses in the police jurisdiction only one-half of the license fee chargeable to similar businesses conducted within the corporate limits.

In 1973 appellants, an unincorporated civic association and seven individual residents of Holt, brought this statewide class action in the United States District Court for the Northern District of Alabama, challenging the constitutionality of these Alabama statutes. They claimed that the city's extraterritorial exercise of police powers over Holt residents, without a concomitant extension of the franchise on an equal footing with those residing within the corporate limits, denies residents of the police jurisdiction rights secured by the Due Process and Equal Protection Clauses of the Fourteenth Amendment.... We now conclude that ... appellants' constitutional claims were properly rejected....

II.

....

A

Appellants focus their equal protection attack on § 11-40-10, the statute fixing the limits of municipal police jurisdiction and giving extraterritorial effect to municipal police and sanitary ordinances. Citing *Kramer v. Union Free School Dist.*, and cases following in its wake, appellants argue that the section creates a classification infringing on their right to participate in municipal elections. The State's denial of the franchise to police jurisdiction residents, appellants urge, can stand only if justified by a compelling state interest.

[The Court discussed the *Kramer, Cipriano* and *Phoenix* cases. It also discussed *Evans v. Cornman*, 398 U.S. 419 (1970). In this case the Court held unconstitutional a ruling "that persons living on the grounds of the National Institutes of Health (NIH), a federal enclave located within the geographical boundaries of the State, did not meet the residency requirement of the Maryland Constitution" and were not entitled to vote in Maryland elections.]

From these and our other voting qualifications cases a common characteristic emerges: The challenged statute in each case denied the franchise to individuals who were physically resident within the geographic boundaries of the governmental entity concerned. No decision of this Court has extended the "one man, one vote" principle to individuals residing beyond the geographic confines of the governmental entity concerned, be it the State or its political subdivisions. On the contrary, our cases have uniformly recognized that a government unit may legitimately restrict the right to participate in its political processes to those who reside within its borders. Bona fide residence alone, however, does not automatically confer the right to vote on all matters, for at least in the context of special interest elections the State may constitutionally disfranchise residents who lack the required special interest in the subject matter of the election.

Appellants' argument that extraterritorial extension of municipal powers requires concomitant extraterritorial extension of the franchise proves too much. The imaginary line defining a city's corporate limits cannot corral the influence of municipal actions. A city's decisions inescapably affect individuals living immediately outside its borders. The granting of building permits for high rise apartments, industrial plants, and the like on the city's fringe unavoidably contributes to problems of traffic congestion, school districting, and law enforcement immediately outside the city. A rate change in the city's sales or ad valorem tax could well have a significant impact on retailers and property values in areas bordering the city. The condemnation of real property on the city's edge for construction of a municipal garbage dump or waste treatment plant would have obvious implications for neighboring nonresidents. Indeed, the indirect extraterritorial effects of many purely internal municipal actions could conceivably have a heavier impact on surrounding environs than the direct regulation contemplated by Alabama's police jurisdiction statutes. Yet no one would suggest that nonresidents likely to be affected by this sort of municipal action have a constitutional right to participate in the political processes bringing it about. And unless one adopts the idea that the Austinian notion of sovereignty, which is presumably embodied to some extent in the authority of a city over a police jurisdiction, distinguishes the direct effects of limited municipal powers over police jurisdiction residents from the indirect though equally dramatic extraterritorial effects of purely internal municipal actions, it makes little sense to say that one requires extension of the franchise while the other does not.

Given this country's tradition of popular sovereignty, appellants' claimed right to vote in Tuscaloosa elections is not without some logical appeal. . . . The line heretofore marked by this Court's voting qualifications decisions coincides with the geographical boundary of the governmental unit at issue, and we hold that appellants' case, like their homes, falls on the farther side.

B

Thus stripped of its voting rights attire, the equal protection issue presented by appellants becomes whether the Alabama statutes giving extraterritorial force to certain municipal ordinances and powers bear some rational relationship to a legitimate state purpose. . . .

Government, observed Mr. Justice Johnson, "is the science of experiment," *Anderson v. Dunn*, 6 Wheat. 204, 226 (1821), and a State is afforded wide leeway when experimenting with the appropriate allocation of state legislative power. This Court has often recognized that political subdivisions such as cities and counties are created by the State "as convenient agencies for exercising such of the governmental powers of the State as may be entrusted to them." *Hunter v. Pittsburgh*, 207 U.S. 161, 178 (1907). . . . While the broad statements as to state control over municipal corporations contained in *Hunter* have undoubtedly been qualified by the holdings of later cases such as *Kramer v. Union Free School Dist.*, we think that the case continues to have substantial constitutional significance in emphasizing the extraordinarily wide latitude that States have in creating various types of political subdivisions and conferring authority upon them.[7]

The extraterritorial exercise of municipal powers is a governmental technique neither recent in origin nor unique to the State of Alabama. See R. Maddox, Extraterritorial Powers of Municipalities in the United States (1955). In this country 35 States authorize their municipal subdivisions to exercise governmental

---

7. In this case residents of the police jurisdiction are excluded only from participation in municipal elections since they reside outside of Tuscaloosa's corporate limits. This "denial of the franchise," as appellants put it, does not have anything like the far-reaching consequences of the denial of the franchise in *Evans v. Cornman*, 398 U.S. 419 (1970). There the Court pointed out that "[i]n nearly every election, federal, state, and local, for offices from the Presidency to the school board, and on the entire variety of other ballot propositions, appellees have a stake equal to that of other Maryland residents." *Id.*, at 426. Treatment of the plaintiffs in *Evans* as nonresidents of Maryland had repercussions not merely with respect to their right to vote in city elections, but with respect to their right to vote in national, state, school board, and referendum elections.

powers beyond their corporate limits. Comment, *The Constitutionality of the Exercise of Extraterritorial Powers by Municipalities*, 45 U. Chi. L. Rev. 151 (1977). Although the extraterritorial municipal powers granted by these States vary widely, several States grant their cities more extensive or intrusive powers over bordering areas than those granted under the Alabama statutes.[8]

In support of their equal protection claim, appellants suggest a number of "constitutionally preferable" governmental alternatives to Alabama's system of municipal police jurisdictions. For example, exclusive management of the police jurisdiction by county officials, appellants maintain, would be more "practical." From a political science standpoint, appellants' suggestions may be sound, but this Court does not sit to determine whether Alabama has chosen the soundest or most practical form of internal government possible. Authority to make those judgments resides in the state legislature, and Alabama citizens are free to urge their proposals to that body. Our inquiry is limited to the question whether "any state of facts reasonably may be conceived to justify" Alabama's system of police jurisdictions, and in this case it takes but momentary reflection to arrive at an affirmative answer.

The Alabama Legislature could have decided that municipal corporations should have some measure of control over activities carried on just beyond their "city limit" signs, particularly since today's police jurisdiction may be tomorrow's annexation to the city proper. Nor need the city's interests have been the only concern of the legislature when it enacted the police jurisdiction statutes. Urbanization of any area brings with it a number of individuals who long both for the quiet of suburban or country living and for the career opportunities offered by the city's working environment. Unincorporated communities like Holt dot the rim of most major population centers in Alabama and elsewhere, and state legislatures have a legitimate interest in seeing that this substantial segment of the population does

---

8. Municipalities in some States have almost unrestricted governmental powers over surrounding unincorporated territories. . . . By setting forth these various state provisions respecting extraterritorial powers of cities, we do not mean to imply that every one of them would pass constitutional muster. We do not have before us, of course, a situation in which a city has annexed outlying territory in all but name, and is exercising precisely the same governmental powers over residents of surrounding unincorporated territory as it does over those residing within its corporate limits. *See Little Thunder v. South Dakota*, 518 F.2d 1253 (CA8 1975). Nor do we have here a case like *Evans v. Cornman, supra*, where NIH residents were subject to such "important aspects of state powers" as Maryland's authority "to levy and collect [its] income, gasoline, sales, and use taxes" and were "just as interested in and connected with electoral decisions as . . . their neighbors who live[d] off the enclave." 398 U.S., at 423, 424, 426. Appellants have made neither an allegation nor a showing that the authority exercised by the city of Tuscaloosa within the police jurisdiction is no less than that exercised by the city within its corporate limits. The minute catalog of ordinances of the city of Tuscaloosa which have extraterritorial effect set forth by our dissenting Brethren, . . . is as notable for what it does not include as for what it does. While the burden was on appellants to establish a difference in treatment violative of the Equal Protection Clause, we are bound to observe that among the powers not included in the "addendum" to appellants' brief referred to by the dissent are the vital and traditional authorities of cities and towns to levy ad valorem taxes, invoke the power of eminent domain, and zone property for various types of uses.

not go without basic municipal services such as police, fire, and health protection. Established cities are experienced in the delivery of such services, and the incremental cost of extending the city's responsibility in these areas to surrounding environs may be substantially less than the expense of establishing wholly new service organizations in each community.

Nor was it unreasonable for the Alabama Legislature to require police jurisdiction residents to contribute through license fees to the expense of services provided them by the city. The statutory limitation on license fees to half the amount exacted within the city assures that police jurisdiction residents will not be victimized by the city government.

"Viable local governments may need many innovations, numerous combinations of old and new devices, great flexibility in municipal arrangements to meet changing urban conditions." *Sailors v. Board of Education*, 387 U.S., at 110–111. This observation in *Sailors* was doubtless as true at the turn of this century, when urban areas throughout the country were temporally closer to the effects of the industrial revolution. Alabama's police jurisdiction statute, enacted in 1907, was a rational legislative response to the problems faced by the State's burgeoning cities. Alabama is apparently content with the results of its experiment, and nothing in the Equal Protection Clause of the Fourteenth Amendment requires that it try something new. . . .

Mr. Justice Stevens, concurring. [Omitted.]

Mr. Justice Brennan, with whom Mr. Justice White and Mr. Justice Marshall join, dissenting. [Omitted.]

Notes and Questions

1. *Residents vs. nonresidents.* If the plaintiffs in Tuskegee (*Gomillion v. Lightfoot*, discussed in Chapter 1) had a right to vote in a city in which they didn't live, why shouldn't the plaintiffs in Tuscaloosa have a right to vote in a city to whose jurisdiction they are more subject than were the *Gomillion* plaintiffs to Tuskegee? Isn't the Court incorrect when it says that the common characteristic in all of its voting rights cases was the fact of residence? Would the Court's decision have been the same if the complaining nonresidents in *Holt* were black? See Note, *Interest Exceptions to One-Resident, One-Vote: Better Results from the Voting Rights Act?*, 74 Tex. L. Rev. 1153 (1996). The author contends that certain of the Court's decisions—the limited purpose *Salyer* exception and the practice of allowing nonresident landowners to vote—would be decided differently under interpretations of the Voting Rights Act where minority vote dilution could be shown. On the other hand, the writer believes that the *Lockport* and *Holt* situations—restricted or weighted voting in annexations and extraterritorial jurisdiction—would survive challenge under the Voting Rights Act.

Even if nonresidents of a municipality have no right to participate generally in municipal elections, could it be argued that a nonresident should be permitted to vote on a specific issue that affects her directly? See *Kollar v. City of Tucson*, 319 F. Supp. 482 (D. Ariz. 1970), *aff'd*, 402 U.S. 967 (1971) (finding no equal protection violation when nonresident user of city water service was denied right to vote in revenue bond referendum despite probable effect on water rates, where under state law municipality had no obligation to extend water utility service to nonresidents). In *Schmidt v. City of Kenosha*, 571 N.W.2d 892 (Wis. App. 1997), the court upheld Kenosha's use of the Wisconsin statute which authorized it to exercise restrictive zoning powers up to three miles from its airport boundary even if the property affected was outside of the city limits. Rejecting the one person-one vote challenge of property owners in the extraterritorial zone that they were denied the right to participate, the court relied on *Holt*.

For an interesting twist on the residents vs. nonresidents question, see *Public Integrity Alliance, Inc. v. City of Tucson*, 836 F.3d 1019 (9th Cir. 2016) (en banc). The case involved a novel hybrid system used by the City of Tucson in selecting local city council members. Council candidates had to reside in one of six wards with roughly equal population. There was an initial first-stage primary in which candidates for council ran in partisan primaries in each ward, and only those living in a given ward could participate in these primaries. Ten weeks after partisan candidates had been selected in each ward's primaries, the general election was held in which all voters in the city vote for their preferred candidate for each ward (that is, had the opportunity to vote for six council candidates, one from each of the six wards, notwithstanding where they lived). Voters challenged this system, saying that the initial primary process allowing only in-ward voters to participate in selecting candidates from a given ward denied them the opportunity to select candidates for whom they would ultimately vote in the general election and who would consequently represent them. The Ninth Circuit, acting en banc, upheld the Tucson system, applying a slightly enhanced standard of review that considered the fit between ends and means and balancing related considerations, rather than rational basis or strict scrutiny review.

2. *Nonresident voting.* On the other side of the coin, extending the right to vote to nonresidents can also give rise to constitutional challenges. Typically, where such extension occurs, it is nonresident property owners who are given the right to vote in a local election. Residents of the local government unit may claim that their vote has been diluted (or in some cases actually denied) by the nonresidents' participation. Recall that in *Salyer* nonresident landowners (and corporate landowners) were entitled to vote in the water storage district elections, but plaintiffs did not directly challenge the provision in that case.

In *Brown v. Board of Comm'rs of Chattanooga*, 722 F. Supp. 380 (E.D. Tenn. 1989), one of the challenges to Chattanooga's local government was that the charter permitted nonresident freeholders to vote in municipal elections in the municipality in which their freehold was situated. Noting that the charter expanded rather than curtailed the franchise and that "[o]ver inclusiveness is a lesser constitutional evil than under inclusiveness," the court applied a rational basis test. In this case, however, the court found the Chattanooga provision too unfocused: while nonresident property owners have a substantial interest in municipal affairs, this provision placed no limit on the number of owners who could "vote" a piece of property and no minimum on the value required. It therefore violates equal protection until it is "more finely tailored." For discussion of *Brown*, see Bahner & Gray, *The Other Brown Case: The Promise of the U.S. Constitution at Work in Chattanooga*, 60-MAY FED. LAW. 27 (2013).

In a New Jersey school board case, the Third Circuit Court of Appeals relied on *Holt* to validate the unequal representation on a high school board. Under New Jersey law a school district may elect to enter into a "send-receive" relationship with a neighboring school district in order to educate its high school students. In reversing a district court opinion which had relied on *Hadley, English v. Board of Educ.*, 135 F. Supp. 2d 588 (D.N.J. 2001), the court of appeals turned to the Supreme Court's conclusion in *Holt* that "a government may legitimately restrict the right to participate in its political process to those who reside within its borders," holding that the unequal voting structure allowed in electing school board members was "the type of complex judgment that a state legislature is entitled to make" and concluding that the decision bore a rational relationship to a legitimate state purpose. *English v. Board of Educ.*, 301 F.3d 69 (3d Cir. 2002).

3. *Standards for Equal Protection analysis. Lockport* and *Holt* suggest that the outcome in a voting rights case depends on the level of Equal Protection review applied a position echoed by many other courts. Looking back at this section as a whole, how does a court decide which standard of review to apply to constitutional challenges?

A Note on Voting Rights in Boundary Changes

Lockport held that it was permissible to create a system that required affirmative votes by both city and county voters to approve a change in the county charter. *Holt* held that those in a municipality's extraterritorial jurisdiction need not be afforded the right to vote notwithstanding the municipality's role in regulating land use in their area. Consider how the logic of these and other cases in this section bears on the constitutionality of various state schemes that might be used to govern municipal annexation.

(a) *Denying those in annexed area the right to vote on annexation.* Annexation statutes commonly provide for an election to be held in the area to be annexed, following adoption by the governing body of the annexing city of a resolution or ordinance proposing the annexation. While the voters of the annexing city do not have a direct vote on the issue, it can be argued that their interests are reflected in the vote of their elected representatives. Contrary approaches are possible, however. In *Murphy v. Kansas City*, 347 F. Supp. 837 (W.D. Mo. 1972), residents of the annexing city could vote on the issue because annexation was accomplished by means of an amendment to the city charter. Residents of the area to be annexed, however, had no vote. The court rejected their equal protection claim, relying principally on *Hunter*.

North Carolina had historically allowed unilateral (involuntary, municipally initiated) annexation of contiguous areas meeting "urban development" standards, without any petition or referendum, but its statutes were substantially modified in 2011 and 2012 to provide a referendum right for those who might otherwise be subject to involuntary annexation. For related discussion, see Cammack, *Municipal Manifest Destiny: Constitutionality of Unilateral Municipal Annexations*, 2013 B.Y.U. L. Rev. 619 (discussing prior North Carolina law and subsequent amendments, arguing that prior provisions violated Equal Protection clause, and suggesting a role for counties as a proxy for the views of those being annexed); Wegner, *North Carolina's Annexation Wars: Whys, Wherefores, and What's Next*, 91 N.C. L. Rev. 165 (2012) (discussing changes in North Carolina annexation law). For an earlier comprehensive discussion of the right to vote in annexation decisions, see Note, *The Right to Vote in Municipal Annexations*, 88 Harv. L. Rev. 1571, 1604–09 (1975).

(b) *Using a petition proxy, not a vote, as a means of demonstrating support within the area annexed. Berry v. Bourne*, 588 F.2d 422 (4th Cir. 1978), is a leading case. One of the optional methods of annexation in South Carolina provided that when a petition was filed signed by 75% of the freeholders in a contiguous area requesting annexation, the city council may complete the annexation simply by adopting a resolution. In this case, registered voters in the area to be annexed claimed a violation of equal protection because they were denied the right to vote on the issue. The court rejected the claim, basing its decision squarely on *Hunter v. Pittsburgh*, whose broad affirmation of state legislative power over annexation was, in the court's judgment, subject to only one exception: challenges resting on racial discrimination. None of the voting rights cases were on point because there was no election provided for there. See also *Torres v. Village of Capitan*, 582 P.2d 1277 (N.M. 1978) (upholding a statute that permitted annexation of contiguous property upon the filing of a petition signed by the owners of a majority of acres in the area proposed to be annexed, and reasoning that petitioning for annexation is not a fundamental voting right and therefore not subject to strict scrutiny).

(c) *Burdening the right to vote or consent to annexation.* In *Hussey v. City of Portland*, 64 F.3d 1260 (9th Cir. 1995), the city attempted to preempt the required approval from potential annexees. Oregon law authorized annexation by either a majority vote in the area to be annexed, or written consent of a majority of voters and of property owners in that area. Portland conditioned a subsidy for nonresidents—who were required by law to connect to Portland's sewer system—on their signing a consent to annex. The Oregon court invalidated that condition. Acknowledging that there is no federal or Oregon constitutional right to vote on annexation (*Hunter*), the court said that, once granted, the exercise thereof was subject to strict scrutiny (*Kramer*).

(d) *Weighing the views of property owners in annexation decisions.* Sometimes owners of property in an area being annexed are given rights to affect annexation decisions that are not accorded to other residents of an area being annexed. For example, a number of state statutes provide that the annexation process is initiated by the filing of a petition signed by a designated portion of those affected. Not infrequently, the petition must be signed by a stated percentage of the property owners or freeholders in the area to be annexed. In some cases, the percentage is measured by the value of the property as well as the number of property owners. Clearly, if these percentages are high enough, this requirement enables the favored group to prevent a boundary change which others who are affected by it may favor—particularly if it is the only method provided for initiating the change. Is this approach permissible? What standard of review would apply in the event of challenges to such provisions? Consider the following cases.

Curtis v. Board of Supervisors, 501 P.2d 537 (Cal. 1972), invalidated a statute that allowed landowners representing 51% of the land within a proposed incorporation to file a protest blocking the incorporation. The court held that voting rights were affected because the right of protest touched upon and burdened the right to vote. The statute did not pass strict scrutiny because the landowners did not have an interest sufficient to justify their right to block an election. Accord *Muller v. Curran*, 889 F.2d 54 (4th Cir. 1989) (statute allowing popular vote on incorporation to be blocked by owners of at least 25% of property in area found to violate Equal Protection Clause). See also *Mayor & Council of Dover v. Kelley*, 327 A.2d 748 (Del. 1974) (applying strict scrutiny; invalidating annexation system that gave every non-property owning vote in the annexation area one vote, and every corporation, firm, and individual owning real estate within the area one vote per $100 of assessed valuation; and holding that the *Salyer* exception did not extend to a unit of general local government such as a city); *Hayward v. Clay*, 573 F.2d 187 (4th Cir. 1978) (invalidating statute providing that annexation had to be approved by a majority of the freeholders in the annexation area and by a majority of the registered voters in the annexation area and the annexing city, counted together).

(e) *Carving out unhappy candidates for annexation?* In an unusual twist to the accommodation of interests, the Alabama Supreme Court set aside an annexation election in which the boundaries of the territory to be annexed had admittedly been drawn to exclude those voters who were opposed to the annexation. *City of Birmingham v. Community Fire Dist.*, 336 So. 2d 502 (Ala. 1976). The court quoted *Kramer* to the effect that absent a compelling state interest, qualified voters may not be excluded from an election unless their stake in the outcome was substantially smaller than that of the ones allowed to vote. But see *City of Birmingham v. Wilkinson*, 516 So. 2d 585 (Ala. 1987) (upholding exclusion of land from voting area in annexation election).

(f) *Weighing views of more remote rural residents?* In *St. Louis County v. City of Town & Country*, 590 F. Supp. 731 (E.D. Mo. 1984), the court upheld an annexation statute that limited the right to vote to voters in the annexing municipality and the area to be annexed. The court rejected a claim that the statute was unconstitutional because it denied residents of the unincorporated areas of St. Louis County the right to vote in annexation elections initiated by suburbs: "The legislature could have rationally determined that residents of the annexing municipality and the area to be annexed are most directly affected by an annexation. The former will have to absorb new territory and provide services for it. The latter will become part of the municipality." *Id.* at 739. The court also rejected a claim that the impact of the annexation on voters in the unincorporated areas of the county was sufficient to establish a constitutional right to vote in annexation elections.

A Note on the Federal Voting Rights Act and Its Significance

The Federal Voting Rights Act: An Introduction

Although this section has focused on constitutional debates concerning the application of the one person-one vote principle, it is also important to appreciate the role of federal statutes in related current debates, particularly since constitutional and statutory issues are often intertwined in recent litigation. The federal Voting Rights Act (VRA), codified at 42 U.S.C. §§ 1973 to 1973aa-6, is of particular significance. Initially adopted more than 50 years ago at a crucial juncture in the civil rights struggle, the VRA has repeatedly been reauthorized at times in response to Supreme Court decisions that have limited its application. The legislation was adopted pursuant to Congress's power under the Fourteenth and Fifteenth Amendments. The Fourteenth Amendment has been discussed earlier. The Fifteenth Amendment provides "The right of citizens of the United States to vote shall not be denied or abridged by the United States or by any State on account of race, color, or previous condition of servitude" and empowers Congress to enforce the Amendment through legislative action.

The VRA has three especially important provisions. Section 5 requires preclearance of actions affecting voting rights in states found to have a history of voting discrimination under Section 4. Section 5 was thus designed as a prophylactic measure that could prevent covered states from instituting practices that created anticipated impediments to voting rights. The United States Supreme Court significantly limited the potential for the federal Voting Rights Act to curb state and local actions that might limit the rights of voters in *Shelby County, Ala. v. Holder*, 570 U.S. 529 (2013). In a decision authored by Chief Justice Roberts, the Court's majority concluded that the formula for determining which jurisdictions would be subject to "preclearance" by the United States Justice Department could no longer be justified in order to impose these requirements on only some of the states, thus obliterating a system that had provided an opportunity for review before action could be taken that would result in discriminatory practices adversely affecting the right to vote. For discussion of this important case, see Charles & Fuentes-Rohwer, *Race, Federalism, and Voting Rights*, 2015 U. Chi. Legal F. 113 (2015). Subsequently, in *Alabama Legislative Black Caucus v. Alabama*, 135 S. Ct. 1257 (2015), minority state legislators challenged legislative redistricting based on Alabama's efforts to among other things minimize districts' deviation from precisely equal population and avoid retrogression as to racial minorities' ability to elect preferred candidates. The Court concluded that racial gerrymandering claims had to be analyzed on a district-by-district basis, equal population goal was not a factor for the purposes at hand, and § 5 of the Voting Rights Act did not require a covered jurisdiction to maintain a particular numerical minority percentage for purposes of redistricting. As a result of *Shelby County*, § 2 of the Voting Rights Act and constitutional challenges now provide the principal bases on which discriminatory practices can be challenged under federal law.

Section 2 of the VRA, 42 U.S.C. § 1973, states that "[n]o voting qualification or prerequisite to voting or standard, practice, or procedure shall be imposed or applied by any State or political subdivision in a manner which results in a denial or abridgement of the right of any citizen of the United States to vote on account of race or color." *Id.* at § 1973(a). It further provides that violations of subsection (a) can be established "if, based on the totality of circumstances, it is shown that the political processes leading to nomination or election in the State or political subdivision are not equally open to participation by members of a class of citizens protected by subsection (a) of this section in that its members have less opportunity than other members of the electorate to participate in the political process and to elect representatives of their choice. The extent to which members of a protected class have been elected to office in the State or political subdivision is one circumstance which may be considered." *Id.* at § 1973(b).

Section 2 of the VRA is a nationwide prohibition against voting practices and procedures that discriminate on the basis of race, color, or membership in a language minority group. Such practices may include redistricting plans and at-large election systems, poll worker hiring, and voter registration procedures. Section 2 prohibits discriminatory election-related practices and procedures. It also monitors elections that are intended to be racially discriminatory and related matters that are shown to have a racially discriminatory result. Section 2 can be used both by the United States Justice Department and by private litigants who seek to enforce the specified rights.

Assume, for example, that a large city is governed by a city council of ten members. The population of the city is 60% white, and 40% black, and both groups live in relatively segregated areas. If the council is elected from single-member districts, the minority black population might well elect four representatives—depending, of course, on how the district lines are drawn and other factors. If, on the other hand, the council members are elected at large—and racial bloc voting occurs—the black population could find itself with no representation on the council. There is no violation of one-person-one-vote in the at-large election: every voter has equal voting power. But every group does not necessarily have equal representation of its interests. A similar practice, which has comparable effects, is the use of multi-member rather than single-member districts for state and local legislative bodies. These types of practices are generally seen as resulting in "dilution" of minority votes and can be challenged under Section 2 of the VRA.

The current text of § 2 was adopted in 1982. The Senate report on this legislation cited approvingly some nine factors which might be probative of a Section 2 violation, developed in an earlier decision, *Zimmer v. McKeithen*, 485 F.2d 1297 (5th Cir. 1973), *aff'd on other grounds*, 424 U.S. 636 (1976). The courts struggled to sort out the priority of factors suggested by Congress. Finally, in 1986, in *Thornburg v. Gingles*, 478 U.S. 30 (1986) the Supreme Court announced three threshold conditions which a challenger must prove to reach a "totality of circumstances" violation of Section 2: "First, . . . that [the minority] is sufficiently large and geographically compact to constitute a majority in a single-member district"; second, "that it is politically cohesive"; and third, "that the white majority votes sufficiently as a bloc to enable it . . . usually to defeat the minority's preferred candidate." 478 U.S. at 50–51. While *Gingles* involved multi-member legislative districts, the Court later held that the *Gingles* preconditions also applied to a Section 2 dilution challenge to single-member districts. *Growe v. Emison*, 507 U.S. 25 (1993).

For discussion of § 2 after *Shelby County*, see Elmendorf & Spender, *Administering Section 2 of the Voting Rights Act After Shelby County*, 115 Colum. L. Rev. 2143 (2015); Tokaji, *Applying Section 2 to the New Vote Denial*, 50 Harv. C.R.-C.L. L. Rev. 439 (2015). See also Fielkow, *Shelby County and Local Governments: A Case Study of Local Governments Diluting Minority Votes*, 14 Nw. J. L. & Soc. Pol'y 348 (2019) (exploring empirical data on local government practices following *Shelby County*); Vandewalker & Bentele, *Vulnerability in Numbers: Racial Composition of the Electorate, Voter Suppression, and the Voting Rights Act*, 18 Harv. Latino L. Rev. 99 (2015).

[2] Educational Funding and Policy Choices

The nation's system of public schools has been a perennial concern for parents, educational advocates, and public policy makers. This section includes two subparts that demonstrate the ways in the courts and legislatures have wrestled with important policy issues relating to public education.

The first tug-of-war concerned systems of school finance that were challenged beginning in the 1970's, as advocates argued that low-wealth school districts and the children they serve should receive more substantial funding. A number of legal theories were developed and deployed over the past half-century in both federal and state courts. Such theories met with varying success and led in many states to serious show-downs between the courts and state legislatures regarding the adequacy and approach to state funding for public education. At this juncture, state courts, legislatures, and governors in nearly all states have grappled with state constitutional challenges relating to public school funding. Theories have evolved over the years, but the core struggle among the different branches of government have persisted, with courts typically relying on state constitutional provisions to force legislatures to address educational inequities. School finance litigation is a prototypical example of the ultimate role of the courts in dealing with legislative inaction in the face of pressing equity issues and budget constraints.

The second tug-of-war, of much more recent vintage, concerns the development of systems of public charter schools, beginning in St. Paul, Minnesota in 1992. The development of such schools can be seen as akin to the "privatization" phenomenon discussed in Chapter 3. Public charter schools are seen by some as "educational laboratories" in which experiments can thrive without the bureaucratic constraints typically associated with other public schools. Such schools receive public funding, and teach students who would otherwise have been enrolled in public schools, but are overseen by independent boards that set educational policy. Not surprisingly, some parents and educational reformers champion public charter schools as a means to provide them with a "choice" of schools, thereby improving the education received by children who they believe may not thrive in traditional public schools, and ratcheting up expectations for public school performance. Others believe that legislative authorization of a growing number of charter schools effectively robs the traditional public schools of much-needed resources while leaving them with a higher proportion of minority students and those with special needs. As the number of charter schools has grown, litigation has flourished, raising significant questions of statutory and constitutional interpretation. Courts are increasingly called upon to mediate competing claims between advocates for public charter schools, and representatives of traditional public school systems. The second subpart of this section considers how these new forms of public education can be meshed with long-standing practices and legal principles, creating a new arena in which legislatures and courts may be at odds.

Problem 9-4

As a special assistant to the Governor of Midwest State, you have been asked to prepare an outline of a long term plan for funding K-12 education in that state. Midwest's current funding structure is generally similar to that described in the text that follows as an example of the Strayer-Haig formula. Assume that District A and District B described in that example are actual school districts in the state.

Midwest has not yet experienced a constitutional challenge to its school finance system, but interested civic groups are considering one. The state's constitution provides that "The legislature shall provide for a thorough and efficient system of free public schools." The state's constitution also contains an equal protection clause. In an earlier decision, the state supreme court enthusiastically endorsed in full the principles adopted by the Vermont Supreme Court in interpreting its equal protection clause equivalent in *Baker v. State*, reproduced in Chapter 1.

Expenditures per pupil in the state vary substantially. The richest school district spends more than twice the amount per pupil annually as the poorest district. Some of the low-spending districts are blue collar bedroom suburbs that have almost no commercial or industrial property and a limited property tax base. Others are rural. Metro City, which is the state's metropolis, has a high property tax base and also ranks higher than the median in annual expenditures per pupil. It also has a higher poverty rate, a larger number of non-English speaking and minority students, and a lower student educational achievement rate than any other city in the state. Its school district has the same boundaries as the city. Elsewhere in the state, school districts are independently organized and may cover several municipalities or even counties. Special programs of various kinds, including a program for disabled students, make up one-third of all spending on K-12 education.

More than half of the school districts, including that of Metro City, were not meeting the standards mandated by the federal No Child Left Behind Act when it was in effect from 2002–2015, and apprehension continues about how subsequent legislation amending the federal Elementary and Secondary Education Act (including the "Every Student Succeeds Act of 2015" and subsequent modifications) will affect the state. The state had requested waiver of some of the requirements under the No Child Left Behind Act, and federal authorities agreed so long as the state agreed to implement Common Core standards that were originally proposed by a coalition of state governors and chief state school officers and were subsequently embraced by federal authorities. More recently, however, some parents and legislators have called for the abolition of Common Core standards in favor of the less stringent state requirements that had previously been in effect. [More details on relevant federal laws are provided below.]

In addition, the state is home to a growing movement ("More Choice for All") favoring parental "choice" of schools. In some instances, proponents of "school choice" are parents who feel that the local schools have been ineffective in serving their children or that the local school to which their children have been assigned are not the ones they would like their children to attend. In other cases, parents would prefer to send their children to schools that reflect an educational philosophy or emphasis different from the practices in use for existing public schools. The More Choice for All group is currently advocating a significant increase in the number of publicly-funded charter schools in the state. As a result of the group's advocacy, a substantial number of state legislators wants to include authorization for an expanded number of charter schools as part of any school finance reform package.

How would you address the Governor's request, keeping in mind educational and legal principles? What if Midwest State did not have the "Thorough and Efficient" Clause in its constitution, or if the state supreme court did not follow *Baker v. State* on the equal protection issues? What legal issues would you expect to arise under state constitutions if the state legislature authorizes an increase in the number of public charter schools?

[a] School Finance and Traditional Public Schools

[i] Introduction

The school finance reform movement that began in the late 1960s and early 1970s focused a spotlight on more issues of fundamental importance to state and local government than perhaps any other dispute in recent history. These issues include the priority of universal public education, the responsibilities of public schools, and the point at which "control" of the school should rest. In addition, they concern funding sources, the balance of state and local power and responsibility, and the roles of the separate branches of government.[5]

Before delving into relevant funding mechanisms and school finance litigation, it is worth considering why issues of school finance have been so vexing. It is worth spending time to gather your own thoughts on this topic and to engage with those whose views may differ. In doing so, you may want to consider matters such as the following:

- *What is an "adequate education" that can reasonably be expected to be available to every child with public support?* Should it matter where a child grows up, whether they face poverty or disability, and whether they live in a poor or affluent neighborhood?
- *Education is among the most important determinants of future personal and economic success. Many would agree that related opportunities should be made available "equitably."* What do we mean by "equitably"? How does "equity" differ from "equality" particularly if students may have different abilities and face different challenges?
- *There is clear evidence that the federal government facilitated years of housing segregation that adversely affected people of color. As a result, many neighborhoods continue to be segregated and many people of color have lacked opportunities to accrue wealth to the extent that majority populations have.* In many places, school districts and neighborhood school catchment areas continue to reflect this history. Should such concerns have a bearing on how courts address

---

5. Influential early scholarship had a significant effect on litigation strategy. See Horowitz, *Unseparate But Unequal—The Emerging Fourteenth Amendment Issue in Public Education*, 13 UCLA L. Rev. 1147 (1966) (concerned primarily with inequalities between individual schools in advantaged and disadvantaged areas within a school district); A. Wise, Rich Schools, Poor Schools (1968), based on his earlier article, *Is Denial of Equal Educational Opportunity Constitutional?* 13 Admin. Notebook 2 (U. Chi. 1965), and his unpublished doctoral dissertation at the University of Chicago, The Constitution And Equality: Wealth, Geography And Educational Opportunity (1967) (the 1965 article was probably the first published challenge to school financing as a violation of equal protection); J. Coons, W. Clune & S. Sugarman, Private Wealth And Public Education (1970) [hereinafter cited as "J. Coons et al., Private Wealth"], and their earlier article, *Educational Opportunity: A Workable Test for State Financial Structures*, 57 Cal. L. Rev. 305 (1969).

educational equity issues that arise in part because of the continued presence of the effects of historic segregation?

- *Assuming we could agree on what is meant by "adequate" and "equitable," how would we know whether these lodestars are in fact being met?* Should the focus be on "inputs" (dollars, teachers, counselors, programming, enrichment opportunities, facilities), or on "outputs" such as scores on achievement tests, successful college placement, or economic success following graduation?
- *How do we fund education?* What responsibilities should be borne by local governments, the states, and the federal government? Should expectations differ depending on local capacity (for example tax base) or state choices (for example whether to implement income taxes)? Who should bear the brunt of enhanced costs facing certain children, for example those who have limited English proficiency, are disabled, or live in urban or rural areas rather than suburbs? What about areas where the federal government has special responsibilities (for example, those with major military bases or Native American reservations)? What about areas of concentrated poverty?
- *What services should be funded in the name of education?* Evidence has shown that poverty, poor nutrition, and exposure to toxins can adversely affect young children's ability to learn. What nutrition and health services should be regarded as part of the "education" mandate? Should schools have to provide transportation? Should extracurricular opportunities be provided at public cost to students whose parents choose to employ "home schooling" strategies?
- *Who should decide and what units are appropriate for decision-making and funding?* We live in an increasingly divided political universe. How should educational decision-making be structured? For example, should politically-constituted state boards get to mandate curriculum, texts and programming (for example, opting for texts that may not fully or accurately accept scientific or historical understandings; or that prohibit schools from teaching "mindfulness techniques" or sex education)? Should states allow or encourage multiple school districts within their counties even if doing so may result in depleted resources due to redundant administrative costs or favor some populations over others? Should parents' organizations in wealthy schools or districts be allowed to raise and retain substantial supplemental funding, despite the unintended effect of comparatively disadvantaging poorer schools nearby whose parents lack the funds or social capital to do the same?

A thoughtful consideration of these vexing matters should suggest why disputes regarding school finance have not been readily resolved over the last several decades. Both the states and the federal government have been embroiled in related debates. Nearly all states have experienced lawsuits challenging their school finance systems. Suits were filed in Michigan, Illinois, Virginia, Texas, and

California, challenging the constitutional validity of those states' school finance systems, as early as 1968. Often such lawsuits continue through multiple rounds, and perhaps with differing plaintiffs, over many years, as occurred in New Jersey. Often recurring constitutional challenges result in standoffs between state supreme courts and state legislatures, such as occurred in Kansas in spring 2014. For a very useful website that monitors ongoing school finance litigation, see http://schoolfunding.info/.

In the nearly 50 years since active debate about school funding entered the public eye and scholarly journals, a number of core questions have persisted, many of which were outlined above to help you get started in your reflection about these challenging matters. As you consider the material that follows, continue to consider a host of questions such as the following. What amount, source and distribution of resources is necessary to satisfy state constitutions? How should accountability for raising and allocating such resources be assigned and measured? What is the appropriate role of the courts in overseeing this most basic of public policies? What are the powers and responsibilities of state and local governments for supporting public schools, and what are the respective roles of the courts and state legislatures in assuring that necessary resources to support public education are available?

[ii] Funding Frameworks

A 2019 study by the Congressional Research Service provides an excellent overview of school funding practices in the United States. See Skinner & Riddle, *State and Local Financing of Public Schools* (Congressional Research Service, R45827, August 26, 2019), available at https://eric.ed.gov/?id=ED597879 (hereinafter referred to as "CRS Report"). It draws on a number of other sophisticated data sources including the following: National Center for Education Statistics (https://nces.ed.gov/programs/digest/2017menu_tables.asp); D. Verstegen, *A Quick Glance at School Finance: A 50 State Survey of School Finance Policies*, 2018 (https://schoolfinancesdav.wordpress.com/); Ed Build, FundEd: State Education Funding Policies for all 50 States, 2019 (http://funded.edbuild.org/); Urban Institute (https://apps.urban.org/features/funding-formulas/); Education Commission of the States, 50-State Comparison: K-12 Funding, August 5, 2019 (https://www.ecs.org/50-state-comparison-k-12-funding/). Students particularly interested in this area would be well-advised to explore these and other relevant sources of data on school funding around the country. This section highlights some key themes.

- *Growing state role*. According to the CRS report, a total of $678.4 billion in revenues was devoted to public elementary and secondary education in the 2015–16 school year. State governments provided $318.6 billion (47.0%) of these revenues, local governments provided $303.8 billion (44.8%), and the federal government provided $56.0 billion (8.3%). This trend compares to the situation in 1965–66, when states provided 39.1% of funding, localities provided 53.0% and the federal government provided 7.9%.

- *Substantial differences across the states.* Putting aside outliers, there are still significant disparaties among states. For example, Vermont covers 89.7% of school funding at the state level, while Illinois only provides 24.1% of funding from state funds. Other states lie between these poles.
- *Elements of typical funding structures.*
    - *Foundation programs.* Foundation programs date back to the 1930s. States typically established an annual target level of funding per pupil applicable to all the states' local education agencies (LEAs). This funding target typically is treated as a minimum level of funding per pupil and in some jurisdictions is regarded as a baseline for providing funding for an "adequate" educational program. This framework is not intended to assure fiscal equity, but as a minimum. Some jurisdictions weight foundation funding requirements to take into account student characteristics (such as grade level, type of educational program, disability, family income, and locality).
    - *Flat grants.* Flat grants have been important since the early 20th century (originally as a primary form of state aid, but subsequently as a supplement to foundation programs). These programs provide grants of an equal amount per pupil to all LEAs in a state (notwithstanding student characteristics or level of property wealth).
    - *District power equalizing.* This form of funding endeavors to equalize the capacity of LEAs to raise revenues, taking into account differences between localities in baseline taxable property values. Under such systems, localities are expected to raise a minimum level of revenue based on local tax rates. If a district cannot raise the anticipated level of revenue due to insufficient taxable property, then state funds will be used to supplement the local effort. Sometimes equalization aid is referred to as embodying the Strayer-Haig formula (named for educational funding reformers who urged its adoption in New York state). States adopting district power equalizing often combine such funding with foundation aid and flat grants, as exemplified below.
    - *Categorical aid.* States (and the federal government) also use categorical grants to augment the funding systems outlined above. Categorical aid typically targets funding toward students with specific needs (those with disabilities, limited English proficiency, low wealth, urban or rural contexts).

Fitting the pieces together. Consider how these diverse elements and funding sources might come together through the following example.

District A has an assessed valuation (AV) of $10,000 per pupil in average daily attendance (ADA) (computed by dividing the total district AV of $10 million by the number of pupils, 1,000, in ADA); District B has an AV of $50,000 per pupil in ADA. The formula would produce these results:

Basic Scenario

District A

$10,000 AV per pupil	
Qualifying tax rate raises (local funds)	$100
Flat grant adds (*state funds*)	50
	$150
Foundation level guarantees	$500
	−150
Equalization aid (*state funds*)	$350
Total available at qualifying rate	= $500

District B

$50,000 AV per pupil	
Qualifying tax rate raises (local funds)	$500
Flat grant adds (*state funds*)	50
	$550
District B receives no *state* equalization aid	
Total available at qualifying rate	= $550

Next, assume both districts choose to impose a 20 mill tax rate, 10 mills in excess of the qualifying rate:

With Additional Property Tax Levy

District A

Qualifying tax rate raises	$100
plus flat grant (*state*)	50
plus equalization (*state*)	350
Additional 10 mills property tax	100
Total available to spend	$600

District B

Qualifying tax rate raises	$500
plus flat grant (*state*)	50
no equalization (*state*)	0
Additional 10 mills property tax	500
Total available to spend	$1050

Note these characteristics of the formula: the foundation plan has some equalizing effect under the figures used in the example; the flat grant adds nothing to District A's state aid because it is effectively absorbed in the equalization aid; indeed, the flat grant serves to dis-equalize; at identical tax rates above the minimum qualifying rate, District A falls farther behind District B in the amount of funds raised, or, to reverse the equation, District B can spend more with the same or less effort. While some states imposed maximum tax rates on school districts, they normally were in excess of the qualifying rate, and, in any event, could usually be overridden by referendum.

In other words, this program type provides for a minimum guaranteed tax base for public elementary and secondary education in the state. It is often said that

District Power Equalizing focuses on equity for taxpayers, while frequently allowing substantial variation in local tax rates and thereby in total state and local funding per pupil, depending on local preferences. Reportedly, fewer states than in the past currently rely primarily on this type of program, though several still incorporate it as part of multifaceted state school finance systems (i.e., in conjunction with Foundation Programs, etc.).

Based on your initial impressions, how would you evaluate the overall system of school finance commonly used in the United States? What recommendations for change might you offer? Why? What political realities might affect the feasibility of implementing your recommendations?

A Note on Recapture ("Robin Hood") Strategies

Occasionally, states have employed quite different approaches to disparities in funding between school districts. A particularly interesting variation has been referred to as the "Robin Hood" approach (or as "recapture"), because it involves taking from richer districts to give to poorer districts. While Wisconsin and Vermont adopted this approach some years ago, Texas became the leading proponent of this funding strategy in more recent years. What questions (legal, policy, and political) would such a strategy raise in a state such as Midwest State?

Wisconsin was one of the early states to include a recapture provision (referred to as a "negative aid" in Wisconsin) in its school financial package. This recapture approach was held to violate the constitutional rule of uniform taxation in *Buse v. Smith*, 247 N.W.2d 141 (Wis. 1976). Vermont also enacted a form of "recapture" under which excess local property taxes raised by property-wealthy districts had to be redistributed to property-poor districts. Vermont's program survived legal challenge in *Stowe Citizens for Responsible Govt. v. State*, 730 A.2d 573 (Vt. 1999), but was eliminated as part of a major compromise revision of Vermont's school funding approach. The revised Vermont program did, however, retain the state property tax while reducing local property taxes, financing the cuts with a state sales tax increase.

The Texas experiment is noteworthy. While not the first to take such steps, Texas subsequently adopted a different type of "equalization" system, one that applied "Robin Hood" principles to recapture and redistribute funds derived from designated "high wealth" school districts to those designated as "low wealth." See Ch. 41, TEXAS EDUCATION CODE ("Equalized Wealth Level"). The recapture structure was set by statute, which provided high-property-value districts with a menu of options for reallocating funds, including paying the state ("purchasing attendance credits") or contracting with partner districts to educate nonresident students. The history behind the Texas "Robin Hood" approach and other similar strategies is worth noting. Other states have experimented with similar strategies. See Reynolds, *Skybox Schools: Public Education as Private Luxury*, 82 WASH. U. L.Q. 755 (2004) (discussing earlier Vermont and Texas practices).

Prior to facing several rounds of school finance litigation, Texas historically employed a system of foundational funding that combined state and local tax revenue, augmented by additional state funding to supplement poor-wealth school districts. Texas had not adopted a state income tax, so its funding of schools relied on other revenue sources (such as taxes on oil). As discussed below, a challenge to Texas' approach to school funding was brought on federal constitutional grounds and proved unsuccessful in *San Antonio Independent School District v. Rodriguez*, 411 U.S. 1 (1973) (rejecting claims by poorly funded school district that sharply disparate funding for Texas school districts violated the federal Equal Protection Clause).

In subsequent rounds of litigation, claims under the state constitution proved more successful. See *Edgewood Indep. Sch. Dist. v. Kirby*, 777 S.W.2d 391 (Tex. 1989) (*Edgewood I*) (successful challenge under a state constitutional provision requiring support for an "efficient system of public free schools," resulting in order by the Texas Supreme Court that the state legislature modify the funding system). After additional unsuccessful efforts to modify the system as required by the state supreme court, the Texas legislature took steps to limit the funding disparities between school districts by imposing a cap on local property taxes, an approach that the state supreme court upheld in 1995. See *Edgewood Indep. Sch. Dist. v. Meno*, 917 S.W.2d 717 (Tex. 1995) *(Edgewood IV)*.

Before long, however, Texas's school finance system was again before the state supreme court, where it was successfully challenged as creating a state-wide property tax system (the result of limiting local discretion in setting property tax levels), something that was prohibited by the state constitution. *Neeley v. West Orange-Cove Consol. Indep. Sch. Dist.*, 176 S.W.3d 746 (Tex. 2005) *(West Orange-Cove II)*. In response, in 2006, the state legislature maintained a cap on local property taxes but adopted a new set of formulas setting maximum per student funding allowances, continued to cap the amount of tax money each school district could collect, and began allocating cigarette and business tax revenues to supplement funding for low-wealth districts. School districts that exceeded the cap were given statutory options (such as consolidating with other districts or educating nonresident students).

Soon, however, the situation changed again. In 2011, during the national economic downturn, the state legislature cut the state education budget by $5.4 billion, notwithstanding significant growth in the school-age population. State constitutional amendments were also passed to provide more flexibility to state agencies responsible for managing and allocating school funds held in endowments. A number of lawsuits were filed, leading to extensive trial proceedings and a trial court decision in 2013 that the state had not made available sufficient funds to meet state constitutional requirements and had not distributed funds equitably. The Texas legislature responded by restoring much of the funding that had been cut. Trial court proceedings resumed early in 2014 to determine whether legislative action in 2013 had resulted in a constitutional funding system.

The Texas Supreme Court again considered the state's funding system in *Morath v. Texas Taxpayer and Student Fairness Coalition*, 490 S.W.3d 826 (Tex. 2016). The Texas Supreme Court noted that more than half of the state's 1,000 plus school districts had joined in the litigation, resulting in a record exceeding 200,000 pages, 1,508 findings of fact and 118 conclusions of law. The school districts' challenge was based on claims that the school system was constitutionally inadequate, unsuitable, and financially inefficient in violation of the state's constitution; the statewide ad valorem tax was unconstitutional; funding for charter schools was constitutionally inadequate; and English language learners and economically disadvantaged students did not receive constitutionally adequate and suitable educations. The Texas Supreme Court upheld the legislature's actions as constitutionally sufficient, concluding that the constitutional requirement of "general diffusion of knowledge" did not require adequate funding, adequacy in class size, tutoring, interventions for special needs students, nurses or security guards. It further held that student achievement generally was adequate to satisfy the "general diffusion of knowledge" requirement, as were English language learners' and economically disadvantaged students' performance, notwithstanding disparities in performance compared to others. The public school system also satisfied the state constitution's "financial efficiency" requirement and "qualitative efficiency" requirement. In the court's view, the Legislative Budget Board's failure to comply with a statute requiring the Board to calculate funding necessary to achieve state educational policies did not violate the state constitution. For a discussion of the Texas school finance system, the *Morath* case, and possible alternative funding strategies that rely on state-wide resources, see Grey, *Remanants of "Separate, But Equal": What Is Wrong with Texas Public School Financing*?, 70 BAYLOR L. REV. 689 (2018).

In 2019, the Texas legislature overhauled the state's education finance system in HB3 (86th Tex. Leg. 2019). The legislation is lengthy and complex. See https://legiscan.com/TX/text/HB3/id/2027986/Texas-2019-HB3-Enrolled.html. The Texas Education Agency has slowly rolled out background materials, guidance documents, and regulations. https://tea.texas.gov/about-tea/government-relations-and-legal/government-relations/house-bill-3. Among important changes were an increase in state funding by more than $600 per average daily attendance, and an increase in teacher pay (with an added bump for those teaching in rural locales and high-need areas). An added allotment was created for early education particularly for students who are educationally disadvantaged, have limited English proficiency, have dyslexia, or need dual-language instruction. Day-long pre-K funding was provided for all four year-olds. The legislation also included an increase in compensatory funding based on density of neighborhood poverty (with the greatest increases going to schools with lowest socio-economic indicators, using census block data). The new system also uses current year property tax values, reduces property tax rates, reduces property tax revenue recapture, and applies recapture only to wealth in excess of base entitlement levels (while eliminating prior "hold harmless" provisions). There are also a number of other nuanced changes as explained on the Texas

Education Agency's website. https://tea.texas.gov/sites/default/files/HB%203%20Master%20Deck%20Final.pdf.

A Note on the Federal Role in School Funding

As a final part of the funding puzzle, it is important to understand the role played by the federal government, pursuant to federal statute and regulations issued by the United States Department of Education.

Relevant federal statutes and strategies have evolved over the years. It is important to realize the extent to which the federal government plays a role in policy-setting and funding of elementary and secondary education in order to gain a full picture of how state and local government policies and funding decisions are made.

The leading federal statute dealing with elementary and secondary school is the Elementary and Secondary Education Act, adopted in 1965, under the leadership of President Lyndon Johnson. Elementary and Secondary Education Act of 1965, Pub. L. No. 89-10, 79 Stat. 27 (1965). In a helpful article tracing the overall history of this legislation (which has been reauthorized and modified several times), Professor Derek Black observed:

> The Act drastically expanded federal funding for schools, which previously was almost nonexistent. Specifically, it drove those funds toward schools serving large percentages of poor students. As a result, the impact on each student and school was more significant than it would have been through a general education aid package. This focused approach on concentrated poverty also meant that, as a practical matter, federal dollars went to the locus of segregation—the South and the North's larger cities. Given the existing education funding practices of states, those funds were sorely needed in poor and predominantly minority communities.... The Elementary and Secondary Education Act was not an attempt to change the teaching profession, reform education standards, or update curricula.

Black, *Abandoning the Federal Role in Education: The Every Student Succeeds Act*, 105 Calif. L. Rev. 1309, 1317–18 (2017) (hereinafter referred to as Black, "*Every Student Succeeds Act*"). Included in the legislation was a provision ("Title I") that allocated supplemental funds to school districts serving students from low-income families, and specified that associated funds be used to "supplement, not supplant" other sources of funding. *Id.* at 1318–19.

Subsequently, the country's commitment to equality and civil rights began to waver. During the 1980s, President Reagan consolidated federal programs into block grants as a way of limiting federal oversight, funding stopped growing, and the ESEA became more akin to general federal aid for education. *Id.* at 1321–1322. Later, during the 1990s, the ESEA was reauthorized as the "Improving America's Schools Act," which changed funding formulas and attempted to encourage states to equalize their funding formulas. The reauthorization also sought to hold states accountable for the education of poor students, and required states to establish standards for math and language arts and to test students periodically on those subjects. *Id.* at 1322–23.

In 2002, President George W. Bush signed the No Child Left Behind Act (NCLB), providing additional federal funding, and in return requiring schools to engage in more intensive testing of students, mandating performance levels by subgroups of students, and setting standards for "highly qualified" teachers. More specifically, the NCLB modified Title I to require that states adopt "challenging" academic standards in English, math and science and admininister recurring tests of student performance. Schools were also obliged to attain "adequate yearly progress" (AYP) levels (racheting up until full proficiency to be achieved in 2014) for all schools in the state. Moreover, proficiency levels had to be shown by disaggregated subgroups (based on gender, race, ethnicity, disability, language status, and socioeconomic status). Failure to achieve AYP had implications for schools, including designation as "in need of improvement," requirements for technical assistance, and possible transfer opportunities. *Id.* at 1324–25. See also Black, *Federalizing Education by Waiver*, 68 VAND. L. REV. 607 (2015).

An increasing number of states have rejected the use of "Common Core" standards under an initiative initially instigated by state superintendents of schools, challenging the venture as reflecting federal intrusion and overreach. For a summary of Common Core standards, see http://www.corestandards.org/. The Common Core standards played an important role in determining waivers or providing supplementing funding to states based on adoption of Common Core standards. The Common Core standards became unpopular in some quarters when they were regarded as a form of federal intrusion with significant implementation challenges. See also Takhar, *No Freedom in a Ship of Fools: A Democratic Justification for the Common Core State Standards and Federal Involvement in K-12 Education*, 26 HASTINGS WOMEN'S L.J. 355 (2015); Kempson, *Star-Crossed Lovers: The Department of Education and the Common Core*, 67 ADMIN. L. REV. 595 (2015).

The latest reauthorization of the ESEA was adopted in 2015 as the "Every Student Succeeds Act" (ESSA). Several key aspects of this legislation should be noted. Standards are expected to be "challenging," and the term is more fully defined as including standards "designed to prepare students for college and careers." ESSA continues to impose testing requirements, but test scores are now treated as one factor among others in assessing student progress, and the focus on low-performing schools is on those in the bottom five percent of performers and high schools with graduation rates below 66 percent. ESSA addresses teacher quality by listing ways in which associated federal funds may be used, requiring teachers to be certified, and prohibiting federal regulators from mandating state teacher evaluation systems. Black, *Every Student Succeeds Act, supra*, at 1332–1338. For further analysis of the ESSA, see Robinson, *Restructing the Elementary and Secondary Education Act's Approach to Equity*, 103 MINN. L. REV. 915 (2018).

There are, of course, other important federal statutes and regulations affecting elementary and secondary education. For example, the federal government has played a crucial role in fostering improved education for students with disabilities. See, e.g., Individuals with Disabilities Education Act, 20 U.S.C. §§ 1400–1482. Various civil rights provisions also apply, including nondiscrimination statutes applicable to programs receiving federal funds (for example Title VI relating to discrimination based on race, and Title IX relating to discrimination based on gender). For a discussion of the federal role generally, see Bowman, *The Failure of Education Federalism*, 51 U. Mich. J.L. Reform 1 (2017) (arguing for larger federal role in elementary and secondary education in order to establish a floor of educational quality; suggesting a litigation strategy that pairs a right to educational quality with substantive due process and equal protection review, and urging development of a more meaningful form of cooperative federalism). See also Shoffner, *Education Reform from the Two-Sided Congressional Coin*, 45 J.L. & Educ. 269 (2016) (discussing increased discretion for the states). For a more general discussion of education federalism, see Robinson, *Disrupting Education Federalism*, 92 Wash. U. L. Rev. 959 (2015) (reviewing historical developments and arguing for a stronger federal role).

Based on your understanding of revenue options as discussed in Chapter 4, and this brief introduction to historical state and local funding strategies, what approach would you take if you were a legislator facing the challenges raised in Problem 9-4?

[iii] The First Wave: Challenges Under Federal Law

Issues of equality were front and center during the civil rights era that played such a crucial role in reshaping the law and public policy during the 1960s. Not surprisingly, those seeking school finance reform initially sought relief in the federal courts and relied upon the federal constitution in developing litigation strategies.

McInnis v. Shapiro, 293 F. Supp. 327 (N.D. Ill. 1968), *aff'd sub nom. McInnis v. Ogilvie*, 394 U.S. 322 (1969), was an important early case that sought financial reform on behalf of high school and elementary school students attending school in four school districts located in Cook County, Illinois. The school finance system in effect relied upon local school districts to raise funds based on property taxation (which constituted approximately 75% of school funds), while the state provided both a flat grant of $400 and an equalization grant for districts that employed a minimum property tax rate. Funds available for expenditure accordingly varied significantly from one district to another. Plaintiffs claimed that the system of school funding that created significant disparities between school districts and thus violated the federal Equal Protection Clause because some students received good educations while others did not, despite the fact that these others had equal or greater educational need.

The three-judge court convened to hear the case determined that plaintiffs had not stated a cause of action. The court concluded that "(1) the Fourteenth Amendment does not require that public school expenditures be made only on the basis of pupils' educational needs, and (2) the lack of judicially manageable standards makes this controversy nonjusticiable." *Id.* at 329.

Similar suits challenging school funding systems that relied heavily on property tax and thus resulted in substantial disparities between districts were filed in nearly half the states. A Texas suit, also filed in 1968, made its way to the United States Supreme Court. The Court was faced with the need to consider whether an elevated level of Equal Protection scrutiny was required under the federal Constitution, in light of the crucial importance of elementary and secondary education and the vast differences in school funding available from one district to the next.

San Antonio Independent School District v. Rodriguez

411 U.S. 1 (1973)

Mr. Justice Powell delivered the opinion of the Court.

This suit attacking the Texas system of financing public education was initiated by Mexican-American parents whose children attend the elementary and secondary schools in the Edgewood Independent School District, an urban school district in San Antonio, Texas. They brought a class action on behalf of school children throughout the State who are members of minority groups or who are poor and reside in school districts having a low property tax base. Named as defendants were the State Board of Education, the Commissioner of Education, the State Attorney General, and the Bexar County (San Antonio) Board of Trustees. The complaint was filed in the summer of 1968 and a three-judge court was impaneled in January 1969. In December 1971 the panel rendered its judgment in a *per curiam* opinion holding the Texas school finance system unconstitutional under the Equal Protection Clause of the Fourteenth Amendment. The State appealed, and we noted probable jurisdiction to consider the far-reaching constitutional questions presented. For the reasons stated in this opinion, we reverse the decision of the District Court. . . .

Until recent times, Texas was a predominantly rural State and its population and property wealth were spread relatively evenly across the State. Sizeable differences in the value of assessable property between local school districts became increasingly evident as the State became more industrialized and as rural-to-urban population shifts became more pronounced. The location of commercial and industrial property began to play a significant role in determining the amount of tax resources available to each school district. These growing disparities in population and taxable property between districts were responsible in part for increasingly notable differences in levels of local expenditure for education. . . .

[The Court traced the development of the Texas school financing system. The Texas Minimum Foundation School Program, while more complex than in many states, had similar characteristics: a combination of local property taxes and state funds. Every school district imposed additional property taxes beyond its share of the Foundation Program. The Edgewood Independent School District, in which appellees resided, was located in the core city of San Antonio in a predominantly

Mexican-American residential neighborhood with little commercial or industrial property. Its assessed valuation per pupil was the lowest in the metropolitan area, as was the median family income. Its tax rate was the highest in the area. It received $222 per pupil from the Foundation Program which, combined with additional property taxes of $26 and federal aid of $108, gave it $356 per pupil. In contrast, Alamo Heights, the most affluent school district in San Antonio, was predominantly "Anglo," had a much higher assessed valuation per pupil, a higher median income and a lower tax rate. The Foundation Program provided Alamo Heights with $225 per pupil; its additional property tax raised $333 and federal aid was $36, for a total of $594.—Eds.]

Despite these recent increases [in state aid], substantial interdistrict disparities in school expenditures found by the District Court to prevail in San Antonio and in varying degrees throughout the State still exist. And it was these disparities, largely attributable to differences in the amounts of money collected through local property taxation that led the District Court to conclude that Texas' dual system of public school financing violated the Equal Protection Clause....

Texas virtually concedes that its historically rooted dual system of financing education could not withstand the strict judicial scrutiny that this Court has found appropriate in reviewing legislative judgments that interfere with fundamental constitutional rights or that involve suspect classifications.... [Indeed, the Court said, under its traditional strict scrutiny analysis, "the Texas financing system and its counterpart in virtually every other State will not pass muster."—Eds.] ...

We are unable to agree that this case, which in significant aspects is *sui generis*, may be so neatly fitted into the conventional mosaic of constitutional analysis under the Equal Protection Clause. Indeed, for the several reasons that follow, we find neither the suspect-classification nor the fundamental-interest analysis persuasive....

The wealth discrimination discovered by the District Court in this case, and by several other courts that have recently struck down school-financing laws in other States, is quite unlike any of the forms of wealth discrimination heretofore reviewed by this Court....

The case comes to us with no definitive description of the classifying facts or delineation of the disfavored class. Examination of the District Court's opinion and of appellees' complaint, briefs, and contentions at oral argument suggests, however, at least three ways in which the discrimination claimed here might be described. The Texas system of school financing might be regarded as discriminating (1) against "poor" persons whose incomes fall below some identifiable level of poverty or who might be characterized as functionally "indigent," or (2) against those who are relatively poorer than others, or (3) against all those who, irrespective of their personal incomes, happen to reside in relatively poorer school districts. Our task must be to ascertain whether, in fact, the Texas system has been shown to discriminate on any of these possible bases and, if so, whether the resulting classification may be regarded as suspect. . . .

Only appellees' first possible basis for describing the class disadvantaged by the Texas school-financing system—discrimination against a class of definably "poor" persons—might arguably meet the criteria established in these prior cases. Even a cursory examination, however, demonstrates that neither of the two distinguishing characteristics of wealth classifications can be found here. First, in support of their charge that the system discriminates against the "poor," appellees have made no effort to demonstrate that it operates to the peculiar disadvantage of any class fairly definable as indigent, or as composed of persons whose incomes are beneath any designated poverty level. Indeed, there is reason to believe that the poorest families are not necessarily clustered in the poorest property districts. A recent and exhaustive study of school districts in Connecticut concluded that "[i]t is clearly incorrect . . . to contend that the 'poor' live in 'poor' districts. . . . Thus, the major factual assumption of *Serrano*—that the education financing system discriminates against the 'poor'—is simply false in Connecticut."

Second, neither appellees nor the District Court addressed the fact that, unlike each of the foregoing cases, lack of personal resources has not occasioned an absolute deprivation of the desired benefit. The argument here is not that the children in districts having relatively low assessable property values are receiving no public education; rather, it is that they are receiving a poorer quality education than that available to children in districts having more assessable wealth. Apart from the unsettled and disputed question whether the quality of education may be determined by the amount of money expended for it, a sufficient answer to appellees' argument is that, at least where wealth is involved, the Equal Protection Clause does not require absolute equality or precisely equal advantages. . . .

For these two reasons—the absence of any evidence that the financing system discriminates against any definable category of "poor" people or that it results in the absolute deprivation of education—the disadvantaged class is not susceptible of identification in traditional terms. . . .

This brings us, then, to the third way in which the classification scheme might be defined—*district* wealth discrimination. Since the only correlation indicated by the evidence is between district property wealth and expenditures, it may be argued that discrimination might be found without regard to the individual income characteristics of district residents. . . .

However described, it is clear that appellees' suit asks this Court to extend its most exacting scrutiny to review a system that allegedly discriminates against a large, diverse, and amorphous class, unified only by the common factor of residence in districts that happen to have less taxable wealth than other districts. The system of alleged discrimination and the class it defines have none of the traditional indicia of suspectness: the class is not saddled with such disabilities, or subjected to such a history of purposeful unequal treatment, or relegated to such a position of political powerlessness as to command extraordinary protection from the majoritarian political process.... [The Court then turned to an examination of appellees' second argument for invoking strict scrutiny; interference with the exercise of a fundamental right.—Eds.]

In *Brown v. Board of Education*, 347 U.S. 483 (1954), a unanimous Court recognized that "education is perhaps the most important function of state and local governments." *Id.* at 493. What was said there in the context of racial discrimination has lost none of its vitality with the passage of time....

Nothing this Court holds today in any way detracts from our historic dedication to public education. We are in complete agreement with the conclusion of the three-judge panel below that "the grave significance of education both to the individual and to our society" cannot be doubted. But the importance of a service performed by the State does not determine whether it must be regarded as fundamental for purposes of examination under the Equal Protection Clause.... It is not the province of this Court to create substantive constitutional rights in the name of guaranteeing equal protection of the laws. Thus, the key to discovering whether education is "fundamental" is not to be found in comparisons of the relative societal significance of education as opposed to subsistence or housing. Nor is it to be found by weighing whether education is as important as the right to travel. Rather, the answer lies in assessing whether there is a right to education explicitly or implicitly guaranteed by the Constitution.

Education, of course, is not among the rights afforded explicit protection under our Federal Constitution. Nor do we find any basis for saying it is implicitly so protected. As we have said, the undisputed importance of education will not alone cause this Court to depart from the usual standard for reviewing a State's social and economic legislation....

[The Court noted that its decision to reject the strict scrutiny test was supported by additional considerations: 1) The Court had traditionally deferred to state legislatures on the subject of how states choose to raise and disburse state and local tax revenues because the Court lacked expertise and the requisite familiarity with local problems; 2) The Court also lacked specialized knowledge in the area of educational policy, leading it to avoid "premature interference with the informed judgments made at the state and local level." "On even the most basic questions in this area the scholars and educational experts are divided. Indeed, one of the major sources of controversy concerns the extent to which there is a demonstrable correlation between educational expenditures and the quality of education—an assumed correlation underlying virtually every legal conclusion drawn by the District Court in this case"; 3) The Court should be cautious where the principles of federalism are involved, and "it would be difficult to imagine a case having a greater potential impact on our federal system than the one now before us." "These same considerations are relevant to the determination whether that [Texas] system, with its conceded imperfections, nevertheless bears some rational relationship to a legitimate state purpose. It is to this question that we next turn our attention." In addressing this question, the Court noted that the Texas plan was based on Strayer-Haig efforts to accommodate the competing forces of a guaranteed statewide minimum educational program and preservation of local participation.—Eds.]

The Texas system of school finance is responsive to these two forces. While assuring a basic education for every child in the State, it permits and encourages a large measure of participation in and control of each district's schools at the local level. In an era that has witnessed a consistent trend to centralization of the functions of government, local sharing of responsibility for public education has survived....

Appellees do not question the propriety of Texas' dedication to local control of education. To the contrary, they attack the school-financing system precisely because, in their view, it does not provide the same level of local control and fiscal flexibility in all districts.... While it is no doubt true that reliance on local property taxation for school revenues provides less freedom of choice with respect to expenditures for some districts than for others, the existence of "some inequality" in the manner in which the State's rationale is achieved is not alone sufficient basis for striking down the entire system.... It is also well to remember that even those districts that have reduced ability to make free decisions with respect to how much they spend on education still retain under the present system a large measure of authority as to how available funds will be allocated.... The people of Texas may believe that along with increased control of the purse strings at the state level will go increased control over local policies.

Appellees further urge that the Texas system is unconstitutionally arbitrary because it allows the availability of local taxable resources to turn on "happenstance." They see no justification for a system that allows, as they contend, the quality of education to fluctuate on the basis of the fortuitous positioning of the boundary lines of political subdivisions and the location of valuable commercial and industrial property. But any scheme of local taxation—indeed the very existence of identifiable local governmental units—requires the establishment of jurisdictional boundaries that are inevitably arbitrary. It is equally inevitable that some localities are going to be blessed with more taxable assets than others.... Moreover, if local taxation for local expenditures were an unconstitutional method of providing for education then it might be an equally impermissible means of providing other necessary services customarily financed largely from local property taxes, including local police and fire protection, public health and hospitals, and public utility facilities of various kinds. We perceive no justification for such a severe denigration of local property taxation and control as would follow from appellees' contentions....

In sum, to the extent that the Texas system of school financing results in unequal expenditures between children who happen to reside in different districts, we cannot say that such disparities are the product of a system that is so irrational as to be invidiously discriminatory.... One also must remember that the system here challenged is not peculiar to Texas or to any other State. In its essential characteristics, the Texas plan for financing public education reflects what many educators for a half century have thought was an enlightened approach to a problem for which there is no perfect solution. We are unwilling to assume for ourselves a level of wisdom superior to that of legislators, scholars, and educational authorities in 50 States, especially where the alternatives proposed are only recently conceived and nowhere yet tested. The constitutional standard under the Equal Protection Clause is whether the challenged state action rationally furthers a legitimate state purpose or interest. We hold that the Texas plan abundantly satisfies this standard. . . .

In light of the considerable attention that has focused on the District Court opinion in this case and on its California predecessor, *Serrano v. Priest* [considered below], a cautionary postscript seems appropriate. It cannot be questioned that the constitutional judgment reached by the District Court and approved by our dissenting Brothers today would occasion in Texas and elsewhere an unprecedented upheaval in public education. . . . Those who have devoted the most thoughtful attention to the practical ramifications of these cases have found no clear or dependable answers and their scholarship reflects no such unqualified confidence in the desirability of completely uprooting the existing system. . . .

These practical considerations, of course, play no role in the adjudication of the constitutional issues presented here. But they serve to highlight the wisdom of the traditional limitations on this Court's function. The consideration and initiation of fundamental reforms with respect to state taxation and education are matters reserved for the legislative processes of the various States, and we do no violence to the values of federalism and separation of powers by staying our hand. We hardly need add that this Court's action today is not to be viewed as placing its judicial imprimatur on the status quo. The need is apparent for reform in tax systems which may well have relied too long and too heavily on the local property tax. And certainly innovative thinking as to public education, its methods, and its funding is necessary to assure both a higher level of quality and greater uniformity of opportunity. These matters merit the continued attention of the scholars who already have contributed much by their challenges. But the ultimate solutions must come from the lawmakers and from the democratic pressures of those who elect them.

Reversed.

[Justice Stewart wrote a separate concurring opinion. Justice White wrote a dissenting opinion, concurred in by Justices Douglas and Brennan, in which he would invalidate the Texas plan because it bore no rational relationship to the legitimate state purpose of maximizing local initiative and choice. Justice Marshall, dissenting, described the majority's holding as "a retreat from our historic commitment to equality of educational opportunity"; and he had no difficulty in finding that "the schoolchildren of property-poor districts constitute a sufficient class for our purposes." With respect to the relationship between money spent and educational quality, he acknowledged that the authorities disagreed as to its significance, but "[i]t is an inescapable fact that if one district has more funds available per pupil than another district, the former will have greater choice in educational planning than will the latter. In this regard, I believe the question of discrimination in educational quality must be deemed to be an objective one that looks to what the State provides its children, not to what the children are able to do with what they receive. That a child forced to attend an underfunded school with poorer physical facilities, less experienced teachers, larger classes, and a narrower range of courses than a school with substantially more funds—and thus with greater choice in educational planning—may nevertheless excel is to the credit of the child, not the State."]

Notes and Questions

1. *Disparities in wealth.* The Court initially grappled with the level of scrutiny to be applied in the face of clear funding disparities between school districts. Equal protection analysis requires a comparison of a favored class with a disfavored class. Did the plaintiffs err in focusing on disparities between school districts? The Court noted that the claim of discrimination based on wealth was either ambiguous or multifaceted insofar as it could refer to discrimination against individuals whose incomes fell below the poverty line, those who were relatively poorer than others, and those who lived in relatively poorer school districts. Which of these claims seems to you to be most powerful? Why did the Court decline to apply enhanced scrutiny? Should the Court instead have treated the challenge as nonjusticiable?

2. *Education as fundamental right?* Why did the Court conclude that elementary and secondary education should not be treated as a fundamental right for purposes of federal Equal Protection analysis? A number of thoughtful commentators have suggested that it is time to re-examine the analysis that led to this conclusion. See, e.g., Friedman & Solow, *The Federal Right to an Adequate Education*, 81 Geo. Wash. L. Rev. 92 (2013) (arguing that there are indeed positive rights created by implication under the federal Constitution's Due Process Clause, and asserting that a right to a minimally adequate education should be recognized as a matter of federal law based on historical developments and recent practice); Rebell, *The Right to Comprehensive Educational Opportunity*, 47 Harv. C.R.-C.L. L. Rev. 47 (2012) (arguing that the federal Elementary and Secondary Education Act should be amended to include a federal right to education, and that a federal constitutional right should be recognized, among other reasons, because of the importance in preparing citizens to vote and exercise First Amendment rights).

Professor Derek Black has offered a new line of argument designed to justify recognition of a federal right to education. See Black, *The Fundamental Right to Education*, 94 Notre Dame L. Rev. 1059 (2019); Black, *The Constitutional Compromise to Guarantee Education*, 70 Stan. L. Rev. 735 (2018). Professor Black argues that there are historical reasons that education should be treated as a fundamental right under the federal Constitution, dating back to the period following the Civil War. He asserts that an originalist interpretation would require greater attention to congressional assumptions that states provide for access to education in post-Civil War state constitutions, and that a driving reason for expecting such provisions was to prepare citizens to participate actively in self-government. Do you agree with this analysis? A right to education would be an unenumerated constitutional right.

That is, the Constitution does not explicitly state it. This makes a difference in the Court's willingness to recognize the right. The fundamental case is *Griswold v. Connecticut*, 381 U.S. 479 (1965).

3. *Comparing voting rights.* An earlier section of this Chapter addressed the approach taken by the Supreme Court in applying close scrutiny in voting rights cases, and allowing only very limited departures from the one person-one vote principle. Why are voting rights regarded as "fundamental" so as to trigger enhanced scrutiny under federal law, but education is not given the same treatment?

4. *Exceptional cases?* Are there any instances in which more intensive scrutiny might be applied to provision of basic education as a matter of federal law? In two decisions subsequent to *Rodriguez*, the Supreme Court upheld equal protection challenges to a state's school policy. In *Plyler v. Doe*, 457 U.S. 202 (1982), the Court held, 5-4, that equal protection prohibited Texas from denying to undocumented school children the free public education it provides to citizens or legally admitted alien children. *Plyler v. Doe* confers important protection for children of undocumented immigrants. For a case study of educational services for unaccompanied migrant children in Oakland, California, see Acosta, *The Right to Education for Unaccompanied Minors*, 43 Hastings Const. L.Q. 649 (2016).

In *Papasan v. Allain*, 478 U.S. 265 (1986), the Court allowed to stand an equal protection challenge to Mississippi's treatment of federal school land grants and its effect on state funding. The Court carefully distinguished *Rodriguez.* Later the Court invoked a rational relation analysis to uphold a North Dakota statute that allowed some school districts to charge a fee for transporting students to school while denying that right to others. *Kadrmas v. Dickinson Public Schools*, 487 U.S. 450 (1988). The Court declined to apply the "heightened scrutiny" analysis it had used in *Plyler.* How do you explain these differing results?

5. *Comparing state constitutional challenges.* Based on what you know so far, how would you expect state courts to respond to challenges similar to those raised in *Rodriguez*, when state rather than federal constitutional principles are at stake? For a fascinating discussion of the role played by Congress in assuring that states included protection for education in their state constitutions, see E. Zakin, Looking for Rights in All the Wrong Places: Why State Constitutions Contain America's Positive Rights 67–105 (2013).

6. *Property tax as essential to school finance systems.* You previously studied the property tax in Chapter 4. The *Rodriguez* case raised important questions about the intersection of local fiscal control (as represented by the property tax) and local educational control (which could have been permitted, even if the state bore a more substantial share of the financing burden for public schools. Since the decision in *Rodriguez*, a number of states, including California and Massachusetts, have imposed significant constraints on the imposition of property taxes, while others have curbed state revenues or expenditures. If these constraints had existed at the

time of *Rodriguez*, would the Court's emphasis on the importance of local control have been less compelling? For a thoughtful consideration of such constraints and potential strategies for constructing a more balanced and effective system of school finance, see Robinson, *It Takes a Federalist Village: A Revitalized Property Tax as the Lynchpin for Stable Effective K-12 Public Education Funding*, 17 Rich. J.L. & Pub. Int. 549 (2014). Other states have embraced property taxes but have adopted statewide rather than local property tax systems. Are such approaches to school finance reform sound? See Reynolds, *Full State Funding of Education as a State Constitutional Imperative*, 60 Hastings L.J. 749 (2009) (arguing for approach that focuses on full state funding of schools based on children's needs and considering implications of state constitutional uniform taxation provisions).

A number of states have faced challenges arising from property tax cuts that have adversely affected education funding. What kinds of challenges might be employed? Cases relying on the First Amendment, among other claims, have been unsuccessful. See *State United Teachers ex rel. Magee v. State*, 31 N.Y.S. 3d 618 (App. Div. 2016) (challenge against statute requiring 60% supermajority of voters to impose property tax levy exceeding specified limit rejected; although taxpayers had standing, they failed to state claim under education article of state constitution, equal protection, fundamental right to vote, and free speech); *Petrella v. Brownback*, 787 F.3d 1242 (10th Cir. 2015) (in case arising from Kansas, challenging state cap on school districts' ability to raise extra money by levying additional property taxes, concluding case was not moot, statutory cap did not violate right to free speech or right to association, cap was subject to rational basis review not strict scrutiny, and cap served legitimate government interest in promoting equity in educational funding). For additional insight about possible property tax reforms, see Gipson, *Attempting to Reform the Use of Local Property Taxes to Finance Education: A Strategic Approach*, 16 Hous. Bus. & Tax. L.J. 147 (2016) (focusing on Alabama).

7. *Rodriguez in retrospect. Rodriguez* was decided more than 40 years ago, and in recent years has been the subject of several retrospectives. See, e.g., Ogletree, *The Legacy and Implications of San Antonio Independent School District v. Rodriguez*, 17 Rich. J.L. & Pub. Int. 515 (2014) (discussing Justice Marshall's dissent that contrasted the importance of local educational control and local fiscal control; considering the implications of the case particularly for Latinos; and suggesting that spending for public safety (including prisons) should be rebalanced with spending for public education); Walsh, *Erasing Race, Dismissing Class: San Antonio Independent School District v. Rodriguez*, 21 Berkeley La Raza L.J. 133, 143–165 (2011) (discussing litigation and judicial review in depth, including importance of concern to uphold property tax and efforts to disentangle issues of race and poverty).

A Note on New Theories Asserting a Federal Right to Education

Initial school finance litigation focused on arguments relating to equal protection. As noted above, leading scholars have continued to plumb the depths of such arguments and marshal additional evidence to support more intensive scrutiny on equal protection grounds.

Are there new litigation strategies that might be employed to advance claims for enhanced educational support under the federal Constitution? Consider the following proposals. Do you think they are justified and viable?

- *Evidence.* See Elmendorf & Shanskea, *Solving "Problems No One Has Solved": Courts, Causal Inference and the Right to Education*, 2018 U. Ill. L. Rev. 693 (2018) (calling for more credible assessment of competing predictions about student performance).
- *Socio-economic status discrimination.* See Peterman, *Socioeconomic Status Discrimination*, 104 Va. L. Rev. 1283 (2018) (calling for reexamination of discrimination on the basis of socioeconomic status as a suspect trait).
- *Structural versus financial issues.* See Koski, *Beyond Dollars? The Promises and Pitfalls of the Next Generation of Educational Rights Litigation*, 117 Colum. L. Rev. 1897 (2017) (arguing for more comprehensive views of educational failure and strategies for reform).
- *Responsible administration.* See Liebman, *Perpetual Evolution: A Schools-Focused Public Law Litigation Model for Our Day*, 117 Colum. L. Rev. 2005 (2017) (arguing for a focus on effective governance of schools and an associated duty that would require school officials to track and respond to deficient and disparate performance).
- *Gerrymandered opportunities.* See Black, *Educational Gerrymandering: Money, Motives, and Constitutional Rights*, 94 N.Y.U. L. Rev. 1385 (2019) (arguing that manipulation of school funding formulas reflect underlying biases including privileging suburban schools, lowering taxes for wealthy individuals, and not "wasting" money on low-income kids; such choices are intentional; and enhanced scrutiny is therefore warranted under federal Equal Protection doctrine and state constitutional provisions guaranteeing a right to education).

[iv] The Second Wave: Inequality and Wealth in State Courts

The case that follows, *Serrano*, was initiated in California in 1968, the same year that saw the commencement of litigation in *McInnis* and *Rodriguez*. While to some observers, that is distant history, to those interested in understanding the evolution and potential for school finance litigation in state courts, it remains a landmark. In *Serrano*, the plaintiffs proceeded in state court, and included state constitutional theories, rather than assuming that their best source of relief would come from the federal courts and the federal Constitution. At the time of the litigation, the California Supreme Court was among the most progressive in the country. Consider how and why the California court reached a different result than was the case in *McInnis* and *Rodriguez*. Was the difference justified? Why or why not?

Serrano v. Priest

487 P.2d 1241 (Cal. 1971)

SULLIVAN, JUSTICE.

We are called upon to determine whether the California public school financing system, with its substantial dependence on local property taxes and resultant wide disparities in school revenue, violates the equal protection clause of the Fourteenth Amendment. We have determined that this funding scheme invidiously discriminates against the poor because it makes the quality of a child's education a function of the wealth of his parents and neighbors. Recognizing as we must that the right to an education in our public schools is a fundamental interest which cannot be conditioned on wealth, we can discern no compelling state purpose necessitating the present method of financing. We have concluded, therefore, that such a system cannot withstand constitutional challenge and must fall before the equal protection clause.

[The court described the parties and the allegations of the complaint. Plaintiffs were public school children and their parents in Los Angeles County, suing as representatives of their class; defendants were certain state and county officials with responsibility for administering the financing of the California public school system. The plaintiff children's complaint was that the state's financing scheme denied them equal protection under the United States and California constitutions because of the substantial disparities in educational resources available to them in contrast to students in wealthier districts. The parents' complaint was that they had to pay higher taxes for less educational opportunities than taxpayers in other districts. The complaint was dismissed by the trial court on demurrer.—Eds.]

I

We begin our task by examining the California public school financing system which is the focal point of the complaint's allegations. At the threshold we find a fundamental statistic—over 90 percent of our public school funds derive from two basic sources: (a) local district taxes on real property and (b) aid from the State School Fund.[2]

By far the major source of school revenue is the local real property tax. Pursuant to article IX, section 6 of the California Constitution, the Legislature has authorized the governing body of each county, and city and county, to levy taxes on the real property within a school district at a rate necessary to meet the district's annual education budget. The amount of revenue which a district can raise in this manner thus depends largely on its tax base—i.e., the assessed valuation of real property within its borders. Tax bases vary widely throughout the state; in 1969–1970, for example, the assessed valuation per unit of average daily attendance of elementary

2. California educational revenues for the fiscal year 1968–1969 came from the following sources: local property taxes, 55.7 percent; state aid, 35.5 percent; federal funds, 6.1 percent; miscellaneous sources, 2.7 percent.

school children ranged from a low of $103 to a peak of $952,156—a ratio of nearly 1 to 10,000.

The other factor determining local school revenue is the rate of taxation within the district. Although the Legislature has placed ceilings on permissible district tax rates, these statutory maxima may be surpassed in a "tax override" election if a majority of the district's voters approve a higher rate. Nearly all districts have voted to override the statutory limits. Thus the locally raised funds which constitute the largest portion of school revenue are primarily a function of the value of the realty within a particular school district, coupled with the willingness of the district's residents to tax themselves for education.

Most of the remaining school revenue comes from the State School Fund pursuant to the "foundation program," through which the state undertakes to supplement local taxes in order to provide a "minimum amount of guaranteed support to all districts. . . ." With certain minor exceptions, the foundation program ensures that each school district will receive annually, from state or local funds, $355 for each elementary school pupil and $488 for each high school student.

The state contribution is supplied in two principal forms. "Basic state aid" consists of a flat grant to each district of $125 per pupil per year, regardless of the relative wealth of the district. "Equalization aid" is distributed in inverse proportion to the wealth of the district. . . . [The formula is similar in operation to that of Illinois as discussed above.—Eds.]

An additional state program of "supplemental aid" is available to subsidize particularly poor school districts which are willing to make an extra local tax effort. . . .

Although equalization aid and supplemental aid temper the disparities which result from the vast variations in real property assessed valuation, wide differentials remain in the revenue available to individual districts and, consequently, in the level of educational expenditures. For example, in Los Angeles County, where plaintiff children attend school, the Baldwin Park Unified School District expended only $577.49 to educate each of its pupils in 1968–1969; during the same year the Pasadena Unified School District spent $840.19 on every student; and the Beverly Hills Unified School District paid out $1,231.72 per child. . . . The source of these disparities is unmistakable: in Baldwin Park the assessed valuation per child totaled only $3,706; in Pasadena, assessed valuation was $13,706; while in Beverly Hills, the corresponding figure was $50,885—a ratio of 1 to 4 to 13. . . . Thus, the state grants are inadequate to offset the inequalities inherent in a financing system based on widely varying local tax bases.

Furthermore, basic aid, which constitutes about half of the state educational funds . . . actually widens the gap between rich and poor districts. . . . Such aid is distributed on a uniform per pupil basis to all districts, irrespective of a district's wealth. Beverly Hills, as well as Baldwin Park, receives $125 from the state for each of its students.

For Baldwin Park the basic grant is essentially meaningless. Under the foundation program the state must make up the difference between $355 per elementary child and $47.91, the amount of revenue per child which Baldwin Park could raise by levying a tax of $1 per $100 of assessed valuation. Although under present law, that difference is composed partly of basic aid and partly of equalization aid, if the basic aid grant did not exist, the district would still receive the same amount of state aid—all in equalizing funds.

For Beverly Hills, however, the $125 flat grant has real financial significance. Since a tax rate of $1 per $100 there would produce $870 per elementary student, Beverly Hills is far too rich to qualify for equalizing aid. Nevertheless, it still receives $125 per child from the state, thus enlarging the economic chasm between it and Baldwin Park. . . .

[In Part II the court rejected plaintiffs' claim that the school financing scheme violated the California constitutional provision requiring the legislature to provide for a system of free common schools.—Eds.]

III

Having disposed of these preliminary matters, we take up the chief contention underlying plaintiffs' complaint, namely that the California public school financing scheme violates the equal protection clause of the Fourteenth Amendment to the United States Constitution.

[In a footnote that turned out to be quite important, the court noted that its analysis of plaintiffs' federal equal protection contention also applied to California's equivalent of equal protection.

[In analyzing the equal protection claim, the court first set up the Supreme Court's two-level test for applying equal protection to legislative classifications: in the case of economic regulation, the legislation need only bear a rational relationship to a legitimate state purpose; legislation involving suspect classifications or touching on fundamental interests are subject to strict scrutiny and must satisfy a compelling state interest.

[The court then examined wealth as a suspect classification, concluding that the system as a whole, with its heavy reliance on locally raised property taxes, "generates school revenue in proportion to the wealth of the individual district." Moreover, "the poorer districts are financially unable to raise their taxes high enough to match the educational offerings of wealthier districts."—Eds.]

Finally, defendants suggest that the wealth of a school district does not necessarily reflect the wealth of the families who live there. The simple answer to this argument is that plaintiffs have alleged that there is a correlation between a district's per pupil assessed valuation and the wealth of its residents and we treat these material facts as admitted by the demurrers.

More basically, however, we reject defendants' underlying thesis that classification by wealth is constitutional so long as the wealth is that of the district, not the individual. We think that discrimination on the basis of district wealth is equally invalid. The commercial and industrial property which augments a district's tax base is distributed unevenly throughout the state. To allot more educational dollars to the children of one district than to those of another merely because of the fortuitous presence of such property is to make the quality of a child's education dependent upon the location of private commercial and industrial establishments.[16]

We turn now to defendants' related contention that the instant case involves at most de facto discrimination. We disagree. Indeed, we find the case unusual in the extent to which governmental action is the cause of the wealth classifications. The school funding scheme is mandated in every detail by the California Constitution and statutes. Although private residential and commercial patterns may be partly responsible for the distribution of assessed valuation throughout the state, such patterns are shaped and hardened by zoning ordinances and other governmental land-use controls which promote economic exclusivity. Governmental action drew the school district boundary lines, thus determining how much local wealth each district would contain. . . .

[The court next determined that despite the absence of any "direct authority," education is a fundamental interest because of the "indispensable role which [it] plays in the modern industrial state." Finally, the court turned to examining whether the California school finance system was necessary to achieve a compelling state interest.—Eds.]

The state interest which defendants advance in support of the current fiscal scheme is California's policy "to strengthen and encourage local responsibility for control of public education." (Ed. Code § 17300.) We treat separately the two possible aspects of this goal: first, the granting to local districts of effective decision-making power over the administration of their schools; and second, the promotion of local fiscal control over the amount of money to be spent on education.

. . . But even assuming arguendo that local administrative control may be a compelling state interest, the present financial system cannot be considered necessary to further this interest. No matter how the state decides to finance its system of public education, it can still leave this decision-making power in the hands of local districts.

The other asserted policy interest is that of allowing a local district to choose how much it wishes to spend on the education of its children. . . .

We need not decide whether such decentralized financial decision-making is a compelling state interest, since under the present financing system, such fiscal free-will is a cruel illusion for the poor school districts. We cannot agree that Baldwin

16. Defendants contend that different levels of educational expenditure do not affect the quality of education. However, plaintiffs' complaint specifically alleges the contrary, and for purposes of testing the sufficiency of a complaint against a general demurrer, we must take its allegations to be true. . . .

Park residents care less about education than those in Beverly Hills solely because Baldwin Park spends less than $600 per child while Beverly Hills spends over $1,200. As defendants themselves recognize, perhaps the most accurate reflection of a community's commitment to education is the rate at which its citizens are willing to tax themselves to support their schools. Yet by that standard, Baldwin Park should be deemed far more devoted to learning than Beverly Hills, for Baldwin Park citizens levied a school tax of well over $5 per $100 of assessed valuation, while residents of Beverly Hills paid only slightly more than $2.

In summary, so long as the assessed valuation within a district's boundaries is a major determinant of how much it can spend for its schools, only a district with a large tax base will be truly able to decide how much it really cares about education. The poor district cannot freely choose to tax itself into an excellence which its tax rolls cannot provide. Far from being necessary to promote local fiscal choice, the present financing system actually deprives the less wealthy districts of that option....

In sum, we find the allegations of plaintiffs' complaint legally sufficient and we return the cause to the trial court for further proceedings....

Wright, C.J., and Peters, Tobriner, Mosk and Burke, JJ., concur.

McComb, Justice (dissenting). [Omitted.]

Notes and Questions

1. *The remand.* Following remand and an extensive trial covering 62 court days, Judge Jefferson of the Los Angeles County Superior Court again held that California's school funding was unconstitutional. Unpublished opinion, Super. Ct., L.A. County No. 938,254, Apr. 10, 1974. (Significant portions of the trial court's findings of fact, conclusions of law and judgment order are described in the subsequent supreme court opinion, 557 P.2d 929, 936–40.) On December 30, 1976, the California Supreme Court, in a 4 to 3 decision, affirmed, holding that the trial court had correctly interpreted and applied the first *Serrano* decision. The court acknowledged that the intervening decision of the United States Supreme Court in *San Antonio Indep. Sch. Dist. v. Rodriguez, infra*, undercut the federal equal protection claim, but it noted that the *Serrano* complaint also rested on state equal protection grounds. Again applying a strict scrutiny test, the court repeated that "(1) discrimination in educational opportunity on the basis of district wealth involves a suspect classification, and (2) education is a fundamental interest." *Serrano v. Priest*, 557 P.2d 929, 951 (Cal. 1976) (*Serrano II*). As documented in later litigation, subsequent legislation changed the legal landscape further. See *Crawford v. Huntington Beach Union High School District*, 121 Cal. Rptr. 2d 96, 104 (Cal. App. 2002).

2. *State funding.* The *Serrano* decisions were only the beginning of a long saga in California involving school finance and property taxation, the legislature, the executive branch and the courts, as well as the voters through the initiative process. The state legislature responded to *Serrano* at first timidly but later more aggressively,

both in the amount and the method of distribution of state aid. A major impetus for change came, however, in the form of Proposition 13, an initiative that was adopted by the voters in 1978. See Chapter 4. That constitutional amendment severely restricted property taxes in California, the principal source of local funding for schools, eliminating possibly as much as 60% of the locally generated revenue. See, e.g., ACIR, *State Constitutional Law and State Educational Policy, in* State Constitutions in the Federal System 114 (1989). In November 1988, voters adopted Proposition 98, an initiative that required that an estimated 40% of the state budget each year be spent on elementary, high school and community college education. Cal. Const. art. XVI, §§ 8, 8.5. In 2013, California adopted the "Local Control Funding Formula" that shifted decision-making more in favor of local districts and provided more funding to districts with higher proportions of low-income and limited English proficiency students. See California Department of Education, Local Control Funding Formula Overview, available at https://www.cde.ca.gov/fg/aa/lc/lcffoverview.asp. Fiscal data and other information about California's school funding are available on-line from EdSource, www.edsource.org.

3. *Disparities.* Of more interest, given the legal premise of *Serrano*, is the effect on disparities. Judge Jefferson, in the 1974 order, required that disparities in expenditure among districts be reduced to less than $100 within six years, exclusive of categorical and special needs programs which are not wealth-related. At the time of a 1986 "compliance hearing" on *Serrano*, the court found that 93.2% of the state's students were in districts within a $100 band adjusted for inflation ($198 in 1982–83); the remaining differences were insignificant and justified by legitimate state interests. *Serrano v. Priest*, 226 Cal. Rptr. 584 (Cal. App. 1986) (*Serrano III*). The *Serrano* band was estimated at $343 per student in 1999; and by 1998–99 very few students were outside the *Serrano* band. However, categorical programs were excluded from the equalization formula, and California's numerous categorical programs accounted for a substantial portion of educational revenues. In addition, some of the "equality" in expenditure may be offset by private fundraising for school extras. See Frisch, *The Class Is Greener on the Other Side: How Private Donations to Public Schools Play into Fair Funding*, 67 Duke L.J. 427 (2017) (arguing for state regulation to balance desires to make private donations and effects on equitable funding of schools).

4. *Ongoing litigation in California.* School finance litigation has continued in California. See *Campaign for Quality Education v. State of California*, 209 Cal. Rptr. 3d 888 (Cal. App. 2016). The case involved claims by school districts, taxpayers and others, seeking injunctive relief on grounds that school children were entitled under the state constitution to "an education of some quality," and alternatively, that the state legislature had failed to meet its obligations since it employed an "irrational" educational funding system. In a divided opinion, the court declined to recognize a "right to education of some quality," and concluded that state constitutional provisions did not constrain how the legislature allocated public school funding. For a very thoughtful analysis of California's right to education, from *Serrano* to

the present, see Gordon, *California Constitutional Law: The Right to an Adequate Education*, 67 Hastings L.J. 323 (2016) (discussing history of California constitution, *Serrano* and subsequent cases, areas of continuing uncertainty, and value of standards-based adequacy requirement).

California has also been on the forefront in addressing challenges to public school teacher tenure, brought on the theory that required retention of inadequate teachers interferes with students' educational rights. See *Vergara v. State*, 209 Cal. Rptr. 3d 532 (Cal. App. 2016) (in case by public school students claiming that teacher tenure statutes violated equal protection, holding that students assigned to grossly ineffective teachers were not a sufficiently identifiable group for equal protection purposes and statutes did not inevitably cause low-income and minority students to be disproportionately assigned to grossly ineffective teachers so as to violate equal protection requirements). For discussion of teacher tenure issues, see Black, *Taking Teacher Quality Seriously*, 57 Wm. & Mary L. Rev. 1597 (2016); Black, *The Constitutional Challenge to Teacher Tenure*, 104 Cal. L. Rev. 75 (2016). Some have suggested that a movement to address teacher quality at the local level could represent a "new wave" of education reform litigation. See Note, *Education Policy Litigation as Devolution*, 128 Harv. L. Rev. 929 (2015).

5. *Other states' experience with equal protection claims.* Some other states adopted the *Serrano* approach focusing on equal opportunity. See, e.g., *Brigham v. State,* 692 A.2d 384 (Vt. 1997) (applying intensified scrutiny under "Common Benefits" clause discussed in *Baker* case presented in Chapter 1); *Tennessee Small School Systems v. McWherter*, 851 S.W.2d 139 (Tenn. 1993); 894 S.W.2d 734 (Tenn. 1995) (applying state equal protection provision to invalidate school finance system). Successful reliance on equal protection claims was the exception rather than the rule, however. See, e.g, *Lujan v. Colorado State Bd. of Educ.*, 649 P.2d 1005 (Colo. 1982) (en banc) (finding no equal protection violation and no violation of state constitution's clause regarding creation of "thorough and uniform system of public schools"); *Kukor v. Grover*, 436 N.W.2d 568 (Wis. 1989) (rational basis applied where no outright denial of educational opportunity and funding system upheld); *City of Pawtucket v. Sundlun*, 662 A.2d 40 (R.I. 1995) (no equal protection violation). For a discussion of equality clauses in state constitutions, see Williams, *Equality Guarantees in State Constitutional Law*, 63 Tex. L. Rev. 1195 (1985); Black, *Unlocking the Power of State Constitutions with Equal Protection: The First Step Toward Education as a Federally Protected Right*, 51 Wm. & Mary L. Rev. 1343 (2010). For additional information on major school finance litigation that has recognized significant state constitutional rights, see *infra*.

To keep up with ongoing developments in school funding litigation, it's worth keeping up with policy-oriented websites. For example, see http://www.schoolfunding.info/ (A Project of the Center for Educational Equity of Columbia Teachers College); Education Law Center, https://www.elc-pa.org/ (nonprofit resource center based in New Jersey). For a discussion of developments in Colorado, see Hunter &

Gebhardt, *State Level School Finance: Legal Precedent and the Opportunity for Educational Equity: Where to Now, Colorado?* 50 U. Rich. L. Rev. 893 (2016).

A Note on State Constitutional Provisions on Education

Overview

State constitutions include a variety of provisions expressly providing for education. It is worth noting the text of these provisions and considering how their specific terms influence court decisions in the face of school finance litigation pursuant to state law. For a compilation of state constitutional provisions relating to education, see Education Commission of the States, 50-State Review: Constitutional Obligations for Public Education (2016), available at https://www.ecs.org/wp-content/uploads/2016-Constitutional-obligations-for-public-education-1.pdf.

An historical study of state constitutions documents related developments. See E. Zakin, Looking for Rights in All the Wrong Places: Why State Constitutions Contain America's Positive Rights 67–105 (2013). Zackin traces the effects of the national "common school" movement that lobbied for inclusion of provisions requiring the creation of publicly funded "common schools" during the nineteenth century. *Id.* at 68–70. Seventeen states had such provisions by the end of the Civil War, 23 more added such provisions by the end of the nineteenth century, and six more states that joined the Union during the twentieth century included "common school" provisions in their state constitutions.

Congress played an important role in urging or forcing states to attend to educational funding. It debated whether to force southern states to include educational provisions in their state constitutions at the time of Reconstruction, giving those states an incentive to do so. *Id.* at 73. It provided many new states (29 in all) with sections of land designated as a means to support schools, *id.* at 74–77. States themselves included provisions regarding financial oversight of school funds in light of histories of mismanagement. *Id.* at 78–83. In response to pressure from teachers and others, they gradually adopted state constitutional provisions requiring mandatory state or local taxation or appropriations in support of public schools. See id. at 84–89 (approximately half the states adopted such provisions in the 19th century). It was not clear that these or other state constitutional provisions were intended to allow litigation, however. See *id.* at 91–93. For a more comprehensive discussion of whether state education clauses should be viewed as authorizing litigation, see Bauries, *The Education Duty*, 47 Wake Forest L. Rev. 705, 719–26 (2012). For a discussion of how theories of constitutional construction might affect judicial views of state constitutional provisions providing a right to public education, see Thro, *Barnett's and Bernick's Theory of Constitutional Construction and School Finance Litigation*, 357 Ed. Law Rep. 464 (2018).

Thorough and efficient

A handful of states whose constitutions mandated the establishment of "thorough and efficient" systems of public schools led the way toward the third wave of school finance litigation. New Jersey's experience should prove helpful in appreciating the significance and character of the state courts' decisions under their state constitutions.

The New Jersey Supreme Court rendered a decision just weeks after *Rodriguez* in which it interpreted its state constitutional provision: "The Legislature shall provide for the maintenance and support of a thorough and efficient system of free public schools for the instruction of all the children in the State." N.J. Const. art. VIII, § 4, par. 1.

In *Robinson v. Cahill*, 303 A.2d 273 (N.J. 1973), the New Jersey court rejected a state equal protection claim but held that the funding system (similar to *Serrano* with even heavier reliance on local property taxes) did not satisfy the state's obligation to provide a "thorough and efficient" system of schools. Unlike the negative fiscal neutrality theory of *Serrano*, the New Jersey court's decision required it to confront the state's responsibility for defining and funding a positive constitutional mandate for equal educational opportunity. It required not only defining the contents of a thorough and efficient education but assuring its funding, especially given the substantial disparities in tax resources that resulted from heavy reliance on local funding. The task was not easy for the court nor for the legislative and executive branches. During a three-year period the state supreme court handed down six opinions or orders,[6] culminating in an order which briefly closed down the entire state common school system until the New Jersey legislature finally bowed to the court's will and enacted a major tax and school reform package—by a one vote margin. The package included enactment, for the first time in New Jersey's history, of a state income tax, which many considered to be the only revenue source sufficient to fund the Public School Education Act, passed by the legislature to comply with *Robinson*, and to provide some property tax relief.

It is fair to say that by the time of the sixth *Robinson v. Cahill* decision, the court had spent as much time in reinterpreting what it had held in *Robinson I* and debating important separation of powers issues as in defining a thorough and efficient education. The dilemma which the court faced as a result of the failure of the other branches to put into effect a school program that would satisfy the constitutional mandate was described by one of the dissenting justices (Justice Mountain) in *Robinson VI*, the decision in which the court enjoined further expenditure of public funds to support the schools. He commented:

---

6. *Robinson v. Cahill, supra* (*Robinson I*); 306 A.2d 65, *cert. denied sub nom. Dickey v. Robinson*, 414 U.S. 976 (1973) (*Robinson II*); 335 A.2d 6 (1975) (*Robinson III*); 351 A.2d 713 (N.J.), *cert. denied sub nom. Klein v. Robinson*, 423 U.S. 913 (1975) (*Robinson IV*); 355 A.2d 129 (1976) (*Robinson V*); 358 A.2d 457 (1976) (*Robinson VI*). A seventh decision resulted in dissolution of the injunction which closed the schools, 360 A.2d 400 (1976).

> Underlying the question of school financing—with which the series of *Robinson* opinions has been chiefly concerned—exists a far more important issue of constitutionalism: to what extent, if at all, should courts affirmatively intrude to rectify perceived instances of unconstitutional conduct which under our system of government should be corrected by one or other of the political branches of government—the executive or legislative. This is the issue we face here. This Court decided in *Robinson I*, that the system of financing public education in this state violated Article 8, §4, 1 of the New Jersey Constitution.... The Constitution places the obligation directly upon the *Legislature*. It is not diffused between or among two or more of the branches of government as are many constitutional obligations; it is imposed squarely upon one of the political branches.
>
> ....
>
> On the other hand it is pointed out that unless the courts will act, no one will act.... [T]here seems no good reason why the citizens of the State should be asked to forego a constitutional right because of governmental inaction. Resort to the ballot box is a last and often ineffectual remedy.
>
> Consideration of the present case in the light of what has been abstractly stated above, convinces me that the action taken by the majority is most unfortunate. The Court has resorted to the equitable remedy of injunction. I have grave misgivings as to the wisdom of this step. This is no ordinary injunction. Its effect will be and is intended to be coercive. It is hoped that by threatening to close the schools this Court will induce the Legislature to raise and appropriate for educational purposes some very large sum of money. Thus the Court is indirectly commanding that a tax be imposed. But the taxing power is legislative and cannot be exercised by the judiciary. Should it seek to do indirectly what all readily admit it cannot do directly? It seems to be agreed that in all probability the money can only be raised by imposing an income tax throughout the state. Should the Court throw its great weight and influence in the scales, upon an issue so deeply controversial which has thus far met consistent legislative rejection? Of course the Legislature may, for whatever reason, fail to respond in the manner the majority must anticipate it will. What would happen then? [358 A.2d at 460–62.]

Notwithstanding (or perhaps because of) this early action by the courts and the state legislature, litigation in New Jersey has continued. In a second round of decisions, the New Jersey Supreme Court held that the school funding system then in place was neither thorough nor efficient and therefore unconstitutional as applied to approximately 28 (later 31) poorer "special needs" urban districts. *Abbott v. Burke*, 575 A.2d 359 (N.J. 1990). In subsequent decisions, the court ordered funding for the special needs districts that would assure them a per pupil spending level equivalent to that of certain wealthy suburban districts, 693 A.2d 417 (1997). It entered a detailed remedial order which mandated whole school reform along with core curriculum standards, pre-school programs for 3 and 4 year old children, on-site health and social services, alternative schools, school-to-work programs, and much more. 710 A.2d 450 (1998); 748 A.2d 82 (2000) (implementation of remedial order). That decision was also one of a growing number to address the inequities and inadequacies in physical facilities; and the court later confirmed that the state was required to fund all of the costs of necessary facilities remediation and construction in the *Abbott* districts. 751 A.2d 1032 (2000). Litigation continued throughout the decade. Finally, after some 20 rulings over two decades in the *Abbott* case, in 2009 the New Jersey Supreme Court held that a new school finance formula satisfied state constitutional mandates and effectively relieved the state from prior remedial orders. *Abbott v. Burke*, 971 A.2d 989 (N.J. 2009). The plan, passed partly in response to changing demographics since the creation of the *Abbott* districts, eliminated the special needs designation for those districts and instead funded all New Jersey school districts uniformly, with a per pupil allocation to be supplemented by special needs funding allowances calculated for each district. The court mandated further review of the plan after three years.

Nonetheless, in 2011, after extensive state budget cuts that affected public education, plaintiffs were back in court. The State Supreme Court remanded for consideration by a special master who found that the state constitutional requirement was not being met. See *Abbott ex rel. Abbott v. Burke*, 20 A.3d 1018 (N.J. 2011). Subsequently, plaintiffs sued based on concerns about treatment of "adjustment aid" (following a study showing that about 30% of New Jersey public schools were being "overfunded" and should have aid cut in favor of the other 70% of schools that were not appropriately funded). In 2020, the New Jersey Commissioner of Education upheld an administrative law judge's dismissal of the challenge based on a lack of standing. See http://schoolfunding.info/news/nj-commissioner-dismisses-funding-cases/. For a review of the *Abbott* litigation from New Jersey, see Higginson, *Abbott Gets an F; Courts Can Provide Extra Credit*, 16 Rutgers Race & L. Rev. 289 (2015) (suggesting changes in New Jersey approach).

[v] The Third Wave: Kentucky, Adequacy, and Beyond

Over the years, 45 of the 50 states have faced litigation regarding school finance. It is not possible to review all these developments here. What is important, however, is to trace the development of a third wave involving new litigation strategies, ones that focused on arguing that state education clauses (whatever their language) were intended to assure that a baseline of adequate educational opportunity was available to all children.

The most dramatic, far-reaching and undoubtedly the most influential of the decisions was that of the Kentucky Supreme Court, which invalidated the state's education system in toto in *Rose v. Council for Better Education, Inc.*, 790 S.W.2d 186 (Ky. 1989). The court focused on the state's school system, and concluded that the system as a whole was flawed:

> Lest there be any doubt, the result of our decision is that Kentucky's *entire system* of common schools is unconstitutional.... This decision applies to the statutes creating, implementing and financing the *system* and to all regulations, etc., pertaining thereto. This decision covers the creation of local school districts, school boards, and the Kentucky Department of Education to the Minimum Foundation Program and Power Equalization Program. It covers school construction and maintenance, teacher certification—the whole gamut of the common school system in Kentucky. [*Rose, infra* at 215. Emphasis in original.]

Excerpts from the opinion follow.

Rose v. Council for Better Education, Inc.

790 S.W.2d 186 (Ky. 1989)

Stephens, Chief Justice.

The issue we decide on this appeal is whether the Kentucky General Assembly has complied with its constitutional mandate to "provide an efficient system of common schools throughout the state."

In deciding that it has not, we intend no criticism of the substantial efforts made by the present General Assembly and by its predecessors, nor do we intend to substitute our judicial authority for the authority and discretion of the General Assembly. We are, rather, exercising our constitutional duty in declaring that, when we consider the evidence in the record, and when we apply the constitutional requirement of Section 183 to that evidence, it is crystal clear that the General Assembly has fallen short of its duty to enact legislation to provide for an efficient system of common schools throughout the state....

The relief sought by the plaintiffs was a declaration of rights to the effect that the system be declared unconstitutional; that the funding of schools also be determined to be unconstitutional and inadequate; that the defendant, Superintendent of Public Instruction be enjoined from further implementing said school statutes; that a mandamus be issued, directing the Governor to recommend to the General Assembly the enactment of appropriate legislation which would be in compliance with the aforementioned constitutional provisions; that a mandamus be issued, directing the President *Pro Tempore* of the Senate and the Speaker of the House of Representatives to place before the General Assembly appropriate legislation which is constitutionally valid; and that a mandamus be issued, directing the General Assembly to provide for an "equitable and adequate funding program for all school children so as to establish an 'efficient system of common schools.'" ...

[The trial court made extensive findings of fact based on the voluminous trial record and concluded that the common school finance system was unconstitutional. An appeal was taken by the President *Pro Tempore* of the Senate (Rose) and the Speaker of the House (Blandford). After reviewing the history of school funding in Kentucky and the trial record, the supreme court continued:]

The overall effect of appellants' evidence is a virtual concession that Kentucky's system of common schools is underfunded and inadequate; is fraught with inequalities and inequities throughout the 177 local school districts; is ranked nationally in the lower 20–25% in virtually every category that is used to evaluate educational performance; and is not uniform among the districts in educational opportunities. . . .

In spite of the Minimum Foundation Program and the Power Equalization Program, there are wide variations in financial resources and dispositions thereof which result in unequal educational opportunities throughout Kentucky. The local districts have large variances in taxable property per student. Even a total elimination of all mismanagement and waste in local school districts would not correct the situation as it now exists. A substantial difference in the curricula offered in the poorer districts contrasts with that of the richer districts, particularly in the areas of foreign language, science, mathematics, music and art.

The achievement test scores in the poorer districts are lower than those in the richer districts and expert opinion clearly established that there is a correlation between those scores and the wealth of the district. Student-teacher ratios are higher in the poorer districts. Moreover, although Kentucky's per capita income is low, it makes an even lower per capita effort to support the common schools.

Students in property poor districts receive inadequate and inferior educational opportunities as compared to those offered to those students in the more affluent districts. . . .

Moreover, most of the witnesses before the trial court testified that not only were the state's educational opportunities unequal and lacking in uniformity, but that *all* were inadequate. Testimony indicated that not only do the so-called poorer districts provide inadequate education to fulfill the needs of the students but the more affluent districts' efforts are inadequate as well, as judged by accepted national standards. . . .

Appellants conceded, the trial court found and we concur that in spite of legislative efforts, the total local and state effort in education in Kentucky's primary and secondary education is inadequate and is lacking in uniformity. It is discriminatory as to the children served in 80% of our local school districts. . . .

Uniform testimony of the expert witnesses at trial, corroborated by data, showed a definite correlation between the money spent per child on education and the quality of the education received. As we have previously stated in our discussion of the history of Kentucky's school finances, our system does not *require* a minimum local effort. The MFP, being based on average daily attendance, certainly infuses more money into each local district, but is not designed to correct problems of inequality and lack of uniformity between local school districts. . . .

[The court denied the contention that the local school boards, being creatures of the state, had no power to sue their "masters, the General Assembly (or the Commonwealth)." The court rejected some *Hunter v. City of Pittsburgh*-like language from a Michigan school funding decision although, curiously, *Hunter* itself was not cited.]

[With respect to the issue of relief against the two legislative-leader appellants, the court noted that the legislative body was properly before the court but that it was not being directed to enact specific legislation or to raise taxes.]

In a few simple, but direct words, the framers of our present Constitution, set forth the will of the people with regard to the importance of providing public education in the Commonwealth.

> "*General Assembly to provide for school system*—The General Assembly shall, by appropriate legislation, provide for an efficient system of common schools throughout the State." [Ky. Const. Sec. 183.]

Several conclusions readily appear from a reading of this section. First, it is the obligation, the sole obligation, of the General Assembly to provide for a system of common schools in Kentucky. The obligation to so provide is clear and unequivocal and is, in effect, a constitutional mandate. Next, the school system must be provided throughout the entire state, with no area (or its children) being omitted. The creation, implementation and maintenance of the school system must be achieved by appropriate legislation. Finally, the system must be an efficient one. . . .

[In approaching its responsibility to define the constitutional requirement of an "efficient" system of education, the court leaned heavily on the West Virginia *Pauley* decision, *supra*. Indeed, it recommended a study of that opinion.]

DEFINITION OF "EFFICIENT"

We now hone in on the heart of this litigation. In defining "efficient," we use all the tools that are made available to us. In spite of any protestations to the contrary, we do not engage in judicial legislating. We do not make policy. We do not substitute our judgment for that of the General Assembly. We simply take the plain directive of the Constitution, and, armed with its purpose, we decide what our General Assembly must achieve in complying with its solemn constitutional duty. . . .

The sole responsibility for providing the system of common schools is that of our General Assembly. It is a duty—it is a constitutional mandate placed by the people on the 138 members of that body who represent those selfsame people.

The General Assembly must not only establish the system, but it must monitor it on a continuing basis so that it will always be maintained in a constitutional manner. The General Assembly must carefully supervise it, so that there is no waste, no duplication, no mismanagement, at any level.

The system of common schools must be adequately funded to achieve its goals. The system of common schools must be substantially uniform throughout the state. Each child, *every child*, in this Commonwealth must be provided with an equal opportunity to have an adequate education. Equality is the key word here. The children of the poor and the children of the rich, the children who live in the poor districts and the children who live in the rich districts must be given the same opportunity and access to an adequate education. This obligation cannot be shifted to local counties and local school districts. . . .

Having declared the system of common schools to be constitutionally deficient, we have directed the General Assembly to recreate and redesign a new system that will comply with the standards we have set out. Such system will guarantee to all children the opportunity for an adequate education, through a *state* system. To allow local citizens and taxpayers to make a supplementary effort in no way reduces or negates the minimum quality of education required in the statewide system.

We do not instruct the General Assembly to enact any specific legislation. We do not direct the members of the General Assembly to raise taxes. It is their decision how best to achieve efficiency. We only decide the nature of the constitutional mandate. We only determine the intent of the framers. Carrying-out that intent is the duty of the General Assembly.

A child's right to an adequate education is a fundamental one under our Constitution. The General Assembly must protect and advance that right. We concur with the trial court that an efficient system of education must have as its goal to provide each and every child with at least the seven following capacities: (i) sufficient oral and written communication skills to enable students to function in a complex and rapidly changing civilization; (ii) sufficient knowledge of economic, social, and political systems to enable the student to make informed choices; (iii) sufficient understanding of governmental processes to enable the student to understand the issues that affect his or her community, state, and nation; (iv) sufficient self-knowledge and knowledge of his or her mental and physical wellness; (v) sufficient grounding in the arts to enable each student to appreciate his or her cultural and historical heritage; (vi) sufficient training or preparation for advanced training in either academic or vocational fields so as to enable each child to choose and pursue life work intelligently; and (vii) sufficient levels of academic or vocational skills to enable public school students to compete favorably with their counterparts in surrounding states, in academics or in the job market.

The essential, and minimal, characteristics of an "efficient" system of common schools, may be summarized as follows:

1) The establishment, maintenance and funding of common schools in Kentucky is the sole responsibility of the General Assembly

2) Common schools shall be free to all.

3) Common schools shall be available to all Kentucky children.

4) Common schools shall be substantially uniform throughout the state.

5) Common schools shall provide equal educational opportunities to all Kentucky children, regardless of place of residence or economic circumstances.

6) Common schools shall be monitored by the General Assembly to assure that they are operated with no waste, no duplication, no mismanagement, and with no political influence.

7) The premise for the existence of common schools is that all children in Kentucky have a constitutional right to an adequate education.

8) The General Assembly shall provide funding which is sufficient to provide each child in Kentucky an adequate education.

9) An adequate education is one which has as its goal the development of the seven capacities recited previously. . . .

SUMMARY/CONCLUSION

We have decided this case solely on the basis of our Kentucky Constitution, Section 183. We find it unnecessary to inject any issues raised under the United States Constitution or the United States Bill of Rights in this matter. We decline to issue any injunctions, restraining orders, writs of prohibition or writs of mandamus.

We have decided one legal issue—and one legal issue only—viz., that the General Assembly of the Commonwealth has failed to establish an efficient system of common schools throughout the Commonwealth. . . .

As we have previously emphasized, the *sole responsibility* for providing the system of common schools lies with the General Assembly. If they choose to delegate any of this duty to institutions such as the local boards of education, the General Assembly must provide a mechanism to assure that the ultimate control remains with the General Assembly, and assure that those local school districts also exercise the delegated duties in an efficient manner.

The General Assembly must provide adequate funding for the system. How they do this is their decision. However, if ad valorem taxes on real and personal property are used by the General Assembly as part of the financing of the redesigned state system of common schools, the General Assembly has the obligation to see that *all such property* is assessed at 100% of its fair market value. *Russman v. Luckett*, 391 S.W.2d 694 (Ky. 1965). Moreover, because of the great disparity of local tax efforts in the present system of common schools, the General Assembly must establish a uniform *tax rate* for such property. In this way, all owners of real and personal property throughout the *state* will make a comparable effort in the financing of the state system of common schools. . . . [The court delayed finality of its decision until 90 days after adjournment of the next session of the General Assembly.]

Notes and Questions

1. *Rationale.* What was the rationale for the court's decision? Did the text of the state constitution matter? What other factors played a role?

2. *Defining an adequate education.* How did the court define the elements of an adequate education? Do you agree with that definition? Why or why not? Does the court's reasoning guarantee individual students' particular educational

opportunities, or does it only assure that students generally have access to such opportunities? Does the definition have a bearing on how schools must be staffed, how their curriculum must be framed, how extra-curricular opportunities should be provided and how student discipline should be managed? What about how their physical facilities are constructed and maintained? For cases that have found that constitutional violates based on disparities and inadequacy of physical facilities, see, e.g., *Roosevelt Elementary Sch. Dist. No. 66 v. Bishop*, 877 P.2d 806 (Ariz. 1994); *Idaho Schools for Equal Educ. Opportunity v. State*, 976 P.2d 913 (Idaho 1998). Should the crucial focus be on educational inputs, or instead on outputs (such as graduation rates)? *Rose* is widely regarded as a very influential opinion even outside the state of Kentucky. For an interesting perspective on the ways in which state courts have influenced each other in the area of school finance litigation, see Gleason & Howard, *State Supreme Courts and Shared Networking: The Diffusion of Education Policy*, 78 Alb. L. Rev. 1485 (2015). For a comprehensive discussion of the backdrop of *Rose*, see A. Newman, Realizing Educational Rights (2013).

3. *Costing-out studies.* Another approach to defining adequate education is to determine the actual cost of a delivering a defined "basket" of needed educational opportunities and support services per student. Costing-out studies can also be used to address costs of special instruction for students with disabilities or those with limited English proficiency. The "costing-out" approach was pioneered in Ohio school finance litigation. The court found the state's system of school finance to be unconstitutional in *DeRolph v. State*, 677 N.E.2d 733 (Ohio 1997) (*DeRolph I*), but declined to specify a precise remedy. Subsequently, the supreme court again considered whether the state's funding met the constitutional standard and found that it did not despite a good faith attempt by the governor and legislature. *DeRolph v. State*, 728 N.E.2d 993 (Ohio 2000) (*DeRolph II*). Subsequently, in *DeRolph v. State*, 780 N.E.2d 529 (Ohio 2002) (*DeRolph III*), the Ohio Supreme Court concluded that a systematic overhaul of the state's school-funding system was required to meet the state constitutional requirement for a "thorough and effective" system of public schools.

4. *Financial challenges.* The *Rose* case was decided prior to the economic meltdown of the "Great Recession," beginning in 2007. Does the "adequacy" framework announced in *Rose* leave any room for state legislatures to make cuts in public education funding during difficult financial times when both state and local tax revenues are likely to decline and individuals may face unemployment? Why or why not? See Rebell, *Safeguarding the Right to a Sound Basic Education in Times of Fiscal Constraint*, 75 Alb. L. Rev. 1855 (2012) (in case study of New York State education funding, arguing that procedures should be developed to identify essential programs for a sound basic education, assess efficiency and cost effectiveness in specific areas, undertake cost analysis, develop foundation funding systems that reflect actual costs of providing educational services in a cost-effective manner, and establish state level accountability for adequacy mechanisms); Harpalani, *Maintaining Educational Adequacy in Times of Recession: Judicial Review of State Education*

Budget Cuts, 85 N.Y.U. L. Rev. 258 (2010) (arguing for application of heightened scrutiny under such circumstances).

5. *Separation of powers.* The Kentucky court was also required to deal with separation of powers issues in passing on the trial court's order. By the time the case reached the supreme court, only two defendant-appellants remained, the President Pro Tempore of the state Senate and the Speaker of the House. The trial court "in effect" required those two defendants to introduce legislation to correct the constitutional defect, an action which the supreme court declined to approve. It also disapproved of the trial court's order to the legislators to report on their progress in overcoming the constitutional deficiencies as "a clear incursion, by the judiciary, of the functions of the legislature." On the other hand, the supreme court noted approvingly that the trial court did not issue writs of mandamus or attempt to order enactment of specific legislation, but only ordered that appellants proceed as rapidly as possible to establish an efficient system of common schools. It was in the latter respect, as the court saw it, that the order correctly drew the line between the judicial duty to determine compliance with the constitution and the legislature's discretion to determine the specifics of the legislative response. Note that one of the concurring justices (Gant) disagreed with the court only in that he would issue writs of mandamus requiring the governor to call a special session of the legislature, requiring the governor and state education officials to recommend corrective measures, and requiring the General Assembly to enact legislation to comply with the constitutional mandate.

Would the Kentucky court's response have been the same if it had endured repeated rounds of litigation? Why or why not? For more detailed discussion of the writ of mandamus, see Chapter 11. Not all courts find school finance challenges to be justiciable. See, e.g., *Nebraska Coal. for Educ. Equity and Adequacy v. Heineman*, 731 N.W.2d 164 (Neb. 2007) (holding challenges to be nonjusticiable, and reviewing examples of protracted litigation); *Oklahoma Educ. Assn. v. State*, 158 P.3d 1058 (Okla. 2007) (holding challenge nonjusticiable). For a subsequent analysis of separation of powers and related political question doctrine issues relating to school finance litigation, see Stern, *Don't Answer That: Revisiting the Political Question Doctrine in State Courts*, 21 U. Pa. J. Const. L. 153, 188–93 (2018) (discussing issues relating to education and spending); Bilan, *The Runaway Wagon: How Past School Discrimination, Finance, and Adequacy Case Law Warrants a Political Question Approach to Education Reform Litigation*, 91 Notre Dame L. Rev. 1225 (2016).

6. *Legislative response.* The Kentucky legislature responded to *Rose* with the Kentucky Education Reform Act of 1990 (KERA), which extensively modified Kentucky's education system. On the funding side, the new law provided for a foundation program consisting of an annually adjusted minimum spending base and a requirement that districts levy a minimum property tax. In addition, a school board could obtain a state-subsidized, guaranteed yield up to 15% of that base amount, and it could by referendum increase revenues an additional 30% entirely from local funds. The board was limited, however, to an expenditure of

45% above the foundation level. State funds were also available for a number of special programs. State and local support increased 38% in just the first full year of KERA, and substantial progress to the equity goal of closing the gap between rich and poor districts was made. Trimble & Forsaith, *Achieving Equity and Excellence in Kentucky Education*, 28 U. Mich. J.L. Ref. 599, 612–13 (1995). Funding reform was, however, only a part of KERA. The act reorganized state and local governance of the schools, addressing "quality" from many perspectives. Probably the most critical was the establishment of a statewide performance-based assessment for students, intended to measure progress to meeting the academic goals. KERA set maximum class sizes, expanded pre-school, established family resource centers with child care and health services, provided extended programs for students, and professional development for teachers. The provisions of KERA are reviewed in Benson, *Definitions of Equity in School Finance in Texas, New Jersey and Kentucky*, 28 Harv. J. Legis. 401, 418–20 (1991); Trimble & Forsaith, *supra* at 609 (analyzing the assessments program in detail).

7. *Gauging progress.* If you were a member of the Kentucky court and faced a subsequent challenge regarding school funding, how would you assess whether a "thorough and effective" system of public schools had been achieved? For a report on subsequent developments, see Wright, *Two Steps Forward, One Step Back: The Kentucky Education Reform Act a Generation Later*, 42 J.L. & Educ. 567 (2013) (reporting that Kentucky students' performance on educational assessments have improved but proposed funding levels have not kept pace with student needs, and some funds have been misdirected into programs unrelated to academics). For a further review of the impact and implications of *Rose*, see Bauries, *Forward: Rights, Remedies, and Rose*, 98 KY. L.J. 703 (2010) (introduction to Kentucky Law Journal symposium on *Rose* at 20). For more analysis of how well Kentucky schools have fared in meeting the *Rose* standards in the aftermath of legislative action, see Collins, *On the Constitutional Sufficiency of the Modern Kentucky School System,* 53 U. Louisville L. Rev. 351 (2015) (contending that the Kentucky funding system presently failed to meet the full requirements of *Rose* and may be subject to future challenges).

Other studies have shown mixed results about whether the post-*Rose* changes in Kentucky have been effective and enduring. See, e.g., A. Newman, *The Rose Case: A Study in Legal Advocacy, in* Realizing Educational Rights: Advancing School Reform through Courts and Communities (2013) (discussing blend of legal and moral advocacy); C. Wilson, *Adequacy Post-Rose v. Council for Better Education in Kentucky in Public Facilities: A Case Study* (2013) (Ph.D. Dissertation), available at https://search.proquest.com/docview/1439139304 (in focused case study of public school facilities, finding that there had been improvements fostering educational adequacy in three out of five key areas); Baumann, *The Funding Gap Between Kentucky's Poor and Wealthy School Districts Continues to Grow* (2017), available at https://kypolicy.org/wp-content/uploads/2017/12/KCEP-equity-gap-report-1.pdf (finding that there has been increased reliance on local rather than state funds in recent years and that a growing gap has arisen in Kentucky between the poorest and wealthiest school districts, resulting in a growing "equity gap" similar to that which fueled the initial *Rose* litigation).

A Note on Other Developments in School Finance Litigation

It is not feasible for this casebook to try to track school finance litigation in all 50 states. At the same time, it may be helpful to provide snapshots of developments in a handful of jurisdictions where major litigation has reached crucial points.

1. *Important state constitutional developments.*

(a) *Connecticut.* Connecticut faced early litigation challenging the state's heavy reliance on local property tax with limited state supplemental funding. See *Horton v. Meskill,* 376 A.2d 359 (Ct. 1977). Notwithstanding legislative reforms of funding structures, further litigation challenged the failure to provide students in Hartford (the state capital) with an adequate education. See *Sheff v. O'Neill,* 678 A.2d 1267 (Ct. 1996). In early 2020, the state trial judge approved a settlement in *Sheff.* The settlement added additional magnet school seats in suburban schools with a substantial proportion reserved for Hartford students. Additional funding is targeted to support magnet schools. See http://schoolfunding.info/litigation-map/connecticut/#1484004342539-fd26c596-a9c0.

(b) *Delaware. See Delawareans for Equal Opportunity v. Carney,* 199 A.3d 109 (Del. Ch. 2018) (holding that education clause of state constitution had qualitative dimension and requiring that political branches create and maintain a system of free public schools that provide education to students attending them; and stating that courts will look to standards established by state legislature and state department of education in interpreting qualitative component).

(c) *Kansas.* Kansas has provided a particularly dramatic story of showdowns between the state supreme court and the state legislature. In *Gannon v. State,* 319 P.3d 1196 (Kan. 2014), the state supreme court held that school districts had standing and could raise justiciable claims that the state constitution specially placed authority and responsibility to finance public school system on the state legislature; state constitution's adequacy provision required that the financing system be reasonably calculated to have all public school students meet or exceed standards set by state board of education; state funding system had established unconstitutional, wealth-based disparities in education funding by withholding all capital outlay state aid payments to which certain school districts would otherwise be entitled and also had created unconstitutional wealth-based disparities by prorating and reducing supplemental general state aid payments to which certain school districts were otherwise entitled. The Kansas state legislature stood firm in the face of the court's mandate. So did the state supreme court. See 402 P.3d 513 (Kan. 2017) (concluding that state failed to meet its burden of establishing that public education system satisfied statutory and constitutional requirements). The Kansas court has retained jurisdiction and entered a number of additional rulings in the case. See *Gannon v. State,* 420 P.3d 477 (Kan. 2018); *Gannon v. State,* 443 P.3d 294 (Kan. 2019) (tying state compliance to *Rose* standard; and concluding state substantially complied with prior court order).

(d) *Detroit, Michigan. See* Bowman, *Education Reform and Detroit's Right to Literacy Litigation*, 75 Wash. & Lee L. Rev. Online 61 (2018), discussing *Gary B. v. Snyder*, 329 F. Supp. 3d 344 (E.D. Mich. 2018) (asserting claim of federal constitutional right of access to literacy). The trial court decision in *Gary B* was affirmed in part and reversed in part, see *Gary B. v. Whitmer*, 957 F.3d 616 (6th Cir. 2020), (rejecting equal protection argument, but concluding that the federal Constitution's Fourteenth Amendment Due Process Clause gave rise to a fundamental right to a basic minimal education meaning one that provided access to literacy, and finding that plaintiff students had stated a claim that they had been deprived of that basic right). Subsequently, in a memorandum opinion, the Sixth Circuit, acting en banc, granted review and vacated the earlier panel decision. See *Gary B. v. Whitmer*, 958 F.3d 1216 (6th Cir. 2020).

(e) *North Carolina.* North Carolina has lingered in its response to long-running litigation challenging compliance with state constitutional requirements. See *Leandro v. State*, 488 S.Ed.2d 249 (N.C. 1997); *Hoke County Bd. of Educ. v. State*, 358 N.C. 605 (N.C. 2004). After completion of a WestEd study, the trial court approved a consent decree that required state defendents to "work expeditiously and without delay to implement a number of requirements." See http://schoolfunding.info/news/north-carolina-court-issues-consent-order-requiring-parties-to-act-to-implement-siginficant-sound-basic-education-reforms/ (requiring attention to teacher development and recruitment; principal development and recruitment; creation of appropriate financial systems; assessment and accountability systems; attention to low-performing schools and districts; attention to early education; and alignment of high school and postsecondary/career expectations).

(f) *Pennsylvania.* In a 2015 decision, the Pennsylvania Commonwealth Court invoked the judicial abstention doctrine applicable to political questions in declining to review the merits of an equal protection and education clause challenge brought under the state constitution. See *William Penn School District v. Pennsylvania Dep't of Educ.*, 114 A.3d 456 (Comm. Pa. 2015). However, the State Supreme Court held that the claims that the system of funding public education violated the state's education clause and equal protection clauses were justiciable. 170 A.3d 414 (Pa. 2017).

(g) *Rhode Island.* There seems to have been a growing reticence among other courts to engage in substantive review of intransigent school finance problems. For example, in a 2014 decision, the Rhode Island Supreme Court concluded that intervening in a public school funding dispute would violate principles of separation of powers. See *Woonsocket School Committee v. Chafee*, 89 A.3d 778 (2014).

(h) *South Carolina.* Some states have tried to take a middle ground in dealing with separation of powers concerns. For example, in 2014, the South Carolina Supreme Court rendered a detailed decision holding the state's educational finance system unconstitutional because it failed to assure children an adequate public education. See *Abbeville County School Dist. v. State*, 767 S.E.2d 157 (S.C. 2014) (concluding that a challenge to the state's funding system was justiciable and that the state funding system violated the state constitution's education clause). The court also ordered both plaintiff school districts and the state to submit periodic updates on their progress in reaching compliance with the court's remedial orders. See *Abbeville County School Dist. v. State*, 780 S.E.2d 609 (S.C. 2015) (indicating that the court would review developments shortly after the end of the 2016 legislative session).

2. *Equality v. adequacy.* Clearly the most important and visible post-*Rose* litigation development has been the increasing emphasis on adequacy more than on fiscal equity. See, e.g., J. Hansen, 21st Century School Finance: How Is the Context Changing? (Educ. Comm. of States, July 2001). Their analysis takes different forms, but in essence, what the "adequacy" courts are saying is that state constitutions guarantee a basic education that will prepare all students for citizenship and a constructive life. Some of these courts may attempt to define in somewhat broad terms the goals and content of an adequate education (as the Kentucky court in *Rose*). A few may enter more detailed remedial orders (as in the New Jersey *Abbott* decisions). While almost all purport to defer to the legislature to design a constitutionally valid system, a finding of constitutional inadequacy pushes the court deeper into educational policy choices than one dealing solely with fiscal equality. Reflect back on the cases in this Chapter that address school finance challenges. At what points do these theories converge? At what points do they differ? See Weishart, *Transcending Equality Versus Adequacy*, 66 Stan. L. Rev. 477 (2014) (arguing that equality of educational opportunity is an "infeasible" standard, "adequacy" is too ambiguous, but that the two standards can effectively be merged).

3. *Special problems: overburden.* Both equality and adequacy theories paint with a broad brush. How should courts approach problems that may face urban or rural school districts in particular, or that affect particular students? These types of problems are often referred to as overburden. "Municipal overburden" refers to added costs facing a locality. "Educational overburden" refers to added costs stemming from needs of particular students (for example, those who need special education or who have limited English proficiency). Often, these types of overburden are compounded. For example, urban school districts may have higher proportions of students with limited English skills or special education needs, and accordingly may face higher costs. Similarly, rural districts may face higher rates of poverty and have greater difficulty recruiting teachers to provide special education, math or science. Should these differences in educational costs have a bearing on judicial analysis of equality or adequacy claims?

Except in unusual cases, courts addressing litigation that relies on an "adequacy" theory have been disinclined to adopt an overburden theory as a means of redirecting funding to especially burdened districts but have instead focused on the need for all children, wherever located, to receive an adequate education. Compare

Leandro v. State, 488 S.E.2d 249 (N.C. 1997) (rejecting claim that certain urban and certain rural districts and counties faced overburden, and instead recognizing individual children's right to a sound, basic education); *Kukor v. Grover*, 436 N.W.2d 568 (Wis. 1989) (in court's view, educational and municipal overburden should be addressed by legislature), with *Campaign for Fiscal Equity, Inc. v. State*, 801 N.E.2d 326, 350 (N.Y. 2003) (recognizing that municipal overburden existed with regard to New York City schools and observing that a unique combination of circumstances had been shown because "New York City schools have the most student need in the state and the highest local costs yet receive some of the lowest per student funding and have some of the worst results"). In your view, is the "overburden" argument a persuasive one? How should "overburden" be analyzed with an eye to state constitutional provisions? More insights regarding overburden can be gained from consideration of thoughtful scholarship. See, e.g., Andersen, *School Finance Litigation — The Styles of Judicial Intervention*, 55 Wash. L. Rev. 137, 161–62 (1979).

For a discussion of the special problems facing urban and migrant school children, see Ostrander, *School Funding: Inequality in District Funding and the Disparate Impact on Urban and Migrant School Children*, 2015 B.Y.U. Educ. & L.J. 271 (2015).

4. *Next waves of litigation*? Based on earlier courts' reasoning, can you anticipate how the next generation of litigation might proceed? Could you foresee challenges to the sufficiency of particular aspects of the public school system, for example, kindergarten or pre-kindergarten programs? After-school extracurricular programs? Should the quality of teachers be assessed separately? How about school facilities such as buildings, laboratories, and other facilities? See, e.g., Snow, *Someone to Watch over Me: A Court Mandated Right to Adequate Extracurricular Activities in California*, 19 Geo. J. on Poverty L. & Pol'y 135 (2012) (arguing that extracurricular activities should be adequate). For scholarly insights on related issues, see Yergin, *Rethinking Public Education Litigation Strategy: A Duty-Based Approach to Reform*, 115 Colum. L. Rev. 1563 (2015) (positing a new approach that might be used in the context of Connecticut school finance litigation, and arguing for a system that would establish a duty for responsible administration of public schools); Davis, *Off the Constitutional Map: Breaking the Endless Cycle of School Finance Litigation*, 2016 B.Y.U. Educ. & L.J. 117 (2016) (reviewing school finance litigation in Ohio, New Jersey, and Washington State, and suggesting alternative litigation strategies); Hinojosa, *"Race-Conscious" School Finance Litigation: Is a Fourth Wave Emerging?* 50 U. Rich. L. Rev. 869 (2016) (suggesting that attention should return to race-based discrimination, using examples from New Mexico and North Carolina).

[b] Charter Schools: New Possibilities, New Challenges

Introduction

Charter schools are an increasingly popular form of public education. As discussed in the introduction to this part of the Chapter, charter schools in the United States have only been in existence for a little more than two decades. The United States Department of Education defines "public charter schools" as ones that are publicly funded, operating under a charter, with their own governing board, and accountability standards set by the state. See United States Department of Education, *The Condition of Education, Public Charter School Enrollment* (2019). https://nces.ed.gov/programs/coe/indicator_cgb.asp. At the time this book went to press, seven states had no charter school laws (Vermont, West Virginia, Kentucky, Nebraska, South Dakota, North Dakota and Wyoming). *Id.* As of fall 2016, 6% of students in elementary and secondary schools attended charter schools, with some states exceeding 10% (Delaware, District of Columbia, Florida, Louisiana, Colorado, Utah and Arizona). The District of Columbia had the highest rate of public charter school attendance (44%), while California had the highest number of public charter school enrollees (more than 600,000). *Id.* On the other hand, six states had 1% or fewer of their students enrolled in public charter schools (Iowa, Kansas, Mississippi, Virginia, Washington, and Wyoming). *Id.*

The number of public charter schools has increased significantly, rising from approximately 2,000 in 2000–01 to 7,000 in 2016–17. *Id.* During this period, public charter school enrollment rose from .4 million in fall 2000 to 3 million in fall 2016. *Id.* Enrollment in public charter schools was particularly high at the elementary school level. *Id.* Between 2000 and 2016, the racial/ethnic composition of public charter schools paralleled that of public schools more generally (with the highest proportions at 32% white, 26% black, and 33% Hispanic). *Id.* In fall 2016, 34% of public charter school students attended high-poverty schools, as compared to 24% of traditional students who attend high-poverty schools. *Id.*

Charter schools form an important element of the "school choice" movement that seeks to give parents and students greater autonomy in selecting their preferred school setting. For a thoughtful analysis of associated issues regarding "choice," see Rauch, *School Choice Architecture*, 34 Yale L. & Pol'y Rev. 187 (2015) (discussing implicit constraints on school choice and possible fixes). For a study of the impacts of charter schools in Virginia, see Lehnen, *Charting the Course: Charter School Exploration in Virginia*, 50 U. Rich. L. Rev. 839 (2016).

Supporters of "school choice" may also support home schooling, and vouchers or tax credits allowing attendance at private schools at public expense. Proponents of charter schools often assert that charter schools can produce better results because they are free from some of the constraints that apply to traditional public schools. See, e.g., Johnson & Medler, *The Conceptual and Practical Development of Charter Schools*, 11 Stan. L. & Pol'y Rev. 291, 292 (2000) (arguments by former U.S. Department of Education officials in favor of charter schools). Do you agree?

For a competing view, see Black, *Preferencing Educational Choice: The Constitutional Limits*, 103 Cornell L. Rev. 1359 (2018) (arguing that expanded charter and voucher programs mean that access to traditional public schools is no longer guaranteed and accordingly violates the constitutional right to public education found in state constitutions; explaining that this argument does not mean that such programs are prohibited entirely or that they are generally unconstitutional; contending instead that state constitutions limit states from giving preference to private choice programs over public education, and that choice programs cannot impede educational opportunities in public schools). Professor Black and others have also argued that the charter school and "choice" movement may atomize the role of public schools in imparting shared public values. See Black, *Charter Schools, Vouchers and the Public Good*, 48 Wake Forest L. Rev. 445 (2013). Others fear that the charter school model may lead to increased risk of segregation and racial subordination. See James, *Opt-Out Education: School Choice as Racial Subordination*, 99 Iowa L. Rev. 1083 (2014); Wilson, *The New White Flight*, 14 Duke J. Const. L. & Pub. Pol'y 233 (2019) (discussing "white charter school enclaves" within predominantly minority school districts, arguing that parental choice is creating new patterns of racial segregation and inequality immune from traditional racial segregation review, and offering arguments for regulating private choices that result in racial segregation in public charter schools).

Still others fear the financial implications of the charter and "choice" model, noting how it has already contributed to the loss of many parochial schools that once provided an option for those who chose to forego public education. See, e.g., Lackman, *The Collapse of Catholic School Enrollment: The Unintended Consequence of the Charter School Movement*, 6 Alb. Gov't L. Rev. 1 (2012). In 2020, the United States Supreme Court concluded that a state scholarship program, limiting eligibility for students attending religiously-affiliated schools, failed to comply with the federal Constitution, notwithstanding state constitutional provisions that limited funding to religious schools to protect principles of separation of church and state (the so-called "Blaine Amendment" common in many states' constitutions). See *Espinoza v. Montana Department of Revenue*, ___S. Ct. ___. 2020 WL 3518364 (2020). The *Espinoza* case therefore puts even more pressure on public educational funding that will need to be made available not only to public schools and public charter schools, but also to students attending parochial and other religiously-affiliated schools.

What will be the role of the courts in navigating these competing views as they play out in legislatures and litigation? The following New Jersey case was decided at an early point in the development of public charter schools. The notes that follow consider subsequent developments.

Grant of Charter School Application of Englewood on the Palisades Charter School

164 N.J. 316, 753 A.2d 687 (2000)

Lavecchia, J.

[Several boards of education brought constitutional and statutory challenges to the creation of charter schools in their districts.—Eds.]

I.

The providing of public education in New Jersey is a state function. Our constitution mandates that the Legislature must "provide for the maintenance and support of a thorough and efficient system of free public schools" for New Jersey's children. N.J. Const. art. VIII, § 4, ¶ 1. Until recently that obligation has been carried out through a system of local school districts functioning as governmental entities. As the challenge of providing a quality education has become more complex and difficult, however, the Legislature has determined to authorize an alternative format, different from the traditional local school district model and known generally as charter schools, for providing public education to New Jersey children. As defined in New Jersey's enabling Act, a charter school is a public school operated pursuant to a charter approved by the Commissioner of Education, which is independent of a local board of education and is managed by a board of trustees. N.J.S.A. 18A:36A.3.

In choosing to experiment with the use of charter schools, New Jersey is not alone. Our state is one of many that has enacted legislation to permit this alternative. The establishment of charter schools across the nation has varied from state to state, but such schools generally share some common characteristics. Charter schools are public schools, which through legislative authorization are free from many state and local regulations. See Kevin S. Huffman, Note, *Charter Schools, Equal Protection Litigation, and the New School Reform Movement*, 73 N.Y.U. L. Rev. 1290, 1294 (1998) (discussing characteristics of charter schools). Charter schools have more autonomy than other public schools in staffing, curriculum and spending choices. Ibid. Generally, if the goals set forth in the school's charter are not fulfilled, the charter is not renewed. [See National Conference of State Legislatures, Education Program: Charter Schools https://www.ncsl.org/research/education/charter-schools-in-the-states-charter-school-fina.aspx (website discussing background on charter school legislation)]. Such schools actually are accountable to several groups for both their academic results and fiscal practices, including the charter schools' governmental approving authority, the individuals who organize the schools and the public that funds them.

The charter school movement in the United States started in 1991, when Minnesota enacted the first charter school law. California followed in 1992. U.S. Dep't of Educ. The State Charter Schools 2000: Fourth-Year Report at 11 (Jan. 2000) (U.S. Dept. of Educ.). By April 1995, when the Act was being considered by the New Jersey Legislature, twelve states authorized the establishment of charter schools, and a number of other states were considering similar legislation during the 1995–1996 session. Public Hearing before Senate Educ. Comm.: Senate Bill No. 1796 (The Charter School Program Act of 1995) (April 28, 1995), 1995–1996 Legislative Session (testimony of Alex Medler, Policy Analyst, Education Commission of the States) at 5X. In 1999 three states, New York, Oklahoma and Oregon, passed charter school legislation, bringing the total number of jurisdictions with charter school laws to thirty-six states and the District of Columbia.

. . . .

New Jersey's Charter School Act shares many of the broader goals voiced by advocates of the charter school movement nationwide. In the Findings and Declarations section of the Act, the Legislature stated that charter schools offer the potential to improve public learning; increase for students and parents the educational choices available when selecting the learning environment which they feel may be the most appropriate; encourage the use of different and innovative learning methods; establish a new form of accountability for schools; require the measurement of learning outcomes; make the school the unit for educational improvement; and establish new professional opportunities for teachers.

The statute further provides that the Legislature "finds that the establishment of a charter school is in the best interests of the students of this State and it is therefore the public policy of the State to encourage and facilitate the development of charter schools." N.J.S.A. 18A:36A-2.

The Act sets forth the procedure for establishing a charter school, N.J.S.A. 18A:36A-4, and the information that must be contained in an application for charter school approval. N.J.S.A. 18A:36A-5. Operating guidelines, admission and enrollment policies, and transportation services are detailed in the Act. N.J.S.A. 18A:36A-7, -8, -11 and -13. As for funding, the Act provides that the district of residence of the charter school shall forward to the school a per-pupil amount set by the Commissioner, but presumptively set by the Legislature at 90% of the local levy budget per pupil for that student's grade level in the district. N.J.S.A. 18A:36A-12. The Commissioner cannot set this amount at a level greater than 100%, and may set it lower than the presumptive 90%. Ibid. The standards and procedures are detailed in duly promulgated regulations of the State Board of Education (State Board). N.J.A.C. 6A:11-1.1 to -8.2. Both the Acts' provisions, as well as the regulations, provide for notice to the local school district when an application for approval of a charter school is filed, and an opportunity to appeal the Commissioner's decision on such an application to the State Board. N.J.S.A. 18A:36A-4(c), (d); N.J.A.C. 6A:11-2.1(b)3, -2.1(e), -2.5.

The three school districts challenging the facial validity of the Act in this consolidated appeal essentially disagree with the legislative decision to allow charter schools to become part of the provision of public education in our state. That argument has been made, and lost, before the Legislature. The choice to include charter schools among the array of public entities providing educational services to our pupils is a choice appropriately made by the Legislature so long as the constitutional mandate to provide a thorough and efficient system of education in New Jersey is satisfied.

Certain principles permeate our school laws. As stated above, one is that the State's obligation to provide a thorough and efficient system of education in our public schools is inviolate. So, too, must the State ensure that no student is discriminated against or subjected to segregation in our public schools. Because of the abiding importance of those two principles and the potential impact of the charter school movement on public education, the Act, and the State's efforts to implement it, require careful scrutiny.

II.

Racial Impact

The Englewood City Board of Education (Englewood) contends that the Act on its face, and as applied, is flawed because the Commissioner is not required to and, in practice, does not assess the effect on racial balance that a charter school may have on a public school district from which it draws its pupils. Englewood asks the Court to require the Commissioner to perform a study of the potential racial imbalancing effects of a charter school on a district of residence before the Commissioner approves a charter school application.

Rooted in our Constitution, New Jersey's public policy prohibits segregation in our public schools:

> The history and vigor of our State's policy in favor of a thorough and efficient public school system are matched in its policy against racial discrimination and segregation in the public schools. Since 1881 there has been explicit legislation declaring it unlawful to exclude a child from any public school because of his race (L. 1881, c. 149; N.J.S.A. 18A:38-5.1), and indirect as well as direct efforts to circumvent the legislation have been stricken judicially. In 1947, the delegates to the Constitutional Convention took pains to provide, not only in general terms that no person shall be denied any civil right, but also in specific terms that no person shall be segregated in the public schools because of his 'religious principles, race, color, ancestry or national origin.' Art. 1, para. 5. [Jenkins v. Township of Morris Sch. Dist. and Bd. of Educ., 279 A.2d 619, 626 (N.J. 1971) (citations omitted).]

New Jersey's abhorrence of discrimination and segregation in the public schools is not tempered by the cause of the segregation. Whether due to an official action, or simply segregation in fact, our public policy applies with equal force against the continuation of segregation in our schools. *Booker v. Board of Educ., Plainfleld*, 212 A.2d 1 (N.J. 1965). We have exhorted the Commissioner to exercise broadly his statutory powers when confronting segregation, whatever the cause. *Jenkins, supra*, 58 N.J. at 506–07, 279 A.2d 619. Responsive to that obligation, the Commissioner has required school districts to monitor racial balance in the public schools. Districts are provided with guidelines to assist them in the review of their schools' pupil populations so they may be vigilant in preventing segregation from occurring and promptly correcting it if it does occur. *New Jersey State Guidelines on the Desegregation and Integration of Public Schools* (*Guidelines*).

The *Guidelines* provide a step-by-step methodology for a school district to use in establishing the ratio between the district's overall pupil population percentages for its racial groups and the population percentages for the same pupil groups for each grade organization level, i.e., elementary, middle, junior high or high school. Once established, all schools within each grade organization level are compared to the expected pupil percentages, allowing for a reasonable deviation. Use of those *Guidelines* provides early warning to school district officials if a school within a particular organizational level, for example an elementary school, begins to have a pupil population that is substantially out of line with that of the other elementary schools in the district. Administrative steps, including but not limited to adjustments in school assignments or instructional clustering of pupils, are then possible to keep the school populations within expected ranges or to otherwise achieve in the students' learning environment appropriate mixtures of pupil populations that reflect the community's pertinent school age population.

The school-to-school comparisons thus promote learning environments in which students are educated among a mix of children that is reflective of the overall district composition for that organizational level. With charter schools, the Legislature sought to achieve a comparable result. Balancing the desire to prevent discrimination on the basis of race in admission policies with a concomitant desire to prevent racial segregation in the charter school, the Act provides:

> The admission policy of the charter school shall, to the maximum extent practicable, seek the enrollment of a cross section of the community's school age population, including racial and academic factors. [N.J.S.A. 18A:36A-8e.]

That language was not included in the original Senate or Assembly versions of the bill. . . .

. . . .

As a result of the comments elicited from the joint hearing, the current language of N.J.S.A. 18A:36A-8e was added, reflecting the importance that the legislators placed on the need to maintain racial balance in the charter schools. In using, as the pertinent reference, "a cross section of the community's school age population including racial and academic factors," the Act requires that a charter school's admission policy seek a pupil population similar to the pupil population that the Guidelines seek for New Jersey's school districts. We see nothing in the Act or its history that is discordant with the State's policy of maintaining nonsegregated public schools in our communities. Nor do we understand the State Board to be suggesting otherwise.

. . . The Commissioner's obligation to oversee the promotion of racial balance in our public schools to ensure that public school pupils are not subjected to segregation includes any type of school within the rubric of the public school designation.

. . . .

Accordingly, we hold that the Commissioner must assess the racial impact that a charter school applicant will have on the district of residence in which the charter school will operate. We express no view on the formality or structure of that analysis except to state that it must take place before final approval is granted to a charter school applicant. We otherwise leave the form and structure of that analysis to the Commissioner and State Board to determine. We simply hold that the Commissioner's obligation to prevent segregation in the public schools must inform his review of an application to approve a charter school, and if segregation would occur the Commissioner must use the full panoply of his powers to avoid that result. . . .

III

Economic Impact

The funding mechanism of the Act provides:

> The school district of residence shall pay directly to the charter school for each student enrolled in the charter school who resides in the district a presumptive amount equal to 90% of the local levy budget per pupil for the specific grade level in the district. At the discretion of the commissioner and at the time the charter is granted, the commissioner may require the school district of residence to pay directly to the charter school for each student enrolled in the charter school an amount equal to less than 90% percent, or an amount which shall not exceed 100% of the local levy budget per pupil for the specific grade level in the district of residence. The per pupil amount paid to the charter school shall not exceed the local levy budget per pupil for the specific grade level in the district in which the charter school is located. The district of residence shall also pay directly to the charter school any categorical aid attributable to the student, provided the student is receiving appropriate categorical services, and any federal funds attributable to the student. [N.J.S.A. 18A:36A-12.]

The three Boards predict that this loss of funds, in the presumptive amount of 90% of the local levy budget per pupil (although the Commissioner may set that amount at a level lower than 90%, or higher, but not to exceed 100%), will cause dire consequences for their respective school districts. None claim, however, that the approval of the charter schools in this consolidated appeal will cause it to cease providing a thorough and efficient education to its remaining pupils. Nevertheless, the Boards argue that the Commissioner should be compelled to examine the economic impact upon a district of residence as a result of the approval of a charter school when the Commissioner determines whether to grant that approval. As with its racial impact argument, Englewood specifically contends that there should be an impact analysis comparable to the type of feasibility study performed when the Commissioner is reviewing a change in a sending-receiving relationship. *See* N.J.SA. 18A:38-13.

The State Board contends that the Commissioner should not be faulted for failing to evaluate expressly the financial consequences to a district of residence that result from the approval of a charter school within its borders. The State's argument is premised on the Act's silence concerning any such requirement in the application process. Moreover, the State Board emphasized that there is no evidence in this record that any district with an approved charter school is unable to provide a thorough and efficient education to its pupils. The Appellate Division concurred with the State Board, observing that it was "the Legislature's choice not to include the [financial] impact on the existing district among the criteria for approval of the charter." . . .

. . . .

While the focus of the examination that the Commissioner must perform in setting the per-pupil amount is on the charter school applicant, the Commissioner cannot reasonably be expected to perform that function in a vacuum. The obligation to supervise the provision of a thorough and efficient system of education in all public schools is omnipresent for the Commissioner. N.J.S.A. 18A:4-23. The Commissioner cannot review the charter school's needs and set a per-pupil amount to be shifted from the district of residence without being circumspect about the district of residence's continuing ability to provide a thorough and efficient education to its remaining pupils. We conclude, however, that the Commissioner is entitled to rely on the district of residence to come forward with a preliminary showing that the requirements of a thorough and efficient education cannot be met.

The Act affirmatively entitles the district of residence to analyze the charter school applicant's submission to the Commissioner and to challenge or augment the applicant's submitted information. N.J.S.A. 18A:36A-4c; N.J.A.C. 6A:11-2.1. Further, the Legislature has put districts on notice that the presumptive per pupil loss shall be 90%. N.J.S.A. 18A:36A-12. Read in combination, those statutory provisions require a district of residence to make an initial showing that imposition of the presumptive amount, or a proposed different amount for the charter school applicant's pupils would impede, or prevent, the delivery of a thorough and efficient education in that district. We note, however, that application of this standard in the context of an *Abbott* district is not part of this case. We leave that question for another day.

We do not regard the discretion allotted to the Commissioner under the Act, when determining whether to apply the presumptive percentage or to apply a different percentage, to be controlled by focusing on the financial consequences to a district of residence. But, if a district of residence demonstrates with some specificity that the constitutional requirements of a thorough and efficient education would be jeopardized by loss of the presumptive amount, or proposed different amount of per-pupil funds to a charter school, then the Commissioner is obligated to evaluate carefully the impact that loss of funds would have on the ability of the district of residence to deliver a thorough and efficient education. The Commissioner is well positioned to analyze such contentions and should do so when they arise.

. . . .

V.

For the foregoing reasons, the judgment of the Appellate Division, as modified by this opinion, is affirmed.

Stein, J., concurring. [Omitted. — Eds.]

Notes and Questions

1. *Facial challenge.* The school districts in the *Englewood* case brought a facial challenge to the charter school legislation, and sought to require charter school applicants to demonstrate that their proposed initiatives would not adversely affect either the racial balance or the economics of the school districts from which charter school students would be drawn. Why did the school districts bring a facial challenge? What about the organizations and community members? For an example of an application that failed on the facts to meet New Jersey's charter school standards, see *In the Matter of the Proposed Quest Academy Charter School of Montclair Founders Group,* 80 A.3d 1120 (N.J. 2013) (upholding Commissioner's denial of application where education plan was weak, content and program were deficient, potential to attract students was limited, charter school might interfere with desegregation, and community criticized proposed school). See also *In re Red Bank Charter School,* 843 A.2d 365 (N.J. App. Div. 2004) (Commissioner required to hold separate hearing to determine whether discrimination or segregation would occur as a result of charter school's proposed policies including enrollment lottery, waiting list, sibling preference, and student withdrawal practices). For a review of issues raised by charter schools in New Jersey, see Barbosa, *An Unfulfilled Promise: The Need for Charter School Reform in New Jersey,* 39 SETON HALL LEGIS. J. 359 (2015) (discussing statutory revisions to charter school legislation in New Jersey).

The principal case addressed public school districts' fears that diversion of public funds to charter schools would impair budgets needed to serve students at traditional public schools in the district. Are such fears justified? For a November 2015 report on New Jersey's funding of traditional and charter public schools, see Farrie & Johnson, *Newark Public Schools Budget Impacts of Underfunding and Rapid Charter Growth* (Education Law Center, 2015), available at https://edlawcenter.org/assets/files/pdfs/Newsblasts/NPS%20Budget%20Impacts%20of%20Underfunding%20and%20Rapid%20Charter%20Growth_hires.pdf (finding that a combination of underfunding and charter school expansion had resulted in 20% decline in spending for Newark's traditional public schools in the period 2008–2015). Another study was done on the impact of charter schools in Ohio. See Cook, *The Effect of Charter Competition on Unionized District Revenues and Resource Allocation,* available from the National Center for the Study of Privatization in Education at Columbia University's Teachers College, https://ncspe.tc.columbia.edu/working-papers/?select=CharterSchools. Cook reviewed budget data from 1982 to 2013 and reached two major conclusions: (1) competition with charter schools reduced federal, state and local support for district schools; and (2) charter competition drove down local funding because residential property values were depressed and schools redirected revenue from instruction expenses to facility improvements.

2. *Washington State and more.* It is worth comparing developments in Washington State where a different story unfolded. See *League of Women Voters of Washington v. State,* 355 P.3d 1131 (Wash. 2015) (en banc) (holding that state charter school

act violated provisions of state constitution relating to common school construction fund, where plaintiffs claimed that these schools were not "common schools" that should received state funding). Notably the legislation challenged in the initial case allowed charter schools to be governed by a "charter school board" rather than the local school board, and were exempt from many state rules. Subsequently, the Washington court upheld revised charter school legislation designed to cure the earlier concerns about constitutionality in *El Centro De La Raza v. State*, 428 P.3d 1143 (Wash. 2018) (concluding that revised state charter school legislation satisfied the constitutional requirement of a general and uniform system of public schools on its face; did not violate requirements relating to supervision by superintendent of public instruction; did not violate constitutional requirement that revenue derived from common school fund and state tax for common schools be exclusively applied to support public schools; but concluding that limitation of charter school employees to bargaining units tied to individual charter schools was unconstitutional but severable).

Courts in other states have allowed charter schools to proceed without imposing limiting constraints sought by school districts. See, e.g., *Richard Allen Preparatory Charter School v. School Dist. of Philadelphia*, 123 A.3d 1101 (Pa. Comm. 2015) (district did not have authority to impose enrollment cap on charter school or dictate system of student assessment). Reflect on the Problem at the outset of this Chapter. What legislative provisions are likely to survive scrutiny under state constitutions, and what provisions might lead to invalidation?

3. *Interpretive standards.* Look closely at the statutory provisions relating to racial balance and economic support in New Jersey, as evident in the principal case. How clear are these provisions? What did the court's interpretation add to the statutory text? Now consider the statutory provisions relating to government funding for "common schools" in Washington State (in the original decision and after 2016 amendments). Do you think the Washington court's interpretation added anything to the text? Are these provisions clear or ambiguous?

A Note on Emerging Issues Relating to Charter Schools

1. *Funding formulas: "educational" costs and more.* As evident in the principal case, charter schools and traditional public schools have often engaged in pulls and tugs over available public financial resources. Often such struggles focus on funding formulas designed to cover certain types of non-core services. See, e.g., *Frederick Classical Charter School, Inc. v. Frederick County Bd. of Educ.*, 164 A.3d 285 (Md. 2017) (under state statute, charter school was entitled to "commensurate" distribution of funds including funds for transportation services, even though public school wanted to provide in kind services instead, and even though the charter school did not provide transportation services to students). See also *School Board of Collier County v. Florida Dep't of Education*, 279 So. 3d 281 (Fla. App. 2019) (holding that school boards lacked standing to challenge creation of independent charter schools and upholding financing system that called for distribution of capital millage

revenue and federal funds to charter schools as constitutional in face of challenges relating to state constitutional provisions regarding ad valorem tax). For an argument that funding for charter schools is inadequate, see Geheb & Owens, *Charter School Funding Gap*, 46 Fordham Urb. L.J. 72 (2019).

2. *Accountability.* When can charter schools' operations be terminated? What ethical standards apply to their personnel? Charter schools generally must meet accountability standards in order to continue to operate in the long term. Depending on the jurisdiction's statutes, their personnel may also be subject to ethics requirements regarding self-dealing and board oversight. See *New Hope Academy Charter School v. School Dist. of City of York*, 89 A.3d 731 (Pa. Commw. 2014) (terminating charter where school's students failed to meet end-of-year performance benchmarks; concluding that contract between school and founder's business had not been appropriately reviewed, and that board violated state ethics act and non-profit corporations law). For an independent review of how charter schools are performing generally, see Center for Research on Education Outcomes, Stanford University, National Charter School Study (2013), available at https://credo.stanford.edu/publications/national-charter-school-study (in study of 26 states and New York City, finding that 25% of charter schools had significantly stronger learning gains in reading than traditional counterparts, 56% were no different and 19% had significantly weaker performance; also finding that in mathematics, 29% had significantly stronger learning gains, 40% were not significantly different than traditional counterparts, and 31% were significantly weaker). This study indicated that since an earlier analysis in 2009 involving 16 states, 8% of charter schools in those states had been terminated. For discussion of charter school revocation, see Grady, *Charter School Revocation: A Method for Efficiency, Accountability and Success*, 41 J. L & Educ. 513 (2013) (including compilation of state revocation statutes and proposing model approach); Eckes, Plucker & Benton, *Charter School Accountability: Legal Considerations Concerning Nonrenewal and Revocation Procedures*, 2006 B.Y.U. Educ. & L.J. 551. For an additional perspective, see Garnett, *Post-Accountability Accountability*, 52 U. Mich. J.L. Reform 157 (2018) (reviewing parental choice, considering academic research on parental choice and charter schools' effects on student performance, addressing accountability issues, and addressing related issues).

3. *"Public" or otherwise*? Charter schools have characteristics of public schools but also characteristics of private entities. As a result, they raise important questions regarding applicable governance models. For example, what are the implications of efforts to divest school boards of traditional governing authority? What issues are likely to be raised? See Garda & Doty, *The Legal Impact of Emerging Governance Models on Public Education and Its Office Holders*, 45 Urb. Law. 21 (2013) (identifying potential equal protection, Voting Rights Act, and state constitutional issues); Kiel, *The Endangered School District: The Promise and Challenge of Redistributing Control of Public Education*, 22 B.U. Pub. Int. L.J. 341 (2013) (considering the implications of charter schools for traditional school districts, drawing on case studies from New Orleans, Louisiana, in the aftermath of Hurricane Katrina);

Green et al., *Having It Both Ways: How Charter Schools Try to Obtain Funding of Public Schools and the Autonomy of Private Schools*, 63 Emory L.J. 303 (2013) (arguing that despite claims of public character for purposes of funding, charter schools have sought to avoid coverage as public entities for purposes of National Labor Relations Act); Davis, *Contracts, Control and Charter Schools: The Success of Charter Schools Depends on Stronger Nonprofit Board Oversight to Preserve Independence and Prevent Domination by For-Profit Management Companies*, 2011 B.Y.U. Educ. & L.J. 1 (discussing role of nonprofit boards).

4. *Liability issues.* How should questions of potential tort or contract liability be handled where charter schools are involved? See Hulden, *Charting a Course to State Action: Charter Schools and § 1983*, 111 Colum. L. Rev. 1244 (2011) (arguing that courts should treat charter schools as state actors for most claims brought by students but not for claims brought by employees); *LTTS Charter School, Inc. v. Palasota*, 362 S.W.3d 202 (Tex. App. 2012) (treating charter school as local governmental unit under state torts claims act, and under statute allowing waiver of sovereign immunity, but finding statutory provision relating to waiver of sovereign immunity did not apply to claim for breach of contract by real estate broker).

5. *Assessing "natural" experiments: New Orleans, post-Katrina.* In the aftermath of Hurricane Katrina, New Orleans endeavored to resurrect its public school system relying on charter schools. How would you assess this natural experiment in implementing major charter school reform? What factors would be particularly important in your analysis? For consideration of the effectiveness of this strategy, see Lay & Bauman, *Private Governance of Public Schools: Representation, Priorities, and Compliance in New Orleans Charter School Boards*, 55 Urban Affairs Rev., No. 4 (2019): 1006–1034 (finding that New Orleans's charter boards are unrepresentative, are focused on fiduciary responsibilities rather than academics, and routinely fail to comply with state transparency laws); Gardia, *Searching for Equity Amid a System of Schools: The View from New Orleans*, 42 Fordham Urb. L.J. 613 (2015) (arguing that immediate post-Katrina decisions were made at the level of autonomous schools resulting in unequal access, retention and service provision; subsequently more centralized policies were developed; and at the date of the article, two paths were emerging in terms of creating equal opportunity including one that relied on centralization and another that relied on market-driven reform to create specialized schools to fill unmet needs of vulnerable populations); K. Buras, Charter Schools, Race, and Urban Space: Where the Market Meets Grassroots Resistance (2015) (in case study of New Orleans, arguing that charter school reforms dispossessed black teachers and students and resulted in privatization of public education).

6. *Advice, please?* Return to the introductory Problem. What would you advise the Governor in terms of policy and legal considerations? Why? If you advise legislation, what legislative model would you suggest? Would you suggest a Robin Hood plan? What would you do about categorical grants and the overburden issue?

Chapter 10

The Chief Executive

The President is a chief executive with major constitutional powers and a wide reach of authority. Governors are not as dominant, and mayors even less so. This Chapter considers these chief executives—the mayor and the governor. Because the separation of powers principle does not usually apply to local governments, most of the interesting law on executive power is at the state level, where the governor plays a role as an important figure in the political process:

> As the central political figure in state government, the governor plays a large role in establishing the state's legislative agenda through such actions as preparation of the executive budget and the state-of-the-state address. The governor also actively participates in the legislative deliberations on both budgetary matters and state policy initiatives. Moreover, state executive departments expect the governor to establish administrative goals and implement strategies, and state residents look to the governor for political leadership and guidance. [Dilger, *A Comparative Analysis of Gubernatorial Enabling Resources*, 27 State & Local Gov't Rev., No. 2 (1995): 118–126.]

Strengthening state executives was a major recommendation of the 1993 Winter Commission report discussed in Chapter One. National Commission on the State and Local Public Service, Hard Truths/Tough Choices: an Agenda for State and Local Reform. The report recommended reducing the number of elected officials, reorganizing state government and limiting legislative amendment of executive budgets. Few states implemented these specific proposals, and the institutional strength of the governor has stabilized in recent years. A measure of institutional strength based on six criteria that include the number of elected officials, veto power and appointment authority showed little change from 1994 to 2006. Beyle, *Being Governor*, in The State of the States 53 (C.E. Van Horn ed., 2006). State attorneys general have also gained prominence as entrepreneurial policy makers whose positions may or may not be in accord with the positions taken by governors and legislatures of opposing parties. For discussion, see Thompson, *State and Local Governance Fifteen Years Later: Enduring and New Challenges*, 68 Pub. Admin. Rev., No. 1 (2008): S8–S19.

Scholarly attention to state governors has increased markedly in recent years. For an in-depth survey of research on governors from 1966 to 2015, see Bernick, *Studying Governors over Five Decades: What We Know and Where We Need to Go?*, 48 State & Local Rev., No. 2 (2016): 132–146. The author detailed trends in scholarship regarding governors, particularly scholarship that significantly proliferated during the period 2006–2015. In particular, he summarized important themes including those relating to governors and budgets, women as governors, state administration, elections and public approval, agendas and policy positions, power, and executive-legislative relations. This Chapter will focus on governors' use of executive orders and veto authority as examples of some of the latter issues.

A major synthesis of gubernatorial authority also provides crucial insights. See Seifter, *Gubernatorial Administration*, 131 HARV. L. REV. 483 (2017). Professor Seifter reviews the historical evolution of governors' roles, from early days in which their powers were relatively limited to present-day practices in which governors hold significant power. She notes that enhanced gubernatorial power provides opportunities for experimentation, but also risks of executive overreach in the absence of effective checks and balances from other branches of government, the media, and interest groups. Professor Seifter also argues that study of state gubernatorial power provides important insights about a variety of important issues such as executive power, federalism, regulatory oversight, local government, and state-local relations. Professor Seifter has continued the important work of exploring how differences in state executive structures and prerogatives create important and frequently underrecognized distinctions when compared to federal government characteristics. See Seifter, *Understanding State Agency Independence*, 117 MICH. L. REV. 1537 (2019) (discussing states' "bespoke approach" to independence that may yield better-tailored and more democratic resolutions, but also noting that states have increasingly been riven by partisanship and strong state governors may limit the independence of state agencies in ways that do not occur in the federal context); Seifter, *Further from the People? The Puzzle of State Administration*, 93 N.Y.U. L. REV. 107 (2018) (challenging traditional wisdom that all of state government is closer to the voters, and asserting that strong factions and failure in civil society checks such as locally-based news coverage may be partly responsible for current patterns at the state level).

The materials that follow focus on the participation of the executive in the legislative process. This can occur in two ways. An executive can issue an executive order that attempts to make law. If the legislature adopts a law that is not to the executive's liking, the executive may veto it. Problems especially arise if the executive attempts to veto a substantive rider in an appropriations act that changes the intent of the legislature in approving the appropriation. These two areas of executive power raise important constitutional questions because they test separation of powers limitations.

Problem 10-1

The governor of West Dakota was elected on an environmental platform, but the legislature has not enacted her program. For example, the governor proposed a program for the protection of endangered species, which the state does not presently have, in her State of the State address. However, the Commissioner of Conservation, an elected official who would administer the program, is opposed to its enactment and has refused to support it. The legislature not only defeated an endangered species act proposed by the governor's office, but added a proviso to the appropriation for the Department of Conservation stating, "No funds appropriated by this act may be used for the designation and protection of endangered species."

You are the governor's legal adviser. She has asked for your advice on the following proposals to break this legislative and political logjam: (1) the governor would like to issue an executive order consolidating the Department of Conservation and an existing Department of Forestry as a new Department of Ecology, and would then like to name the Director of the new department. (2) The governor would like to issue an executive order directing all state agencies to take all steps necessary within their legislative authority to protect endangered species. (3) The governor would like to veto the condition attached to the Department of Conservation appropriation. What would you advise? The governor does not have constitutional or statutory authority to reorganize, and the state constitution contains the usual provision that the governor "shall faithfully execute" the laws of the state. It also contains a provision allowing the governor to veto an "item" in a law.

A. Executive Orders

What they are. The Executive Order is not authorized nor even acknowledged in the United States Constitution or the constitutions of the states—except for a few relatively recent and limited references in state constitutions. Yet the practice of chief executives in issuing what came to be known as "executive orders" or "proclamations" has existed from the earliest days of the Republic at the federal level, and very likely also at the state level—although the recorded history of gubernatorial executive orders is sparse.

The terms executive order and proclamation do not have established meaning, form, or subject matter. The range encompasses such diverse uses as a proclamation establishing Be Kind to Animals Week, a proclamation declaring the results of an election, a memorandum requesting executive offices to conserve energy, an order requiring state offices to close one hour early in winter to conserve energy, an order authorizing collective bargaining for public employees, and an order requiring state agencies to enforce a policy of nondiscrimination by government contractors.

A congressional staff study of presidential executive orders and proclamations described them as follows:

> Executive orders and proclamations are directives or actions by the President. When they are founded on the authority of the President derived from the Constitution or statute, they may have the force and effect of law.
>
> There is no law or even Executive order which attempts to define the terms "Executive order" or "proclamation." In the narrower sense Executive orders and proclamations are written documents denominated as such. . . .

> Executive orders are generally directed to, and govern actions by, Government officials and agencies. They usually affect private individuals only indirectly.
>
> Proclamations in most instances affect primarily the activities of private individuals.
>
> Since the President has no power or authority over individual citizens and their rights except where he is granted such power and authority by a provision in the Constitution or by statute, the President's proclamations are not legally binding and are at best hortatory unless based on such grants of authority. [HOUSE COMM. ON GOVERNMENT OPERATIONS, EXECUTIVE ORDERS AND PROCLAMATIONS: A STUDY OF A USE OF PRESIDENTIAL POWERS, 85th Cong., 1st Sess. I (Comm. Print 1957).]

One study found 3,456 executive orders issued in 2004–2005 in 49 states. It examined the use of executive orders in 13 categories. Appointments took up the largest percentage. Disaster relief and emergency procedures, advisory boards and task forces, and directions for program actions were also common. Ferguson & Bowling, *Executive Orders and Administrative Control*, 68 PUB. ADMIN. REV., No. S1 (2008): S20–S28. Some states have adopted statutes authorizing executive orders. The basis for executive orders, their provisions and procedures are summarized in 31 BOOK OF THE STATES 24, Table 2.5 (1996–97). The Maryland statute is more detailed than most:

> In this subtitle, "executive order" means an order or an amendment or rescission of an order that, over the signature of the Governor:
>
> (1) proclaims or ends a state of emergency or exercises the authority of the Governor during an emergency . . . ;
>
> (2) adopts guidelines, rules of conduct, or rules of procedure for:
>
> (i) State employees
>
> (ii) units of the State government; or
>
> (iii) persons who are under the jurisdiction of those employees or units or who deal with them;
>
> (3) establishes a unit, including an advisory unit, study unit, or task force; or
>
> (4) changes the organization of the Executive Branch of the State Government. [MD. STATE GOV'T CODE § 3-401.]

The statute also provides for the codification of executive orders. § 3-404. For a discussion of executive orders in Maryland, see Zarnoch, *Gubernatorial Executive Orders: Legislative or Executive Power*, 44 MD. B.J. 48 (May/June 2011). For a discussion of executive orders in other specific states, see, e.g., Herman, *Gubernatorial Executive Orders*, 30 RUTGERS L.J. 987 (1999) (New Jersey); Hunter, *Sound and Fury*,

Signifying Northing: Nullification and the Question of Gubernatorial Executive Power of Idaho, 49 IDAHO L. REV. 659 (2013).

Bear in mind that distinctions in case law across jurisdictions may arise due to differences in source, extent of authority, and procedures for issuing executive orders. For a chart outlining details regarding authorization, use and procedures relating to gubernatorial executive orders in individual states, see Council of State Governments, THE BOOK OF THE STATES, Table 4.5 (2019), available at http://knowledgecenter.csg.org/kc/system/files/4.5.2019.pdf. A study of 49 states in 2004 and 2005 found considerable variation in the use and function of executive orders. Many allowed the governor more direction and control of the state bureaucracy. Ferguson & Bowling, *Executive Orders and Administrative Control, supra*. See Note, *Gubernatorial Executive Orders as Devices for Administrative Direction and Control*, 50 IOWA L. REV. 78, 97 n.109 (1964) (also finding variance in form and content of executive orders, and patterns in many state statutes that confined them to ceremonial proclamations and perfunctory and mandatory statutory requirements).

Also bear in mind that the operating assumptions governing state-level powers do not necessarily correlate with those governing the federal government (since the federal government's powers are limited and specifically detailed in the United States Constitution).

How they are used. From the perspective of executive-legislative separation of powers, the major uses of executive orders might be classified by whether the governor's action can be said to be purely executive or to involve elements of law making. The following classification scheme may be helpful.

1. *Ceremonial proclamations, in which the governor designates a group, an individual or a cause to be honored, e.g.*, Senior Citizens Week. The bulk of gubernatorial proclamations and orders is of this type. Normally they have no legal impact—unless the proclamation "triggers a holiday," as it might in the case of a day of mourning. See *Pullano v. City of Springfield*, 342 S.E.2d 164 (W. Va. 1986).

2. *Directives relating to internal administrative matters.* For example, the governor issues an order requiring that state employees observe the 55 mile-per-hour speed limit in state cars in order to conserve fuel. This exercise of a governor's authority to administer executive agencies under his or her jurisdiction would normally be unquestioned.

3. *Executive orders creating committees to investigate and advise the governor on personnel practices or computer utilization within the executive department.* The creation of the committee would seem to fall within the governor's prerogatives, but the expenditure of state funds for that purpose might be questioned unless the governor had an unrestricted contingency fund. See *Markham v. Wolf*, 190 A.3d 1175 (Pa. 2018) (upholding action by governor in creating committee to advise executive branch on home care policies where action could have been taken without executive order, did not violate separation of powers principles, and

did not violate state legislation regarding home attendants or state labor relations act).

4. *Executive orders and proclamations in which the governor's action affects persons or events outside of his or her own executive departments but is specifically authorized, or in some cases mandated, by statute or constitution.* An example might be a statute empowering the governor to call a special election to fill vacancies. Because the governor's action is specifically authorized, the order or proclamation is not objectionable on grounds the governor usurped legislative authority. The statute might be challenged, however, on grounds that the legislature invalidly delegated its legislative powers.

5. *Executive orders or proclamations in which the chief executive makes policy decisions which, whatever the governor's claimed source of authority, the legislature would ordinarily make.* These decisions may be essentially administrative or they may affect third persons. In either case, they pose the issue of what is the scope of the governor's lawmaking power

Notes and Questions

1. *Is plenary constitutional authority enough?* An initial question is the extent to which a governor's power to issue executive orders can rest solely on his plenary power as governor, and the extent to which it requires statutory authority. Some courts uphold an executive order based on a governor's plenary power if it does not exceed the boundaries of gubernatorial authority. In *Kenny v. Byrne*, 365 A.2d 211 (N.J. App. Div. 1976), *aff'd mem.*, 383 A.2d 428 (N.J. 1978), the governor issued an executive order requiring all employees of the executive branch to file financial disclosure statements. The court rejected the contention the executive order was beyond the governor's "constitutional powers" as "manifestly without merit." It added:

> The Governor is vested with the executive power of the State. . . . As head of the Executive Branch of government he has the duty and power to supervise all employees in each principal department of that branch. . . . Of necessity, this includes the inherent power to issue directives and orders by way of implementation in order to insure efficient and honest performance by those state employees within his jurisdiction. [*Id.* at 215.]

The court also noted that the "objective of the 1947 [state] Constitution was the creation of a strong executive." It held that "the executive power reposed in the Governor under the Constitution . . . must be given life and meaning."

Executive orders must be within the executive authority, however. *Fletcher v. Office of the AG. ex rel. Stumbo*, 163 S.W.3d 852 (Ky. 2005), held the governor invaded legislative authority to make appropriations when he adopted a budget for the executive department by executive order. *Buettell v. Walker*, 319 N.E.2d 502 (Ill. 1974), held invalid an executive order requiring state suppliers and state-regulated businesses to provide a statement of political contributions because it applied to entities outside the executive branch and did not fall within the governor's constitutional executive authority. An executive order that violates a provision of the state constitution is clearly invalid. *Stone v. State*, 664 S.E.2d 32 (N.C. App. 2008) (diversion of contributions for pension retirement fund to general fund).

2. *Gubernatorial powers under supplementary statutory authority.* Statutes also play a role in defining gubernatorial executive authority, and can supplement executive authority conferred by the constitution. Fiscal crises in the states provide examples. *Perth Amboy Bd. of Educ. v. Christie*, 997 A.2d 262 (N.J. App. Div. 2010), upheld an executive order freezing state aid to school districts for the remainder of Fiscal Year 2010 in an amount equal to each district's anticipated surplus funds, but allowed transfers from the surplus to meet a school district's current year's operating costs. The court held the order justified by the governor's constitutional authority to balance the budget as well as constitutional plenary authority, and by statutory authority to deny fiscal appropriations under certain circumstances. There was no violation of separation of powers. Many other jurisdictions recognize the authority of the governor to balance the state budget and grant associated flexibility in acting on that authority. See, e.g., *Brouillette v. Wolf*, 213 A.3d 341 (Pa. Comm. 2019) (concluding that governor and other executive branch officers did not unconstitutionally incur debt by authorizing transfer of Commonwealth revenue between Commonwealth entities within relevant fiscal years to facilitate operation of Commonwealth government for those fiscal years). The courts have also recognized governors' authority to act by executive order in other contexts that bridge constitutional and statutory authority. See *Abelove v. Cuomo*, 57 Misc. 3d 668, 61 N.Y.S.3d 837 (N.Y. Sup. Ct. 2017) (in challenge brought by district attorney against governor's executive order that authorized state attorney general to act as special prosecutor in matters involving unarmed civilian's death caused by law enforcement officer, holding that executive order was valid exercise of governor's superseder authority embodied in statute but derived from governor's constitutional obligation to take care that the laws are faithfully executed).

If there is a clear conflict between an executive order and a statute, however, the executive order cannot stand because the governor, under the separation of powers doctrine, cannot override legislative choice. *Communications Workers of America, AFL-CIO v. Christie*, 994 A.2d 545 (N.J. App. Div. 2010), held invalid an executive order that extended legislation prohibiting political campaign contributions to labor organizations that entered into collective bargaining agreements with the state or other public entities. The court held the order was so "fundamentally incompatible" with existing laws that it impaired the constitutional integrity of the legislature. Any change in political contribution legislation would require substantial revision and amendment of existing statutes, which were clearly limited to state procurement. "An executive order cannot bypass the Legislature and carry out what would be, in effect, an implied repealer of existing legislation." See also *Torres v. Commonwealth Utils. Corp.*, 2009 WL 3156492 (Sept. 28, 2009) (executive order invalid that transferred the functions of one agency to another because it considerably altered the transferred agency's administration, nullifying statutes that gave the legislature the power to create executive branch agencies).

Assume a governor wants to strengthen antidiscrimination legislation by adding new offenses and extending it to new entities. Assume the state antidiscrimination law is silent on both issues. Can the governor issue an executive order that implements these changes? See *Louisiana Dep't of Justice v. Edwards*, 233 So. 3d 76 (La. App. 2017) (concluding that governor's executive order, requiring that all state contracts for purchase of services include language that the contractor not discriminate based on sexual orientation or identity, violated separation of powers principles because relevant powers were vested only in state legislature).

What about an order like one issued by a California governor that required an 80% decrease in greenhouse gas emissions from 1990 to 2050? The statutes are silent on this problem. *Fischer-McReynolds v. Quasim*, 6 P.3d 30 (Wash. App. 2000), held the governor could not authorize suits against state agencies by employees to secure compliance with an executive order when no statute or constitutional provision authorized the order. For recent articles exploring the use of state executive orders in environmental and public health contexts, see Walline, *Executive Power and Regional Climate Change Agreements*, 31 Pace Envtl. L. Rev. 804 (2014) (discussing sources of power and methods through which some governors have been pursuing multi-jurisdictional strategies to address climate change); Lock, *The Role of State Emergency Powers in Curbing the Opioid Epidemic: A Case Study in Lessons Learned*, 51 Ariz. St. L.J. 629 (2019) (discussing the legal issues relating to the opioid crisis that had to be considered in eight states, litigation challenging action by one governor, and resulting lessons learned).

These issues are examined in the next case, which considered whether an executive order was supported by constitutional and statutory authority:

Kinder v. Holden

92 S.W.3d 793 (Mo. App. 2002)

Harold L. Lowenstein, P.J.

Overview

A group of plaintiffs consisting of Missouri state legislators, organizations, and individual state employees sought a judicial declaration that an executive order issued by Governor Holden violated laws of Missouri and the United States.

At the core of this declaratory judgment action is whether a Missouri Governor's executive order dealing with binding arbitration in labor negotiations between state employees and executive agencies and departments, as to wages, hours, and working conditions, usurps what is a strictly legislative function and may, therefore, be declared invalid. While emotions and opinions in this area of public sector labor law readily appear, Missouri case precedent evaluating the extent of a Governor's power to issue executive orders is scarce and almost non-existent with regard to the issue of labor negotiation between the executive department and its employees.

To better understand the issue at bar, a brief summary of Missouri public sector labor law is in order. . . . [The state Public Sector Labor Law is typical and authorizes the right to join labor organizations, the right to present proposals and the right to bargain.] This statutory scheme has been described as a "meet, confer, and discuss law," and has been upheld by our Supreme Court. . . .

The Court in *City of Springfield v. Clouse*, 206 S.W.2d 539 (Mo. banc 1947), acknowledged that, while the United States and Missouri Constitution gave public employees the right to organize and to speak freely to public officers or the legislature, those constitutional rights did not extend to collective bargaining as to qualifications, tenure, compensation, and working conditions, because those matters were strictly legislative and could not be delegated or contracted away by administrative or executive officers. . . .

I. Procedural and Factual History

A. The Executive Order

On June 29, 2001, the defendant, Governor Robert Holden, issued Executive Order 01-09 ("Order"). Paraphrased, and set out in pertinent part below, the Order established a mechanism for negotiation between state agencies and the employees of those agencies.

Paragraph one of the Order requires executive branch departments and agencies, which are directly under the control of the Governor, to meet and confer in good faith with the certified bargaining representatives of the public employees to resolve disputes and to reach a written memorandum of understanding as to agreed upon items.

Paragraph two states that if unresolved issues remain after sixty days, then "impasse negotiation" procedures are instituted which include: (1) assistance by an impartial person or representative from the Federal Mediation and Conciliation Service who will render "non-binding advice"; and, if that is not successful, then (2) submission of those unresolved issues to an arbitrator to conduct hearings and render "a final and determinative recommendation." Paragraph three lists factors the arbitrator should consider in making a recommendation.

Paragraph four states that all memoranda of agreement must contain a grievance procedure and must provide for binding arbitration of issues arising under the agreement "that may be legally binding under the Missouri Constitution and laws. . . ." This paragraph also contains language that no arbitration award under this section shall require any additional appropriation of funds.

Paragraph five provides that, where the state and the employees have reached a negotiated agreement, "any provision of the agreement which requires an additional appropriation of funds or which is found to be in conflict with the Missouri Constitution or laws shall take effect only on required approval of the appropriation of such funds or required legislative or Constitutional enactment." Paragraph five also states that if a recommendation of an arbitrator made pursuant to the second paragraph: (1) requires legislative approval; (2) requires an appropriation; (3) is "contrary to law"; or (4) requires action by the executive or legislative branch, then the recommendation "shall be of no force and effect until such action is taken."

Paragraph six provides that state agencies "may" include in memoranda provisions requiring employees to remit dues and service fees to the certified bargaining representative.

Finally, paragraphs seven through nine state that failure of the General Assembly to approve any portion of a memorandum agreed to by the state agency will not constitute bad faith negotiation. The Order also has a severability clause so that if any portion of the Order is invalidated by the courts or the General Assembly, the rest of the order is to remain in force. . . .

B. Plaintiffs and their Petition

On September 24, 2001, plaintiffs filed a four-count petition seeking a declaratory judgment that the Order violated various Missouri statutes and provisions of the Missouri and United States Constitutions. . . . [The plaintiffs were two Missouri state legislators, individual executive department employees, and a number of organizational plaintiffs. The complaint stated in part the executive order was invalid because of lack of constitutional authority and because provisions of the order conflicted with statutory and constitutional provisions. The trial court granted the governor's motion to dismiss, holding the executive order was not actionable because it was within the Governor's discretion and authority.]

III. Analysis

. . . .

[The court next considered "whether the Order was legally actionable and presented a justiciable controversy must be reviewed."] . . .

[An earlier Missouri case, *Stein v. James*, 651 S.W.2d 624 (Mo. App. 1983), applied the analysis of executive orders in a Pennsylvania case, *Shapp v. Butera*, 348 A.2d 910 (Pa. Commw. Ct. 1975).] The *Stein* opinion acknowledged there are three categories of executive orders.

The first category consists of formal, ceremonial, and political orders. These types of orders are usually issued as proclamations to declare some special day or week in honor of or in commemoration of some special thing or event and have no legal effect. The second category includes communications to subordinate executive branch officials regarding the execution of their executive branch duties. This second category is also not legally enforceable, and the Governor could not seek a court order to enforce that aspect of the executive order. Rather, the executive order would only carry the implication of a penalty for noncompliance. The third category consists of orders which implement or supplement the state's constitution or statutes. The third category of executive orders have the force of law. *Shapp* gives the example of the Governor issuing an executive order based on article IV, section 10 of the Pennsylvania Constitution which states that the Governor may require information from officers of the Executive Department regarding any subject relating to the duties of their respective offices. If the Governor issued an order requiring information from an officer of the Executive Department and such officer refused, the Governor could obtain a court order and the sanctions of noncompliance with a court order to enforce the executive order. "The distinction between this third classification and the second classification is based upon the presence of some constitutional or statutory provision, which authorizes the executive order either specifically or by way of necessary implication."[8]

This court agreed with the analysis contained in *Shapp*, and determined that "absent some constitutional or statutory basis for an executive order, it cannot be considered more than a directive from the governor to his subordinates in the executive branch for the carrying out of their official duties." The court in *Stein* concluded that because the executive order in that case lacked a constitutional or statutory basis, it did not create a legal cause of action.

The Executive Order at issue in this case falls within the second classification of executive orders because there are no constitutional or statutory provisions which authorize the Order either specifically or by implication. This conclusion becomes apparent when compared to the similar factual scenario in *McCulloch v. Glendening*, 701 A.2d 99 (Md. 1997). Although the executive order in *McCulloch* was not categorized by the court in that case, it seems clear that it would have been considered in the third classification of executive orders that have the force of law due to the constitutional and statutory provisions authorizing it.

In *McCulloch*, Maryland taxpayers filed a complaint and request for declaratory and injunctive relief, seeking to prevent the implementation of an executive order granting unionization and collective bargaining rights to executive branch employees. Some of the issues raised in *McCulloch* were: (1) whether the executive order issued by the Governor of Maryland exceeded his power to issue executive orders; (2) whether he had the constitutional and statutory authority to issue the order; and (3) whether the issuance of the order violated Maryland's constitutional separation of powers doctrine.

8. The court stated in *Stein*: "Because there is no constitutional or statutory provision authorizing Executive Order 81-2 and because it directs the execution of the duties of executive branch officials, it falls under the second class enumerated in *Shapp*. *Shapp* held that this category of executive orders is not legally enforceable and that the governor cannot seek a court order to enforce them. The *Shapp* court further concluded that noncompliance with this type of order would result only in a penalty such as possible removal from office, demotion or reprimand as to the executive branch official disobeying the rule."

First, the Court in *McCulloch* found that the Governor's executive power was expressly provided in the Maryland Constitution. Article II, section 1, vests the executive power of the state in the Governor, including the execution of the laws of Maryland, and Article II, section 9, directs the Governor to take care that the laws are faithfully executed. Further, Article II, section 24, gives the Governor broad authority to reorganize and reassign functions among executive branch agencies. It provides, in pertinent part:

> The Governor may make changes in the organization of the Executive Branch of the State Government, including establishment or abolition of departments, offices, agencies, and instrumentalities, and the reallocation or reassignment of function, powers, and duties among the departments, offices, agencies, and instrumentalities of the Executive Branch. *Where these changes are inconsistent with existing law, or create new governmental programs they shall be set forth in executive orders in statutory form which shall be submitted to the General Assembly* within the first ten days of regular session.[9]

701 A.2d at 105.

Second, the Court in *McCulloch* found that Maryland's statutory scheme concerning the executive branch gave the Governor a significant role in setting policies to govern the management and supervision of Maryland employees. "[Section] 3-302 of the State Govt. Article, entrusted to the Governor the power to establish personnel policies and to require executive agency heads to carry out those policies." Section 3-302 states that the Governor is the head of the executive branch of Maryland's government and, except as otherwise provided by law, "shall supervise and direct the officers and units in the executive branch." *Id. McCulloch* also lists executive orders the Maryland legislature has authorized the Governor to issue in § 2-101 and § 3-401(2), (3) and (4), which include: [The statute is reproduced, *supra*.] . . .

The court in *McCulloch* determined that given the breadth of the authority that the Legislature had bestowed on the Governor in the statutes cited *supra*, a strong argument could be made that the executive order could be upheld on the statutory authority alone. "In any event, when the statutory and constitutional provisions are considered together, it becomes crystalline that the Governor has broad power and authority over Executive Branch employees and their working conditions." *Id.*[10]

---

9. Section 8-301 of the State Government Article states that "in addition to any reorganization under Article II, § 24 of the Maryland Constitution, the Governor may order any other reorganization of the Executive Branch that is considered by the Governor to be necessary and desirable and that is not inconsistent with the law."

10. It was ultimately held in *McCulloch* that the executive order met Maryland's constitutional and statutory requirements and was not in violation of the separation of powers. The Governor's broad authority to issue executive orders for the guidance and direction of units and employees of the executive branch "necessarily permits the promulgation of an executive order authorizing the limited collective-bargaining rights for Executive Branch employees contained in the subject Order. This act is an exercise of executive function, not a usurpation of legislative function."

As such, it is easy to conclude that had the executive order in *McCulloch* been categorized, it would have been considered in the third category. Whereas the court in *McCulloch* found Maryland's Constitution and statutes to be "crystalline" as to the Governor's power and authority to issue an executive order concerning executive branch employees and their working conditions, this court's research shows that Missouri's Constitution and statutes are virtually silent in this regard.

The Governor's executive power is expressly provided in the Missouri Constitution. Article 4, section 1, provides that "The supreme executive power shall be vested in a governor[;]" and article 4, section 2, states that: "The governor shall take care that the laws are distributed and faithfully executed, and shall be a conservator of the peace throughout the state."

As for statutory authority, section 105.969.1, which gives the Governor the authority to adopt by executive order a code of conduct applicable to state employees of the executive branch on or before February 1, 1992, is the only provision in § 105.500 *et seq.*, the Public Sector Labor Law, that gives the Governor any express statutory authority to issue executive orders concerning executive branch employees and their working conditions.

In regard to reorganization plans such as the one analyzed in *McCulloch*, section 26.500 authorizes the Governor to submit plans for the reorganization of executive agencies. A reorganization plan submitted would become effective by executive order unless it is disapproved by the legislature. § 26.510. As stated *supra*, however, the Maryland Legislature granted the Governor much more specific express statutory and constitutional power in this area than the Missouri legislature. Furthermore, in *Moore v. Pelzer*, 710 S.W.2d 416, 421 (Mo. App. 1996), this court commented that neither a reorganization plan for state government nor an executive order issued by the Governor in approval of such a plan "ever attains the status of a law within the meaning of article III, § 21." Indeed, executive orders must be "*within* the grant of authority from the General Assembly." *Rider v. Julian*, 282 S.W.2d 484, 489 (Mo. banc 1955). It must be noted that the Order in this case contained language clearly recognizing that legislative approval and/or appropriations will be needed on certain matters addressed in the Order.

The purpose of the comparison between the case at bar and *McCulloch* is to show the distinction between an executive order that clearly is in the third category of executive orders because it was authorized by constitutional and statutory authority, and an executive order such as the one here that clearly is not. *See also Nass v. State ex rel. Unity Team, Local 9212*, 718 N.E.2d 757, 763 (Ind. App. 1999) (Governor's authority to issue executive orders regulating the terms and conditions of employment for executive branch employees is inherent in a number of statutes).

Based upon the foregoing analysis, this court finds that Executive Order 01-09 is merely a category two directive order and, therefore, not legally actionable. As such, the plaintiffs cannot maintain this suit and alternatively, the Governor could not seek a court order to enforce Executive Order 01-09.

This is not to say that all executive orders issued by the Governor fall within the second category and are not legally actionable. For example, article IV, section 6, of the Missouri Constitution provides that, "The governor shall be the commander in chief of the militia, except when it is called into the service of the United States, and may call out the militia to execute the laws, suppress actual and prevent threatened insurrection, and repel invasion." Section 41.480 also provides that the Governor may call out the militia when, in his opinion the circumstances so warrant. Thus, "the power to decide whether a public exigency exists such as justifies the calling out of the militia is vested solely in the Governor." *McKittrick ex rel. Donaldson v. Brown*, 85 S.W.2d 385, 388 (Mo. banc 1935). If the Governor were to issue an executive order calling up the Missouri military reserves due to a public emergency, the order would be a type three order and would be enforceable in court because the Governor has constitutional and statutory authority to issue such an executive order.

As stated *supra*, the law pertaining to declaratory judgment actions based on executive orders is sparse; statutory and constitutional declarations on the matter are virtually non-existent. In fact, as pointed out in the Wisconsin Law Review article cited in footnote seven, [Comment, *Gubernatorial Executive Orders in Wisconsin: The Case for Judicial Enforcement*, 2000 Wis. L. Rev. 1323,] the dearth of law on enforcement of executive orders makes it unclear "when, if ever, a Wisconsin gubernatorial executive order is judicially enforceable." Had this court not adopted the analyses of the three types of orders in *Stein*, such a differentiation would have to be established.

Although the Order here utilizes mandatory-style language as to the bargaining scheme and resulting contract, it is still nothing more than a directive from the chief executive (sans constitutional or legislative approval) to his appointed executive department head. Thus, in effect it is a type two directive. The court in *Shapp*, the case that formed the foundation for *Stein*, stated that, had the Governor in that case attempted to issue an order pursuant to a section of the Constitution or a section of a statute, "a different question might have been presented." Although the Governor does have authority to deal with departments and agencies under his direct control, a Missouri Governor does not have constitutional or statutory authority to set up a mechanism which results in a state employee collective bargaining agreement which must be acted upon or paid for by the appropriation process. Despite intent or language, this Order is not actionable because it lacks constitutional or statutory authority. Even if the deferential language in the Order as to legislative action and funding were not present, this order lacks the underpinnings to be a type three order; it is not enforceable and the court's duty is to dismiss this suit....

Notes and Questions

1. *Finding authority for executive orders.* The *Holden* case shows how the mix of constitutional and statutory authority determines the scope of the governor's power to issue executive orders. Review the discussion of the *McCulloch* case and decide what additional authority in that case led the court to uphold the order. The *Nass*

case, discussed in the principal opinion, also upheld a gubernatorial executive order that provided for collective bargaining. After quoting the constitutional provision on gubernatorial authority and several state statutes giving the governor authority over the terms and conditions of employment of state employees, the court held that "[t]he order was within the broad authority granted the Governor by article 5, section 1 of the Indiana Constitution and gave effect to various statutory enactments." *State v. Maryland State Family Child Care Ass'n*, 966 A.2d 939 (Md. App. 2009), followed *McCulloch* to uphold an executive order providing for the designation of a bargaining unit for a state agency. The court also held an executive order is not a regulation subject to the state Administrative Procedure Act.

2. *Enforceability.* The enforceability of executive orders is a difficult question. The court in the principal case dodged this issue because it found the executive order was not mandatory. Aside from declaratory judgment, an action in mandamus to compel compliance with an executive order is another option. Chapter 11 discusses mandamus actions. Remember that a governor's control over his cabinet and executive branch may be limited. The student Note cited in *Holden* suggests the following non-legal options:

> There are several non-legal tools with which a Wisconsin governor could effect compliance with an executive order. First, if the non-compliant official were the secretary of an administrative agency, the governor could simply remove him. Second, the governor could apply political pressure to the individual or agency at whom the order is directed by making pro-enforcement statements in the press. Third, the mere threat of a lawsuit might be sufficient to entice compliance, particularly in the case of a less consequential order. Regardless of method, a governor's decision to pursue legal or non-legal avenues of enforcement will depend upon his own political calculation of the relative risks and benefits of litigation. [2000 Wis. L. Rev. at 1341.]

3. *Reorganization.* Governors often seek to reorganize state government, either partially through the creation of new agencies or the transfer of agency functions, or through a comprehensive reorganization plan. Powers of reorganization may be granted by the constitution or statute, and may require legislative approval or by subject to legislative veto. See Benjamin & Zack, *Executive Orders and Gubernatorial Authority to Reorganize State Government*, 74 Alb. L. Rev. 1613, 1632–1634 (2010/2011). For a case upholding a reorganization under the Missouri statute, see *State ex rel. Dep't of Social Servs. v. K.L.D.*, 118 S.W.3d 283 (Mo. App. 2003). Compare *In re Plan for the Abolition of the Council on Affordable Housing*, 70 A.3d 559, 214 N.J. 444 (N.J. 2013) (finding that governor lacked statutory authority to abolish state agency that was "in, but not of" the executive branch). In some instances, legislative efforts to reorganize executive branch agencies may be found to violate separation of powers insofar as they impinge on a governor's executive authority. See, e.g., *Cooper v. Berger*, 809 S.E.2d 98 (N.C. 2018) (in challenge by governor against legislative action consolidating the functions relating to elections, campaign finance,

lobbying, and ethics under newly-created bipartisan State Board of Elections and Ethics Enforcement, concluding that legislation usurped governor's constitutional authority to take care that the laws be faithfully executed and thus violated doctrine of separation of powers).

4. *Testing the impact of legislative authority.* Justice Jackson's concurring opinion in *Youngstown Sheet & Tube Co. v. Sawyer*, 343 U.S. 579 (1951), provided the following guidelines that summarize the impact of legislation on presidential executive orders:

> 1. When the President acts pursuant to an express or implied authorization of Congress, his authority is at its maximum, for it includes all that he possesses in his own right plus all that Congress can delegate. In these circumstances, and in these only, may he be said (for what it may be worth) to personify the federal sovereignty. If his act is held unconstitutional under these circumstances, it usually means that the Federal Government as an undivided whole lacks power....
>
> 2. When the President acts in absence of either a congressional grant or denial of authority, he can only rely upon his own independent powers, but there is a zone of twilight in which he and Congress may have concurrent authority, or in which its distribution is uncertain. Therefore, congressional inertia, indifference or quiescence may sometimes, at least as a practical matter, enable, if not invite, measures on independent presidential responsibility. In this area, any actual test of power is likely to depend on the imperatives of events and contemporary imponderables rather than on abstract theories of law.
>
> 3. When the President takes measures incompatible with the expressed or implied will of Congress, his power is at its lowest ebb, for then he can rely only upon his own constitutional powers minus any constitutional powers of Congress over the matter. Courts can sustain exclusive Presidential control in such a case only by disabling the Congress from acting upon the subject. Presidential claim to a power at once so conclusive and preclusive must be scrutinized with caution, for what is at stake is the equilibrium established by our constitutional system? [*Id.* at 635–38.]

How would you apply these guidelines at the state level? See *Chang v. University of Rhode Island*, 375 A.2d 925 (R.I. 1977). The court there held invalid an executive order extending the state Fair Employment Practices Act to nonprofit educational institutions. The order expressly excluded such institutions. The court held the executive order fell within the category identified by Justice Jackson consisting of orders incompatible with legislative intent. Because the legislature had excluded nonprofit educational institutions from the Act, the executive order could be "supported only if regulation of the university's employment practices was exclusively within the executive domain and beyond the control of the legislature." That was not the case, as the state constitution had reserved the control of education to the legislature, which had delegated control over state educational institutions to a state board of regents.

5. *Governors, executive orders, and the pandemic.* Litigation has arisen on various fronts when governors have issued executive orders that address public health concerns relating to the COVID pandemic. Legislatures have also sought to constrain governors' actions, whether relating to holding primaries safely, wearing masks, or declining to authorize bars and gyms to reopen. Assume that existing statutes give the governor explicit authority relating to public health and emergencies. How would you expect courts to proceed when faced with challenges such as these, whether presented through litigation by private parties or legislative interventions intended to curb gubernatorial action?

A Note on Local Executive Orders

At the local government level, executive authority to adopt executive orders is governed by statute or, in the case of home-rule governments, by the home-rule charter, but courts are again concerned with the separation of executive and legislative functions. In *County Executive v. Doe*, 436 A.2d 459 (Md. 1981), the county executive issued an order prohibiting abortions in county owned or operated hospitals except when necessary to save the life of the mother. The court held the order was unauthorized by the charter, which made all county agencies "subject to the direction, supervision, and control of the County Executive." The charter also created a "system of county government in which the executive branch and the legislative branch were separate and distinct." The executive was in charge of general administration, but the council was authorized to assign duties and responsibilities to executive branch agencies. The council had allocated management and policy-making authority over county hospitals to designated entities. The county executive's executive power did not constitute a grant of unbridled authority permitting him to usurp, nullify or supersede, at his pleasure, functions and duties committed by law to other executive branch officers, or to refuse to observe existing laws enacted by the Council. *Id.* at 463.

Compare *Leskovar v. Nickels*, 166 P.3d 1251 (Wash. App. 2007). The court upheld an executive order issued by the mayor of a home rule city that extended benefits to city employees in same sex marriages. The court did not find a conflict with state marriage statutes, as the order did not give legal effect to same sex marriages. Neither was the field of benefits for public employees preempted by statute. The order did not purport to confer legal status on same-sex marriages. Home rule cities had wide discretion to legislate on benefits for city employees as a matter of local concern. What distinguishes these cases?

B. Veto Powers

The nature of veto power. The veto power of the chief executive is often described as an exception to the separation of powers doctrine, but that characterization is accurate only if separation of powers is taken as an absolute in American government, which it is not. In both cases—the doctrine and the exception—the source is the same: the constitution. Many of the first state constitutions did not authorize an executive veto. According to a 1950 study, however, by 1812 eight of the 18 states provided for it, and thereafter no new state except West Virginia (which has since adopted it) entered the union without some form of executive veto. Prescott, *The Executive Veto in American States*, 3 W. Pol. Q. 98, 98–100 (1950). Briffault, *The Item Veto in State Courts*, 66 Temp. L. Rev. 1171, 1177 (1993) points out that "[t]he item veto represents the coming together of three widespread state constitutional policies: the rejection of legislative logrolling; the imposition of fiscal restrictions on the legislature; and the strengthening of the governor's role in budgetary matters."

The veto clearly thrusts the chief executive into the legislative process by giving him or her the power to deny approval to bills enacted by the legislature. While the power is conditional in the sense that the legislature is constitutionally entitled to override the executive's action, historically gubernatorial vetoes are overridden in a small percentage of the cases. There are various reasons for this: The difficulty of assembling an extraordinary majority, which most states require, to overturn the governor; the opportunity for the legislature to reconsider an issue in a less charged atmosphere at a later time; and the fact that many vetoes may reflect technical errors or other matters about which there is no real dispute.

The gubernatorial veto power is strengthened in a number of states by the requirement that bills be confined to a single subject, and in a few states, by the additional requirement that appropriation bills be confined to the subject of appropriations. Where these provisions exist, they reduce the legislative practice of attaching an unacceptable "rider" to a bill that the executive feels compelled to sign.

How veto powers work. The veto powers available to most state governors are more varied and more sophisticated than the presidential veto. Under Article I, § 7, the president is limited to approving or disapproving a bill in its entirety, or to withholding action and thereby achieving the same result as disapproval when the adjournment of Congress prevents return of the bill (the pocket veto). The latter has the additional advantage to the President that Congress has no power to attempt to override the veto. Congress gave the President line-item veto authority for appropriations, but the Supreme Court held it unconstitutional. *Clinton v. City of New York*, 524 U.S. 417 (1998).

In addition to a general veto power similar to the President's, and the pocket veto which is available in a number of states, many state governors have the power to veto items, or parts, or sections of a bill, usually limited to appropriations. For a table showing line-item veto powers in the states, see 2019 Book of the States

95–96, Table 4.4. For a study of the six states that do not give their governors line-item veto power over budget legislation, see Lauth, *The Other Six: Governors without the Line-Item Veto*, 36 PUBLIC FINANCE & BUDGETING, No. 4 (Winter 2016): 26–49 (discussing Indiana, Nevada, New Hampshire, North Carolina, Rhode Island and Vermont). The item veto first appeared in the constitution of the Confederacy as an attempt to introduce aspects of the parliamentary system by enhancing the role of the executive in the appropriations process. It was widely adopted by the states in the latter part of the 19th century, and has generated the most controversy and the most litigation.

The typical line-item veto provision in state constitutions is quite simple:

> The governor may approve appropriation bills in whole or in part and may disapprove any item of an appropriation bill; and the part approved shall become a law. [Iowa Const. art. III, § 16.]

The line-item veto takes its importance from the tendency of legislatures to vote appropriations by line or item, e.g., $80,000,000 for the state university system. A governor has the authority under the line-item veto provision of the constitution to veto this item. Problems arise when the legislature attempts to make policy in an appropriations bill by adding conditions that limit or direct how the appropriate should be spent. For example, in the appropriation for the university system it might attach a proviso stating that tenure shall not be granted to any professor who has taught for less than ten years. Assume this proviso overrules present policy, and is opposed by the governor. The legislature could have enacted this restriction into law, but the governor could then have vetoed it and the legislature might not have had the votes to override. Putting it into an appropriation bill saves it from a veto, unless the governor vetoes the entire appropriation for universities, which may be politically difficult. The governor's alternative is to accept the appropriation but veto the attached language as an "item," which may or may not be constitutionally possible, as the cases that follow indicate.

Abney & Lauth, *Gubernatorial Use of the Item Veto for Narrative Deletion*, 62 PUB. ADMIN. REV., No. 4 (2002): 492–503, examine this problem and argue that legislators include substantive narrative in appropriations bills because a governor may hesitate to negotiate or item veto a bill that contains appropriations. Legislative leadership also has more control over an appropriations bill because they can insert substantive narrative without going through the committee system. For consideration of how legislative coalitions affect the exercise of veto powers, see McGrath, Rogowski & Ryan, *Gubernatorial Veto Powers and the Size of Legislative Coalitions*, 40 LEG. STUD. Q. 571 (2015).

The budgetary process. This example illustrates the use of the budget as a policy-making rather than a fiscal measure. The line-item veto presents the governor with an opportunity to intervene in the policy-making process by rejecting policy measures that are inserted in appropriations. A study of the item veto in Wisconsin explains:

> The budgetary process can appropriately be described as *the* policy-making process in Wisconsin. Governors in Wisconsin have traditionally included major policy items in the budget ... [such as] equalization of major local assistance programs, including aid to primary and secondary school districts ... and state general revenue sharing to counties and municipalities.... [T]hese heavily policy-laden policy initiatives could have been alternatively routed through the traditional, substantive legislative process....
>
> [T]he practice of including policy in the budget ... permits the governor to exercise the item veto over policy initiatives having no associated appropriation, since—once included in the budget bill—they are subject to the item veto. [Gosling, *Wisconsin Item-Veto Lessons*, 46 PUB. ADMIN. REV., No. 4 (1986): 292–300.]

The governor has been given the authority to prepare the budget in 42 states, but the legislature has unlimited power to change the budget, and legislative committees have budget staff to assist them. Since about half the states often have divided government, legislative modification of the executive budget can be expected in these jurisdictions.

Problem 10-2

For reasons of economy and policy, e.g., the governor does not believe in large custodial institutions located far from population centers, she announces a program to phase out two of the state's antiquated mental health hospitals. Legislators from the areas in which the institutions are located, responding to the fears of residents that the closings will have a negative effect on the economies of the areas, enlist the support of their colleagues in the legislature to oppose the governor's program. In the appropriations for the mental health department, the legislature attaches a proviso that none of the amounts appropriated in that act may be used for any purpose in connection with the closing of the named institutions or any other institutions within the department's jurisdiction. Can the governor veto this provision?

Rush v. Ray

362 N.W.2d 479 (Iowa 1988)

SCHULTZ, JUSTICE.

In this appeal a legislator challenges the legality of the governor's action exercising his item veto power. The basic issue is whether use of the governor's item veto power to eliminate a provision in an appropriation bill which prohibits the expenditure or transfer of appropriated funds from one department of state government to another is proper. The trial court held that such a veto is proper. We conclude such a provision is a qualification or limitation on the appropriation, rather than an item, and reverse.

During the 68th session of the Iowa General Assembly, the legislature enacted five appropriation bills for specific purposes. The bills in question are senate files 471, 497 and 2241 and house files 764 and 2580. Each bill contains a provision that either provided "notwithstanding section eight point thirty-nine (8.39) of the Code, funds appropriated by this Act shall not be subject to transfer or expenditure for any purpose other than the purposes specified" or recited a phrase similar in language and content.

Governor Robert D. Ray exercised his item veto power to excise the quoted and similar phrases from each act. The legislature did not override the governor's item vetoes. We find it unnecessary to set out details concerning each specific bill or give the governor's message concerning the reasons for the individual vetoes. Our opinion concerning the wisdom of either the original enactments or the vetoes does not enter into our judicial evaluation of the legality of the governor's action.

The constitutional provision which gives the governor item veto authority provides in pertinent part:

> The governor may approve appropriation bills in whole or in part and may disapprove any item of an appropriation bill; and the part approved shall become a law. Any item of an appropriation bill disapproved by the governor shall be returned.... Any such item of an appropriation bill may be enacted into law notwithstanding the governor's objections, in the same manner as provided for other bills. [Iowa Const. art. III, § 16 (1857, amended 1968).]

On September 18, 1980, Robert Rush, a state senator, filed an action in district court against the governor challenging the vetoes. . . . [T]he parties moved for summary judgment. The district court granted the governor's motion and denied appellant's motion; this ruling is the subject of the appeal. Appellant asserts that the vetoed portions of these five acts are provisos or limitations, not items; thus, they were not subject to the governor's item veto power. On the other hand, the governor asserts that the language stricken from the five appropriation bills constituted distinct, severable "items" within the meaning of article III, section 16 of the Iowa Constitution that could be removed from the appropriation bills by the use of the item veto.

We have twice passed on the legality of the governor's exercise of the item veto power. On each occasion, we discussed whether the vetoed portion of the legislative bill was a condition or qualification of the appropriation, not subject to veto, or an item, properly deleted. *Welden v. Ray*, 229 N.W.2d 706, 710 (Iowa 1975); *State ex rel. Turner v. Iowa State Highway Comm'n*, 186 N.W.2d 141, 151 (Iowa 1971). In these cases we have extensively discussed the history and phraseology of our constitutional item veto provision and decisions from other jurisdictions interpreting and construing similar language and provisions. We need not repeat these discussions at length, but consider only the general principles announced.

The problem presented in *Turner* arose when the legislature appropriated funds to the primary road fund, and the governor vetoed a portion of the bill that additionally prohibited removing certain established offices from their present location. 186 N.W.2d at 143. When this item veto was challenged, we upheld the veto. We established certain principles to be used in interpreting the term "item" and distinguished items, which are subject to veto, from provisos or conditions inseparably connected to an appropriation, which are not subject to veto. We approved another court's statement that an "item" is "something that may be taken out of a bill without affecting its other purposes and provisions. It is something that can be lifted bodily from it rather than cut out. No damage can be done to the surrounding legislative tissue, nor should any scar tissue result therefrom." *Id.* at 151 (*quoting Commonwealth v. Dodson*, 11 S.E.2d 120, 124 (Va. 1940)). While we did not provide a specific definition of those provisos or conditions which are not subject to veto, we did quote the following language: "It follows conclusively that where the veto power is attempted to be exercised to object to . . . language qualifying an appropriation or directing the method of its uses, he exceeds the constitutional authority vested in him. . . ." *Id.* at 150 (*quoting Fulmore v. Lane*, 140 S.W. 405, 412 (1911)). While we surmised that the legislature may have intended to make the challenged language a limitation or proviso on the expenditure of funds, we held the act as drawn and enacted did not restrict the use of the appropriated funds for the purposes and uses referred to in the deleted language. We held the deleted language was an item rather than a qualification.

When the governor's authority to exercise his item veto power was challenged in *Welden*, we reached a different result than in *Turner*, holding that the attempted vetoes by the governor were beyond the scope of his constitutional power. 229 N.W.2d at 715 (two justices dissenting). The vetoed items in the appropriation bills provided limitations on how the money appropriated for each department was to be spent. Specifically, these provisions included limitations on the number of employees in a department, limitations on the percent of the appropriation that could be used for salaries, prohibition against construction of buildings, prohibition against spending beyond budget, and elimination of matching fund grants if the federal funds were discontinued—with the further provision that unused state matching funds would revert to the general fund. We held that these clauses were lawful qualifications upon the respective appropriations rather than separate, severable provisions.

In *Welden* we again approved the use of the severability test announced in *Turner* to determine whether language constitutes an item. We further discussed and explained the nature of the governor's role in the separation of powers and the prohibition against using the veto to destroy the remaining legislative provision by altering the legislative intent. We quoted a law review article with approval as follows:

> It is obvious that the item veto power does not contemplate striking out conditions and restrictions alone as items, for that would be affirmative legislation, whereas the governor's veto power is a strictly negative power, not a creative power. [*Id.* at 713 (*quoting* Note, *Item Veto Amendment to the Iowa Constitution*, 18 Drake L. Rev. 245, 249–50 (1969)).]

We also quoted a New Mexico ruling that stated:

> The power of partial veto is the power to disapprove. This is a negative power, or a power to delete or destroy a part or item, and is not a positive power, or a power to alter, enlarge or increase the effect of the remaining parts or items. . . . Thus, a partial veto must be so exercised that it eliminates or destroys the whole of an item or part and does not distort the legislative intent, and in effect create legislation inconsistent with that enacted by the Legislature, by the careful striking of words, phrases, clauses or sentences. [*Id.* at 711 (*quoting State ex rel. Sego v. Kirkpatrick*, 524 P.2d 975, 981 (N.M. 1974).]

Additionally, we referred to language from a Virginia case as follows:

> We think it plain that the veto power does not carry with it power to strike out conditions or restrictions. That would be legislation. Plainly, money devoted to one purpose cannot be used for another, and it is equally plain that power to impose conditions before it can become available is legislation. [*Id.* at 712 (*quoting Commonwealth v. Dodson*, 11 S.E.2d 120, 127 (1940)).]

The message of these cases and others reviewed in *Welden* is that the governor's power is a negative one that does not allow him to legislate by striking qualifications in a manner which distorts legislative intent. Thus, he cannot strike a provision that would divert money appropriated by the legislature for one purpose so that it may be used for another. Finally, we held in *Welden* that the governor's veto of a legislatively-imposed qualification upon an appropriation must also include a veto of the appropriation.

In the present case the trial court determined that the vetoed portion of each appropriation bill did not change the basic purpose of the legislation; thus, the provision is properly considered a severable item rather than a legislatively-imposed condition. We agree with appellant's contention that "the effect of this veto was to make money from the treasury available for purposes not authorized by the legislation as it was originally written, contrary to the clear intent of the legislature." The governor has used the item veto power affirmatively to create funds not authorized by the legislature. The vetoed language created conditions, restricting use of the money to the stated purpose. It is not severable, because upon excision of this language, the rest of the legislation is affected. The appropriated money is no longer required to be used only for the stated purpose; it could be used for other purposes. Thus, these are not items which are subject to veto.

This case is unlike *Turner* in which the deletion of directions concerning office changes had no effect on the appropriation of funds. We find it closer akin to *Welden* in which the governor had deleted provisions which dictated how and for what purposes the appropriated funds were to be expended. In the present case the legislature clearly limited the expenditure of the appropriated funds to specified purposes. The veto distorted the obvious legislative intent that the funds only be spent for the appropriated purposes and created additional ways the funds might be spent. This was use of the veto power to create rather than negate. We hold that the language vetoed constituted qualifications on the appropriations rather than separate items subject to veto.

We are not unmindful that the governor maintains the stricken language merely "sought to override Iowa Code section 8.39, an independent subject of legislative concern that possessed only a figurative relationship with the subject of appropriation." It is claimed the effect of the stricken language was to accomplish a distinct legislative goal wholly unrelated to the underlying appropriation, or the recipient's use of the appropriated funds, and as such, the language constituted separate, severable items. We do not agree.

The purpose of the language was to limit and qualify the use of the funds, an appropriate legislative function. The stricken clauses, standing by themselves, would have no independent purpose if the governor had vetoed the appropriations. Such clauses only have purpose and effect when they stand in conjunction with the appropriations. The avoidance of section 8.39 was not the motivating purpose of these stricken sections. Rather, this avoidance was necessary to effectuate the language's main thrust, qualifying and restricting the use of the appropriations. Thus, the language "[n]otwithstanding the provisions of section 8.39" did not represent an independent legislative goal, but merely was used to facilitate the legislature's goal in designating the way the appropriations were to be spent.

In summary, we hold the language stricken was an outgrowth of the legislature's power to appropriate funds. "Inherent in the power to appropriate is the power to specify how the money shall be spent." *Welden*, 229 N.W.2d at 710. We construe the stricken language to qualify the appropriation by limiting its expenditure. We do not consider the vetoed language an item that is the proper subject of the governor's item veto power.

In the governor's motion for summary judgment, he maintained the legislative action is an unconstitutional restriction since it attempts to prevent gubernatorial exercise of the transfer power previously delegated in section 8.39. The trial court did not reach this issue, and the governor did not specifically address this issue on appeal. Although article III, section 1 of the Iowa Constitution provides for separation of powers and various constitutional provisions provide executive authority, we find no merit in these claims. We do not condone an invasion of the executive function. Section 8.39 which authorizes the comptroller, with the approval of the governor, to transfer funds from the appropriation of one department, institution, or agency to another is a limited and qualified delegation of a legislative power. An impingement on that authority, restricting its exercise against qualifications to appropriations, cannot be construed as a violation of an executive power. It did not invade or prevent the governor's exercise of his constitutional veto power. As we have discussed, the matters vetoed were qualifications rather than items. "The authorities hold that an attempted veto of a qualification on an appropriation is not within the scope of the item veto." *Welden*, 229 N.W.2d at 710. Thus, the executive power was not invaded....

Reversed.

All Justices concur except HARRIS, J., REYNOLDSON, C.J., and MCGIVERIN, J., who dissent.

HARRIS, J. (dissenting).

The majority holding is a rejection of the definition of "item" which we established in *State ex rel. Turner v. Iowa State Highway Comm'n* and a far-flung expansion of our majority holding in *Weldon v. Ray.* The result at once deprives the executive branch of a proper item veto and the right to veto legislation that repeals the operation of an existing statute. I respectfully dissent....

The experience in other states shows that, at best, there tends to be a blurred line between an "item" (which can be vetoed from an appropriation bill) and a proviso or condition on how the funds are to be spent (which cannot). It does however seem clear that the line, no matter how blurred, is crossed when legislation (even if labeled a proviso or condition) is appended to an appropriation bill in violation of the single subject provision of a state constitution.

The cases recognize a difficulty faced by governors when presented with appropriation bills which have been infused with legislation, going beyond the appropriation, which impacts either on existing statutes or upon purely executive functions. Some governors are unprotected even by a single-subject constitutional provision. It is quite common to find provisions such as Art. III, § 29 of the Iowa Constitution which provide that "every act shall embrace but one subject...." Single subject provisions offer some protection but it is limited. If a provision is attached to an appropriation bill in violation of the single-subject provision the whole act could be challenged as void. But a governor is usually in a poor position to ask for an appropriation bill to be declared void. This would be the case when the government could not continue to function without the funds from the appropriation. Legislation attached by means of proviso or condition labels to crucial appropriation bills might thus become impervious to veto. The upshot was a liberal definition of an item, mentioned by the majority, which we adopted in *Turner.* We said: "... should the ... [l]egislature attempt to coerce the [g]overnor into approving a lump sum appropriation by combining purposes and amount the court [will] interpret the term 'item' liberally to preserve the purpose of the item veto amendment." 182 N.W.2d at 152 (*quoting* Note, *Item Veto Amendment to the Iowa Constitution*, 18 DRAKE L. REV. 245, 250 (1969)).

Moreover, in *Weldon*, this court stated what it would do when faced with a legislative appropriation unneeded for the specific enactment; we said we would apply the "scar tissue" test:

> We would have a different case if the clauses involved here came under the rule relating to separate, severable provisions under which appropriations

were not dependent for passage by the legislature. [*Weldon*, 229 N.W.2d at 714 (citing *Turner*).]

The scar tissue test certainly did not originate in our *Turner* opinion. Again, it is a well established response by the courts to a legislature's temptation to append controversial bills to appropriation measures.

Plaintiffs no doubt think the scar tissue rule is an unwarranted expansion of the originally intended scope of an item veto, which they see as the mere authority to strike individual dollar amounts. But courts elsewhere commonly apply it. . . .

The majority recites, and seems to acknowledge the validity of, the "scar-tissue test," but does not follow it. Under the test the provisions in question here were proper subjects of item vetoes. Each appropriation was earmarked to a department of government which could use the funds only for the purpose specified by the legislature. The vetoes here in no way modified the legislative plan of how the department could use the funds. The vetoed provisions related only to funds which might remain unused. The power of the governor to transfer unused funds under section 8.39, acting after notice to and "review and comment by" appropriate legislative chairpersons, has been statutorily provided for more than forty years. *See* Iowa Acts (49 G.A.) ch. 62, § 5 (1941). All branches of Iowa government have become quite used to it. It is, to put it in simple terms, the way our state government works.

If the legislature were to pass an act calling for the repeal or suspension of section 8.39 the act would be subject to an executive veto. Under the scar tissue rule the governor should not be robbed of this veto power by the simple process of attaching the repeal or suspension of this existing statute to an appropriation bill. This is a textbook example of why we and states elsewhere adopted the scar tissue rule. The trial court should be affirmed.

REYNOLDSON, C.J., and MCGIVERIN, J., join this dissent.

Notes and Questions

1. *What can be vetoed?* The governor's authority to veto conditioning language in appropriations is critical. Without this power, the legislature can include substantive legislation in appropriations and force the governor to veto a popular appropriation to eliminate provisions he considers objectionable. Abney & Lauth, *The Line-Item Veto in the States: An Instrument for Fiscal Restraint or an Instrument for Partnership?*, 45 PUB. ADMIN. REV., NO. 3 (1985): 372–377, note responses from a number of governors who reported that their legislatures had successfully written appropriation bills to limit their veto opportunities.

At one extreme, some states hold that the governor does not have the authority to veto descriptive language in appropriations. *Alaska Legislative Council v. Knowles*, 21 P.3d 367 (Alaska 2001); *Drummond v. Beasley*, 503 S.E.2d 455 (S.C. 1998) (holding the governor could not veto sentences and phrases in an appropriations bill but must veto whole parts distinctly labeled by the legislature). Other states have navigated more complex combinations of issues. See *North Dakota Legislative Assembly v. Burgum*, 916 N.W.2d 83 (N.D. 2018) (in challenge by legislators against five partial vetoes, concluding that governor's veto of workplace safety provisions was within his item veto authority, governor lacked authority to partially veto statement of legislative intent, and veto modifying condition on appropriated funds was ineffective; bill conditioning appropriation to the water commission on the approval of the budget section as to the transferring of funds was unconstitutional; and bill conditioning a portion of an appropriation to the commissioner of university and school lands on approval of budget section was unconstitutional).

The Iowa rule allows the legislature to attach conditions to appropriations that in fact write new substantive law, thereby preventing the governor from disapproving these conditions. The provision in a number of state constitutions that limits every bill to one subject and its stricter counterpart, limiting appropriation bills to the subject of appropriations, are designed in part to protect the integrity of the gubernatorial veto; but it does not serve that purpose if the added matter is read as a condition on the appropriation and not subject to the item veto.

2. *Defining an "item."* In a comprehensive review of the item veto power, the Iowa court recognized it is difficult to decide whether an item can be vetoed and offered the following summary:

> We generally recognize three types of items that may be item vetoed. The first is a specific appropriation made on the face of the bill. The second is a rider, "an unrelated substantive piece of legislation incorporated in the appropriation bill." The third is a condition, "a provision in a bill that limits the use to which an appropriation may be put," which may be vetoed only if the appropriation accompanying it is vetoed as well. However, a condition, standing apart from its appropriation, may not be item vetoed because such a veto would invade the legislative prerogative to "specify how money shall be spent," granted through the general appropriation power. A provision must fall within one of these three types and circumstances to be subject to the item veto power. [*Rants v. Vilsack*, 684 N.W.2d 193, 206, 207 (Iowa 2004).]

How would you apply this test to the following examples:

(a) An appropriation for a state lottery contained a condition, vetoed by the governor, that limited expenditures for advertising. *Opinion of the Justices to the Senate*, 643 N.E.2d 1036 (Mass. 1994).

(b) A condition to an appropriation for tourism and export trade activities vetoed by the governor. It stated that "as a condition, limitation, and qualification, any official Iowa trade delegation led by the governor which receives financial or other support from the appropriation in this subsection shall be represented by a bipartisan delegation." *Welsh v. Branstad*, 470 N.W.2d 644 (Iowa 1991).

(c) The legislature appropriated $1.1 million to the office of administration "For Capitol Building Renovation (West Side)." The governor vetoed out the words West Side. See *State ex rel. Cason v. Bond*, 495 S.W.2d 385 (Mo. 1973).

(d) The appropriation to the attorney general's office for operating expenses contained language, specifically declared by the legislature to be an integral part of the appropriation and not a separate item, which provided that the appropriation was also available to permit the secretary of state to hire independent counsel to defend certain lawsuits. The governor vetoed that provision. See *State ex rel. Brown v. Ferguson*, 291 N.E.2d 434 (Ohio 1972).

(e) The governor item-vetoed the definition of "field office" in an appropriation without vetoing an "appropriation for field offices." The provision defined "field office" as requiring the physical presence of an employee at each field office. *Homan v. Branstad*, 812 N.W.2d 623 (Iowa 2012).

(f) Are there times when a governor's veto of appropriations so implicates the operation of another branch of government that the veto may be unconstitutional? See *Barrett v. Greitens*, 542 S.W.3d 370 (Mo. App. 2018) (governor's withholding of funds from the public defender's appropriation did not violate separation of powers requirements where public defender's office was a "state agency" subject to veto and not part of the judicial branch); *Ninetieth Minnesota State Senate v. Dayton*, 903 N.W.2d 609 (Minn. 2017) (in legislative challenge against line-item veto of legislative appropriations, concluding that line-item veto complied with plain language of state constitution, state constitution did not authorize judiciary to order funding for legislature in absence of an appropriation, governor's exercise of line-item veto power did not violate separation of powers, and pursuant to principles of judicial restraint, judiciary should decline to determine whether governor's exercise of line-item veto power violated separation of powers principles).

3. *When is there an appropriation?* Can a governor item veto a substantive provision that amounts to an appropriation? In *Johnson v. Carlson*, 507 N.W.2d 232 (Minn. 1993), the court upheld the governor's veto of language stating a tax increase was to be paid into a special fund for higher education. The provision was an appropriation because the funds were for the specific purpose of paying the cost of providing higher education services under a contract with the state university system. The appropriation was not merely a "transfer" of funds that diverted money from a legislative purpose to a purpose desired by the governor, distinguishing *Rush v. Ray.* Accord *Rios v. Symington*, 833 P.2d 20 (Ariz. 1992) (upholding veto of fund transfer from special accounts to a general account). For a discussion of whether gubernatorial vetoes in reality tend to reduce expenditures, see Douglas, *Maintaining Higher Taxes and Spending More with the Line-Item Veto: Uncommon Events that Sting,* 38 Public Budgeting & Finance, No. 2 (2018): 3–22 (based on data from four states, concluding that governors at times use veto power to maintain, not just to reduce higher taxes and spending).

Other courts may not be as willing to characterize substantive language as an appropriation. In *Forty-Seventh Legislature of State of Arizona v. Napolitano*, 143 P.3d 1023 (Ariz. 2006), the governor vetoed a provision in a bill that exempted certain employees from the civil service. The court held this provision was not an "item of appropriation or money" for which the constitution authorized an item veto because it failed to specify any fund from which payment to exempt employees would be made. The governor argued the provision specified a fund because exempt employees accrue more leave than merit system employees and must be paid for this when separated. The court held, however, that the governor "incorrectly equates the *obligation* imposed by the statutes with an *appropriation* to fulfill the obligation." Accord *State Legislative Council v. Knowles*, 86 P.3d 891 (Alaska 2004) (nonmonetary asset transfer held not an appropriation).

4. *Lump sum appropriations*. A variation of the condition-versus-separate-item issue is presented by the practice of lump sum appropriations, which has given rise to considerable litigation. To illustrate: the legislature appropriates $2 million to the state personnel department, to be used for the following purposes: $1 million for in-service training programs for state employees; $500,000 for tuition and other expenses of state employees on authorized leave to seek additional education; $500,000 for advertising and other expenses in connection with state recruitment of employees. Can the governor item veto the $500,000 allocation for recruitment expenses? If not, then lumping the appropriations in this fashion frustrates the governor's veto power, as confirmed in a Texas study, Thompson & Boyd, *Use of the Item Veto in Texas—1940–1990*, 26 State & Local Gov't Rev., No. 1 (1994): 38–45. For a holding that lump sum appropriation can be vetoed, see *Washington State Legislature v. Lowry*, 931 P.2d 885 (Wash. 1997). Other similar issues can arise because of unique aspects of state appropriations practices. See, e.g., *Wielechowski v. State*, 403 P.3d 1141 (Alaska 2017) (governor could exercise veto power with regard to distributions from the "Permanent Fund," notwithstanding claims by legislature that dividends from that fund automatically transferred funds without need for legislative appropriations).

5. *State-specific analysis*. While some scholars endeavor to draw lessons that encompass practices involving multiple states, others focus on specific factors affecting the use of vetoes and judicial review in individual states. Significant lessons can be learned from case studies such as these. See, e.g., Schratz, *How a Bill Becomes a Law in Maine: Governor LePage, the State Legislature, and the 2015 Opinion of the Justices on the Veto Question*, 69 Me. L. Rev. 199 (2017) (Maine).

State ex rel. Wisconsin Senate v. Thompson

144 Wis. 2d 429, 424 N.W.2d 385 (1988)

Heffernan, Chief Justice.

This is an original action for declaratory judgment and supplemental injunctive relief. We declare the rights of the parties and declare that the petitioners are not entitled to the prayer for relief. . . .

[Petitioners are the Wisconsin Senate and its president, the Assembly and its speaker, and the Joint Committee on Legislative Organization.]

This declaratory judgment action challenges the validity of 37 of the 290 partial vetoes the governor exercised in acting on 1987 Wisconsin Act 27, the biennial omnibus budget bill. The petitioners' primary contention is that the governor's vetoes were invalid because the governor has no authority under art. V, sec. 10 of the Wisconsin Constitution to veto individual letters, digits or words, and has no authority to reduce appropriate amounts. The governor, on the other hand, maintains that under the constitution and the standards set forth in *State ex rel. Kleczka v. Conta*, 264 N.W.2d 539 (1978), and its progenitors, he can veto any part of an appropriation bill, including words, letters, or numbers, even if that veto results in a reduction in an appropriation, as long as what remains after the veto is a "complete, entire, and workable law." . . .

We conclude that the governor properly exercised his partial veto authority pursuant to art. V, sec. 10 of the Wisconsin Constitution with respect to the 37 specifically identified vetoes challenged in this case. We consider that this result has been presaged by our prior decisions regarding the scope of the governor's partial veto authority. Thus, in this opinion, we break no new ground except as we now, on the facts before us, have the obligation to clarify that the governor may, in the exercise of his partial veto authority over appropriation bills, veto individual words, letters and digits, and also may reduce appropriations by striking digits, as long as what remains after veto is a complete, entire, and workable law. We also accept, and for the first time in this case give explicit judicial recognition to, the long-standing practical and administrative interpretation of *modus vivendi* between governors and legislatures, that the consequences of any partial veto must be a law that is germane to the topic or subject matter of the vetoed provisions. . . . [The constitution provides that "[a]ppropriation bills may be approved in whole or in part by the governor."]

The latest case dealing with the governor's partial veto authority, *State ex rel. Kleczka v. Conta*, 264 N.W.2d 539 (1978), . . . upheld the governor's exercise of his partial veto authority which had resulted in changing a legislatively proposed "add-on" to a "check-off" system on taxpayers' returns to finance the state public campaign fund. This court once again reaffirmed the broad power granted to the governor to veto parts of appropriation bills.

Furthermore, the *Kleczka* decision is significant for our present analysis because it finally jettisoned the idea that the governor's partial veto could not operate on "provisos or conditions" the legislature had placed upon an appropriation. . . . This court clarified that under Wisconsin law, the governor may exercise his partial veto power by removing provisos and conditions to an appropriation "so long as the net result of the partial veto is a complete, entire and workable bill which the legislature could have passed in the first instance." *Id.* at 539. . . . [The court then considered whether there was a "germaneness" limitation on the partial veto:]

[F]ocusing on the 37 specifically challenged partial vetoes involved in the instant case, it is clear that all of the new provisions resulting from those vetoes involve the same subject matter as the original legislative enactment. From this it can be inferred that all chief executives of this state, including the present incumbent, have perceived and recognized an implicit "topicality" or "germaneness" limitation on their partial veto authority. We deem the long-standing recognition of this limitation to be a practical construction of the relations between the governor and legislature....

This broad and expansive interpretation of the governor's partial veto authority as mandated by the constitution has, in effect, impelled this court's rejection of any separation of powers-type argument that the governor cannot affirmatively legislate by the use of the partial veto power. Instead, this court had adopted an objective test permitting the affirmative use of the partial veto power as long as the parts remaining after the veto are a complete and workable law. This objective test has been called an "attractive alternative" to the subjective test used in other jurisdictions, *see* Harrington, *supra*, at 825. Under this objective test the governor can initially determine whether the parts of an appropriation bill remaining after a partial veto will be a "complete and workable" law. On the other hand, the subjective test, which holds that the governor's item veto can only be used negatively, often necessitates court action in order to determine whether an item veto has an affirmative or negative effect. Again, it must be noted that Wisconsin's objective test is premised on the language of our constitution giving the governor of this state the authority to veto parts of an appropriation bill, as distinguished from other states which grant their governors the authority to veto items of appropriations....

The petitioners identify 16 instances in the 1987–89 budget bill where the governor, purporting to exercise his partial veto authority, reduced the appropriation. In four of those instances, the governor reduced the appropriation by striking digits, and in twelve instances the governor eliminated the appropriation entirely.

We conclude, consistent with the broad constitutional power we have recognized the governor possesses with respect to vetoing single letters, words and parts of words in an appropriation bill, that the governor has similar broad powers to reduce or eliminate numbers and amounts of appropriations in the budget bill....

We recognize that the majority of the jurisdictions that have considered this issue—under an "item" veto constitutional provision—have concluded that the governor has no such authority on the rationale that a reduction in an appropriation is, in effect, a veto of part of an item, and thus a type of veto not authorized. *See* Committee Print, *supra*, at 157. Contrarily, in Wisconsin, where the veto authority is phrased in terms of disapproving parts of an appropriation bill, we conclude that the governor has the power to reduce appropriations by striking the numbers or digits he deems appropriate as well as to eliminate the appropriation entirely.

Moreover, although our constitution does not specifically provide the governor with authority to reduce items of appropriation, that power is implicit. *See Karcher v. Kean*, 479 A.2d 403 (N.J. 1984). The New Jersey Constitution, analogous to that of Wisconsin, provides that if any bill is presented to the governor which contains one or more items of appropriation, the governor may object "in whole or in part to any such items or items while approving the other portions of the bill. . . ." New Jersey Constitution, art. V, sec. 1, para. 15. In *Karcher*, the New Jersey Supreme Court upheld the governor's vetoes which had the effect of reducing state aid appropriations to municipalities. The New Jersey court stated:

> In sum, because the provisions relating to state aid to municipalities are appropriations, they are subject to the governor's line item veto power. The governor exercised this power with respect to these appropriations in the most traditional and long sanctioned sense. His effectuation of a reduction of a state aid appropriation to eligible municipalities represents precisely the sort of measure that the line item veto power was intended to permit. . . .

[The majority referred to the claim made by the concurring-dissenting opinion that the partial veto was subject to abuse. The majority replied:] Act 399 is loaded with non-fiscal legislative policy determinations, all of which have been interjected into an appropriation bill. Clearly, the legislature faces a dilemma. From its point of view there are obviously good reasons to do exactly that—some are political, some practical, and some make good sense administratively—to "jumble together" unrelated bits of legislation. But the legislature cannot have it both ways. Practical and sensible expediency may in fact dictate a continuation of the present practice, but it is this practice, the "jumbling together" of unrelated pieces of legislation—as demonstrated in the concurring-dissenting opinion's example—that is the invitation to "terrible abuse." . . .

The solution is obvious and simple: Keep the legislature's internally generated initiatives out of the budget bill (unless the legislature is prepared to face the possibility of a partial veto), or amend the constitution to provide for an "item" veto, and not a veto of "parts" of an appropriation bill. It is fantasy to continue to adhere to the notion that the governor's partial veto power is of "items" only. . . .

Relief denied.

Bablitch, J. (dissenting in part, concurring in part). . . .

I dissent to that portion of the majority opinion which allows a gubernatorial veto of individual letters. Article V, sec. 10 of the Wisconsin Constitution gives the governor the power to "approve" and the power to "veto." It does not give the governor the power to create. The power to create is so far removed from the plain meaning of the words "approve" and "veto" that to so interpret art. V, sec. 10 strains the English language beyond the breaking point. Yet that is precisely the result of the majority's opinion. The veto of single letters can have but one purpose: to create new words. These new words when joined with others, necessarily create new legislation that in turn becomes law with the approval of as few as 12 members of the legislature. The majority opinion allows the governor to creatively legislate with a few strokes of his pen and the approval of one-third plus one member of one house of the legislature. That simply could not have been the intent of the framers of art. V, sec. 10, nor the voters who approved it. It is an invitation to terrible abuse. [The rest of the opinion is omitted.]

Notes and Questions

1. *Making law.* The *Thompson* decision is unique. In a later case, the court upheld the governor's authority to strike dollar amounts in appropriations and insert a smaller and different amount. *Citizens Utility Bd. v. Klauser*, 534 N.W.2d 608 (Wis. 1995). What distinguishes these decisions? The *Turner* case, discussed in the *Rush* opinion, could find no difference between the Iowa and Wisconsin constitutions. 186 N.W.2d at 149. After the decision in *Thompson*, the Wisconsin constitution was amended to provide that "in approving an appropriation bill in part, the governor may not create a new word by rejecting individual letters." Art. V, § 10(1)(c), held constitutional in *Risser v. Thompson*, 930 F.2d 549 (7th Cir. 1991). A 2008 amendment added the words "and may not create a new sentence by combining parts of 2 or more sentences of the enrolled bill" at the end of the subsection.

For discussion of the item veto in Iowa and Wisconsin, see Note, *After Rants v. Vilsack: An Update on Item-Veto Law in Iowa and Elsewhere*, 91 Iowa L. Rev. 373 (2005); Comment, *Wisconsin's Chief Legislator: The Governor's Partial Veto Authority and the New Tipping Point*, 90 Marq. L. Rev. 739 (2007); Comment, *Tipping the Balance of Power: A Critical Survey of the Gubernatorial Line Item Veto*, 50 S.C. L. Rev. 503 (1999).

2. *Power to reduce.* In somewhat less than one-fifth of the states, the power to reduce appropriations is granted to the governor by the constitution. Where it is not authorized, the courts have almost always rejected the governor's attempt to reduce an appropriation as an act of creative lawmaking, inconsistent with the separation of powers. See, e.g., *State ex rel. Smith v. Martinez*, 265 P.3d 1276 (N.M. 2011) (invalidating veto that reduced an appropriation by striking the digit 1 from the appropriation amount; veto distorted legislative intent). Did the Wisconsin *Thompson* case successfully handle the separation of powers issue?

3. *Effect of invalid veto.* When the governor's attempt to exercise item veto power is held invalid, what is the status of the resulting bill? Some courts hold the improperly exercised veto is ineffectual, and the entire bill becomes law, including the vetoed part. See, e.g., *State ex rel. Turner v. Iowa Highway Comm'n*, 186 N.W.2d 141 (Iowa 1971) (if affirmative action not required); *State ex rel. Peterson v. Olson*, 307 N.W.2d 528 (N.D. 1981). Others hold that the failure of the veto results in failure of the entire bill. *Rants v. Vilsack*, 684 N.W.2d 193 (Iowa 2004). The reason most often assigned for the differing results is the difference in the constitutional language covering executive vetoes. Generally, in the first group of states, the constitution provides that a bill becomes law unless the governor takes affirmative action to veto all or part of it; the ineffective veto is thus ignored. In the second group, a bill

does not become law unless approved by the governor within certain time limits: the governor not having approved all of the bill, it fails. Can either or both of these explanations be said confidently to reflect the governor's probable intent? Does it make any difference why the governor misjudged the scope of his power: e.g., the bill was not an appropriation bill; the language vetoed was found to be a condition, not a separate item, etc.?

4. *Unconstitutional legislation.* What if the governor believes a bill is unconstitutional because, e.g., it violates the one-subject requirement or encroaches on his executive power? Some courts have allowed a veto for this reason. *Harbor v. Deukmejian*, 742 P.2d 1290 (Cal. 1987) (court upheld veto of a bill because it violated one-subject requirement, but did not decide this question); *State ex rel. Coll v. Carruthers*, 759 P.2d 1380 (N.M. 1988) (bills intruded into the executive managerial function, violated a prohibition against special legislation or left no meaningful executive discretion to exercise).

With these cases compare *Romer v. Colorado General Assembly*, 810 P.2d 215 (Colo. 1991) (governor may not veto allegedly unconstitutional provision in appropriation bill; only a court can declare legislation unconstitutional). Is deciding whether a statute is constitutional a legitimate part of the executive power? *Florida Senate v. Harris*, 750 So. 2d 626 (Fla. 1999), holds a governor may bring a declaratory judgment action if he believes a law is unconstitutional.

5. *Amendatory vetoes.* In the separation of powers lexicon, the amendatory veto presents the most interesting challenge. While differing in detail among the seven states which have adopted it, typically the amendatory or conditional veto permits the governor to return a bill to the legislature with specific recommendations for change which would make the bill acceptable to him. The legislature may adopt the governor's recommended changes or reenact the bill by the same vote required for initial passage. The bill then returns to the governor for his approval or certification that the legislature's action was in accordance with his proposals. The legislature generally has the option of treating the governor's action as an outright veto and moving to override it in the usual manner. See *Application of McGlynn*, 155 A.2d 289 (N.J. App. Div. 1959). Studies indicate that most amendatory vetoes have been accepted by the legislature. *See* J. Kallenbach, THE AMERICAN CHIEF EXECUTIVE 365–66 (1966).

6. *Evaluating the item veto.* One study concluded that institutional rather than personal reasons determined how often the veto power is used. Substantial use of the veto was influenced by the presence of greater formal gubernatorial powers, a higher number of legislators necessary to override vetoes, the existence of a divided legislature, and the fact that the governor was a lame duck. Klarney & Karch, *Why Do Governors Issue Vetoes? The Impact of Individual and Institutional Influences*, 61 POL. RES. QTLY, No. 4 (2018): 574–584. Some studies have found the item veto does not encourage fiscal restraint in state spending. See, e.g., Berch, *The Item Veto in the*

States: An Analysis of the Effects Over Time, 19 Soc. Sci. J. No. 3 (1992): 335–347. See also Alm & Evers, *The Item Veto and State Government Expenditures*, 68 Pub. Choice, No.1/3 (1991): 1–15 (expenditures lowered only when governor and majority of state legislature belong to different political parties); Carter & Schap, *Line Item Veto: Where Is Thy Sting?*, 4 J. Econ. Perspectives, No. 2 (Spring 1990): 103–118 (political preferences and attitude toward spending are critical factors).

7. *Local vetoes.* A statute or home rule charter may authorize a mayor or executive officer to veto ordinances. *Municipality of Anchorage v. Repasky*, 34 P.3d 302 (Alaska 2001). However, a charter may not confer mayoral veto power if it is inconsistent with a statute. *Detroit City Council v. Detroit* Mayor, 770 N.W.2d 117 (Mich. App. 2009) (statute authorizing city council to reject convention center transfer to regional authority invalidated charter veto provision). The veto authority is limited to legislative, as distinguished from administrative, acts. *D.R. Horton, Inc. v. Peyton*, 959 So. 2d 390 (Fla. App. 2007), held a council's decision to approve a contract with a developer to provide its fair share of transportation improvements, in order to qualify for approval of its planned development, was a legislative act. The court held that in approving the contract "the Council and mayor necessarily were required to evaluate the impact of the proposed development on the City's overall transportation facilities and expenditures, including its ability to provide for future growth."

Another issue at the local level is whether a veto concerns local matters. In *County Comm'rs v. County Executive*, 296 N.W.2d 621 (Mich. App. 1980), the court upheld the county executive's veto of resolutions calling for the withdrawal of the county from a regional transportation authority. The veto was a matter affecting the county even though it had regional applications. The resolution "could only bind Oakland County and would not operate beyond its boundaries," even though it might have an indirect inter-county effect.

Problem 10-3

You are an adviser to the governor of your state, who is planning a State of the State address in which he will propose an amendment to the item veto provision in the state constitution following a defeat in the supreme court on a recent veto. Assume the state constitution has a veto provision identical to that in the Wisconsin constitution. What would you recommend assuming 1) the cases allow the governor to veto substantive conditions to a veto but apply the Iowa severability rule; 2) the cases do not allow the governor to veto substantive conditions to an appropriation; and 3) either of the above, but the cases define an appropriation to include only specific quantitative amounts.

A Note on Executive Impoundment and Reduction in Appropriations

Executive impoundment of legislative appropriations led to dramatic confrontations between the President and Congress which culminated in the Nixon Administration. Although numerous lawsuits were brought challenging President Nixon's impoundment of appropriated funds, the only case that reached the Supreme Court was decided on statutory grounds. See *Train v. City of New York*, 420 U.S. 35 (1975), holding that the impoundment was unauthorized by statute, and not reaching the constitutional question. See Brownell, *The Constitutional Status of the President's Impoundment of National Security Funds*, 12 Seton Hall Const. L.J. 1 (2001).

The executive impoundment issue also arises at the state level. An understanding of the constitutional issues presented first requires a definition. The term "impoundment" does not have an accepted meaning, and may be defined narrowly or broadly. In its broadest sense impoundment occurs whenever the executive spends less than the legislature appropriated for a given period of time, which can be temporary or permanent. *See* Mikva & Hertz, *Impoundment of Funds—The Courts, the Congress, and the President: A Constitutional Triangle*, 69 Nw. U. L. Rev. 335 (1974).

As in other areas in which the governor's executive authority is at issue, the ability of a governor to impound funds depends on how a court views his inherent authority, and on whether a statute has conferred the impoundment power. Some courts find no inherent authority to impound. *County of Oneida v. Berle*, 404 N.E.2d 133 (N.Y. 1980) (holding governor does not have implicit constitutional obligation to maintain balanced budget). Compare *Caputo v. Halpin*, 575 N.E.2d 784 (N.Y. 1991), where the court held a hiring freeze imposed by a county executive was authorized under the charter and the executive's inherent powers. An executive does not have the authority to transfer funds appropriated by the legislature. *State ex rel. Condon v. Hodges*, 562 S.E.2d 623 (S.C. 2002). Compare *Matter of Dutchess County Legislature v. Steinhaus*, 866 N.Y.S.2d 753 (App. Div. 2008) (county executive cannot delegate to Budget Director the discretionary authority to abolish vacant budgeted positions by refusing to fill them).

Some courts take an intermediate view. The Arizona court held the governor had the power to manage the government in a fiscally responsible fashion. This power allowed him to "revert" funds still available at the end of a fiscal year. However, he could not substitute his judgment for that of the legislature except through the veto power. *Rios v. Symington*, 833 P.2d 20 (Ariz. 1992). For example, the court held the governor could not order an unspecified blanket reversion in advance, and had to target specific funds. Accord *Opinion of the Justices*, 376 N.E.2d 1217 (Mass. 1978).

State statutes may confer the power to reduce appropriations. Judicial reaction to claims that that statute violates the separation of powers is mixed. *New Hampshire Health Care Assoc. v. Governor*, 13 A.3d 145 (N.H. 2011), upheld an executive order requiring spending reductions under a statute that allowed the governor to order them if projected state revenues could not maintain a balanced budget, and a "serious deficit" was likely. The court held there was no delegation of authority because the legislature was responsible for adopting a balanced budget, and the governor was responsible for keeping it balanced. The statute authorizing reductions also concerned the governor's implied constitutional authority not to spend state revenue recklessly. Accord *Judy v. Schaefer*, 627 A.2d 1039 (Md. 1993) (upholding statute authorizing governor, with the approval of the Board of Public Works, to reduce any appropriation she considers "unnecessary" but not by more than 25 percent); *New Eng. Div. of the Am. Cancer Soc'y v. Commissioner of Admin.*, 769 N.E.2d 1248 (Mass. 2002) (upholding statute authorizing governor to reduce appropriation by amount of revenue deficiency).

Some courts invalidated similar statutes as a violation of separation of powers. See *State v. Fairbanks N. Star Borough*, 736 P.2d 1140 (Alaska 1987) (invalid delegation of power); *Chiles v. Children A et al.*, 589 So. 2d 260 (Fla. 1991) (invalidating statute authorizing governor to make reductions as violation of separation of powers).

Gubernatorial authority is not the only measure available for handling budget deficits. *Hunter v. State*, 865 A.2d 381 (Vt. 2004), upheld a statute that authorized the state Secretary of Administration and the Joint Finance Committee of the legislature to reduce appropriations when there were budget deficits. The court rejected delegation and separation of power arguments.

Chapter 11

Judicial Relief and Citizen Control of Governmental Action

Scope of Chapter

Litigation is at the center of this book, which has focused on cases that establish the basic principles of state and local government law. This Chapter looks at how citizens can control what their local governments do through litigation, and how and when they can get into court. The cases and problems in this chapter involve local government primarily. Decisions and actions by state agencies are reviewable under state administrative procedure acts based on a similar federal act. Local governments do not usually come under these acts unless they are expressly made to apply. *Hanselman v. Killeen*, 351 N.W.2d 544 (Mich. 1984). Local governments must be sued under judicial writs and procedures that had their origins at common law. Their reach is limited. In the Bean Town problem, stopping a municipality from taking an action can be difficult, and the circumstances in which an action by a municipality can be compelled by judicial action are limited. A final section looks at the initiative and referendum as an alternate means through which citizens and voters can have an influence on local government policymaking.

Problem 11-1 An Uprising in Bean Town

The citizens of Bean Town are unhappy. The city is planning to build new fire stations, but nobody is happy about where they are going to be. A protest meeting was held in a local hall, but the city does not seem to be listening, and a question was raised whether something could be done about it. Somebody suggested suing the city to make them change their minds, but it was not clear whether this could be done.

Another group of citizens is unhappy because the city is not doing enough. Heavy winter storms left the streets in bad condition and full of potholes, but there is not enough money in the city budget to get everything fixed. A delegation went to a council budget meeting, but they were told that more money could not be spent unless taxes were raised, which was prohibited by a state law. Though it seems a long shot, some citizens are talking with a lawyer to see if some kind of lawsuit could bring the city around.

Statutes provide the authority for government responsibilities and the basis for litigation when statutory responsibilities are not fulfilled. The Problem that follows is illustrative.

Problem 11-2

A state statute contains the following provisions:

> § 1. All cities shall establish pension systems for employees appointed under municipal civil service ordinances. Pension plans established under this section shall comply with the requirements for state civil service employee pensions established by the state civil service pension law.
>
> § 2. A city, by ordinance, may extend an approved pension system to officials appointed by the mayor and city council.
>
> § 3. The State Department of Labor shall have jurisdiction to determine, in a contested case hearing, whether any violations of Sections 1 or 2 have occurred.

What remedies, if any, are available to challenge the following actions in court? (1) A city refuses to adopt a pension system for its civil service employees. (2) A city refuses to extend an approved pension system to its appointed officials. (3) A city adopts a pension system for civil service employees that do not comply with the state pension law. (4) The State Department of Labor files notice that it intends to review a decision by a city not to extend its approved pension system to appointed officials. Assuming a remedy is available in any of these situations, who can sue? If a city adopts an ordinance extending a pension system for civil service employees to appointed officials, is it subject to referendum?

A. Through the State Courts

Citizen access to the courts to sue local governments is by no means always guaranteed or universal. Judicial review is expressly provided by some statutes. For example, most zoning laws provide for certiorari review on the record of zoning board decisions. If statutory judicial review is not available, a litigant who wants to sue a local government must use the judicial review opportunities provided by what are called the extraordinary or "high prerogative" writs. This section reviews the use of these writs and closes with a review of taxpayer and citizen standing to sue. For an excellent review of this subject, see Bruff, *Judicial Review in Local Government Law: A Reappraisal*, 60 Minn. L. Rev. 669 (1976).

An important and distinctive characteristic of the extraordinary writs must first be noted. The writs are similar to the early private causes of action. Remember that litigants at one time could not walk into court and simply file a suit in civil litigation, such as an action in tort. A plaintiff had to identify a specifically named cause of action that would allow recovery for the particular damage he had suffered. If a litigant selected the wrong cause of action, she was out of court.

The extraordinary writs operate in much the same way. The court first decides whether the writ selected by a plaintiff is the appropriate writ to review the local government action she has challenged. If a plaintiff has selected the correct writ, the court then considers the merits of her action. If the plaintiff did not select the correct writ, she is usually (but not always) out of court. The decision on what writ to use is thus very important in actions against local governments. The writ of mandamus may operate differently than the other writs, however. In mandamus cases, the court often decides the merits of the action when it considers whether the writ is appropriate. The next section indicates why this is so.

The extraordinary writs originally were court-created at common law. Today statutes in most states have codified the writs but with no change in their use or character. *O'Neill v. Kallsen*, 24 N.W.2d 715 (Minn. 1946) (prohibition).

[1] Mandamus

Mandamus is a remedy that is available to compel the performance of ministerial as compared with discretionary actions. It is a potentially important remedy that can compel a local government or its officials to take an action that will give specific remedial relief. An example is the issuance of a license when all of the requirements for a license have been met. As one court put it:

> The writ of mandamus is the highest judicial writ known to the law.... The primary purpose or function of a writ of mandamus is to enforce an established right, and to enforce a corresponding imperative duty created or imposed by law. It is designed to promote justice, subject to certain well-defined qualifications. Its principal function is to command and execute, and not to inquire and adjudicate. [*Willimon v. City of Greenville*, 132 S.E.2d 169, 170–71 (S.C. 1963).]

State ex rel. Parks v. Council of the City of Omaha

277 Neb. 919, 766 N.W.2d 134 (2009)

GERRARD, J.

Charles O. Parks, Jr., and Edward Rollerson (Relators) brought this action for a writ of mandamus against the Omaha City Council, seeking an order requiring the city council to employ and appropriate funds for a public safety auditor (Auditor). We conclude that the Relators have no clear legal right to the relief they seek. Accordingly, the district court did not err in denying the writ of mandamus. We affirm.

BACKGROUND

The Relators are citizens, taxpayers, registered voters, and residents of Omaha, Nebraska. They also belong to the "Coalition Against Injustice," which is an unincorporated association of Omaha citizens who are concerned with identifying and correcting injustices, including those related to police misconduct and oversight.

The city council is the elected legislative body of the city of Omaha. It has the power to pass ordinances and adopt the budget for expenditures.

In July 2000, the city council adopted ordinance No. 35280, codified at Omaha Mun. Code, ch. 25, art. I, § 25-9 (2005), which establishes the office of Auditor. The function of the Auditor is to review all citizens' complaints against any city of Omaha police officer or firefighter. Section 25-9F(2) provides that the Auditor "shall be appropriated funds in the normal city budgeting process similar to other city departments, and shall be included within the police department and fire department budget." The city council had not appropriated funds in the 2008 budget for an Auditor, and no Auditor has been employed by the city of Omaha since November 2006.

The Relators filed a petition for a writ of mandamus seeking to compel the city council to comply with § 25-9 by immediately appropriating funds for the office of the Auditor and employing an Auditor for as long as required by law. The district court issued an alternative writ of mandamus ordering the city council to carry out its obligations under § 25-9 or to show cause why a writ of mandamus should not issue. A hearing to show cause was held. After the hearing, the court denied the petition for writ of mandamus, concluding that the Relators lacked standing and that in any event, § 25-9 does not impose a ministerial duty on the city council to employ and appropriate funding for an Auditor. The Relators appeal.

ASSIGNMENTS OF ERROR

The Relators assign, restated, that the district court erred in (1) determining that the Relators did not have standing to bring a mandamus action, (2) determining that § 25-9 did not impose a legal duty on the city council to employ and appropriate funding for an Auditor, and (3) receiving certain evidence offered by the city council to aid in the interpretation of § 25-9.

STANDARD OF REVIEW

The meaning of a statute is a question of law. When reviewing questions of law, an appellate court has an obligation to resolve the questions independently of the conclusion reached by the trial court.

ANALYSIS

The Relators' first argument is that the district court erred in concluding that they lacked standing. For purposes of this appeal, we assume, without deciding, that the Relators have alleged facts sufficient to permit them to bring the action. Instead, we turn to whether the Relators alleged facts sufficient to establish that they have a clear legal right to a writ of mandamus.

In their second assignment of error, the Relators argue that the district court erred when it concluded that the city council did not have a ministerial duty to employ and fund an Auditor. Mandamus is a law action and is defined as an extraordinary remedy, not a writ of right, issued to compel the performance of a purely ministerial act or duty, imposed by law upon an inferior tribunal, corporation, board, or person, where (1) the relator has a clear right to the relief sought, (2) there is a corresponding clear duty existing on the part of the respondent to perform the act, and (3) there is no other plain and adequate remedy available in the ordinary course of law. In a mandamus action, the party seeking mandamus has the burden of proof and must show clearly and conclusively that such party is entitled to the particular thing the relator asks and that the respondent is legally obligated to act.

At issue in this case is whether, under § 25-9, the city council is legally obligated to employ and appropriate funding for an Auditor. The Relators argue that it is. The language of § 25-9, the Relators contend, creates a ministerial duty to employ and appropriate funds for an Auditor. Based on the plain and unambiguous language of § 25-9, however, we conclude that employing and appropriating funds for an Auditor is a discretionary function, not a ministerial act that can be compelled by mandamus.

Section 25-9 provides in part that "[t]he [A]uditor committee shall retain the services of [an A]uditor and his or her support staff...." In addition, § 25-9F(2) provides:

> *Preliminary budgeting.* Initial budget obligations shall be provided before January 1, 2001, by city council fund transfer ordinances to sustain the initial startup expenditures as required. Thereafter, and in subsequent years, the ... [A]uditor shall be appropriated funds in the normal city budgeting process similar to other city departments, and shall be included within the police department and fire department budget.

When analyzing the Omaha Municipal Code, a legislative enactment, we follow the same rules as those of statutory analysis. Absent anything to the contrary, statutory language is to be given its plain meaning, and a court will not look beyond the statute or interpret it when the meaning of its words is plain, direct, and unambiguous.

Section 25-9 was adopted on July 25, 2000, during budget preparations for the fiscal year 2001. Because § 25-9 was adopted in the middle of budget preparations, the first sentence of § 25-9F(2), entitled "*Preliminary budgeting*," provides that the preliminary budget obligations shall be provided by fund transfer ordinances. The clear import of the first sentence of § 25-9F(2) is to establish initial budgeting for the office of the Auditor by fund transfer notices. The second sentence of § 25-9F(2), however, establishes the process by which an Auditor shall be funded in subsequent years. The plain and unambiguous language provides that after the initial budgeting process, the Auditor, like other employment positions, would be appropriated funds in the normal city budgeting process. Contrary to the Relators' assertion, § 25-9F(2) does not mandate funding for the Auditor—it mandates how the position is to be funded, if the city council, in its normal budgeting process, allocates such funding. We do not read § 25-9 as compelling the employment of, or an appropriation for, an Auditor.

Mandamus lies only to enforce the performance of a mandatory ministerial act or duty and is not available to control judicial discretion. Mandamus is available to enforce the performance of ministerial duties of a public official but is not available if the duties are quasi-judicial or discretionary. A duty imposed by law which may be enforced by writ of mandamus must be one which the law specifically enjoins as a duty resulting from an office, trust, or station. The general rule is that an act or duty is ministerial only if there is an absolute duty to perform in a specified manner upon the existence of certain facts. A duty or act is ministerial when there is *no room* for the exercise of discretion, official or otherwise, the performance being required by direct and positive command of the law. A ministerial duty is not dependent upon a public officer's judgment or discretion—it is performed under the conditions specified in obedience to the mandate of legal authority, without regard for the exercise of the officer's judgment upon the propriety of the act being done.

Here, § 25-9 does not create an absolute duty to perform in a specified manner. As explained above, the plain and unambiguous language of § 25-9 states that the employment and funding of an Auditor is subject to the normal budgeting process of the city of Omaha. The city's budgeting process is a discretionary activity and not subject to mandamus. While the word "shall" may render a particular provision mandatory in character, when the spirit and purpose of the legislation require that the word "shall" be construed as permissive rather than mandatory, such will be done. Because a legislative body cannot bind its successors, we do not read the statement in § 25-9F(2) that the Auditor "shall be appropriated funds in the normal city budgeting process similar to other city departments" as mandating an allocation of funds, as opposed to a permissive exercise of the discretion associated with the normal budgeting process.

And it is clear that whether the city of Omaha should employ and fund an Auditor is a discretionary public policy decision that is entrusted to the city, as are the myriad of policy decisions involved in setting the city's budget. The decision whether to have an Auditor, and whether or how to fund the position of Auditor, requires a policy determination that is, in the absence of a constitutional question, clearly for the legislative branch. That legislative discretion is recognized by state law, which affords a metropolitan class city council the power and duty to appoint a chief of police, "and all other members of the police force *to the extent that funds may be available* to pay their salaries, and *as may be necessary* to protect citizens and property, and maintain peace and good order." Although it is certainly a laudatory goal to "increase public confidence in the internal investigations process" of Omaha citizens' complaints against police officers and firefighters, it is beyond our judicial authority to force the city, by granting the writ of mandamus, to appoint and fund the Auditor. The employment and funding of an Auditor is a discretionary function, not a ministerial act that can be compelled by mandamus.

This is made plain by the fact that § 25-9 expressly incorporates the normal city budgeting process, instead of establishing a separate appropriation process, or specifying an amount to be appropriated. By contrast, the cases relied upon by the Relators involve circumstances in which the amount of public funds to be expended in the performance of a ministerial duty were specified by the same law that created the ministerial duty in the first place. For example, in *State ex rel. Agricultural Extension Service v. Miller*, [154 N.W.2d 469, 471 (Neb. 1967),] we found a ministerial duty to have been created when the state statutes establishing a budget for the county agricultural extension service created a process "different than the method provided by law for the preparation of the general county budget." We noted that the county board had "a general duty and power to coordinate and to reduce, alter, or amend the county budget," but that the statute at issue in that case had the "obvious intent" to specify funding and "not vest it in the county board under its general budget-making powers." In other words, the duty of the county board in *Miller* was ministerial precisely *because* it had been removed from the normal budgeting process. The ordinance at issue in this case, by contrast, expressly incorporates the normal budgeting process—and therefore is subject to the discretion that is inherently part of that process.

And the Relators' petition necessarily implicates judicial involvement in the city's budgeting process. The Relators petitioned the court to issue a writ "commanding" the city council to comply with § 25-9 "by immediately appropriating funding for the office of the . . . Auditor, and to employ and appropriate funding for the . . . Auditor so long as required by law, or be held in contempt by this Court." The court could not enforce such a writ unless it was willing to determine, not only whether funding has been appropriated for an Auditor, but whether that funding is sufficient to support the office. This is not a case in which the respondent's legal duty was clearly articulated—for example, filling a vacancy in an office created by state law, or abiding by merit selection or civil service rules. The duty at issue in this case requires the exercise of discretion that cannot be commanded by a court.

In this mandamus action, the Relators bear the burden of demonstrating clearly and conclusively that they are entitled to the particular thing they want—the funding and appointment of the Auditor—and that the city council is legally obligated to act. The Relators have failed to carry their burden of demonstrating that § 25-9 imposes a clear legal duty on the city council to employ and appropriate funding for an Auditor. Because the Relators have not demonstrated that they had a clear right to the relief they sought, we conclude that the district court did not err in denying the Relators their requested writ of mandamus. . . .

Notes and Questions

1. *When mandamus is available.* The court in the principal case resolves a tension in the ordinance. Appropriations are to be made in the "normal budgeting process," but the ordinance also provided that the Auditor "shall be appropriated funds." The command "shall" is usually mandatory. How does the court resolve this tension? Mandamus is available, however, to compel the making of an appropriation if the legislature imposes a mandatory obligation. *Perron v. Evangeline Parish Police Jury*, 798 So. 2d 67 (La. 2001) (funding for coroner's office mandated). In the Bean Town Problem above, what would a statute have to provide in order to form the basis for a writ of mandamus to compel the city to fix the streets?

Edelstein v. Ferrell, 295 A.2d 390 (N.J.L. Div. 1972), illustrates the difference between a duty to act and the exercise of discretion in carrying out a duty. A member of a voter registration drive sought to mandamus the county superintendent of elections to hold increased off-premises registration, particularly in minority areas. The applicable statute provided that the superintendent "shall receive the application for registration of all eligible voters who shall personally appear for registration during office hours at the office of the commissioner . . . or at such other place or places as may from time to time be designated by him . . . for registration." The court first defined "ministerial" as follows:

> If a statute imposes a command to act or the performance of a positive duty in compliance with defined standards, the matter is ministerial and mandamus would be available to compel obedience. [*Id.* at 396.]

The court found the choice of registration locations to be within the superintendent's discretion. Since he had exercised his discretionary authority in scheduling off-premises registration, and there was no showing that he had abused his discretion, mandamus was inappropriate. "All the plaintiff has shown is that she thinks Ferrell should have performed his statutory duty differently." *Id.* Does the statute impose a duty to conduct at least some off-premises registration? If the superintendent refused to take any registrations off-premises, would an action in mandamus lie to require him to do so? See also *Falls Rd. Cmty. Ass'n v. Baltimore County*, 85 A.3d 185 (Md. 2014) (zoning enforcement discretionary because "[t]here are a myriad of discretionary decisions made in determining how to employ limited resources").

2. *Arbitrary and capricious decisions.* Mandamus is not available to direct the exercise of a discretionary duty in a particular manner, but is available to review an arbitrary and capricious exercise of discretion. Do you see the difference? How does a court decide whether a decision was arbitrary and capricious? In *California Correctional Supervisors Organization, Inc. v. Department of Corrections*, 117 Cal. Rptr. 2d 595 (Cal. App. 2002), the plaintiff brought an action in mandamus to compel the state corrections agency to discontinue certain staffing practices which allegedly violated its duty to provide prison employees with safe working conditions. The court held the agency had not properly exercised its discretion in adopting these practices, and explained:

> Where a statute leaves room for discretion, a challenger must show the official acted arbitrarily, beyond the bounds of reason or in derogation of the applicable legal standards. Where only one choice can be a reasonable exercise of discretion, a court may compel an official to make that choice. . . . In some cases, reasonable minds could not differ. But where reasonable minds can and do differ about a workplace safety issue, a discretionary call by the employer should not be disturbed. [*Id.* at 596, 600.]

How would you apply this test in the principal case?

If a court finds an exercise of discretion was arbitrary and capricious, the usual remedy is a remand to the agency to decide the case again, but a court may grant relief to a plaintiff if he is clearly entitled to it. *Bower Assocs. v. Planning Bd.*, 735 N.Y.S.2d 806 (App. Div. 2001) (decision denying subdivision approval was without support and developer met all criteria). Specific relief is critical because an agency on remand may make the same decision, and another appeal will be necessary.

3. *The magic word "shall."* The magic word "shall" can be decisive. In *United Mine Workers v. Miller*, 291 S.E.2d 673 (W. Va. 1982), the court granted a writ of mandamus to compel the director of the state department of mines to allow miners to accompany state inspectors during mine inspections. The statute stated "authorized representatives of the miners . . . shall be given an opportunity to accompany" inspectors during inspections. The court held the word "shall," in the absence of language showing a contrary intent, should be afforded a "mandatory connotation." It is often said that the word "shall" does not signify a mandatory intent if the context in which it is used indicates otherwise. How does this maxim affect this case? The principal case? See also *Fagan v. Smith*, 41 A.3d 816 (Pa. 2012) (constitutional provision that presiding officer of either house of legislature shall call election to fill vacancy is mandatory); *Shadid v. State*, 421 P.3d. 160 (Ariz. App. 2018) (denying mandamus in case by inmate seeking to have term of community supervision rounded down, where statute provided that term "shall be rounded to the nearest month" and that "all fractions of the month may be increased or decreased to the nearest month").

4. *Mandamus against the legislature and the governor. Legislature.* Courts usually will not interfere with legislative bodies by issuing a mandamus to compel the adoption of legislation. In an action brought against the Lincoln City Council to compel it to repeal a zoning ordinance and reenact an earlier one, the Nebraska Supreme Court stated one reason for this judicial restraint as follows:

> Obviously the action of the members of the legislative body of the city is a matter of discretion and is not the subject of mandatory control by the courts. [*Kurth v. Lincoln*, 76 N.W.2d 924, 926 (Neb. 1956).]

Mandamus will issue if the duty is mandatory. *Chanceford Aviation Properties, LLP v. Chanceford Twp. Bd. of Supervisors*, 923 A.2d 1099 (Pa. 2007), held the Airport Zoning Act required townships to adopt, administer, and enforce airport zoning regulations for hazard areas. The ordinance did not comply with Act, and mandamus was appropriate to compel compliance. As an independent branch of government, the judiciary has the inherent power to compel the legislative branch to furnish sufficient funds, but only in exceptional cases where underfunding is a genuine threat to the judiciary's ability to adequately administer justice. See *Medico v. Makowski*, 793 A.2d 167 (Pa. Commw. 2002).

Compare the situation in which a state statute requires the enactment of a local ordinance. Is the act of legislating still discretionary? In *Taylor v. Abernathy*, 222 A.2d 863 (Pa. 1966), a state statute required municipalities to adopt pension plans for retired police and firefighters. Mandamus was used to compel the local council to provide such a plan, leaving the amounts and recipients of the benefits to their discretion.

Once legislation is enacted, mandamus may be used to compel its enforcement. At this point the object of the writ is generally an executive, not a legislative body. For example, in *Council of Philadelphia v. Street*, 856 A.2d 893 (Pa. Commw. 2004), the mayor refused to enforce an ordinance claiming the council did not have the authority to adopt it. The court found otherwise and ordered enforcement.

Mandamus can be an important tool in bringing institutional reform litigation at the state level. See *West Virginia Dep't of Health and Human Services v. E.H.*, 778 S.E.2d 643 (W. Va. 2015) (finding that where state had granted rights to patients in mental health institutions, mandamus could issue against state agency to identify requisite resources to provide services anticipated by grant of rights). On the other hand, state legislators have not been successful in employing mandamus as a tool to force an executive agency to issue regulations. See *Scarnati v. Dep't of Environmental Protection*, 220 A.3d 723 (Pa. Commw. 2019) (finding that legislators lacked standing since they did not identify any direct interest distinct from that of individual citizens, had not alleged that timely issuance of regulations impaired their ability to legislate or vote, and did not involve internal affairs of senate).

Governor. The courts disagree on whether mandamus will lie against a governor in the exercise of his ministerial or mandatory duties. Those favoring mandamus follow the view that the writ will issue when the duty is clearly ministerial, no discretion is involved, and there is no alternate remedy to protect individual rights. *Edwards v. State*, 678 S.E.2d 412 (S.C. 2009), held the governor had a mandatory duty to apply for federal stimulus package funds when the legislature had appropriated the federal stimulus package funds and had overridden the governor's veto of the appropriation. The court held "[t]he duty to execute the Budget, as properly enacted by the General Assembly, is a ministerial duty of the Governor."

Courts holding that mandamus will not lie to compel action by a governor say that judicial inquiry into the nature of an act as political or ministerial is itself an interference with the separation of powers. *Town of Milton v. Commonwealth*, 623 N.E.2d 482 (Mass. 1993) (cannot compel payment of incentive funds for hiring of police officers).

5. *Adequacy of remedies.* Courts in mandamus cases apply the usual rule that the writ will not issue if another remedy is adequate. *Muschiano v. Travers*, 973 A.2d 515 (R.I. 2009) (appeal to zoning board provided adequate remedy for denial of building permit). The rule is not absolute, as the alternate remedy must be plain, speedy and adequate. Compare *Krivitsky v. Town of Westerly*, 849 A.2d 359 (R.I. 2004) (appeal to town council adequate), with *State ex rel. Ohio General Assembly v. Brunner*, 872 N.E.2d 912 (Ohio 2007) (remedy by declaratory judgment inadequate when writ of mandamus needed to reinstate law improperly vetoed by governor).

6. *Converting the action.* Pleading is very important in extraordinary writ cases. If a plaintiff pleads an incorrect writ, she runs the risk of being thrown out of court. A court may save the case, however, if it looks to substance rather than form and re-characterizes the action as one it can consider. This can happen with any of the

extraordinary writs. See *In Interest of Doe*, 691 P.2d 1163 (Haw. 1984) (charactering a plea for a writ of mandamus as a writ of prohibition); *State ex rel. Dispatch Printing Co. v. Louden*, 741 N.E.2d 517 (Ohio 2001) (converting a writ of prohibition into a writ of mandamus). There is still a risk, however, as conversion rests in the discretion of the judge.

[2] Prohibition, Certiorari, and Quo Warranto

The writ of mandamus is used to compel government to act. Some other writs are used either to prohibit governmental action or to review decisions taken by governmental agencies. The first of these is the writ of prohibition.

Prohibition is the converse of mandamus; the former prohibits action, the latter orders it. Mandamus most commonly issues to compel the performance of a ministerial act, but prohibition is limited to excesses of a judicial nature. It will not lie to prevent ministerial action. See, e.g., *Giacopelli v. Clymer*, 521 S.W.2d 196 (Mo. App. 1975) (writ will not issue to prohibit county clerk from administering oath for county legislators). The following case explains when prohibition will lie:

Family Court v. Department of Labor & Industrial Relations

320 A.2d 777 (Del. Ch. 1974)

OPINION AND ORDER ON MOTION TO DISMISS

Quillen, Chancellor:

This is an action for declaratory judgment and injunctive relief brought by the Family Court of the State of Delaware (Family Court). The respondent is the Department of Labor (Department), an agency of the State of Delaware; and Council #81, American Federation of State, County, and Municipal Employees AFL-CIO (Council 81) is an intervening respondent. The issue presented is whether the Department has the jurisdiction under 19 Del. C., Ch. 13 to certify a bargaining representative for public employees with which a branch of the State Judiciary must collectively bargain.... [The court considered whether the writ of prohibition provided an alternate legal remedy and required transfer to a court with equity jurisdiction.]

Although the Superior Court may issue a writ of prohibition to an inferior court, the question arises whether such a writ may issue to an administrative body such as the Department of Labor. In *Knight v. Haley*, 176 A. 461, 464 (Del. Super. 1934), Chief Justice Layton stated that a writ of prohibition may issue to a "tribunal, possessing judicial powers." This phrase is certainly of broad scope and could reasonably be taken to include administrative bodies exercising judicial or quasi-judicial functions. But the question has not been expressly determined by any Delaware case brought to the Court's attention.

The general rule in other jurisdictions is that a writ of prohibition may issue to an inferior administrative body where that body is performing a judicial or quasi-judicial function. Of particular application to our situation is *In re First Congressional District Election*, 144 A. 735 (Pa. 1928), where it was held that:

> The writ of prohibition lies from a superior court, not only to inferior judicial tribunals, but also to inferior ministerial tribunals, possessing incidentally judicial powers, and known as quasi-judicial tribunals." . . . This writ is very generally used in other jurisdictions . . . it is an ancient common-law process employed by the Court of King's Bench in the exercise of its supervisory powers over subordinate tribunals . . . and the Supreme Court of Pennsylvania is possessed of the common-law powers of the Court of King's Bench, except where such powers have been taken from us by constitutional or statutory provisions. [144 A. at 739. . . .]

The question now becomes is this legal remedy an adequate one? If it is, its existence will deprive this court of jurisdiction. It has been held that to be adequate the legal remedy must be available as a matter of right. The legal remedy must be full, fair and complete. And it must be as practical to the ends of justice and to its prompt administration as the remedy in equity.

It is with these principles in mind that the current situation must be judged. A writ of prohibition is an extraordinary legal remedy, the issuance of which rests within the sound discretion of the Court. Like the writs of mandamus, certiorari, and quo warranto, it is termed prerogative writ.

In evaluating the sufficiency of the legal remedy, prerogative writs are somewhat awkward because of their own equitable nature. But such writs, despite their prerogative nature, are capable of affording complete and adequate relief to a petitioner, and, if such is the case, resort may not be had to a court of equity. . . .

Under certain circumstances the writ of prohibition is available as a matter of right:

> While the writ should be used with caution and only in cases of great necessity, and not in doubtful cases, yet narrow, technical rules should not govern its use; nor should the scope of the remedy be abridged, as it is better to prevent the exercise of unauthorized power than to be driven to the correction of error after it has been committed. . . . It is a discretionary writ in a sense that it will not issue where the facts do not appear to justify the resort to such remedy, as where there is another adequate remedy available, or where the question of jurisdiction is doubtful; but where it is clear that the court whose action is sought to be prohibited has no jurisdiction of a cause originally, or in some collateral matter arising therein, a party who has objected seasonably to the jurisdiction and has no other remedy is entitled to the writ as a matter of right. [*Knight v. Haley, supra*, at 464–65.]

The availability of an appeal is an important factor in determining this right. In the case at bar, the statute does not provide the petitioner with a remedy by way of an appeal from a decision of the Department. Moreover, such a remedy evidently is not constitutionally required. The right to have such a question reviewed by way of a petition for a writ of prohibition often depends upon the inadequacy of ordinary appellate review. Furthermore, it has been held that, where no right of an appeal exists, prohibition will lie to bar the lower court.

It therefore appears to this Court that petitioner has a right to a writ of prohibition, assuming of course that he can successfully establish the absence of jurisdiction in the Department. The right exists because the petitioner has asserted that the respondent is acting in excess of its jurisdictional power and because the petitioner has no remedy at law either by way of appeal or by any other legal remedy.

The next question is whether petitioner's legal remedy is full, fair, and complete, and as practical to the administration of justice as the remedy in equity. Petitioner's sole objection to the administrative proceedings is jurisdictional, and it is the thrust of his petition that the Department has attempted to assume power over matters not legally within its cognizance. It is for the cure of such objections that prohibition is peculiarly appropriate.

The Court finds somewhat disturbing the prospect that the respondent, an administrative agency, may potentially decide questions of its jurisdiction and not be subject to judicial scrutiny. . . . [I]t seems clear to this Court that if the respondent is correct as to his interpretation of . . . [the statute] he will be entitled to a writ of prohibition as a matter of right. . . .

I conclude that the Court of Chancery has no jurisdiction in this case. The case is therefore dismissed subject to plaintiff's right to transfer the case to the Superior Court under 10 Del. C. § 1901. . . .

Notes and Questions

1. *Basis for writ.* Prohibition lies to prohibit an illegal exercise of jurisdiction, and the absence of jurisdiction must be clear. The principal case, where the writ was used to prevent a state agency from improperly asserting jurisdiction, is an example. Can you think of any other similar circumstances where the writ might be allowed? For a case that discusses when the writ can be used, and illustrating the need to interpret statutes to determine whether there is an unauthorized exercise of power, see *State ex rel. Tucker County Solid Waste Auth. v. West Virginia Div. of Labor*, 668 S.E.2d 217 (W. Va. 2008). See also *State ex rel. Dir., Ohio Dep't of Agriculture v. Forchione*, 69 N.E.3d 636 (Ohio 2016) (in case concerning seizure of animals under the Ohio Dangerous Wild Animals and Restricted Snakes Act, where owner had not secured requisite permit, concluding that agency director had sole discretion to determine whether dangerous animals should be returned to owner, and issuing writ of prohibition to trial judge denying trial judge's claim of jurisdiction to return animals).

The writ lies to prevent an illegal exercise of jurisdiction. It does not lie to prevent an abuse of discretion in the exercise of jurisdiction. With the principal case compare *Milford School Dist. v. Whiteley*, 401 A.2d 951 (Del. Super. 1979). The district sought a writ of prohibition claiming the state secretary of labor had improperly determined the appropriate bargaining unit for the district's custodial staff. The court held the secretary had the authority to make the determination. The writ of prohibition could not be used to review the merits of the secretary's decision, even though the district claimed the secretary had abused his discretion. See also *Galin v. Chassin*, 629 N.Y.S.2d 247 (App. Div. 1995) (investigation into doctor's misconduct; writ does not lie to seek review of administrative proceeding).

2. *Judicial or quasi-judicial?* The key to the availability of prohibition is the exercise of a judicial or quasi-judicial function. In defining the scope of "judicial" or "quasi-judicial," a court effectively sets the limits of its power to intervene. Consider the following: *Nemo v. Local Joint Exec. Bd.*, 35 N.W.2d 337 (Minn. 1948) (duties of a labor conciliator held quasi-judicial); *State ex rel. Wright v. Cuyahoga County Bd. of Elections*, 896 N.E.2d 706 (Ohio 2008) (Board of Elections did not exercise quasi-judicial authority in placing proposed charter amendment on ballot; hearing not required, no sworn evidence introduced in proceeding).

3. *Adequate remedy.* As usual, prohibition will not lie when an alternate remedy is adequate, *State ex rel. Miller v. Reed*, 510 S.E.2d 507 (W. Va. 1998) (revocation of driver's license), but will lie when the remedy is inadequate. *State ex rel. Finkbeiner v. Lucas County Bd. of Elections*, 912 N.E.2d 573 (Ohio 2009) (writ of prohibition to prevent Board of Election from placing mayoral recall petition on ballot). If the jurisdictional violation is clear, a court may allow the writ even though an appeal is available. *State ex rel. Marsteller v. Maloney*, 2005 WL 911140 (Ohio App. 2005).

A Note on Certiorari and Quo Warranto

Certiorari. The writ of certiorari is a common law writ, often codified by statute that provides a right of appeal on the merits of a quasi-judicial decision once it is made. The appeal is on the record, and the usual rule is that a court will uphold a decision if it is based on substantial evidence. A typical example is § 7 of the Standard Zoning Act, which allows an appeal by way of certiorari from decisions of zoning boards of appeal, which hear variances and other zoning matters. Certiorari will not lie from a quasi-legislative decision, such as a rezoning of a single parcel of land in most states. *Neddo v. Schrade*, 200 N.E. 657 (N.Y. 1932) (certiorari will not lie in case involving zoning map amendment).

In certiorari, the agency has made a decision, and the critical question is to determine the scope of judicial review. The Florida Supreme Court has explained the "competent substantial evidence" standard that applies:

> We reiterate that the "competent substantial evidence" standard cannot be used by a reviewing court as a mechanism for exerting covert control over the policy determinations and factual findings of the local agency. Rather, this standard requires the reviewing court to defer to the agency's superior technical expertise and special vantage point in such matters. The issue before the court is not whether the agency's decision is the "best" decision or the "right" decision or even a "wise" decision, for these are technical and

> policy-based determinations properly within the purview of the agency. The circuit court has no training or experience-and is inherently unsuited-to sit as a roving "super agency" with plenary oversight in such matters. [*Dusseau v. Metropolitan Dade County Bd. of County Comm'rs*, 794 So. 2d 1270, 1275–1276 (Fla. 2001).]

Compare this standard of judicial review with judicial review in mandamus of actions that are arbitrary and capricious. Is there a difference? In the Bean Town problem at the beginning of this chapter, if the city held a hearing to decide where to locate fire stations, what evidence would you present at the hearing in opposition to locating a fire station in your neighborhood that would stand up in court?

Quo Warranto. This writ is often used to test the right to public office and oust any usurpers. At early common law, the function of the writ was to protect the crown from the unlawful usurpation of government office or franchise. For a fascinating study of the history of the quo warranty writ and its role in history, see Bowie, *Why the Constitution Was Written Down*, 71 Stan. L. Rev. 1397, 1421–56 (2019). Quo warranto remains essentially a "public" action, usually brought by a representative of the state, such as the attorney general or the county attorney. See, e.g., *Detzner v. Anstead*, 256 So. 3d 820 (Fla. 2018) (challengers seeking to strike proposed amendment from general election ballot were not entitled to quo warranto relief where ballot language was not defective or misleading); *Israel v. DeSantis*, 269 So. 3d 491 (Fla. 2019) (governor's executive order discharging Broward County sheriff following two mass shootings articulated factual allegations reasonably related to neglect of duty and incompetence, and quo warranto petition was therefore dismissed).

What if the attorney general refuses to bring an action? *International Ass'n of Fire Fighters v. City of Oakland*, 220 Cal. Rptr. 256 (Cal. App. 1985), suggested bringing a writ of mandamus to prevent arbitrary or capricious action in control of the litigation. Is this enough? For use of quo warranto in another context, see *State ex rel. Schmidt v. City of Wichita*, 367 P.3d 282 (Kan. 2016) (granting writ of quo warranto in suit by state to declare null and void a city ordinance that reduced severity level of first-offense convictions for possession of 32 grams or less of marijuana and related drug paraphernalia if defendant was 21 years of age or older).

The right to bring the action has generally been extended by statute to individuals claiming title to the office, and in some states may be brought by taxpayers. *Bateson v. Weddle*, 48 A.3d 652 (Conn. 2012) (challenging appointment to office). Unless otherwise provided by statute, quo warranto is generally treated as an exclusive remedy when it is adequate to resolve the issues at hand. *State ex rel. New Mexico Judicial Standards Comm'n v. Espinosa*, 73 P.3d 197 (N.M. 2003) (need not bring mandamus or prohibition).

Exercise of power. Most courts do not allow the use of quo warranto to challenge the exercise of a governmental power. For example, in *State ex rel. Wagner v. St. Louis County Port Auth.*, 604 S.W.2d 592 (Mo. 1980), quo warranto was brought to challenge the state port authority act. The court held that quo warranto could be used to challenge the state's authority to delegate the power of eminent domain and whether the act served a public purpose. Quo warranto could not be used to challenge an exercise of the power of eminent domain. Do you see the basis for this distinction? In a subsequent action, a county counselor brought suit in his official capacity using a petition in quo warranto to prevent city from engaging in tax increment financing (TIF) projects for five years. The court concluded that the counselor lacked authority to bring the quo warranto action against the city and that the city's purported failure to comply with the TIF statute's reporting requirements did not support use of the writ. See *State ex inf. Dykhouse v. City of Columbia*, 509 S.W.3d 140 (Mo. App. 2017).

Public office. In most jurisdictions, a "public office" must be involved for the writ to issue in cases challenging the right to office. Quo warranto has been held to be the proper remedy to contest the right to the office of mayor, *State v. Jones*, 219 P.2d 706 (Kan. 1950); city council member, *State ex rel. Gains v. Rossi*, 716 N.E.2d 204 (Ohio 1999); sheriff, *State ex rel. Varnau v. Wenninger*, 962 N.E.2d 790 (Ohio 2012); state supreme court judge, *State v. Crawford*, 295 P.2d 174 (Or. 1956); and city superintendent of treatment plants, *Carleton v. Civil Service Comm'n*, 522 A.2d 825 (Conn. 1987).

Election contest statutes. At common law a quo warranto action was the only means to contest the results of an election. Now there are statutory and constitutional provisions for election contests. The question often arises whether these provisions preclude or supplement the remedy of quo warranto. See *Dunlap v. State ex rel. Durrett*, 622 So. 2d 1305 (Ala. 1993) (quo warranto available because election code does not cover mistake in counting votes). The two proceedings differ in purpose. An election contest allows the unsuccessful candidate to lay claim to the office, while quo warranto is brought on behalf of the public to determine whether the office is properly held. For further distinctions, see *Tiegs v. Patterson*, 318 P.2d 588 (Idaho 1957).

Legislatures. Most state constitutions contain provisions that each house of the state legislature shall judge the qualifications and election of its own members. The general view is that these constitutional provisions vest the legislature with the sole power to judge the qualifications of its members, leaving the judiciary with no jurisdiction to decide such issues. *Heller v. Legislature of Nevada*, 93 P.3d 746 (Nev. 2004) (mandamus case). The courts take a different view at the local level. In *State ex rel. Repay v. Fodeman*, 300 A.2d 729 (Conn. Sup. 1972), quo warranto was found to be the proper remedy to oust an alderman who moved away from his ward, thereby becoming disqualified to hold office.

[3] Taxpayer Standing and Injunction

The standing problem. A litigant who sues a state or local government must have standing, a link between her personal claim and the government action in question sufficiently concrete to convince a court she is entitled to judicial review. For most of the writs discussed in this section the plaintiff has a personal claim because she is the person injured by the governmental action. In mandamus cases, for example, the plaintiff wants some action done in her favor by government and brings an action to compel government to carry it out, such as the issuance of a building permit.

Members of the general public can also sue their government when they do not have a personal stake in the outcome, but seek judicial relief to remedy illegal governmental action. Because plaintiffs in these cases assert a general public interest in the controversy rather than judicial relief that will benefit them, the question is whether their interest is sufficient and tangible enough to confer standing to sue. This is a justiciability question. Courts insist that litigants have a real interest in a controversy so that the issues in the case will be adequately presented and contested.

Taxpayer's suits. A taxpayer's suit is a common action used by members of the general public for challenging government conduct. The taxpayers' suit is a representative suit filed by a taxpayer on behalf of all similarly situated taxpayers. A taxpayer can claim standing to sue based on his pecuniary interest in the payment of taxes. One might ask why taxpayer standing is allowed at all, since the actual pecuniary injury to any one taxpayer is usually negligible, and the connection between any injury and the alleged illegal act is tenuous at best. Commentators suggest the real basis for granting taxpayer standing is the recognition of a general cause of action to test the legality of governmental acts which otherwise might remain unreviewable:

> Taxpayers' litigation seems designed to enable a large body of the citizenry to challenge governmental action which would otherwise go unchallenged in the courts because of the standing requirement. Such litigation allows the courts, within the traditional notion of "standing," to add to the controls over public officials inherent in the elective process the judicial validity of their acts. Taxpayers' suits also extend the uniquely American concept of judicial review of legislative action by allowing minorities ineffective at the ballot box to invalidate statutes or ordinances on constitutional grounds. [Davis, *Taxpayers' Suits: A Survey and Summary*, 69 Yale L.J. 895, 904 (1960).]

On the municipal level, the typical analogy likens city officials to trustees of the municipal corporation. Taxpayers, as cestuis que trust, may sue for a breach of that trust. Their interest in the "corporation" is objectively demonstrated by their tax contributions. Taxpayers may also have a non-derivative suit in which they sue on their behalf and that of other taxpayers, not the municipality. In this type of suit the taxpayer must have an interest which is distinct from that of the general public. See *City of Appleton v. Town of Menasha*, 419 N.W.2d 249 (Wis. 1988) (claim that statute apportioning assets and liabilities after annexation was unconstitutional).

Some state courts are reluctant to allow taxpayer standing to challenge financial levies or expenditures for reasons such as the following: (a) a multiplicity of suits will result so that both the court system and governmental operation are hampered; (b) the balance of power is upset in favor of the judiciary if it is to review executive and legislative action at the whim of a taxpayer; and (c) taxpayer suits generally are not justiciable because no real adversary context can be achieved where no significant injury is demonstrable. Other courts may allow such standing under certain circumstances. See *Michigan Association of Home Builders v. City of Troy*, 934 N.W.2d 713 (Mich. 2019) (in action challenging increase in building fees to be used to cover past deficits, stating that "under general standing principles, a taxpayer has no standing to challenge the expenditure of public funds if the threatened injury to him or her is no different than that to taxpayers generally"; finding that state constitutional amendment expressly allowed for taxpayer standing relating to local funding and taxation; and permitting suit for declaratory judgment). See also *J.F. Ahern Co. v. Wisconsin State Bldg. Com'n*, 336 N.W.2d 679, 686 (Wis. App. 1983) (in action challenging waiver of public bidding requirements for construction of state building, finding that taxpayers had standing to bring declaratory relief action challenging the constitutionality of statutes that result in public expenditures, whether or not the taxpayers had suffered an actual loss, since "[h]ow or why a taxpayer came to be a party is irrelevant to the standing issue.") It seems eminently reasonable for states to adopt legislation clarifying issues of taxpayer standing. See, e.g., N.Y. State Finance Law § 123-b(1):

> Action for declaratory and equitable relief. 1. Notwithstanding any inconsistent provision of law, any person, who is a citizen taxpayer, whether or not such person is or may be affected or specially aggrieved by the activity herein referred to, may maintain an action for equitable or declaratory relief, or both, against an officer or employee of the state who in the course of his or her duties has caused, is now causing, or is about to cause a wrongful expenditure, misappropriation, misapplication, or any other illegal or unconstitutional disbursement of state funds or state property, except that the provisions of this subdivision shall not apply to the authorization, sale, execution or delivery of a bond issue or notes issued in anticipation thereof by the state or any agency, instrumentality or subdivision thereof or by any public corporation or public benefit corporation.

There is no federal or state taxpayer standing in federal courts to bring constitutional challenges to federal or state taxes and expenditures. The exception is *Flast v. Cohen*, 392 U.S. 83 (1968), which granted standing to bring Establishment Clause challenges to direct financial outlays. However, municipal taxpayers have plenary standing that allows them to contest local taxes and budgetary outlays in federal courts. For discussion see Urquhart, *Disfavored Constitution, Passive Virtues? Linking State Constitutional Fiscal Limitations and Permissive Taxpayer Standing Doctrines*, 81 Fordham L. Rev. 1263 (2012), who argues that this situation improperly shifts constitutional decisions on state tax and spending policies to the state courts.

For a suggestion that additional tools might be useful in holding local governments to account, based on theories similar to class actions and derivative suits, see Kimhi, *Private Enforcement in the Public Sphere—Towards a New Model of Residential Monitoring of Local Governments,* 18 NEV. L.J. 657 (2018).

Taxpayer suits often ask for an injunction to stop governmental conduct claimed to be illegal, as in the following case:

Rath v. City of Sutton

267 Neb. 265, 673 N.W.2d 869 (2004)

GERRARD, J.

The City of Sutton, Nebraska (City), sought to make improvements to its wastewater treatment facility. The City received bids from a number of construction companies, including JJ Westhoff Construction Company, Inc. (Westhoff), and Van Kirk Sand & Gravel, Inc. (Van Kirk). The Sutton City Council (City Council) awarded the contract for the project to Van Kirk, a local contractor, despite the fact that Westhoff's bid was $16,000 lower. The question presented on appeal is whether the City impermissibly awarded the contract to someone other than the lowest responsible bidder in contravention of Neb. Rev. Stat. §§ 17-918 and 18-507.

FACTUAL AND PROCEDURAL BACKGROUND

In September 2001, the City advertised an invitation for bids for the construction of certain improvements to its wastewater treatment facility. The City's invitation for bids stated that the City would receive bids until October 3, 2001, at 1:30 p.m., at which time all bids would be publicly opened and read aloud. . . .

The invitation for bids also stated that the City reserved "the right to reject any and all bids and to waive informalities in bids submitted and to accept whichever bid that is in the best interest of the City, at its sole discretion." Likewise, article 19 of the "Instructions to Bidders" purported to give the City, as the "Owner," nearly unbounded discretion in the bidding process. . . .

Van Kirk, a contractor located in Sutton, and Westhoff, a contractor located in Lincoln, Nebraska, submitted bids on the project. On October 3, 2001, the bids were opened and Westhoff's bid ($1,274,000) was lower than Van Kirk's bid ($1,290,000) by $16,000. Per the bid specifications, both Westhoff and Van Kirk listed August 15, 2002, as the substantial completion date and September 15 for the project's final completion date. . . . A public meeting to award the project was scheduled for October 9, 2001.

After the bids were unsealed, but before the October 9, 2001, meeting of the City Council, the president of Van Kirk sent a letter to the City urging the City Council to award the project to Van Kirk. The letter noted the amount of personal property taxes Van Kirk had paid in 2000 and the amount Van Kirk estimated it would pay in 2001. In addition, the letter stated the amount of money Van Kirk spent annually within the City and estimated the amount Van Kirk contributed to the City's economy each year. Van Kirk recognized that it was not the low bidder, but argued that the $16,000 difference in bids would be more than made up in overall economic benefits to the City if the project were awarded to a local contractor.

During the public meeting on October 9, 2001, the City Council noted the $16,000 difference in bids. The minutes of the meeting show that one council member stated that the difference in bids was not substantial and that by choosing Van Kirk, the wages would stay in the City. All four members of the City Council voted in favor of awarding the contract to Van Kirk, and the motion carried.

Westhoff protested this decision through a letter to the clerk of the City. In the letter, dated October 11, 2001, Westhoff argued that it was the lowest responsible bidder and threatened to pursue legal action if it were not awarded the contract. On October 23, Marlowe Rath, a taxpayer and resident of the City, instituted this action, at the request and with the funding of Westhoff, against the City, the City Council, the mayor, and Van Kirk (collectively the appellees). Essentially, Rath's petition claimed that the City failed to award the contract to the lowest responsible bidder.

After the lawsuit was filed, the City Council called a "special meeting" for October 31, 2001, to reconsider their decision. . . .

Westhoff presented no supporting evidence at the special meeting. Rather, it merely reminded the City Council that a lawsuit had been filed over the matter and restated its position that the award to Van Kirk was inappropriate and contrary to law. In response, the president of Van Kirk reiterated Van Kirk's status as a local contractor and argued that by selecting Van Kirk, the City would reap a variety of savings and economic benefits. Additionally, various persons presented oral testimony in favor of awarding the bid to Van Kirk, specifically emphasizing the positive economic impact its selection would have on the community.

The City Council then voted in favor of reconsidering the original award of the contract. During the subsequent discussion, each of the three present members of the City Council stated their support for awarding the contract to a local business. Generally speaking, they argued that awarding the contract to a local business would offset the $16,000 difference in bids and contribute positive economic benefits to the community. The City Council then voted 3 to 0 to award the contract to Van Kirk.

Rath's operative amended petition, filed December 3, 2001, sought to temporarily and permanently enjoin the City from (1) awarding the project to Van Kirk and (2) spending any public funds on the project until it was awarded to the lowest responsible bidder. In addition, the amended petition sought an order declaring the contract between Van Kirk and the City null and void. . . .

[On February 7, 2002, the district court found that both bidders were responsible, that Westhoff was the low bidder by $16,000, and that Westhoff did not receive the contract because the City thought it would be best to award the project to a local bidder. The court denied Rath's motion because Rath failed to show he would suffer irreparable injury if the injunction were not granted.]

Rath filed a timely notice of appeal, but did not request a stay or supersedeas bond. Therefore, because there was no court order prohibiting Van Kirk from proceeding with construction, Van Kirk began the work and, on September 30, 2003, completed the improvements to the wastewater treatment facility. The City remitted final payment to Van Kirk on July 23. On October 6, 1 day prior to oral argument in this court, the appellees, by way of separate motions, moved to dismiss Rath's appeal as moot. Rath opposed these motions, and we granted the parties additional time to brief the issue of mootness.

ASSIGNMENTS OF ERROR

Rath claims, renumbered and restated, that the district court erred in (1) finding that a resident taxpayer claiming the illegal expenditure of public funds is required to prove more than the illegality of the expenditure in order to show irreparable harm; (2) construing the bidding statutes, §§ 17-918 and 18-507, to allow a city of the second class to have discretion in awarding a contract for the construction of a wastewater treatment facility or the improvement thereof; . . . .

[The court held it must reach a conclusion independent of the lower court's decision, and that an action for injunction sounds in equity so that "an appellate court tries the factual questions de novo on the record and reaches a conclusion independent of the findings of the trial court." The court also held the case was moot but that it would consider it on its merits under a public interest exception to mootness.]

IRREPARABLE HARM

Rath's amended petition requested temporary and permanent injunctive relief to prevent the City from (1) awarding the project to Van Kirk and (2) spending any public funds on the project until it was awarded to the lowest responsible bidder. In its order, the district court quoted *Central Neb. Broadcasting v. Heartland Radio*, 560 N.W.2d 770, 771–72 (Neb. 1997), for the standard for granting an injunction.

> As an injunction is an extraordinary remedy, it ordinarily should not be granted except in a clear case where there is actual and substantial injury. . . . Stated otherwise, injunctive relief should not be granted unless the right is clear, the damage is irreparable, and the remedy at law is inadequate to prevent a failure of justice. . . . As an injunction is an extraordinary remedy, it is available in the absence of an adequate remedy at law and where there is a real and imminent danger of irreparable injury.

(Citations omitted.) Initially, the court determined that Rath "failed to produce any evidence of substantial or irreparable injury" and denied his request for a temporary injunction. Nearly 8 months later, the court made the same determination and denied Rath's request for permanent injunctive relief. The court explained:

> The evidence to date is that money to pay off the debt on this project will come from rate payers. There was no additional evidence presented at final hearing as to whether the rates would increase or if so how much, by a $16,000.00 difference in bid price. The evidence could conceivably be that it will not increase rates due to certain economies of having a local contractor. There was no showing of irreparable injury to rate payers or Mr. Rath as a taxpayer. The request for permanent injunction and other relief should therefore be denied.

On appeal, Rath argues the district court erred in holding that a taxpayer has to prove more than an illegal expenditure of public funds in order to establish irreparable injury. According to Rath, taxpayers have the right to enjoin the government's illegal expenditure of funds without any showing of individual financial loss. Rath relies exclusively on the following oft-cited rules of standing:

> . . . A resident taxpayer, *without showing any interest or injury peculiar to itself*, may bring an action to enjoin the illegal expenditure of public funds raised for governmental purposes.

(Emphasis supplied.) *Chambers v. Lautenbaugh*, 644 N.W.2d 540, 547–48 (Neb. 2002). Essentially, Rath argues that his right to injunctive relief is established by proof that (1) he is a resident taxpayer and (2) taxpayer funds are being expended contrary to law. . . .

It is clear, and no one argues otherwise, that Rath has standing to maintain the action. Likewise, it is clear that taxpayers have an equitable interest in public funds and their proper application. . . . It is not clear, however, what a resident taxpayer alleging the illegal expenditure of public funds needs to show in order to establish irreparable harm.

We conclude that the injury that flows from an illegal expenditure of public funds is inherently irreparable. An injury is irreparable "when it is of such a character or nature that the party injured cannot be adequately compensated therefor in damages, or when the damages which may result therefrom cannot be measured by any certain pecuniary standard." [Citing cases]

Obviously, plaintiff taxpayers have no problem determining the amount of money that was illegally expended. However, an eventual declaration of illegality does not void the obligations a municipal corporation has incurred for services expended on its behalf under the illegal contract. Thus, the taxpayer will not be made whole, i.e., the public coffer will not return to its original level. "Where a municipal corporation receives and retains substantial benefits under a contract which it was authorized to make, but which was unenforceable because irregularly executed, it is liable in an action brought to recover the reasonable value of the benefits received." *Gee v. City of Sutton*, 31 N.W.2d 747, 751 (Neb. 1948). In other words, if an action is "void not because of a lack of power but because of a failure to properly exercise existing power[,] the organization is bound to the extent that it has received the benefits of the action." *Fulk v. School District*, 53 N.W.2d 56, 63 (Neb. 1952).

For example, if a city acts within its power to enter into a contract for a construction project, as soon as a contractor expends efforts on behalf of the city, the contractor becomes entitled to compensation for those efforts, even if the contract is eventually declared null and void for failure to follow the applicable bidding statutes. This leaves the taxpayer with unavoidable and unrecoverable obligations and establishes the existence of irreparable harm.

Moreover, the district court's ruling suggests that before taxpayers are able to obtain an injunction to prevent an illegal expenditure of public funds, they have to quantify the amount the expenditure will increase their rates or taxes. Yet, even if we assume a taxpayer action gives rise to a private claim for damages, it would be nearly impossible for an aggrieved taxpayer to quantify his or her pro rata share of damages. For example, an illegal expenditure of $500 would have almost no budgetary or tax consequences for a city with a multimillion-dollar budget. In fact, while it may be easy to determine the amount of the illegal expenditure, the true fiscal impact of the expenditure will often be indeterminable because of the myriad of fiscal and political choices that follow an expenditure of public funds.

Finally, if an absence of irreparable harm (beyond the illegality of the expenditure itself) prevents a court from deciding if an illegal expenditure of public funds has occurred, following the law becomes irrelevant to those entrusted to uphold it. This cannot be the case. If the inscription on the State Capitol Building is true and "the salvation of the state is watchfulness in the citizen" (inscribed by Hartley Burr Alexander), legitimate taxpayer suits should not be unduly hindered and empty formalism should not prevent a determination on the merits.

In sum, we hold that a taxpayer seeking to enjoin an alleged illegal expenditure of public funds needs to prove only that the funds are being spent contrary to law in order to establish an irreparable injury. Stated otherwise, irreparable harm should be assumed whenever a plaintiff proves an expenditure of public funds is contrary to law. See, *White v. Davis*, 68 P.3d 74, 93 (Cal. 2003) ("a taxpayer's general interest in not having public funds spent unlawfully" is "sufficient to afford standing to bring a taxpayer's action . . . and to obtain a permanent injunction after a full adjudication on the merits"); *Kendall Appraisal Dist. v. Cordillera Ranch, Ltd.*, 2003 Tex. App. LEXIS 6293 (Tex. App. July 23, 2003) (standing is "conferred on the taxpayer, despite the absence of a distinct injury, precisely because imminent and irreparable harm will likely befall the taxpayer in the absence of equitable intervention").

LOWEST RESPONSIBLE BIDDER

[The court held that "when responsible bidders submit identical bids, the public body's freedom of action is curtailed, and it must award the contract to the lowest of the responsible bidders. Contracts let in contravention of this rule, i.e., in contravention of §§ 17-918 and 18-507, are illegal and can be enjoined."]

Appeal dismissed.

Notes and Questions

1. *When an injunction is available.* It is available to prevent a violation of law when the action taken is not quasi-judicial. For example, in *Hames v. Polson*, 215 P.2d 950, 955 (Mont. 1950), the Montana court said: "That public bodies and public officers may be restrained by injunction from proceeding in violation of law, to the prejudice of the public, or to the injury of individual rights, cannot be questioned." In that case, the city park board was enjoined from diverting publicly owned property to private uses. The *Rath* case demonstrates a common example of improper official behavior which is challenged by injunction—the misuse of public funds. For a thorough analysis of taxpayer injunction suits, in a case adopting a lenient injury requirement where plaintiffs charged a violation of a competitive bidding statute, see *State Center v. Lexington Charles Ltd. P'ship*, 92 A.3d 400 (Md. App. 2014). When there is no illegality in an expenditure, an injunction cannot issue. *Cota v. County of Los Angeles*, 164 Cal. Rptr. 323 (Cal. App. 1980). For a case considering the intersection of taxpayer standing, remedial injunctions, and state ballot initiatives, see *Huff v. Wyman*, 361 P.3d 727 (Wash. 2015) (en banc) (in suit to enjoin statutory initiative regarding state taxes and fees from being placed on the ballot, holding that plaintiffs had taxpayer standing, action was justiciable, but plaintiffs lacked a clear legal right to relief as required to obtain injunction).

Relief through injunction is limited by the separation of powers. In *Lap v. Thibault*, 348 So. 2d 622 (Fla. App. 1977), the court held:

> [T]he doctrine of separation of powers must restrict the judicial branch of government, when faced, as here, with the question of issuing a mandatory injunction to require a municipality to file legal action to recover city property, to a determination of whether the municipality's action involves illegality of a palpable abuse of authority amounting to illegality or is fraudulent or clearly oppressive.

Although discretionary action may not be enjoined, an abuse of discretion is an illegal act subject to injunction. See *City of Huntsville v. Smartt*, 409 So. 2d 1353 (Ala. 1982) (selection process for promotion held not arbitrary). As the New York court put it, an injunction cannot be brought on a claim that funds have not been spent wisely, only on a claim the expenditure is illegal. *Saratoga County Chamber of Commerce, Inc. v. Pataki*, 798 N.E.2d 1047 (N.Y. 2003). Compare the similar rule that applies to the writ of mandamus.

2. *Pecuniary loss not required.* Chilakamarri, *Taxpayer Standing: A Step toward Animal-Centric Litigation*, 10 Animal L. 251 (2004), discusses the judicial rules governing taxpayer's suits, and includes an appendix listing the rules in each state on the need for pecuniary loss. It finds three categories: "General distinctions can be drawn between (1) states that require some pecuniary loss as well as additional criteria to be met by the taxpayer before granting standing, (2) states requiring only pecuniary loss, and (3) states requiring only a monetary connection, but no actual

loss." *Id.* at 259. California is in the third category, as the court holds that illegal expenditure is not required.

Other courts, like *Rath*, also take a lenient view of the injury necessary for taxpayer standing without the benefit of a statute. They stress that public injury comes from the mere misuse of public funds (whatever the actual pecuniary result of their mishandling), rather than from a misuse that leads necessarily to additional public expenditure. *Alabama State Florists Ass'n v. Lee County Hosp.*, 479 So. 2d 720 (Ala. 1985) (florists allowed to challenge use of county money to run gift and flower shop in hospital as ultra vires though shop profitable); *City of Wilmington v. Lord*, 378 A.2d 635 (Del. 1977) (court allowed taxpayer to challenge building of water tower in city park as improper use of publicly held property).

The Texas court explained:

> As a general rule of Texas law, to have standing, unless it is conferred by statute, a plaintiff must demonstrate that he or she possesses an interest in a conflict distinct from that of the general public, such that the defendant's actions have caused the plaintiff some particular injury. Taxpayers, however, fall under a limited exception to this general rule. Taxpayers in Texas have standing to enjoin the illegal expenditure of public funds, and need not demonstrate a particularized injury. Implicit in this rule are two requirements: (1) that the plaintiff is a taxpayer; and (2) that public funds are expended on the allegedly illegal activity. (citing cases) [*Williams v. Huff*, 52 S.W.3d 171, 179 (Tex. 2001).]

In other courts, the amount of loss is irrelevant if some pecuniary loss or injury is alleged. In *Gordon v. Mayor & City Council*, 267 A.2d 98 (Md. 1970), for example, a taxpayer was allowed to maintain a taxpayer's suit to challenge the receipt by a private, but municipally supported, library of a collection of books, because the transfer would in fact require the taxpayer to assume the costs of preserving the collection. Consider the comparable use of § 1983 of the Federal Civil Rights Act to enforce federal statutes, which is discussed in Chapter 6. See also Parsons, *Taxpayers' Suits: Standing Barriers and Pecuniary Restraints*, 59 Temple L.Q. 951 (1986).

3. *Pecuniary loss required.* Some states require a showing of an actual pecuniary loss in addition to an expenditure of public funds. *Murphy v. City of Stamford*, 974 A.2d 68 (Conn. App. 2009) (not enough for plaintiff to show tax dollars have contributed to challenged project; must prove that project has directly or indirectly increased its taxes or, in some other fashion, caused it irreparable injury in its capacity as a taxpayer). Accord *Henderson v. McCormick*, 215 P.2d 608 (Ariz. 1950) (city automobile sold to highest bidder even though violation of state conflict of interest law alleged); *Weber v. St. Louis County*, 342 S.W.3d 318 1564 (Mo. 2011) (county expanded trash collection without giving notice to trash haulers currently handling trash, as required by statute; plaintiffs did not have standing to bring a declaratory judgment action challenging the county, because failure to give notice did not result in expenditure of tax dollars, increase in tax dollars, or pecuniary

loss). Other states fall in the first category and have additional requirements. For example, some require that the illegal spending be an act of public significance, such as economic or constitutional significance, that damages the public interest. *Friends of Willow Lake, Inc. v. State of Alaska*, 280 P.3d 542 (Alaska 2012) (use plan violated protected common use of and free access to public waters under Alaska constitution).

4. *Public interest standing.* Some courts allow standing on public interest grounds when the taxpayer's interest is not substantial and immediate. See *Brouillette v. Wolf*, 213 A.3d 341 (Pa. Comm. 2019) (in action challenging unbalanced budgets and loans to cover deficits beyond fiscal year, allowing taxpayer standing where government officials allegedly were involved in asserted violations of the state constitution and were unlikely to challenge practices, actions would otherwise likely go unchallenged, other formers of redress were unavailable, and no others were better situated than petitioners as taxpayers to raise constitutional issues). See also *Bodman v. State of S. Carolina*, 742 S.E.2d 363 (S.C. 2013) ("Standing may be conferred upon a party when an issue is of such public importance as to require its resolution for future guidance.").

5. *Standing based on taxes other than real property taxes.* This can be more tenuous. A California court rejected a claim that payment of state income taxes conferred standing under the statute considered in the principal case. The suit claimed a local affirmative action program for awarding construction contracts was unconstitutional. *Cornelius v. Los Angeles County Metropolitan Transp. Auth.*, 57 Cal. Rptr. 2d 618 (Cal. App. 1998). The court held the extensive nature of the authority's construction activities, and the pervasive nature of the construction industry, gave reason to believe the program would be challenged by someone suffering actual injury. Compare *California DUI Lawyers Ass'n v. California Department of Motor Vehicles*, 229 Cal. Rptr. 3d 787 (Cal. App. 2018) (interpreting state statute that relaxed traditional taxpayer standing requirements and concluding that taxpayer standing could be asserted based on "waste" that resulted from alleged violation of motorists' due process rights). *Williams v. Huff, supra*, held that payment of a sales tax does not confer standing because this "would mean that even a person who makes incidental purchases while temporarily in the state could maintain an action. This would eviscerate any limitation on taxpayer suits."

Could a taxpayer challenge the statute quoted in Problem 11-2 at the beginning of this chapter under the cases discussed in this Note?

6. *Other aspects of the taxpayer's suit.* Laches or estoppel may sometimes defeat a taxpayer suit if the court finds that there has been acquiescence in the conduct, or if the taxpayer is suing on a municipal cause of action and the municipality would be estopped to sue. However, courts usually look at the merits of most taxpayer suits before they give weight to defenses. As in all injunction cases, the action challenged must not be discretionary so that a violation of law is clear. If the action is taken

to implement a discretionary power, it follows that no injunction may issue even though extremely poor judgment was used unless the decision was arbitrary and capricious.

Several states require the posting of bonds by plaintiffs in taxpayer suits. See, e.g., ARIZ. REV. STAT. § 11-642; N.Y. STATE FIN. LAW § 123-d. The courts have upheld bonding requirements against claims they violate due process. *Gram v. Village of Shoreview*, 106 N.W.2d 553 (Minn. 1960). Although bond requirements may serve to deter frivolous lawsuits, they can also be a substantial deterrent to bringing legitimate injunctive actions against government officials and units.

Brent v. City of Detroit

27 Mich. App. 628, 183 N.W.2d 908 (1970)

J.H. GILLIS, PRESIDING JUDGE

Plaintiffs appeal from a summary judgment issued by the lower court in favor of defendant. Plaintiffs, property owners, complaint prayed for injunctive relief against defendant City to prevent it from building an outdoor swimming pool in Palmer Park near plaintiffs' property. A temporary restraining order was issued. At the "show cause" hearing the court dissolved the restraining order and entered summary judgment for defendant. Plaintiffs' complaint was dismissed because it failed to state a cause of action upon which relief could be granted.

Plaintiffs allege that construction of the proposed swimming pool on the site selected by defendant will constitute a public nuisance. Plaintiffs argue that there are more suitable sites for the swimming pool elsewhere in the park area.

Defendant testified that a public meeting was held on the pool situs before the City's Common Council, and plaintiffs' objections were heard. As a result of that meeting, the original situs was moved to a new location, over 400 feet from plaintiffs' nearest property.

It has been a long-standing rule in Michigan that the judiciary will not interfere in the discretionary acts of municipal governments, absent fraud or a clear abuse of discretion. The Michigan Supreme Court articulated this judicial attitude when they said:

> So long as the power to govern the city and control its affairs is vested by the people in local municipal officers in pursuance of law, neither this court nor any other may assume to dictate the local governmental policy of the municipality. The power and authority is vested in the commission to govern as its discretion dictates so long as its action is not contrary to law or opposed to sound public policy. So long as the city commission acts within the limits prescribed by law, the court may not interfere with its discretion. The judiciary is not charged with supervisory control over the exercise of governmental functions by the city commission. . . . It is not the business of

> courts to act as city regulators and, unless the authority of the representatives of the citizens . . . has been illegally exercised, their action cannot be interfered with merely because it may not seem to other persons to have been as wise as it ought to have been.

Courts are reluctant to enjoin anticipatory nuisances absent a showing of actual nuisance or the strong probability of such result. This has been true with proposed uses of children's playgrounds and park areas. *See* Annotation, 32 A.L.R.3d 1127. It is especially true in cases where anticipatory nuisance claims have been leveled against proposed municipal swimming pool sites. . . .

Michigan law is replete with applications of the equity maxim that:

> Equity, as a rule, will not interfere in advance of the creation of a nuisance where the injury is doubtful or contingent, and anticipated merely from the use to which the property is to be put. [*Plassey v. S. Lowenstein & Son* (Mich. 1951), 48 N.W.2d 126, 128.]

See also Warren Township School District v. City of Detroit (Mich. 1944), 14 N.W.2d 134 (proposed use of nearby property as airport); *Village of St. Clair Shores v. Village of Grosse Pointe Woods* (Mich. 1947), 29 N.W.2d 860 (apprehension that use of beach as municipal park will pollute the waters of plaintiff village); *Foster v. County of Genesee* (Mich. 1951), 46 N.W.2d 426 (proposed use of nearby property as animal shelter); *Brown v. Shelby Township* (Mich. 1960), 103 N.W.2d 612 (proposed use of nearby property as automobile race track); *Falkner v. Brookfield* (1962), 117 N.W.2d 125 (proposed use of nearby property as an automobile junk yard); *Oak Haven Trailer Court, Inc. v. Western Wayne County Conservation Association* (Mich. App. 1966), 141 N.W.2d 645 (proposed use of nearby property by a gun club), and cases cited therein.

This is not to say that such swimming pool is forever insulated from becoming a nuisance. However, plaintiffs have pleaded nothing at this time which indicates that increased noise, traffic and parking problems will necessarily result with its construction.

> [T]o secure an injunction against a neighbor's prospective use of his property, *more must be shown than the mere possibility or even probability of harm resulting from that use.* [*Commerce Oil Refining Corp. v. Miner* (CA 1, 1960), 281 F.2d 465, 474. (Emphasis supplied.)]

Therefore, the order entered in the circuit court granting summary judgment to defendant is affirmed.

Costs to defendant.

Notes and Questions

1. *Anticipatory nuisances.* The *Brent* case was an attempt to influence future events. Consider the *Brent* case as it might apply to the fire station problem in Bean Town. As this case shows, equity principles will often lead a court to refuse an

injunction against an anticipatory nuisance by a governmental unit, but not always. In *Keiswetter v. City of Petoskey*, 335 N.W.2d 94 (Mich. App. 1983), plaintiffs who were residents in a single-family residential area brought an action claiming that the proposed construction of a fire training facility was a nuisance in fact. The court held that the complaint stated a cause of action as it alleged an intentional invasion of plaintiffs' residential area with knowledge on the city's part that substantial harm was likely to result. Was this a "clear illegality" sufficient for an injunction? The court distinguished *Brent* because the plaintiffs in that case did not allege a sufficient injury. What could the plaintiffs in *Brent* have alleged to overcome this deficiency? See generally Comment, *An Ounce of Prevention: Rehabilitating the Anticipatory Nuisance Doctrine*, 15 B.C. Envtl. Aff. L. Rev. 627 (1988).

2. *Adequate legal remedy and balancing of interests.* As with the other extraordinary writs, a court may grant an injunction only if the legal remedy is inadequate. *Fulton County Bd. of Tax Assessors v. Marani*, 683 S.E.2d 136 (Ga. App. 2009) (granting injunction to taxpayers challenging tax calculation because legal remedy inadequate). The relationship between an injunction and the legal remedy in an action for inverse condemnation discussed in Chapter 6 is illustrated by *Nueces County Drainage & Conserv. Dist. No. 2 v. Bevly*, 519 S.W.2d 938 (Tex. Civ. App. 1975). Plaintiff sued to enjoin the enlargement of an existing drainage ditch by the district, claiming that the enlargement would flood his land and thus would constitute an illegal and enjoinable taking under the Texas constitution. The court refused the injunction, noting that injury to property of this kind was compensable as a constitutional damaging rather than a taking, and that plaintiff had an adequate remedy at law for any resulting damage. The court also discussed the balance of interests raised by the injunction remedy:

> Injunctions may be denied even in cases where irreparable injury is shown and where no adequate remedy at law exists, if it is reasonably clear that the injury or damage to the party who seeks the relief will be much less if the writ is refused than that which would result to the party restrained if the relief be granted. [*Id.* at 947.]

The court held the ditch extension was necessary to prevent serious flooding in the city of Robstown, which had resulted in damage to the public streets requiring substantial repairs. An injunction would result "in public inconvenience to a large number of persons not parties to the suit which is disproportionate to the damage . . . suffered by [plaintiff]." *Id.* at 949.

It may be strategic to seek an injunction to prevent a course of potentially illegal conduct rather than bring an injunction against individual violations as they occur. The anticipatory conduct rule may prevent this kind of action. In *Borom v. City of St. Paul*, 184 N.W.2d 595 (Minn. 1971), for example, plaintiffs as taxpayers sought an injunction to restrain the city from entering into contracts with contractors who discriminated on the basis of race, creed, or color in the hiring or recruitment of common or skilled labor. No specific instances of discrimination were alleged.

The court dismissed their suit, noting that adequate legal remedies were available to establish discrimination by a contractor under state law and a comparable city ordinance. What advantages might there be to possible victims of discrimination from a blanket injunction order in a situation such as this? Assuming lack of effective enforcement could be shown, what relief might be open to a litigant by way of injunction? Mandamus?

3. *Legislation.* As in the case of mandamus, a court cannot enjoin the enactment of legislation when to do so would interfere with legislative discretion and decisions. Once legislation is passed, an injunction is the proper remedy to enjoin enforcement if the legislation or its implementation is claimed to be invalid. A court can enjoin a tax increase, for example, if it was invalidly enacted. *Levinson v. City of Kansas City*, 43 S.W.3d 312 (Mo. App. 2001). An injunction may be the only remedy available to challenge a local ordinance because it is not possible to appeal a legislative act through the usual appeal process. See *Copple v. City of Lincoln*, 274 N.W.2d 520 (Neb. 1979). Do you see why?

A Note on Citizen Standing

If there is no pecuniary or other basis for a taxpayer's suit, a citizen who wishes to challenge government must do so as a citizen third party plaintiff. Under the standard rule, a general interest as a member of the public is not enough for standing. See *Kendall v. Howard County*, 66 A.3d 684 (Md. 2013) (citizens did not have standing to challenge county avoidance of legislation that would have triggered right to referendum; claim amounted to abstract generalized interest in failure to comply with charter). A court wishing to grant standing must find some other reason for granting standing.

State versus federal standing rules. There are important differences in citizen standing to sue in federal and state courts. At the federal level, standing is based on the Case and Controversy Clause in Article III of the federal Constitution. This clause requires a showing of injury in fact as the basis for standing, but the Supreme Court in an early environmental case expanded this basis for standing by interpreting it to include environmental as well as tangible economic injury. *Sierra Club v. Morton*, 405 U.S. 727 (1972). Later cases toughened this requirement, see *Lujan v. Defenders of Wildlife*, 504 U.S. 555 (1992), but the Court took a more generous view of citizen standing in *Friends of the Earth, Inc. v. Laidlaw Envtl. Servs.*, 528 U.S. 167 (2000), where it held that only an injury to the plaintiff was necessary for standing, not an injury to the environment.

State constitutions usually do not have a case and controversy requirement, but state courts apply separation of powers principles to limit citizen standing. As the court pointed out in *Jenkins v. Swan*, 675 P.2d 1145 (Utah 1983):

> Unlike the federal system, the judicial power of the state of Utah is not constitutionally restricted by . . . [the case and controversy requirement in the federal Constitution] since no similar requirement exists in the Utah

> constitution. . . . However, the requirement that the plaintiff have a personal stake in the outcome of a legal dispute is rooted in the historical and constitutional role of the judiciary in Utah. . . .
>
> The requirement that a plaintiff have a personal stake in the outcome of a dispute is intended to confine the courts to a role consistent with the separation of powers, and to limit the jurisdiction of the courts to those disputes which are most efficiently and effectively resolved through the judicial process. . . . A plaintiff with a direct and personal stake in the outcome of a dispute will aid the court in its deliberations by fully developing all the material factual and legal issues in an effort to convince the court that the relief requested will redress the claimed injury. [*Id.* at 1149.]

See also *Pence v. State*, 652 N.E.2d 486 (Ind. 1995) (same, in action challenging statute redefining the salary paid to legislators).

State courts adopting federal standing rules. Some state courts recognize that the federal standing rules are based on the case and controversy clause of the federal Constitution, but nevertheless look to the federal decisions as instructive. See *Glengary-Gamlin Protective Ass'n, Inc. v. Bird*, 675 P.2d 344 (Idaho 1983); *Godfrey v. State*, 752 N.W.2d 413 (Iowa 2008).

The federal standing rules do not necessarily preclude standing even though an injury in fact must be found. Some state courts apply federal standing rules from the early environmental cases to grant standing to citizen plaintiffs. See *In re Lappie*, 377 A.2d 441 (Me. 1977), adopting the "private attorney general" rationale of *Sierra Club, supra*, and holding that an abutting landowner had standing to challenge a state permit for a waste disposal facility. *State v. Lewis*, 559 P.2d 630 (Alaska 1977), relied on *Sierra Club* to grant standing to citizens challenging the constitutionality of a major land exchange which plaintiffs claimed would result in large financial losses to the state.

State courts adopting public interest standing rules. Some state courts have adopted a public interest exception to allow citizen standing. As the Ohio court stated:

> "Unlike the federal courts, state courts are not bound by constitutional strictures on standing; with state courts standing is a self-imposed rule of restraint. State courts need not become enmeshed in the federal complexities and technicalities involving standing and are free to reject procedural frustrations in favor of just and expeditious determination on the ultimate merits" [quoting American Jurisprudence]. This court has long taken the position that when the issues sought to be litigated are of great importance and interest to the public, they may be resolved in a form of action that involves no rights or obligations peculiar to named parties. [*State ex rel. Ohio Academy of Trial Lawyers v. Sheward*, 715 N.E.2d 1062, 1081, 1082 (Ohio 1999).]

Dimanno, *Beyond Taxpayers' Suits: Public Interest Standing in the States*, 41 Conn. L. Rev. 639 (2008), discusses the state rules:

> [State taxpayers] have standing to sue in public action cases, with variations by jurisdiction in terms of the source and content . . . [M]any states also have common law-derived alternative standing doctrines that allow citizens or taxpayers to sue on behalf of the public interest in [certain] cases. . . .
>
> . . . [T]hese jurisdictions focus on . . . the character of the issue and [that of] the [taxpayer or citizen] . . . to determine whether . . . to grant standing. . . . The character of the issue factor queries whether the issue is of great public or constitutional importance and whether there is a pressing need to get the particular public interest vindicated by the judiciary. The character of the litigant factor deals with the capacity of the putative plaintiff to be the best advocate for the public interest involved, [because] . . . she [is connected] with the question presented, and . . . possesses the competence . . . necessary to be a good advocate . . . [as well as] whether the provision in question would go unchallenged if . . . plaintiff were denied standing. [*Id.* at 656–57.]

For a different perspective, see Harmanis, *States' Stances on Public Interest Standing*, 76 Ohio St. L.J. 729 (2015) (arguing that actual injury is warranted and that state courts should more clearly define standing doctrine while limiting the use of public interest standing).

New Mexico's public importance doctrine grants standing to citizens or voters who otherwise lack standing under traditional doctrines, if the case raises issues of great public importance. *State ex rel. Coll v. Johnson*, 990 P.2d 1277 (N.M. 1999). These cases usually involved clear threats to the essential nature of state government that the state constitution guaranteed to New Mexico citizens. *Id.* at 1284. *Gregory v. Shurtleff*, 299 P.3d 1098 (Utah 2013), held that plaintiffs had public interest standing to claim violations of the constitutional one subject rule, because its limits were important, they were "appropriate" parties united to bring the case, their issues were unlikely to be raised if the court denied standing, and they sought to enforce an explicit, mandatory constitutional provision on form and process. See also *Rialto Citizens for Responsible Growth v. City of Rialto*, 146 Cal. Rptr. 3d 12 (Cal. App. 2012). Could the citizens in Bean Town, in the problem at the beginning of this chapter, get standing to sue under the public interest doctrine?

Citizen suits and the judicial function. The acceptance of citizen suits to challenge public actions in some state courts raises questions about the judicial function and the role of courts in adjudicating matters of public interest. Professor Hershkoff examined this issue in *State Courts and the "Passive Virtues": Rethinking the Judicial Function*, 114 Harv. L. Rev. 1833 (2001). She asks whether federal justiciability doctrine should apply to state judicial systems, and concludes that federal doctrine rests on common law, separation of powers and federalism concerns that do not apply completely to state courts. She argues that state courts should construct their own independent judicial access rules, and notes that:

> [S]tate and local decisionmaking is both populist and private, challenging the major premises of federal justiciability doctrine. Structurally, local government lacks many of the checks and balances that the federal model assumes: local governance structures are not always elected bodies, may be unicameral, often do not meet in public, and are not easily monitored. In addition, the current governance trend toward privatization and public-private partnerships . . . may tend to exacerbate latent antidemocratic tendencies by sanctioning novel forms of private delegation and sublocal structure. Moreover, in some states, the people retain control over the processes of constitutional revision through such devices as the initiative and the referendum, causing further deviation from the federal model. [*Id.* at 1925.]

For an argument that looser justiciability rules at the state level should support state statutes granting citizen standing, see Doggett, *"Trickledown" Constitutional Interpretation: Should Federal Limits on Legislative Conferral of Standing Be Imported into State Constitutional Law?*, 108 Colum. L. Rev. 839 (2008).

B. Through Local Initiative and Referendum

At the end of the nineteenth and at the beginning of the twentieth century, many states adopted constitutional and statutory provisions that established a direct democracy by authorizing the initiative and referendum at both state and local levels. This reform reflected the dominant populism of that period, which favored a variety of changes that would return the management of government to the people, as well as serious concern about the domination of state legislatures by interest groups and lobbyists. Today almost all states have constitutional provisions authorizing the referendum at the state level, most authorize referendums at the local level, and about half authorize the initiative for both state and local governments. The initiative or referendum can be available for constitutional amendments, state legislation or local ordinances, or local charters. They are used more extensively in some states than others, and are more frequently in the west coast states. The International City and County Management Association collects information about use of local initiatives and referenda. See, e.g., International City/County Management Association, County Form of Government 2014 Survey Results, http://icma.org, at 5 (35% of counties report having authority for initiatives), *id.* (38% have provisions for legislative referenda), *id.* at 6 (34% have provisions for citizen referenda); 2018 Municipal Form of Government Survey—Summary of Survey Results. Washington, DC: ICMA, 2019, http://icma.org, at 5 (34% of respondents have provisions for local referenda).

At the state level, 19 states have constitutional provisions authorizing direct or indirect initiatives, with five more allowing initiatives by statute. See National

Conference of State Legislatures, http://www.ncsl.org/research/elections-and-campaigns/chart-of-the-initiative-states.aspx. The Initiative and Referendum Institute at the University of Southern California Gould School of Law, reports that states with the largest number of initiatives since 1904 were California and Oregon, followed by Colorado, North Dakota and Washington. http://www.iandrinstitute.org/docs/IRI-Initiative-Use-(2019-2).pdf. This section discusses the use of the initiative and referendum at the local government level, where it presents issues concerning its relationship to state legislation and the scope of the initiative and referendum power.

As applied to the legislative process, an initiative measure is a voter-initiated piece of legislation placed on the ballot following submission of a petition carrying the required number of voter signatures. If the initiative is passed, the measure becomes law. Under a variant of this process, the legislative body is first given an opportunity to accept or reject an initiative measure before an election is held. A referendum is an election on a legislative measure which is called after the legislative body has adopted a law. The legislation may again be taken to the electorate following the submission of the requisite petition, or the legislative body may itself propose that a referendum be held. The vote on an initiative or referendum may take place at a special election or at a regularly scheduled election, depending on the governing statute. An initiative can accomplish the same purpose of a referendum by repealing an existing law. *Brendtro v. Nelson*, 720 N.W.2d 670, 682 (S.D. 2006) (overruling earlier case).

Leading books and studies treat initiatives and referenda as significant aspects of direct democracy. See J. Zimmerman, The Initiative: Citizen Lawmaking (2d ed. 2014) (discussing state and local initiative provisions and evaluating initiative processes); L. Morel & M. Qvortrub (eds.), The Routledge Handbook of Referenda and Direct Democracy (2017) (providing comparative perspectives on many aspects of referenda). For competing views, see Nat'l Conference of State Legislatures, Final Report and Recommendations of the NCSL I&R Task Force, Initiative and Referendum in the 21st Century (2002) (disapproving initiative and referendum). For thoughtful scholarship on initiatives and referenda, see Noyes, *Direct Democracy as a Legislative Act*, 19 Chap. L. Rev. 199 (2016) (discussing history of initiative and referendum in the United States, and asserting that such ventures are "legislative acts" in some cases); Dinan, *State Constitutional Initiative Processes and Governance in the Twenty-First Century*, 19 Chap. L. Rev. 61 (2016) (reviewing constitutional initiative processes in a number of states, associated experiences, and scholarly analyses); Bishop, *Standing in for the State: Defending Ballot Initiatives in Federal Court Challenges*, 2015 B.Y.U. L. Rev. 121 (2015) (discussing *Hollingsworth v. Perry*, 570 U.S. 693 (2013), decision on standing of proponents to defend referendum validity); Levinson & Blake, *What Americans Think about Constitutional Reform: Some Data and Reflections*, 77 Ohio St. L.J. 211 (2016) (discussing popular interest in state constitutions and analyzing patterns evident in state referenda). Close analysis of individual states' experience with initiatives and referenda can prove particularly helpful in evaluating the strengths and weaknesses of such systems. See Carrillo et al., *California Constitutional Law: Direct Democracy*, 92 S. Cal. L. Rev. 557 (2019) (tracing history of direct democracy in California and concluding that related strategies are a "net positive force" in state government).

Notes and Questions

1. *Authorizing the initiative and referendum.* There must be authority for the use of the initiative and referendum. This authority can be provided by the state constitution, by statute, or by charter. For examples of state constitutional provisions authorizing initiatives or referenda, see Colo. Const. art. V, § 1; Mo. Const. art. 3, §§ 49–53; Ohio Const. art. II, §§ 1a–1g. Most of these provisions provide that the power of initiative and referendum is a power "reserved" to the people rather than a power granted to them. In some states, a constitutional provision is required authorizing the state legislature to provide for a referendum or initiative. *People ex rel. Thomson v. Barnett*, 176 N.E. 108 (Ill. 1931). A charter cannot confer the power to hold an initiative or referendum if legislation is necessary; voters cannot confer the power by amending a municipal charter. *Holzendorf v. Bell*, 606 So. 2d 645 (Fla. App. 1992). Likewise, if a charter places authority for certain actions in the city council, citizens cannot overtake that allocation of authority by using an initiative. See, e.g., *Vasseur v. City of Minneapolis*, 887 N.W.2d 467 (Minn. 2016) (proposed local minimum wage standard could not be adopted by initiative where charter in plain language allocated general legislative authority and responsibility for general welfare of citizens to the city council); *Protect Public Health v. Freed*, 430 P.3d 640 (Wash. 2018) (proposed initiative by nonprofit organization to prohibit county from putting on ballot proposed ban on "community health engagement" (injection) sites was impermissible given council's authority over budget). See also *Spokane Entrepreneurial Center v. Spokane Moves to Amend the Constitution*, 369 P.3d 140 (Wash. 2016) (en banc) (concluding that city and county residents seeking to challenge proposed local initiative relating to zoning changes, water rights, workplace rights and rights of corporations had standing to challenge initiative and that initiative exceeded scope of local legislative initiative authority).

Moreover, an initiative may not enact an invalid law. *Desjarlais v. State*, 300 P.3d 900 (Alaska 2013) (ban on abortion); *Jackson v. District of Columbia Bd. of Education & Ethics*, 999 A.2d 89 (D.C. App. 2010) (initiative providing that only marriage between a man and a woman is valid would authorize discrimination prohibited by law).

State legislation may preempt the use of initiatives or referenda. For example, authority to act may be delegated solely to the legislative body, as in *Mukilteo Citizens for Simple Gov't v. City of Mukilteo*, 272 P.3d 227 (Wash. 2012) (use and operation of automated traffic safety cameras). *1000 Friends of Wash. v. McFarland*, 149 P.3d 616 (Wash. 2006), held that land use ordinances enacted under the state's Growth Management Act were not subject to referendum because the Act delegated authority to adopt them only legislative bodies. It was "a clear example of legislation that creates public policy to be implemented in large part at the local level, by representatives more attuned to the individual needs, wants, and characteristics of their areas." But see *Clark v. City of Saint Paul*, 934 N.W.2d 334 (Minn. 2019) (city residents authorized to bring forward ballot referendum on contractual arrangements relating to solid waste management where there was no conflict with state statute nor impairment of contracts).

As a New Jersey court explained,

> in finding a legislative intent to foreclose referendum or initiative, the courts there considered such matters as whether the ordinance would have regional impact, whether any municipal action is subject to state approval, whether the ordinance is 'legislative' or 'administrative' in nature, whether action of the electorate would represent uncoordinated tampering with a comprehensive scheme, and whether action of the electorate would subvert or bypass procedures mandated by the legislature. [*Tumpson v. Farina*, 573 A.2d 472 (N.J. App. Div.), *aff'd*, 575 A.2d 1368 (N.J. 1990).]

The legislative-administrative distinction is considered in the next principal case.

2. *Good or bad?* Initiatives and referenda can be used for many reasons, and there is a spirited debate over whether they are beneficial or destructive. Examples at the local level include restrictive measures, such as not putting flourides in the public water supply, and protective measures, such a growth management controls. Critics argue that initiatives and referenda suffer from a host of flaws including voter lack of information, low and uneven voter turnout, voters' failure to deliberate, excessive influence of money and interest groups, and voter anonymity, which is claimed to result in greater enthusiasm for legislation hostile to minorities. Baker, *Direct Democracy: Preferences, Priorities, and Plebiscites*, 13 J. Contemp. Legal Issues 317 (2004). A Ninth Circuit panel struck down a voter-passed state initiative that amended the constitution because they found it ambiguous, and had the following to say:

> Before an initiative becomes law, no committee meetings are held; no legislative analysts study the law; no floor debates occur; no separate representative bodies vote on the bill; no reconciliation conferences are held; no amendments are drafted; no executive official wields a veto power and reviews the law under that authority; and it is far more difficult for the people to "reconvene" to amend or clarify the law if a court interprets it contrary to the voters' intent. The public also generally lacks legal or legislative expertise—or even a duty (as legislators have under [the constitution]) to support the Constitution. It lacks the ability to collect and to study information that is utilized routinely by legislative bodies. [*Jones v. Bates*, 127 F.3d 839, 860 (9th Cir. 1997), *judgment rev'd*, 131 F.3d 843 (1997).]

Clark, *A Populist Critique of Direct Democracy*, 112 Harv. L. Rev. 434 (1998), takes a somewhat different view. He claims initiatives and referenda restrict choice because they are limited to one issue at a time. The representative process is preferable because it allows voters to select priorities among issues as well as express preferences for single issues.

Defenders also claim the legislative representative process has faults equally as severe as those claimed for the initiative and referendum. See Baker, *supra*. They argue that direct democracy can be seen as a useful supplement to that process. Gillette, *Is Direct Democracy Anti-Democratic*, 34 Willamette L. Rev. 609 (1998), rebuts three of the arguments made by the attackers against the use of initiatives. He argues that capture by special interests through logrolling is actually more likely in legislatures. He claims initiatives will not have an adverse effect on minorities, arguing that many issues that affect minorities entail legitimately held different views rather than prejudice, that the success of initiatives concerning minorities has been mixed, and that prejudice will not be present in municipalities with homogenous populations. Finally, he rejects claims the initiative is unacceptable because it is not deliberative, arguing that deliberation does occur and that deliberation through discussion prior to adoption of an initiative is sufficient. He provides examples where deliberation does not occur at the time of adoption in legislatures, such as the rule that a conference committee report in Congress cannot be debated. Who is right? Does the availability of judicial review affect your answer to this question? As you consider these questions, you may wish to explore examples of policy issues that have been addressed by initiatives and referenda. See 5 McQuillin Mun. Corp. § 16:55 (3d ed. 2019) (considering cases involving reorganization of city government, transfer of school grades to particular school, licensing of saloons, contracts for lease-purchase of parking meters, and ban on importation or sale of alcohol).

3. *Exclusions.* The power of initiative and referendum is often explicitly limited by statutory or constitutional provisions, see, e.g., Ohio Const. art. II, § 1e, to exclude certain types of legislation, such as laws on the "classification of property for the purposes of levying different rates" and emergency measures and appropriations for ordinary and common government expenditures. See generally Annot., 100 A.L.R.2d 314 (1965). The emergency exception enables the legislature to respond immediately whenever the public health, safety or welfare is endangered without waiting for popular approval. For a discussion of Washington's experience, see Sharf, *Rethinking Emergency Legislation in Washington State*, 94 Wash. L. Rev. 1477 (2019).

The appropriations exception is designed to prevent political interference with the funding of state and local government. In *State ex rel. Card v. Kaufman*, 517 S.W.2d 78 (Mo. 1974), a proposed ordinance that would have set firemen's salaries as not less than those of a neighboring municipality was held to be within the appropriations exception, and therefore not a proper subject for an initiative. Compare *Arizona Chamber of Commerce & Industry v. Kiley*, 399 P.3d 80 (Ariz. 2017) (rejecting challenge against voter-approved initiative under state's "Revenue Source Rule," where initiative provided for minimum-wage increase and mandatory sick leave and imposed civil penalty on employers who did not pay earned sick time). See also *Alaska Action Ctr., Inc. v. Municipality of Anchorage*, 84 P.3d 989 (Alaska 2004) (initiative for the designation of parkland held an appropriation because it designated the use of public assets). But see *State ex rel. LetOhioVote.org v. Brunner*, 916 N.E.2d 462, 472 (Ohio 2009) (legislation requiring video lottery terminals not an appropriation even though it raises revenue).

4. *Can a court hear a pre-election challenge to an initiative?* Many courts hold no because lack of justiciability means the case is not ripe, and a court may not give an advisory opinion. *City of Memphis v. Shelby County Election Comm'n*, 146 S.W.3d 531 (Tenn. 2004); *State ex rel. Althouse v. City of Madison*, 255 N.W.2d 449 (Wis. 1977). Free speech values are also implicated because an initiative sends a message to legislators, as is the doctrine of necessity holding that constitutional issues should not be decided in advance of a strict necessity for deciding them.

There are exceptions. Courts usually allow pre-election review if procedures have not been followed, if there is a content problem, or if there is a conflict with a statute or charter. Some may allow judicial review of a constitutional challenge, but may require clear unconstitutionality. See *Berent v. City of Iowa City*, 738 N.W.2d 193 (Iowa 2007) (reviewing cases). For example, *State ex rel. Hazelwood Yellow Ribbon Comm. v. Klos*, 35 S.W.3d 457 (Mo. App. 2000), found an exception when a law was unconstitutional on its face. In this situation the "substantive legality" is so clear and unsettled that it is "tantamount to" a mere matter of form. As the Alaska court explained, allowing limited judicial review "balance[s] competing policies—allowing expansive direct democracy through the initiative process, and withholding prohibited questions from the electorate when" it would be useless to allow a vote, only to be confronted by a decision that the initiative is invalid. *Pebble L.P. v. Lake & Peninsula Borough*, 262 P.3d 598, 599 (Alaska 2011) ("Save our Salmon" initiative).

For a case rejecting pre-election review of a substantive challenge, see *Herbst Gaming, Inc. v. Heller*, 141 P.3d 1224 (Nev. 2006) (reviewing cases). The court noted that such reviews "lack a concrete factual context in which a provision may be evaluated, and any harm is highly speculative since the measure may not even pass at election time." *Id.* at 1231. How would you draw the line? See Gordon & Magleby, *Pre-Election Review of Initiatives and Referendums*, 64 NOTRE DAME L. REV. 298 (1989); Kafker &. Rosscol, *The Eye of a Constitutional Storm: PreElection Review by the State Judiciary of Initiative Amendments to State Constitutions*, 2012 MICH. ST. L. REV. 1279 (2012).

Additional complications can arise with regard to state referenda on particularly controversial topics, such as the legality of cannabis use under state law. See, e.g., *Grant v. Herbert,* 449 P.3d 122 (Utah 2019) (after successful state-wide initiative legalizing cannabis use, governor convened legislature which voted by supermajority to modify cannabis legislation; citizens filed an application to mount a referendum to reject the newly adopted legislation; Supreme Court granted extraordinary review and concluded that governor's action in convening the legislature did not constitute an illegal veto of the original initiative, and that the resulting legislation was exempt from review by referendum).

Another restriction on the use of the initiative and referendum is that it is available only for legislative, not administrative, acts. The following case considers this question:

Witcher v. Canon City

716 P.2d 445 (Colo. 1986)

REVERE, JUSTICE.

This case is an appeal from the district court for Fremont County, challenging an amendment to the Royal Gorge Bridge and Park Lease entered into between Canon City (City) and the Royal Gorge Company of Colorado (Company). The district court held, on summary judgment, that the amendment was not subject to referendum under either the Colorado Constitution or the City Charter of Canon City, and that the amendment was not unconstitutional under article XI, sections 1 and 2, of the Colorado Constitution. We affirm.

I

In 1906, certain lands surrounding and including the Royal Gorge Canyon were conveyed by the United States to the City to be used exclusively for park purposes. The major feature of the park is a canyon cut by the Arkansas River, which is known as the Royal Gorge. In 1929, the City leased a portion of the park to Lot Piper for twenty years, subject to an agreement by Piper to build a suspension bridge across the Royal Gorge (Original Lease). At the end of the term, the City could either buy the bridge from the lessee, or extend the lease for an additional twenty years, at the end of which time the City would own the Bridge without further payment. In 1947, the Company purchased the Original Lease from Piper. After an election in 1949 determined that Canon City residents did not wish to purchase the bridge, the Original Lease was extended for twenty years pursuant to its terms.

The lease under which the Company is presently operating the bridge and park was entered into in 1967, after a second election indicated that the electors did not want the City to operate the bridge directly. Between 1967 and 1981, six amendments to the lease were entered into between the City and the Company. In 1981, the term of the lease was extended, by the Seventh Amendment, to October 31, 2001. None of these seven amendments were submitted to the voters for approval. When the City determined in early 1982 that extensive modernization of the bridge was necessary, and that proposed improvements would extend the life of the bridge for at least fifty years, the City entered into negotiations with the Company regarding the City's role in the cost of the modernization. These negotiations culminated in the Eighth Amendment to the lease in August 1983.

Since the contemplated modernization would extend the useful life of the bridge for at least thirty-one years beyond the expiration date of the Company's lease, the City Council decided to encourage the Company to undertake the long-term modernization by reducing the City's percentage of the tolls collected by the Company from 25% to 20% until 62% of the cost of reanchoring the Bridge or $1,015,412, whichever is less, has been retained by the Company. In addition, the City agreed that the Company will impose a new 2 and one half percent fee on concessions and all other retail sales made at the park, 80% of which will be retained by the Company until the Company has recovered the sum of $567,412, which is 62% of the actual cost of the wind cable system installed in the modernization, with the balance of the new fee to be paid to the City. . . .

[S]everal residents filed an action in the district court challenging the decision of the City Council that the Eighth Amendment was not subject to the referendum power. . . .

Subsequently, the Company filed a motion for summary judgment. . . .

Relying on *City of Aurora v. Zwerdlinger*, 571 P.2d 1074 (Colo. 1977), the trial court determined that the action by the City Council was not legislative in nature and the referendum process does not "apply to administrative or executive matters addressed by a city council." . . .

II

Plaintiffs argue that both the City Council and the district court erred in concluding that the resolution adopting the Eighth Amendment was not subject to the referendum power. They first contend that the resolution was a legislative act, and therefore subject to referendum under article V, section 1, of the Colorado Constitution.

A. The Constitutional Referendum Power

Article V, section 1, of the Colorado Constitution provides, in pertinent part, that

> [t]he people reserve to themselves the power to propose laws and amendments to the constitution and to enact or reject the same at the polls independent of the general assembly, and also reserve power at their own option to approve or reject at the polls any act, item, section or part of any act of the general assembly. . . .
>
> The initiative and referendum powers reserved to the people by this section are hereby further reserved to the legal voters of every city, town and municipality as to all local, special and municipal legislation of every character in or for their respective municipalities. The manner of exercising said powers shall be prescribed by general laws, except that cities, towns and municipalities may provide for the manner of exercising the initiative

> and referendum powers as to their municipal legislation. . . . [Colo. Const. art. V, sec. 1.]

As a reservation of power, the terms of this article are to be liberally construed to effectuate their purpose. In *Zwerdlinger*, we held that the structure of article V made it clear that the referendum provision was intended to apply only to legislative actions. *Accord Margolis v. District Court*, 638 P.2d 297 (Colo. 1981).

On a day-to-day basis, elected city officials are required to make decisions on administrative functions facing the city, such as purchase of city vehicles, establishment of parking fees, and the proper maintenance of city-owned lands and buildings. In *Zwerdlinger*, we concluded that to subject each such decision to referendum would result in chaos and bring the machinery of government to a halt. The rule that administrative functions are not subject to referendum is therefore both logical and well grounded in common sense. Moreover, even to the extent that it excludes the referendum, this limitation on the referendum power does not leave citizens without remedy. Citizens who disagree with the manner in which their municipal government is administered are free to elect new officials or recall those who are currently in office. We therefore conclude, as we did in *Zwerdlinger* and *Margolis*, that plaintiffs are only entitled to a referendum if the action of which they complain is legislative in character.

In *Zwerdlinger* and *Margolis*, three tests for determining whether a specific municipal act is legislative or administrative were set out. First, actions that relate to subjects of a permanent or general character are legislative, while those that are temporary in operation and effect are not. Second, "acts that are necessary to carry out existing legislative policies and purposes or which are properly characterized as executive are deemed to be administrative, while acts constituting a declaration of public policy are deemed to be legislative." Third, if an original act was legislative, then an amendment to the original act must also be legislative. In order to determine whether the resolution in question was legislative or administrative in character, we must apply the first and second tests to the lease amendment, and the third test to the lease itself.

Under the first test, the Eighth Amendment is clearly an administrative act. The language of the Eighth Amendment specifically limits the operation of the reduction in tolls to the period which is necessary for the lessee to recoup 62% of the costs of certain capital improvements made to the Royal Gorge Bridge. Plaintiffs argue that the Council's action will have the effect of raising citizens' tax burdens, so as to offset the decreased bridge revenues. This is pure supposition on the plaintiffs' part, since a city can respond to a decrease in a revenue source in a number of ways, only one of which is to increase taxes. Moreover, plaintiffs' argument begs the issue, for it is one of Council's administrative tasks to expend money to further legislatively declared policies. The question of whether a subsequent measure to raise taxes, resulting from any revenue loss produced by the Eighth Amendment, would be referable is a very different issue that is not before us here. The effect of the

Eighth Amendment is the same as that of any other spending decision by the Council, whether for a contract for professional services or for a roof on a police station. It is the administrative task of elected municipal officials to, among other things, collect and expend monies for the protection or enhancement of public properties. As such, the amendment is administrative in character.

Moreover, in the context of a lessor-lessee relationship, changing circumstances often require amendments to an original agreement between parties. In making changes to a lease, neither party presumes an amendment to be permanent in nature or effect. The adoption of the previous seven amendments and the Eighth Amendment itself indicates that the lease is subject to modification as circumstances dictate.

Plaintiffs cite several cases that involve acts which are not analogous to the amendment of a lease between a municipality and a private concern in an attempt to demonstrate that the effect of the Eighth Amendment is permanent or general. For example, *Burks v. City of Lafayette*, 349 P.2d 692 (Colo. 1960), involved creation of a special improvement district. There is little doubt that creation of an improvement district is a permanent decision, but there is no logical connection between the creation of an improvement district and the amendment of a lease with a fixed termination date. Similarly, the decisions of this Court, holding that zoning decisions are permanent or general in nature, *see, e.g., Margolis*, are not analogous to the amendment of a lease.

The second test, that an action, in order to be considered legislative, must declare new public policy, also supports the conclusion that the Eighth Amendment is administrative. Two elections have established the public policy of leasing the bridge, rather than operation of the bridge by the City. The question of approval of the specific terms and conditions of the lease is not a matter of public policy. The negotiation of the leases and the amendments thereto are administrative acts, undertaken to carry out the policy decision to lease, rather than operate, the bridge.

When it was determined that replacement of the existing bridge cable anchors and wind stay system with more modern components would be appropriate in light of both the bridge's condition and developments in the technology of bridge construction since the original erection of the bridge, the Company proposed major capital improvements to the structure rather than simply repairing areas where damage had been discovered. The City Council determined that this proposal contained a package of improvements which would extend the life of the existing bridge for at least 50 years, resulting in an unencumbered capital improvement for 34 years beyond the term of the existing Lease Agreement.

Plaintiffs assert that the action of the Council was legislative, because it reversed the existing legislative policy evidenced by the Original Lease, the 1967 Lease, and the first seven amendments to the 1967 Lease by providing that the City should bear a portion of the maintenance costs which would otherwise be borne by the lessee. However, that decision did not result in the City's assuming the lessee's maintenance obligation, but rather, it authorized the lessee to make certain capital improvements to the Royal Gorge Bridge that were not provided for in the 1967 Lease. The trial court found that the existing policy that maintenance and repair of the Bridge is the responsibility of the lessee is not changed by the Eighth Amendment. Since neither the 1967 Lease nor its first seven amendments speak to either the necessity for, or allocation of the costs of, capital improvements made to the structure that exceed the life of the Lease, the trial court's finding is in accord with the evidence.

We also note that the lessee is financing the entire cost of the capital improvements, with the City to receive a reduction of rent equivalent to the costs expended by lessee, for the benefit of the City, and reflecting the actual costs expended on such improvements, exclusive of interest. There is no provision in the Lease Agreement that requires the Company to make capital improvements, particularly improvements determined to have a useful life extending 34 years beyond the term of the Lease.

The action of the City Council carried out the continuing obligation placed upon it to preserve the property of the City and beyond that, chose a method of financing the capital improvements to the bridge without municipal borrowing. Improvements to municipal facilities are specifically provided for in the Canon City Charter, article XIII, section 13. . . . Since the bridge itself will eventually provide the revenues to pay for the capital improvements, this action is specifically within the discretion of the Council, as no bonds were authorized, issued or sold to raise funds to defray the costs of the capital improvements.

Further, Canon City voters established a clear policy when they twice defeated proposals that the City operate the bridge and park itself. Thus, under the second test, the negotiations for the Lease and its amendments were administrative acts undertaken to carry out the public policy decision to lease rather than operate the bridge and other concessions in the Royal Gorge Park.

Since we conclude that the Lease itself merely carried out the previously established policy of transferring all operational and maintenance responsibilities for the bridge to a private company, and is therefore administrative in character, it is clear that the Eighth Amendment is also administrative under the third test. Because the amendment is administrative under each of the three tests set forth in *Zwerdlinger* and *Margolis*, it falls outside of the reservation of the referendum power in article V, section 1, of the Colorado Constitution. . . .

LOHR, JUSTICE, concurring in part and dissenting in part: . . .

I believe . . . that the standards governing the characterization of a governmental action as either legislative or administrative have been improperly applied to the facts by the majority, with the consequence that the result reached is incorrect.

At the outset, the majority fundamentally misconceives the nature of the action taken by the city council. By approving the amendment, the council did more than amend a lease. It decided to undertake a significant capital improvement at a cost to the city of $1.5 million. The capital improvement involves a structure that generates at present approximately $0.5 million dollars of revenue per year for the city, an amount that constitutes approximately fifteen percent of the city's budget. The amount of revenue derived by the city from the bridge is projected to increase to approximately $1.5 million dollars per year by the year 2000. Moreover, the improvements are calculated to extend the life of the bridge for at least thirty-one years beyond the expiration of the lease in 2001. Approval of the lease amendment was simply the vehicle through which the city council expressed its decision to undertake this improvement and provided the mechanism by which the city will finance the improvement. The decision by the city to undertake something of such significance can only be characterized as a legislative policy decision, not merely administrative action. In an affidavit attached to their response to the defendants' motions for summary judgment and at oral argument on the summary judgment motions, the plaintiffs represented that the amount of revenue derived by the city from the lease payments totaled approximately fifteen to seventeen percent of the city's budget. This is not otherwise corroborated. However, the city did not protest this representation, and it is accepted for the purposes of this dissent.

As noted by the majority, one of the "tests" for determining whether an act is legislative or administrative is whether the act constitutes a declaration of public policy or whether passage of the act simply carries out existing legislative policies. In applying this standard, the plaintiffs argue that the council's action was legislative because it reversed a purported policy expressed in the lease that the city would not bear any of the costs of maintenance or modification of the bridge. The city responds, and the district court and the majority agree, that there is no merit to this argument because the lease did not require the lessee to make capital improvements to the bridge of the nature contemplated here. But, this is precisely the reason why this action is legislative. Accepting the district court's reasonable construction of the lease as not requiring the lessee to make capital improvements means that the city has made a new policy decision—not expressed by the city in the lease or elsewhere before the passage of the Eighth Amendment—to undertake the substantial capital improvement of an important city asset. . . .

Another of the "tests" for determining whether an action is legislative or administrative is whether the action relates to a subject of a permanent or general character or a subject of a temporary or special nature. . . . The majority's analysis [of this test] is unpersuasive. This is not simply a lease amendment with little effect beyond the life of a relatively short leasehold. Instead, the lease amendment is a financing mechanism by which the city has committed itself to acquire and pay for a capital improvement of vast significance to the affairs of the city, its people and its government—an improvement that will have a life and an effect for at least thirty years beyond the life of the existing lease. This is not an action of a temporary or special character, and the duration of its impact should not be measured solely by the time in which the bridge will generate sufficient income to cover the costs of the improvements. It is a legislative act of a substantial and general nature, having a long-term impact on city finances. This is hardly comparable to a decision concerning "a contract for professional services or for a roof on a police station." . . .

Notes and Questions

1. *Legislative vs. administrative.* The limitation of the initiative and referendum to legislative acts is so ingrained that some courts adopt it even if the statute or constitutional provision authorizing these measures does not specifically require it. *Town of Whitehall v. Preece*, 956 P.2d 743 (Mont. 1998). For discussion of the rules adopted by different states, see *Friends of Congress Square Park v. City of Portland*, 91 A.3d 601 (Me. 2014).

Where should the line be drawn? Actions that simply apply existing laws are clearly administrative. *State ex rel. Committee for the Referendum of Ordinance No. 3844-02 v. Norris*, 792 N.E.2d 186 (Ohio 2003) (application of zoning regulations to property). Some courts provide a bright line rule by holding that actions based on statutory authority are always administrative. See *Lane Transit Dist. v. Lane County*, 957 P.2d 1217 (Or. 1997), holding the power to set the salary of the district's general manager was an administrative act because a statute gave the district board the power to appoint a general manager and fix the terms of employment, including compensation. The *Whitehall* case, *supra*, pointed out, however, that this rule is "practically meaningless, because virtually all municipal actions are, either directly or indirectly, taken pursuant to statutory authority." A water conservation project that included a water metering plan was held administrative.

Sometimes initiatives appear to blend policy-making and administrative dimensions, making judicial decisions especially challenging. See, e.g., *Global Neighborhood v. Respect Washington*, 434 P.3d 1024 (Wash. App. 2019) (based on finding that initiative was administrative in character, upholding challenge to proposed Spokane city initiative that would have allowed city employees, including law enforcement officers, to question individuals about immigration and citizenship status, assemble and share that information with others).

2. *When does policy-making make an act legislative?* Consider the following cases. What factors seem especially important in determining that an act is legislative?

(a) *Funding considerations. Concerned Citizens v. Pantalone*, 447 A.2d 200 (N.J. App. Div. 1982). An initiative ordinance was proposed to repeal a borough ordinance imposing a beach fee. The court held that an initiative was proper. "[W]e have a local question of a basic policy nature. The issue is long-term in effect. It cannot be fairly deemed highly technical in nature." *Id.* at 205. See also *Wilde v. City of Dunsmuir*, 240 Cal. Rptr. 3d 88 (Cal. App. 2018) (resolution adopting new water rates was legislative in character).

(b) *Public buildings and enterprises. Moore v. School Comm.*, 378 N.E.2d 47 (Mass. 1978), held a decision to close a school was legislative, because it was a "policy determination." "Before voting to close and consolidate, the school committee weighed the costs of the closing on the pupils and community against the economic savings and other gains to be realized." *Id.* at 50. Isn't a similar cost-benefit calculus struck for every governmental decision? See also *Swetzof v. Philemonoff*, 203 P.3d 471 (Alaska 2009) (holding initiative proposing that city get out of electricity generating business was legislative as a permanent policy decision even though it involved "difficult and complex choices").

(c) *Design selection. Vagneur v. City of Aspen*, 295 P.3d 493 (Colo. 2013), held that initiatives proposing a design for the entrance to the city of Aspen were administrative. They mandated through municipal ordinance a specific proposal for the location, design, and construction of a state highway corridor. They directly circumvented a complex and multi-layered administrative process that included a federal environmental review involving the city and county and state and federal highway agencies. This process required a case-specific evaluation based on careful study and specialized expertise. The initiatives would legislate alternatives rejected in this process. They also would require the amendment of contractual agreements, as well as changes to right-of-way easements previously conveyed.

(d) *Water fluoridation. City of Port Angeles v. Our Water–Our Choice!*, 239 P.3d 589 (Wash. 2010), held 5-4 that initiatives to prohibit the fluoridation of water in a municipal water utility were not allowable because they "explicitly seek to administer the details of the city's existing water system," and modify a plan already in effect. The court noted that water quality in the United States is highly regulated, and that state regulations allow "water systems to administratively adopt water fluoridation programs." The dissent would have held the initiative involved a legislative matter, because state regulations did not "determine whether fluoride should be added in the first place." *Carter v. Lehi City*, 269 P.3d 141 (Utah 2012), provides an extensive discussion of legislative power, and holds that initiatives regulating salaries and residency requirements for city employees were legislative.

3. *Temporary vs. permanent.* A finding that a proposal is permanent helps support a holding that it is legislative. In *Save Our Fire Dep't Paramedics Comm. v. City of Appleton*, 389 N.W.2d 43 (Wis. App. 1986), the court held a proposed charter amendment requiring the city to provide emergency medical services through its fire department was legislative. The amendment would establish a "permanent rule regarding emergency medical services." *Id.* at 48. The proposal did not encroach on administrative personnel matters because it did not specify the individuals who would perform the services and did not specify conditions of employment. See also *Berent v. City of Iowa City*, 738 N.W.2d 193 (Iowa 2007) (proposal for Police Citizens Review Board held permanent).

Compare *Fite v. Lacey*, 691 P.2d 901 (Okla. 1984). An initiative was filed calling for adoption of the state law concerning collective bargaining and arbitration for firefighters and police officers. Unlike the state law, the initiative required binding arbitration. The court held that an initiative was not available because the bargaining and arbitration process was temporary, not permanent. "Collective bargaining with compulsory binding arbitration is a tool of personnel management which involves the consideration of a number of factors which are subject to change." *Id.* at 905.

4. *Judicial review.* Should the adoption of a law by initiative or its repeal by referendum change the basis for judicial review? A student Note, *Judicial Approaches to Direct Democracy,* 118 Harv. L. Rev. 2748 (2005), points out that "the wholesale incorporation of interpretive canons and theories into the realm of direct democracy is problematic because these canons and theories are based on assumptions about the legislative process that do not fit in this different context." *Id.* at 2754. It notes that some commentators believe adoption by popular vote should not change the basis for judicial review, others argue that voter-adopted legislation required greater deference to give expression to the popular will, while others argue that voter-adopted legislation requires greater scrutiny because of the deficiencies of direct democracy.

The California court stated the case for deference:

> The exercise of initiative and referendum is one of the most precious rights of our democratic process. Since under our theory of government all the power of government resides in the people, the power of initiative is commonly referred to as a "reserve" power and it has long been our judicial policy to apply a liberal construction to this power wherever it is challenged in order that the right be not improperly annulled. If doubts can reasonably be resolved in favor of the use of this reserve power, our courts will preserve it. [*Mervynne v. Acker,* 11 Cal. Rptr. 340, 344 (Cal. App. 1961).]

Eule, *Judicial Review of Direct Democracy,* 99 Yale L.J. 1503 (1990), disagrees and calls for a "hard judicial look" at legislation adopted by popular vote because there are no checks, balances, and deliberation in direct democracy. Charlow, *Judicial Review, Equal Protection and the Problem with Plebiscites,* 79 Cornell L. Rev. 527 (1994), faults Eule's analysis and argues that reforms in the referendum and initiative process, rather than heightened judicial review, might be more appropriate responses to the problems present by voter-approved legislation. For analysis revisiting questions posed by Professor Eule, see Solimine, *Judicial Review of Direct Democracy: A Reappraisal,* 104 Ky. L.J. 671 (2015–16). See also Johanningmeier, *Law & Politics: The Case Against Judicial Review of Direct Democracy,* 82 Ind. L.J. 1125 (2007) (defending popular democracy and opposing judicial review).

5. *Amendment or repeal.* In the absence of special limiting constitutional provisions, either the legislative body or the people through the initiative and referendum process can amend or repeal legislation enacted by the other. See the extensive discussion in Annot., 33 A.L.R.2d 1118 (1965). However, in order to restrict the power of the legislative body to nullify any legislation enacted by the people through the power of initiative or referendum, constitutional, statutory or charter provisions may require that such legislation may be repealed or amended only by a vote of the electorate. See, e.g., Cal. Const. Art. II, § 10(c) ("Legislature . . . may amend or repeal an initiative statute by another statute that becomes effective only when

approved by the electors unless the initiative statute permits amendment or repeal without their approval.") See, e.g., *Howard Jarvis Taxpayers Association v. Newsom*, 252 Cal. Rptr. 3d 106 (Cal. App. 3d Dist. 2019) (court invalidated legislative amendment after concluding that the amendment was barred by language in the original constitutional initiative that limited changes in public campaign funding system unless adopted by action of the voters or by a supermajority of the legislature acting "to further its purposes").

A Note on Racial Discrimination in the Initiative and Referendum Process

Critics argue that the initiative and referendum process is racially discriminatory. For a summary of these arguments, see Traub, *Discrimination in Plebiscites: Discursive Irrationality*, 6 Temple Pol. & Civ. Rts. L. Rev. 99 (1996–97). The classic article is Bell, *The Referendum: Democracy's Barrier to Racial Equality*, 54 Wash. L. Rev. 1 (1978). An example is *United States v. City of Birmingham*, 727 F.2d 560 (6th Cir. 1984), which invalidated as racially discriminatory under the Fair Housing Act a referendum that attempted to block a subsidized housing project. However, the literature on the effect of racial composition on the use of the initiative is mixed. See Filla & DeLong, *Race and the Use of Local Initiatives in American Cities*, 46 State & Local Gov't Rev. No. 1 (2014): 3–12 (study finding initiative used more often in cities with higher level of white racial prevalence, but used more in racially homogenous than in racially diverse cities).

The Supreme Court dealt with this problem in several cases. In *Hunter v. Erickson*, 393 U.S. 385 (1969), the city of Akron, Ohio, enacted a fair housing ordinance that prohibited discrimination in the sale or rental of housing. After plaintiff filed a complaint under the ordinance, the city charter was amended to require a referendum on any ordinance of this type. The city also had a long-standing referendum procedure under which a referendum could be had on almost any city ordinance following the filing of a petition by ten percent of the electors.

The charter provision mandating a referendum on fair housing ordinances was held unconstitutional, as it was "an explicitly racial classification treating racial housing matters differently from other racial and housing matters." *Id.* at 389. The Court noted that while the law applied on its face to both majority and minority groups its "impact" fell on the minority. *Id.* at 391. Because the mandatory referendum was based on a racial classification, it bore a heavier burden of justification than other classifications. It was not justified by "insisting that a State may distribute legislative power as it desires and that the people may retain for themselves the power over certain subjects . . . [as there is a violation of] the Fourteenth Amendment." *Id.* at 392.

The Court backtracked in *James v. Valtierra*, 402 U.S. 137 (1971). It upheld an amendment to the California state constitution that mandated a referendum on all local public housing projects. These projects are built by local agencies and governments and receive federal subsidies. The Court distinguished *Hunter* because the

California procedure "requires referendum approval for any low-rent public housing project, not only for projects which will be occupied by a racial minority." There was no support in the record for "any claim that a law seemingly neutral on its face is in fact aimed at a racial minority." *Id.* at 141.

However, in *Washington v. Seattle School Dist. No. 1*, 458 U.S. 457 (1982), the Court invalidated a referendum on school desegregation as racially discriminatory. The district had adopted a school desegregation plan that included mandatory busing. State voters then adopted a statute by initiative that prohibited school boards from requiring any student to attend a school which was not geographically nearest or next to his place of residence. The statute contained a number of exceptions that allowed school boards to assign students away from their neighborhood school for virtually all purposes except racial desegregation.

Applying *Hunter*, the Court held that "the political majority may generally restructure the political process to place obstacles in the path of everyone seeking to secure the benefits of governmental action. But a different analysis is required when the State allocates governmental power non-neutrally, by explicitly using the racial nature of a decision to determine the decisionmaking process." *Id.* at 470. Although the initiative was facially neutral, the Court was convinced that it "was effectively drawn for racial purposes," and was "condemned" by *Hunter.* "The initiative removes the authority to address a racial problem—and only a racial problem—from the existing decisionmaking body, in such a way as to burden minority interest." *Id.* at 474.

Compare *Crawford v. Board of Educ.*, 458 U.S. 527 (1982), decided the same day. The Court upheld an amendment to the California constitution adopted by initiative that limited court-ordered busing for school desegregation purposes to cases in which a federal court would order busing to remedy a Fourteenth Amendment violation.

If the initiative or referendum is "facially neutral" because it does not discriminate on its face, the question now is whether proof of racial discrimination turns on proof of "disparate" racial impact or racial motivation. After *Hunter* and *Valtierra*, the Supreme Court in *Washington v. Davis*, 426 U.S. 229 (1976), held that "disparate impact" was not enough to prove a Fourteenth Amendment racial discrimination claim, and that proof of racial motivation was necessary when legislation was facially neutral. Addressing this problem in *Seattle*, the Court said:

> [W]hen the political process or the decisionmaking process used to *address* racially conscious legislation—and only such legislation—is singled out for peculiar and disadvantageous treatment, the governmental action plainly "rests on 'distinctions based on race.'" [*Id.* at 485 (emphasis in original).]

Seattle distinguished *Hunter* from *Washington v. Davis.* "[T]he charter amendment at issue in *Hunter* dealt in explicitly racial terms with legislation designed to benefit minorities 'as minorities,' not legislation intended to benefit some larger group of underprivileged citizens among whom minorities were disproportionately represented." What is needed to make the *Hunter* rule apply?

Subsequently, in a Michigan case addressing affirmative action in higher education, the Court held that nothing in the federal Constitution allowed it to overturn a state referendum that had prohibited use of affirmative action to diversify state public school districts, community colleges, and universities. See *Schuette v. Coal. to Defend Affirmative Action, Integration & Immigrant Rights & Fight for Equal. by Any Means Necessary (BAMN)*, 572 U.S. 291 (2014) (plurality decision by Justice Kennedy, Chief Justice Roberts and Justice Alito with Justices Scalia, Thomas and Breyer concurring in the judgment). The Court stressed that it was not deciding on the constitutionality of affirmative action in general, but rather addressing the question of the legitimacy of a state referendum that reflected state voters' views on that subject. The Court characterized its prior holdings in the following terms: "*Seattle* is best understood as a case in which the state action in question (the bar on busing enacted by the State's voters) had the serious risk, if not purpose, of causing specific injuries on account of race, just as had been the case in [earlier cases including *Hunter v. Erickson*]." *Id.* at 305. In narrowing the *Seattle* decision, the Court also reshaped the "political process" doctrine reflected in the earlier caselaw by deferring to the right of the state's voters to engage in democratic dialogue and engage in related decision-making. Justices Ginsberg and Sotomayor dissented, and Justice Kagan took no part in the decision.

Index

[References are to sections.]